Vietnam

Nick Ray, Wendy Yanagihara

Contents

NORTHEAST VIETNAM P118

NORTHWEST VIETNAM P147

✪ HANOI P74

NORTH-CENTRAL VIETNAM P171

CENTRAL VIETNAM P187

SOUTH-CENTRAL COAST P249

CENTRAL HIGHLANDS P288

AROUND HO CHI MINH CITY P367

○ HO CHI MINH CITY P319

MEKONG DELTA P391

Destination Vietnam

Prepare for sensory overload, as Vietnam is one long trip of sights, sounds and smells.

The sights are spectacular, thanks to a rich civilisation that has left its temples and traditions throughout the land, and a lucky hand with nature, which has dealt Vietnam breathtaking mountains, a killer coastline and sublime scenery. A place of blessed beauty, Vietnam is blanketed from top to toe with a patchwork of emerald-green rice paddies, timelessly tended by farmers in conical hats.

There is no volume control on the soundtrack to Vietnam – it is the story of a people on the move, the bustle of the cities as they rush towards the future. The buzz of bikes, the cries of sellers, the hum of voices and the clink of beer glasses collide head-on with the tinkle of the past in the pagodas, the swish of the scythe or the haunting music that accompanies sadness or success. Vietnam's cuisine is a cracker, a wonderful world of pungent herbs and secret spices, a treasure chest of 500 different dishes. Overstimulating perhaps is the smell of *nuoc mam*, a fish sauce that is as compulsory for the Vietnamese as ketchup. And don't forget the *xeo* (rice wine), which is as varied as Scotch.

'Nam to a generation, the long history of war continues to weigh heavily on the consciousness of all who can remember, but here the Vietnamese side of the story is told at poignant sites throughout the country. Fiercely protective of their independence and sovereignty, the Vietnamese are graciously welcoming to those who come in peace.

In short, Vietnam is defiantly different…hardly surprising, as it has had to defy so many to get to where it is today.

SIMON ROWE

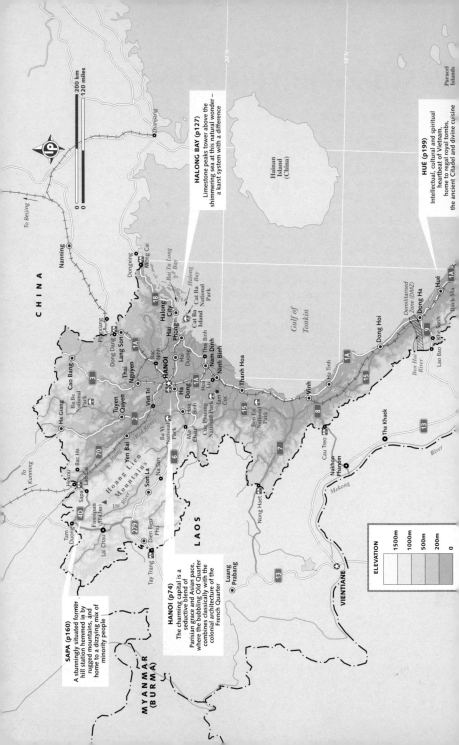

SAPA (p160)
A stunningly situated former hill station hemmed in by rugged mountains, and home to a dizzying mix of minority people

HANOI (p74)
The charming capital is a seductive blend of Parisian grace and Asian pace, where the bubbling Old Quarter combines classically with the colonial architecture of the French Quarter

HALONG BAY (p127)
Limestone peaks tower above the shimmering sea at this natural wonder – a karst system with a difference

HUÉ (p199)
Intellectual, cultural and spiritual heartbeat of Vietnam, home to regal royal tombs, the ancient Citadel and divine cuisine

CHINA

To Beijing

Nanning

Zhanjiang

Hainan Island (China)

Gulf of Tonkin

Parcel Islands

26°N

18°N

Bai Tu Long Bay

Halong Bay

Mong Cai

Dongxing

Pingxiang

Dong Dang
Lang Son
Bac Ninh
Thai Nguyen
Viet Tri
HANOI
Ha Dong
Hoa Binh
Bac Ha
Lao Cai
Sapa
Fansipan (3143m)
Tam Duong
Lai Chau
Dien Bien Phu
Tay Trang
Son La
Na San
Yen Bai
Tuyen Quyen
Ha Giang
Cao Bang
Ba Be National Park

Ba Vi National Park
Cuc Phuong National Park
Mai Chau
Tam Coc
Ninh Binh
Nam Dinh
Hai Duong
Hai Phong
Cat Ba Island
Cat Ba National Park
Halong City

Thai Binh

Thanh Hoa

Ben En National Park

Vinh

Ha Tinh

Cau Treo

Dong Hoi

Demilitarised Zone (DMZ)
Dong Ha
Ben Hai River
Lao Bao
Phong Nha
Bach Ma
Hué

Gulf of Tonkin

LAOS

VIENTIANE
Nong Haet
Nakhon Phanom
Tha Khaek
Luang Prabang

Mekong River

MYANMAR (BURMA)

To Kunming

Hekou

Song Hong (Red River)

Da River

Hoang Lien Mountains

1D
4D
279
6
70
2
3
1A
1A
1A
8
5
15
6
7
15
8
1A
9
1A
13
13

ELEVATION

	1500m
	1000m
	500m
	200m
	0

200 km
120 miles
0

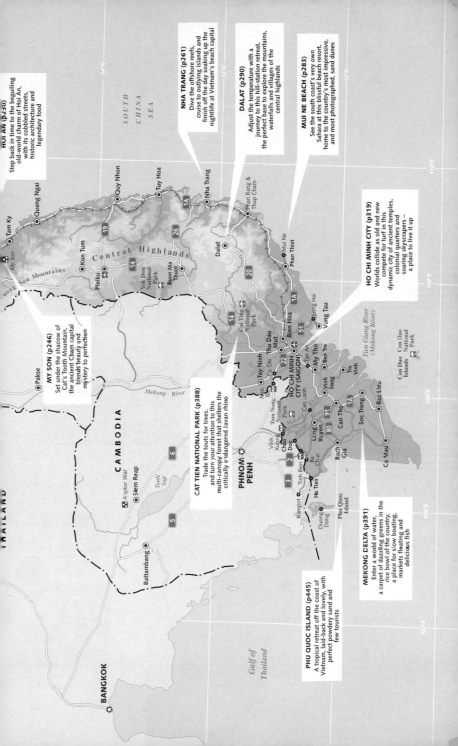

HOI AN (p230)
Step back in time to the beguiling old-world charm of Hoi An, with its cobbled streets, historic architecture and legendary food

NHA TRANG (p261)
Dive the offshore reefs, cruise to outlying islands and finish off the day soaking up the nightlife at Vietnam's beach capital

DALAT (p290)
Adjust the temperature with a journey to this hill-station retreat, the perfect base to explore the mountains, waterfalls and villages of the central highlands

MUI NE BEACH (p283)
See the south coast's very own Sahara at this blissful beach resort, home to the country's most impressive, and most photographed, sand dunes

HO CHI MINH CITY (p319)
Worlds collide as old and new compete for turf in this dynamic city of ancient temples, colonial quarters and soaring skyscrapers – a place to live it up

MY SON (p246)
Set under the shadow of Cat's Tooth Mountain, the ancient Cham capital blends beauty and mystery to perfection

CAT TIEN NATIONAL PARK (p388)
Trade the touts for trees, and turn your attention to this multi-canopy forest that shelters the critically endangered Javan rhino

PHU QUOC ISLAND (p445)
A tropical retreat off the coast of Vietnam, laid-back and lovely, with perfect powdery sand and few tourists

MEKONG DELTA (p391)
Enter a world of water, a carpet of dazzling greens in the rice bowl of the country, a place for slow boating, markets floating and delicious fish

It is to the cities you must go to get beneath the skin of Vietnam. Their intoxicating contradictions are hypnotising: the headlong rush towards the future while hanging on tight to the past; the motorbikes, mobiles and miniskirts of the new generation side by side with the politics, pagodas and piety of the old. Marx one minute, MTV the next; Vietnam is evolving fast and the cities are the only place to hitch a ride.

Hué (p199) is the city for culture vultures, the old imperial capital with a flair for food. Dash through **Danang** (p220) to discover the Museum of Cham Sculpture – the finest collection of Cham art in the world.

Wander past a Chinese temple on Pho Hang Quat on your way to Hanoi's Old Quarter (p83)

RICHARD I'ANSON

OLIVER STREWE

Live it up in one of Hanoi's many bars (p104)

Watch students in *ao dai* (Vietnamese national dress) zoom by in Ho Chi Minh City (p319)

JOHN BANAGAN

ALAIN EVARD

Consider a cut in Hanoi (p109)

GREG ELMS

Take in Ho Chi Minh City by night, from the balcony of the Rex Hotel (p351)

Get caught in the hurly-burly of Hanoi's Old Quarter (p83)

MANFRED GOTTSCHALK

With more than 3450km of coastline, Vietnam is no novice when it comes to brilliant beaches. And just off the coast are idyllic tropical islands in the south and rugged, jungle-clad mountains of rock in the north, perfect for the beach bum or the action addict. Snorkelling and surfing, diving and boating, there is plenty of action under and above the water.

Enjoy an afternoon drinking at the floating bar of Mama Linh's boat, a legend throughout Asia, off the coast of **Nha Trang** (p261). Trek through the jungle amid lost-world scenery on **Cat Ba Island** (p130). Chill out on **Cua Dai Beach** (p245), the perfect excuse to stay in Hoi An a few more days.

Catch a wave at China Beach (p226) – surf capital of Vietnam

PHIL WE

ANDERS BLOMQVIST

Size up the awesome sand dunes and colourful waters of Mui Ne Beach (p283)

Relax on tranquil Lang Co Beach (p218)

NOBORU KOMINE

JOHN BANAGAN

Hop off and enjoy the sunset at Nha Trang (p261)

JOHN ASHBURNE

LInger over the evening tide on Phu Quoc Island (p445)

Savour the delicious, freshly caught seafood of Halong Bay (p127)

RICHARD I'ANSON

Marvel at the majesty of Halong Bay (p127)

MICHAEL GEBICKI

In the interests of preserving our culture and heritage for future generations, Unesco has been awarding World Heritage–site status to the most important treasures on the planet. Vietnam is no slouch when it comes to such treasures, some made by the hand of humans, others the work of nature that knows no bounds.

Cruise along the river into Vietnam's biggest underground complex at **Phong Nha Cave** (p185). Succumb to the charms of **Hoi An** (p230), where successive cultures have left their legacy in a beautiful blend of buildings.

Revel in royalty at the tomb of Minh Mang (p215) in Hué.

NOBORU KOMINE

MARK KIRBY

Explore the stunning illuminated caves of Halong Bay (p127)

Ponder an ancient kingdom at the Cham temples at My Son (p246)

NOBORU

Natural highs are numerous in Vietnam and opportunities for adventures are never far away. The network of national parks is the perfect place to trek in the jungle, encounter an ape or ride an elephant. The mountains of the northwest are one long adventure and that's just the road trip.

Swoon at the views around **Sapa** (p160), home to a wealth of minority peoples, and a base for exploring the Tonkinese Alps. Boat, bike and hike your way around **Ba Be National Park** (p144), a serene and scenic spot. For a truly colourful experience, meet the Flower H'mong of **Bac Ha** (p168). See elephants in their element at beautiful **Yok Don National Park** (p311). Discover a different world with a dive under the waters off **Nha Trang** (p261). Abseil down a waterfall or rock climb up one near **Dalat** (p290).

Greet the gibbons at Cuc Phu-ong National Park (p177)

Cavort among the karsts at Halong Bay (p127)

Paddle your way through awesome caves at Tam Coc (p175)

Taste the best of Vietnam in a culinary caper around the country. Vietnamese cuisine is heaven sent and the divine flavours are as diverse as the destinations in which they are dished up. The seafood is spectacular thanks to an endless coastline, and vegetarians will love the magical 'mock meat' that the Vietnamese have mastered.

Taste the secrets of the Ba Le Well in a plate of *cao lau* in **Hoi An** (p230). Fire up a fresh seafood barbecue in **Nha Trang** (p261). Do the one dollar pub crawl through the **bia hoi bars** (p105) of Hanoi's Old Quarter.

Discover *pho bo* – the breakfast that built a nation (p62)

GREG ELMS

RICHARD I'ANSON

Get fresh at Binh Tay Market in Cholon (p362)

GARRETT C

Taste the treats of the hawkers at Hué (p199)

Soak up the atmosphere at a night market in Dalat (p290)

Getting Started

Vietnam is one of the *in* places in Asia thanks to its vibrant yet traditional cities, unashamedly idyllic coastline, incredible scenery, pulsating history and culture, and potpourri of people. Vietnam has everything, but it's also raw in places, so pack some flexibility, humour and patience. Come expecting the unexpected, be ready for an adventure as much as a holiday, and Vietnam will deliver.

WHEN TO GO

When it comes to weather, it's a tough call, as Vietnam's climate is so diverse. Think frosts and occasional snow in the mountains of the north, and temperatures soaring to 40°C in the dry season of the south.

Vietnam's weather is dictated by two monsoons. The winter monsoon comes from the northeast between October and March, bringing wet cold winters to all areas north of Nha Trang, and dry and warm temperatures to the south. From April or May to October, the southwestern monsoon brings warm, humid weather to the whole country except for those areas sheltered by mountains. For the best balance, try the months of April, May or October. For those sticking to the south, November to February is dry and a touch cooler. From July to November, violent and unpredictable typhoons hit central and northern Vietnam.

See Climate Charts (p455) for more information.

It gets pretty crowded from November to March and in July and August. Prices tend to peak over the Christmas and New Year period, but if you don't fancy sharing the sites with the masses, try to avoid these busy times.

Some travellers like to time a visit with Tet (Vietnamese New Year; see the special section on p53), which is the biggest festival in the calendar in late January or early February. A nice idea but not ideal, as the whole country is on the move.

COSTS & MONEY

The cost of travel in Vietnam varies from next to nothing to the sky is the limit, depending on taste and comfort. Ascetics can get by on US$10 a day, while a conventional budget traveller can live it up on US$20 to US$25. Mid-range travellers can have a ball with US$75 to US$100 a day, staying comfortably, eating well and travelling in style. At the top end, spending US$200 or more a day, anything is possible.

DON'T LEAVE HOME WITHOUT...

Bring as little as possible; Vietnam has pretty much anything you can find back home. All the soaps and smellies are cheap and plentiful, and clothing, shoes and backpacks are all manufactured in Vietnam and available at a fraction of the price in the West. Tampons are available in all major towns and cities, but not in more remote areas.

A Swiss army knife or equivalent comes in handy, but you don't need 27 separate functions, just one blade and an opener. A torch (flashlight) and compass are also useful.

Other handy things to bring are name cards, as Vietnamese deal them out like a deck of cards; ear plugs to block the ever-present noise; a universal plug adaptor; a rain cover for the backpack; a sweater for the highlands and air-con bus trips; and mosquito repellent to keep the bugs at bay.

Finally, the secret of successful packing: plastic bags – not only do they keep things separate and clean, but also dry. That means a lot at the end of a long, wet day.

HOW MUCH?

Litre of petrol
US$0.40

Litre of water
US$0.35-0.70

Big BGI beer
US$1

Souvenir T-shirt
US$2

Pho bo from a street stall
US$0.50

Restaurant meal
US$3.50-7

Hotel room with air-con
US$6-20

Internet access
US$0.30-0.70 per minute

Print film
US$2.50-3.50

Two-kilometre taxi ride
US$1

Foreigners are frequently overcharged, particularly when buying souvenirs and occasionally in restaurants. Rapacious bus and taxi drivers will often bump up their rates to several times the Vietnamese price. However, don't assume that everyone is trying to rip you off. Despite severe poverty, many Vietnamese will only ask the local price for most goods and services.

Rooms start from as little as US$3 to US$5 in busy tourist centres. Spending US$10 to US$20 will boost the comforts quickly, and rooms will generally include air-con, satellite TV, a fridge and hot water. Make the step up to US$50 and three-star standards are available. At US$100 and above it's five-star territory. Don't be afraid to negotiate for a discount if it is low season or if traffic is down.

Dining out is where Vietnam comes into its own. Surfing the street stalls and markets, meals can be found for between US$0.35 and US$0.70. Local restaurants are more comfortable and you can eat well for between US$1 and US$3.50. Then there are the Vietnamese gourmet restaurants, where you can still only spend around US$10 with drinks; with the right wines you could easily spend US$50.

Domestic flights are relatively expensive compared with some countries in the region. A one-way ticket from Hanoi to Ho Chi Minh City (HCMC) is around US$100. Trains are great value and overnight sleepers are a good way to cover long distances like Hanoi to Hué or HCMC to Nha Trang.

Bus travel is a bargain. Public buses between major destinations have fixed fares, but when travelling by bus in remote areas, overcharging is the rule. For maximum flexibility, many prefer to rent a car or 4WD to explore with a guide. Costs run from about US$25 around town to as much as US$70 a day upcountry (including the driver's food and lodging). A guide costs from US$20 to US$40, depending on the destination.

Whatever your budget might be, Vietnam is a dream deal. Live it up while you can.

TRAVEL LITERATURE

Vietnam: A Traveller's Literary Companion (1996), edited by Nguyen Qui Doc, is an engaging collection of stories by various Vietnamese writers, ranging from folklore and the tragedy of war to love and family ties, set against evocative backdrops from Hanoi to Dalat.

Fragrant Palm Leaves (1998) is a remarkable, poetic collection of journal entries by Zen monk and peace crusader Thich Nhat Hanh, written in Vietnam and the USA during the 1960s. As the American War in Vietnam rages on, he tries to make sense of it all, and there are some vivid scenes from South Vietnam in the 1960s.

Sparring with Charlie: Motorbiking down the Ho Chi Minh Trail (1996), by Christopher Hunt, is a light-hearted travelogue about modern Vietnam that takes the reader off the tourist trail and into some less-travelled parts of the country.

In a similar vein is *Ten Years After* (1987) by Tim Page. This impressive book boasts '12-months worth of photos taken 10 years after the war'. The author also returned to Vietnam to write *Derailed in Uncle Ho's Victory Garden* (1995), the story of his quest to erect a war memorial in the Demilitarised Zone (DMZ) to honour the fallen war correspondents on all sides.

A Dragon Apparent (1952) is Norman Lewis' fascinating account of his journeys through Vietnam, Laos and Cambodia in 1950, and is a good insight into the last days of French rule.

TOP TENS

WAR IN WORDS

The American War captivated a generation and has inspired endless accounts of the tragedies and triumphs that took place. There are some classic accounts by US soldiers who came home to tell the tale, some poignant and human stories written by Vietnamese on the other side and some definitive pieces of reportage by the finest journalists of the time. Pick up one or two of these before hitting 'Nam.

- *Bright Shining Lie* (1989) Neil Sheehan
- *Dispatches* (1977) Michael Herr
- *The Girl in the Picture* (2001) Denise Chong
- *If I Die in a Combat Zone* (1973) Tim O'Brien
- *Novel Without a Name* (1996) Duong Thu Huong
- *The Quiet American* (1955) Graham Greene
- *Requiem* (1997) Tim Page
- *A Rumour of War* (1978) Phillip Caputo
- *The Sorrow of War* (1996) Bao Ninh
- *Street Without Joy* (1961) Bernard Fall

MUST-SEE MOVIES

Filmmakers have found a rich vein of material in the turbulent tales of Vietnamese history, and both foreign and local directors have tapped it well. There are some moody, atmospheric movies from a time before the torment, a whole host of films dealing with the American experience in Vietnam, and some that deal with both Americans and Vietnamese coming to terms with life after so much death.

- *Apocalypse Now* (1979)
  Director: Francis Ford Coppola
- *Born on the Fourth of July* (1989)
  Director: Oliver Stone
- *Cyclo* (1995) Director: Tran Anh Hung
- *The Deer Hunter* (1978)
  Director: Michael Cimino
- *Heaven and Earth* (1993)
  Director: Oliver Stone
- *The Lover* (1992)
  Director: Jean-Jacques Annaud
- *Platoon* (1986) Director: Oliver Stone
- *The Quiet American* (2002)
  Director: Phillip Noyce
- *The Scent of Green Papaya* (1992)
  Director: Tran Anh Hung
- *We Were Soldiers* (2002)
  Director: Randall Wallace

BEST BREWS

Bia hoi (beer) is the new tea in Vietnam and everyone is drinking it. It doesn't come much cheaper than this, from 10 cents a glass to a large local bottle for less than US$1. Seize the day and sample a selection as you travel through the country, a sure-fire way to find some Vietnamese friends. Just remember that down-in-one is a national pastime in Vietnam, so bring your beer goggles.

- **Bia Hoi** The world's cheapest beer keeps on flowing
- **BGI** The Big Groovy I, popular in the south
- **Halida** North Vietnam's finest, a smooth pilsner
- **Hanoi** Another northern favourite in handy half-litre bottles
- **Huda** Hué meets Denmark, Central Vietnam's ultimate joint venture
- **Larue** A hangover from the French, the Export is a cracker
- **Red Horse** Strong as an ox, this helps pass the time in Nha Trang
- **Saigon** A longrunning southern tipple, the Export has gone national
- **333** *Ba ba ba*, the saviour of the south
- **Tiger** Strictly speaking a Singaporean interloper, but brewed locally

Karin Muller's *Hitchhiking Vietnam* (1998) is a travelogue detailing one woman's tumultuous seven-month journey through Vietnam.

Part memoir and part travel narrative, *Catfish and Mandala* (1999) is Vietnamese-American Andrew X Pham's fascinating account of his escape from the war-torn Vietnam of 1977 and his subsequent return two decades later, equipped with a bicycle and a need to work out his mixed-up cultural identity.

INTERNET RESOURCES

Jewels of the Mekong Delta (www.travelmedia.com/mekong/) Features travel information and news about countries along the Mekong River.

Lonely Planet (www.lonelyplanet.com) Summaries on travelling to Vietnam, the Thorn Tree bulletin board, travel news and the Subwwway section for links to other useful travel resources.

Things Asian (www.thingsasian.com) Bubbling with information on the culture of Vietnam, this site has everything from architecture to literature and fashion.

Vietnam Adventures Online (www.vietnamadventures.com) Another fine site full of practical travel information that features monthly adventures and special travel deals.

Vietnam Online (www.vietnamonline.com) Loaded with useful travel lore and handy coverage of employment and business opportunities in Vietnam.

Vietnam Travel (www.vietnam-travel.com) Dedicated to travel in Vietnam, this website has an interesting selection of links for further exploration.

Itineraries
CLASSIC ROUTES

COASTAL CLASSIC
Three to Four Weeks

Kick off in the capital, **Hanoi** (p74); soak up the sights, dine in style and prepare for the long ride south. A short hop south is **Ninh Binh** (p174), gateway to the surreal scenery of **Tam Coc** (p175) and **Hoa Lu** (p176), and the animals of **Cuc Phuong National Park** (p177).

Visit **Hué** (p199), imperial capital of old, then take the awesome Hai Van Pass to **Danang** (p220), home to the **Museum of Cham Sculpture** (p221) – a must before encountering the legacy of their ancient empire. **Hoi An** (p230) is the place for some time out – sightseeing, shopping and sunning yourself on the beach. Spend a day at **My Son** (p246), the best preserved of the many Cham temple cities that dot the coastal regions south of here.

Enter **Nha Trang** (p261), the biggest, possibly brashest, beach resort in Vietnam, and try a hedonistic boat trip to nearby islands. If it's all too much, carry on south to **Mui Ne Beach** (p283), a tropical idyll with smart resorts, blissed-out budget options, and towering sand dunes.

Wind up in **Ho Chi Minh City** (p319), where you can spend any excess cash in the best restaurants and bars in the country.

Many tour companies offer this trip in a two-week timeframe, but this barely allows enough time to unpack your bags in each place. Train, bus or opt for a car and driver for this 1710km epic.

THE BIG ONE   One Month

Run this one in reverse, starting out in the cauldron of commerce that is
Ho Chi Minh City (p319). Hit the markets, browse a couple of museums and
take a day trip to the underground world that is the **Cu Chi Tunnels** (p369).
Carry on to **Tay Ninh** (p373), headquarters of the Cao Dai sect and their
rococo temple, for a morning service.

Delve into the delta for a day or two...Mekong, that is. Try an overnight or two at **Can Tho** (p414), the social and commercial heart of the
region, and take to the water to cruise through the incredible world of
the floating markets.

For a complete change from the pancake-flat delta, head up into the
central highlands to the romantic hill station of **Dalat** (p290). Back down
on the coast, take in the stops from the Coastal Classic itinerary (see p17),
including the beach resort of **Nha Trang** (p261), the cultured charmer that is
Hoi An (p230) and the old imperial capital of **Hué** (p199). North of Hué
is the former Demilitarised Zone (DMZ) that divided North and South
Vietnam. All around this area are famous sites from the American War,
including **Khe Sanh Combat Base** (p194) and the **Vinh Moc Tunnels** (p191). All
aboard the night train to **Hanoi** (p74), gateway to the north.

To the east of the capital lies **Halong Bay** (p127), with more than 3000
limestone outcrops dotting the scenic bay. Cruise through the bay to the
rugged, foreboding **Cat Ba Island** (p130) before looping back to the capital
through **Hai Phong** (p121), for a slice of the atmosphere of old Hanoi.

To top it off, take a night train to **Sapa** (p160), unofficial capital of the
northwest hill-tribe region and a beautiful base for hiking and biking.

**Trains and buses
stop at most
destinations, but to
cover this huge dis-
tance a Hué–Hanoi
flight could save
time. Travel by boat
around the Halong
Bay area – the only
way to get a good
look at the crazy
karsts.**

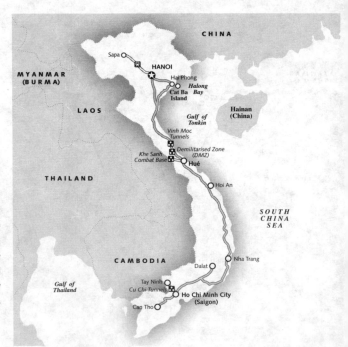

ROADS LESS TRAVELLED

AIN'T NO MOUNTAIN HIGH ENOUGH   One to Three Weeks

Northwest Vietnam is a land of looming mountains, a mosaic of ethnic minorities, a region of overwhelming beauty – very much a world unto itself. Hit the road by 4WD or motorbike for an adventure more than a holiday – an experience that will stay with you forever.

Leaving the capital, head west to the villages of **Mai Chau** (p152), which are home to the White Thai people and a perfect introduction to the life of the minorities. Northwest of here, where the road begins to climb into the Hoang Lien Mountains, a logical stop is **Son La** (p153).

Dien Bien Phu (p155) is a name that resonates with history; it was here that the French colonial story ended with their overwhelming defeat at the hands of the Viet Minh in one of the most celebrated military victories. In the remote northeast is **Lai Chau** (p158), at the heart of a patchwork of Thai communities and a staging post to Sapa. The road weaves through **Tam Duong** (p160) before climbing over the mighty **Tram Ton Pass** (p164).

Sapa (p160) is the most popular destination in the northwest, thanks to the infinite views (on a clear day!), the amazing array of minority peoples and some of the region's most colourful markets. Bail out here by train from **Lao Cai** (p167), or continue east to **Bac Ha** (p168), home to the Flower H'mong. And for the ultimate end to the adventure, head into **Ha Giang** (p170), a realm of mythical landscapes and unchartered territory.

The snaking roads on this journey are some of the most treacherous in Vietnam, and landslips and floods are common. The motorbiking here is pure heaven for seasoned two-wheelers, but for the majority a 4WD is the sanest way to go.

DELTA DELIGHTS

Two Weeks

With their own wheels, travellers can tear up the three-day tourist trail through the Mekong byways and delve deeper into the delta to be rewarded with its rhythms, fragrances and colours. For anyone battling the insane highways of the delta by motorcycle, a helmet is a wise accessory (and required by law)!

Beginning in **Ben Tre** (p400), take a boat trip to nearby islands for an overnight in a bungalow set in a small longan orchard. From Ben Tre, a trek to **Can Tho** (p414) takes you to the home of the famous Ho Chi Minh 'Tin Man' statue and the delta's most commercial and cosmopolitan city.

It's easy to hop onto boat tours of the local floating markets before moving on to charming **Chau Doc** (p429), a border-crossing town for those pushing westward into Cambodia via river or road.

The departure from the road more travelled starts here, heading southwest to **Ba Chuc** (p435) and its bone pagoda, and then through **Ha Tien** (p440), another border town with a beach to boot. Even more bucolic a beach can be found at **Hon Chong** (p443), where the sunset meets the South China Sea and the rocky coastal geography contrasts sharply with the sandy beaches east of HCMC.

From here, travellers can take the highway along the southern wedge of the delta region to **Rach Gia** (p436), the jumping-off point for boats bound for serene **Phu Quoc Island** (p445). Phu Quoc affords rest and relaxation, *nuoc mam* (fish sauce) and forest reserves – a spectacular ending point for the Mekong Delta experience.

Down to Chau Doc, public transport is a breeze; after that, it's sparse and requires flexibility. Flights from Phu Quoc Island to HCMC run three times a week; if flying back to HCMC, book return flights well before hitting the delta to guarantee a quick getaway.

TAILORED TRIPS

NATURAL ADVENTURES

For adrenaline junkies or nature lovers, Vietnam has plenty to offer. Start out with a visit to **Halong Bay** (p127) for some sea kayaking among the karsts. Experienced climbers with their own gear might leave the water far below, as these limestone outcrops offer some excellent ascents.

Further northeast in **Bai Tu Long Bay** (p135), take to the water by local boat to see the 'new' Halong Bay without the tourists. Take a trip north of the capital to **Ba Be National Park** (p144) – three beautiful lakes set amid verdant forest with some great opportunities for hiking and biking. Heading south to central Vietnam, **Bach Ma National Park** (p216) is well geared up for walkers and has a series of marked trails to waterfalls. Down on the coast below Bach Ma is **China Beach** (p226).

Go under the waves at **Nha Trang** (p261), dive capital of Vietnam, with several international-standard operators, before heading out of Ho Chi Minh City (HCMC) up towards the hills of the central highlands, where there are two of Vietnam's best-known national parks: the birding hot spot of **Cat Tien** (p388), with a population of rare Javan rhinos, and **Yok Don** (p311), home to elephants, elephants and more elephants.

Wind up, or down, in **Dalat** (p290), a base for abseiling, cycling or rock climbing.

BEACH BLISS

Beach lovers should start in the south, as just a short drive from HCMC are some unexpected beach retreats, including the busy bars of **Vung Tau** (p379), and the quieter hideaways of **Loc An Beach** (p387), **Ho Coc Beach** (p387) and **Long Hai** (p385). Or jump on a plane or helicopter and leave the mainland behind with a trip to the remote **Con Dao Islands** (p382) or perfect **Phu Quoc Island** (p445).

Make for **Mui Ne Beach** (p283), the prettiest of Vietnam's beach resorts. Windsurf, sandboard, kite sail or just chill out before heading to **Ca Na** (p281), where the boulder formations are the perfect backdrop. Further north is **Nha Trang** (p261), Vietnam's honky-tonk beach capital. There are peaceful paradises near here, including **Doc Let Beach** (p260), **Jungle Beach** (p261), **Whale Island** (p261) and **Dai Lanh Beach** (p260).

Central Vietnam has a 30km beach running from Danang to Hoi An. Call it **China Beach** (p226) to the north, **Cua Dai Beach** (p245) to the south – either way it's paradise. And running hundreds of kilometres north and south are hidden coves and secluded bays, suggesting a bright beach future for Vietnam.

There are some fine beaches around **Cat Ba Island** (p130) and **Bai Tu Long Bay** (p135).

The Authors

NICK RAY   Coordinating Author & Hanoi, Northeast Vietnam, Northwest Vietnam, North-Central Vietnam, Central Vietnam

A Londoner of sorts, Nick comes from Watford, the sort of town that makes you want to travel. He has been visiting Vietnam for more than a decade now, first just passing through and later leading people astray as a tour guide for adventure travel companies. Living in nearby Phnom Penh, Vietnam is his backyard of sorts and he has co-authored *Cycling Vietnam, Laos* and *Cambodia* for Lonely Planet. Nick has been to almost every province from north to south, but it is the mountains of the northwest and the laid-back loveliness of Hoi An that really fire him up. His motto in Vietnam: don't be coy, drink *bia hoi*!

My Favourite Trip...

Riding the coastline along Hwy 1 is hard to beat, stopping off at obscure beaches like Dai Lanh (p260) and Doc Let (p260).

Taking on the mighty mountains of the northwest on a Minsk is one of the most memorable road trips in Asia. Dropping down to Muong Thanh Valley around Dien Bien Phu (p155) at night was insane, but more fun was heaving over the mountains into Sapa (p160), where you run out of superlatives to describe the scenery. The finale was the best... Deep into northern Ha Giang (p170) on the mind-blowing road to Meo Vac (p170). Blew the good vibes by stumbling on military exercises in Khau Vai District. Back to Ha Giang city to buy a permit please... On your bike, we thought, and escaped over the mountains eastward, with a midnight ride along a cliffside footpath. Anything to avoid a run-in with the police!

WENDY YANAGIHARA   South-Central Coast, Central Highlands, Ho Chi Minh City, Around Ho Chi Minh City, Mekong Delta

Curiosity compelled Wendy Yanagihara to live in Ho Chi Minh City for a year, during which she taught English, learned more than could be crammed into one glib sentence, and attained (slightly) higher levels of peace and patience. Wendy has updated slices of LP's *Southeast Asia on a Shoestring* and *Mexico* and covered southern Vietnam for this book. Confounded by and enamoured of Vietnam, she currently contemplates its complex psyche from California while dreaming of doing so over a glass of pastis in Saigon.

CONTRIBUTING AUTHORS

Dr Trish Batchelor wrote the Health chapter (p485). Trish is a general practitioner and travel-medicine specialist who works at the CIWEC Clinic in Kathmandu, Nepal, as well as being a Medical Advisor to the Travel Doctor New Zealand clinics. Trish teaches travel medicine through the University of Otago, and is interested in underwater and high-altitude medicine, and in the impact of tourism on host countries. She has travelled extensively through Southeast and East Asia and particularly loves high-altitude trekking in the Himalayas.

Snapshot

Vietnamese society has undergone a profound transition in the past decade, even if the politics hasn't come along for the ride. Communism, the mantra for a generation, has taken a back seat to capitalism and the rush to embrace the market. Following the Chinese road to riches espoused by Deng Xiaoping, the Vietnamese have taken the brakes off the economy while keeping a firm hand on the steering wheel. The result is a contradictory blend of ultra-liberal economics and ultra-conservative politics that has left many Vietnamese confused about what sort of country they live in. They have the freedom to make money but not the basic freedom to voice a political opinion. And the more the average Vietnamese person engages with the outside world – through business, tourism, the Internet – the harder this contradiction is to swallow.

For now, the economy keeps the communist show on the road. It's one of the new generation of Asian tigers, growing at nearly 8% a year, one of the few countries capable of keeping the Chinese juggernaut in their sights. Political power may be held by a small elite, but economic power is firmly in the hands of the middle classes. The government is buying the popularity it hasn't tested at the ballot box by embarking on a building spree of immense proportions. Roads, bridges, tunnels, civic buildings – the scale is enormous, but it has to be, otherwise questions could start to be asked.

And some have already been asked. The trial of local crime lord Nam Can in Ho Chi Minh City was quite an embarrassment for the government, given how many police and officials turned out to be on his payroll. Corruption is a cancer undermining the good intentions of some within the government.

The minorities are revolting, or that is what the central government seems to think. Vietnamisation is in full swing in the central highlands and the northwest; when the central highlanders said enough is enough, their protests provoked a repressive reaction. Engaging the minority people on equal terms is something the party has yet to grapple with.

Disease has put Vietnam back on the media map in the past couple of years. First came SARS in 2003, which killed five people and massacred tourist arrivals for most of the year. Just as the country and its tourism industry appeared to be back on their feet, along came bird flu and another round of bad publicity. The way in which the Vietnamese government and health-care system dealt with these outbreaks was extremely professional.

Marx and Lenin may have been laid to rest in their homeland, but they are alive and well in Vietnam. Just how tenable this is as Vietnam engages with its neighbours and plugs into the world economy is anyone's guess. Whatever the Vietnamese may make of communism in private, Ho Chi Minh remains a man for all seasons. Politics aside, he was a nationalist and patriot who delivered Vietnam its independence. Come what may to the party, Ho's place in history as a hero is assured.

FAST FACTS

Population: 82.7 million (2004)

Life expectancy: 68 for men, 73 for women

Infant mortality: 30 per 1000 births

GDP: $34.6 billion (2002)

Adult literacy rate: 94%

Annual rice production: 32.3 million tonnes

Tonnage of bombs dropped on Vietnam: 15 million

Number of motorbikes: 9.4 million and counting

Litres of *nuoc mam* (fish sauce) produced per year: 200 million

Members of communist party: 2 million

History

Vietnam has a history as rich and evocative as anywhere on earth. Sure, the American War in Vietnam captured the attention of the West, but centuries before that Vietnam was scrapping with the Chinese, the Khmers, the Chams and the Mongols. Vietnamese civilisation is as sophisticated as that of its mighty northern neighbour China, from where it drew many of its influences under a thousand-year occupation. Later came the French and the humbling period of colonialism from which Vietnam was not to emerge until the second half of the 20th century. The Americans were simply the last in a long line of invaders who had come and gone through the centuries and, no matter what was required or how long it took, they too would be vanquished. If only the planners in Washington had paid a little more attention to the history of this proud nation, then Vietnam might have avoided the trauma and tragedy of a brutal war.

Visitors to Vietnam can't help but notice that the same bunch of names pops up again and again on streets of every city and town. These are Vietnam's greatest national heroes who, over the last 2000 years, have led the country in its repeated expulsions of foreign invaders and whose exploits have inspired subsequent generations of patriots.

EARLY DAYS

Recent archaeological finds date the earliest human habitation of northern Vietnam to about 500,000 years ago. Neolithic cultures were romping around the same area just 10,000 years ago and engaged in primitive agriculture as early as 7000 BC. The sophisticated Bronze Age Dong Son culture, famous for its drums, emerged sometime around the 3rd century BC.

From the 1st to 6th centuries AD, southern Vietnam was part of the Indianised Cambodian kingdom of Funan – famous for its refined art and architecture. The Funanese constructed an elaborate system of canals both for transportation and the irrigation of rice. The principal port city of Funan was Oc-Eo in the Mekong Delta and archaeological excavations here tell us of contact between Funan and China, Indonesia, Persia and even the Mediterranean.

For a closer look at China's thousand-year occupation of Vietnam, which so much shaped the country's outlook and attitude today, try *The Birth of Vietnam* by Keith Weller Taylor.

The Hindu kingdom of Champa emerged around present-day Danang in the late 2nd century AD (see the boxed text on p245). Like Funan, it adopted Sanskrit as a sacred language and borrowed heavily from Indian art and culture. By the 8th century Champa had expanded southward to include what is now Nha Trang and Phan Rang. The Cham were a feisty bunch who conducted raids along the entire coast of Indochina, and so found themselves in a perpetual state of war with the Vietnamese to the north and the Khmers to the southwest. Check out some brilliant Cham sculptures in the Museum of Cham Sculpture in Danang (p221).

1000 YEARS OF CHINESE DOMINATION

The Chinese conquered the Red River Delta in the 2nd century BC and, over the next few centuries, significant numbers of Chinese settlers, officials and scholars imposed a centralised state system on the Vietnamese.

40	938
The Trung Sisters (Hai Ba Trung) lead a rebellion against the Chinese occupiers	The Chinese are kicked out of Vietnam after more than a thousand years of occupation

Local rulers didn't take this sitting down and in the most famous act of resistance, in AD 40, the Trung Sisters (Hai Ba Trung) rallied tribal chieftains, raised an army and led a revolt that sent the Chinese governor fleeing. The sisters proclaimed themselves queens of an independent Vietnam. In AD 43 the Chinese counterattacked and, rather than surrender, the Trung Sisters threw themselves into the Hat Giang River.

During this era, Vietnam was a key port of call on the sea route between China and India. The Chinese introduced Vietnam to Confucianism, Taoism and Mahayana Buddhism, while the Indians brought Theravada Buddhism. Monks carried with them the scientific and medical knowledge of these two great civilisations, and Vietnam was soon producing its own great doctors, botanists and scholars.

The early Vietnamese learned a lot from the Chinese, including the construction of dikes and irrigation works. These innovations established a reliance on rice growing, which remains the foundation of the Vietnamese way of life to this day. As food became more plentiful the population grew, forcing the Vietnamese to seek new lands.

INDEPENDENCE FROM CHINA

The collapse of the Tang dynasty in China in the early 10th century provoked a long overdue revolt against Chinese rule in Vietnam. In 938 AD popular patriot, Ngo Quyen, finally vanquished the Chinese armies at a battle on the Bach Dang River, ending 1000 years of Chinese rule.

From the 11th to 13th centuries, Vietnamese independence was consolidated under the emperors of the Ly dynasty, founded by Ly Thai To. During the Ly dynasty repeated attacks on Vietnam by the Chinese, Khmers and Chams were repelled. Meanwhile, the Vietnamese continued their expansion southwards and instituted an aggressive policy of colonisation of the Cham kingdom.

After the Mongol warrior Kublai Khan had completed his conquest of China in the mid-13th century, he demanded the right to cross Vietnamese territory on his way to attack Champa. The Vietnamese refused him, but the Mongols – 500,000 of them – pressed on anyway. Tran Hung Dao defeated them in the battle of Bach Dang River, one of the most celebrated scalps among many the Vietnamese have taken. See the boxed text 'Playing for High Stakes' (p130) for more on this big win and soak up some of the story in Halong Bay (p127).

DID YOU KNOW?

In AD 679 the Chinese changed the name of Vietnam to Annam, which means the 'Pacified South'. Ever since this era, the collective memory of Chinese domination has played an important role in shaping Vietnamese identity and attitudes towards their northern neighbour.

CHINA BITES BACK

The Chinese seized control of Vietnam once more in the early 15th century, carting off the national archives and some of the country's intellectuals to China – an irreparable loss to Vietnamese civilisation. Of this period, poet Nguyen Trai (1380–1442) wrote: 'Were the water of the Eastern Sea to be exhausted, the stain of their ignominy could not be washed away; all the bamboo of the Southern Mountains would not suffice to provide the paper for recording all their crimes.'

LE LOI ENTERS THE SCENE

In 1418 wealthy philanthropist Le Loi kick-started the Lam Son Uprising, travelling the countryside to rally the people against the Chinese. Victory

1010	1076
Thanh Long, or City of the Soaring Dragon, known today as Hanoi, becomes Vietnam's capital	Vietnam's first university, the Temple of Literature in Hanoi, opens its doors to scholars

came in 1428, after which Le Loi declared himself Emperor Ly Thai To. To this day, Le Loi is riding high in the Top Ten of the country's all-time national heroes.

After Le Loi's victory over the Chinese, Nguyen Trai, a scholar and Le Loi's companion in arms, wrote his famous *Great Proclamation* (Binh Ngo Dai Cao), which is memorable for the compelling voice it gave to Vietnam's fierce spirit of independence:

> Our people long ago established Vietnam as an independent nation with its own civilisation. We have our own mountains and our own rivers, our own customs and traditions, and these are different from those of the foreign country to the north…We have sometimes been weak and sometimes powerful, but at no time have we suffered from a lack of heroes.

Le Loi and his successors launched a campaign to take over Cham lands to the south, wiping the kingdom of Champa from the map, and parts of eastern Laos were forced to kowtow to the might of the Vietnamese.

EARLY CONTACT WITH THE WEST

The first Portuguese sailors hit Danang in 1516 and were soon followed by a proselytizing party of Dominican missionaries. During the following decades the Portuguese began to trade with Vietnam, setting up a commercial colony alongside those of the Japanese and Chinese at Faifo (present-day Hoi An, p230). The Catholic Church eventually had a greater impact on Vietnam than on any country in Asia save the Philippines, which was ruled by the Spanish for 400 years.

LORDING IT OVER THE PEOPLE

Throughout the 17th and 18th centuries, Vietnam was divided between the Trinh Lords, who ruled in the North, and the Nguyen Lords, who controlled the South. The powerful Trinh failed in their persistent efforts to subdue the Nguyen, in part because their Portuguese weaponry was far inferior to the Dutch armaments supplied to the Nguyen. For their part, the Nguyen expanded southwards again, absorbing the Khmer territories of the Mekong Delta.

TAY SON REBELLION

In 1765 a rebellion erupted in the town of Tay Son near Qui Nhon. The Tay Son Rebels, as they were popularly known, were led by the brothers Nguyen who by 1773 controlled the whole of central Vietnam. In 1783 they captured Saigon from the Nguyen Lords and the rest of the South, killing the reigning prince and his family. Nguyen Lu became king of the South, while Nguyen Nhac was crowned king of central Vietnam.

Meanwhile, the Tay Son Rebels overthrew the Trinh Lords in the North. The Chinese moved in to take advantage of the power vacuum, provoking the third brother, Nguyen Hue, to proclaim himself Emperor Quang Trung. In 1789, Nguyen Hue's armed forces overwhelmingly defeated the Chinese army at Dong Da in another of the most celebrated military achievements in Vietnamese history.

DID YOU KNOW?

Saigon began life as humble Prey Nokor in the 16th century, a backwater of a Khmer village in what was then the eastern edge of Cambodia.

1428	1516
Le Loi's uprising brings victory over the Chinese	Portuguese traders land at Danang, sparking the start of European interest in Vietnam

In the South, Nguyen Anh, a rare survivor from the original Nguyen Lords – yes, there are a lot of Nguyens in Vietnamese history – gradually pushed back the rebels. In 1802, Nguyen Anh proclaimed himself Emperor Gia Long, thus beginning the Nguyen dynasty. When he captured Hanoi, his victory was complete and, for the first time in two centuries, Vietnam was united, with Hué as its new capital city.

THE LAST OF THE NGUYENS

Emperor Gia Long looked back to Confucian values to consolidate his shaky position. He appealed to the conservative elements of the elite, who had been undermined by the dizzying atmosphere of reform stirred up by the Tay Son Rebels.

Gia Long's son, Emperor Minh Mang, worked to strengthen the state. He was profoundly hostile to Catholicism, which he saw as a threat to Confucian traditions, and extended this antipathy to all Western influences.

The early Nguyen emperors continued the expansionist policies of the preceding dynasties, pushing into Cambodia and westward into the mountains along a wide front. They seized huge areas of Lao territory and clashed with Thailand for control of the lands of the fractured Khmer Empire.

DID YOU KNOW?

One of the most illustrious of the early missionaries was the brilliant French Jesuit Alexandre de Rhodes (1591–1660), widely lauded for his work in devising *quoc ngu*, the Latin-based phonetic alphabet in which Vietnamese is written to this day.

FRENCH RULE

France's military activity in Vietnam began in 1847, and after the Revolution of 1848 significant interest began to bubble. But over the next four decades the French colonial venture in Indochina was carried out haphazardly and without any preconceived plan. It repeatedly faltered and at times only the reckless adventures of a few mavericks kept it going.

In 1847 the French Navy attacked Danang harbour in response to Thieu Tri's suppression of Catholic missionaries. Saigon was seized in early 1859 and, in 1862, Emperor Tu Duc signed a treaty that gave the French the three eastern provinces of Cochinchina.

The next chapter in French colonisation began in 1872, when Jean Dupuis, a merchant seeking to supply salt and weapons to a Yunnanese general by sailing up the Red River, seized the Hanoi Citadel. Captain Francis Garnier, ostensibly dispatched to rein in Dupuis, instead took over where Dupuis left off and began a conquest of the north.

A few weeks after the death of Tu Duc in 1883, the French attacked Hué and imposed the Treaty of Protectorate on the imperial court. There then began a tragicomic struggle for royal succession that was notable for its palace coups, mysteriously dead emperors and heavy-handed French diplomacy.

The Indochinese Union proclaimed by the French in 1887 may have ended the existence of an independent Vietnamese state, but active resistance continued in various parts of the country for the duration of French rule. The expansionist era came to an end and the Vietnamese were forced to give back territory taken from Cambodia and Laos.

The French colonial authorities carried out ambitious public works, such as the construction of the Saigon–Hanoi railway, but to fund these activities the government taxed the peasants heavily, devastating the traditional rural economy. And since colonialism was supposed to be a profitable

1802	1883
Emperor Gia Long takes the throne and the Nguyen dynasty is born; it rules until 1945	The French impose the Treaty of Protectorate on the Vietnamese, marking the start of 70 years of colonial control

proposition, operations became notorious for the abysmal wages paid by the French and the subhuman treatment of Vietnamese workers. Out of the 45,000 indentured workers at one Michelin rubber plantation, 12,000 died of disease and malnutrition between 1917 and 1944.

VIETNAMESE ANTICOLONIALISM

Throughout the colonial period, the vast majority of Vietnamese retained a strong desire for independence. Seething nationalist aspirations often broke out into open defiance of the French, which ranged from the publishing of patriotic periodicals to an attempt to poison the French garrison in Hanoi.

The imperial court in Hué, although quite corrupt, was a centre of nationalist sentiment and the French orchestrated a game of musical thrones as one emperor after another turned against their patronage. This comical caper culminated in the accession of Emperor Bao Dai in 1925, who was just 12 years old at the time and studying in France!

Ultimately, the most successful of the anticolonialists were the communists, who were able to tune into the frustrations and aspirations of the population – especially the peasants – and effectively channel their demands for fairer land distribution.

The story of Vietnamese communism, which in many ways is also the political biography of Ho Chi Minh (see the boxed text opposite), is complicated. Keeping it simple, the first Marxist grouping in Indochina was the Vietnam Revolutionary Youth League, founded by Ho Chi Minh in Canton, China, in 1925. This was succeeded in February 1930 by the Vietnamese Communist Party. In 1941, Ho formed the League for the Independence of Vietnam, much better known as the Viet Minh, which resisted the Japanese and carried out extensive political activities during WWII. Despite its broad nationalist programme and claims to the contrary, the Viet Minh was, from its inception, dominated by Ho's communists.

WWII

When France fell to Nazi Germany in 1940, the Indochinese government of Vichy France collaborators acquiesced to the presence of Japanese troops in Vietnam. For their own convenience the Japanese left the French administration in charge of the day-to-day running of the country. The only group that did anything significant to resist the Japanese occupation was the Viet Minh.

A FALSE DAWN

By the spring of 1945 the Viet Minh controlled large parts of the country, particularly in the north. In mid-August, Ho Chi Minh formed the National Liberation Committee and called for a general uprising, later known as the August Revolution, to take advantage of the power vacuum. In central Vietnam, Bao Dai abdicated in favour of the new government, and in the South the Viet Minh soon held power in a shaky coalition with non-communist groups. On 2 September 1945, Ho Chi Minh declared independence at a rally in Hanoi's Ba Dinh Square. Throughout this period, Ho wrote no fewer than eight letters to US

1887	1925
The French proclaim the Indochinese Union, which sees active resistance by some Vietnamese	Ho Chi Minh establishes the Vietnam Revolutionary Youth League in Canton, later to morph into the Vietnamese Communist Party

UNCLE OF THE PEOPLE

Ho Chi Minh (Bringer of Light) is the best known of some 50 aliases assumed by Nguyen Tat Thanh (1890–1969) over the course of his long career. He was founder of the Vietnamese Communist Party and president of the Democratic Republic of Vietnam from 1946 until his death. Born the son of a fiercely nationalistic scholar-official of humble means, he was educated in the Quoc Hoc Secondary School in Hué.

In 1911, he signed on as a cook's apprentice on a French ship, sailing the seas to North America, Africa and Europe. He stopped off in Europe where, while working various jobs such as a gardener, snow sweeper, waiter, photo retoucher and stoker, his political consciousness began to develop.

Ho Chi Minh moved to Paris, where he adopted the name Nguyen Ai Quoc (Nguyen the Patriot). During this period, he mastered a number of languages (including English, French, German and Mandarin) and began to write about and debate the issue of Indochinese independence. During the 1919 Versailles Peace Conference, he tried to present an independence plan for Vietnam to US President Woodrow Wilson.

Ho Chi Minh was a founding member of the French Communist Party, which was established in 1920. In 1923 he was summoned to Moscow for training by Communist International and from there to Guangzhou (Canton), China, where he founded the Revolutionary Youth League of Vietnam.

During the early 1930s, the English rulers of Hong Kong obliged the French government by imprisoning Ho for his revolutionary activities in France, Indochina, China and Hong Kong. After his release, he travelled to the USSR and China. In 1941 Ho Chi Minh returned to Vietnam – for the first time in 30 years. That same year, at the age of 51, he helped found the Viet Minh, the goal of which was the independence of Vietnam from French colonial rule and Japanese occupation. In 1942 he was arrested and held for a year by the Nationalist Chinese. As Japan prepared to surrender in August 1945, Ho Chi Minh led the August Revolution, which took control of much of Vietnam.

The return of the French shortly thereafter forced Ho Chi Minh and the Viet Minh to flee Hanoi and take up armed resistance. Ho spent eight years conducting a guerrilla war until the Viet Minh's victory against the French at Dien Bien Phu in 1954. He led North Vietnam until his death in September 1969 – he never lived to see the North's victory over the South. Ho is affectionately referred to as 'Uncle Ho' (Bac Ho) by his admirers.

The party has worked hard to preserve the image of Bac Ho who, like his erstwhile nemesis South Vietnamese president Ngo Dinh Diem, never married. His image dominates contemporary Vietnam more than three decades after his death and no town is complete without a statue of Ho, no city complete without a museum in his name. This cult of personality is in stark contrast to the simplicity with which Ho lived his life.

However, a surprise spate of sensationalist stories published in Vietnamese newspapers during the early 1990s alleged that Ho had had numerous lovers, two wives – one French! – and a son born to a Tay minority woman. She later died in mysterious circumstances. Perhaps time will reveal the true story. For the fullest picture of Ho's legendary life, check out *Ho Chi Minh*, the excellent biography by William J Duiker.

The Vietnamese government has so far refused anyone permission to capitalise on Ho Chi Minh's name. A proposed American joint venture called 'Uncle Ho's Hamburgers' flew like a lead balloon, although Kentucky Fried Chicken successfully entered Vietnam. The Vietnamese joint-venture partner, however, was not amused when the American business rep pointed out that Ho Chi Minh does vaguely resemble Colonel Sanders. 'No' said the frowning Vietnamese, 'Ho Chi Minh was a general.'

1941	1945
Ho Chi Minh forms the Viet Minh	Ho Chi Minh proclaims Vietnamese independence on 2 September, but the French have other ideas

president Harry Truman and the US State Department asking for US aid, but received no replies.

A minor item on the agenda of the Potsdam Conference of 1945 was the disarming of Japanese occupation forces in Vietnam. It was decided that the Chinese Kuomintang would accept the Japanese surrender north of the 16th Parallel and that the British would do the same south of that line.

When the British arrived in Saigon, chaos reigned. Defeated Japanese troops were turned loose to help the Brits restore order and 1400 armed French paratroopers were also released from prison and immediately went on a rampage around the city, breaking into the homes and shops of the Vietnamese and indiscriminately clubbing men, women and children. The Viet Minh responded by calling a general strike and by launching a guerrilla campaign against the French. On 24 September, French general Jacques Philippe Leclerc arrived in Saigon, with the declaration 'We have come to reclaim our inheritance'. The end of the war had brought liberation for France, but not, it seemed, for its colonies.

In the north, Chinese Kuomintang troops were fleeing the Chinese communists and pillaging their way southward towards Hanoi. Ho tried to placate them, but as the months of Chinese occupation dragged on, he decided 'better the devil you know' and accepted a temporary return of the French. For the Vietnamese, even the French colonisers were better than the Chinese. The French were to stay for five years in return for recognising Vietnam as a free state within the French Union.

WAR WITH THE FRENCH

The French had managed to regain control of Vietnam, at least in name. But when the French shelled Hai Phong in November 1946, killing hundreds of civilians, the patience of the Viet Minh snapped. Only a few weeks later fighting broke out in Hanoi, marking the start of the Franco–Viet Minh War. Ho Chi Minh and his forces fled to the mountains, where they would remain for the next eight years.

In the face of determined Vietnamese nationalism, the French proved unable to reassert their control. Despite massive US aid and the existence of significant indigenous anti-communist elements, it was an unwinnable war. As Ho said to the French at the time, 'You can kill 10 of my men for every one I kill of yours, but even at those odds you will lose and I will win.'

After eight years of fighting, the Viet Minh controlled much of Vietnam and neighbouring Laos. On 7 May 1954, after a 57-day siege, more than 10,000 starving French troops surrendered to the Viet Minh at Dien Bien Phu (p155) – a catastrophic defeat that totally shattered France's remaining public support for the war. The following day, the Geneva Conference opened to negotiate an end to the conflict. Resolutions included an exchange of prisoners; the temporary division of Vietnam into two zones at the Ben Hai River (near the 17th Parallel); the free passage of people across the 17th Parallel for a period of 300 days; and the holding of nationwide elections on 20 July 1956. In the course of the Franco–Viet Minh War, more than 35,000 French fighters had been killed and 48,000 wounded; there are no exact numbers for Vietnamese casualties but they were certainly far higher.

DID YOU KNOW?

Between 1944 and 1945, the Viet Minh received funding and arms from the US Office of Strategic Services (OSS). When Ho Chi Minh declared independence in 1945, he had OSS agents at his side and borrowed liberally from the American Declaration of Independence. Such irony.

1946	1954
Fighting breaks out in Hanoi, marking the start of the Franco–Viet Minh War	French forces surrender en masse to Viet Minh fighters at Dien Bien Phu on 7 May, marking the end of colonial rule in Indochina

SOUTH VIETNAM

After the signing of the Geneva Accords, the South was ruled by a government led by Ngo Dinh Diem, a fiercely anticommunist Catholic. His power base was significantly strengthened by 900,000 refugees – many of them Catholics – who'd fled the communist North during the 300-day free-passage period.

During the first few years of his rule, Diem consolidated power fairly effectively, defeating the Binh Xuyen crime syndicate and the private armies of the Hoa Hao and Cao Dai religious sects. During Diem's 1957 official visit to the USA, President Eisenhower called him the 'miracle man' of Asia. As time went on Diem became increasingly tyrannical in dealing with dissent. Running the government became a family affair.

In the early 1960s, the South was rocked by anti-Diem unrest led by university students and Buddhist clergy, which included several highly publicised self-immolations by monks that shocked the world (see the boxed text 'Thien Mu Pagoda' p211). The US decided he was a liability and threw its support behind a military coup; in November 1963, Diem was overthrown and killed. He was followed by a succession of military rulers who continued his erratic policies.

NORTH VIETNAM

The Geneva Accords allowed the leadership of the Democratic Republic of Vietnam to return to Hanoi and assert control of all territory north of the 17th Parallel. The new government immediately set out to eliminate those elements of the population that threatened its power. Tens of thousands of 'landlords', some with only tiny holdings, were denounced to 'security committees' by envious neighbours and arrested. Hasty 'trials' resulted in between 10,000 and 15,000 executions and the imprisonment of thousands more. In 1956, the party, faced with serious rural unrest, recognised that things were out of control and began a Campaign for the Rectification of Errors.

THE NORTH-SOUTH WAR

The campaign to 'liberate' the South began in 1959. The Ho Chi Minh Trail, which had been in existence for several years, was expanded, and in April 1960 universal military conscription was implemented in the North. Eight months later, Hanoi announced the formation of the National Liberation Front (NLF), which came to be known, derogatorily, as the Viet Cong or the VC. Both are abbreviations for Viet Nam Cong San, which means Vietnamese communist. American soldiers nicknamed the VC 'Charlie'.

When the NLF campaign got under way, the military situation of the Diem government rapidly deteriorated. To turn things around, the Strategic Hamlets Program began in 1962, based on British tactics in Malaya, forcibly moving peasants into fortified 'strategic hamlets' in order to deny the VC bases of support. This programme was abandoned with the death of Diem, but years later the VC admitted that it had caused them major headaches.

And for the South it was no longer just a battle with the VC. In 1964 Hanoi began infiltrating regular North Vietnamese Army (NVA) units

DID YOU KNOW?

In May 1954, the Viet Minh dug a tunnel network under the French defences on Hill A1 and rigged it with explosives. Comrade Sapper Nguyen Van Bach volunteered himself as a human fuse in case the detonator failed. Luckily for him it didn't and he is honoured as a national hero.

DID YOU KNOW?

In Hanoi and the North, Ho Chi Minh created a very effective police state. The regime was characterised by ruthless police power; denunciations by a huge network of secret informers; and the blacklisting of dissidents, their children and their children's children.

1956	1960
Vietnam remains divided at the 17th Parallel into communist North Vietnam and 'free' South Vietnam	Civil war erupts in the south and the Ho Chi Minh Trail opens for business

into the South. By early 1965 the Saigon government was in desperate straits; desertions from the Army of the Republic of Vietnam (ARVN), whose command was notorious for corruption and incompetence, had reached 2000 per month. The South was losing a district capital each week, yet in 10 years only one senior South Vietnamese army officer had been wounded. The army was getting ready to evacuate Hué and Danang, and the central highlands seemed about to fall. It was clearly time for the Americans to 'clean up the mess'.

ENTER THE AMERICANS

The Americans saw France's colonial war in Indochina as an important part of a worldwide struggle against communist expansion. By 1954, US military aid to the French topped US$2 billion. In 1950, the US Military Assistance Advisory Group (MAAG) rocked into Vietnam, ostensibly to instruct local troops in the efficiency of US firepower; there would be American soldiers on Vietnamese soil for the next 25 years.

A decisive turning point in US strategy was precipitated by the August 1964 Tonkin Gulf Incident, in which two US destroyers, the *Maddox* and the *Turner Joy*, claimed to have come under 'unprovoked' attack while sailing off the North Vietnamese coast. Subsequent research indicates that there was plenty of provocation; the first attack took place while the *Maddox* was in North Vietnamese waters assisting a secret South Vietnamese commando raid and the second one never happened.

However, on US President Johnson's orders, 64 sorties rained bombs on the North – the first of thousands of such missions that would hit every single road and rail bridge in the country, as well as 4000 of North Vietnam's 5788 villages. Two US aircraft were lost and the pilot of one, Lieutenant Everett Alvarez, became the first American prisoner of war (POW) of the conflict; he would remain in captivity for eight years.

A few days later, an indignant (and misled) US Congress overwhelmingly passed the Tonkin Gulf Resolution, which gave the president the power to 'take all necessary measures' to 'repel any armed attack against the forces of the United States and to prevent further aggression'. Until its repeal in 1970, the resolution was treated by US presidents as carte blanche to do whatever they chose in Vietnam without any congressional control.

As the military situation of the Saigon government reached a new nadir, the first US combat troops splashed ashore at Danang in March 1965. By December 1965, there were 184,300 US military personnel in Vietnam and 636 Americans had died. By December 1967, there were 485,600 US soldiers in the country and 16,021 had died. There were 1.3 million men fighting for the Saigon government, including the South Vietnamese and other allies.

By 1966 the buzz words in Washington were 'pacification', 'search and destroy' and 'free-fire zones'. Pacification involved building a pro-government civilian infrastructure in each village, and soldiers to guard it. To protect the villages from VC raids, mobile search and destroy units of soldiers moved around the country hunting VC guerrillas. In some cases, villagers were evacuated so the Americans could use heavy weaponry like napalm and tanks in areas that were declared free-fire zones.

OK, so we are recommending it in every shape and size (p15), but the 2002 remake of *The Quiet American*, starring Michael Caine, is a must. Beautifully shot, it is a classic introduction to Vietnam in the 1950s, as the French disengaged and the Americans moved in to take their place.

DID YOU KNOW?

The USA closed its consulate in Hanoi on 12 December 1955 and would not officially reopen an embassy in the Vietnamese capital for more than 40 years.

1962	1963
The Strategic Hamlets Program is initiated in order to deny the Viet Cong support systems	South Vietnam's president Ngo Dinh Diem is overthrown and killed in a coup backed by the USA

TRACKING THE WAR

The American war in Vietnam was *the story* for a generation. Follow in the footsteps of soldiers, journalists and politicians on all sides with a visit to the sites where the story unfolded.

- **China Beach** (p226) The strip of sand near Danang where US soldiers dropped in for some rest and relaxation.
- **Cu Chi Tunnels** (p369) The Vietnamese dug an incredible and elaborate tunnel network to evade American forces, just 30km from Saigon and right under the noses of a US base.
- **Demilitarised Zone** (p190) The no-man's land at the 17th Parallel dividing North and South Vietnam from 1954 soon became one of the most heavily militarised zones in the world.
- **Dien Bien Phu** (p155) The ultimate battle site, where the French colonial story came to a close in May 1954.
- **Ho Chi Minh Trail** (p194) The supply route for the South; the North Vietnamese moved men and munitions down this incredible trail through the Truong Son Mountains in an almost unparalleled logistical feat.
- **Hué Citadel** (p203) The ancient citadel was razed to the ground in street-to-street fighting in early 1968 when the Americans retook the city from the communists after a three-week occupation.
- **Khe Sanh** (p194) This was the biggest diversion of the war, as the North Vietnamese massed forces around this US base in 1968 to draw attention away from the coming Tet Offensive.
- **Long Tan Memorial** The Australian contingent who fought in Vietnam, mostly based near Vung Tau in the south, is remembered at this moving memorial. The Long Tan Memorial Cross was erected by Australian survivors of a fierce 1967 battle. The original is now in Bien Hoa Military Museum. The Vietnamese erected a memorial cross in 2002, but you need to arrange a permit to visit (for more details see www.diggerhistory.info/pages-memorials/longtan.htm).
- **My Lai** (p252) The village of My Lai is infamous as the site of one of the worst atrocities in the war, when American GIs massacred hundreds of villagers in March 1968.
- **Vinh Moc Tunnels** (p191) The real deal, these tunnels haven't been surgically enlarged for tourists and mark yet another feat of infrastructural ingenuity.

These strategies were only partially successful: US forces could control the countryside only by day, while the VC usually controlled it by night. Although lacking heavy weapons, VC guerrillas continued to inflict heavy casualties in ambushes and by using mines and booby traps. Although free-fire zones were supposed to prevent civilian casualties, plenty of villagers were nevertheless shelled, bombed, strafed or napalmed to death – their surviving relatives soon signed up to join the VC.

THE TURNING POINT

In January 1968 North Vietnamese troops launched a major attack at Khe Sanh in the Demilitarised Zone. This battle, the single largest of the war, was in part a massive diversion for what was to follow one week later: the Tet Offensive.

The Tet Offensive marked a decisive turning point in the war. On the evening of 31 January, as the country celebrated the Lunar New Year, the VC launched a stunning offensive in more than 100 cities and towns,

1964	1965
The US bombs North Vietnam for the first time	The first US marines wade ashore at Danang

Neil Sheehan's account of the life of Colonel John Paul Vann, *Bright Shining Lie*, won the Pulitzer Prize and is the portrayal of one man's disenchantment with the war, mirroring America's realisation it could not be won.

including Saigon. As the TV cameras rolled, a VC commando team took over the courtyard of the US embassy in central Saigon.

US forces had long been itching to engage the VC in open battle and the Tet Offensive delivered. Although taken by complete surprise – a major failure of US military intelligence – the South Vietnamese and Americans immediately counterattacked with massive firepower, bombing and shelling heavily populated cities as they had the open jungle. The effect was devastating on the VC, but also on the civilian population. In Ben Tre, a US officer bitterly explained that they 'had to destroy the town in order to save it'.

The Tet Offensive killed about 1000 US soldiers and 2000 ARVN troops, but VC losses were more than 10 times higher, at around 32,000 deaths. In addition, some 500 American and 10,000 North Vietnamese troops had died at the battle of Khe Sanh a week before.

If the VC lost the battle, they were far from losing the war. After years of hearing that they were winning, many Americans – having watched the killing and chaos in Saigon beamed into their living rooms – stopped believing the hype. While US generals were proclaiming a great victory, public tolerance of the war and its casualties reached breaking point. For the VC the Tet Offensive ultimately proved a success – it made the cost of fighting the war unbearable for the Americans.

Simultaneously, stories began leaking out of Vietnam about atrocities and massacres carried out against unarmed Vietnamese civilians, including the infamous My Lai Massacre (p253). This helped turn the tide and a coalition of the conscientious emerged that threatened the establishment. Antiwar demonstrations rocked American university campuses and spilled onto the streets.

Hitch a ride with Michael Herr and his seminal work *Dispatches*. A correspondent for *Rolling Stone* magazine, Herr tells it how it is as some of the darkest events of the American War unfold around him, including the siege of Khe Sanh.

NIXON & HIS DOCTRINE

Richard Nixon was elected president in part because of a promise that he had a 'secret plan' to end the war. The Nixon Doctrine, as it was called, was unveiled in July 1969 and it called on Asian nations to be more 'self-reliant' in defence matters. Nixon's strategy called for 'Vietnamisation', which meant making the South Vietnamese fight the war without US troops.

Nixon Doctrine or not, the first half of 1969 saw yet greater escalation of the conflict. In April the number of US soldiers in Vietnam reached an all-time high of 543,400. While the fighting raged, Nixon's chief negotiator, Henry Kissinger, pursued talks in Paris with his North Vietnamese counterpart Le Duc Tho.

In 1969 the Americans began secretly bombing Cambodia and the following year US ground forces were sent into Cambodia to extricate ARVN units, whose fighting ability was still unable to match the enemy's. The North Vietnamese moved deeper into Cambodian territory and together with their Khmer Rouge allies controlled half of the country by the summer of 1970.

The American War in Vietnam claimed the lives of countless journalists. For a look at the finest photographic work from the battlefront, *Requiem* is an anthology of work from fallen correspondents on all sides of the conflict and a fitting tribute to their trade.

This new escalation provoked yet more bitter antiwar protests. A peace demonstration at Kent State University in Ohio resulted in four protesters being shot dead by National Guard troops. The rise of organisations like Vietnam Veterans Against the War demonstrated that

1967	1968
By December there are 1.3 million soldiers fighting for the South; nearly half a million of these are US soldiers	The Viet Cong launch the Tet Offensive, an attack on towns and cities throughout the South that catches the Americans unaware

it wasn't just 'cowardly students fearing military conscription' who wanted the USA out of Vietnam. It was clear that the war was ripping America apart.

In the spring of 1972 the North Vietnamese launched an offensive across the 17th Parallel; the USA responded with increased bombing of the North and by laying mines in North Vietnam's harbours. The 'Christmas bombing' of Hai Phong and Hanoi at the end of 1972 was meant to wrest concessions from North Vietnam at the negotiating table. Eventually, the Paris Peace Accords were signed by the USA, North Vietnam, South Vietnam and the VC on 27 January 1973, which provided for a cease-fire, the total withdrawal of US combat forces and the release of 590 American POWs. The agreement made no mention of approximately 200,000 North Vietnamese troops then in South Vietnam.

In total, 3.14 million Americans (including 7200 women) served in the US armed forces in Vietnam during the war. Officially, 58,183 Americans were killed in action or are listed as missing in action (MIA). Pentagon figures indicate that by 1972, 3689 fixed-wing aircraft and 4857 helicopters had been lost and 15 million tonnes of ammunition had been expended. The direct cost of the war was officially put at US$165 billion, though its real cost to the economy was double that or more.

By the end of 1973, 223,748 South Vietnamese soldiers had been killed in action; North Vietnamese and VC fatalities have been estimated at one million. Approximately four million civilians (or 10% of the Vietnamese population) were injured or killed during the war, many of them in the North as a result of US bombing. At least 300,000 Vietnamese and 2200 Americans are still listed as MIA (see the boxed text 'Missing in Action' p191).

The ultimate American War movie has to be *Apocalypse Now*. Marlon Brando plays renegade Colonel Kurtz who has gone AWOL, and native, in the wilds of northeast Cambodia. Martin Sheen is sent to bring him back and the psychotic world into which he is drawn is one of the most savage indictments of war ever seen on screen.

OTHER FOREIGN INVOLVEMENT

Australia, New Zealand, South Korea, the Philippines and Thailand also sent military personnel to South Vietnam as part of what the Americans called the 'Free World Military Forces', whose purpose was to help internationalise the American war effort and thus confer upon it some legitimacy. Sound familiar?

Australia's participation in the conflict constituted the most significant commitment of its military forces since the 1940s. Overall, 46,852 Australian military personnel served in the war; the Australian casualties totalled 496 dead and 2398 wounded.

Most of New Zealand's contingent, which numbered 548 at its high point in 1968, operated as an integral part of the Australian Task Force, which was stationed near Baria, just north of Vung Tau.

For a human perspective on the North Vietnamese experience during the war, read *The Sorrow of War* by Bao Ninh, a poignant tale of love and loss that shows the soldiers from the North had the same fears and desires as most American GIs.

THE FALL OF THE SOUTH

Apart from a small contingent of technicians and CIA agents, all US military personnel had departed Vietnam by 1973. The bombing of North Vietnam had ceased and the US POWs were released, but the war raged on – the only difference was that the South Vietnamese were fighting alone.

In January 1975 the North Vietnamese launched a massive ground attack across the 17th Parallel using tanks and heavy artillery. The invasion

1973	1975
All sides put pen to paper to sign the Paris Peace Accords on 27 January 1973	On 30th April 1975, Saigon falls to the North Vietnamese and is renamed Ho Chi Minh City

> **INNOCENT VICTIMS OF THE WAR**
>
> One tragic legacy of the American War was the plight of thousands of Amerasians. Marriages, relationships and prostitution between Americans and Vietnamese were common during the war. But when the Americans headed home, often they abandoned their 'wives' and mistresses, leaving them to raise children who were half-American or half-Vietnamese in a society not particularly tolerant of such racial intermingling.
>
> After reunification, the Amerasians – living reminders of the American presence – were often mistreated by Vietnamese and even abandoned, forcing them to live on the streets. They were also denied educational and vocational opportunities, and were sadly referred to as 'children of the dust'.
>
> At the end of the 1980s, the Orderly Departure Program (ODP) was designed to allow for the orderly resettlement in the West (mostly in the USA) of Amerasians and political refugees who otherwise might have tried to flee the country by land or sea.
>
> Unfortunately, many Amerasian children were adopted by Vietnamese eager to emigrate, but were then dumped after the family's arrival in the USA. **Asian American LEAD** (☎ 202-518 6737; www.aalead.org; 1323 Girard St NW, Washington, DC 20009, USA) is an organisation that has been doing fine work training and mentoring Amerasian kids as they adapt to life in the USA.

panicked the South Vietnamese army, which had always depended on the Americans. In March, the NVA occupied a strategic section of the central highlands at Buon Ma Thuot. South Vietnam's president, Nguyen Van Thieu, decided on a strategy of tactical withdrawal to more defensible positions. This proved to be a spectacular military blunder.

Whole brigades of ARVN soldiers disintegrated and fled southward, joining hundreds of thousands of civilians clogging Hwy 1. City after city – Hué, Danang, Quy Nhon, Nha Trang – were simply abandoned with hardly a shot fired. So quickly did the ARVN troops flee that the North Vietnamese army could barely keep up.

Nguyen Van Thieu, in power since 1967, resigned on 21 April 1975 and fled the country, allegedly taking with him millions of dollars in ill-gotten wealth. The North Vietnamese pushed on to Saigon and on the morning of 30 April 1975 tanks smashed through the gates of Saigon's Independence Palace (now called Reunification Palace). General Duong Van Minh, president for just 42 hours, formally surrendered, marking the end of the war.

Just a few hours before the surrender the last Americans were evacuated by helicopter from the US embassy roof to ships stationed just offshore. Thus more than a decade of American military involvement came to a close. Throughout the entire episode, the USA never actually declared war on North Vietnam.

The Americans weren't the only ones who left. As the South collapsed, 135,000 Vietnamese also fled the country; in the next five years, at least 545,000 of their compatriots would do the same. Those who left by sea would become known to the world as 'boat people'.

Mostly neglected by writers is the painful experience of the fatherless Amerasian children left behind in Vietnam after 1975. The sordid tale is told in unforgettable detail in *Vietnamerica* by Thomas Bass.

REUNIFICATION

On the first day of their victory, the communists changed Saigon's name to Ho Chi Minh City (HCMC). That proved to be only the first of many changes.

1978	1979
Vietnam invades Cambodia on Christmas Day, overthrowing the Khmer Rouge government	China invades northern Vietnam in February to 'punish' the Vietnamese for attacking Cambodia

The sudden success of the 1975 North Vietnamese offensive surprised the North almost as much as it did the South. As a result, Hanoi had no specific plans to deal with the integration of the two parts of the country, which had totally different social and economic systems.

The North was faced with the legacy of a cruel and protracted war that had literally fractured the country; there were high levels of understandable bitterness on both sides, and a mind-boggling array of problems. Damage from the fighting extended from unmarked minefields to war-focused, dysfunctional economies; from a chemically poisoned countryside to a population who had been physically or mentally battered. Peace may have arrived but in many ways the war was far from over.

Until the formal reunification of Vietnam in July 1976, the South was ruled by the Provisional Revolutionary Government. The Communist Party did not trust the Southern urban intelligentsia, so large numbers of Northern cadres were sent southward to manage the transition. This fuelled resentment among Southerners who had worked against the Thieu government and then, after its overthrow, found themselves frozen out.

A rapid transition to socialism in the South was the adopted policy, but it proved disastrous for the South's economy. Reunification was accompanied by widespread political repression. Despite repeated promises to the contrary, hundreds of thousands of people who had ties to the previous regime had their property confiscated and were rounded up and imprisoned without trial in forced-labour camps, euphemistically known as re-education camps. Tens of thousands of businesspeople, intellectuals, artists, journalists, writers, union leaders and religious leaders – some of whom had opposed both Thieu and the war – were held in horrendous conditions.

Contrary to its economic policy, Vietnam sought some sort of *rapprochement* with the USA and by 1978 Washington was close to re-establishing relations with Hanoi. But the China card was ultimately played: Vietnam was sacrificed for the prize of US relations with Beijing and Hanoi was pushed into the arms of the Soviet Union, on whom it was to rely for the next decade.

Relations with China to the north and its Khmer Rouge allies to the west were rapidly deteriorating and war-weary Vietnam seemed beset by enemies. An anticapitalist campaign was launched in March 1978, seizing private property and businesses. Most of the victims were ethnic-Chinese – hundreds of thousands soon became refugees and relations with China soured further.

Meanwhile, repeated attacks on Vietnamese border villages by the Khmer Rouge forced Vietnam to respond. Vietnamese forces entered Cambodia on Christmas Day 1978. They succeeded in driving the Khmer Rouge from power in 1979 and set up a pro-Hanoi regime in Phnom Penh. China viewed the attack on the Khmer Rouge as a serious provocation. In February 1979, Chinese forces invaded Vietnam and fought a brief, 17-day war before withdrawing (see the boxed text 'Neighbouring Tensions' p140).

Author and documentary filmmaker John Pilger was ripping into the establishment long before Michael Moore rode into town. Get to grips with his hard-hitting views on the American War at http://pilger.carlton .com/vietnam.

Oliver Stone has never been one to shy away from political point-scoring and in the first of his famous trilogy about Vietnam, *Platoon*, he earns dix points. A brutal and cynical look at the conflict through the eyes of rookie Charlie Sheen, with great performances from Tom Berenger and Willem Dafoe.

OPENING THE DOOR

The relatively recent liberalisation of foreign investment laws and the relaxation of visa regulations for tourists are part of a general opening up of Vietnam to the world.

1986	1989
Doi moi (economic reforms), the first step towards re-engaging with the West, are launched	Vietnamese forces pull out of Cambodia and Vietnam is at peace for the first time in decades

The USSR began its first cautious opening to the West in 1984 and Vietnam followed suit in 1986 by choosing reform-minded Nguyen Van Linh to lead the Vietnamese Communist Party. However, dramatic changes in Eastern Europe and the USSR were not viewed with favour in Hanoi. The party denounced the participation of non-communists in Eastern Bloc governments, calling the democratic revolutions 'a counter-attack from imperialist circles' against socialism.

Relations with Vietnam's old nemesis, the USA, have improved over the last decade. In early 1994, the USA finally lifted its economic embargo, which had been in place since the 1960s. Full diplomatic relations with the USA have been restored and Bill Clinton, who didn't fight in the war (and didn't inhale!), became the first US president to visit northern Vietnam in 2000.

Relations have also improved with the historic enemy China, and trade and tourism are booming. Vietnam is an active member of Asean, an organisation originally established as a bulwark against communism, and this is all adding up to a rosy economic picture. The future is bright, but ultimate success depends on how well the Vietnamese can follow the Chinese road to development: economic liberalisation without political liberalisation. With only two million paid-up members of the Communist Party and 80 million Vietnamese, it is a road they must tread carefully.

1995	2000
Vietnam joins the Association of South-East Asian Nations (Asean)	Bill Clinton visits Vietnam and becomes the first American president to set foot in Hanoi

The Culture

THE NATIONAL PSYCHE

The Vietnamese have been shaped by their history, which is littered with the scars of battles against enemies old and new. The Chinese have been the traditional threat and the proximity of this northern giant has cast a long shadow over Vietnam and its people. They respect but fear China, and in the context of 2000 years of history, the French and the Americans are but a niggling annoyance that were duly dispatched. The Vietnamese are battle-hardened, proud and nationalist, as they have earned their stripes in successive skirmishes with the world's mightiest powers.

But that's the older generation, who remember every inch of the territory for which they fought and every bomb and bullet that rained upon them during the long, hard years. For the new generation, Vietnam is a different place: a place to succeed, a place to ignore the rigid structures set in stone by the communists, and a place to go out and have a good time. While Uncle Ho is respected and revered across the generations for his dedication to the national cause, the young are more into David Beckham's latest haircut than the party's latest pronouncements.

It is not only young and old who are living a life apart, but also the urban and rural populations, and the rich and poor. Communism is dead; long live the one-party capitalist dictatorship where survival of the fittest is the name of the game. Some have survived the transition better than others, and this has created strains in the shape of rural revolts and political backlash. One of the great ironies of the Vietnamese revolution is that it strove to impose a communist system on a people seemingly born with a commercial gene, a competitive instinct to do business and to do it at any hour of the day or night. To the Vietnamese, business, work, commerce – call it what you like – is life.

Finally, don't forget 'face' – or more importantly the art of not making the locals lose face. Face is all in Asia, and in Vietnam it is above all. Having 'big face' is synonymous with prestige, and prestige is particularly important in Vietnam. All families, even poor ones, are expected to have big wedding parties and throw their money around like it is water in order to gain face. This is often ruinously expensive but far less important than 'losing face'. And it is for this reason that foreigners should never lose their tempers with the Vietnamese; this will bring unacceptable 'loss of face' to the individual involved and end any chance of a sensible solution to the dispute.

LIFESTYLE

Traditionally, Vietnamese life has revolved around family, fields and faith, the rhythm of rural existence continuing for centuries at the same pace. For the majority of the population still living in the countryside, these constants have remained unchanged, with several generations sharing the same roof, the same rice and the same religion. But in recent decades these rhythms have been rocked to the core by war and ideology, as the peasants were dragged from all they held dear to defend their motherland, and later herded into cooperatives as the party tried to take over as the moral and social beacon in the lives of the people.

The party failed to move the masses in the post-war period. Communism only converted a few, just as the French and Americans had only corrupted a few before it, and, for the majority, it was to the familiar

Shadows and Wind (1999) by journalist Robert Templer is a snappily written exploration of contemporary Vietnam, from Ho Chi Minh personality cults to Vietnam's rock-and-roll youth.

For an in-depth insight into the culture of Vietnam, including fashion, film and music, check out www.thingsasian.com.

they looked to define their lives. But this is beginning to change and it's not due to Uncle Ho (Chi Minh) or Tricky Dicky (Nixon), but to a combination of a population shift from the countryside to the cities and a demographic shift from old to young.

Like Singapore and Thailand before it, Vietnam is experiencing its very own '60s swing, as the younger generation stand up for a different lifestyle than that of their parents. This is creating plenty of feisty friction in the cities, as sons and daughters dress as they like, date who they want and hit the town until all hours. But few live on their own and they still come home to mum and dad at the end of the day, where arguments might arise, particularly about marriage and settling down.

Extended family is important to the Vietnamese and that includes second or third cousins, the sort of family that many Westerners may not even realise they have. The extended family comes together during times of trouble and times of joy, celebrating festivals and successes, mourning deaths or disappointments. This is a source of strength for many of the older generation, while for the younger generation it's likely to be friends, girlfriends or gangs who are more important.

With so many family members under one roof, the Vietnamese don't share Western concepts of privacy and personal space. Don't be surprised if people walk into your hotel room without knocking. You may be sitting starkers in your hotel room when the maid unlocks the door and walks in unannounced.

DID YOU KNOW?

Failing businesses often call in a geomancer (feng shui expert). Sometimes the solution is to move a door or a window. If this doesn't do the trick, it might be necessary to move an ancestor's grave. Distraught spirits may have to be placated with payments of cash.

DO THE RIGHT THING!

Dress Code
Respect local dress standards, particularly at religious sites. Always remove your shoes before entering a temple. Nude sunbathing is considered *totally* inappropriate, even on beaches.

Meet & Greet
The traditional Vietnamese form of greeting is to press your hands together in front of your body and bow slightly. These days, the Western custom of shaking hands has almost completely taken over.

It's on the Cards
Exchanging business cards is an important part of even the smallest transaction or business contact. Get some printed before you arrive in Vietnam and hand them out like confetti.

Deadly Chopsticks
Leaving a pair of chopsticks sitting vertically in a rice bowl looks very much like the incense sticks that are burned for the dead. This is a powerful sign and is not appreciated anywhere in Asia.

Mean Feet
Like the Chinese and Japanese, Vietnamese strictly maintain clean floors and it's usual to remove shoes when entering somebody's home. It's rude to point the bottom of your feet towards other people. Never, ever point your feet towards anything sacred, such as a Buddha image.

Hats Off to Them
As a form of respect to elderly or other esteemed people, such as monks, take off your hat and bow your head politely when addressing them. In Asia, the head is the symbolic highest point – never pat or touch an adult on the head.

As in many parts of Asia, Vietnamese women take a lot of pain for little gain, with plenty of hard work to do and little authority at the decision-making level. Vietnamese women were highly successful as guerrillas in the American War and brought plenty of grief to US soldiers. After the war, their revolutionary contributions were given much fanfare, but all the important government posts were given to men. In the countryside, you'll see women doing backbreaking jobs, such as crushing rocks at construction sites and carrying baskets weighing 60kg. It's doubtful that many Western men would be capable of such strenuous activity.

The country's two-children-per-family policy is boosting the independence of Vietnamese women, and more are delaying marriage to get an education. Around 50% of university students are female, but they're not always given the same opportunity as males to shine after graduation.

One of the sadder realities of the recent opening up to the West has been the influx of pimps posing as 'talent scouts'. Promises of lucrative jobs in developed countries are dangled in front of naive Vietnamese women who later find themselves enslaved as prostitutes. The trafficking of poor, rural women into the sex industry in Cambodia has been a huge problem and in many cases this involves the connivance of family members selling one of their daughters for the rest to survive.

The Vietnamese consider pale skin to be beautiful. On sunny days, trendy Vietnamese women can often be seen strolling under the shade of an umbrella in order to keep from tanning. Women who work in the fields will go to great lengths to preserve their pale skin by wrapping their faces in towels and wearing long-sleeved shirts, elbow-length silk gloves and conical hats. To tell a Vietnamese woman that she has white skin is a great compliment; telling her that she has a 'lovely suntan' is a grave insult.

One tradition that remains central to Vietnamese life is geomancy, or 'feng shui' as most of us know it today. Known as *phong thuy* to the locals, this is the art (or science) of living in tune with the environment. The orientation of houses, tombs, *dinh* (communal meeting halls) and pagodas is determined by geomancers. The location of an ancestor's grave is an especially serious matter: if the grave is in the wrong spot or facing the wrong way, there's no telling what trouble the spirits might cause. Ditto for the location of the family altar, which can be found in nearly every Vietnamese home.

POPULATION

Vietnam's population hovers at nearly 83 million, making it the 13th most populous country in the world, and with its population growth rate it might soon make the top ten. Vietnam is a young country, with an incredible 65% of the population under the age of 30, and after years of revolutionary initiatives encouraging large families, a two-child policy is now enforced in urban areas.

Traditionally a rural agrarian society, the race is on for the move to the cities. Like Thailand and Malaysia before it, Vietnam is experiencing a tremendous shift in the balance of population, as increasing numbers of young people desert the fields in search of those mythical streets paved with gold in Hanoi or Ho Chi Minh City (HCMC). The population of HCMC and its suburbs is already approaching six million, Hanoi has more than three million, and both Danang and Hai Phong are millionaires. As economic migrants continue to seek their fortune, these numbers look set to soar.

For a look at the impact of *doi moi* (economic reform) on some Vietnamese women, Vu Xuan Hung's film *Misfortune's End* (1996) tells the tale of a silk weaver deserted by her husband for an upwardly mobile businesswoman.

DID YOU KNOW?

Vietnamese who have emigrated are called Viet Kieu. They have traditionally been maligned by locals as cowardly, arrogant and privileged. In the '90s, returning Viet Kieu were often followed by police but now official policy is to welcome them, and their money, back to the motherland.

THE PEOPLE OF VIETNAM

Vietnamese culture and civilisation have been profoundly influenced by the Chinese, and to many observers of Vietnamese history, China has long treated Vietnam as some sort of renegade province rather than an independent entity. However, the Vietnamese existed as a people in the Red River Delta region long before the first waves of Chinese arrived more than 2000 years ago.

However, history has influenced the mix of Vietnamese minorities. The steady expansion southwards in search of cultivable lands absorbed first the Kingdom of Champa and later the eastern extent of the Khmer empire, and both the Chams and the Khmers are sizeable minorities today. There are perhaps one million Khmers inhabiting the Mekong Delta, or what they refer to as Kampuchea Krom (lower Cambodia), and almost as many Chams living along the coastal regions between Phan Rang and Danang.

Traffic was not only one way. Many of the 50 or more ethno-linguistic minority groups that inhabit the far northwest only migrated to these areas from Yunnan (China) and Tibet in the last two centuries. They moved into the mountains that the lowland Vietnamese considered uncultivable and help make up the most colourful part of the ethnic mosaic that is Vietnam today.

While the invasions and occupations of old may be over, the largest minority group in Vietnam has always been the ethnic-Chinese community, which makes up much of the commercial class in the cities. While the current government has traditionally viewed them with suspicion, and drove many of them out of the country as 'boat people' in the late 1970s, many are now comfortably resettled and play a major part in driving economic development.

The Hill Tribes

While the ethnic-Vietnamese and ethnic-Chinese live mainly in urban centres and coastal areas, the remaining 10% of Vietnam's population live primarily in the high country. While some of these minorities number as many as a million people, others are feared to have dwindled to as few as 100.

Most hill-tribe communities are seminomadic, cultivating crops such as 'dry' rice and using slash-and-burn methods, which have taken a heavy

---

ONG TAY & BA TAY

The main reason that children shout *ong tay!* (Mr Westerner) and *ba tay!* (Mrs Westerner) at white Westerners is similar to why people tap on aquarium fish tanks: they want to be recognised by an exotic being and provoke some kind of reaction. This is particularly the case in remote areas. Often, children will unabashedly come up to you and pull the hair on your arms or legs or dare each other to touch your skin.

In the past, the term *lien xo!* (Soviet Union) was often shouted at Westerners, all of whom were assumed to be the legendary and very unpopular Russians residing in Vietnam.

In the markets, vendors may try to woo you by calling you *dong chi!* (comrade) on the assumption that you will find this a kindred term of endearment. Depending on your age and how sloppy you look, a more common name you may be called behind your back is *tay balo!* (literally, 'Westerner backpack'), a relatively recent term for scruffy-looking backpackers.

If you are cycling, you may also hear people call *tay di xe dap* at you, which means 'Westerner travelling by bicycle'. Until recently, locals have only been used to seeing foreigners travelling in Citroëns, Jeeps, Volgas and Toyotas.

toll on the environment. The government has been trying to encourage the hill tribes to adopt standard agriculture at lower altitudes, but a long history of independence coupled with a general distrust of the ethnic-Vietnamese majority keeps many away from the lowlands.

As in other parts of Asia, the culture of Vietnam's ethnic minorities is gradually giving way to a variety of outside influences. While factors such as the introduction of electricity, modern medicine and education improve the standard of living, they have also contributed to the abandonment of many age-old traditions.

A more recent, and perhaps equally threatening, outside influence is tourism. It has resulted in some children, particularly in Sapa, expecting hand-outs of money or sweets. Worse, domestic tourism has created a market for karaoke, massage and sex, and in some areas unscrupulous ethnic-Vietnamese are luring minority women into this trade.

Vietnam's hill-tribe minorities have substantial autonomy and, though the official national language is Vietnamese, children still learn their local languages (see the Language chapter on p497 for useful phrases). Hanoi is far away and it seems that if the Montagnards don't interfere with the political agenda, they can live as they please. But if they choose to interfere, it's a different story, as the harsh suppression of demonstrations in the central highlands during 2001 and 2002 over language rights in schools and against the Vietnamisation of their culture, showed.

While there may be no official discrimination system, cultural prejudice against hill-tribe people helps ensure they remain at the bottom of the educational and economic ladder.

DID YOU KNOW?

The French dubbed the hill-tribe peoples 'Montagnards' (highlanders or mountain people). The Vietnamese generally refer to them as *moi*, a derogatory term that means 'savages', which unfortunately reflects all-too-common attitudes.

BAHNAR

The Bahnar are believed to have migrated long ago to the central highlands (p316) from the coast. They are animists and worship trees such as the banyan and ficus. The Bahnar keep their own traditional calendar, which calls for 10 months of cultivation, with the remaining two months set aside for social and personal duties such as marriage, weaving, ceremonies and festivals. They wear similar dress to the Jarai.

DZAO

The Dzao (or Zao/Dao) are one of the most colourful of Vietnam's ethnic groups and live in the northwestern provinces (p160) near China and Laos. The Dzao practise ancestor worship of spirits or 'Ban Ho' (no relation to Uncle Ho!) and hold elaborate rituals with sacrifices of animals.

The Dzao are famous for their elaborate dress. Women's clothing typically features intricate weaving and silver-coloured beads and coins – the wealth of a woman is said to be in the weight of coins she carries. Their long flowing hair, shaved above the forehead, is tied up into a large red turban.

H'MONG

Since migrating from China in the 19th century, the H'mong have grown to become one of the largest ethnic groups in Vietnam. Numbering around half a million, they are spread across the far north, but most visitors will run into them in Sapa (p160) or Bac Ha (p168). The H'mong are animists, and worship spirits.

The H'mong live at high altitudes and cultivate dry rice and medicinal plants (including opium), and raise animals. There are several groups within the H'mong, including Black, White, Red, Green and Flower, each of which has its own subtle dress code. One of the most recognisable are

For a lavish introduction to the landscapes of the northwest, check out *The Colours of Sapa*, a photographic portrait of the incredible people and breathtaking scenery around this old French hill station.

To get up close and personal with the north-western hill tribes, Tim Doling's *Mountains and Ethnic Minorities: North West Vietnam*, available in most Hanoi bookshops, is an essential companion for a tour of the region.

the Black H'mong, who wear indigo-dyed linen clothing, with women typically wearing skirts, aprons, retro leggings and cylindrical hats. The Flower H'mong women wear extroverted outfits, with bright rainbow banding and '70s-style sequins from head to toe. Many H'mong women wear large silver necklaces, earrings and clusters of silver bracelets.

JARAI
The Jarai are the most populous minority in the central highlands, numbering about 200,000 people, many living around Pleiku (p313). Jarai women typically propose marriage to men through a matchmaker, who delivers the prospective groom a copper bracelet. Animistic beliefs and rituals still abound, and the Jarai pay respect to their ancestors and nature through a host or *yang* (genie).

Perhaps more than any of Vietnam's other hill tribes, the Jarai are renowned for their indigenous musical instruments, from stringed 'gongs' to bamboo tubes, which act as wind flutes and percussion. Jarai women typically wear sleeveless indigo blouses and long skirts.

MUONG
Mainly concentrated in Hoa Binh province (p149), the male-dominated Muong live in small stilt-house hamlets. Though their origins lie close to the ethnic-Vietnamese, the Muong have a culture similar to the Thai.

They are known for producing folk literature, poems and songs, much of which have been translated into Vietnamese. Musical instruments such as the gong, drums, pan pipes, flutes and two-stringed violin are popular. Muong women wear long skirts and short blouses, while the men traditionally wear indigo tops and trousers.

NUNG
The Nung, numbering about 700,000, inhabit the far northeastern provinces near the Chinese border. From ardent ancestral worship to traditional festivities, the Nung are spiritually and socially similar to the Tay. Nung brides traditionally command high dowries from prospective grooms.

Most Nung villages still have medicine men, called upon to help get rid of evil spirits and cure the ill. The Nung are also known for their handicrafts such as bamboo furniture, basketry, silverwork and paper making. The Nung primarily wear black and indigo clothing with elaborate headdresses.

SEDANG
Native to the central highlands, the Sedang do not carry family names, and there is said to be complete equality between the sexes. The children of one's siblings are also given the same treatment as one's own, creating a strong fraternal tradition. The Sedang practise unique customs, such as grave abandonment, sharing of property with the deceased and giving birth at the forest's edge. Sedang women traditionally wear long skirts and a sarong-like top wrap.

TAY
The Tay, the most populous of the hill tribes at 1.2 million people, live at low elevations and in valleys between Hanoi and the Chinese border. They adhere closely to Vietnamese beliefs but also worship genies and local spirits. Since they developed their own script in the 16th century, Tay literature and arts are famous throughout Vietnam. Tay people wear distinctive indigo-blue and black clothes.

THAI

Like the Tay, the Thai originated in southern China before settling along the fertile riverbeds of the northwest from Hoa Binh (p149) to Lai Chau (p167). Thai people worship spirits in an animist sense. The Thai minority, numbering about one million, are usually categorised by colour, including the Red, Black and White Thai. Black Thai women wear vibrantly coloured blouses and headgear, while the White Thai tend to dress in contemporary clothing.

The Thai, using a script developed in the 5th century, have produced literature ranging from poetry and love songs to folk tales. Travellers staying overnight in Mai Chau (p152) can see the Thai's renowned music and dance.

RELIGION

Four great philosophies and religions have shaped the spiritual life of the Vietnamese: Buddhism, Confucianism, Taoism and, later, Christianity. Over the centuries, Confucianism, Taoism and Buddhism have fused with popular Chinese beliefs and ancient Vietnamese animism to create the Tam Giao (Triple Religion). If asked about religion, most Vietnamese people are likely to say that they are Buddhist, but when it comes to family or civic duties they are likely to follow the moral and social code of Confucianism, and turn to Taoist concepts to understand the nature of the cosmos.

Although the majority of the population has only a vague notion of Buddhist doctrines, they invite monks to participate in life-cycle ceremonies such as funerals. Buddhist pagodas have come to be seen by many Vietnamese as a physical and spiritual refuge from an uncertain world.

Buddhism

Buddhism, like all great religions, has been through a messy divorce, and arrived in Vietnam in two flavours. Mahayana Buddhism (the Northern school) proceeded north into Nepal, Tibet, China, Korea, Mongolia, Vietnam and Japan, while Theravada Buddhism (the Southern school) took the southern route from India, Sri Lanka, Myanmar and Cambodia.

The Theravada school of Buddhism is an earlier and, according to its followers, less corrupted form of Buddhism than the Mahayana schools found around East Asia and the Himalayan regions. As Therevada followers tried to preserve and limit the Buddhist doctrines to only those canons codified in the early Buddhist era, the Mahayana school gave Theravada Buddhism the name 'Hinayana' (meaning 'Lesser Vehicle'). They considered themselves 'Greater Vehicle' because they built upon the earlier teachings.

The predominant school of Buddhism, and indeed religion, in Vietnam is Mahayana Buddhism (Dai Thua, or Bac Tong, meaning 'From

---

PAGODA OR TEMPLE?

Travelling around Vietnam, there are a lot of 'pagodas' and 'temples', but how does the average person know which is which? The Vietnamese regard a *chua* (pagoda) as a place of worship where they make offerings or pray. A Vietnamese *den* (temple) is not really a place of worship, but rather a structure built to honour some great historical figure (Confucius, Tran Hung Dao, even Ho Chi Minh).

The Cao Dai temple seems to somehow fall between the cracks. Given the mixture of ideas that is part and parcel of Cao Daism, it's hard to say if it's a temple, pagoda, church or mosque!

the North'). The largest Mahayana sect in the country is Zen (Dhyana; Thien), also known as the school of meditation. Dao Trang (the Pure Land school), another important sect, is practised mainly in the south.

Theravada Buddhism (Tieu Thua, or Nam Tong) is found mainly in the Mekong Delta region, and is mostly practised by ethnic-Khmers.

Vietnamese Buddhist monks *(bonze)* minister to the spiritual needs of the peasantry, but it is largely up to the monks whether they follow the lore of Taoism or the philosophy of Buddhism.

Taoism
Taoism (Lao Giao, or Dao Giao) originated in China and is based on the philosophy of Laotse (The Old One), who lived in the 6th century BC. Little is known about Laotse and there is some debate as to whether or not he actually existed. He is believed to have been the custodian of the imperial archives for the Chinese government, and Confucius is supposed to have consulted him.

Understanding Taoism is not easy. The philosophy emphasises contemplation and simplicity. Its ideal is returning to the Tao (The Way, or the essence of which all things are made), and it emphasises *am* and *duong*, the Vietnamese equivalents of Yin and Yang. Much of Taoist ritualism has been absorbed into Chinese and Vietnamese Buddhism, including, most commonly, the use of dragons and demons to decorate temple rooftops.

Confucianism
While it is more a philosophy than an organised religion, Confucianism (Nho Giao, or Khong Giao) has been an important force in shaping Vietnam's social system and the lives and beliefs of its people.

Confucius (Khong Tu) was born in China around 550 BC. He saw people as social beings formed by society yet also capable of shaping their society. He believed that the individual exists in and for society and drew up a code of ethics to guide the individual in social interaction. This code laid down a person's obligations to family, society and the state, which remain the pillars of Vietnamese society today.

Ancestor Worship
Vietnamese ancestor worship dates from long before the arrival of Confucianism or Buddhism. Ancestor worship is based on the belief that the soul lives on after death and becomes the protector of its descendants. Because of the influence the spirits of one's ancestors exert on the living, it is considered not only shameful for them to be upset or restless, but downright dangerous.

Traditionally, the Vietnamese worship and honour the spirits of their ancestors on a regular basis, especially on the anniversary of their death. To request help for success in business or on behalf of a sick child, sacrifices and prayers are offered to the ancestral spirits. Important worship elements are the family altar and a plot of land whose income is set aside for the support of the ancestors.

Cao Daism
Cao Daism is a Vietnamese sect that seeks to create the ideal religion by fusing the secular and religious philosophies of both East and West. It was founded in the early 1920s based on messages revealed in seances to Ngo Minh Chieu, the group's founder. At present there are about two million followers of Cao Daism in Vietnam. The sect's colourful headquarters is in Tay Ninh (p373), 96km northwest of HCMC.

DID YOU KNOW?

Cao Daism is a cocktail of the world's faiths and philosophies and its prophets include Buddha, Confucius, Jesus Christ, Moses and Mohammed, and some wacky choices like Joan of Arc, Shakespeare and Victor Hugo.

LUNAR CALENDAR
The Vietnamese lunar calendar closely resembles that of the Chinese. Year one of the Vietnamese lunar calendar corresponds to 2637 BC and each lunar month has 29 or 30 days, resulting in years with 355 days.

Approximately every third year is a leap year; an extra month is added between the third and fourth months to keep the lunar year in time with the solar year. If this was not done, the seasons would shift around the lunar year, playing havoc with all elements of life linked to the agricultural seasons. To check the Gregorian (solar) date corresponding to a lunar date, pick up any Vietnamese or Chinese calendar.

The Vietnamese have 12 zodiacal animals, each of which represents one year in a 12-year cycle. If you want to know your sign in the Vietnamese zodiac, look up your year of birth in the following chart. Don't forget that the Vietnamese New Year falls in late January or early February. If your birthday is in the first half of January it will be included in the zodiac year before the calendar year of your birth.

Rat *(tý)*	1924	1936	1948	1960	1972	1984	1996
Cow *(suu)*	1925	1937	1949	1961	1973	1985	1997
Tiger *(dan)*	1926	1938	1950	1962	1974	1986	1998
Rabbit *(mao)*	1927	1939	1951	1963	1975	1987	1999
Dragon *(thin)*	1928	1940	1952	1964	1976	1988	2000
Snake *(ty)*	1929	1941	1953	1965	1977	1989	2001
Horse *(ngo)*	1930	1942	1954	1966	1978	1990	2002
Goat *(mui)*	1931	1943	1955	1967	1979	1991	2003
Monkey *(than)*	1932	1944	1956	1968	1980	1992	2004
Rooster *(dau)*	1933	1945	1957	1969	1981	1993	2005
Dog *(tuat)*	1934	1946	1958	1970	1982	1994	2006
Pig *(hoi)*	1935	1947	1959	1971	1983	1995	2007

Hoa Hao Buddhism
The Hoa Hao Buddhist sect (Phat Giao Hoa Hao) was founded in the Mekong Delta in 1939 by Huynh Phu So. After he was miraculously cured of an illness, So began preaching a reformed Buddhism based on the common people and embodied in personal faith rather than elaborate rituals. His Buddhist philosophies involve simplicity in worship and no intermediaries between humans and the Supreme Being. Hoa Hao Buddhists are thought to number approximately 1.5 million.

Christianity
Catholicism was introduced in the 16th century by missionaries. Today, Vietnam has the highest percentage of Catholics (8% to 10% of the population) in Asia outside the Philippines. Under the communist government, Catholics faced severe restrictions on their religious activities. As in the USSR, churches were viewed as a capitalist institution and a rival centre of power that could subvert the government. Since 1990, the government has taken a more liberal line and Catholicism is making a comeback.

Protestantism was introduced to Vietnam in 1911 and most of the 200,000 today are Montagnards living in the central highlands. Protestants were doubly unfortunate in that they were persecuted first by the pro-Catholic regime of Diem and later by the communists.

Islam
Muslims, mostly ethnic-Chams, make up about 0.5% of the population. The Chams consider themselves Muslims, but in practice they follow a localised adaptation of Islamic theology and law. Though Muslims

usually pray five times a day, the Chams pray only on Fridays and celebrate Ramadan (a month of dawn-to-dusk fasting) for only three days. In addition, their Islam-based religious rituals co-exist with animism and the worship of Hindu deities. Circumcision is symbolically performed on boys at age 15, when a religious leader makes the gestures of circumcision with a wooden knife.

Hinduism

Champa was profoundly influenced by Hinduism and many of the Cham towers, built as Hindu sanctuaries, contain lingas that are still worshipped by ethnic-Vietnamese and ethnic-Chinese alike. After the fall of Champa in the 15th century, most Chams who remained in Vietnam became Muslims but continued to practise various Hindu rituals and customs.

ARTS
Music
TRADITIONAL

Heavily influenced by the Chinese to the north and Indian-influenced Khmer and Cham musical traditions to the south, this blend has produced an original style and instrumentation for Vietnamese music. Written music and the five note (pentatonic) scale may be of Chinese origin, but Vietnamese choral music is unique, as the melody and the tones must move as one; the melody cannot rise during a verse that has a falling tone.

Vietnamese folk music is usually sung without any instrumental accompaniment and was adapted by the communist party for many a patriotic marching song.

Classical, or 'learned music', is rather formal and frigid. It was performed at the imperial court for the entertainment of the mandarin elite. There are two main types of classical chamber music: *hat a dao* from the north and *ca Hue* from central Vietnam.

Traditional music is played on a wide array of indigenous instruments, dating back to the ancient *do son* drums that are sought after works of art. The best known traditional instrument in use is the *dan bau*, a single-stringed lute that generates an astounding array of tones. Also common at performances of traditional music is the *dan tranh*, a 16-string zither that is mesmerising, and *to rung*, a large bamboo xylophone.

Each of Vietnam's ethno-linguistic minorities has its own musical traditions that often include distinctive costumes and instruments, such as reed flutes, lithophones (similar to xylophones), bamboo whistles, gongs and stringed instruments made from gourds.

CONTEMPORARY/POP

Like the rest of Southeast Asia, Vietnam has a thriving domestic pop scene. The most celebrated artist is Khanh Ly, who left Vietnam in 1975 for the USA. She is massive both in Vietnam and abroad. Her music is widely available in Vietnam, but the government frowns on her recently composed lyrics that recall the trials of her life as a refugee.

Vietnam's number one domestic heart-throb is Hué-born Quang Linh, a former Hanoi banker, whose early popularity among Saigonese shot him up the local pop charts. He is adored by Vietnamese of all ages for his radiant love songs.

Other celebrated local pop singers include sex symbol Phuong Thanh, Vietnam's answer to Madonna or Britney Spears, only with more clothes. Vietnamese girls are seriously into heart-throb Lam Truong.

Of the legion of legendary Vietnamese contemporary-music composers, the leader of the pack was Trinh Cong Son, who died in HCMC in 2001. A former literature student from Hué, he wrote more than 500 songs, making him perhaps the most prolific Vietnamese composer in history.

Dance

Traditionally reserved for ceremonies and festivals, tourism has brought Vietnamese folk dance back to the mainstream. The Conical Hat Dance is one of the most visually stunning dances, in which a group of women wearing *ao dai* (the national dress of Vietnam) shake their stuff and spin around, whirling their classic conical hats like Fred Astaire used his cane.

Vietnam's ethnic minorities have their own dancing traditions, which are distinctly different from the Vietnamese majority. A great deal of anthropological research has been carried out in recent years in order to preserve and revive important indigenous traditions.

Theatre & Puppetry

Vietnamese theatre fuses music, singing, recitation, dance and mime into an artistic whole. These days, the various forms of Vietnamese theatre are performed by dozens of state-funded troupes and companies around the country.

Classical theatre is known as *hat tuong* in the north and *hat boi* in the south and is based on Chinese opera. Classical theatre is very formal, employing fixed gestures and scenery similar to the Chinese classics. The accompanying orchestra, which is dominated by the drum, usually has six musicians. Often, the audience also has a drum so it can pass judgement on the onstage action. It has a limited cast of characters, each of whom is easily identifiable through their make-up and costume. Red face paint represents courage, loyalty and faithfulness, while traitors and cruel people have white faces. A male character expresses emotions (pensiveness, worry, anger) by fingering his beard in different ways.

Popular theatre *(hat cheo)* expresses social protest through satire, although there has been less protest and more satire since 1975. The singing and verse are in everyday language and include many proverbs and sayings, accompanied by folk melodies.

Modern theatre *(cai luong)* originated in the South in the early 20th century and shows strong Western influences. Spoken drama *(kich noi* or *kich)*, with its Western roots, appeared in the 1920s. It's popular among students and intellectuals.

Conventional puppetry *(roi can)* and the uniquely Vietnamese art form of water puppetry *(roi nuoc)*, draw their plots from the same legendary and historical sources as other forms of traditional theatre. It is believed that water puppetry developed when determined puppeteers in the Red River Delta managed to continue performances despite annual flooding (see the boxed text on p108).

Cinema

One of Vietnam's earliest cinematographic efforts was a newsreel of Ho Chi Minh's 1945 Proclamation of Independence. Later, parts of the battle of Dien Bien Phu were restaged for the benefit of movie cameras.

Prior to reunification, the South Vietnamese movie industry produced a string of sensational, low-budget flicks. Conversely, North Vietnamese film-making efforts were dedicated to 'the mobilisation of the masses for economic reconstruction, the building of socialism and the struggle for national reunification'.

Returning to Ngo Thuy (1977), directed by Le Manh Thich and Do Khanh Toan, pays homage to the women of Ngo Thuy village. In 1971, these women were the subject of a propaganda film to encourage people to sign up for the war effort.

Dancing Girl, directed by Le Hoang, caused a major splash with its release in 2003. Telling the story of two HIV-positive prostitutes, Hoa, played by My Duyen, is seen mainlining heroin.

In recent years Vietnamese cinema has evolved from the realm of propaganda to a world that more closely reflects the lives of modern Vietnamese people and the issues they face. Contemporary films span a wide range of themes, from warfare to modern romance.

In Nguyen Khac's *The Retired General* (1988), the central character copes with adjusting from his life as a soldier during the American War to life as a civilian family man, symbolising Vietnam's difficult transition to the post-war era.

Dang Nhat Minh is perhaps Vietnam's most prolific film maker. In *The Return* (1993), Minh hones in on the complexities of modern relationships, while *The Girl on the River* (1987) tells the stirring tale of a female journalist who joins an ex-prostitute in search of her former lover, a Viet Cong soldier whose life she had saved and whose heart she'd been promised.

Young overseas-Vietnamese film directors are steadily carving a niche for themselves in the international film industry and snapping up awards at film festivals worldwide.

Paradise of the Blind, the first Vietnamese novel to be published in the USA, is set in a northern village and a Hanoi slum and recalls the lives of three women and the hardships they faced over some 40 years.

Tran Anh Hung's touching *The Scent of Green Papaya* (1992), filmed in France, celebrates the coming of age of a young girl working as a servant for an affluent Saigon family during the 1950s. *Cyclo* (1995), Tran Anh Hung's visually stunning masterpiece, charges to the core of HCMC's gritty underworld and its violent existence.

Vietnamese-American Tony Bui made a splash in 1999 with his exquisite feature debut *Three Seasons* (1999). Set in present-day HCMC, this beautifully made film weaves together the lives of four unlikely characters with a US war veteran, played by Harvey Keitel, who comes to Vietnam in search of his long lost daughter.

Literature

There are three veins of Vietnamese literature. Traditional oral literature *(truyen khau)* began long before recorded history and includes legends, folk songs and proverbs. Sino-Vietnamese literature was written in Chinese characters *(chu nho)*. Dominated by Confucian and Buddhist texts, it was governed by strict rules of metre and verse. Modern Vietnamese literature *(quoc am)* includes anything recorded in *nom* characters. The earliest text written in *nom* was the late-13th-century *Van Te Ca Sau* (Ode to an Alligator).

The Sacred Willow (2000) by Duong Van Mai Elliot spans four tumultuous generations of an upper-class Vietnamese family. This enlightening historical memoir traces French colonisation, WWII and the wars with the French and Americans.

One of Vietnam's literary masterpieces, *Kim Van Kieu* (The Tale of Kieu) was written during the first half of the 19th century by Nguyen Du (1765–1820), a poet, scholar, mandarin and diplomat.

Architecture

The Vietnamese have not been prolific builders like their Khmer neighbours, who erected the monuments of Angkor in Cambodia, and the Chams, whose graceful brick towers adorn many parts of the southern half of the country. For more on the Chams, check out the boxed text on p245.

Traditionally, most Vietnamese constructions were made of wood and other materials that decayed in the tropical climate. This, coupled with the fact that almost all stone structures erected by the Vietnamese have been destroyed in countless feudal wars and invasions, means that very little pre-modern Vietnamese architecture remains.

Plenty of pagodas and temples founded hundreds of years ago are still functioning, but they have usually been rebuilt many times with little concern for the original. As a result, many modern elements have been

THE CULTURE ·· Arts 51

casually introduced into pagoda architecture – those garish neon haloes for statues of Buddha are a shining example.

Because of the custom of ancestor worship, many graves from previous centuries survive today. These include temples erected in memory of high-ranking mandarins, royal-family members and emperors.

Memorials for Vietnamese who died in the wars against the Chinese, French and Americans usually contain cement obelisks inscribed with the words *to quoc ghi cong* ('the country will remember their exploits').

Painting & Sculpture

Painting on frame-mounted silk dates from the 13th century and was at one time the preserve of scholar-calligraphers, who painted grand scenes from nature. Before the advent of photography, realistic portraits for use in ancestor worship were produced. Some of these – usually of former head monks – can still be seen in certain Buddhist pagodas.

During the past century, Vietnamese painting has been influenced by Western trends. Much recent work has had political rather than aesthetic or artistic motives. These propagandist pieces are easy to spot at the Fine Arts Museum (p90) in Hanoi.

The recent economic liberalisation has convinced many young artists to abandon the revolutionary themes and concentrate on producing commercial paintings. Some have gone back to the traditional-style silk or lacquer paintings, while others are experimenting with contemporary subjects.

The Chams produced spectacular carved sandstone figures for their Hindu and Buddhist sanctuaries. Cham sculpture was profoundly influenced by Indian art but over the centuries it managed to also incorporate Indonesian and Vietnamese elements. The largest single collection of Cham sculpture in the world is found at the Museum of Cham Sculpture (p221) in Danang. For the lowdown on Cham architecture, see the listing for Po Klong Garai Cham Towers on p278.

Vietnamese Painting – From Tradition to Modernity, by Corinne de Ménonville, is a lush look at Vietnamese contemporary painting. For the contribution of women to the art scene, check out *Vietnamese Women Artists* (2004).

Lacquerware & Ceramics

The art of making lacquerware was brought to Vietnam from China in the mid-15th century. During the 1930s, the Fine Arts School in Hanoi had several Japanese teachers who introduced new styles and production methods.

Lacquer, or *cay son*, is made from resin extracted from the rhus tree. It is creamy white in raw form, but is darkened with pigments in an iron container for 40 hours. After the object has been treated with a glue, the requisite 10 coats of lacquer are applied. Each coat must be dried for a week and then thoroughly sanded with pumice and cuttlebone before the next layer can be applied. A specially refined lacquer is used for the 11th and final coat, which is sanded with a fine coal powder and lime wash before the object is decorated. Think over this process before you bargain too hard! Designs include engraving in low relief, or inlaying mother-of-pearl, egg shell or precious metals.

The production of ceramics *(gom)* has a long history in Vietnam. In ancient times, ceramic objects were made by coating a wicker mould with clay and baking it. Later, ceramic production became very refined, and each dynastic period is known for its particular techniques and motifs.

It's possible to view ancient ceramics in museums throughout Vietnam. Excavations of archaeological sites are still revealing ancient examples, as are the ongoing discoveries of shipwreck treasures.

Bat Trang (p114), located near Hanoi, is famous for its contemporary ceramic industry.

If you're crazy about your china, or pots about your pottery, try to find a copy of *Viet Nam Ceramics*, an illustrated insight into Vietnamese pottery over the centuries.

SPORT

Football (soccer) is Vietnam's number-one spectator sport and the country is mad for it. During the World Cup, the European Champions League or other major clashes, half the country stays up all night to watch live games in different time zones around the world. Post-game fun includes hazardous high-speed motorbike cruising in the streets of Hanoi and HCMC. Sadly the national team has not kept pace with this obsession and although one of the strongest in Southeast Asia, they remain minnows on the international stage. Think World Cup 2022 or beyond.

Tennis has considerable snob appeal these days and trendy Vietnamese like to both watch and play. Similarly, golf has taken off as a way to earn brownie points with international investors or local movers and shakers. The Vietnamese are a nation of badminton players and every street is a potential court. Other favourite sports include volleyball and table tennis.

Tet Festival

The Tet Nguyen Dan (Festival of the First Day) announces the Lunar New Year and is the most important date in the Vietnamese festival calendar. Commonly known as Tet, it is much more than your average Gregorian New Year's celebration; it's a time when families reunite in the hope of good fortune for the coming year, and ancestral spirits are welcomed back into the family home. And Tet is everybody's birthday; on this day everyone becomes one year older.

The festival falls some time between 19 January and 20 February on the Western calendar, the same time as Chinese New Year. The exact dates vary from year to year due to differences between the lunar and solar calendars. New Year's Day will fall on the following dates: 9 February 2005, 29 January 2006 and 18 February 2007. The first three days after New Year's Day are the official holidays but many people take the whole week off, particularly in the south.

Tet rites begin seven days before New Year's Day. This is when the Tao Quan – the three Spirits of the Hearth, found in the kitchen of every home – ascend to the heavens to report on the past year's events to the Jade Emperor. Often these kitchen gods are described as a single person and may be called Ong Tao, Ong Lo or Ong Vua Bep. The Tao Quan ride fish on their journey to heaven, so on this day people all over Vietnam release live carp into rivers and lakes. Altars, laden with offerings of food, fresh water, flowers, betel and live carp for celestial transport, are assembled in preparation for the gods' departure, all in the hope of receiving a favourable report and ensuring good luck for the family in the coming year.

Other rituals performed during the week before Tet include visiting cemeteries and inviting the spirits of dead relatives home for the celebrations. Absent family members start to make their way home so that the whole family can celebrate Tet under the same roof. All loose ends are tied up so that the new year can be started with a clean slate; debts are paid and everything is cleaned, including ancestors' graves.

SPIRITS OF THE HEARTH

One legend behind the Tao Quan is based on the story of a woodcutter and his wife. The couple lived happily together until the man was driven to drink by the worry of being unable to provide enough food for them both. He became violent towards his wife and eventually she could no longer bear it and left him. After some time she met and married a local hunter, forgetting the terrors of her previous marriage.

A few days before the Vietnamese New Year the woman received a beggar at the front door while the hunter was searching for game. She offered the beggar a meal and soon realised that he was her former husband. Panicked by the sound of her current husband returning, she hid the beggar under a pile of hay. The hungry hunter promptly set the hay alight and placed his recently caught game on it to roast, unaware that there was someone there. Fearing that the hunter might kill the woman if he cried out, the beggar remained silent. The woman was torn with grief, realising that her former husband was dying for her sake. With little hesitation, she threw herself onto the fire to die with him. The confused hunter thought that he must have driven her to such desperation, so he too jumped into the fire, unable to contemplate life without her.

All three perished, an act of devotion which so deeply touched the Jade Emperor that he made them gods. In their new role, they were to look out for the wellbeing of the Vietnamese people from the vantage point of the hearth.

Much like the tradition of Christmas trees in the West, Vietnamese homes are decorated with trees at this time. A New Year's tree (cay neu) is constructed to ward off evil spirits. Kumquat trees are popular throughout the country, while branches of pink peach blossoms (dao) grace houses in the north, and yellow apricot blossoms (mai) can be found in southern and central Vietnamese homes.

For a spectacular sight, go to ĐL Nguyen Hue in Ho Chi Minh City, much of which is taken over by the annual Tet flower market at this time of year. In Hanoi, the area around Pho Hang Dau and Pho Hang Ma is transformed into a massive peach-blossom and kumquat-tree market. Or be dazzled by the blocked-off streets near the Dong Xuan Market, ablaze with red and gold decorations for sale. A few days before the New Year is heralded in, the excitement at these markets is almost palpable, as people rush to buy their food and decorations, and motorbikes laden with blossoms and two or three kumquat trees jam the streets.

This is an expensive time of year for most families (the kumquat trees alone cost around US$20). In addition, children are given red envelopes containing substantial amounts of li xi (lucky money). The Vietnamese see this expense as being necessary to gain favour with the gods for the coming year.

Like special events anywhere, a large part of the celebrations revolve around food. A Tet staple is banh chung (see the boxed text opposite). These intriguing square parcels are made of fatty pork and bean paste, sandwiched between two layers of glutinous nep rice. They're wrapped in green dong, a leaf resembling that of a banana tree, and tied with bamboo twine, giving them the appearance of a present. You'll see mountains of them everywhere and will no doubt be invited to taste one. Banh day, a similar food which is round in shape, is served in the south.

Banh chung is often accompanied by mang, a dish made with boiled bamboo shoots and fried pork marinated in nuoc mam (fish sauce). Many visitors don't appreciate these dishes but they have a symbolic significance for Vietnamese people: their simple ingredients are reminders of past hard times. Popular sweets include mut (candied fruit, such as sugared apples, plums and even tomatoes). Fresh fruit is another essential element of Tet: red dragon fruit and watermelon are big favourites.

On New Year's Eve, the Tao Quan return to earth. At the stroke of midnight, all problems from the previous year are left behind and jubilant celebrations ensue. The goal seems to be to make as much noise as possible: drums and percussion are popular, and so were firecrackers until they were banned in 1995 (although you might still hear recordings of exploding firecrackers blaring from cassette players). Any noise will do really, as long as it provides a suitable welcome back for the gods, while scaring off any evil spirits that may be loitering.

The events of New Year's Day are very important as it's believed they affect the course of life in the year ahead. People take extra care not to be rude or show anger. Other activities that are believed to attract bad spirits and hence avoided include sewing, sweeping, swearing and breaking things.

It's crucial that the first visitor of the year to each household is suitable. They're usually male – best of all is a wealthy married man with several children. Foreigners are sometimes welcomed as the first to enter the house, although not always, so it's wise not to visit any Vietnamese house on the first day of Tet, unless you are explicitly invited (and make sure you confirm the time they want you to arrive). Those blacklisted as first visitors include single middle-aged women, and anyone who has lost their job, had an accident or lost a family member during the previous

BANH CHUNG

The fable behind *banh chung* originated with King Hung Vuong the Sixth, who fathered 22 sons, all worthy heirs. In order to select his successor, the king instructed them to search the globe for delicacies unknown to him. Whoever returned with the best dish would rule the kingdom. Twenty-one of them did as they were told, but one young prince, Lang Lieu, remained in the palace with no idea of where to start looking. He was filled with gloom until one night a genie appeared in his dreams. 'Man cannot live without rice', she said, and told him the recipe for *banh chung*. When the time came for the king to taste the 22 dishes, he was bitterly disappointed with the 21 from the princes who had travelled abroad. Finally he tasted the rice creations of Lang Lieu and was amazed at how delicious they were. When told of the genie's assistance with the recipe, the king was impressed with this divine support and named Lang Lieu his successor.

year – all signs of bad luck. Such unfortunates and their families can be ostracised from their community and sometimes stay home during the whole Tet period.

Unique to the south is the Unicorn Dance – a procession led by people carrying brightly coloured square flags followed by the unicorn itself (several men dressed up in tight uniforms) and then another mythical creature called Ong Dia (a man wearing a moon-like face mask). At the tail end come the drums and cymbals. The procession begins early on the first morning of Tet, and systematically visits every home and shop in its area, looking for donations. The Vietnamese are generous in their gifts, as the unicorn is regarded as a symbol of wealth, peace and prosperity. However, they make the unicorn work for its rewards: homeowners or shopkeepers often present their donations tied to a pole, suspended from the first-floor balcony or window. To reach the gifts, the unicorn is elevated through a human pyramid until it can swallow the prize in its mouth.

In Hanoi, a popular activity during the weeks that follow Tet is *co nghoi* (human chess). All the human chess pieces come from the same village, Lien Xa, in the northern province of Ha Tay. They're chosen because they're attractive, young, unmarried and have had no recent deaths in their families or other signs of bad luck. The form of chess played is Chinese. Although the pieces and moves are different from Western chess, the objective remains the same: to capture the opposing leader, in this case the 'general'.

Apart from New Year's Eve itself, Tet is not a particularly boisterous celebration. It's like Christmas Day: a quiet family affair. Difficulty in booking transport and accommodation aside, this is an excellent time to visit the country, especially to witness the contrasting frenzied activity before the New Year and the calm (and quiet streets!) afterwards. Wherever you're staying, it's more than likely you'll be invited to join in the celebrations.

If you are visiting Vietnam during Tet, be sure you learn this phrase: *chúc mùng nam mói* – Happy New Year!

Environment

THE LAND

Vietnam is a land shaped by its history. Dominated by the Chinese for a thousand years, the Vietnamese pushed southwards seeking new lands for cultivation and to put a bit of distance between them and their northern neighbour. Hemmed in by the Truong Son Mountains to the west, they had little choice but to head on down the coast, eating up the Kingdom of Champa and taking a bite-sized chunk out of Cambodia.

The result is the map of Vietnam today. As the Vietnamese are quick to point out, it resembles a *don ganh*, or the ubiquitous bamboo pole with a basket of rice slung from each end. The baskets represent the main rice-growing regions of the Red River Delta in the north, and the Mekong Delta in the south. The country is S-shaped, broad in the north and south and very narrow in the centre, where at one point it is only 50km wide.

Vietnam stretches more than 1600km along the eastern coast of the Indochinese peninsula. The country's land area is 326,797 sq km, making it a bit bigger than Italy and slightly smaller than Japan. Vietnam has 3451km of coastline and 3818km of land borders.

The coastline is one of the big draws for tourists and it doesn't disappoint, with sweeping beaches, towering cliffs, undulating dunes and countless uninhabited islands along its length. The largest of these islands is Phu Quoc (p445), off the coast of Cambodia in the Gulf of Thailand. Other major islands include Cat Ba (p130) and Van Don (p135) in the Halong Bay area and a splattering of dots off Nha Trang (p261).

Both the Red River Delta and the Mekong Delta are pancake flat and prone to flooding. Silt carried by the Red River and its tributaries, confined to their paths by 3000km of dykes, has raised the level of the river beds above the surrounding plains. Breaches in the dykes result in disastrous flooding. The Mekong Delta has no such protection and when *cuu long* (the nine dragons – the nickname for the nine tributaries of the Mekong where it splits in the delta) burst their banks it creates havoc for communities and crops. The Mekong Delta continues to expand at a rate of about 100m per year, though global warming and the consequent rise in sea levels around the world could one day submerge it.

The Vietnamese are starting to take environmental protection seriously, particularly as the popularity of national parks soars. The Vietnam Environmental Protection Agency has the tough task of environmental watchdog; see its website at www.nea.gov.vn/english.

Three-quarters of the country consists of rolling hills and mighty mountains, the highest of which is 3143m-high Fansipan (p163) in the far northwest. The Truong Son Mountains, which form the central highlands, run almost the full length of Vietnam along its borders with Laos and Cambodia.

The most striking geological features in Vietnam are the karst formations. Karst consists of limestone in which erosion has produced fissures, sinkholes, caves and underground rivers. Northern Vietnam is a showcase for these outcrops, with stunning examples at Halong Bay (p127) and Bai Tu Long Bay, (p135) and around Ninh Binh (p175) and the Perfume Pagoda (p112). At Halong and Bai Tu Long Bays, an enormous limestone plateau has steadily sunk into the ocean and the old mountain tops stick out of the sea like bony vertical fingers pointing towards the sky.

Not all of Vietnam's mountains are limestone. The coastal ranges near Nha Trang and those at Hai Van Pass (Danang) are composed of granite, and the giant boulders littering the hillsides are a surreal sight.

The western part of the central highlands, near Buon Ma Thuot and Pleiku, is well known for its red volcanic soil, which is incredibly fertile.

The highlands are, of course, high above sea level, but are mostly flat and not particularly scenic.

WILDLIFE

Despite some disastrous bouts of deforestation, Vietnam's flora and fauna is as exotic, abundant and varied as any tropical country. Scientists are only just beginning to effectively catalogue the country's plant and animal life, and the government is showing some determined enthusiasm for ecological conservation.

Animals

On paper, Vietnam has plenty to offer those who are wild about wildlife, but in reality many of the animals live in remote forested areas and an encounter is extremely unlikely. A lot of the wildlife is rapidly disappearing, thanks to population pressures and the destruction of habitats. Hunting, poaching and pollution have taken their toll, too.

With a wide range of habitats – from equatorial lowlands to high, temperate plateaus and even alpine peaks – the wildlife of Vietnam is enormously diverse. It is home to 275 species of mammal, more than 800 species of bird, 180 species of reptile, 80 species of amphibian, hundreds of species of fish and thousands of species of invertebrates.

Every now and then, Vietnam throws up a new creature that manages to elude scientific classification. Since Vietnam reopened for business around 1990, zoologists have discovered several previously unknown species of large mammal in Vietnam, including a new breed of muntjac deer in 1998. The scientific and conservation value of these recent discoveries has not been lost on authorities, and the Vietnamese government has been expanding the size of national parks and nature reserves, and banning logging within these areas. As research and conservation efforts gather pace, Vietnam may turn out to be a treasure chest of undiscovered species.

Rare and little-known birds previously thought to be extinct have been spotted and no doubt there are more in the extensive forests along the Lao border. Edwards' pheasant, previously believed to be extinct, was found on a scientific expedition, and other excursions have yielded the white-winged wood duck and white-shouldered ibis.

Even casual visitors will spot a few bird species: swallows and swifts flying over fields and along watercourses; flocks of finches at roadsides and in paddies; and bulbuls and mynahs in gardens and patches of forest. Vietnam is on the east-Asian flyway and is an important stopover for migratory waders en route from Siberian breeding grounds to their Australian winter quarters.

Twitchers with a serious interest in the birdlife of Vietnam should seek out a copy of *A Field Guide to the Birds of South-East Asia* (1982) by Ben King, Martin Woodcock & Edward Dickinson, which has thorough coverage of Vietnam.

ENDANGERED SPECIES

Tragically, Vietnam's wildlife has been in deadly decline as forest habitats are destroyed and waterways polluted. In addition, widespread illegal hunting has exterminated local animal populations, in some cases wiping out entire species. Continued deforestation and poaching means that many endangered species are on a one-way ticket to extinction. Captive-breeding programmes may be the only hope for some.

Officially, the government has recognised 54 species of mammal and 60 species of bird as endangered. The tapir and Sumatran rhinoceros are already extinct in Vietnam. In the early 1990s a small population of Javan rhinos, the world's rarest rhinoceros, was discovered in the Cat Tien National Park (p388), southwest of Dalat, and there are probably between 20 and 30 left in the entire country.

Larger animals crucial to the country's conservation efforts include the elephant, tiger, leopard, black bear, honey bear, snub-nosed monkey, flying squirrel, crocodile and turtle.

In a positive sign, some wildlife populations are re-establishing themselves in reforested areas. Birds, fish and crustaceans have reappeared in replanted mangrove forests. Areas in which large animals were thought to have been wiped out by war are now hot spots of biodiversity and abundance. The extensive forests of the central highlands and far north remain a home to some of nature's most noble creatures, such as the tiger, Asian elephant, clouded leopard and sun bear. Their chance of survival rests in the balance, as Vietnam's population continues to expand, eating up more and more of the remaining wilderness areas.

Plants

Years ago Vietnam was blanketed in forest, from vast mangrove fringing the coast to dense rainforest in the mountainous regions. Over the centuries, the forests have progressively been pushed back: first by the clearing of land for cultivation, and later by a booming population and the ravages of war.

Although the scars of war are still visible and much of the damage is irreversible, reforestation programmes have been implemented and today the landscape is showing signs of recovery. Natural forests at higher elevations, such as those in the northwest, feature wild rhododendrons, dwarf bamboo and many varieties of orchid; the central coast is drier and features stands of pine; while the river deltas support mangrove forests, which are valuable nurseries for fish and crustaceans as well as feeding sites for many bird species.

The remaining forests of Vietnam are estimated to contain more than 12,000 plant species, only around 7000 of which have been identified and 2300 of which are known to be valuable to humanity. Recently the islands and caves of Halong Bay yielded seven previously unknown plants – the largest and most conspicuous of the new flora has been christened the Halong Fan Palm.

The Vietnamese make good use of the plants around them for medicines and remedies. Locals forage in the forests for barks, roots, herbs and flowers, which go into making cures for all sorts of ailments.

NATIONAL PARKS

Vietnam currently has 13 national parks and an expanding array of nature reserves. There are plans to increase and improve existing parks and nature reserves, and also to establish new ones.

DID YOU KNOW?

Ho Chi Minh, taking time off from the war in 1963 to dedicate Cuc Phuong National Park, said: 'Forest is gold. If we know how to conserve it well, it will be very precious. Destruction of the forest will lead to serious effects on both life and productivity'.

Most of Vietnam's national parks are seldom visited by travellers, who tend to get stuck on the 'must-see' tourist trail, without the time or wanderlust to explore the parks. Access can be problematic with some parks hidden in remote areas, but others are easy to reach. For those who make the effort to seek them out, national parks reveal a whole different face to Vietnam. They also have the added appeal of being among the few places in Vietnam where tourists are unlikely to be hassled to buy anything. However, if you are wanting a bit of peace and quiet to soak up the serenity and splendour, it is better to visit parks during the week, as hordes of Vietnamese descend during the weekend.

The most interesting and accessible parks are Cat Ba (p130), Ba Be (p144) and Cuc Phuong (p177) in the north; Bach Ma (p216) in the centre; and Cat Tien (p388) and Yok Don (p311) in the south. All of the parks levy some sort of admission charge, but it is usually very reasonable at around

NATIONAL PARK HIGHLIGHTS

Park (size in hectares)	Features	Activities	Best time to visit	Page
Ba Be (7610)	lakes, rainforest, waterfalls, towering peaks, bears, monkeys	hiking, boating, birding	Apr-Nov	p144
Bach Ma (22,000)	hiking, waterfalls, tigers, primates	hiking, birding	Mar-Sep	p216
Cat Ba (15,200)	hiking, ethnic groups, caves, monkeys, boars, deer, waterfowl	hiking, swimming, birding	Apr-Aug	p131
Cat Tien (73,878)	primates, elephants, birdlife, rhinos, tigers	hiking, jungle exploration	Nov-Feb	p388
Cuc Phuong (22,200)	jungle, grottoes, primates, birding centre, caves	hiking, endangered-primate viewing	Oct-Mar	p177
Yok Don (115,545)	ethnic groups, stilt houses	elephant rides, hiking	Nov-Feb	p311

10,000d or less than US$1. Most of the parks have accommodation available, most often a mix of rooms and bungalows, and camping is possible if you have your own gear.

Cat Ba National Park is on a beautiful island and during the summer months it attracts a steady stream of foreign travellers willing to make the boat journey. In 2000, Vietnam also created Bai Tu Long National Park, a protected reserve situated to the east of Halong Bay, which includes more than 15,000 hectares of tropical evergreen forest.

Ba Be National Park features spectacular waterfalls and is accessible by hired 4WD or motorbike from Hanoi. Cuc Phuong National Park is less visited, but easily reached from Hanoi and offers great hiking, plus an amazing array of rescued primates that are being rehabilitated. Bach Ma National Park, near Hué, receives far fewer visitors than its attractions deserve, but is demonstrating good potential for responsible ecotourism.

Cat Tien National Park, in the southern part of the central highlands, is relatively easy to reach from Ho Chi Minh City or Dalat, and very popular with bird-watchers. Also in the central highlands is Yok Don National Park, which is home to many elephants and local minority tribes.

ENVIRONMENTAL ISSUES

Vietnam's environment is not teetering on the brink, but there are some worrying signs. Vietnam is a poor, densely populated, agricultural country, so humans are competing with native plants and animals over the same limited resources.

Deforestation is the most serious problem facing the country today. Originally, almost all of Vietnam was covered with dense forests. Since the arrival of human beings many millennia ago, Vietnam has been progressively denuded of forest cover. While 44% of the original forest cover was extant in 1943, by 1983 only 24% was left and in 1995 it was down to 20%. In a positive turnaround, recent reforestation projects by the Forest Ministry, including the banning of unprocessed timber exports in 1992, have seen a slight rise in the amount of forest cover here.

DOING YOUR BIT

■ Vietnam has a low level of environmental awareness and responsibility, and many people remain unaware of the implications of littering. Try and raise awareness of these issues by example, and dispose of your litter as responsibly as possible.

■ Vietnam's faunal populations are under considerable threat from domestic consumption and the illegal international trade in animal products. Though it may be 'exotic' to try wild meat such as muntjac, bats, deer, sea horses, shark fins and so on – or to buy products made from endangered plants and animals – doing so will indicate your support or acceptance of such practices and add to the demand for them.

■ When visiting coral reefs and snorkelling or diving, or simply boating, be careful not to touch live coral or anchor boats on it, as this hinders the coral's growth. If your tour operator does this and it's possible to anchor in a sandy area, try to convince the operator to do so and indicate your willingness to swim to the coral. Don't buy coral souvenirs.

■ When visiting limestone caves, be aware that touching the formations hinders growth and turns the limestone black. Don't break off the stalactites or stalagmites as they take lifetimes to regrow. Don't carve graffiti onto limestone formations, cave walls or other rock.

■ Do not remove or buy 'souvenirs' that have been taken from historical sites and natural areas.

In addition, the Ministry of Education has made the planting and taking care of trees part of school curricula. However, even at this rate, reforestation cannot keep up with forest losses. Each hectare of land stripped of vegetation contributes to a multitude of environmental problems, including the flooding of areas downstream from catchment areas; irreversible soil erosion; the silting up of rivers, streams, lakes and reservoirs; the loss of wildlife habitat; and unpredictable climatic changes.

Vietnam has so far suffered little industrial pollution largely because there has been little industry. However, the nation's rapid economic and population growth indicates environmental trouble ahead. The dramatic increase in the number of noisy, smoke-spewing motorbikes in recent years should be taken as a sign of abominations to come.

Ecotourism is increasingly on the rise, with trekking and other outdoor activities becoming more and more popular with travellers. The government has set aside tens of thousands of square kilometres of forest land with plans to create around 100 protected areas in the form of national parks and nature reserves. Local ecologists hope that as tropical ecosystems have highly diverse species but low densities of individual species, reserve areas will be large enough to contain viable populations of each species. However, there are development interests that are not particularly amenable to boosting the size of Vietnam's national parks and nature reserves. As in the West, even the best-laid plans can sometimes go awry. Massive infrastructure projects such as new highways are threatening protected areas, as it is cheaper for the government to use park land than compensate villagers for farm land. A case in point is the new Ho Chi Minh road, Hwy 14, which cuts through Cuc Phuong National Park.

Much has been said about the human and economic devastation wrought by the USA during the American War, but there was also ecocide – the war saw the most intensive attempt to destroy a country's natural environment the world has ever seen. American forces sprayed 72 million litres of herbicides (named Agents Orange, White and Blue after the colour of their canisters) over 16% of South Vietnam to destroy the Viet Cong's natural cover.

DID YOU KNOW?

Some 13 million tonnes of bombs – equivalent to 450 times the energy of the atomic bomb used on Hiroshima – were dropped on the Indochina region. This equates to 265kg for every man, woman and child in Vietnam, Cambodia and Laos.

Another environmentally disastrous method of defoliation employed during the war involved the use of enormous bulldozers called 'Rome ploughs' to rip up the jungle floor. Large tracts of forest, agricultural land, villages and even cemeteries were bulldozed, removing both the vegetation and topsoil. Flammable melaleuca forests were ignited with napalm. In mountain areas, landslides were deliberately created by bombing and spraying acid on limestone hillsides. Elephants, useful for transport, were attacked from the air with bombs and napalm. By the war's end, extensive areas had been taken over by tough weeds (known locally as 'American grass'). The government estimates that 20,000 sq km of forest and farmland were lost as a direct result of the American War.

Scientists have yet to conclusively prove a link between the residues of chemicals used by the USA and spontaneous abortions, stillbirths, birth defects and other human health problems. However, the circumstantial evidence is certainly compelling. In 2002, on the heels of a landmark Agent Orange conference in Hanoi, the USA and Vietnam initiated a joint investigation into the health effects of this damaging herbicide. Delegates from Vietnam's National Environmental Agency and the US National Institute of Environmental Health Sciences cosigned a directive for scientists to explore possible links between Agent Orange and various physical illnesses.

Ecotourism is increasingly popular in Vietnam and more and more companies are launching environmentally friendly biking and hiking tours. Vietnam Ecotours (www .ecotourisminvietnam .com) is dedicated to promoting ecotourism.

Food & Drink

One of the delights of visiting Vietnam is the cuisine, and there are said to be about 500 traditional dishes. Eating is such an integral part of the culture that a time-honoured Vietnamese proverb, 'hoc an, hoc noi', dictates that people should 'learn to eat before learning to speak'.

Vietnamese cuisine is the sum of many parts. Vietnam has an enviable natural prosperity, and the cooking techniques showcase the bounty from land and sea to great advantage. Colonialism and foreign influences led to a marrying of techniques and ingredients. The result? The Vietnamese table.

Famous dishes such as *pho* and fresh spring rolls are but the tip of a gastronomic iceberg. In addition to a myriad of foods and preparations, there is a staggering number of sauces and dips limited only by the imagination of each cook. If cooking were painting, Vietnam would have one of the world's most colourful palettes. The Vietnamese themselves have no culinary inhibitions and are always willing to try something new. When you combine the two, nothing is ruled out.

STAPLES & SPECIALITIES

From the land comes rice, and from the sea and waterways fresh fish for *nuoc mam* (fish sauce; see the boxed text opposite). Together they form the bedrock of Vietnamese cuisine. In supporting roles are the myriad pungent roots, leafy herbs and aromatic tubers, which give Vietnamese salads, snacks, soups and stews their distinctive fragrance and kick. But there are constants: for the Vietnamese cook, freshness and a balanced combination of flavours and textures are paramount.

For the full caboodle of Vietnamese specialities, see the Menu Decoder on p70.

Pho

You can have *pho* (rice noodles) everywhere in Vietnam, but it is almost a cult in Hanoi. This full and balanced meal in a bowl will cost you less than 10,000d. In the north the people eat it at any time of day or night, while in the south it's popular for breakfast. It is artistry, practicality and economy.

Com

Vietnamese have a reverence for *com* (rice). It is the 'staff of life', not only at the table but in the economy and culture. Rice can be made into almost anything – wrappers, wine and noodles. *Banh trang* (rice paper) is something of a misnomer. This stuff is not very good for writing on, but is very good for eating. People use it to wrap Vietnamese spring rolls.

Vegetarian cookery uses a lot of glutinous rice, *gao nep,* a 'sticky rice' with a slightly sweet flavour when cooked. Stuffed with mung-bean paste or other savouries, it is the backbone of a variety of rice cakes.

Nem

One of the most popular dishes is *nem* (Vietnamese spring rolls), which are known as *cha gio* in the south and *nem Sai Gon* or *nem ran* in the north. They are made of rice paper, and are filled with minced pork, crab, vermicelli, onion, mushroom and eggs. *Nem rau* are vegetable spring rolls.

NUOC MAM

Nuoc mam is the one ingredient that is quintessentially Vietnamese and it lends a distinctive character to Vietnamese cooking. The sauce is made by fermenting highly salted fish in large ceramic vats for four to 12 months. Connoisseurs insist the high-grade rocket fuel has a much milder aroma than the cheaper variety, though most foreigners will find it hard to tell the difference. It is very often used as a dipping sauce, and takes the place of salt on a Western table. It can be mixed with garlic, chilli, sugar, vinegar and fresh lime to make the dipping sauce *nuoc cham*. Insist on the real thing (rather than the lighter stuff) – you will not have been to Vietnam otherwise.

If *nuoc mam* isn't strong enough for you, try *mam tom*, a powerful shrimp paste that American soldiers sometimes called 'Viet Cong tear gas'. It's often served with dog meat – foreigners generally find it far more revolting than the dog itself.

A variation on the theme are the delicious larger 'fresh' spring rolls called *banh trang* in the south and *banh da* in the north. With these you put the ingredients together yourself and roll your own. The outer shell is a translucent rice crepe.

Herbs & Spices

While rice and *nuoc mam* define Vietnamese 'food', it is spices that define Vietnamese 'cuisine' – the study, practice and development of the kitchen arts. There could be no *pho bo* without them, just plain beef noodle soup, and nothing to wax rhapsodic about.

Fruits & Vegetables

After rice, fruits and vegetables make up the bulk of the Vietnamese diet. If given the choice of abandoning vegetables or abandoning meat, virtually all Vietnamese would eschew flesh and keep the vegies. And they would not be the inveterate snackers and grazers that they are were it not for the gift of fruit.

Fish, Meat & Fowl

Thanks to Vietnam's long coastline, seafood has always been a major source of protein. Crabs, prawns, shrimps, cuttlefish, clams, eel, shellfish and many species of fin fish can be found up and down the coast. For seafood lovers a coastal culinary cruise is one of the highlights of a trip through Vietnam.

In Vietnam chickens, as well as other fowl, are produced in barnyards where they grow up fit, happy and tasty. Beef tends to be expensive as there is not much suitable land for cattle to graze. It can be tough but usually has a good flavour. Pork is one of the favourite meats. Frogs' legs are good but lamb and mutton are rarely seen. Chinese-style sausages are common in the markets. Then there are those, shall we say, 'unusual' meats (see the boxed text 'Travel Your Tastebuds' on p64).

Desserts

Do ngot (Vietnamese sweets) and *do trang mieng* (desserts) are popular everywhere, and are especially prevalent during festivals, when *danh* (traditional cakes) come in a wide variety of shapes and flavours.

Regional Specialities

For such a long country, the way that the people treat their produce is bound to differ according to where they are. Northern food displays a

DID YOU KNOW?

According to some veterans, American troops fighting in Vietnam could detect Viet Cong guerrillas by the lasting aroma of *nuoc mam*. For their part, the Vietnamese were said to be able to detect the Americans by the smells of tobacco and chewing gum.

DID YOU KNOW?

In accordance with international aviation regulations against taking strong-smelling and corrosive substances on board, *nuoc mam* joined the nasally obnoxious durian fruit among the food substances banned on Vietnam Airlines flights.

TRAVEL YOUR TASTEBUDS

No matter what part of the world you come from, if you travel much in Vietnam you are going to encounter food that to you might seem unusual. The fiercely omnivorous Vietnamese find nothing strange in eating insects, algae, offal or fish bladders. They'll feast on the flesh of dogs, they'll eat a crocodile, or a dish of cock's testicles. They'll kill a venomous snake before your eyes, cut out its still-beating heart, feed it to you with a cup of the serpent's blood to wash it down, and say it increases your potency. They'll slay a monkey and then barbecue it at your tableside.

To the Vietnamese there is nothing 'strange' about anything that will sustain the body. To them a food is either wholesome or it isn't; it's nutritious or it isn't; it tastes good or it doesn't. And that's all they worry about. They'll try anything once, even Kentucky Fried Chicken.

During your travels, avoid eating endangered species, as this will only further endanger them. If you are keen for some canine chow, or keen to avoid it, look out for the words *thit cho* in the north, *thit cay* in the south.

We Dare You! The Top Five

crickets	dog	duck embryo	field mouse	king cobra

Chinese heritage, but in the south, where the weather is more tropical, the dishes have a more aromatic, spicy nose. In the middle lies Hué, the home of Vietnamese imperial cooking, which features a range of sophisticated, refined dishes designed to tempt jaded royal appetites of yore.

Pleasures of the Vietnamese Table (2001), by Mai Pham, owner of the renowned Lemon Grass Restaurant in Sacramento, California, sees the author returning to Vietnam to reconnect with her family and food.

THE NORTH

We are forever thankful to the capital for *pho*, but there are other tasty teasers in the north. *Banh cuon* (rice rolls) are produced everywhere in Vietnam, but those that are made in Hanoi have special characteristics, with wrappings as thin as a sheet of paper.

In Hanoi there is a type of *oc* (snail) living in ponds and lakes that grows to the size of a golf ball, has a streaked colour and, while chewy, is very tasty. *Bun oc* are boiled snails dipped in *nuoc cham*.

THE CENTRE

Emperor Tu Duc was a demanding diner, but Hué should be thankful as his legacy is some of the best food in Vietnam.

Appearance is very important, not only in the use of colour and the arrangement of food on the plate, but also in the manner of serving. The menu for an imperial-style banquet today, whether in a fine restaurant or hotel banquet room or even a private home, might include up to a dozen dishes.

DID YOU KNOW?

Thanh long (dragon fruit) grows on a kind of creeping cactus – resembling a green dragon – that climbs up the trunks and branches of trees and flourishes on parched hillsides that get little water.

Hoi An is best known for *cao lau* (doughy flat noodles mixed with croutons, bean sprouts and greens and topped off with pork slices). Word has it among foreign tourists that true *cao lau* can only be made from water drawn from the Ba Le Well (p241), and that you can taste the difference if someone tries to sneak a bastardised version by you.

THE SOUTH

With the cultivation of a greater range of tropical and temperate fruits and vegetables, and more varieties of spice, the south favours spicy dishes. Curries have been around since earliest times, although – unlike the Indian originals – they are not hot but aromatic, influenced by Cambodia. Almost anything cooked in coconut milk is a typical southern dish.

DRINKS

Vietnam has a healthy drinking culture, and the heat and humidity will ensure that you hunt out anything on offer to slake your thirst. Widely available are coffee, tea, beer, soft drinks, fresh fruit juices and some of the more exotic 'fire waters' (strong local spirits). Tea is traditionally the preferred drink of the Vietnamese, but these days it is just as likely to be beer in the glass.

Beer

You will never be more than a few minutes from beer. There is no 'national brand', but a rip-roaring selection of regional beers, some of them distributed countrywide. Some of the best beers to look out for include the ubiquitous Ha Noi and Halida in the north; Hué's finest, Huda, and Biere Larue in central Vietnam (Larue Export is currently taking the nation by storm); and 333 *(ba ba ba)* and Saigon Export in the south.

Memorise the words *bia hoi,* which mean 'draught beer'. There are signs advertising it everywhere and most cafés have it on the menu. 'Fresh beer' *(bia tuoi)* is similar to draught beer. See the boxed text on p105 for the full picture on this Vietnam institution.

Xeo

Xeo (rice wine) is as old as the hills. Formerly seen as a sort of cider for country bumpkins, it is gaining new kudos in the cities as a cheap and cheerful route to oblivion.

Most ethnic minorities in the central highlands make *xeo,* and use it for all kinds of celebrations, religious rituals, weddings, and simply for receiving guests. Its taste and alcohol content will vary, like moonshine anywhere, according to the maker and the season.

Another Vietnamese speciality is *ruou ran* (snake wine). This is basically rice wine with a pickled snake floating in it. This elixir is considered a tonic and allegedly cures everything from night blindness to impotence.

Wine

Since the French arrived in the 19th century Vietnam has not been without wine. All major tourist centres have a good selection of wine these days.

Vietnamese-made wine? Vines have been introduced to the highlands of Vietnam where the cooler temperatures and plentiful light *could* produce very good wines. But it will take years for local growers to learn the vintner's arts.

Tea

The preparation, serving and drinking of tea has a social importance seldom appreciated by Western visitors. Serving tea in the home or office is more than a gesture of hospitality, it is a ritual.

Tea requires time. Time to prepare it, time to contemplate it, time to talk about it, time to savour it. It is to the average Vietnamese what the finest wines are to the Western connoisseur.

Coffee

Vietnamese coffee is fine stuff. There is, however, one qualifier: most drinkers need to dilute it with hot water. The Vietnamese prefer their coffee so strong and sweet that it will strip the enamel from your teeth. Ordering 'white coffee' *(ca phe sua da)* usually results in coffee with about 30% to 40% sweet condensed milk.

DID YOU KNOW?

Bia hoi (draught beer) is probably the best lager in the world... sorry, we meant the cheapest beer in the world. Starting at just 1500d a glass, anyone can afford a round and you can get off yer head for just US$1!

For the full take on Vietnamese cuisine, check out *Authentic Vietnamese Cooking: Food from a Family Table* (1999) by Corinne Trang. Illustrated with captivating black and white images, this is an entertaining way to learn the art of cooking.

Instant coffee *(ca phe tan)* made its debut in 1996 – a disaster! Many cafés assume Westerners prefer instant coffee because it's 'modern' and comes from the West. Demand fresh-brewed Vietnamese coffee *(ca phe phin)*, not imported instant powder.

Rather than prepare coffee in a pot, the Vietnamese prefer to brew it right at the table, French-style – a dripper with coffee grounds is placed over the cup and hot water poured in.

Some consider *chon* to be the highest grade of Vietnamese coffee. It is made of beans fed to a certain species of weasel and later collected from its excrement. Try a cup of this stuff at Trung Nguyen, Vietnam's answer to Starbucks, found throughout the country.

Mineral Water

The selection of mineral water *(nuoc suoi)* has been expanding rapidly ever since the Vietnamese realised that tourists were willing to pay good money for water sealed in plastic bottles. It costs anything from 3000d a bottle on the street to US$3 in the fancy hotels.

Smoothies & Juices

We're not talking the smoothies back home. We're talking about something that, in our humble opinion, can only be produced by the smoothie meisters of Vietnam. Pick your fruit and enjoy!

There is nothing more refreshing on a hot day than *nuoc dua* (chilled baby coconut), but for a natural glucose high hit the sugar-cane juice, freshly pressed through a mangle at street-side stalls across the land. This is the ultimate pick-me-up in the scorching sun.

CELEBRATIONS

Vietnam, for all its poverty, is a land rich with abundant natural resources and potential. There are many holidays and feasts accompanied by special food on its calendar, as well as weddings and other family celebrations.

DID YOU KNOW?

Emperor Tu Duc (1848–83) expected 50 dishes to be prepared by 50 cooks to be served by 50 servants at every meal. And his tea had to be made from the dew that accumulated on leaves overnight. Not too demanding then!

For a festival, the family coffers are broken open and no matter how much they hold, it is deemed insufficient. But they will be well used for racks of roasted squabs and game birds. They will go towards the Vietnamese version of Peking duck, sliced into juicy slabs, drizzled with a piquant sauce. The more highly prized species of fish will be steamed or braised whole, and the cooks will give themselves over to the Chinese penchant for elaborate decoration.

In the highly structured Vietnamese society, the standard meal is knocked askew for the feast, symbolising the fact that during the feast the world is a different, better, place. People north and south recall the emperors at Hué and nibble tidbits, perhaps with sips of whisky, before the main repast. And dishes may be brought forth and consumed individually so that they can be savoured and duly commented upon and praised. Attendance at a festive meal in Vietnam will convince you, should you even need it, that the Vietnamese do not eat to live, but live to eat.

WHERE TO EAT & DRINK

Whatever your taste, one eatery or another in Vietnam is almost certain to handle it, be it the humble peddler with his yoke, a roadside stall, a simple *pho* shop or a fancy-pants restaurant.

In almost any district you will pass restaurants of every kind. There are lots of speciality restaurants. You'll pass by any number of *pho* houses from grand to grotty. Also popular are 'pancake houses'. Not American style, but a savoury dish more like a crepe or Indian *dhosa*.

Barbecue is a speciality and many such restaurants are easy to locate by the aroma wafting through the streets. Also popular is the dish known as *bo bay mon*, which is beef prepared in seven different ways – a good feed when you're feeling protein-impaired.

The micro-restaurant set in the family home is taking off in Vietnam, as people become more entrepreneurial. Some can only accommodate a few diners, others can take a crowd.

Don't neglect the remaining French and Chinese restaurants. They are not as common as they used to be, but they are an important part of Vietnam's culinary and cultural legacy. And they have now been supplemented by Indian and Italian, Turkish and Thai, as the cities of Vietnam boast truly international cuisine.

There are often no set hours for places to eat, but as a general rule of thumb, cafés are open most of the day and into the night. Street stalls are open from very early in the morning until late at night. Restaurants usually open for lunch (between 11am and 2pm) and dinner (between 5pm or 6pm and 10pm or 11pm).

Quick Eats

Street food is an important part of everyday life. Like much of Southeast Asia, the Vietnamese people are inveterate snackers. They can be found in impromptu stalls at any time of day or night, delving into a range of snacky things. Whether you want your tidbit wrapped, unwrapped, spicy, sweet, cakey or crunchy, chances are it is somewhere in the streets of Vietnam. It's cheap, it's cheerful and it's a cool way to get up close and personal with Vietnamese cuisine.

VEGETARIANS & VEGANS

The good news is that there is now more choice than ever before when it comes to vegetarian dining. The bad news is that you have not landed in Veg Heaven, for the Vietnamese are voracious omnivores. While they dearly love their vegies, they also dearly love anything that crawls on the ground, swims in the sea or flies in the air.

In keeping with Buddhist precepts, many restaurants go vegie on the 1st and 15th of each lunar month, and this is a great time to scour the markets. Otherwise, be wary. Any dish of vegetables is likely to have been cooked with fish sauce or shrimp paste. The Vietnamese are very willing

---

FESTIVAL FOOD

Tet brings out the Vietnamese sweet tooth and all over the towns and villages shops sell assorted candies packaged in elegant boxes. Dried watermelon seeds or sweet green-bean candies are served to visitors with their tea. To the foreign visitor some of the most unusual treats are the sugared, dried fruits and vegetables called *mut*. Ginger, persimmons, bananas, lemons, tangerines, lotus seeds and sugared winter melons are common, as are the salted dried fruits called *o mai*.

Other festivities involve *banh troi* (floating cake), made of glutinous rice flour encasing a pellet of brown sugar. The egg-like shape of the dumpling on the outside represents the heavens and the square pellet of sugar on the inside represents the earth. *Banh chay* are round with a depressed centre and float in a thick, clear yellowish soup which has sesame seeds sprinkled on top. This combination represents the trinity of the sun, the moon and the earth (the three cakes), the earth's water (the surrounding fluid) and the stars (the sesame seeds).

to help, but you've got to speak up. If you're vegan, you've got a bigger challenge. Eggs are easy to spot, and the Vietnamese rarely, if ever, cook with dairy, though they do enjoy yogurt and ice cream, and use milk in their coffee.

'Mock meat' restaurants are an exquisite experience for those who want to remain true to their vegetarian principles, but secretly miss their bacon butties. Found throughout Vietnam, they use tofu and pulses to cook up magic meat-like dishes that even hardened carnivores enjoy.

Most of the major tourist centres have one or two dedicated vegetarian restaurants these days, and Indian restaurants can always be called upon in an emergency, as they usually understand vegetarian principles better than the *nuoc mam*–loving Vietnamese.

WHINING & DINING

Family is at the centre of life in Vietnam, so it is hardly surprising to find family-oriented restaurants throughout the country. Most local restaurants will welcome children with open arms, particularly foreign kiddies, as staff don't get a chance to see them up close very often. Sometimes the welcome will be too much, with pinches and pats coming left, right and centre, but there is no need to overreact, just set some boundaries.

Ironically, it is often the upmarket Western restaurants where the welcome may be terse if the children are playing up, as some stiff expats seem to have forgotten that they started out life that small. That said, there are plenty of excellent, child-friendly cafés and restaurants in tourist centres up and down Vietnam that serve a slice of the action from home. There are rarely children's menus in any places, but with food so affordable there is little room to quibble.

Most of the snacks children are accustomed to back home are available in Vietnam. It is a great country for fruit, and the sweetness of mangosteens or the weirdness of dragon fruit or rambutan is a sure way to get them interested. There is also an incredible selection of vegetarian creations for parents who prefer their children to avoid meat.

There is a lot of monosodium glutamate (MSG) in local Vietnamese food. If your child has problems digesting it or you prefer to avoid it, it is better to stick to restaurants with an English menu that are used to dealing with tourists.

HABITS & CUSTOMS

Enter the Vietnamese kitchen and you will be convinced that good food comes from simplicity. Essentials consist of a strong flame, clean water, basic cutting utensils, a mortar and pestle, and a well-blackened pot or two. The kitchen is so sacred that it is inhabited by its own deities. The spiritual guardian of the hearth must have its due and the most important object in the kitchen is its altar.

The Vietnamese like to eat three meals a day. Breakfast is simple and may be *pho* or *congee* (rice porridge). Baguettes are available at any time of day or night, and go down well with a cup of coffee.

Lunch starts early, around 11am. People traditionally went home to eat with their families, but many locals now eat at nearby street cafés, washing the food down with lashings of *bia hoi*. Major markets are popular at lunchtime for cheap eats.

Dinner is a time for family bonding. The dishes are arranged around the central rice bowl and diners each have a small eating bowl. The procedure is uncomplicated: spoon some rice into your bowl and lay 'something else' on top of it.

'Anyone who wants to see the Vietnamese at their gregarious best and to find out what the public is saying about current events need only to go on a gastronomical excursion among the soup stands. It's a delicious way to take a political survey.'

EDWARD LANSDALE, CHIEF OF US PSY OPS IN VIETNAM IN THE 1950s

DOS & DON'TS

- Do wait for your host to sit first.
- Don't turn down food placed in your bowl by your host.
- Do learn to use chopsticks.
- Don't leave them in a v-shape in the bowl (a symbol of death).
- Do use the cold towel that is usually provided.
- Don't jump out of your seat when the Vietnamese pop open the cold towel.
- Do tip about 10% in restaurants, as wages are low.
- Don't tip if there is already a service charge on the bill.
- Do drink every time someone offers a toast.
- Don't be sick or pass out face down on the table if it goes on all night.

Vietnamese are not fond of desserts after meals, preferring fruit, but they do like sweets as a snack. Rice cookies, fried bananas, sweet potatoes and coconut candy are all popular snacks. And people will go a long way for ice cream if they have to.

When ordering from a restaurant menu don't worry – don't even think – about the proper succession of courses. All dishes are placed in the centre of the table as soon as they are ready. Diners help themselves to whatever appeals to them regardless of who ordered what. It may seem like gastronomic Russian roulette, but just spin the cylinder, pull the trigger and take your chance. The worst blast you can get will come from the spices.

Table Etiquette

Sit at the table with your bowl on a small plate, chopsticks and a soup spoon at the ready. Each place setting will include a small dipping bowl at the top right-hand side of the bowl for the *nuoc mam*, *nuoc cham* or other dipping sauces.

When serving yourself from the central bowls, use the communal serving spoon so as not to dip your chopsticks into it. To begin eating, just pick up your bowl with the left hand, bring it close to your mouth and use the chopsticks to spoon in the food.

It is polite for the host to offer more food than the guests can eat, and it is polite for the guests not to eat everything in sight!

COOKING COURSES

The best way to tackle Vietnamese cuisine head on is to sign up for a cooking course during your stay. For those who fall in love with the food, there is no better experience than re-creating the real recipes back home. It's also a great way to introduce your Vietnam experience to friends; they may not want to hear the stories or see the photos, but offer them a mouthwatering meal and they will all come running!

Cooking courses have really taken off in the last few years as more and more travellers combine the twin passions of eating and exploring. Courses range from budget classes in the local specialities of Hoi An to gastronomic gallops through the country's classic cuisine at some of the luxury hotels in Hanoi and Ho Chi Minh City. If you are set on something longer, try a short course in Hoi An and negotiate for something longer once you've tasted the experience.

For some of the most authentic Vietnamese recipes, grab a copy of *The Classic Cuisine of Vietnam* (1986) by Bach Ngo and Gloria Zimmerman. More than a glossy cookbook, this is a treasure chest of old Vietnamese recipes for future generations.

EAT YOUR WORDS

Speaking some of the local lingo always helps and never more than when it's time for a meal. Locals will appreciate your efforts, even if your pronunciation is off the mark, and might just introduce you to some regional specialities you would otherwise never have discovered.

Useful Phrases

restaurant
nhà hàng — nyà hàng

Do you have a menu in English?
Bạn có thực đơn bằng tiếng Anh không? — bạn kó turk dern bùng tíng ang kom

I'm a vegetarian.
Tôi ăn chay. — doy un chay

I'd like ...
Xin cho tôi ... — sin jaw doy ...

What's the speciality here?
Ở đây có món gì đặc biệt? — èr day kó món zèe dạk bee·et

Not too spicy please.
Xin đừng cho cay quá. — sin dùrng jaw kay gwá

No sugar.
Không đường. — kom dur-erng

No salt.
Không muối. — kom moo-ée

Can I get this without the meat?
Cho tôi món này không thịt được không? — jaw doi món này kom tịt dur-ẹrk kom

I'm allergic to ....
Tôi bị dị ứng với ... — doy bẹe zẹe úrng ver-ee ...

I don't eat ...
Tôi không được ăn ... — doy kom dur-ẹrk un ...

beef
thịt bò — tịt bàw

chicken
thịt gà — tịt gà

fish
cá — ká

fish sauce
nước mắm — nur-érk múm

pork
thịt heo — tịt hay-o

peanuts
đậu phọng — dọw fọm

Can you please bring me ...?
Xin mang cho tôi...? — sin mang jaw doy ...

a spoon
cái thìa — kái tèe-a

a knife
con dao — kon zow

a fork
cái nĩa — kái nẽe-a

chopsticks
đôi đũa — doh-ee dõo-a

a glass
  cái ly   kái lee

Can I have a (beer) please?
  Xin cho tôi (chai bia)?   sin cho doy (chai bee-a)
Thank you, that was delicious.
  Cám ơn, ngon lắm.   kám ern, ngon lúm
The bill, please.
  Xin tính tiền.   sin dín dee-èn

Menu Decoder
TYPICAL DISHES
bánh bao (bán bow) – sweet, doughy Chinese pastry filled with meat and vegetables and dunked in soy sauce
bánh chưng (bán churng) – square cakes made from sticky rice and filled with beans, onion and pork, boiled in leaves for 10 hours
bánh cuốn (bán koo-ón) – steamed rolls with minced pork
bò bảy món (bàw bảy món) – sweet beef dishes
bún bò huế (bóon bàw hwáy) – spicy beef noodle soup
bún chả (bóon chả) – rice vermicelli with roasted pork and vegetables
bún thịt nướng (bóon tịt nur-érng) – rice vermicelli with char-grilled pork
cánh khổ qua (káng kổh gwa) – a bitter soup
chả (chả) – pork paste fried in fat or grilled over hot coals
chả cá (chả ká) – filleted fish slices grilled over charcoal
chả quế (chả gwáy) – cha prepared with cinnamon
chạo tôm (chọw dom) – grilled sugar cane rolled in spiced shrimp paste
ếch tẩm bột rán (ék tửm bọt rán) – frog meat soaked in a thin batter and fried in oil
giò (zàw) – pork paste packed into banana leaves and boiled
gỏi ngó sen (gỏy ngáw sen) – lotus stem salad
lẩu (lów) – Vietnamese hotpot, served with fish *(lau ca)* or goat *(lau de)* or vegetables only *(lau rau)*
khoai rán/chiên (N/S) (kwai rán/chee-en) – french fries
ốc nhồi (óp nyòh-ee) – snail meat, pork, chopped green onion, fish sauce and pepper rolled up in ginger leaves and cooked in snail shells
rau muống xào (row moóng sòw) – stir-fried water spinach

NOODLES
bún bò (bóon bàw) – braised beef with rice vermicelli
hủ tiếu bò kho (hỏo tee-óo bàw kaw) – beef stew with flat rice noodles
mì gà (mèe gà) – chicken soup with thin egg noodles
miến cua (mée-en koo-a) – cellophane noodle soup with crab
phở gà/bò (fér gà/bàw) – rice noodle soup with chicken/beef

VEGETARIAN
đậu hũ kho (dọw hõo kaw) – braised tofu
đậu hũ xào xả ớt (dọw hõo sòw sả ért) – tofu fried with lemon grass and chilli
gỏi cuốn chay (gỏy koón chay) – vegetarian rice-paper rolls
nấm rơm kho (núm rerm kaw) – braised straw mushrooms
rau cải xào thập cẩm (row kải sòw tụp kảm) – stir-fried mixed vegetables
súp rau (sóop row) – vegetable soup

DESSERTS
bánh đậu xanh (bán dọw sang) – mung-bean cake
bánh ít nhân đậu (bán ít nyan dọw) – pastry made of sticky rice, beans and sugar that's steamed in a banana leaf folded into a triangular pyramid
chè (jàir) – served in a tall ice-cream sundae glass containing beans, fruit, coconut and sugar

kem dừa (kem zùr-a) – mix of ice cream, candied fruit and the jellylike flesh of young coconut

mút (móot) – candied fruit or vegetables, made with carrot, coconut, kumquat, gourd, ginger root, lotus seeds and tomato

sữa chua (sữr-a choo-a) – little jars or plastic cups of sweetened frozen yogurt

Glossary

RICE

rice	*cơm*	kerm
steamed rice	*cơm trắng*	kerm cháng
mixed fried rice	*cơm rang thập cẩm* (N)	kerm rang tụp kúm
	cơm chiên (S)	kerm chee-en
rice porridge	*cháo*	jów

MEAT & SEAFOOD

beef	*thịt bò*	tịt bàw
chicken	*thịt gà*	tịt gà
crab	*cua*	koo-a
eel	*lươn*	lur-ern
fish	*cá*	ká
frog	*ếch*	áyk
goat	*thịt dê*	tịt zay
offal	*thịt lòng*	tịt lòm
pork	*thịt lợn/heo*	tịt lẹrn/hay-o
shrimp/prawns	*tôm*	dohm
snail	*ốc*	óp
squid	*mực*	mụrk

FRUIT

apple	*táo/bơm* (N/S)	dów/berm
banana	*chuối*	chóo-ee
coconut	*dừa*	zừr-a
grapes	*nho*	nyaw
lemon	*chanh*	chan
lychee	*vải*	vải
mandarin	*quýt*	gwéet
mango	*xoài*	swài
orange	*cam*	kam
papaya	*đu đủ*	doo dỏo
pineapple	*dứa*	zứr-a
strawberry	*dâu*	zow
watermelon	*dưa hấu*	zur-a hów

VEGETABLES

cabbage	*bắp cải*	búp kải
carrot	*cà rốt*	kà rót
corn	*bắp/ngô*	búp/ngo
cucumber	*dưa leo/dưa chuột*	zur-a lay-o/zur-a ?tlit?
eggplant	*cà tím*	kà téem
green beans	*đậu xanh*	dọw sang
green pepper	*ớt xanh*	ét sang
lettuce	*rau diếp*	row zee-ép
mushrooms	*nấm*	núm
peas	*đậu bi*	dọw bee
potato	*khoai tây*	kwai tay
pumpkin	*bí ngô*	bée ngo

sweet potato	*khoai lang*	kwai lang
tomato	*cà chua*	kà choo-a

DRINKS

coffee	*cà phê*	kà fay
hot black coffee	*cà phê đen nóng*	kà fay den nóm
hot milk coffee	*nâu nóng* (N)	now nóm
	cà phê sữa nóng (S)	kà fay sữr-a nóm
iced black coffee	*cà phê đá*	kà fay dá
iced milk coffee	*nâu đá* (N)	now dá
	cà phê sữa đá (S)	kà fay süa dá
tea	*chè/trà* (N/S)	jàir/chà
hot black tea	*chè đen nóng* (N)	jàir den nóm
	trà nóng (S)	chà nóm
hot milk black tea	*chè đen sữa* (N)	jàir den sữr-a
	trà pha sữa (S)	chà ?tlit? sữr-a
milk	*sữa*	sữr-a
hot milk	*sữa nóng*	sữr-a nóm
iced milk	*sữa đá*	sữr-a dá
iced chocolate	*cacao đá*	ka-kow dá
soy milk	*sữa đậu nành*	sữr-a dọw nàn
iced lemon juice	*chanh đá*	chan dá
orange juice	*cam vắt*	kam vút
fruit shake	*sinh tố*	sin dóh
mineral water	*nước khoáng* (N)	nur-érk kwáng
	nước suối (S)	nur-érk sóo-ee
soda water & lemon	*soda chanh*	saw-da chan
beer	*bia*	bi-a
ice	*đá*	dá
No ice.	*không đá*	kom dá

Hanoi

CONTENTS

The capital of Vietnam is a city of timeless grace, a grand old dame of Asia who is ageing better than most of her contemporaries. Hanoi lay in a deep slumber after Vietnam's partition in 1954, until the effects of economic reforms began to kick in four decades later. The city and its inhabitants survived American bombs and Russian planners to emerge relatively unscathed in the early 1990s as a superb example of a French colonial city.

Hanoi's centre today is a quixotic blend of Parisian grace and Asian pace, an architectural museum piece evolving in harmony with its history, rather than bulldozing through it like many of the region's capitals. The bustling Old Quarter has been a cauldron of commerce for 800 years and is still the best place to check the pulse of this resurgent city. Elsewhere, towering mansions line grand, tree-lined boulevards, and lakes and parks dotting the city provide the local people with the perfect place for a spot of dawn exercise. There are still fleeting moments of Paris, as the smell of warm baguettes permeates street corners, the beret is as common as the baseball cap and a 'bonjour' is as likely as a 'hello'.

Hanoi was slow to get into the tourism thing, as the authorities here were suspicious of economic reforms and foreign influences in the early days of opening up. Attitudes have changed and Hanoi today is dramatically different from just a few years ago. Visitors are flooding in to soak up the atmosphere, browse the museums, chill out in the cafés and sample the nightlife. Investors are looking at Hanoi with the same enthusiasm that only a few years ago was reserved exclusively for Ho Chi Minh City (HCMC). Known by many names down the centuries, Thanh Long (City of the Soaring Dragon) is the most evocative, and let there be no doubt that this dragon is on the up once more.

HIGHLIGHTS

- Delve into the hectic but historic streets of the bustling **Old Quarter** (p83)
- Step back in time to the **Temple of Literature** (p88), a world away from the busy streets
- Enjoy Punch and Judy in a pool at a performance of the city's famed **water puppets** (p107)
- Pay your respects to 'Uncle Ho' at **Ho Chi Minh's Mausoleum** (p86)
- Piece together the country's ethnic mosaic at the wonderful **Vietnam Museum of Ethnology** (p90)

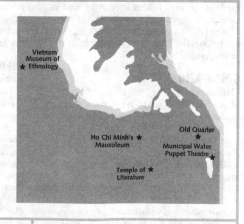

Vietnam Museum of ★ Ethnology

Ho Chi Minh's ★ Mausoleum

Old Quarter ★

Municipal Water Puppet Theatre ★

Temple of ★ Literature

- TELEPHONE CODE: 04   - POPULATION: 3.5 MILLION

HISTORY

The site where Hanoi now stands has been inhabited since the Neolithic period. Emperor Ly Thai To moved his capital here in AD 1010, naming it Thang Long (City of the Soaring Dragon). The decision by Emperor Gia Long, founder of the Nguyen dynasty in 1802, to rule from Hué relegated Hanoi to the status of a regional capital.

Over the centuries Hanoi has been called many names, including Dong Kinh (Eastern Capital), from which the Europeans derived the name they eventually applied to all of northern Vietnam – Tonkin. The city was named Hanoi (The City in a Bend of the River) by Emperor Tu Duc in 1831. From 1902 to 1953, Hanoi served as the capital of French Indochina.

Hanoi was proclaimed the capital of Vietnam after the August Revolution of 1945, but it was not until the Geneva Accords of 1954 that the Viet Minh, driven from the city by the French in 1946, were able to return.

During the American War, US bombing destroyed parts of Hanoi and killed many hundreds of civilians; almost all the damage has since been repaired. One of the prime targets was the 1682m-long Long Bien Bridge, originally built between 1888 and 1902 under the direction of the same architect who designed the Eiffel Tower in Paris. US aircraft repeatedly bombed the strategic bridge, yet after each attack the Vietnamese somehow managed to improvise replacement spans and return it to road and rail service. It is said that when US prisoners of war (POWs) were put to work repairing the bridge, the US military, fearing for their safety, ended the attacks.

ORIENTATION

Hanoi sprawls along the banks of the Song Hong (Red River), which is spanned by two bridges – the Long Bien Bridge (now used only by nonmotorised vehicles and pedestrians) and, 600m south, the newer Chuong Duong Bridge.

The attractive centre of Hanoi is built around Hoan Kiem Lake. Just north of this lake is the Old Quarter (known to the French as the Cité Indigène), which is characterised by narrow streets whose names change every one or two blocks. Most visitors prefer to base themselves in this part of town.

Along the western periphery of the Old Quarter is the ancient Hanoi Citadel, which was originally constructed by Emperor Gia Long. Unfortunately, the citadel is now a military base and also the residence of high-ranking officers and their families – in other words, closed to the public. Most of the ancient buildings were tragically destroyed by French troops in 1894 – US bombing during the American War took care of the rest.

Further west is Ho Chi Minh's Mausoleum. Most of the foreign embassies, which are housed in classical architectural masterpieces from the French-colonial era, are found in this neighbourhood and posh joint-venture hotels have also sprung up here. Ho Tay (West Lake), Hanoi's largest lake, is north of Ho Chi Minh's Mausoleum and is also the site of many pleasure palaces for tourists.

Taxis, an airport minibus and local buses link Hanoi's Noi Bai International Airport with the city centre. From bus and train stations, there are metered taxis, xe om (motorbike taxis) or cyclos to ferry you to your destination.

Maps

Hanoi city maps come in every size and scale. Some are freebies subsidised by advertising and others precise works of cartography.

Pretty much all the leading maps are produced by **Ban Do** (☎ 344 108) and include detailed ones at a scale of 1:10,000 or 1:17,500, both costing around 6000d; and a hand-drawn 3D map of Old Hanoi which makes a nice souvenir. They are available at all leading bookshops in Hanoi.

INFORMATION
Bookshops

If you're out of reading material, Hanoi's a good place to stock up. Many of the budget hotels and travellers cafés in the Old Quarter have small book exchanges.

Bookworm (Map pp80-1; ☎ 943 7226; bookworm@fpt .vn; 15a Ngo Van So; ☒ 10am-7pm Tue-Sun) The best selection of English-language books in Hanoi. It's mostly fiction here, but there's also some good travel stock; choose from new or second-hand books.

Foreign Language Bookshop (Map p84; ☎ 825 7376; 64 Pho Trang Tien) Does what it says on the packet…stocks a healthy selection of foreign language titles, particularly in French.

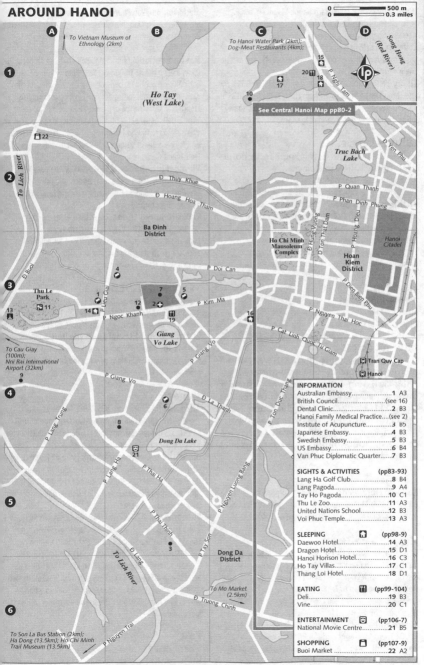

AROUND HANOI

0 — 500 m
0 — 0.3 miles

To Vietnam Museum of Ethnology (2km)

To Hanoi Water Park (2km);
Dog-Meat Restaurants (4km)

Song Hong (Red River)

Ho Tay (West Lake)

See Central Hanoi Map pp80-2

Truc Bach Lake

To Lich River

Đ Thuy Khue

Đ Hoang Hoa Tham

P Quan Thanh

P Phan Dinh Phung

Ba Đinh District

Ho Chi Minh Mausoleum Complex

Hoan Kiem District

Hanoi Citadel

P Doi Can

Thu Le Park

P Lieu Giai

P Kim Ma

P Ngoc Khanh

Giang Vo Lake

P Dien Bien Phu

P Nguyen Thai Hoc

P Cat Linh-Quoc Tu Giam

Tran Quy Cap

Hanoi

To Cau Giay (100m);
Noi Bai International Airport (32km)

P Giang Vo

Đ La Thanh

Dong Da Lake

P Lang Trung

P Lang Ha

P Thai Ha

P Nguyen Luong Bang

P Thai Thinh

Dong Da District

To Lich River

P Tay Son

To Mo Market (2.5km)

Đ Truong Chinh

To Son La Bus Station (2km);
Ha Dong (13.5km); Ho Chi Minh Trail Museum (13.5km)

P Nguyen Trai

INFORMATION	
Australian Embassy	1 A3
British Council	(see 16)
Dental Clinic	2 B3
Hanoi Family Medical Practice	(see 2)
Institute of Acupuncture	3 B5
Japanese Embassy	4 B3
Swedish Embassy	5 B3
US Embassy	6 B4
Van Phuc Diplomatic Quarter	7 B3

SIGHTS & ACTIVITIES	(pp83-93)
Lang Ha Golf Club	8 B4
Lang Pagoda	9 A4
Tay Ho Pagoda	10 C1
Thu Le Zoo	11 A3
United Nations School	12 B3
Voi Phuc Temple	13 A3

SLEEPING	(pp98-9)
Daewoo Hotel	14 A3
Dragon Hotel	15 D1
Hanoi Horison Hotel	16 C3
Ho Tay Villas	17 C1
Thang Loi Hotel	18 D1

EATING	(pp99-104)
Deli	19 B3
Vine	20 C1

ENTERTAINMENT	(pp106-7)
National Movie Centre	21 B5

SHOPPING	(pp107-9)
Buoi Market	22 A2

Hanoi Bookstore (Hieu Sach Hanoi; Map p84; ☎ 824 1616; 34 Pho Trang Tien) A good place for coffee-table classics and other souvenir books.

Love Planet (Map p84; ☎ 828 4864; 25 Pho Hang Bac) Big second-hand bookshop with a wide selection of mostly English paperbacks.

Thang Long Bookshop (Map p84; ☎ 825 7043; 53-55 Pho Trang Tien) A stroll away from Hoan Kiem Lake, it's a big bookshop with English and French titles, plus some international newspapers and magazines.

Cultural Centres

For periodicals and newspapers from home, head to the following places.

American Club (Map p84; ☎ 824 1850; amclub@fpt.vn; 19-21 Pho Hai Ba Trung)

British Council (Map p77; ☎ 843 6780; www.british council.org/vietnam; 40 Pho Cat Linh) Right next to the Hanoi Horison Hotel.

Centre Culturel Française de Hanoi (Map p84; ☎ 936 2164; 24 Trang Tien) In the L'Espace building, a great new venue opposite the Dan Chu Hotel.

Emergency

Ambulance (☎ 115)
Fire (☎ 114)
Police (☎ 113)

Internet Access

It's hard to go more than a few hundred metres anywhere in the city without stumbling across an Internet café, in particular those at backpacker cafés and travel agents along Pho Hang Bac and Pho Hang Be in the Old Quarter. Many places do not display prices, so check before you notch up a couple of hours online: overcharging isn't unheard of in some places.

Libraries

National Library and Archives (Map p84; ☎ 825 3357; 31 Pho Trang Thi) Some English and French material available, but mostly Vietnamese.

Medical Services

Bach Mai Hospital (Benh Vien Bach Mai; Map pp80-1; ☎ 869 3731; Đ Giai Phong) Includes an international department with English-speaking doctors.

Dental Clinic (Map p77; ☎ 846 2864; thedental@netnam.vn) Can't live with the tooth? Deal with it here, part of the Hanoi Family Medical Practice.

French Embassy Clinic (Map pp80-1; ☎ 825 2719; 49 Pho Ba Trieu) A 24-hour clinic for French nationals.

Hanoi Family Medical Practice (Map p77; ☎ 843 0748, 24hr emergency service ☎ 0903-401 919; www

.doctorkot.com; Van Phuc Diplomatic Compound, Bldg A1, Ste 109-112, Pho Kim Ma) Boasts a team of well-respected international physicians. It's pricey so make sure your medical insurance is in order.

SOS International Clinic (Map p84; ☎ 934 0555; fax 934 0556; 31 Pho Hai Ba Trung; ⌚ 8am-7pm Mon-Fri, 8am-2pm Sat, emergency 24hr) Expensive international chain of clinics with annual policies for expats living in Vietnam. English, French and Japanese spoken. Evacuation specialists.

Viet Duc Hospital (Benh Vien Viet Duc; Map p84; ☎ 825 3531; 40 Pho Trang Thi; ⌚ 24hr) Old Quarter unit for emergency surgery; the doctors here speak English, French and German.

Vietnam International Hospital (Map pp80-1; ☎ 574 0740, 24hr emergency service ☎ 547 1111; Đ Giai Phong) A good international-standard facility staffed by French doctors.

Vietnam-Korea Friendship Clinic (Map pp80-1; ☎ 843 7231; 12 Chu Van An; ⌚ 9am-noon & 2-5pm Mon-Fri) If you're crazy enough to travel without insurance, this high standard nonprofit clinic is the least expensive in Hanoi; consultations US$5.

TRADITIONAL MEDICINE

Institute of Acupuncture (Map p77; ☎ 853 3881; H3 Pho Vinh Ho & 49 Pho Thai Thinh) Holistic medicine? Well, very small holes anyway.

Institute of Traditional Medicine (Map pp80-1; ☎ 943 1018; 26-29 Pho Nguyen Binh Khiem) Check out some Vietnamese solutions to what might be Vietnamese problems.

Money

ANZ Bank (Map p84; ☎ 825 8190; 14 Pho Le Thai To; ⌚ 8.30am-4pm Mon-Fri) On the western edge of Hoan Kiem Lake, it does cash advances in dong and dollars, plus has a 24-hour ATM.

Industrial & Commercial Bank (Map p84; ☎ 825 4276; 37 Pho Hang Bo) Convenient location in the Old Quarter; it cashes travellers cheques at the standard 0.5% commission for dong, 1.25% for US dollars and 3% for credit-card cash advances.

Vietcombank Pho Hang Bai (Map p84; ☎ 826 8031; 2 Pho Hang Bai); Pho Tran Quang Khai (Map p84; ☎ 826 8045; 198 Pho Tran Quang Khai; ⌚ 7.30-11.30am & 1-3.30pm Mon-Fri, 7.30-11.30am Sat) The towering HQ is located a few blocks east of Hoan Kiem Lake and it has an ATM and offers most currency services. Several smaller branches are scattered around town, including a handy one on Pho Hang Bai, near the southeast corner of Hoan Kiem Lake.

Post

There are small post-office kiosks all over the city that do the basics. Go to the main

HANOI IN...

A Day

Begin with breakfast in an Old Quarter café before jumping on a *cyclo* to **Ho Chi Minh's Mausoleum** (p86), where you might be lucky enough to catch a changing of the guard. Check out the surreal **museum** (p88) and the balancing act that is the **One Pillar Pagoda** (p88) before moving on to the **Temple of Literature** (p88). This is a great escape from the hustle and bustle of Hanoi and just opposite is **KOTO** (p99), an essential lunch stop as all proceeds from this great restaurant go towards helping street children. In the afternoon, it is time to take a serious look at the **Old Quarter** (p83), browsing its buildings, shops or bars to soak up the unique atmosphere. If you haven't already been tempted, stop for a *bia hoi* (fresh beer) around sunset and watch Hanoi shift from work to play. Catch a performance of the wonderful **water puppets** (p107) before enjoying a local meal and some beers in nearby Pho Bao Khanh.

Two Days

After the fun of day one, it is time to amuse yourself in some museums. This morning head out of town to the excellent **Museum of Ethnology** (p90) to discover the ethnic mosaic that makes up Vietnam today. Have a local lunch in **Nha Hang Lan Chin** (p105), tucked away next to the **Museum of Vietnamese Revolution** (p90) and hop across the road to the **History Museum** (p90). The building is stunning and the contents a fine introduction to 2000 years of ups and downs. Head back to the Old Quarter for a look at **Memorial House** (p90) and then kick back in a café and contemplate the next part of your journey.

domestic and international post office in the event that you need to do anything complicated.

Domestic post office (Buu Dien Trung Vong; Map p84; ☎ 825 7036; 75 Pho Dinh Tien Hoang; ☒ 7am-9.30pm) Occupies a full city block facing Hoan Kiem Lake. You can send letters, pick up domestic packages and purchase philatelic items.

International postal office (☎ 825 2030; cnr Pho Dinh Tien Hoang & Pho Dinh Le; ☒ 7am-8.30pm) Has its own entrance to the right of the domestic office.

Private document and parcel carriers in Hanoi:

DHL (Map pp80-1; ☎ 733 2086; 49 Pho Nguyen Thai Hoc)
Federal Express (Map p84; ☎ 824 9054; 6C Pho Dinh Le)
UPS (Map p84; ☎ 824 6483; 4C Pho Dinh Le)

Telephone

For domestic telephone calls, the post offices throughout town are as good as anywhere. Guesthouses and Internet cafés are also a convenient option for local calls within Hanoi. For international telephone calls and faxes, hit the international postal office (p78). The cheapest international telephone calls are available at most Internet cafés, but the connection is not always as clear as from a standard phone.

Tourist Information

Even though this is the capital of the country, forget anything really useful like a helpful tourism office that dishes out free information. The best source of tourism information in Hanoi, as in the rest of Vietnam, is asking around at different guesthouses, travel agencies and bars, and talking to your fellow travellers.

Travel Agencies

There are plenty of travel agencies in Hanoi, both government-run and privately owned, which can book tours, provide cars and guides, issue air tickets and arrange visa extensions.

Several budget agencies also double as restaurant-cafés, which offer cheap eats, rooms for rent and Internet access. The mighty alliance between HCMC's Sinh Café and state-run Hanoi Toserco captures a large share of the local 'fast-food' tourist market, in particular the dirt-cheap 'open tours', which shuttle travellers in buses along Hwy 1 between Hanoi and HCMC. The proliferation, however, of 'fake' Sinh Cafés in Hanoi has confused more than a few travellers. And it's not only fake Sinh Cafés, but several of the other leading local agents have been cloned over the years. Check the

HANOI

CENTRAL HANOI

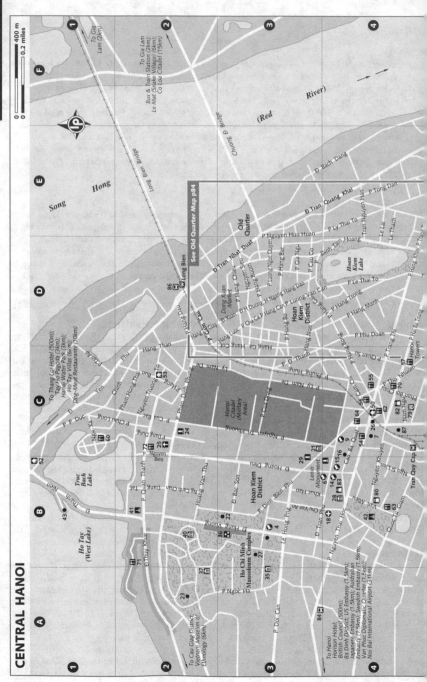

400 m
0.2 miles

To Gia
Lam (2km)

To Gia Lam (2km);
Le Mat (Snake Village) (6km);
Bus & Train Station (2km);
Co Loa Citadel (15km)

Song   Hong   (Red   River)

Long Bien Bridge

Chuong D Bridge

To Thang Loi Hotel (500m);
Tay Ho Pagoda (3km);
Hanoi Water Park (3km);
Ho Tay Villas (6km);
Dog-Meat Restaurants (10km)

Ho Tay
(West Lake)

Trac
Bach Lake

See Old Quarter Map p84

Old
Quarter

D Tran Quang Khai
P Tong Dan
P Ly Thai To
Tran Nguyen Han
Le Lai
Le Thach

Long Bien

Đ Tran Nhat Duat

P Nguyen Huu Huan

Dong Xuan Market

Hang Than

Hoan
Kiem
Lake

Hoan
Kiem
District

P Le Thai To

P Hang Trong

Hanoi District
Towers

Hanoi Citadel
(Military Area)

Lenin Monument

Hoan Kiem
District

Ho Chi Minh
Mausoleum Complex

P Ngoc Ha

P Doi Can

To Cau Giay District;
Vietnam Museum of
Ethnology (6km)

To Hanoi Hotel;
Horison Hotel;
British Council (500m);
Ba Dinh District; US Embassy (1.5km);
Japanese Embassy (1.5km); Australian
Embassy (1.5km); Swedish Embassy (1.5km);
Van Phuc Diplomatic Quarter (3km);
Noi Bai International Airport (35km)

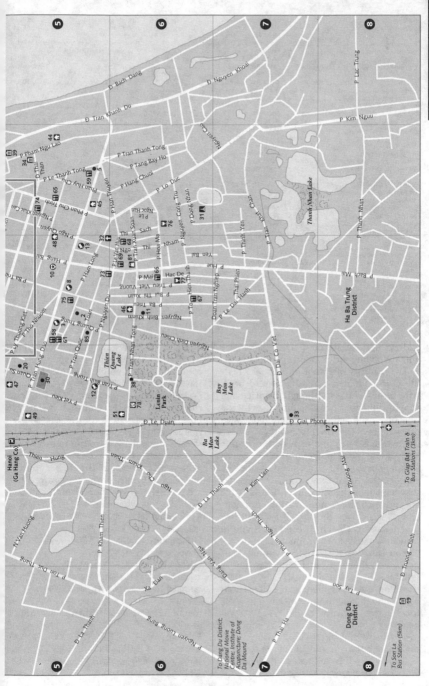

address and website carefully to make sure you are buying the authentic product.

The majority of Hanoi's hotels also peddle tours, but it is not advisable to book trips through hotels: although the prices are roughly the same, booking directly with the tour operators will give a much better idea of what you'll get for your money.

There has been a stream of complaints lately about some budget tour operators in Hanoi. The biggest issue seems to be the gap between what they promise and what they actually deliver. Competition is fierce and price-cutting among various tour operators has driven the cost of tours so low that in some cases it has become difficult to provide a satisfactory product.

You can buy a two-day/one-night, all-inclusive excursion to Halong Bay for as little as US$16, but do you really want to travel on a 45-seat bus and be herded en masse onto a boat to tour the bay and grottoes? In the long run, the dollars saved will probably not be remembered as much as the quality of the trip itself. It's your choice of course, but if you buy the cheapest thing out there, you'll have to share the blame if you don't come away satisfied.

We suggest seeking out tour operators who stick to small groups and use their own vehicles and guides. **Handspan Adventure Travel** (Map p84; ☎ 926 0581; www.handspan.com; 80 Pho Ma May) at the Tamarind Café is a long-running favourite that consistently generates positive feedback from readers. **Kangaroo Café** (Map p84; ☎ 828 9931; kangaroo@hn.vnn.vn; 18 Pho Bao Khanh) is a popular Aussie-run tour company that also has a very good reputation.

New places open all the time, and existing places change, so the suggestions here are not exhaustive. Shop around and consider the following places:
A to Z Queen Café (Map p84; ☎ 826 0860; www.queencafé.com.vn; 65 Pho Hang Bac)
ET Pumpkin (Map p84; ☎ 926 0739; www.et-pumpkin.com; 85 Pho Ma May)
Explorer Tours (Map p84; ☎ 923 0713; www.explorer.com.vn; 75 Pho Hang Bo)
Fansipan Tours (Map p84; ☎ /fax 926 0910; www.fansipantours.com.vn; 24a Pho Hang Bac)
Footprint Travel (Map p84; ☎ /fax 826 0879; 116 Pho Hang Bac)
Kim Café (Map p84; ☎ 824 9049; www.kimcafe79travel.com; 79 Pho Hang Bac)
Lotus Travel (Map p84; ☎ 826 8642; Lotus Guesthouse, 42V Pho Ly Thuong Kiet)

Love Planet Café (Map p84; ☎ 828 4864; loveplanet@hn.vnn.vn; 25 Pho Hang Bac)
ODC Travel (Formerly Old Darling Café; Map p84; ☎ 824 3024; www.odctravel.com; 43 Pho Hang Bo & 142 Pho Hang Bac)
Red River Tours (Map p84; ☎ 826 8427; fax 828 7159; redrivertours.hn.vn@fpt.vn; www.redrivertours .com.vn; 73 Pho Hang Bo)
Sinh Café (Map p84; ☎ 926 0646; sinhcafé@hn .vnn.vn; 52 Pho Hang Bac)

DANGERS & ANNOYANCES

Far fewer than Saigon is the quick answer! Some western women have been hassled by young men around town who follow them home. Walking alone in well-lit areas of the Old Quarter is usually safe, but it pays to stay alert. Getting from one part of town to the other at night, particularly from late-night spots, it is more sensible for solo women to take a metered taxi or *xe om*.

Scams

One unfortunate development in Hanoi has been hustlers moving into the hotel market. They rent a building, appropriate the name of another hotel, and then work with touts to bring unwitting tourists to their 'chosen' accommodation. Visitors who question the alternative location are told the hotel has moved and it is not until they check the next day that they realise they have been had. And these fly-by-night hotels overcharge for any extras (like US$1 for a bottle of water and so on). Airport taxis and minibuses often work in partnership with these copycat hotels, as they give the biggest commissions.

Gay men should be aware of a scam going on around the Hoan Kiem Lake. It starts with a friendly stranger approaching a foreigner and suggesting a night out. This leads to a karaoke bar and a private room for a few drinks and some songs. The bill arrives and it's miraculously US$100 or more. The situation deteriorates from here and ends in extortion. Be careful and follow your instincts.

SIGHTS
Old Quarter

Hanoi's Old Quarter, with more than a thousand years of history, remains one of Vietnam's most lively and unusual places. The commercial quarter of the city evolved alongside the Red River and the smaller To Lich River, which once flowed through the city centre in an intricate network of canals and waterways teeming with boats. As the waters could rise as high as 8m during the monsoon, dikes, which can still be seen along Tran Quang Khai, were constructed to protect the city.

In the 13th century Hanoi's 36 guilds established themselves here, each taking a different street – hence the original name '36 Streets'; there are more than 50 streets in today's Old Quarter. *Hang* means 'merchandise' and is usually followed by the name of the product that was traditionally sold in that street. Thus, Pho Hang Gai translates as 'Silk Street' (see the boxed text 'Old Quarter Street Names', p87, for the rest); these days the street name may not indicate what's sold there, otherwise there would be loads of Pho Hang Du Lich (Tourism Streets).

Exploring the maze of back streets is fascinating; some streets open up while others narrow into a warren of alleys. The area is known for its tunnel (or tube) houses – so called because of their narrow frontages and long rooms. These tunnel houses were developed to avoid taxes based on the width of their street frontage. By feudal law, houses were also limited to two storeys and, out of respect for the king, could not be taller than the Royal Palace. These days there are taller buildings, but no real high-rise buildings.

Opportunities to lighten your load of dong are almost endless. As you wander around you'll find clothes, cosmetics, fake sunglasses, luxury food, T-shirts, musical instruments, plumbing supplies, herbal medicines, jewellery, religious offerings, spices, woven mats and much, much more (see Shopping, p107).

Some of the specialised streets include Pho Hang Quat, with its red candlesticks, funeral boxes, flags and temple items; and the more glamorous Pho Hang Gai, with its silk, embroidery, lacquerware, paintings and water puppets – silk sleeping-bag liners and elegant *ao dai* are very popular here. Finally, no trip to the Old Quarter would be complete without a visit to **Dong Xuan Market** (cnr Pho Hang Khoai & Pho Dong Xuan), which was rebuilt after a fire in 1994.

A stroll through the historic Old Quarter can last anywhere from a few minutes to the better part of a day, depending on your pace

HANOI

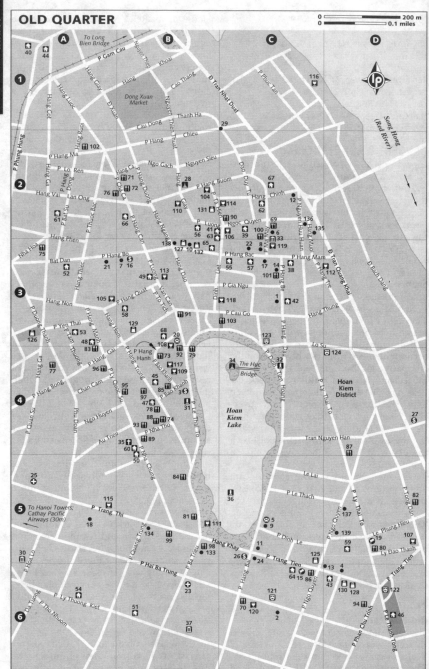

OLD QUARTER

and how well you navigate the increasing motor traffic plaguing the streets. However long, or whatever detours you might take, the suggested route in the Walking Tour (p93) will provide you with a good dose of Vietnamese culture and some insight into the country's long history.

Lakes

HOAN KIEM LAKE

Right in the heart of Hanoi, **Hoan Kiem Lake** (Map p84) is an enchanting body of water. Legend has it that, in the mid-15th century, Heaven sent Emperor Ly Thai To (Le Loi)

a magical sword, which he used to drive the Chinese out of Vietnam. One day after the war he stumbled upon a giant golden tortoise swimming on the surface of the water; the creature grabbed the sword and disappeared into the depths of the lake. Since that time, the lake has been known as Ho Hoan Kiem (Lake of the Restored Sword) because the tortoise restored the sword to its divine owners.

Ngoc Son Temple (p89) sits on an island near the northern end of Hoan Kiem Lake; and forlorn **Thap Rua** (Tortoise Tower), on an islet near the southern end, is topped with

HANOI

a red star and is often used as an emblem of Hanoi. Every morning around 6am, local residents can be seen doing their traditional t'ai chi, jogging and playing badminton around the lake.

HO TAY (WEST LAKE)

Two legends explain the origins of **Ho Tay** (Map p77), also known as the Lake of Mist and the Big Lake. According to one legend, Ho Tay was created when the Dragon King drowned an evil nine-tailed fox in his lair, which was in a forest on this site. Another legend relates that in the 11th century, a Vietnamese Buddhist monk, Khong Lo, rendered a great service to the emperor of China, who rewarded him with a vast quantity of bronze from which he cast a huge bell. The sound of the bell could be heard all the way to China, where the Golden Buffalo Calf, mistaking the ringing for its mother's call, ran southward, trampling on the site of Ho Tay and turning it into a lake.

The boring explanation is that the lake was created when the Song Hong (Red River) overflowed its banks. Indeed, the river has changed its course numerous times, alternately flooding some land and creating some through silt build-up. The flood problem has been partially controlled by building dikes, and the highway along the eastern side of Ho Tay is built upon one.

The lake was once ringed by magnificent palaces and pavilions that were destroyed throughout the course of various feudal wars. The circumference of West Lake is about 13km.

On the southern side of the lake is a popular strip of outdoor seafood restaurants (see p102), while the northern side has been earmarked for a development of luxurious villas and hotels.

TRUC BACH LAKE

This **lake** (Ho Truc Bach; Map p77) is separated from Ho Tay by Ð Thanh Nien, which is lined with flame trees. During the 18th century the Trinh lords built a palace on the lakeside; it was later transformed into a reformatory for wayward royal concubines, who were condemned to spend their days weaving a very fine white silk.

Ho Chi Minh Mausoleum Complex

To the west of the Old Quarter is the **Ho Chi Minh mausoleum complex** (Map pp80-1; cnr Pho Ngoc Ha & Pho Doi Can), an important place of pilgrimage for many Vietnamese, combining the secular and the spiritual. A traffic-free area of parks, monuments, memorials and pagodas, it's usually crowded with groups of all ages who have come to pay their respects.

HO CHI MINH'S MAUSOLEUM

In the tradition of Lenin and Stalin before him, and Mao after, the **final resting place of Ho Chi Minh** (Map pp80-1; admission free; ☒ 8-11am Tue-Thu, Sat & Sun Dec-Sep, last entry usually 10.15am) is a glass sarcophagus set deep in the bowels of a monumental edifice that is Vietnam's number one place of pilgrimage. Ho Chi Minh's Mausoleum – built contrary to his desire for a simple cremation – was constructed, between 1973 and 1975, of native materials gathered from all over Vietnam. The roof and peristyle are said to evoke either a traditional communal house or a lotus flower, though to many tourists it looks like a concrete cubicle with columns.

THE TORTOISES OF HOAN KIEM LAKE: FACT OR FICTION?

Unbelievably, there *are* tortoises in the mysterious and murky waters of Hoan Kiem Lake.

Surfacing on rare occasions, and bringing luck to anyone fortunate enough to see one, the Sword Lake tortoise *Rafetus leloii* is not just your common garden-variety tortoise – it is a huge animal. A specimen that died in 1968 weighed in at 250kg and was 2.1m long! Its preserved remains are on show in the Ngoc Son Temple complex (p89), together with a photo taken of a tortoise that appeared in the lake in 2000. No-one is sure how many there still are, or how they have survived in this urban setting. Rumours abound.

Are these really the lake-dwelling descendants of the golden tortoise of Le Loi? Or are they safeguarded in enclosures elsewhere and transported to the lake from time to time, where their occasional appearance is simply an orchestrated ploy to keep the legend of the lake alive?

Those ripples on the lake surface will never seem so innocent again.

OLD QUARTER STREET NAMES

Street name	Description	Street name	Description
Bat Dan	wooden bowls	Hang Giay	paper or shoes
Bat Su	china bowls	Hang Hanh	onions
Cha Ca	roasted fish	Hang Hom	cases
Chan Cam	string instruments	Hang Huong	incense
Cho Gao	rice market	Hang Khay	trays
Gia Ngu	fishermen	Hang Khoai	sweet potatoes
Hai Tuong	sandals	Hang Luoc	combs
Hang Bac	silversmiths	Hang Ma	votive Papers
Hang Be	rafts	Hang Mam	pickled fish
Hang Bo	baskets	Hang Manh	bamboo screens
Hang Bong	cotton	Hang Muoi	salt
Hang Buom	sails	Hang Ngang	transversal street
Hang But	brushes	Hang Non	hats
Hang Ca	fish	Hang Phen	alum
Hang Can	scales	Hang Quat	fans
Hang Chai	bottles	Hang Ruoi	clam worms
Hang Chi	threads	Hang Than	charcoal
Hang Chieu	mats	Hang Thiec	tin
Hang Chinh	jars	Hang Thung	barrels
Hang Cot	bamboo Lattices	Hang Tre	bamboo
Hang Da	leather	Hang Trong	drums
Hang Dao	(silk) dyers	Hang Vai	cloth
Hang Dau	beans or oils	Lo Ren	blacksmiths
Hang Dieu	pipes	Lo Su	coffins
Hang Dong	copper	Ma May	rattan
Hang Duong	sugar	Ngo Gach	bricks
Hang Ga	chicken	Thuoc Bac	herbal medicine
Hang Gai	silk		

It's closed for about three months each year while Ho Chi Minh's embalmed corpse goes to Russia for maintenance. Some sceptics have suggested Madame Tussaud's has the contract these days.

The queue, which moves quite quickly, usually snakes for several hundred metres to the mausoleum entrance itself. Inside, more guards, regaled in snowy-white military uniforms, are posted at intervals of five paces, giving an eerily authoritarian aspect to the macabre spectacle of the embalmed body with its wispy white hair.

The following rules are strictly applied to all visitors to the mausoleum:

- People wearing shorts, tank tops etc will not be admitted.
- Nothing (including day packs and cameras) can be taken into the mausoleum.
- A respectful demeanour must be maintained at all times.
- For obvious reasons of decorum, photography is absolutely prohibited inside the mausoleum.
- It is forbidden to put your hands in your pockets.
- Hats must be taken off inside the mausoleum building.

Most of the visitors are Vietnamese and it's interesting to watch their reactions. Most show deep respect and admiration for Ho Chi Minh, who is honoured for his role as the liberator of the Vietnamese people from colonialism, as much as for his communist ideology. This view is reinforced by Vietnam's educational system, which emphasises Ho's deeds and accomplishments.

If you're lucky, you'll catch the changing of the guard outside Ho's mausoleum – the pomp and ceremony displayed here rivals the British equivalent at Buckingham Palace.

HANOI

Photography is permitted outside the building but not inside and visitors must leave their bags at a counter just inside the entrance. The soundtrack for a 20-minute video about Ho Chi Minh is available in Vietnamese, French, English, Khmer, Lao, Russian and Spanish.

HO CHI MINH'S STILT HOUSE & THE PRESIDENTIAL PALACE
Behind Ho Chi Minh's Mausoleum is a **stilt house** (Nha San Bac Ho; Map pp80-1; admission 5000d; 🕑 8-11am & 2-4pm), where Ho lived on and off from 1958 to 1969. The house is built in the style of Vietnam's ethnic minorities, and has been preserved just as Ho left it. It's set in a well-tended garden next to a carp-filled pond. Just how much time he actually spent here is questionable – the house would have been a tempting target for US bombers had it been suspected that Ho was hanging out here.

Near the stilt house is the **Presidential Palace** (Map pp80-1), a beautifully restored colonial building constructed in 1906 as the Palace of the Governor General of Indochina. It is now used for official receptions and isn't open to the public. There is a combined entrance gate to the stilt house and Presidential Palace grounds on Pho Ong Ich Kiem, inside the mausoleum complex; when the main mausoleum entrance is closed, enter from Đ Hung Vuong near the palace building.

HO CHI MINH MUSEUM
The two separate sections of the **Ho Chi Minh Museum** (Bao Tang Ho Chi Minh; Map pp80-1; admission 5000d; 🕑 8-11am & 1.30-4.30pm Tue-Thu, Sat & Sun) relate to the past and future. You start in the past and move to the future by walking in a clockwise direction downwards through the museum, starting from the right-hand side of the top of the stairs. The modern displays all have messages, such as 'peace', 'happiness' and 'freedom'.

It's probably worth taking an English-speaking guide, since some of the symbolism is hard to figure out. The 1958 Ford Edsel bursting through the wall – a US commercial failure to symbolise its military failure – is a knockout.

The museum is the huge cement structure next to Ho Chi Minh's Mausoleum. Photography is forbidden and, upon entry, you must leave bags and cameras at reception.

ONE PILLAR PAGODA
Hanoi's famous **One Pillar Pagoda** (Chua Mot Cot; Pho Ong Ich Kiem; Map pp80-1) was built by the Emperor Ly Thai Tong, who ruled from 1028 to 1054. According to the annals, the heirless emperor dreamed that he had met Quan The Am Bo Tat, the Goddess of Mercy, who, while seated on a lotus flower, handed him a male child. Ly Thai Tong then married a young peasant girl he met by chance and had a son and heir by her. As a way of expressing his gratitude for this event, he constructed this pagoda in 1049.

One Pillar Pagoda, built of wood on a single stone pillar 1.25m in diameter, is designed to resemble a lotus blossom, symbol of purity, rising out of a sea of sorrow. One of the last acts of the French before quitting Hanoi in 1954, malicious and pointless, was to destroy the One Pillar Pagoda; the structure was rebuilt by the new government. The pagoda is between the mausoleum and the museum.

DIEN HUU PAGODA
The entrance to **Dien Huu Pagoda** (Map pp80-1) is a few metres from the staircase of the One Pillar Pagoda. This small pagoda, which surrounds a garden courtyard, is one of the most delightful in Hanoi. The old wood and ceramic statues on the altar are distinctively northern. An elderly monk can sometimes be found performing acupuncture on the front porch.

Temples & Pagodas
TEMPLE OF LITERATURE
A relaxing retreat from the streets of Hanoi, the **Temple of Literature** (Van Mieu; Map pp80-1; Pho Quoc Tu Giam; admission 20,000d; 🕑 8am-5pm) is a rare example of well-preserved traditional Vietnamese architecture and is well worth a visit.

It was founded in 1070 by Emperor Ly Thanh Tong, who dedicated it to Confucius (Khong Tu) in order to honour scholars and men of literary accomplishment. Vietnam's first university was established here in 1076 to educate the sons of mandarins. In 1484 Emperor Le Thanh Tong ordered that stelae be erected on the temple premises, recording the names, places of birth and achievements of men who received doctorates in each triennial examination from 1442. Although 116 examinations were held between 1442 and 1778, when the practice was discontinued, only 82 stelae are extant. In 1802 Emperor Gia Long transferred the National University to his new capital, Hué. Major renovations were carried out here in 1920 and 1956.

The Temple of Literature is made up of five separate courtyards. The central pathways and gates between them were reserved for the king. The walkways on one side were solely for the use of administrative mandarins, while those on the other side were for military mandarins.

The main entrance is preceded by a gate, on which there's an inscription requesting that visitors dismount their horses before entering. Khué Van Pavilion, at the far side of the second courtyard, was constructed in 1802 and is a fine example of Vietnamese architecture. The 82 stelae, considered to be the most precious artefacts in the temple, are arrayed to either side of the third enclosure; each one sits on a stone tortoise.

The Temple of Literature is about 2km west of Hoan Kiem Lake.

NGOC SON TEMPLE

Founded in the 18th century, **Ngoc Son Temple** (Jade Mountain Temple; Map p84; admission 2000d; 8am-5pm) is on an island in the northern part of Hoan Kiem Lake. Surrounded by water and shaded by trees, it is a delightfully quiet place to rest. The temple is dedicated to the scholar Van Xuong, General Tran Hung Dao, who defeated the Mongols in the 13th century, and La To, the patron saint of physicians.

Ngoc Son Temple is reached via the red The Huc (Rising Sun) Bridge, which was constructed in 1885.

AMBASSADORS' PAGODA

The official centre of Buddhism in Hanoi, the **Ambassadors' Pagoda** (Chua Quan Su; Map pp80-1; ☎ 825 2427; 73 Pho Quan Su) attracts quite a crowd on holidays. During the 17th century there was a guesthouse here for the ambassadors of Buddhist countries. Today there are about a dozen monks and nuns based at the Ambassadors' Pagoda. Next to the pagoda is a store selling Buddhist ritual objects.

The Ambassadors' Pagoda is located between Pho Ly Thuong Kiet and Pho Tran Hung Dao.

BACH MA TEMPLE

Nestled in a corner of the Old Quarter, the small **Bach Ma Temple** (Map p84; Pho Hang Buom & Pho Hang Giay; admission free) is the oldest in the city. Built by King Ly Thai To to honour a white horse that guided him to the site to construct his city walls, the pagoda includes a statue of the legendary horse, as well as a beautiful red-lacquered funeral palanquin. Donations are very welcome.

HAI BA TRUNG TEMPLE

Two kilometres south of Hoan Kiem Lake, this **temple** (Map pp80-1; Pho Tho Lao) was founded in 1142. A statue shows the two Trung sisters (who lived in the 1st century AD) kneeling with their arms raised in the air, as if they are addressing a crowd. Some people say the statue shows the sisters, who had been proclaimed the queens of the Vietnamese, about to dive into a river. They are said to have drowned themselves rather than surrender following their defeat at the hands of the Chinese.

QUAN THANH TEMPLE

Shaded by huge trees, **Quan Thanh Temple** (Map pp80-1) was established during the Ly dynasty (1010–1225) and was dedicated to Tran Vo (God of the North), whose symbols of power were the tortoise and the snake. A bronze statue and bell date from 1677. The temple is on the shores of Truc Bach Lake, near the intersection of Ð Thanh Nien and Pho Quan Thanh.

TAY HO PAGODA

The most popular spot for worship in Hanoi is at **Tay Ho Pagoda** (Pho Tay Ho; Map p77). Throngs of people come here on the first and 15th day of each lunar month in the hope of receiving good fortune. The walk in is along a colourful lane of stalls selling temple offerings and food; and a line of good fresh seafood restaurants fronts the lake. It's a great place to watch the world go by.

TRAN QUOC PAGODA

One of the oldest in Vietnam, **Tran Quoc Pagoda** (Map pp80-1) is on the eastern shore of Ho Tay, just off Ð Thanh Nien, which divides Ho Tay from Truc Bach Lake. A stele here, dating from 1639, tells the history of this site. The pagoda was rebuilt in the 15th century and again in 1842. There are

HANOI

a number of monks' funerary monuments in the garden.

Museums

It's worth noting that in addition to the usual two-hour lunch break, many of the museums in Hanoi are closed on Monday.

VIETNAM MUSEUM OF ETHNOLOGY

The Musée de l'Homme in Paris helped design the wonderful **Vietnam Museum of Ethnology** (Map p113; ☎ 756 2193; Đ Nguyen Van Huyen; admission 10,000d; ☺ 8.30am-5.30pm Tue-Sun). It features a fascinating collection of art and everyday objects gathered from Vietnam and its diverse tribal people.

The museum has excellent maps and the displays are well labelled in Vietnamese, French and English. Interesting dioramas portray a typical village market, the making of conical hats and a Tay shamanic ceremony, while videos show the real life contexts. There are fabulous displays of weaving and fabric motifs. Visitors can also enter a traditional Black Thai house reconstructed within the museum, and there are outdoor exhibits in the landscaped grounds. A craft shop – affiliated with Craft Link, which is a fair trade organisation – sells books, beautiful postcards, and arts and crafts from ethnic communities.

The museum is quite a way from central Hanoi, but it shouldn't be missed.

Getting There & Away

The museum is in the Cau Giay district, about 7km from the city centre. A good way to get here is by rented bicycle (30 minutes). If you're short of time or energy, an air-con metered taxi costs around 40,000d each way. The cheapest way to get here is to take local bus No 14 (2500d) from Hoan Kiem Lake and get off at the junction between Đ Hoang Quoc Viet and Đ Nguyen Van Huyen.

MEMORIAL HOUSE

It's well worth stopping at this delightful **house** (Map p84; 87 Pho Ma May; admission 5000d; ☺ 9-11.30am & 2-5pm) north of Hoan Kiem Lake in the Old Quarter. This thoughtfully restored traditional Chinese-style dwelling is sparsely but beautifully decorated, and gives an excellent idea of how local merchants used to live in the Old Quarter. The

restoration of the house was carried out in 1999 in cooperation with the city of Toulouse, France. While there are many such houses open to the public in Hoi An, there is nothing else like this in Hanoi.

HISTORY MUSEUM

Once the museum of the École Française d'Extrême Orient, the **History Museum** (Bao Tang Lich Su; Map pp80-1; 1 Pho Pham Ngu Lao; admission 15,000d; ☺ 8-11.30am & 1.30-4.30pm Tue-Sun) is an elegant, ochre-coloured structure built between 1925 and 1932. French architect Ernest Hebrard was among the first in Vietnam to incorporate a blend of Chinese and French design elements in his creations, and this particular building remains one of Hanoi's most stunning architectural showpieces.

Exhibited here are some artefacts from the country's turbulent past, including: prehistory (Palaeolithic and Neolithic periods); proto-Vietnamese civilisations (1st and 2nd millennia BC); the Dong Son culture (3rd century BC to 3rd century AD); the Oc-Eo (Funan) culture of the Mekong Delta (1st to 6th century AD); the Kingdom of Champa (2nd to 15th century); the Khmer kingdoms; various Vietnamese dynasties and their resistance to Chinese attempts at domination; the struggle against the French; and the inevitable history of the Communist Party.

MUSEUM OF VIETNAMESE REVOLUTION

The history of the Vietnamese Revolution is creatively presented by this **museum** (Bao Tang Cach Mang; Map pp80-1; 25 Pho Tong Dan; admission 10,000d; ☺ 8-11.45am & 1.30-4.15pm Tue-Sun). It's diagonally across the road from the History Museum.

FINE ARTS MUSEUM

The former French Ministry of Information now houses Hanoi's **Fine Arts Museum** (Bao Tang My Thuat; Map pp80-1; 66 Pho Nguyen Thai Hoc; admission 10,000d; ☺ 9.15am-5pm Tue-Sun). Here you can see some very intricate sculptures, paintings, lacquerware, ceramics and other traditional Vietnamese fine arts. Reproductions of antiques are on sale here, but be sure to ask for a certificate to clear these goods through customs when you leave Vietnam.

The Fine Arts Museum is on the corner of Pho Cao Ba Quat, across the street from the back wall of the Temple of Literature.

WOMEN'S MUSEUM

There are some fascinating displays in the excellent **Women's Museum** (Bao Tang Phu Nu; Map p84; 36 Pho Ly Thuong Kiet; admission 10,000d; 8am-4pm). The inevitable tribute to women soldiers is balanced by some great exhibits from the international women's movement protesting the American War. And there's much more in terms of cultural and political information. On the 4th floor you can see different costumes worn by the women of the ethnic-minority groups, and examples of tribal basket ware and fabric motifs. This is one place where many of the exhibits have multilingual explanations.

ARMY MUSEUM

Outside the **Army Museum** (Bao Tang Quan Doi; Map pp80-1; Pho Dien Bien Phu; admission 10,000d; 8-11.30am & 1.30-4.30pm Tue-Sun), Soviet and Chinese weaponry supplied to the North is displayed alongside French- and US-made weapons captured in the Franco–Viet Minh and American Wars. The centrepiece is a Soviet-built MiG-21 jet fighter, triumphant amid the wreckage of French aircraft downed at Dien Bien Phu, and a US F-111. The displays include scale models of various epic battles from the long military history of Vietnam, including Dien Bien Phu and the capture of Saigon.

Next to the Army Museum is the hexagonal Flag Tower, which has become one of the symbols of Hanoi. Some museum guards may offer to show you this tower, but will then ask for a large sum of cash to pay for the privilege.

HOA LO PRISON MUSEUM

This provocative site is all that remains of the former **Hoa Lo Prison** (Map p84; 1 Pho Hoa Lo, cnr Pho Hai Ba Trung; admission 5000d; 8-11.30am & 1.30-4.30pm Tue-Sun), ironically nicknamed the 'Hanoi Hilton' by US POWs during the American War. Those incarcerated at Hoa Lo included Pete Peterson, who would later become the first US Ambassador to Vietnam following the re-establishment of diplomatic ties between the two countries in 1995.

The vast prison complex was built by the French in 1896. Originally intended to house around 450 inmates, records indicate that by the 1930s there were close to 2000 prisoners inside! Much of the prison was razed to make room for the Hanoi Towers

skyscraper, though the section at the front of the site has been thoughtfully preserved and restored as a museum – look for the sign over the gate reading 'Maison Centrale'. There are some English and French labels corresponding with the displays, and you may be able to find an English-speaking guide on site.

The bulk of the exhibits here relate to the prison's use up to the mid-1950s, focusing on the Vietnamese struggle for independence from France. Notable tools of torture on display in the dark chambers include an ominous French guillotine that was used to behead Vietnamese revolutionaries during the colonial period, and the fetters with which prisoners were chained to the bunks. It has to be said that, even allowing for the propaganda, it looks like the treatment of Americans by the Vietnamese was infinitely better than that of Vietnamese nationalists by the French.

There are also mug shots on display of Americans and Vietnamese who served time at Hoa Lo. Propaganda photos of cheerful-looking American prisoners are shown with a placard reading:

> From August 5, 1964 to January 24, 1973, US government carried out two destruction wars by air and navy against Northern Vietnam. The Northern Army and people brought down thousands of aircrafts and captured hundreds of American pilots. Though having committed untold crimes on our people, but American pilots suffered no revenge once they were captured and detained. Instead they were well treated with adequate food, clothing and shelter. According to the provisions of Paris Agreement, our government had in March 1973 returned all captured pilots to the US government.

AIR FORCE MUSEUM

This is one of the larger museums in the country and, though seldom visited by foreigners, it's very worthwhile if you are a war history junkie or an aircraft buff.

Exhibits at the **Air Force Museum** (Bao Tang Khong Quan; Map pp80-1; Đ Truong Chinh; admission 10,000d; 8-11am & 1-4.30pm Tue-Sat) include a number of Soviet-built MiG fighters, reconnaissance planes, helicopters and anti-aircraft equipment. Inside the hall are other weapons, including mortars, machine guns and some US-made bombs. There is a partially truncated MiG with a ladder so that you can climb up into the cockpit and have your photo taken. The museum has other war memorabilia, including paintings of obvious Soviet design and portraits of Ho Chi Minh.

The Air Force Museum is in the Dong Da district, in central Hanoi's far southwest.

St Joseph Cathedral

Stepping inside the Old Quarter's neo-Gothic **St Joseph Cathedral** (Map p84; Pho Nha Tho; ☺ main gate 5-7am & 5-7pm) is like being transported to medieval Europe. The cathedral, inaugurated in 1886, is noteworthy for its square towers, elaborate altar and stained-glass windows. It is in dire need of a paint job these days. The first Catholic mission in Hanoi was founded in 1679. The cathedral stands facing the western end of Pho Nha Tho, which is a fashionable strip of restaurants, cafés and boutiques.

The main gate to St Joseph Cathedral is open when Mass is held. Guests are welcome at other times of the day, but must enter the cathedral via the compound of the Diocese of Hanoi, the entrance to which is a block away at 40 Pho Nha Chung. After walking through the main gate, go straight and then turn right. When you reach the side door to the cathedral, ring the small bell high up to the right-hand side of the door so the priest can let you in.

Thu Le Park & Zoo

With its vast expanses of shaded grass and ponds, **Thu Le Park and Zoo** (Bach Thu Le; Map p77; admission 2000d; ☺ 4am-10pm) is about 4km west of Hoan Kiem Lake. While it's not Singapore Zoo, it is not one of Asia's horror shows either, and children will enjoy the fun park and swan pedal boats. The easiest way to get here is by metered taxi.

ACTIVITIES
Fitness Clubs

A number of international hotels open their exercise centres to the public for a fee. Among these is the top-of-the-market **Clark Hatch Fitness Centre** (☎ 826 6919 ext 8881) in the Sofitel Metropole Hotel and Sofitel Plaza, which has a day-use fee of US$15 for the

gym, including pool access. Similar is the **Daewoo Hotel Fitness Centre** (☎ 835 1000), which has a day-use fee of US$20 for all facilities including the pool.

Golf

King's Island (☎ 733 2459; www.kingsislandgolf.com) is an 18-hole golf course 45km west of Hanoi, close to the base of Ba Vi Mountain. Membership is a whopping US$5000, but the club is open to visitors.

On the western side of Hanoi, but still within the city limits, is the **Lang Ha Golf Club** (Map p77; ☎ 835 0909; 16A Pho Lang Ha; nonmembers fee US$20; ☺ 6am-10pm), opposite the TV tower. Basically, this is just a driving range – you'll have to go to King's Island if you want to pursue a white ball over hills and fields.

Hash House Harriers

The 'hash', as all expats refer to it, has two chapters in Hanoi, one running Saturday and one running Tuesday. Hit the Moca Café (p103) for a low-down on the latest schedule. Don't worry if you're not a runner: it's more about beer-swilling at the end of the run anyway. It costs around US$5 and includes the drinks.

Massage

The government has severely restricted the number of places licensed to give massages because of the concern that naughty 'extra services' might be offered (as indeed they are at many places). At present, you can get a good legitimate massage at the **Hoa Binh Hotel** (Map pp80-1; per hr US$7) and **Dan Chu Hotel** (Map p84; ☎ 825 4937; www.danchuhotel .com; 29 Pho Trang Tien) for about US$7 per hour, including some sauna time. The upmarket **Guoman** (Map pp80-1; ☎ 822 2800; 83A Pho Ly Thuong Kiet) and **Sofitel Metropole Hotel** (Map p84; ☎ 826 6919; 15 Pho Ngo Quyen) charge nearer US$15 and US$25 per hour, respectively, for this service.

Swimming

Several upmarket hotels have swimming pools, but most are for hotel guests and members only. For the general public, the **Army Hotel** (Map pp80-1; Pho Pham Ngu Lao), near the History Museum, charges US$3.50 for day use of its pool, which is big enough to do laps and is open all year. Just about big enough to do laps – but a much nicer place to lounge around afterwards – is the pool at the **Melia Hotel** (Map p84; Pho Ly Thuong Kiet), where 'walk-in-members' pay US$6 to swim, or US$10 to swim and use the gym. Some other hotels charge a US$10 day-use fee.

Out by Ho Tay (West Lake), the **Ho Tay Villas** (Map p77; ☎ 804 7772) charges US$2 per day to swim. Also by Ho Tay is the **Thang Loi Hotel** (Cuban Hotel; Map p77; ☎ 829 4211; Đ Yen Phu), which has a swimming pool in a nicer location that's open to the public for just US$1. These two pools are open only in the summer months, from about May to October.

Hanoi Water Park (Map p113; ☎ 753 2757; ⏱ 9am-9pm Wed-Mon Apr 15-Nov) is about 5km north of the city centre and offers a fun selection of pools, slides and splashing opportunities. Entry costs 50,000d for those over 110cm tall, and 30,000d for shorter people.

WALKING TOUR

Start at the **Ngoc Son Temple** (**1**; p89) at the northern end of Hoan Kiem Lake. After crossing back over bright-red **Huc Bridge (2)**,

stop for a quick look at the **Martyrs' Monument (3)**, erected to those who died fighting for Vietnam's independence. Follow the lake around on Pho Dinh Tien Hoang and walk past the **Water Puppet Theatre** (**4**; p107) on So Lau. Head north on Pho Hang Dau and you'll soon be surrounded by **shoe shops (5)** selling every shape, size and style – demonstrating how serious Hanoians are about their footwear. Cross over Pho Cau Go to Pho Hang Be, and pop into the colourful **market (6)**, which occupies the narrow eastern terminus of Pho Gia Ngu.

Back on Pho Hang Be, continue north to the 'T' junction with Pho Hang Bac. Near here are several shops where artisans carve intricate **gravestones (7)**, most bearing an image of the deceased, by hand. A short detour north on Pho Ma May will lead you to the **Memorial House** (**8**; p90) at No 87, an exquisite Chinese merchant's home that has been restored as a museum.

Return to Pho Hang Bac and head west past a strip of snazzy **jewellery shops (9)**, then right onto Pho Hang Ngang past a row of **clothing shops (10)**, and right again

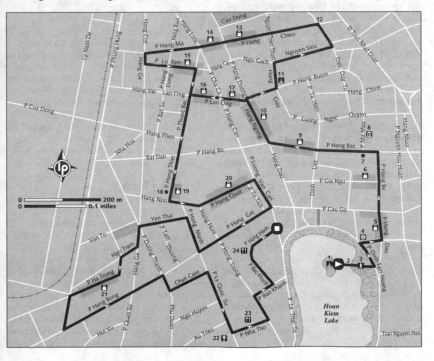

onto Pho Hang Buom; this will take you past the small **Bach Ma Temple** (11; p89). As you pass the pagoda, with its red funeral palanquin, look for its white-bearded guards, who spend their days sipping tea.

Legend has it that Ly King used the pagoda to pray for assistance in building the city walls because they persistently collapsed, no matter how many times he rebuilt them. His prayers were finally answered when a white horse appeared out of the temple and guided him to the site where he could safely build his walls. Evidence of his success is still visible at **Cua O Quan Chuong (12)**, the quarter's well-preserved Old East Gate at the eastern end of Pho Hang Chieu, near the intersection with Pho Tran Nhat Duat.

Head west back along Pho Hang Chieu, past a handful of **shops (13)** selling straw mats and rope, to one of the most interesting streets, **Pho Hang Ma (14)** – the name translates as Counterfeit Street – where imitation 'ghost money' is sold for burning in Buddhist ceremonies – there are even US$5000 bills! Loop around and follow your ears to the sounds of skilful **blacksmiths (15)** pounding away on metal on the corner of Pho Lo Ren and Pho Thuoc Bac. Moving south on Pho Thuoc Bac, head left past the **towel shops (16)** onto Pho Lan Ong, where a fantastic row of **herb sellers (17)** fill the street with succulent aromas.

Double back and head south past the **tin-box makers (18)**, opposite the **mirror shops (19)** on Pho Hang Thiec, then turn left towards the interesting **shops selling Buddhist altars and statues (20)** along Pho Hang Quat.

Time permitting, loop around and zigzag west to check out the **leather and PVC shops (21)** along Pho Ha Trung, then head east again to the superb neo-Gothic **St Joseph Cathedral** (22; p92). If you're feeling a bit breathless from the walk, a few steps from the church, along Pho Nha Tho, you'll find that there's a cluster of stylish **restaurants and cafés (23)**.

If you're looking for something a bit more local in flavour, turn left at the end of Pho Nha Tho onto Pho Hang Trong, right onto Pho Bao Khanh and left at Pho Hang Hanh. This street is chock-a-block with **Vietnamese coffee shops (24)** and is a good place to stop, rest your weary legs and watch the world go by.

COURSES

Hanoi Foreign Language College (Map pp80-1; ☎ 826 2468; 1 Pho Pham Ngu Lao), housed in the History Museum compound, is a branch of Hanoi National University is where foreigners can study Vietnamese for about US$7 per lesson.

HANOI FOR CHILDREN

Hanoi is a fun city for children thanks to the all-action Old Quarter (p83) and the city's many parks and lakes. Wandering the Old Quarter can be tiring for young ones, but there are enough diversions to keep them entertained, and plenty of ice-cream shops and fruit markets for those little treats along the way.

Boating is a fun family activity and there is the choice of bigger boats on Ho Tay (p86) or pedal-powered boats in Thu Le Park (p92). Hanoi Water Park (p93) is a great place to take children to cool off, but it is only open half the year. Come the evening, there is only one place for any self-respecting child to be, and that is at the water puppets (p107), a Punch and Judy pantomime on the water.

TOURS

Anyone arriving in Hanoi on an organised trip will have a city tour included. If you're travelling independently, Hanoi is a city best enjoyed at your own pace without the timetable of a tour. If you really want an organised city tour, contact one of the travel agencies recommended on p79. Prices start from US$12 for a group tour, including guide, transport and entrance fees. For a private tour by car, expect to pay more like US$40 to US$50.

Motorbike Tours

If you're a competent motorbiker, it's easy to organise a trip on your own. For general information about motorbike rental in Hanoi, see p110.

There are a handful of companies in Hanoi running motorbike tours who know secret road routes and can open doors that you would never imagine from a cursory scan of the map. Foreign guides charge considerably more than local Vietnamese guides. Based on a group of four people, you can expect to pay around US$100 per day per person for an all-inclusive tour

GAY & LESBIAN HANOI

By Vietnam's standards there's a lively gay scene in Hanoi, but there are few, if any, gay venues, just some places that are more gay-friendly than others. There is a bustling cruising area along Pho Bao Khanh, plus nearby Hoan Kiem Lake, although gay males should watch out for an extortion scam linked to the latter (see p83).

Official attitudes are still fairly conservative and Hanoi is home to these official attitudes. Police raids in the name of 'social reform' aren't unknown and that tends to ensure gays and lesbians keep a low profile. **GC Pub** (Map p84; ☎ 825 0499; 5 Pho Bao Khanh) is a gay-friendly pub with a pool table, while **Apocalypse Now** (Map pp80–1; ☎ 971 2783; 5C Pho Hoa Ma) draws a gay crowd that hangs out at the back bar – although you should keep the antennae up for hustlers.

providing motorbike rental, guide, food, drink (it's true!) and accommodation.

Explore Indochina (☎ 0913-524 658; www.explore indochina.com) is run by Digby and Dan, a pair of biking connoisseurs from Oz and the UK respectively. You can usually find one or both of them at Highway 4 (Map p84), a bar on Pho Hang Tre.

Alternatively, try **Free Wheelin Tours** (☎ 747 0545; www.freewheelin-tours.com), run by Fredo (Binh in Vietnamese), who speaks French, English and Vietnamese. He also has Vietnamese guides on call.

FESTIVALS & EVENTS

Tet (Tet Nguyen Dan/Vietnamese Lunar New Year; late January or early February) A flower market is held on Pho Hang Luoc during the week preceding Tet. There's also a colourful two-week flower exhibition and competition, beginning on the first day of the new year, that takes place in Lenin Park near Bay Mau Lake. For much, much more on Tet, see the 'Tet Festival' special section (p53).

Quang Trung Festival (February/March) Wrestling competitions, lion dances and human chess take place on the 15th day of the first lunar month at Dong Da Mound, site of the uprising against Chinese invaders led by Emperor Quang Trung (Nguyen Hue) in 1788.

Vietnam's National Day (2 September) Celebrated in Hanoi at Ba Dinh Square – the expanse of grass in front of Ho Chi Minh's Mausoleum – with a rally and fireworks; boat races are held on Hoan Kiem Lake.

SLEEPING

The majority of Hanoi's budget accommodation is within walking distance of Hoan Kiem Lake. Unlike HCMC's Pham Ngu Lao district, where the cheapies are lined up wall-to-wall, lodgings here are more scattered, though they're mostly in and around the Old Quarter.

There are several budget places around with both dorm beds (around US\$3) and cheap rooms (under US\$10), but for between US\$10 and US\$20 the choice includes a wide selection of 'minihotels', which offer clean, air-con rooms, satellite TV and hot water.

In the US\$20 to US\$50 range, there is usually a step up in the service, and the rooms may be larger than those in the mini-hotels or guesthouses.

Above and beyond US\$50, it is possible to stay in posh four- and five-star hotels that in cities like Hong Kong or Bangkok would cost around double. Keep an eye out in *Vietnam News*, the *Guide* and *Time Out* for the latest deals, and always ask about current 'promotions' at reception.

Old Quarter
BUDGET

Stars Hotel (Map p84; ☎ 828 1911; hoalinhhotel@hn .vnn.vn; 26 Pho Bat Su; r US\$10-20; ☒) This place gets a steady stream of favourable feedback for its clean, comfortable rooms and friendly service. Rooms include satellite TV, fridge and bathtub and some have balconies; all include breakfast.

Prince Hotel (Map p84; ☎ 828 0155; ngo dzung@hn .vnn.vn; 51 Pho Luong Ngoc Quyen; r US\$14/20; ☒) The name is now borrowed by countless other hotels, but this is the original Prince. The clean, spacious doubles here have character-laden Chinese-style furniture and balconies. Breakfast and Internet access are included in the rate.

Prince 79 Hotel (Map p84; ☎ 926 0628; www .kimcafé79travel.com; 79 Pho Hang Bac; r US\$8-15; ☒ 🖳) A smart spot among the many other Princes. The more expensive rooms include bathtub and balcony. Friendly folk run this place.

Van Minh Hotel (Map p84; ☎ 926 0150; nngocminh@fpt.vn; 88 Pho Hang Bac; r US\$10-20; ☒) Just along the road from Prince 79, this is

THE AUTHOR'S CHOICE

Viet Anh Hotel (Map P84; ☎ 926 1302; www
.vietanhhotel.com; 11 Pho Ma May; r US$8-20;
❄ 🖳) A new hotel on the ever more fashionable Ma May strip. Rooms include wood
trim, TV, fridge and bathtub, plus there's a
lift. Well worth checking out.

great value. Spotless rooms feature all the
typical touches and big hot-water tanks give
a longer power shower.

Venus Hotel (Map p84; ☎ 826 1212; venus
.hotel@fpt.vn; 10 Pho Hang Can; r US$8-10; ❄) The
kitsch carpeted interior is decidedly dated,
but the rooms are a good deal with TV and
hot water. Breakfast is included.

Thu Giang Guesthouse (Map p84; ☎ 828 5734;
thuygiangn@hotmail.com; 5A Pho Tam Thuong; r US$6-8;
❄) A friendly little place that is popular
with budget travellers for its compact but
comfortable rooms. Tucked away down a
narrow alley between Pho Yen Thai and
Pho Hang Gai, this is a good hunting
ground for cheap rooms.

Manh Dung Guesthouse (Map p84; ☎ 826 7201;
tranmanhdungvn@yahoo.com; 2 Pho Tam Thuong; r US$4-
8; ❄ 🖳) A small place with a big heart,
thanks to a friendly family that can't do
enough for its guests. TV, fridge and hot
water make for a real deal and there's now
a second building nearby with bigger,
brighter rooms.

Thuy Nga Guesthouse (Map p84; ☎ 826 6053;
thuyngahotel@hotmail.com; 24C Pho Ta Hien; r US$9-10;
❄) A bright, airy, family-run place with
small but smart rooms including extras like
TV, fridge and IDD telephone.

Hanoi Spirit Club (Map p84; ☎ 826 7356; www
.azqueencafé.com; 50 Pho Hang Be; dm US$2, r US$4-7;
❄ 🖳) Probably the cheapest place in town,
but in keeping with the 'get what you pay
for' maxim, it is as basic as it comes. Not far
to the bar though!

Binh Minh II Hotel (Map p84; ☎ 825 0728; 31 Pho
Hang Mam; r US$10; ❄) The classic tall, thin
structure of this building epitomises the
hotels of Saigon. Good value rooms with
TV and hot water, but it's a steep climb to
the higher floors.

Real Darling Café (Map p84; ☎ 826 9386; darling
_café@hotmail.com; 33 Pho Hang Quat; dm US$3, r US$5-
12; ❄ 🖳) One of the few places with dorms
for those on a breadline budget. The range

of rooms is reasonable and the staff speaks
good English.

Lotus Guesthouse (Map p84; ☎ 934 4197; lotus
-travel@hn.vnn.vn; 42V Pho Ly Thuong Kiet; r US$6-15;
❄) A warren of a place with low ceilings
and plenty of passages, so it might be a
bit cramped for claustrophobes or big folk.
Once inside, the rooms are. There's an
equally small café downstairs.

MID-RANGE

Sunshine Hotel (Map p84; ☎ 926 1559; fax 926 1558;
42 Pho Ma May; r US$10-22; ❄) A super spot on
the mighty Ma May strip. The big, bright
bedrooms have tasteful furnishings and
some have balconies with great street view.
Friendly and helpful staff, plus breakfast
included at the popular Sunshine Restaurant downstairs.

Classic Street Hotel (Map p84; ☎ 825 2421;
hohoa@hn.vnn.vn; 41 Pho Hang Be; r US$20-30; ❄) A
stylish hotel in the bustling heart of old
Hanoi. All rooms have air-con and satellite
TV, and some have fantastic views of the
quarter's higgledy-piggledy rooftops. Fancy
toilets as well, if that's the sort of touch that
tickles your fancy.

Queen Hotel (Map p84; ☎ 826 0860; www
.azqueentravel.com; 65 Pho Hang Bac; r US$30-35; ❄ 🖳)
This place has really turned on the style,
graduating from a backpacker crash pad
to one of the best mid-range deals in town.
The rooms are delightfully decorated with
wooden furnishings and silk lamps, and
those little extras come big here, including
DVD players in each room. Only 10 rooms
so it might be wise to book ahead.

Camellia Hotel (Map p84; ☎ 828 3583; www
.camellia-hotels.com; 13 Pho Luong Ngoc Quyen; r US$15-22;
❄ 🖳) An old favourite that remains great
value for money. The rooms are cavernous
and the price includes satellite TV, a buffet
breakfast and free Internet access.

Lucky Star Hotel (Map p84; ☎ 923 1781; www
.luckystarhotel.com; 11 Pho Bat Dan; r US$12-30; ❄) A
plush new place on the eastern side of the
Old Quarter. Large rooms are well-fitted –
'works of art' according to the marketing
munchkins – and the bathrooms big.

Hong Ngoc Hotel 1 (Map p84; ☎ 828 5053;
hongngochotel@hn.vnn.vn; 34 Pho Hang Manh; r US$25-
30; ❄) A short stroll northwest from Hoan
Kiem Lake, this is a smart hotel with spacious rooms, big beds, solid furnishings and
breakfast thrown in.

Hong Ngoc Hotel 2 (Map p84; ☎ 923 0000; hongngochotel@hn.vnn.vn; 14 Pho Luong Van Can; r US$25; ❄) Hong Ngoc has been expanding and several more properties, including this one – another good deal in a central location.

Ho Guom Hotel (Map p84; ☎ 825 2225; hoguomtjc@hn.vnn.vn; 76 Pho Hang Trong; s US$18-30, d $US20-35; ❄) This is that rare breed: a state-run hotel that's clean and quiet, with friendly staff and in a good location. The rooms with balconies overlooking the inner courtyard are good value.

There's a cluster of cheap hotels in a good location in the artsy quarter near the cathedral on Pho Nha Chung:

Spring Hotel (Map p84; ☎ 826 8500; spring .hotel@fpt.vn; 8a Pho Nha Chung; r US$10-30; ❄) Run by a helpful family that speaks fluent English. Some of the rooms are on the small side, but dish out the dollars and they'll have nicer furniture and extras such as a balcony.

Hotel Thien Trang (Map p84; ☎ 826 9823; thientranghotel24@hotmail.com; 24 Pho Nha Chung; r US$10-20; ❄) Thien Trang offers a warm welcome to guests and has good-value rooms for this popular location.

Win Hotel (Map p84; ☎ 826 7150; winhotel@yahoo .com; 34 Pho Hang Hanh; r US$20-30; ❄) A friendly place set amid a slew of happening local cafés on 'coffee street'. The rooms are well finished but some are a touch on the tiny side.

Nam Phuong Hotel (Map p84; ☎ 928 5085; fax 825 8964; 16 Pho Bao Khanh; r US$12-20; ❄) Just around the corner, Nam Phuong offers a good deal, with satellite TV, minibar and copious amounts of hot water.

Chains First Eden Hotel (Map p84; ☎ 828 3896; cfeden@hn.vnn.vn; 3A Pho Phan Dinh Phung; r US$25-35; ❄) Up near the Hanoi Citadel, this large

---

THE AUTHOR'S CHOICE

Dan Chu Hotel (Map p84; ☎ 825 4937; www .danchuhotel.com; 29 Pho Trang Tien; r from US$40; ❄ 🖳) An elegant building from the late 19th century that has an attractive air of delicately decaying grandeur. One day it will be renovated and room rates will rocket, so enjoy it while you can. Great location between the Opera House and the lake, and legitimate massage for 80,000d per hour.

---

business hotel has a health club, sauna, business centre and pretty plush rooms for the money. Deluxe rooms used to be double this price.

Galaxy Hotel (Map p84; ☎ 828 2888; galaxy htl@netnam.org.vn; 1 Phan Dinh Phung; s/d US$40/45; ❄ 🖳) A hearty hotel that is deservedly popular with tour groups. Based around the original 1918 building, it has a business centre and a popular café-restaurant; all rooms feature satellite TV and a safe.

Still want more? Try these wholesome hotels:

Classic Hotel (Map p84; ☎ 826 6224; 22A Pho Ta Hien; r US$15-22; ❄) Sister hotel to the Sunshine; same rooms, same great deal, almost the same location.

Golden Buffalo Hotel (Trau Vang Hotel; Map p84; ☎ 928 6979; goldenbuffalohotel@fpt.vn; 35 Pho Hang Trong; r US$17-25; ❄) New hotel with smart rooms near the popular Bao Khanh area.

Trang Tien Hotel (Map p84; ☎ 825 6115; fax 825 1416; 35 Pho Trang Tien; r US$15-30; ❄) Sprawling hotel worth considering for the location – between Hoan Kiem Lake and the Opera House.

TOP END
Hilton Hanoi Opera (Map p84; ☎ 933 0500; www .hanoi.hilton.com; 1 Le Thanh Tong; r from US$95; ❄ 🖳 🏊) Situated in a prime location beside Hanoi's grand Opera House, this hotel looks stunning from the outside and is everything you'd expect from a Hilton on the inside. It is possibly the best all-rounder for location and comfort at this end of the scale. Treat yourself to day-use of the luxurious health club and swimming pool for US$11.

Melia Hotel (Map p84; ☎ 934 3343; solmelia@ meliahanoi.com.vn; 44B Pho Ly Thuong Kiet; r US$79-149; ❄ 🖳 🏊) Home to some of the best views in Hanoi if you ask for an upper floor – yes, of course there's a lift! Unappealing from the outside, it's very appealing inside, with all the five-star features you are familiar with.

Central Hanoi
BUDGET
Hotel Memory (Map pp80-1; ☎ 934 9909; memory hotel@fpt.vn; 25 Pho Nguyen Thai Hoc; r US$13-20; ❄) An alternative to the Old Quarter if you want to be near the train station. Rates include breakfast and satellite TV and it's near Cam Chi (p103), the speciality-food street.

HANOI

Hotel 30/4 (Map pp80-1; ☎ 942 0807; 115 Pho Tran Hung Dao; r US$10-20; ✂) Right opposite Hanoi train station and named after 30 April 1975, the date of Saigon's liberation. Unsurprisingly, it's state-owned. Large rooms, but the staff aren't exactly helpful and friendly.

MID-RANGE

Thien Thai Hotel (Paradise Hotel; Map pp80-1; ☎ 716 4126; 45 Pho Ngyuen Truong To; r US$30-40; ✂) A smart, modern three-star hotel with a colonial trim. All rooms have balconies and all the creature comforts. Rates include breakfast.

Army Hotel (Khach San Quan Doi; Map pp80-1; ☎ 825 2896; armyhotel@fpt.vn; 33C Pho Pham Ngu Lao; r US$30-40; ✂) This place is owned by the army, but looks nothing like a barracks – it is a rather splendid old colonial building. A popular place for tour groups, it has its own gym and salt-water swimming pool. Access to the pool for nonguests is just US$3.50 per day.

Green Park Hotel (Map pp80-1; ☎ 822 7725; www.hanoi-greenpark-hotel.com; 48 Pho Tan Nhan Tong; r from US$45; ✂ 🖥) Just a short stroll from Lenin Park, this place is, well, big and green from the outside. If you can handle the colour scheme, it is a good place to stay once you're safely in the rooms. There are good vistas from the hotel's Park View Restaurant.

De Syloia Hotel (Map pp80-1; ☎ 824 5346; www.desyloia.com; 17A Pho Tran Hung Dao; s/d US$80/90; ✂ 🖥) One of the best boutique hotels in Hanoi, with a decidedly French theme. There is a fitness centre and sauna here, and the in-house Vietnamese restaurant, Cay Cau, is a popular place for a power lunch.

Guoman Hotel (Map pp80-1; ☎ 822 2800; guoman hn@hn.vnn.vn; 83A Pho Ly Thuong Kiet; r US$70-180; ✂ 🖥 🖾) A stately place that maintains an international four-star standard and often offers special deals on the rates quoted here. Facilities include a sleek health club, fine dining, two good bars and staff who remember your name.

Sofitel Plaza (Map pp80-1; ☎ 823 8888; www.accor.com; 1 Đ Thanh Nien; r US$89-299; ✂ 🖥 🖾) A gigantic joint-venture boasting every possible amenity, including Southeast Asia's first ever indoor-outdoor swimming pool with a retractable roof. The Summit Lounge Bar on the 20th floor has a daily happy hour (4.30pm to 8pm) and great sunset views across West Lake and the city.

Greater Hanoi
MID-RANGE

Thang Loi Hotel (Cuban Hotel; Map p77; ☎ 829 4211; thangloihtl@hn.vnn.vn; Đ Yen Phu; r from US$40; ✂ 🖾) Nicknamed the Cuban Hotel because it was built in the mid-1970s with Cuban assistance, the floor plan of each level is said to have been copied from a one-storey Cuban building, which explains the doors that lead nowhere. The hotel is built on pylons over the water, and is surrounded by attractive landscaping. The hotel also has a swimming pool, tennis courts, a sauna and a massage service. It is 3.5km from the city centre on the shores of Ho Tay (West Lake).

Dragon Hotel (Map p77; ☎ 829 2955; dragon co@hn.vnn.vn; 48 Pho Xuan Dieu; s/d US$30/35; ✂) This is a Chinese-themed hotel overlooking Ho Tay. The rooms are good value given the features and the US$60 apartments are well worth considering if you are thinking of sticking around a while.

Ho Tay Villas (Map p77; ☎ 804 7772; hotay villas@fmail.vnn.vn; r US$45-50; ✂ 🖾) These spacious villas, set on Ho Tay, were once the Communist Party Guesthouse and the exclusive preserve of top party officials. These days dollar-toting tourists are welcome to use the once-splendid facilities, and even if you don't stay, it's instructive to visit to see how the 'people's representatives' lived in one of Asia's poorest countries. The hotel is 5.5km north of central Hanoi.

TOP END

Hanoi Horison Hotel (Map p77; ☎ 733 0808; hhh_sale@netnam.org.vn; 40 Pho Cat Linh; r US$70-135; ✂ 🖥 🖾) A swish hotel featuring a brick smokestack in front, which was preserved from an old brick factory that once stood on the site. It also has an excellent health club and swimming pool, with a US$7 day-use fee.

Daewoo Hotel (Map p77; ☎ 831 5000; info@daewoohotel.com.vn; Pho Ngoc Khanh; r from US$199; ☒ ☐ ☑) The style at this South Korean joint venture – Hanoi's largest and most expensive hotel – is most definitely *not* French colonial. This 15-storey behemoth offers everything you could want in life, including a vast landscaped swimming pool, a nightclub, health club, business centre and three restaurants. You can use the pool for only US$10 per day.

EATING
In recent years Hanoi has undergone a miraculous transformation from a culinary wasteland to a premier city for eating and drinking. The city boasts everything from cheap backpacker joints (yes, *more* banana pancakes) to exquisite Vietnamese restaurants and a growing legion of chic cafés.

Restaurants, bars and cafés have a strong tendency to change names, location, management and just about everything else, so ask around and keep an eye out in for current listings in the *Guide* and *Time Out*.

Dining for a cause
Combine food for the body with food for the soul at restaurants and cafés that run vocational training programmes for street kids. Good cause, good food, good idea.

Hoa Sua (Map p80-1; ☎ 824 0448; www.hoasuaschool.com; 28A Pho Ha Hoi; Vietnamese/French set lunch 35,000/65,000d; ☑ 11am-10pm) A fine place to dine, day or night, with a balanced menu of Vietnamese and international cuisine. The set menus are a good deal, or go à la carte for some DIY fusion. Recently relocated, the new home has a lush garden terrace and an indoor retreat for those rainy days. Hoa Sua is a successful goodwill project that takes in and trains a steady stream of disadvantaged kids for culinary careers. It often holds musical performances or themed nights.

Baguette & Chocolat (Map p84; ☎ 923 1500; 11 Pho Cha Ca; cakes from 6000d; ☑ 7am-10pm) Another branch in the Hoa Sua family tree, this is a bewitching bakery with divine (or devilish) cakes and pastries, depending on your calorie count. Remember those patisseries in Paris, with artistic creations at €3 a pop? Try them here for less than US$1.

Vietnamese
For some of the tastiest, and certainly cheapest Vietnamese food, stroll up to some of the street stalls around town. The food is as fresh as it comes and the kitchen is right there in front of you. Most of Vietnam's greatest hits are available if you shop around, and it's a great way to plug the hole after a long night on the town. Almost every corner and alley in the Old Quarter has street stalls. Check out how many locals are eating there; the more, the merrier, as the food must be good. Overcharging is the norm rather than the exception at many of these places, so it is worth checking the price before you order a spread.

Another excellent and inexpensive fast track to a feed is to visit one of the innumerable *bia hoi* around the city. All of them have mini-menus to help hold off the hangover. For more on the national institution that is the *bia hoi* scene in Hanoi, see the boxed text 'Bia Ahoy!' (p105).

For other Vietnamese options, see p103, and don't forget Highway 4 (p106) for some mouth-watering dishes favoured by the minority peoples of north Vietnam.

OLD QUARTER
There are plenty of Vietnamese restaurants to choose from in the Old Quarter.

Little Hanoi 1 (Map p84; ☎ 926 0168; 25 Pho Ta Hien; meals from 20,000d) A cosy, friendly little eatery that's worth seeking out; in fact, it's so cosy and so little that it has expanded into a second building across the road.

HANOI

Popular specialities are do-it-yourself fish spring rolls – seriously tasty!

69 Bar-Restaurant (Map p84; ☎ 926 0452; 69 Pho Ma May; meals from 40,000d) An ideal bolthole from the bustle of the Old Quarter, set in a beautifully restored old Vietnamese house. The menu draws on influences beyond Vietnam and it is open later than many places – the perfect place for a nightcap.

Hanoi Garden (Map p84; ☎ 824 3402; 36 Pho Hang Manh; set menus from 80,000d, à la carte from 40,000d) A smart setting for lunch or dinner, Hanoi Garden serves southern Vietnamese and spicy Chinese dishes in an elegant building with an open-air courtyard for steamy summer nights.

Dinh Lang Restaurant (Map p84; ☎ 828 6290; 1 Pho Le Thai Tho; meals 50,000-150,000d) This place has a great location on the northwest shore of Hoan Kiem Lake. It serves Chinese and Vietnamese cuisine with a backdrop of traditional music. Kitsch but likeable.

Pho Bo Dac Biet (Map p84; 2B Pho Ly Quoc Su; soups 10,000d) This is a good place to go for a bowl of beef noodle soup (*pho bo*), but virtually any of the restaurants or street stalls are fine for *pho* as long as you can see that the soup is still on the boil.

One of Hanoi's most famous food specialities is *cha ca*, perhaps best thought of as sumptuous little fish burgers. **Cha Ca La Vong** (Map p84; ☎ 825 3929; 14 Pho Cha Ca; meals from 50,000d), the *cha ca* capital of the Old Quarter, has been family-run for five generations. Other worthy (and cheaper) places at which to try this local delicacy include **Cha Ca 66** (Map p84; ☎ 826 7881; 66 Pho Hang Ga), located upstairs, and **Thang Long** (Map p84; ☎ 824 5115; 40 Pho Hang Ma).

CENTRAL HANOI

Quan Com Pho (Map pp80-1; ☎ 943 2356; 29 Pho Le Van Huu; dishes from 25,000d) A great concept – bringing street and market food to the middle class masses. Minikitchens turn out terrific food, including a delicious honey-barbecued squid. Dining is spread over several levels and lunchtime is particularly busy with Vietnamese and expats from nearby offices.

Tiem Pho (Map pp80-1; 48-50 Pho Hué; dishes 10,000d) Serves up great chicken noodle soup (*pho ga*) and keeps late hours.

Restaurant 1,2,3 (Map pp80-1; ☎ 822 9100; 55 Pho Hué; meals 30,000d) Diagonally across from

Tiem Pho, this place feels like a fancy-pants fast-food restaurant. The barbecued fish, and 'fish porridge' (*chao*), are scrumptious selections.

Gourmet Vietnamese
OLD QUARTER

Club Opera (Map p84; ☎ 824 6950; 59 Pho Ly Thai To; mains from US$6) Right opposite the Sofitel Metropole Hotel, Club Opera offers delectable Vietnamese dining in an elegant European atmosphere. The menu changes seasonally, but always includes an impressive array of seafood.

CENTRAL HANOI

Brothers Café (Map pp80-1; ☎ 733 3866; 26 Pho Nguyen Thai Hoc; lunch/dinner buffet US$6/11.50) For something completely different – Brothers is set in the courtyard of a carefully restored 250-year-old Buddhist temple. The nightly dinner buffet is the affordable approach and includes one drink; the lunch special is a bargain. The Zen atmosphere is simply serene, even when it's busy.

Emperor (Map pp80-1; ☎ 826 8801; 18B Pho Le Thanh Tong; mains from US$5) Stylish Vietnamese cuisine with an emphasis on presentation. This is a good place for live traditional music (7.30pm to 9.30pm) on Wednesday and Saturday, and Latino music on Tuesday and Friday.

Nam Phuong (Map pp80-1; ☎ 824 0926; 19 Pho Phan Chu Trinh; mains 60,000d) A chic setting in a charming villa with authentic and delicious Vietnamese food. Traditional music is played for a couple of hours from 7.30pm and there's an impressive wine list.

Seasons of Hanoi (Map pp80-1; ☎ 843 5444; 95B Pho Quan Thanh; dishes 40,000-100,000d) Another of Hanoi's *haute cuisine* venues for a lavish Vietnamese spread. It is in a classic French villa delightfully decorated with an eclectic collection of Vietnamese and colonial-era antiques.

Le Tonkin (☎ 943 3457; 14 Pho Ngo Van So; meals 40,000-120,000d) In a similar vein, with a flourishing garden for an outdoor dinner. Sensibly priced for an introduction to the gourmet Vietnamese experience.

Other Asian
OLD QUARTER

Baan Thai Restaurant (Map p84; ☎ 828 1120; 3B Pho Cha Ca; mains 30,000-90,000d) One of the longer-running Thai places in town, with a loyal following among the growing Thai community in Hanoi. For those who have forgotten their Thai favourites, there is a handy photo-illustrated menu at the door.

Tandoor (Map p84; ☎ 824 5359; 24 Pho Hang Be; mains from 40,000d) A great place to spice up your life in the heart of the Old Quarter. All the old favourites appear here, including good value *thali* if you can't decide.

Dakshin (Map p84; ☎ 928 6872; 94 Pho Hang Trong; meals 25,000-60,000d) The sister restaurant to Tandoor, Dakshin is all vegetarian and enjoys a great reputation among the curry crew in Hanoi. Good southern Indian food, as well, including delicious *dosas*.

Khazaana (formerly Revival; Map p84; ☎ 824 1166; 41B Pho Ly Thai To; vegetation/meat dishes 39,000d/59,000d) A sophisticated Indian restaurant with a handy chilli index on the menu to remind you what you should, or shouldn't, be ordering.

Saigon Sakura (Map p84; ☎ 825 7565; 17 Pho Trang Thi) One of the more central places to experience good Japanese cooking. Expect to pay around US$10 to US$15 for sushi and miso soup.

CENTRAL HANOI

Benkay Restaurant (Map pp80-1; ☎ 822 3535; 84 Tran Nhan Tong; set lunches from US$7) According to Hanoi's resident Japanese, Benkay can't be beaten for food. Location is another matter, as it's on the 2nd floor of the ugly Hotel Nikko.

Van Anh (Map pp80-1; ☎ 928 5163; 5a Pho Tong Duy Tan) A Thai restaurant with a Thai chef that has dared to take on the mass of Vietnamese restaurants in speciality food street Pho Cam Chi (p103).

Foodshop 45 (Map pp80-1; ☎ 716 2959; 11B Pho Tran Te Xuong St) This place has earned a loyal following thanks to its excellent and affordable Indian food. Out of the way, but worth going out of the way for.

International
OLD QUARTER

Café des Arts (Map p84; ☎ 828 7207; 11B Pho Bao Khanh; mains from US$5; ☺ 9am-late) A self-styled gastronomic grill modelled on a Parisian brasserie. The ambience is alluring and the menu great for lovers of fine French food. Art exhibitions and cultural events are held here.

Stop Café (Map p84; ☎ 828 7207; 11A Pho Bao Khanh; steaks 60,000d; ☺ 9am-late) A great little secret next door, although the phone number sort of gives it away. This informal café is the place to sample Café des Arts cuisine at cheaper prices.

Restaurant Bobby Chinn (Map p84; ☎ 934 8577; www.bobbychinn.com; 1 Pho Ba Trieu; mains US$6-10; ☺ 10am-late) A top spot for flavours blending the best of East and West. Hardly surprising given owner-chef Bobby Chinn is part Chinese and part Egyptian, and brings all his influences to bear in this classy setting. Try the superb salads or the fish with flair, chased down with a chocolate bomb. For an aperitif or a coffee, move through the silk drapes to the chill-out cushions at the back where smokers can stoke up a *sheesha* (water pipe) with fruit-flavoured tobacco.

Cyclo Bar & Restaurant (Map p84; ☎ 828 6844; 38 Pho Duong Thanh; mains from 60,000d) This is one restaurant everyone remembers…not necessarily for the lively Vietnamese and French food, but thanks to the *cyclos* that have been creatively transformed into tables. The set lunch is good value.

Green Tangerine (Map p84; ☎ 825 1286; 48 Pho Hang Be) The latest offering from the team that brought you Cyclo. Set in a superb structure from the French period, this place has a mixed menu of European and Vietnamese food. Worth a drink to soak up the atmosphere.

La Salsa (Map p84; ☎ 828 9052; 25 Pho Nha Tho; ☺ 10.30am-midnight) This tapas bar on the trendy strip opposite St Joseph Cathedral has earned a steady following among tourists and expats. Thursday is paella day.

Restaurant (Press Club; Map p84; ☎ 934 0888; 59a Pho Ly Thai To; mains around US$15) Long considered one of Hanoi's leading wining and dining venues, this place has stylish surroundings and makes innovative use of fine local and imported foods. Try the splendid signature sauce of black bean and Cabernet Sauvignon with seafood.

Le Beaulieu Restaurant (Map p84; ☎ 826 6919 ext 8028; 15 Pho Ngo Quyen) At the elegant Sofitel Metropole Hotel, Le Beaulieu is the fanciest French restaurant in town. This is the place for authentic French cooking, regular regional specialities and a romantic atmosphere.

There are several Italian restaurants around the Old Quarter:

Mama Rosa (Map p84; ☎ 825 8057; 6 Pho Le Thai To; pasta & pizza from 50,000d) This place has a prime location across from Hoan Kiem Lake but feels a little formal. Genuine Italian menu if you don't mind staff with bow ties and all.

Mediterraneo (Map p84; ☎ 826 6288; 23 Pho Nha Tho; mains US$5-7) Pasta, pizza and salads are all on offer, but the portions are a touch on the tapas side; be prepared to order more.

Al Fresco's (Map p84; ☎ 826 7782; 23L Pho Hai Ba Trung; meals US$5-15; ⊙ from lunch) A good place for juicy Tex-Mex ribs, fish fajitas and plenty of pizzas and salad. Al Fresco's has a legion of loyal followers and is well known for its margaritas.

Pepperoni's Pizza & Café (Map p84; ☎ 928 5246; 29 Pho Ly Quoc Su; mains from 40,000d; ⊙ from lunch) This is a legendary lunch stop, thanks to the 25,000d all-u-can-eat weekday lunchtime pasta and salad bar. It also has authentic pizzas and takeaway. Try the newer **branch** (☎ 928 7030; 31 Pho Bao Khanh) on the popular Bao Khanh strip.

For budget Western food, many of the travellers cafés listed under Travel Agencies (p79) can deliver. Among them is the **Kangaroo Café** (Map p84; ☎ 828 9931; 18 Pho Bao Khanh), just around the corner from Bao Khanh strip. This welcoming place is run by an Australian couple and serves filling Western food at Vietnamese prices.

CENTRAL HANOI

Jacc's (Map pp80-1; ☎ 934 8325; 4th fl Hanoi Towers, 49 Hai Ba Trung; ⊙ 6.30am-midnight) This busy bar and restaurant is popular with expats, thanks to a creative à la carte menu and some cheaper bar snacks. One of the places to watch international sporting events.

Verandah Bar & Café (Map pp80-1; ☎ 825 7220; 9 Pho Nguyen Khac Can; mains from US$5) Located in a stylish French villa, Verandah's menu includes chicken enchiladas and smoked salmon; or else you can just swing by for a relaxed drink. Try for a table on the very verandah that gives this place its name.

Luna d'Autumno (Map pp80-1; ☎ 823 7338; 11B Dien Bien Phu; pizza from 60,000d, fresh pasta from 90,000d; salads from 33,000d) A very strong contender for Hanoi's best Italian restaurant. The menu includes a superb selection of home-made antipasto and some of the only fresh pasta in town. The attractive villa includes a large outdoor terrace and upstairs is the Luna Lounge, a happening drinking spot for the after-dinner crowd. Call for takeaways.

Vine (Map p77; ☎ 719 8000; 1A Xuan Dieu) On the shore of West Lake, Vine is a richly decorated restaurant with a serious selection of international food. The menu includes a great rib eye steak with blue cheese, and the wine list doesn't get any longer than this, thanks to Vine's sister distribution business. Select wine from countries as varied as Argentina and Hungary.

Seafood

OLD QUARTER

La Brique (Map p84; ☎ 928 5638; 6 Pho Nha Tho; fish dishes from 60,000d; ⊙ 9am-midnight) Along the trendy strip opposite St Joseph Cathedral, La Brique is set amid the walls of what was once a wholesale fish market. It's a relaxed restaurant serving a simple but excellent selection of local seafood. The *cha ca* barbecued fish, and fish wrapped in banana leaf, remain favourites.

CENTRAL HANOI

Sam Son Seafood Market (☎ 825 0780; 77 Pho Doc Bac) A giant fish-market-cum-restaurant on the banks of Song Hong (Red River), this is fish fantasy. Choose your live fish and eat it several minutes later – that's fresh!

San Ho Restaurant (Map pp80-1; ☎ 934 9184; 58 Pho Ly Thuong Kiet; meals around 200,000d) Set in an attractive villa, San Ho has a reputation as one of the best seafood restaurants in Hanoi. It sells seafood at market prices.

Vegetarian

Tamarind Café (Map p84; ☎ 926 0580; 80 Pho Ma May; meals US$2-4; ⊙ 6am-midnight) Virtuoso vegetarian food, and a blend of fresh flavours bringing together Asian and European elements. One of the trendsetters on Ma May, the shakes and smoothies here are some of the best pick-me-ups in town.

Whole Earth Restaurant (Map p84; ☎ 926 0696; 7 Pho Dinh Liet; set menus from 25,000d; ⊙ 8am-11pm) Offers a healthy choice of vegetarian 'meat' dishes and is in the lively Dinh Liet strip with other cafés and bars.

Com Chay Nang Tam (Map pp80-1; ☎ 826 6140; 79A Pho Tran Hung Dao; meals from 20,000d) About 1km southwest of Hoan Kiem Lake, this is a smoke-free Hanoi hotspot. It is famed for creative vegetarian dishes, some of which are named after, and look like, meat. Some vegetarians may find this a contradiction, but it's an ancient Buddhist tradition that is designed to make meat-eating guests feel at home. Yes, it really is down that unlikely-looking alley behind those buildings. There's also a **branch** (79 Pho Hang Bac) of Com Chay Nang Tam in the Old Quarter.

Cafés & Ice Cream
OLD QUARTER

Little Hanoi 2 (Map p84; ☎ 928 5333; 21 Pho Hang Gai; sandwiches from 25,000d; ☷ 7.30am-11pm) On a corner crossroads near Hoan Kiem Lake, Little Hanoi 2 is no relation to Little Hanoi 1. This is a lovely open-plan café, with a mouthwatering selection of baguettes, pastas and salads. French breakfast is a steal at 30,000d.

Puku (Map p84; ☎ 928 5244; upstairs 60 Pho Hang Trong; light bites 25,000-35,000d; ☷ 7am-10pm) A cool little café with a good vibe, fine food and a tiny balcony. The brilliant business card makes a good mini-Frisbee if you left yours at home.

No Noodles (Map p84; ☎ 928 5969; 20 Pho Nha Chung; sandwiches from 22,000d; ☷ 9am-9pm) A sandwich bar with a serious selection of baguettes and bread. Eat in or take away for a snack on the shores of Hoan Kiem Lake.

Moca Café (Map p84; ☎ 825 6334; 14-16 Pho Nha Tho; espresso 20,000d; ☷ 7.30am-11pm) Prime for people-watching, thanks to its huge windows. Tuck into affordable Vietnamese, Western and Indian food.

Café Le Malraux (Map p84; ☎ 928 6203; 6 Pho Nha Tho; French breakfast 55,000d; ☷ all day) A funky French-run café-bar serving everything from cakes to culinary extravaganzas. It doubles as a furniture shop, so the seating comes in many shapes and sizes.

Au Lac (Map p84; ☎ 825 7807; 57 Pho Ly Thai To) This café is set in the comfy courtyard of a French villa. It serves light bites and the coffee has a radical reputation among caffeine cravers.

Diva (Map p84; ☎ 934 4088; 57 Pho Ly Thai To; light meals from 35,000d; ☷ 7am-midnight) A few steps away from Au Lac, Diva is in another charming French-period villa, and has a big outdoor terrace for leisurely lunches or a sneaky sundowner at the end of the day.

Press Club Deli (Map p84; ☎ 934 0888; 59A Pho Ly Thai To; sandwiches from US$3, set lunch from US$5) This is a breadhead's heaven, with quiches, cakes

and pastries to set the pulse racing. Eat-in or take away.

Paris Deli (Map p84; ☎ 934 5269; 2 Pho Phan Chu Trinh; meals from 30,000d; ☷ 7.30am-11pm) This is a Parisian-style café-restaurant that enjoys a premium position opposite the Opera House. It serves bulging baguettes and delicate pastries.

Fanny Ice Cream (Map p84; ☎ 828 5656; 48 Pho Le Thai To) The most celebrated ice cream shop in town. Sniggering about the name aside, it serves great 'Franco-Vietnamese' ice cream and crepes. During the right season try the *com*, a delightful local flavour extracted from young sticky rice; otherwise try the ginger for the flavour of Asia.

Kem Trang Tien (Map p84; 54 Pho Trang Tien) Between the Opera House and Hoan Kiem Lake, this is probably the most popular ice-cream shop with Hanoians. You'll spot the crowd long before you see the café, which has air-con inside if you don't think the ice cream will last five minutes in the Hanoi heat.

CENTRAL HANOI

Café Pho Cu Xua (Map pp80-1; ☎ 928 5749; 195 Pho Hang Bong) It's popular with young Vietnamese professionals, but has a forgettable shop front. Walk through to the back where there's a lush garden oasis serving coffee, ice cream and cocktails.

Kinh Do Café (Map pp80-1; ☎ 825 0216; 252 Pho Hang Bong; light meals 20,000d; ☷ 7am-10pm) This place serves some of the best yoghurt in Vietnam, plus tasty French pastries and coffee with a kick. For movie buffs, this was the simple setting where Catherine Deneuve had her morning cuppa during the making of the film *Indochine*, and the owner speaks good French.

GREATER HANOI

Deli (Map p77; ☎ 846 0007; 18 Pho Tran Huy Lieu) Out of town near Giang Vo Lake, Deli whips up tasty sandwiches from 20,000d should you happen to be passing this way.

Speciality Food Streets
If you would like to combine eating with exploration, most of the following food streets are in central Hanoi.

CAM CHI

This is about 500m northeast of Hanoi train station. Cam Chi is a super-small street – actually an alley – that's crammed full of lively street stalls (Map pp80-1) serving budget-priced, delicious food. Forget about English menus and don't expect comfortable seating. Still, there's no room to complain when you get a small banquet for US$2. Cam Chi translates as 'Forbidden to Point' and dates from centuries ago. It is said that the street was named as a reminder for the local residents to keep their curious fingers in their pockets when the king and his entourage went through the neighbourhood.

PHO MAI HAC DE & PHO TO HIEN THANH

Located in the south-central area, Pho Mai Hac De has several blocks of restaurants (Map pp80-1), running south from the northern terminus at Pho Tran Nhan Tong. It intersects with a street that specialises in seafood, Pho To Hien Thanh.

DUONG THUY KHUE

On the south bank of Ho Tay, Đ Thuy Khue (Map pp80-1) features a strip of 30 or more outdoor seafood restaurants with a peaceful lakeside setting, popular with locals. The level of competition is evident by the daredevil touts who literally throw themselves in front of oncoming traffic to steer people to their tables. You can eat well here for about 100,000d a head.

PHO NGHI TAM

About 10km north of central Hanoi, Pho Nghi Tam has a 1km-long stretch of about 60 **dog-meat restaurants** (Map p113; meals from 30,000d). The street runs along the embankment between West Lake and the Red River. Even if you have no interest in eating dog meat, it's interesting to cruise this stretch of road on the last evening of the lunar month. Hanoians believe that eating dog meat in the first half of the lunar month brings bad luck. As a consequence, these restaurants are deserted at that time and most of them shut down. Business picks up in the second half of the lunar month and the last day is particularly auspicious so the restaurants are packed. Cruise by in the evening and you'll see thousands of motorbikes parked here. As you drive along, hawkers practically leap out in front of you to extol the virtues of their cuddly canine specialities.

Self-Catering
OLD QUARTER
Fivimart (Map p84; 210 Tran Quang Khai) One of the best ranges of Western supermarket supplies in the city.

Trung Tam Thuong Mai (Map p84; 7 Pho Dinh Tien Hoang) A well-located supermarket-cum-department store with plenty of imported food and drinks. Enter from the lakeside or out back.

Citimart (Map pp80-1; Hanoi Towers, 49 Hai Ba Trung) A supermarket with a teasing range of treats for the many expats that live in the skyscraper above.

Intimex (Map p84) supermarket is a good alternative for any creature comforts you might need. It's on the western side of Hoan Kiem Lake, tucked down a driveway behind the Clinique beauty shop.

CENTRAL HANOI
Western Canned Foods (Map p84; Pho Ba Trieu) This place carries a good range of exactly what the name suggests, plus other imported items.

More determined self-caterers can buy fresh vegetables at the Hom Market (Map pp80-1), just south of the city centre near the intersection of Pho Hué and Pho Tran Xuan Soan.

DRINKING
Bars
There is a drink for every occasion in Hanoi, with sophisticated bars, congenial pubs and grungy clubs. Don't forget to warm up with some quality time drinking *bia hoi*, the world's cheapest beer: see the boxed text 'Bia Ahoy!' opposite for more. And busy Bao Khanh has a cheery choice of bars and is a hit with hip Vietnamese.

Bear in mind that the fun police supervise a fairly strict curfew of midnight during the week and 1am at the weekend, which takes the edge off the nightlife. There are a few late-night lock-ins; read on for the rub.

Quan Bia Minh (Map p84; ☎ 934 5233; 7A Pho Dinh Liet) A backpacker favourite, thanks to some of the cheapest Hanoi beer in town. There is a great balcony terrace overlooking Dinh Liet and at 8000d for a big beer, stumbling is the most popular way home.

Red Beer (Map p84; ☎ 826 0247; 97 Pho Ma May) Totally the opposite, this is a local microbrewery that is earning a following among

BIA AHOY!

'Tram phan tram!' Remember these words well as all over Vietnam, glasses of *bia hoi* are raised and emptied, cries of '100%' or 'bottoms up' echo around the table.

Bia hoi (fresh beer) is Vietnam's very own draft beer or microbrew. This refreshing, light-bodied Pilsener was first introduced in Vietnam by the Czechs. Decades later *bia hoi* is still brewed and delivered daily to drinking establishments throughout HCMC, Hanoi and all points between. Brewed without preservatives, it is meant to be enjoyed immediately. And enjoyed it is! Many tourists and expats have never heard of this nectar, but that's their loss, especially given it costs just 1500d a glass!

If you think you're ready to try *bia hoi,* be prepared – drinking with the pros is not for the meek! A Western face is a bit unusual at any *bia hoi* establishment and inevitably attracts curious attention from fellow patrons. Raising your glass in toast more often than not results in an invitation to join a group.

Hanoi is the *bia hoi* capital of Vietnam and there are microbars on almost every street corner. Hitting the Old Quarter for a *bia hoi* crawl is a brilliant way to get beneath the skin of the capital. Put US$10 in your pocket and you will be able to afford 100 beers, so you'll soon make lots of friends. One of the best places to sample this bargain beer is 'bia hoi junction' (Map p84) in the heart of the Old Quarter where Pho Ta Hien meets Pho Luong Ngoc Quyen. Here are three bustling *bia hoi* places occupying different corners, all packed with backpackers and locals every night and knocking out the ale at just 1500d a glass.

For the best quality *bia hoi,* try **Bia Hoi Viet** Ha (Map p84; 24 Pho Tong Dan), which is well loved by Hanoi insiders, as it has the biggest chillers in town. Check out the toilets, a legend in themselves.

Other good spots to sample the brew include **Bia Hoi 68 Hang Quat** (Map p84; Pho Hang Quat), which we have been drinking at for a decade now, and **Nha Hang Lan Chin** (Map pp80-1; 2 Pho Trang Tien), one of the most popular local lunch spots in town, which is a good reminder to mention that most *bia hoi* also serve delicious and inexpensive food.

Vietnamese beer drinkers. It has two types of home brew for those who have had enough of the standard beers.

Funky Monkey (Map p84; ☎ 928 6113; 15b Pho Hang Hanh; beers from 15,000d) This place leads the pack in Bao Khanh: a long, narrow bar with some of the best beats in town. Crazy cocktails, dark décor and occasional dancing on a busy Friday or Saturday.

Polite Pub (Map p84; ☎ 825 0959; 5 Pho Bao Khanh) Not for the impolite…well, unless there's a big game on in the Premier League – then it's everyone for themselves. A popular pub for inexpensive drinks and all the major sports.

GC Pub (Map p84; ☎ 825 0499; 5 Pho Bao Khanh) Right next door, GC has a more mellow vibe, complete with a pool table in the middle of things. One of the more gay-friendly places in town.

Bar Le Maquis (Map p84; ☎ 928 2618; 2A Pho Ta Hien) This teeny-tiny bar on lively Ta Hien doesn't need a crowd to make it feel busy and is one of the few places open later into the night.

Labyrinth (Map p84; ☎ 926 0788; 7 Pho Ta Hien) There's a minute and missable entrance on Ta Hien, but inside Labyrinth takes after its name, opening up into a series of small rooms. Cool rather than kickin', a good middle-of-the-evening spot.

Half Man, Half Noodle (Map p84; ☎ 926 1943; 52 Dao Duy Tu, off Pho Hang Giay) The dream of a former barman from Labyrinth, this place proves that it is people that help make a place – he has taken a lot of regulars with him. Dix points for the name!

Met Pub (Map p84; ☎ 826 6919 ext 8857) A refined bar in the Sofitel Metropole Hotel. The Met is a lovely place with fine food and Hanoi's best beer selection, but it's also expensive unless you hit the happy hour.

Spotted Cow (Map p84; ☎ 824 1028; 23C Pho Hai Ba Trung) This popular Aussie-run pub is a loud place with such intellectual pursuits as frog racing. Also a gathering point for Hash House Harrier runs (p92).

Phuc Tan Bar (Map p84; ☎ 932 3244; 49 Phuc Tan; ☺ early til late) Definitely *the* place to be in the early hours of the morning come the

HANOI

THE AUTHOR'S CHOICE

Highway 4 (Map p84; ☎ 926 0639; 5 Pho Hang Tre) A popular rallying point for members of Hanoi's infamous Minsk Club (a motorbike club for riders of the legendary mule of the mountains, the Russian Minsk). This is the place to discover the mystical, medicinal (and intoxicating) qualities of Vietnamese rice wine *(xeo)* – take it straight, fruity or 'five times a night', the possibilities are endless.

The bar boasts a rugged mountain decor and a rooftop terrace, and is an excellent place to find information on motorbiking Vietnam. There is also an innovative menu of Montagnard specialities and Vietnamese favourites. There's a new upmarket **Highway 4** (Map pp80-1; ☎ 976 2647; 5 Pho Mai Hac De) that's very popular with Vietnamese.

---

weekend. Striking out on its own, Phuc Tan is in a weird part of town – beyond the dike on the banks of the Red River – but don't let this stop you hanging here. Punk and rock classics on the approach to midnight; Leftfield, The Prodigy and friends on the night shift. Small bar at the front with a popular pool table and huge terrace bars out the back overlooking the river. Sunday recovery breakfasts mean it never really shuts at the weekend.

Coffee Shops
Thuy Ta Café (Map p84; ☎ 828 8148; 1 Pho Le Thai To; pastries from 5000d; ☑ 6am-11pm) One of the best settings in Hanoi for a cuppa is Thuy Ta's shady garden, right on the edge of Hoan Kiem Lake.

Highlands Coffee (Map p84; ☎ 828 7043) At the opposite end of Hoan Kiem Lake, this café offers a prime patio for drinks and is an ideal place to watch the world go by on a warm day.

There is a lively, packed and chaotic cluster of coffee shops on the Old Quarter's Pho Hang Hanh; relax on one of the upstairs balconies and watch the bustle below on one of Hanoi's most happening streets.

ENTERTAINMENT
Cinemas
National Movie Centre (Map p77; ☎ 514 1114; 87 Pho Lang Ha) One of the best venues to catch

foreign films in Hanoi – the equivalent of an arts cinema back home.

Cinematheque (Map p84; 22a Hai Ba Trung; ☎ 936 2648) The latest cinema to open, Cinematheque is earning rave reviews for its adventurous choice of films – from shorts to a mixed selection of arthouse films.

Fanslands Cinema (Map pp80-1; ☎ 825 7484; 84 Pho Ly Thuong Kiet) For a more standard selection of Western movies.

Centre Culturel Française de Hanoi (Map p84; ☎ 936 2164; 24 Trang Tien) Set in the sublime L'Espace building near the Opera House, it offers a regular programme of French flicks.

Circus Troupes
Central Circus (Rap Xiec Trung Uong; Map pp80-1; admission US$2.50; shows 8-10pm Tue-Sun, 9am Sun) The circus is one Russian entertainment tradition that has survived and thrived in Vietnam. Performers – gymnasts, jugglers, animal trainers – were originally trained in Eastern Europe, though today's new recruits learn their skills from their Vietnamese elders.

Performances are held in a huge tent near the northern entrance to Lenin Park. A special show is staged for children on Sunday morning.

Nightclubs
If you want to see the beautiful people of Vietnam cutting their moves, there are several local clubs to check out. New clubs tend to go in and out of favour like Beckham's haircuts, so ask around for what's hot or not before venturing forth.

Apocalypse Now (Map pp80-1; ☎ 971 2783; 5C Pho Hoa Ma; ☑ 8pm-1am) A popular place of pilgrimage for Hanoi's hedonists. It really fires up on weekends, and is known for its loud and raucous music and street-wise swillers. It used to close when the last customers trickled away, but now the fun police crash the party around 1am.

New Century Nightclub (Map p84; ☎ 928 5285; 10 Pho Trang Thi) The place to be seen for young Vietnamese who love to flash the cash. Dress to impress, as this club is right out of New York, London or Paris.

Live Music
CLASSICAL
Hanoi Opera House (Nha Hat Lon; Map p84; ☎ 825 4312; Pho Trang Tien) This magnificent 900-seat

venue looks along Pho Trang Tien to Hoan Kiem Lake. It was built in 1911 and a painstaking, three-year renovation has restored it to its former glory. It was from a balcony on this building that the Viet Minh–run Citizens' Committee announced, on 16 August 1945, that it had taken over the city. Performances of classical music are periodically held here in the evenings and the atmosphere is incredible. The theatre's Vietnamese name appropriately translates to 'House Sing Big'.

Check the listings in the *Guide* or *Time Out* to find out if anything is happening here during your stay.

JAZZ & MODERN
Jazz Club By Quyen Van Minh (Cau Lac Bo; Map p84; ☎ 825 7655; 31-33 Pho Luong Van Can; ☼ performances 9-11.30pm) *The* place in Hanoi to catch hot, live jazz (well, mostly jazz). Bar owner Minh teaches saxophone at the Hanoi Conservatory and moonlights here, jamming with a variety of musicians ranging from his talented son to top-notch international jazz players.

R&R Tavern (Map p84; ☎ 934 4109; 47 Pho Lo Su) One of the best bars for live music in Hanoi, with a Vietnamese band running through counter-culture '60s classics at the weekend, and a string quartet on Thursday. Bargain beer compared with many expat haunts, and some of the best burgers in town.

Terrace Bar (Press Club; Map p84; ☎ 934 0888; 59a Pho Ly Thai To) This place is frenetic on Friday, when half of Hanoi's high-flyers seem to descend here for the happy hour (6pm). Drink specials from 20,000d include access to the roving platters of finger food and a soundtrack of live music – rock'n'roll, '70s disco, Latin – it's a lucky dip.

TRADITIONAL
Some of the best places to catch live traditional music are upmarket Vietnamese restaurants in central Hanoi, like **Cay Cau** (Map pp80-1; ☎ 824 5346; 17A Pho Tran Hung Dao) in the De Syloia Hotel, **Club Opera** (Map p84; ☎ 824 6950; 59 Pho Ly Thai To), **Dinh Lang Restaurant** (Map p84; ☎ 828 6290; 1 Pho Le Thai Tho) and **Nam Phuong** (Map p84; ☎ 928 5085; fax 825 8964; 16 Pho Bao Khanh). It can feel kind of touristy, but close your eyes and the music is hauntingly beautiful.

There is also live music performed daily at the Temple of Literature (p88).

Water Puppets
This fantastic art form (see the boxed text 'Punch & Judy in a Pool', p108) originated in northern Vietnam, and Hanoi is the best place to see it.

At the **Municipal Water Puppet Theatre** (Roi Nuoc Thang Long; Map p84; ☎ 825 5450; 57B Pho Dinh Tien Hoang; admission 20,000-40,000d, still-camera fee 10,000d, video fee 50,000d; ☼ performances at 6.30pm & 8pm, 9.30am Sun), the higher admission price buys the best seats and a take-home cassette of the music; fans and multilingual programmes are free – it helps to read up on each vignette as it's performed. Check out the faces of enthralled Vietnamese kids in the audience – they're magic!

SHOPPING
Designer Boutiques
La Boutique and the Silk (Map p84; ☎ 928 5368; 6 Pho Nha Tho) Near St Joseph Cathedral, this place is well worth a look. The original designs are inspired by Vietnamese ethnic-minority clothing and are made from high-quality Lao silk.

Khai Silk (Map p84; ☎ 825 4237; khaisilk@fpt.vn; 96 Pho Hang Gai) Offers funky, fashionable silk clothing, as well as more austere classical creations. The proprietor, Khai, is fluent in both French and English, and has an eye for turning on the style.

Ipa-Nima (Map pp80-1; ☎ 942 1872; 59G Pho Hai Ba Trung) A boutique that aims for 'smart humour, bright colours, subtle satire'. A cute collection of clothes includes designer-kitsch beaded tops and accessories.

There are several beautiful furnishings shops on Pho Nha Tho if you are in the mood for shipping stuff back home or setting up house.

Galleries
Aspiring young artists display their works in Hanoi's private art galleries in the hope of attracting a buyer. The highest concentration of upmarket galleries is on Pho Trang Tien, between Hoan Kiem Lake and the Opera House – just stroll down the strip. Most art galleries have some English-speaking staff, and are open daily until 8pm or 9pm. Prices range from a few dollars to a few thousand and polite bargaining is the norm.

HANOI

PUNCH & JUDY IN A POOL

The ancient art of water puppetry (roi nuoc) was virtually unknown outside of northern Vietnam until the 1960s. Depending on which story you believe, it originated with rice farmers who worked the flooded fields and either saw the potential of the water as a dynamic stage or adapted conventional puppetry during a massive flood of the Red River Delta. Whatever the true history, it is at least 1000 years old.

The farmers carved the puppets from water-resistant fig-tree timber (sung) in forms modelled on the villagers themselves, animals from their daily lives and more fanciful mythical creatures such as the dragon, phoenix and unicorn. Performances were usually staged in ponds, lakes or flooded paddy fields.

Contemporary performances use a square tank of waist-deep water for the 'stage'; the water is murky to conceal the mechanisms that operate the puppets. The wooden puppets can be up to 50cm long and weigh as much as 15kg; they're painted with a glossy vegetable-based paint. Each lasts only about three to four months if used continually, so puppet production provides several villages outside Hanoi with a full-time industry.

Eleven puppeteers, trained for a minimum of three years, are involved in each performance. They stand in the water behind a bamboo screen and have traditionally suffered from a host of water-borne diseases – these days they wear waders to avoid this nasty occupational hazard.

Some puppets are simply attached to a long pole, while others are set on a floating base, in turn attached to a pole. Most have articulated limbs and heads, some also have rudders to help guide them. In the darkened auditorium it looks as if they are literally walking on water.

The considerable skills required to operate the puppets were traditionally kept secret and passed only from father to son; never to daughters through fear that they would marry outside the village and take the secrets with them.

The music, which is provided by a band, is as important as the action on stage. The band includes wooden flutes (sao), gongs (cong), cylindrical drums (trong com), bamboo xylophones and the fascinating single-stringed dan bau.

The performance consists of a number of vignettes depicting pastoral scenes and legends. One memorable scene tells of the battle between a fisherman and his prey, which is so electric it appears as if a live fish is being used. There are also fire-breathing dragons (complete with fireworks) and a flute-playing boy riding a buffalo.

The performance is a lot of fun. The water puppets are both amusing and graceful, and the water greatly enhances the drama by allowing the puppets to appear and disappear as if by magic. Spectators in the front row seats can expect a bit of a splash.

Hanoi Gallery (Map p84; 110 Pho Hang Bac; 9am-8pm) stocks a great selection of old propaganda posters, with translations of the slogans, and mailing tubes for easy carrying or posting.

In a cluster around the Old Quarter corner of Pho Trang Tien and Pho Ngo Quyen are Gallery Huong Xuyen (Map p84), which also stocks some beautiful greetings cards; **A Gallery** (Map p84; www.vietnamesepainting.com), with both permanent and visiting exhibitions; and **Hanoi Contemporary Art Gallery** (Map p84; www.hanoi-artgallery.com), with some ceramics as well as paintings.

Situated close to Dan Chu Hotel on Pho Trang Tien are the well-established Hanoi Studio (Map p84) and the **Van Gallery** (www.vangallery.com).

Handicrafts & Antiques

There are quite a few stores in Hanoi that offer new and antique Vietnamese handicrafts (lacquerware, mother-of-pearl inlaid furniture, ceramics, sandalwood statuettes etc), as well as watercolours, oil paintings, prints and assorted antiques (real and fake). Pho Hang Gai, Pho To Tich, Pho Hang Khai and Pho Cau Go are happy hunting grounds.

Viet Hien (Map pp80-1; ☎ 826 9769; 8B Pho Ta Hien) An enormous warehouse of antiques, paintings, furniture and handicrafts, including rattan creations that are a hell of a lot cheaper than at home.

Vietnamese House (Map p84; ☎ 826 2455; 92 Pho Hang Bac) A small but attractive shop dealing in a mix of old and new treasures.

MASON FLORENCE

Funeral procession, Hanoi (p74)

JOHN BANAGAN

Lotus flowers, Temple of
Literature (p88), Hanoi

Canoes await passengers for the trip to
the Perfume Pagoda (p112), near Hanoi
CRAIG PERSHOUSE

RICHARD I'ANSON

Two-wheel traffic, Hanoi (p74)

Street vendor, Hanoi (p74)

MICHAEL COYNE

JULIET COOMBE

Water puppets, Municipal Water Puppet
Theatre (p107), Hanoi

Huc Bridge over Hoan Kiem Lake (p85), Hanoi

ANDERS BLO

There is a strip of antique shops located on Le Duan, across from the Hotel Nikko on Tran Nhan Tong, but most tend to be overpriced.

Markets

Dong Xuan Market (Map p84) is a three-storey market in the Old Quarter, 900m north of Hoan Kiem Lake. The market burned down in 1994, killing five people, all of whom had entered the building after the fire started, to either rescue goods or steal them. It has now been rebuilt and is a tourist attraction in its own right. There are hundreds of stalls here, employing around 3000 people.

Hang Da Market (Map p84) is a relatively small market, but it is good for imported foods, wine, beer and flowers. The 2nd floor is good for fabric and ready-made clothing. It is very close to the Protestant Church.

Hom Market (Map p84), on the northeast corner of Pho Hué and Pho Tran Xuan Soan, is a good general-purpose market with lots of imported food items. It's a good place to buy fabric if you plan to have clothes made.

Cua Nam Market (Map pp80-1) is a few blocks north of the Hanoi train station. The market is itself of no great interest (except maybe for the flowers), but Ð Le Duan between the market and the train station is a treasure-trove of household goods, such as electronics and plastic ware.

Buoi Market (Map p77) is located out in the far northwest; it is notable for live animals (chickens, ducks, pigs and so on), but also features ornamental plants.

Salons & Spas

Note that many of Hanoi's beauty salons offer – ahem – 'extra services' as standard.

Vu Doo Salon (☎ 823 3439; 32c Pho Cao Ba Quat) If you feel in need of sprucing, Vu Doo is a good, legitimate hairdresser with a steady following among Hanoi's expat community. It charges a mere US$9/10 for men/women, including a wash, head massage, cut and blow dry. Manicures and pedicures cost about US$4.

QT Salon (Map p84; ☎ 928 6166; 28 Pho Le Thai To; ❤️ 10am-8pm) For a spa splurge on facials or body treatments, head to this place overlooking Hoan Kiem Lake. There are additional

outlets at the Hilton (Map p84) and Horison (Map p77) hotels.

Souvenirs & Other Shops

Around Pho Hang Bong and Pho Hang Gai, just northwest of Hoan Kiem Lake, are plenty of souvenir shops selling T-shirts and Viet Cong (VC) headgear. It might be worth noting, however, that neither Ho Chi Minh T-shirts nor VC headgear are very popular apparel with Vietnamese refugees and certain war veterans living in the West. Wearing such souvenirs while walking down a street in Los Angeles or Melbourne might offend someone and result in a costly trip to the dentist.

Pho Hang Gai and its continuation, Pho Hang Bong, are a good place to look for embroidered tablecloths, T-shirts and wall hangings. Pho Hang Gai is also a good place to have clothes custom-made. Take a look along Pho Hang Dao, just north of Hoa Kiem Lake, for souvenir Russian-made watches.

If you don't make it up to Sapa (p160), there is a wide selection of ethnic-minority garb and handicrafts available in Hanoi; a stroll along Pho Hang Bac or Pho To Tich will turn up close to a dozen places. **Craft Link** (Map pp80-1; ☎ 843 7710; 43 Pho Van Mieu) is a not-for-profit organisation that buys good quality tribal handicrafts and weavings at fair-trade prices, and funds community development initiatives for the artisans.

There is an outstanding **shoe market** (Map p84; Pho Hang Dau) at the northeast corner of Hoan Kiem Lake; however, it can be difficult to find large sizes for big Western feet.

For the best in CDs and DVDs, there are several shops along Pho Hang Bong and Pho Trang Tien. Be aware that they're bootleg, though, so not strictly legal.

On Pho Trang Tien you'll also find many shops willing to make dirt-cheap eyeglasses in a mere 10 minutes, using decent imported lenses from France or Japan.

GETTING THERE & AWAY
Air

Hanoi has fewer direct international flights than HCMC, but with a change of aircraft in Hong Kong or Bangkok you can get to almost anywhere. For further information about international flights, see p468.

Vietnam Airlines (Map p84; ☎ 943 9660; www
.vietnamair.com.vn; 25 Pho Trang Thi; ⏱ 7am-6.30pm
Mon-Fri, 8-11.30am & 1.30-5pm Sat & Sun & hols) links
Hanoi to destinations throughout Vietnam.
Popular routes include Hanoi to Danang,
Dien Bien Phu, HCMC, Hué and Nha
Trang, all served daily.

Pacific Airlines (Map pp80-1; ☎ 851 5356; 100
Đ Le Duan) has daily flights to Danang and
HCMC.

For further information about domestic
flights from Hanoi, see p475.

Bus & Minibus

Hanoi has several main long-distance bus
stations and each one serves a particular
area. They are fairly well organised, with
ticket offices and printed schedules and
prices. You'd be well advised to check information and buy tickets the day before
you plan to travel.

In central Hanoi, **Kim Ma bus station** (Map
pp80-1; cnr Pho Nguyen Thai Hoc & Pho Giang Vo) has
buses to the northwestern part of Vietnam,
including Lao Cai (53,000d, 10 hours) and
Dien Bien Phu (100,000d, 16 hours).

Gia Lam bus station is the place for
buses to points northeast of Hanoi. These
include Halong Bay (35,000d, 3½ hours),
Hai Phong, and Lang Son (30,000d, three
hours), near the Chinese border. The bus
station is 2km northeast of the centre –
cross the Red River to get there. *Cyclos*
can't cross the bridge, so take a taxi (around
30,000d) or motorbike.

Giap Bat bus station (Đ Giai Phong) serves
points south of Hanoi, including HCMC
(49 hours). It is 7km south of the Hanoi
train station.

Son La bus station (Km8, Pho Nguyen Trai), southwest of Hanoi (near Hanoi University), can
be reached by motorbike or taxi. It is a departure point for buses to destinations in
the northwest, such as Hoa Binh, Son La
(63,000d, 12 to 14 hours), Dien Bien Phu
(100,000d, 16 hours) and Lai Chau. Most
travellers find Kim Ma bus station more
convenient for these destinations.

Tourist-style minibuses can be booked
through most hotels and cafés. Popular destinations include Halong Bay and Sapa. See
p79 for operators.

Many open-ticket tours through Vietnam start or finish in Hanoi – for more
details see p478.

Car & Motorbike

To hire a car with a driver, contact a hotel,
travellers café or travel agency. The main
roads in the northeast are generally OK,
but in parts of the northwest they can be
awful. For this reason, you may need a high
clearance vehicle or a 4WD.

The average cost for a six-day trip in a
Russian jeep is about US$200, including the
jeep, a driver and petrol. These old jeeps fit
only two passengers and are pretty uncomfortable: they're dusty and hot, or damp and
cold, depending on the weather. For a fancier Japanese or Korean air-con 4WD you
are looking at paying around double. The
price usually includes the driver's expenses,
but it's a good idea to clarify this.

A long-distance journey from Hanoi into
the mountainous hinterland of the north
is exciting, though slightly risky in terms
of traffic accidents, and definitely tiring.
You probably wouldn't want to do it during
the coldest months (January and February),
and in mid-summer you have to contend
with occasionally heavy rains. Despite such
annoyances, many travellers prefer motorbike travel to all other forms of transport.

If you plan to tour the north by bike, see
p94. There are several good outfits that can
arrange guides and rentals and help with
itinerary planning.

The 125cc Russian-made Minsk is the
best overall bike for touring the north – you
will need this kind of power for the mountainous regions, and all mechanics know
how to fix them. Quality of rental motorbikes can be extremely variable, so try to
find a reputable dealer, especially if you're
planning long trips.

For the most reliable Minsk rental in
town, make for **Cuong's Motorbike Adventure**
(Map p84; ☎ 926 1534; 1 Pho Luong Ngoc Quyen).
Cuong rents out bikes for US$5 a day, in-
cluding a full range of spares and a repair
manual. It offers top service and is a good
place to buy if you are in the market for a
Minsk.

Train

The main **Hanoi train station** (Ga Hang Co; Map
pp80-1; ☎ 825 3949; 120 Đ Le Duan; ⏱ ticket office
7.30am-12.30pm & 1.30-7.30pm) is at the western
end of Pho Tran Hung Dao; trains from
here go to destinations south. Foreigners
can buy tickets for southbound trains at

counter 2, where the staff speaks English. It's often best to buy tickets at least one day before departure to ensure a seat or sleeper.

To the right of the main entrance of the train station is a separate ticket office for northbound trains to Lao Cai (for Sapa) and China. Tickets to China must be bought from counter 13.

However, the place where you purchase the ticket is not necessarily where the train departs! Just behind the main 'A Station' on Đ Le Duan is **Tran Quy Cap station** (B Station; Pho Tran Qui Cap; ☎ 825 2628) and all northbound trains leave from there.

To make things even more complicated, some northbound (Lao Cai and Lang Son included) and eastbound (Hai Phong) trains depart from Gia Lam on the east side of the Red River, and **Long Bien** (Map pp80-1; ☎ 826 8280) on the western (city) side of the river. Be sure to ask just where you need to go to catch your train. Tickets can be bought at the main station until about two hours before departure; if it's any closer to the departure time, go to the relevant station and buy tickets there.

Check with **Vietnam Rail** (Duong Sat Viet Nam; www.vr.com.vn) for current timetables. For more information on trains see p482.

GETTING AROUND
To/From the Airport

Hanoi's Noi Bai International Airport is about 35km north of the city and the journey takes from 45 minutes to an hour. The airport freeway is one of the most modern roads in Vietnam, although you'll see oxen herded by farmers dressed in rags crossing it. The freeway suddenly terminates in the suburbs north of Hanoi.

Vietnam Airlines minibuses between Hanoi and Noi Bai airport charge US$2 a seat. There are few information signs inside the new terminal building; you need to go outside and look for the signs for taxis and minibuses. Coming from the airport, the driver is supposed to drop you at the office of Vietnam Airlines at Pho Trang Thi, but the drivers usually tour the Old Quarter on the chase for commissions. If you end up dropped somewhere you don't want to be, just arrange a metered taxi to your destination: they are the easiest option if you have heavy bags, and there is no need to haggle.

The airport minibus service works reasonably well, but there are a few scams, especially at the airport. Normally, local touts (well dressed and posing as employees of Vietnam Airlines) board the official minibuses. They are skilled at befriending newly arrived passengers and by the time you reach the city will offer to recommend a 'good, cheap hotel'. If you want to avoid the sales pitch, just tell them that you've already got a hotel reservation, even if you don't.

To get to the airport from town, you can take one of the minibuses that depart roughly every half-hour from opposite the same Vietnam Airlines office on Pho Trang Thi. It's best – though not essential – to book the day before.

The cheapest way to get between Noi Bai airport and central Hanoi is to use public bus No 7, which runs all the way to the northern end of Hoan Kiem Lake, right on the edge of the Old Quarter. Services depart every 15 minutes from around 5am to 9pm and tickets are just 2500d – perhaps the cheapest airport run in the world. It can take more than an hour, however.

Airport Taxi (☎ 873 3333) charges US$10 for a taxi ride door-to-door to or from Noi Bai airport. They do *not* require that you pay the toll for the bridge you cross en route. Some other taxi drivers require that you pay the toll, so ask first.

Inside the terminal, touts will offer taxi services. Don't use the meter with a tout, as it may well be rigged. The 'official' taxi rank is outside the concourse and you buy tickets from the seller at the head of the taxi line.

In central Hanoi, there is always a collection of taxi drivers just outside the Vietnam Airlines office or at the northern end of Hoan Kiem Lake – it doesn't take much effort to find one. Don't pay more than US$10, including the toll.

There are also share cabs/private minibuses from travellers' cafés for about US$2 per person.

Bicycle

A good way to get around Hanoi is by bicycle. Many hotels and cafés offer these for rent for about 10,000d per day.

Bus

There are 31 public bus lines in Hanoi. Figuring out exactly where the buses go can be a challenge, and service on some of the lines is infrequent. Still, when it comes to economy, only walking is cheaper. Bus fares are typically 2000d or so, depending on the route.

A long-awaited city bus-route guide was published in 2001. Presently, the only place to get a copy is from the **Traffic Management Center** (Map pp80-1; ☎ 747 0403; hncauduong@fpt.vn; 16 Cao Ba Quat). The guide also shows interprovincial routes and bus interchanges.

Car & Motorbike
Though many travellers have rented motorbikes and scooters to tour Hanoi, it is *not* the best place for beginners. Traffic conditions are definitely not the same as home and driving after some drinks at night can be very dangerous, particularly crossing the busy junctions with no traffic lights. Then there are the hassles of dealing with traffic, parking and possible theft. It's also easy to unknowingly violate road rules. That said, if you are well versed in the ways of Asian cities, it can be a lot of fun. Most guesthouses and hotels can arrange new motorbikes for around US$5 a day.

Cyclo
The *cyclos* in Hanoi are wider than the HCMC variety, making it possible for two people to fit in one and share the fare. One common *cyclo* driver's ploy when carrying two passengers is to agree on a price, and then *double* it upon arrival gesturing 'no, no, no…that was per person'.

Aim to pay around 5000d per person for a journey in the city centre. Longer rides or night rides are double that or more. Try to negotiate in dong, not dollars. You'll also find that a little bit of Vietnamese goes a long way when talking about prices.

The *cyclo* drivers in Hanoi are even less likely to speak English than in HCMC, so take a map of the city with you. A notebook and pencil to write your destination and to negotiate prices is useful. It's a thankless job, so don't agonise too much about giving a *cyclo* driver that extra few thousand dong.

Motorbike Taxi
You won't have any trouble finding a *xe om* in Hanoi. Just stroll along any major street and you'll get an offer from a driver almost every 10 seconds.

The official cost for a *xe om* is 2000d per kilometre. In reality, tourists are expected to pay around 5000d per person for rides in the city centre, or 10,000d and up for longer rides.

Taxi
There are several companies in Hanoi offering metered taxi services. All charge similar rates. Flag fall ranges from 5000d to 10,000d, which takes you one or two kilometres; every kilometre thereafter costs about 5000d. Competitors in this business include the following companies.
Airport Taxi (☎ 873 3333)
City Taxi (☎ 822 2222)
Red Taxi (☎ 856 8686)
Taxi PT (☎ 856 5656)
Viet Phuong Taxi (☎ 828 2828)

AROUND HANOI

HO CHI MINH TRAIL MUSEUM
If you're interested in this amazing feat of human determination, the **Ho Chi Minh Trail Museum** (Bao Tang Duong Ho Chi Minh; Hwy 6; admission 10,000d; ☯ 7.30-11am & 1.30-4pm Tue-Sun) is an introduction to the famous supply route from the communist north to the occupied south of Vietnam. It is located about 13km southwest of Hanoi and can be combined with a visit to Van Phuc handicraft village (p113), or visited on the way to the Perfume Pagoda.

PERFUME PAGODA
A complex of pagodas and Buddhist shrines built into the limestone cliffs of Huong Tich Mountain (Mountain of the Fragrant Traces) makes up the **Perfume Pagoda** (Chua Huong; admission 17,000d plus 8000d return boat trip). Among the better-known sites here are Thien Chu (Pagoda Leading to Heaven); Giai Oan Chu (Purgatorial Pagoda), where the faithful believe deities purify souls, cure sufferings and grant offspring to childless families; and Huong Tich Chu (Pagoda of the Perfumed Vestige).

The entertaining boat trip along the scenic waterways between limestone cliffs takes about two hours return; allow an additional two or three hours return to climb to the top. A word of warning: bring good walking shoes! The path to the top is steep

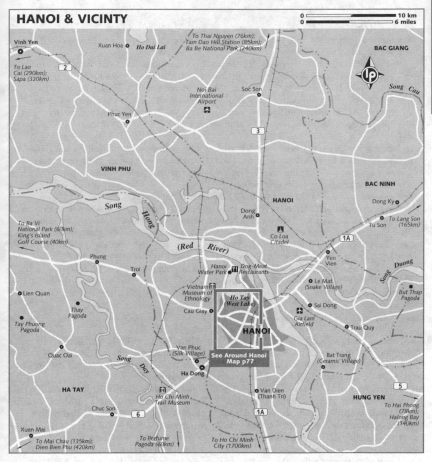

HANOI & VICINITY

0 — 10 km
0 — 6 miles

Vinh Yen

Xuan Hoa   Ho Dai Lai

To Thai Nguyen (76km);
Tam Dao Hill Station (85km);
Ba Be National Park (240km)

BAC GIANG

To Lao
Cai (290km);
Sapa (320km)

2

Noi Bai
International
Airport

Soc Son

Song   Cau

Phuc Yen

3

VINH PHU

Song   Hong

(Red   River)

Dong
Anh

HANOI

Dong Ky

BAC NINH

To Lang Son
(165km)

Tu Son

To Ba Vi
National Park (60km);
King's Island
Golf Course (40km)

Co Loa
Citadel

1A

Phung

Troi

Hanoi
Water Park

Dog-Meat
Restaurants

Yen
Vien

Song   Duong

Le Mat
(Snake Village)

But Thap
Pagoda

Lien Quan

Vietnam
Museum of
Ethnology

Ho Tay
(West Lake)

Sai Dong

Thay
Pagoda

Cau Giay

Gia Lam
Airfield

Trau Quy

Tay Phuong
Pagoda

HANOI

Quac Oai

Van Phuc
(Silk Village)

Song   Day

See Around Hanoi
Map p77

Bat Trang
(Ceramic Village)

5

Ha Dong

HA TAY

Ho Chi Minh
Trail Museum

Van Dien
(Thanh Tri)

HUNG YEN

To Hai Phong
(78km);
Halong Bay
(140km)

Chuc Son

6

1A

Xuan Mai

To Mai Chau (135km);
Dien Bien Phu (420km)

To Perfume
Pagoda (60km)

To Ho Chi Minh
City (1700km)

in places and if it's raining the ground can get *very* slippery.

Great numbers of Buddhist pilgrims come here during a festival that begins in the middle of the second lunar month and lasts until the last week of the third lunar month (usually corresponding to March and April). It's *very* busy during this period, especially on the even dates of the lunar month; you'll have a much easier time if you establish the lunar date and plan to go on an odd date. In 2002, on the particularly auspicious sixth day of the first lunar month, 3000 boats crammed the waterway and there was a boat jam that lasted from noon until 9pm! Weekends tend to draw crowds all year, when pilgrims and other

visitors spend their time boating, hiking and exploring the caves. Litter and noisy stalls and hawkers are part and parcel of the visit, and some hawkers are persistent enough to hassle you all the way to the top; you have been warned!

Getting There & Away

The Perfume Pagoda is about 60km southwest of Hanoi by road. Getting there requires a journey first by road, then by river, then on foot.

First, travel from Hanoi by car for two hours to the township of My Duc. Vehicles usually drop you about a 15-minute walk from the boat ramp, or you can hop on a *xe om* for a few thousand dong. Then take a

HANOI

MRS THUYEN, BOAT WOMAN

Anyone who visits the Perfume Pagoda will approach the sacred mountain by rowing boat. Here, one of the rowers tells her story:

'I've rowed tourists to the Perfume Pagoda for about two years now. Our boat group is made up of 27 boats rowed by women who all belong to martyr's families – our husbands or fathers or children were killed or injured in the war. There are more than 100 of us in the same group, but only 27 of us are allowed to work at one time, so there's an annual lottery to establish which of us will row each year. So I may not work every year, but when I do it's consistent and I get paid 15,000d every day, regardless of how many trips I do, or even if there's no work for day or two.

'You see our group of martyrs' families has priority for rowing all the foreigners. It's easier because there are fewer people in the boat and if we're lucky we get tips. Other boats have to compete on their own for customers and sometimes might not have any and might not make any money. A boat costs about one million dong, and we all save to buy our own. Every three or four years we have to change the floor of the boat and that costs 250,000d.

'We all also have a plot of land nearby, and we grow and sell things when we're not working on the boats. I grow longan fruit. My husband raises bees; he moves his hives around other people's plantations depending on what's flowering, and pays for the bees' use of the flowers with a litre or two of honey. Honey sells for about 70,000d a litre. Last year was a bad year; my husband only made 50L all year, but in the first three months of this year he's already made 30L.

'I used to be a soldier; that's how I met my husband. Our children are 19, 16 and 14 years old and when they were little I didn't row the boat, I sold jewellery and incense at the pagoda. It's hard work but I think about my children finishing their study and becoming successful and that keeps me going.'

small boat, usually rowed by women, for one to 1½ hours to the foot of the mountain.

The main pagoda area is about a 4km steep hike up from where the boat lets you off. Allow yourself at least two hours to make the return trip, longer if it's been raining and is slippery. The combined fee for the boat journey and general admission ticket is 28,000d; if you want to charter a boat to go up and back at your convenience, it will cost you an extra 45,000d. Negotiate this while still at the boat ramp itself – the ticket office at the main entrance tries to charge 200,000d! The return trip to your vehicle is also by rowboat.

Most of the travellers' cafés in Hanoi offer inexpensive tours to the pagoda. You can find day trips as cheap as US$9 or US$10, inclusive of transport, guide and lunch. For a better quality tour (with a smaller group and a more comfortable vehicle) expect to spend around US$14 to US$16. Take a tour! Unless you charter a vehicle, it's a real pain trying to do this trip by public transport.

HANDICRAFT VILLAGES

There are numerous villages surrounding Hanoi that specialise in particular cottage industries. Visiting these villages can make for a rewarding day trip, though you will need a good guide to make the journey worthwhile.

Bat Trang is known as the 'ceramic village'. Here artisans mass-produce ceramic vases and other pieces in their kilns. It's hot, sweaty work, but the results are superb and very reasonably priced. There are masses of ceramic shops but poke around down the lanes and behind the shops to find the kilns. Bat Trang is 13km southeast of Hanoi.

So is known for its delicate noodles. The village even produces the flour from which the noodles are made. The flour is made from yams and cassava (manioc) rather than wheat. So is in Ha Tay province, about 25km southwest of Hanoi.

Van Phuc is a silk village. Silk cloth is produced here on looms and lots of visitors like to buy or order tailor-made clothes. Many of the fine silk items you see on sale in Hanoi's Pho Hang Gai originate here. There's a small daily fruit-and-vegetable market here in the morning, and a village pagoda with a lily pond. Van Phuc is 8km southwest of Hanoi in Ha Tay province.

Dong Ky was known as the 'firecracker village' until 1995, when the government banned firecrackers. With that industry now extinguished, the village survives by producing beautiful traditional furniture inlaid with mother-of-pearl. You can have handcrafted furniture custom-made here and exported directly to your address abroad. Dong Ky is 15km northeast of Hanoi.

Le Mat, 7km northeast of central Hanoi, is a snake village. The locals raise snakes for upmarket restaurants in Hanoi, and for producing medicinal spirits. Fresh snake cuisine and snake elixir is available at this village, and for around 100,000d to 150,000d you can try a set course consisting of snake meat prepared in around 10 different ways. On the 23rd day of the third lunar month is the very interesting Le Mat Festival, featuring 'snake dances' and other activities.

Other handicraft villages in the region produce conical hats, delicate wooden bird cages and herbs.

THAY & TAY PHUONG PAGODAS

Clinging to the sides of stunning limestone outcrops that emerge suddenly from the surrounding flat rice fields, these pagodas are about 20 minutes apart from each other by road.

Thay Pagoda (Master's Pagoda; admission 3000d), also known as Thien Phuc (Heavenly Blessing), is dedicated to Thich Ca Buddha (Sakyamuni, the historical Buddha) and 18 arhats appear on the central altar. On the left is a statue of the 12th-century monk Tu Dao Hanh, the master after whom the pagoda is named; on the right is a statue of King Ly Nhan Tong, who is believed to have been a reincarnation of Tu Dao Hanh.

In front of the pagoda is a small stage built on stilts in the middle of a pond; water-puppet shows are staged here for festivals. Follow the path around the outside of the main pagoda building, and take a steep 10-minute climb up to a beautiful smaller pagoda perched high on the rock. Thay Pagoda is a big and confusing complex for non-Buddhists – you may want to hire a pagoda guide to get the most from a visit.

The pagoda's annual festival is held from the fifth to the seventh days of the third lunar month. Pilgrims and other visitors enjoy watching water-puppet shows, hiking and exploring caves in the area.

Tay Phuong Pagoda (Pagoda of the West; admission 3000d), also known as Sung Phuc Pagoda, consists of three single-level structures built in descending order on a hillock said to resemble a buffalo. The figures representing 'the conditions of man' are carved from jackfruit wood, many dating from the 18th century, and are the pagoda's most celebrated feature. The earliest construction here dates from the 8th century. Take the steep steps up to the main pagoda building, then find a path at the back that loops down past the other two pagodas and wanders through the hillside village that surrounds the complex. At the base, return to the car park a couple of hundred metres to your right.

Getting There & Away

The pagodas are about 30km west of Hanoi in Ha Tay province. Hanoi's cafés catering to budget travellers can arrange combined day tours of the Thay and Tay Phuong Pagodas. Alternatively, you could hire a car and driver for US$30, and make a good day tour combining the pagodas and Ba Vi National Park.

BA VI NATIONAL PARK
☎ 034
Centred on scenic Ba Vi Mountain (Nui Ba Vi), Ba Vi National Park (☎ 881 205; admission 10,000d, motorbike 5000d) attracts Hanoians looking for a weekend escape from the city. The park has several rare and endangered plants in its protected forest, and its mammals include two species of rare 'flying' squirrel. Human encroachment on the area has made the chances of seeing any of them pretty rare.

There's an orchid garden and a bird garden, and hiking opportunities through the forested slopes of the mountain. There's a temple to Uncle Ho at the mountain's summit (1276m) – it's a hard but beautiful 30-minute climb up 1229 steps through the forest – with spectacular views of the Red River valley and Hanoi in the distance. At least there are views between April and December when the air is clear; at other times it's damp and misty but eerily atmospheric. The road to the summit car park is seriously steep, slippery and narrow, but road widening is ongoing.

Sleeping & Eating

Ba Vi Guesthouse (☎ 881 197; r 120,000-150,000d) spreads over several blocks in the heart of the park. Prices are an extra 50,000d per room on weekends and there's a big swimming pool that is chaos in the summer months. Go for one of the less-noisy guesthouses away from the pool and restaurant area if you're here on a weekend. You *must* have your passport with you to check into the guesthouse here.

Despite its unpromising appearance, the park restaurant serves good, cheap, fresh-cooked food; a tasty meal for two costs around 35,000d, so make this your lunch stop if you're on a day tour combining the park with Thay and Tay Phuong Pagodas. The toilets are terrible – pee behind a tree.

Getting There & Away

Ba Vi National Park is about 65km west of Hanoi, and presently the only practical option for visiting is by hired vehicle from Hanoi. Travelling by motorbike, it is possible to visit Ba Vi before taking a beautiful riverside road down to Hoa Binh and onwards into the northwest.

There has been some confusion between attractions near Ba Vi town, which is well away from the park boundaries, and Ba Vi National Park. Make sure your driver knows you want the national park.

CO LOA CITADEL

Dating from the 3rd century BC, **Co Loa Citadel** (Co Loa Thanh; admission per person 2000d, per car 5000d; ⏰ 8am-5pm) was the first recorded fortified citadel in Vietnamese history and became the national capital during the reign of Ngo Quyen (AD 939–44). Only vestiges of the ancient ramparts, which enclosed an area of about 5 sq km, remain.

In the centre of the citadel are temples dedicated to the rule of King An Duong Vuong (257–208 BC), who founded the legendary Thuc dynasty, and his daughter My Nuong (Mi Chau). When My Nuong showed her father's magic crossbow trigger, which made the Vietnamese king invincible in battle, to her husband (who was the son of a Chinese general), he stole it and gave it to his father. With its help, the Chinese were then able to defeat An Duong Vuong and his forces, thus depriving Vietnam of its independence.

Co Loa Citadel is 16km north of central Hanoi in Dong Anh district, and can be visited as a short detour while on the way to or from Tam Dao.

TAM DAO HILL STATION

☎ 0211 / elevation 930m

Founded in 1907 by the French, who named it 'La Cascade d'Argent' (Silver Waterfall; Thac Bac in Vietnamese), **Tam Dao Hill Station** was a popular place of escape from the heat of the Red River Delta. Most of the grand old colonial villas were destroyed during the Franco–Viet Minh War in the 1950s and the ruins have since been replaced by Soviet-inspired, concrete-box architecture. A somewhat belated effort to restore some of the colonial villas is now under way.

Hanoi residents sometimes call Tam Dao 'the Dalat of the north'. This has more to do with its high elevation and cool climate than any resemblance to Dalat. If you're living in Hanoi and would like to find a summer weekend retreat, it's worth heading up for the cool weather and a change of pace. However, unless you plan to do some serious hiking or bird-watching, there really isn't that much to see and do here. Except, that is, to spend hours listening to loud karaoke ricochet around the valley from the bars. If you are planning to visit the mountains elsewhere in Vietnam, you won't miss much by passing up Tam Dao.

Tam Dao National Park was designated in 1996 and covers much of the area. Tam Dao means 'Three Islands', and the three summits of Tam Dao Mountain, all about 1400m in height, are sometimes visible to the northeast of the hill station, floating like islands in the mist. The relative dampness and altitude makes the area particularly rich in rainforest and associated animals. There are at least 64 mammal species, including langurs, and 239 bird species in the park, but you'll need a good local guide and be prepared to do some hiking to find them. Illegal hunting remains a big problem. Many of the bars in Tam Dao offer rice wines with, variously, whole birds, reptiles or small mammals from the park pickled in it; it's not uncommon for tourists to be offered live wildlife for sale. Logging, both legal and otherwise, has also had a serious impact on the environment. Some hill-tribe people live in the Tam Dao region, though the communities are less prominent than they used to be.

Remember that it is cool up in Tam Dao and that this part of Vietnam has a distinct winter. Don't be caught unprepared. Hikes vary from half an hour return to the **waterfall**, to eight hours into **primary rainforest**. A guide is essential for the longer treks and can be hired from 50,000d; inquire about these at the Mela Hotel (p117). Generally the best time to visit is between late April and mid-October, when the mist sometimes lifts and the weather can be fine. As with other popular sites in Vietnam, weekends can be packed with Vietnamese tour groups, so try to make your visit during the week if possible.

Sleeping & Eating

There's a host of hotels and guesthouses in Tam Dao, charging anything from 80,000d to US$65. You can walk around the town quite easily, so look around, negotiate and watch out for neighbouring karaoke bars.

Huong Lien Hotel (☎ 824 282; r 150,000d) A friendly, family-run place that offers good value. There is no English spoken, so pack your phrasebook.

Green World Hotel (☎ 824 315; r 180,000-350,000d) This big, new hotel has plush rooms for the price. It has all wood furnishings and balconies with a view at the front, plus a tennis court.

Mela Hotel (☎ /fax 824 352; r US$45-65) As stylish and elegant as the price suggests, Mela is a favoured haunt for Hanoi expats. In fact it's the only stylish and elegant place in town and is a great spot to huddle up around the fire.

There are hotel restaurants galore and several rows of *com-pho* places in town. Try to avoid eating the local wildlife if you can.

Getting There & Away

Tam Dao is 85km northwest of Hanoi in Vinh Phuc province. Buses run from Kim Ma bus station in Hanoi (p110) to Vinh Yen (around 15,000d, one hour). From there you can hire a motorbike (about 40,000d one way) to travel the 24km single-lane road that leads to the national park.

Hiring a car and driver for the day from Hanoi will cost about US$40. If you rent a motorbike in Hanoi, the journey time is about two hours, and the last part of the ride into the park is beautiful.

Northeast Vietnam

NORTHEAST VIETNAM

NORTHEAST VIETNAM

The surreal seascape of Halong Bay is one of Vietnam's most magical sights and the main reason that most make their way to the northeast. Bizarre but beautiful, this is geology gone wild, with hundreds and thousands of limestone pinnacles protruding from the waters. North of Halong Bay is the seldom visited Bai Tu Long Bay, where nature's splendid show continues all the way to the Chinese border. To the south of Halong Bay is Cat Ba Island, a 'lost world' landscape with hiking, biking or just hanging around the order of the day. And just a hydrofoil away is Hai Phong, the north's major port and a step back in time with wide boulevards and elegant architecture.

Up, up and away from the coast is the rugged interior, home to Ba Be National Park and its beautiful lakes, and the stark mountains around Cao Bang, a base for meeting the Montagnard minorities who have made it their home. The highlands of the northeast are well off the tourist trail and a good place to do some exploring as much as travelling.

On a more practical note, it's also a popular route for travelling overland between China and Vietnam. There are two border crossings, one on the coast at Mong Cai that is seldom used, and a second crossing near the bustling town of Lang Son. With all this border traffic, life is looking good for the locals and the northeast is riding high on a boom, as the gateway to Hanoi, by land and by sea.

HIGHLIGHTS

- Set sail amid the spectacular scenery of **Halong Bay** (p127), a Unesco World Heritage site of more than 3000 islands

- Check out **Cat Ba Island** (p130) for a beach retreat or some jungle trekking in the national park

- Step back in time in **Hai Phong** (p121), a sleepy city that feels like the Hanoi of old

- Take in the lakes, rivers and waterfalls of **Ba Be National Park** (p144) from the blissfulness of a boat

- Step off the tourist trail at the waterfalls, caves and historical sites around **Cao Bang** (p141)

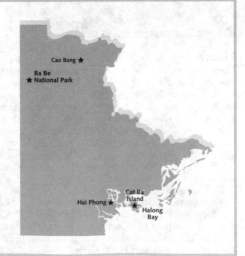

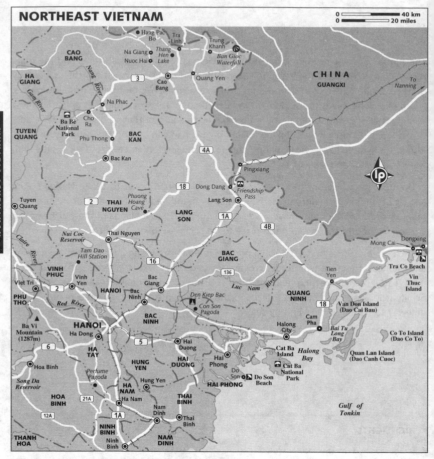

History

Dominated by the Red River basin and the sea, the fertile northeast is the cradle of Vietnamese civilisation. Much of Vietnamese history, not all of it happy, was made here. Vietnam has had less than cordial relations with the Chinese, who invaded in the 2nd century BC and stuck around for about 1000 years. They were finally vanquished in the 10th century (for more on this story, see the boxed text on p130).

Any time the Chinese wanted to interfere in Vietnam's affairs, it was through the northeast that they approached, the last time as recently as 1979, ostensibly to punish the Vietnamese for invading Cambodia; see the boxed text on p140 for more.

As well as invasions, this region has also witnessed an exodus during the late 1970s and early 1980s, as thousands of ethnic-Chinese and later thousands more Vietnamese took to the mountains or the seas to search for a better life in China, Hong Kong and beyond.

CON SON & DEN KIEP BAC

Con Son and Den Kiep Bac are more appealing to domestic travellers than foreigners, but are potential diversions en route to Hai Phong or Halong City.

Con Son was home to Nguyen Trai (1380–1442), the famed Vietnamese poet, writer and general. Nguyen Trai assisted Emperor Le Loi in his successful battle against the

Chinese Ming dynasty in the 13th century. **Con Son pagoda complex** (admission per person/vehicle 3000/5000d) has a temple honouring Nguyen Trai atop a nearby mountain. It's a 600-step climb to reach it – a serious workout. Alternatively, take the loop walk past a spring, heading up through pine forests, and return down the steps.

Several kilometres away, **Den Kiep Bac** (Kiep Bac Temple; admission per person/vehicle 2000/5000d) is dedicated to Tran Hung Dao (1228–1300). He was an outstanding general of renowned bravery, whose armies defeated 300,000 Mongol invaders in the mid-1280s. Perhaps second only to Ho Chi Minh in the pecking order, he is a revered Vietnamese folk hero.

This beautiful temple was founded in 1300 and built on the site where Tran Hung Dao is said to have died. The temple was built not only for the general, but also to honour other notable members of his family. One was the general's daughter, Quyen Thanh, who married Tran Nhat Ton, who was credited with founding the Truc Lam sect of Vietnamese Buddhism.

Within the temple complex there's a small exhibition on Tran Hung Dao's exploits, but a Vietnamese speaker is needed to translate the details. The **Tran Hung Dao Festival** is held at Den Kiep Bac every year from the 18th to the 20th day of the eighth lunar month.

Den Kiep Bac and Con Son are in Hai Duong province, about 80km from Hanoi. With wheels, it is easy to visit on the way to Hai Phong or Halong Bay. There are several hotels and guesthouses in the immediate area.

HAI PHONG
☎ 031 / pop 1,667,600
Hai Phong is a graceful city that feels much like the Hanoi of a decade ago. Bicycles outnumber motorbikes and the verdant tree-lined boulevards conceal some classic colonial-era structures. Stroll around the centre and soak up the atmosphere.

Despite being one of the country's most important seaports and industrial centres, and officially Vietnam's third-largest city, Hai Phong today seems a somnolent place with clean streets and an understated air of prosperity. In general, the city is far less hassle than major tourist magnets, though as usual keep your wits about you around the train station and ferry landing.

Hai Phong makes a sensible stopover for travellers making their own way to/from Cat Ba Island or Halong Bay. A combination of bus, boats and train make an economical and easy way to link the popular places of the northeast.

History
The French took possession of Hai Phong, then a small market town, in 1874. The city developed rapidly, becoming a major port; heavy industry was a natural choice thanks to its proximity to coal supplies.

One of the most immediate causes of the Franco–Viet Minh War was the infamous French bombardment of the 'native quarters' of Hai Phong in 1946, in which hundreds of civilians were killed and injured. A contemporary French account estimated civilian deaths at more than 6000.

Hai Phong came under US air and naval attack between 1965 and 1972. In May 1972 President Nixon ordered the mining of Hai Phong Harbour to cut the flow of Soviet military supplies to North Vietnam. As part of the Paris cease-fire accords of 1973, the USA agreed to help clear the mines from Hai Phong Harbour – 10 US navy minesweepers were involved in the effort.

Since the late 1970s Hai Phong has experienced a massive exodus, including many ethnic-Chinese refugees, who have taken much of the city's fishing fleet with them.

Information
EMERGENCY
If you need medical treatment it is best to head to Hanoi. **Vietnam-Czech Friendship Hospital** (Benh Vien Viet-Tiep; Pho Nha Thuong) should be considered for emergencies only.

INTERNET ACCESS
There are centrally located **Internet cafés** (Pho Dien Bien Phu; per hr around 6000d), and there seems to be at least one Internet café on most other streets in the city.

MONEY
Vietcombank (11 Pho Hoang Dieu) Not far from the post office, this bank in a beautiful building can deal with cash and cheques, and has an ATM.

POST
Main post office (3 Pho Nguyen Tri Phuong) A grand old yellow dame on the corner of Pho Hoang Van Thu.

NORTHEAST VIETNAM

HAI PHONG

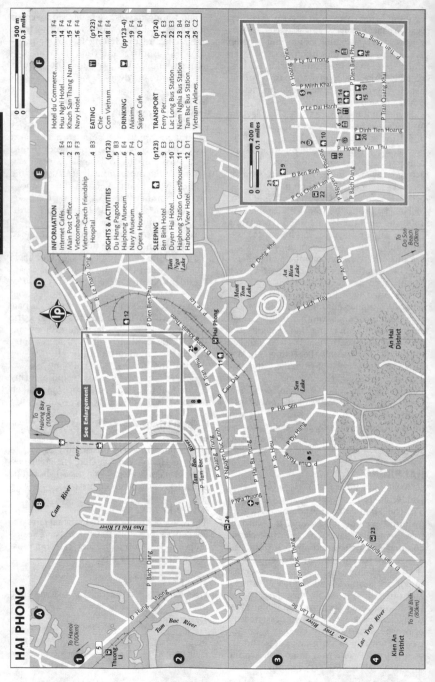

INFORMATION	
Internet Cafés..................................1	E4
Main Post Office.............................2	E3
Vietcombank..................................3	F3
Vietnam-Czech Friendship	
Hospital.......................................4	B3

SIGHTS & ACTIVITIES	(p123)
Du Hang Pagoda.............................5	B3
Haiphong Museum...........................6	E4
Navy Museum.................................7	F4
Opera House..................................8	C2

SLEEPING	(p123)
Ben Binh Hotel...............................9	E3
Duyen Hai Hotel............................10	E3
Haiphong Station Guesthouse........11	C2
Harbour View Hotel.......................12	D1

Hotel du Commerce........................13	F4
Huu Nghi Hotel.............................14	F4
Khach San Thang Nam...................15	F4
Navy Hotel....................................16	F4

EATING	(p123)
Chie..17	F4
Com Vietnam................................18	E4

DRINKING	(pp123-4)
Maxims..19	F4
Saigon Cafe...................................20	E4

TRANSPORT	(p124)
Ferry Pier......................................21	E3
Lac Long Bus Station.....................22	E3
Niem Nghia Bus Station..................23	B4
Tam Bac Bus Station......................24	B2
Vietnam Airlines............................25	C2

TOURIST INFORMATION
Vietnam Tourism (☎ 747 216; vntourism.hp@bdvn
.vnmail.vnd.net; 55 Pho Dien Bien Phu) Located at the
Khach San Thang Nam hotel.

Sights & Activities
Half a day on your hands in Hai Phong?
There are a few low-key sights to keep you
busy, but the museums have limited opening times.

Haiphong Museum (Pho Dien Bien Phu; admission
free; ☼ 8-10.30am Tue & Thu, 8-9.30pm Wed & Sun) is
in a splendid colonial building and has a
small collection. Nearby, opposite the Navy
Hotel, is the **Navy Museum** (Bao Tang Hai Quan; Pho
Dien Bien Phu; ☼ 8-11am Tue, Thu & Sat), popular
with visiting sailors and veterans.

Check out the **Opera House** (Pho Quang Trung)
when the refurbishment is finished. Smaller
than the Hanoi Opera House from the outside, the interior is lavish.

Du Hang Pagoda (Chua Du Hang; 121 Pho Chua Hang)
was founded three centuries ago. Though
it has been rebuilt several times, it remains
a fine example of traditional Vietnamese
architecture and sculpture. Pho Chua Hang
itself is narrow and bustling with Hai Phong
street life, and is fun to wander along.

Sleeping
Hai Phong hosts up to a thousand Chinese
tourists per day. To guarantee a bed in one
of the more expensive hotels, you'd do well
to book ahead. There are no real budget
options in Hai Phong.

Harbour View Hotel (☎ 827 827; www.harbour
viewvietnam.com; 4 Pho Tran Phu; s/d US$75/85; ☒
🖵 🖳) The leading hotel in town, designed in classic colonial style, the rooms
are smart and stylish, while the facilities
include a swimming pool, gym and spa.
The hotel is popular with European tour
groups, discount rates are sometimes half
of the prices quoted here.

Ben Binh Hotel (☎ 842 260; fax 842 524; 6 Đ Ben
Binh; r US$15-25; ☒) Slap bang opposite the
ferry pier, this is a cavernous old place set
in large gardens. The cheaper rooms are
ageing, though the larger US$25 pads are
in good shape.

Duyen Hai Hotel (☎ 842 157; fax 841 140; 5 Pho
Nguyen Tri Phuong; r 100,000-200,000d; ☒) One
of the cheaper deals, the least-expensive
rooms here are tiny, but all come with TV
and bathtubs with hot water.

Hotel du Commerce (☎ 842 706; fax 842 560; 62
Pho Dien Bien Phu; r US$10-20; ☒) Set in a ven-
erable old building, the rooms here are
slowly being upgraded and improved, and
have high ceilings and gigantic bathrooms.
Think atmosphere above amenities.

Khach San Thang Nam (☎ 747 216; vntourism
.hp@bdvn.vnmail.vnd.net; 55 Pho Dien Bien Phu; rooms
US$15-18; ☒) This place is great value, with
bright, clean rooms and all mod cons, including satellite TV.

Navy Hotel (Khach San Hai Quan; ☎ 842 856; fax
842 278; 27C Pho Dien Bien Phu; r US$20-25; ☒) A
spacious hotel on the main strip that is
very popular with tour groups. Rooms are
shipshape…that's colloquial clean and tidy
rather than like a frigate.

Huu Nghi Hotel (☎ 823 244; fax 823 245; 62 Pho Dien
Bien Phu; r US$20-60; ☒ 🖵 🖳) It may be one of
the more hideous buildings in Hai Phong,
but this ugly duckling has great value, four-
star rooms with individual shower and
bathtub, and facilities like swimming pool
and tennis courts.

Haiphong Station Guesthouse (☎ 855 391; 75 Đ
Luong Khanh Thien; r 150,000-180,000d; ☒) Rather
overpriced given its musty and mothballed
rooms, but it's right in the train station for
an early ride.

Eating
Hai Phong is noted for its sumptuous fresh
seafood, which is available at most hotel
restaurants.

Com Vietnam (☎ 841 698; 4 Pho Hoang Van Thu;
mains 20,000-60,000d) This is a little courtyard
restaurant serving affordable local seafood
and Vietnamese specialities.

Chie (☎ 821 018; 64 Pho Dien Bien Phu; meals around
US$10) Good Japanese food that's worth your
while if you're hanging out for sushi and the
like.

The best options for cheap eats are the
glut of eateries on Pho Minh Khai. Another
good hunting ground is Pho Quang Trung,
brimming with popular *bia hoi* bars and
cafés. Speaking of which, Bia Hai Phong
is the local brew and it gets the thumbs up
from aficionados of the amber nectar.

Drinking
Saigon Cafe (cnr Pho Dien Bien Phu & Pho Dinh Tien
Hoang) A loungey café-bar with an extensive
food and drinks menu, plus live music most
evenings.

Maxims (☎ 822 934; 51B Pho Dien Bien Phu) A sort of distant relation to the famous Maxims in Saigon, it has live music from classical to jazz most nights.

Getting There & Away
AIR
Vietnam Airlines (☎ 921 137; www.vietnamair.com.vn; 30 Pho Tran Phu) serves the Hai Phong–Ho Chi Minh City (HCMC) and the Hai Phong–Danang routes.

BOAT
All boats leave from the **ferry pier** (Đ Ben Binh), 10 minutes' walk from the centre of town.

Hydrofoils leave for Cat Ba (90,000d, 45 minutes) at 8.20am, 8.50am and 9am. **Tahaco** (☎ 822 141) has the fastest boats, according to regulars. There are no longer hydrofoils operating to Halong City, as the road journey is faster. **Greenlines** (☎ 747 370) has a hydrofoil to Mong Cai (US$15, 4½ hours) at 7.30am.

Slow boats to Mong Cai via Cat Ba (70,000d) also leave from here, but it is an insanely long journey compared with a bus to Halong City and hydrofoil from there.

BUS
Hai Phong has three long-distance bus stations. Buses to Hanoi (25,000d, two hours) leave from **Tam Bac bus station** (Pho Tam Bac) about every 10 minutes throughout the day. Buses to points south such as Ninh Binh leave from **Niem Nghia bus station** (Đ Tran Nguyen Han).

The new **Lac Long bus station** (Pho Cu Chinh Lan) has buses to Bai Chay (Halong City; 25,000d, 1½ hours), and from there connections to Mong Cai on the Chinese border by boat or road. Lac Long also has buses to/from Hanoi for those connecting with the Cat Ba hydrofoil.

CAR & MOTORBIKE
Hai Phong is 103km from Hanoi on Hwy 5. This expressway (Vietnam's first) between the two cities was completed in 1999 and is one of the biggest and busiest roads in the country.

TRAIN
Hai Phong is not on the main line between Hanoi and HCMC, but there is a spur line connecting it to Hanoi. There's one express train daily to Tran Quy Cap station (22,000d, two hours) at 6.10pm and

several others to Hanoi's Long Bien station (22,000d, 2½ hours), on the eastern side of the Red River.

There are two train stations within the Hai Phong city limits. Thuong Li train station is in the western suburbs of the city, while Hai Phong train station is right in the city centre.

Getting Around
Hai Phong is serviced by several companies that use metered, air-con taxis. Try **Haiphong Taxi** (☎ 838 383) or **Taxi Mai Linh** (☎ 833 833). There are also plenty of *cyclos* (pedicabs) and *xe om* (motorbike taxis) cruising around town (between 5000d and 10,000d, depending on distance).

AROUND HAI PHONG
Do Son Beach
Do Son Beach, 21km southeast of central Hai Phong, is a seaside resort that is popular with Vietnamese for wailing and sex (euphemistically known as karaoke and massage). The hilly, 4km-long promontory ends with a string of islets, and the peninsula's nine hills are known as Cuu Long Son (Nine Dragons). There are plenty of colourful fishing boats on the water and a long promenade lined with oleander bushes, but the beaches are disappointingly small and disappear completely at high tide. The resort is not all it's cracked up to be – or should that be, it's more cracked up than it used to be. Many hotels are looking rather forlorn.

In 1994 the first **casino** to open in Vietnam since 1975 commenced operation as a joint venture between the government and a Hong Kong company. Foreigners are welcome to win or lose their fortunes here, but Vietnamese are barred from entering the casino.

Do Son town is famous for its ritual **buffalo fights**, the finals of which are held annually on the 10th day of the eighth lunar month, commemorating the date when the leader of an 18th-century peasant rebellion was killed here.

HALONG CITY
☎ 033 / pop 149,900
The majority of food, accommodation and other life-support systems for Halong Bay are found in Halong City, the capital of Quang Ninh province and Vietnam's new sin city – the number of signs advertising

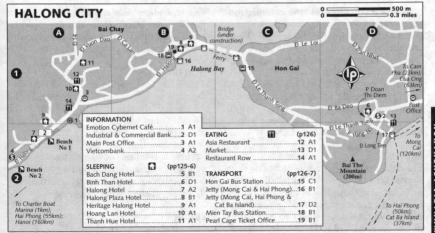

NORTHEAST VIETNAM

'Thai Massage' gives a good indication of the size of the prostitution market. In more recent years this once-peaceful outpost has developed into a pleasure den for package tourists, both domestic and international, with a large following of border-hopping Chinese.

There aren't a whole lot of reasons to stay in Halong City itself, although most visitors transit the city on the way to Halong Bay. Many people end up booking tours from Hanoi, as they feel travelling independently is tough. This is no longer the case, as buses from Hanoi (35,000d, 3½ hours) are fast and regular and the boat dock at Bai Chay lists fixed prices for Halong Bay cruises, including an afternoon tour to Cat Ba (70,000d, five hours) from where you can loop back to Hanoi via Hai Phong. This means you no longer have to run the gauntlet of freelance touts who prowl along the waterfront. If you are booking a tour, opt for those with an overnight in the bay.

Orientation

Halong City is bisected by a bay, and the most important district for travellers is called Bai Chay. Accommodation can be found on both sides of the bay, but Bai Chay, on the western side, is more scenic, closer to Hanoi and much better endowed with hotels and restaurants. Bai Chay is also where the majority of tourist boats are moored.

A short ferry ride (500d) across the bay takes you to the Hon Gai district. Hon Gai

is the main port district for coal exports, which means it's a bit dirty, but at least there is some local flavour.

There is a bridge under construction to finally link Bai Chay and Hon Gai, which is good news for everyone (except perhaps the ferry captains).

District names are important: most long-distance buses will be marked 'Bai Chay' or 'Hon Gai' rather than 'Halong City'.

Information

Emotion Cybernet Café (Đ Halong) Small beachfront spot for getting that online fix.

Industrial & Commercial Bank (Đ Le Thanh Tong) Useful ATM for those staying in Hon Gai.

Main post office (Đ Halong) Along with the usual postal services, there's cheap and fast Internet access with plenty of webcams.

Vietcombank (Đ Halong) A new and more convenient branch in Bai Chay with the usual exchange and ATM.

Beaches

The 'beaches' around Halong City are basically mud and rock – a problem the authorities are trying to 'correct'. A Taiwanese company has built two beaches in Bai Chay with imported sand, but they are not at all attractive for swimming as the water is pretty murky.

Sleeping

The majority of visitors stay in Bai Chay. There are more than 100 hotels located here, and keen competition keeps prices down, especially if you can avoid the commission-seeking touts. Prices rise in the peak season (summer) or during the Tet festival. There are also accommodation options in Hon Gai, but it's noisier and dustier across the water… coal dust that is!

The nearby island of Dao Tuan Chau (p129) is currently under massive redevelopment as a luxury resort retreat, an attempted antidote to the mistakes made in the development of Halong City.

BAI CHAY

The heaviest concentration of hotels is in town, in the aptly named 'hotel alley'. This is where you'll find over 50 minihotels, most of them almost identical (a guidebook author's nightmare). Expect to pay something between US$8 and US$12 for a double room with private bathroom and air-con. The following places are standouts.

Hoang Lan Hotel (☎ 846 504; 17 Đ Vuon Dao; r US$10-12; 🔀) Friendly hosts and the usual suspects: hot water, satellite TV and a fridge, plus breakfast is thrown in for good measure.

Thanh Hue Hotel (☎ 847 612; 17 Đ Vuon Dao; r US$10-12; 🔀) Right at the top of the same hill as Hoang Lan, this place offers some cracking views of the bay as a reward for the climb. Rooms aren't bad either, with hot water, TV and balcony.

Bach Dang Hotel (☎ 846 330; bachdanghotelqn@hn.vnn.vn; 2 Đ Halong; r 239,000-299,000d; 🔀) The furthest northeast of the hotels, it has comfortable and clean rooms set on seven floors…with a lift. Near both the ferry and Mien Tay bus station.

Halong Plaza Hotel (☎ 845 810; www.halongplaza.com; 8 Đ Halong; r from US$140; 🔀 🖳 🐾) A high-end hotel looming over the car-ferry landing, with all the facilities a four-star delivers. Discounts of around 50% of the published price are usually offered.

Halong Hotel (☎ 846 320; fax 846 318; Đ Halong; r US$20-100; 🔀 🖳) This is a huge complex divided into hotels 1, 2 and 3. There is something for everyone here: 1 offers a pseudo-colonial experience in the most expensive villa-style rooms; 2 delivers deluxe rooms in a modern government block; and 3 is the most basic, but still complete with TV, fridge, IDD phone and so on.

Heritage Halong Hotel (☎ 846 888; Đ Halong; r US$80-90; 🔀 🖳 🐾) Another huge hotel, this

one is a glitzy Singaporean joint venture packing four stars. The rooms are sophisticated, with fine views, and it's popular with international tour groups.

HON GAI

There are fewer options in Hon Gai, but demand is low so prices are static. The hotels are clustered mainly along Đ Le Thanh Tong, which runs on an east–west axis, but it is a noisy strip.

A good option here is the **Binh Than Hotel** (☎ 621 668; 4 Pho Doan Thi Diem; r 180,000d; 🔀), one of the newest and best tended of the Hon Gai hotels. Not much English is spoken, but it is right in the middle of town.

Eating

Minihotels aside, most hotels have restaurants. If you're on a tour, it's likely that meals will be included.

For independent travellers, the area just west of central Bai Chay, along Đ Halong contains a reliable row of cheap restaurants, all of which serve up seafood daily. All have tables inside and spill out onto the pavement at night. These are good places to indulge in a beer in the absence of any real bars in town.

Asia Restaurant (☎ 846 927; Đ Vuon Dao; mains 20,000-40,000d) Located on 'hotel alley' slope, this is a popular place. The owner used to run a restaurant in East Berlin and speaks excellent German and pretty good English. The Vietnamese food here is tasty and prices are reasonable.

In Hong Gai, check out the string of local eateries along Pho Ben Doan, or try the stalls in and around the market.

Getting There & Away
BOAT

There are daily slow boats connecting Hon Gai with Hai Phong (30,000d, three hours). Boats depart Hon Gai at 6.30am, 11am and 4pm. There are no longer hydrofoils linking Halong and Hai Phong as travel by road is cheaper and just as fast.

The best way to get to Cat Ba Island is to hop onto the regular tourist boats from Bai Chay tourist-boat dock. It costs 70,000d one way, including a leisurely cruise through the most beautiful parts of the bay. An extra 30,000d brings entry to the most important caves and grottoes in the bay. The whole trip takes about five hours, but there are no precise departure times, as it depends on numbers.

From Bai Chay, **Pearl Cape** (☎ 847 888; Đ Halong) operates hydrofoils to Mong Cai (US$12, three hours) leaving at 8am and 1pm; the ticket office is almost next door to the Mien Tay bus station. The trip is definitely preferable to the long road journey.

As always, be prepared for changes to these schedules.

BUS
Buses from Halong City to Hanoi (35,000d, 3½ hours) leave from **Mien Tay bus station** (Đ Ca Lan) in Bai Chay every 15 minutes. Buses to Hai Phong (22,000d, 1½ hours) depart every 20 minutes from here.

Most buses to northeastern destinations start from Mien Tay bus station before passing through **Hon Gai bus station** (Đ Le Loi). Buses for Mong Cai (35,000d, six hours) and Cua Ong (9000d, 1½ hours) for Van Don Island (Dao Cai Bau) depart regularly during daylight hours.

CAR & MOTORBIKE
Halong City is 160km from Hanoi and 55km from Hai Phong. The one-way trip from Hanoi to Halong City takes about three hours by private vehicle.

HALONG BAY
☎ 033
Magnificent Halong Bay is undoubtedly the natural wonder of Vietnam. Picture 3000 or more incredible islands rising from the emerald waters of the Gulf of Tonkin and you have a vision of greatness. In 1994 it was designated Vietnam's second World Heritage site. Visitors have compared the area's magical landscape of limestone islets to Guilin in China and Krabi in southern Thailand. These tiny islands are dotted with beaches and grottoes created by wind and waves, and have sparsely forested slopes ringing with birdsong.

Besides the breathtaking vistas, visitors to Halong Bay come to explore the caves – some of which are beautifully illuminated for the benefit of tourists – and to hike in Cat Ba National Park. There are few 'proper' beaches in Halong Bay itself, except for those on Cat Ba Island, but in Lan Ha Bay (off Cat Ba Island) there are over 100 sandy strips.

As the number-one tourist attraction in the northeast, Halong Bay draws a steady stream of visitors year-round. From February to April, the weather in this region is often cool and drizzly. The ensuing fog can make visibility low, although the temperature rarely falls below 10°C. During the summer months tropical storms are frequent, and tourist boats may have to alter their itineraries, depending on the weather.

Halong translates as 'where the dragon descends into the sea'. Legend has it that the islands of Halong Bay were created by a great dragon that lived in the mountains. As it ran towards the coast, its flailing tail gouged out valleys and crevasses; as it plunged into the sea, the areas dug up by the tail became filled with water, leaving only the high land visible.

Dragons aside, the biggest threat to the bay may be from souvenir-hunting tourists. Rare corals and seashells are rapidly being stripped from the sea floor, and stalactites and stalagmites are being broken off from the caves. These items get turned into key rings, paperweights and ashtrays, which are on sale in the local souvenir shops. Obviously the fewer people buy, the less the local people will take to sell: so please don't!

There's an excellent map (8000d) of Halong Bay, shown together with neighbouring Bai Tu Long Bay, published in 1998 by the Management Department of Halong Bay. Look for it at souvenir stalls at the cave sites, or ask your tour guide where you can find a copy.

Sights & Activities
GROTTOES
Halong Bay's limestone islands are dotted with caves of all shapes and sizes. Most of these are accessible only by charter boat, but some can easily be visited on a tour.

Hang Dau Go (Cave of Wooden Stakes), known to the French as the Grotte des Merveilles (Cave of Marvels), is a huge cave consisting of three chambers, which you reach via 90 steps. Among the stalactites of the first hall, scores of gnomes appear to be holding a meeting. The walls of the second chamber sparkle if bright light is shone on them. The cave derives its Vietnamese name from the third chamber. This chamber is said to have been used during the 13th

HALONG BAY & BAI TU LONG BAY

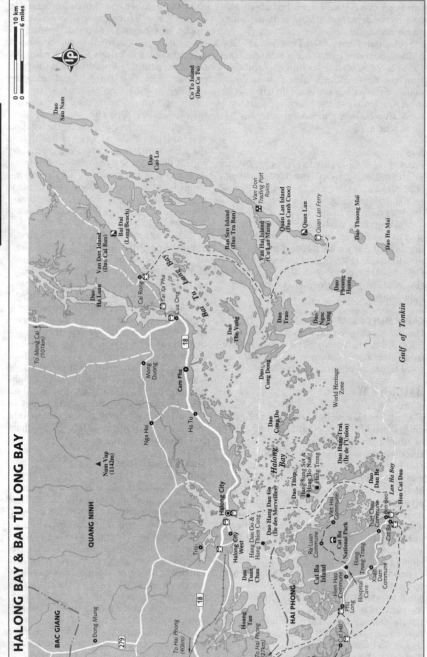

HALONG BAY'S VERY OWN LOCH NESS MONSTER

The dragon that gave birth to Halong Bay may be legend, but sailors have often reported sightings of a mysterious marine creature of gargantuan proportions known as the tarasque. The more paranoid elements of the military suspect it's an imperialist spy submarine, while eccentric travellers believe they have discovered Vietnam's version of the Loch Ness monster. Meanwhile, the monster – or whatever it is – continues to haunt Halong Bay, unfettered by the marine police, Vietnam Tourism and the immigration authorities. Enterprising Vietnamese boat owners have made a cottage industry out of the creature, offering cash-laden tourists the chance to rent a junk and pursue the tarasque before it gets bored and swims away.

century to store the sharp bamboo stakes that Vietnamese folk hero and war general, Tran Hung Dao, planted in the bed of the Bach Dang River to impale Mongolian general Kublai Khan's invasion fleet. It's the closest cave site to the mainland. Part of the same system, the nearby cave **Hang Thien Cung** has 'cauliflower' limestone growths as well as stalactites and stalagmites.

Hang Sung Sot is a popular cave to visit. It too has three vast and beautiful chambers, in the second of which there's an astonishing pink-lit 'penis rock' (really, it's the only way to describe it), which is regarded as a fertility symbol. It too requires a hike up steps to reach it, and a loop walk through the cool interior takes you back to the bay. **Hang Bo Nau**, another impressive cave, can be visited nearby.

Hang Trong (Drum Grotto) is so named because when the wind blows through its many stalactites and stalagmites, visitors think they can hear the sound of distant drumbeats.

Exactly which of these – or other – caves you visit will probably be decided on the day you travel. It depends on several factors, including the weather, number of other boats in the vicinity, and the number of people putting environmental pressure on the caves.

There is a 30,000d entry charge that applies to these sights whether you visit one or all – buy the ticket at the tourist boat dock in Bai Chay.

ISLANDS
Dao Tuan Chau (Tuan Chau Island), just 5km west of Bai Chay, is one of the few islands in Halong Bay that has seen any development. For many years, the only accommodation was in Ho Chi Minh's former summer residence, an elegant but decaying structure.

However, all this has changed as the island is being remodelled into **Tuan Chau International Recreation Complex** (☎ 842 159; aulaco@hn .vnn.vn; r US$80-110;), complete with aquarium, circus, golf course and private villas. The beachside rooms are tasteful and the top rate includes steam baths and saunas in the rooms!

Dao Titop (Titop Island) has a small beach where you can swim or hike to the top of the islet. **Cat Ba Island** (p130) is the best-known and most developed of Halong Bay's islands.

For details of operators in Hanoi that run tours to Halong Bay, see p79.

KAYAKING
A leisurely paddle among the karsts is an activity that has taken off in recent years and Halong Bay is now following hard on the heels of Krabi in Thailand as kayaking capital of Southeast Asia. There are several travel agencies (p79) in Hanoi that can arrange kayaking trips through the bay, including overnight camping on one of the many islands.

Getting There & Away
AIR
At present, **Northern Airport Flight Service Company** (☎ 04-827 4409; fax 827 2780; 173 Pho Truong Chinh, Hanoi) offers a helicopter charter service from Hanoi to Halong Bay on Saturday from 7.15am. The cost for the charter service is US$195 per person, but it only runs with a minimum of six guests. The same helicopters can be privately chartered for US$2000 an hour.

BUS & BOAT
Most travellers to this part of the country book a one- or two-night Halong Bay tour at cafés or hotels in Hanoi. The trips are

NORTHEAST VIETNAM

very reasonably priced, starting from as little as US$12 to US$16 per person (on a jam-packed 45-seat bus), and rising to between US$40 and US$55. The latter will buy you a small-group tour on which you can sleep out on a boat on the bay, an overnight stay that is highly recommended.

Most tours include transport, meals, accommodation and activities such as boat tours of Halong Bay and island hikes. Drinks are extra. Also increasingly popular are tours that incorporate sea kayaking around the outcrops.

It is hard to do it any cheaper on your own, but for those who prefer to steer their own course, it can be done without the hair-greying hassle of the old days. Travelling independently allows you to take more or less time in places, depending on the weather. Take a bus to Halong from Hanoi (35,000d, 3½ hours) and book a passage on a Cat Ba tourist boat (100,000d including entry ticket, five hours). This boat takes in the main sites and drops you at Ben Beo harbour. Chill out on Cat Ba before taking a hydrofoil to Hai Phong and a bus to Hanoi.

If you book a tour, there is always a small chance that the boat-trip part may be cancelled due to bad weather. This may actually entitle you to a partial refund, but remember that the boat trip is only a small portion of the cost of the journey (it is the hotels, food and transport along the way that really add up). Depending on the number of people in your group, you probably won't get back more than US$5 to US$10 if the boats don't sail.

Getting Around
BOAT
You won't see much unless you take a boat tour of the islands and their grottoes. For those travelling independently, life has got much easier under the watch of **Halong Bay Management Department** (☎ 824 467; http://halong .org.vn/; 166 Đ Le Thanh Tong). It regulates pricing for cruises on the bay and has a published list in its office at the Bai Chay tourist dock.

There is no need to rent a whole boat for yourself, as there are plenty of other travellers, Vietnamese and foreign, to share with. The official prices are ridiculously reasonable at 20,000/25,000/30,000d for a four-/six-/eight-hour cruise. Whole boats can be chartered starting with 25-seaters for 280,000/400,000/500,000d respectively – an affordable indulgence for those wanting some privacy. Boats to Cat Ba Island cost 70,000d per person or 700,000d for a charter.

Once aboard, be very careful with your valuables. Sleep-over boats have lockable cabins, but ask someone to keep an eye on your things if you're swimming off a day-tour boat.

CAT BA ISLAND
☎ 031 / pop 7000
Rugged, craggy and jungle-clad Cat Ba, the largest island around Halong Bay, is straight out of Jurassic Park. **Lan Ha Bay**, off the eastern side of the island, is especially scenic and offers numerous beaches to explore. While the vast majority of Halong Bay's islands are uninhabited vertical rocks, Cat Ba has a few tiny **fishing and farming villages** as well as a fast-growing town.

PLAYING FOR HIGH STAKES

A military general and one of Vietnam's greatest heroes, Tran Hung Dao (1226–1300) three times defeated the Mongol warriors of the Chinese army as they attempted to invade Vietnam.

His most famous victory was at the Bach Dang River in northeast Vietnam in 1288 where, copying the military strategy of Ngo Quyen (who had regained Vietnam's independence in 939, after 1000 years of Chinese rule), he retained the country's independence.

After dark, sharpened bamboo poles – of a length designed to remain hidden underwater at high tide – were set vertically in the river, near the bank where it was shallow. On high tide, Tran Hung Dao sent small boats out – passing easily between the posts – to goad the Chinese warships to approach, which they duly did. As the tide receded, the Chinese boats were left high and dry, and flaming arrows destroyed the fleet. In Halong Bay you can visit the Cave of Wooden Stakes (Hang Dau Go), where Tran Hung Dao's forces are said to have prepared and stored the bamboo poles.

So that's why he is commemorated in all of those Tran Hung Dao streets in every Vietnamese town, and why every street parallel to a river is called Bach Dang, in memory of the victory.

Except for a few fertile pockets, the terrain is too rocky for serious agriculture; most residents earn their living from the sea, while others cater to the tourist trade. Life has always been hard here and many Cat Ba residents joined the exodus of Vietnamese boat people in the 1970s and '80s. Although the island lost much of its fishing fleet this way, overseas Vietnamese have sent back large amounts of money to relatives on the island, thus financing the new hotels and restaurants here. Cat Ba is still relatively laid-back, despite about a 20-fold increase in hotel rooms (and karaoke machines!) since 1996.

About half of Cat Ba Island (which has a total area of 354 sq km) and 90 sq km of the adjacent waters were declared a national park in 1986, to protect the island's diverse ecosystems. These include subtropical evergreen forests on the hills, freshwater swamp forests at the base of the hills, coastal mangrove forests, small freshwater lakes and coral reefs. Most of the coastline consists of rocky cliffs, but there are a few sandy beaches tucked into small coves.

There are numerous lakes, waterfalls and grottoes in the spectacular limestone hills, the highest of which rises 331m above sea level. The largest permanent body of water on the island is **Ech Lake**, which covers an area of three hectares. Almost all of the surface streams are seasonal; most of the island's rainwater flows into caves and follows underground streams to the sea, which creates a shortage of fresh water during the dry season. Although parts of the interior of the island are below sea level, most of the island is between 50m and 200m in elevation.

The waters off Cat Ba Island are home to 200 species of fish, 500 species of mollusc and 400 species of arthropod. Larger marine animals in the area include seals and three species of dolphin.

Ho Chi Minh paid a visit to Cat Ba Island on 1 April 1951 and there is a large annual festival on the island to commemorate the event. A **monument** to Uncle Ho stands on Mountain No 1, the hillock across from the pier in Cat Ba town.

The best weather on Cat Ba Island is from late September to November, particularly the latter, when the air and water temperature is mild and skies are mostly clear. December to February is cooler, but still pleasant. From February to April, rain is common, while the summer months, from June through August, are hot and humid.

Cat Ba National Park

This **national park** (admission 15,000d, guide fee per day US$5; dawn-dusk) is home to 32 types of mammals – including François monkeys, wild boar, deer, squirrels and hedgehogs – and more than 70 species of birds have been sighted, including hawks, hornbills and cuckoos. Cat Ba lies on a major migration route for waterfowl, which feed and roost on the beaches in the mangrove forests. There are 745 species of plants recorded on Cat Ba, including 118 timber species and 160 plants with medicinal value. The park is home to a species of tree called Cay Kim Gao. In ancient days, kings and nobles would eat only with chopsticks made from this timber, as anything poisonous it touches is reputed to turn the light-coloured wood to black!

A guide is not mandatory, but is definitely recommended if you want to go walking; otherwise, all you are likely to see is a canopy of trees. Camping is also allowed in the park, but you'll need to bring your own gear or hire it from Cat Ba town.

Two caves in the national park are open to visitors. **Hospital Cave** oozes historical significance, as it served as a secret, bombproof hospital during the American War. **Hang Trung Trang** (Trung Trang Cave) is easily accessible, but bring a torch (flashlight) as it is gloomy inside. The cave is just south of the park entrance along the main drag, and there's a small entry fee.

There is a *very* challenging 18km (five to six hour) hike through the park and up to one of the mountain summits. Take a guide, and arrange bus or boat transport to the trailhead and a boat to return. All of this can be easily organised at the hotels in Cat Ba if you're travelling independently, and is usually included on group tours. Many hikes end at Viet Hai, a remote minority village just outside the park boundary, from where boats shuttle back to Cat Ba town. Take proper hiking shoes, a raincoat and a generous supply of water for this hike. Independent hikers can buy basic snacks at the kiosks in Viet Hai, which is where many hiking groups stop for lunch. This is *not* an easy walk, and is much harder and more slippery after rain. There are shorter hiking options that are less hardcore.

To reach the national park headquarters at Trung Trang, take a minibus from one of the hotels in Cat Ba town (8000d, 30 minutes). All restaurants and hotels should be able to sell you minibus tickets. Another option is to hire a motorbike (one way 20,000d).

Beaches

The white-sand Cat Co beaches (simply called Cat Co 1, Cat Co 2 and Cat Co 3) used to be great places to lounge around for the day. However, Cat Co 1 is being transformed into a gigantic resort and Cat Co 3 looks set to follow. Cat Co 2, less busy and more attractive, remains a sane and safe haven and also offers simple accommodation and camping. It is accessible via a wooden cliffside walkway around the mountain from Cat Co 1.

On weekends the beaches fill up with Vietnamese tourists and become messy with litter, but during the week the crowds diminish.

The beaches are about 1km southeast from Cat Ba town over a steep headland,

and can be reached on foot or by motorbike (about 5000d).

Other beaches include Cai Vieng, Hong Xoai Be and Hong Xoai Lon.

Cat Ba Town

A sleepy fishing village just a decade ago, it is now Costa del Cat Ba! Since being 'discovered' by Hanoi residents, Cat Ba has turned into a highly popular summer getaway, filling up on weekends and holidays, when the town is jumping. This has been a boon for the range of amenities available, from hotels to restaurants, but the downside is a boom in karaoke joints and the tuneless wailing they often emit. During the summer, the town also fills up with cars, as Hanoi residents use the car ferries to come via Cat Hai. Weekdays are saner, as is just before or just after the peak summer season.

INFORMATION
Internet Access

Located on 'hotel alley', **Pacific Internet Café** (per min 200d) has terminals galore.

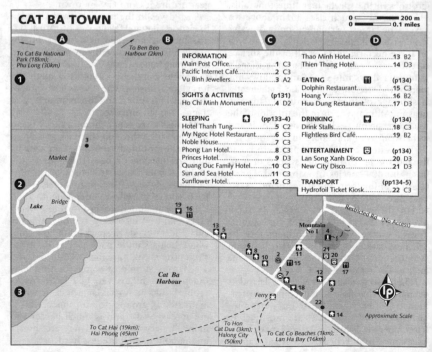

CAT BA TOWN

| 0 | 200 m |
| 0 | 0.1 miles |

To Cat Ba National Park (18km); Phu Long (30km)

To Ben Beo Harbour (2km)

INFORMATION
Main Post Office.....................1 C3
Pacific Internet Café..............2 C3
Vu Binh Jewellers...................3 A2

SIGHTS & ACTIVITIES   (p131)
Ho Chi Minh Monument.............4 D2

SLEEPING   (pp133-4)
Hotel Thanh Tung.....................5 C2
My Ngoc Hotel Restaurant........6 C3
Noble House.............................7 C3
Phong Lan Hotel......................8 C3
Princes Hotel............................9 D3
Quang Duc Family Hotel.........10 C3
Sun and Sea Hotel..................11 C3
Sunflower Hotel.......................12 C3

Thao Minh Hotel.....................13 B2
Thien Thang Hotel..................14 D3

EATING   (p134)
Dolphin Restaurant................15 C3
Hoang Y.................................16 B2
Huu Dung Restaurant.............17 D3

DRINKING   (p134)
Drink Stalls.............................18 C3
Flightless Bird Café................19 B2

ENTERTAINMENT   (p134)
Lan Song Xanh Disco..............20 D3
New City Disco.......................21 D3

TRANSPORT   (pp134-5)
Hydrofoil Ticket Kiosk............22 C3

Market

Lake   Bridge

Cat Ba Harbour

Restricted Rd (No Access)

Mountain No 1

Ferry

To Cat Hai (19km); Hai Phong (45km)

To Hon Cat Dua (3km); Halong City (50km)

To Cat Co Beaches (1km); Lan Ha Bay (16km)

Approximate Scale

Money

There are no banks on Cat Ba Island, but **Vu Binh Jewellers** (☎ 888 641) can change cheques at 3% commission and does credit card cash advances at 5%.

Post

The main post office is the place to make international telephone calls.

Tourist Information

There is no official tourist information office, but most guesthouses and hotels can 'help' with tourist information (booking you on their trips or tours in other words).

SLEEPING

Over the past few years the number of accommodation offerings in Cat Ba has risen dramatically, while development continues apace, feeding an expanding tourist market. Look around, as the quality of hotels varies widely.

Most hotels are situated on the waterfront in Cat Ba town. The ones to the east, built right up against the hillside, tend to offer better cross-breezes and less of the seedy, karaoke call-girl scene. Most hotels have at least one staff member who speaks English.

Room rates fluctuate greatly. In the high-season summer months (May to September) you can expect to pay a minimum of US$15 per room. During the slower winter months (October to April) you can find decent rooms for between US$5 and US$10. The rates given here are for winter, when there's usually the opportunity for negotiation.

Budget

Quang Duc Family Hotel (☎ 888 231; fax 888 423; r US$10; ✦) Cat Ba's original friendly 'family hotel' is still very popular. Rooms come with satellite TV and hot water. A good place to arrange tours as well.

Thien Thang Hotel (☎ /fax 888 568; r US$10; ✦) A swish new place offering mid-range standards at budget prices. Satellite TV, big bathrooms and seaview balconies available.

My Ngoc Hotel Restaurant (☎ 888 199; fax 888 422; r US$5-7; ✦) This hotel delivers value for money with its simple, clean rooms and a little restaurant spilling out onto the waterfront pathway. Kayaks are available for US$6 per day.

Phong Lan Hotel (☎ 888 605; r US$6-10; ✦) In a good location in the middle of the seafront strip, the front rooms have balconies overlooking the harbour, as well as some unique tile designs in the bathrooms.

Thao Minh Hotel (☎ /fax 888 630; r US$5-10; ✦) A hotel with small waterfront rooms, but the balcony views are worth the walk for those staying on higher floors.

Hotel Thanh Tung (☎ 888 364; r US$6-10; ✦) Next door to Thao Minh, this place has 'bed rooms forward sea', which are seaview rooms to the uninitiated. Same story as the other budget places, and very clean.

There are several hotels on the waterfront west of these two, which are flanked by a row of karaoke bars and massage joints, so it's not the quietest part of town.

To avoid the hoopla in town, try a night at the rustic (read basic) two-room **guesthouse** (r 50,000d) over on Cat Co 2. The manager also rents out tents for guests to camp on the beach.

If you really want to get away from it all, the National Parks Department has a basic four-room **beach guesthouse** (rooms US$10) on the nearby island of **Hon Cat Dua** (Pineapple Island). It is also possible to camp on the beach, provided you bring your own gear. Come prepared to be self-sufficient. Hon Cat Dua is about 30 minutes by private boat (one way per boat US$6) from Cat Ba town. To make arrangements, ask at **My Ngoc Hotel Restaurant** (☎ 888 199) or **Quang Duc Family Hotel** (☎ 888 231). Handspan Adventure Travel also operates a kayaking **base camp** here, where you can stay for US$10 a night in bamboo huts on a private beach; see (p79) for contact details.

Mid-Range

Sun and Sea Hotel (☎ 888 315; sunseahotel@mail.ru; r US$15; ✦) Ultimately clean rooms here, the sort you could eat your breakfast off, which happens to be included. TV, fridge and hot water complete the picture. It's just off the waterfront.

Princes Hotel (☎ 888 899; princeshotel@yahoo .com; r US$16-25; ✦) A new kid on the block, arguably the best hotel in town right now. Smart if slightly soulless rooms feature all mod-cons.

Noble House (☎ 888 363; thenoblehousevn@yahoo .com; r US$10; ✦) This is a small guesthouse with some big differences, like thoughtful

---

FLOATING RESTAURANTS

There are numerous 'floating' seafood restaurants just offshore in Cat Ba Harbour. There have been several stories of overcharging, so be sure to work out in advance the price, as well as the cost of a boat to get you out there and back. Locals advise heading around the bay to the couple of floating restaurants in Ben Beo Harbour; the water's cleaner and it's less touristy. A boat ride there and back, including waiting time, should cost around 15,000d. Ask your hotel to recommend a boatman.

One of these restaurants is **Xuan Hong** (☎ 888 485), a fish-farm-cum-restaurant at Ben Beo Pier, just next to the passenger jetty, where you can tread on the edges of the large fish cages and get a close look at the workings of the 'farm'. You will know that the fish is fresh when it is plucked from the cages *after* you've ordered. Prices simply go by weight and type of seafood; you can eat your fill of a selection of fish for around 100,000d.

---

decoration and elegant bathrooms. Prices leap to US$30 during peak season.

Sunflower Hotel (☎ 888 215; sunflowerhotel@hn .vnn.vn; r US$18-25; 🗷) This place has a whopping 104 rooms located within its two properties. They are some of the smartest on Cat Ba and the rates include breakfast.

EATING
Unsurprisingly, fresh and delicious seafood is the smart choice in Cat Ba town, and there are lots of restaurants along the length of the waterfront.

Hoang Y (dishes 10,000-50,000d), towards the western end of the waterfront, serves a top selection of seafood dishes. Fresh grilled shrimp or squid with garlic costs around 50,000d for a huge helping. There are also good vegetarian dishes on offer. No frills, but always packed.

Huu Dung Restaurant (dishes 10,000-40,000d) continues to be popular, but eat early: two discos have opened nearby and it's hard to hear anything once the music starts. Formerly known as the Coka Cola Restaurant, the roof was painted like a Coke billboard, locals still refer to it by this name. The house special is whole steamed fish.

Dolphin Restaurant (☎ 888 804; mains 20,000-50,000d) A good place that's just a short stroll from the seafront, serving dishes from all over the globe. Don't worry though, no dolphin!

DRINKING
One of the most enjoyable ways to spend time in the evening is to sit at tables on the waterfront towards the eastern end of the harbour, order a drink from one of the stalls, and watch the world and the water go by.

Noble House (☎ 888 363) has a lively 2nd floor bar-restaurant. There's a free pool table, board games and plenty of drinks flowing. Throw in the good grub and it's a great place to get the evening started.

As the night draws on, a lot of foreigners make for the **Flightless Bird Café** (☎ 888 517; 🕑 from 6.30pm), run by a congenial Kiwi expat. This homely little bar is a good place for drinks, drinks and more drinks, plus there's darts, music and movies. There is a pleasant 2nd-floor balcony overlooking the harbour, and a small book exchange.

ENTERTAINMENT
There are presently two thumping (literally!) discos on the slope behind town. New City Disco is in an enormous purple building, and has the strange sales technique, on quiet nights, of refusing to play any tunes until you buy a drink. Next door is Lan Song Xanh Disco, which plays music for its customers regardless.

Getting There & Away
Cat Ba Island is 45km east of Hai Phong and 20km south of Halong City. Be aware that there are several piers on Cat Ba Island. Most handy is the jetty directly in front of Cat Ba town from where the hydrofoils to Hai Phong depart. A second popular one is at Ben Beo, about 2km from Cat Ba town where most of the tourist boats berth. The other pier is at Phu Long, 30km from Cat Ba, where boats from Cat Hai dock. At Phu Long, motorbike drivers wait to whisk passengers to town (or the 15km to Cat Ba National Park) for about 50,000d. There is also a public bus that meets the boats, but this takes longer to get across the island.

Good news for independent travellers are the Russian hydrofoils linking Cat Ba to Hai Phong. These air-con rockets reduce the journey to just 45 minutes. There are three hydrofoils to Hai Phong (90,000d), but all depart at 3.15pm, which is maddeningly daft! Coming the other way, hydrofoils depart Hai Phong at 8.20am, 8.50am and 9am. Tahaco has the fastest boats, according to regulars. In general, but especially on peak-season summer weekends, book tickets in advance and get there early, as boats tend to run as soon as they are full.

There are currently no hydrofoils operating to Halong City, but this could change, as it was a mighty convenient service. The easiest way to get from Halong City to Cat Ba is to hop on the tourist boats (70,000d, five hours) that leave several times a day. This is less organised going in the other direction to Halong City, but your guesthouse or hotel should be able to hook you up with a boat going that way.

There are plenty of slow, chartered tourist boats making the run from Halong City to Cat Ba Island; check with the cafés and travel agencies in Hanoi about tour options. Such trips generally include all transport, accommodation, food and a guide, but ask to make sure.

An alternative way to reach Cat Ba town is via the island of Cat Hai, which is closer to Hai Phong. A boat departs Hai Phong and makes a brief stop in Cat Hai on the way to the port of Phu Long on Cat Ba Island. It is also possible to drive a motorbike or car to Hai Phong, from where you can get the ferry to Cat Hai, then drive 15 minutes across the island to a pier from where you take a ferry to Phu Long. This accounts for all those surreal traffic jams during the summer season!

Getting Around
Rented bicycles are a great way to explore the island and several of the hotels can arrange cheap Chinese bikes.

Minibuses with driver are easily arranged. Motorbike rentals (with or without a driver) are available from most of the hotels (from US$5 without a driver). If you are heading out to the beaches or national park, pay the 2000d parking fee to ensure that your vehicle is still there when you return: there have been reports of theft and vandalism.

You'll get plenty of offers to tour Cat Ba Harbour in a small rowboat (around 20,000d), or hire a kayak from one of the hotels.

Tours of the island and national park, boat trips around Halong Bay and fishing trips are being peddled by nearly every hotel and restaurant in Cat Ba town. The cost depends on the number of people, but typical prices are US$8 for day trips and US$20 for two-day, one-night trips.

Among the consistently reputable tour operators, we can recommend **My Ngoc Hotel Restaurant** (☎ 888 199) and **Quang Duc Family Hotel** (☎ 888 231).

BAI TU LONG BAY
☎ 033
There's more to northeastern Vietnam than Halong Bay. The sinking limestone plateau, which gave birth to the bay's spectacular islands, continues for some 100km to the Chinese border. The area immediately northeast of Halong Bay is known as Bai Tu Long Bay.

Bai Tu Long Bay is every bit as beautiful as its famous neighbour. Indeed, in some ways it's more beautiful, since it has scarcely seen any tourist development. This has its positives and negatives. The bay is unpolluted and undeveloped, but there's little tourism infrastructure. It's pretty hard travelling around and staying here, and unless you speak Vietnamese, it's difficult to get information.

Charter boats can be arranged to Bai Tu Long Bay from Halong Bay; a boat suitable for 20 passengers costs US$10 per hour and the one-way journey takes about five hours. A cheaper alternative is to travel overland to Cua Ong pier, catch a public ferry to Van Don Island and visit the remote outlying islands by boat from Cai Rong pier.

Van Don Island (Dao Cai Bau)
Van Don is the largest and most populated and developed island in the archipelago. However, there is only very limited tourism development here to date.

Cai Rong is the main town on the island, which is about 30km in length and 15km across at the widest point. **Bai Dai** (Long Beach) runs along much of the southern side of the island and is hard-packed sand with some mangroves. Just offshore, almost touching distance away, there are stunning **rock formations** similar to those in Halong Bay.

SLEEPING & EATING
The only hotels are at Cai Rong pier, about 8km from Tai Xa Pha, which is where ferries from the mainland dock. Cai Rong is a colourful, busy area, with lots of fishing boats and passenger vessels, and a backdrop of limestone mountains in the bay. It's also full of karaoke bars and motorbikes. You might want to get a room with air-con to block out some of the noise. There's no beach.

Hung Toan Hotel (☎ 874 220; r 120,000d; ✷) The three rooms on the top floor are best – they share a huge balcony – and the place has been given a bit of a makeover, making it a good deal. It's about 100m before the pier.

Duyen Huong Guesthouse (☎ 874 113; r 80,000-120,000d; ✷) A clean little place, its decent-sized rooms have attached bathroom with hot water, and some have balconies.

Nha Nghi Nhu Hoa (r 80,000-120,000d; ✷) Right next door and pretty much the same in style as the Duyen Huong. It's fine, but watch out for the excruciatingly loud karaoke room on the 2nd floor.

Bai Tu Long Ecotourism Resort (☎ 793 156; www.ati-tourism.com; r 180,000-250,000d; ✷) A new resort up on Long Beach, it's a much nicer alternative to the places in Cai Rong. There are attractive beachside bungalows or more basic rooms in stilt houses, and the beach has a beautiful backdrop.

GETTING THERE & AWAY
For the moment, the island's inhabitants mostly rely on ferries that run between Cua Ong Pha (Cua Ong Pier) on the mainland and Tai Xa Pha (Tai Xa Pier) on Van Don Island. The passenger ferry (which also carries bicycles, motorbikes and chickens) runs every 30 minutes (1000d, 20 minutes) from 6am to 5pm. The car ferry (per car 15,000d; 15 minutes) leaves Cua Ong every two hours (between 6.30am and 4.30pm from 1 October to 31 March; and between 5am and 5pm from 1 April to 30 September).

The fastest way to get to Van Don is by hydrofoil from Halong City (US$6, 8am, one hour). In the other direction, it leaves for Halong City at 3pm.

Note that these boat schedules may change and are dependent on the weather. Be prepared to hang around here a day or so.

Frequent buses run between Hon Gai (Halong City) and Cua Ong bus station, 1km from the pier on the mainland. You'll pass plenty of coal mines en route – your face (and lungs) will receive a fine coating of black coal dust before the journey is completed. Just pity the folks who live here and have to breathe this in every day.

Motorbikes run the 8km between Tai Xa Pha and Cai Rong town (15,000d, 15 minutes).

Other Islands
Cai Rong Pier (Cai Rong Pha) is just on the edge of Cai Rong town. This is the place for boats to the outlying islands. Chartering a boat from here to Hon Gai or Bai Chay costs around US$10 per hour (the one-way journey takes five hours).

Tourist boats can be chartered at Cai Rong to cruise the nearby islands for a few hours. Ask at the pier. The hourly rate is between 70,000d and 80,000d.

Quan Lan Island (Dao Canh Cuoc)
The main attraction here is a beautiful, 1km-long **white-sand beach** shaped like a crescent moon. The water is clear blue and the waves are suitable for surfing. The best time to play in the water is from about May to October – winter is too chilly.

The northeastern part of the island has some battered **ruins** of the old Van Don Trading Port. There is little to show that this was once part of a major trading route between Vietnam and China. Deep-water ports, such as Hai Phong and Hon Gai, long ago superseded these islands in importance.

The rowing-boat festival **Hoi Cheo Boi** is held here from the 16th to the 18th day of the sixth lunar month. It's the biggest festival in the bay area, and thousands of people turn out to see it.

Quan Lan Ecotourism Resort (☎ 033-877 417; www.ati-tourism.com; bungalows 150,000d) has a fine location on the beach, with a choice of four basic bungalows or a large stilt house for big groups.

There are a couple more cheapies on the island: **Phuong Hoang Guesthouse** (☎ 877 345) and **Ngan Ha Guesthouse** (☎ 877 296), both with solar-powered hot water and rooms around the 100,000d mark.

A ferry service between Quan Lan and Van Don Islands runs daily (17,000d, two hours), departing Van Don at 2pm and Quan Lan at 7am; in other words, a trip to the island requires an overnight stay.

Van Hai Island (Cu Lao Mang)
Ancient Chinese graves have been found in this area, indicating that this region has seen considerable maritime trade. There are many good beaches, but a sand-mining pit (used to make glass) is destroying the place. There are boats to and from Van Don Island at 7am and 2pm (17,000d, 80 minutes).

Ban Sen Island (Dao Tra Ban)
Also known as Tra Ban Island, this is the closest major island to Van Don Island, making it easy to visit. However, there are no tourist facilities on the island and as a visit will mean an overnight stay, be prepared to be self-sufficient.

Boats depart from Van Don Island at 2pm and arrive on the northern side of Ban Sen between 3pm and 3.30pm (10,000d). Going the other way, boats leave daily at 7am and arrive at Van Don between 8am and 8.30am.

Co To Island (Dao Co To)
In the northeast, Co To Island is the furthest inhabited island from the mainland. Its highest peak reaches a respectable 170m. There are numerous other hills, and a large lighthouse atop one of them. The coastline is mostly cliffs and large rocks, but there's at least one fine sandy **beach**. Fishing boats

usually anchor just off here, and you can walk to some of the boats during low tide. There is a small and very basic guesthouse on the island.

Ferries bound for Co To Island depart Van Don Island on Monday, Wednesday and Friday at unspecified times – check the schedule in Cai Rong. They return from Co To Island on Tuesday, Thursday and Friday. The one-way fare is 30,000d and the journey takes about five hours, depending on the wind.

MONG CAI & CHINESE BORDER
☎ 033 / pop 48,100

Mong Cai is located on the Chinese border in the extreme northeastern corner of Vietnam. Previously the border gate (Cua Khau Quoc Te Mong Cai) was only open to Vietnamese and Chinese, but today it is an official international overland border crossing. It's open from 7.30am to 4.30pm daily. However, your Chinese visa *must* be issued in Hanoi only, or your Vietnam visa issued by the embassy in Beijing only (if you're coming the other way).

It would take a real optimist to think Mong Cai is an attractive place. For the Vietnamese, the big draw here is the chance to purchase low-priced (and low-quality) Chinese-made consumer goods. For the Chinese, the attraction is mostly gambling and girls.

Chinese speakers will find plenty of opportunity to practice in Mong Cai. Most of the market stalls are run by Chinese. This

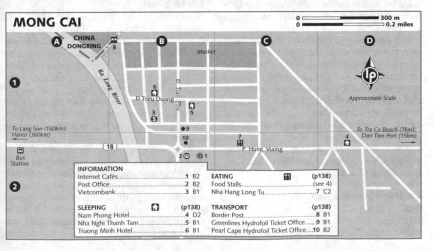

MONG CAI

0 —————— 300 m
0 —————— 0.2 miles

Approximate Scale

To Lang Son (160km);
Hanoi (360km)

To Tra Co Beach (7km);
Dan Tien Port (15km)

Bus Station

INFORMATION		EATING	🍴	(p138)
Internet Cafés	1 B2	Food Stalls		(see 4)
Post Office	2 B2	Nha Hang Long Tu		7 C2
Vietcombank	3 B1			
		TRANSPORT		(p138)
SLEEPING 🛏	(p138)	Border Post		8 B1
Nam Phong Hotel	4 D2	Greenlines Hydrofoil Ticket Office		9 B1
Nha Nghi Thanh Tam	5 B1	Pearl Cape Hydrofoil Ticket Office		10 B2
Truong Minh Hotel	6 B1			

NORTHEAST VIETNAM

explains why the market shuts so early – the Chinese have to head back across the border before it closes at 4.30pm. It also means it's easy to offload any leftover Chinese yuan.

Other than the prospect of crossing the border, Mong Cai is of little interest to tourists. The town is dusty, the buildings are ramshackle, and there's construction-site chaos everywhere. Dongxing (on the Chinese side) is arguably worse.

Information

Vietcombank, in the centre of town, can change travellers cheques and also has a handy ATM.

Internet access (Pho Hung Vuong) is available in a cluster of places near the post office.

Sleeping & Eating

Many travellers prefer to spend the night in the nearby beach retreat of Tra Co (see right). There are masses of hotels in Mong Cai; some more-inspiring choices:

Nha Nghi Thanh Tam (☎ 881 373; Đ Trieu Duong; r 120,000d; 🔀) A small, spotless place that charges a sensible price. Local TV only for those learning the lingo.

Truong Minh Hotel (☎ 883 368; 202 Đ Trieu Duong; r 120,000d; 🔀) Just to the west of the market, this place is marginally quieter than the hotels on the main drag. TV, fridge and hot water are all part of the deal.

Nam Phong Hotel (☎ 887 775; fax 887 779; Pho Hung Vuong; r from 240,000d; 🔀) Currently the classiest joint in town, this is a modern business hotel with well-tended rooms and attentive staff.

Nha Hang Long Tu (☎ 770 489; Pho Hung Vuong; mains from 20,000d) One of the best restaurants in town with a plastic-fantastic simple set-up downstairs and a more refined dining room upstairs. Good table-top barbecues and steamboats, plus stacks of seafood.

There are currently a couple of five-star casino resorts under construction to cater to Chinese high rollers.

There are plenty of **food stalls** (Pho Hung Vuong) including several good spots near the Nam Phong Hotel.

Getting There & Away
BOAT

High-speed hydrofoils run daily from Mong Cai to Bai Chay (US$12, three hours)

in Halong City at 9am and 2pm, and 8am and 1pm from Halong City. They leave for Hai Phong at 12.30pm (US$15, 4½ hours). From Mong Cai, shuttle vans leave the hydrofoil ticket offices in town, for the pier at Dan Tien Port, about 15km away. Arriving in Mong Cai, the hydrofoils often berth in the middle of the open sea; don't worry, you haven't broken down! Low tides require a transfer by small boat.

There are several hydrofoil ticket offices in town. Try **Pearl Cape** (☎ 883 988; Pho Hung Vuong) or **Greenlines** (☎ 881 214; 43 Pho Tran Phu).

For masochists, there's also a daily slow ferry between Hon Gai and Mong Cai (about 12 hours); check schedules locally.

Hydrofoil services to Van Don Island were not operating at the time of writing, but may start up again.

BUS

Mong Cai is 360km from Hanoi. Buses to/from Hanoi (62,000d, 10 hours) leave five times a day between 5.30am and 7.30am. Many buses and minibuses connect Mong Cai and Hon Gai (35,000d, six hours) between 5.30am and 4.30pm. Smart folk take the hydrofoil!

Mong Cai to Lang Son is a five-hour journey. However, buses on this route leave only once or twice a day, early, if at all, and require a change at Tien Yen. Much of the road is unpaved – expect plenty of dust or mud.

AROUND MONG CAI
Tra Co Beach
☎ 033

Lying 7km southeast of Mong Cai is Tra Co, an oddly shaped peninsula ranking as the northernmost beach resort in Vietnam. It's a fine beach of hard-packed sand with shallow water, and, at 17km in length, it's one of the longest stretches of sandy beachfront real estate in Vietnam. Painted wooden fishing boats are pulled up on shore, or illuminate the water during night catches.

It's still a small-scale resort, but there's a high season between May and August, with many Vietnamese and Chinese tourists and the usual swathe of karaoke bars and massage parlours. Out of season it's delightful: peaceful, clean and beautiful. It's a more tranquil option for an overnight stay than Mong Cai itself.

SLEEPING & EATING

There are plenty of hotels and guesthouses; those described here are, at present, the only ones with direct beach frontage. Low-season rates are given; expect inflation in high season.

Hotel Gio Bien (☎ 881 635; r 120,000-150,000d; ❄) A newish, family-run minihotel. Rooms at the top have shared balconies and a bird's-eye panorama over the beach.

Sao Bien Hotel (☎ 881 243; r 140,000-180,000d; ❄) Pick of the pack, but a new pool and park on the seafront have wiped out any sea views. Clean rooms with TV, fridge and hot water.

Tra Co Beach Hotel (☎ 881 264; r 100,000-150,000d; ❄) Boasting the ultimate location right on the beach, but crying out for a renovation. For now, mildew and mothballs are the main amenities.

Opposite the Tra Co Beach Hotel, on the edge of the beach, are some great little **restaurants** (dishes 15,000-50,000d) knocking up fresh seafood.

GETTING THERE & AWAY

A one-way metered taxi from Mong Cai will be about 75,000d. A motorbike taxi is cheaper at 20,000d.

LANG SON

☎ 025 / pop 62,300 / elevation 270m

Capital of mountainous Lang Son province, the town of Lang Son is in an area populated largely by Tho, Nung, Man and Dzao Montagnards, many of whom continue living their traditional way of life.

Lang Son was partially destroyed in February 1979 by invading Chinese forces (see the boxed text on p140); the ruins of the town and the devastated frontier village of Dong Dang were frequently shown to foreign journalists as evidence of Chinese aggression. Although the border is still heavily fortified, both towns have been rebuilt and Sino-Vietnamese trade is in full swing again.

Close to Lang Son, there are a couple of impressive caves in the surrounding limestone hills, and remnants of the ruined 16th-century Mac Dynasty Citadel. Most travellers come to Lang Son when crossing between Vietnam and China: the border is actually just outside Dong Dang, a village 18km to the north. It's not a town to linger

in, but if you find yourself with a few hours to spare there's enough to explore.

Information
INTERNET ACCESS

The main concentration of Internet cafés is on Đ Le Loi.

MONEY

Change your US dollars to dong at **Vietcombank** (51 Đ Le Loi).

POST

Use up the last of your Vietnamese stamps at the **main post office** (Đ Le Loi).

Sights & Activities

There are two large and beautiful **caves** (admission 5000d; ❄ 6am-6pm) just 2.5km from the centre of Lang Son. Both are illuminated, which makes for easy exploration, and both have Buddhist altars inside. **Tam Thanh Cave** is vast and seductive. There's an internal pool and a viewing point or natural 'window' offering a sweeping view of the surrounding rice fields. Just 100m up a stone staircase are the

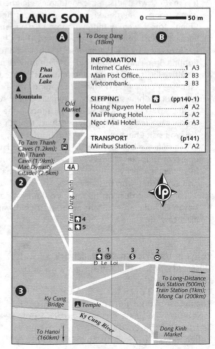

NEIGHBOURING TENSIONS

Mong Cai is a free-trade zone with plenty of frenetic activity in the city's booming markets. It wasn't always so. From 1978 to 1990 the border was virtually sealed. How two former friends became such bitter enemies and then 'friends' again is an interesting story.

China was on good terms with North Vietnam from 1954 (when the French left) until the late 1970s. But relations began to sour shortly after reunification, as the Vietnamese government became more and more friendly with China's rival, the USSR. There's good reason to believe that Vietnam was simply playing them off against each other, while receiving aid from both.

In March 1978 the Vietnamese government launched a campaign in the south against 'commercial opportunists', seizing private property in order to complete the country's 'socialist transformation'.

The campaign hit the ethnic-Chinese particularly hard. It was widely assumed that the Marxist–Leninist rhetoric veiled ancient Vietnamese antipathy towards the Chinese.

The anti-capitalist and anti-Chinese campaign caused up to 500,000 of Vietnam's 1.8 million ethnic-Chinese to flee the country. Those in the north fled overland to China, while those in the south left by sea. The creation of Chinese refugees in the south proved to be lucrative for the government – to leave, refugees typically had to pay up to US$5000 each in 'exit fees'. Chinese entrepreneurs in Ho Chi Minh City (HCMC) had that kind of money, but refugees in the north were mostly dirt poor.

In response, China cut all aid to Vietnam, cancelled dozens of development projects and withdrew 800 technicians. Vietnam's invasion of Cambodia in late 1978 was the final straw: Beijing – alarmed because the Khmer Rouge was its close ally, and worried by the huge build-up of Soviet military forces on the Chinese–Soviet border – became convinced that Vietnam had fallen into the Russian camp, which was trying to encircle China with hostile forces.

In February 1979, China invaded northern Vietnam at Lang Son 'to teach the Vietnamese a lesson'. Just what lesson the Vietnamese learned is not clear, but the Chinese learned that Vietnam's troops – hardened by many years of fighting the USA – were no pushovers. Although China's forces were withdrawn after 17 days, and the operation was officially declared a 'great success', most observers soon realised that China's People's Liberation Army (PLA) had been badly mauled by the Vietnamese. It is believed to have suffered 20,000 casualties in 2½ weeks of fighting. Ironically, China's aid to Vietnam was partially responsible for China's humiliation.

Officially, these 'misunderstandings' are considered ancient history – trade across the Chinese–Vietnamese border is booming and both countries profess to be 'good neighbours'. In practice, China and Vietnam remain highly suspicious of each other's intentions. Continued conflicts over who owns oil-drilling rights in the South China Sea are exacerbating tensions. The border area remains militarily sensitive, though the most likely future battleground is at sea.

If you visit China and discuss this border war, you will almost certainly be told that China acted in self-defence because the Vietnamese were launching raids across the border and murdering innocent Chinese villagers. Virtually all Western observers, from the US government's Central Intelligence Agency to historians, consider China's version of events to be nonsense. The Chinese also claim they won this war – nobody outside of China believes that, either.

For the real deal on how the communist comrades fell out, read *Brother Enemy* (1988) by Nayan Chanda, an excellent account of cold war power plays and the making and breaking of alliances.

ruins of the **Mac Dynasty Citadel**. It's a lovely, deserted spot, with stunning views across the countryside.

The Ngoc Tuyen River flows through **Nhi Thanh Cave**, 700m beyond Tam Thanh. The cave entrance has a series of carved poems written by the cave's discoverer, a soldier called Ngo Thi San, in the 18th century.

There's also a carved stone plaque commemorating an early French resident of Lang Son, complete with his silhouette in European clothing.

Sleeping & Eating

Hoang Nguyen Hotel (☎ 870 349; 84 Pho Tran Dang Ninh; s/d US$10/15; 🕸) A friendly, privately

MANFRED GOTTSCHALK

Halong Bay (p127)

Local boy on sampan, Halong Bay (p127)

RICHARD I'ANSON

Halong Bay (p127)

White-sailed junk, Halong Bay (p127)

Sampans, Halong Bay (p127)

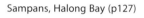

Karst mountains viewed through the mouth of a cave, Halong Bay (p127)

owned place, it is one of the cleanest hotels in town. Take a room at the back overlooking the rice fields. There's an Internet café a couple of doors away.

Mai Phuong Hotel (☎ 870 458; 82 Pho Tran Dang Ninh; r 120,000-150,000d; 🗙) Right next door to the Hoang Nguyen Hotel, the rooms here are fine, if you can make it past the strange smell in the lobby.

Ngoc Mai Hotel (☎ 871 837; 25 Pho Le Loi; r 80,000d; 🗙) Big, bright but musty rooms. There's also an Internet café next door.

There are plenty of other hotels and guesthouses in town, of much the same standard. Few have restaurants, but there are some *com pho* places in town and a couple of cheap restaurants near the bus station.

Getting There & Away
Buses heading to Hanoi's Long Bien bus station (30,000d, three hours) depart regularly from the **long-distance bus station** (Đ Le Loi). A daily bus leaves Lang Son for Cao Bang (47,000d, five hours) at 5am. Minibuses heading to Cao Bang via That Khe and Dong Khe leave regularly from the **minibus station** (Pho Tran Dang Ninh).

Three daily trains run between Lang Son and Hanoi (56,000d, five hours) at 2.20am, 6.40am and 2.10pm.

Getting Around
There are plenty of *xe om* (motorbike taxis) around the post office and the market.

On Pho Tran Dang Ninh you'll see minibuses looking for passengers who are heading to the border at Dong Dang.

DONG DANG & FRIENDSHIP PASS (CHINESE BORDER)
There is nothing in Dong Dang to hold the traveller's interest, except its position as a border town. The border post itself is at Huu Nghi Quan (Friendship Gate), 3km north of town; a *xe om* will take you there for 10,000d. The border is open from 7am to 5pm daily, and there's a 500m walk between the Vietnamese and Chinese frontiers. There's a train from Hanoi to Dong Dang (61,000d), via Lang Son, three times a day, if you want to make your own way across the border.

Trains from Hanoi to Beijing via the Friendship Pass depart the capital on Tues-

day and Friday at 6.30pm, a 48-hour journey that involves a three-hour stop for border formalities. You cannot board this international train in Lang Son or Dong Dang. Check the schedule in Hanoi, as it may change.

CAO BANG
☎ 026 / pop 45,500
The dusty capital of Cao Bang province, Cao Bang town is high above sea level and has a pleasant climate. The main reason to come here is to go on excursions into the surrounding scenic countryside. This is the most beautiful mountain area in the northeast and is worth exploring.

While in Cao Bang town, hit the hill leading up to the **War Memorial**; head up the

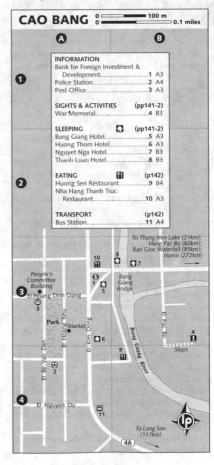

second lane off Đ Pac Bo, go under the entrance to a primary school, and you'll see the steps. There are great 360-degree views from the summit, and it's very peaceful, not to mention good exercise.

Information

Internet access has come to Cao Bang and there are several places to get an online fix on Pho Vuon Cam.

The Bank for Foreign Investment and Development will change US dollars but it's a major exercise, undertaken by sleepy staff. Try to arrive with enough cash to cover your stay.

Sleeping & Eating

Thanh Loan Hotel (☎ 857 026; fax 857 028; 159 Pho Vuon Cam; r US$15; ☒) A bright and clean place to stay, the staff are friendly here. All rooms are the same price, irrespective of size, so opt for one at the front or back which are lighter and bigger than those in the middle. Pity the poor old stuffed eagle in the lobby. Rates include breakfast.

Huong Thom Hotel (☎ 855 888; Đ Kim Dong; r 180,000d; ☒) Another good option, near the market, some of the rooms have river views and all have TV and hot water. Rates include breakfast.

Bang Giang Hotel (☎ 853 431; r 150,000-200,000d; ☒) This is an enormous state-run hotel that's better than some, located near the bridge in the north of town. Rooms on the upper floors in the rear of the building have sweeping views overlooking the river.

Nguyet Nga Hotel (☎ 856 445; r 100,000-140,000d; ☒) Diagonally opposite the Bang Giang Hotel, across the bridge, this is arguably the best of the cheaper hotels.

Besides the hotel restaurants, there are plenty of good **food stalls** (meals 5000-10,000d) near the market, and **Huong Sen Restaurant** (meals 10,000-30,000d) is a decent *com binh dan* place on the riverbank.

Nha Hang Thanh Truc Restaurant (meals 8000-20,000d) serves good, cheap local food; if you don't have someone who speaks Vietnamese with you, the staff will take you into the kitchen to show you what's on the menu and you can use the 'point and eat' technique.

It is best to eat early, as most eateries are closed by 8pm.

Getting There & Away

Cao Bang is 272km north of Hanoi, along Hwy 3. This is a sealed road, but due to the mountainous terrain, it's a full day's drive. There are several direct buses daily from Hanoi (70,000d, 10 hours) and Thai Nguyen. There is also a daily bus to/from Lang Son (47,000d, five hours) at 5am, departing from the **bus station** (Đ Kim Dong).

AROUND CAO BANG
Thang Hen Lake

This is a large lake that can be visited year-round; however, what you get to see varies according to the seasons. During the rainy season, from about May to September, the 36 lakes in the area are separated by convoluted rock formations. In the dry season, most of the lakes – except Thang Hen itself – are dry. However, during this time of year the lake level drops low enough to reveal a large **cave**, which can be explored by bamboo raft; that is, if you can locate anyone at all in the vicinity to ask. There are opportunities for good day **walks** throughout this area, but you'll need a local guide; try the hotels in Cao Bang for assistance.

As yet there are no restaurants or hotels at Thang Hen, nor is there any public transport. To get here from Cao Bang, drive 20km to the top of Ma Phuc Pass. From there carry on for 1km to the fork in the highway – take the left branch and continue another 4km.

Hang Pac Bo

Hang Pac Bo (Water-Wheel Cave) is just 3km from the Chinese border. The cave and the surrounding area is sacred ground for Vietnamese revolutionaries. Here, on 28 January 1941, Ho Chi Minh re-entered Vietnam ready to lead the revolution that he had long been planning while living abroad for 30 years.

Ho Chi Minh lived in this cave, writing poetry while waiting for WWII to end. He stuck close to China so that he would be able to flee across the border if French soldiers discovered his hiding place. He named the stream in front of his cave Lenin Creek and a nearby mountain Karl Marx Peak.

There's an Uncle Ho **museum** (admission free; ⏲ 7.30-11.30am & 1.30-4.30pm) at the entrance to the Pac Bo area. About 2km beyond this is a parking area. The cave is a 10-minute walk

NORTHEAST VIETNAM

THE LEGEND OF THE LAKES

The charming setting of Thang Hen wouldn't be complete without a depressing legend to go with it. It seems that there was a very handsome and clever young man named Chang Sung. His mother adored him and deemed that he should become a mandarin and then marry a beautiful girl.

Under Confucian tradition, the only way to become a mandarin was to pass a competitive examination – Chang Sung, being a clever boy, sat the exam and passed. He received an official letter bearing the good news and ordering him to report to the royal palace just one week later.

With her son virtually guaranteed admission to mandarinhood, Chang Sung's mother completed her plan – a beautiful girl, Biooc Luong (Yellow Flower), was chosen to marry Chang Sung and a big wedding was hastily arranged.

Chang Sung couldn't have been happier. In fact, he and Biooc were having such a great time on their honeymoon that he forgot all about his crucial appointment at the royal palace until the night before the deadline.

Knowing how disappointed his mother would be if he missed his chance to be a mandarin, Chang Sung summoned magical forces to help him hop in great leaps and bounds to the palace. Unfortunately, he messed up the aerodynamics and leapt 36 times, with no control over his direction or velocity, and wound up creating 36 craters, finally landing at the top of Ma Phuc Pass, where he died of exhaustion and became a rock. The craters filled up with water during the rainy season and became the 36 Lakes of Thang Hen.

away, and a **jungle hut**, which was another of Ho's hideouts, is about 15 minutes' walk in the opposite direction, across a paddy field and in a patch of forest. On the way to the hut is a rock outcrop used as a 'dead-letter box', where he would leave and pick up messages. It's a lovely, quiet spot and presently almost wholly undeveloped.

Hang Pac Bo is about 60km northwest of Cao Bang; allow three hours to make the return trip by road, plus 1½ hours to poke around. To do this as a return half-day trip by *xe om*, expect to pay around US$10. No permits are currently needed, despite the proximity to the Chinese border.

Ban Gioc Waterfall

This scenic spot, on the border with China, sees very few visitors. The name Ban Gioc is derived from the Montagnard languages spoken in the area, and is sometimes spelt Ban Doc.

The waterfall is the largest, although not the highest, in the country. The vertical drop is 53m, but it has an impressive 300m span; one end of the falls is in China, the other is in Vietnam. The water volume varies considerably between the dry and rainy seasons: the falls are most impressive from May to September, but swimming during this period in the waterholes below may be difficult due to turbulence. The falls have

three levels, creating a sort of giant staircase, and there's enough water any time, most years, to make the trip worthwhile. Half the pleasure of the visit is walking across paddy fields to reach the base of the falls.

The falls are fed by the Quay Son River. An invisible line halfway across the river marks the border, and **rafts** (per trip 30,000d) pole out the few metres to exactly the halfway mark – and no further! – from each side. There's been some development of tourist facilities on the Chinese side in recent years, but almost nothing except a bamboo footbridge and a couple of bamboo rafts on the Vietnamese side.

There is no official border checkpoint here, but a police permit is required to visit – you cannot simply rent a motorbike and go there on your own. The permit is officially US$10, but hotels in Cao Bang will do the paperwork for between 100,000d and 200,000d. Let them do it – it's much less hassle than doing it yourself at the Cao Bang police station.

About 10km before the falls, show the permit – and leave your passport – at a roadside checkpoint. An official at the parking area at the falls will then take your permit. You collect each from the same place on return. It was all very straightforward at the time of writing, but be prepared for changes to the regulations.

NGUOM NGAO CAVE

The main entrance to this **cave** (admission & guide 50,000d) is 2km from Ban Gioc Waterfall, just off the road to Cao Bang. The cave is enormous (about 3km long) and one branch reaches almost all the way to the waterfalls, where there is a 'secret' entrance. Normally a guided tour will take about an hour and will only go about 400m into the cave; ask if you want to see more. The price remains the same, and a full tour takes about two hours. Mains electricity is due to be installed, but it's probably sensible to take a torch.

SLEEPING & EATING

At the time of writing, there were no hotels located on the Vietnamese side of the border. Cao Bang is really the closest option for accommodation.

There is limited food available in Trung Khanh, and nothing at all in Ban Gioc. Prepare a picnic in Cao Bang.

GETTING THERE & AWAY

The road between Cao Bang and Ban Gioc via Quang Yen is in good nick, and is presently fine for 2WD. The 87km trip will take you about 2½ hours each way; it's mountainous and winding and very beautiful. If you take the loop route to and from the falls, the section between Tra Linh and Trung Khanh is still very bumpy, and 4WD is recommended for this stretch, especially after rain. There is public transport between Cao Bang and Trung Khanh but nothing beyond that; negotiate for a *xe om* in Trung Khanh to take you to the falls.

Montagnard Markets

In the province of Cao Bang, Kinh (ethnic-Vietnamese) are a distinct minority. The largest ethnic groups are the Tay (46%), Nung (32%), H'mong (8%), Dzao (7%) and Lolo (1%). Intermarriage, mass education and 'modern' clothing is gradually eroding tribal and cultural distinctions.

Check out Tim Doling's *Mountains and Ethnic Minorities: North East Vietnam* for detailed accounts of tribal people in the region It's available from the Vietnam Museum of Ethnology (p90) and bookshops in Hanoi.

Most of Cao Bang's Montagnards remain blissfully naive about the ways of the outside world. Cheating in the marketplace,

for example, is virtually unknown and even tourists are charged the same price as locals without bargaining. Whether or not this innocence can withstand the onslaught of even limited tourism remains to be seen.

The following big Montagnard markets in Cao Bang province are held every five days, according to lunar calendar dates.

Trung Khanh 5th, 10th, 15th, 20th, 25th and 30th day of each lunar month

Tra Linh 4th, 9th, 14th, 19th, 24th and 29th day of each lunar month

Nuoc Hai 1st, 6th, 11th, 16th, 21st and 26th day of each lunar month

Na Giang 1st, 6th, 11th, 16th, 21st and 26th day of each lunar month. Attracting Tay, Nung and H'mong, this is one of the best and busiest markets in the provinces.

BA BE NATIONAL PARK

☎ 0281 / elevation 145m

Sometimes referred to as Ba Be Lakes, **Ba Be National Park** (☎ 894 014; fax 894 026; admission per person 10,000d, per car 10,000d, plus 1000d insurance fee) is in Bac Kan province and was established in 1992 as Vietnam's eighth national park. It's a beautiful region that covers more than 7,000 hectares and boasts waterfalls, rivers, deep valleys, lakes and caves set amid towering peaks. The surrounding area is home to members of the Tay minority, who live in stilt homes.

The park is a tropical-rainforest area with over 550 named plant species, and the government subsidises the villagers not to cut down the trees. The 300 or so wildlife species in the forest include 65 (mostly rarely seen) mammals, 214 bird species, butterflies and other insects. Hunting is forbidden, but villagers are permitted to fish.

The park is surrounded by steep mountains, up to 1554m in height. The 1939 *Madrolle Guide to Indochina* suggests to travel around Ba Be Lakes 'in a car, on horseback, or, for ladies, in a chair', meaning, of course, a sedan chair.

Ba Be (Three Bays) is in fact three linked lakes, which have a total length of 8km and a width of about 400m. The deepest point in the lakes is 35m, and there are nearly 50 species of freshwater fish.

Two of the lakes are separated by a 100m-wide strip of water called Be Kam, sandwiched between high walls of chalk rock. The **Thac Dau Dang** (Dau Dang or Ta Ken Waterfall) consists of a series of spectacular

> ### THE LEGEND OF WIDOW'S ISLAND
>
> A tiny islet in the middle of Ba Be Lakes is the source of a local legend. The Tay people believe that what is a lake today was once farmland, and in the middle was a village called Nam Mau.
>
> One day, the Nam Mau residents found a buffalo wandering in the nearby forest. They caught it, butchered it and shared the meat. However, they didn't share any with a certain lonely old widow.
>
> Unfortunately for the villagers, this wasn't just any old buffalo. It belonged to the river ghost. When the buffalo failed to return home, the ghost went to the village disguised as a beggar. He asked the villagers for something to eat, but they refused to share their buffalo buffet and ran the poor beggar off. Only the widow was kind to him and gave him some food and a place to stay for the night.
>
> That night the beggar told the widow to take some rice husks and sprinkle them on the ground around her house. Later in the evening, it started to rain, and then a flood came. The villagers all drowned, the flood washed away their homes and farms, thus creating Ba Be Lakes. Only the widow's house remained: it's now Po Gia Mai (Widow's Island).

cascades between sheer walls of rock, and is accessible by boat and on foot during day trips. Just 200m below the rapids is a small Tay village called Hua Tang.

Hang Puong (Puong Cave) is visited on day tours. It's about 30m high and 300m long, and completely passes through a mountain. A navigable river flows through the cave, making for an interesting boat trip.

Renting a boat is *de rigueur*, and costs about 40,000d per hour. The boats can carry maybe eight people (but it's the same price if there are just two), and you should allow at least seven hours to take in most sights. Enjoy the ride: it's lovely despite the noisy engines. An optional guide (recommended) costs US$10 per day. The boat dock is about 2km from park headquarters.

The park staff can organise several **tours**. Costs depend on the number of people, but expect to pay at least US$25 per day if you're travelling alone. There's the option of a one-day tour by boat; a one-day tour combining motorboat, a 3km or 4km walk, and a trip by dugout canoe; and there are also combination cycling, boating and walking possibilities. Homestays can be arranged at several of the villages in the park, and longer treks can also be arranged.

The park entrance fee is payable at a checkpoint on the road into the park, about 15km before the park headquarters, just beyond the town of Cho Ra.

Sleeping & Eating

Not far from the park headquarters are two accommodation options. Rooms in the newly built **guesthouses** (r US$20) are fine, if a bit pricey. There are also pleasant air-con two-room **cottages** (r US$25). There's a reasonable **restaurant** (dishes 10,000-30,000d) – note that you'll need to place your order an hour or so before you want to eat. There is even Internet access available for 10,000d per hour.

It's also possible to stay in **stilt houses** (per person US$3) at a couple of hamlets in the park. The park office can organise this. Food is available at the homestays, which can include fresh fish from the lake, and prices are reasonable.

Take enough cash for your visit – there are no money-exchange facilities, although there are banks in Bac Kan, the provincial capital en route from Hanoi.

Getting There & Away

Ba Be National Park is in Bac Kan province not far from the borders of Cao Bang province and Tuyen Quang province. The lakes are 240km from Hanoi, 61km from Bac Kan (also known as Bach Thong) and 18km from Cho Ra.

Most visitors to the national park get there by chartered vehicle from Hanoi. Since the 2000 opening of a new road into the park, 4WD is no longer necessary. The one-way journey from Hanoi takes about six hours; most travellers allow three days and two nights for the entire excursion.

Reaching the park by public transport is possible, but not easy. Take a bus from Hanoi to Phu Thong (30,000d, six hours) via Thai Nguyen and/or Bac Kan, and from there take another bus to Cho Ra (10,000d, one hour). In Cho Ra arrange a motorbike (about 30,000d) to cover the last 18km.

THAI NGUYEN

☎ 028 / pop 171,400

Definitely not northeast Vietnam's most interesting city, but Thai Nguyen is home to the **Museum of the Cultures of Vietnam's Ethnic Groups** (Bao Tang Van Hoa Cac Dan Toc; admission 10,000d; ☟ 7-11am & 2-5.30pm Tue-Sun). It's worth a stop on the way to Ba Be National Park. It is the largest Montagnard museum in Vietnam. The giant pastel-pink building houses a wide array of colourful exhibits representing the 50-odd hill tribes residing in Vietnam. There is an interesting English booklet about the displays for US$2.

Thai Nguyen is 76km north of Hanoi, and the road here is in good shape. Buses and minibuses to Thai Nguyen (15,000d, two hours) depart from Hanoi's Gia Lam station regularly between 5am and 5pm.

AROUND THAI NGUYEN
Phuong Hoang Cave

Phuong Hoang Cave is one of the largest and most accessible caverns in northeastern Vietnam. There are four main chambers, two of which are illuminated by the sun when the angle is correct. Most of the stalactites and stalagmites are still in place, although quite a few have been broken off by thoughtless souvenir hunters. Like many caves in Vietnam, this one served as a hospital and ammunition depot during the American War. If you want to see anything, bring a good torch.

The cave is a 40km motorbike ride over a bumpy road from Thai Nguyen.

Nui Coc Reservoir

A scenic spot popular with locals, **Nui Coc Reservoir** (admission 6000d; hotel rooms 80,000-250,000d) is 25km west of Thai Nguyen. It's a pretty stretch of water, and is a major drawcard for Hanoi residents looking to get away from it all. On summer weekends it can get particularly crowded. A one-hour, circular motorboat tour of the lake is *the* thing to do and costs about 200,000d. You can use the water park's swimming pool for 20,000d, and also rent rowboats. It could be worth a visit if you're travelling to Ba Be National Park, with your own wheels, and fancy a dip.

Northwest Vietnam

NORTHWEST VIETNAM

Northwest Vietnam is home to the country's most spectacular scenery, the mountains of the Tonkinese Alps looming large over the land and providing a haven for an incredible mix of hill tribes. Many of these Montagnards continue to live as they have for generations despite coming into contact with outside influences.

Sapa is the gateway to the northwest, an atmospheric old hill station set amid stunning scenes of near-vertical rice terraces and towering peaks. But beyond Sapa the voluptuous views continue, and other options to come face to face with the bold landscapes and colourful inhabitants of this region include Bac Ha, Dien Bien Phu and Mai Chau. For the ultimate adventure head to Ha Giang, the final frontier in northern Vietnam, but road conditions, bureaucracy and a lack of facilities make it missable for most.

Hwy 6 winds through majestic mountains and high plains, which are inhabited by minorities, notably the Thai, the H'mong and the Dzao. The Thai live mostly in the lower lands, where they cultivate tea and fruit and live in smart stilt houses. The Dzao and H'mong live in the harsher highlands above 1000m.

Although many of the roads in this region are surfaced, many are dangerous cliffhangers that are regularly wiped out by landslides in the wet season. The stretch from Lai Chau into Sapa offers some of the best mountain vistas in Southeast Asia, as the road climbs more than 1000m over the Tram Ton Pass. The northwestern roads are always improving, but if you suffer from vertigo, backache or (God forbid) haemorrhoids, you might want to stick to the shorter trips. Many travel only as far as Mai Chau or Sapa before turning back.

The most rewarding journey in this region is the 'northwest loop'. Head for Mai Chau, followed by Son La and Dien Bien Phu, then north to Lai Chau, Sapa and back to Hanoi. The loop is best with a 4WD or motorbike, in case the roads are cut and you need to do some bush-bashing. Allow at least a week for this journey, and considerably more time if braving the local buses. And three cheers for the hardy cyclists who pump up and down these roads.

HIGHLIGHTS

- Take on the **northwest loop** (above), the ultimate road trip for a close encounter with Vietnam's mighty mountains
- Stick around **Sapa** (p160), the perfect base for meeting Montagnards, trekking through valleys to villages or just soaking up the scenery
- Step back in history at **Dien Bien Phu** (p155), where French colonial might met its match
- Browse the minority markets around **Bac Ha** (p168), home to the colour-crazy Flower H'mong
- Rise to the challenge of **Fansipan** (p163) on a three-day ascent of Vietnam's highest mountain

History

The history of the northwest is a separate saga from that of lowland Vietnam. The Vietnamese steered clear of the mountains, as the unforgiving terrain was not seen as suitable for large-scale rice production. For many centuries the area remained inhabited by small groups of minority people who were later joined in the 19th century by new migrants from Yunnan, China and Tibet. During Ho Chi Minh's leadership of the north, the Vietnamese experimented with limited autonomy in 'special zones', but these were abolished after reunification.

Life for the minorities has been hard, as their most profitable crop is opium, which doesn't go down well with the Vietnamese authorities. Educational and economic opportunities have been more limited, and creeping Vietnamisation of towns and villages is only likely to make things worse. Ironically, it is tourism in centres like Sapa and Bac Ha that is finally bringing independent means of income to the minority people.

Getting There & Away

Remote and mountainous, the northwest is the one region of Vietnam where it pays to consider the `ins and outs' carefully. The most comfortable way to reach the region is to take the train from Hanoi to Lao Cai, gateway to Sapa and the Tonkinese Alps. Day train for some scenery or night train for convenience, this is the gentle entry. Or it's the mountain roads, which can be very unforgiving on a public bus, not to mention more than a little dangerous in the wet season. Try 16 hours to Dien Bien Phu if you don't believe us. Better is the option of a private 4WD vehicle if you have the funds or can muster a group. Lastly, for the adventurous, there is the Russian Minsk motorbike, the mule of the mountains that

can get pretty much anywhere. Only for experienced bikers, this is the way to get up close and personal with the northwest.

HOA BINH
☎ 018 / pop 75,000
The city of Hoa Binh (Peace) is the capital of Hoa Binh province, home to many hill-tribe people, such as the H'mong and Thai. Locals have adopted modern Vietnamese garb, but some Montagnards venture into the town's market. Hoa Binh is a stop on the long drive towards Dien Bien Phu via Mai Chau, but most don't stay overnight.

Information
POST
Main post office Internet access is available here, plus international phone services.

TOURIST INFORMATION
Hoa Binh Tourism Company (☎ 854 374; fax 854 372) No walk-in office, but staff at the company's Hoa Binh hotels can help with information.

Sights
In Hoa Binh there is a small **museum** (admission free; 🕑 8-10.30am & 2-4.30pm Mon-Fri) that has French–Viet Minh and American Wars memorabilia, including a rusty French amphibious vehicle.

Cross the new bridge towards Phu Tho and to the right you will see the **dam wall** of a vast and impressive hydroelectric station; across the river is a massive shrine to the 161 workers who died during its construction.

Sleeping & Eating
Hoa Binh Hotels I & II (☎ 854 374; fax 854 372; s/d US$23/28; 🔀) Rooms here are built in pseudo-Montagnard stilt-house style with comfortable non-traditional amenities like hot water and TV. They're on the road heading out of town towards Mai Chau, but are starting to feel a little musty around the edges.

Thap Vang Hotel (☎ 852 864; 213 Đ Cu Chinh Lan; r 150,000d; 🔀) A smart new alternative in the centre of town, with hot water and satellite TV to complete a comfortable setup.

Cuisine is not Hoa Binh's trump card, but there are many *com pho* places lining Hwy 6 in the centre of town. Locals venture across the new bridge to a string of *bia hoi* shacks along the riverbank.

NORTHWEST VIETNAM

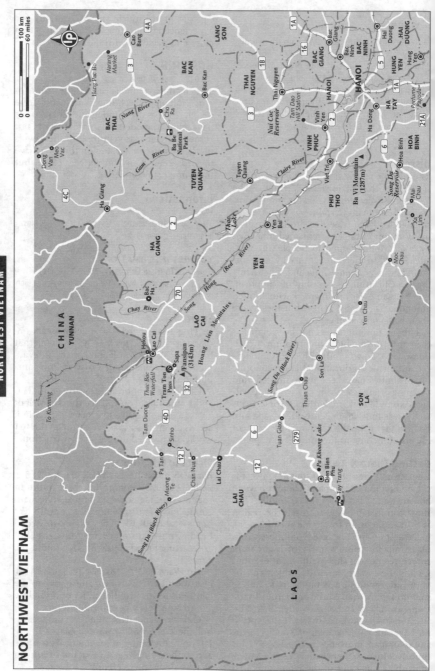

100 km
60 miles

Cao Bang
Hang Pac Bo
Narang Market
4A
LANG SON
1A
Hai Duong
HAI DUONG
3
BAC KAN
Bac Giang
Bac Ninh
BAC NINH
Hung Yen
HUNG YEN
BAC KAN
Bac Kan
1B
THAI NGUYEN
Thai Nguyen
16
BAC GIANG
HANOI
HANOI
5
HA TAY
1A
21A
Perfume Pagoda
Nang River
Cho Ra
3
Tam Dao Hill Station
Nui Coc Reservoir
Vinh Yen
2
Ha Dong
BAC THAI
Ba Be National Park
Gam River
Dong Van
Meo Vac
4C
Ha Giang
TUYEN QUANG
Tuyen Quang
Claire River
VINH PHUC
Viet Tri
PHU THO
Ba Vi Mountain (1287m)
Song Da Reservoir
Hoa Binh
HOA BINH
Mai Chau
6
2
HA GIANG
Thac Ba Lake
Hong (Red River)
YEN BAI
Yen Bai
Xa Linh
Moc Chau
Bac Ha
70
Chay River
Song
LAO CAI
Hoang Lien Mountains
6
Yen Chau
CHINA YUNNAN
Hekou
Lao Cai
Sapa
Fansipan (3143m)
Thac Bac Waterfall
Tram Ton Pass
32
Song Da (Black River)
Thuan Chau
Son La
SON LA
To Kunming
Tam Duong
4D
Sinho
12
Pa Tan
Chan Nua
6
Tuan Giao
279
Lai Chau
12
Pa Khoang Lake
Dien Bien Phu
Muong Te
Song Da (Black River)
LAI CHAU
Tay Trang
LAOS

THE ROADS WELL TRAVELLED: CONVERSATIONS WITH JEEP DRIVERS

I didn't plan to be a tourist driver. In the early 1980s I went to Moscow on a scholarship, to take a degree in civil engineering, and hoped to make that my career. Many of us Vietnamese went to study in Russia during that time. I learned to speak Russian, too, of course. That lasted three years, but by the time I came back the political climate here had changed, a Russian education was not highly valued and my degree didn't count for much.

My extended family pooled our money and bought this 4WD. It's a 1993 model and we bought it second-hand in a shipment that came from the US. It registers miles, not kilometres, which was a bit confusing for me at first!

I drive all over the country, but the northwest is the area that tourists want most to see and I go there most often, I suppose at least 30 times a year. Yes, they're long days, but as long as I can have an hour at lunch to eat and rest that's fine. And the tourists usually bring snacks to share during the journey; I really like those M&Ms.

Mostly when I drive foreigners there's a guide/interpreter with them, so I don't need to speak another language. You can understand a lot just by gestures and tone of voice and expressions. But I know it would be sensible to learn more English. I can understand some, but I'm not good at speaking it. My last passenger and I had fun learning to say things from the phrase book; I taught her how to pronounce the Vietnamese and she taught me how to pronounce the English, then we'd test each other on the longer road trips. Foreigners always find it really hard to pronounce Vietnamese, though – too many tones. She left the book with me, so I must keep practising.

I'm usually home in Hanoi for one night and one day a week if I'm lucky. My wife works full-time in an office, but our children are almost teenagers so they can pretty well look after themselves when we're busy. We spend a lot on mobile phone calls though!

Getting There & Away

Hoa Binh is 74km southwest of Hanoi and accessible by public bus. Those with transport can visit Ba Vi National Park (p115) and follow a river road to Hoa Binh.

SONG DA RESERVOIR

West of Hoa Binh is Song Da Reservoir (Ho Song Da), Vietnam's largest. The flooding of the Da River has displaced a large number of farmers for about 200km upstream, and is part of a major hydroelectric scheme that generates power for northern Vietnam. In 1994 a 500kV power line was extended to the south, freeing Ho Chi Minh City (HCMC) from seasonal power shortages.

Easiest access to the reservoir is by taking a spur road that cuts off from Hwy 6 at Dong Bang Junction (60km west of Hoa Binh and just outside Mai Chau). From the junction it's about a 5km drive to Bai San Pier. There's no obvious jetty here – hang around and someone will come out from a house and ask where you want to go. You'll need a Vietnamese speaker to help make arrangements.

One of the trips you can take is to the **Ba Khan Islands**. The islands are the tops of submerged mountains. The return trip to the islands takes three hours and costs about 150,000d per boat (each boat can seat 10).

Another possible boat trip is to **Than Nhan village**, home to members of the Dzao tribe. The two-hour return trip costs about 100,000d. The boat leaves you at a pier from where it's a steep 4km uphill walk to the village. If you'd like to stay in the village, take the boat one way for 50,000d and get a return boat to Bai San Pier the next day.

The last option is to charter a boat from Bai San Pier to Hoa Binh (400,000d, six hours).

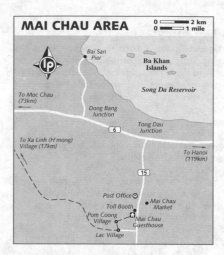

MAI CHAU AREA

To Moc Chau (73km)

Bai San Pier

Ba Khan Islands

Song Da Reservoir

Dong Bang Junction

Tong Dau Junction

6

To Xa Linh (H'mong) Village (17km)

To Hanoi (119km)

15

Post Office

Toll Booth

Mai Chau Market

Pom Coong Village

Mai Chau Guesthouse

Lac Village

MAI CHAU

☎ 018 / pop 47,500 / elevation 300m

Mai Chau is rural with no town centre – rather, it's a collection of villages, farms and huts spread out through a large valley. It's a beautiful area, and most people here are ethnic White Thai, said to be distantly related to tribes in Thailand, Laos and China.

Although most local people no longer wear traditional dress, the Thai women are masterful weavers who ensure that there is plenty of traditional-style clothing to buy in the village centre. You will probably see women weaving on looms under or inside their houses in the village. The Thai of Mai Chau are less likely to employ strong-arm sales tactics than their H'mong counterparts in Sapa: polite bargaining is the norm.

Sights & Activities

This is one of the closest places to Hanoi where you can visit a 'real' **Montagnard village**. Other attractions here include staying overnight in one of the Thai stilt houses (see Sleeping & Eating above), **walking** through the beautiful valley through the rice fields and **trekking** to minority villages. A typical trek further afield covers 7km to 8km; a local guide can be hired for about US$5.

There is a popular 18km trek from **Lac village** (Ban Lac) in Mai Chau, to **Xa Linh village**, near a mountain pass (elevation 1000m) on Hwy 6. Lac village is home to the White Thai people, while the inhabitants of Xa

Linh are H'mong. The trek is too strenuous to be done in a day, so it's necessary to spend the night in a village along the way. Arrange a local guide and a car to meet you at the mountain pass for the journey back to Mai Chau. Be warned that there is a 600m climb in altitude and the trail can be slippery in the rain.

Longer treks of three to seven days are possible. Ask around in the Mai Chau villages of Lac or Pom Coong. Many cafés and travel agencies in Hanoi run inexpensive trips to Mai Chau (see p79). These include all transport, food and accommodation.

Sleeping & Eating

Mai Chau Guesthouse (☎ 851 812; r from 120,000d) This is a decent, if basic, state-run guesthouse on the main road through the valley. Rooms at the back have balconies and views across the rice fields to the mountains.

However, most travellers choose to walk a few hundred metres back from the 'main' roadside and stay in the **Thai stilt houses** (50,000d per person) of Lac or Pom Coong villages. Lac is the busier of the two, and villagers will sometimes organise traditional song-and-dance performances in the evenings. See the boxed text opposite for more on the experience.

Getting There & Away

Mai Chau is 135km from Hanoi and just 5km south of Tong Dau junction on Hwy 6. There's no direct public transport to Mai Chau from Hanoi; however, buses to nearby Hoa Binh (15,000d, two hours) are plentiful. From Hoa Binh there are several scheduled buses to Mai Chau (20,000d, two hours) daily. Usually these stop at Tong Dau junction; a *xe om* from there to Mai Chau proper will cost about 10,000d.

Theoretically, foreigners must pay a 5000d entry fee to Mai Chau; there's a toll booth at the state-run guesthouse on the 'main' road. Sometimes it's staffed, sometimes not.

MOC CHAU

☎ 022 / pop 113,100 / elevation 1500m

This highland town produces some of Vietnam's best tea and is a good place to stock up. The surrounding area is also home to several ethnic minorities, including Green H'mong, Dzao, Thai and Muong.

Moc Chau boasts a pioneering dairy industry that started in the late 1970s with

SLEEPING ON STILTS

If you are anticipating an exotic Indiana Jones encounter – sharing a bowl of eyeball soup, taking part in some ancient fertility ritual and so on – think again. Spending a night in one of Mai Chau's minority villages is a very 'civilised' experience: the local authorities have made sure that the villages are up to tourist standards, so electricity flows, modern amenities abound and there are hygienic Western-style toilets. Mattresses and mosquito nets are provided. While this is not a bad thing per se, it may not live up to your rustic hill-tribe trekking expectations. Tour operators are not helping the situation: somehow they cannot seem to resist slapping up their oversized stickers wherever their groups stop to eat or drink, even if that happens to be on these lovely wooden stilt houses.

Despite – or perhaps because of – modern amenities, most people come away pleased with the experience. The Thai villages are exceedingly friendly and, when it's all said and done, even with TV and the hum of the refrigerator, it *is* a peaceful place and you're still sleeping in a thatched-roof stilt house on split-bamboo floors.

Reservations are not necessary; you can just show up, but it's advisable to arrive before dark. You can book a meal at the house where you're staying for around 20,000d, depending on what you require. The women here have learned to cook everything from fried eggs to French fries, but try to eat the local food – it's more interesting.

Australian and, later, UN assistance. The dairy provides Hanoi with such delectable luxuries as fresh milk, sweetened condensed milk and little tooth-rotting bars called *banh sua*. Not surprisingly, Moc Chau is a good place to sample some fresh milk and yogurt. Indulge yourself at one of the dairy shops that line Hwy 6 as it passes through Moc Chau.

Duc Dung Guesthouse (☎ 866 181; r 120,000d; ⚡), about 100m from the post office on Hwy 6, is the best choice for those planning to overnight here. A family-run pad, it is basic but friendly.

Moc Chau is 200km from Hanoi, and the journey takes about six hours by private car. The road is in good condition. It's another 120km from Moc Chau to Son La.

YEN CHAU

☎ 022 / pop 50,800

This agricultural district is known for fruit-growing. Apart from bananas, all fruits grown here are seasonal – mangoes, plums and peaches are harvested from April to June, longans in July and August, and custard apples in August and September.

The mangoes, in particular, are considered to be some of the tastiest in Vietnam, although travellers may find them disappointing at first, as they are small and green rather than big, yellow and juicy as in the tropical south. However, many Vietnamese prefer the somewhat tart taste and aroma

of the green ones, especially dipped in fish sauce (*nuoc mam*) and sugar.

Yen Chau is 260km from Hanoi, approximately eight hours by road.

SON LA

☎ 022 / pop 61,600

Son La makes a logical overnight stop for travellers doing the run between Hanoi and Dien Bien Phu. While not one of Vietnam's big hitters, the surrounding scenery is impressive and there are enough diversions to keep you busy for half a day.

The area is populated predominantly by Montagnards, notably the Black Thai, Meo, Muong and White Thai. Vietnamese influence in the area was minimal until the 20th century; from 1959 to 1980 the region was part of the Tay Bac Autonomous Region.

Sights & Activities

The **Old French Prison & Museum** (Nha Tu Cu Cua Phap; admission 5000d; ⏱ 7.30-11am & 1.30-5pm) in Son La was once the site of a French penal colony where anticolonial revolutionaries were incarcerated. It was destroyed by the infamous 'off-loading' of unused ammunition by US warplanes returning to their bases after bombing raids, but has been partially restored. Rebuilt turrets and watchtowers stand guard over the remains of cells, fetters, inner walls and a famous lone surviving peach tree. The tree, which blooms with traditional Tet flowers, was

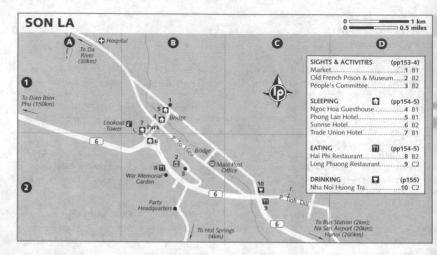

SON LA

SIGHTS & ACTIVITIES	(pp153-4)
Market.............................1	B1
Old French Prison & Museum......2	B2
People's Committee..................3	B2
SLEEPING	(pp154-5)
Ngoc Hoa Guesthouse.............4	B1
Phong Lan Hotel.....................5	B1
Sunrise Hotel.........................6	B2
Trade Union Hotel..................7	B1
EATING	(pp154-5)
Hai Phi Restaurant...................8	B2
Long Phuong Restaurant...........9	C2
DRINKING	(p155)
Nha Noi Huong Tra..................10	C2

NORTHWEST VIETNAM

planted in the compound by To Hieu, a former inmate from the 1940s. To Hieu has subsequently been immortalised, with various landmarks named after him.

A narrow road leads uphill to the prison, off the main highway. At the end of a road is a People's Committee office with a small **museum** on the top floor, where there are some interesting hill-tribe displays and a good bird's-eye view of the prison ruins. The prison itself is at the back, the entrance beneath a faded sign marked 'Penitencier'.

Perched above the town, a **lookout tower** offers a sweeping overview of Son La and the surrounding area. The climb is steep and takes about 20 minutes, but the view from the top is well worth it. The stone steps leading up to the tower are immediately to the left of the Trade Union Hotel.

You can find a small selection of colourful woven shoulder bags, scarves, silver buttons and necklaces, clothing and other Montagnard crafts at Son La's **market**.

A few kilometres south of town are **hot springs** (Suoi Nuoc Nong). There's a rather soupy small communal **pool** (admission free), and several privately run concrete **cubicles** (admission 5000d) where water is pumped into private bathtubs. To get here, start opposite the museum road. The road leads past the party headquarters building, after which there's 1km or so of bumpy track before the road is sealed for the final 5km to the springs.

Sleeping & Eating

Almost all travellers journeying between Hanoi and Dien Bien Phu spend the night in Son La. There are plenty of hotels in town, some of which double as brothels; the following are currently exceptions.

Trade Union Hotel (Khach San Cong Doan; ☎ 852 804; fax 855 312; s/d/t US$10/15/20; ✺) For a government-run place, this remains a rare gem. The staff are genuinely friendly and prices are reasonable. Large rooms come with hot water and include a hearty breakfast. There's a good restaurant upstairs.

Sunrise Hotel (☎ 858 798; fax 859 799; 53 Đ 26/8; r US$10-15; ✺) A smart new pad just across the road from the Trade Union Hotel, the rooms come with all the trimmings like hot water and TV, and it's sparkling clean.

Ngoc Hoa Guesthouse (☎ 853 993; 3 Đ Cho Moi; dm US$3, s/d US$10/15; ✺) Tucked away down an alley off the main drag, it is the best of the cheaper options in town and run by a friendly family.

Phong Lan Hotel (☎ 853 516; fax 852 318; 1 Đ Nguyen Luong Bong; r US$17; ✺) The rooms are large, but the main road setting can be noisy. It is just opposite the market and breakfast is included.

Long Phuong Restaurant (☎ 852 339; Pho Thinh Doi) Located at the main junction, this restaurant offers a menu of diverse dishes. Try the sour *mang dang* (bamboo shoots) soup, a speciality of the Thai minority people, helped down with sticky rice dipped in sesame seed salt.

Hai Phi Restaurant (Hwy 6) Here they dish up Son La's speciality – *lau* (goat meat). Try the highly prized *tiet canh*, a bowl of goat's-blood curd dressed with a sprinkling of peanuts and veggies. Or go for the more conventional, but tasty, goat-meat steamboat.

Nightlife is not Son La's selling point, but a local crowd gathers at **Nha Noi Huong Tra** (Đ Nguyen Luong Bong), a Trung Nguyen café built over an ornamental pond.

Getting There & Away
Son La's airport, called Na San, is 20km southeast of Son La along the road towards Hanoi.

Buses run from 4am to noon between Son La and Hanoi (63,000d), taking 12 to 14 hours assuming there are no serious breakdowns. Regular morning buses also run to Dien Bien Phu (38,000d, eight hours).

Son La lies 320km from Hanoi and 150km from Dien Bien Phu. By 4WD or motorbike, the Hanoi–Son La run typically takes 10 hours. Son La to Dien Bien Phu takes another six hours.

THUAN CHAU
☎ 022
The township of Thuan Chau is about 35km northwest of Son La. Try to pass through it early in the morning; the small daily local market is full of wonderfully garbed hilltribe women. From about 9am, for about an hour, a steady stream of women can be seen walking, cycling and motorbiking home to their villages along the main road.

TUAN GIAO
☎ 023 / pop 94,900 / elevation 600m
This remote town is at the junction of Hwy 42 to Dien Bien Phu (three hours, 80km) and Hwy 6 to Lai Chau (four hours, 98km). Not many people spend the night unless they are running behind schedule and can't make it to Dien Bien Phu, though if you are taking your time through the northwest it is a logical place to bed down for the night.

Sleeping & Eating
People's Committee Guesthouse (Nha Khach Uy Ban Nhan Dan Huyen; ☎ 862 391; r 100,000-150,000d; ✷) Try out the recently renovated section for a good, clean setup. The cheaper rooms are

dark and dingy. The guesthouse is set back behind the post office in a green and leafy courtyard.

Tuan Giao Hotel (☎ 862 613) Under renovation when we passed through town, but this has traditionally been a warm and welcoming place. It is about 150m from the main junction in the direction of Lai Chau.

Hoang Quat Restaurant (☎ 862 582; dishes 10,000-30,000d) About 300m from the junction towards Dien Bien Phu, this is the best place to eat in town, and deservedly popular with travellers passing through.

Getting There & Away
Most travellers approach from Son La (three hours, 75km). Few travellers use the direct road from Tuan Giao to Lai Chau, as most are visiting Dien Bien Phu. It's a wild road, and a wild ride, for experienced motorbikers.

PA KHOANG LAKE
A beautiful body of water, Pa Khoang Lake is 17km east of Dien Bien Phu, on the road from Son La, and 4km off the highway. About 15km drive around the lake's edge, or an hour's boat ride plus a 3km forest walk, is the **bunker of General Giap**, Vietnamese commander of the Dien Bien Phu campaign. There is also a remote **Thai village** that can be visited across the lake.

There is accommodation at Pa Khoang in the 1997-built but rapidly disintegrating **Pa Khoang Hotel** (☎ 926 552; r US$10-12); it's in a gorgeous setting, but the cobwebby and musty rooms are falling apart. While the hotel might not cry out for overnight guests, it's a good venue in which to spend a few hours en route to or from Dien Bien Phu. Hire a motor boat (US$10 return) to the bunker or villages, and stay for a spot of lunch.

DIEN BIEN PHU
☎ 023 / pop 25,000
Dien Bien Phu is famous the world over as the site of a battle that can truly be called decisive. The French colonial forces were roundly defeated at the hands of the Viet Minh on 7 May 1954 and the days of their Indochina empire were finally numbered.

Dien Bien Phu, recently granted the prestigious status of provincial city like Hanoi and Ho Chi Minh City, is in one of the most remote parts of Vietnam. The town

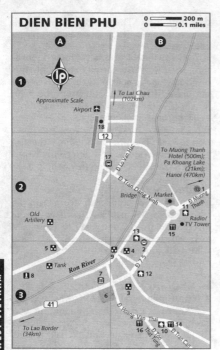

is 34km from the Lao border in the flat, heart-shaped Muong Thanh Valley, which is about 20km long and 5km wide and surrounded by steep, heavily forested hills. The size and look of the city is surprising considering the remote location, especially if you survived getting here overland.

History is the main attraction here and the scenery is more stunning on the journey to or from Dien Bien Phu than around town itself. Not surprisingly, the majority of travellers who come here now are French – Dien Bien Phu seems to hold the same sort of fascination for them as the Demilitarised Zone (DMZ) does for Americans.

For centuries Dien Bien Phu was a transit stop on the caravan route from Myanmar and China to northern Vietnam. The town itself was established in 1841 by the Nguyen dynasty to prevent raids on the Red River Delta by bandits.

The area is inhabited by Montagnards, most notably the Thai and H'mong. The government has been encouraging ethnic Vietnamese to settle in the region and they currently make up about half of the Muong Thanh Valley's total population.

Tourism is having quite an impact on Dien Bien Phu, with a building boom underway in the past few years. Domestic tourism went through the roof in the first half of 2004, as the whole of Vietnam geared up to celebrate the 50th anniversary of the French defeat at Dien Bien Phu.

Orientation & Information

It may enjoy the same status as metropolises such as Ho Chi Minh City and Danang, but in reality it's an overgrown village when it comes to navigating. The Ron River splits the town in half, but most of the accommodation and attractions are on the east bank. To the west is the airport and what might pass as suburbs.

Internet access is available at several little cafés along Đ Muong Thanh.

Sights & Activities

The site of the battle is now marked by the **Dien Bien Phu Museum** (☎ 824 971; admission 5000d; ⏱ 7.30-11am & 1.30-4.30pm), an informative if dry look at one of Vietnam's finest hours. The **bunker headquarters** (admission 5000d; ⏱ 7.30-11am & 1.30-4.30pm) of the French commander, Colonel Christian de Castries, has been re-created, and there are old French tanks and artillery pieces nearby. There is a monument to Viet Minh casualties on the site of the former French position, known to the French as Eliane and to the Vietnamese as **A1 Hill** (admission 5000d; ⏱ 7.30-11am & 1.30-4.30pm), where bitter fighting took place. The

MASON FLORENCE

Black Thai women, Son La (p153)

Black Thai child, Cat Cat village (p163),
near Sapa

ALISON WRIGHT

OLIVER STREWE

Colonial-style house, Sapa
(p160)

MASON FLORENCE

Water-powered rice thrashers,
Lai Chau (p158)

Traditional homes near Sapa
(p160)

H'mong girl, Tram Ton Pass (p164)

Worker in fields, Lao Cai (p167)

Tram Ton Pass (p164), approaching Sapa

THE SIEGE OF DIEN BIEN PHU

In early 1954 General Henri Navarre, commander of the French forces in Indochina, sent 12 battalions to occupy the Muong Thanh Valley to prevent the Viet Minh from crossing into Laos and threatening the former Lao capital of Luang Prabang. The French units, of which about 30% were ethnic Vietnamese, were soon surrounded by a Viet Minh force under General Vo Nguyen Giap that consisted of 33 infantry battalions, six artillery regiments and a regiment of engineers. The Viet Minh force, which outnumbered the French by five to one, was equipped with 105mm artillery pieces and anti-aircraft guns, carried by porters through jungles and across rivers in an unbelievable feat of logistics. The guns were emplaced in carefully camouflaged positions dug deep into the hills that overlooked the French positions.

A failed Viet Minh human-wave assault against the French was followed by weeks of intense artillery bombardments. Six battalions of French paratroopers were parachuted into Dien Bien Phu as the situation worsened, but bad weather and the Viet Minh artillery, impervious to French air and artillery attacks, prevented sufficient French reinforcements and supplies from arriving. An elaborate system of trenches and tunnels allowed Viet Minh soldiers to reach French positions without coming under fire. The trenches and bunkers were overrun by the Viet Minh after the French decided against the use of US conventional bombers – and the Pentagon's proposal to use tactical atomic bombs. All 13,000 men in the French garrison were either killed or taken prisoner; Viet Minh casualties were estimated at 25,000.

Just one day before the Geneva Conference on Indochina was set to begin half a world away, Viet Minh forces overran the beleaguered French garrison at Dien Bien Phu after a 57-day siege. This shattered French morale and forced the French government to abandon its attempts to re-establish colonial control of Indochina. For the full story of this incredible siege, pick up a copy of *Hell in a small place – The siege of Dien Bien Phu* by legendary French reporter Bernard S Fall.

elaborate trenches at the heart of the French defences have recently been re-created.

The old **Muong Thanh Bridge** is preserved and closed to four-wheeled traffic. Near the southern end of the bridge – though not much more than a crater in the ground overgrown with weeds – is the **bunker** where Chief Artillery Commander Pirot committed suicide.

A **memorial** to the 3000 French troops buried under the rice paddies was erected in 1984 on the 30th anniversary of the battle. The stylishly designed **Dien Bien Phu Cemetery** commemorates the Vietnamese dead, and you can catch a good view over it by climbing the stairs inside the main entry gate. Looking over the endless headstones begs the question: are there any victors in war?

Sleeping

Beer Factory Guesthouse (Khach San Cong Ty Bia; ☎ 824 635; r 150,000-180,000đ; ☒) This illustriously named guesthouse has smartened up its popular rooms to include hot water and TV. A must for beer heads, there are countless *bia hoi* pubs lining the nearby streets.

Binh Long Hotel (☎ 824 345; 429 Đ Muong Thanh; tw US$12; ☒) Run by a friendly family, this place has clean, though a touch tiny, twin-bedded rooms with bathrooms. Rates include breakfast.

Muong Thanh Hotel (☎ 810 043; fax 810 713; Đ Muong Thanh; r US$15-20; ☒ ☒) Probably the plushest place in town, but it often fills up with tour groups so book ahead. Go for the new wing if it is available, as the standard rooms are smarter for the same price. There's a swimming pool, bar, large restaurant, karaoke and 'Thai Massage', making it a veritable entertainment Mecca in this part of the world. Rates include breakfast.

Dien Bien Phu–Hanoi Hotel (☎ 825 103; fax 826 290; 279 Đ 7.5; r US$13-28; ☒) Currently in the middle of a major facelift, the cheapest rooms are not great, as they only have a fan, but top-priced VIP rooms are suites with beguiling bathrooms.

Lottery Hotel, close to the post office, was undergoing a major renovation during our recent visit, but gamblers might like to take a chance and stay here.

Eating

As far as eating goes, **Lien Tuoi Restaurant** (☎ 824 919; Đ Hoang Van Thai; mains around 30,000đ) is

BORDER CROSSING: TAY TRANG

The Lao border is only 34km from Dien Bien Phu and there has been much speculation about this crossing being opened to foreign tourists. As of Visit Dien Bien Phu Year and the grand fanfare of the 50th anniversary of the French defeat, it was still *not* open to foreigners, but it is surely coming soon. Keep your ear to the ground and do your homework in Hanoi.

the best stop in town for good Vietnamese and good Chinese after a long day on the road. The menu is in English and French with some wacky translations. It is about 400m up the road from the cemetery.

There is a superb little café opposite the Beer Factory Hotel, turning out some of the tastiest *pho* in the northwest and it is always heaving with locals. There are also a few decent local *com pho* joints on Ð 7.5.

Getting There & Away

The overland trip to Dien Bien Phu can be more intriguing than the actual battlefield sites for which the town is so celebrated. Of course, you miss out on this if you fly.

AIR

Vietnam Airlines (☎ 824 948; fax 825 536; ☷ 7.30-11.30am & 1.30-4.30pm) operates daily flights between Dien Bien Phu and Hanoi, costing 465,000d one way. The new office is just before the airport, about 1.5km from the town centre, along the road towards Lai Chau.

BUS

There is a direct bus service that runs from Hanoi to Dien Bien Phu (100,000d, 16 hours) and the bus leaves at 4.30am, 8.30am and 10.30am.

Buses to Lai Chau (25,000d, three hours) leave at 6am and 7am. Daily buses to Son La (38,000d, five hours) start at 4.30am, but for normal folk there are regular departures until noon.

Although the bus is cheap, it's not really much fun. Buses are so packed that the only scenery you get to admire is the armpit of the person sitting next to you. If overloaded vehicles, bad roads and bad brakes worry you, definitely fly or travel overland by 4WD or motorbike.

CAR & MOTORBIKE

The 470km drive from Hanoi to Dien Bien Phu on Hwys 6 and 42 takes 16 hours (if you're lucky). Conceivably it could be done in a single direct journey, but almost everyone stays overnight in Son La. Speaking from experience, it's no picnic handling the hairpins on a motorbike in the dark!

LAI CHAU

☎ 023 / pop 19,600 / elevation 600m

This small town is nestled in a pretty valley carved from spectacular mountains by the Da River, and makes a good lunch or overnight stop for people travelling between Dien Bien Phu and Sapa.

Beneath Lai Chau's beauty lies a difficult existence for locals. Despite a marked increase in tourist numbers, for most of the people it's a hard living. Far from busy trade routes, normal commerce is limited and the town has only been really successful in harvesting particularly valuable cash crops, including opium and timber. Needless to say, opium harvesting does not find favour with the central government, which has been trying to discourage the Montagnards from producing opium poppies.

If the opium business is falling on hard times, the same must be said for the timber industry. In recent years the forest cover has been reduced and flooding has increased dramatically. Around 140 people lost their lives in 1990 in a devastating flood on the Da River that swept through the narrow valley. An even worse flood in 1996 killed 100 people and cut all roads into town for two months; the ruins of the flooded former cultural hall can be seen in town.

It seems that this kind of flooding could become a permanent feature of Lai Chau. There are government plans to place a dam just above the current Song Da Reservoir, and this will fill the Lai Chau valley with water. If and when this comes to pass (not before 2010), this will be the largest hydroelectric station in Southeast Asia. It also could mean that in the future the only way to visit Lai Chau will be by submarine.

Being underwater, however, would at least keep things cooler. Odd as it might seem, in summer Lai Chau is one of the hottest places in Vietnam. June and July temperatures can soar as high as 40°C.

Sleeping & Eating

Lan Anh Hotel (☎ 852 682; fax 852 370; r US$10-20; 🕄)
This is one of the most switched-on hotels in
provincial Vietnam, with tourism information aplenty, a good restaurant and a steady
stream of cold beer. The wooden Thai-style
stilt houses are pretty, with wide fan-cooled
verandas, and the hotel is steadily expanding
with a mishmash of buildings dotting the
nearby street. More expensive rooms come
with air-con and hot water. The hotel also
offers an extensive programme of tours and
boat trips around Lai Chau. It's just past the
market, to the right before the bridge.

Song Da Hotel (☎ 852 527; r 120,000d; 🕄) These
guys face an uphill struggle to take on the
Lan Anh, especially with the relatively run-
down rooms. They do offer hot water and
air-con and might be the place for those
wanting to avoid other tourists. It's located
on the road to Dien Bien Phu.

Getting There & Away

Most travellers will arrive from Dien Bien
Phu (three hours, 103km), although there's
also the rocky road option of Hwy 6 from
Tuan Giao (four hours, 96km). The road
from Lai Chau to Sapa and Lao Cai (seven
hours, 180km) is one of the most beautiful
drives in Vietnam, particularly the final climb
up over the Tram Ton Pass. Remember that
all of the travel times listed here are pretty
much hypothetical – it only takes a single
landslide to cause considerable delays.

Public buses make the run to/from
Hanoi, as well as to points in the northwest
like Dien Bien Phu, Son La and Sapa.

MUONG TE

☎ 023 / pop 43,900 / elevation 900m
Muong Te is one of Vietnam's most remote outposts, 98km northwest of Lai Chau
along the scenic Da River. The majority of
the population is ethnic Thai, although they
have assimilated and are nearly indistin-
guishable from the Vietnamese. Other minority groups found in the area include the
Lahu (Khau Xung), Si La and Ha Nhi.

Apart from a small Sunday **market** and
some nearby **villages**, there is not much to
see or do in Muong Te. The only accommodation available in town is the shabby
People's Committee Guesthouse, which
also has a small restaurant.

SINHO

☎ 023 / pop 8500 / elevation 1054m
Sinho is a scenic mountain village that is
home to a large number of ethnic minorities. It should attract more tourists, but the
police have a bad reputation here and there
is a 'You ain't from around here look' on
the faces of many locals. Strange, but true.
There is a colourful Sunday **market**, although
the dingy People's Committee Guesthouse
has the only beds in town and they have to be
pressured into accepting foreigners.

Sinho is a 38km climb on an abysmal dirt
road (that has beautiful scenery) off Hwy
12, which takes about 1½ hours each way.
The turn-off is about 1km north of Chan
Nua, on the road from Lao Cai. A road
through to Hwy 4D is nearly completed,
which will put Sinho right on the map and
may help thaw the frosty welcome.

GET OFF MY LAND!

Follow the road from the signposted turn-off on Hwy 12 towards Muong Te for about 8km to
encounter a peculiar historical relic: an ancient poem carved in stone by 15th-century emperor Le
Loi, who had succeeded in expelling the Chinese from the region. The poem was left as a warning
for any other potential invaders not to mess with Le Loi. The translation from Chinese reads:

Hey! The humble, coward and frantic rebels, I come here to counter-attack for the
sake of the border inhabitants. There existed the betrayed subjects since the beginning
of human history. The land is no longer dangerous. The plants' figures, the whisper of
the wind, and even the singing of the songbirds startle the mean enemy. The nation is
now integrated and this carved poem an amulet for Eastern peace of the country.
An Auspicious Day of December, The Year of the Pigs (1432)

To find this vestige, look for the narrow flight of steps marked by a small stone placard reading
'Di Tich Lich Su – Bia Le Loi' on the roadside overlooking the river.

TAM DUONG
☎ 023 / pop 94,400

This remote town lies between Sapa and Lai Chau and is set in a verdant valley of conical peaks, like diminutive volcanoes that pose no threat. While the town is nothing special, it's a handy lunch stop between Dien Bien Phu or Lai Chau and Sapa.

The local **market**, about midway through the town on Hwy 12, is worth a visit. The majority of people are Montagnards from nearby villages, although ethnic Vietnamese make up the largest single group. If you're not in a rush to get to Sapa or Lai Chau, you could base yourself in Tam Duong for a day or so and explore the surrounding areas.

The drive from Tam Duong to Sapa along Hwy 4D, threading through the Fansipan Mountain Range and the Chinese border, is a beautiful stretch of road.

Sleeping & Eating

Tay Bac Hotel (☎ 875 879; r US$10; 🌀) The most atmospheric beds in town are found here, in an attractive Thai-style wooden house at the rear. Rooms come with air-con and hot water, and they boast a 'safe big car park'.

Tuan Anh Restaurant offers the best food in town for those on a lunch run. Other nearby *com pho* spots like Phuong Thanh are cheap and cheerful. Be aware that Kieu Trinh is known for its canine fare.

SAPA
☎ 020 / pop 36,200 / elevation 1650m

The premier destination of northwest Vietnam, Sapa is a former hill station built in 1922. Nestled in a beautiful valley close to the Chinese border, the spectacular scenery that surrounds Sapa includes cascading rice terraces that hug the heights looming over town. The mountains are often cloaked in mist that rolls back and forth along the mountaintops, offering tantalising glimpses of what lies in wait on a clear day. The valleys and villages around Sapa are home to a host of hill-tribe people who wander in to town to buy, sell and trade.

History has not always been kind to Sapa, and the long series of conflicts that swept over Vietnam left it on its last legs. From

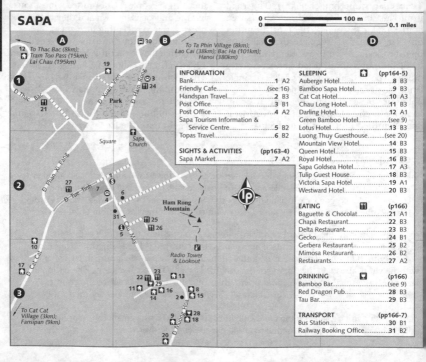

SAPA

0 ——————— 100 m
0 ——————— 0.1 miles

INFORMATION	
Bank	1 A2
Friendly Cafe	(see 16)
Handspan Travel	2 B3
Post Office	3 B1
Post Office	4 A2
Sapa Tourism Information & Service Centre	5 B2
Topas Travel	6 B2

SIGHTS & ACTIVITIES	(pp163-4)
Sapa Market	7 B3

SLEEPING 🏠	(pp164-5)
Auberge Hotel	8 B3
Bamboo Sapa Hotel	9 B3
Cat Cat Hotel	10 A3
Chau Long Hotel	11 B3
Darling Hotel	12 A1
Green Bamboo Hotel	(see 9)
Lotus Hotel	13 B3
Luong Thuy Guesthouse	(see 20)
Mountain View Hotel	14 B3
Queen Hotel	15 B3
Royal Hotel	16 B3
Sapa Goldsea Hotel	17 A3
Tulip Guest House	18 B3
Victoria Sapa Hotel	19 A1
Westward Hotel	20 B3

EATING 🍴	(p166)
Baguette & Chocolat	21 A1
Chapa Restaurant	22 B3
Delta Restaurant	23 B3
Gecko	24 B1
Gerbera Restaurant	25 B2
Mimosa Restaurant	26 B2
Restaurants	27 A2

DRINKING 🍷	(p166)
Bamboo Bar	(see 9)
Red Dragon Pub	28 B3
Tau Bar	29 B3

TRANSPORT	(pp166-7)
Bus Station	30 B1
Railway Booking Office	31 B2

Map labels: 12 To Thac Bac (8km); Tram Ton Pass (15km); Lai Chau (195km); To Ta Phin Village (8km); Lao Cai (38km); Bac Ha (101km); Hanoi (380km); Park; Ð Xuan Vien; Ð Ham Rong; Ð Thac Bac; Square; Sapa Church; Ð Pham Xu Panh; Ð Tue Tinh; Ham Rong Mountain; Ð Cau May; Radio Tower & Lookout; Ð Cat Cat; To Cat Cat Village (3km); Fansipan (9km); Ð Muong Hoa

NORTHWEST VIETNAM

WWII, through the wars against the French and the USA, to the border skirmish with China in 1979, the old hotels built by the French were allowed to fall into disrepair, and Sapa was pretty much forgotten.

Recently the place has been rediscovered, and the subsequent tourist boom has caused a sea change in Sapa's fortunes. Bad roads have been upgraded, many streets have been given names, countless new hotels have popped up, the electricity supply is reliable and the food has improved immeasurably. Inherent in all of this prosperity is cultural change for the Montagnards, many of whom are now well versed in the ways of the cash economy and are reaping the financial rewards of the tourism influx.

One inconvenience that will not change is the weather. If you visit off-season, don't forget your winter woollies. Not only is it cold (0°C), but winter brings fog and drizzle. Quite why the French alighted on this spot is difficult to comprehend: it must have been one of those rare clear days when the views are to die for. The chilly climate does have a few advantages, though – the area boasts temperate-zone fruit trees bearing fruit such as peaches and plums, and gardens for raising medicinal herbs.

The dry season in Sapa lasts from around January to June. January and February are the coldest (and foggiest) months. From March to May the weather is often excellent, and the summer is warm despite the rains between June and August. The window from September to mid-December is a pleasant time to be in Sapa, though there is a bit of lingering rain at the start and the temperature dips by December.

If possible, try to visit during the week, when the prices are cheaper and Sapa is less crowded and more manageable. Crowds flock to Sapa for the Saturday market, but a smaller market is held every day. There is plenty to see on weekdays, and there are many interesting villages within walking distance of the centre.

Sapa would be of considerably less interest without the H'mong and Dzao people, the largest ethnic groups in the region. Mostly they're very poor, but are rapidly learning the spirit of free enterprise. Most of the Montagnards have had no formal education and are illiterate, yet many of the youngsters have a good command of English and French.

Lots of the women and young girls have gone into the souvenir business; the older women in particular are known for their strong-armed selling tactics. One frequent Sapa sight is a frenzy of elderly H'mong women clamouring around hapless backpackers to hawk their goods, which range from colourful ethnic garb to little pouches of opium stashed away in matchboxes. When negotiating prices, you do need to hold your ground, but go easy when it comes to bargaining. They may be persistent, but are not nearly as rapacious as Vietnamese vendors.

A word of warning on the clothes: as beautiful and cheap as they are, the dyes used are natural and not set. Much of the stuff sold has the potential to turn anything it touches (including your skin) an unusual blue/green colour – check out the hands and arms of the H'mong for an idea. Wash the fabric separately in cold salt water – it helps stop the dye from running. Wrap anything you buy in plastic bags before stuffing it in your luggage.

Orientation
MAPS
The following maps can be obtained from the Sapa Tourism Information & Service Centre (p163).
Sapa Tourist Map (20,000d) An excellent 1:60,000 scale map of the walking trails and attractions around Sapa, plus an inset of the town.
Sapa Trekking Map (20,000d) A nice little hand-drawn map showing trekking routes and the town.

Information
INTERNET ACCESS
Internet access is available in many hotels and travel offices around town, usually for 500d per minute.

MONEY
There is a small bank in Sapa, but it doesn't do anything useful like handle foreign-currency exchange. The nearest ATM is currently in Lao Cai. Most hotels accept US dollars, but expect a worse exchange rate than in Hanoi. Travellers cheques can also be changed at Royal Hotel and Victoria Hotel, but command a commission of around 5%.

POST
Phone calls can be made at the two post offices in Sapa, but for postal services it's

TREAD LIGHTLY IN THE HILLS

For the world's indigenous people, tourism is a mixed blessing.

Studies show indigenous cultures are a major drawcard for travellers and attract substantial revenue, yet little of it directly benefits these minority groups, who are often among their country's poorest and most disadvantaged.

Hill-tribe communities in Vietnam have generally not initiated tourist activities, are not the major economic beneficiaries of it, are unable to stop it and have little say in its management.

Tourism can bring many benefits to its highland communities. These include cross-cultural understanding; improved infrastructure like roads; cheaper market goods; and tourist dollars supporting handicraft industries and providing employment opportunities for locals as guides and hospitality workers.

However, there are also negative side-effects. Tourism creates or contributes to overtaxing of natural resources; increased litter and pollutants; dependency on tourist dollars; proliferation of drug use and prostitution; and erosion of local values and practices.

If you travel to these regions, the good news is that you can make a positive contribution and ensure that the benefits of your stay outweigh the costs.

Behaviour

- Be polite and respectful
- Dress modestly
- Minimise your litter
- Do not urinate or defecate near villagers' households; bury faeces
- Do not take drugs – young children tend to imitate tourists' behaviour
- Do not engage in sexual relationships with local people, including prostitutes
- Try to learn something about the community's culture and language and teach something good about yours

Gifts

- Do not give children sweets or money; it encourages begging and paves the way for prostitution for 'gifts' and money. Sweets also contribute to tooth decay.
- Do not give clothes – communities are self-sufficient
- Don't give medicines – it erodes traditional healing practices and the medicine may not be correctly administered
- Individual gifts create jealousy and create expectations. Instead make donations to the local school, medical centre or community fund.
- No matter how poor they are, villagers are extremely hospitable; however, feeding a guest can result in food shortages. If you accept an invitation to share a meal, be sure to bring a generous contribution.

Shopping

- Haggle politely and always pay the agreed (and fair) price for goods and services
- Do not ask to buy a villager's personal household items or the jewellery or clothes they are wearing
- Don't buy village treasures, such as altar pieces

Photographs

- Do not photograph without first asking permission – this includes children. Some hill tribes (particularly the Dzao people) believe the camera will capture their spirit. Don't photograph altars.
- If you take a picture, do it quickly and avoid using a flash. It is polite to send copies (if possible) – if you promise to do so, keep your word.

Travel

- Travel in small, less disruptive groups
- Stay, eat and travel with local businesses
- Try to book tours with responsible tourism outlets who employ hill-tribe people or contribute to community welfare

Compiled with assistance from Oxfam Community Aid Abroad

better to hang on and post things from Hanoi as it is much faster.

TOURIST INFORMATION
Sapa Tourism Information & Service Centre (TISC; ☎ 871 975; www.sapatourism.info in Vietnamese; Pho Cau May) promotes sustainable tourism development in and around Sapa. As well as providing information, the centre can book guides and arrange community-based treks. There is also a branch of Craft Link not-for-profit handicrafts.

TRAVEL AGENCIES
There are several reliable travel companies in Sapa for trekking, mountain biking and other fun activities, as well as those recommended in the Trekking to Local Villages (below) and Fansipan (see right) sections.
Handspan Travel (8 Pho Cau May; ☎ /fax 872 110; www.handspan.com) Reliable outfit for trekking and mountain biking.
Topas Travel (28 Pho Cau May; ☎ 871 331; www .topas-adventure-vietnam.com/) Specialises in trekking, biking and horse riding. It operates a booking desk at the Victoria Sapa Hotel.

Sights & Activities
If you've got only an hour or so to kill, it is worthwhile following the steps up to the **Sapa radio tower** (admission 15,000d); the views of the valley from here are breathtaking.

SAPA MARKET
Montagnards from surrounding villages don their best clothes and go to **market** most days. Saturday is the busiest day, and the town is choking with tourists as the market is a big magnet for organised tour groups from Hanoi. If you'd rather enjoy Sapa at a more sedate pace, avoid the Saturday market.

TREKKING TO LOCAL VILLAGES
The nearest village within walking distance is **Cat Cat** (admission 5000d), 3km south of Sapa. Like everywhere in this area, it's a steep and very beautiful hike down; if you're too exhausted or unfit to hike back up, there are plenty of *xe om* ready and willing to cart you back to your hotel.

Another popular hike is to **Ta Phin village** (admission 5000d), about 10km from Sapa. Most people take a *xe om* to a starting point about 8km from Sapa, and then make a 14km loop walk of the area. Most hotels offer guided day and half-day treks; depending on the number of people and what, if any, vehicles are needed, expect to pay somewhere between US$4 and US$10.

The Sapa TISC can arrange community-based tours to the nearby H'mong village of **Sin Chai** with an overnight in the village to learn about textiles or music and dance.

Long-standing (and still recommended) places to ask about guided treks include **Auberge Hotel** (☎ 871 243), **Mountain View Hotel** (☎ 871 334) and the **Friendly Cafe** (Royal Hotel; ☎ 871 313). There are also many tour-booking offices on the main street.

FANSIPAN
Surrounding Sapa are the Hoang Lien Mountains, nicknamed the Tonkinese Alps by the French. These mountains include Fansipan, which at 3143m is Vietnam's highest peak. The summit towers above Sapa, although it is often obscured by clouds and is occasionally dusted with snow. The peak is accessible all year to those in good shape and properly equipped, but don't underestimate the challenge. It is very wet, can be perilously slippery and generally cold, so you must be prepared. Do not attempt an ascent if the weather is terrible in Sapa, as limited visibility on Fansipan could be treacherous.

The summit of Fansipan is 19km from Sapa and can be reached only on foot. The terrain is rough and adverse weather is frequent. Despite the short distance, the round trip usually takes three to four days; some very fit and experienced hikers have made it in two days, but this is rare. After the first morning you won't see any villages; just the forest, striking mountain vistas and perhaps some local wildlife such as monkeys, mountain goats and birds.

No ropes or technical climbing skills are needed, just endurance. There are no mountain huts or other facilities along the way (yet), so you need to be self-sufficient. This means taking a sleeping bag, waterproof tent, food, stove, raincoat or poncho, compass and other miscellaneous survival gear. Bring your own gear. Hiring a reputable guide is vital and, unless you are a seriously experienced mountaineer, finding porters who will carry your gear is also strongly recommended.

Good places to inquire about trekking guides include the **Auberge Hotel** (☎ 871 243), **Mountain View Hotel** (☎ 871 334), **Friendly Cafe**

ALL STITCHED UP

Like many hill-tribe women, those of the Yao of Ta Phin – a community about 10km from Sapa – are expert at embroidery, an art handed down through generations. Traditionally, only silk thread is used. Unprocessed silk is bought at the market, boiled to make it smooth, and then dyed with natural colours extracted from plants like turmeric and tea leaves.

Embroidery is done in segments. Items of everyday clothing include the *luy khia*, a densely embroidered lower back flap on a jacket. Trousers, *la peng*, are decorated with distinctive stripes of colour rather than blocks of pattern. *La peng pe* are cloths used to bind the lower legs, like leggings straight out of *Fame*. *La sin* is a belt used to hoist up the back flap of the jacket when women work in the fields. *Chap hoong* is the bib of red cotton behind the opening of a jacket, and may be studded with silver ornaments. The red head-covering worn by Dzao women is called a *hong*, and is usually made up of at least seven layers of cotton scarves.

There are many recurring motifs in Dzao embroidery and many are associated with nature, from gibbon hands or cabbages to thunder deities. Like all cultures, Dzao culture is dynamic and ever-changing. Women 'borrow' or copy motifs from other tribal groups and incorporate them with their own; H'mong flower motifs are common. It may not be long before Western images, such as backpacks and hiking boots, turn up on traditional clothing.

Source: A Yao Community in Sapa, Vietnam
by Vo Mai Phuong & Claire Burkert, 2001.

(Royal Hotel; ☎ 871 313), and **Chapa Restaurant** (☎ 871 245). If you organise the climb through a local operator, you'll find yourself paying an all-inclusive rate of around US$60 per person for a couple, US$50 per person for a group of four and US$45 per person for the sensible maximum group size of six.

Weather-wise the best time for making the ascent is from mid-October to mid-December, and again in March, when wild-flowers are in bloom.

TRAM TON PASS

The road between Sapa and Lai Chau crosses the Tram Ton Pass on the northern side of Fansipan, 15km from Sapa. At 1900m this is the highest mountain pass in Vietnam. On the Sapa side of the mountain the weather is often cold, foggy and generally nasty. Drop down a few hundred metres below the pass on the Lai Chau side and it will often be sunny and warm. Ferocious winds come ripping over the pass, which is not surprising given the temperature differences – Sapa is the coldest place in Vietnam while Lai Chau is the warmest. Tram Ton Pass is the dividing line between two great weather fronts – who says you can't see air?

Alongside the road, about 5km towards Sapa, is **Thac Bac**, the Silver Waterfall. With a height of 100m, it's a big one, and the **loop track** (admission 3000d) is steep and spectacular.

Sleeping

Accommodation will be pre-arranged for travellers on a tour booked through a café or travel agency in Hanoi. However, self-propelled travellers need to know that prices can fluctuate wildly according to the volume of tourist traffic. On weekends prices can skyrocket to at least double that of the week. Look around and negotiate. Needless to say, it's wise to avoid the weekend rush.

Beware of hotels using old-style charcoal burners for heat – the fumes can cause severe breathing problems if the room's not well ventilated. Many hotels now offer electric heaters instead, or open fireplaces during the winter.

There are now dozens of accommodation options, from a solid string of cheap guesthouses to a luxury resort. The hotels named here generally offer rooms and/or balconies with views – the scenery is, after all, one of the main reasons for visiting Sapa. However, be aware that the building boom can wipe out a view overnight; always check the view before you rent the room. It is a real shame the local government hasn't done more to impose height restrictions on the valley edge.

This is not an exhaustive list: there are *plenty* of other hotels in town that are also good value, especially along the main street, but they lack the scenic setting.

BUDGET

Auberge Hotel (☎ 871 243; auberge@sapadiscovery .com; Pho Cau May; r US$6-28; 🖳) The Auberge is a Sapa institution notable for its valley views and bonsai garden. Some upper-floor rooms have fireplaces and fine furnishings; cheaper rooms are in an older section of the hotel that lost their mountain views during the building boom. It's a good place to find travel and trekking information. Credit cards are accepted.

Queen Hotel (☎ 871 301; fax 871 783; Pho Cau May; r US$4-12) Next door to the Auberge, this hotel has friendly, fun staff to keep you entertained. Size matters when it comes to price, but all rooms have hot water and TV; some have fireplaces. Aim high for views.

Westward Hotel (☎ 871 481; Đ Muong Hoa; r US$6) This is the real deal for those venturing to the edge of town. Spick and span rooms with hot water and uninterrupted views are well worth the money.

Luong Thuy Guesthouse (☎ 871 446; Đ Muong Hoa; r 70,000đ) Almost next door to the Westward, this is another bargain with small rooms, but big views from the balconies.

Mountain View Hotel (☎ 871 334; fax 871 690; r US$6-15) A friendly little place occupying a prime corner of town. Owner Mrs Hong speaks fluent English, and was one of the first female trekking guides in Sapa. Pay the US$15 for doubly dramatic views from corner rooms, or US$12 for a basic balcony room with hot water and TV.

Other good possibilities:

Lotus Hotel (☎ 871 308; 5 Đ Muong Hoa; r US$4-8) Cracking value at these prices, rooms have hot water, TV and a fireplace.

Tulip Guest House (☎ 871 914; Pho Cau May; r 90,000-180,000đ) Small, simple, clean and boasts some terrific views.

MID-RANGE

Cat Cat Hotel (☎ 871387; catcatht@hn.vnn.vn; Pho Cat Cat; r US$7-30) This sprawling place is a multilevel maze that gets top marks for its sweeping views from the terraces and upper rooms. The new wing across the road has cheaper rooms, while those way above reception with all the trimmings demand more dollars. Pack your climbing gear, it's a long haul up.

Royal Hotel (☎ 871 313; royalhotel_sapa@yahoo .com; Pho Cau May; r US$12-20) Occupying a good location, there are only a few rooftops obscuring the view from the more expensive rooms at this smart place. The rooms are in good shape, and the long-standing Friendly Cafe, a good source for trekking information, has relocated here.

Chau Long Hotel (☎ 871 245; www.chaulonghotel .com; 24 Dong Loi; r US$32-65), Looking more like a castle than a hotel, it has the high standards you would expect for the price, including fine furnishings. The location was magnificent, but it is now necessary to head to the highest floors to get the views as new guesthouses crowd it in.

Bamboo Sapa Hotel (☎ 871 076; bamboosapa@hn .vnn.vn; Pho Cau May; r US$30-55) There are really two parts to this hotel. This part is a smart three-star option with large, airy rooms and breezy balconies with extensive views.

Green Bamboo Hotel (r US$15-20) Part two of the Bamboo Sapa, this is the old wing and is set in one of the finest French villas in town. Rooms are basic for the price, so it's crying out for a tasteful renovation.

Baguette & Chocolat (☎ 871 766; hoasuaschool sp@hn.vnn.vn; Đ Thac Bac; r US$14) A tiny four-bedroom offshoot of the popular bakery to help disadvantaged youth, the elegant little rooms with nice touches are popular enough to make bookings essential. Rates include a great breakfast downstairs.

Other places with potential:

Sapa Goldsea Hotel (☎ 871 869; sapagoldsea@hn .vnn.vn; Pho Cat Cat; r US$15-65) A brand new place on the road to Cat Cat offering comfortable, rather than cosy, rooms.

Darling Hotel (☎ 871 349; fax 871 963; Đ Thac Bac; r US$10-70) A long-running place with some decorative flair for those budgeting around the US$20 mark.

TOP END

Victoria Sapa Hotel (☎ 871 522; www.victoria hotels-asia.com; r from US$115; 🍴 🖳 🌊) This is a delightful place to rest your weary head. Located on its own commanding hillock, Victoria Sapa has it all – tastefully decorated rooms, sweeping views from the restaurant, two bars, a heated indoor swimming pool, a fitness centre and a tennis court. Consider booking one of its many two- or three-day discount deals for a real steal. As part of these packages, hotel guests can travel between Hanoi and Lao Cai in the resort's *Victoria Express*, the luxurious, private train carriages, a la Orient Express, attached to the regular train. Return berths start from US$90, or US$145 for deluxe twin share.

Eating

Most of the busier hotels have reasonably priced cafés, which get more popular as the weather worsens! There's a string of popular restaurants worth checking out below the market as you head in the direction of Cat Cat village.

Auberge Hotel (Pho Cau May; meals 10,000-30,000d) The hotel's popular terrace restaurant has affordable prices and some vegetarian dishes.

Mimosa Restaurant (☎ 871 377; Pho Cau May; mains 15,000-30,000d) Above the main drag, this family-run eatery has a terrace and serves good and reasonably-priced barbecue beef, wild boar and venison, as well as pasta, salad and a variety of Vietnamese dishes.

Gerbera Restaurant (☎ 871 064; Pho Cau May; mains from 20,000d) Located close to Mimosa, this restaurant has a similar range of dishes and amenities. There are some great views over town from the upstairs panorama room.

Chapa Restaurant (☎ 871 045; 40 Pho Cau May; mains around 20,000d) A true travellers' café, this small spot serves up a steady diet of banana pancakes and spring rolls. Peek in the front door and the place may appear full, but there are more tables upstairs.

Gecko (☎ 871 504; Đ Ham Rong; mains around US$5) A fine French-run restaurant where you can sip espressos, pick up picnic lunches or treat yourself to a sumptuous set menu. The bar is a good gathering place if you've had enough of the main strip.

Delta Restaurant (☎ 871 799; Pho Cau May; mains US$5) This was Sapa's first (and still the town's only) predominantly Italian restaurant. It turns out good pizzas and pastas, but at higher, Hanoi, prices.

Baguette & Chocolat (Đ Thac Bac; cakes 6000-15,000d) Definitely a very blissful retreat on a chilly day; tuck into a hot chocolate and the finest pastries in town. Picnics and light meals are also available.

Drinking

Considering the number of travellers to Sapa, organised entertainment is relatively scarce and the bar scene slow. For most, an evening out is the guesthouse balcony, particularly if the fog rolls in.

Bamboo Bar (Green Bamboo Hotel; Pho Cau May) The first Western-style watering hole to open in Sapa and it's still going strong in the basement of a grand building.

Bamboo Sapa (Pho Cau May) Next door to the Bamboo Bar, there's a free traditional hill-tribe music-and-dance show here from 8.30pm Friday and Saturday.

Red Dragon Pub (☎ 872 085; 23 Pho Muong Hoa) Downstairs is a tiny little tearoom; upstairs a British pub. They knock out a serious range of beers, as any good pub should, including ginseng flavour.

Tau Bar (☎ 871 322; 42 Pho Cau May) Claiming to be 'slightly lounge', Tau brings a different kind of cool to the mountains of the north. A lengthy bar to lean on, great tunes and a pool table suggest this place will prosper.

Victoria Sapa Hotel (☎ 871 522) Offers two bars or a terrace for a sundowner in style. Drinks cost more than elsewhere in town, but the ambience is alluring on a cold night.

Getting There & Away
BUS, MINIBUS & MOTORBIKE

Sapa's proximity to the border region makes it a possible first or last stop for travellers crossing between Vietnam and China.

The gateway to Sapa is Lao Cai, 38km away on the Chinese border. Buses to points west such as Lai Chau and Dien Bien Phu come through once or twice a day from Lao Cai, the main bus hub.

Minibuses make the trip from Lao Cai regularly between 5am and 5pm (10,000d, one to two hours depending on roadworks). In Sapa minibuses wait in front of the church but do not run on any particular schedule. However, in Lao Cai minibuses wait for the train that arrives from Hanoi and charge a tourist price of 25,000d.

The advertised hotel minibus services to Bac Ha (110km) for the Sunday market is around US$10 per person; departure from Sapa is at 6am and from Bac Ha at 1pm. It's cheaper to go to Bac Ha by public minibus and change buses in Lao Cai.

Driving a motorbike from Hanoi to Sapa is feasible, but it's a very long trip, so start early. The total distance between Hanoi and Sapa is 380km. The last 38km are straight uphill – unless you've been training for the Olympics, it's hell on a bicycle.

Cafés in Hanoi offer weekend trips to Sapa for around US$40, usually combining train and minibus transport, for those who are willing to sacrifice independence for convenience. See Travel Agencies in the Hanoi chapter (p79) for more information.

TRAIN

The train trip between Lao Cai (gateway station to Sapa) and Hanoi has become much more comfortable with the advent of a soft-sleeper class. At the moment, a sleeper ticket between Hanoi and Sapa can be booked only through hotels and agencies in Sapa, but in Hanoi you can book at the station. There is an official **Railway Booking Office** (☎ 871 480; 7.30-11am & 1.30-4pm) on Pho Cau May which charges a 7000d service fee.

Ticket prices start at 65,000d for a hard seat (bad choice!) to around 169,000d for an air-conditioned soft sleeper, and rise by about 10% at weekends. There are now two private companies, Tulico and Ratraco, operating special carriages with comfortable sleepers.

The day train (LC4) leaves Lao Cai at 10.20am, while the night trains leave at 7pm (LC2) and 8.50pm (SP2). The journey takes about 10 hours. From Hanoi the all-stations day train (LC3) departs at 6.15am and the night trains at 9.30pm (SP1) and 10.10pm (LC1).

Getting Around

The best way to get around Sapa is to walk, and almost everywhere it's steep! For excursions further out you can hire a self-drive motorbike for about US$6 a day, or take one with a driver for about US$10.

LAO CAI

☎ 020 / pop 35,100 / elevation 650m

Lao Cai, the end of the line so to speak, is right on the Vietnam-China border. The town was razed in the Chinese invasion of 1979, so most of its buildings are new. The border crossing here slammed shut during the 1979 war and only reopened in 1993.

Today Lao Cai is a major destination for travellers journeying between Hanoi or Sapa and Kunming in China, but Lao Cai is no place to linger.

Orientation & Information

The border town on the Chinese side is called Hekou – you would have to be an enthusiast of Chinese border towns to want to hang out there.

MONEY

Be wary of black marketeers, especially on the Chinese side – they frequently short-change

tourists. If you do black-market dealings, it's best to change only small amounts.

Directly across the bridge on the west bank of the river, the **BIDV Bank** (Đ Thuy Hoa) can exchange cash and travellers cheques, and also has an ATM... there are no ATMs in Sapa yet!

Sleeping & Eating

Gia Nga Guest House (☎ 830 459; Pho Moi; r 80,000-120,000d;) A typical tall, thin tower, this place has very clean rooms. The enthusiastic owner, who doesn't speak a word of English, has sensibly set aside a shower (15,000d with towel and soap) and luggage room behind reception, for freshening up after the night train.

BORDER CROSSING

The Lao Cai–Hekou crossing is popular with travellers making their way between Yunnan and northern Vietnam. The border is open daily between 7am and 5pm. China is separated from Vietnam by a road bridge and a separate rail bridge over the Red River. Pedestrians pay a toll of 3000d to cross.

The border is about 3km from Lao Cai train station. This journey is easily done on a motorbike (5000d).

Thuy Hoa Guesthouse (☎ 826 805; fax 824 689; 118 Đ Thuy Hoa; r 170,000; ☒) Looking across the Red River to China, this is a smart little establishment and rooms come with hot water, TV and IDD telephone.

Lao Cai International Resort (☎ 826 668; 88 Đ Thuy Hoa; laocaihotel@hn.vnn.vn; r US$70-85; ☒ ☒) Claims to be the 'ultimate choice', although not if you travel the 38km uphill to the Victoria Sapa. High standards, with a casino, and they accept Chinese currency.

Nhat Linh Restaurant (☎ 835 346; Pho Nguyen Hué) This spot is a hugely popular little travellers' café outside Lao Cai station. Fun-loving staff and a cheap, eclectic menu make this a good stop before or after a long train ride.

Viet Hoa Restaurant (☎ 830 082; Đ Phan Dinh Phung; mains from 25,000d) This big, brash Vietnamese place relocated, as the old incarnation was bulldozed for border redevelopment. As well as weddings, they accept 'merry making party'. Good Vietnamese grub.

Getting There & Away
Minibuses to Sapa (10,000d) leave regularly until mid-afternoon. The tourist bus from the train station charges 25,000d. Minibuses to Bac Ha (20,000d, two hours) leave twice daily; the last at 1pm.

Lao Cai is 340km from Hanoi. Buses make the run (53,000d, 10 hours), leaving at 4am and 5am from the **long distance bus station** (Pho Nguyen Hué), but most travellers prefer the train. See Getting There & Away under Sapa (p167) for details on train travel between Hanoi and Lao Cai.

BAC HA
☎ 020 / pop 70,200 / elevation 700m
In the last few years this small highland town has emerged as a weekend alterna-

tive to Sapa. Compared with Sapa, tourism is still on a small scale here and during the week the town has a deserted feel. But things haven't stood still – new hotels are under construction and restaurants have mastered banana pancakes.

Long slowing down the tourist boom in Bac Ha were two sets of loudspeakers, which used to relay the clamorous and crackly Voice of Vietnam from 5am to 6am and again from 6pm to 7pm every day. Thankfully these appeared to have been given the red card on our last visit, but it doesn't hurt to have a pair of earplugs handy just in case.

The highlands around Bac Ha are about 900m above sea level, making it noticeably warmer than Sapa. There are 10 Montagnard groups that live around Bac Ha: the colourful Flower H'mong are the most visible, but other groups include Dzao, Giay (Nhang), Han (Hoa), Xa Fang, Lachi, Nung, Phula, Thai and Thulao.

One of Bac Ha's main industries is the manufacture of alcoholic brews (rice wine, cassava wine and corn liquor). The corn stuff

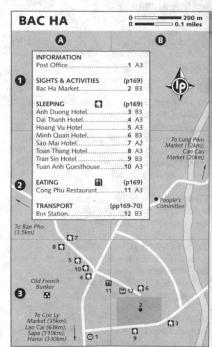

produced by the Flower H'mong is so potent it can ignite! Bac Ha is the only place in Vietnam where you'll find this particular ferment; there's an entire area devoted to it at the Sunday market. Swill some down before deciding whether to buy a buffalo or cow.

Sights & Activities
MONTAGNARD MARKETS
There are several interesting markets in and around Bac Ha, most within 20km of each other.

Bac Ha Market
This lively and crowded concrete bazaar is the main market in Bac Ha proper. You'll see plenty of Flower H'mong – so-named because the women embroider elaborate floral motifs on their skirts. Items on sale include water buffaloes, pigs, horses, dogs and chickens: a forlorn bunch as they seem to know what is coming. Tourists, however, stick to buying handicrafts, textiles and the local firewater. The market operates on Sunday. Get here early to experience it without the razzamatazz of day-trippers from Sapa.

Can Cau Market
This is one of the most fascinating open-air markets in the region, specialising in livestock. It's 20km north of Bac Ha and just 9km south of the Chinese border. Can Cau attracts a large number of Chinese traders, evidenced by the booming dog trade here. The market is only open on Saturday.

Lung Phin Market
This small market is between Can Cau market and Bac Ha town, about 12km from the town. It's less busy than other markets, and is open on Sunday. It is a good place to move onto once the tour buses arrive in Bac Ha from Sapa, and has a very real feel.

Coc Ly Market
This Tuesday market is about 35km from Bac Ha. You can get here via a fairly good road, or by road and river; hotels in Sapa and Bac Ha can organise trips.

TREKKING TO LOCAL VILLAGES
Villages around Bac Ha provide a good opportunity to see how Montagnard people live. **Ban Pho** is nearest, and the villagers live simply. The Flower H'mong villagers are extremely hospitable and some of the kindest people you'll meet in Vietnam. Ban Pho is a 7km return trip from Bac Ha. Take a loop route to get there and back.

Other nearby villages include: **Trieu Cai**, an 8km return walk; **Na Ang**, a 6km return walk; and **Na Hoi**, a 4km return walk. Ask at your hotel for directions.

Sleeping & Eating
Room rates tend to increase on weekends when tourists flock to town for the Sunday market; it can be hard to find a room.

Sao Mai Hotel (☎ /fax 880 288; r US$10-25) The beds of choice with tour groups, as this hotel offers the smartest rooms in town. The cheaper rooms in the older concrete building are poor value compared with elsewhere, but things smarten considerably in the newer wooden houses. There is also a popular restaurant-bar here, where they hold occasional dance shows for visiting groups.

Toan Thang Hotel (☎ 880 444; r 80,000d) Right opposite the Sao Mai, this place offers much better value for money at the budget end for rooms set in a solid wooden house.

Dai Thanh Hotel (☎ 880 448; r 60,000d) The place to help your dong last long, without compromising comfort, as rooms have hot water, TV, mozzie net and ceiling fan.

Hoang Vu Hotel (☎ 880 264; r 120,000d) This hotel has large rooms with balconies, although the view of the town is not outstanding. Hot water and TV are standard, and good tour information is available.

Minh Quan Hotel (☎ 880 222; r 120,000-150,000d) A good hotel offering a bird's eye view of Bac Ha market and the mountains beyond.

Other options:

Anh Duong Hotel (☎ 880 329; r 80,000d) Clean and quiet; good price, good place.

Tran Sin Hotel (☎ 880 240; r 100,000d) Overlooking the market, get a balcony to catch the action.

Tuan Anh Guesthouse (☎ 880 377; r 120,000d) No-frills family-run place, but fine for the price.

Other than the hotel restaurants, the best place for a feed is **Cong Phu Restaurant** (☎ 880 254; mains 15,000-25,000d) with tasty, low-priced meals on large photocopied English menus; just tick the boxes!

Getting There & Away
Minibuses depart from Lao Cai for Bac Ha (20,000d, two hours) around 6.30am and

NORTHWEST VIETNAM

1pm daily. Buses from Bac Ha leave for Lao Cai around 5.30am, 11.30am and 1pm. The road is well maintained and the rural scenery gorgeous.

Locals on motorbikes will do the Lao Cai–Bac Ha run for about US$5, or even Sapa–Bac Ha (110km) for US$12. Sunday minibus tours from Sapa to Bac Ha cost around US$10, including transport, guide and trekking to a minority village. On the way back to Sapa you can bail out in Lao Cai and catch the night train back to Hanoi.

Bac Ha is about 330km (10 hours) from Hanoi. Some cafés in Hanoi offer four-day bus trips to Bac Ha for around US$60, usually with a visit to Sapa included.

HA GIANG PROVINCE

Ha Giang is the final frontier in northern Vietnam, a lunar landscape of limestone pinnacles and granite outcrops. The far north of the province has some of the most spectacular scenery in all of Vietnam and the road trip between Dong Van and Meo Vac is a mind-blower for motorbikers, but not much fun on public buses. It should be one of the most popular destinations in this region, but is one of those rare provinces that still requires travel permits and the bureaucratic bullshit here keeps most at bay.

Ha Giang

☎ 019

Ha Giang is somewhere to recharge the batteries on the long road north. The scenery is a good taste of things to come, with limestone outcrops looming large over the town. Those heading further north to explore the districts of Yen Minh, Dong Van, Meo Van and Bac Me need to arrange a permit (per person US$10) with the local police.

SLEEPING & EATING

There are some great value hotels in Ha Giang: because there are few foreigners, foreigner pricing doesn't seem to exist.

Sao Mai Hotel (☎ 863 019; Pho Nguyen Trai; r US$10) One of the first places when approaching on the road from Hanoi, this is probably the best value in town. Enjoy the hot water, TV and comfortable beds. There's karaoke at all hours, though.

Hai Dang Hotel (☎ 866 863; 15 Pho Nguyen Trai; r 100,000d) A good value cheapie right opposite the bus station. Normally this could be a negative, but for those making the road trip north, the buses pull out very early so convenience is king.

Huy Hoan Hotel (☎ 861 288; 14 Pho Nguyen Trai; r 100,000-250,000d) The smartest place in town with slick rooms, big beds and a lift, not something you'd expect in these parts.

Thanh Thu Restaurant (Pho Tran Hung Dao) One of the best eateries in town, it's run by a friendly family who really look after diners. Bring a Vietnamese phrasebook, as there is no English menu.

GETTING THERE & AWAY

Ha Giang is 290km north of Hanoi on Hwy 2 and buses take about six hours to cover the distance. It is also possible to get here from Bac Ha, but the tough road is only for the strongest 4WD or very experienced bikers.

Around Ha Giang

It's all about the motorbike trip north to the districts of **Dong Van** and **Meo Vac**, nestled against the border with China. Leaving Ha Giang town, the road climbs over the Quan Ba Pass (Heaven's Gate) and the wow factor just keeps on growing. Dropping into Yen Minh through pine forests, it is worth stopping for a drink before the final leg into the surreal scenery near China. Dong Van is just a small, dusty outpost, but don't be disappointed as it is the gateway to the best road trip in Vietnam, the 22km that snakes its way along the mountainside to Meo Vac. The road has been cut into the side of a cliff face and far below are the distant waters of the Nho Que River and, towering above, the rock face of this mighty gorge. Take your time and soak it up, as this journey is one to savour.

Meo Vac is a district capital hemmed in by mountains and, like many towns in the northwest, it is steadily being settled by Vietnamese from elsewhere. There are several small faceless guesthouses in town, charging 60,000d for a basic room with shared bathroom. Best is the **Viet Hung Guesthouse** (r 60,000d) with comfy beds and a TV, located on the road to Khau Vai district. You need to show your travel permit when checking in at any guesthouse. There are a couple of *com pho* places around town, plus the market has some food stalls.

North-Central Vietnam

NORTH-CENTRAL VIETNAM

Often overlooked by tourists treading the trail, north-central Vietnam offers a handful of worthy sites just a couple of hours from Hanoi. Some visitors do the hit-and-run on a day trip, but for a fuller flavour it is better to make an overnight journey from the capital. Tam Coc is an area of extraordinary beauty, where limestone pinnacles rise from the heart of the rice paddies, while nearby the ancient capital of Hoa Lu is impressively atmospheric. The floating village of Kenh Ga gives a glimpse of life on the water, and the cathedral at Phat Diem brings European and Vietnamese religious architecture together in a unique blend. Cuc Phuong National Park offers the opportunity to get close to nature at its best. And the good news is that all these teasers are a short distance from Ninh Binh, itself less than 100km south of Hanoi.

The north-central region remains one of the poorest areas of Vietnam and is still the least visited by foreign tourists. Most travellers make a beeline between Hué and Hanoi, choosing to spend more time in places like Hoi An. Fair enough if you are racing against time, but for those who are taking it slowly but surely through the country, the attractions here have the added appeal of far fewer tourists than the more popular spots to the north and south.

The coastal highway is heaving with traffic and the beaches of north-central Vietnam, though popular with domestic tourists, pale in comparison to those further south. What better excuse for a spot of adventure than the new Ho Chi Minh Rd, Hwy 14, which runs along the spine of the country, traversing some wild and beautiful stretches of the Truong Son Mountains in north-central Vietnam? Motorbikers or fit cyclists will love the stunning section north of the Phong Nha Cave, but remember that little traffic means little in the way of facilities.

NORTH-CENTRAL VIETNAM

HIGHLIGHTS

- Paddle about **Tam Coc** (p175), the hauntingly beautiful 'Halong Bay on the rice fields'
- Go bananas at the Endangered Primate Rescue Centre at **Cuc Phuong National Park** (p177)
- Temple hop amid the atmospheric ruins of the ancient capital of **Hoa Lu** (p176)
- Check out the funky fusion architecture of the Sino-Vietnamese **Phat Diem Cathedral** (p177)
- Go underground at the mighty **Phong Nha Cave** (p185), a World Heritage–site grotto at Son Trach village

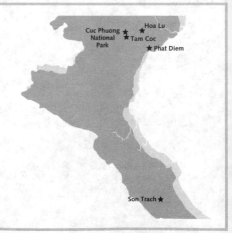

JULIET COOMBE

Boaters passing the Tam Coc caves (p175)

MATT DARBY

Temple, Ninh Binh (p176)

CRAIG PERSHOUSE

Farmer in rice paddy,
Ninh Binh (p174)

Rice fields, Hoa Lu (p176)

THOMAS DOWNS

JULIET COOMBE

Hang Nga Gallery & Guesthouse (p293), Dalat

K

Traditional Bahnar thatched-roof house, Kon Tum village (p316)

JOHN BANAGAN

Silk worms; silk production is a major industry in Bao Loc (p305)

Central highlands (p288)

MARK ANDF

History

The region has more historical importance than it might appear at first glance. One of Vietnam's earliest capitals was at Hoa Lu, where magnificent temples are strategically set amid a dramatic landscape of limestone cliffs and rice paddies.

In the 13th and 14th centuries, Tran dynasty kings ruled from the capital of Thang Long (present-day Hanoi). This was the only period in Vietnamese history when the heirs to the throne partially succeeded their fathers, taking the official role of king, while the older generation shared power in a second unofficial capital in Tuc Mac, about 5km from Nam Dinh. This prevented the traditional practice of feuding brothers killing each other off for the throne, making the Tran dynasty one of the most politically stable and prosperous periods in Vietnamese history.

During the American War, north-central Vietnam suffered great damage from US bombing, notably in Thanh Hoa. Further south, Vinh marked the start of the Ho Chi Minh Trail, as supplies passed through the docks on the way inland to the Truong Son Mountains.

THAI BINH

☎ 036 / pop 135,000

Few travellers taste Thai Binh, because it is not on Hwy 1A. People really only pass through when travelling on the spur route

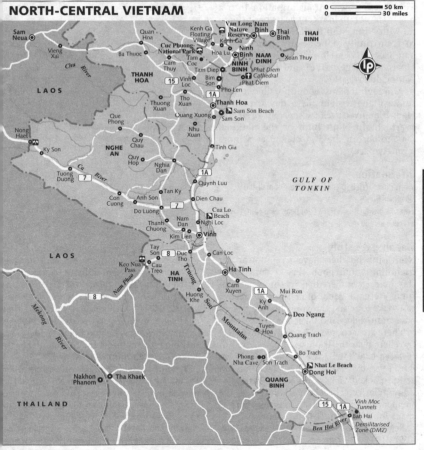

NORTH-CENTRAL VIETNAM

that connects Ninh Binh and Hai Phong. The only sight of interest around here is nearby **Keo Pagoda**.

Founded in the 12th century, Keo Pagoda was built to honour Buddha and the monk Khong Minh Khong, who miraculously cured Emperor Ly Thanh Ton (r 1128–38) of leprosy. The finely carved wooden bell tower is considered a masterpiece of traditional Vietnamese architecture. The nearby dike is a good place to get a general view of the pagoda complex.

Keo Pagoda is in Thai Binh province, 9.5km from Thai Binh. Take a motorbike taxi (10,000d) from Thai Binh to the pagoda.

NINH BINH
☎ 030 / pop 53,000

This sleepy town's transformation into a major travel hub in recent years has little to do with Ninh Binh itself. Rather, it is due to its proximity to the nearby attractions of Tam Coc (p175), Hoa Lu (p176), Kenh Ga Floating Village (p176) and Cuc Phuong National Park (p177).

Although it is just about possible to visit some of these sights as a day trip from Hanoi, many travellers sensibly prefer to overnight in Ninh Binh or the national park to absorb the atmosphere at a more leisurely pace.

Information
Main Post Office (Đ Tran Hung Dao) For mail and telephone fixes.
Vietcombank (Đ Tran Hung Dao) Deals with cash, travellers cheques and most plastic.

Sleeping & Eating
Ninh Binh hoteliers have a reputation for friendliness and good service, making a stay here smoother than in some parts of rural Vietnam. Most offer Internet access, can make tour and transport bookings, and have motorbikes and bikes for hire.

There are a couple of bargains for budget travellers near the train station.

Queen Mini-Hotel (☎ 871 874; 3 Đ Hoang Hoa Tham; r from US$3-15; ☒) This place has an action-packed visitors book that attests to its popularity. The cheaper the price, the smaller the room, but as long as there is space for a bed, who's complaining?

New Guesthouse (☎ 872 137; 3 Đ Hoang Hoa Tham; r US$3-15; ☒) A few strides closer to the station

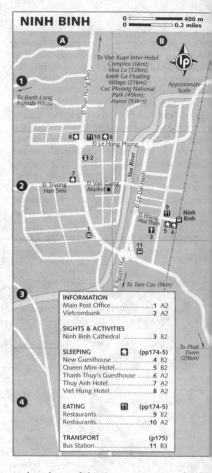

NINH BINH

INFORMATION
Main Post Office.....................1 A2
Vietcombank..........................2 A2

SIGHTS & ACTIVITIES
Ninh Binh Cathedral 3 B2

SLEEPING ☐ (pp174-5)
New Guesthouse......................4 B2
Queen Mini-Hotel....................5 B2
Thanh Thuy's Guesthouse 6 A2
Thuy Anh Hotel.......................7 A2
Viet Hung Hotel......................8 A2

EATING ☐ (pp174-5)
Restaurants............................9 B2
Restaurants............................10 A2

TRANSPORT (p175)
Bus Station...........................11 B3

is this clone of the Queen Mini-Hotel. The more expensive rooms come with four or more beds, so are good if you have a posse.

Thanh Thuy's Guesthouse (☎ 871 811; tuc@hn .vnn.vn; 128 Đ Le Hong Phong; old wing US$3-6, new wing US$8-15; ☒ ☐) Another popular spot that has been reinvesting its profits. The cheapies in the old wing are a good deal, while those seeking more comfort can head to the back. There's a restaurant downstairs.

Viet Hung Hotel (☎ 872 002; viethunghotel.nb@hn .vnn.vn; 2 Đ Tran Hung Dao; r US$10-35; ☒) One of the newest hotels in town, located on the main drag, it's clean, bright and good value with rates including breakfast.

Thuy Anh Hotel (☎ 871 602; www.thuyanhhotel .com; 55A Đ Truong Han Sieu; old wing US$7-25, new wing

US$35-40; ⚭ 🖳) This is the smartest operation in town. The old wing offers spotless rooms of varying shapes and sizes, while the slick new wing, complete with lift, pulls in the tour groups. Good restaurant downstairs and a rooftop bar for drinkers.

Out of town, **Van Xuan Inter-Hotel Complex** (☎ 622 615; fax 622 616; r US$25-35; ⚭) is a slightly surreal, suburban place that is quieter than places in town. Wearing an air of torpor, the rooms are cavernous. It's on the road to Hoa Lu, so best for those with transport.

Ninh Binh is not exactly the gastronomic heart of Vietnam, so most people end up eating at their guesthouse or hotel. There are a couple of clusters of *com pho* restaurants, one on the corner of Ð Le Hong Phong and Ð Tran Hung Dao, and the other near the railway station.

Getting There & Away
BUS
The bus station in Ninh Binh is located across the Van River from the post office. Regular public buses (25,000d, two hours) leave from the Giap Bat bus station in Hanoi. Ninh Binh is 93km south of Hanoi.

Ninh Binh is also a hub on the north–south open-tour bus route (p478), which drops off and picks up passengers at some of the hotels (eg Thuy Anh Hotel and Thanh Thuy's Guesthouse). Seats on the smarter buses running to/from the Old Quarter in Hanoi cost US$3.

TRAIN
Ninh Binh is a scheduled stop for the *Reunification Express* trains travelling between Ho Chi Minh City (HCMC) and Hanoi, but only the slow services stop here (p482).

AROUND NINH BINH
Tam Coc
Poetically penned 'Halong Bay on the rice paddies', the area around Tam Coc boasts stunning scenery. While Halong Bay (p127) has huge rock formations jutting out of the sea, at Tam Coc they soar skywards from a sea of green. Travellers who have passed through China will notice a remarkable resemblance to those classic landscapes around Guilin and Yangshou.

The ideal way to see Tam Coc – which translates as 'Three Caves' – is by **rowboat** (per person incl entry fee 55,000d) on the Ngo Dong River.

It all looks a bit Disneyesque, like you're lining up for some 'Pirates of the South China Sea' ride, but don't be put off as the boats are rowed into the caves – a serene and scenic trip. Hang Ca, the first cave, is 127m long; Hang Giua, the second, is 70m long; and the third and smallest, Hang Cuoi, is only 40m. The boat trip to all three caves takes about two hours and tickets are sold at the small booking office by the new car park. Even on cloudy days, bring sunscreen and a hat or umbrella, as there's no shade in the boats. Umbrellas can be rented at the pier.

Bring a healthy dose of patience and good humour to Tam Coc. The prime problem is that boat owners are constantly pushing their embroidery and no doesn't seem to mean no to these good folk. There are also boat vendors who paddle alongside and try to sell drinks. Not thirsty? They will strongly 'suggest' that you buy a Coke for the person rowing your boat. Many travellers do this only to find that the oarsperson sells the Coke back to the drink vendors for half the price.

The area behind the Tam Coc restaurants is **Van Lan village**, which is famous for its embroidery. Here local artisans make napkins, tablecloths, pillowcases and T-shirts. A lot of these items wind up being sold on Hanoi's Pho Hang Gai (p108), but it is cheaper to buy them here directly from the artisan. The village has a much better selection and slightly lower prices than those available from the boat vendors.

BICH DONG PAGODA
This charming cave pagoda is just a couple of kilometres north of Tam Coc and worth a visit if you have your own wheels. The scenic road winds through rice fields hemmed in by karsts and ends in a dusty village. Bich Dong or 'Jade Grotto' is cut into the caves of a karst and is a holy site of pilgrimage for Vietnamese. The smoke of burning incense and the gloom of the caves give this place an earthy atmosphere.

GETTING THERE & AWAY
Tam Coc is 9km southwest of Ninh Binh. Follow Hwy 1 south and turn west at the Tam Coc turn-off (note that Hwy 1 is in the process of becoming Hwy 1A). Ninh Binh hotels run day tours, but it is more fun to make your own way by bicycle or motorbike. Hotel staff can also advise about some

beautiful back roads that link Tam Coc with Hoa Lu. Budget cafés in Hanoi book day trips to Tam Coc and Hoa Lu; the fast-food version goes for about US$12, but it's closer to US$20 with a smaller group, comfortable vehicle and professional guide.

Hoa Lu

The scenery here is similarly spectacular to Tam Coc and comes with an interesting historical twist. Hoa Lu was the capital of Vietnam during the Dinh (968–80) and early Le (980–1009) dynasties. The site was a smart choice for a capital city because of the natural protection afforded by the region's bizarre landscape.

The **ancient citadel of Hoa Lu** (admission 10,000d), most of which has been destroyed, covered an area of about 3 sq km. The outer ramparts encompassed temples, shrines and the king's palace. The royal family lived in the inner citadel.

Yen Ngua Mountain provides a scenic backdrop for Hoa Lu's two remaining temples. The first, **Dinh Tien Hoang**, was restored in the 17th century and is dedicated to the Dinh dynasty. Out the front is the stone pedestal of a royal throne; inside are bronze bells and a statue of Emperor Dinh Tien Hoang with his three sons. The second temple, **Le Dai Hanh** (or Duong Van Nga), commemorates the rulers of the early Le dynasty. Inside the main hall are an assortment of drums, gongs, incense burners, candle holders and weapons. On the hillside above the temples is the tomb of Dinh Tien Hoang. It's a good climb up 207 steps, but your efforts will be rewarded with great views.

In 1998, archaeologists unearthed a 'new' section of the old citadel, which was dated to the 10th century. This, and some associated artefacts, have been preserved on site and are on show in a display room built around them.

There are guides at the temples who work for free (don't forget to tip) or wander about alone. Once you've navigated the hassle of persistent sellers on the way in, it's very peaceful inside the complex, especially in the late afternoon when the crowds head back to Hanoi.

GETTING THERE & AWAY

Hoa Lu is 12km northwest of Ninh Binh; turn left 6km north of town on Hwy 1A.

There is no public transport, so most travellers get there by bicycle (US$1 per day from Ninh Binh), motorbike or car. Ask your hotel about the blissful back roads linking Hoa Lu to Tam Coc.

Kenh Ga Floating Village

The village of Kenh Ga (Chicken Canal) gets its name apparently from the number of wild chickens that used to live in the area. It's essentially a floating village on the Hoang Long River, with just a few permanent buildings on the riverbanks. About the only other place in Vietnam where you can see anything like this is in the Mekong Delta. On the other hand, nowhere in the Mekong Delta will you find a stunning mountain backdrop like the one at Kenh Ga. Another difference: people in Kenh Ga row boats with their feet, leaning back and watching the world go by.

It's a lovely area, and one of the best places in northern Vietnam to see river life. People here seem to spend most of their lives floating on water: at their floating fish-breeding pens, harvesting river grass to feed the fish, trawling in the muddy shallows for shellfish or selling veggies boat-to-boat. Even the children commute to school by boat.

From the pier you can hire a motorboat to take you for an hour or so touring around the village for 40,000d per person. The boat trips are organised through the local government tourism agency and, thankfully, they've managed to keep the operation relatively low-key and hassle-free. How much longer can it last?

The locals are very friendly. The children gleefully shout 'tay oi' (Westerner) at every tourist they see, even Vietnamese tourists!

GETTING THERE & AWAY

The Kenh Ga floating village is 21km from Ninh Binh on the road to Cuc Phuong National Park. Follow Hwy 1 north for 11km, then it's a 10km drive west to reach the boat pier. Hotels and guesthouses in Ninh Binh can arrange tours. There are some fantastic back roads through wonderful scenery, which also lead to the pier, but it's best to take a local guide from Ninh Binh to find them.

Van Long Nature Reserve

Set amid yet more of the limestone pinnacles that characterise this region, **Van**

Long (entry 20,000d) is a reedy wetland that draws the birds. The fee includes a punt through the shallow waters and with your eyes peeled, you just might see a Delacour's langur lurking in the outcrops. Van Long can be easily combined with a visit to Kenh Ga and, at a stretch, both can be visited en route to Cuc Phuong National Park.

Van Long is 2km east of Tran Me, a small town 23km from Ninh Binh along the road to Cuc Phuong.

PHAT DIEM

The Tay Ninh (p373) of the north, Phat Diem is the home of a celebrated **cathedral**, which is remarkable for its vast dimensions and superb Sino-Vietnamese architecture – with a dash of European dressing for good measure. During the French era, the cathedral was an important centre of Catholicism in the north and there was a seminary here. The 1954 division of Vietnam caused Catholics to flee south en masse and the cathedral was closed. It is now functional again and there are also several dozen other churches in the Phat Diem district. Current estimates suggest that there are about 120,000 Catholics in the area.

The vaulted ceiling is supported by massive wooden columns that are almost 1m in diameter and 10m tall. In the lateral naves, there are a number of curious wood and stone sculptures. The main altar is made of a single block of granite.

The cathedral complex comprises a number of buildings; the main one was completed in 1891. The whole project was founded by a Vietnamese priest named Six, whose tomb is in the square fronting the cathedral.

Behind the main building is a large pile of limestone boulders – Father Six piled them up to test whether the boggy ground would support his planned empire. Apparently the test was a success.

Opposite the main entrance at the back of the cathedral is the bell tower. At its base lie two enormous stone slabs, one atop the other. Their sole purpose was to provide a perch for the mandarins to sit and observe – no doubt with great amusement – the rituals of the Catholics at mass. All the big carved stones here were transported from some 200km away with only very rudimentary equipment.

Atop the cathedral's highest tower is such an enormous bell that Quasimodo's famous chimer at Paris' Notre Dame Cathedral pales significantly in comparison. This bell, and all the other heavy metal, was pushed and pulled to the cathedral's top via an enormous earth ramp. After construction was completed, the earth was used to raise the whole site about 1m higher than the surrounding terrain.

Near the main cathedral is a small chapel built of large carved stone blocks and inside it's as cool as a cave. Also not far from this cathedral is a covered bridge dating from the late 19th century.

Hordes of Vietnamese tourists come to this place. Few of them are Catholic, but many of them are extremely curious about churches and Christianity in general. Admission to the complex is free, but you may have to negotiate hordes of sellers and beggars at busy times. Daily mass is celebrated at 5am and 5pm.

Getting There & Away

Phat Diem, sometimes known by its former name, Kim Son, is 121km south of Hanoi and 29km southeast of Ninh Binh. There are direct buses from Ninh Binh to Phat Diem (one hour), or you can go by bicycle or motorbike.

There are no regular tours to Phat Diem, though any of the budget agents in Hanoi should be able to offer a customised day trip by private car, with or without a guide.

CUC PHUONG NATIONAL PARK

☎ 030 / elevation 648m

Established in 1962, **Cuc Phuong National Park** (☎ 846 006; admission adult/child 40,000/20,000d) is one of Vietnam's most important protected areas. Ho Chi Minh personally took time off from the war in 1963 to dedicate this, Vietnam's first national park. He offered a short dedication speech: 'Forest is gold. If we know how to conserve it well, it will be very precious. Destruction of the forest will lead to serious effects on both life and productivity.'

This national park is 70km from the coast and covers an area about 25km in length and 11km in width, spanning the provinces of Ninh Binh, Hoa Binh and Thanh Hoa. The elevation of the park's highest peak, Dinh May Bac (Silver Cloud Peak) is 648m.

NORTH-CENTRAL VIETNAM

ENDANGERED PRIMATE RESCUE CENTER

One of the highlights of a visit to Cuc Phuong is the **Endangered Primate Rescue Center** (www .primatecenter.org). The facility, run by German biologists and local Vietnamese, is a laudable endeavour to improve the wellbeing of Vietnam's primates.

What started out as a small-scale operation in 1995 with just a handful of animals has grown into a highly productive centre, where today about 85 creatures are cared for, studied and bred. There are around 14 species of gibbon and langur on site. The langur is a long-tailed, tree-dwelling monkey; the gibbon is a long-armed, fruit-eating ape. There are also lorises (smaller nocturnal primates) at the centre.

There are estimated to be only about 20 species of primate remaining in the wild in Vietnam, most of which are threatened by hunters and/or habitat destruction. Some people attempt to keep these animals as pets, which is almost impossible. Langurs survive exclusively on fresh-cut leaves and their digestive systems will not tolerate anything else. By feeding them incorrectly, people usually discover they've murdered their new 'pet' before they can even show it off to their friends. All the animals in the centre were rescued either from cages or from illegal traders, who transport them mostly to China to become medicinal ingredients. Such rare animals can fetch anywhere between US$200 and US$1000 from buyers looking to cash in on their 'medicinal worth', be it for gallstone relief or as an aphrodisiac.

In cooperation with the Vietnamese authorities, the centre has had some major recovery and breeding successes. When we visited, we saw a world-first: a week-old grey-shanked Douc langur, the first ever bred in captivity. (The proud new father did the protective male thing by sticking his neck out and frowning fiercely at observers while exposing his long, erect pink penis!) The red-shanked Douc langurs are breeding fantastically and are fascinating animals that look as though they are wearing red shorts (their Vietnamese name translates as 'monkeys wearing shorts'). It's a treat to be able to see these remarkable – and seriously cute – animals. Some southern species of langur at the centre even have heated sleeping quarters in winter, which is more than can be said for the human residents.

One of the larger aims of the centre is to re-introduce these primates into their natural habitat. Currently hunting pressures are still too high, but as a preliminary step, some gibbons and a group of Hatinh langurs have been released into a two-hectare, semi-wild area adjacent to the centre; and a group of Douc langurs are in a second, four-hectare, semi-wild enclosure. If you're keen to look for langurs in the wild, ask at the centre about the best places to spot them; for obvious reasons we won't publicise their possible locations here.

The stone tools of prehistoric humans have been discovered in Con Moong Cave, one of the park's many grottoes.

The park is home to the excellent **Endangered Primate Rescue Center** (www.primatecenter .org; admission free; ☺ 9-11am & 1-4pm) – see the boxed text above. The centre is located about 500m before the national park reception centre. You can't wander around the centre alone, so if you're travelling independently you need first to go to the national park reception area and arrange a guide. Entry is free, but you might consider purchasing some postcards or a poster, or making a donation.

Though wildlife has suffered a precipitous decline in Vietnam in recent decades, the park's 222 sq km of primary tropical forest remains home to an amazing variety of animal and plant life. There are 320 species of bird, 97 species of mammal including bats, and 36 species of reptile identified so far. Of the 1983 known plant species, 433 have medicinal properties and 299 are food sources. The park is also home to a species of tree called Cay Kim Gao – for aspiring horticulturists, the scientific name is *Podocarpus fleuryi hickel*. In ancient times, kings and mandarins would only eat with chopsticks made from this lumber – it was said that anything poisonous it touches turns the light-coloured wood to black! These chopsticks make a nice souvenir.

Poaching and habitat destruction are a constant headache for the park rangers. Many native species, such as the black bear, wild cats, birds and reptiles, have perished in the park as a result of human impact. Episodes of violence have erupted between the Muong and park rangers who have tried to stop logging in the park. The government has responded by relocating the villagers further from the park's boundary. Hopefully the park authorities will be able to create opportunities for local people to participate in the ecotourism ventures, thereby giving conservation an economic value that will benefit the environment. Ask at park headquarters about homestays with the minority people who inhabit the park.

Hwy 14, the new Ho Chi Minh Rd, bisects the park in the west and has led to increased illegal logging, which in turn is having a huge impact on the growth, movement and conservation of plants and animals.

The best time of year to visit the park is in the dry months from October to March. From April to June it becomes increasingly hot and wet, and from July to September the rains arrive, bringing ,lots of leeches. Visitors in April and May should be lucky enough to see literally millions of butterflies that breed here.

There is a low-key, informative **visitor centre** a few hundred metres before the park entrance, sponsored by the Australian government.

Hiking in Cuc Phuong

Excellent hiking opportunities abound in the park and you could spend several days trekking through the forest here.

Short walks include a large, enclosed **botanic garden** near the park headquarters where some native animals – deer, civets, gibbons and langurs – have been released. Another short trail leads to a steep stairway up to the archaeologically significant **Cave of Prehistoric Man**, where tools were found (now housed in Hanoi).

Popular day-trails include an 8km return walk to the massive, 1000-year-old **Big Tree** (*Tetrameles nudiflora*); and a longer hike to **Silver Cloud Peak**. There's also a strenuous five-hour hike to **Kanh**, a Muong village. You can overnight here and also raft on the Buoi River.

Park staff can provide you with basic maps to find the well-marked trail heads, but a guide is recommended for day trips and is mandatory for longer treks. A guide will cost a minimum of US$5 per day for up to five people, plus US$1 for each extra person.

Sleeping & Eating

There are two accommodation areas in the park, with a complicated range of prices and options.

The centre of the park, 18km from the gate, is the best place to be for an early morning walk or bird-watching. Here there are basic rooms in a **pillar house** (per person US$6), or a couple of self-contained **bungalows** (s/d US$15/25). There's also an enormous river-fed swimming pool.

At park headquarters, there are self-contained **bungalows & guesthouse rooms** (s/d US$15/20). There are also rooms in a **pillar house** (per person US$5). The smarter rooms at park headquarters are the new ones that have recently been constructed around an artificial lake just inside the park boundary. You can **camp** (per person US$2) at either location, but need to bring your own gear. **Meals** (10,000-25,000d) are available from reception, including a vegetarian option.

It can get very busy here at weekends and during Vietnamese school holidays; avoid these times if you are seeking a peaceful retreat! Reservations can be made by contacting the national park office.

Getting There & Away

Cuc Phuong National Park is 45km from Ninh Binh. The turn-off from Hwy 1 is north of Ninh Binh and follows the road that goes to Kenh Ga and Van Long Nature Reserve. There is no public transport all the way to the park.

THANH HOA
☎ 037

The eponymous capital of Thanh Hoa province has little to offer the visitor, except for a large and attractive **church** on the northern outskirts of town. Most people zoom through Thanh Hoa on the way to somewhere else.

Thanh Hoa province was the site of the Lam Son Uprising (1418–28), in which Vietnamese forces led by Le Loi (who later became Emperor Ly Thai To) expelled the Chinese and re-established the country's independence. Muong and Red Thai hill tribes live in the western part of the province.

Sleeping & Eating

Thanh Cong Hotel (☎ 710 224; fax 710 656; 29 Đ Trieu Quoc Dat; r US$17-27; 🕸) A swish new high-rise,

> **BORDER CROSSING: NAM CAN/NA MEO**
>
> Take a deep breath: this is an endurance test and a half. Catch a morning bus from Vinh to Muang Xen (29,000d, seven hours), which departs when full. Grab a motorbike for the 25km run to the border (50,000d) and get ready to wait around on the Lao side. Local transport on to Nong Haet is about 5000k if anything shows up. From Nong Haet, there are several buses a day on to Phonsavan (20,000k, four hours) starting from 7am sharp. It might also be possible to charter a private car from US$30. From Phonsavan, it is easy to connect to Luang Prabang or Vientiane.

its prominent sign is visible from Hwy 1A as you pass through town. Rooms come with all the gadgets, including large bathrooms with tubs.

Loi Linh Hotel (☎ 851 667; 22 Đ Tran Phu; r US$10; 🔀) This family-run hotel is rather oddly designed above a sort of massive entry hall. Rooms are small and dark but clean.

Soup shops, cafés and a few restaurants can be found along Hwy 1, in particular around the southern entrance to town.

Getting There & Away

Thanh Hoa is a stop for *Reunification Express* trains (p482). The city is 502km from Hué, 139km from Vinh and also 153km from Hanoi by road.

SAM SON BEACH
☎ 037

Vietnamese tourists love Sam Son for its pine forests, enormous granite boulders, sweeping views and long stretches of white sand. But love has its price and that is a concrete jungle of hotels, karaoke bars and massage parlours. It's not to everyone's taste, but could break the road trip between Ninh Binh and Vinh if you've got your own transport.

Sam Son was long the most popular beach resort in the north, but like Do Son and Cua Lo, it is losing local business to the slick south. It's too far from Hanoi for day-trippers, but during summer (May to September) the place is chock-a-block with weekenders escaping the oven-hot capital. During winter,

Sam Son is pretty much deserted and only a few hotels bother to stay open.

There are two **beaches** here, separated by a rocky headland. The main beach, which is beautiful out of season, is on the north side of the headland. The southern beach is mostly undeveloped, but can still fill up with picnickers.

Sleeping

Most of Sam Son's ugly state-run hotels offer luxury hotel prices without the luxury. Be aware that prices shoot up between June and August. It's possible to negotiate discounts in winter, though there's not much point visiting at that time with only the wind and rain for company.

Most hotels are state run but **Hoa Dang Hotel** (☎ 821 288; r low/high season 100,000/350,000d; 🔀) is a smaller private hotel. Don't expect too much for the price, but at least you can sit on the balcony overlooking the beach and escape the room.

There are wall-to-wall **hotels** (r US$10-50) along the beachfront.

Getting There & Away

Access to Sam Son is from the Thanh Hoa road and railway junction. It's only 16km to Sam Son, a short enough trip by motorbike.

VINH
☎ 038 / pop 205,000

Budding Marxists might like the lashings of Soviet-realist architecture here, but otherwise Vinh is an uninspiring place with just a few 'almost attractions' nearby, including Ho Chi Minh's birthplace Kim Lien and the beach resort of Cua Lo.

A port city, Vinh is the capital of Nghe An province. Recently its economic fortunes have been on the rise thanks to more traffic on Hwy 1A. For travellers, the town is a convenient place to stop for the night on the overland route between Hué and Hanoi. Vinh is also a transit town on the overland trail to/from Tha Khaek in Laos via the Cau Treo border crossing (p183), although not if you have opted for the 24-hour Hanoi–Vientiane bus from hell.

History

Vinh's more recent history has not been the happiest. It was a pleasant citadel city during its colonial days, but was destroyed

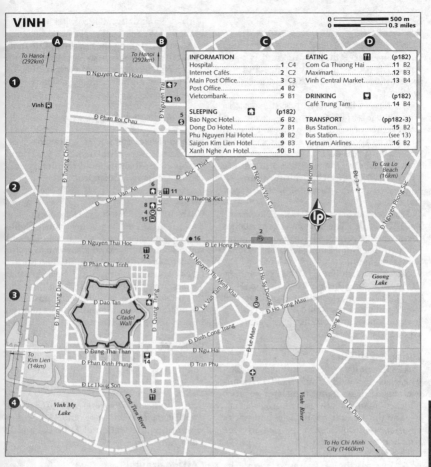

VINH

INFORMATION		EATING	🍴	(p182)
Hospital..........................1 C4		Com Ga Thuong Hai.......11 B2		
Internet Cafés.................2 C2		Maximart.........................12 B3		
Main Post Office.............3 C3		Vinh Central Market........13 B4		
Post Office.....................4 B2				
Vietcombank...................5 B1		DRINKING	🍷	(p182)
		Café Trung Tam..............14 B4		
SLEEPING	(p182)			
Bao Ngoc Hotel................6 B2		TRANSPORT	(pp182-3)	
Dong Do Hotel.................7 B1		Bus Station.....................15 B2		
Phu Nguyen Hai Hotel.......8 B2		Bus Station................(see 13)		
Saigon Kim Lien Hotel.......9 B3		Vietnam Airlines..............16 B2		
Xanh Nghe An Hotel........10 B1				

in the early 1950s as a result of French aerial bombing and the Viet Minh's scorched-earth policy. Later, a huge fire finished off anything that was left standing.

The Ho Chi Minh Trail began in Nghe An province, and many of the war supplies sent south were shipped via the port of Vinh. Not surprisingly, the US military obliterated the city in hundreds of air attacks and naval artillery bombardments from 1964 to 1972, which left only two buildings intact. The Americans paid a high price for the bombings – more US aircraft and pilots were shot down over Nghe An and Ha Tinh provinces than over any other part of North Vietnam. The heavy loss of planes and pilots was one reason why the USA

later brought in battleships to pound North Vietnam from offshore.

Orientation & Information

As Hwy 1 enters Vinh from the south, it crosses over the mouth of the Lam River (Ca River), also known as the Cua Hoi Estuary. Street address numbers are rarely used in Vinh.

There are several Internet cafés on Đ Le Hong Phong. For medical emergencies, head to the **hospital** (cnr Đ Tran Phu & Đ Le Mao). The **Vietcombank** (Đ 9 Nguyen Sy Sach) has an ATM and exchange services. There is a second ATM next to the Saigon Kim Lien Hotel. For postal services, visit the **Main post office** (Đ Nguyen Thi Minh Khai; ⏰ 6.30am-9pm).

Sleeping

Bao Ngoc Hotel (☎ 569 999; fax 585 097; 99 Đ Le Loi; r 120,000-160,000d; 🅰) This hotel delivers 'bed room airy, serve thought ful' and is great value. All rooms have TV, fridge and hot water, plus it has a lift to avoid a nightly workout.

Phu Nguyen Hai Hotel (☎ 848 429; ctpnh@hn .vnn.vn; 81 Đ Le Loi; r US$15-20; 🅰) As clean as it comes, the rooms here are big and bright. The pricier rooms are virtual suites and this adds up to a real deal.

Dong Do Hotel (☎ 846 989; 9 Đ Nguyen Trai; r 100,000-140,000d; 🅰) Uninspiring rooms at slightly inspiring prices, all with TV and hot water.

Xanh Nghe An Hotel (☎ 844 788; 2 Đ Nguyen Trai; r US$17-26; 🅰 🅰) The hideous exterior belies the attractive rooms, all furnished in pine. Formerly the Nang Luong Hotel, it even has a swimming pool.

Saigon Kim Lien Hotel (☎ 838 899; sgklna@hn .vnn.vn; 25 Đ Quang Trung; s US$20-55; d US$24-55; 🅰 🅰 🅰) A smart business hotel, part of the Saigon Tourist family, facilities here include a pool and a buffet breakfast in-cluded in the rates.

Eating & Drinking

Com Ga Thuong Hai (99 Đ Le Loi; mains 10,000-40,000d) The place for good Chinese and Vietnam-ese cuisine. The name translates as 'Rice Chicken Shanghai', the tasty house special-ity, and the menu has some wild and wacky translations into English, particularly the frog and snake dishes.

Vinh Market has food stalls around the back, towards the central bus station. The market is at the end of Đ Cao Thang, which is the southern continuation of Đ Quang Trung. Another good option for self-caterers or anyone contemplating a long public bus journey is **Maximart** (Đ Nguyen Thai Hoc), a big branch of the national supermarket chain.

The top drinking spot in town, **Café Trung Tam** (1 Đ Quang Trung) is heavily plastered with Trung Nguyen coffee marketing. Coffee by day, beer by night, it attracts a steady local crowd.

Getting There & Away

AIR

Vietnam Airlines (☎ 595 777; 2 Đ Le Hong Phong) connects Vinh with Danang (US$32) and HCMC (US$70.50) should the dreary sur-rounds demand a quick exit.

BUS

There are two bus stations in Vinh. The station on Đ Le Loi is where most Hanoi and HCMC buses leave and arrive. The bus station behind the market is where to go for buses to Tay Son, and on to the Lao border (see the boxed text opposite). Be aware that Tay Son was formerly called Trung Tam, and this is usually what you'll see signposted on the bus. Some northbound and southbound buses also use this bus station.

CAR & MOTORBIKE

From Vinh it's 96km to the Lao border, 96km to Dong Hoi and 319km to Hanoi.

TRAIN

The *Reunification Express* (p482) stops here. The **Vinh train station** (Ga Vinh; ☎ 824 924) is 1km west of the intersection of Đ Le Loi and Đ Phan Boi Chau.

Getting Around

Despite its small size, Vinh has plenty of taxi companies: among them, **Mai Linh Taxi** (☎ 522 666), **Phu Nguyen Taxi** (☎ 833 333) and **Viet Anh Taxi** (☎ 843 999).

WEATHERING THE STORM

Nghe An and neighbouring Ha Tinh provinces have been lumped with poor soil and some of the worst weather in Vietnam; the area frequently suffers from severe floods and devastating typhoons. The locals say, 'The typhoon was born here and comes back often to visit.' The sum-mers are very hot and dry, while in winter the cold and rain are made all the more unpleasant by biting winds from the north.

As a result of the poor climate and many years of ill-managed collectivised farming policies, Nghe An and Ha Tinh provinces are among the most destitute regions in Vietnam. The recent economic reforms have greatly improved things, but nobody has yet figured out a way to reform the lousy weather.

BORDER CROSSING: NAM PHAO/CAU TREO

The **border** (🕒 7am-5pm) at Nam Phao (Laos) and Cau Treo (Vietnam) is 96km west of Vinh and about 30km east of Lak Sao in Laos. Fifteen-day Lao visas (US$30) are available on arrival in Nam Phao, but Vietnamese visas still need to be arranged in advance; try the Vietnamese embassy in Vientiane.

Vinh is the junction for transport to the border. Buses for **Tay Son** (formerly Trung Tam; 10,000d) leave from the central market bus station 10 times a day between 6am and 2pm. A lot of travellers have reported bad experiences on this local bus, including chronic overcharging and being kicked off in the middle of nowhere. From Tay Son, it's a further 26km to the border. Take a minibus or hire a motorbike to cover the last stretch; both cost 50,000d. The last 25km or so climbs through some spectacular steep and forested country. There is absolutely nothing here except the border post itself, so stock up on water and snacks in Tay Son when passing through. From the Vietnamese side it's a short walk to the Laos border.

Once in Laos, *jumbo* (three-wheeled taxis) and *sawngthaew* (pick-up trucks) to Lak Sao leave the border when full or cost about US$10 to charter. If you plan to continue on from Lak Sao to Tha Kaek, try to cross the border as early as possible.

Coming the other way from Laos to Vietnam, *sawngthaew* (US$1, 45 minutes) depart regularly from the market. Once in Vietnam the vultures begin circling to arrange transport to Vinh. Many will try and charge US$20 per person to Vinh, but $5 is more sensible. Try to hook up with as many other people as possible as you cross the border to improve your bargaining position.

Motorbike taxis charge about 5000d to most places in town.

AROUND VINH
Cua Lo Beach
This is one of the three 'old school' beach resorts in the northern half of the country: 'old school' as in government-approved holidays in government-run hotels! In the new Vietnam, most vote with their feet and head south. It's designed for Vietnamese taste and won't suit many travellers' style.

The beach here is beautiful, with white sand, clean water and a shady grove of pine trees along the shore, but in high season (May to September) there's litter everywhere. Nevertheless, if you're in the area and the weather is warm, Cua Lo could be worth a visit to cool off and to eat a good seafood lunch at one of the restaurants on the beach.

There are masses of **guesthouses** (r from US$5) along the waterfront there's huge **government enterprises** (r US$30). Most offer 'massage' and karaoke, and most have prostitutes hanging around outside, even in low season. Hotel rates drop considerably during the winter months – the name of the game is negotiation if for some reason you really want to stay here.

Cua Lo is 16km northeast of Vinh and can be reached easily by motorbike or taxi.

Kim Lien
Just 14km northwest of Vinh is **Ho Chi Minh's birthplace** in the village of Hoang Tru. The house in which he was born in 1890 is maintained as a sacred shrine, and it is a popular pilgrimage spot for Vietnamese tourists. Ho Chi Minh's childhood home is a simple farmhouse that's made of bamboo and palm leaves, reflecting his humble beginnings, although what you see today is a 1959 recreation. He was raised in this house until 1895, when the family sold it and moved to Hué so that his father could study.

In 1901, Ho Chi Minh's family returned to a **house** in Kim Lien, about 2km from Hoang Tru. Not far from this house, there is a **museum**, complete with the usual black-and-white photos of Ho's life in politics.

Admission to all the **sites** (🕒 7.30-11am & 1.30-5pm) is free. However you are obliged to buy three bouquets of flowers (10,000d each) from the reception desk and place one by each of the three altars. No English-language information is available.

There is no public transport to Kim Lien, but it's easy enough to hire a motorbike or taxi in Vinh.

DONG HOI
☎ 052 / pop 95,000
From a pretty fishing port, Dong Hoi, the capital of Quang Binh province, has

expanded into a major transit town on Hwy 1A. The town has lost much of its charm for foreign visitors but, with lengthy stretches of beautiful beach to the north and south of town, it is being earmarked as the north's latest, greatest beach resort for Vietnamese tourists.

During the American War, the city suffered extensive damage from US bombing. When you travel along Hwy 1, north of the DMZ, note the old French **bunkers** and US **bomb craters** lining the route; they're especially common near road and rail bridges.

The Nhat Le River flows along the eastern side of town; if you're staying overnight head 200m or so east of Hwy 1 to this area, where there are plenty of hotels and guesthouses along the waterfront.

Most travellers only spend the night in Dong Hoi if they are going underground at the **Phong Nha Cave** (see opposite). The cave is 55km from Dong Hoi, so it can be visited as a day trip; some hotels in Dong Hoi book pricey trips to the cave.

Beaches

Most of Quang Binh province is lined with sand dunes and beaches. These spread for dozens of kilometres north of town and also on a long spit of sand south of town. **Nhat Le Beach** is at the mouth of the Nhat Le River, about 2.5km north of central Dong Hoi, and some serious resort construction is underway here – watch this space, it's a big one!

If you're heading north along Hwy 1 from Dong Hoi, it's possible to follow the beautiful coast road for a few kilometres and then branch left to rejoin the highway.

Sleeping & Eating

The best places to stay are on the west bank of the Nhat Le River, just east of Hwy 1.

Khach San Mau Hong (☎ 821 804; Đ Truong Phap; r 100,000-140,000d; ☒) The friendliest of the riverfront cheapies, it's a small guesthouse run by a delightful family (who speak almost no English), with bright and clean rooms with hot water.

Khach San Tu Quy (☎ 829 909; Đ Truong Phap; r 150,000-200,000d; ☒) This is a smart little riverfront hotel, with well-equipped rooms. Splash the dong and you'll get something approaching a suite, although there is no English spoken here.

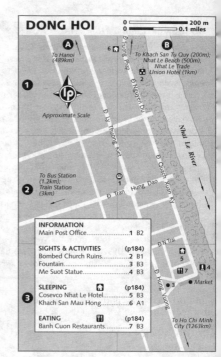

Nhat Le Trade Union Hotel (☎ 822 369; Đ Truong Phap; r 160,000-300,000d; ☒) One of a new breed of government getaways on Nhat Le Beach. Large, smart rooms with all mod cons are temptingly affordable and the beach is on the doorstep.

Cosevco Nhat Le Hotel (☎ 840 088; 16 Đ Quach Xuan Ky; r US$35-60; ☒ ☐ ☒) The big player in town, although the charges rather outweigh the comfort. Carpets are the obvious extra, if you happen to miss such things, plus it has a swimming pool and tennis court.

The list goes on…There are stacks of other hotels and guesthouses along the waterfront, as well as along Hwy 1 if you like lucky dips.

Dining out is not *de rigueur* in Dong Hoi, so the restaurant choice is limited. There is a cluster of good **local restaurants** (meals around 15,000d) near the market specialising in delicious pancake-like *banh cuon*.

Getting There & Away

Dong Hoi is on Hwy 1, 166km north of Hué and 197km south of Vinh, and is serviced by regular bus traffic from Vinh or Dong Ha.

BETEL NUT

One thing you'll undoubtedly see for sale at street stalls everywhere in Vietnam is betel nut. This is not a food – swallow it and you'll be sorry! The betel nut is the seed of the betel palm (a beautiful tree, by the way) and is meant to be chewed. The seed usually has a slit in it and is mixed with lime and wrapped in a leaf. Like tobacco, it's strong stuff that you can barely tolerate at first, but eventually you'll be hooked.

The first time you bite into betel nut, your whole face gets hot – chewers say it gives them a buzz. Like chewing tobacco, betel nut causes excessive salivation and betel chewers must constantly spit. The reddish-brown stains you see on footpaths are not blood, but betel-saliva juice. Years of constant chewing cause the teeth to become stained progressively browner, eventually becoming nearly black.

Dong Hoi is also a stop for the *Reunification Express* train service (p482).

PHONG NHA CAVE

Formed approximately 250 million years ago, give or take a few million years, **Phong Nha Cave** (☎ 823 424; admission 20,000d, charter boat 60,000d; ☯ 6am-4pm daily) is the largest and most beautiful cave in Vietnam. Located in the village of Son Trach, 55km northwest of Dong Hoi, it was designated a Unesco World Heritage site in 2000. It's remarkable for its thousands of metres of **underground passageways** and **river caves** filled with abundant stalactites and stalagmites. In November and December the river is prone to flooding and the underground cave may be closed.

In 1990, a British caving expedition explored 35km of the cave and made the first reliable map of Phong Nha's underground (and underwater) passageways. They discovered that the main cavern is nearly 8km long, with 14 other caves nearby.

Phong Nha means 'Cave of Teeth', but, unfortunately, the 'teeth' (or stalagmites) that were by the entrance are no longer there. Once you get further into the cave, it's mostly unspoiled. There's also a **dry cave** in the mountainside just above Phong Nha Cave. You can walk to it from the entrance to Phong Nha Cave (10 minutes) – look for the sign to Tien Son at the foot of the stairs.

The Chams used the cave's grottoes as Hindu sanctuaries in the 9th and 10th centuries; the remains of their altars and inscriptions are still here. Vietnamese Buddhists continue to venerate these sanctuaries, as they do other Cham religious sites.

More recently, this cave was used as a hospital and ammunition depot during the American War. The entrance shows evidence of aerial attacks. That US warplanes spent considerable time bombing and strafing the Phong Nha area is really hardly surprising: this was one of the key entrance points to the Ho Chi Minh Trail. Some overgrown remains of the trail are still visible, though you'll need a guide to point them out to you.

You should be aware that Phong Nha is heavily visited by Vietnamese groups. The cave itself is fantastic, the experience less so. That is unless you like your World Heritage sites to incorporate litter, noise, people climbing on stalagmites and cigarette smoke in the underground caverns. Of course these things are prohibited, but enforcement appears to be lax to say the least. Presumably these distractions can be avoided if you arrive early in the morning. The toilets might be less putrid then, too.

The Phong Nha Reception Department, an enormous complex in **Son Trach village**, organises tourist access to the cave. You buy your admission ticket here and organise a boat to take you to the cave. Boats seat about 10, so it's cheaper to share. The cave system is electrically lit, but you may want to bring a torch (flashlight), as some of the paths are poorly illuminated.

Sleeping & Eating

There's a **government guesthouse** (☎ 052-675 004; r 100,000-180,000d; ☒) in Son Trach, but it tends to fill up with local school parties and the like. The cave is an easy day trip from Hwy 1 and better accommodation options in Dong Hoi.

In Son Trach itself, there are plenty of cheap *com pho* places. Don't expect *haute cuisine*.

Getting There & Away

Some hotels in Dong Hoi (20km south of Bo Trach) offer pricey tours to Phong Nha. There are now infrequent public buses direct to Son Trach, but they tend to leave at the crack of dawn.

The actual cave entrance is 3km by river from Son Trach. The one-way ride takes about 30 minutes and gives a great glimpse of the life of river people. Overall, it takes about two hours to visit the river cave, or about four hours with a trip to the dry cave too.

Central Vietnam

CONTENTS

Central Vietnam plays host to many of the most memorable sights the country has to offer. Historic towns, ancient empires, beautiful beaches, wild landscapes… Central Vietnam has all this and more; take your pick, then take your time.

The historic towns of Hué and Hoi An are both World Heritage sites and ideal places to soak up the culture and indulge in the cuisine. Hué breathes history at every turn, having served as Vietnam's capital from 1802 to 1945 under the 13 emperors of the Nguyen dynasty, and there are many regal remnants from this time. The old port of Hoi An is a real charmer and the perfect spot to take some time out, with its inspired blend of fusion architecture, fantastic food and serious shopping.

Echoes of the American War in Vietnam ring loudly through the mountains that rise towards the Lao border and many visitors make a poignant pilgrimage through the Demilitarised Zone (DMZ). Stepping further back in time, the most important Cham sites in Vietnam are found in this region, including My Son, which is set in a stunning location under Cat's Tooth Mountain. Put the Chams in some context with a trip to the classic Museum of Cham Sculpture in Danang. Vietnam's third city is refreshing and reinvigorated and China Beach is a great place to surf or soak up the sun.

And the list goes on: popular Marble Mountains is a natural stop between Danang and Hoi An; beautiful Bach Ma National Park offers the chance to catch up with nature at its best; plus one of the most radical road trips in the country, over the Hai Van Pass from Danang to Hué. Do the maths: it all adds up to make this region a *must* on any trip through Vietnam.

HIGHLIGHTS

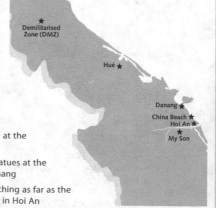

- Cruise down the picturesque Perfume River in **Hué** (p199) to the majestic Royal Tombs of the emperors of old
- Fall in love with the old-world atmosphere of **Hoi An** (p230), *the* place in Vietnam to take your time
- Learn some lessons from the past at the battlefields of the **Demilitarised Zone** (DMZ; p190)
- Strike out early for the solitude of a sunrise at the incredible Cham ruins at **My Son** (p246)
- Check out the classic collection of Cham statues at the **Museum of Cham Sculpture** (p221) in Danang
- Beat a retreat to **China Beach** (p226), stretching as far as the eye can see from Danang to Cua Dai Beach in Hoi An

History

History hangs heavy over the central Vietnam region and the Vietnamese are only one element of the successive stories that have unfolded here. This region was the heartland of the ancient kingdom of Champa (see the boxed text on p245), and the Chams left their mark in the shape and form of the many towers dotting the landscape here, the most renowned of which are at My Son, a day trip away from Hoi An.

As the Vietnamese pushed southwards, pacifying the Chams, the first Europeans, who were Portuguese traders, set foot in Vietnam in Danang in the 16th century.

The French would come to dominate Vietnam, but not before the balance of power shifted decisively to central Vietnam under the last royal dynasty, the Nguyens, who ruled from 1802 to 1945. Successive emperors established a lavish imperial court at Hué, which became the centre of political intrigue, intellectual excellence and spiritual guidance in Vietnam. The French broke the will of later emperors and the balance of power shifted back to Hanoi by the time of independence.

History was not to ignore this once proud region, but this time it was a tale of tragedy. As Vietnam found itself engulfed in the American War, central Vietnam was the scene of the heaviest fighting around the DMZ. The North Vietnamese sought to infiltrate the south along the Ho Chi

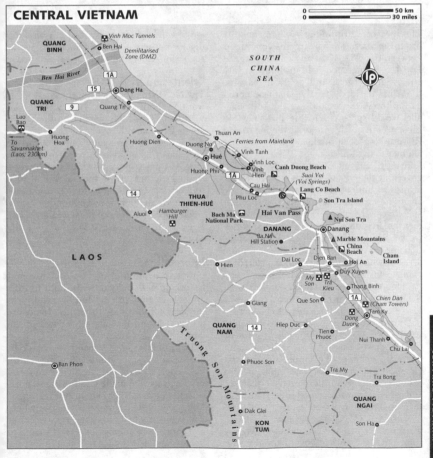

CENTRAL VIETNAM

Minh Trail, while American forces and their South Vietnamese allies tried their best to disrupt supplies. Thousands of lives were lost in bloody battles for strategic hills and valleys, and names like Khe Sanh and Hamburger Hill were forever etched into the consciousness of the West.

DEMILITARISED ZONE (DMZ)

From 1954 to 1975, the Ben Hai River served as the demarcation line between the Republic of Vietnam (RVN; South Vietnam) and the Democratic Republic of Vietnam (DRV; North Vietnam). On either side of the river was an area 5km wide that was known as the Demilitarised Zone (DMZ). Ironically, as the conflict escalated, it became one of the most militarised zones in the world.

History

The idea of partitioning Vietnam had its origins in a series of agreements concluded between the USA, UK and the USSR at the Potsdam Conference, held in Berlin in July 1945. For logistical and political reasons, the Allies decided that the Japanese occupation forces to the south of the 16th Parallel would surrender to the British while those to the north would surrender to the Kuomintang (Nationalist) Chinese army led by Chiang Kaishek.

In April 1954 at Geneva, Ho Chi Minh's government and the French agreed to an armistice; among the provisions was the creation of a demilitarised zone at the Ben Hai River. The agreement stated explicitly that the division of Vietnam into two zones was merely temporary and that the demarcation line did not constitute a political boundary. But when nationwide general elections planned for July 1956 were not held, Vietnam found itself divided into two states with the Ben Hai River, which is almost exactly at the 17th Parallel, as their de facto border.

During the American War, the area just south of the DMZ was the scene of some of the bloodiest battles of the conflict. Quang Tri, The Rockpile, Khe Sanh, Lang Vay and Hamburger Hill became household names in the USA as, year after year, TV pictures and casualty figures provided Americans with their evening dose of war.

Since 1975, 5000 people have been injured or killed in and around the DMZ by mines and ordnance left over from the war.

> **WARNING**
>
> The war may be over, but death and injury are still fairly easy to come by in the old DMZ. At many of the places listed in this section there may be live mortar rounds, artillery projectiles and mines strewn about. Watch where you step and don't leave the marked paths. As tempted as you might be to collect souvenirs, *never* touch any leftover ordnance. If the locals have not carted it off for scrap it means that even they are afraid to disturb it. White phosphorus shells – whose contents burn fiercely when exposed to air – are remarkably impervious to the effects of prolonged exposure and are likely to remain extremely dangerous for many more years.

Despite the risk, impoverished peasants still dig for chunks of leftover metal to sell as scrap, for which they are paid a pittance.

Orientation

The old DMZ extends from the coast westward to the Lao border; Hwy 9 (Quoc Lo 9) runs more or less parallel to the DMZ, about 10km south.

The old US bases along Hwy 9 can be visited as a long day trip from Hué, or as a long half-day trip from Dong Ha. The road leading southeast from the Dakrong Bridge on Hwy 9 goes to Aluoi and the Ashau Valley (site of the infamous Hamburger Hill).

The DMZ sites of significance along Hwy 1 are more easily accessed, and generally easier to find.

Information

For an in-depth tour of the DMZ, it is best to link up with a good guide, both to fully appreciate the history and, critically, to physically find some of the sites. Many are unmarked, and it's easy to get lost in the labyrinth of dirt tracks.

Day tours are most readily available in Hué, and the same tours will also pick up passengers as they pass through Dong Ha. Bookings can be made at almost any hotel or café in town. There are only a few agencies running the tours, so no matter where you sign up you'll still wind up as part of a group. There are also two great places to book tours in Dong Ha (see p197).

Expect to pay around US$8 to US$15 for a day-long outing into the DMZ. Most of these tours have English-speaking guides, but some speak French. Don't book a half-day tour from Hué as you'll see almost nothing.

MILITARY SITES ON HIGHWAY 1
Vinh Moc Tunnels
The incredible tunnels of **Vinh Moc** (admission plus guided tour 25,000d; ☼ 7am-4.30pm) are a monument to the determination of the North Vietnamese to persevere and triumph – at all costs and despite some incredible sacrifices – in the American War. A visit to the tunnels can be combined with bathing at the beautiful beaches that extend for many kilometres to the north and south of Vinh Moc.

The 2.8km of tunnels here, all of which can be visited, are the real thing and unadulterated for viewing by tourists, unlike the tunnels at Cu Chi (p369), near Ho Chi Minh City (HCMC). Vinh Moc's underground passageways are also larger and taller than those at Cu Chi, which makes for an easier and less claustrophobic visit.

There are lights installed inside the tunnels, but you may also want to bring a torch (flashlight). Although a guide is included in the entrance fee, it is quite an evocative experience to explore on your own.

Offshore is Con Co Island, which during the war was an important supply depot. Today the island, which is ringed by rocky beaches, houses a small military base.

MISSING IN ACTION

An issue that continues to plague relations between the USA and Vietnam is that of US military personnel officially listed as 'missing in action' (MIA). There are still more than 2000 American soldiers officially 'unaccounted for' and many of their families are adamant that their loved ones are prisoners of war (POWs) in secret prison camps deep in the jungles of Vietnam. POW-MIA groups in the USA continue to lobby Congress to 'do something'. It remains a highly emotive issue.

Others believe the POW-MIA groups are flogging a dead horse. They believe the figure of 2265 MIAs is almost certainly too high. About 400 flight personnel were killed when their planes crashed into the sea off the coast of Vietnam, others died when their aircraft went down in flames or in ground combat – the tropical jungle quickly reclaims a human corpse. However, when Vietnam returned the last 590 American POWs, 37 soldiers believed to have been captured were not among them. The Vietnamese government adamantly denies that there are MIAs still in Vietnam; it would make no logical sense for Vietnam to continue holding American POWs.

Not much is said about the 300,000 Vietnamese who are also MIAs – they are difficult to identify because they didn't wear ID tags. However, the Vietnamese do feel just as strongly about their MIAs, particularly as they consider it their duty to perform ancestor worship – a difficult task without a corpse.

In the meantime, MIA teams continue to comb the Vietnamese countryside – at an ongoing cost of millions of dollars to American taxpayers. Investigative crews carry out assessments, based on wartime records and interviews with local villagers; once they have enough evidence to warrant a search, a recovery team conducts an on-site excavation. Any remains discovered are flown home for forensic identification analysis based on dental records and DNA, which has sparked a cottage industry in villagers foraging for any sort of bones they can dig up.

Many Vietnamese are also employed in the search teams, with 75% of their salaries going to the government. Not surprisingly, the Vietnamese government is in no hurry to see the MIA teams leave, despite the Americans raising this issue in diplomatic negotiations. The fact that the MIA teams have been digging through Vietnamese cemeteries looking for American bones has also irritated many locals who would rather see their dead rest in peace.

Meanwhile, the sad saga continues to play itself out. During the 1980s, when private POW-MIA groups started circulating photographs showing US soldiers being held as prisoners in a Vietnamese camp, there was a flurry of official investigations. The photos proved to be fakes, but groups such as the National League of Families of American Prisoners and Missing in Southeast Asia were very effective at stalling the US government's attempts to forge diplomatic relations with Vietnam. Despite protests, diplomatic relations were finally established in 1995, and serving US President Bill Clinton visited in 2000.

GOING UNDERGROUND

In 1966 the USA began a massive aerial and artillery bombardment of North Vietnam. Just north of the DMZ, the villagers of Vinh Moc found themselves living in one of the most heavily bombed and shelled strips of land on the planet. Small family shelters could not withstand this onslaught and villagers either fled or began tunnelling by hand into the red-clay earth.

The Viet Cong (VC) found it useful to have a base here and encouraged the villagers to stay. After 18 months of work, during which the excavated earth was camouflaged to prevent its detection from the air, an enormous VC base was established underground. Civilians were employed in the digging and were accommodated in new underground homes. Whole families lived here and 17 babies were born in the underground delivery room.

Later, the civilians and VC were joined by North Vietnamese soldiers, whose mission was to keep communications and supply lines to nearby Con Co Island open. A total of 11,500 tonnes of military supplies reached Con Co Island and a further 300 tonnes were shipped to the South, thanks to the Vinh Moc Tunnels.

Other villages north of the DMZ also built tunnel systems, but none were as elaborate as Vinh Moc. The poorly constructed tunnels of Vinh Quang village (at the mouth of the Ben Hai River) collapsed after repeated bombing, killing everyone inside.

The tunnel network at Vinh Moc remains essentially as it looked in 1966, though some of the 12 entrances – seven of which open onto the palm-lined beach – have been retimbered and others have become overgrown. The tunnels were built on three levels ranging from 15m to 26m below the crest of the bluff.

The tunnels were repeatedly hit by American bombs, but the only ordnance that posed a real threat was the feared 'drilling bomb'. Only once did such a bomb score a direct hit, but it failed to explode and no-one was injured; the inhabitants adapted the bomb hole for use as an air shaft. Occasionally the mouths of the tunnel complex, which faced the sea, were struck by naval gunfire.

The turn-off to Vinh Moc from Hwy 1 is 6.5km north of the Ben Hai River in the village of Ho Xa. Vinh Moc is another 13km east from Hwy 1.

Cua Tung Beach

This long, secluded stretch of sand, where Vietnam's last emperor, Bao Dai, used to holiday, is just north of the mouth of the Ben Hai. There are beaches on the southern side of the Ben Hai River as well. Every bit of land in the area not levelled for planting is pockmarked with big bomb craters.

There are no buses to Cua Tung Beach, which can be reached by turning right (east) off Hwy 1 at a point 1.2km north of the Ben Hai River. Cua Tung Beach is about 7km south of Vinh Moc via the dirt road that runs along the coast.

Doc Mieu Base

Doc Mieu Base, next to Hwy 1 on a low rise 8km south of the Ben Hai River, was once part of an elaborate electronic system (McNamara's Wall, named after the US Secretary of Defence between 1961 and 1968) intended to prevent infiltration across the DMZ. Today, it is a lunar landscape of bunkers, craters, shrapnel and live mortar rounds. Bits of cloth and decaying military boots are strewn about on the red earth. This devastation was created not by the war, but by scrap-metal hunters, who have found excavations at this site particularly rewarding.

Ben Hai River

Twenty-two kilometres north of Dong Ha, Hwy 1 crosses the Ben Hai River, once the demarcation line between North and South Vietnam. Check out the old wartime bridge; until 1967, when it was bombed by the Americans, the northern half of the bridge that stood on this site was painted red, while the southern half was yellow. Following the signing of the Paris cease-fire agreements in 1973, the present bridge and the two flag towers were built.

Truong Son National Cemetery

Truong Son National Cemetery is a sobering memorial to tens of thousands of North

AROUND THE DMZ

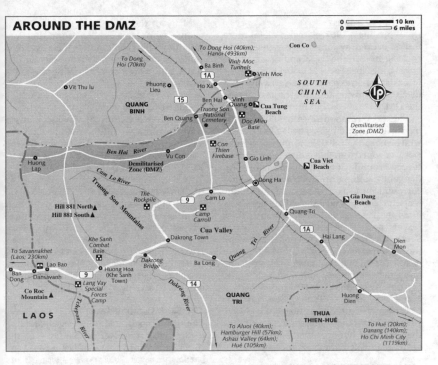

Vietnamese soldiers from transport, construction and anti-aircraft units who were killed in the Truong Son Mountain Range (Annamite Cordillera) along the Ho Chi Minh Trail. Row after row of white tombstones stretch across the hillsides and the cemetery is maintained by disabled war veterans.

The soldiers are buried in five zones, according to the part of Vietnam they came from; each zone is further subdivided into provinces. The gravestones of five colonels and seven decorated heroes (Trung Ta and Dai Ta represent the ranks of the martyrs), including one woman, are in a separate area. Each headstone bears the inscription 'Liet Si', which means 'Martyr'. The remains of soldiers interred here were originally buried near the spot where they were killed and were brought here after reunification. Many graves are empty, simply bearing the names of a small number of Vietnam's 300,000 MIAs.

On the hilltop above the sculpture garden is a three-sided stele. One face has engraved tributes from high-ranking Vietnamese leaders to the people who worked on the Ho Chi Minh Trail. At the bottom is a poem by To Huu. Another side tells the history of the May 1959 Army Corps (Doang 5.59), which is said to have been founded on Ho Chi Minh's birthday in 1959 with a mission to construct and maintain a supply line to the South. The third side lists the constituent units of the May 1959 Army Corps, which eventually included five divisions. The site where the cemetery now stands was used as a base by the May 1959 Army Corps from 1972 to 1975.

The road to Truong Son National Cemetery intersects Hwy 1 13km north of Dong Ha and 9km south of the Ben Hai River; the distance from the highway to the cemetery is 17km along the excellent new Ho Chi Minh road.

A rocky cart path that is passable by motorbike links Cam Lo (on Hwy 9) with Truong Son National Cemetery (18km). This track passes rubber plantations and also the homes of Bru (Van Kieu) people, who cultivate, among many other crops, black pepper.

Con Thien Firebase

In September 1967, North Vietnamese forces, backed by long-range artillery and rockets, crossed the DMZ and besieged the US Marine Corps base of Con Thien, which was established as part of McNamara's Wall in an attempt to stop infiltrations across the DMZ.

The USA responded with 4000 bombing sorties (including 800 by B-52s), during which more than 40,000 tonnes of bombs were dropped on the North Vietnamese forces around Con Thien, transforming the gently sloping brush-covered hills that surrounded the base into a smoking moonscape of craters and ashes. The siege was lifted, but the battle had accomplished its real purpose: to divert US attention from South Vietnam's cities in preparation for the Tet Offensive. The area around the base is still considered too dangerous, even for scrap-metal hunters, to approach.

Con Thien Firebase is 10km west of Hwy 1 and 7km south of Truong Son National Cemetery along the road that links Hwy 1 with the cemetery. Concrete bunkers mark the spot a few hundred metres to the south of the road where the base once stood.

MILITARY SITES ON HIGHWAY 9

The Ho Chi Minh Trail (Duong Truong Son) – actually a series of roads, trails and paths – ran between North and South Vietnam (perpendicular to Hwy 9) through the Truong Son Mountains and eastern Laos; it was used by the Viet Cong to transport troops and equipment.

To disrupt the flow of troops and supplies along the Ho Chi Minh Trail, the Americans established a line of bases along Hwy 9, including (from east to west) Cua Viet, Gio Linh, Dong Ha, Con Thien, Cam Lo, Camp Carroll, The Rockpile, Ca Lu (now called Dakrong Town), Khe Sanh and Lang Vay.

Huong Hoa (Khe Sanh Town)

This town has now been officially renamed Huong Hoa, but the Western world will forever remember it as Khe Sanh. Set amid beautiful hills, valleys and fields at an elevation of about 600m, it is a verdant district capital. The town is known for its coffee plantations, which were originally cultivated by the French.

Many of the inhabitants are Bru tribal people who moved here from the surrounding hills. You'll notice their different clothing, with women wearing sarong-like skirts, and woven baskets taking the place of plastic bags.

SLEEPING

About the only reason for staying here is if you're planning to hit the road to Laos the next morning. At the time of writing the **People's Committee Guesthouse** (☎ 053-880 563; r 100,000-150,000d; ❀) is the sole option.

GETTING THERE & AWAY

About 600m southwest (towards the Lao frontier) of the triangular intersection, where the road to Khe Sanh Combat Base branches off, is Khe Sanh bus station, on Hwy 9. Buses to Dong Ha (15,000d, 1½ hours) and Lao Bao (10,000d, one hour) depart regularly. Change at Dong Ha for all other destinations.

Khe Sanh Combat Base

The site of the most famous siege – and one of the most controversial battles – of the American War in Vietnam is **Khe Sanh Combat Base** (admission 25,000d; ⊙ 7am-4.30pm). It sits silently on a barren plateau, surrounded by vegetation-covered hills that are often obscured by mist and fog. It is hard to imagine as you stand in this peaceful, verdant land – with the neat homes and vegetable plots of local people all around – that in early 1968 the bloodiest battle of the war took place here. About 500 Americans (the official figure of 205 was arrived at by statistical sleight of hand), 10,000 North Vietnamese troops and uncounted civilian bystanders died amid the din of machine guns and the fiery explosions of 1000kg bombs, white-phosphorus shells, napalm, mortars and artillery rounds of all sorts.

The site includes the recent addition of a small memorial museum. A couple of bunkers have been recreated and some photos and other memorabilia are on show. Behind the main site, the outline of the airfield remains distinct – to this day nothing will grow on it. Some of the comments in the visitors' book, especially those written by visiting war veterans, can make for emotional reading.

The MIA team still visits the area regularly to search for the bodies of Americans

DISPATCHES FROM KHE SANH

Despite opposition from marine corps brass, the small US Army Special Forces (Green Beret) base at Khe Sanh, built to recruit and train local Montagnards, was turned into a marines stronghold in late 1966. In April 1967 there began a series of 'hill fights' between US forces and the well dug-in North Vietnamese infantry, who held the surrounding hills. In only a few weeks, 155 marines and thousands of North Vietnamese were killed. The fighting centred on hills 881 South and 881 North, both of which are about 8km northwest of Khe Sanh Combat Base.

In late 1967, American intelligence detected the movement of tens of thousands of North Vietnamese regulars armed with mortars, rockets and artillery into the hills around Khe Sanh. General Westmoreland became convinced that the North Vietnamese were planning another Dien Bien Phu (the decisive battle in the Franco–Viet Minh War in 1954). This was a misleading analogy given American firepower and the proximity of Khe Sanh to supply lines and other US bases. President Johnson himself became obsessed by the spectre of 'Din Bin Foo', as he famously referred to it. To follow the course of the battle, he had a sand-table model of the Khe Sanh plateau constructed in the White House situation room and took the unprecedented step of requiring a written guarantee from the Joint Chiefs of Staff that Khe Sanh could be held.

Westmoreland, determined to avoid another Dien Bien Phu at all costs, assembled an armada of 5000 planes and helicopters and increased the number of troops at Khe Sanh to 6000. He even ordered his staff to study the feasibility of using tactical nuclear weapons.

The 75-day siege of Khe Sanh began on 21 January 1968 with a small-scale assault on the base perimeter. As the marines and the South Vietnamese Rangers braced for a full-scale ground attack, Khe Sanh became the focus of global media attention. It was the cover story for both *Newsweek* and *Life* magazines and appeared on the front pages of countless newspapers around the world. During the next two months, the base was subject to continuous ground attacks and artillery fire. US aircraft dropped 100,000 tonnes of explosives on the immediate vicinity of Khe Sanh Combat Base. The expected attempt to overrun the base never came and, on 7 April 1968 after heavy fighting, US troops reopened Hwy 9 and linked up with the marines to end the siege.

It now seems clear that the siege of Khe Sanh, in which an estimated 10,000 North Vietnamese died, was merely an enormous diversion intended to draw US forces and the attention of their commanders away from the South Vietnamese population centres, in preparation for the Tet Offensive, which began a week after the siege started. However, at the time, Westmoreland considered the entire Tet Offensive to be a 'diversionary effort' to distract attention from Khe Sanh!

A few days after Westmoreland's tour of duty in Vietnam ended in July 1968, US forces in the area were redeployed. Policy, it seemed, had been reassessed and holding Khe Sanh, for which so many men had died, was deemed unnecessary. After everything at Khe Sanh was buried, trucked out or blown up (nothing recognisable that could be used in a North Vietnamese propaganda film was to remain), US forces upped and left Khe Sanh Combat Base under a curtain of secrecy. The American command had finally realised what a marine officer had expressed long before: 'When you're at Khe Sanh, you're not really anywhere. You could lose it and you really haven't lost a damn thing.'

who disappeared during the fierce battles in the surrounding hills. Most remains they find are Vietnamese.

GETTING THERE & AWAY

To get to Khe Sanh Combat Base from Huong Hoa bus station, head 600m towards Dong Ha then turn northwest at the triangular intersection; there's a small sign. The base is 2.5km further, 500m off the right-hand (east) side of the road.

Lang Vay Special Forces Camp

In February 1968, Lang Vay Special Forces Camp, established in 1962, was attacked and overrun by North Vietnamese infantry backed by nine tanks. Of the base's 500 South Vietnamese, Bru and Montagnard defenders, 316 were killed. Ten of the 24 Americans at the base were killed and 11 were wounded.

All that's left of dog bone–shaped Lang Vay Combat Base are the overgrown remains of numerous concrete bunkers, and a rusty tank memorial.

The base is on a ridge southwest of Hwy 9, between Khe Sanh bus station (9.2km) and Lao Bao (7.3km).

Camp Carroll

Established in 1966, Camp Carroll was named after a Marine Corps captain who was killed while trying to seize a nearby ridge. The gargantuan 175mm cannons at Camp Carroll were used to shell targets as far away as Khe Sanh. In 1972 the South Vietnamese commander of the camp, Lieutenant Colonel Ton That Dinh, surrendered and joined the North Vietnamese Army.

These days there is not that much to see at Camp Carroll, except for a Vietnamese memorial marker, a few overgrown trenches and the remains of their timber roofs. Bits of military hardware and rusty shell casings can still be found. The concrete bunkers were destroyed by local people seeking to extract the steel reinforcing rods to sell as scrap; concrete chunks from the bunkers were hauled off for use in construction.

The area around Camp Carroll now belongs to State Pepper Enterprises. On the road in, you'll see pepper plants trained so that they climb up the trunks of jackfruit trees. There are also rubber plantations nearby.

The turn-off to Camp Carroll is 10km west of Cam Lo and 23km northeast of Dakrong Bridge. The base is 3km from Hwy 9.

The Rockpile

The Rockpile was named after what can only be described as a 230m-high pile of rocks. There was a US Marine Corps lookout on top of The Rockpile and a base for American long-range artillery was nearby.

Today there isn't much left of The Rockpile and you will probably need a guide to point it out to you. The Rockpile is 26km west of Dong Ha on Hwy 9.

Dakrong Bridge

Crossing the Dakrong River 13km east of the Khe Sanh bus station, Dakrong Bridge was rebuilt in 2001. The road to Aluoi that heads southeast from the bridge passes by the stilted homes of the Brus and was once a branch of the Ho Chi Minh Trail.

Aluoi

Located approximately 65km southeast of Dakrong Bridge and 60km southwest of Hué is Aluoi. There are a number of waterfalls and cascades in the surrounding area. Tribes living in the mountainous Aluoi area include the Ba Co, Ba Hy, Ca Tu and Taoi. US Army Special Forces bases in Aluoi and Ashau were overrun and abandoned in 1966; the area then became an important transshipment centre for supplies coming down the Ho Chi Minh Trail.

Among the better-known military sites around Aluoi are **landing zones Cunningham**, **Erskine** and **Razor**, as well as **Hill 1175** (west of the valley) and **Hill 521** (in Laos). Further south, in the Ashau Valley, is **Hamburger Hill** (Apbia Mountain). In May 1969, US forces on a search-and-destroy operation near the Lao border fought in one of the fiercest battles of the war. In less than a week of fighting, 241 US soldiers died at Hamburger Hill – a fact that was very well publicised in the US media. A month later, after the US forces withdrew from the area to continue operations elsewhere, the hill was reoccupied by the North Vietnamese Army.

DONG HA
☎ 053 / pop 65,200

The capital of the reconstituted Quang Tri province, Dong Ha is at the busy intersection of Hwys 1 and 9. Dong Ha served as a US Marine Corps command and logistics centre from 1968 to '69. In the spring of 1968, a division of North Vietnamese troops crossed the DMZ and attacked Dong Ha. The city was later the site of a South Vietnamese army base. Today, there is no conceivable reason to visit, save as a stopover on the way to the DMZ and/or the Lao border. Hwy 1 thunders through town, dust blowing and horns blaring, and almost all the hotels are close by. The public loudspeakers start their broadcasting at 5am.

Orientation

Hwy 1 is called Ð Le Duan as it passes through Dong Ha. Hwy 9, signposted as going to Lao Bao, intersects Hwy 1 next to the bus station. Ð Tran Phu (which is the old Hwy 9) intersects Ð Le Duan 600m north of the bus station (towards the river). Ð Tran Phu then runs south for 400m before turning west.

There is a market area along Hwy 1 between Đ Tran Phu and the river.

Information

There are a couple of good places to book more personalised DMZ tours in Dong Ha than those on offer in Hué. The **DMZ Café** (☎ 857 026; dmzcafédongha@yahoo.com; 88 Đ Le Duan; 🖳) is run by a south Vietnamese veteran who lived through many of the monumental events associated with the DMZ. His guides take in places many other tours don't visit; it is US$7 per guide and US$8 for a motorbike. The DMZ Café is also a good place to arrange transport to Lao Bao, plus it offers Internet access (300d per minute).

About a kilometre north of the bridge heading out of town, **Dong Que Restaurant** (☎ 852 303; dongqueqt@dng.vnn.vn; 159 Đ Le Duan) is run by a charming and helpful family who can book DMZ tours, and bus and train tickets.

Bus tours cost around US$10 per person, but you'll be added to a tour group coming from Hué. If you are heading south, you can hitch a ride on to Hué.

Sleeping

DMZ Café (☎ 857 026; dmzcafédongha@yahoo.com; 88 Đ Le Duan; r US$4-5; 🖳) This is as cheap and cheerful as it gets. Cheap as the price suggests and cheerful thanks to the energetic supervision of Mr Tinh. Clean beds and cold water, but near the noise of the main road.

Nha Nghi Mai Yen (☎ 551 750; 24 Đ Nguyen Trai; r 60,000-130,000d; 🆒) A brand spanking new little guesthouse, this dishes up a real deal. Scrupulously clean rooms that include a bathroom start from 70,000d (60,000d rooms have shared bathrooms), and little touches like toothbrushes are more than this money warrants.

Khach San Duong 9 Xanh (Highway 9 Hotel; ☎ 550 991; 4 Đ Nguyen Trai; r US$9-15; 🆒) This is on the same quiet strip as the Nha Nghi Mai Yen. All rooms come with TV, fridge and hot water and the helpful staff speak good English.

Phung Hoang Hotel (☎ 854 567; victoryqt@dng.vnn.vn; 146 Đ Le Duan; r US$10-25; 🆒) Don't be put off by the large *Guide Routard* sign here, as it really is a good place. The rooms are fully furnished and the more expensive ones are virtual suites complete with big baths. A new restaurant-bar has just opened downstairs.

Hieu Giang Hotel (☎ 855 856; highotel@dng.vnn.vn; 183 Đ Le Duan; s US$19-35, d US$22-40; 🆒) Supposedly the smartest place in town, but this hotel is not such good value as the Phung Hoang. Located right where Hwy 9 intersects Hwy 1, the rooms are pleasant but predictable.

Eating

Trung Tan Quan Restaurant (Đ Le Loi; meals around 20,000d) Right in the middle of town, this hole in the wall has a mean little menu. The 'Vietnamese Food' – as proclaimed on the menu here – is a good, freshly cooked meal of fish or meat, vegetables, rice and condiments.

Dong Que Restaurant (☎ 852 303; 159 Đ Le Duan; meals 10,000-40,000d) Also does fine fresh food with a Vietnamese and Chinese accent, plus there are clean bathrooms for those holding out for such things.

Besides the dining rooms in Dong Ha's hotels, there's a slew of roadside **com pho restaurants** (Hwy 1; meals around 10,000d) along the main drag, particularly in the vicinity of the bus station and the intersection of Hwy 9.

Getting There & Away

BUS

Dong Ha bus station (Ben Xe Khach Dong Ha; 122 Đ Le Duan) is near the intersection of Hwys 1 and 9. Vehicles to Hué (14,000d, 1½ hours), Khe Sanh (15,000d, 1½ hours) and Lao Bao (20,000d, two hours) depart regularly. These are local prices; foreigners are unfailingly charged more.

It is sometimes necessary to change buses in Khe Sanh for Lao Bao. Buses also link Dong Ha with Ho Xa, along Hwy 1, about 13km west of Vinh Moc.

CAR & MOTORBIKE

Road distances from Dong Ha are: Danang (190km), Dong Hoi (94km), Hué (72km), Khe Sanh (65km), Lao Bao (80km) and Vinh Moc (41km).

Motorbike hire with driver to the DMZ starts from US$10. A one-way car trip to the Lao Bao border will set you back US$25.

TRAIN

Reunification Express trains stop in Dong Ha (see p482).

To get to the Dong Ha train station from the bus station, head 1km southeast on Hwy

1 to a big guesthouse called Nha Khach 261. Turn right here and the back of the train station is about 150m along a track.

LAO BAO (LAOS BORDER)
☎ 053

Lao Bao is becoming an important border crossing for trade and tourism between Laos, Thailand and central Vietnam. Lao Bao is on the Sepon River (Song Xe Pon), which marks the Vietnam–Laos border. Towering above Lao Bao on the Lao side of the border is Co Roc Mountain, once a North Vietnamese artillery stronghold.

There is a huge border market on the Vietnamese side, where Thai goods smuggled through the bush from Laos are readily available. Merchants accept either Vietnamese dong or Lao kip. Don't change US dollars at the border unless you have to: the rate can be about 50% less than the bank's.

There's absolutely no reason to linger in Lao Bao, but if you miss the border opening hours (see the boxed text below) and need to stay, **Bao Son Hotel** (☎ 877 848; r US$12-18; 🗙) is a smart business hotel and good value for

the money. There is the inevitable row of *com pho* places in the centre of town.

Lao Bao town is 18km west of Khe Sanh, 80km from Dong Ha, 152km from Hué, 45km east of Sepon (Laos) and 255km east of Savannakhet (Laos).

QUANG TRI
☎ 053 / pop 15,400

Quang Tri was once an important citadel city. In the spring of 1972, four divisions of North Vietnamese regulars, backed by tanks, artillery and rockets, poured across the DMZ into Quang Tri province in what became known as the Eastertide Offensive. They laid siege to the city of Quang Tri, shelling it heavily before capturing it along with the rest of the province.

During the next four months, the city was almost completely obliterated by South Vietnamese artillery and massive carpet bombing by US fighter-bombers and B-52s. The South Vietnamese army suffered 5000 casualties in the rubble-to-rubble fighting to retake the city.

Today, there is little to see in the town of Quang Tri except a few remains of the

---

BORDER CROSSING: LAO BAO/DANSAVANH

The **Lao Bao border** (⏲ 7am-5pm) is the most popular crossing between Laos and Vietnam. You can get a 15-day Lao visa (US$30) on arrival in Dansavanh, but Vietnamese visas still need to be arranged in advance; drop in on the Vietnamese consulate in Savannakhet.

Dong Ha is the junction town for Lao Bao. Regular public buses go from Dong Ha to Khe Sanh (15,000d, 1½ hours) and Lao Bao (20,000d, two hours). You may need to change buses in Khe Sanh for Lao Bao. Overcharging is a distinct possibility on either of these local buses. Travellers coming from Laos should be aware that no public buses go directly to Hué, despite what drivers may tell you! Buses only go as far as Dong Ha.

The border post used to be 2km from Lao Bao town, but the town has expanded so fast it runs almost up to the border. From the bus station, the local price for a *xe om* (motorbike taxi) to the border is 5,000d (foreigners pay about 10,000d), or walk it in about 20 minutes. From the Vietnam border post to the Laos border post is a short walk of a few hundred metres.

Once in Laos, there is only one bus a day direct to Savannakhet, which leaves when full. *Sawngthaew* (pick-up trucks) leave fairly regularly to Sepon, from where you can get a bus or further *sawngthaew* to Savannakhet.

Coming the other way, Rte 9 from Savannakhet to the border is now one of the best roads in Laos. From Savannakhet, buses (US$3, 255km, 5 hours) leave at 7am and noon for the border. Alternatively, take a *sawngthaew* to Sepon (US$3, 210km, four hours) and another from there to the border (US$1.20, 45km, one hour). If you're passing this way it's worth breaking the journey for a night in Sepon as a base for seeing the Ho Chi Minh Trail.

If you're travelling by tourist bus between Savannakhet and Hué or Danang, expect a wait at the border while documents are checked. Be aware that some through buses arrive at the border in the middle of the night – this means that you may have a fun wait until the border post opens at 7am.

moat, ramparts and gates of the Citadel, which once served as a South Vietnamese army headquarters. The remnants are 1.6km north from Hwy 1. Along Hwy 1, on the Hué side of Quang Tri, is the skeleton of a church that was chillingly scarred with bullet holes and mortar shells.

The **bus station** (Đ Tran Hung Dao) is about 1km from Hwy 1. However, locals suggest that rather than wait at the bus station for north- or southbound buses, stand on the highway and flag them down.

HUÉ

☎ 054 / pop 286,400

Historically, Hué has been the heartbeat of Vietnam, a centre of political intrigue, cultural innovation, religious worship and educational excellence. Today, its main attractions are the splendid tombs of the Nguyen emperors, several notable pagodas and the remains of the Citadel. In May 2001 the first Festival of Hué was celebrated, with local and international cultural performers at locations throughout the city, and this is now a biennial event in the calendar (to be held next in 2006). Hotel accommodation is at a premium at this time, so book ahead if you can.

Tourism may just have saved Hué's cultural sites from oblivion. Between 1975 and 1990, all the old buildings were regarded as politically incorrect, signs of the 'feudal Nguyen dynasty'. Everything was left to decay. It was only in 1990 that the local government recognised the potential of the place and declared these sites 'national treasures'. In 1993 Unesco designated the complex of monuments in Hué a World Heritage site, and restoration and preservation work continues.

Most of the city's major sights have an admission charge of 55,000d; often there is an additional charge for video cameras.

History

The citadel city of Phu Xuan was originally built in 1687 at Bao Vinh Village, 5km northeast of present-day Hué. In 1744 Phu Xuan became the capital of the southern part of Vietnam, which was under the rule of the Nguyen lords. The Tay Son Rebels occupied the city from 1786 until 1802, when it fell to Nguyen Anh. He crowned himself Emperor Gia Long, thus founding the Nguyen dynasty, which ruled the country – at least in name – until 1945.

In 1885, when the advisers of 13-year-old Emperor Ham Nghi objected to French activities in Tonkin, French forces encircled the city. Unwisely, the outnumbered Vietnamese forces launched an attack; the French responded mercilessly. According to a contemporary French account, the French forces took three days to burn the imperial library and remove from the palace every single object of value, including everything from gold and silver ornaments to mosquito nets and toothpicks. Ham Nghi fled to Laos, but he was eventually captured and exiled to Algeria. The French replaced him with the more pliable Dong Khanh, thus ending any pretence of genuine independence for Vietnam.

The city's present name probably evolved from its former name, Thanh Hoa. The word *hoa* means 'peace' or 'harmony' in Vietnamese. The city has been called Hué for more than two centuries now.

Hué was the site of the bloodiest battles of the 1968 Tet Offensive and was the only city in South Vietnam to be held by the communists for more than a few days. While the American command was concentrating its energies on relieving the siege of Khe Sanh, North Vietnamese and VC troops skirted the American stronghold and walked right into Hué, South Vietnam's third-largest city. When the communists arrived, they hoisted their flag from the Citadel's Flag Tower, where it flew for the next 25 days; the local South Vietnamese governmental apparatus completely collapsed.

Immediately on taking Hué, communist political cadres implemented detailed plans to liquidate Hué's 'uncooperative' elements. Thousands of people were rounded up in extensive house-to-house searches, conducted according to lists of names meticulously prepared months before.

During the 3½ weeks Hué remained under communist control, approximately 3000 civilians – including merchants, Buddhist monks, Catholic priests, and intellectuals, as well as people with ties to the South Vietnamese government – were summarily shot, clubbed to death or buried alive. The victims were buried in shallow mass graves that were discovered at various spots around the city over the following few years.

HUÉ

A **B** **C** **D**

1

Cua Hau Canal

Đ Tang Bat Ho

Luong Ngoc Quyen

Nha Do Gate

Đ Đinh Tien Hoang

To Mang Ca

Thanh Long Bridge

Nga Ha Canal

Tang Tau Lake

● 32

The Citadel

Tinh Tam Lake

● 34

To An Hoa Bus Station (200m);
Dong Ha (72km);
DMZ (90km); Vinh (363km);
Hanoi (689km)

Đ Thai Phien

Đ Nguyen Trai

Đ Ngo Duc Ke

Đ 1968

2

Chanh Tay Gate

Đ Tran That Thiep

Đ Phung Hung

Đ Le Thanh Ton

Đ Tinh Tam

Đ Ngo Si Lien

Đ Mai Thuc Loan

Nga Ha Canal

Đ Nguyen Dieu

Kẻ Van Canal

Đ Le Duan

Đ Trieu Quang Phuc

Đ Nhat Le

Đ Đang Dung

● 62

Đ Nguyen Chi Dieu

Đ Thach Han

Đ Tue Tinh

Đ Đang Thai Than

Đ Doan Thi Diem

Đ Han Thuyen

Hoa Binh Gate

3

Đ Nguyen Chi Trinh

Đ Tran Nguyen Dan

Đ Yet Kieu

Đ Le Huan

● 12

Hien Nhon Gate

17

14

Đ Đinh Cong Trang

🏛 15

Đ Le Truc

● 81 🏛

21

19

🏛 33

18 🏛

Chuong Duc Gate

36

Thuong Tu Gate

Đ Ngo

Thoi Nhiem

Đ Nguyen Thien Thuat

35

26

25

28

Đ Tran Nguyen Han

27

30

23 Thang 8

16

24

4

Đ Le Duan

To Thien Mu
Pagoda (3.5km)

Đ Kim Long

Song Huong
(Perfume River)

River Boats 🚢

5

River Boats 🚢

20

Đ Le Loi

Gia Vien
Island

38 🏛

65 🍴

54

23

Đ Tran Thuc

Đ Bui Thi Xuan

🚂 Hué

Đ Bui Thi Xuan

8

Đ Dien Bien Phu

Đ Phan Boi Chau

6

37

22

To Nam Giao;
Royal Tombs (2-16km)

CENTRAL VIETNAM

0   400 m
0   0.2 miles

Phu Hiep Subdistrict

Đ Ho Xuan Huong

To Ferry (800m)

To Duong No Village (4.5km); Thuan An Beach (14.5km)

Phu Cat Subdistrict

Đ Nguyen Chi Thanh

Đ Nguyen Binh Khiem

Đ Chung Dong

Đ Bach Dang

Chi Lang

Dong Ba Canal

Đ Nguyen Du

Đ Huynh Thuc Khang

River Boats

Đ Le Loi

Đ Doc Chua

Đ Phuong Hung

Đ Vo Thi Sau

Đ Nguyen Thai Hoc

Dong Ba Gate

Đ Dinh De

Đ Phan Dang Luu

Đ Huong Vuong

Đ Tran Cao Van

Đ Tran Quang Khai

Đ Ly Quy Don

Đ Hoang

Đ Hoa Xuan

Đ Nguyen Tri Phuong

Đ Ben Nghe

St Xavier Church

Đ Hanoi

Ferry Dock

Song Huong (Perfume River)

River Boats

Dap Da Dam

Nhung River

0   200 m
0   0.1 miles

Đ Tong Duy Tan

Đ Tran Hung Dao

River Boats

See Enlargement

Đ Le Loi

Đ Doc Chua

Đ Vo Thi Sau

Trang Tien Bridge

Đ Nguyen Dinh Chieu

Đ Nguyen Cong Tru

Phu Xuan Bridge

Đ Le Loi

Đ Tran Cao Van

Đ Ben Nghe

Đ Nguyen Thai Hoc

Đ Phan Boi Chau

Đ Hanoi

Đ Nguyen Tri Phuong

Đ Tran Quang Khai

Đ Ly Quy Don

Đ Nguyen Huy Tu

Đ Ngo Quyen

Đ Ly Thuong Kiet

Đ Hai Ba Trung

Đ Dong Da

Đ Hung Vuong

To Thanh Toan Bridge (6km)

Đ Le Loi

Đ Nguyen Hue

Đ Phan Dinh Phung

Kenh Phu Cam

Đ Phan Chu Trinh

An Cuu Bridge

Đ Nguyen Truong To

Đ Doan Huu Trinh

Phu Cam Cathedral

To Phu Bai Airport (13km); Danang (108km); Ho Chi Minh City (1097km)

CENTRAL VIETNAM

When the South Vietnamese army units proved unable to dislodge the occupying North Vietnamese and VC forces, General Westmoreland ordered US troops to recapture the city. Over the next few weeks, whole neighbourhoods were levelled by VC rockets and US bombs. In 10 days of combat, the VC were forced to retreat from the 'New City'.

Over the next two weeks, most of the area inside the Citadel was battered by the South Vietnamese air force, US artillery and brutal house-to-house fighting. Approximately 10,000 people died in Hué during the Tet Offensive. Thousands of VC troops, 400 South Vietnamese soldiers and 150 US marines were among the dead, but most of those killed were civilians.

Long after the American War ended, one American veteran is said to have returned to Hué and, upon meeting a former VC officer, commented that the USA never lost a single major battle during the entire war. 'You are absolutely correct', the VC officer agreed, 'but that is irrelevant, is it not?' Journalist Gavin Young's 1997 memoir *A Wavering Grace* is a moving account of his 30-year relationship with a family from Hué, and with the city itself, during and beyond the American War. It makes a good literary companion for a stay in the city.

Orientation

The city of Hué lies along either side of the Perfume River. The north side of the river has the Citadel and a few places to stay, making for a pleasant and quiet stop. However, it is the south side that has most facilities and a greater selection of hotels and restaurants.

The island on which Phu Cat and Phu Hiep subdistricts are located can be reached by crossing the Dong Ba Canal near Dong Ba Market.

MAPS

The fold-up *Hué Tourism Map* (5000d) is available in town. Not much detail, but handy to stuff in the pocket.

Information

INTERNET ACCESS

There are lots of Internet cafés on the tourist strips of Đ Hung Vuong and Đ Le Loi, and they charge about 100d per minute. You will find that most hotels in the city also offer Internet access for around 300d per minute.

MEDICAL SERVICES

Hué Central Hospital (Benh Vien Trung Uong Hué; ☎ 822 325; 16 Đ Le Loi) For medical treatment, this place is close to Phu Xuan Bridge.

MONEY

Vietcombank (54 Đ Hung Vuong) offers the usual kinds of services, such as exchanging travellers cheques, and has an ATM. There's another handy **branch** (Hotel Saigon Morin, 30 Đ Le Loi; 7am-10pm Mon-Sat), which also has an ATM. Close by to Vietcombank is **Industrial Development Bank** (41 Đ Hung Vuong), which has the same services.

POST

The **main post office** (Đ Ly Thuong Kiet) offers postal and telephone services; there's a smaller **branch** (Đ Le Loi) near the river.

TRAVEL AGENCIES

Official tourism information is in slim supply, but guesthouses, hotels and travel cafés plug the gap.

Café on Thu Wheels (832 241; 1/2 Đ Nguyen Tri Phuong) Immensely popular cycling and motorbiking tours round Hué with a large dose of laughs.

Le Loi Hué Hotel (824 668; 2 Đ Le Loi) Well-organised travel office at this big hotel.

Mandarin Café (821 281; mandarin@dng.vnn vn; 3 Đ Hung Vuong) Watched over by the eagle eyes of photographer Mr Cu, this place is great for information, transport and tours.

Stop and Go Café (827 051; 10 Đ Ben Nghe) Silver-haired Mr Do is a can-do kind of guy for travel and tour arrangements.

Sights

CITADEL

Construction of the moated **Citadel** (Kinh Thanh), which has a 10km perimeter, was begun in 1804 on a site chosen by Emperor Gia Long's geomancers. The Citadel was originally made of earth, but tens of thousands of workers laboured to cover the ramparts, built in the style of the French military architect Vauban, with a layer of bricks 2m thick.

Three sides of the Citadel are straight; the fourth is rounded slightly to follow the curve of the river. The ramparts are encircled by a zigzag moat, which is 30m across and about 4m deep. In the northern corner of the Citadel is Mang Ca Fortress, once known as the French Concession, which is still used as a military base. The Citadel has 10 fortified gates, each reached via a bridge across the moat.

Wide areas within the Citadel are now devoted to agriculture, a legacy of the destruction of 1968.

Flag Tower

The 37m-high **Flag Tower** (Cot Co), also known as the King's Knight, is Vietnam's tallest flagpole. Erected in 1809 and extended in 1831, a terrific typhoon, which devastated the whole city, knocked it down in 1904. The tower was rebuilt in 1915, only to be destroyed again in 1947. It was erected once again, in its present form, in 1949. During the VC occupation of Hué in 1968, the National Liberation Front flag flew defiantly from the tower for 3½ weeks.

Nine Holy Cannons

Located just inside the Citadel ramparts near the gates to either side of the Flag Tower, the Nine Holy Cannons, symbolic protectors of the palace and kingdom, were cast from brass pieces captured from the Tay Son Rebels. The cannons, which were cast on the orders of Emperor Gia Long in 1804, were never intended to be fired. Each is 5m long, has a bore of 23cm and weighs about 10 tonnes. The four cannons near Ngan Gate represent the four seasons, while the five cannons next to Quang Duc Gate represent the five elements: metal, wood, water, fire and earth.

IMPERIAL ENCLOSURE

The emperor's official functions were carried out in the **Imperial Enclosure** (admission 55,000d; 6.30am-5.30pm), a citadel-within-a-citadel with 6m-high walls that are 2.5km in length. The Imperial Enclosure has four gates, the most famous of which is Ngo Mon Gate.

Ngo Mon Gate

The principal entrance to the Imperial Enclosure is **Ngo Mon Gate** (Noontime Gate), which faces the Flag Tower.

The central passageway with its yellow doors was reserved for the use of the emperor, as was the bridge across the lotus pond. Others had to use the gates to either side and the paths around the lotus pond.

On top of the gate is **Ngu Phung** (Belvedere of the Five Phoenixes), where the emperor appeared on important occasions, most notably for the promulgation of the lunar calendar. On 30 August 1945, Emperor Bao Dai ended the Nguyen dynasty here when he abdicated to a delegation sent by Ho Chi Minh's Provisional Revolutionary Government.

Thai Hoa Palace

Built in 1803 and moved to its present site in 1833, **Thai Hoa Palace** (Palace of Supreme Harmony) is a spacious hall with an ornate timber roof supported by 80 carved and lacquered columns. Accessible from Ngo Mon Gate via Trung Dao Bridge, it was used for the emperor's official receptions and other important court ceremonies, such as anniversaries and coronations. During state occasions, the king sat on his elevated throne and his mandarins paid homage. Nine stelae divide the two-level courtyard into separate areas for officials in each of the nine ranks of the mandarinate; administrative mandarins stood to one side while the military mandarins stood to the other.

Halls of the Mandarins

The buildings in which the mandarins prepared for court ceremonies, held in Can Chanh Reception Hall, were restored in 1977. The structures are directly behind Thai Hoa Palace on either side of a courtyard, where there are two gargantuan bronze *vac dong* (cauldrons), dating from the 17th century.

Nine Dynastic Urns

These *dinh* (urns) were cast between 1835 and 1836. Traditional ornamentation was chiselled into the sides of the urns, each dedicated to a different Nguyen sovereign. The designs, some of which are of Chinese origin and date back 4000 years, include the sun, moon, meteors, clouds, mountains, rivers and various landscapes. About 2m in height and weighing 1900kg to 2600kg each, the urns symbolise the power and stability of the Nguyen throne. The central urn, which is the largest and most ornate, is dedicated to Gia Long.

Forbidden Purple City

Reserved solely for the personal use of the emperor, the only servants allowed into this compound were eunuchs, who would pose no threat to the royal concubines.

The **Forbidden Purple City** (Tu Cam Thanh) was almost entirely destroyed during the Tet Offensive. The area is now given to vegetable plots, between which touch-sensitive mimosa plants flourish. The two-storey **Emperor's Reading Room** (Thai Binh Lau) has been partially restored in its landscaped surrounds

and now houses a small photographic exhibition. The foundations of the **Royal Theatre** (Duyen Thi Duong), begun in 1826 and later home of the National Conservatory of Music, can also be seen nearby.

Dien Tho Residence

In the western corner of the Imperial Enclosure is the stunning Dien Tho Residence. This comprises the apartments and audience hall of the Queen Mothers of the Nguyen dynasty. The audience hall now houses an exhibition of photos showing its former use, and there is a beautiful display of embroidered royal garments. Just outside is their Highnesses' enchanting pleasure pavilion, a carved wooden building set above a lily pond.

To Mieu Temple

Close to Chuong Duc Gate is To Mieu Temple and its associated buildings, constructed in 1821. It's dedicated to the Nguyen emperors, and restoration work on the wooden structures was completed in 1998.

TINH TAM LAKE

In the middle of Tinh Tam Lake, which is 500m north of the Imperial Enclosure, are two islands connected by bridges. The emperors used to come here with their retinues to relax.

TANG TAU LAKE

An island on Tang Tau Lake, which is northeast of Tinh Tam Lake, was once the site of a royal library. It is now occupied by a small Theravada Buddhist pagoda, called Ngoc Huong Pagoda.

MUSEUMS
Fine Arts Museum

The beautiful hall that houses the **Fine Arts Museum** (3 Đ Le Truc; admission 22,000d; ⏰ 7am-5pm) was built in 1845 and restored when the museum was founded in 1923. The walls are inscribed with poems written in *nom* (Vietnamese script). The most precious artefacts were lost during the American War, but the ceramics, furniture and royal clothing that remain are well worth the visit.

On the left side of the hall is a royal sedan chair, a gong and a musical instrument consisting of stones hung on a two-level rack. On the other side of the hall is he equipment for a favourite game of the mperors – the idea was to bounce a stick ff a wooden platform into a tall, thin jug.

General Museum Complex

The equally lovely building across the street was once a school for princes and the sons f high-ranking mandarins. It's now a gallery, and forms part of the **General Museum complex** (enter from Đ Le Truc or Đ 23 Thang 8; admission free; 7.30am-5pm Fri-Wed). It combines, in n odd juxtaposition, the **Military Museum**, with its usual assortment of US- and Soviet-made weapons, and a small **Natural History Museum**.

Ho Chi Minh Museum

On display at this **museum** (9 Đ Le Loi) are photographs, some of Ho Chi Minh's personal effects, and documents relating to his life and accomplishments.

PAGODAS & CHURCHES

Bao Quoc Pagoda

Last renovated in 1957, **Bao Quoc Pagoda** (Pagoda Which Serves the Country; Ham Long Hill) was founded in 1670 by Giac Phong, a Buddhist monk from China. It was given its present name in 1824 by Emperor Minh Mang, who celebrated his 40th birthday here in 1830. A school for training monks was opened here in 1940.

The central altar in the main sanctuary contains three identical Buddha statues, which represent (from left to right) Di Lac, Thich Ca and A Di Da, and behind these is a memorial room for deceased monks. Around the main building are the tombs of monks, including a three-storey, red-and-grey stupa built for the pagoda's founder.

Bao Quoc Pagoda is on Ham Long Hill in Phuong Duc district. To get here, head south from Đ Le Loi on Đ Dien Bien Phu and turn right immediately after crossing the railway tracks.

Tu Dam Pagoda

About 400m south of Bao Quoc Pagoda is **Tu Dam Pagoda** (cnr Đ Dien Bien Phu & Đ Tu Dam), one of Vietnam's best-known pagodas. Unfortunately, the present buildings are recent additions that date from 1936.

Tu Dam Pagoda was founded around 1695 by Minh Hoang Tu Dung, a Chinese monk. It was given its present name by Em-peror Thieu Tri in 1841. It was here that the Unified Vietnamese Buddhist Association was established at a meeting in 1951. During the early 1960s, Tu Dam was a major centre of the Buddhist anti-Diem and antiwar movements, and in 1968 it became the scene of heavy fighting, scars of which remain.

Today, Tu Dam Pagoda, home to a handful of monks, is the seat of the provincial Buddhist Association. The peculiar bronze Thich Ca Buddha in the sanctuary was cast locally in 1966.

Just east of the pagoda is **Linh Quang Pagoda** (Đ Tu Dam) and the **tomb** of the scholar and anticolonialist revolutionary Phan Boi Chau (1867–1940).

Dieu De National Pagoda

The entrance to **Dieu De National Pagoda** (Quoc Tu Dieu De; 102 Đ Bach Dang), built under Emperor Thieu Tri's rule (1841–47), is along Dong Ba Canal. It is one of the city's three 'national pagodas', which were once under the direct patronage of the emperor. Dieu De is famous for its four low towers, one to either side of the gate and two flanking the sanctuary. There are bells in two of the towers; the others contain a drum and a stele dedicated to the pagoda's founder.

During the regime of Ngo Dinh Diem (1955–63) and through the mid-1960s, Dieu De National Pagoda was a stronghold of Buddhist and student opposition to the South Vietnamese government and the war. In 1966 the pagoda was stormed by police, who confiscated the opposition movement's radio equipment and arrested many monks, Buddhist laypeople and students.

The pavilions on either side of the main sanctuary entrance contain the 18 La Ha, whose rank is just below that of Bodhisattva, and the eight Kim Cang, protectors of Buddha. In the back row of the main dais is Thich Ca Buddha flanked by two assistants, Pho Hien Bo Tat (to his right) and Van Thu Bo Tat (to his left).

Other Pagodas

Founded by the Hainan Chinese Congregation in the mid-19th century, **Chieu Ung Pagoda** (Chieu Ung Tu; opposite 138 Đ Chi Lang) was rebuilt in 1908. The pagoda's sanctuary retains its original ornamentation, which is becoming faded but has been mercifully unaffected by the third-rate modernistic renovations that have marred other such structures. The pagoda was built as a memorial to 108 Hainan merchants, who were mistaken for pirates and killed in Vietnam in 1851.

Down the alley opposite 80 Đ Nguyen Chi Thanh, **Tang Quang Pagoda** (Tang Quang Tu) is the largest of the three Theravada pagodas in Hué. Built in 1957, it owes its distinctive architecture to Theravada Buddhism's historical links to Sri Lanka and India.

Founded by the Hainan Chinese Congregation almost a century ago, **Chua Ba** (opposite 216 Đ Chi Lang) was damaged in the Tet Offensive and subsequently reconstructed. On the central altar is Thien Hau Thanh Mau, Goddess of the Sea and Protector of Fishermen and Sailors.

Chua Ong Pagoda (opposite 224 Đ Chi Lang) was founded by Hué's Fujian Chinese Congregation during the reign of Vietnamese emperor Tu Duc (1848–83). This building was severely damaged during the Tet Offensive, when a nearby ammunition ship blew up. A gold Buddha sits in a glass case opposite the main doors of the sanctuary. The left-hand altar is dedicated to Thien Hau Thanh Mau, who is flanked by her two assistants, 1000-eyed Thien Ly Nhan and red-faced Thuan Phong Nhi, who can hear for 1000 miles. On the altar to the right is Quan Cong.

Notre Dame Cathedral

This **cathedral** (Dong Chua Cuu The; 80 Đ Nguyen Hue) is an impressive modern structure that combines the functional aspects of a European cathedral with traditional Vietnamese architecture, including a decidedly Asian spire. The huge cathedral, which was constructed between 1959 and 1962, has around 1600 members. Two French-speaking priests hold mass daily, at 5am and 5pm, with an extra 7am service on Sunday. Visitors who find the front gate locked should ring the bell of the yellow building next door.

Phu Cam Cathedral

Construction of this **cathedral** (20 Đ Doan Huu Trinh) began in 1963 and was halted in 1975, before the completion of the bell tower. It is the eighth church to be built on this site since 1682 and the Hué diocese, which is based here, hopes eventually to find the funds to complete the structure. Mass is

held at 5am and 6.45pm from Monday to Saturday and at 5am, 7am, 2pm and 7pm on Sunday.

NATIONAL SCHOOL

One of the most famous secondary school in Vietnam, the **National School** (Quoc Hoc; 10 Đ L Loi; 🕑 after 3pm) was founded in 1896 and ru by Ngo Dinh Kha, the father of South Viet namese president Ngo Dinh Diem. Man of the school's pupils later rose to prom inence in both North and South Vietnam Numbered among the National School' former students is General Vo Nguye Giap, strategist of the Viet Minh victory a Dien Bien Phu and North Vietnam's long serving deputy premier, defence ministe and commander-in-chief. Pham Van Dong North Vietnam's prime minister for ove a quarter of a century, and the secretary general and former prime minister D Muoi also studied here. Even Ho Chi Min attended the school briefly in 1908.

The school was given a major renovatio in 1996 to celebrate its 100th anniversar and a statue of Ho Chi Minh was erected The National School cannot be visited unti after classes finish at about 3pm.

THANH TOAN BRIDGE

If you miss the famous Japanese bridge i Hoi An, or prefer to get off the beaten track there is a classic covered footbridge abou 7km east of central Hué well worth seek ing out. Thanh Toan Bridge is architectur ally similar to its cousin in Hoi An, though it receives far fewer visitors – it's mostl used by local villagers for naps in the shad walkway.

The bridge is best reached by motorbik or bicycle. Finding it is a bit tricky, but toler able if you consider getting lost part of th excursion. Head north for a few hundre metres on Đ Ba Trieu until you see a sign t the Citadel Hotel. Turn right here and fol low the delightful (and bumpy) dirt road fo another 6km past villages, rice paddies an several pagodas until you reach the bridge.

Sleeping
BUDGET
East Đ Le Loi Area

A good place to find basic, cheap room near the river is in the narrow alley off Đ L Loi between Đ Pham Ngu Lao and Đ Chu

Van An. Many budget hotels offer pick-ups from the airport if you book in advance.

Guesthouse Hoang Huong (☎ 828 509; 46/2 Đ Le oi; dm US$2.50, r $3.50-6; ✘) Occupying a tiny space on 'budget alley', this is one of the only places with dorms. It often fills up, but here are plenty of places nearby.

Mimosa Guesthouse (☎ 828 068; fax 823 858; 46/6 Đ Le Loi; r US$3-8; ✘) A popular pad run by Mr Tran Van Hoang, a former French teacher and author of several books written in French. It's quiet and has cool common balconies. Book ahead to be sure of a bed.

Thanh Thuy's Guesthouse (☎ 824 585; thanhthuy 56@dng.vnn.vn; 46/4 Đ Le Loi; r US$4-7; ✘) Blink and you'll miss this six-room family-run guest-house. Most of the higher-priced rooms come with balcony.

Phuong Hoang Hotel (Phoenix Hotel; ☎ 826 736; phoenixhotel@dng.vnn.vn; 48/3 Đ Le Loi; r US$10-20; ✘) A definite step up in comfort along this strip, it offers roomy rooms with satellite TV and bathtubs. There's a popular little restaurant here.

A Dong Hotel (☎ 824 148; adongcoltd@dng.vnn.vn; 8 Đ Chu Van An; s US$6-8, d US$8-15; ✘) A reli-able hotel that offers those extra comforts that distinguish hotels from guesthouses. Doubles include breakfast.

A Dong II Hotel (☎ 822 765; 7 Đ Doi Cung; r US$8-20; ✘) This is another step up in comfort.

Guesthouse Van Xuan (☎ 826 567; 10 Đ Pham Ngu Lao; s/d US$5/7; ✘) This is a fine, friendly family-run budget place that's low-key and low-rise, and has big, breezy verandas. Hot water and satellite TV are also part of the package.

Other promising places in this area:

An Phuoc Hotel (☎ 824 925; fax 826 090; 26 Đ Pham Ngu Lao; s/d/t US$10/12/15; ✘) Fresh and friendly feel at this hotel and all rooms have TV, fridge and hot water.

Minh Hien Hotel (☎ 828 725; 3 Đ Chu Van An; r US$10-15; ✘) New place with nifty amenities; breakfast is included.

Đ Hung Vuong Area

There's another cluster of budget hotels lo-cated around the junction of Đ Nguyen Tri Phuong and Đ Hung Vuong.

Binh Duong Hotel II (☎ 833 298; 8 Ngo Gia Tu; r US$7-15; ✘ 🖳) Near the post office, this place can take up the slack if the mid-range original is full.

Hai Dang Hotel (☎ 824 755; 43 Đ Hung Vuong; s/d US$8/10; ✘) This hotel sets a serious standard

for value for money. All rooms are equipped with TV, telephone, fridge and hot-water bathtubs. To top it all off, it has a friendly feel.

Also worth a look here:

Huong Vuong Inn (☎ 821 068; fax 827 899; 20 Đ Hung Vuong; r US$7-9; ✘) New guesthouse in good shape that has a little bakery downstairs.

Saigon Hotel (☎ 821 007; fax 821 009; 32b Đ Hung Vuong; r US$10-15; ✘) Large, well-tended rooms, all including breakfast.

Other Areas

Le Loi Hué Hotel (Khach San Le Loi; ☎ 822 153; fax 824 527; 2 Đ Le Loi; r US$5-20; ✘ 🖳) Simply enor-mous, this place boasts 172 rooms. It's also been hugely successful at attracting back-packers, thanks to low prices, good rooms – budget rooms are tiny and tatty but do the trick – and its location, just a 100m walk from the train station. Satellite TV is on tap, there's Internet access, and it's a good place for booking transport and tours.

MID-RANGE
North Bank

Over in the Citadel lies the **Thanh Noi Hotel** (☎ 522 478; thanhnoi@dng.vnn.vn; 57 Đ Dang Dung; r US$20-30; ✘ 🖳 🖳), a popular hotel in a lovely location. The quiet, tree-shaded com-pound has its own restaurant, ample parking and a fair-sized swimming pool with water jets. All rooms have satellite TV, fridge and hot water and more money buys more space. Enter from Đ Doan Thi Diem. The hotel is being rebranded as the Imperial Hué.

South Bank

Binh Minh Hotel (☎ 825 526; binhminhhue@dng .vnn.vn; 12 Đ Nguyen Tri Phuong; r US$12-25; ✘ 🖳) A fancy, family-run place that earns rave re-views from travellers. This hotel has a good range of rooms with touches like bathtubs and big balconies. It also has a lift.

Binh Minh 2 (☎ 849 007; 45 Đ Ben Nghe; r US$12-25) A second branch of the Binh Minh, for spillovers.

Ngoc Huong Hotel (☎ 830 111; www.ngochuong hotels.com; 32b Đ Hung Vuong; r US$25-80; ✘) Located in a popular part of town, this is a smart new hotel. The large rooms include all the crea-ture comforts one might want, plus there's a Jacuzzi and sauna for winding down.

Duy Tan Hotel (☎ 825 001; nkduytan@dng.vnn .vn; 12 Đ Hung Vuong; r US$10-25; ✘ 🖳) About as

CENTRAL VIETNAM

central as it gets, with plenty of parking available, the rates are right on the mark. The more expensive rooms are large and bright and have balconies.

Thai Binh Hotel (☎ 828 058; ksthaibinh@dng.vnn .vn; 10/9 Đ Nguyen Tri Phuong; r US$6-30; 🏵 🖳) Just across the alley from Binh Duong Hotel, this is a popular option, and has old and new wings. The old wing is at the back and offers the quieter, cheaper rooms. There's a lift to avoid the workout necessary at many budget guesthouses. Internet access is available in the lobby.

L'Indochine Hotel (Dong Duong Hotel; ☎ 823 866; indochine-hotel@dng.vnn.vn; 2 Đ Hung Vuong; r US$10-30; 🏵 🖳) There is something for everyone here, with well-equipped standard, superior and deluxe rooms. Even the budget rooms have air-con and hot water, plus there's a lift.

Binh Duong Hotel (☎ /fax 833 298; binh duong1@dng.vnn.vn; 10/4 Đ Nguyen Tri Phuong; r US$5-30; 🏵) It may have a small exterior, but this belies a warren of an interior with 24 rooms. It is often chock-full and especially popular with Japanese backpackers. Most of the clean rooms are at the cheaper end and good value, all with satellite TV and hot water.

Thuan Hoa Hotel (☎ 822 553; t_hoahtl@dng.vnn .vn; 7 Đ Nguyen Tri Phuong; r US$25-50; 🏵) It may look more like a large bank, but the US$25 rooms are sensible value, with tasteful trimmings and most mod cons.

5 Le Loi Hotel (☎ 822 155; 5leloihotel@dng.vnn.vn; 5 Đ Le Loi; r US$30-60; 🏵) Housed in a stately old villa, this place has lovely river views and lush gardens. It was just about to close for renovations when we visited, so it may be more expensive and more luxurious when it reopens.

Also worth a look in this range:

Phu Xuan Hotel (☎ 823 278; pxhotel@dng.vnn.vn; 9 Đ Ngo Quyen; r US$12-30; 🏵) Recently relocated to the south bank, it's a smart, central option.

Thanh Lich Hotel (☎ 825 973; thanhlichks@dng.vnn .vn; 33 Đ Hai Ba Trung; r US$20-30; 🏵) Elegant by name, elegant by nature, but not so central.

TOP END

Hotel Saigon Morin (☎ 823 526; sgmorin@dng.vnn .vn; 30 Đ Le Loi; r US$50-100; 🏵 🖳 🏊) A grand historic hotel, this impressive building occupies an entire city block near the south bank of the Perfume River. The hotel offers all the features of a four-star, and has three restaurants, a lovely courtyard café bar with a very reasonably priced bar-food menu, and a swimming pool in the shape of a gourd. A new 4th-floor extension has been added to cope with demand for a slice of history.

Century Riverside Hotel (☎ 823 390; cenhotvn@ dng.vnn.vn; 49 Đ Le Loi; r US$50-170; 🏵 🖳 🏊) A huge hotel on the banks of the Perfume River, where comfort comes at a price, but discounts of about 30% are common, especially during quiet periods. There's a US$5 fee to use the pool for the day.

Huong Giang Hotel (☎ 822 122; hghotel@dng.vnn .vn; 51 Đ Le Loi; r US$50-180; 🏵 🖳 🏊) An identikit image of Century Riverside, this place has plush rooms with pine finishes. The riverside terrace is a top spot to watch river life float by, and nonresidents can use the landscaped pool for US$3.

Eating

Hue is a famed culinary city and has set many trends in Vietnamese cooking. See the Food & Drink chapter (p62) for leads on what to try.

NORTH BANK

Lac Thanh Restaurant (☎ 524 674; 6A Đ Dinh Tien Hoang; dishes 7000-20,000d) This is an in spot for travellers venturing over the river. The congenial owner, Mr Lac, is deaf and mute, so everything is communicated with sign language. However, his daughter speaks English well. It looks a bit run-down at first glance, but is spread over four floors for some balcony dining.

Lac Thien Restaurant (☎ 527 348; 6B Đ Dinh Tien Hoang) This place has cloned Lac Thanh's motif. Deaf people working here also produce fine food, plus an entertaining atmosphere.

Lac Thuan (☎ 531 362; 6 Đ Dinh Tien Hoang) In true Vietnamese fashion, yet a *third* clone of the same name pulls the punters and is just on the other side of Lac Thanh.

Tinh Gia Vien (☎ 522 243; 20/3 Đ Le Thanh Ton; set-course meals US$10-15) The garden setting here plays host for dishes in the traditional style of Hue's imperial court. The artistic presentation of the food is more interesting than its taste. Too many tour groups for some, but, yes, it really is down that unlikely looking lane.

Y Thao Garden (☎ 523 018; hoacuchue@dng.vnn .vn; 3 Đ Thach Han; set-course meals US$7-10) An altogether more charming choice for Citadel dining. Set in a private house brimming with antiques, the set menus here are beautifully presented and replicate those of the royal court of old. Best to book ahead, as it can get busy.

Adventurous diners might explore the **Dong Ba Market** (Đ Tran Hung Dao; ☺ 6am-6pm). Food here is so cheap they might as well give it away, but it's fresh and flavoursome. The only real problem will be finding comfortable chairs (or, for that matter, any chairs) to sit down and enjoy a meal.

SOUTH BANK

The cafés along Đ Hung Vuong are good places to meet people and swap travellers' tales.

Mandarin Café (☎ 821 281; mandarin@ dng.vnn .vn; 12 Đ Hung Vuong; dishes 5000-50,000d; ☺ 6.30am-10.30pm) A magnet for travellers, it recently moved down the road to make way for a five-star hotel. The cheerful owner, Mr Cu, speaks English and French and is full of useful travel advice; he's also been consistently improving his services since the first LP mention – a rare breed indeed.

Minh & Coco Mini Restaurant (☎ 821 822; 1 Đ Hung Vuong; mains 10,000-30,000d; ☺ 6.30am-late) Run by two lively sisters, this hole in the wall is fast gaining a reputation as a fun place to get an inexpensive feed.

Xuan Trang Cafeteria (☎ 832 480; 14A Đ Hung Vuong; mains 10,000-30,000d) Come here for cheap and filling food. There's a good vegetarian selection and there's usually a crowd.

Phuong Nam Café (☎ 827 037; 5 Đ Hung Vuong; mains 10,000-30,000d) This little eatery claims to have been voted 'best food in Hué by international travellers'. A little pre-ordained, perhaps? But it is always busy and has good, cheap food.

Stop & Go Café (☎ 889 106; 4 Đ Ben Nghe; mains 10,000-70,000d) A sort of indoor-outdoor café run by Mr Do, a silver-haired painter who ensures the café's slightly eccentric air. The house specialities are *banh khoai* (savoury rice pancakes) and *nem lui* (grilled kebabs that you roll yourself and dip into peanut sauce). Fish and meat dishes are pretty pricey, but it's a good spot for a beer.

Tropical Garden Restaurant (☎ 847 143; 27 Đ Chu Van An; mains 30,000-80,000d; ☺ from 6.30pm) This is a popular place with a choice of dining in the attractive main building, or outdoors in a delightful garden. It specialises in central-Vietnamese cuisine, and is presently the best place in Hué to catch a traditional music performance (from 7pm nightly).

Club Garden (☎ 826 327; 8 Đ Vo Thi Sau; mains 30,000-80,000d; ☺ from 6.30pm) So popular has Tropical Garden proved that the owners have opened this place, dishing up the same diet.

Song Huong Floating Restaurant (☎ 823 738; dishes 20,000-50,000d; ☺ 8am-9pm) Top location for this place, right on the bank of the Perfume River, just north of Trang Tien Bridge. The food includes Vietnamese and other Asian standards, but it's not bad for a sundowner, soaking up the river breeze.

Tinh Tam (☎ 823 572; 12 Đ Chu Van An; dishes 10,000-25,000d) Here they take mock meat to new places, with a signature 'deer' with black pepper and lemongrass or 'tuna' with tomato. Even die-hard meat eaters will appreciate the meals here.

Dong Tam (☎ 828 403; 48/7 Đ Le Loi; set lunch or dinner 25,000d) Set in a garden on 'budget alley', this low-key place has some of the best Vietnamese vegetarian fare in town and prices remain really low.

Rice-resistant after a few weeks incountry? There is also the choice of French, Italian and Indian on this side of the river.

La Carambole (☎ 810 491; 19 Đ Pham Ngu Lao; meals 25,000-75,000d) Try this extravagantly decorated place for a good range of French-style dishes, including steaks and grills. Good Vietnamese dishes and seafood to keep everyone happy, plus a healthy wine list.

Little Italy (☎ 826 928; 2A Đ Vo Thi Sau; pastas 35,000d, pizzas 45,000d) Set in one of Hué's hangovers from the Soviet era, don't be put off by the exterior, as inside await the best pizzas and pasta in town.

Omar Khayyam's Indian Restaurant (☎ 821 616; 10 Đ Nguyen Tri Phuong; curries 30,000-60,000d) On the verge of becoming a national curry house in Vietnam, there are branches in several cities. Low on atmosphere, but high on flavours for those craving a curry.

There's a **café** (2 Đ Le Loi; dishes 10,000-30,000d) in the grounds of Le Loi Hué Hotel, and **Café 3 Le Loi** (☎ 824 514; dishes 7000-20,000d), just across the street, also serves up fine food. They're both near the train station and especially handy to cram in the calories before a long train ride.

Vegetarian food has a long tradition in Hué. Stalls in the **markets** (dishes 5000-10,000d) serve lots of vegetarian food on the first and 15th days of the lunar month. You'll find several vegie options on most menus in town, many using soya-bean mock meat.

Drinking

DMZ Bar & Cafe (44 Đ Le Loi) Long the leading late-night spot, the beer flows on into the night, the tunes match the mood and there is a popular pool table in the middle of things.

Café on Thu Wheels (☎ 832 241; 1/2 Đ Nguyen Tri Phuong) It's a tiny little bar with a big personality in the shape of owner Thu. Graffiti galore to gaze at if you've left the guidebook at home and a rowdy crowd most nights.

B4 Bar-Café (75 Đ Ben Nghe) A Belgian-run bar that takes its beers as seriously as you would expect, including a delicious draft Huda. Great spot with bar games galore, free pool and an endless music selection.

Bar Why Not? (☎ 824 793; 21 Đ Vo Thi Sau) This is a new place with classic cocktails for those who want a drink with a kick. There are also plenty of beers and some good bar food, plus the predictable pool table.

Shopping

Hué is known for producing the finest conical hats in Vietnam. The city's speciality is 'poem hats', which, when held up to the light, reveal shadowy scenes of daily life.

Hué is also home to one of the largest and most beautiful selections of rice-paper and silk paintings available in Vietnam, but the prices quoted are usually inflated to about four times the real price.

Dong Ba Market (Đ Tran Hung Dao; ☿ 6am-6pm), on the north bank of the Perfume River a few hundred metres north of Trang Tien Bridge, is Hué's largest market, where anything and everything can be bought. It was rebuilt after much of the structure was destroyed by a typhoon in 1986.

Getting There & Away

AIR

The booking office of **Vietnam Airlines** (☎ 823 249; 12 Đ Hanoi; ☿ 7-11am & 1.30-5pm Mon-Sat) handles reservations. Several flights a day connect Hué to both Hanoi and HCMC; check out the latest schedule at www.vietnamairlines.com.vn.

BUS

Hué has three main bus stations. **An Cuu bus station** (Đ Hung Vuong), which is behind the Mobil garage, serves southern destinations. Public buses leave from this bus station for Danang (22,000d, three hours) every half-hour between 6am and 4.30pm.

There is also an international bus service to Savannakhet (US$15, 13 hours, departing 6am or 6pm daily), crossing via the Lao Bao border.

An Hoa bus station (Hwy 1), northwest of the Citadel, serves northern destinations, including Dong Ha (14,000d, 1½ hours) and Hanoi (75,000d, around 14 hours).

Dong Ba bus station (Đ Tran Hung Dao), for short-haul bus trips, is next to Dong Ba Market.

CAR & MOTORBIKE

A car with driver is available from US$25 per day. Self-drive motorbikes are available from US$5.

Principal destinations from Hué include Danang (108km), Dong Ha (72km), Hanoi (689km), HCMC (1097km) and Lao Bao (152km).

MINIBUS

Hué is a major target for tourist minibus companies and most backpackers travel this way. The Hué–Hoi An run (tickets US$2) is popular; it also stops in Danang.

Tickets for the minibuses are sold at some hotels and guesthouses or open ticket offices – staff will tell you where the minibuses pick up from. Departure from either end is twice daily at 8am and 1pm, and there are usually scenic stops at Lang Co Beach and Hai Van Pass.

TRAIN

Reunification Express trains stop in Hué. For information on ticket prices and schedules, see p482.

The **Hué train station** (☎ 822 175; ticket office ☿ 7.30am-5pm) is on the south bank, at the southwestern end of Đ Le Loi.

Getting Around

TO/FROM THE AIRPORT

Hué is served by Phu Bai Airport, once an important US air base, which is 14km south of the city centre. Taxi fares there are typically around US$8. Share-taxis to the airport cost as little as US$2 – inquire at

THIEN MU PAGODA

Thien Mu Pagoda was a hotbed of antigovernment protest during the early 1960s. Surprisingly, it also became a focus of protest in the 1980s when someone was murdered near the pagoda and anticommunist demonstrations started here, closing traffic around Phu Xuan Bridge. Monks were arrested and accused of disturbing the traffic and public order. Things calmed down and a small group of monks, novices and nuns now live at the pagoda.

Behind the main sanctuary of the Thien Mu Pagoda is the Austin motorcar that transported the monk Thich Quang Duc to the site of his 1963 self-immolation. Thich Quang Duc travelled to Saigon and publicly burned himself to death to protest the policies of President Ngo Dinh Diem. A famous photograph of his act was printed on the front pages of newspapers around the world. His death soon inspired a number of other self-immolations.

Many Westerners were shocked less by the suicides than by the reaction of Tran Le Xuan (Madame Nhu, the president's notorious sister-in-law), who happily proclaimed the self-immolations a 'barbecue party' and said, 'Let them burn and we shall clap our hands'. Her statements greatly added to the already substantial public disgust with Diem's regime; the US press labelled Madame Nhu the 'Iron Butterfly' and 'Dragon Lady'. In November, both President Diem and his brother Ngo Dinh Nhu (Madame Nhu's husband) were assassinated by Diem's own military. Madame Nhu was overseas at the time.

A memorial to Thich Quang Duc (Dai Ky Niem Thuong Toa Thich Quang Duc) can be found at the intersection of Đ Nguyen Dinh Chieu and Đ Cach Mang Thang Tam, around the corner from the Xa Loi Pagoda, in Ho Chi Minh City.

hotels to find these vehicles. **Vietnam Airlines** (☎ 823 249; 12 Đ Hanoi; ☼ 7-11am & 1.30-5pm Mon-Sat) runs its own minibus from its office to the airport, a couple of hours before flight times (tickets 20,000d).

BICYCLE

Pedal power is a fun way to tour Hué and the nearby Royal Tombs if you can cope with the traffic. Many hotels rent out bicycles for about US$1 per day.

BOAT

A boat ride down the Perfume River is a must in Hué. Tours typically take in the tombs of Tu Duc, Thieu Tri, Minh Mang (see Royal Tombs on p213) and the Thien Mu Pagoda; any hotel or travellers café can make bookings. Prices vary, but are generally implausibly cheap at US$1 to US$2 per person (which includes lunch but not entry fees). The journey takes about six hours, and usually runs from 8am to 2pm.

Many sights in the vicinity of Hué, including Thuan An Beach, Thien Mu Pagoda and several of the Royal Tombs, can be reached by boat. Rates for chartering a boat are around 60,000d for an hour's sightseeing on the river; a half-day charter to one or more sites will cost around 150,000d. Ask directly at any of the four main river-boat moorings; it's cheaper than chartering through an agency and you can negotiate your own route.

CYCLO & MOTORBIKE

A typical scene in Hué is a foreigner walking down the street with two *cyclos* and a motorbike in hot pursuit, the drivers yelling, 'hello *cyclo*' and 'hello motorbike' and the foreigner yelling, 'no, thank you, no!' There's a pretty standard fare for both of 10,000d per kilometre.

Self-drive motorbikes can be hired from some guesthouses, hotels and restaurants. Think 50,000d to 70,000d per day.

For a top motorbike tour around Hué, contact **Cafe On Thu Wheels** (☎ 832 241; 1/2 Đ Nguyen Tri Phuong).

TAXI

There are several metered taxi companies in Hué. Try the following:

Co Do Taxi (☎ 830 830)
Gili (☎ 828 282)
Mai Linh (☎ 898 989)
Thanh Do (☎ 858 585)

AROUND HUÉ
Thien Mu Pagoda

Built on a hillock overlooking the Perfume River, 4km southwest of the Citadel, this

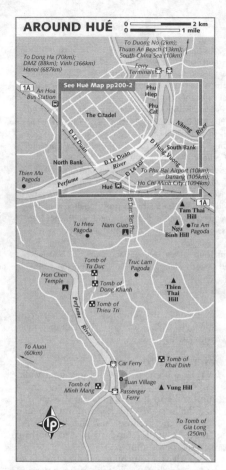

AROUND HUÉ

0 —————— 2 km
0 —————— 1 mile

To Dong Ha (70km);
DMZ (88km); Vinh (366km)
Hanoi (687km)

To Duong No (2km);
Thuan An Beach (13km);
South China Sea (10km)

Ferry
Terminals

1A An Hoa
Bus Station

See Hué Map pp200-2

Phu
Hiep

Phu
Cat

The Citadel

Nhung River

D Le Duan

South Bank

D Le Duan
River

North Bank

D Le Loi

D Hung Vuong

To Phu Bai Airport (10km);
Danang (105km);
Ho Chi Minh City (1094km)

Thien Mu
Pagoda

Perfume

Hué

1A

D Dien Bien Phu

Tam Thai
Hill

Tu Hieu
Pagoda

Nam Giao

Ngu
Binh Hill

Tra Am
Pagoda

Tomb of
Tu Duc

Truc Lam
Pagoda

Hon Chen
Temple

Tomb of
Dong Khanh

Thien
Thai
Hill

Tomb of
Thieu Tri

Perfume River

To Aluoi
(60km)

Car Ferry

Tomb of
Khai Dinh

Tomb of
Minh Mang

Tuan Village

Passenger
Ferry

Vung Hill

To Tomb of
Gia Long
(250m)

pagoda (admission free) is an icon of Vietnam. The existing 21m-high octagonal tower, the seven-storey Thap Phuoc Duyen, was constructed under the reign of Emperor Thieu Tri in 1844 and has become the unofficial symbol of the city of Hué. Each of the seven storeys is dedicated to a *manushi-buddha*, which is a Buddha that appeared in human form.

Thien Mu Pagoda was originally founded in 1601 by Nguyen Hoang, governor of Thuan Hoa province. According to legend, a Fairy Woman (Thien Mu) appeared and told the people that a lord would come to build a pagoda for the country's prosperity. On hearing this, Nguyen Hoang ordered a pagoda to be constructed here. Over the centuries, its

buildings have been destroyed and rebuilt several times. During the 1960s and 1980s, it became a flashpoint of antigovernment demonstrations – see the boxed text on p211.

To the right of the tower is a pavilion containing a stele dating from 1715. It is set on the back of a massive marble turtle, a symbol of longevity. To the left of the tower is another six-sided pavilion, this one sheltering an enormous bell, Dai Hong Chung, which was cast in 1710 and weighs 2052kg; it is said to be audible 10km away. In the main sanctuary, in a case behind the bronze laughing Buddha, are three statues: A Di Da, the Buddha of the Past; Thich Ca, the historical Buddha (Sakyamuni); and Di Lac Buddha, the Buddha of the Future.

For a nice bicycle ride, head southwest (parallel to the Perfume River) on riverside Đ Tran Hung Dao, which turns into Đ Le Duan after passing Phu Xuan Bridge. Cross the railway tracks and keep going on Đ Kim Long. Thien Mu Pagoda can also be reached by dragon boat and a visit is included in most city tours.

Duong No Village

The peaceful village of Duong No makes for a refreshing trip from Hué. The main attraction here is the well-preserved, modest and beautiful **Ho Chi Minh's House** (Nha Bac Ho; admission free), where Uncle Ho lived from 1898 to 1900. Walk a few metres further along the riverbank to **Ben Da**, the steps down to the water where Ho bathed. Another 300m or so beyond them, over a quaint bridge, is an **Am Ba** ('female spirit' temple). It's in some disrepair, but it's quiet and contemplative, with ceramic mosaic work decorating the walls.

Duong No, 6km northeast of Hué, can easily be reached by bicycle or motorbike. Look for a small wooden sign on the left at a bridge off the main road; cross over the bridge and turn immediately right. Ho Chi Minh's House is a few hundred metres along the riverbank. A loop can be made by following the path beside the house to a road at the end; turn left and continue through a pretty rural village for a couple of kilometres. Turn left again, and the road rejoins the bridge to the main road.

Thuan An to Vinh Hien

Thuan An Beach, 15km northeast of Hué, is on a splendid lagoon near the mouth of the Perfume River, at the tip of a long, thin island. It's lovely for beach-combing, and quite undeveloped except for a few kiosks, but between September and April the water's often too rough to swim in.

It is joined to the mainland by a short bridge, and beyond the beach a 50km scenic road (actually Hwy 49, though you'd never guess) stretches the length of the undeveloped island (no maps give it a name) from Thuan An to Vinh Hien. This makes a great day trip by motorbike or car from Hué. It also offers an alternative route to or from Hué for travellers making their way on two wheels along the coast road.

Coming from Thuan An, the island is skinny and the road winds along the lagoon with fishing activity on one side and the ocean on the other. There are several villages on the way with stacks of enormous *nuoc mam* (fish sauce) jars lining the outer walls of many houses, and miles of fertile raised vegetable gardens. But most extraordinary are the vast, colourful and opulent graves and family temples lining the ocean side of the road; there are thousands upon thousands of them. In Vietnam the area is known as the 'city of tombs', with families vying to outdo their neighbours' ancestral monuments. There was a huge outflow of boat people from this area and the overseas Vietnamese now provide the funds to construct these astonishing buildings.

GETTING THERE & AWAY

There are at least three options for driving this road: two for day-trippers from Hué, and one for through travellers.

Those on day trips can just drive as far as they like and then return to Thuan An. An alternative is to drive to Vinh Tanh, about halfway along the road, turn right and head to a wharf where a ferry runs back and forth across the lagoon until about 4pm. The 20-minute crossing costs 5000d for motorbikes, 30,000d for cars, and moors 13km from Hwy 1, a little south of Phu Bai Airport.

An option for through travellers – on motorbikes and bicycles only – is to make your way to Vinh Hien and, from there, catch a public boat to Cau Hai on the mainland, close to the Bach Ma National Park access road. The cost for two people and a motorbike is 5000d, and the journey takes an hour or so.

Be aware that weather conditions affect the running of the boats, so be prepared to backtrack if necessary.

Royal Tombs

The **tombs** (6.30am-5.30pm, in winter 7am-5pm) of the rulers of the Nguyen dynasty (1802–1945) are extravagant mausoleums that were constructed along the banks of the Perfume River. They are situated between 2km and 16km south of Hué.

TEMPLE OF NAM GIAO

The **temple of Nam Giao** (Temple of Heaven; admission free) was once the most important religious site in all of Vietnam. It was here that, every three years, the emperor solemnly offered elaborate sacrifices to the All-Highest Emperor of the August Heaven (Thuong De). The topmost esplanade, which represents heaven, is round; the middle terrace, representing earth, is square, as is the lowest terrace.

After reunification, the provincial government erected an obelisk in memory of soldiers killed in the war against the South Vietnamese government and the Americans on the site where the sacrificial altar had once stood. There was strong public sentiment in Hué against the obelisk and it was finally torn down in 1993. Nam Giao remains unrestored and crumbling.

TOMB OF TU DUC

The majestic and serene **tomb of Emperor Tu Duc** (admission 55,000d) is set amid frangipani trees and a grove of pines. Tu Duc designed the exquisitely harmonious tomb, which was constructed between 1864 and 1867, for use both before and after his death. The enormous expense of the tomb and the forced labour used in its construction spawned a coup plot that was discovered and suppressed in 1866.

It is said that Tu Duc, who had the longest reign of any Nguyen monarch (1848–83), lived a life of ultimate imperial luxury. Though Tu Duc had 104 wives and countless concubines, he had no offspring. One theory has it that he became sterile after contracting smallpox.

Tu Duc's tomb, which is surrounded by a solid octagonal wall, is entered from the southeast via Vu Khiem Gate. A path paved with *bat trang* tiles leads to Du Khiem Boat

TOMBS FIT FOR KINGS

Although all are unique in structure and design, most of the mausoleums consist of five parts:

- A stele pavilion in which the accomplishments, exploits and virtues of the deceased emperor are engraved on a marble tablet. The testaments were usually written by the dead ruler's successor, although Tu Duc chose to compose his own.
- A temple for the worship of the emperor and empress. In front of each altar, on which the deceased ruler's funerary tablets were placed, is an ornate dais that once held items the emperor used every day, such as his tea and betel-nut trays and cigarette cases.
- A sepulchre, usually inside a square or circular enclosure, where the emperor's remains are buried.
- An honour courtyard paved with dark-brown *bat trang* bricks, along the sides of which stand stone elephants, horses, and civil and military mandarins. The civil mandarins wear square hats and hold the symbol of their authority: an ivory sceptre; the military mandarins wear round hats and hold swords.
- A lotus pond surrounded by frangipani and pine trees.

Almost all of the tombs, which are in walled compounds, were planned by the Nguyen emperors during their lifetimes. Many of the precious ornaments that were once reposited in the tombs disappeared during Vietnam's wars.

Landing, which is on the shore of Luu Khiem Lake. From the boat landing, Tinh Khiem Island, where Tu Duc used to hunt small game, is to the right. Across the water to the left is Xung Khiem Pavilion, where the emperor would sit among the columns with his concubines, composing or reciting poetry. The pavilion, built over the water on piles, was restored in 1986.

Across Khiem Cung Courtyard from Du Khiem Boat Landing are steps leading through Khiem Cung Gate to Hoa Khiem Temple, where Emperor Tu Duc and Empress Hoang Le Thien Anh are worshipped. Before his death, Tu Duc used Hoa Khiem Temple as a palace, staying here during his long visits to the complex.

The temple contains a number of interesting items, including a mirror used by the emperor's concubines; a clock and other objects given to Tu Duc by the French; the funerary tablets of the emperor and empress; and two thrones, the larger of which was for the empress (Tu Duc was only 153cm tall).

Minh Khiem Chamber, just to the right behind Hoa Khiem Temple, was originally built for use as a theatre. Tu Duc's mother, the Queen Mother Tu Du, is worshipped in Luong Khiem Temple, directly behind Hoa Khiem Temple.

At the bottom of the stairway, the brick path continues along the shore of the lake to the Honour Courtyard. Across the lake from there are the tombs of Tu Duc's adopted son, Emperor Kien Phuc, who ruled for only seven months (1883–84), and Empress Hoang Le Thien Anh, Tu Duc's wife. After walking between the honour guard of elephants, horses and diminutive civil and military mandarins (the stone mandarins were made even shorter than the emperor), you reach the Stele Pavilion, which shelters a massive stone tablet weighing about 20 tonnes. It took four years to transport the stele, the largest in Vietnam, from the area of Thanh Hoa, 500km to the north. Tu Duc drafted the inscriptions on the stele himself in order to clarify certain aspects of his reign. He freely admitted that he had made mistakes and chose to name his tomb Khiem, which means 'modest'. The two nearby towers symbolise the emperor's power.

Tu Duc's sepulchre, enclosed by a wall, is on the other side of a half-moon-shaped lake. In fact, Tu Duc was never actually interred here. The site where his remains were buried (along with great treasure) is not known. Because of the danger of grave robbers, some extreme measures were taken to keep the location secret – every one of the 200 servants who buried the king was beheaded.

Tu Duc's tomb is about 5km south of Hué on Van Nien Hill in Duong Xuan Thuong Village.

TOMB OF DONG KHANH

The smallest of the Royal Tombs, **Dong Khanh's mausoleum** (admission 22,000d) was built in 1889. Emperor Dong Khanh was the nephew and adopted son of Tu Duc, and was placed on the throne by the French after they captured his predecessor, Ham Nghi. Predictably, Dong Khanh proved docile; he ruled from 1885 until his death three years later.

Seldom visited, there is a certain serenity here. It is just over 5km from the city, 500m behind the tomb of Tu Duc.

TOMB OF THIEU TRI

Construction of the **tomb of Thieu Tri** (admission free), who ruled from 1841 to 1847, was completed in 1848. It is the only Royal Tomb not enclosed by a wall. The tomb has a similar floorplan to Minh Mang's tomb (see right), but is substantially smaller. Thieu Tri's tomb is about 7km from Hué, in a peaceful rural landscape, and is off the tour-bus trail. If you're walking, cycling or on a motorbike, there's a pretty 2km or so cross-country track that leads here from the tomb of Dong Khanh.

TOMB OF KHAI DINH

The hillside **tomb of Emperor Khai Dinh** (admission 55,000d), who ruled from 1916 to 1925, is perhaps symptomatic of the decline of Vietnamese culture during the colonial era. Begun in 1920 and completed in 1931, the grandiose concrete structure is completely unlike Hué's other tombs, being a synthesis of Vietnamese and European elements. Even the stone faces of the mandarin honour guards are endowed with a mixture of Vietnamese and European features.

After climbing 36 steps between four dragon banisters, you reach the first courtyard, flanked by two pavilions. The Honour Courtyard, with its rows of elephants, horses, and civil and military mandarins, is 26 steps further up the hillside. In the centre of the courtyard is an octagonal Stele Pavilion.

Up three more flights of stairs is the main building, Thien Dinh, which is divided into three halls. The walls and ceiling are decorated with murals of the Four Seasons, Eight Precious Objects and Eight Fairies. Under a graceless, one-tonne concrete canopy is a gilt bronze statue of Khai Dinh in regalia. Behind the statue is the symbol of the sun. The emperor's remains are interred 18m below the statue. Khai Dinh is worshipped in the last hall.

The tomb of Khai Dinh is 10km from Hué, in Chau Chu Village.

TOMB OF MINH MANG

Perhaps the most majestic of the Royal Tombs is that of **Minh Mang** (admission 55,000d), who ruled from 1820 to 1840. Renowned for its architecture, which harmoniously blends into the natural surroundings, the tomb was planned during Minh Mang's lifetime and built between 1841 and 1843 by his successor.

The Honour Courtyard is reached via three gates on the eastern side of the wall: Dai Hong Mon (Great Red Gate; centre), Ta Hong Mon (Left Red Gate); and Huu Hong Mon (Right Red Gate). Three granite staircases lead from the courtyard to the square Stele Pavilion, Dinh Vuong. Nearby there once stood an altar on which buffaloes, horses and pigs were sacrificed.

Sung An Temple, dedicated to Minh Mang and his empress, is reached via three terraces and Hien Duc Gate. On the other side of the temple, three stone bridges span Trung Minh Ho (Lake of Impeccable Clarity). The central bridge, Cau Trung Dao, constructed of marble, was for the emperor's use only. Minh Lau Pavilion stands on the top of three superimposed terraces that represent the 'three powers': the heavens, the earth and water. Visible to the left is the Fresh Air Pavilion; the Angling Pavilion is to the right.

From a stone bridge across crescent-shaped Tan Nguyet Lake (Lake of the New Moon), a monumental staircase with dragon banisters leads to the sepulchre, which is surrounded by a circular wall symbolising the sun. In the middle of the enclosure, reached through a bronze door, is the emperor's burial place: a mound of earth covered with mature pine trees and dense shrubbery.

The tomb of Minh Mang, which is on Cam Ke Hill in An Bang Village, is on the west bank of the Perfume River, about 12km from Hué. There is now a bridge across the river here, so it is no longer necessary to take a ferry.

TOMB OF GIA LONG

Emperor Gia Long, who founded the Nguyen dynasty in 1802 and ruled until 1819, ordered the construction of his tomb in 1814. According to royal annals, the emperor himself chose the site after scouting the area on the back of an elephant. The rarely visited **tomb** (admission free), which is presently in a state of ruin, is around 14km south of Hué and 3km from the west bank of the Perfume River. You can take a motorbike across with you on the boat for about US$1 but, again, be prepared to negotiate.

BACH MA NATIONAL PARK

☎ 054 / elevation 1200m

A French-era hill station known for its cool weather, **Bach Ma National Park** (Vuon Quoc Gia Bach Ma; ☎ 871 330; www.bachma.vnn.vn; admission 10,500d) is 1200m above sea level, but only 20km from Canh Duong Beach. It's simply gorgeous. The French started building villas here in 1930; by 1937 the number of holiday homes had reached 139 and it became known as the 'Dalat of central Vietnam'. Most of the visitors were high-ranking French VIPs. Not surprisingly the Viet Minh tried hard to spoil the holiday – the area saw some heavy fighting in the early 1950s. After independence from the French, Bach Ma was soon forgotten and the villas abandoned; today they are in total ruin and only a few stone walls remain.

Bach Ma has some stunning views across the coastline near Hai Van Pass, which the Americans used to their advantage; during the war, US troops turned the area into a fortified bunker. The VC did their best to harass the Americans, but couldn't dislodge them. Between the eerie remains and memories of the American War, spooky stories abound among locals, who maintain that the park is a realm of ghosts.

In 1991, 22,000 hectares of land were set aside as a nature preserve and designated Bach Ma National Park. Efforts are now fast under way to regenerate patches of forest that were destroyed by clear-felling and defoliation during the American War.

Ninety-three species of mammal have been recorded within the boundaries of the park, including tigers, bears and several species of primate. A recent victory in the wildlife stakes came with the discovery

---

WALKING TRAILS IN BACH MA NATIONAL PARK

There are several hiking opportunities through this beautiful forest. The national park's map describes several nature trails, but check with the rangers for the current condition of each track.

- **Pheasant Trail** is named after the rare and beautiful crested argus pheasant; you're more likely to hear the birds calling than see them, unless you have lots of time and patience. The 2.5km track starts 5km along the summit-access road, and leads through forest to a series of waterfalls and pools. You can cool off here before the return hike.

- **Five Lakes Cascade Trail** starts 1km beyond the national-park guesthouse. A 2km walk takes you through forest and follows a series of cascades. The water is so cold that not much is living in it – just a recently discovered species of frog.

- **Rhododendron Trail** can be walked as an extension of the Five Lakes Cascade Trail, or can be reached by a separate track from km16 on the summit-access road. Spring is the best time to walk this trail, when the rhododendrons are in bloom. At the end of the trail is a spectacular waterfall, and you can get to the bottom if you're fit enough to climb the 650 steps that lead down! The water here eventually makes its way down to join up with the Perfume River in Hué.

- **Summit Trail** is a steep but short 500m walk to Hai Vong Dai, the 1450m summit of Bach Ma. Today visitors simply enjoy the stunning views, but in 1968 a helicopter base was maintained at this strategic spot. The white streams of cloud (bach ma) often seen at the summit are thought to look like the hair of a white horse, and inspired the park's name.

These trails and others are described more fully in the national park's map, which you get with your ticket; further information is found in the *Bach Ma National Park* booklet, available for 12,000d at the park entrance.

in 1992 of evidence of *sao la*, a previously unknown antelope-like creature whose footprints and horns were found in the Bach Ma domain. Two other animals were discovered in the late 1990s: the deer-like Truong Son muntjac and the giant muntjac. And with enforced protection from poachers, there is some hope that wild elephants, currently restricted to the Lao side of the border, will return to seek the sanctuary of Bach Ma.

As most of the park's resident mammals are nocturnal, sightings demand a great deal of effort and patience. Bird-watching is fantastic here, but of course you need to be up at dawn to get the best sightings. Of the 800-odd species of bird known to inhabit Vietnam, the park is home to some 330, including the fabulous crested argus pheasant and the tenacious Edwards' pheasant – unseen and thought to be extinct for 70 years, it was recently discovered in the park's buffer zone.

More than 1150 species of plant have been discovered in the park, though this figure is estimated to be just half of the actual number. Among these, at least 338 species are medicinal plants, 33 produce essential oils, 26 are used for weaving and 22 bear edible fruit.

It was not until March 1998 that Bach Ma National Park began receiving visitors. Despite its tender age, the efforts of the park's staff are laudable and they are hard at work protecting the area, working on community development with the ethnic minorities in the area and promoting sustainable ecotourism. Several young rangers here speak English well and there is an interesting display in the visitor centre. As well as plenty of natural-history information, there's a huge crate of confiscated hunting tools, weaponry and the remains of a crashed helicopter.

Bach Ma is very foggy and wet from July to February, and the rains in October and November bring plenty of leeches. Still, these winter months are not out of the question for visiting. The best time to visit Bach Ma is from March to September, particularly between April and June, for what's likely to be the best weather.

Sleeping & Eating
National Park Guesthouse (☎ /fax 871 330; camp sites per person 3000d, 6-person tents 80,000d, r 100,000-150,000d) This is a prime place, rebuilt from one of the French ruins that was originally part of Emperor Bao Dai's summer retreat here. The more expensive twin-bed rooms are in a separate building and are a better bet for views and facilities. Give at least four hours' notice for meal requirements, as fresh food is brought up to the park from the market on demand.

Several private companies are building low-key accommodation in the park. Near the summit trail, **Morin-Bach Ma Hotel** (☎ 871 199; r US$15-20) has already opened and is smart for the money. All new places are being constructed under the watchful eye of the park authorities, so hopefully a sympathetic eco-friendly standard will be maintained.

Getting There & Away
Bach Ma is 28km west of Lang Co and 45km southeast of Hué. The narrow road into the park was originally built by the French in 1932, was rebuilt in 1993 and is now sealed all the way to the summit.

The entrance and visitors centre is 3km along the summit road, the turn-off for Bach Ma is signposted in the town of Phu Loc on Hwy 1. It's another steep and meandering 16km from the gate to the summit, and unless you have your own vehicle or are willing to walk, you'll need to hire private transport from the park. Four-seater 4WDs rent for around 250,000d per same-day return, 300,000d next-day return or 150,000d one way. Be aware that motorbikes and bicycles are no longer allowed on the summit road.

Walking takes about three to four hours down, so carry plenty of water and wear a hat, as there is little canopy protection on the lower part of the road.

Getting Around
Your visit will be much easier if you can hire a vehicle to keep with you for your time in the park, especially if you plan to walk some of the trails, as they are spread along the 16km of the summit-access road.

SUOI VOI (HOT SPRINGS)
About 15km north of Lang Co Beach is the inland turn-off to **Suoi Voi** (Elephant Springs; admission per person 10,000d, plus per car/motorbike 10,000/5000d). This is a secluded recreation area, where you can easily spend a half-day traipsing through the forest and swimming in cool, crystal-clear streams. It's a

pleasant detour and is recommended for motorbikers and cyclists who are braving their way north or south along Hwy 1.

The main springs are a short walk from the parking area. This is a bumpy 1.5km from the entry gate, which is 2.3km from the main road. The springs feature huge boulders – one vaguely in the shape of an elephant's head, and cosmetically enhanced to look more like it – and the stunning backdrop of the Bach Ma National Park in the distance. Further exploration will lead to less-populated swimming holes, including the **Vung Do Pool**, about 200m beyond the main area.

Foreign visitors here are scarce (most seem to be rushing in one direction or another along the coast), and on weekdays you may have the whole place to yourself. Weekends, however, are jam-packed with Vietnamese, notably young couples exploring the birds and bees.

To reach the springs from Hwy 1, look for a large faded sign reading 'Suoi Voi'. You will see the 19th-century Thua Lau Church just ahead of you, after making a turn-off to the west. From here, follow the dirt road for 2.3km to the entry gate.

Buy an entry ticket here and hold onto it as you may be asked to show it more than once. There are some basic food stalls near the springs, but it's better to bring a picnic.

About another 15km north of this turn-off is the village of Phu Loc, and the turn-off to reach Bach Ma National Park.

LANG CO BEACH
☎ 054

Lang Co is an attractive, island-like stretch of palm-shaded sand with a crystal-clear, turquoise lagoon on one side and many kilometres of beachfront facing the South China Sea on the other. It's a tranquil spot where lots of travellers make a lunch stop and some spend the night. If you're travelling on one of the 'open tours' along the coast, this makes a fine place to hop off for a night or two, depending on the weather.

The beach here is best enjoyed between April and July. From late August till November, rains are frequent, and during the chilly months, from December to March, it may serve best as just a lunch stop.

There are spectacular views of Lang Co, just north of Hai Van Pass, from both Hwy 1 and the trains linking Danang and Hué.

Sleeping & Eating

Lang Co Hotel (☎ 874 426; codolangco@dng.vnn.vn; r US$15; 🍴) This beachside pad has just been given a much needed facelift and is excellent value. Big beachfront rooms include TV, fridge and bathtubs with hot water. It is set in a shaded garden compound and the staff are always willing to assist. Bicycles can be hired for 10,000d a day. The restaurant was still being rebuilt at the time of writing but has traditionally offered good seafood.

Thanh Tam Seaside Resort (☎ 874 456; fax 873 762; r US$10-20; 🍴) About 1km north of Lang Co Hotel, this 'resort' has basic beachfront cottages with no hot water for US$10; curiously, the more expensive rooms look onto a patch of concrete that doubles as a parking area. The outdoor terrace restaurant has great views and is a very popular seafood stop for tourists travelling between Hué and Danang.

Lang Co Beach Resort (☎ 873 555; langco@dng.vnn.vn; r US$50-60; 🍴 💻 🏊) Set amid lavishly landscaped gardens, this is a stylish beachfront resort. Rooms are nice at this price and facilities include a pool and a fitness centre.

New guesthouses are springing up on the lagoon side of the road and it's only a short stroll to the beach. **Chi Na Guesthouse** (☎ 874 597; r US$5-10; 🍴) is the best of these, and offers cheap rooms with TV and fan or air-con. The friendly family speak some English.

Getting There & Away

Lang Co is 35km north of Danang over the Hai Van Pass (or under, with the tunnel being built at the time of writing). Tourist buses pass through daily, en route for Hué, Danang and Hoi An, all tickets costing just US$2. Thrillseekers might prefer to take a motorbike over the Hai Van pass for some top views.

Served by non-express trains, Lang Co train station is 3km from the beach. Finding someone to take you by motorbike from the train station to the beach shouldn't be difficult.

HAI VAN PASS

The Hai Van (Sea Cloud) Pass crosses over a spur of the Truong Son Mountain Range that juts into the South China Sea. About

30km north of Danang, Hwy 1 climbs to an elevation of 496m, passing south of the Ai Van Son peak (1172m). It's an incredibly mountainous stretch of highway with spectacular views. The railway track, with its many tunnels, goes around the peninsula, following the shoreline to avoid the hills.

In the 15th century, Hai Van Pass formed the boundary between Vietnam and the Kingdom of Champa. Until the American War, the pass was heavily forested. At the summit is an old French fort, later used as a bunker by the South Vietnamese and US armies.

If you cross in winter, the pass serves as something of a visible dividing line between the climates of the north and south. Acting as a virtual wall, the pass protects the area to the south of it from the fierce 'Chinese winds' that sweep in from the northeast. From about November to March the exposed side on the north of the pass (including Lang Co Beach) can be uncomfortably wet and chilly, while just to the south (on the beaches around Danang and Hoi An) it's warm and dry. Generally, when the winter weather is lousy in Hué, it is usually good in Danang.

Most buses make a 10-minute rest stop at the top of the pass. You'll have to fight off a rather large crowd of very persistent souvenir vendors. You would be wise not to change money with anyone on the pass, as you're more than likely to get short-changed.

In June 2000 construction began on a US$150 million tunnel under Hai Van Pass to improve traffic flow on Hwy 1. The project is nearing completion and should open during the lifetime of this book, shaving as much as one hour off the journey time between Danang and Hué.

BA NA HILL STATION

☎ 0511 / elevation 1485m

Optimistically deemed 'the Dalat of Danang province' by the provincial government, **Ba Na** (admission 10,000d, per motorbike/car 5000/10,000d) is a former French hill station along the crest of Mt Ba Na (Nui Chua). The 360-degree view is truly spectacular and the air is fresh and cool. When it's 36°C on the coast, it's likely to be between 15°C and 26°C at Ba Na. Rain often falls between 700m and 1200m above sea level, but around the hill station itself, the sky is usually clear. Mountain tracks in the area lead to a variety of waterfalls and viewpoints.

Ba Na was founded in 1919 and, until WWII, the French were carried up the last 20km of rough mountain road by sedan chair! Of the 200-odd villas that originally stood, a few tattered, atmospheric ruins remain. The provincial government has high hopes of once again making Ba Na a magnet for tourists and is in the process of developing the site to suit domestic visitors. This means a variety of accommodation and restaurants, all good news, but also lots of karaoke, music for all from a loud PA and litter, which are not such good news.

Views from the Le Nim restaurant (see below) balcony are fantastic and worth a stop in themselves; it's a great place for lunch. The Ba Na By Night Resort (don't be fooled by the name, it's open by day as well) has preserved an old French wine cellar in its foundations – walk in and feel the cool (see below). You can also walk along a marked track, just behind the plushest accommodation section, to the atmospheric ruins of one of the French villas. An enormous Buddha that's visible for miles around has also been constructed here.

Sleeping & Eating

Each resort has an extraordinarily complex system of different room standards and prices depending on season, day of the week, number of people, length of stay and so on. Note that rates here are very general guidelines.

Le Nim (☎ 670 026; r 200,000-350,000d) For sweeping views over Ba Na, look no further than the Le Nim, which is located down a slope near the post office. All rooms are set around an open courtyard where karaoke campfires take place of a weekend – you have been warned! The restaurant serves up terrific fresh seafood dishes and has an unsurpassed daytime view.

Ba Na By Night Resort (☎ 671016; bananight@dng .vnn.vn; r 200,000-500,000d) Probably the best choice of rooms at Ba Na, set in *rong* houses (thatched-roof houses on stilts) or various villas, but you miss out on the views. The remnants of a colonial-era wine cellar and French villa at this place are interesting to check out. Facilities include a popular bar and tennis courts.

CENTRAL VIETNAM

Ba Na Resort (☎ 818 054; banatourist@dng.vnn.vn; r 200,000-300,000d, bungalows 50,000-100,000d) This is a curious fusion of a 30-room hotel and 40 teeny-weeny, triangular bungalows that just about accommodate two. There is also a large restaurant located here.

Ba Na Tourist also operate the overspill **Hoa Rung Hotel** (banatourist@dng.vnn.vn; r 200,000-300,000d, bungalows 50,000-100,000d), just along the road from Ba Na Resort (and with the same contact details and rates).

Getting There & Away

Ba Na is 42km west of Danang along a beautiful winding road that can be dangerous on a foggy day. Pay the admission fee at the bottom of the access road. Arriving by public bus from Danang, shuttle buses take passengers up the mountain for an extra 15,000d.

If you don't want to drive all the way – or if you want the thrill – there is a **cable car** (return tickets 35,000d) that whisks visitors up from a free parking lot a few kilometres below the hill station. The vistas are huge.

SUOI MO

A pleasant detour for an hour or so on the way to Ba Na, the waterfall at **Suoi Mo** (Dream Springs; admission 3000d) has some clear swimming holes for a dip. It's a pretty, undeveloped spot, if you can ignore the litter; go on a weekday to avoid the crowds.

To get here, turn right just before the Ba Na access-road entry gate. There's another entry gate here, where you pay the entry fee. Continue up the bumpy track for 2km or so and look for a small arrowed sign 'Suoi Mo' on the left. Park here and walk along the track that leads off to the right, beside a few houses. A 20-minute climb – slippery when wet – brings you to the waterfall.

DANANG

☎ 0511 / pop 1,100,000

Vietnam's fourth-largest city, Danang is the economic powerhouse of central Vietnam. After a long period of slumber, the city is once again awaking and has been given a total makeover in the past few years. With new roads, new bridges and new buildings, it is starting to act like a city of its size, although with Hué to the north and Hoi An to the south, it's never going to make the major league for tourism. Travellers pass through Danang to visit the Museum of Cham Sculpture or to make transport connections. Most people prefer to stay in Hoi An or out at nearby China Beach, but for city slickers who like to soak up the atmosphere of bustling centres, it's an endearing enough place to idle a night or two away.

Back in the heady days of the American War, Danang was often referred to as the 'Saigon of the North'. This held a note of both praise and condemnation: like its big sister to the south, Danang was notable for its booming economy, fine restaurants, busy traffic and glittering shops. Entertaining the military was also a profitable business – bars and prostitution were major industries, and that legacy lingers. As in Saigon, corruption also ran rampant. Liberation arrived in 1975, promptly putting a sizable dent in the city's economy until the good old days came back again a few years ago.

Danang also marks the northern limits of Vietnam's tropical zone and boasts a pleasant climate all year round.

History

Known during French colonial rule as Tourane, Danang succeeded Hoi An as the most important port in central Vietnam during the 19th century, and it remains the principal port for central Vietnam.

In late March 1975 Danang, the second-largest city in South Vietnam, was the scene of utter chaos. Saigon government forces were ordered to abandon Hué, while Quang Ngai had fallen to the communists, cutting South Vietnam in two. Desperate civilians tried to flee the city, as some soldiers of the disintegrating South Vietnamese army engaged in looting, pillage and rape. On 29 March 1975, two truckloads of communist guerrillas, more than half of them women, drove into what had been the most heavily defended city in South Vietnam and, without firing a shot, declared Danang 'liberated'.

Orientation

Danang is on the western bank of the Han River. The eastern bank is accessible via the Song Han Bridge or Nguyen Van Troi Bridge further south. The city is part of a long, thin peninsula, at the northern tip of which is Nui Son Tra (called Monkey Mountain by US soldiers). A new road encircles Nui Son Tra, and it's slowly opening to tourism. China

FIGHTING TO FLEE

Almost the only fighting that took place as Danang fell was between South Vietnamese soldiers and civilians battling for space on flights and ships out of the city. On 27 March the president of World Airways, Ed Daly, ignored explicit US government orders and sent two 727s from Saigon to Danang to evacuate refugees. When the first plane landed, about a thousand desperate and panicked people mobbed the tarmac. Soldiers fired assault rifles at each other and at the plane as they tried to shove their way through the rear door. As the aircraft taxied down the runway trying to take off, people climbed up into the landing-gear wells and someone threw a hand grenade, damaging the right wing.

Those who managed to fight their way aboard, kicking and punching aside anyone in their way, included over 200 soldiers, mostly members of the elite (Vietnamese) Black Panthers company. The only civilians on board were two women and one baby – and the baby was only there after being thrown aboard by its desperate mother, who was left on the tarmac. Several of the stowaways in the wheel wells couldn't hold on and, as the plane flew southward, TV cameras on the second 727 filmed them falling into the South China Sea.

Beach and the Marble Mountains lie south of the city, and Hai Van Pass overlooks Danang from the north.

MAPS
Look out for the *Danang Tourist Map*, a pocket-sized foldout that is available for about 8000d in bookshops and hotels in Danang and Hoi An.

Information
INTERNET ACCESS
There is plenty of Internet access in Danang, including a gaggle of **Internet cafés** (Đ Tran Quoc Toan) between Đ Yen Bai and Đ Nguyen Chi Thanh. The standard charge per hour is about 6000d.

MEDICAL SERVICES
Danang Family Medical Practice (☎ 582 700; 50 Đ Nguyen Van Linh) Newest branch of Vietnam's long-running foreign-owned family clinic.
Hospital C (Benh Vien C; ☎ 822 480; 35 Đ Hai Phong) The most advanced medical facility among the four hospitals in town.

MONEY
VID Public Bank (2 Đ Tran Phu) Exchanges cash and can arrange cash advances.
Vietcombank (140 Đ Le Loi) Near the corner of Đ Hai Phong, this is the best place to change travellers cheques and it has an ATM.

POST
Main post offices 1 & 2 (Đ Bach Dang) Split into two branches flanking the Song Han Bridge, No 1 is for international services and No 2 is for domestic services.

TRAVEL AGENCIES
An Phu Tourist (☎ 818 366; 5 Đ Dong Da) Office for open tickets for those wanting to hop on a bus to Hué or Hoi An.
Dana Tours (☎ 825 653; danamarle@dng.vnn.vn; 76 Đ Hung Vuong) Danang's main tour agency is enlightened compared with most of the state-run agencies. It is a good place to ask about car rentals, boat trips, visa extensions and treks in nearby Ba Na or Bach Ma.
Truong Van Trong's Tour (☎ 0903-597 971; trongn59@yahoo.com) Sightseeing with a difference, Trong conducts tours of the central highlands by motorbike or day trips around Danang. He and his co-bikers, between them, speak good English, French, Japanese, German and Italian and they get rave reviews from travellers.

Sights
MUSEUM OF CHAM SCULPTURE
The leading sight in Danang is the internationally renowned **Museum of Cham Sculpture** (Bao Tang Cham; cnr Đ Trung Nu Vuong & Đ Bach Dang; admission 20,000d; ⏰7am-5pm). Founded in 1915 by the École Française d'Extrême Orient, this collection of Cham sculpture is the finest in the world. Many of the sandstone carvings, including altars, lingas, garudas, Ganeshas, and images of Shiva, Brahma and Vishnu, are exquisitely detailed; take time to soak it up.

The museum's artefacts, which date from the 7th to 15th centuries, were discovered at Dong Duong (Indrapura), Khuong My, My Son, Tra Kieu (Simhapura) and other sites, mostly in Quang Nam and Danang provinces. The museum's rooms are named after the localities in which the objects displayed were found.

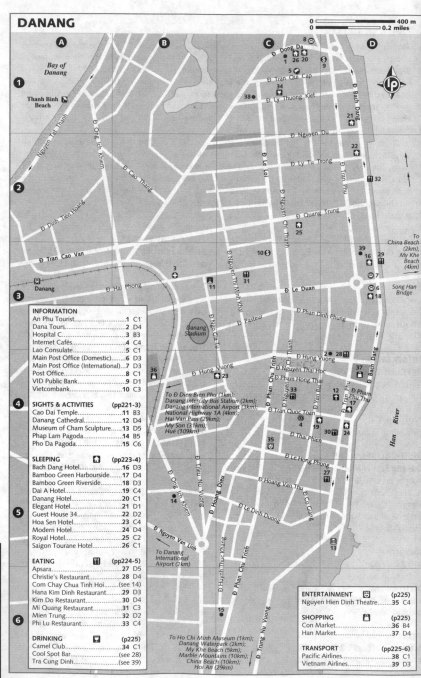

DANANG

0	400 m
0	0.2 miles

INFORMATION
An Phu Tourist......................**1**	C1
Dana Tours...........................**2**	D4
Hospital C............................**3**	B3
Internet Cafés......................**4**	C4
Lao Consulate......................**5**	C1
Main Post Office (Domestic)...**6**	D3
Main Post Office (International)...**7**	D3
Post Office..........................**8**	C1
VID Public Bank...................**9**	D1
Vietcombank.......................**10**	C3

SIGHTS & ACTIVITIES (pp221-3)
Cao Dai Temple..................**11**	B3
Danang Cathedral...............**12**	D4
Museum of Cham Sculpture...**13**	D5
Phap Lam Pagoda................**14**	B5
Pho Da Pagoda...................**15**	C6

SLEEPING (pp223-4)
Bach Dang Hotel.................**16**	D3
Bamboo Green Harbourside...**17**	D4
Bamboo Green Riverside......**18**	D3
Dai A Hotel........................**19**	C4
Danang Hotel.....................**20**	C1
Elegant Hotel.....................**21**	D1
Guest House 34..................**22**	D2
Hoa Sen Hotel....................**23**	C4
Modern Hotel.....................**24**	D4
Royal Hotel........................**25**	C2
Saigon Tourane Hotel..........**26**	C1

EATING (pp224-5)
Apsara...............................**27**	D5
Christie's Restaurant...........**28**	D4
Com Chay Chua Tinh Hoi.......(see 14)	
Hana Kim Dinh Restaurant....**29**	D3
Kim Do Restaurant..............**30**	D4
Mi Quang Restaurant...........**31**	C3
Mien Trung........................**32**	D2
Phi Lu Restaurant................**33**	C4

DRINKING (p225)
Camel Club........................**34**	C1
Cool Spot Bar.....................(see 28)	
Tra Cung Dinh.....................(see 39)	

ENTERTAINMENT (p225)
Nguyen Hien Dinh Theatre....**35**	C4

SHOPPING (p225)
Con Market........................**36**	B4
Han Market........................**37**	D4

TRANSPORT (pp225-6)
Pacific Airlines...................**38**	C1
Vietnam Airlines.................**39**	D3

Bay of Danang

Thanh Binh Beach

Đ Nguyen Tat Thanh

Đ Ong Ich Khiem

Đ Cao Thang

Đ Dinh Tien Hoang

Đ Tran Cao Van

Danang

Đ Hai Phong

Đ Dong Da

Đ Tran Qui Cap

Đ Ly Thuong Kiet

Đ Nguyen Du

Đ Ly Tu Trong

Đ Le Loi

Đ Nguyen Chi Thanh

Đ Quang Trung

Đ Bach Dang

Đ Tran Phu

Đ Nguyen Thi Minh Khai

Đ Pasteur

Đ Le Duan

Đ Phan Dinh Phung

Danang Stadium

Đ Ngo Gia Tu

Đ Hung Vuong

Đ Hung Vuong

Đ Phan Chu Trinh

Đ Nguyen Chi Thanh

Đ Nguyen Thai Hoc

Đ Pham Hong Thai

Đ Yen Bai

Đ Tran Phu

Đ Pham Phu Thu

Đ Bach Dang

Đ Tran Quoc Toan

Đ Le Hong Phong

Đ Thai Phien

Đ Ong Ich Khiem

Đ Trieu Nu Vuong

Đ Hoang Dieu

Đ Hoang Van Thu

Đ Co Giang

Đ Le Dinh Duong

Đ Nguyen Van Linh

Đ Huynh Thuc Khang

Đ Phan Chu Trinh

Đ Trung Nu Vuong

Han River

Song Han Bridge

To China Beach (2km); My Khe Beach (4km)

To Đ Dien Bien Phu (1km); Danang Intercity Bus Station (2km); Danang International Airport (3km); National Highway 1A (4km); Hai Van Pass (31km); My Son (31km); Huế (109km)

To Danang International Airport (2km)

To Ho Chi Minh Museum (1km); Danang Waterpark (2km); My Khe Beach (5km); Marble Mountains (10km); China Beach (10km); Hoi An (29km)

The four scenes carved around the base of the 7th-century Tra Kieu Altar tell parts of the Ramayana epic and are influenced by the Amaravati style of South India. Scene A tells the story of Prince Rama, who broke the sacred bow (Rudra) at the citadel of Videha, thus winning the right to wed King Janak's daughter, Princess Sita.

Scene B shows the ambassadors sent by King Janak to Prince Rama's father, King Dasaratha, at Ayodhya. The emissaries inform King Dasaratha of his son's exploits, present him with gifts and invite him to Videha to celebrate the wedding.

Scene C shows the royal wedding ceremony, including three of Prince Rama's brothers, who are marrying three of Princess Sita's cousins.

In Scene D, 11 *apsaras* (heavenly maidens) dance and present flowers to the newlyweds under the guidance of the two *gandhara* musicians who appear at the beginning of Scene A.

A trilingual guidebook about the museum, *Museum of Cham Sculpture – Danang*, was written by its director, Tran Ky Phuong, who is Vietnam's most eminent scholar of Cham civilisation. The book provides excellent background on the art of Champa; it also includes details on the museum's exhibits. The book is usually on sale at the entrance.

Guides wait at the entrance of the museum to offer their services, but agree on a price before you begin.

DANANG CATHEDRAL

Known to locals as Con Ga Church (Rooster Church) because of the weathercock on top of the steeple, **Danang Cathedral** (Đ Tran Phu) was built for the city's French residents in 1923. Today, it serves a Catholic community of 4000. The cathedral's candy-pink architecture is interesting, as are the medieval-style stained-glass windows featuring various saints.

Next door to the cathedral are the offices of the diocese of Danang and the St Paul Convent. About 100 nuns – who wear white habits in summer and black in winter – divide their time between here and another convent building across the Han River.

Mass is usually held from Monday to Saturday at 5am and 5pm, and on Sunday at 5am, 6.30am and 4.30pm.

CAO DAI TEMPLE

Built in 1956, **Cao Dai Temple** (Đ Hai Phong) is the largest such structure outside the sect's headquarters in Tay Ninh (p373). There are 50,000 Cao Dai faithful in Quang Nam and Danang provinces – 20,000 in Danang itself. The temple is across the street from Hospital C. As with all Cao Dai temples, prayers are held four times a day: at 6am, noon, 6pm and midnight.

The left-hand gate to the complex, marked *nu phai*, is for women; the right-hand gate, marked *nam phai*, is for men. The doors to the sanctuary are also segregated: women to the left, men to the right, and priests of either sex through the central door. Behind the main altar sits an enormous globe with the 'divine eye', a symbol of Cao Daism, on it.

A sign reading *van giao nhat ly*, which means 'All religions have the same reason', hangs from the ceiling in front of the altar. Behind the gilded letters is a picture of the founders of five of the world's great religions. From left to right are Mohammed, Laotse (wearing blue robes cut in the style of the Greek Orthodox), Jesus (portrayed as he is in French icons), Buddha (who has a distinctly Southeast Asian appearance) and Confucius (looking as Chinese as could be).

Portraits of early Cao Dai leaders, dressed in turbans and white robes, are displayed in the building behind the main sanctuary. Ngo Van Chieu, the founder of Cao Daism, is shown standing, wearing a pointed white turban and a long white robe with blue markings.

PAGODAS

Built in 1936, **Phap Lam Pagoda** (Chua Tinh Hoi; 500 Đ Ong Ich Khiem) has a brass statue of Dia Tang, the King of Hell, near the entrance.

Pho Da Pagoda (opposite 293 Đ Phan Chu Trinh) was built in 1923 in a traditional architectural configuration. Today, about 40 monks (most of them young) live and study here. Local people and their children participate actively in the pagoda's lively religious life.

Sleeping

There are almost no genuine budget options in Danang and, compared with the bargains in Hoi An, rooms seem expensive here. For information on accommodation at My Khe and China Beaches, see p228.

The riverfront revamp means this is now the best area of the city in which to stay and it is worth making for the hotels on this strip. There are plenty of places running northwards along Đ Bach Dang.

Modern Hotel (☎ 820 113; fax 821 842; 186 Đ Bach Dang; r US$15-30; 🔀) It's just that – a new hotel in a super central location that boasts a wide range of amenities. Rooms have all the bells and whistles you'd expect.

Bamboo Green Riverside (☎ 832 592; riversidets@ dng.vnn.vn; 68 Đ Bach Dang; r US$30-50; 🔀 🖳) This is the best located of the Bamboo Green family of smart business hotels. Overlooking the Song Han Bridge, the rooms have three-star touches and it's worth paying a touch more for the view.

Bamboo Green Harbourside (☎ 822 722; bamboo green2@dng.vnn.vn; 177 Đ Tran Phu; s/d US$35/40; 🔀 🖳) Another of the Bamboo Green family, it has a good location opposite Danang Cathedral.

Bach Dang Hotel (☎ 823 649; bdhotel@dng.vnn.vn; 50 Đ Bach Dang; s US$18-40, d US$25-50; 🔀 🖳 🖭) A towering tourist complex, this place boasts big river views from the upper-floor rooms. Cavernous cheaper rooms are at the back, where it can be quieter. There's a swimming pool and tennis court.

Elegant Hotel (☎ 892 893; elegant@dng.vnn.vn; 22A Đ Bach Dang; s US$25-50, d US$35-60; 🔀 🖳) Living up to its name, this is the best of the boutique business hotels in town and the shiny, smart rooms include touches such as hairdryers.

Guest House 34 (☎ 822 732; 34 Đ Bach Dang; r US$8; 🔀) A step down in comfort, but it's probably the best bargain in town. The basic-looking rooms are set around a quiet garden courtyard on the waterfront, and all have TV, fridge and hot water.

Danang Hotel (☎ 834 662; dananghotel@dng.vnn .vn; 3 Đ Dong Da; r US$15-28; 🔀) This used to be the budget deal in town, but successive renovations have pushed up prices. All rooms come with TV, IDD phone and hot water, but it's a long way from the action.

Saigon Tourane Hotel (☎ 821 021; sgtouran@dng .vnn.vn; 5 Đ Dong Da; r US$60-150; 🔀 🖳) One of the smartest hotels in Danang, there is also a breezy roof-top terrace restaurant overlooking the river. Rates for well-appointed rooms include breakfast, and drop-in deals can be as low as US$30, which is well worth it.

Royal Hotel (☎ 823 295; royalhotel@dng.vnn.vn; 17 Đ Quang Trung; r US$25-45; 🔀 🖳) Away from the

river, this is the best choice. It's stylish and has free Internet access in the sophisticated rooms. Breakfast included, plus there's an in-house Japanese restaurant.

Other options for those who want the widest choice:

Dai A Hotel (☎ 827 532; daiahotel@dng.vnn.vn; 27 Đ Yen Bai; r US$15-30; 🔀) Small, friendly and central, a sound choice.

Hoa Sen Hotel (☎ 829 000; fax 829 001; 101-105 Đ Hung Vuong; r US$15-25; 🔀) Close to the train station, look out for the profundities behind reception and enjoy the lift.

Eating

Christie's Restaurant (☎ 824 040; 112 Đ Tran Phu; meals 20,000-80,000đ; 🕑 10am-10pm) This 2nd-storey bar-restaurant has an international menu, including authentic Japanese and Vietnamese food, big burgers and steaks, as well as pizza and pasta to round off the picture.

Apsara Restaurant (☎ 561 409; www.apsara-da nang.com; 222 Đ Tran Phu; mains 25,000-75,000đ) The latest in opulent dining in Danang, it is set in a grand villa, the garden complete with a replica Cham temple. The extensive seafood menu is popular for power-dining at lunch.

Hana Kim Dinh Restaurant (☎ 830 024; 15 Đ Bach Dang; dishes 25,000-100,000đ) A Japanese joint venture, this is a riverside restaurant-bar with an extensive menu of Asian and Western cuisine. Cool cocktail menu and refreshing outdoor area above the river.

Kim Do Restaurant (☎ 821 846; 174 Đ Tran Phu; mains 20,000-80,000đ) This huge Chinese restaurant has a faithful following among the northern neighbours who have settled in Danang.

Mi Quang Restaurant (1A Đ Hai Phong; dishes 5000-15,000đ) Near the Cao Dai Temple, this is a popular daytime place serving filling and tasty bowls of *mi quang* (yellow-noodle soup with salad greens).

Com Chay Chua Tinh Hoi (500 Đ Ong Ich Khiem; dishes from 3000đ) Legendary among locals for the best vegetarian food in town; it's just inside the entrance gate to the Phap Lam Pagoda. There are more vegie places in the streets outside the pagoda.

Other central places to chow down:

Mien Trung (9 Đ Bach Dang; dishes 10,000-50,000đ) Vietnamese, Chinese and Western dishes served up in a great location on the river.

Phi Lu Restaurant (☎ 823 772; 225 Đ Nguyen Chi Thanh; meals 15,000-150,000d) A lack of atmosphere aside, it dishes up excellent Chinese food.

Drinking

Cool Spot Bar (below Christie's Restaurant, 112 Đ Tran Phu) The main gathering point for Danang's small gang of expats. Narrow and dark, it is the easiest place to strike up a conversation in town, but isn't oozing atmosphere.

Tra Cung Dinh (35 Đ Tran Phu) Try Danang's very own jazz café for something a little more sophisticated. No alcohol available, but the shakes, teas and coffees more than make up for it.

Camel Club (Đ Ly Thuong Kiet; entry 20,000d; 7pm-1am) This is where Danang's beautiful people hang out, some because they're working here, others so they can flash their cash. Pricey drinks from 30,000d and up, plus heavy beats.

Entertainment

Traditional Vietnamese music and dance is performed at the new **Nguyen Hien Dinh Theatre** (cnr Đ Le Hong Phong & Đ Phan Chu Trinh; admission 20,000d; 7.30pm Fri, Sat & Sun). Bookings aren't necessary, just turn up.

Shopping

Han Market (Cho Han; cnr Đ Hung Vuong & Đ Tran Phu; 6am-9pm) is a fine place for a casual stroll or to shop in the evenings.

The **Con Market** (Cho Con; Đ Ong Ich Khiem) is Danang's largest, but is mainly a daytime affair. This huge, colourful market has a selection of just about everything that can be bought in Vietnam.

Getting There & Away

AIR

During the American War, Danang had one of the busiest airports in the world. It still distinguishes itself by having one of Vietnam's three international airports.

Airlines around town:

Pacific Airlines (☎ 886 799; 6 Đ Le Loi) Flights from Danang to Hong Kong.

Vietnam Airlines (☎ 821 130; 35 Đ Tran Phu) Connects Danang with destinations throughout Vietnam (see p475).

BUS

The **Danang intercity bus station** (Map p227; Đ Dien Bien Phu; ticket office 7-11am & 1-5pm) is about 3km from the city centre in the direction

of Hué. The efficient ticket office here is one of the most helpful in Vietnam, with some English spoken and prices clearly displayed.

Buses leave for Hué (22,000d, three hours), Hanoi (87,000d, 16 hours) and HCMC (102,000d, 24 hours) regularly throughout the day.

There are services to Vientiane (US$25, 24 hours) departing at 3pm daily, but this is overpriced for what is a rickety old bus that you wouldn't choose to spend more than an hour on.

Regular buses to Hoi An (5000d, one hour) depart from a local bus station 200m away from the intercity bus station. Foreigners tend to be overcharged.

CAR & MOTORBIKE

The simplest way to get to Hoi An (30km) is to hire a car for around US$10 from a local travel agency (see p221), or a motorbike for around US$6 from one of the guys on the street corners. For a slightly higher fee you can ask the driver to stop off and wait for you while you visit Marble Mountains and China Beach.

You can also reach My Son by motorbike (US$12) or car (US$35), with the option of being dropped off in Hoi An on the way back.

Distances to major destinations from Danang include Hanoi (764km), Hué (108km) and HCMC (972km).

MINIBUS

Most travellers prefer to stay in Hoi An rather than Danang, and Hoi An has better minibus services. Try An Phu Tourist (p221) to hop aboard an open-ticket bus heading to Hoi An or Hué. It will be a flat US$2 in either direction.

TRAIN

Danang is served by all *Reunification Express* trains (see p482) and there are several trains daily to HCMC, Hanoi and points in between.

Danang train station (Đ Hai Phong) is about 1.5km from the city centre, at the northern end of Đ Hoang Hoa Tham. The train ride to Hué (20,000d) is short but sweet, one of the best in the country. Watch your belongings as you pass through the pitch-black tunnels.

Getting Around
TO/FROM THE AIRPORT
Danang's airport is just 2km west of the city centre, close enough to reach by *xe om* (motorbike taxi) in 10 minutes (around 10,000d). A metered taxi to the centre is about 20,000d.

CYCLO & MOTORBIKE
Danang has plenty of motorbike taxis and *cyclo* drivers; take the usual caution and be prepared to bargain the fare. The **Tourism Pedicab Team** (☎ 887 722; 118 Đ Le Loi) is an organised outfit, charging US$2 an hour for comfortable *cyclos*.

TAXI
Both **Airport Taxi** (☎ 825 555) and **Dana Taxi** (☎ 815 815) provide modern vehicles with air-con and meters.

AROUND DANANG
Ho Chi Minh Museum
There are three sections to the **Ho Chi Minh Museum** (Đ Nguyen Van Troi; ☿ 7-11am & 1.30-4.30pm). There's a museum of military history in front of which US, Soviet and Chinese weaponry is displayed; a replica of Ho Chi Minh's house in Hanoi (complete with a small lake); and, across the pond from the house, a museum about Uncle Ho.

The replica house is a must-see for anyone who won't make it to the bona fide stilt house in Hanoi (or to one of the many other reproductions scattered throughout the country).

The museum is 250m west of Đ Nui Thanh.

Danang Waterpark
The enormous **waterpark** (admission 5000d, slide use 30,000d; ☿ 9am-9pm Wed-Mon) opened in early 2002 and it's on the riverbank, 2km beyond the Ho Chi Minh Museum.

Nui Son Tra (Monkey Mountain)
Much of Son Tra peninsula is a military and naval base, and still off-limits. However, there's a winding, rural road partway around the coast, a very low-key beach area and a memorial to a forgettable episode of colonial history.

Spanish-led Filipino and French troops attacked Danang in August 1858, ostensibly to end Emperor Tu Duc's mistreatment of Vietnamese Catholics and Catholic missionaries. The city quickly fell, but the invaders had to contend with cholera, dysentery, scurvy, typhus and mysterious fevers. By the summer of 1859, the number of invaders who had died of illness was 20 times the number of those who had been killed in combat.

Many of the **tombs** (admission free) of the Spanish and French soldiers are below a chapel about 15km north of the city. The names of the dead are written on the walls. To get here, cross Song Han Bridge and turn left onto Đ Ngo Quyen. Continue north to Tien Sa Port (Cang Tien Sa). The ossuary, a small white building, stands on the right on a low hill, about 500m before the gate of the port and below the chapel.

The sheltered **Tien Sa Beach**, behind the port and the chapel, is quiet and calm, with clear water. It's good for a swim if you can ignore the litter, and there are great views across to the Hai Van Pass.

Heading east around the coast you'll probably smell the *nuoc mam* factories before you see them. After a few bumpy kilometres you come to the beachside settlement of **Bai But**. It's something of a surreal place of tiny **bungalows** (50,000-100,000d) that dot the hillside above the beach. They look great from below, but are basic inside – take a sleeping mat if you choose to stay. There are also a few ramshackle restaurants here, all set in a placid and gorgeous bay. It's a nice spot to while away an hour or so.

Nam O Beach
Nam O Beach is on the Bay of Danang about 15km northwest of the city. The small community of Nam O supported itself for years by producing firecrackers. Unfortunately, since the ban on firecrackers by the government in 1995, the community has fallen on hard times. However, the resourceful locals have recently gone into making *nuoc mam* instead – and while it's not as profitable as firecrackers, it's better than nothing.

There is another local speciality here called *goi ca*, which is fresh, raw fish fillets marinated in a special sauce and coated in a spicy powder – something like Vietnamese sushi.

China Beach
Famous the world over thanks to the American TV series of the same name, China Beach stretches for many kilometres north

AROUND DANANG

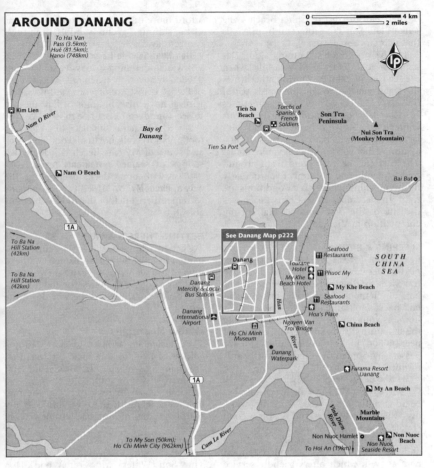

To Hai Van
Pass (3.5km);
Hué (81.5km);
Hanoi (748km)

Kim Lien

Nam O River

Bay of
Danang

Tien Sa
Beach

Tombs of
Spanish &
French
Soldiers

Son Tra
Peninsula

Nui Son Tra
(Monkey Mountain)

Tien Sa Port

Bai But

Nam O Beach

1A

To Ba Na
Hill Station
(42km)

To Ba Na
Hill Station
(42km)

See Danang Map p222

Danang

SOUTH
CHINA
SEA

Seafood
Restaurants

Touranne
Hotel
My Khe
Beach Hotel

Phuoc My

My Khe Beach

Danang
Intercity & Local
Bus Station

Seafood
Restaurants

Hoa's Place

Danang
International
Airport

Nguyen Van
Troi Bridge

China Beach

Ho Chi Minh
Museum

Han River

Danang
Waterpark

Furama Resort
Danang

1A

My An Beach

Marble
Mountains

Vinh Dien River

To My Son (50km);
Ho Chi Minh City (962km)

Cam Le River

Non Nuoc Hamlet

To Hoi An (19km)

Non Nuoc
Seaside Resort

Non Nuoc
Beach

and south of the Marble Mountains. During the American War, US soldiers were airlifted here for rest and relaxation (R&R), which often included a picnic on the beach. For some, it was their last meal before their return to combat by helicopter.

The jumbo beach stretches some 30km south from Son Tra almost all the way to Hoi An. It has become a very popular seaside escape for both domestic and foreign tourists, and is now home to one of Vietnam's plushest resort hotels and many more are under construction all the way to Cua Dai Beach near Hoi An.

Though the entire stretch of oceanfront here is collectively known as China Beach, the name is a relatively recent creation. The beachfront is, in fact, divided into sections, each with its own local name.

The most populated areas are **My Khe Beach**, where the Americans did most of their R&R, and the strip of seashore by the Non Nuoc Seaside Resort (p228). Expect an onslaught of vendors flogging 'China Beach' baseball caps and other tourist paraphernalia, but there are plenty of other peaceful, secluded areas to explore along the coastline.

Many people insist that My Khe Beach was the real China Beach of wartime fame and that the present China Beach is a fake. My Khe is about 3km by road from central Danang. The beach has a dangerous undertow, especially in winter. However, it is safer than the rest of China Beach – the bulk of Nui Son Tra protects it from winds that whip up rough surf.

The best time for swimming along Danang's beaches is from May to July, when the sea is at its calmest. During other times the water can get rough; lifeguards patrol only Non Nuoc, My An and sometimes My Khe Beaches. Ironically, the dangerous winter conditions go hand in hand with large breakers, which are ideal for surfing – assuming that you know what you're doing. The surf can be very good from around mid-September to December, particularly in the morning when wind conditions are right. In December 1992, China Beach was the site of the first international surfing competition in Vietnam.

SLEEPING & EATING

Hoa's Place (☎ 969 216; hoasplace@hotmail.com; r U$4-6) Deservedly a local legend among travellers that have spent any time in this part of Vietnam. Small-scale, low-key and laid-back, Hoa and his wife ensure their home is your home. Good food, including the signature shrimp spring rolls, and cheap beer (6000d) make it a smart lunch stop for passers-by. Sometimes there are surfboards for hire.

My Khe Beach Hotel (☎ 836 125; fax 836 123; s/d/t from US$12/16/20; 🏊) This beach pile has been steadily renovated, wing by wing, over the past few years and is now a good choice. Prices rise with size and views, but all rooms have the obvious, like TV, fridge and hot water. There's a good restaurant here as well, which offers friendly service and donates 10% of its proceeds to a local charity.

Tourane Hotel (☎ 932 666; touranehotel@dng .vnn.vn; r US$25-30; 🏊) It's no relation to the swish Saigon Tourane in town, and while just across the road from the beach, it is rapidly showing signs of age. Pay the extra US$5 for a suite with two rooms.

Furama Resort Danang (☎ 847 333; furamadn@hn .vnn.vn; r US$160-500; 🏊 🖥 🍴) This is Danang's luxury hotel. In fact, for a long time it was Vietnam's luxury hotel. Perched on a private slice of China Beach, this lavish resort features a diving facility, a golf driving range and two landscaped swimming pools. Rooms include opulent bathrooms and the finest five-star trim. If you can't

afford more than a taste of luxury, day-use of the stunning grounds, pools and fitness centre is available for around US$10.

Non Nuoc Seaside Resort (☎ 836 214; fax 836 335) was undergoing a massive and much-needed renovation when we visited. Fans of Soviet-realist architecture will be sad to witness its demise, but most will be pleased to see a modern resort rise in its place.

My Khe Beach is the place to go for seafood. A short walk north of Tourane Hotel, and south of My Khe Beach Hotel, are two strings of **seafood restaurants** (meals 25,000-100,000d) with open decks overlooking the ocean. **Phuoc My** (☎ 831 962) is an easy name to remember! Luckily the food is memorable, too.

GETTING THERE & AWAY

To get to China Beach from central Danang, cross the Song Han Bridge and head toward the sea. A *xe om* can take you, and wait for a couple of hours, for about US$3. The beach continues all the way down the coast to Hoi An.

Marble Mountains

These **mountains** (admission 10,000d; ⏱ 7am-5pm) consist of five sizeable rock outcrops that are made of…marble. Ironically, most of the marble is now shipped in from China, as locals began to realise that at the rate they were using it, there wouldn't be any marble, or any mountains, left for visitors to see.

Each mountain is said to represent a natural element and is named accordingly: Thuy Son (Water), Moc Son (Wood), Hoa Son (Fire), Kim Son (Metal or Gold) and Tho Son (Earth). The largest and most famous, Thuy Son, has a number of natural caves in which first Hindu, and later Buddhist, sanctuaries have been built over the centuries. Thuy Son is a popular pilgrimage site, especially on days of the full and sliver moons and during Tet, when it's a very beautiful place to visit.

Of the two paths leading up Thuy Son, the one closer to the beach (at the end of the village) makes for a better circuit once at the top. So, unless you want to walk the following route in reverse, don't go up the staircase that has concrete kiosks. The admission fee is collected at either entrance.

At the top of the staircase is a gate, Ong Chon, which is pockmarked with bullet holes. Behind Ong Chon is Linh Ong Pagoda. Entering the sanctuary, look to the left to see a fantastic figure with a huge tongue. To the right of Linh Ong are monks' quarters and a small orchid garden.

Behind Linh Ong, a path leads left through two short tunnels to several caverns known as Tang Chon Dong. There are several concrete Buddhas and blocks of carved stone of Cham origin in these caves. Near one of the altars is a flight of steps leading up to another cave, partially open to the sky, with two seated Buddhas in it.

Immediately to the left as you enter Ong Chon Gate is the main path to the rest of Thuy Son. Stairs off the main pathway lead to Vong Hai Da, a viewpoint for a brilliant panorama of China Beach and the South China Sea.

The stone-paved path continues to the right and into a canyon. On the left is Van Thong Cave. Opposite the entrance is a cement Buddha, and behind that there is a narrow passage that leads up to a natural chimney open to the sky.

Exit the canyon and pass through a battle-scarred masonry gate. There's a rocky path to the right, which goes to Linh Nham, a tall chimney-shaped cave with a small altar inside. Nearby, another path leads to Hoa Nghiem, a shallow cave with a Buddha inside. If you go down the passageway to the left of the Buddha, you come to cathedral-like Huyen Khong Cave, lit by an opening to the sky. The entrance to this spectacular chamber is guarded by two administrative mandarins (to the left of the doorway) and two military mandarins (to the right).

Scattered about the cave are Buddhist and Confucian shrines; note the inscriptions carved into the stone walls. On the right, a door leads to two stalactites, dripping water that local legend describes as coming from heaven. Actually, only one stalactite drips; the other one supposedly ran dry when Emperor Tu Duc touched it. During the American War, this chamber was used by the VC as a field hospital. Inside is a plaque dedicated to the Women's Artillery Group, which destroyed 19 US aircraft from a base below the mountains in 1972.

Just to the left of the battle-scarred masonry gate is Tam Thai Tu, a pagoda restored by Emperor Minh Mang in 1826. A path heading obliquely to the right goes to the monks' residence, beyond which are two shrines. From there, a red dirt path leads to five small pagodas. Before you arrive at the monks' residence, stairs on the left-hand side of the path lead to Vong Giang Dai, which offers a fantastic 180-degree view of the other Marble Mountains and the surrounding countryside. To get to the stairway down, follow the path straight on from the masonry gate.

A torch (flashlight) is handy for exploring the caves. Local children have learned that foreigners buy souvenirs and leave tips for unsolicited guided tours, so you won't begin your visit alone. And watch your wallets! The local government adopted a regulation (which it sternly enforces) that the children cannot take tips, but can sell souvenirs. This seems counterproductive; most travellers would rather tip the kids for the guided tours than buy the sorry souvenirs on offer. In general, the kids are good-natured, if extremely persistent, and some of the caves are difficult to find without their assistance.

Non Nuoc Hamlet

Non Nuoc Hamlet is on the southern side of Thuy Son and is a few hundred metres west of Non Nuoc Beach. The marble carvings made here by skilled (and not-so-skilled) artisans would make great gifts if they didn't weigh so much. It's fun to watch the carvers at work, and there are some tiny carved figures that make nice presents.

The town has been spruced up for tourism. During the war, the Americans referred to the shantytown near here as 'Dogpatch', after a derelict town in the comic strip *L'il Abner*. Most of the residents living here at the time were refugees fleeing the fighting in the surrounding countryside.

GETTING THERE & AWAY

Local buses between Danang and Hoi An (tickets 5000d) can drop you at Marble Mountains. The Marble Mountains are 19km north of Hoi An and the road is rapidly being turned into a highway.

It is possible to get to the Marble Mountains from Danang by chartered boat. The 8.5km trip up the Han and Vinh Diem Rivers takes about 1¼ hours.

HOI AN

☎ 0510 / pop 75,800

A living museum, the riverside town of Hoi An oozes charm and culture from every corner. Emphatically the most enchanting place along the coast, this is one spot worth lingering in.

Known as Faifo to early Western traders, it was one of Southeast Asia's major international ports from the 17th to 19th centuries. In its heyday Hoi An, a contemporary of Macau and Melaka, was an important port of call for Dutch, Portuguese, Chinese, Japanese and other trading vessels. Vietnamese ships and sailors based in Hoi An sailed to all corners of Vietnam, as well as Thailand and Indonesia. Perhaps more than any other place in Vietnam, Hoi An retains a sense of history that envelops you as you explore the town.

Every year during the rainy season, particularly in October and November, Hoi An has problems with flooding, especially in areas close to the waterfront. The greatest flood ever recorded in Hoi An took place in 1964, when the water reached all the way up to the roof beams of the houses.

'Hoi An Legendary Night' takes place on the 14th day of every lunar month (full moon) from 5.30pm to 10pm. This colourful monthly event features traditional food, song and dance, and games along the lantern-lit streets in the town centre. All motorised traffic is banned from the streets, including motorbikes.

Hoi An is pedestrian-friendly: the Old Town is closed to cars, and the distances from all the town hotels to the centre are walkable. There's plenty to do in Hoi An. For a relaxed half-day walk, follow the Hoi An walking tour (p234) and enjoy the cultural sites – and sights – of the town.

Other activities to while away a day include taking a Vietnamese cooking class

ARCHITECTURE OF HOI AN

A number of Hoi An's wooden buildings date from the first half of the 19th century or earlier. Imaginative visitors feel that they have been transported back a couple of centuries to a time when the wharf was crowded with sailing ships, the streets teemed with porters transporting goods to and from warehouses, and traders from a dozen countries haggled in a babble of different languages.

Because Hoi An was relatively untouched by the American War, it serves as a museum piece of Vietnamese history. More than 800 structures of historical significance have been officially identified in Hoi An, including houses and shops, wells, family chapels for ancestor worship, pagodas, Vietnamese and Chinese temples, bridges, communal buildings, assembly halls of various Chinese congregations, and tombs (Vietnamese, Chinese and Japanese; no original European tombs survive).

Many of Hoi An's older structures exhibit features of traditional architecture rarely seen today. As they have for centuries, some shopfronts (which are open during the day to display their wares) are shuttered at night by the shopkeepers, who insert horizontal planks into grooves that cut into the columns that support the roof. Some of the buildings' roofs are made up of thousands of brick-coloured am and duong (Yin and Yang) roof tiles – so called because of the way the alternating rows of concave and convex tiles fit snugly together. During the rainy season, the lichens and moss that live on the tiles spring to life, turning entire rooftops bright green.

A number of Hoi An's houses have round pieces of wood with an am and duong symbol in the middle surrounded by a spiral design over the doorway. These mat cua (watchful eyes) are supposed to protect the residents of the house from coming to any harm.

Hoi An's historic structures are gradually being restored and there is a sincere effort being made to preserve the unique character of the city. The local government has put some thought into this: old houses must be licensed for restoration work, which must be done in a tasteful manner.

Many of the house owners also charge for the invasion of their privacy – as much as US$3 for a guided tour of the building – but this is negotiable. The government permits this on the basis that the funds will be used for renovation of the homes.

Assistance in historical preservation is being provided to local authorities by the Archaeological Institute in Hanoi, the Japan-Vietnam Friendship Association, and experts from Europe and Japan.

watching local artisans working with wood, paint, ceramics and fabrics; taking a boat ride on the river; hiring a bike and cycling to the beach; or browsing the tailors' shops and ordering a new set of clothes. Plan on spending a few days here!

History

Recently excavated ceramic fragments from around 2200 years ago constitute the earliest evidence of human habitation in the Hoi An area. They are thought to belong to the late–Iron Age Sa Huynh civilisation, which is related to the Dong Son culture of northern Vietnam.

From the 2nd to the 10th centuries, this region was the heartland of the Kingdom of Champa – when the Cham capital of Simhapura (Tra Kieu) as well as the temples of Indrapura (Dong Duong) and My Son were built (see the boxed text on p245) – and there was a bustling seaport at Hoi An. Persian and Arab documents from the latter part of the period mention Hoi An as a provisions stop for trading ships. Archaeologists have uncovered the foundations of numerous Cham towers around Hoi An: the bricks and stones of the towers were reused by Vietnamese settlers.

In 1307 the Cham king married the daughter of a monarch of the Tran dynasty and presented Quang Nam province to the Vietnamese as a gift. When the Cham king died, his successor refused to recognise the deal and fighting broke out; for the next century, chaos reigned. By the 15th century, peace had been restored, allowing normal commerce to resume. During the next four centuries Chinese, Japanese, Dutch, Portuguese, Spanish, Indian, Filipino, Indonesian, Thai, French, British and American ships called at Hoi An to purchase high-grade silk (for which the area is famous), fabrics, paper, porcelain, tea, sugar, molasses, areca nuts, pepper, Chinese medicines, elephant tusks, beeswax, mother-of-pearl, lacquer, sulphur and lead.

The Chinese and Japanese traders sailed south in the spring, driven by winds from the northeast. They would stay in Hoi An until the summer, when southerly winds would blow them home. During their four-month sojourn in Hoi An, the merchants rented waterfront houses for use as warehouses and living quarters. Some traders began leaving full-time agents in Hoi An to take care of off-season business affairs. This is how foreign colonies got started, although the Japanese ceased coming to Hoi An after 1637, when the Japanese government forbade all contact with the outside world.

Hoi An was the first place in Vietnam to be exposed to Christianity. Among the 17th-century missionary visitors was the French priest Alexandre de Rhodes, who devised the Latin-based *quoc ngu* script for the Vietnamese language.

Hoi An was almost completely destroyed during the Tay Son Rebellion in the 1770s and 1780s. It was rebuilt and continued to serve as an important port for foreign trade until the late 19th century, when the Thu Bon River (Cai River), which links Hoi An with the sea, silted up and became too shallow for navigation. During this period Danang (Tourane) began to eclipse Hoi An as a port and centre of commerce. In 1916 a rail line linking Danang with Hoi An was destroyed in a terrible storm; it was never rebuilt.

During French colonisation Hoi An served as an administrative centre. During the American War the city, with the cooperation of both sides, remained almost completely undamaged.

Hoi An was the site of the first Chinese settlement in southern Vietnam. The town's Chinese *hoi quan* (congregational assembly halls) still play a special role among southern Vietnam's ethnic-Chinese, some of whom come to Hoi An from all over to participate in congregation-wide celebrations. Today, 1300 of Hoi An's population of 75,800 are ethnic-Chinese. Relations between ethnic-Vietnamese and ethnic-Chinese in Hoi An are excellent, partly because the Chinese here have become assimilated to the point where they even speak Vietnamese among themselves.

Information

BOOKSHOPS

Second-hand books are available in several shops and travel agents along Đ Le Loi.

Hoi An Bookstore (☎ 916 272; 6 Đ Nguyen Thi Minh Khai) The leading bookstore for cultural and historic tomes on Hoi An and the rest of Vietnam.

EMERGENCY

Hoi An Hospital (☎ 861 364; 10 Đ Tran Hung Dao) If it's anything serious, make for Danang.

Hoi An Police Station (☎ 861 204; 84 Đ Hoang Dieu)

CENTRAL VIETNAM

HOI AN

0   200 m
0   0.1 miles

To Green Field Hotel (100m);
Phu Tinh Hotel II (250m);
Ancient House Resort (350m);
Hoi An Riverside Resort (4km);
Red Bridge Cooking School (4km);
Victoria Hoi An Resort (5km);
Hoi An Beach Resort (5km);
Cua Dai Beach (5km)

To South China
Sea (5km);
Cham Island

Cam Nam
Island

To Cam Nam
Village (50m)

Cam Nam
Bridge

Thu Bon River

To Cam Kim
Island

An Hoi Peninsula

To Vinh Hung
Resort (300m)

An Hoi
Footbridge

Central
Market

Đ Trương Minh Lương
Đ Phan Bội Châu
Đ Nguyễn Duy Hiệu
Đ Cửa Đại
Đ Hoàng Diệu
Đ Nguyễn Huệ
Đ Trần Phú
Đ Hoàng Văn Thụ
Đ Nguyễn Thái Học
Đ Bạch Đằng
Đ Nguyễn Thái Học
Đ Lê Lợi
Đ Trần Hưng Đạo
Đ Thái Phiên
Đ Nguyễn Trường Tộ
Đ Lý Thường Kiệt
Đ Nẻo Gia Tu
Đ Lê Hồng Phong
Đ Thái Phiên
Đ Nhị Trung
Đ Nhị Trung
Đ Trần Cao Vân
Đ Phan Đình Phùng
Đ Nguyễn Huệ
Đ Phan Chu Trinh
Đ Nguyễn Thị Minh Khai
Đ Huỳnh Thúc Kháng

Chinese-style
War Memorial

To Northern Bus Station (200m);
Marble Mountains (12km);
China Beach (19km);
Danang (30km);
My Son (35km)

To Chúc Thánh
Pagoda (200m);
Phước Lâm Pagoda
(1.3km)

To Thanh Ha (2km);
Tra Kieu (20km);
Tam Ky (43km)

INTERNET ACCESS

You will trip over Internet cafés on every street in Hoi An. Most charge around 100d to 200d per minute, with a minimum 10-minute charge.

Min's Computer (☎ 914 323; 131 Đ Nguyen Duy Hieu) One of the few places with high-speed broadband access.

INTERNET RESOURCES

Hoi An Old Town (www.hoianworldheritage.org) The official World Heritage website for Hoi An's old town.

MONEY

Incombank (9 Đ Le Loi) Central place to change cash.

Vietcombank (Đ Tran Hung Dao) Exchange office, plus there's a handy ATM.

Vietincombank (4 Đ Hoang Dieu) Best all-rounder: changes cash and travellers cheques, offers cash advances and has an ATM.

POST

Main post office (48 Đ Tran Hung Dao) International post and telecommunications services, located at the junction with Đ Ngo Gia Tu.

TRAVEL AGENCIES

These days there are almost as many travel agencies as historic buildings in Hoi An!

Check out the strip of agencies opposite the Hoi An Hotel on Đ Tran Hung Dao. It's difficult to recommend one over the other, as most agencies offer the same services, including tours to My Son, bus and plane ticketing, and visa extensions. Competition is pretty fierce, so for expensive or complicated arrangements it's probably worth checking out a few options and negotiating.

Dangers & Annoyances

Generally speaking, Hoi An is one of the safer towns in Vietnam, but there have been stories of late-night bag-snatching in the poorly lit market area of town. Try to avoid this area at night or make sure you are not alone.

We have also heard accounts of women being followed to their hotels and assaulted on very rare occasions. If you are a lone female, try and make sure you walk home with somebody. In the very unlikely event that something like this happens, shout and scream as Hoi An is a very quiet town by night and the noise will reverberate all over.

Touts and their hard-sell used to be a constant companion in Hoi An, but this had been cracked down on during our last

HOI AN WALKING TOUR

Follow this tasty little trail to see Hoi An's main sights in a half-day amble.

The trail starts at **Phac Hat Pagoda** (**1**; opposite). Heading east along Ð Phan Chu Trinh, turn right into the alley next to street number 69. Here lies the **Truong Family Chapel** (**2**; opposite). Back on the main road, look out for the **Tran Family Chapel** (**3**; opposite) in the northeast corner of Ð Phan Chu Trinh. Head south now on Ð Le Loi and turn left at the next junction onto Ð Tran Phu. Visit the **Museum of Trading Ceramics** (**4**; opposite). Opposite the museum is the historic **House at 77 Ð Tran Phu** (**5**; opposite). Continuing along Ð Tran Phu, there is a cluster of interesting buildings on the left side of the road, including the **Chinese All-Community Assembly Hall** (**6**; opposite) and the **Assembly Hall of the Fujian Chinese Congregation** (**7**; opposite). Back on the road, keep heading east and at the next junction you'll see the **Quan Cong Temple** (**8**; p236). Take a short detour north on Ð Nguyen Hue to the **Quan Am Pagoda & History Museum** (**9**; p236). Back on Ð Tran Phu, still walking east, the **Assembly Hall of the Hainan Chinese Congregation** (**10**; p236) is on the left. Cross the next junction and the road becomes Ð Nguyen Duy Hieu. On the left is the **Assembly Hall of the Chaozhou Chinese Congregation** (**11**; p236).

Take the second right and turn right again onto Ð Phan Boi Chau. There is a whole city block of colonnaded French buildings here between Nos 22 and 73, among them the 19th-century **Tran Duong House** (**12**; p236). Wander along Ð Phan Boi Chau, take the fourth street on your right, turn left into Ð Nguyen Thai Hoc and soak up the ambience of this street. Turn right onto Ð Le Loi, then left onto Ð Tran Phu. Almost immediately on the left is the **Old House at 103 Tran Phu** (**13**; p237). Keep heading west now and you'll pass the **Assembly Hall of the Cantonese Chinese Congregation** (**14**; p237). A little further along on the left is the **Museum of Sa Huynh Culture** (**15**; p237). Beyond the museum is the famed **Japanese Covered Bridge** (**16**; p237), which connects Ð Tran Phu with Ð Nguyen Thi Minh Khai. Continue westward and keep an eye out for **Phung Hung Old House** (**17**; p237). Also check out **Cam Pho Temple** (**18**; p237).

From here, either retrace your steps or continue on to the **Cao Dai Pagoda** (**19**; p237). Then, back across the Japanese bridge, turn right and follow the road onto Ð Nguyen Thai Hoc, where you'll see the **Tan Ky House** (**20**; p237) at No 101. On the left before the next junction is the **Diep Dong Nguyen House** (**21**; p238). Settle down for a long, cool drink – you've earned it!

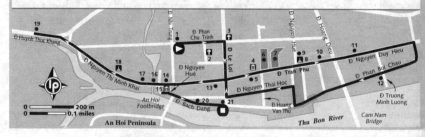

visit. No-one was allowed to solicit on the street and it made for a very peaceful place. How long this lasts is anyone's guess, but enjoy it while it does!

Sights

Now a Unesco World Heritage site, **Hoi An Old Town** (www.hoianworldheritage.org; entrance ticket 50,000d) is governed by preservation laws that are well up to speed. Several buildings of historical and cultural significance are open for public viewing, a number of streets in the centre of town are off-lim-

its to cars, and building alterations and height restrictions are well enforced. If only Hanoi would follow suit in its historic Old Quarter.

The admission fee goes towards funding this conservation work. This ticket gives you a rather complicated choice of heritage attractions to visit. You can visit all of the old streets, and one each of the five types of attractions: museums; assembly halls; old houses; 'intangible culture', such as a traditional music concert or handicraft workshop; and 'other', which means Quan

Cong's Temple or the temple within the Japanese Covered Bridge. If you want to visit additional attractions, then it is necessary to buy another ticket; there are ticket offices dotted around the town.

But for those who only want to buy one ticket, what are the best options? The most interesting museum is that of Trading Ceramics, not only thanks to the fine porcelain collection, but also for the building itself. Among the assembly halls, the Fujian folk probably have the edge. When it comes to old houses, Tan Ky House is a trip back in time to the early 19th century. Intangible culture is a musical performance or a handicrafts workshop in plain English and comes down to a matter of taste. Finally there is that obscure 'other' category: the Japanese Bridge or Quan Cong Temple. Choose the temple, as you can enjoy the experience of the Japanese Bridge without a ticket. The ticket just gets you into a small shrine that is very much second-best to the bridge itself.

The system doesn't seem to be well-monitored, but hopefully the fees do get collected and end up as part of the restoration and preservation fund. Despite the number of tourists who come to Hoi An, it is still a very conservative town, and visitors should dress modestly when touring the sites.

PHAC HAT PAGODA
This modern **pagoda** has a colourful façade of ceramics and murals and is an active place of worship.

TRUONG FAMILY CHAPEL
Founded two centuries ago, the **Truong Family Chapel** is a shrine dedicated to the ancestors of the ethnic-Chinese Truong family. A number of the memorial plaques were presented by emperors of Vietnam to honour members of the Truong family, who served as local officials and also as mandarins at the imperial court. To get here, turn into the alley next to 69 Đ Phan Chu Trinh.

TRAN FAMILY CHAPEL
At the northeast corner of Đ Phan Chu Trinh is the **Tran Family Chapel** (21 Đ Le Loi). This house for worshipping ancestors was built about 200 years ago with donations from

family members. The Tran family moved from China to Vietnam around 1700. The architecture of the building reflects the influence of Chinese and Japanese styles. The wooden boxes on the altar contain the Tran ancestors' stone tablets, and feature chiselled Chinese characters.

MUSEUM OF TRADING CERAMICS
Showcasing a collection of blue and white ceramics of the Dai Viet period, the delightful **Museum of Trading Ceramics** is in a simply restored house. In particular, check out the great ceramic mosaic that's set above the pond in the inner courtyard.

HOUSE AT 77 Đ TRAN PHU
This private **house** (77 Tran Phu; 7am-5pm) is about three centuries old. There is some especially fine carving on the wooden walls of the rooms around the courtyard, on the roof beams and under the crab-shell roof (in the salon next to the courtyard). Look out for the green ceramic tiles built into the railing around the courtyard balcony. The house is open to visitors for a small fee.

CHINESE ALL-COMMUNITY ASSEMBLY HALL
Founded in 1773, the **Chinese All-Community Assembly Hall** (Chua Ba) was used by Fujian, Cantonese, Hainan, Chaozhou and Hakka congregations in Hoi An. The pavilions off the main courtyard incorporate elements of 19th-century French architecture.

The main entrance to the assembly hall is located on Đ Tran Phu. However, the only way to get inside these days is to enter from around the back at 31 Đ Phan Chu Trinh.

ASSEMBLY HALL OF THE FUJIAN CHINESE CONGREGATION
Founded as a place to hold community meetings, this **assembly hall** (opposite 35 Đ Tran Phu) was later transformed into a temple for the worship of Thien Hau, the deity who was born in Fujian province. The triple gate to the complex was built in 1975.

The mural near the entrance to the main hall, on the right-hand wall, depicts Thien Hau, her way lit by lantern light, crossing a stormy sea to rescue a foundering ship. On the wall opposite is a mural of the heads of the six Fujian families who fled from China to Hoi An in the 17th century, following the overthrow of the Ming dynasty.

The penultimate chamber contains a statue of Thien Hau. To either side of the entrance stand red-skinned Thuan Phong Nhi and green-skinned Thien Ly Nhan. When either sees or hears sailors in distress, they inform Thien Hau, who sets off to effect a rescue. The replica of a Chinese boat along the right-hand wall is 1:20 scale.

The central altar in the last chamber contains seated figures of the heads of the six Fujian families. The smaller figures below them represent their successors as clan leaders. In a 30cm-high glass dome is a figurine of Le Huu Trac, a Vietnamese physician renowned in both Vietnam and China for his healing powers.

Behind the altar on the left is the God of Prosperity. On the right are three fairies and smaller figures representing the 12 *ba mu* (midwives), each of whom teaches newborns a different skill necessary for the first year of life: smiling, sucking, lying on their stomachs and so forth. Childless couples often come here to pray for offspring. The three groups of figures in this chamber represent the elements most central to Chinese life: ancestors, children and financial wellbeing.

The middle altar of the room to the right of the courtyard commemorates deceased leaders of the Fujian congregation. On either side are lists of contributors – women on the left and men on the right. The wall panels represent the four seasons.

The Fujian assembly hall is fairly well lit and can be visited after dark. Shoes should be removed upon mounting the platform just past the naves.

QUAN CONG TEMPLE
Founded in 1653, **Quan Cong Temple** (Chua Ong; 24 Đ Tran Phu) is a Chinese temple that is dedicated to Quan Cong, whose partially gilt statue, made of papier-mâché on a wooden frame, is in the central altar at the back of the sanctuary. On the left is a statue of General Chau Xuong, one of Quan Cong's guardians, striking a tough-guy pose. On the right is the rather plump administrative mandarin Quan Binh. The life-size white horse recalls a mount ridden by Quan Cong, until he was given a red horse of extraordinary endur-

ance, representations of which are common in Chinese pagodas.

Stone plaques on the walls list contributors to the construction and repair of the temple. Check out the carp-shaped rain spouts on the roof surrounding the courtyard. The carp is a symbol of patience in Chinese mythology and is popular in Hoi An.

Shoes should be removed when mounting the platform in front of the statue of Quan Cong. Note that according to the old numbering system, the address is 168 Đ Tran Phu.

QUAN AM PAGODA & HISTORY MUSEUM
The comparatively austere **Quan Am Pagoda & History Museum** (7 Đ Nguyen Hue; 8am-5pm) houses a small collection of bronze temple bells, gongs and cannon. There's also a display of Cham artefacts.

ASSEMBLY HALL OF THE HAINAN CHINESE CONGREGATION
Built in 1883, this **assembly hall** (Đ Tran Phu, 8am-5pm) is a memorial to the 108 merchants from Hainan Island who were mistaken for pirates and killed in Quang Nam province during the reign of Emperor Tu Duc. The elaborate dais contains plaques in their memory. In front of the central altar is a fine gilded woodcarving of Chinese court life.

ASSEMBLY HALL OF THE CHAOZHOU CHINESE CONGREGATION
The Chaozhou Chinese in Hoi An built their **congregational hall** (opposite 157 Đ Nguyen Duy Hieu; 8am-5pm) in 1776. Some outstanding woodcarvings are on the beams, walls and altar. On the doors in front of the altar are carvings of two Chinese girls wearing their hair in a Japanese style.

TRAN DUONG HOUSE
There is a whole city block of colonnaded French-colonial buildings on Đ Phan Boi Chau, between Nos 22 and 73, among them the 19th-century **Tran Duong House** (25 Đ Phan Boi Chau; admission free, donations welcome; 9am-6pm). Mr Duong, a friendly retired mathematics teacher, speaks English and French, and is happy to explain the history of his 62m-long house and its contents to visitors.

MARK ANDREW KIRBY

Ben Hai River (p192), Demilitarised Zone

Vinh Moc Tunnels (p191)
PETER PTSCHELINZEW

Boy mixing herbal medi-
cines, Hué (p199)
PHIL WEYMOUTH

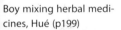

Fading façade of houses, Hoi An (p230)
MICHELLE BENNETT

Traditional Chinese lanterns, Hoi An (p230)

NOBORU KOMINE

Tan Ky House (p237), Hoi An

JOHN ELK III

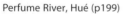

Marble Mountains (p228), near Danang

WAYN

Perfume River, Hué (p199)

ALA

OLD HOUSE AT 103 TRAN PHU

The wooden frontage and shutters make a good photographic backdrop to this eclectic **shop** (103 Đ Tran Phu), where women make silk lanterns. There are ornamental aquarium fish for sale and you can also buy shampoo.

ASSEMBLY HALL OF THE CANTONESE CHINESE CONGREGATION

Founded in 1786, this **assembly hall** (176 Đ Tran Phu; ⏱ 8am-5pm) has a main altar that is dedicated to Quan Cong. Note the long-handled brass 'fans' to either side of the altar. The lintel and door posts of the main entrance and a number of the columns supporting the roof are made of single blocks of granite. The other columns were carved out of the durable wood of the jackfruit tree. There are some intricate carvings in the wooden beams that support the roof in front of the main entrance.

MUSEUM OF SA HUYNH CULTURE

Artefacts from the early Dong Son civilisation of Sa Huynh are displayed at this **museum** (149 Đ Tran Phu; ⏱ 8am-5pm). The building itself is not that interesting; visit for the collection of objects it houses.

JAPANESE COVERED BRIDGE

This famed **bridge** (Cau Nhat Ban or Lai Vien Kieu) connects 155 Đ Tran Phu with 1 Đ Nguyen Thi Minh Khai. The first bridge on this site was constructed in the 1590s. It was built by the Japanese community of Hoi An in order to link them with the Chinese quarters across the stream. The bridge was constructed with a roof so that it could be used as a shelter from both the rain and sun.

The Japanese Covered Bridge is very solidly constructed; apparently the original builders were concerned about the threat of earthquakes. Over the centuries the ornamentation of the bridge has remained relatively faithful to the original Japanese design. Its understatement contrasts greatly with the Vietnamese and Chinese penchant for wild decoration. The French flattened out the roadway to make it more suitable for their motor vehicles, but the original arched shape was restored during major renovation work carried out in 1986.

Built into the northern side of the bridge is a small **temple** (Chua Cau). The writing over the door of the temple is the name given to the bridge in 1719 to replace the name meaning Japanese Covered Bridge. However the new name, Lai Vien Kieu (Bridge for Passers-By from Afar), never quite caught on.

According to legend, there once lived an enormous monster called Cu, who had its head in India, its tail in Japan and its body in Vietnam. Whenever the monster moved, terrible disasters such as floods and earthquakes befell Vietnam. This bridge was built on the monster's weakest point and killed it, but the people of Hoi An took pity on the slain monster and built this temple to pray for its soul.

The entrances of the bridge are guarded by a pair of monkeys on one side and a pair of dogs on the other. According to one story, these animals were popularly revered because many of Japan's emperors were born in years of the dog and monkey. Another tale relates that construction of the bridge started in the year of the monkey and was finished in the year of the dog.

The stelae, listing all the Vietnamese and Chinese contributors to a subsequent restoration of the bridge, are written in *chu nho* (Chinese characters) – the *nom* script had not yet become popular in these parts.

PHUNG HUNG OLD HOUSE

In a lane full of beautiful buildings, this old **house** (4 Đ Nguyen Thi Minh Khai; ⏱ 8am-7pm) stands out. At present it houses a bookshop and showcases designer ceramics; wander through and enjoy the ambience.

CAM PHO TEMPLE

This less-ornate, newish **temple** (52 Đ Nguyen Thi Minh Khai; ⏱ 8am-5pm) is notable mainly for its ceramic dragon roof line.

CAO DAI PAGODA

Serving Hoi An's Cao Dai community is the small **Cao Dai Pagoda** (btwn Nos 64 & 70 Đ Huynh Thuc Khang), near the bus station. Only one priest, who grows sugar and corn in the front yard to make some extra cash, lives here. It was built in 1952.

TAN KY HOUSE

Built two centuries ago as the home of a well-to-do ethnic-Vietnamese merchant, **Tan Ky House** (☎ 861 474; 101 Đ Nguyen Thai Hoc;

8am-noon & 2-4.30pm) has been lovingly preserved and today looks almost exactly as it did in the early 19th century.

The design of Tan Ky House shows some evidence of the Japanese and Chinese influence on local architecture. Japanese elements include the ceiling (in the area immediately before the courtyard), which is supported by three progressively shorter beams, one on top of the other. There are similar beams in the salon. Under the crab-shell ceiling there are carvings of crossed sabres wrapped in silk ribbon. The sabres symbolise force; the silk represents flexibility.

Chinese poems written in inlaid mother-of-pearl are hung from a number of the columns that hold up the roof. The Chinese characters on these 150-year-old panels are formed entirely of birds gracefully portrayed in various positions of flight.

The courtyard here has four functions: to let in light, provide ventilation, bring a glimpse of nature into the home and collect rainwater and provide drainage. The stone tiles covering the patio floor were brought from Thanh Hoa province in north-central Vietnam. The carved, wooden balcony supports around the courtyard are decorated with grape leaves, which are a European import and further evidence of the unique blending of cultures that took place in Hoi An.

The back of the house faces the river. In the past, this section of the building was rented out to foreign merchants. That the house was a place of commerce, as well as a residence, is indicated by the two pulleys attached to a beam in the storage loft just inside the front door.

The exterior of the roof is made of tiles; inside, the ceiling consists of wood. This design keeps the house cool in summer and warm in winter. The floor tiles were brought from near Hanoi.

Tan Ky House is a private home, but is one of the choices on the Hoi An Old Town entrance ticket (see p237). The owner, whose family has lived here for seven generations, speaks fluent French and English.

DIEP DONG NGUYEN HOUSE

Built for a Chinese merchant, an ancestor of the current inhabitants, in the late 19th century is **Diep Dong Nguyen House** (58 Đ Nguyen Thai Hoc; admission free; 8am-noon & 2-4.30pm). The front room on the ground floor was once a dispensary for *thuoc bac* (Chinese medicine); the medicines were stored in the glass-enclosed cases lining the walls. The owner's private collection of antiques, which includes photographs, porcelain and furniture, is on display upstairs. The objects are not for sale! Two of the chairs were once lent by the family to Emperor Bao Dai.

HOI AN CHURCH

The only tombs of Europeans in Hoi An are found in the yard of this **church** (cnr Đ Nguyen Truong To & Đ Le Hong Phong). This modern building was built to replace an earlier structure at another site. Several 18th-century missionaries were exhumed from tombs at the original site and reburied here.

CHUC THANH PAGODA

Founded in 1454 by Minh Hai, a Buddhist monk from China, **Chuc Thanh Pagoda** (Khu vuc 7, Tan An; 8am-6pm) is the oldest pagoda in Hoi An. Among the antique ritual objects still in use are several bells, a stone gong that is two centuries old and a carp-shaped wooden gong said to be even older. Today, several elderly monks live here.

In the main sanctuary, the gilt Chinese characters inscribed on a red roof beam give details of the pagoda's construction. An A Di Da Buddha flanked by two Thich Ca Buddhas sits under a wooden canopy on the central dais. In front of them is a statue of a boyhood Thich Ca flanked by his servants.

To get to Chuc Thanh Pagoda, go all the way to the end of Đ Nguyen Truong To and turn left. Follow the sandy path for 500m.

PHUOC LAM PAGODA

Founded in the mid-17th century is **Phuoc Lam Pagoda** (Thon 2A, Cam Ha; 8am-5pm). The head monk at the end of that century was An Thiem, a Vietnamese prodigy who had become a monk at the age of eight. When he was 18, the king drafted An Thiem's brothers into his army to put down a rebellion. An Thiem volunteered to take the places of the other men in his family and eventually rose to the rank of general. After the war, he returned to the monkhood, but felt guilty about the many people he had slain. To atone for his sins, he volunteered to clean

he Hoi An Market for 20 years. When that
ime was up, he was asked to come to Phuoc
Lam Pagoda as head monk.

To reach the pagoda, continue past Chuc
Thanh Pagoda for 400m. The path passes
an obelisk that was erected over the tomb
of 13 ethnic-Chinese, who had been de-
capitated by the Japanese during WWII for
resistance activities.

Cooking Courses
Many of the most popular cafés offer cooking classes, where you learn how to make
two or three dishes and then – the best bit –
sit down to enjoy them. Dinner is usually
the most popular, but lunch classes with a
morning trip to the market are also taking
off. A small group class costs about US$5
per person, but you can tailor a longer class
if you find a favourite spot.

For a cooking class with a difference,
check out **Red Bridge** (☎ 933 222; www.visithoian
com). Starting out with a trip to the local
market, you then cruise down the river to
this relaxing retreat about 4km from Hoi
An. The class includes leading local dishes
as well as some decorative touches. The
class costs US$12; it starts at 8.45am and
finishes at 1pm.

Sleeping
Hoi An used to be notorious for room
shortages in the peak seasons from August to October and December to February. That has all changed with a building
boom beyond belief that added 1000 beds
alone in a six-month period in 2003! From
a town you might have been turned away
from during the peak period, you'll find
yourself turning down cheap deals galore
instead. Demand should once again catch
up with supply in a few years, but for now
Hoi An has the best bargain bedrooms in
Asia. Still, if you have your heart set on a
particular hotel, you should probably book
ahead at busy times.

Many of the new hotels are second or
third incarnations of old favourites, with
innovative names like II and III. They all
seem to follow the same architectural blue-
print first made famous by the Vinh Hung 2
and many include central swimming pools.
Most of these places advertise two rates for
rooms: with or without air-con. You can
get a room with satellite TV, fridge, hot-

water bathtub and access to a pool for just
US$6!

Most travellers want to find a room right
in the town centre, so not surprisingly these
central places fill up quickly. The quieter
and more spacious hotels tend to be on the
outskirts of town. Considering how small
Hoi An is, and how easy it is to navigate on
foot, there should be no great compulsion
to find a place in the bustling heart of town.
Plus the older hotels in town tend to charge
the same as the nicer new ones on the edge,
but lack the extras like a swimming pool.

Đ Nhi Trung (New St) is overflowing
with options that, for the moment at least,
have rare rear views over the rice fields.
On the eastern edge of town, towards Cua
Dai Beach, are a host of hotels. Restaurants,
Internet cafés and travel agencies have
sprung up nearby, but it's a 10-minute walk
to the real action.

Prices listed here are standard rates. It
was common for rates to rise during the
peak December and January period, but
now with such over-supply it is generally
no longer the case. In fact, you may find the
opposite; the struggle to survive for some of
the new places has led to cut-throat competition and even cheaper prices.

BUDGET & MID-RANGE
Vinh Hung 1 Hotel (☎ 861 621; vinhhung.ha@dng.vnn
.vn; 143 Đ Tran Phu; r US$15-45; ✷) Set in a classic
Chinese trading house, this is an atmospheric hotel. Splash the cash for one of two
rooms used as dressing rooms by Michael
Caine while filming *The Quiet American*;
each is decorated with antiques and a beautiful canopy bed. Perfect setting in the heart
of the old town.

Vinh Hung 2 Hotel (☎ 863 717; quanghuy.ha@dng
.vnn.vn; Đ Nhi Trung; r US$15-35; ✷ 🖳 ☲) This
was the first of the new breed of annex
hotels and has comfortable Chinese-themed
rooms and a swimming pool in the central
courtyard.

Phu Tinh Hotel (☎ 861 297; fax 861 757; 144 Đ
Tran Phu; r US$8-12; ✷) One of the best loca-
tions of any hotel, the rates are enticing at
this place, as all rooms have TV, fridge and
hot water.

Phu Tinh Hotel II (☎ 923 923; minhthaoha@dng
.vnn.vn; 144 Đ Cua Dai; r US$12-30; ✷ ☲) A newer
relation on the beach road, with fancier
rooms and a pool.

Minh A Ancient Lodging House (☎ 861 368; 2 Đ Nguyen Thai Hoc; r US$7-12; 🌀) This could start a new trend in town – a small, family-owned historic house that feels more like a B&B, only without the breakfast. Just three rooms, including a sort of suite upstairs.

Ha An Hotel (☎ 863 126; tohuong@fpt.vn; 6 Đ Phan Boi Chau; r US$20-30; 🌀) A hotel that is definitely different, something that can't be said about many places in town. A strip of buildings built in Hoi An style (one French, one Chinese and so on), all set in a lush, lush garden. Decorative flair inside and breakfast is included.

Thanh Binh 1 Hotel (☎ 861 740; vothihong@dng .vnn.vn; 1 Đ Le Loi; r US$10-25; 🌀) An old favourite near the old town, the rooms are largish for the location, with average amenities.

Thanh Binh 2 Hotel (☎ 863 715; vothihong@dng .vnn.vn; Đ Nhi Trung; r US$7-20; 🌀 🖥 🏊) This is a better deal if you don't mind a walk into town, and has elegant rooms and a pool.

Huy Hoang 1 Hotel (☎ 861 453; kshuyhoang1@dng .vnn.vn; 73 Đ Phan Boi Chau; r US$7-25; 🌀 🖥) A popular place by Cam Nam Bridge, where breakfast on the riverside balcony is included.

Huy Hoang 2 Hotel (☎ 916 234; kshuyhoang2@dng .vnn.vn; 87 Đ Huynh Thuc Khang; r US$6-15; 🌀 🖥) This is better value, with big, clean rooms, satellite TV and a garden restaurant.

Thien Trung Hotel (☎ 861 720; thientrungha@dng .vnn.vn; 63 Đ Phan Dinh Phung; r US$7-15; 🌀 🖥) This hotel has had a makeover, but the prices have stayed the same. The cleaners are conscientious and the price is right.

Thuy Duong Hotel I (☎ 861 574; thuyduongco@dng .vnn.vn; 11 Đ Le Loi; r US$7-10; 🌀 🖥) It's looking a touch tatty these days, but is very central and a good place to get online.

Thuy Duong Hotel III (☎ 916 565; Đ Nhi Trung; r US$20-40; 🌀 🖥 🏊) This is a smart new place on Đ Nhi Trung (New St), but there are better value options on the same strip.

Thanh Xuan Hotel (☎ 916 696; www.thanhxuan hotel.com; 22 Đ Nhi Trung; r US$10-20; 🌀 🖥) A nifty new place with the best bathtubs you are likely to find for this sort of money. Nice design, nice rooms, nice price.

Thien Thanh Hotel (☎ 916 545; www.hoianthien thanhhotel.com; 6 Đ Nhi Trung; r US$8-15; 🌀 🖥) This is an obliging option with breezy balconies at the back and the typical trimmings like TV, fridge and hot water.

Nhi Trung Hotel (☎ 863 436; 13 Đ Nhi Trung; r US$7-10; 🌀 🖥) A friendly, family-run pad that has cheap rooms. Air-con costs US$2 extra if you want to chill out here.

Hop Yen Hotel (☎ 863 153; 16 Đ Nhi Trung; r US$6-10; 🌀 🖥) A minihotel that employs helpful staff who speak good English. Internet access downstairs for quick communications.

Sao Bien Hotel (Sea Star Hotel; ☎ 861 589; fax 861 382; 15 Đ Cua Dai; r US$8-12; 🌀) One of the older places in town, but the budget rooms at the top have fine views over Hoi An's red-brick roofs. Friendly French-speaking owner.

Green Field Hotel (Dong Xanh Hotel; ☎ 863 484; www.greenfieldhotel.com; dm US$3, r US$15-24, 🌀 🖥 🏊) The place to find the cheapest beds in town, with its popular dorms, and access to the pool is included! The normal rooms are comfortable, the staff ready to assist and there is an ATM outside.

Cua Dai Hotel (☎ 862 231; cuadaihotel@dng.vnn.vn; 18 Đ Cua Dai; s/d/tr US$20/25/30; 🌀 🖥) A popular place, but the rates are a touch out-of-touch given what is on offer elsewhere. Comfy rattan chairs in the communal areas and a good balcony.

Ancient House Resort (☎ 923 377; www.ancient houseresort.com; 61 Đ Cua Dai; r US$40-55; 🌀 🖥 🏊) This hotel stands out from the crowd, as it is designed in keeping with the ageing architecture of Hoi An. In fact, there is an ancient house at the heart of the complex and the elegant rooms are complemented by a large swimming pool.

Among the mushrooming minihotels on Đ Nhi Trung, consider the following:
Hoi Pho Hotel (☎ 916 382; 4 Đ Nhi Trung; r US$7-10; 🌀) Straightforward value for money with clean rooms and attentive service.
Thien Nga Hotel (☎ 916 330; thiennga_hotel@pmail .vnn.vn; Đ Nhi Trung; s/d US$12/15; 🌀 🖥) One of the oldest on this street, and still a popular place.

TOP END

Hoi An Hotel (☎ 861 373; hoianhotel@dng.vnn.vn; 6 Đ Tran Hung Dao; r US$40-100; 🌀 🖥 🏊) A grand colonial-style building that was once, believe it or not, the only place to stay in town. One of the largest hotels in Vietnam, room rates range widely and there's a good-sized swimming pool. Very popular with tour groups.

Vinh Hung Resort (☎ 910 577; www.vinhhung hotels.com; An Hoi Islet; r US$70-110; 🌀 🖥 🏊) The fourth and latest member of the Vinh Hung family has a lovely location and a lush garden. Rooms are enormous and set around a central swimming pool. Discounts of up to 40% during quiet periods.

Hoi An Riverside Resort (☎ 864 800; hoian river@dng.vnn.vn; Ð Cua Dai; r from US$129; 🍴 🖳 🕭) An elegant series of villas in a rustic setting overlooking the river and rice fields, this is a lovely place to wind down. Choose from the beach to the east or the huge pool. Expect discounts of 50% or so off these published rates.

Victoria Hoi An Resort (☎ 927 040; hoian@ victoriahotels-asia.com; r from US$115; 🍴 🖳 🕭) Sitting on a huge slice of Cua Dai Beach, about 5km east of town, this resort boasts all the stylish facilities you'd expect for the price, including a pristine pool. Unique hotel transport includes old Renault buses and motorbikes and sidecars. Low-season discounts are usually available.

Hoi An Beach Resort (☎ 927 011; hoianbeach resort@dng.vnn.vn; Cua Dai Beach; r from US$100; 🍴 🖳 🕭) Large and lavish rooms with big balconies to catch a breeze are the order of the day here. Better to avoid those on the noisy beachfront road. There are two swimming pools, Jacuzzi, steam bath and plenty of other diversions.

Many more swanky hotels are under construction; **Hoi An Life Resort** (www.life-resorts.com) should be well worth a look.

Eating

Hoi An's contribution to Vietnamese cuisine is *cao lau*, doughy flat noodles mixed with croutons, bean sprouts and greens and topped off with pork slices. It is mixed with crumbled, crispy rice paper immediately before eating. *Cao lau* pops up on menus all over Hoi An, which is the only place genuine *cao lau* can be made because the water used in its preparation must come from **Ba Le Well**. The well itself, which is said to date from Cham times, is square in shape. To get there, turn down the alley opposite 35 Ð Phan Chu Trinh and hang a right before reaching number 45/17 (you might need to ask someone for directions).

Other Hoi An specialities are fried won ton and the delicate 'white rose' (steamed shrimp wrapped in rice paper), available in most local eateries.

Many types of cuisine are available, including Vietnamese, Chinese, Western and vegetarian. Unless otherwise stated, expect to get a filling feed for 25,000d or so. Around 50,000d will buy a good three-course set menu in many of the restaurants.

There are heaps of restaurants on Ð Nguyen Hue, Ð Tran Phu and, on the waterfront, along Ð Bach Dang where you can enjoy a leisurely meal or linger over drinks.

Hong Phuc Restaurant (☎ 862 567; 86 Ð Bach Dang; dishes 15,000-40,000d) One of the best, this place is famous for its fish wrapped in banana leaf. Often copied but never bettered, it's a divine dish with garlic, lemongrass, pepper and a dash of lime.

Café des Amis (☎ 861 616; 52 Ð Bach Dang; 4-course veg menus 50,000d, seafood menus 60,000d; ⏱ from 5pm) This gastronomic hideaway has earned a loyal following over the past decade thanks to fine food. There is no menu; the set dinner is whatever the chef, Mr Kim, feels like cooking that day, but it is always delicious.

Café Can (☎ 861 525; 74 Ð Bach Dang; dishes 15,000-60,000d) Housed in a grand old French building, this café has a wide sundeck out front for a breezy bite to eat. Vietnamese and international dishes or just dabble with the drinks.

Hoi An Hai San (☎ 861 652; 64 Ð Bach Dang; mains around 50,000d) This seafood restaurant serves innovative Vietnamese concoctions and some Swedish dishes to keep the chef-owner in touch with his roots.

Han Huyen Restaurant (Floating Restaurant; ☎ 861 462; meals from 20,000d) Berthed on the banks of the river, it serves good food, better views, and it's a top spot to watch Hoi An life drift by.

Hyn Na Restaurant (☎ 863 736; 1 Ð Cong Dong; dishes 10,000-40,000d) For an alternative view of Hoi An, try life on the other side of the river at this little local eatery.

Miss Ly Cafeteria 22 (☎ 861 603; 22 Ð Nguyen Hue; dishes 15,000-40,000d) A Hoi An institution, this place has some of the best Hoi An specialities in town. The restaurant closes when empty (and that's usually late) and is nearly always crowded.

Mermaid Restaurant (☎ 861 527; 2 Ð Tran Phu; dishes 10,000-35,000d) One of the original Hoi An eateries, this is still a favourite for its sensational, three-course set menus during the evening.

Ba Le Well Restaurant (☎ 864 443; 51 Ð Tran Hung Dao; dishes 5000-20,000d) Named after and located near the well that provides the water for Hoi An's *cao lau*, so what better place to sample the speciality than this little family-run place.

Café Bobo (☎ 861 939; 18 Đ Le Loi; dishes 7000-25,000đ) When it comes to a traditional traveller café and a bit of backpacker cuisine, this place is hard to beat. It's still churning out the banana pancakes, and is a good source of travel information.

Banana Split Cafe (☎ 861 136; 53 Đ Hoang Dieu; 🖳) Cloned direct from the beaches of Nha Trang, this is where sweet-tooths can relieve a sudden craving for ice cream, fresh fruit juices and, of course, banana splits.

Cargo Club (☎ 910 489; 107 Đ Nguyen Thai Hoc; cakes 5000-15,000đ) This is the latest, greatest spot on Đ Nguyen Thai Hoc, one of the most happening streets in Hoi An. Mouthwatering pastries downstairs and distinguished dining upstairs, plus a balcony terrace overlooking the river.

Yellow Star Café (☎ 910 430; 73 Đ Nguyen Thai Hoc; dishes 20,000-60,000đ) This place has an eclectic menu of delicious dishes from around the world. Great steaks, succulent seafood and home comforts like fruit crumbles. About as central as it gets, so a good spot for an early evening drink to see who is out and about.

Brothers Café (☎ 914 150; 27 Đ Phan Boi Chau; set lunch US$12; 🕙 10am-10pm) Looking like a film set in one of the finest French-colonial buildings in town, it has a gorgeous garden that runs down to the river. The setting is superb and the attention to designer detail perfect. It is properly pricey by Hoi An standards, so many just drop by for a drink.

Omar Khayyam's Indian Restaurant (☎ 864 538; 14 Đ Phan Dinh Phung; veg/nonveg thalis 39,000/49,000đ; 🕙 9am-10pm) The place for curry connoisseurs, it's a small slice of the Subcontinent here in Hoi An.

Good Morning Vietnam (☎ 910 227; 34 Đ Le Loi; pizzas from 35,000đ) This is a Hoi An outpost of the celebrated Saigon spot. The best pizzas and pastas in town, as this is the real thing.

SEWING UP A STORM *Juliet Coombe*

From dawn until dusk the whirring of sewing machines resounds through Hoi An. The town itself is a virtual treasure-trove, with fabric of every shape and size stacked to the ceilings of the myriad cloth shops.

Spending a morning being pampered in any of the dressmakers' shops in and around the market is a great experience. Choose your new wardrobe from endless rolls of material and, for a little over the cost of the cloth, you'll soon have tailor-made shirts, trousers, dresses and skirts.

A completely new wardrobe, including material, can cost as little as US$100. An evening dress starts at around US$15, a summer dress at US$8 and a suit at US$20.

Incredibly, the master tailors here can whip together anything from slinky silk pyjamas to a formal Japanese kimono, and are even able to copy designs straight out of fashion magazines – anything from a copy of a designer ball gown to a top city-slicker suit in just a couple of hours. Whether silk, cotton or linen, people rave about the clothes they had made in Hoi An.

When buying silk, it is important to ascertain that the material is real silk and not 'Vietnamese silk' – a term often used to describe polyester and other synthetic fabrics that look and feel like silk. The only real test is with a cigarette or match (synthetic fibres melt and silk burns), but be careful not to set the shop on fire! Ask for a cut-off sample of the material you are thinking of buying and go outside to test it if you're concerned about its authenticity.

It is also important to check the seams of the finished garment: a single set of stitching along the inside edges will soon cause fraying and, in many cases, great big gaping holes. All well-tailored garments have a second set of stitches (known in the trade as blanket stitching), which binds the edge, oversewing the fabric so fraying is impossible. Ask the person tailoring the outfit to use the same colour cotton as the material – otherwise they will use white cotton throughout. Where possible, also insist on the clothes being lined, as it helps them move and fall in the right direction.

A few hours after your initial consultation, when you will be measured from every angle, you can return for your final fitting session and adjustments. Your only concern will be whether to carry your new gear around or make a dash to the post office to send it home.

Other good places:

Fukien Restaurant (☎ 861 326; 28 Ð Tran Phu) Bird's-eye view of the bustling market from the balcony.

Thanh Binh Restaurant (☎ 862 920; 94 Ð Le Loi) Chinese-influenced eatery right in the middle of the action that is well regarded by travellers.

Thanh Thanh Restaurant (☎ 861 308; 152 Ð Tran Phu) Traditional house with traditional food.

Drinking

Tam Tam Cafe & Bar (☎ 862 212; tamtam.ha@dng .vnn.vn; 110 Ð Nguyen Thai Hoc) Tam Tam has its home in a lovingly restored tea warehouse. Expanding downstairs, the heart and soul of this place remains upstairs, where there is a large lounge and dining area as well as a popular pool table. Great European and Vietnamese food is on offer here, and there's a fine wine list and bar snacks for those just wanting something to partner a pitcher of beer. A definitive stop on the night train.

Lounge Bar (☎ 910 480; 102 Ð Nguyen Thai Hoc) Just along the road from Tam Tam, this place has yet to draw the drinkers it deserves. A stylish conversion of an ancient house, the drinks menu is huge and there are some fun bar games. Out back are cushions and a chill-out area.

Hai's Scout Café (☎ 863 210; 98 Ð Nguyen Thai Hoc; sandwiches around 30,000d; 💻) A dimly lit local café on the Ð Nguyen Thai Hoc side, this becomes a courtyard café if you make a grand entrance from Ð Tran Phu. It serves sandwiches, light meals, real cappuccinos and lattes. Breaks into a bar by night and has information on WWF projects in central Vietnam.

Champa Bar (☎ 862 974; 75 Ð Nguyen Thai Hoc) Another drinking den on this neat street, it has a pool table, cheap local cocktails and a traditional show every night.

Treat's Café (☎ 861 125; 158 Ð Tran Phu) The backpacker bar of old Hoi An, this place is regularly full to bursting. It is a sprawling place with a restaurant-café upstairs. The oh-so-happy happy hours between 5pm and 9pm include two-for-one spirits and bargain beer.

Re-Treat Café (☎ 910 527; 23 Ð Phan Dinh Phung) Recreates Treat's recipe in the newer part of town, 'same same but better'. Not quite, but saves a walk if you're staying here.

Other options for a swift one on Ð Phan Dinh Phung:

Bamboo Bar (15b Ð Phan Dinh Phung) Popular place in the thick of the action.

Camel Bar (☎ 861 203; 9 Ð Phan Dinh Phung) Dark interior, light garden, plus a penchant for rock music.

Shopping

Hoi An is a shoppers' haven, and though the air of commercialism has increasingly taken a toll on the mellowed charm of the town, it is nowhere near as overwhelming as many other tourist centres in Vietnam.

Reaching Out (☎ 910 168; 103 Ð Nguyen Thai Hoc; 🕙 8am-9pm) is a great place to spend your dong. It is a fair-trade gift shop with a little bit of everything you see on sale in Hoi An. Profits go towards assisting disabled artisans.

Hoi An is known for its production of cotton cloth. All over the city there are cotton mills with rows of fantastic wooden looms that make a rhythmic 'clackety-clack, clackety-clack' sound as a whirring, cycloidal drive wheel shoots the shuttle back and forth under the watchful eyes of the machine attendant. The classic technology used in building these domestically produced machines dates from the Industrial Revolution. This is probably what mills in Victorian England must have looked like.

Tailor-made clothing is one of Hoi An's specialities (see the boxed text opposite). In the space of just a few years the number of tailor shops has grown from dozens to hundreds! It's fair to say that you can't tour the town without bumping into them at every turn. Recommending one tailor over another is a difficult proposition, as most shops outsource their tailoring to cutting centres anyway. Before the ban on touts, the killer competition for limited tourist dollars saw touts out in full force (most of them cute young girls who used the 'What's your name? Where are you from? Would you like to come and see my auntie's shop?' approach), but this had all stopped during our visit. Many of the tailors carry the same catalogues and turn out the latest designs. Most are fine, whether you're looking for alterations or a whole new wardrobe. They're very good at copying, so take any favourite clothes you want replicated. The most important thing to remember is to leave yourself time for adjustments to be made, and for a final fitting. Those with more time on their hands might like to try and get a few things made in different shops before taking the plunge.

For a look at the various materials available locally, take a peek at the **Hoi An Cloth Market** (Đ Tran Phu).

It is not only clothes that are being turned out in numbers, shoes are now a popular purchase. The cobblers here can copy anything from trainers (sneakers) to the highest heels or the coolest Cubans. Prices are very low, so it's a great place to pick up sandals, copycat Campers or anything else that takes your fancy.

The presence of numerous tourists has turned the fake-antique business into a major growth industry for Hoi An. Theoretically you could find something here that is really old, but it's hard to believe that all the genuine stuff wasn't scooped up long ago. Proceed with scepticism.

On the other hand, there is some really elegant artwork around, even if it was turned out only yesterday. Paintings are generally of the mass-produced kind, but are still hand-painted; for a few US dollars you can't complain. A row of **art galleries** (Đ Nguyen Thi Minh Khai) inside the gorgeous old buildings just across from the Japanese Covered Bridge are great to browse through.

And now that you've bought that lovely piece of artwork, you need to light it properly. Lighting is a major growth industry in Hoi An and lanterns lead the way. Popular Chinese lanterns come in various shapes and sizes, and some shops are now bringing in elegant new designs, all easily foldable.

Woodcarvings are also a local speciality. Cross Cam Nam Bridge to **Cam Nam Village**, a lovely spot where woodcarvings are made. Woodcarving is also a speciality on Cam Kim Island (opposite). Across the An Hoi footbridge is the **An Hoi Peninsula**, which is known for its boat and mat-weaving industries.

Vietnam has a great reputation for its ceramics, and while much of what is on sale here comes from further north, around the Hanoi region, it is worth stocking up if you are only visiting central Vietnam. The black pottery with a glassy glaze is particularly striking. It's best to browse the strip of small **ceramics shops** (Đ Bach Dang) along the riverfront.

Getting There & Away

BOAT

Small, motorised ferries leave Hoi An for nearby districts and Cham Island from the landing at the end of Đ Hoang Van Thu. There are daily boats to Cham Island (usually departing between 7am and 8am), weather-dependent; foreigners need permits to make this trip on a public boat (see opposite). There is also frequent service to Cam Kim Island.

BUS

The main **Hoi An bus station** (74 Đ Huynh Thuc Khang) is 1km west of the centre of town. Buses from here go to Danang (5000d, one hour), Quang Ngai and other points. More frequent services to Danang leave from the **northern bus station** (Đ Le Hong Phong). The cost is about 5000d and services begin at 5am; the last Danang bus departs in the late afternoon.

CAR & MOTORBIKE

The quickest way between Danang and Hoi An is via the Marble Mountains, which takes 45 minutes. The going rate for a motorbike taxi between Danang and Hoi An is about US$6. A taxi costs from US$8 to US$10.

MINIBUS

Virtually every hotel in Hoi An can sell you a minibus ticket to either Nha Trang or Hué. The Hoi An–Hué minibus goes through Danang (US$2) and you can be dropped off there if you like. Heading south, jump out at Nha Trang (from US$5) or My Lai (US$4). Most minibuses leave from the cafés on the corner of Đ Phan Dinh Phung and Đ Nhi Trung at around 8am; there's often a mid-afternoon service too.

Getting Around

Anywhere within town can be reached on foot. To go further afield, rent a bicycle from 10,000d per day. A motorbike without/with a driver will cost around US$5/10 per day. Hire places are located all over town.

BOAT

A paddle-boat trip on the Thu Bon River – the largest in Quang Nam province – is something different. A simple rowing boat with someone to row it costs something like US$2 per hour, and one hour is probably long enough for most travellers. Some My Son tours offer the return trip to Hoi An by boat, which is a fun way to travel.

Boats that carry up to five people can be hired to visit handicraft and fishing villages in the area; expect to pay around US$4 per hour. Look for the boats near the rowboat dock close to the market.

AROUND HOI AN
Cua Dai Beach
The fine sands of palm-lined Cua Dai Beach (Bai Tam Cua Dai) are popular at weekends, but can often be deserted at other times. Safe swimming is usually only possible between April and October, but it's nice to walk or just hang out here. This is a monster beach that continues all the way up to Danang, an incredible 30km of pristine white sands. During the full moon, people wander around until late at night. Fresh seafood and refreshments are sold at a line of kiosks that lead to the beachfront.

Cua Dai Beach is 5km east of Hoi An on Đ Cua Dai, which is the continuation of Đ Tran Hung Dao.

For information about accommodation at Cua Dai Beach, see Sleeping (p239).

Cam Kim Island
The master woodcarvers, who in previous centuries produced the fine carvings that graced the homes of Hoi An's merchants and the town's public buildings, came from Kim Bong Village on Cam Kim Island.

These days, most of the woodcarvings on sale in Hoi An are produced here. Some of the villagers also build wooden boats.

To reach the island, catch one of the frequent boats that leave from the boat landing at Đ Hoang Van Thu in Hoi An.

Cham Island
Also known as Culao Cham, Cham Island is 21km from Hoi An in the South China Sea. The island is famous as a source of swiftlet nests, which are exported to Hong Kong, Singapore and elsewhere for use in bird's-nest soup.

Permits are needed to visit Cham Island, and the weather determines when boats can run. Public boats leave from the landing at Đ Hoang Van Thu in Hoi An between 7am and 8am and the one-way journey takes three hours, but it's difficult for foreigners to organise the paperwork to travel on one of these boats. It's best to go with a tour guide (around US$20), which includes the permit as well as boat, guide and lunch.

Thanh Ha
Sometimes called the 'pottery village', Thanh Ha is 3km west of Hoi An. Not so long ago, there were many pottery factories here, but the industry has been in decline. Still, some artisans are employed in this hot and sweaty work. The locals don't mind if you visit their factories to watch them at work, though they'd be happier if you bought them something in exchange for showing

---

KINGDOM OF CHAMPA

The kingdom of Champa flourished from the 2nd to the 15th centuries. It first appeared around present-day Danang and later spread south to what is now Nha Trang and Phan Rang. Champa became Indianised through commercial relations with India: the Chams adopted Hinduism, employed Sanskrit as a sacred language and borrowed from Indian art.

The Chams, who lacked enough land for agriculture along the mountainous coast, were semi-piratic and conducted attacks on passing trade ships. As a result, they were in a constant state of war with the Vietnamese to the north and the Khmers to the southwest. The Chams successfully threw off Khmer rule in the 12th century, but were entirely absorbed by Vietnam in the 17th century.

The Chams are best known for the many brick sanctuaries (Cham towers) they constructed throughout the south. The greatest collection of Cham art is in the Museum of Cham Sculpture (p221) in Danang. The major Cham site is at My Son (p246), and other Cham ruins can be found in Nha Trang (p266), Phan Rang (p278) and Thap Cham (p278).

Elements of Cham civilisation can still be seen in the life of the people of Quang Nam, Danang and Quang Ngai provinces, whose forebears assimilated many Cham innovations into their daily lives. These include techniques for pottery, fishing, sugar production, rice farming, irrigation, silk production and construction.

you around. Many tours to My Son make a stop here on the way back to Hoi An.

MY SON

One of the most stunning sights to see in the Hoi An area is **My Son** (admission 50,000d; ⏱ 6.30am-4.30pm), Vietnam's most important centre of the ancient kingdom of Champa and a Unesco World Heritage site.

During the centuries when Tra Kieu (which was then known as Simhapura) served as the political capital of the kingdom of Champa, My Son was the site of the most important Cham intellectual and religious centre, and also may have served as a burial place for Cham monarchs.

My Son is considered to be Champa's smaller counterpart to the grand cities of Southeast Asia's other Indian-influenced civilisations: Angkor (Cambodia), Ayuthaya (Thailand), Bagan (Myanmar) and Borobudur (Java).

The monuments are set in a verdant valley surrounded by hills and overlooked by the massive Cat's Tooth Mountain (Hon Quap). Clear streams run between the structures and past nearby coffee plantations.

History

My Son became a religious centre under King Bhadravarman in the late 4th century and was occupied until the 13th century – the longest period of development of any monument in Southeast Asia. Most of the temples were dedicated to Cham kings associated with divinities, particularly Shiva, who was regarded as the founder and protector of Champa's dynasties.

Champa's contact with Java was extensive. Cham scholars were sent to Java to study and there was a great deal of commerce between the two empires – Cham pottery has been found on Java and, in the 12th century, the Cham king wed a Javanese woman.

Because some of the ornamentation work at My Son was never finished, archaeologists know that the Chams first built their structures and only then carved decorations into the brickwork. Researchers have yet to figure out for certain how the Chams managed to get the baked bricks to stick together. According to one theory, they used a paste prepared with a botanical oil that is indigenous to central Vietnam. During one period in their history, the summits of some of the towers were completely covered with a layer of gold.

During the American War, this region was completely devastated and depopulated in extended bitter fighting. Finding it to be a convenient staging ground, the VC used My Son as a base; in response the Americans bombed the monuments. Traces of 68 structures have been found, of which 25 survived repeated pillaging in previous centuries by the Chinese, Khmer and Vietnamese. The American bombings spared about 20 of these, some of which sustained extensive damage. Today, Vietnamese authorities are attempting to restore as much as possible of the remaining sites.

Information

The entry fee includes local transport from the parking area to the sites, about 2km away. By departing from Hoi An at about 5am, you will arrive to wake up the gods (and the guards) for sunrise and could be leaving just as the tour groups reach the area! It gets very busy at My Son; if you can go early or late do so, and soak up the scenery and atmosphere in relative peace and quiet.

The Site

Archaeologists have divided My Son's monuments into 10 main groups, uninspiringly named A, A', B, C, D, E, F, G, H and K. Each structure has been given a name consisting of a letter followed by a number.

The first structure you encounter along the trail is the false gate K, which dates from the 11th century. Between K and the other groups is a coffee plantation begun in 1986.

GROUP B

The main *kalan* (sanctuary), **B1**, was dedicated to Bhadresvara, which is a contraction of the name of King Bhadravarman, who built the first temple at My Son, combined with '-esvara', which means Shiva. The first building on this site was erected in the 4th century, destroyed in the 6th century and then again rebuilt in the 7th century. Only the 11th-century base, made of large sandstone blocks, remains; the brickwork walls have disappeared. The niches in the wall were used to hold lamps (Cham sanctuaries had no windows). The linga inside was discovered during excavations in 1985, 1m below its current position.

B5, built in the 10th century, was used for storing sacred books and precious objects (some made of gold), which were used in ceremonies performed in B1. The boat-shaped roof (the 'bow' and 'stern' have fallen off) demonstrates the influence of Malayo-Polynesian architecture. Unlike the sanctuaries, this building has windows and the fine Cham masonry inside is original. Over the window on the wall facing B4 is a brick bas-relief of two elephants under a tree with two birds in it.

The ornamentation on the exterior walls of **B4** is an excellent example of a Cham decorative style, typical of the 9th century, said to resemble worms. This style is unlike anything found in other Southeast Asian cultures.

B3 has an Indian-influenced pyramidal roof typical of Cham towers. Inside **B6** is a bath-shaped basin for keeping sacred water that was poured over the linga in B1; this is the only known example of a Cham basin. **B2** is a gate.

Located around the perimeter of Group B are small temples, **B7** to **B13**, dedicated to the gods of the directions of the compass (*dikpalaka*).

GROUP C

The 8th-century **C1** was used to worship Shiva, portrayed in human form (rather than in the form of a linga, as in B1). Inside is an altar where a statue of Shiva, now in the Museum of Cham Sculpture in Danang, used to stand. On either side of the stone doorway it's possible to see, bored into the lintel and the floor, the holes in which two wooden doors once swung. Note the motifs, characteristic of the 8th century, carved into the brickwork of the exterior walls.

GROUP D

Buildings **D1** and **D2**, which were once meditation halls, now house small displays of Cham sculpture.

GROUP A

The path from Groups B, C and D to Group A leads eastward from near D4.

Group A was almost completely destroyed by US attacks. According to locals, massive **A1**, considered the most important monument at My Son, remained impervious to aerial bombing and was finally finished off by a helicopter-borne sapper team. All that remains today is a pile of collapsed brick walls. After the destruction of A1, Philippe Stern, an expert on Cham art and curator of the Guimet Museum in Paris, wrote a letter of protest to the US president, Nixon, who ordered US forces to continue killing the VC, but not to do any further damage to Cham monuments.

A1 was the only Cham sanctuary with two doors. One faced east, in the direction of the Hindu gods, the other faced west towards Groups B, C and D and the spirits of the ancestor kings that may have been buried there. Inside A1 is a stone altar pieced together in 1988. Among the ruins, some of the brilliant brickwork, which is of a typical 10th-century style, is still visible. At the base of A1 on the side facing A10 (decorated in 9th-century style) is a carving of a worshipping figure, flanked by round columns, with a Javanese sea-monster god (*kala-makara*) above. The presence of these Javanese motifs highlights the connection between Champa and Java. There are plans to partially restore A1 and A10 in the future.

OTHER GROUPS

Dating from the 8th century, **Group A'** is at present overgrown and inaccessible. **Group E** was built from the 8th to 11th centuries, while **Group F** dates to the 8th century. **Group G**, which has been damaged by time rather than war, dates to the 12th century. There are long-term plans to restore these monuments.

Getting There & Away
CAR

A hire car with driver from Hoi An to My Son costs around US$20. Going under your own steam gives you the option of arriving before or after the tour groups, and My Son is quite spectacular and atmospheric when you're one of only a few people there.

MINIBUS

Numerous hotels in Hoi An can book a day trip to My Son that includes a stop-off at Tra Kieu. At US$2 to US$3 per person, you could hardly do it cheaper unless you walked. The minibuses depart from Hoi An at 8am and return at 2pm. Some agencies offer the option of returning to Hoi An by boat.

MOTORBIKE

It's possible to get to the sites by rented motorbike. Make sure you park in the official parking area. Otherwise, get somebody else to drive you on their motorbike and then ask them to wait for you.

TRA KIEU (SIMHAPURA)

Formerly called Simhapura (Lion Citadel), Tra Kieu was the first capital city of Champa, serving in that capacity from the 4th to the 8th centuries. Today, nothing remains of the ancient city except the rectangular ramparts. A large number of artefacts, including some of the finest carvings in the Museum of Cham Sculpture in Danang (p221), were found here.

Mountain Church

You can get a good view of the city's outlines from the **Mountain Church** (Nha Tho Nui), on the top of Buu Chau Hill in Tra Kieu. This modern, open-air structure was built in 1970 to replace an earlier church destroyed by time and war. A Cham tower once stood on this spot.

The Mountain Church is 6.5km from Hwy 1 and 19.5km from the start of the footpath to My Son. Within Tra Kieu, it is 200m from the morning **market**, Cho Tra Kieu, and 550m from Tra Kieu Church.

Tra Kieu Church

This **church** (Dia So Tra Kieu), which serves the town's Catholic population of 3000, was built a century ago. There's a fantastic ceramic mosaic dragon on the external stairs. A priest working here, who died in 1989, was interested in Cham civilisation and amassed a collection of Cham artefacts found by local people. A 2nd-floor room in the building to the right of the church opened as a **museum** in 1990. The round ceramic objects with faces on them, which date from the 8th and 10th centuries, were affixed to the ends of tiled roofs. The face is of Kala, the God of Time. Tra Kieu Church is 7km from Hwy 1 and 19km from the trail to My Son. It is down an alley opposite the town's **Clinic of Western Medicine** (Quay Thuoc Tay Y).

Getting There & Away

Most day trips to My Son from Hoi An include a stop-off at Tra Kieu. Otherwise you'll need to rent a bike or a car (with driver); see p247.

TAM KY

Tam Ky, the capital of Quang Nam province, is a nondescript town on the highway between Quang Ngai and Danang. However, travellers are drawn to the Cham towers at nearby **Chien Dan** (Chien Dan Cham), 5km north of Tam Ky.

The three towers are enclosed by a wall, and a broken stele here dates from the 13th-century reign of King Harivarman. Many of the Cham statues you can see on display at Chien Dan were collected from other parts of the country after the American War, and show signs of war-related damage. Expect to have to make a donation to the site's insistent custodian; there were no tickets or price lists when we visited, but 5,000d per person is probably a fair amount to give.

South-Central Coast

CONTENTS

Along this stretch of coastline lie some of Vietnam's most beautiful beaches, as well as many Cham ruins. Most travellers in southern Vietnam will hit Nha Trang or Mui Ne for beach time, ocean sports and party boats, but the region also offers sedate coastal towns for those interested in a more local or low-key experience. Additionally, those with an eye towards cultural edification will find a wealth of Cham towers and what remains of the Cham population in this region. Worth seeking out in the northern reaches of the south-central coast is the Son My Memorial, dedicated to the villagers who perished there in the My Lai Massacre of the American War.

The south-central coast is logically best known for its excellent seafood, which you may see being hauled off colourful fishing boats in various harbours, or being dragged in by fisherpeople in basket boats. Another regional treat is green dragon fruit *(thanh long)*, which is grown widely around Phan Rang; you'll see the snaking branches of the dragon fruit plant growing on stakes along highways. The southernmost province, Binh Thuan, is one of the most arid regions of Vietnam, particularly north of Phan Thiet. The nearby plains, dominated by rocky, roundish mountains, support some marginal irrigated rice farms.

The South-Central Coast chapter covers the littoral provinces of Binh Thuan, Ninh Thuan, Khanh Hoa, Phu Yen, Binh Dinh and Quang Ngai. The cities, towns, beaches and historical sites in this region, most of which are along National Hwy 1, referred to by many foreign tourists as the 'Ho Chi Minh Trail' (the real one is actually further inland), appear in this chapter from north to south. There's easy access in and out of the mountainous regions inland from several points along the coast.

HIGHLIGHTS

- Soak up sun and pick up kite-surfing at peaceful **Mui Ne Beach** (p283)
- Seek out impressive Cham ruins around **Phan Rang and Thap Cham** (p277)
- Island-hop and snorkel away in the turquoise waters off **Nha Trang** (p261)
- Scuba dive off the coast of peaceful **Whale Island** (p261)
- Meditate with the largest reclining Buddha in Vietnam, at **Ta Cu Mountain** (p287)

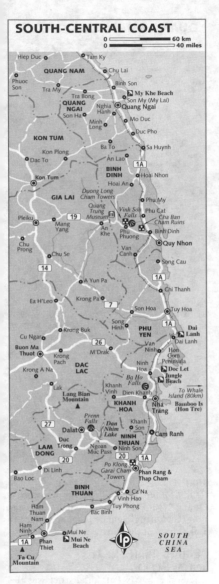

SOUTH-CENTRAL COAST

During the Franco–Viet Minh War, the area was a Viet Minh stronghold. In 1962, the South Vietnamese government introduced its ill-fated Strategic Hamlets Program to the area. Villagers were forcibly removed from their homes and resettled in fortified hamlets, infuriating and alienating the local population and increasing popular support for the Viet Cong (VC). Some of the most bitter fighting of the American War took place in Quang Ngai province.

Son My subdistrict (p252), 14km north of Quang Ngai, was the scene of the infamous My Lai Massacre of 1968, in which hundreds of civilians were slaughtered by US soldiers. A memorial has been erected on the site of the killings.

As a result of war, very few of the older bridges in Quang Ngai province remain intact. At many river crossings, the rust-streaked concrete pylons of the old French-built bridges, probably destroyed by the Viet Minh, stand next to the ruins of their replacements, blown up by the VC.

Orientation & Information

Built on the southern bank of the Tra Khuc River (known for its oversized water wheels), the city is about 15km from the coast. The city and province of Quang Ngai are also known as Quang Nghia; the name is sometimes abbreviated to Quangai.

Hwy 1 is called Đ Quang Trung as it passes through Quang Ngai. The train station is 1.5km west of the town centre, on Đ Hung Vuong.

The **main post office** (80 Đ Phan Dinh Phung) is 150m west of Đ Quang Trung, several metres up from a beautifully incongruous, colonial-yellow water tower.

You'll find a speedy ADSL connection at **Pu Internet** (☎ 824 959; 102 Đ Phan Dinh Phung).

Sleeping

Hotel 502 (☎ 822 656; 28 Đ Hung Vuong; r US$6-10; ❄) Worth a try if you're looking for a peaceful night's sleep, Hotel 502 has a gated courtyard down a quiet alley. The rooms are simple and clean.

Kim Thanh Hotel (☎ 823 471; fax 826 134; 19 Đ Hung Vuong; r 150,000-250,000đ; ❄) This family-run spot seems fairly well attuned to the backpacker market. Very clean, comfortable rooms include TV and minibar, and bathrooms have tubs.

QUANG NGAI

☎ 055 / pop 108,200

Although it's the capital of Quang Ngai province, Quang Ngai offers very little to see or do, but it makes a convenient stopover for travellers along Hwy 1.

Even before WWII, Quang Ngai was an important centre of resistance to the French.

Central Hotel (☎ 829 999; www.vidc.com.vn/central hotel; 784 Đ Quang Trung; r US$45-95; 🅿 🛗 🏊) The classiest joint in Quang Ngai, the Central Hotel is located at the southern end of town. This fancy place boasts facilities such as a tennis court and swimming pool. Even-numbered rooms in the back have lovely views of Quang Ngai's red-tiled roofs. Breakfast is included in the price, and the hotel even accepts credit cards.

Eating

Mimosa (☎ 822 438; 21 Đ Hung Vuong; mains 15,000d) This busy family-run restaurant bustles with friendly service and asks great prices for well-prepared Vietnamese food.

An Lac (☎ 822 566; 54 Đ Tran Hung Dao; meals 7000d) For good, cheap vegetarian grub, try this shopfront across from the pink church.

Quang Ngai province is famous for a local delicacy called *com ga*, which actually originates further north at Tam Ky. It consists of boiled chicken over yellow rice (the colour comes from being steamed with chicken broth) with a mint leaf garnish, plus egg-drop soup and pickled vegies on the side. It is indeed delicious and something any chicken lover should try. At about 7000d per plate, you might even have two. There are several places in town to try this treat (just look for signs reading *com ga*), including **Hue Restaurant** (☎ 821 037; 314 Đ Nguyen Nghiem).

If you arrive in town after dark, the **food stalls** (Đ Quang Trung) just south of the Tra Khuc River tend to stay open later than restaurants in town.

Getting There & Away

BUS

Express buses depart from **Quang Ngai bus station** (Ben Xe Khach Quang Ngai; opposite 32 Đ Nguyen Nghiem), about 100m east of Đ Quang Trung (Hwy 1); see p477 for more information.

CAR & MOTORBIKE

From Quang Ngai road distances are: 131km to Danang, 860km to Ho Chi Minh City (HCMC), 412km to Nha Trang and 174km to Quy Nhon.

MINIBUS

Plenty of tourist minibuses (US$5, about two hours) travel between Quang Ngai and Hoi An. Quang Ngai is about 100km from Hoi An.

QUANG NGAI

INFORMATION	
Main Post Office	1 A3
Pu Internet	2 A4

SIGHTS & ACTIVITIES	(p251)
Church	3 A3
Market Buildings	4 B4
Old Church	5 A4
Water Tower	(see 1)

SLEEPING 🏠	(pp251-2)
Hotel 502	6 A4
Kim Thanh Hotel	7 B3

EATING 🍴	(p252)
An Lac	8 B4
Hue Restaurant	9 B4
Mimosa	10 B3

TRANSPORT	(p252)
Quang Ngai Bus Station	11 B4

TRAIN

Reunification Express (p482) trains stop at Quang Ngai. The Quang Ngai train station (Ga Quang Nghia, Ga Quang Ngai) is 1.5km west of the town centre.

AROUND QUANG NGAI
Son My (My Lai)

The Son My (My Lai) subdistrict was the site of the most horrific war crimes committed by US troops during the American War.

The My Lai Massacre consisted of a series of atrocities carried out all over the subdistrict, which is divided into four hamlets, including the now-infamous My Lai. The largest mass killing took place in Xom Lang

MY LAI MASSACRE

Son My subdistrict was a known Viet Cong (VC) stronghold, and it was widely believed that villagers in the area were providing food and shelter to the VC (if true, the villagers would have had little choice – the VC was known for taking cruel revenge on those who didn't 'cooperate'). Just whose idea it was to 'teach the villagers a lesson' has never been determined. What is known is that several US soldiers had been killed and wounded in the area in the days preceding the search-and-destroy operation that began on the morning of 16 March 1968.

The operation was carried out by Task Force Barker – three companies of US infantry. At about 7.30am – after the area around Xom Lang had been bombarded with artillery, and the landing zone raked with rocket and machine-gun fire from helicopter gunships – Charlie Company (commanded by Captain Ernest Medina) landed by helicopter. They encountered no resistance during the 'combat-assault', nor did they come under fire at any time during the entire operation; but as soon as their sweep eastward began, so did the atrocities.

As Lieutenant William Calley's 1st Platoon moved through Xom Lang, they shot and bayoneted fleeing villagers, threw hand grenades into houses and bomb shelters, slaughtered livestock and burned dwellings. Somewhere between 75 and 150 unarmed villagers were rounded up and herded to a ditch, where they were mowed down by machine-gun fire.

In the next few hours, as command helicopters circled overhead and American navy boats patrolled offshore, the 2nd Platoon (under Lieutenant Stephen Brooks), the 3rd platoon (under Lieutenant Jeffrey La Cross) and the company headquarters group also committed unspeakable crimes. At least half a dozen groups of civilians, including women and children, were assembled and executed. Villagers fleeing towards Quang Ngai along the road were machine-gunned, and wounded civilians (including young children) were summarily shot. As these massacres were taking place, at least four girls and women were raped or gang-raped by groups of soldiers.

One soldier is reported to have shot himself in the foot to get himself out of the slaughter; he was the only American casualty in the entire operation. Troops who participated were ordered to keep their mouths shut, but several disobeyed orders and went public with the story after returning to the USA. When it broke in the newspapers, it had a devastating effect on the military's morale and fuelled further public protests against the war. Unlike WWII veterans, who returned home to parades and glory, soldiers coming home from Vietnam often found themselves ostracised by their fellow citizens and taunted as 'baby killers'.

A cover-up of the atrocities was undertaken at all levels of the US army command, eventually leading to several investigations. Lieutenant Calley was made chief ogre and was court-martialled and found guilty of the murders of 22 unarmed civilians. He was sentenced to life imprisonment in 1971 and spent three years under house arrest at Fort Benning, Georgia, while appealing his conviction. Calley was paroled in 1974 after the US Supreme Court refused to hear his case. Calley's case still causes controversy – many claim that he was made a scapegoat because of his low rank, and that officers much higher up ordered the massacres. What is certain is that he didn't act alone.

For the full story of this horrendous event and its aftermath, pick up a copy of *Four Hours in My Lai* by Michael Bilton and Kevin Sim, a stunning piece of journalism.

(Thuan Yen) subhamlet, where the Son My Memorial was later erected.

The site of the My Lai Massacre is 14km from central Quang Ngai. To get here from town, head north (towards Danang) on Đ Quang Trung (Hwy 1) and cross the long bridge over the Tra Khuc River. Metres from the northern end of the bridge, you will come to a triangular concrete stele indicating the way to the Son My Memorial. Turn right (eastward, parallel to the river)

on the dirt road and continue for 12km. The road to Son My passes through particularly beautiful countryside: rice paddies, manioc patches and vegetable gardens shaded by casuarinas and eucalyptus trees.

The Son My Memorial is set in a park where the Xom Lang subhamlet once stood (see the 'My Lai Massacre' boxed text, above). Around it, among the trees and rice paddies, are the graves of some of the victims, who were buried in family groups.

Near the memorial is a **museum** (admission 14,000d; ⊗ 8-11.30am & 1-4.30pm Mon-Fri), which opened in 1992.

If you don't have a car, the best way to get to Son My district from Quang Ngai is to hire a *xe om* (motorbike taxi) near the bus station or along Ð Quang Trung. The return trip should cost around 30,000d.

My Khe Beach

Secluded **My Khe Beach** (Bai Bien My Khe) is a long, fine-sand beach 17km from Quang Ngai and several kilometres east of the Son My Memorial. The beach stretches for many kilometres along a long, thin, casuarina-lined spit of sand. It is separated from the mainland by Song Kinh Giang, a body of water about 150m inland from the beach. There's no public transport to the beach, but a *xe om* ride from Quang Ngai will cost you about 15,000d.

A new resort on the beach was under construction when we visited.

SA HUYNH
☎ 055

The little seaside town of Sa Huynh has a beautiful semicircular beach bordered by rice paddies and coconut palms. The town is also known for its salt marshes and salt-evaporation ponds.

Archaeologists have unearthed remains from the Dong Son civilisation dating from the 1st century AD in the vicinity of Sa Huynh.

Sleeping & Eating

Sa Huynh Hotel (☎ 860 311; fax 860 661; r US$6-15; ⊠), a crumbling concrete hotel right on the beach, is the only place to stay in town. It doesn't offer much more than a pleasant setting and friendly staff, but the beach is lovely and uncrowded.

The **restaurant** (mains 10,000d) on the hotel grounds is OK, with leisurely service. There are also a number of roadside restaurant-cafés a few hundred metres away, out on Hwy 1. One of the best is called Vinh.

Getting There & Away

Sa Huynh is on Hwy 1, about 114km north of Quy Nhon and 60km south of Quang Ngai.

Some nonexpress trains stop at the Sa Huynh train station (Ga Sa Huynh), but it will be slow going.

QUY NHON
☎ 056 / pop 260,000

The capital of Binh Dinh province and one of Vietnam's more active second-string seaports, Quy Nhon (Qui Nhon) is a great spot to sample some fresh local seafood. It's a pleasant place to break the long journey from Nha Trang to Danang and an easy detour away from heavy foreign-tourist traffic.

The beaches in the immediate vicinity of the city are nothing special, but south of Quy Nhon there are some nice ones to explore, notably on the newly built coastal road to Song Cau.

On the outskirts of Quy Nhon there are numerous Cham towers to visit, including some along Hwy 1, about 10km north of the Quy Nhon turn-off.

During the American War, there was considerable South Vietnamese, US, VC and South Korean military activity in the Quy Nhon area. Refugees dislocated by fighting and counter-insurgency programmes built whole slums of tin-and-thatch shacks around the city. During this period, the mayor of Quy Nhon, hoping to cash in on the presence of US troops, turned his official residence into a large massage parlour.

There's an obscure historical connection between Quy Nhon and New Zealand dating back to the early 1960s, when funds from New Zealand were provided to build the provincial hospital and later to aid refugees. The New Zealand connection continues with volunteers working on development projects in the province.

Orientation

Quy Nhon is on the coast 10km east of Hwy 1. The highway junction where you turn off to Quy Nhon is called Phu Tai.

Quy Nhon proper is on an east–west orientated peninsula, shaped like an anteater's nose. The tip of the nose (the port area) is closed to the public. The municipal beach (opposite) is on the peninsula's south coast.

From the municipal beach, Cu Lao Xanh Island is visible offshore, as is a rusting US Army tank lying half submerged closer to the shore. Due east of the beach you can see, in the distance, an oversize statue of Tran Hung Dao, erected on a promontory overlooking the fishing village of Hai Minh.

The streets around Lon Market constitute Quy Nhon's town centre.

Information

Barbara's Backpackers (☎ 892 921; nzbarb@yahoo .com; 18 Đ Nguyen Hue) A budget travellers guesthouse that also organises unique regional tours and boat trips.
Binh Dinh Internet (☎ 823 055; vtnghi@dng.vnn.vn; 245 Đ Le Hong Phong; per min 100d)
Binh Dinh Tourist (☎ 892 329; fax 894 544; 25 Đ Nguyen Hue) For tours to the Cham ruins of Thap Doi, Cha Ban, and Duong Long.
Vietcombank (☎ 822 266; 148 Đ Le Loi) On the corner of Đ Tran Hung Dao; has a 24-hour ATM.

Sights

BINH DINH MUSEUM

This small **museum** (cnr Đ Nguyen Hue & Đ Le Loi; admission free; ☻ 8-11.30am Mon-Fri) features exhibits on regional history, and includes some Cham statues and ancient bronze drums. Hours tend to be spotty.

LONG KHANH PAGODA

You'll find Quy Nhon's main pagoda, **Long Khanh Pagoda**, down an alley opposite 62 Đ Tran Cao Van and next to 143 Đ Tran Cao Van. A 17m-high Buddha (built in 1972) is visible from the street, and presides over a lily pond that's strongly defended (against surprise attack?) by barbed wire. To the left of the main building is a low tower sheltering a giant drum; to the right, its twin contains an enormous bell, which was cast in 1970.

The main sanctuary was completed in 1946, but was damaged during the Franco–Viet Minh War; repairs were completed in 1957. In front of the large copper Thich Ca Buddha (with its multicoloured neon halo) is a drawing of multiarmed and multi-eyed Chuan De (the Goddess of Mercy); the numerous arms and eyes symbolise her ability to touch and see all. There is a colourfully painted Buddha at the edge of the raised platform. In the corridor that passes behind the main altar is a bronze bell that dates from 1805 and has Chinese inscriptions on it.

Under the eaves of the left-hand building in the courtyard, behind the sanctuary, hangs a blow-up of the famous photograph of the monk Thich Quang Duc, taken in Saigon in June 1963 as he immolated himself to protest the policies of the Diem regime. The second level of the two-storey building behind the courtyard contains memorial plaques for deceased monks (on the middle altar) and lay people.

Long Khanh Pagoda was founded around 1700 by a Chinese merchant, Duc Son (1679–1741). The monks who reside here preside over the religious affairs of Quy Nhon's relatively active Buddhist community. Single-sex religious classes for children are held here on Sunday.

THAP DOI CHAM TOWERS

The two **Cham towers** (admission free; ☻ 8-11am & 1-6pm) of Thap Doi have curved pyramidal roofs rather than the terracing typical of Cham architecture. The larger tower, whose four granite doorways are oriented towards the cardinal directions, retains some of its ornate brickwork and remnants of the granite statuary that once graced its summit. The dismembered torsos of garuda (griffin-like sky beings that feed on *naga*, or divine serpents) can be seen at the corners of the roofs of both structures.

The upper reaches of the small tower are home to several flourishing trees, whose creeping tendrilous roots have forced their way between the bricks, enmeshing parts of the structure in the sort of netlike tangle for which the monuments of Angkor in Cambodia are famous.

To get here, head out of town on Đ Tran Hung Dao and turn right after street number 886 onto Đ Thap Doi; the towers are about 100m from Đ Tran Hung Dao.

TAM AN PAGODA

Quy Nhon's second most active pagoda, **Chua Tam An**, is a charming little place that attracts mostly female worshipers.

LON MARKET

Quy Nhon's central market, **Lon Market** (Cho Lon), is in a large modern building enclosed by a courtyard. Fruit and vegetables are sold here.

BEACHES

Extending along the southern side of the 'anteater's nose', Quy Nhon **municipal beach** consists of a few hundred metres of sand shaded by a coconut grove. The nicest section of beach is across from the Quy Nhon Hotel. Further west, the shore is lined with the boats and shacks of fishing families.

The longer, quieter **Queen's Beach** begins about 2km southwest of the municipal beach. To get here, follow Đ Nguyen Hue

QUY NHON

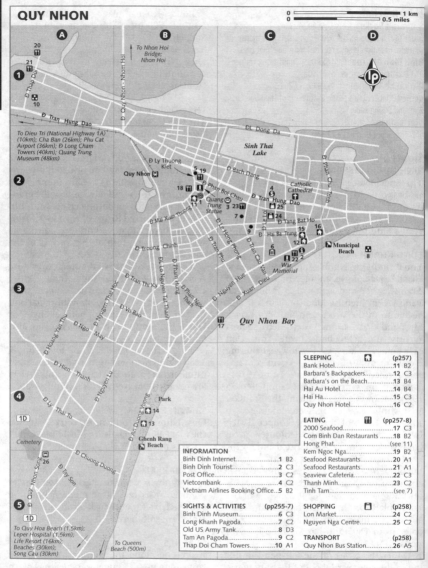

To Nhon Hoi
Bridge;
Nhon Hoi

Sinh Thai
Lake

To Dieu Tri (National Highway 1A)
(10km); Cha Ban (26km); Phu Cat
Airport (36km); Ð Long Cham
Towers (40km); Quang Trung
Museum (48km)

Ð Thap Doi

Ð Tran Hung Dao

Ð Ly Thuong
Kiet

Quy Nhon

Ð Bach Dang

Catholic
Cathedral

Ð Phan Boi Chau

Quang
Trung
Statue

Ð Tran Hung Dao

Ð Tang Bat Ho

Ð Mai Xuan Thuong

Ð Le Hong Phong

Ð Hai Ba Trung

Municipal
Beach

Ð Troung Chinh

Ð Tran Phu

Ð Tran Cao Van

War
Memorial

Ð Phan Dang Luu

Ð Nguyen Hue

Ð Xuan Dieu

Quy Nhon Bay

Ð Hoang Van Thu

Ð Nguyen Thai Hoc

Ð Ngo May

Ð Lo Nguyen Tai Thanh

Ð Phan Ngoc Thach

Ð Vo Bao

Ð Lo Thai To

Ð Hien Thanh

Ð Nguyen Lu

Park

Ð An Duong Vuong

Ghenh Rang
Beach

Cemetery

Ð Chuong Duong

Ð Quy Nhon-Song Cau

Ð Tay Son

To Quy Hoa Beach (1.5km);
Leper Hospital (1.5km);
Life Resort (16km);
Beaches (30km);
Song Cau (30km)

To Queens
Beach (500m)

INFORMATION	
Binh Dinh Internet.....................1	B2
Binh Dinh Tourist.......................2	C3
Post Office.................................3	C2
Vietcombank..............................4	C2
Vietnam Airlines Booking Office..5	B2

SIGHTS & ACTIVITIES	(pp255-7)
Binh Dinh Museum.....................6	C3
Long Khanh Pagoda....................7	C2
Old US Army Tank......................8	D3
Tam An Pagoda..........................9	C2
Thap Doi Cham Towers..............10	A1

SLEEPING	(p257)
Bank Hotel................................11	B2
Barbara's Backpackers...............12	C3
Barbara's on the Beach.............13	B4
Hai Au Hotel.............................14	B4
Hai Ha....................................15	C3
Quy Nhon Hotel........................16	C2

EATING	(pp257-8)
2000 Seafood...........................17	C3
Com Binh Dan Restaurants 18	B2
Hong Phat..............................(see 11)
Kem Ngoc Nga.........................19	B2
Seafood Restaurants.................20	A1
Seafood Restaurants.................21	A1
Seaview Cafeteria.....................22	C3
Thanh Minh.............................23	C2
Tinh Tam...............................(see 7)

SHOPPING	(p258)
Lon Market..............................24	C2
Nguyen Nga Centre...................25	C2

TRANSPORT	(p258)
Quy Nhon Bus Station...............26	A5

away from the tip of the peninsula westward. Further south there are several good
beaches on the recently completed coastal
road to Song Cau.

QUY HOA BEACH & LEPER HOSPITAL
Visitors are welcome, for a small entrance
fee, to enjoy the beach here. As leper hos-

pitals go, this one is highly unusual. Rather
than being a depressing place, it's a sort
of model village near the seafront, where
treated patients live together with their
families in small, well-kept houses. Depending on their abilities, the patients work
in the rice fields, in fishing, and in repair-
oriented businesses or small craft shops

(one supported by Handicap International produces prosthetic limbs).

The grounds of the **hospital** (☎ 646 343; admission 3000d; 🕙 8-11.30am & 1.30-4pm) are so well maintained that it looks a bit like a resort, complete with numerous busts of distinguished and historically important doctors (both Vietnamese and foreign) scattered around the property.

Fronting the village is **Quy Hoa Beach**, one of the nicer stretches of sand around Quy Nhon and a popular weekend hang-out of the city's expat community. Just up from the beach, there's a dirt path to the hillside **Tomb of Han Mac Tu**, a mystical poet who died in 1940.

The village and beach are about 1.5km south of town and easily accessible from the road to Song Cau. If coming from Quy Nhon, turn left (down to the village) at the top of the first hill; there's a sign for the hospital at the junction.

Sleeping

Barbara's on the Beach (☎ 846 992; 492 Đ An Duong Vuong; dm US$3, r US$10-12; 🌐) Run by congenial Kiwi Barbara – who is also Quy Nhon's travel expert – this bright blue-and-yellow haven sits right on the lovely golden beachfront south of the city centre. Inside the house, with its wooden staircase and pool table downstairs, there are four dorm-style rooms with shared bathroom and four doubles with private bathrooms. The restaurant downstairs features a full Vietnamese and Western menu, served on the breezy beachside terrace. There are also indie-travel services on offer: you want to do it, Barbara's will arrange it.

Barbara's Backpackers (☎ 892 921; nzbarb@yahoo .com; 18 Đ Nguyen Hue; r US$6-7) Barbara's original establishment is a venerable travellers' favourite. It's directly across from the beach and exudes a certain antiquated charm, with rounded walls and wood-panelled ceilings. The place is clean and well run, and the friendly staff create a lovely atmosphere. Various types of tours and transport can be arranged here, and the in-house Kiwi Cafe features cheap home-style international food.

Life Resort (☎ 840 132; www.life-resorts.com /quy-nhon/html/index.htm; Ghenh Rang, Bai Dai; r US$138-161, ste US$196-202; 🌐 🖥 🏊) A breath of salty, life-affirming air in Quy Nhon is the Life Resort, 16km south of town. Spacious, bright

rooms here are unfussily elegant and can be procured with most major credit cards. If you're looking to treat yourself, this is Quy Nhon's answer to what you seek.

Hai Ha Mini Hotel (☎ 891 295; fax 892 300; 5 Đ Tran Binh Trong; r US$15-35; 🌐) One block from the municipal beach, the Hai Ha is a friendly place with decent rooms. There's a lovely shared terrace, and rooms on that floor are the best deal. Breakfast is included.

Quy Nhon Hotel (☎ 892 401; hotelquynhon@dng .vnn.vn; 8 Đ Nguyen Hue; r US$16-35; 🌐 🖥) One of the more upmarket, bigger places in town, the Quy Nhon Hotel is directly opposite the municipal beach. Though it's nothing to rave about, even older-wing rooms are set back from the street and quite pleasant – 2nd-storey rooms have sea views. The hotel features massage and sauna, and a buffet breakfast is included in rates.

Hai Au Hotel (Seagull Hotel; ☎ 846473; ks.haiau@dng .vnn.vn; 489 Đ An Duong Vuong; r US$30-45; 🌐 🖥) Hai Au is undergoing some major monolithic development, after which it will also have a swimming pool. Popular with foreign tour groups and right on the beach, this hotel currently has uninspiring, musty-smelling rooms. A simple breakfast is included in the rates, and the in-house restaurant is notable for its ocean-view bar shaped like a large tree, complete with shady canopy.

Bank Hotel (☎ 823591; fax 821013; 257-259 Đ Le Hong Phong; r US$10-15; 🌐) The ageing Bank Hotel is central and accustomed to hosting foreign guests. Rooms in front have nice terraces looking onto a park and trees – pleasant, nothing special. Interior rooms are positively depressing and the bathrooms could use remodelling (they just look dirty).

Eating

2000 Seafood (☎ 812 787; 1 Đ Tran Doc) Among the most popular seafood restaurants in Quy Nhon – it tends to be packed with locals. Recommended is its seafood hotpot *(lau)* for 45,000d.

Hong Phat (☎ 811 550; 261 Đ Le Hong Phong; mains 20,000d) This place just beside the Bank Hotel does respectable Thai and Vietnamese dishes.

Seaview Cafeteria (☎ 891 791; 25 Đ Nguyen Hue) A pleasant beachfront place that's outdoors and next to the local tourist office, the Seaview offers a selection of cold drinks and coffee (5000d).

Thanh Minh (☎ 821 749; 151 Đ Phan Boi Chau; mains 4000-12,000đ) and **Tinh Tam** (141 Đ Tran Cao Van; mains 4000-12,000đ), right next to Long Khanh Pagoda, both serve amazingly good vegetarian dishes.

In the town centre, look for the local point-and-eat *com binh dan* restaurants near the Bank Hotel. Nearby, check out the tasty bakery items and excellent ice cream at **Kem Ngoc Nga** (☎ 821 562; 326 Đ Phan Boi Chau).

About 100m down Đ Thap Doi, near Thap Doi Cham towers, are some local **seafood restaurants** (mains around 20,000đ) on both sides of the channel.

Shopping
Nguyen Nga Centre (☎ 825 115; nngacenter@dng.vnn .vn; 100 Đ Phan Boi Chau) is a workshop for physically disabled children and young people, and is well worth stopping in for a look. The centre provides vocational training, music and art lessons, room and board – it also has another branch in town for hearing-impaired children. The shop sells lovely Bahnar weavings, handicrafts and clothing made in-house.

It's a cause worth supporting, and a good place to look for gifts.

Getting There & Away
AIR
Vietnam Airlines flights link HCMC with Quy Nhon six times weekly; see p475 for more information on flights.

Quy Nhon has a **Vietnam Airlines booking office** (☎ 822 953, 823 125; 2 Đ Ly Thuong Kiet; ☺ 8am-5pm Mon-Fri) offering minibus transport (25,000đ) for airline passengers between the office and Phu Cat airport. Call ahead for current information.

Phu Cat airport is 36km north of Quy Nhon.

BUS
There are express buses to Buon Ma Thuot, Dalat, Danang, Dong Hoi, Hanoi, Hué, Nha Trang, Ninh Binh, Quang Tri, HCMC, Thanh Hoa and Vinh.

Quy Nhon bus station (Ben Xe Khach Quy Nhon; ☎ 822 246; Đ Tay Son) is on the south side of town, across from the local cemetery.

CAR & MOTORBIKE
Road distances from Quy Nhon are: 677km to HCMC, 238km to Nha Trang, 186km to

Pleiku, 198km to Kon Tum, 174km to Quang Ngai and 303km to Danang.

TRAIN
The nearest the *Reunification Express* trains get to Quy Nhon is Dieu Tri, 10km from the city. **Quy Nhon train station** (Ga Quy Nhon; ☎ 822 036) is at the end of a 10km spur line off the main north–south track. Only very slow local trains stop at Quy Nhon train station and they are not worth bothering with. It's better to get to/from Dieu Tri by taxi or *xe om* for around 50,000đ.

Tickets for trains departing from Dieu Tri can be purchased at the Quy Nhon train station, though if you arrive in Dieu Tri by train, your best bet is to purchase an onward ticket before leaving the station.

AROUND QUY NHON
There are half a dozen or so groups of Cham structures in the vicinity of Quy Nhon.

Cha Ban
The ruins of the former Cham capital of **Cha Ban** (also known at various times as Vijaya and Quy Nhon) are 26km north of Quy Nhon and 5km from Binh Dinh. The city was built within a rectangular wall measuring 1400m by 1100m. Canh Tien Tower (Tower of Brass) stands in the centre of the enclosure. The tomb of General Vu Tinh is nearby.

Cha Ban, which served as the seat of the royal government of Champa from the year 1000 (after the loss of Indrapura, also known as Dong Duong) until 1471, was attacked and plundered repeatedly by the Vietnamese, Khmers and Chinese.

In 1044, the Vietnamese Prince Phat Ma occupied the city and carried off a great deal of booty as well as the Cham king's wives, harem and female dancers, musicians and singers. Cha Ban was under the control of a Khmer overseer from 1190 to 1220.

In 1377, the Vietnamese were defeated and their king was killed in an attempt to capture Cha Ban. The Vietnamese emperor Le Thanh Ton breached the eastern gate of the city in 1471 and captured the Cham king and 50 members of the royal family. During this, the last great battle fought by the Cham, 60,000 Cham were killed and 30,000 more were taken prisoner by the Vietnamese.

During the Tay Son Rebellion, Cha Ban served as the capital of the central Vietnam region, and was ruled by the eldest of the three Tay Son brothers. The capital was attacked in 1793 by the forces of Nguyen Anh (later Emperor Gia Long), but the assault failed. In 1799, the forces of Nguyen Anh, under the command of General Vu Tinh, laid siege to the city and captured it. The Tay Son soon reoccupied the port of Thi Nai (modern-day Quy Nhon) and then lay siege to Cha Ban themselves. The siege continued for over a year, and by June 1801, Vu Tinh's provisions were gone. Food was in short supply; all the horses and elephants had long before been eaten. Refusing to consider the ignominy of surrender, Vu Tinh had an octagonal wooden tower constructed. He filled it with gunpowder and, arrayed in his ceremonial robes, went inside and blew himself up. Upon hearing the news of the death of his dedicated general, Nguyen Anh wept.

Duong Long Cham Towers

About 15km west of Cha Ban are the **Duong Long Cham towers** (Thap Duong Long, meaning Towers of Ivory). The largest of the three brick towers is embellished with granite ornamentation representing *naga* and elephants. Over the doors are bas-reliefs of women, dancers, standing lions, monsters and various other animals. The corners of the structure are formed by enormous dragon heads.

Quang Trung Museum

Nguyen Hue, the second-oldest of the three brothers who led the Tay Son Rebellion, crowned himself Emperor Quang Trung in 1788. In 1789 Quang Trung led the campaign that overwhelmingly defeated a Chinese invasion of 200,000 troops near Hanoi. This epic battle is still celebrated as one of the greatest triumphs in Vietnamese history. Quang Trung died in 1792 at the age of 40. The **Quang Trung Museum** (admission 10,000d; ☑ 8-11.30am & 1-4.30pm Mon-Fri) is dedicated to him.

During his reign, Quang Trung was something of a social reformer. He encouraged land reform, revised the system of taxation, improved the army and emphasised education, opening many schools and encouraging the development of Vietnamese

poetry and literature. Indeed, communist literature often portrays him as the leader of a peasant revolution whose progressive policies were crushed by the reactionary Nguyen dynasty, which came to power in 1802 and was overthrown by Ho Chi Minh in 1945.

The Quang Trung Museum, 48km from Quy Nhon, displays various statues, costumes, documents and artefacts from the 18th century, most of them labelled in English. Especially notable are the elephant skin-wrapped battle drums and gongs from the Bahnar tribal people in Gia Lai province. The museum is also known for its demonstrations of *vo binh dinh*, a traditional martial art that is performed with a bamboo stick.

GETTING THERE & AWAY
To get here, take Hwy 19 west towards Pleiku. The museum is about 5km north off the highway – the turn-off is sign-posted) in the Tay Son district.

Vinh Son Falls

Eighteen kilometres off Hwy 19, which links Binh Dinh and Pleiku, you'll find the **Vinh Son Falls**. It's an OK stop combined with a trip to the Quang Trung Museum or Duong Long Cham Towers.

SONG CAU
☎ 057
The village of Song Cau is an obscure place that you could easily drive past without ever noticing, but it's worth stopping here if you have the time. Near the village is an immense bay, a beautiful rest stop that attracts both foreign and domestic tourists.

Tourists doing the Nha Trang–Hoi An run often make a stop off for brunch in Song Cau, and some visitors decide to spend the night. Song Cau is along a notorious stretch of Hwy 1 dubbed the 'Happy 16 Kilometres' by long-distance truck drivers. It was so named for the vast number of 'taxi girls' who ply their trade by the roadside along this stretch.

An amusing thing to do here is to take a **boat trip** around the bay. Stop by the harbour to arrange a boat, which should cost about 30,000d per hour for six people. There are some lovely secluded beaches in the area, including **Bai Tro** (Tro Beach), which can be reached by boat or a scenic drive south of Song Cau through rice fields, fish farms and over rickety wooden bridges. Ask for directions at the restaurant.

Getting There & Away
Song Cau is 170km north of Nha Trang and 43km south of Quy Nhon. Highway buses can drop off and pick up here (with luck), but most travellers will probably arrive by chartered minibus.

If travelling with your own wheels, consider taking the newly completed coastal road between Song Cau and Quy Nhon; the scenery is stunning, and there are several good beaches en route.

TUY HOA
☎ 057 / pop 185,700
The capital of Phu Yen province, Tuy Hoa, is a nondescript little town on the coast between Dai Lanh Beach and Quy Nhon. A navigable river justifies Tuy Hoa's existence, but there isn't much else to the place, not even a good beach. One minor attraction is the **Nhan Cham Tower**, perched on a hill in the southern part of town, just off Hwy 1. There's also a Seated Buddha on a hillside north of town.

The main appeal of Tuy Hoa for travellers is that it has decent accommodation, which could be useful if you have a late start heading north or south along Hwy 1.

Sleeping & Eating
Huong Sen Hotel (☎ 823 775; fax 823 460; 22B Hwy 1A; r US$20-25; ✷) This large hotel with attached restaurant near the centre of town is your best bet in Tuy Hoa. Rooms have TV and hot water. Though there's not much English spoken here, staff are helpful and friendly.

Hung Phu Hotel (☎ 824 349; km2 Hwy 1A; r 50,000-100,000d; ✷) A cheaper option than Huong Sen, this is an old state-run place about 500m north of the bus station.

Getting There & Away
Vietnam Airlines operates two flights weekly between Tuy Hoa and HCMC. You can also reach Tuy Hoa by bus or local train.

BEACHES NORTH OF NHA TRANG
☎ 058
There are four noteworthy beach spots north of Nha Trang. Dai Lanh Beach (right) is a popular place, though is largely geared

toward Vietnamese holiday makers. If you're not into crowds, try to avoid visiting on weekends.

Of considerably more interest than these, however, and definitely worth finding your way to, are Jungle Beach (opposite) and Whale Island (opposite), two of Vietnam's most secluded and peaceful beach venues.

Dai Lanh Beach
Semicircular, casuarina-shaded **Dai Lanh Beach** is a gorgeous spot 83km north of Nha Trang and 150km south of Quy Nhon, right on Hwy 1. Other than the turquoise water, soft cream-coloured sand and quiet, there's a whole lot of nothing around.

About 1km south of Dai Lanh Beach is a vast sand-dune causeway worth exploring; it connects the mainland to Hon Gom, a mountainous peninsula almost 30km in length. The main village on Hon Gom is **Dam Mon** (known to the French as Port Dayot), which is on a sheltered bay facing the island of Hon Lon.

At the northern end of Dai Lanh Beach is Dai Lanh Promontory (Mui Dai Lanh), which was named Cap Varella by the French.

Keep a close eye on your gear if you're overnighting at Dai Lanh Beach; we've heard a few reports of theft.

SLEEPING & EATING
Thuy Ta Restaurant (☎ 842 117; tents 15,000d; r 70,000-120,000d) Midway down the beach, Thuy Ta has tents for rent, as well as some ultra-simple straw-roof beach bungalows with brick floors and fans. Toilets are shared, and for nonguests there's a charge of 3000d for the use of cold showers. Fresh seafood features prominently on the menu here; expect mains to cost about 30,000d.

GETTING THERE & AWAY
Dai Lanh Beach runs along Hwy 1, so any vehicle travelling along the coast between Nha Trang and Tuy Hoa (or Quy Nhon) will get you here. The coastal scenery is stunning, in particular north of Dai Lanh Beach.

Local trains stop directly across from the beach.

Doc Let Beach
Domestic tourists have gradually claimed **Doc Let Beach** (pronounced yop-lek locally)

away from foreign backpackers, who once had free range of this lovely stretch of beachfront. The beach is long and wide, with chalk-white sand and shallow water. Doc Let is easily accessible from Nha Trang, and worth considering as a day trip or overnight stop.

The 3000d beach-entry fee is waived for resort guests.

SLEEPING

Paradise Resort (☎ 670480; paradise_doclech@hotmail com; s/d bungalows US$9/14) Run by a blustery septuagenarian and his young Vietnamese family, the Paradise Resort occupies a gorgeous – and rustic – stretch of beach, with a terrace above and bungalows built around the palm trees. Rates include three meals, as well as free bottled water, tea, coffee and fruit. From the highway leading to Doc Let Beach, continue about 2km northward past the turn-off for Doc Let Resort and follow the blue arrows to Paradise.

Doc Let Resort (☎ 849663; fax 849506; docletresort@ dng.vnn.vn; bungalows 150,000-320,000d; 🔀 💻) This resort has 28 concrete beach-bungalows, each with private toilet and fridge, and is close to the beach; air-con bungalows have hot water. Other facilities include tennis courts (30,000d per hour), two restaurants, a bar and, of course, karaoke and massage facilities.

GETTING THERE & AWAY

Doc Let Beach is 30km north of Nha Trang on Hwy 1; just north of the Hyundai Shipyards take the right fork (east) and continue for 10km past photogenic salt fields until you reach Doc Let Beach. A sign in English marks the turn-off. There is no public transport to this spot. Some people take day tours from Nha Trang (US$6) – inquire at Mr Vu's Tour Adventures (p263) – while others hire a vehicle or drive themselves.

Whale Island

This is a lovely and secluded French-run beach retreat. Electricity is supplied to the **Whale Island Resort** (☎ /fax 840501; www.whaleisland resort.com; per person US$35) by generator, thankfully out of earshot of the simple wooden beachfront bungalows. Rates include accommodation, all meals and boat transfers.

Scuba-diving season on the island ends in mid-October, starting up again in mid-

February. The best season for diving is from April to September. Despite the damaging effects of dynamite fishing, environmental-protection efforts (including the transplanting of sea coral) around the resort bay have brought about a marked increase in the number of marine species – from 40 to over 170.

To reach Whale Island, follow Hwy 1 to Van Ninh, 60km north of Nha Trang and 64km south of Tuy Hoa. From there, it's a two-hour trip by **boat** (in Nha Trang ☎ 811607; fax 822 251; 11B Đ Nguyen Thien Thuat) to the island.

Jungle Beach

This rustic spot sits on 3 hectares of land where jungle-clad mountains converge with 550m of pristine beach front. **Jungle Beach Resort** (☎ 622 384, 0913-429 144; syl@dng.vnn .vn; per person US$15) is a quiet, communal sort of retreat for those looking to do a little hillside exploration or sunning on the deserted beach.

In addition to several rooms in the main house or bungalow building, basic dome-tent or mattress-plus-mosquito-net camping is also possible here – but sleeping alfresco still costs US$15. We strongly recommend calling ahead to book a room, as you may have no choice but to sleep outside (and there are no nearby alternatives) if you simply turn up.

The per-person rate includes three simple meals daily, served family-style in the main house.

Jungle Beach is about halfway between Doc Let Beach and Nha Trang, 59km by road from Nha Trang via Hwy 1, but just 15km as the crow flies (or by boat). Though there is no public transportation here, motorbike drivers from Dalat and Nha Trang know the place.

NHA TRANG

☎ 058 / pop 315,200

Nha Trang, the capital of Khanh Hoa province, has one of the most popular municipal beaches in all of Vietnam. Club Med hasn't arrived yet, and there are still no Monte Carlo–style casinos, but the resort town has rapidly developed into a bustling destination for sun and fun.

Nha Trang is a place to come and party, and the service on the beach is incredible – massage, lunch, cold beer, manicure, beauty

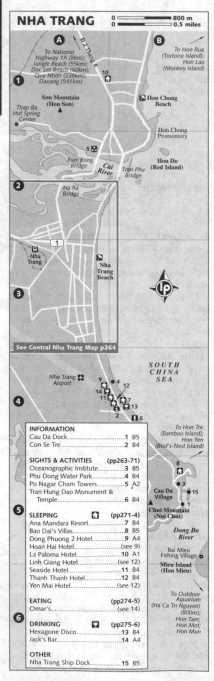

NHA TRANG

0 — 800 m
0 — 0.5 miles

To National
Highway 1A (8km);
Jungle Beach (55km);
Doc Let Beach (60km);
Quy Nhon (238km);
Danang (541km)

To Hon Rua
(Tortoise Island);
Hon Lao
(Monkey Island)

Son Mountain
(Hon Son)

Thap Ba
Hot Spring
Center

Hon Chong
Beach

Hon Chong
Promontory

Xom Bong
Bridge

Cai
River

Tran Phu
Bridge

Hon Do
(Red Island)

Ha Ra
Bridge

Nha
Trang

Nha
Trang
Beach

See Central Nha Trang Map p264

Nha Trang
Airport

SOUTH
CHINA
SEA

To Hon Tre
(Bamboo Island);
Hon Yen
(Bird's-Nest Island)

Cau Da
Village

Chut Mountain
(Nui Chut)

Dong Bo
River

Bai Mieu
Fishing Village

Mieu Island
(Hon Mieu)

To Outdoor
Aquarium
(Ha Ca Tri Nguyen)
(800m);
Hon Tam;
Hon Mot;
Hon Mun

INFORMATION	
Cau Da Dock	1 B5
Con Se Tre	2 B4

SIGHTS & ACTIVITIES	(pp263-71)
Oceanographic Institute	3 B5
Phu Dong Water Park	4 B4
Po Nagar Cham Towers	5 A2
Tran Hung Dao Monument & Temple	6 B4

SLEEPING	(pp271-4)
Ana Mandara Resort	7 B4
Bao Dai's Villas	8 B5
Dong Phuong 2 Hotel	9 A4
Hoan Hai Hotel	(see 9)
La Paloma Hotel	10 A1
Linh Giang Hotel	(see 12)
Seaside Hotel	11 B4
Thanh Thanh Hotel	12 B4
Yen Mai Hotel	(see 12)

EATING	(pp274-5)
Omar's	(see 14)

DRINKING	(pp275-6)
Hexagone Disco	13 B4
Jack's Bar	14 A4

OTHER	
Nha Trang Ship Dock	15 B5

treatments etc. If you're after something more tranquil, however, consider heading for Mui Ne Beach (p283) further south or to some of the beaches north of Nha Trang (p260).

The clear turquoise waters around Nha Trang make for excellent fishing, snorkelling and scuba diving. However, you aren't likely to enjoy these pursuits in the off-season months of November and December, when the rains come. During heavy rains, run off from the rivers at each end of the beach flows into the bay, which can turn a murky brown. Most of the year, however, the water is as it appears in the tourist brochures.

Nha Trang's dry season runs from June to October. The wettest months are October and November, but rain usually falls only at night or in the morning. The best beach weather is generally before 1pm; the afternoon sea breezes can make things unpleasant until the wind dies back down around 8pm. Although well within the tropics, Nha Trang has cool evenings.

The area's seafood products include abalone, lobster, prawns, cuttlefish, mackerel, pomfret, scallops, shrimps, snapper and tuna. Nha Trang's fishing fleet operates mostly at night, using the days in port for rest and equipment repair. Agricultural products exported from the area include cashew nuts, coconuts, coffee and sesame seeds. Salt production is also large, employing over 4000 people; a good place to observe some photogenic salt fields is on the access road leading to Doc Let Beach (p260).

Boat trips are a real highlight of Nha Trang (p269).

Information
BOOKSHOPS
Mr. Lang's Book Exchange (Map p264) Outdoors, near the War Memorial; stocks a good collection of used books in a variety of languages.

Shorty's Bar (Map p264; ☎ 810 985; 45 Đ Biet Thu) Carries a great selection of mostly English-language books.

INTERNET ACCESS
As well as the places listed here, many hotels also offer Internet access, as do travellers cafés.

La Fregate Internet (Map p264; ☎ 829 011; fregate@dng.vnn.vn; 4 Đ Pasteur; per min 100d) There is plenty of fast ADSL Internet access available here.

Thanh's Family Booking Office (Map p264; 2 Đ Hung Vuong; per min about 100d) In the town centre.

MONEY

Vietcombank Đ Quang Trung (Map p264; ☎ 822 720; 17 Đ Quang Trung; ☼ Mon-Fri) Changes travellers cheques and gives cash advances; Đ Hung Vuong (Map p264; ☎ 524 500; 5 Đ Hung Vuong) Has an ATM, and exchanges cash and travellers cheques.

POST

Main post office (Map p264; ☎ 821 271; 4 Đ Le Loi; ☼ 6.30am-10pm) Near the northern end of Nha Trang Beach. Has EMS and DHL desks.

Post office branch (Map p264; ☎ 823 866; 50 Đ Le Thanh Ton; ☼ 7am-11pm)

TRAVEL AGENCIES

Découvrir Whale Island (Map p264; ☎ 811 607; fax 822 251; 11B Đ Nguyen Thien Thuat) Stop by this office to get more information about visiting beautiful Whale Island.

Khanh Hoa Tourist (Map p264; ☎ 823 709; fax 824 206; 1 Đ Tran Hung Dao) The provincial tourism authority is beside the Vien Dong Hotel. It offers various tour programmes, but you'll likely find it cheaper and more interesting to book elsewhere.

Mr Vu's Tour Adventures (Map p264; ☎ 828 996; www.vutouradventure.com; 2D Đ Biet Thu) Recommended for inland 4WD/motorbike excursions to the Central Highlands.

The following are a few of Nha Trang's budget-traveller cafés-cum-travel-agencies (all of which sell bottom-of-the-barrel 'fast food' tours).

Hanh Cafe (☎ 827 814; hanhcafé@dng.vnn.vn; 22 Đ Tran Hung Dao)

Sinh Cafe (Map p264; ☎ 811 981; sinhcafént@dng.vnn .vn; 10 Đ Biet Thu)

TM Brothers Cafe (Map p264; ☎ 814 556; fax 815 366; hoanhaont@dng.vnn.vn; 22 Đ Tran Hung Dao)

Dangers & Annoyances

Although Nha Trang is generally a safe place, be careful at night, especially on the beach and along Đ Tran Phu. Though the waterfront has been refurbished, we've heard a few stories of thievery and rip-offs along the beach.

Sights
BEACHES

Coconut palms provide shelter for both bathers and strollers along most of Nha Trang's 6km of beachfront. Beach chairs are available for rent – you can just sit and enjoy the drinks and light food that the beach vendors have on offer. About the only

time you need to move is to use the toilet or when the tide comes up.

Hon Chong Beach (Bai Tam Hon Chong) is a series of beaches that begin just north of Hon Chong Promontory; fishing families live here among the coconut palms, but the refuse makes the place unsuitable for swimming or sunbathing. Behind the beaches are steep mountains whose lower reaches support crops that include mangoes and bananas.

About 300m south of Hon Chong (ie, towards Nha Trang) and a few dozen metres from the beach is tiny **Hon Do** (Red Island), which has a Buddhist temple on top.

ISLANDS

Khanh Hoa province's 71 offshore islands are renowned for the remarkably clear water surrounding them. A trip to these islands is one of the best reasons for visiting Nha Trang, so try to schedule at least one day for a boat journey. If you're interested in overnighting offshore, consider Whale Island (p261) or Hon Tre.

Hon Mieu

All the tourist literature touts **Hon Mieu** (also called Tri Nguyen Island) as the site of an outdoor aquarium (Ho Ca Tri Nguyen). In fact, the 'aquarium' is an important fish-breeding farm, where over 40 species of fish, crustacean and other marine creatures are raised in three separate compartments. There is also a café built on stilts over the water. Ask around for canoe rentals.

The main village on Hon Mieu is Tri Nguyen. Bai Soai is a gravel beach on the far side of Hon Mieu from Cau Da. There are a few rustic **bungalows** (US$6) on the island.

Most people will take some sort of boat tour booked through a hotel, café or Khanh Hoa Tourist (left). Impoverished and less-hurried travellers might catch one of the regular ferries that go to Tri Nguyen village from Cau Da dock.

Hon Tre (Bamboo Island)

Several kilometres from the southern part of Nha Trang Beach is **Bamboo Island**, the largest island in the Nha Trang area. **Tru Beach** is at the northern end of the island. Boats can be hired to take you there, and we can also recommend the day and overnight trips offered by Con Se Tre (left).

SOUTH-CENTRAL COAST

CENTRAL NHA TRANG

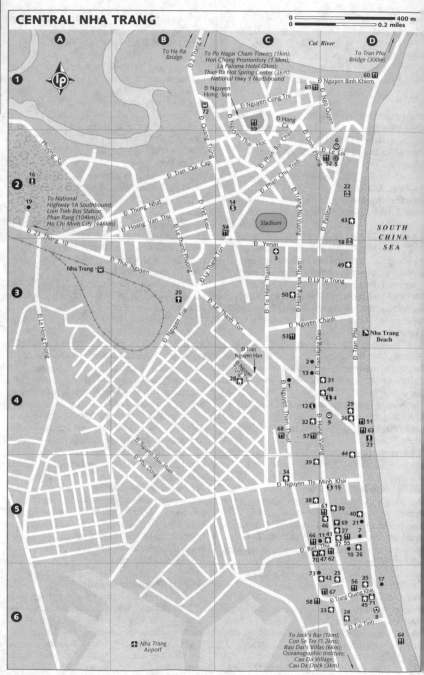

0 ⎯⎯⎯⎯⎯⎯ 400 m
0 ⎯⎯⎯⎯⎯⎯ 0.2 miles

A · **B** · **C** · **D**

Cai River

To Ha Ra
Bridge

To Po Nagar Cham Towers (1km);
Hon Chong Promontory (1.6km);
Thap Ba Hot Spring Center (3km);
National Hwy 1 Northbound

To Tran Phu
Bridge (300m)

Đ 2 Thang 4

Đ Nguyen
Hong Son

72

Đ Nguyen Thai Hoc

59

Đ Nguyen Cong Tru

Đ Hang
Ca

Đ Phan Boi Chau

Đ Quang Trung

Đ Tran Qui Cap

Đ Phan Chu Trinh

Đ Dinh Phung

Đ Ngo Quyen

65

Đ Nguyen Binh Khiem

60

6
Đ Le Loi
52 5

22

To National
Highway 1A Southbound;
Lien Tinh Bus Station;
Phan Rang (104km);
Ho Chi Minh City (448km)

16

19

Đ Thong Nhat

Đ Hoang Van Thu

Đ Yet Kieu

Đ Le Thanh Phuong

Đ Ly Thanh Ton

Đ Tran Nu Vuong

Đ Pasteur

43

SOUTH
CHINA
SEA

14

54

Stadium

Đ Yersin

3

18

49

Đ 23 Thang 10

Đ Thai Nguyen

Nha Trang

Đ Le Hong Phong

Đ Nguyen Trai

Đ Le Thanh Ton

20

Đ To Hien Thanh

Đ Hoang Hoa Tham

Đ Ly Tu Trong

50

Đ Nguyen Chanh

53

Đ Tran Phu

Nha Trang
Beach

Đ Tran
Nguyen Han

Đ Nguyen
Trung Truc

28

Đ Nguyen Thien Thuat

2
13

31

1

48
4

Đ Tran Hung Dao

12
32

9

29

36

51
63
23

68
57

Đ Hung Vuong

44

39

34

15

Đ Nguyen Thi Minh Khai

38

61
46

30

66 11 41
70 47 62

69

40
21

27
37 55

7

10 26

Đ Biet Thu

73

42

25

56

35
17

67

45 71

58

33

Đ Trang Quang Khai

24
8

Đ Tu Tinh

Nha Trang
Airport

To Jack's Bar (1km);
Con Se Tre (1.2km);
Bao Dai's Villas (6km);
Oceanographic Institute;
Cau Da Village;
Cau Da Dock (3km)

64

Hon Mun

Also called Ebony Island, **Hon Mun** is just southeast of Bamboo Island and is known for its snorkelling. To get here, you'll probably have to hire a boat.

Hon Mot

Sandwiched neatly between Ebony Island and Hon Tam is tiny **Hon Mot**; it's another great place for snorkelling.

Monkey Island

Called Hon Lao in Vietnamese, **Monkey Island** is named after its large contingent of resident monkeys, and has become a big hit with tourists. Most of the monkeys have grown quite accustomed to receiving food handouts from the tourists, providing ample opportunity to take a memorable photo. However, these are wild animals and should be treated as such. Monkey bites are a fairly reliable source of rabies.

Aside from being unwilling to cuddle, the monkeys are materialistic! They'll grab the sunglasses off your face or snatch a pen from your shirt pocket and run off. So far, we haven't heard of monkeys slitting open travellers' handbags with a razor blade, but keep a close eye (and hand) on your possessions.

A word of warning: though the island itself can make for a fun visit, there's also a bear-and-monkey 'show' held there that you may want to avoid. Travellers have reported seeing the animals beaten by their trainers during performances.

Monkey Island is 12km north of Bamboo Island, and one-day boat tours can easily be arranged in Nha Trang. A faster way to get here is to take a motorbike or car 15km north of Nha Trang on Hwy 1 – near a pagoda and the pleasant Nha Trang Restaurant, from where boats will ferry you to the island in 15 minutes for 50,000d. Other destinations from here include Hoa Lan Springs on Hon Heo (40,000d, 45 minutes), and Hon Thi (20,000d, 20 minutes).

Bird's-Nest Island

Salangane Island (Hon Yen or Dao Yen) is the name applied to two lump-shaped islands visible from Nha Trang Beach. These and other islands off Khanh Hoa province are the source of Vietnam's finest swiftlet (*salangane*) nests. The nests are used in bird's-nest soup as well as in traditional medicine, and are considered an aphrodisiac. It is said that the extraordinary virility of Emperor Minh Mang, who ruled Vietnam

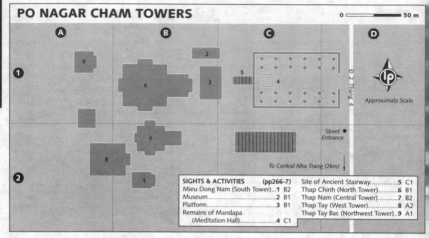

PO NAGAR CHAM TOWERS

0 ————— 50 m

Approximate Scale

Street Entrance

To Central Nha Trang (2km)

SIGHTS & ACTIVITIES	(pp266-7)		
Mieu Dong Nam (South Tower)...1 B2		Site of Ancient Stairway..............5 C1
Museum.....................................2 B1		Thap Chinh (North Tower)..........6 B1
Platform...................................3 B1		Thap Nam (Central Tower)..........7 B2
Remains of Mandapa		Thap Tay (West Tower)...............8 A2
(Meditation Hall)..................4 C1		Thap Tay Bac (Northwest Tower)..9 A1

from 1820 to 1840, was derived from the consumption of swiftlet nests.

The nests, which the swiftlets build out of silklike salivary secretions, are semioval and about 5cm to 8cm in diameter. They are usually harvested twice a year. Red nests are the most highly prized. Annual production in Khanh Hoa and Phu Yen provinces is about 1000kg. At present, swiftlet nests fetch US$2000 per kilogram in the international marketplace!

There is a small, secluded beach at Salangane Island. The 17km trip out to the islands takes three to four hours by small boat from Nha Trang.

PO NAGAR CHAM TOWERS

The Cham towers of **Po Nagar** (Thap Ba, The Lady of the City; Maps p262 & above; admission 4500d; ☾ 6am-6pm) were built between the 7th and 12th centuries. The site was used for Hindu worship as early as the 2nd century AD. Today, both ethnic Chinese and Vietnamese Buddhists come to Po Nagar to pray and make offerings, according to their respective traditions. This site has a continuing religious significance, so do remember to remove your shoes before entering.

The towers serve as the Holy See, honouring Yang Ino Po Nagar, the goddess of the Dua (Liu) clan, which ruled over the southern part of the Cham kingdom covering Kauthara and Pan Duranga (present day Khanh Hoa and Thuan Hai provinces). The original wooden structure was razed

to the ground by attacking Javanese in AD 774 but was replaced by a stone-and-brick temple (the first of its kind) in 784. There are stone slabs scattered throughout the complex, most of which relate to history or religion, and provide insight into the spiritual life and social structure of the Cham.

Originally the complex covered an area of 500 sq metres and there were seven or eight towers, four of which remain. All of the temples face east, as did the original entrance to the complex, which is to the right as you ascend the hillock. In centuries past, a person coming to pray passed through the pillared meditation hall, 10 pillars of which can still be seen, before proceeding up the staircase to the towers.

The 28m-high **North Tower** (Thap Chinh), with its terraced pyramidal roof, vaulted interior masonry and vestibule, is a superb example of Cham architecture. One of the tallest Cham towers, it was built in AD 817 by Pangro, a minister of King Harivarman I, after the original temples here were sacked and burned. The raiders also carried off a *linga* made of precious metal. In AD 918 King Indravarman III placed a gold *mukha-linga* in the North Tower, but it too was taken, this time by the Khmers. This pattern of statues being destroyed or stolen and then replaced continued for some time until 965, when King Jaya Indravarman I replaced the gold *mukha-linga* with the stone figure, Uma (*shakti*, or a feminine manifestation of Shiva), which remains to this day.

Above the entrance to the North Tower, two musicians flank a dancing four-armed Shiva, one of whose feet is on the head of the bull Nandin. The sandstone doorposts are covered with inscriptions, as are parts of the walls of the vestibule. A gong and a drum stand under the pyramid-shaped ceiling of the antechamber. In the 28m-high pyramidal main chamber, there is a black stone statue of the goddess Uma (in the shape of Bhagavati) with 10 arms, two of which are hidden under her vest; she is seated and leaning back against some sort of monstrous animal.

The **Central Tower** (Thap Nam) was built partly of recycled bricks in the 12th century on the site of a structure dating from the 7th century. It is less finely constructed than the other towers and has little ornamentation; the pyramidal roof lacks terracing or pilasters, although the interior altars were once covered with silver. There is a *linga* inside the main chamber. Note the inscription on the left-hand wall of the vestibule.

The **South Tower** (Mieu Dong Nam), at one time dedicated to Sandhaka (Shiva), still shelters a *linga*. The richly ornamented **Northwest Tower** (Thap Tay Bac) was originally dedicated to Ganesha. The pyramid-shaped summit of its roof has disappeared. The **West Tower**, of which almost nothing remains, was constructed by King Vikrantavarman during the first half of the 9th century. Near the North Tower is a small **museum** with a few mediocre examples of Cham stonework; the explanatory signs are in Vietnamese only. At one time there was a small temple on this site.

The towers of Po Nagar stand on a granite knoll, 2km north of central Nha Trang and on the banks of the Cai River. To get here from central Nha Trang, take Đ Quang Trung (which becomes Đ 2 Thang 4) north across Ha Ra and Xom Bong Bridges, which span the mouth of the Cai River. Po Nagar can also be reached via the new Tran Phu Bridge along the beachfront road.

LONG SON PAGODA

Perhaps the most impressive sight in Nha Trang, aside from the beach and Cham towers, is **Long Son Pagoda** (Map p264; 7.30am-8pm), also known as Tinh Hoi Khanh Hoa Pagoda and An Nam Phat Hoc Hoi Pagoda. It's about 500m west of the train station.

The pagoda, which has resident monks, was founded in the late 19th century and has been rebuilt several times over the years. The entrance and roofs are decorated with mosaic dragons constructed of glass and bits of ceramic tile. The main sanctuary is an attractive hall adorned with modern interpretations of traditional motifs. Note the ferocious nose hairs on the colourful dragons wrapped around the pillars on either side of the main altar.

At the top of the hill, behind the pagoda, is a huge white **Buddha** (Kim Than Phat To; Map p264) seated on a lotus blossom and visible from all over the city. The platform around the 14m-high figure, which was built in 1963, has great views of Nha Trang and nearby rural areas. As you approach the pagoda from the street, the 152 stone steps up the hill to the Buddha begin to the right of the structure. You should take some time to explore off to the left, where there's an entrance to another impressive hall of the pagoda.

PASTEUR INSTITUTE

Dr Alexandre Yersin (1863–1943) founded Nha Trang's **Pasteur Institute** (Map p264; 822 355; fax 824 058; 10 Đ Tran Phu; 8-11am & 2-4.30pm Mon-Fri, 2-4.30pm Sat) in 1895. He was, from among the tens of thousands of colonists who spent time in Vietnam, probably the Frenchman most loved by the Vietnamese. Vietnam's two other Pasteur Institutes are in HCMC and Dalat.

Born in Switzerland, Dr Yersin came to Vietnam in 1889 after working under Louis Pasteur in Paris. He learned to speak Vietnamese fluently, and spent the next few years travelling throughout the central highlands and recording his observations. During this period he came upon the site of what is now Dalat and recommended to the government that a hill station be established there. Dr Yersin also introduced rubber and quinine-producing trees to Vietnam. In 1894, while in Hong Kong, he discovered the rat-borne microbe that causes bubonic plague.

Today, the Pasteur Institute in Nha Trang coordinates vaccination and hygiene programmes for the country's southern coastal region. The institute produces vaccines (eg for rabies and Japanese B encephalitis) and carries out medical research and testing

LONG THANH – PHOTOGRAPHER

Most of the 500-odd members of the National Association of Photographers are based in Hanoi or HCMC, and most choose colour film as their medium. Long Thanh, a photographer born in Nha Trang in 1951, is a rare exception. A family man, Long Thanh has managed, with limited resources and a geographical disadvantage, to establish himself as Nha Trang's most acclaimed local shutterbug. He has been taking pictures since the 1960s, when at the age of 13 he learned to use a camera while working in a local photo shop.

Purist that he is, Long Thanh religiously uses black-and-white film and laments the fact that so many great photographers prefer to shoot in colour. He works out of a makeshift darkroom in his simple kitchen, mixes his own chemicals, and awaits the day when professional quality black-and-white photographic paper will be sold in Vietnam (for now, he relies on friends from abroad to keep him stocked).

If you've got the time, it may be possible to visit Long Thanh's home-studio and talk photography; that is, if he's not out on the road looking to capture the next great shot. Long Thanh is an incurable traveller and has been known to happily accompany new friends on excursions into the Vietnamese countryside. For fellow photographers, who could be a better travel companion?

to European standards. Physicians at the clinic here offer medical advice to around 70 patients a day.

Dr Yersin's library and office are now an interesting **museum** (Map p264; admission 26,000d; 7-11am & 2-4.30pm Mon-Fri, 2-4.30pm Sat), on the 2nd floor in an adjacent building. Items on display include laboratory equipment (such as his astronomical instruments), books from his library, a fascinating 3-D photo viewer and some of the thousand or so letters written to his mother! The model boat was given to him by local fishermen with whom he spent a great deal of his time. Tours of the museum are guided in French, English and Vietnamese, and a short film on Dr Yersin's life is also shown.

At his request, Dr Yersin was buried near Nha Trang.

KHANH HOA MUSEUM

This sleepy local **museum** (Map p264; ☎ 882 227; 16 Đ Tran Phu; admission free; 8-10am & 2-4pm Mon, Wed, Thu & Sun) features displays such as Cham statutes and costumes, and artefacts of the ethnic minorities in the province. The Uncle Ho room features several of Ho Chi Minh's personal effects, such as clothing and the actual microphone with which he made his famous independence speech in Hanoi on 2 September 1945.

LONG THANH GALLERY

The work of Nha Trang's most prominent photographer, Long Thanh, is shown at **Long Thanh Gallery** (☎ 824 875; lvntrang50@hotmail.com; 126 Đ Hoang Van Thu; 8.30-11.30am & 1-6pm Mon-Sat). Long Thanh shoots extraordinary black-and-white images of everyday Vietnamese moments. Though he has shown his photos in group exhibitions abroad more than 50 times and had his first international solo exhibition in Hamburg, Germany in 1999, Long Thanh's talents remain relatively undiscovered outside Vietnam.

Long Thanh's powerful images capture the heart and soul of Vietnam. Among his most compelling works, *Under the Rain* is a perfectly timed shot of two young girls caught in a sudden downpour, with a mysterious beam of sunlight streaming down on them. *Afternoon Countryside* is another rare scene – a boy dashing across the backs of a herd of water buffalos submerged in a lake outside Nha Trang.

For more information see above. You can also view Long Thanh's photos on the walls of his favourite watering hole, the **Nha Trang Sailing Club** (Map p264; ☎ 826 528; 72 Đ Tran Phu), which features an ongoing exhibition of his work.

NHA TRANG CATHEDRAL

Built in the French Gothic style, complete with medieval-looking stained glass windows, **Nha Trang Cathedral** (Map p264) stands on a small hill overlooking the train station. It was constructed of simple cement blocks between 1928 and 1933. Today, the cathedral is the seat of the bishop of Nha Trang. In 1988 a Catholic cemetery not far from the church was disinterred to make room

GIẦY DÉP ĐỂ TẠI ĐÂY
QUÝ KHÁCH VUI LÒNG TỰ GIỮ LẤY
PLEASE LEAVE YOUR SHOES HERE

TOM SMALLMAN

Temple steps to the North Tower, Po Nagar Cham Towers (p266), Nha Trang

NOBORU KOMINE

Nha Trang Cathedral (p268)

Đ Tran Phu, Nha Trang (p261)

MATT DARBY

Nha Trang (p261)

SARA-JANE CLELAN

Woman exercising on one of Nha Trang's beaches (p263)

JOHN BANAGAN

JOHN BANAGAN

Inhabitants of Monkey Island (p265), near Nha Trang

MARK AND

Hon Chong Promontory (p263), Nha Trang

or a new train-station building. The ashes were brought to the cathedral and reburied in the cavities behind the wall of plaques that line the ramp up the hill.

Masses are held daily.

HON CHONG PROMONTORY

The narrow granite promontory of **Hon Chong** (Map p262) juts into the turquoise waters of the South China Sea. The views of the mountainous coastline north of Nha Trang and the nearby islands are fine, and the beach here offers a more local flavour than the main beach in the town centre.

There's a gargantuan handprint on the massive boulder balanced at the tip of the promontory. According to local legend, a drunk giant male fairy made it when he fell while spying a female fairy bathing nude at Bai Tien (Fairy Beach), the point of land closest to Hon Rua. They fell in love and began a life together, but the gods intervened, punishing the male fairy by sending him away.

The lovesick female fairy waited patiently for her husband to come back, but after a very long time, despairing that he might never return, she lay down in sorrow and turned into Nui Co Tien (Fairy Mountain). Looking to the northeast from Hon Chong Promontory, the peak on the right is supposed to be her face, gazing up towards the sky; the middle peak is her breasts; and the summit on the left (the highest) forms her crossed legs.

To the northeast is **Hon Rua** (Tortoise Island), which really does resemble a tortoise. The two islands of **Hon Yen** are off in the distance to the east.

OCEANOGRAPHIC INSTITUTE

Housed in a grand French-colonial building 6km south of Nha Trang's main post office in the port district of Cau Da (also called Cau Be) is the **Oceanographic Institute** (Vien Nghiem Cuu Bien; Map p262; ☎ 590 037; haiduong@dng .vnn.vn; 1 Cau Da; adult/child 10,000/5000d; guide 30,000d; ☼ 7.30am-noon & 1-4.30pm). Founded in 1923, it has an aquarium and specimen room open to the public; it also has a library. The 23 tanks on the ground floor are home to a variety of colourful live specimens of local marine life, including seahorses.

Behind the main building and across the volleyball court is a large hall filled with 60,000 dead specimens of sea life, including stuffed seabirds and fish, corals and the corporeal remains of other marine creatures preserved in glass jars.

As nice as the Oceanographic Institute is, if you really want to see an aquarium take a boat across to nearby Hon Mieu (p263).

BAO DAI'S VILLAS

These **villas** (Biet Thu Cau Da; Map p262; admission 2000d, usually free for restaurant patrons) were formerly the retreats of Bao Dai, Vietnam's own 'last emperor', who abdicated in 1945. Between the mid-1950s and 1975, the villas were used by high-ranking officials of the South Vietnamese government, including President Thieu. This all changed in 1975, when the villas were taken over for use by high-ranking communist officials, including the prime minister, Pham Van Dong. Today, low-ranking 'capitalist tourists' can rent a room in the villas (see p272).

Built in the 1920s, Bao Dai's five villas are set on three hills south of town, and have brilliant views of the South China Sea, Nha Trang Bay (to the north) and Cau Da dock (to the south). Between the buildings are winding paths lined with tropical bushes and trees. Most of the villas' furnishings have not been changed in decades.

To get to Bao Dai's Villas from Nha Trang, turn left off Đ Tran Phu just past the white cement oil-storage tanks (but before reaching Cau Da village). These villas are several hundred metres north of the Oceanographic Institute.

Activities

BOAT TOURS

Virtually every hotel in town books island boat tours. You can pay more for a less-crowded and more luxurious boat that takes you to more islands. Indeed, you'll have to do this if you want to get in much snorkelling. The place to charter boats is at the Cau Da dock, south of Nha Trang. If you're not with an organised group, you'd better book the day before or go to Cau Da dock early in the morning – by 10am all the boats are gone. One attractive alternative is joining up with one of the local dive boats, most of which will take nondivers along for a discounted rate.

Shallow water prevents boats from reaching shore at some of the fishing villages on the islands. In this case, you must walk perhaps several hundred metres across floats. The floats were designed for Vietnamese people, and weightier Westerners might get wet – balance carefully and take care with your camera. Nevertheless, it's all good fun and a visit to these fishing villages is highly recommended.

Mama Linh's Boat Tours (Map p264; ☎ 826 693; fax 815 365; 2A Đ Hung Vuong; ⏰ 8am-6pm) are now the hottest ticket for island hopping, guzzling fruit wine at the impromptu 'floating bar', and deck-side dancing. Daily trips last from 8.45am until 4.30pm, and typically include stops on Hon Mun (Salangane Island), Hon Mot, Hon Tam and Hon Mieu – see p263. Tickets (US$5) are sold at the office, but you can easily book at your hotel for a dollar or two more.

Of course all of this fun in the sun, let's just say, might not be the best environment for families with children (or for recovering alcoholics). If the cultural fanfare of the Mama Linh experience does not sound up your alley, there are other more orthodox boat tours around.

Con Se Tre (Map p262; ☎ /fax 811 163; 100/16 Đ Tra Phu; ⏰ 8am-6pm) offers interesting boat tour to peaceful Hon Tre (Bamboo Island). Full day tours cost US$5/10 with/without lunch and the popular dinner trips (US$8) are also worth looking into.

In the interests of environmental preservation, when booking a boat tour you might consider asking if the captain anchors his boat to a buoy, as opposed to dropping anchor directly on the coral. Of course, when booking a tour through a hotel or tourist operator it's hard to know if you'll get a truthful or informed answer to this question.

DIVING
Nha Trang is Vietnam's premier scuba diving locale. Visibility averages 15m but can be as much as 30m, depending on the

---

CONSIDERATIONS FOR RESPONSIBLE DIVING
The popularity of diving is placing immense pressure on many sites. Please consider the following tips when diving and help preserve the ecology and beauty of Vietnam's reefs.

- Do not use anchors on the reef, and take care not to ground boats on coral. Encourage dive operators and regulatory bodies to establish permanent moorings at popular dive sites.
- Avoid touching living marine organisms with your body or dragging equipment across the reef. Polyps can be damaged by even the gentlest contact. Never stand on corals, even if they look solid and robust. If you must hold on to the reef, touch only exposed rock or dead coral.
- Be conscious of your fins. Even without contact, the surge from heavy fin strokes near the reef can damage delicate organisms. When treading water in shallow reef areas, take care not to kick up clouds of sand. Settling sand can easily smother the delicate organisms of the reef.
- Practise and maintain proper buoyancy control. Major damage can be done by divers descending too fast and colliding with the reef. Make sure you are correctly weighted and that your weight belt is positioned so that you stay horizontal. If you have not dived for a while, have a practice dive in a pool before taking to the reef. Be aware that buoyancy can change over the period of an extended trip: initially you may breathe harder and need more weight; a few days later you may breathe more easily and need less weight.
- Resist the temptation to collect or buy coral or shells. Aside from the ecological damage, taking home marine souvenirs depletes the beauty of a site and spoils the enjoyment of others. The same goes for marine archaeological sites (mainly shipwrecks). Respect their integrity; some sites are even protected from looting by law.
- Ensure that you take home all your rubbish and any litter you may find as well. Plastics in particular are a serious threat to marine life. Turtles can mistake plastic for jellyfish and eat it.
- Resist the temptation to feed fish. You may disturb their normal eating habits, encourage aggressive behaviour or feed them food that is detrimental to their health.
- Minimise your disturbance of marine animals.

eason (late October to early January is the worst time of year).

There are around 25 dive sites in the area, both shallow and deep. There are no wrecks to dive on, but some sites have good drop-offs and there are a few small underwater caves to explore. The waters support a good variety of soft and hard corals, and a reasonable number of small reef fish.

A full-day outing including boat transport, two dives and lunch typically costs between US$40 and US$60. Most dive operators also offer a range of dive courses, including a 'discover diving' programme for uncertified, first-time divers to experience the thrill under the supervision of a qualified dive master.

It is difficult to recommend one dive operator over another: our best advice is to shop around, speak to a few different operators and use your better judgement. With that caveat in mind, consider the following outfits, all long-running operators with environmentally responsible diving practices.

Blue Diving Club (Map p264; ☎ 825 390; www .vietnamdivers.com; 12B Đ Biet Thu; ⌚ 7.30am-9pm) French-British owned and operated.

Jeremy Stein's Rainbow Divers (Map p264; ☎ 829 946; www.divevietnam.com; Nha Trang Sailing Club; ⌚ 7am-10pm) Run by Briton Jeremy Stein, who also just happens to be a dead ringer for Chuck Norris.

Octopus Diving (Map p262; ☎ 810 629; octopusdivingclub@yahoo.com; 62 Đ Tran Phu; ⌚ 7.30am-9pm) Brit- and Japanese-run club; guides speak 11 languages; certified to train instructors.

SWIMMING & WATER SPORTS

Right on the beach front, **Phu Dong Water Park** (Map p262; admission 20,000d; ⌚ 9am-5pm) has water slides, shallow pools and fountains if salt water is not your thing.

If salt water *is* your thing, check out **Manamana Beach Club** (Map p264; ☎ 812 948; fax 821 977; La Louisiane Café, 29 Đ Tran Phu). Offering windsurfing, sea kayaking, wakeboarding and sailing lessons, Manamana uses state-of-the-art equipment and makes safety a priority.

Sleeping

Nha Trang is a trendy place for both domestic and foreign tourists, so that there are around 100 hotels to choose from. Several of the state-run hotels occupying prime beachfront property have become markedly run-down, and most are not worth considering. For the same money you can do much better at one of the countless private minihotels, which even if not on the beach, will be within a few minutes' walk.

For secluded beach accommodation alternatives outside of Nha Trang, try Whale Island (p261) or Jungle Beach (p261).

BUDGET

Ha Huong Hotel (Map p264; ☎ 512 069; hahuongnt@ dng.vnn.vn; 26 Đ Nguyen Trung Truc; dm US$2, r US$6-15; ▨) With a tiny, pretty koi pond and orchids hanging in the front courtyard, this friendly hotel is on a quiet street about five minutes' walk from the beach. The rooms are clean and the air-con rooms have satellite TV and balconies.

Yen My Hotel (☎ 829 064; yenmyhotel@hotmail .com; 22 Đ Hoang Hoa Tham; r US$4-8; ▨) A good budget place run by a friendly man named Mr Duan. It's small and clean.

Blue Star Hotel (Map p264; ☎ 826 447; quangc@ dng.vnn.vn; 1B Đ Biet Thu; r US$8-15; ▨) Offering the basic amenities, the Blue Star is pretty clean, and has nice seaviews from the upper floors. Corner rooms have great big balconies. It's a good budget choice close to the beach; rates include breakfast.

Phong Lan Hotel (Orchid Hotel; Map p264; ☎ 811 647; orchidhotel2000@yahoo.com; 24/44 Đ Hung Vuong; r US$5-10; ▨) The bright, small rooms here are immaculate and cosy. This quiet minihotel is in a small alley off Đ Hung Vuong and is run by a friendly family.

Thien Tan Hotel (New Sky Hotel; Map p264; ☎ 816 455; newskyhotel@dng.vnn.vn; 78 Đ Hung Vuong; r US$7-18; ▨) Thien Tan offers up sparkly, comfortable and bright rooms. It's set back from the street a little and there's a small sitting area in the parking courtyard out front.

Phu Quy Mini-Hotel (Map p264; ☎ 810 609; phuquy hotel@dng.vnn.vn; 54 Đ Hung Vuong; r US$6-20; ▨ ▣) The best part about this minihotel is its rooftop terrace – it has awesome views and is great for dining or sunning. All rooms are quite comfortable, and the more expensive ones have tubs and balconies. The in-room safes here don't seem pilfer-proof, so consider leaving your valuables at reception.

Bang Khuong Hotel (Map p264; ☎ 813 516; 1 Đ Quan Tran; r US$6-10; ▨) Tucked into a quiet alley near the Chanh Quan Pagoda on Đ Hung Vuong, the Bang Khuong is central and offers all the usual comforts.

Sun Hotel (Map p264; ☎ 814 428; kshoangvan@dng .vnn.vn; 1 Đ Tran Quang Khai; r US$7-15; ﹗) Sun provides a welcoming reception, satellite TV and bathtubs in most rooms. It's a stone's throw away from the beach.

Thuan An Hotel (Map p264; ☎ 815 577; thuanan hotel@dng.vnn.vn; 1A Đ Tran Quang Khai; r US$5-12; ﹗ ▯) Close to the beach, this friendly place offers Internet access in the lobby. It was being remodelled at the time of research, so expect rates to be slightly higher than listed here.

Sao Mai Hotel (Map p264; ☎ 827 412; saomaiht@dng .vnn.vn; 99 Đ Nguyen Thien Thuat; dm US$2-3, r US$5-10; ﹗ ▩) With its pretty rooftop terrace adorned with potted plants, this is a good budget place with dorm accommodation. Rooms have hot water and TV.

Huu Nghi Hotel (Map p264; ☎ 826 703; huunghi hotel@dng.vnn.vn; 3 Đ Tran Hung Dao; r 140,000-270,000d; ﹗) A time-honoured backpackers haunt, Huu Nghi offers rooms with satellite TV; the older, cheery rooms outside are also comfortable, though bathrooms could be a bit cleaner. Breakfast will set you back an extra 10,000d.

Other reliable budget options:

Hotel Canary (Kim Tuoc; Map p264; ☎ 828 679; kimtuochotel@dng.vnn.vn; 27C Đ Hung Vuong; r 100,000-180,000d; ﹗) Nice place; has a lift.

Hotel O-Sin 2 (Map p264; ☎ 822 902; 15 Đ Hung Vuong; dm US$2, r US$4-20; ﹗ ▩) With a steady following among backpackers, the O-Sin 2 will soon have the added attractions of a swimming pool and small café.

My Long Hotel (Map p264; ☎ /fax 814 451; mylonghotel@yahoo.com; 26A Đ Nguyen Thien Thuat; r US$7-15; ﹗) Centrally located; a clean and friendly choice.

Yen Mai Hotel (Map p262; ☎ 815 589; fax 825 746; 98A Đ Tran Phu; r US$8-10; ﹗)

MID-RANGE

La Paloma Hotel (Map p262; ☎ 831 216; datle@dng .vnn.vn; 1 Đ Hon Chong; r US$10-25; ﹗ ▯) A commendable little family-run oasis on the northern outskirts of town, near the Hon Chong Promontory. Fronting the hotel is a pleasant outdoor dining area in a palm garden, where meals are served family-style. The friendly owner Mr Bu offers guests free 4WD shuttles to/from the train station and airport, as well as between the hotel and downtown. There's a small beach nearby with good local flavour.

Perfume Grass Inn (Map p264; ☎ 826 345; www .perfume-grass.com; 4A Đ Biet Thu; r US$10-25; ﹗ ▯)

The best rooms at this lovely inn have wood floors, wood-panelled walls, and bathtubs. Even the bright, comfortable US$10 far rooms have great sea views. The nice folk running the place offer Internet access in the breezy, open-air lobby. Breakfast is $ extra and there's a pleasant restaurant/ba downstairs.

La Suisse Hotel (Map p264; ☎ 524 353; lasuisse hotelnt@dng.vnn.vn; 34 Đ Tran Quang Khai; r US$15-30 ﹗ ▯) Down a quiet street, yet central and close to the beach, this sparkly new place is friendly and spotless. Room numbers ending in 01 boast gorgeous round wrought-iron balconies, but all rooms are pleasingly comfortable.

Truc Linh Villa Resort (Map p264; ☎ 820 089 Internet_bt@yahoo.com; 21 Đ Biet Thu; bungalows US$15- 25; ﹗) This appealing little stucco place has clean, bright rooms around a relaxing courtyard. The staff is attentive and the place boasts a central location.

Nha Trang Beach Hotel (Map p264; ☎ 524 468 nt_beachhotel@dng.vnn.vn; 4 Đ Tran Quang Khai; r US$12- 20; ﹗) Another relatively new spot on Đ Tran Quang Khai, Nha Trang Beach Hotel has a lift, cool granite lobby and echoing hallways. All rooms are twins, and breakfast is included.

Que Huong Hotel (Map p264; ☎ 825 047 quehuong60@dng.vnn.vn; 60 Đ Tran Phu; r US$50-100 ﹗ ▩) Boasting a swimming pool (which nonguests can use for US$1!) and tennis court, Que Huong looks a bit better on the outside than it does on the inside. There's a lift, and sitting areas on the shared terraces; the hotel is on the small, intimate side. Breakfast is included and some rooms have sea-view balconies.

Hai Yen Hotel (Map p264; ☎ 822 828; haiyen hotel@dng.vnn.vn; 40 Đ Tran Phu; r US$10-52; ﹗ ▩) Notable for its swimming pool and balcony sea views, the Hai Yen also has perks like a lift and tennis courts. All of the very spacious rooms have hot water, satellite TV and free breakfast. Villa rooms in the back have all-tile floors and small terraces, as well as a vaguely colonial feel.

Bao Dai's Villas (Map p262; ☎ 590 148; baodai@dng .vnn.vn; Cau Da village; r US$25-80; ﹗ ▯) Furthest from the town centre, Bao Dai's Villas are 6km south of the train station. The spacious top-end rooms are classic, with high ceilings, huge bathrooms and prime views of the bay, though are perhaps not worth the price tag. This is where Vietnam's ruling elite has rested itself since the days of French rule. There's a private beach below the hotel and two good restaurants, one with fine bay views. Credit cards are accepted and private boats do tours to nearby islands (also available to nonguests). Rates include breakfast.

Vien Dong Hotel (Map p264; ☎ 821 606; viendong htl@dng.vnn.vn; 1 Đ Tran Hung Dao; r 275,000-825,000d; ✗ 🖳 🔊) Long a travellers' favourite, this large old place has a swimming pool, lift, tennis courts, currency exchange, photo-processing facilities and bicycle rentals (US$5 per day). All red-carpeted rooms come with free breakfast.

Sea View Hotel (Map p264; ☎ 524 333; seaview hotel@dng.vnn.vn; 4B Đ Biet Thu; r US$12-15; ✗ 🔊) All rooms have balconies, fridge, TV, two beds and carved wooden furniture. This hotel has a lift and a swimming pool, and pricier rooms have – surprise! – sea views.

Rainbow Hotel (Map p264; ☎ 810 501; rainbow hotel@dng.vnn.vn; 10A Đ Biet Thu; r US$6-20; ✗) The Rainbow's pastel-green building is hard to miss. Near the beach, it has a lift and satellite TV. The cheapest rooms, windowless singles, are worth a miss. More-spacious rooms have wide balconies.

T78 Hotel (Map p264; ☎ 822 445; fax 825 395; 44 Đ Tran Phu; r 60,000-800,000d; ✗) Formerly the Grand and now named like a chemical compound, this big beachfront place is housed in a stately French colonial-style building. It recently had an underwhelming restoration job, and although the cheapest rooms are dismal, the upper-end ones are huge and high-ceilinged. With its deserted tennis courts and large driveway in front, the setup is slightly bizarre for a place with so much potential.

Hoan Hai Hotel (Map p262; ☎ 821 262; hoanhai 96tp@dng.vnn.vn; 96 Đ Tran Phu; r US$15-20; ✗) Squeaky-clean Hoan Hai offers satellite TV, a lift and minibars. All rooms are fairly spacious, and the more expensive rooms have sea views.

Dong Phuong 1 Hotel (Map p264; ☎ 825 986; dong phuongnt@dng.vnn.vn; 103 Đ Nguyen Thien Thuat; r in old wing US$6-10, in new wing US$10-30; ✗) The spacious rooms here feature the thickest mattresses in Nha Trang. The new-wing minihotel next door features a lift and sea views from the upper-floor rooms. It's clean

and the service is briskly efficient. Rooms have bathtubs, satellite TV and two beds. Air-con room rates include breakfast.

There's a strip of fine oceanfront mini-hotels along the southern part of Đ Tran Phu; some rooms feature balconies overlooking the sea. Worth checking out:
Seaside Hotel (Map p262; ☎ 821 178; fax 828 038; 96B Đ Tran Phu; r US$12-16; ✗) The slightly more upscale of the bunch, with red-carpeted halls, balconies, distinctive carved wooden furniture.
Thanh Thanh Hotel (Map p262; ☎ 824 657; thanhthanhhotel@dng.vnn.vn; 98A Đ Tran Phu; r US$10-20; ✗)
Linh Giang Hotel (Map p262; ☎ 816 454; linhgianghotelkh@dng.vnn.vn; 98A Đ Tran Phu; r US$15-20; ✗)

More mid-range possibilities:
Indochine Hotel (Map p264; ☎ 815 333; indochinehotel@yahoo.com; 14 Đ Hung Vuong; r US$12-25; ✗) With terrace and lift; credit cards accepted.
Dong Phuong 2 Hotel (Map p262; ☎ 814 580; dongphuong2@dng.vnn.vn; 96A Đ Tran Phu; r US$7-15; ✗) Big, blue, nicely basic rooms, quiet and set back from the main road.
Ban Me Hotel (Map p264; ☎ 829 500; fax 810 035; 3/3 Đ Tran Quang Khai; r 253,000-418,000d; ✗) A large place a few hundred metres from the beach.

TOP END
It's worth calling or emailing ahead to see if these top end places have promotions going; it's often possible to negotiate steep discounts.

Ana Mandara Resort (Map p262; ☎ 829 829; resvana@dng.vnn.vn; Đ Tran Phu; bungalows US$236-468; ✗ 🖳 🔊) A gorgeous complex of open timber-roofed beach villas south of town, this exquisite resort is hands-down Nha Trang's classiest accommodation offering. The décor is simple and elegant, and luxuries include two restaurants (one with 24-hour service), two swimming pools and a serene spa area offering beachfront massages and treatments. The sumptuous buffet breakfast is extra.

Nha Trang Lodge Hotel (Map p264; ☎ 810 500; www.nt-lodge.com; 42 Đ Tran Phu; r US$58-169; ✗ 🖳 🔊) With 13 floors, the Lodge is one of Nha Trang's tallest and fanciest high-rises. Views from upper floors are sweeping, taking in Đ Tran Phu and Nha Trang's long beach. A buffet breakfast is included. Nonguests can use the pool for 50,000d.

Customer service is not the hotel's strong suit, and the pricier rooms aren't worth the expense.

Yasaka 'Saigon Nha Trang Hotel (Map p264; ☎ 820 090; www.yasanhatrang.com; 18 Đ Tran Phu; r & ste US$113-403; ❈ ⚊) Another snazzy skyscraper, this hotel is a glitzy joint-venture between Saigon Tourist and the Japanese. Facilities include a health club and swimming pool. The posh suites have sitting rooms, office space, a full bathroom and another separate toilet.

Sunrise Beach Resort (Map p264; ☎ 820 999; www .sunrisebeachresortnhatrang.com; 12 Đ Tran Phu; r & ste US$147-573; ❈ ⚊) This behemoth was under construction when we visited, but it's slated to be a five-star resort with business facilities, swimming pool, several international restaurants and prime beachfront real estate.

Eating

Nha Trang is naturally a seafood haven and there's a wide variety of excellent eateries. If you've been enjoying the fresh baguettes in Vietnam, you're in for a treat – Nha Trang has its own unique variety of French bread, a heavier loaf that is closer in consistency (and taste) to a New York City hot pretzel. Proud locals say the bread is more filling for Nha Trang's hard-working fishermen.

VIETNAMESE

Dua Xanh Restaurant (Map p264; ☎ 823 687; fax 821 880; 189 Đ Nguyen Binh Khiem; mains 35,000d) A pleasant spot with many seafood dishes, Dua Xanh (Green Coconut) has outdoor garden tables in addition to its indoor dining room. Leave room for dessert. The owner speaks English and French.

Truc Linh (Map p264; ☎ 820 089; 21 Đ Biet Thu; mains 20,000-100,000d) Popular and festive, Truc Linh has a garden setting and indoor-outdoor seating. In the evening you can choose fresh seafood from a table in front of the restaurant and enjoy a beer while you wait.

Lac Canh Restaurant (Map p264; ☎ 821 391; 44 Đ Nguyen Binh Khiem; mains 35,000d) A Nha Trang institution, Lac Canh is one of the busiest local eateries in town. Here, on the street level or upstairs, beef, squid, giant shrimps, lobsters and the like are grilled right at your table.

Cyclo Café (Map p264; ☎ 524 208; khuongthuy@ hotmail.com; 5A Đ Tran Quang Khai; mains 30,000d) Run by a local couple with years of experience in the restaurant business, the Cyclo Café has an intimate atmosphere, excellent Vietnamese and Italian dishes, great service and pleasing décor.

Red Star (Map p264; ☎ 812 790; 14 Đ Biet Thu; mains 25,000d) This no-frills place serves excellent seafood. Try the crab or clams with ginger, lemongrass and chilli, or the fish hotpot.

Cafe des Amis (Map p264; ☎ 813 009; 2D Đ Biet Thu; mains 25,000d) A popular spot with good vegetarian fare. The walls here are covered with an interesting collection of works by Vietnamese painters.

Then there's **Dam Market** (Map p264), which has a colourful collection of stalls in the covered semicircular food pavilion.

INTERNATIONAL

Nha Trang Sailing Club (Map p264; mains 50,000-90,000d) One of the most popular hangouts in Nha Trang, the Sailing Club serves a variety of cuisines from Vietnamese and European to Indian and Japanese. It has a wide terrace on the beach – good for people-watching during the day and ocean breezes at night.

El Coyote (Map p264; ☎ 820 202; coyote-nt@caramail .com; 76 Đ Hung Vuong; mains 40,000-60,000d) This Coyote does authentic Tex-Mex food like chilli con carne and *pato con coca* (duck leg with Coca-Cola sauce). The owner has perhaps the most curious ethnic roots in town: he's a mixture of French, Vietnamese, Lao and Cheyenne Indian.

Good Morning Vietnam (Map p264; ☎ 815 071; 19B Đ Biet Thu; mains 20,000-50,000d) The Nha Trang branch of this Italian-run chain does good and reasonably priced pizza, pasta and salads, plus a bit of Thai and Vietnamese to spice things up. Upstairs you can kick back on cosy Thai cushions to eat or watch movies (shown at 5pm and 8pm).

7C Biergarten (Map p264; ☎ 828 243; 7C Đ Le Loi; mains 20,000-25,000d) This is *the* place to head if you're craving an authentic German sausage. This expat-run place serves up excellent bratwurst and schnitzel, plus home-baked brown bread. Prices are reasonable: the good local Viet Duc beer is on tap for 12,000d.

La Bella Napoli (Map p264; ☎ 829 621; labellanapol iviet@hotmail.com; Đ Tran Phu; mains 60,000d) Congenial owners Marinella and Gigi specialise in home-cooked southern Italian dishes and great brick-oven pizzas; they make their own mozzarella and gnocchi. Inquire a day ahead about their special fish dishes (the sea bass cooked in salt crust is divine!).

Thanh Thanh Cafe (Map p264; ☎ 824 413; 10 Đ Nguyen Thien Thuat; food 30,000d) A travellers' café serving pizza, Vietnamese dishes and other standard backpacker fare, Thanh Thanh has a pretty terracotta patio surrounded by plants. And if you feel like staying in, deliveries can be made.

Same Same But Different Café (Map p264; ☎ 524 079; ssbdcafé@yahoo.com; 111B Đ Nguyen Thien Thuat; mains 30,000d) Another good travellers' café run by cool people, this place serves Vietnamese and Western food (including vegie dishes and tasty muesli for breakfast) at reasonable prices.

Candle Light Cafe (Map p264; ☎ 813 133; candlelightcafé2001@yahoo.com; 6 Đ Tran Quang Khai; mains 30,000d) Last but not least is this place that serves decent Vietnamese and international-style food.

CAFÉS

La Louisiane (Map p264; ☎ 812 948; fax 821 977; 29 Đ Tran Phu; ⏰ 7.30am-midnight; 🏊) This attractive beachfront bar/café has been done in a stylish Mediterranean blue motif. Guests can indulge themselves in the use of the swimming pool and beach chairs here in exchange for patronising the restaurant, bakery or bar. The cakes and pastries (10,000d) are superb.

4 Seasons Café (Map p264; ☎ 825 229; 40 Đ Tran Phu) If you're on this end of the beach, the simple 4 Seasons (across from Hai Yen Hotel) is a good place to have some coffee or a reasonably priced light meal. It even has beach chairs and thatched umbrellas on the quiet, clean stretch of beach in front.

Banana Split Cafés (Map p264; 58 & 60 Đ Ly Thanh Ton) For some great ice cream, try one of the remarkable little Banana Split Cafés near the roundabout where Đ Quang Trung meets Đ Ly Thanh Ton. Both are long-time rivals, evidenced by their strong-arm tactics for luring customers inside.

OTHER ASIAN

Omar's (Map p262; ☎ 814 489; omarnewdelhi@yahoo.com; 96A/8 Đ Tran Phu; meals 60,000d) The best Indian food in Nha Trang.

Bombay (Map p264; ☎ 812 557; 15 Đ Biet Thu) and **Chau Café** (Map p264; ☎ 826 336; chaucafé@hotmail.com; 42 Đ Hung Vuong; mains 30,000d) also do good Indian food that's worth a try.

VEGETARIAN

Two places serving excellent vegetarian food are **Au Lac** (Map p264; ☎ 813 946; 28C Đ Hoang Hoa Tham) and **Bo De** (Map p264; ☎ 810 116; 28A Đ Hoang Hoa Tham), neighbouring restaurants near the corner of Đ Nguyen Chanh.

Vegetarian food (com chay) can also be found at Dam Market.

Drinking

Guava (Map p264; ☎ 524 140; www.clubnhatrang.com; 17 Đ Biet Thu; cocktail specials 15,000-25,000d) Cool, clean-lined and atmospheric, this lounge bar is run by a trio of hip Canadians. Outside is a yellow-walled patio shaded with trees; inside, pillow-laden sofas and chairs furnish the bar. There's a pool table and several TVs for watching major sports events. And the substantial 'hangover breakfasts' are conveniently served all day.

Jack's Bar (Map p262; ☎ 813 862; 96A/8 Đ Tran Phu; bar food 10,000-30,000d) This is a fine place to get the night started. Run by a congenial young Brit named, you guessed it, Jack, the bar boasts a roof terrace overlooking Nha Trang Bay, two pool tables, good music and cheap cold beer (happy hour is from 6pm until 10pm). A full menu is offered from 8am to 10pm.

Crazy Kim Bar (Map p264; ☎ 816 072; crazykim99@hotmail.com; 19 Đ Biet Thu) This cool pub is run by a Vietnamese-Canadian woman named Kimmy, and is a vehicle for her commendable 'Hands off the Kids!' campaign, which works to thwart the growing problem of paedophilia in Nha Trang. Part of the proceeds from the food, booze and T-shirt sales go towards the cause. Sign up at the bar if you're interested in volunteering to teach English to local street kids (10.30am to 11.30am).

Nha Trang Sailing Club (Map p264; ☎ 826 528; 72 Đ Tran Phu) A very popular, Aussie-run, open-air beach bar where most of the hard-core party crowd ends up at some point in the evening. It's best known for thumping music, wild dancing, flowing shots, pool and general mayhem. You can escape the madness (sort of) outside on the large beachside terrace.

Shorty's Cafe & Bar (☎ 810 985; 45 Đ Biet Thu) There's a pool table here, and a small terrace out front; it's also got a book exchange if you're in need of a new read.

Cool Kangaroo (Map p264; ☎ 826 520; 17C Đ Hung Vuong) In addition to serving good Australian food and cold beer, this friendly bar shows free movies in the evening.

Entertainment

Hexagone Disco (Map p262; ☎ /fax 826 782; Huong Duong Centre, Đ Tran Phu; ☼ 8pm-midnight) This is a long running dance spot right on the beach near the Ana Mandara Resort.

Vien Dong Hotel (Map p264; ☼ shows 7.30pm) Free ethnic-minority song and dance performances are held here nightly.

Shopping

Along with Hanoi, HCMC and Hoi An, Nha Trang has emerged as a reasonable place to look for art. Though actual galleries are scant, there are several local painters and photographers who display their work on the walls of Nha Trang's resorts, restaurants, cafés and bars.

Bambou Company (Map p264; ☎ 910 774; bambou-company@hotmail.com; 15 Đ Biet Thu) Run by a French expat, Bambou Company produces high-quality T-shirts (75,000d to 100,000d) featuring cool original designs.

XQ Nha Trang Arts & Crafts Centre (Map p264; ☎ 826 879; www.xqhandembroidery.com; 64 Đ Tran Phu; ☼ 8am-8pm) You can watch the artisans at work at this embroidery workshop and gallery, where intricate embroidery 'paintings' are painstakingly worked by hand.

Also worth checking out are the handpainted T-shirts done by a friendly local painter named **Kim Quang** (☎ 0913-416 513). Quang works every night from his wheelchair at the Nha Trang Sailing Club (p275).

Hung Hara Photo Lab (Map p264; ☎ 828 030; 2C Đ Biet Thu) is a reliable local photo lab.

Getting There & Away

AIR

There are regular flights by **Vietnam Airlines** (Map p264; ☎ 826 768; fax 825 956; 91 Đ Nguyen Thien Thuat) connecting Nha Trang with HCMC, Hanoi and Danang. See p475 for more information on flights.

There's another **branch** of Vietnam Airlines (Map p264; ☎ 822 753; ☼ 7-11.30am & 1.30-5pm) at 1 Đ Tran Hung Dao.

BUS

Express and regular buses (p477) depart from Mien Dong bus station in HCMC to Nha Trang. The express bus trip takes 11 to 12 hours and costs around US$7.

Lien Tinh bus station (Ben Xe Lien Tinh; ☎ 822 192; Đ 23 Thang 10) is Nha Trang's main intercity bus terminal, and is 500m west of the train station. The short-haul bus station is for local routes only.

CAR & MOTORBIKE

Road distances from Nha Trang are: 205km to Buon Ma Thuot, 541km to Danang, 448km to HCMC, 104km to Phan Rang, 424km to Pleiku, 412km to Quang Ngai and 238km to Quy Nhon.

A series of roughly parallel roads heads inland from near Nha Trang, linking Vietnam's deltas and coastal regions with the central highlands.

MINIBUS

The preferred option, chartered minibuses are easy to book at most places where travellers congregate.

TRAIN

Hotels and travellers cafés all book train tickets, and it's worth paying the small commission to use these booking services.

The **Nha Trang train station** (Ga Nha Trang; ☎ 822 113; opposite 26 Đ Thai Nguyen; ☼ ticket office 7am-2pm) is overlooked by the nearby cathedral.

Nha Trang is well served by express trains connecting Hanoi and HCMC, and a daily local train between HCMC and Nha Trang; see p483 for more information.

Getting Around

TO/FROM THE AIRPORT

The airport is on the southern side of town and is so close to many of the hotels that you can actually walk.

Cyclos can get you to the airport for about US$1. They're good for around town, but limit your *cyclo* riding to the daytime.

Nha Trang Taxi (☎ 824 000) and **Khanh Hoa Taxi** (☎ 810 810) have air-con cars with meters.

BICYCLE

Most major hotels have bicycle rentals. The cost is around US$1 per day.

AROUND NHA TRANG
Dien Khanh Citadel

This **citadel** dates from the 17th-century Trinh dynasty. It was rebuilt by Prince Nguyen Anh (later Emperor Gia Long) in 1793 during his successful offensive against the Tay Son Rebels. Only a few sections of the walls and gates are extant. Dien Khanh Citadel is 11km west of Nha Trang near the villages of Dien Toan and Dien Khanh.

Ba Ho Falls

The three waterfalls and pools at **Ba Ho Falls** (Suoi Ba Ho) are in a forested area about 20km north of Nha Trang and about 2km west of Phu Huu village. Turn off Hwy 1 just north of Quyen restaurant.

Fairy Spring

The enchanting little spring seems to pop out of nowhere as you approach it. Like a small oasis, the **Fairy Spring** (Suoi Tien) is decorated with its own natural garden of tropical vegetation and smooth boulders.

You'll need to rent a motorbike or car to reach the spring. Driving south on Hwy 1, you come to a spot 17km from Nha Trang where there is a signpost to your left (the east side of the highway). Turn off the highway here and go through the village. The road twists and winds its way for 8km through the hills until it reaches a valley. Just as the road starts to get bad, you come upon the spring. You'll probably see some other vehicles parked here as it's a popular spot with locals.

PHAN RANG & THAP CHAM

☎ 068 / pop 143,700

The twin cities of Phan Rang and Thap Cham, which are famous for their production of table grapes, are in a semiarid region. The sandy soil supports scrubby vegetation; local flora includes poinciana trees and prickly-pear cacti with vicious thorns. Many of the houses on the outskirts of town are decorated with Greek-style grape trellises.

Also worth sampling in this area is the green dragon fruit *(thanh long)*. The mild, kiwi-like taste of this juicy fruit is especially refreshing when chilled. You'll find it in the Phan Rang market, or in grocery shops along Đ Thong Nhat.

The area's best-known sight (and a common stop on the Dalat–Nha Trang route) is the group of Cham towers known as Po Klong Garai (p278), from which Thap Cham (Cham Tower) derives its name.

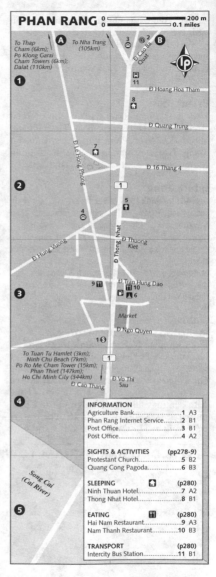

PHAN RANG

To Thap Cham (6km); Po Klong Garai Cham Towers (6km); Dalat (110km)

To Nha Trang (105km)

Đ Cảo Bá Quát

Đ Hoang Hoa Tham

Đ Quang Trung

Đ Le Hong Phong

Đ 16 Thang 4

Đ Thong Nhat

Đ Thuong Kiet

Đ Hung Vuong

Đ Trần Hung Đao

Market

Đ Ngo Quyen

To Tuan Tu Hamlet (3km); Ninh Chu Beach (7km); Po Ro Me Cham Tower (15km); Phan Thiet (147km); Ho Chi Minh City (344km)

Đ Cao Thang

Đ Vo Thi Sau

Song Cai (Cai River)

INFORMATION	
Agriculture Bank	1 A3
Phan Rang Internet Service	2 B1
Post Office	3 B1
Post Office	4 A2

SIGHTS & ACTIVITIES	(pp278-9)
Protestant Church	5 B2
Quang Cong Pagoda	6 B3

SLEEPING	(p280)
Ninh Thuan Hotel	7 A2
Thong Nhat Hotel	8 B1

EATING	(p280)
Hai Nam Restaurant	9 A3
Nam Thanh Restaurant	10 B3

TRANSPORT	(p280)
Intercity Bus Station	11 B1

You can see Cham towers dotted about the countryside 20km north of Phan Rang.

Ninh Thuan province is home to tens of thousands of descendants of the Cham people, many of whom live in and around Phan Rang and Thap Cham. There are also 3000 or 4000 Chinese descendants in the area, many of whom come to worship at the

135-year old Chua Quang Cong, a colourful Chinese temple in the town centre.

Phan Rang and Thap Cham are a good base for visiting the local sights; nearby Ninh Chu Beach (p280) is another, quieter alternative.

Orientation

Hwy 1 is Phan Rang's main commercial street (called Đ Thong Nhat). Thap Cham, about 7km from Phan Rang, is strung out along Hwy 20, which heads west from Phan Rang towards Ninh Son and Dalat.

Information

Agriculture Bank (☎ 824 619; fax 822 716; 540-544 Đ Thong Nhat; ☺ Mon-Fri) Exchanges currency.

Internet service (ttbttbth@ninhthuanpt.com.vn; 6 Đ Nguyen Van Troi; per min 500d; ☺ 7am-5pm Mon-Fri) The post office's Internet service is available just up the street.

Main post office (☎ 824 430; 217A Đ Thong Nhat) In the north of town at the corner of Đ Thong Nhat and Đ Nguyen Van Troi.

Sights

PO KLONG GARAI CHAM TOWERS

Phan Rang and Thap Cham's most famous landmark is **Po Klong Garai** (Map below; admission 5000d; ☺ 7.30am-6pm), also known as Po Klong Girai – *girai* means 'dragon'. The four brick towers were constructed at the end of the 13th century, during the reign of the Cham monarch Jaya Simhavarman III. The towers were built as Hindu temples and stand on a brick platform at the top of Cho'k Hala, a crumbly granite hill covered with some of the most ornery cacti this side of the Rio Grande.

Over the entrance to the largest tower (the *kalan*, or sanctuary) is a carving of a **dancing Shiva** with six arms. This bas-relief is known locally as Po Klaun Tri – the Guardian of the Temple Tower – and is famous for its beauty. Note the inscriptions in the ancient Cham language on the doorposts. These tell of past restoration efforts and offerings of sacrifices and slaves made to the temple towers.

Inside the vestibule is a statue of the bull Nandin (also known as the Kapil Ox), symbol of the agricultural productivity of the countryside. To ensure a good crop, farmers would place an offering of fresh greens, herbs and areca nuts in front of Nandin's muzzle.

Under the main tower is a *mukha-linga*, a *linga* with a human face painted on it. A wooden pyramid has been constructed above the *mukha-linga*.

Inside the tower, opposite the entrance to the sanctuary, you can get a good look at some of the Chams' sophisticated building technology; the wooden columns that support the lightweight roof are visible. The structure attached to it was originally the main entrance to the complex.

On a nearby hill is a rock with an inscription from the year 1050, commemorating the erection of a *linga* by a Cham prince.

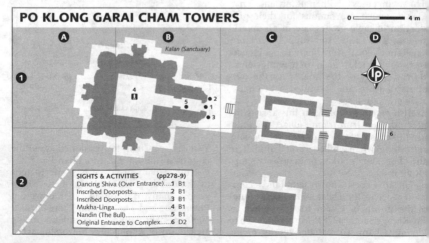

PO KLONG GARAI CHAM TOWERS

0 —— 4 m

Kalan (Sanctuary)

SIGHTS & ACTIVITIES	(pp278-9)
Dancing Shiva (Over Entrance)....**1**	B1
Inscribed Doorposts....................**2**	B1
Inscribed Doorposts....................**3**	B1
Mukha-Linga...............................**4**	B1
Nandin (The Bull)........................**5**	B1
Original Entrance to Complex......**6**	D2

CHAM NEW YEAR

The Cham New Year *(kate)* is celebrated at the towers in the seventh month of the Cham calendar (around October in the Gregorian calendar). The festival commemorates ancestors, Cham national heroes and deities such as the goddess Po Ino Nagar, who assisted the Chams with their farming.

On the eve of the festival, a procession guarded by the mountain people of Tay Nguyen carries King Po Klong Garai's clothing to the accompaniment of traditional music. The procession lasts until midnight. The following morning the garments are carried to the tower, once again accompanied by music, along with banners, flags, singing and dancing. Notables, dignitaries and village elders follow behind. This colourful ceremony continues into the afternoon.

The celebrations then carry on for the rest of the month, as the Cham attend parties and visit friends and relatives. They also use this time to pray for good fortune.

On the hill directly south of Cho'k Hala is a concrete water tank built by the Americans in 1965. It is encircled by French pillboxes built during the Franco–Viet Minh War to protect the nearby rail yards. To the north of Cho'k Hala, you can see the concrete revetments of Thanh Son Airbase, used since 1975 by the Vietnamese Air Force.

Po Klong Garai is several hundred metres north of Hwy 20, at a point 6km west of Phan Rang towards Dalat. The towers are on the opposite side of the tracks to Thap Cham train station. If you're travelling between Dalat and Nha Trang or Mui Ne Beach, you will pass the site. Most of the open-tour buses shuttling people between Dalat and the coast make a requisite pit stop here.

PO RO ME CHAM TOWER

Among the newest of Vietnam's Cham towers, **Po Ro Me Cham Tower** (Thap Po Ro Me) is about 15km south of Phan Rang on a rocky hill 5km west of Hwy 1. The ruins are very interesting, but are also difficult to reach and your own motorbike or a *xe om* is required. The trip is guaranteed to be worthwhile as long as getting lost is a part of your agenda.

The sanctuary, which is decorated with numerous paintings and occupied by bats, has two inscribed doorposts; two stone statues of the bull Nandin; a bas-relief representing a deified king in the form of Shiva; and two statues of queens, one of whom has an inscription on her chest. The towers are named after the last ruler of an independent Champa, King Po Ro Me (r. 1629–51), who died as a prisoner of the Vietnamese.

To get here, take Hwy 1 south from Phan Rang, about 1km into the town of Phuoc Dan. A narrow sealed road just after the Petrolimex (petrol) station on the right takes you to a T-junction, where you should turn left. Stay on the road meandering through a dusty village, and you'll see the towers ahead. A sign at the base of a hill points the way towards the last 500m. This dirt track may be negotiable on a motorbike, but it is deeply rutted, and studded with rocks and cacti.

If you're lucky, the Cham caretaker of the ruins, Mr Truong Dai Tho, will be around to hike up the steps and unlock the temple door for you. The temple affords a wonderful view of the surrounding countryside and is blessedly quiet.

TUAN TU HAMLET

There is a minaret-less Cham mosque, closed to visitors, in the Cham hamlet of Tuan Tu (population 1000). This Muslim community is governed by elected religious leaders (Thay Mun), who can easily be identified by their traditional costume, which includes a white robe and an elaborate white turban with red tassels. In keeping with Islamic precepts governing modesty, Cham women often wear head coverings and skirts. The Cham, like the other ethnic minorities in Vietnam, suffer from discrimination and are even poorer than their ethnic-Vietnamese neighbours.

To get to Tuan Tu Hamlet, head south from Phan Rang along Hwy 1. Go 250m south of the large bridge to a small bridge. Cross it and turn left (to the southeast) onto Đ Tran Nhat Duat, a dirt track. At the Buddhist pagoda on the right, turn right and follow the road – part of which is lined with cacti – for about 2km, crossing a white concrete footbridge. Tuan Tu is 3km from Hwy 1.

CAM RANH BAY

The gorgeous natural harbour of Cam Ranh Bay is 56km north of Phan Rang and Thap Cham, in Khanh Hoa province. The strategic naval base here has long been considered one of Asia's prime deep-water anchorages.

The Russian fleet of Admiral Rodjestvenski used it in 1905 at the end of the Russo-Japanese War, as did the Japanese during WWII, when the area was still considered an excellent place for tiger hunting. In the mid-1960s, the Americans constructed a vast base here, including an extensive port, ship-repair facilities and an airstrip.

After reunification the Russians and their fleet came back, enjoying far better facilities than they had found seven decades before. For a while this became the largest Soviet naval installation outside the USSR. With the collapse of the Soviet Union in 1991 and the end of the Cold War, economic problems forced the Russians to cut back vastly on their overseas military facilities. Although the initial contract for Cam Ranh Bay was due to expire in 2004, the Russian military agreed to vacate their position, the last hurrah for the Russian navy in Asia, by the end of 2002.

Though plans for the bay were in limbo for several years, an international airport is now in the works for Cam Ranh Bay to help serve the beach resort town of Nha Trang. It also appears that the bay – with its beautiful beaches and gorgeous harbour – will be developed and promoted as a tourist destination in its own right. Stay tuned.

Sleeping

Ninh Thuan Hotel (☎ 827 100; fax 822 142; 1 Đ Le Hong Phong; r US$22-35; ✷) A pleasant place with satellite TV, this hotel is on the north side of town, opposite a small park.

Thong Nhat Hotel (☎ 827 201; thongnhathotel _pr@hcm.vnn.vn; 343 Đ Thong Nhat; r US$15-32; ✷) All rooms at this friendly and comfortable place have bathtubs, satellite TV and minibars. Rates include breakfast.

Eating

One of the local delicacies here is roasted or baked gecko (ky nhong), served with fresh green mango. If you prefer self-catering and have fast reflexes, you could consider catching your own gecko from the ceiling in your hotel room!

Some good, centrally located places to eat Vietnamese dishes include **Hai Nam** (meals around 20,000d) and **Nam Thanh** (meals around 20,000d).

Phan Rang is the grape capital of Vietnam. Stalls in the market sell fresh grapes, grape juice and dried grapes (too juicy to be called raisins).

Getting There & Away
BUS

Buses from HCMC to Phan Rang and Thap Cham depart from Mien Dong bus station.

Phan Rang intercity bus station (Ben Xe Phan Rang; opposite 64 Đ Thong Nhat) is on the northern outskirts of town.

The **local bus station** (opposite 426 Đ Thong Nhat) is at the southern end of town.

CAR & MOTORBIKE

Phan Rang is about 344km from HCMC, 147km from Phan Thiet, 105km from Nha Trang and 110km from Dalat.

TRAIN

The Thap Cham train station is about 6km west of Hwy 1, within sight of Po Klong Garai Cham towers.

NINH CHU BEACH
☎ 068

South of Phan Rang, Ninh Chu Beach (Bai Tam Ninh Chu) has a decent beach and a few places to stay. It makes a pleasant alternative to Phan Rang as a base for visiting the local Cham ruins.

Sleeping & Eating

Den Gion Resort (☎ 874 223; dongthuantourist@hcm .vnn.vn; r 220,000-600,000d, camping per person 30,000d; ✷ 🖳) The upper-end rooms are on the small side, but have lovely details like glassed-in showers and wooden ceiling fans. There's even dome-tent camping near the beach. There's an on-site, open-air restaurant (mains 30,000d), and the place is nicely landscaped with flowers and small wooden footbridges.

Hoan Cau Resort (☎ 890 077; dlhoancaunt@hcm .vnn.vn; r 160,000-180,000d; ✷) If you're into theme parks, stay at Hoan Cau, where the bunga-lows are built to resemble squat treehouses. The rooms are comfortable, with TV, tele-phone and hot water, but even better are the odd Disney-meets-Vietnamese-folklore plaster statues adorning the grounds. There's a restaurant (mains around 25,000d) near re-ception, and a **water park** (adult/child 10,000/5000d) next door.

Ninh Chu Hotel (☎ 873 900; ninhchuhotel@hcm .vnn.vn; r US$20-45; ❄) This government-run place is in decent shape, has all the usual amenities and is on the beachfront; how-ever, the rates seem a bit inflated. There's also a restaurant here.

Getting There & Away
Ninh Chu Beach is about 7km south of Phan Rang, off Hwy 1. Unless you're driv-ing yourself, it's probably easiest to arrive here via *xe om* (30,000d).

CA NA
☎ 068
During the 16th century, princes of the Cham royal family would fish and hunt tigers, elephants and rhinoceroses here. Today Ca Na is better known for its white-sand beaches dotted with huge granite bould-ers – it's a beautiful spot, but it's tough to ignore the rumble of trucks drifting over from nearby Hwy 1. You're probably bet-ter off continuing south to Mui Ne Beach (p283) or north to Nha Trang (p261).

The terrain is studded with magnificent prickly-pear cacti. A small pagoda on the hillside makes for an interesting, but steep, climb over the boulders (see 'Lizard Fish-ing', below).

Rau Cau Island is visible offshore, and there is a well-outfitted scuba-diving centre a few

kilometres south of Ca Na in Vinh Hao (below).

Further afield, **Tra Cang Temple** is about midway between Ca Na and Phan Rang. Unfortunately, you have to sidetrack over an abysmal dirt road in order to reach it. Many ethnic Chinese from Cholon visit the temple.

Sleeping & Eating
Ca Na Hotel (☎ /fax 861 320; r 150,000-180,000d) This place rents crusty rooms in an ancient ferro-concrete hotel near the highway; the quieter beach bungalows are a better choice.

Haison Hotel (☎ 861 312; fax 861 339; r US$15; ❄) A decent motel-style place, across from the Lac Son Pagoda but also close to the highway.

Both hotels have restaurants that are popular lunch spots on the HCMC–Nha Trang route.

Getting There & Away
Ca Na is 114km north of Phan Thiet and 32km south of Phan Rang. Many long-haul buses cruising Hwy 1 can drop you here. No train service is available.

VINH HAO
☎ 062
Vinh Hao is an obscure town just off Hwy 1 between Phan Thiet and Phan Rang. The town's claim to fame is its celebrated min-eral waters, which are bottled and sold all over Vietnam. If you spend any length of time in the country, you are almost certain to sip water from a bottle of Vinh Hao.

Diving
Vietnam Scuba (☎ 853 919, in HCMC ☎ 08-925 4301; fax 853 918; www.vietnamscuba.com) This is an

---

LIZARD FISHING

When most people think of fishing in the mountains they conjure up images of hooking river trout or lake bass. But in the arid foothills of the south-central coast (notably around places like Ca Na, Phan Rang, Phan Thiet and Mui Ne) there is whole other kind of angling, and a walk in these hills can yield one of the strangest sights in Vietnam – lizard fishing!

These lizards, called *than lan nui*, are members of the gecko family and good for eating – some say they taste like chicken. The traditional way of catching the lizards is by setting a hook on a long bamboo fishing pole and dangling bait from the top of a boulder until the spunky little reptiles strike.

In local restaurants lizards could be served grilled, roasted or fried, and are often made up into a paté (complete with their finely chopped bones) and used as a dip for rice-paper crackers. Yum.

attractive and well-appointed Korean-run dive centre on a private beach about 3.5km south of Ca Na. The resort is simple to spot on the sea side of Hwy 1.

Vietnam Scuba is very much a by-Koreans for-Koreans resort, but serious scuba divers (and *kimchi* lovers) will appreciate the setup and some of the best diving in Vietnam. Marine life includes big fish, manta rays, barracuda and sharks.

Daily dive packages (US$130, nondivers US$50) include accommodation in nice beachfront villas, boat trips and guides, and three meals a day. A BC and regulator can be rented for an extra US$50 a day. All dive sites are offshore, anywhere from 30 to 90 minutes from the resort's private jetty.

PHAN THIET
☎ 062 / pop 168,400

Although Phan Thiet is traditionally known for its fish sauce *(nuoc mam)*, tourism is playing an increasingly larger role in the local economy today. The population includes descendants of the Cham, who controlled this area until 1692. During the colonial period, the Europeans lived in their own segregated ghetto stretching along the northern bank of the Phan Thiet River, while the Vietnamese, Cham, Southern Chinese, Malays and Indonesians lived along the southern bank.

Besides the excellent golfing and a relatively nice beach, there is little to do in Phan Thiet itself. Most travellers head for nearby Mui Ne Beach (p283), 11km away.

Orientation & Information

Phan Thiet is built along both banks of the Phan Thiet River, which is also known as the Ca Ti River and the Muong Man River. Hwy 1 runs right through town; south of the river it is known as Đ Tran Hung Dao, while north of the river it is called Đ Le Hong Phong.

Stop by **Binh Thuan Tourist** (☎ 816 821; www .binhthuantourist.com; 82 Đ Trung Trac; ☽ 7-11am & 1.30-5pm Mon-Fri, 8-10.30am Sat & Sun). This agency can arrange transport and also has tourist maps of Phan Thiet.

Sights & Activities
PHAN THIET BEACH

To get to Phan Thiet's **beachfront**, turn east at Victory Monument, an arrow-shaped con-

crete tower with victorious cement people at the base.

FISHING HARBOUR

The river flowing through the centre of town creates a small fishing **harbour**, which is always chock-a-block with boats. It makes for charming photos.

GOLF

The **Ocean Dunes Golf Club** (☎ 823 366; odgc@hcm .vnn.vn; 1 Đ Ton Duc Thang) is a top-notch 18-hole golf course near the beachfront at the Novotel (below).

To drum up business, very reasonably priced golf package tours are available if you book from HCMC. Per-golfer deals are as inexpensive as US$76/82 on weekdays/ weekends, including one round of golf, a night at the stylish Novotel and breakfast. There is a minibus shuttle service between the golf course and HCMC.

For information, contact the resort's HCMC **marketing office** (☎ 08-824 3460; www .vietnamgolfresorts.com; New World Hotel, 76 Đ Le Lai).

Sleeping

Unless you're bypassing Mui Ne Beach and just looking for a place to sleep (or play golf), don't bother staying in Phan Thiet. Much better deals can be found in Mui Ne.

Thanh Cong Hotel (☎ 825 016; fax 823 905; 49-51 Đ Tran Hung Dao; r 70,000-225,000d; ✽) This is a good budget minihotel conveniently located near Hwy 1 and the bus station.

Binh Minh Hotel (☎ 823 344; fax 823 354; 405 Đ Vo Thi Sau; r 135,000-225,000d; ✽) The clean Binh Minh is right across the street from cafés and food vendors along the palm-lined beachfront.

Novotel Coralia Ocean Dunes & Golf Resort (☎ 822 393; novpht@hcm.vnn.vn; 1 Đ Ton Tuc Thang; r US$127-194; ✽ ⊠) A luxurious option for golfers. Facilities include a golf course, several restaurants, a swimming pool, a private beach, tennis courts and a fitness centre. Rack rates are usually heavily discounted.

Eating

Hoang Yen Restaurant (☎ 821 614; 51 Đ Tran Hung Dao) is a good eatery about midway through Phan Thiet. It's popular with tour groups passing through town. Ask here about bicycle rental if you're thinking of heading out to Mui Ne Beach (opposite).

Getting There & Around

BUS

The buses from HCMC to Phan Thiet depart from Mien Dong bus station.

Phan Thiet bus station (Ben Xe Binh Thuan; Đ Tu Van Tu; 5.30am-3.30pm) is on the northern outskirts of town, just past 217 Đ Le Hong Phong (Hwy 1).

CAR & MOTORBIKE

Phan Thiet is on Hwy 1, 198km east of HCMC, 250km from Nha Trang and 247km from Dalat.

When driving, be careful of the fish-sauce trucks – hit one of these and the odour may follow you for life.

TRAIN

The nearest train station to Phan Thiet is 12km west of town in dusty little Muong Man. The *Reunification Express* train between Hanoi and HCMC stops here.

MUI NE BEACH

☎ 062

Peaceful Mui Ne Beach is a long and beautiful stretch of white sand 22km east of Phan Thiet on Route 706, near a fishing village at the tip of Mui Ne Peninsula. It's a lovely spot with swaying palm trees, and for traffic-weary travellers and residents of HCMC, Mui Ne offers a relaxed and welcome change of pace.

Mui Ne sees only about half the rainfall of nearby Phan Thiet. The sand dunes help protect Mui Ne's unique microclimate, and even during the wet season (from June to September) rains tend to be fairly light and sporadic.

There is no scuba diving in Mui Ne, but when Nha Trang and Hoi An get the rains, Mui Ne gets the waves. Surf's up from August to December. For windsurfers, the gales howl as well, especially from late October to late April, when swells stir over from the Philippine typhoons.

Orientation

A narrow palm-lined road runs for about 10km along the Mui Ne seafront. Local addresses are designated by a kilometre mark measuring the distance along Rte 706 from Hwy 1 in Phan Thiet; Route 706 is also sometimes referred to as Đ Nguyen Dinh Chieu.

Information

Hanh Cafe/Ha Phuong Tourist (☎ 847 347; km13) caters mainly to backpackers, with cheap transportation, fast food and Internet access. There's a similar setup just down the road at **TM Brothers Cafe** (☎ 847 359; km13). If you arrive by open tour it's likely you'll be delivered to one of these places.

You can also find Internet access at **Happy Café** (☎ 847 561; km19) and Coco Café, near Hiep Hoa Tourism on the hill side of the highway.

At the Tropico Resort, a branch of **Incombank** (68 Đ Nguyen Dinh Chieu; Sun-Fri) can exchange currency and travellers cheques.

Sights

Mui Ne is famous for its enormous **sand dunes**. These have been a favourite subject matter for many a Vietnamese photographer, including some who sit like camels on the blazing hot sand for hours, waiting for the winds to sculpt the dunes into that perfect 'Kodak moment'. If you visit, be sure to try the **sand-sledding**!

Also of interest is the **Fairy Spring** (Suoi Tien), which is really a stream that flows through a patch of dunes with interesting sand and rock formations. It's a beautiful trek to follow from the sea to its source, though it might be wise to hire a local guide. You can do the trek barefoot, but if you're heading out into the big sand dunes, this is out of the question unless you have leather soles on your feet; sandals are even questionable during the midday sun.

On Rte 706 heading towards Phan Thiet, the small **Po Shanu Cham Tower** (km5; admission 2000d; 7.30-11.30am & 1.30-4.30pm) occupies a hill with sweeping views of Phan Thiet, the river mouth filled with boats and a cemetery filled with candy-like tombstones.

Activities

Jibes (☎ 847 405; www.windsurf-vietnam.com; 90 Đ Nguyen Dinh Chieu; 7.30am-6pm) is a surf watersports haven next to Full Moon Resort. Run by an expat Frenchman, it rents state-of-the-art gear like windsurfers (US$5/10/25/45 for 30 minutes/one hour/half-day/full-day), surfboards (US$5 per hour) and kitesurfing boards (US$10 per hour). Check out its website for package deals.

Airwaves (☎ 847 440; airwaveskitesurfing.com), based at Mui Ne Sailing Club, is another

MUI NE BEACH

0 — 6 km
0 — 4 miles

INFORMATION	
Coco Cafe	(see 1)
Hanh Cafe/Ha Phuong Tourist....**1**	B2
Happy Café	**2** D2
Incombank	**3** B2
Post Office	**4** C2
Post Office	**5** D3
TM Brothers Cafe	(see 1)

SIGHTS & ACTIVITIES	(pp283-4)
Airwaves	(see 17)
Chua Phuoc Thien	**6** C2
Jibes	(see 10)

SLEEPING	(pp284-6)
Mui Ne Sailing Club	(see 17)
Po Shanu Cham Tower	**7** A3
Bamboo Village Beach Resort	**8** B2
Blue Ocean Resort	**9** B2
Canary Resort	(see 18)
Full Moon Resort	**10** B2
Hiep Hoa Tourism	(see 12)
Hoang Kim	**11** C2
Hong Di Guesthouse	**12** B2
Indochina Dreams	(see 12)
Little Mui Ne Cottages	**13** C2

Lucy Hotel	**14** A3
Mai Khanh	(see 10)
Red Sun	**15** C2
Sanctuary Resort	**16** C2
Sea Breeze Resort	(see 15)
Seahorse Resort	**17** B2
Song Hai	(see 12)
Swiss Village Resort	(see 8)
Thai Hoa Mui Ne Resort	**18** C2
Beach Resort	(see 17)
Tropico Resort	(see 3)
Victoria Phan Thiet Resort	**19** A3
Vietnam-Austria House	(see 10)
Xuan Uyen	(see 10)

To Lake (20km)
Bridge
Fairy Spring (Suoi Tien)
To Sand Dunes (5km)
To National Highway 1A (4km); Phan Thiet (5km)
706
707
People's Committee
To Fishing Village; Market (11km)

SOUTH CHINA SEA

EATING	(p286)
Dung Su	(see 14)
Good Morning Vietnam	(see 20)
Hoang Vu	(see 21)
Luna d'Autunno	**20** B2
Rung	(see 20)

DRINKING	(p287)
Hot Rock	**21** B2
Sheridan's Irish House	(see 9)

outfit offering kite-surfing, windsurfing and sailing lessons and equipment rentals.

Sleeping

Mui Ne has seen an extraordinary increase in the number of beach resorts in the last several years, and nearly all local accommodation is right on the beachfront.

For budget travellers there are several cheap places to stay. In the mid-range, nice bungalows can be found for between US$20 and US$70. At Mui Ne's pricier resorts you can expect all the trimmings, including satellite TV, IDD phones and minibars, plus breakfast included in the room rate.

High-/low-season dates vary from resort to resort and rates are typically higher on weekends.

BUDGET

Thai Hoa Mui Ne Resort (☎ 847 320; dtp@hcm.vnn.vn; km18; r 120,000-180,000d) A cheap and tidy place with two rows of bungalow-style rooms separated by a sandy courtyard and volleyball net; Thai Hoa also has a good, shady café on site. Cheaper rooms have shared bathroom.

Canary Resort (☎ 847 258; www.canaryresort.com; km18; r US$5-20; ❇) There's a pleasant café here, and rooms range from cheap sharedbathroom spots to more-expensive bungalow rooms. It does a brisk business, and while the accommodation is comfortable, the staff can be a bit surly.

Hong Di Guesthouse (☎ 847 014; hdhongdi@yahoo.com; 70 Đ Nguyen Dinh Chieu; bungalows US$10; ❇ 🖳) With several bamboo bungalows and a small café on the beach, this is an intimate little place. There's Internet access available in front, at 200d per minute.

Hiep Hoa Tourism (☎ 847 262; hiephoatourism@yahoo.com; 80 Đ Nguyen Dinh Chieu; r US$10-15; ❇) Calm and lovely, the family-run Hiep Hoa is sandwiched between big resorts but is still a good deal, with a beautiful slice of beach. There's also a small café in front.

Song Hai (☎ 847 015; songhairesort@yahoo.com; 72 Đ Nguyen Dinh Chieu; r US$10-15, f US$40; ❇) All rooms have hot water and bamboo-bead curtains. There's a shared terracotta terrace on the beach, with chickens and songbirds adding to the ambience. There's also a restaurant in front.

Hoang Kim (☎ 847 689; 140 Đ Nguyen Dinh Chieu; r US$4-15; ☒ ☐) Hoang Kim is run by a congenial family. The cheapie rooms here are very basic with very clean shared bathrooms nearby. Pricier ones are clean and of a good budget standard. There's a lot of bamboo decoration, plants in the courtyard, and two restaurants, one of which is on the beach.

Red Sun (☎ 847 387; caféloumi@hcm.vnn.vn; km13; r US$8-15; ☒) With a brick courtyard and terrace and plenty of shade, the Red Sun is a good option. Room rates include a breakfast of an omelette and fresh-baked pastries.

Lucy Hotel (☎ 847 017; lucy_hotelvn@yahoo.com; km10; r 400,000d; ☒) With only four comfortable, small rooms, and unattached to the string of guesthouses and restaurants lining Rte 706, you're sure to avoid crowds here. It's right next to two good restaurants and has a nice aesthetic.

Vietnam-Austria House (☎ 847 047; ngothi kimhong@hotmail.com; km13.5; r US$10, bungalows US$15-20; ☒ ☒) This established place has wooden bungalows or squeaky-clean rooms in a modern villa; there's also a small swimming pool.

Xuan Uyen (☎ 847 476; km13.3; r US$8-12) These bungalow rooms are very simple and clean.

MID-RANGE
Mui Ne Sailing Club (☎ 847 440; www.sailingclub vietnam.com; 24 Đ Nguyen Dinh Chieu; r US$30-90; ☒ ☒) Popular for its wide open bar overlooking the sea, the Sailing Club also has spacious rooms in its garden setting. The resort blends Asian and European architecture, and the comfortable, clean rooms are designed with bamboo and dark, matte wood. In addition to the restaurant and bar, there's a swimming pool and water sports (see p283). Breakfast is included and major credit cards are accepted.

Full Moon Resort (Trang Tron; ☎ 847 008; full moon@windsurf-vietnam.com; km13; bungalows US$20-40, r US$45; ☒) Simple bungalows, some with large corner bathtubs, are set around the garden here. Decorative details include bamboo-screen partitions, low square tables, wooden ceiling fans and slatted sliding doors. Rooms in the house have huge bathtubs and sofa beds to accommodate extra guests. All rates include breakfast.

Mai Khanh (☎ 847 177; cheznina@hcm.vnn.vn; km13; r US$20-25; ☒) Rooms at charming Mai Khanh have wooden floors and simple bamboo décor. There's a restaurant and café on site, massage (60,000d for 50 minutes) on the beach and bikes and motorbikes for rent. It's set in a bright garden environment and is central.

Indochina Dreams (☎ 847 271; fax 832 174; 74 Đ Nguyen Dinh Chieu; r US$20-25; ☒) This dreamy place is on a small scale, but it's well-designed and very comfortable. Rooms are cool and well-appointed, and there's a good restaurant in front.

Bamboo Village Beach Resort (☎ 847 007; www .bamboovillageresort.com; km11.8; bungalows US$35-85; ☒ ☐ ☒) This low-key, beautifully landscaped resort has attractive round bamboo bungalows with small concrete terraces. There's a clean beach, a small swimming pool and a good restaurant on the premises with 24-hour service.

Little Mui Ne Cottages (☎ 847 550; www.little muine.com; km18; r US$50-80; ☒ ☒) Lots of perks warrant the higher prices here: comfortable, well-appointed cottages have lots of space around them, and the pool is big enough for swimming laps. Other special touches are a welcome drink upon arrival and daily complimentary fresh fruit. The sea-view restaurant is upstairs, at reception, and breakfast is included in rates.

Beach Resort (☎ 847 626; www.thebeachresort.com. vn; 18 Đ Nguyen Dinh Chieu; r US$60-75; ☒ ☒) Clean, simple design in a lushly landscaped setting characterise this new resort. Rooms have ethnic fabric accents and the place looks green and unobtrusive from the road. Breakfast is included, all major credit cards are accepted and the restaurant is open 24 hours.

Sea Breeze Resort (☎ 847 373; fax 847 430; sea breeze-lanno@hcm.vnn.vn; km13.7; r US$25-40; ☒) A cosy place with finely manicured gardens, the Sea Breeze has comfy rooms and A-frame bungalows featuring terracotta floors. The beach, however, disappears at high tide. There's a restaurant here and breakfast is included.

Blue Ocean Resort (Bien Xanh; ☎ 847 322; www .blueoceanresort.com; km12.2; bungalows US$55; ☒ ☒) This is another established, stylish choice, with thatched cottages, a bar in the swimming pool and an Irish pub. There's an intimate garden and pool area, beach volleyball, and a beachfront restaurant. The service here is terrific and the beach is beautiful.

GO FLY A KITE

If sunning on the serene shores of Mui Ne doesn't do anything for you and you're jonesing for an adrenaline fix, you're in the right place (er, drag-racing along the lonely unlit highway is strongly not recommended). Kite-surfing should administer a good jolt to ennui.

Mui Ne is Vietnam's premier kite-surfing venue; on average, about two-thirds of each month is blessed with winds of over 12 knots. The dry season – between mid-October and May – also coincides with good wind weather. Word to the wise: bronzing on the beach is better in the morning, before the wind kicks up in the early afternoon.

The uncrowded turquoise waters of Mui Ne's bay are also prime for windsurfing, and can even work up a just-surfable swell – best from August to December.

Naturally, these favourable conditions have attracted a small enclave of well-trained fanatics who are more than happy to induct you into their cult of the kite. The best place to rent equipment, take lessons from the knowledgeable (and cute!) staff, or suss out the secret spots, is Jibe's (p283).

Swiss Village Resort (☎ 847 399; www.svr-vn.com; km12; r & bungalows US$50-120; ✂ Ⓟ ⚈) Rooms and bungalows here are fairly spacious and comfortable, with Vietnamese architecture and a pool with the Swiss flag emblazoned on the floor tile. Other facilities include a tennis court and a Jacuzzi.

TOP END

Victoria Phan Thiet Resort (☎ 847 170; fax 847 174; victoriapt@hcm.vnn.vn; www.victoriahotels-asia .com; km9; bungalows US$138-196; ✂ ⚈) Thatched cottages at this stylish resort are outfitted with terracotta tile and dark wood, and shaded with eucalyptus trees. There's a nice terrace restaurant, two bars, tennis courts, a swimming pool, a fitness club, a massage room, a sauna and an indoor-outdoor Jacuzzi. Excursions from the hotel can be arranged by 4WD, classic sidecar or Minsk motorbike. Internet bookings garner steep discounts.

Seahorse Resort (☎ 847 507; www.seahorsere sortvn.com; km11; r US$80-150; ✂ ⚈) Gorgeously designed, the flagstone pathways and narrow pond at the Seahorse follow the natural contours of the land. Each building has four separate rooms surrounding an interior garden. The rooms themselves are elegantly decorated with Vietnamese art and furnishings, and have open-air bathrooms. There's also a restaurant and swimming pool.

Sanctuary Resort (☎ 847 232; sanctuaryvietnam@ yahoo.com; km19; r US$75-230; ✂ ⚈) Entry here is via a long driveway, and cows wander the property. There are only two luxurious villas and one bungalow, with two shallow pools on the shared terraces. Appropriately named, it's got a decidedly 'away from it all' feel.

Eating

Besides the ubiquitous in-house restaurants at the beach resorts (which are open to non-guests too), a handful of interesting eateries in Mui Ne are open for lunch and dinner.

Rung (Forest Restaurant; ☎ 847 589; 65B Đ Nguyen Dinh Chieu; mains 50,000d) Rung has both indoor and outdoor seating at its landscaped spot above the road. It serves up traditional Vietnamese dishes, and is worth visiting in the evenings, when the atmosphere is sort of romantic and Cham music is performed.

Luna d'Autunno (Autumn Moon; ☎ 847 330; hagi@hn .vnn.vn; km12; mains 30,000-70,000d) An unexpected retreat serving authentic Italian fare like antipasto, salads, fresh pasta and great wood-fired pizza. There's also a decent wine list.

Hoang Vu (Double Wheels Restaurant; ☎ 847 525; km12.2; seafood 30,000d) Within its cosy wood-and-rattan interior, the staff provides casually attentive service and delicious, beautifully presented Vietnamese food at reasonable prices.

Good Morning Vietnam (☎ 847 342; www.good morningviet.com; km11.8; mains around 45,000d) This is another in the popular chain of Italian eateries, but don't say 'good morning' until lunchtime; it doesn't do breakfast.

Dung Su (☎ 847 310; km10; seafood per person around 40,000d) Located near the western end of the beach, Dung Su is raised on stilts and sits over the water. It's highly popular with Vietnamese, and tasty seafood is sold by the kilo here, plucked fresh from tanks across the back wall.

Drinking

Beach bars that get hopping at night include the **Mui Ne Sailing Club** (☎ 847 440; www.sailingclubvietnam.com; 24 Đ Nguyen Dinh Chieu) and **Jibes** (☎ 847 405; www.windsurf-vietnam.com; 90 Đ Nguyen Dinh Chieu), which has a pool table. Both of these places also serve food and place a decided emphasis on good times. Start your evening at the **Hot Rock** (km 12.1) and catch some breezes in the tropical garden here. If you're craving a Guinness, head for **Sheridan's Irish House** (Blue Ocean Resort; km12.2).

Getting There & Away

Mui Ne is 200km (three hours' drive) from HCMC. Many of the open-tour buses cruising Hwy 1 make a detour to Mui Ne; the cost from HCMC or Nha Trang is US$6. From Tuesday to Sunday there's a comfortable shuttle service (one way/return US$9/16) by Mercedes van between the Blue Ocean Resort and Sheridan's Irish Pub in HCMC.

A local bus makes trips between Phan Thiet bus station and Mui Ne, but it is irregular and slow. The best way to reach the beach from the highway in Phan Thiet is by xe om (50,000d) or you can rent your own bike for around US$6 a day (ask at the Hoang Yen Restaurant, p282).

Getting Around

Mui Ne is small enough to get around on foot if you're staying in the central beach area, or you can rent a bicycle from most hotels.

TA CU MOUNTAIN

The highlight here is the **white reclining Buddha** (Tuong Phat Nam). At 49m, it's the largest in Vietnam. The pagoda was constructed in 1861, during the Nguyen dynasty, but the Buddha is a much more recent addition (1972). It has become an important pilgrimage centre for Buddhists, who stay overnight in the pagoda's dormitory. Foreigners can't do this without police permission, but there's now a **guesthouse** (☎ 867 484; tacu@hcm.vnn.vn; r 200,000d; 🅿) on the mountain.

The mountain is just off Hwy 1, 28km south from Phan Thiet, from which the Buddha is a beautiful two-hour trek, or a two-minute cable-car ride (50,000d return) and a short, but steep, hike.

Central Highlands

CONTENTS

Renowned for its cool climate, mountain scenery and innumerable streams, lakes and water-falls, the central highlands cover the southern section of the Truong Son Mountain Range (Annamite Cordillera). This region is home to many hill-tribe minority groups, or Montagnards (French for highlanders). Although these groups aren't as colourful as the tribes in the deep north of Vietnam, they are diverse and maintain fascinating cultural traditions.

Though the western highlands have lost much of their natural beauty from agricultural clear-cutting and Agent Orange poisoning from the American War, the region still retains some remnant of forests and the landscape is a green patchwork of agriculture. During the early months of the year you'll see the puffy white blooms of coffee bushes along the roads, as well as neat rows of rubber trees and climbing pepper vines.

The western edge of the central highlands, along the border with Cambodia and Laos, is a vast, fertile plateau with red volcanic soil. The good soil and sparse population has made it a government target for a massive resettlement programme. Most of the new settlers are farmers from the crowded Red River Delta area in the north; the local hill tribes have been less than thrilled by the sudden influx of northern Vietnamese.

In February 2001 the government forbade travellers from visiting the central highlands because of local uprisings over land distribution. By early June 900 local minority people who had fled to Cambodia were granted refugee status and relocated to the USA, much to the chagrin of the Vietnamese authorities. In March 2004 another clash in Buon Ma Thuot precipitated another brief closure of the area, so before heading to the hills make local inquires to confirm that your destinations are accessible.

For some outdoor adventure, both Cat Tien National Park and Yok Don National Park are easily accessible from the central highlands.

HIGHLIGHTS

- Explore the cool-climate kitsch of **Dalat** (p290), the old French hill station
- Rock-climb, mountain-bike or hike the hills around Dalat or rappel the many **waterfalls** (p305)
- Visit Bahnar, Jarai, M'nong and Ede hill-tribe villages around **Buon Ma Thuot** (p307) and **Kon Tum** (p315)
- Get off the beaten track and onto the back of an elephant at **Yok Don National Park** (p311)
- Hit the road on two wheels and follow the rugged and historic **'Ho Chi Minh Trail'** (p315)
- Trek into the jungle outside of Kon Tum, and overnight at a **hill-tribe village** (p316)

CENTRAL HIGHLANDS

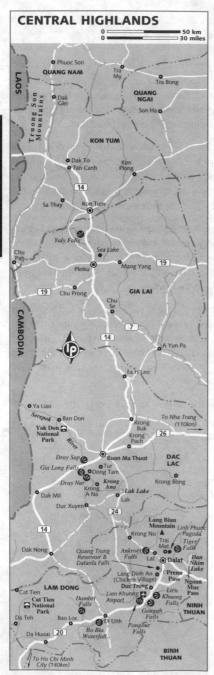

CENTRAL HIGHLANDS

0 ———————— 50 km
0 ———————— 30 miles

Getting There & Away

The central highlands is easily approached from the south, and from points along the eastern coast. From Ho Chi Minh City (HCMC) and Nha Trang, private open-tour buses to Dalat are cheap and frequent, but to reach places further afield such as Buon Ma Thuot, Pleiku and Kon Tum you'll either have to depend on rattletrap public buses – some of which may only run once a day – or arrange some form of private transport.

The central highlands is one area where having the right guide and vehicle can make all the difference, especially for visiting national parks and hill-tribe villages. **Sinhbalo Adventures** (☎ 08-837 6766, 836 7682; www.sinhbalo .com; 283/20 Đ Pham Ngu Lao) in HCMC and **Mr Vu's Tour Adventures** (☎ 058-828 996; www.vutour adventure.com; 2D Đ Biet Thu) in Nha Trang know the region very well and can be recommended for customised trips into the highlands. Another interesting option is to hire one of the popular motorbike drivers who work in Dalat (see 'Easy Riders' on opposite page).

DALAT

☎ 063 / pop 130,000 / elevation 1475m
The jewel of the central highlands, Dalat is in a temperate region dotted with lakes, waterfalls, evergreen forests and gardens. The cool climate and the park-like environment make this one of the most delightful places in all of Vietnam.

The city was once called Le Petit Paris, and to this day there is a miniature replica of the Eiffel Tower behind the main post office. Dalat is also the favourite haunt of Vietnamese artists and avant-garde types, many of whom have made it their permanent home. It is also the country's most popular honeymoon spot, and although the locals are thankfully scaling back on circus-style 'tourist attractions', Dalat still remains the final word in Vietnamese kitsch.

Local industries include growing garden vegetables and flowers (especially beautiful hydrangeas), which are sold all over southern Vietnam. But the biggest contribution to the economy of Dalat is tourism: more than 800,000 domestic tourists and another 80,000 or so foreign tourists visit here every year.

The Dalat area was once famous for its big-game hunting and a 1950s brochure boasted that 'a two-hour drive from the town leads to several game-rich areas abounding in deer, roe, peacocks, pheasants, wild boar, black bear, wild caws, panthers, tigers, gaurs and elephants'. So successful were the hunters that all of the big game is now extinct. However, you will get a whiff of Dalat's former glory by viewing some of the taxidermied specimens about town.

The city's population includes about 5000 members of hill tribes, which make up 33 distinct communities in Lam Dong province. Members of these hill tribes, who still refer to themselves as Montagnards, can occasionally be seen in the market places in their traditional dress. Hill-tribe women of this area carry their infants on their backs in a long piece of cloth worn over one shoulder and tied in the front.

Dalat is often called the City of Eternal Spring. The average maximum daily temperature here is a cool 24°C and the average minimum daily temperature is 15°C. The dry season runs from December to March, and even during the rainy season, which lasts more or less from April to November, it is sunny most of the time.

History

The local area has been home to various Montagnard groups for centuries. In the local Lat language, 'Da Lat' means 'River of the Lat Tribe'.

The first European to claim the 'discovery' of Dalat was Dr Alexandre Yersin in 1893, who was a protégé of Louis Pasteur and the first person to identify the plague bacillus. The city itself was established in 1912 and quickly became popular with Europeans as a cool retreat from the sweltering heat of the coastal plains and the Mekong Delta. At one point during the French colonial period some 20% of Dalat's population was foreign, as evidenced by the 2500-odd chalet-style villas scattered around the city.

During the American War Dalat was, by the tacit agreement of all parties concerned, largely spared the ravages of war. Indeed, it seems that while South Vietnamese soldiers were being trained at the city's military academy and affluent officials of the Saigon regime were relaxing in their villas, Viet Cong (VC) cadres were doing the same thing not far away in *their* villas. Dalat fell to North Vietnamese forces without a fight on 3 April 1975. There is no problem with leftover mines and ordnance in the Dalat area.

Dalat was the first city in Vietnam to introduce a city water purification system that provides potable water from the tap (an 80% Danish government-funded project).

Orientation

Dalat's sights are very spread out, and the terrain in and around the city is hilly. Still, tramping around in Dalat is made easier by the cool temperatures. The city centre is around Rap 3/4 cinema (named after the date on which Dalat was liberated in 1975), up the hill from the central-market building.

EASY RIDERS

Dalat's notorious Easy Riders are a witty, informal crew of freelance motorbike guides who were truly born to be wild. Most of the 30-odd members carry their clients on the back of vintage Russian and East German motorcycles, and their popularity is reaching cult proportions among travellers seeking an exciting alternative to being herded around on the Sinh Café tourist trail.

The Easy Riders can be hired for fun day trips around Dalat, and the cost is very reasonable (about US$8 a day around the city, or US$10 a day around the outskirts). You can also make arrangements with them for longer trips around the central highlands (Lak Lake is a popular spot) or down to the coast. Some travellers have even adopted their drivers and ridden with them all the way north to Hanoi! We've received countless letters recommending these guys.

Travelling with the Easy Riders is a great way to explore the region, and having a friendly and articulate guide along can really help put things into perspective. You can usually find the Easy Riders hanging around the hotels in Dalat, but don't worry about looking; they'll find you. All of them speak English, and some can speak French and German. Most of the Easy Riders carry portable guestbooks containing raving testimonials from past clients.

CENTRAL DALAT

INFORMATION

Agriculture Bank of Vietnam	1 B1
Agriculture Bank of Vietnam	2 B2
Dalat Travel Service	3 B2
Groovy Gecko Tour	4 A1
Incombank	(see 2)
Photo-Processing Shops	(see 31)
TM Brothers	5 B2
Viet Hung Internet Cafe	6 B2
Vietcombank	7 C2
Youth Action Tour	(see 4)

SIGHTS & ACTIVITIES (pp293-8)

Dalat Holidays/Phat Tire Ventures	8 A1
Dalat Sailing and Fishing Club	(see 10)
Hardy Dalat	9 B1
Paddleboat Hire	10 D2

SLEEPING (pp298-9)

A Chau Hotel	11 B1
Dai Loi Hotel	12 D1
Dreams Hotel	13 A1
Empress Hotel	14 C2
Golf 3 Hotel	15 C2
Hotel Chau Au Europa	16 B3
Lyla Hotel	17 B2
Mimosa Hotel	18 A1
Peace Hotel	19 A1
Peace Hotel II	(see 20)
Phuong Thanh Hotel	20 A1

EATING (pp299-301)

An Lac	21 A2
Art Café	(see 19)
Café 100 Roofs	22 B2
Cafe Tung	23 B1
Food Stalls	24 C2
Long Hoa	25 B2
Minh Uyen	26 A1
Restaurants	27 A1
Stop & Go Cafe	28 C1
V Cafe	29 D1

DRINKING (p301)

Saigon Nite Bar	30 A1

TRANSPORT (p301-2)

Taxi Stand	31 B2

OTHER

Rap 3/4 Cinema	32 B2

Information

INTERNET ACCESS

Internet cafés can be found along either side of Đ Nguyen Chi Thanh.

Viet Hung Internet Cafe (Map above; ☎ 835 737; 7 Đ Nguyen Chi Thanh) At this place you can sip an iced coffee and check email.

MEDICAL SERVICES

Lam Dong Hospital (Map pp304-5; ☎ 822 154; 4 Đ Pham Ngoc Thach)

MONEY

The following banks exchange money and travellers cheques and do credit card cash advances. Between them are several foreign-exchange offices.

Agriculture Bank of Vietnam (Map above; Ngan Hang Nong Nghiep Vietnam; ☎ 822 535; 9 Đ Nguyen Van Troi & 22 Hoa Binh Sq)

Incombank (Map above; ☎ 822 496; fax 822 782; 46-48 Hoa Binh Sq; ☯ closed Sat)

Vietcombank (Map above; ☎ 510 478; fax 510 480; 6 Đ Nguyen Thi Minh Khai)

POST

Main post office (Map pp304-5; ☎ 836 638; fax 835 888; 14 Đ Tran Phu) Opposite the Novotel Dalat; has international telephone, fax and email facilities.

TRAVEL AGENCIES

Dalat Travel Service (Map above; ☎ 822 125; ttdhhd@hcm.vnn.vn; 7 Đ 3 Thang 2) Visit Dalat's state-run travel agency for tour bookings or vehicle rentals.

Groovy Gecko Tour (Map opposite; ☎ 836 521; ggtour@yahoo.com; 65 Đ Truong Cong Dinh; ⏱ 7.30am-8.30pm) Usual trips, a couple of good trekking options.

TM Brothers (Map opposite; ☎ 828 383; dalat_tm brother@yahoo.com; 9 Đ Nguyen Chi Thanh) A smaller outfit selling open-tour bus tickets and fast-food tours.

Youth Action Tour (Map opposite; ☎ 510 357; youthactiontour@hcm.vnn.vn; 49A Đ Truong Cong Dinh; ⏱ 7.30am-8.30pm)

For chauffeured tours by motorbike, see the boxed text 'Easy Riders' (p291).

Sights & Activities

XUAN HUONG LAKE

Created by a dam in 1919, **Xuan Huong Lake** is in the centre of Dalat. It is named after a 17th-century Vietnamese poet known for her daring attacks on the hypocrisy of social conventions and the foibles of scholars, monks, mandarins, feudal lords and kings. The lake can be circumnavigated along a 7km sealed path.

Paddle boats that look like giant swans can be rented at the edge of the lake near Thanh Thuy Restaurant and the Dalat Sailing and Fishing Club rents a wide selection of water craft, from kayaks and two-person sail boats to electric motorboats. The fishing club has netted off an area of the lake and stocked it with fish; it also rents equipment, and has a per-kilo catch rate, as well as catch-and-release rules for sport. Shade umbrellas are supplied.

The Dalat Palace Golf Club occupies 50 hectares on the northern side of the lake near the Dalat Flower Gardens. The majestic hill-top Hotel Sofitel Dalat Palace overlooks Xuan Huong Lake from the south.

A delightful walk or jog around the 7km lake road provides an excellent city orientation and a very nice overview of Dalat, including the French influence. Along the way are the Dalat Flower Gardens, views of the golf course and the grand old villas on Đ Tran Hung Dao. A stroll up the steps to the Hotel Sofitel Dalat Palace garden provides spectacular views. From there, head up to the post office and the higher quality buildings of old and new along Đ Tran Phu.

HANG NGA GALLERY & GUESTHOUSE

Nicknamed the **'Crazy House'** (Map pp304-5; ☎ 822 070; fax 831 480; 3 Đ Huynh Thuc Khang; admission 5000d) by locals, this guesthouse, café and art gallery is about 1km southwest of Xuan Huong Lake. The architecture is something straight out of *Alice in Wonderland* and cannot easily be described: there are caves, giant spider webs made of wire, concrete 'tree trunks', a nude female statue (a rarity in Vietnam), a concrete giraffe (with a tearoom built inside) and caged turkeys providing the surreal soundtrack. Yes it's tacky, and exceedingly commercialised, but many are astounded to find such a countercultural construction in Dalat.

The gallery's designer, Mrs Dang Viet Nga, is from Hanoi and lived in Moscow for 14 years, where she earned a PhD in architecture. She dresses in pure 1960s hippie garb, burns incense and has something of an air of mystery about her. Hang Nga, as she's known locally, has designed a number of other buildings, which dot the landscape around Dalat, including the Children's Cultural Palace and the Catholic church in Lien Khuong.

The Dalat People's Committee has not always appreciated such innovative designs. An earlier Dalat architectural masterpiece, the 'House with 100 Roofs', was torn down as a 'fire hazard' because the People's

SUGGESTED SIGHTSEEING ROUTES

The best way to enjoy the forests, sites and cultivated countryside around Dalat is by foot, motorbike or bicycle.

- Head out on Đ 3 Thang 4, which becomes Hwy 20, to the pine forests of Prenn Pass and Quang Trung Reservoir.
- Go via the Governor-General's Residence and up Đ Khe Sanh to Thien Vuong Pagoda.
- Take Đ Phu Dong Thien Vuong from Dalat University to the Valley of Love.
- Go out to Bao Dai's Summer Palace and from there, after stopping at Lam Ty Ni Pagoda, head via Đ Thien My and Đ Huyen Tran Cong Chua to Du Sinh Church.

Committee thought it looked 'antisocialist'. However, there is little chance that Hang Nga will have such trouble with the authorities (her father, Truong Chinh, was Ho Chi Minh's successor). He served as Vietnam's second president from 1981 until his death in 1988.

If you'd like to stay in one of the cave-like, quirky rooms (see p299), booking in advance is recommended.

CRÉMAILLÈRE RAILWAY STATION

About 500m east of Xuan Huong Lake is a **cog-railway station** (Map pp304-5; ☎ 834 409; return US$5; departs 8am, 9.30am, 2pm & 3.30pm) and, although you aren't likely to arrive in Dalat by train, the station is worth a visit. There is an old Russian steam train on display here.

The *crémaillère* linked Dalat and Thap Cham from 1928 to 1964, when it was closed because of VC attacks. The line has been partially repaired and is now operated as a tourist attraction. You can't get to anywhere useful (like HCMC) on this train, but you can ride 8km (30 minutes) down the tracks to Trai Mat village and back again.

Once in Trai Mat, most travellers make a requisite stroll over to visit the ornate **Linh Phuoc Pagoda**. This colourful pagoda was originally built between 1949 and 1952, and recent renovations included the installation of an 8½-tonne bell (cast in 1999) in a seven-tiered tower. You must remove your shoes when entering the main temple building, where an amusement-park dragon guards the gate. Once inside visitors are greeted by a 5m-high Buddha statue seated under a Bodhi Tree painting – this Buddha even sports a five-ringed neon halo! The statue is flanked by Pho Hien riding an elephant, and Van Thu riding a tiger. From the ground floor, take the left-hand staircase up to the 2nd-level balcony area for great views. In a small room here another Buddha statue with multiple heads and arms sits surrounded by 108 Bodhisattvas painted on the wall.

LAM DONG MUSEUM

This hill-top **museum** (Map pp304-5; ☎ 822 339; 4 Đ Hung Vuong; admission 10,000d; 7.30-11.30am & 1.30-4.30pm Tue-Sat) displays stone artefacts and pottery excavated from an ancient Oc-Eo archaeological site, costumes and musical instruments of local ethnic minorities, and artefacts relating to the struggles against the French and Americans.

The museum is housed in a lovely French-style villa, once the abode of Nguyen Huu Hao, father of Empress Nam Phuong, Bao Dai's wife. Nguyen Huu Hao, who died in 1939, was the richest person in the Go Cong district of the Mekong Delta. His **tomb** lies on a hilltop near Dalat, 400m west of Cam Ly Falls. Walk around the valley side of the villa to discover an interesting fusion of Chinese-style longevity symbols on the side of the building.

BAO DAI'S SUMMER PALACE

This **villa** (Biet Dien Quoc Truong, or Dinh 3; Map pp304-5; Đ Le Hong Phong; admission 5000d; 7-11am & 1.30-4pm), with 25 rooms, was constructed in 1933. The decor has not changed in decades, except for the addition of Ho Chi Minh's portrait over the fireplace, but the palace is filled with artefacts from decades and governments past and is extremely interesting.

For instance, the engraved-glass map of Vietnam was given to Emperor Bao Dai in 1942 by Vietnamese students in France. In Bao Dai's office, the life-sized white bust above the bookcase is of Bao Dai himself; the smaller gold and brown busts are of his father, Emperor Khai Dinh. Note the heavy brass royal seal (on the right) and military seal (on the left). The photographs over the fireplace are of (from left to right) Bao Dai; his eldest son, Bao Long (in uniform); and Empress Nam Phuong, who died in 1963.

Upstairs are the royal living quarters. The room of Bao Long, who now lives in France, is decorated in yellow, the royal colour. The huge semicircular couch was used by the emperor and empress for family meetings, during which their three daughters were seated in the yellow chairs and their two sons in the pink chairs. Check out the ancient tan Rouathermique infrared sauna machine near the top of the stairs.

Bao Dai's Summer Palace is set in a pine grove 500m southeast of the **Pasteur Institute** (Đ Le Hong Phong), 2km southwest of the city centre. The palace is open to the public and shoes must be removed at the door. There is an extra charge for cameras and videos.

LAM TY NI PAGODA

This **pagoda** (Quan Am Tu; Map pp304-5; 2 Đ Thien My; 8.30am-6.30pm) was founded in 1961.

The decorative front gate was constructed by the pagoda's only monk, Vien Thuc, an industrious man who learned English, French, Khmer and Thai at Dalat University. During his time here he built flowerbeds and gardens in several different styles, including a miniature Japanese garden complete with a bridge. Nearby are trellis-shaded paths decorated with hanging plants. Signs list the Chinese name of each garden. Vien Thuc also built much of the pagoda's wooden furniture.

But more than the pagoda and its gardens, the attraction here is Mr Thuc himself and his mind-boggling collection of self-brushed art works. It would be a gross understatement to call him prolific. By his own estimates he has churned out more than 100,000 works of art, piles and piles of which hang in and around the pagoda – even out in the rain!

So industrious is this eccentric local celebrity that since he began selling his paintings to tourists he has become, some say, the wealthiest person in Dalat. Judging by the astounding number of 'instant paintings' he sells, you could believe it. The one-time hermit monk has today earned himself the esteemed title of 'the business monk' by local motorbike guides (many of whom resent his financial success, not to mention having to wait for hours while their customers linger at the pagoda). Others call him 'the crazy monk', in keeping with the kooky theme of Dalat's sights.

Paintings sell anywhere from a dollar or two to whatever smooth-talking Mr Thuc can take you for. These days the monk is saving those dollars while waiting for his long-awaited around-the-globe journey. His plans include visiting travellers who have been to see him, and the homes where his paintings hang.

Lam Ty Ni Pagoda is about 500m north of the Pasteur Institute. A visit here can easily be combined with a stop at Bao Dai's Summer Palace.

DALAT FLOWER GARDENS

These beautiful **gardens** (Vuon Hoa Dalat; Map pp304-5; ☎ 822 151; 2 Đ Phu Dong Thien Vuong; admission 8000d; ☒ 7.30am-4pm) were established in 1966 by the South Vietnamese Agricultural Service, renovated in 1985, and have been greatly refined in recent years.

Flowers here include hydrangeas, fuchsias and orchids (hoa lan). Most of the latter are in special shaded buildings to the right of the entrance. The orchids are grown in blocks of coconut-palm trunk and in terracotta pots with lots of ventilation holes.

Hasfarm, a local Dutch-run nursery, has chipped in with some displays. All in all it's a very nice and well-kept cross section of Dalat foliage. The plants still have a lot of space in which to grow, and before long they may be calling it a botanic garden.

A few monkeys live in cages on the grounds of the Dalat Flower Gardens, and a warning to any feeble-minded tourists who might enjoy tormenting the monkeys by throwing things at them – these clever monkeys have learned to throw back!

Near the gate you can buy cu ly (reddish-brown animal-shaped pieces of fern stems whose fibres are used to stop bleeding in traditional medicine). Plants and flowers are also for sale.

The Dalat Flower Gardens front Xuan Huong Lake, on the road that leads from the lake to Dalat University.

DALAT UNIVERSITY

Dalat is actually something of an education centre. The reason for this is its climate: before air-con, it was one of the few places in Vietnam where it was possible to study without working up a sweat. Therefore, a number of educational institutions were located in town, with **Dalat University** (Map pp304-5; 1 Đ Phu Dong Thien Vuong) being the most famous.

Dalat University was founded as a Catholic university in 1957 by Hué Archbishop Ngo Dinh Thuc, the older brother of President Ngo Dinh Diem (assassinated in 1963), with the help of Cardinal Spelman of New York. The university was seized from the church in 1975 and closed, but it reopened two years later as a state-run institution.

There are presently more than 13,000 students studying here, although they all live in off-campus boarding houses. The university library contains 10,000 books, including some in English and European languages.

The 38-hectare campus can easily be identified by the triangular tower topped by a red star, which was stuck over the cross originally erected by the church. The fact that the cross was never actually removed has led some to speculate that the church may some day get the campus returned to it.

Foreign visitors are generally welcome to visit the campus.

VALLEY OF LOVE
Named the Valley of Peace by Emperor Bao Dai, this **valley** (Thung Lung Tinh Yeu, or Vallée d'Amour; Map pp304-5; Đ Phu Dong Thien Vuong; admission adult/child 6000/3000d; 7am-5pm) had its name changed in 1972 (the year Da Thien Lake was created) by romantically minded students from Dalat University.

Today this ever-tacky place has taken on a carnival atmosphere and now local tour guides call it the Valley of Shops! Tourist buses line up to regurgitate visitors and boats line up to accommodate them. Get into the spirit with some aquatic activities: paddle boats, 15-person canoes and obnoxious noise-making motorboats can be hired to tour the lake.

This is a good place to see the 'Dalat cowboys', Vietnamese guides dressed as American cowboys. We've also seen locals dressed as bears; can Mickey Mouse and Donald Duck costumes be far behind? The cowboys rent horses to tourists for a guided tour around the lake. The Dalat cowboys and bears expect cash if you take their picture – they want about 5000d per photo!

Refreshments and local delicacies (such as jams and candied fruits) are on sale at the lookout near where the buses disgorge tourists.

The Valley of Love is 5km north of Xuan Huong Lake.

GOVERNOR-GENERAL'S RESIDENCE
Built in 1933, the **French Governor-General's Residence** (Dinh Toan Quyen, or Dinh 2; Map pp304-5; 822 092; Đ Tran Hung Dao) is a dignified building of modernist design. Today it's used as a guesthouse for the local People's Committee and for official receptions, and the original style of furnishing has been retained in most of its 25 rooms. At the time of writing it was closed to the public, and plans for renovation are in the works (inquire locally).

The Governor-General's Residence is about 2km east of the centre of town, up the hill from the intersection of Đ Tran Hung Dao and Đ Khoi Nghia Bac Son.

PETIT LYCÉE YERSIN
The former school is now a **teacher training college** (Map pp304-5; 822 511; 1 Đ Hoang Van Thu) run by the provincial government. Music lessons in electric and acoustic musical instruments are held here, making this a good place to meet local musicians. This building's older sister, the former **Grand Lycée Yersin**, is located east of Xuan Huong Lake.

DOMAINE DE MARIE CONVENT
The pink tile-roofed structures of this hilltop **convent** (Nha Tho Domaine; Map pp304-5; 6 Đ Ngo Quyen; admission free; 7-11.30am & 2-5pm), constructed between 1940 and 1942, were once home to 300 nuns. Today the remaining nuns support themselves by making ginger candies and selling the fruit grown in the orchard out the back.

Suzanne Humbert, wife of Admiral Jean Decoux (French Governor-General of Indochina from 1940 to 1945) is buried at the base of the outside back wall of the chapel. A benefactor of the chapel, she was killed in a car accident in 1944.

The French-speaking nuns are pleased to show visitors around and explain the work they do for orphans, the homeless and handicapped children. The shop sells handicrafts made by the children and nuns.

Masses are held in the large chapel Sunday to Friday.

LINH SON PAGODA
Built in 1938, this **pagoda** (Chua Linh Son; Map pp304-5; 120 Đ Nguyen Van Troi) is a lovely ochre-coloured building that fuses French and Chinese architecture. The giant bell is said to be made of bronze mixed with gold, its great weight making it too heavy for thieves to carry off. Behind the pagoda are coffee and tea plants tended by 20 monks, who range in age from 20 to 80, and half a dozen novices.

Linh Son Pagoda is about 1km from the town centre, near the corner of Đ Phan Dinh Phung. The sign on the front gate reads 'Phat Giao Viet-Nam' (Vietnam Buddhist Association).

DALAT CATHEDRAL
Next to the Novotel Dalat, this gingerbread **cathedral** (Map pp304-5; Đ Tran Phu) was built between 1931 and 1942 for use by French residents and holiday-makers. The cross on

the spire is 47m above the ground. Inside, the stained-glass windows bring a hint of medieval Europe to Dalat. The first church built on this site (in the 1920s) is to the left of the cathedral; it has a light-blue arched door.

There are three priests here, and masses are held daily.

DU SINH CHURCH

This **church** (Map pp304–5) was built in 1955 by Catholic refugees from the north. The four-post, Sino-Vietnamese steeple was constructed at the insistence of a Hué-born priest of royal lineage. The church is on a hilltop with beautiful views in all directions, making this a great place for a picnic.

To get to Du Sinh Church, walk 500m southwest along Đ Huyen Tran Cong Chua from the former **Couvent des Oiseaux**, which is now a teachers' training high school.

THIEN VUONG PAGODA

This **pagoda** (Chua Tau; Map pp304–5; Đ Khe Sanh) is popular with domestic tourists, especially ethnic Chinese. Set on a hilltop amid pine trees, the pagoda was built by the Chaozhou Chinese Congregation. Tho Da, the monk who initiated the construction of the pagoda in 1958, emigrated to the USA; there are pictures of his 1988 visit on display. The stalls out the front are a good place to buy local candied fruit and preserves.

The pagoda itself consists of three yellow buildings made of wood. In the first building is a gilded, wooden statue of Ho Phap, one of the Buddha's protectors. On the other side of the glass case is a gilded wooden statue of Pho Hien, a helper of A Di Da Buddha (Buddha of the Past). Remove your shoes before entering the third building, in which there are three 4m-high standing Buddhas, donated by a British Buddhist and brought from Hong Kong in 1960. Made of gilded sandalwood and weighing 1400kg each, the figures (which are said to be the largest sandalwood statues in Vietnam) represent Thich Ca Buddha (the historical Buddha Sakyamuni; in the centre); Quan The Am Bo Tat (Avalokiteçvara, the Goddess of Mercy; on the right); and Dai The Chi Bo Tat (an assistant of A Di Da; on the left).

Thien Vuong Pagoda is about 5km southeast of the centre of town.

MINH NGUYET CU SY LAM PAGODA

A second Chinese Buddhist pagoda, **Minh Nguyet Cu Sy Lam Pagoda** (Map pp304–5), can be reached by a path beginning across the road from the gate of the Thien Vuong Pagoda. It was built by the Cantonese Chinese Congregation in 1962. The main sanctuary of the pagoda is a round structure constructed on a platform representing a lotus blossom.

Inside the pagoda (remove shoes before entering) is a painted cement statue of Quan The Am Bo Tat flanked by two other figures. Notice the repetition of the lotus motif in the window bars, railings and gateposts. There is a giant, red, gourd-shaped incense-burning oven near the main sanctuary.

VIETNAMESE EVANGELICAL CHURCH

Dalat's pink **Evangelical Church** (Map pp304–5; 72 Đ Nguyen Van Troi), the main Protestant church in the city, was built in 1940. Until 1975 it was affiliated with The Christian and Missionary Alliance.

Since reunification Vietnam's Protestants have been persecuted even more than the Catholics, in part because many Protestant clergymen were trained by US missionaries. Although religious activities at this church are still restricted by the government, Sunday is a busy day with Bible study, worship and a youth service.

Most of the 25,000 Protestants in Lam Dong province, who are served by more than 100 churches, are hill-tribe people. Dalat's Vietnamese Evangelical Church is one of only six churches in the province whose membership is ethnic Vietnamese.

The Vietnamese Evangelical Church is 300m north of Rap 3/4.

GOLF

The **Dalat Palace Golf Club** (Map pp304–5; ☎ 821 201; www.vietnamgolfresorts.com; Đ Phu Dong Thien Vuong), established in 1922, was once used by Bao Dai, the last Vietnamese emperor. Visitors can play 18-hole rounds here for US$65, but the more affordable 'twilight gold specials' practically make golfing an option for budget travellers. These rates are just US$35 after 2.30pm, or US$25 after 3.30pm, including play until sundown, caddy fees, rental clubs, rental shoes and six used golf balls.

Happy hour at the club house is from 4pm to 7pm and worth checking out just for the guacamole and home-baked tortilla chips!

To lure the customers up to Dalat, very reasonably priced golf-package tours are available if you book from HCMC. Per-golfer deals are as inexpensive as US$59, including a round of golf, a night at the elegant Novotel Dalat and breakfast. Tack on around US$30 to these rates and you can upgrade to the Sofitel Dalat Palace.

For information, contact the golf club's **marketing office** (☎ 08-824 3640; www.vietnam golfresorts.com) in HCMC.

Tours

Nature lovers looking for their outdoor-adventure fix should check out the activities offered by these agencies.

Dalat Holidays/Phat Tire Ventures (Map p292; ☎ 829 422; www.phattireventures.com; 73 Đ Truong Cong Dinh; ⏰ 7.30am-8.30pm) Unlike many operators in Vietnam, who cluelessly throw the terms 'eco' and 'environment' around for the sake of profit, these folks take the term ecotourism seriously. This agency employs knowledgeable English-, French- and Japanese-speaking guides, all of whom are Red Cross certified.

It offers canyoning, abseiling (rappelling), technical rock climbing and treks to the minority villages in the mountains surrounding Dalat. It also runs a range of ass-kicking 'fat tire' tours of the Dalat area, as well as a ride 120km *downhill* to the sand dunes at Mui Ne Beach (see p283). Trips range in price from US$10 to US$100, and the agency maintains a fleet of high-quality imported mountain bikes as well as rappelling equipment from Europe and the US.

Hardy Dalat (Map p292; ☎ 836 840; hardydl@hcm .vnn.vn; 66 Đ Phan Dinh Phung; ⏰ 7.30am-8.30pm) With an experienced team of French- and English-speaking tour guides, Hardy Dalat offers abseiling trips to local waterfalls, local trekking, swimming and bird-watching tours.

Sleeping

Owing to its popularity with domestic tourists, Dalat has an extensive network of excellent lodgings, from backpacker dives and private villas to elegant luxury hotels.

Few hotels in cool Dalat have air-con and it's hard to imagine why anyone would want it!

BUDGET

Dreams Hotel (Map p292; ☎ 833 748; dreams@hcm .vnn.vn; 151 Đ Phan Dinh Phung; s US$8, d US$12-15; 💻) Dreams wins hands-down when it comes to value for dollar. This friendly place offers tidy rooms, some with balconies, and a family-style breakfast is included. Musical instruments in the lobby are available for use, and it even accepts credit cards.

Peace Hotel (Map p292; ☎ 822 787; peace12@hcm .vnn.vn; 64 Đ Truong Cong Dinh; r US$8-15) The Peace Hotel is a long-time favourite with backpackers, and its café downstairs is a popular gathering place for travellers and motorbike guides. There's another villa-style branch up the street known as **Peace Hotel II** (Map p292 67 Đ Truong Cong Dinh).

Phuong Thanh Hotel (Map p292; ☎ 825 097; fax 836 521; 65 Đ Truong Cong Dinh; r US$3-6) A friendly, attractive villa-style place, this mini-hotel has wooden floors and a shared terracotta terrace. The cheapest rooms are located in the basement.

Mimosa Hotel (Map p292; ☎ 822 656; fax 832 275 170 Đ Phan Dinh Phung; r US$4-12) Rooms at the Mimosa are tidy and sunny, and some have balconies. Though it's slightly away from the centre and breakfast isn't included, it's a good budget standby.

Lyla Hotel (Map p292; ☎ 834 540; lylahotel@hcm .vnn.vn; 18 Đ Nguyen Chi Thanh; s US$10 d US$15-20) A stylish, central place with an in-house restaurant serving Vietnamese and European fare, the Lyla Hotel has comfy furnished rooms with raised-level bathrooms. Breakfast costs an extra US$1 to room rates.

Hotel Chau Au Europa (Map pp304-5; ☎ 822 870 europa@hcm.vnn.vn; 76 Đ Nguyen Chi Thanh; s/d US$10/15 A friendly, family-run place, the Europa has satellite TV, a shared terrace overlooking town and big shower stalls (with a step) The doubles are very spacious and have electric kettles. The in-house restaurant is also good.

A Chau Hotel (Map p292; ☎ 823 974; 13 Đ Tang Ba Ho; s/d US$8/10) The quiet, centrally located A Chau is on a more out-of-the-way street and has big airy rooms. Doubles are spacious, and all rooms are clean and blandly comfortable with hot water but without mosquito nets.

MID-RANGE

Empress Hotel (Map p292; ☎ 833 888; empresdl@hcm .vnn.vn; 5 Đ Nguyen Thai Hoc; r US$70-230) Befitting the name, this is an elegant hotel set on Xuan

Huong Lake. The Empress has some of the most beautiful rooms in Dalat, some with great views. Rates include a buffet breakfast, and discounts can usually be negotiated. Aesthetic details include wood-slatted window shades, terracotta tile floors and wicker furniture. There's a bar downstairs and an intimate, quiet restaurant at reception.

Hang Nga Gallery & Guesthouse (Map pp304-5; ☎ 822 070; fax 831 480; 3 Đ Huynh Thuc Khang; r US$19-40) Named after aspects of their interior design, these cozy little cavelike rooms come without modern annoyances like phones and TVs. Some rooms have skylights, while others have big tubs or small sitting areas in front of them; all are distinctively different. With only 10 rooms it's wise to book in advance. Our favourites are the Kangaroo and the Gourd.

Golf 1 Hotel (Map pp304-5; ☎ 824 082; golf1@hcm nn.vn; 11 Đ Dinh Tien Hoang; r US$30-45; 💻 🅿) On the more rural outskirts of central Dalat, the Golf 1 boasts helpful staff and a quieter setting than its downtown sisters. On the back side the comfortable rooms have gorgeous views of agricultural fields; at the front, 2nd-storey rooms have sweet, round-shaped wrought-iron balconies. Breakfast is included in room rates, and there's a lift here.

Dal Loi Hotel (Fortune Hotel; Map p292; ☎ 837 333; fax 837 474; 3A Đ Bui Thi Xuan; r US$14-25) Rooms here are spacious and comfortable, with cool tile floors and fairly high ceilings; some have balconies and whirlpool baths. The hotel, run by a friendly couple, also features a lift and in-house restaurant, and the breakfast buffet is included in room rates.

Villa Hotel 28 Tran Hung Dao (Map pp304-5; ☎ 822 764; fax 835 639; 28 Đ Tran Hung Dao; r US$12-20) This charming place, resembling a British country inn, occupies a lovely garden setting. Rooms feature wooden trim, and most have garden views. The 'family room' in the main house has a fireplace and can sleep up to six (US$5 per person). The main house has a huge, shady sitting room, which is carpeted like the individual rooms; the annexe has terracotta tile floors.

Minh Tam Villas (Map pp304-5; ☎ 822 447; fax 824 20; 20A Đ Khe Sanh; r/cottages US$18/15) Set amid lovely **flower gardens** (admission nonguests 4000d) km out of town, this place proffers good views of the surrounding landscape. The house originally belonged to a French archi-

tect, who sold it to a well-to-do Vietnamese family in 1954. It underwent several major renovations and in 1975 was 'donated' to the victorious communist government. The place was under renovation at the time we visited.

Golf 3 Hotel (Map p292; ☎ 826 042; golf3hot@hcm .vnn.vn; 4 Đ Nguyen Thi Minh Khai; r US$42-80) This centrally located property has a rooftop café commanding great views of Dalat and the best steam bath facilities in town. The top-end rooms have wood and tile floors, with views of the lake. It's also equipped with a lift.

TOP END

Discounted rates can usually be negotiated at both of these glorious hotels. If you golf, it's well worth looking into their reasonably priced package deals (see p297).

Hotel Sofitel Dalat Palace (Map pp304-5; ☎ 825 444; sofitel@bdvn.vnd.net; 12 Đ Tran Phu; r US$149-414; 💻) This grand old place was built between 1916 and 1922. Major renovation work has turned it into Dalat's premier luxury accommodation, where most rooms have working fireplaces in addition to the usual amenities. Panoramic views of Xuan Huong Lake can be enjoyed in the expansive ground-floor public areas, where one can sit in a rattan chair, sip iced tea and gaze out through a wall of windows. The nearby tennis courts are owned by the hotel.

Novotel Dalat (Map pp304-5; ☎ 825 777; novotel@ bdvn.vnd.net; 7 Đ Tran Phu; r US$55-92) Nearly opposite the Sofitel, the Novotel is another large vintage hotel. It was constructed in 1932 as the Du Parc Hotel and has undergone extensive renovation work. Today it retains much of the original French-colonial air, with an old-fashioned gated lift, elegant wood floors and carpeted halls. Rates include breakfast; deluxe rooms are probably the best deal for the dong.

Eating

The stairway down to Đ Nguyen Thi Minh Khai turns into a big food stall area in the late afternoon and early evening. Women sell all sorts of precooked home-made dishes or prepare them on a portable charcoal stove. The prices are amazingly cheap. Of course, other vendors with more permanent stalls in the market sell similar things, but at higher prices.

DALAT SPECIALITIES

Dalat is a paradise for lovers of fresh garden vegetables, which are grown locally and sold all over the south. The abundance of just-picked peas, carrots, radishes, tomatoes, cucumbers, avocados, green peppers, lettuce, Chinese cabbages, bean sprouts, beets, green beans, potatoes, corn, bamboo shoots, garlic, spinach, squash and yams makes for meals unavailable elsewhere in the country.

The Dalat area is justifiably famous for its strawberry jam, dried blackcurrants and candied plums, persimmons and peaches, all of which can be purchased from food stalls in the market area west of the lake. Other local delicacies include avocado ice cream, sweet beans *(mut dao)* and strawberry, blackberry and artichoke extracts (for making drinks). The strawberry extract is great in tea. The region also produces grape, mulberry and strawberry wines. Vang Dalat, a brand of local wine, is not bad tasting and it's cheap at around 45,000d a bottle. Artichoke tea, another local speciality, is said to lower blood pressure and benefit the liver and kidneys. Most of these products can be purchased at the central market and at stalls in front of Thien Vuong Pagoda.

Dau hu, a type of pudding made from soy milk, sugar and a slice of ginger, is one of Dalat's specialities, as is hot soy milk *(sua dau nanh)*. Both are sold by itinerant female vendors, who walk around carrying a large bowl of the stuff and a small stand suspended from either end of a bamboo pole.

Most vendors in the central market will let you sample a bit of something before you buy.

RESTAURANTS

Several restaurants on Đ Phan Dinh Phung dish up inexpensive Vietnamese, Chinese, Western and vegetarian cuisine, just down the street from Hardy Dalat.

V Cafe (Map p292; ☎ 837 576; 1 Đ Bui Thi Xuan; mains around 40,000d) This is a fine place to begin a culinary exploration of Dalat. The friendly proprietor Vy (with her American husband singing back-up) dishes up great home-style Vietnamese food, as well as respectable soups, salads, burgers, tacos and quesadillas with home-made flour tortillas. The roasted pork loin with mashed potatoes and gravy is divine. Top it all off with Vy's home-made lemon meringue – yum! V Cafe is also an excellent place to pick brains for travel tips.

Art Café (Map p292; ☎ 510 089; 70 Đ Truong Cong Dinh; mains 30,000d) Owned by an artist whose work adorns the walls, this elegant, bamboo-lined little spot has intimate tables sporting white tablecloths and wineglasses. The menu features mostly Vietnamese dishes with a few Western curveballs thrown in for good measure. Food, presentation, prices and service are excellent, and it's perfect for a relaxed dinner.

Quan Diem Tam (Map pp304-5; ☎ 820 104; 217 Đ Phan Dinh Phung; noodle soup 7000d) Be sure to try this long-running Chinese-style soup shop serving up delicious yellow-noodle won ton soup *(mi hoanh thanh)*.

Trong Dong (Map pp304-5; ☎ 821 889; 220 Đ Phan Din Phung; mains 20,000-45,000d) Another good place t sample superb Vietnamese food served o white tablecloths. House specialities includ grilled shrimp paste on sugar cane, fish in clay pot and minced beef wrapped in lalc leaves. Trong Dong is a bit outside the centre but it's well worth walking over to.

Long Hoa (Map p292; ☎ 822 934; 6 Đ 3 Thang ; mains 15,000-30,000d) Long in vogue with trav ellers, Long Hoa proves to be consistent. I does great sautéed dishes and hotpot. Yo might opt for the rear seating, away fron the street noise.

Minh Uyen (Map p292; meals 10,000d) For some thing more local, head to Dalat's bes budget hole-in-the-wall. Its *com thap can* a mixture of rice, chicken, beef, pork, eg and vegies, is a guaranteed filler!

The Sofitel Dalat Palace (p299) has sev eral dining options. For fine French dining **Le Rabelais** (Map pp304-5; set dinner US$19-29) canno be beat, but bring a credit card or a whee barrow full of dong. Downstairs, **Larry's Ba** (Map pp304-5; mains around 45,000d) serves respect able pub grub and the best pizza in town Lastly, the bright-yellow **Café de La Poste** (Ma pp304-5; set lunch without/with starter US$4.50/6.50, se dinner without/with starter US$12.50/15.50), acros from the post office, is a casual bistro wit a pool table. Waitresses dressed like Pro vençal barmaids serve up good light meal and exquisite pastries and desserts.

VEGETARIAN

There are vegetarian food stalls (signposted *com chay*) in the market area, northwest of Xuan Huong Dam. All serve up delicious 100% vegetarian food, some prepared to resemble and taste like traditional Vietnamese meat dishes.

An Lac (Map p292; ☎ 822 025; 71 Đ Phan Dinh Phung; meals 10,000d) Another cheap vegie restaurant worth checking out is An Lac. There's an English menu here, and options range from noodle soups to rice plates to *banh bao* (steamed rice-flour dumplings stuffed with savoury vegetarian filling).

CAFÉS

Coffee and cake in Dalat is some of the best in Vietnam and a visit to any of the town's finer cafés should make you an instant addict of both.

Stop & Go Cafe (Map p292; ☎ 828 458; 2A Đ Ly Tu Trong; coffee 5000d) This little bohemian oasis is run by a delightful former journalist named Duy Viet. He speaks English and French, and always sports a French beret and a smile. Duy Viet is a notable poet and, judging by the gorgeous bonsai and orchids in the gardens outside the villa, a man with a green thumb. Check out the books of poems and the paintings for sale, or read the comments in the guestbooks that date back to 1989.

Café 100 Roofs (Way to the Moon; Map p292; ☎ 822 780; puppy@hcm.vnn.vn; 57 Đ Phan Boi Chau; ice cream 5000d) Have a little ice cream inside this labyrinthine café created by a friend and colleague of the Crazy House's architect. Constantly evolving, the wet concrete of the interior even smells like a limestone cave. A gem of a place to marvel at and explore.

Cafe Tung (Map p292; 6 Khu Hoa Binh Sq; coffee 5000d) During the 1950s Cafe Tung was a famous hang-out of Saigonese intellectuals. Old-timers swear that the place remains exactly as it was when they were young. As it did then, Cafe Tung serves only tea, coffee, hot cocoa, lemon soda and orange soda to the accompaniment of mellow French music. This is a marvellous place to warm up and unwind on a chilly evening.

Drinking

Dalat has an interesting variety of watering holes, and more happy hours per capita than any other place in Vietnam!

Saigon Nite Bar (Map p292; ☎ 820 007; 11A Đ Hai Ba Trung; happy hour ☯ 5-8pm) Run by zany Mr Dung and his friendly daughter, this lively little place has a billiards table and is a fun place to hang out.

Larry's Bar (Map pp304-5; happy hour ☯ 5-7pm) This cosy little tavern has exposed wooden rafters and stone walls; happy hour specials also apply to food on the bar menu.

The busy market area, to the northwest of Xuan Huong Dam, provides another form of entertainment. Here you can hang out drinking coffee and chatting with the locals at a strip of local cafés near the Viet Hung Internet Cafe.

Shopping

In the past few years the Dalat tourist-kitsch market has really come into its own. Without any effort at all you'll be able to find that special something for your loved ones at home – perhaps a battery-powered stuffed koala that sings 'Waltzing Matilda' or a lacquered alligator with a light bulb in its mouth.

In addition to these useful items, Dalat is known for its *kim mao cau tich*, a kind of fern whose fibres are used to stop bleeding in traditional Chinese medicine. The stuff is also known as *cu ly* because the fibrous matter is sold attached to reddish-brown branches pruned to resemble hairy animals.

The hill tribes of Lam Dong province make handicrafts. Lat products include dyed rush mats and rice baskets that roll up when empty. Koho and Chill people produce the split-bamboo baskets used by all the Montagnards in this area to carry things on their backs. The Chill also weave cloth, including the dark blue cotton shawls worn by some of the Montagnard women. The hill-tribe people carry water in a hollow gourd, with a corn-cob stopper that is sometimes wrapped in a leaf for a tighter fit. If you are interested in Montagnard handicrafts, try Chicken village (p304) or Lat village (p303).

Hoa Binh Square (Map p292), along with the central-market building that's adjacent to it, is one big buy and sell, and a good place to pick up clothing at a reasonable price.

Getting There & Away
AIR

A short walk from the Hotel Sofitel Dalat Palace, **Vietnam Airlines** (Map pp304-5; ☎ 822 895; 40 Đ Ho Tung Mau) has daily services that connect Dalat and HCMC (see p475). Dalat's Lien Khuong Airport is located 30km south of the city.

BUS & MINIBUS

Although there are plenty of public buses to/from Dalat, it's nearly as cheap (and far more comfortable and convenient) to use the private tourist buses and minibuses. Another thing to take into consideration is that the long-distance public bus station is 1km south of Xuan Huong Lake, while most private services will (if asked) pick up and drop off at the hotel of your choice.

The fare for HCMC–Dalat and Nha Trang–Dalat is US$5. Most of the private buses and minibuses travelling between Dalat and Nha Trang/Mui Ne make a stop at the impressive Po Klong Garai Cham towers in Thap Cham, a few kilometres from the junction of Hwys 1 and 20 (see p278).

CAR & MOTORBIKE

From HCMC, taking the inland route to Dalat via Bao Loc and Di Linh is faster than taking the coastal route via Ngoan Muc Pass.

The following are road distances from Dalat: Di Linh (82km), Nha Trang (205km), Phan Rang (101km), Phan Thiet (247km) and HCMC (308km). There are roads connecting Dalat to Buon Ma Thuot and other parts of the central highlands.

Getting Around
TO/FROM THE AIRPORT

The Vietnam Airlines shuttle bus between Lien Khuong Airport and Dalat cost US$3 per person, including door-to-door drop off at your hotel. Private taxis can be hired to make the trip for around US$10, while a motorbike taxi should cost from US$3 to US$5.

BICYCLE

Pedal power is a great way of seeing Dalat, but the hilly terrain and long distances between the sights make it both time and energy consuming. Still, if you're not in a rush and have the stamina, it's a good option.

Several hotels around town rent out bicycles to tourists. It's also well worth looking into the cycling tours offered by Phat Tire Ventures (see p298).

MOTORBIKE

Dalat is much too hilly for *cyclos*, but motorbike is a popular way of touring the environs. For short point-to-point trips around town *xe om* drivers can be flagged down around the central market area for around 5000d.

Self-drive motorbikes can be rented for around US$6 to US$8 a day, but for a dollar or two more we highly recommend hiring one with a driver, leaving the navigation to someone else. Countless motorbike drivers in Dalat offer their services, though you'd be better off finding an Easy Rider (see p291).

TAXI & CAR

Dalat Tourist now has a reliable fleet of taxis. One way, to just about anywhere in Dalat, costs $2 or less. Daily rentals (with driver) cost around US$25.

AROUND DALAT
Lake of Sighs

The **Lake of Sighs** (Ho Than Tho; Map pp304-5; admission 5000d) is a natural lake enlarged by a French-built dam; the forests in the area are hardly Dalat's finest.

According to legend, Mai Nuong and Hoang Tung met here in 1788 while he was hunting and she was picking mushrooms. They fell in love and sought their parents' permission to marry. But at that time Vietnam was threatened by a Chinese invasion and Hoang Tung, heeding the emperor's call to arms, joined the army without telling Mai Nuong. Mai Nuong sent word for him to meet her at the lake, and when he did not come she was overcome with sorrow and threw herself into the lake. Thereafter, the lake has been known as the Lake of Sighs.

There are several small restaurants up the hill from the dam. Horses can be hired for 80,000d an hour, while a ride in a horse drawn carriage costs 140,000d per hour.

The Lake of Sighs is 6km northeast of the centre of Dalat via Đ Phan Chu Trinh.

Tiger Falls

These **falls** (Thac Hang Cop; Map pp304-5; admission 4000d) are named from the local legend of a ferocious tiger living in a nearby cave. This helps to explain the huge ceramic tiger statue, as well as the nearby statue of a hill tribe hunter. The falls themselves are set in a quiet pine forest, and are very photogenic.

You'll also find that there are good hiking trails in the area.

Tiger Falls is about 14km east of Dalat and can be easily reached by bicycle or motorbike. Follow Đ Hung Vuong to Trai Mat village. From the train station there, continue for another 3.5km to the left-hand turn (signposted). From here it's another 5km along a dirt road to the falls. It is also possible to trek to the falls from Dalat, but you'll need to allow a full day.

Quang Trung Reservoir

Created by a dam in 1980, **Quang Trung Reservoir** (Tuyen Lam Lake; Map pp304-5) is an artificial lake that was named after Emperor Quang Trung (also known as Nguyen Hue), a leader of the Tay Son Rebellion. Paddle boats, rowboats and canoes can be rented nearby. The hills around the reservoir are covered with pine trees. There is a switchback path up the hill southwest of the water-intake tower. Ethnic-minority farmers live and raise crops in the vicinity of the lake.

To get to Quang Trung Reservoir, head out of Dalat on Hwy 20. At a point 5km from town turn right and continue for 2km.

Datanla Falls

The nice thing about **Datanla Falls** (admission 5000d) is the short but pleasant walk to get here. The cascade is 350m from Hwy 20 on a path that first passes through a forest of pines and then continues steeply down the hill into a rainforest. The other good thing is the wildlife – lots of squirrels, birds and butterflies. This may have much to do with the fact that hunting is prohibited in the area, so the creatures are less scared of humans.

To get to Datanla Falls, turn off Hwy 20 about 200m past the turn-off to Quang Trung Reservoir. There is a second entrance to the falls several hundred metres further down the road.

Lat Village

pop 6000

The nine hamlets of **Lat village**, whose name is pronounced 'lak' by the locals, are about 12km north of Dalat at the base of Lang Bian Mountain. The inhabitants of five of the hamlets are of the Lat ethnic group; the residents of the other four are members of the Chill, Ma and Koho tribes, each of which speaks a different dialect.

Traditionally, Lat houses are built on piles with rough plank walls and a thatched roof. The people of Lat Village eke out a living growing rice, coffee, black beans and sweet potatoes; the villages have 300 hectares of land and produce one rice crop per year. Many residents of Lat have been economically forced into producing charcoal, a lowly task often performed by Montagnards. Before 1975 many men from Lat worked with the Americans, as did Montagnards elsewhere in the central highlands.

Classes in the village's primary and secondary schools, successors of the École Franco-Koho established in Dalat in 1948, are conducted in Vietnamese rather than tribal languages. Lat has one Catholic and one Protestant church. A Koho-language Bible (Sra Goh) was published by Protestants in 1971; a Lat-language Bible, prepared by Catholics, appeared a year later. Both Montagnard dialects, which are quite similar, are written in a Latin-based script.

To visit the village, you may need to obtain a permit (US$5). Inquire at **Dalat Travel Service** (Map p292; ☎ 822 125; ttdhhd@hcm.vnn.vn; 7 Đ 3 Thang 2). If you book a day tour, the permit should be arranged by the tour operator. There are no restaurants in Lat, just a few food stalls.

To get to Lat from Dalat, head north on Đ Xo Viet Nghe Tinh. At Trung Lam Hamlet there is a fork in the road marked by a street sign. Continue straight on (northwest) rather than to the left (which leads to Suoi Vang, the Golden Stream, 14km away). By bicycle the 12km trip from Dalat to Lat takes about 40 minutes. On foot it's a two-hour walk.

Lang Bian Mountain

Lang Bian Mountain (also called Lam Vien Mountain) has five volcanic peaks ranging in altitude from 2100m to 2400m. Of the two highest peaks, the eastern one is known to locals by the woman's name K'Lang; the western one bears a man's name, K'Biang. The upper reaches of the mountain are forested. Only half a century ago the verdant foothills of Lang Bian Mountain, now defoliated, sheltered wild oxen, deer, boars, elephants, rhinoceroses and tigers.

The hike up to the top of Lang Bian Mountain, from where the views are truly spectacular, takes three to four hours from Lat village. The path begins due north of Lat and is easily recognisable as a red gash in the green mountainside.

You do not need a permit to visit Lang Bian Mountain, though taking a guide along will certainly make the trip more interesting. Consider contacting **Dalat Holidays** (Map p292; ☎ 829 422; www.phattireventures.com; 73 Đ Truong Cong Dinh) to see what outdoor programmes they are offering to Lang Bian.

Chicken Village

Famous for its **giant concrete chicken** caught mid-strut in the village centre, **Lang Dinh An** (Chicken village) has become very popular with travellers because it's conveniently situated on the Dalat–Nha Trang highway 17km from Dalat.

The village is home to the Koho minority who, to a certain extent, have been assimilated into Vietnamese society. Most no longer live in stilt houses and they wear Vietnamese-style clothing. Several stories explain why the statue of the chicken is situated in the centre of the village – one is yet another doomed romance with its lovelorn heroine dying in the forest – but apparently the statue is a gift from the government.

Though the residents of Chicken village are extremely poor, we'd like to suggest that you do *not* give sweets or money to the

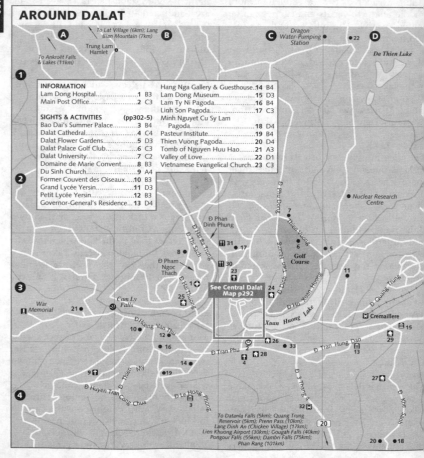

AROUND DALAT

To Lat Village (6km); Lang Bian Mountain (7km)

Trung Lam Hamlet

To Ankroët Falls & Lakes (11km)

Dragon Water-Pumping Station

Da Thien Lake

• 22

Nuclear Research Centre

Đ Phu Dong

Đ Phan Dinh Phung

Đ Thi Sach

Đ Ba Trung

Đ Pham Ngoc Thach

Đ Hai Thuong

Golf Course

Thien Vuong

Đ Duong Dinh Dong

See Central Dalat Map p292

Đ Ho Xuan Huong

Cam Ly Falls

War Memorial

21 ●

Xuan Huong Lake

Cremaillere

Đ Quang Trung

Đ Hoang Van Thu

10 ●

12 ●

● 16

● 26

● 33

Đ Tran Hung Dao

Đ Tran Phu

28

Đ 3 Thang 4

14 ●

●19

9

Đ Thien My

Đ Huyen Tran Cong Chua

Đ Le Hong Phong

27

Đ Khe Sanh

32

To Datanla Falls (5km); Quang Trung Reservoir (5km); Prenn Pass (10km); Lang Dinh An (Chicken Village) (17km); Lien Khuong Airport (30km); Gougah Falls (40km); Pongour Falls (55km); Dambri Falls (75km); Phan Rang (101km)

20

20 ● ●18

children. If you want to help the villagers, there are a couple of shops where you can buy simple things like drinks and biscuits. There are also beautiful weavings for sale near the highway.

Waterfalls

ANKROËT FALLS & LAKES

The two **Ankroët Lakes** were created as part of a hydroelectric project. The waterfall, **Thac Ankroët**, is about 15m high. The Ankroët Lakes are 18km northwest of Dalat in an area inhabited by hill tribes.

DAMBRI FALLS

This is one of the highest (90m) and most magnificent and easily accessible **waterfalls** (admission 10,000d) in Vietnam. The views are positively breathtaking – the steep walk up the path to the top of the falls will almost certainly take your breath away (unless you opt to ride the cable car for 5000d).

If you continue walking upstream from the top of the falls you reach 'Monkey Island', a mini-zoo filled with monkeys and reindeer living at the usual captive standard (ie poor) of Vietnam. The Dambri Restaurant, which adjoins the car park, is cheap and good.

Dambri Falls is close to the town of **Bao Loc** in an area populated chiefly by Montagnards. To reach Dambri Falls, turn off the main highway before Bao Loc as you approach from Dalat and follow the road for 18km. As you're driving towards the falls you can see plentiful tea and mulberry plantations; the high peak off to your right is May Bay Mountain.

Tea and silk (mulberry leaves make up the silkworms' diet) are the major local industries in Bao Loc, and free samples of the local tea can be had at a couple of the roadside rest stops in town. There are also a couple of guesthouses here, making it a practical place to break the journey between HCMC and Dalat.

PONGOUR, GOUGAH & LIEN KHUONG FALLS

The largest in the Dalat area, **Pongour Falls** (admission 5000d) is about 55km towards HCMC from Dalat and 7km off the highway. During the rainy season the falls form a full semicircle, but even during the dry season their stepped formation is beautifully impressive.

Gougah Falls (admission 4000d) is approximately 40km from Dalat towards HCMC. It is only 500m from the highway so it's easy to get to.

At **Lien Khuong Falls**, the Dan Nhim River, 100m wide at this point, drops 15m over an outcrop of volcanic rock. The site, which can be seen from the highway, is 25km towards HCMC from Dalat. Lien Khuong Falls is not far from Lien Khuong airport.

DI LINH

The town of Di Linh (pronounced zee-ling), also known as Djiring, is 1010m above sea level. The area's main product is tea, which is grown on giant plantations founded by

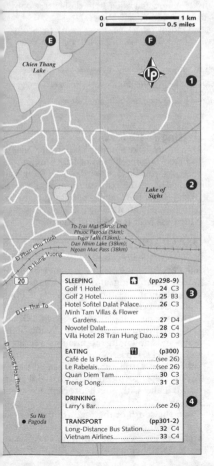

SLEEPING 🏠 (pp298-9)
Golf 1 Hotel...........................24 C3
Golf 2 Hotel...........................25 B3
Hotel Sofitel Dalat Palace.........26 C3
Minh Tam Villas & Flower
    Gardens.............................27 D4
Novotel Dalat.........................28 C4
Villa Hotel 28 Tran Hung Dao....29 D3

EATING 🍴 (p300)
Café de la Poste.....................(see 26)
Le Rabelais...........................(see 26)
Quan Diem Tam......................30 C3
Trong Dong...........................31 C3

DRINKING
Larry's Bar............................(see 26)

TRANSPORT (pp301-2)
Long-Distance Bus Station........32 C4
Vietnam Airlines.....................33 C4

FULRO

The Front Unifié de Lutte des Races Opprimées (FULRO), or the United Front for the Struggle of the Oppressed Races, was for decades a thorn in the side of successive Vietnamese regimes. FULRO, a band of well-organised guerrillas, drew recruits mainly from the Montagnards, who had no love for the Vietnamese majority. Much as it was then, nowadays FULRO's focus is on two key issues: the return of ancestral lands to the Montagnards and allowing them the freedom of religious practice, both of which are strictly controlled by the Vietnamese government.

While the old South Vietnamese government suppressed the Montagnards, the US military exploited their valuable skills in jungle survival during the American War. When the communists took over in 1975, they sought retribution against FULRO rather than attempting to make peace. The guerrillas continued their insurrection for years, but by the mid-1980s they were considered a spent force, with most of their guerrilla bands either dead, captured, living abroad or having given up the fight. In 1992 the surrender of a lone band of FULRO adherents, conducting raids from the remote northeastern corner of Cambodia, appeared to confirm this appraisal.

The insurrection issue would seem to be dead and buried, but as Montagnard demonstrations turned violent in 2001 and 2004, the Vietnamese government is still very sensitive about FULRO. Because the area was immediately closed to outside visitors following both clashes, the only reports released about the events were from Vietnamese government sources.

In contrast to the far north, where minorities are mostly left alone, the government keeps a very tight grip on the Montagnards of the central highlands. Hanoi's policies in this region include:

- populating the highlands with ethnic-Vietnamese settlers, especially in New Economic zones
- encouraging the replacement of traditional slash-and-burn agriculture with sedentary farming
- promoting (in the form of re-education) Vietnamese language, religion and culture.

the French. The Di Linh Plateau, sometimes compared to the Cameron Highlands of Malaysia, is a great place for day hikes. Only a few decades ago the region was famous for its tiger hunting.

The 32m-high **Bo Bla Waterfall** is 7km southwest of Di Linh, close to Hwy 20.

Di Linh is 226km northeast of HCMC and 82km southwest of Dalat on the main HCMC–Dalat highway. The town is 96km from Phan Thiet by a secondary road.

DAN NHIM LAKE
elevation 1042m

Dan Nhim Lake was created by a dam built between 1962 and 1964 by Japan as part of its war reparations. The huge Dan Nhim hydroelectric project supplies electricity to much of the south.

The lake is often used by HCMC movie studios for filming romantic lake scenes. The lake's surface area is 9.3 sq km.

The power station is at the western edge of the coastal plain. Water drawn from Dan Nhim Lake gathers speed as it rushes almost a vertical kilometre down from Ngoan Muc Pass in two enormous pipes.

Getting There & Away

Dan Nhim Lake is about 38km from Dalat in the Don Duong district of Lam Dong province. As you head towards Phan Rang and Thap Cham, the dam is about a kilometre to the left of the Dalat–Phan Rang highway. The power station is at the base of Ngoan Muc Pass near the town of Ninh Son.

NGOAN MUC PASS

Known to the French as Bellevue Pass, **Ngoan Muc Pass** (altitude 980m) is about 5km towards Phan Rang and Thap Cham from Dan Nhim Lake and 64km west of Phan Rang. On a clear day you can see all the way across the coastal plain to the Pacific Ocean (an aerial distance of 55km)! As the highway winds down the mountain in a series of switchbacks, it passes under two gargantuan water pipes – still guarded by armed troops in concrete fortifications – that link Dan Nhim Lake with the hydroelectric power station.

To the south of the road (to the right as you face the ocean) you can see the steep tracks of the *crémaillère* linking Thap Cham with Dalat (see p294).

If you're leaving Dalat for Phan Rang, sites of interest at the top of Ngoan Muc Pass include a waterfall next to the highway, pine forests and the old Bellevue train station.

BUON MA THUOT
☎ 050 / pop 186,600 / elevation 451m

Buon Ma Thuot (or Ban Me Thuot) is the capital of Dac Lac province and the largest town in the western highlands. Before WWII the city was a centre for big-game hunting, but the animals have all but disappeared – along with most of the region's rainforest.

The region's main crop is coffee, and it's the coffee industry that accounts for Buon Ma Thuot's current prosperity. If you can find a good guide, visiting the coffee plantations and processing plants could be interesting.

A large percentage of the area's population is made up of Montagnards. The government's policy of assimilation has been effective: nearly all of the Montagnards now speak Vietnamese fluently.

The rainy season around Buon Ma Thuot lasts from May to October, though downpours are usually short. Because of its lower elevation, Buon Ma Thuot is warmer and more humid than Dalat; it is also very windy.

Buon Ma Thuot is mostly of interest to travellers for being the gateway to Yok Don National Park, but the town also makes a pleasant enough stop between Dalat and Kon Tom or Pleiku.

Information
MEDICAL SERVICES
Dak Lak General Hospital (☎ 852 665; 2 Đ Mai Hac De)

MONEY
Agriculture & Rural Development Bank (☎ 853 930; 37 Đ Phan Boi Chau) This branch can make foreign-currency exchanges.
Vietcombank (1 Nguyen Tat Thanh) ATM near the Victory Monument.

POST
Main Post Office (☎ 852 612; 6 Đ Le Duan) This branch also offers Internet access from around 8am to 5pm.

TRAVEL AGENCIES
Dak Lak Tourist (☎ 852 108; daklaktour@dng.vnn .vn; 3 Đ Phan Chu Trinh; ☼ 7.30-11am & 1.30-5pm) The provincial tourism authority is next to the Thang Loi Hotel.

Dam San Tourist (☎ 851 234; damsantour@dng .vnn.vn; 212-214 Đ Nguyen Cong Tru; ☼ 7am-6pm) This private company based at the excellent Dam San Hotel specialises in tours to the local waterfalls. It also organises trips to Yok Don National park; guides speak English, French and Japanese.
Nguyen Van Mui (☎ 856 085, 0914-010 411) One of many local English-speaking guides who can be hired for trips outside the city, notably to Yok Don National Park.

TRAVEL PERMITS
Permits are still required to visit certain minority villages in the area surrounding Buon Ma Thuot. Contact Dak Lak Tourist to get these valuable bits of paper.

Sights
VICTORY MONUMENT
You can hardly miss this one, as it dominates the square in the centre of town. The **victory monument** commemorates the events of 10 March 1975, when VC and North Vietnamese troops 'liberated' the city. It was this battle that triggered the complete collapse of South Vietnam.

As an interesting footnote, there was formerly a real army tank here facing south, but when it was later replaced with a concrete replica, it was turned north (toward Pleiku), to indicate the correct direction during Ho Chi Minh's campaign to 'liberate' Saigon.

AKO DHONG VILLAGE
Between the northern end of Buon Ma Thuot and outlying coffee plantations, the Ede village of **Ako Dhong** is a neat little community of stilt-house suburbia. Strolling the village makes for a pleasant break from the downtown din (such as it is), and you may be able to find some locals at work weaving traditional fabrics – which might also be for sale.

The village is located about 1½km from the centre of town and makes an easy walk; to get to the village take Đ Phan Chu Trinh northward and hang a left on Đ Tran Nhat Duat. On the way back, stop in at Quan Café Po Lang (p310) for coffee and see if you can catch some live music.

MUSEUM OF DAK LAK PROVINCE
The Dak Lak Province Museum (Bao Tang Tinh Dak Lak) is in fact two separate museums, the Ethnographic Museum and the

CENTRAL HIGHLANDS

BUON MA THUOT

To Quan Café Po Lang (1km); Ako Dhong Village (1.5km)

To Vietnam Airlines Office (2.5km); Bus Station (3km); Ban Me Hotel (3km); Dak Lak Water Park (4km); Pleiku (197km); Nha Trang (205km)

To Yok Don National Park (42km); Ban Don (45km)

Buon Ma Thuot Market

Catholic Church

Stadium

Ho Chi Minh Monument

War Monument

To Tur Village (13km); Dray Nur (20km); Gia Long Falls (20km); Dray Sap (27km)

INFORMATION
Agriculture & Rural
   Development Bank..............1 B2
Dak Lak General Hospital.........2 A4
Dak Lak Tourist......................3 B2
Dam San Hotel.......................4 D2
Dam San Tourist..............(see 4)
Main Post Office....................5 B3
Post Office............................6 B2
Vietcombank.........................7 B2

SIGHTS & ACTIVITIES (pp307-8)
Ethnographic Museum...............8 A4
Revolution Museum..................9 B3
Victory Monument..................10 B2

SLEEPING (p309)
Cao Nguyen Hotel..................11 B1
Duy Hoang Hotel...................12 B2
Tay Nguyen Hotel..................13 B1
Thang Loi Hotel....................14 B2
Thanh Binh Hotel..................15 B2
Thanh Phat Hotel..................16 B2
White Horse Hotel.................17 B1

EATING (pp309-10)
Bon Trieu Restaurant..............18 B2
Cafe 54.............................19 B2
Hanoi Bakery.......................20 A3
Noodle Soup Shops................21 B2
Quan Ngon..........................22 C2
Spring-Roll Stalls.................23 B2

SHOPPING (p310)
Retail Coffee Shops................24 B1

Revolution Museum. The latter is possibly of less interest to foreign tourists.

There are said to be 31 distinct ethnic groups in Dac Lac province, and the **Ethnographic Museum** (☎ 850 426; cnr Đ Nguyen Du & Đ Le Duan; admission 10,000d; ⏱ 7.30-11am & 1.30-5pm) is one place to get some understanding of these disparate groups. Displays at the museum feature traditional Montagnard dress, as well as agricultural implements, fishing gear, bows and arrows, weaving looms and musical instruments. There is a photo collection with accompanying explanations about the historical contacts between the Montagnards and the rest of Vietnam – some of the history is plausible, some is pure fiction.

The Ethnographic Museum is in the former reception of the Bao Dai Villa, a grand French colonial building. A local guide can show you around the exhibits for around 5000d.

The **Buon Ma Thuot Revolution Museum** (☎ 852 527; 1 Đ Le Duan; admission 10,000d; ⏱ 7.30-11am & 2-5pm) focuses on the city's role during the American War.

DAK LAK WATER PARK
If sampling the local rocket-fuel coffee doesn't raise your heart rate, then perhaps waterslides will at **Dak Lak Water Park** (☎ 950 381; Đ Nguyen Tat Thanh; admission 30,000d; ⏱ 9am-6pm). It's about 1km past the bus station, northeast of town.

Sleeping

BUDGET

Ban Me Hotel (☎ 951 001; fax 954 741; 9 Đ Nguyen Chi Thanh; r US$15-20; 🗙) About 3km north of the centre, but within walking distance of the bus station, is this large, friendly motel with a tidy, garden-like setting. A *xe om* from the centre to here costs about 5000d. Air-con rates include breakfast, but fan rooms are more spacious and arguably more comfortable, with bigger terraces upstairs.

Thanh Phat Hotel (☎ 854 857; fax 813 366; 41 Đ Ly Thuong Kiet; r 120,000-180,000d; 🗙) This clean, central budget place has fan rooms with shared bathroom; air-con rooms have a private bathroom and are much nicer, with fridges and TVs. Street-facing rooms have balconies but get very noisy.

Thanh Binh Hotel (☎ 853 812; fax 811 511; 24 Đ Ly Thuong Kiet; r 150,000-170,000d; 🗙) The rooms here are spotless, but they don't come with breakfast. Some have air-con, and it's a good deal if you go for the more luxurious rooms.

Duy Hoang Hotel (☎ /fax 858 020; 30 Đ Ly Thuong Kiet; r 170,000-200,000d; 🗙) Fan rooms share a cold-water bathroom; air-con rooms come complete with hot water, TV and fridge.

MID-RANGE

Dam San Hotel (☎ 851 234; damsantour@dng.vnn.vn; 212-214 Đ Nguyen Cong Tru; r hotel/valley view US$25/30; 🗙 🗙) The Dam San is the best deal in town, with gorgeous views and mellow staff. This quiet, attractive hotel features clean rooms with wooden floors, bathtubs and satellite TV, plus a good restaurant (breakfast is included). Rooms at the back of the building overlook the swimming pool, tennis court and neighbouring coffee plantations.

White Horse Hotel (Khach San Bach Ma; ☎ 851 656; www.bachma.com.vn; 9-11 Đ Nguyen Duc Canh; r US$20-40; 🗙) Sparkling with varnished surfaces and marble, the White Horse is full of immaculate, comfortable rooms with satellite TV. The hotel has a lift, a restaurant, pool tables and the requisite karaoke and massage. Staff are eager to please and friendly; breakfast is included in rates.

Thang Loi Hotel (☎ 857 615; thangloihotelbmt@dng .vnn.vn; 1 Đ Phan Chu Trinh; r US$30-40; 🗙) You'll find most amenities at this government-run tourist hotel, including satellite TV and bathtubs. *Thang loi* means 'victory', so it's not surprising that the hotel faces the local Victory Monument. Some rooms have good city views, and all rooms come with breakfast.

Tay Nguyen Hotel (☎ 851 009; taynguyenhotel@dng .vnn.vn; 110 Đ Ly Thuong Kiet; r US$10-23; 🗙) This is another large, decent place with satellite TV, fridges and minibars. Comfortable doubles have terraces and are more spacious than the singles. It has a large restaurant on the ground floor; breakfast is included. Though staff speak a limited amount of English, they're friendly and eager to help.

Cao Nguyen Hotel (☎ 851 913; daklaktour@dng .vnn.vn; 65 Đ Phan Chu Trinh; r US$40-45; 🗙) Operated by Dak Lak Tourist, the Cao Nguyen is a few years old now but still fairly luxurious. It's known for its dance hall, karaoke and massage service; there's also a restaurant, and the place is equipped with a lift. Rates include breakfast.

Eating

Quan Ngon (☎ 851 909; 72-74 Đ Ba Trieu; mains around 35,000d) Buon Ma Thuot's most remarkable eatery, this large indoor-outdoor place offers seating in a pleasant courtyard garden, or in a wooden stilt house. It has an extensive menu with a wide range of Vietnamese dishes, and to add to the flavour there is an astonishing display of home-made rice wine. Large wine bottles lining the walls inside the restaurant contain everything from snakes, geckos and birds to large reptiles. There is even a small wild cat in a fish tank filled with rice wine. It accepts most major credit cards.

If Quan Ngon doesn't sound like your cup of tea, **Bon Trieu Restaurant** (33 Đ Hai Ba Trung; mains around 20,000d) is known for its delicious beef dishes.

For excellent *nem ninh hoa* – grilled pork wrapped in dried rice paper – head for the bustling fresh **spring-roll stalls** (20-22-26 Đ Ly Thuong Kiet; spring rolls 10,000d) near the Victory Monument. There are also good **noodle-soup shops** (soup 7000d) on Đ Hai Ba Trung.

Travellers looking for something sweet should head straight for **Hanoi Bakery** (☎ 853 609; 123-125 Đ Le Hong Phong; pastries 5000d). Not only are there shelves of freshly-baked pastries, but it also carries snack foods like cheese and chocolate.

CAFÉS

Buon Ma Thuot is justifiably famous for its coffee, which is the best in Vietnam. As usual, the Vietnamese serve it so strong it will make your hair stand on end, and typically in a very tiny cup that allows you no room to add water or milk. Most coffee shops in Buon Ma Thuot also throw in a free pot of tea – be sure you don't mistake it for water and use it to dilute your coffee!

Try **Cafe 54** (54 Đ No Trang Long) for strong coffee, blaring Viet-pop and good people-watching near the Victory Monument. For something more atmospheric, check out **Quan Café Po Lang** (☎ 953 322; cafépolang@pmail.vnn .vn; G26 Đ Tran Khanh Du), about 1km from the city centre. There's an open-air upstairs terrace above the garden setting accented by ethnic fabric-covered chairs and furnishings modelled after branches and tree stumps. The café features live music on Tuesday, Thursday, Friday and Sunday. To get there take Đ Phan Chu Trinh northward, turning right on Đ Tran Khanh Du. The café is several blocks down, on the left.

Shopping

If you like the coffee enough to take some home, be sure to pick up a bag here because the price is lower and quality higher than in HCMC or Hanoi. You can buy whole beans or coffee already ground to a fine powder. Coffee is for sale everywhere in Buon Ma Thuot, and prices average around 15,000d per 500g. Good places to buy coffee beans include the shops around the corner of Đ Hoang Dieu and Đ Phan Chu Trinh, as well as along the guesthouse strip on Đ Ly Thuong Kiet.

Getting There & Away

AIR

There are **Vietnam Airlines** (☎ 955 055; fax 956 265; 65-67 Đ Nguyen Tat Thanh; ☯ 8am-5pm) flights between Buon Ma Thuot and HCMC, as well as Danang (see p475).

BUS

Buon Ma Thuot's bus station is at 71 Đ Nguyen Tat Thanh, about 3km outside of the centre. There are bus services to Buon Ma Thuot from HCMC, Danang, Nha Trang, Dalat, Pleiku and Kon Tum. The Buon Ma Thuot–HCMC buses take 20 hours.

CAR & MOTORBIKE

The road linking the coast with Buon Ma Thuot intersects Hwy 1 at Ninh Hoa

(160km from Buon Ma Thuot), which is only 34km north of Nha Trang. The road is surfaced and in good condition, though a bit steep. Buon Ma Thuot to Pleiku is 197km on an excellent highway.

There's a scenic sealed road connecting Buon Ma Thuot with Dalat (via Lak Lake). Though full of twists and turns, it's in great condition.

AROUND BUON MA THUOT
Dray Sap

The spectacular **Dray Sap** (admission 10,000d), about 27km from Buon Ma Thuot, is in the middle of a hardwood rainforest. The name, fittingly, means 'smoky waterfall'; unfortunately, the beauty of the 100m-wide falls is a bit marred by the trash tossed around with alacrity by visitors.

Along with the new road under construction, plans are in the works for a cliffside restaurant.

Dray Nur & Gia Long Falls

Both of these waterfalls, 3km apart on the Krong Ana River, are stunning and offer good riverside trekking opportunities. Ruins of ramparts ordered by the French during the colonial period can be seen near the falls.

Both can be done as day trips, but you can also consider camping out. Entry to **Gia Long Falls** (admission US$2) includes the right to camp (tents US$5). Simple food (noodle soup, rice etc) is also available.

To reach the falls, follow Hwy 14 south from Buon Ma Thuot to a fork about 8km south of town; bear left there and continue for 6.5km to the small village of Dong Tam. Turn right at the village centre and continue another 10.5km to a lonely dirt crossroads; turn left here and travel the final 300m to a gate. These days the landscape viewed from the red-dirt road is largely a product of slashing and burning for the coffee and sugarcane plantations.

In Buon Ma Thuot **Dam San Tourist** (☎ 851 234; damsantour@dng.vnn.vn; 212-214 Đ Nguyen Cong Tru) is the place to inquire about information and tours to the waterfalls.

Tur Village

The Rhade (or Ede) hamlet of **Tur** is 13km south from Buon Ma Thuot. The people raise animals and grow cassava (manioc), sweet potatoes and maize. This village has become one of the most heavily 'Vietnamised' in the region, but along with the loss of cultural identity it has earned a higher standard of living.

Rhade society is matrilineal and matrilocal (centred on the household of the wife's family). Extended families live in longhouses – each section of which houses a nuclear family. Each longhouse is presided over by a man, often the husband of the senior woman of the family. The property of the extended family is owned and controlled by the oldest woman in the group.

The religion of the Rhade is animistic. In the past century many Rhade have converted to Christianity.

Yok Don National Park
☎ 050

The largest of Vietnam's nature preserves, Yok Don National Park (Vuon Quoc Gia Yok Don; ☎ 783 049; yokdon@dng.vnn.vn) has been gradually expanded and today encompasses 115,545 hectares. There is excellent forest trekking in Yok Don and the beautiful Serepok River flows through the park and has several waterfalls and good fishing holes.

Yok Don is home to 67 mammal species, 38 of which are listed as endangered in Indochina, and 17 of those endangered worldwide. The park habitat accommodates elephants, tigers and leopards, as well as nearly 200 different species of bird, including peacocks. Other common wildlife in the park includes deer, monkeys and snakes. In recent years previously unknown animals like the *Canisauvus,* a species of wild dog, have been discovered in the park. In 2003 a pair of critically-endangered giant ibis *(Thaumatibis gigantea)* was sighted in the park.

The delicate balance between ecological conservation and the preservation of local cultures is a challenge, considering the poverty of the region's people and their traditional means of survival (eg hunting). However, the Vietnamese government is working with international agencies such as the United Nations Development Programme (UNDP) to manage this ongoing balance, aiming towards education and community participation towards conservation practices.

There are 17 ethnic groups in the region, including a significant number that have recently migrated from northern Vietnam.

The locals are mostly Ede and M'nong, a matrilineal tribe so the family name is passed down through the mother and children are considered members of their mother's family. The M'nong are known for their fiercely belligerent attitude towards other tribes in the area, as well as towards ethnic Vietnamese.

The M'nong are also known for their astute skills in capturing wild elephants, dozens of which live in the area (see p312). Traditional elephant-racing festivals are put on from time to time. Visitors can arrange elephant rides through some beautiful forests. Elephants typically carry three people, but for heavier Westerners two is usually the limit. Elephant rides can be arranged through Dak Lak Tourist in Buon Ma Thuot, but you can also simply turn up and make arrangements. Booking direct costs from 100,000 to 200,000d per hour.

SIGHTS & ACTIVITIES

Most of the domestic tourist action in the area centres on the village of **Ban Don** in Ea Sup district, 45km northwest of Buon Ma Thuot. The village, 5km beyond the turn-off into the national park, has unfortunately become overrun with bus loads of tourists.

Traditional activities in Ban Don involve **gong performances** and drinking wine from a **communal jug**. Everybody gathers around the wine jug and drinks at the same time through very long straws – it makes for good photos.

There are the neglected ruins of a 13th-century Cham tower called **Yang Prong** 50km north of Ban Don at Ya Liao, near the Cambodian border. A permit and guide are necessary to visit this spot.

SLEEPING & EATING

At the national park headquarters, **Yok Don Guesthouse** (☎ 853 110; r 150,000d; ☒) has four basic rooms (cold water only), each with two beds.

Camping in the park is possible, but you must have a guide with you in order to do so, due to Yok Don's proximity to the Cambodian border. Overnight treks with a guide cost 350,000d, and longer treks can also be arranged. You'll need to bring your own food on all trips.

Though it can be a bit of a circus, there is a good restaurant in Ban Don. If you're

---

THE ELEPHANT MAN

Throughout history kings from Thailand, Vietnam, Cambodia and Laos have come to the area around present-day Yok Don National Park in search of elephants. To this day the tradition of elephant trapping continues, and no-one else knows more about it than local legend Yprong Eban.

Yprong Eban, a gentle 89-year-old, is Vietnam's greatest living elephant hunter. Born of a M'nong father and Lao mother, Yprong Eban spent his childhood years riding on the backs of elephants with his uncle, the late Khun Su Nop. Also known as Y'thu, Khun Su Nop was so renowned that he is hailed as Kuru, or King of the Elephant Hunters. Khun Su Nop's old tribal house still stands in the village of Ban Don, and his grave is also nearby.

Yprong Eban spent most of his life in the forest, and by the time he retired in 1996 he had captured more than 300 elephants. Typically, hunters use two domesticated elephants in order to catch one wild calf. Only elephants under the age of three are targeted, otherwise they are too wild, hard to train, and run a higher risk of returning to the jungle.

One interesting local custom is that men must abstain from sex for a week or more before preparing for the hunt. The hunts involve a series of quick attacks and retreats, and their energy needs to be saved in case they are chased down by a herd of stampeding elephants! Unlike the evil elephant poachers in Africa, the elephant hunters of Ban Don never cause physical harm to the parents when capturing their young.

Despite his desire to head back into the forest in search of elephants, these days Yprong Eban spends his time hanging around the park headquarters chatting with curious tourists and sharing his stories of love and respect for these intelligent and faithful creatures. He still dresses in traditional M'nong garb and enjoys blowing the old buffalo horn he used to alert the village with when an elephant had been caught. Yprong Eban speaks French, Vietnamese, Lao and several hill-tribe languages, and is happy to entertain visitors to the park with elephant-hunting stories.

---

lucky you might catch a local performance of gong music and dancing put on for a group tour.

In Ban Don contact Banmeco Travel Agency or **Ban Don Tourist** (☎ 798 119) about overnighting in minority **stilt houses** (US$5 per person). Another option is the **bungalows** (US$12) out on nearby Aino Island, reached via a rickety series of bamboo suspension bridges.

GETTING THERE & AROUND

There's no public transport to Yok Don National Park, but it's easily reached by car or motorbike. Local motorbike guides in Buon Ma Thuot can take you to the park for around US$7 one way, or US$10 round trip.

Elephants can be hired overnight for 600,000d per day.

Lak Lake

Emperor Bao Dai built a small palace at **Lak Lake** (Ho Lak), but it is now a ruin. Nevertheless, the lake views are fantastic and the climb up the adjacent hills is well worthwhile. The nearby M'nong village is a unique experience.

Lak Lake is 50km south of Buon Ma Thuot, along a sealed and relatively flat road. The hillier stretch of road from the lake to Dalat, 154km on Rte 27, is breathtaking in spots, with some nice forest patches and jungle. There's a good deal of evidence of slashing-and-burning, and clear-cutting. There is little in the way of facilities en route. Krong No has a couple of *com pho* restaurants; it's a small town 41km from Lak Lake in the direction of Dalat.

SLEEPING & EATING

In a peaceful lake setting, **Khu Dulich Ho Lak** (☎ 586 184; r US$7-10, shared longhouse US$5) was built under the shade of jackfruit trees. Sleeping in the fragrant rattan M'nong longhouse is a simple treat; all accommodations share clean showers and toilets. There's a floating restaurant nearby that does decent food.

A more authentic accommodation alternative is the **stilt houses** (☎ 586 268; fax 586 343; per person US$5) in the pleasant lakeside village of the Ede minority group. **Jun village** is surrounded by plush green rice paddies and the Ede-style stilt longhouses are indeed atmospheric. There are some souvenir shops selling hill-tribe handicrafts. Two-hour elephant rides can be arranged in June for around US$30.

PLEIKU

☎ 059 / pop 141,700 / elevation 785m

Pleiku (or Playcu) is the major market town of the western highlands, but a tourist destination it's not. Although it's not the most compelling town, there are a couple of sights worth checking out if you're breaking a journey here. The city is 785m above sea level, which makes the climate cool.

In February 1965 the VC shelled a US compound in Pleiku, killing eight Americans. Although the USA already had more than 23,000 military advisers in Vietnam, their role was supposed to be noncombative at the time. The attack on Pleiku was used as a justification by US President Johnson to begin a relentless bombing campaign against North Vietnam and the rapid build-up of US troops.

When US troops departed in 1973, the South Vietnamese kept Pleiku as their main combat base in the area. When these troops fled the advancing VC, the whole civilian population of Pleiku and nearby Kon Tum fled with them. The stampede to the coastline involved over 100,000 people, but tens of thousands died along the way.

The departing soldiers torched Pleiku, but the city was rebuilt in the 1980s with assistance from the Soviet Union. As a result, the city has a large collection of ugly, Soviet-style buildings and lacks much of the colour and antiquity you find elsewhere in Vietnamese towns.

Information

INTERNET ACCESS

Internet Café (☎ 875 986; Internet_pleiku@yahoo.com; 80 Đ Nguyen Van Troi)

MONEY

Vietcombank (☎ 828 593; vcbgialai@vietcombank.com.vn; 12 Đ Tran Hung Dao & 33 Đ Quang Trung) Both branches offer foreign currency exchanges and credit card advances and cash travellers cheques.

POST

Main Post Office (☎ 824 011; 69 Đ Hung Vuong)

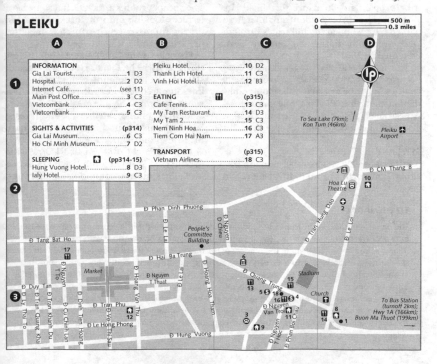

TRAVEL AGENCIES

Gia Lai Tourist (☎ 874 571; gialaitourist@hotmail.com; 215 Đ Hung Vuong) Located beside the Hung Vuong Hotel, Gia Lai offers a wide variety of tours including trekking, elephant riding and programmes catering to war veterans.

TRAVEL PERMITS

You don't need a permit to stay overnight in Pleiku itself, or to travel the major highways, but you are likely to need one to visit villages in Gia Lai province. The permits cost money and you'll be required to hire a guide in Pleiku. This puts off many travellers, who usually just skip Pleiku entirely and head north to Kon Tum, where the authorities are more hospitable. Gia Lai Tourist can arrange the permit.

Sights
MUSEUMS

Pleiku has two museums, neither of them remarkable and both often closed.

The **Ho Chi Minh Museum** (☎ 824 276; 1 Phan Dinh Phuong; admission free; ◷ 8-11am & 1-4.30pm Mon-Fri) displays documents and photos to demonstrate Uncle Ho's affinity for hilltribe people, and their love for Uncle Ho. There are also displays about a Bahnar hero named Nup who led the hill tribes through wars with both the French and the USA. Nup died in 2001.

The **Gia Lai Museum** (☎ 824 520; 28 Đ Quang Trung; admission 10,000d; ◷ 8-11am & 1-4.30pm Mon-Fri) features hill-tribe artefacts and photographs that memorialise Pleiku's role during the American War. Check in first at Gia Lai Tourist to get a ticket and an appointment.

SEA LAKE

Bien Ho, or Sea Lake, is a deep mountain lake about 7km north of Pleiku. It is believed to have been formed from a prehistoric volcanic crater. Both the lake itself and the surrounding area boast beautiful scenery and, thankfully, there's little in the way of development, apart from a tiered viewing terrace. This makes a pleasant bike ride and picnic from Pleiku.

Sleeping

Ialy Hotel (☎ 824 843; fax 827 619; 89 Đ Hung Vuong; r 220,000-400,000d; ✕) The Ialy is a solid choice in Pleiku – bright and airy rooms come with air-con and hot water, and the lobby boasts a Vietcombank ATM and lift. First-class rooms are suite-style and very comfortable. Rates include a Vietnamese breakfast, tax and service.

Hung Vuong Hotel (☎ 824 270; fax 827 170; 2 Đ Le Loi; tw US$10-24; ✕) With an attractive lobby, this large hotel has a range of comfortable rooms featuring satellite TV and minibars. As it's on a busy intersection, try to get a room facing the back.

Thanh Lich Hotel (☎ 824 674; fax 828 319; 86 Đ Nguyen Van Troi; r US$7-15; ✕) This place is most successful at attracting the backpacker set. The cheaper rooms are small, but some have terraces looking onto the back alley roofs; pricier rooms have air-con and amenities like fridge and TV.

Pleiku Hotel (☎ 824 628; fax 822 151; 124 Đ Le Loi; r US$22-30; ✕) The Pleiku Hotel is a big, old, state-run concrete hunk of impressive Stalinesque architecture. All rooms have hot water, and rates include breakfast. Perks include IDD phone, satellite TV and fridges. Some rooms around the courtyard have nice views of town.

Vinh Hoi Hotel (☎ 824 644; fax 871 637; 39 Đ Tran Phu; r US$17-24; ✕) The Vinh Hoi is OK as one of Pleiku's nicer accommodation offerings,

---

TO DIE JARAI

The Jarai minority live in the Pleiku area and have an unusual burial custom: each deceased gets a grave marked with a shelter or bordered with stakes of bamboo, with carved wooden figures sometimes placed along the borders of the grave. Though these figures are carved simply, they're quite expressive, often carved in a squatting position with hands on the person's face in an attitude of mourning. Graves are set up much like a miniature village, with several people buried in one graveyard.

For years relatives bring food to the grave and pass the death anniversaries at the gravesite. Death anniversaries are spent feasting, drinking rice wine and mourning – as well as celebrating – the deceased. After several years the grave is abandoned, the spirit having moved on from the village.

but you can probably find a better deal for upper-end prices. Fan rooms have a shared bathroom.

Eating

My Tam Restaurant (Đ Quang Trung; mains 10,000-20,000đ) This Chinese family-run place is a hit with locals. It has perhaps the best fried chicken in the central highlands, but the menu is only in Vietnamese. Also good is its other branch, **My Tam 2** (☎ 824 730; 6 Đ Quang Trung).

Cafe Tennis (☎ 874 532; 61 Đ Quang Trung; coffee 5000đ) Next to the local tennis court, this café serves good local coffee in a fake bamboo stilt house near the Gia Lai Museum. The pleasant garden setting – with small pond and plants – and muffled *thwacks* of tennis balls provide an interesting ambience.

Nem Ninh Hoa (80 Đ Nguyen Van Troi) does tasty and fresh spring rolls, while **Tiem Com Hai Nam** (☎ 883 128; 140 Đ Hai Ba Trung; mains 10,000-20,000đ) is a good spot for chicken-and-rice dishes.

Getting There & Away
AIR
The local office of **Vietnam Airlines** (☎ 823 058; fax 825 096; 55 Đ Quang Trung) is near the corner of Đ Tran Hung Dao. Flights connect Pleiku with HCMC and Danang.

BUS
There are bus services to Pleiku from HCMC and most coastal cities between Nha Trang and Danang. The bus station is just over 2km east of town.

CAR & MOTORBIKE
Pleiku is linked by road to Buon Ma Thuot (197km), Quy Nhon (166km) and Kon Tum (49km). There is a particularly barren stretch of land on the road from Buon Ma Thuot, probably the result of Agent Orange use and overlogging.

Road distances from Pleiku are 550km to HCMC and 424km to Nha Trang.

KON TUM
☎ 060 / pop 89,800 / elevation 525m
This sleepy mountain town is the capital of Kon Tum province, the northernmost region of the central highlands. It's a region inhabited primarily by Montagnards, including the Bahnar, Jarai, Rengao and Sedang communities. Relatively little English is spoken in Kon Tum, and the relative lack of foreign tourists also means that overcharging is equally uncommon.

So far Kon Tum remains largely unspoiled and the authorities remain blessedly invisible. Some may argue that Dalat offers more things to see and do, but Dalat is very touristy and if you're trying to avoid the beaten track, this is one place to do it. Kon Tum is on the original (and seldom-travelled) Ho Chi Minh Trail.

The Vietnamese government is currently undertaking a major renovation of the Ho Chi Minh Trail, from the Hoa Binh province in the north to Ca Mau in the south. At the time of writing, these projects were still underway and these regions quite untrammelled by the tourist trail. Motorcycle and mountain-bike tours can be arranged to explore this historical road-less-travelled; customised tours are most easily arranged at the adventure agencies in Dalat (see p292) or at Sinhbalo in HCMC (see p328).

There are plenty of minority villages in the area, including several that are right on the edges of town. One interesting aspect of village life that you will not see in the north are the communal *rong* houses: tall and impressive thatched-roof buildings on stilts. If your timing is right, you may be able to catch a local festival with gong playing and rice-wine drinking from ceramic jars.

Like elsewhere in the highlands, Kon Tum saw its share of combat during the war. A major battle between South Vietnamese forces and the North Vietnamese took place in and around Kon Tum in the spring of 1972 – the area was devastated by hundreds of American B-52 raids.

Information
MEDICAL SERVICES
Kon Tum General Hospital (☎ 862 573; 224 Đ Ba Trieu)

MONEY
There's no place to cash travellers cheques in Kon Tum; the nearest place to accomplish this is in Pleiku.
BIDV (☎ 862 340; 1 Đ Tran Phu; ☒ closed Sat) Exchanges US dollars and Euros, and makes cash advances on major credit cards.

POST
Main post office (☎ 862 361; 250 Đ Le Hong Phong)

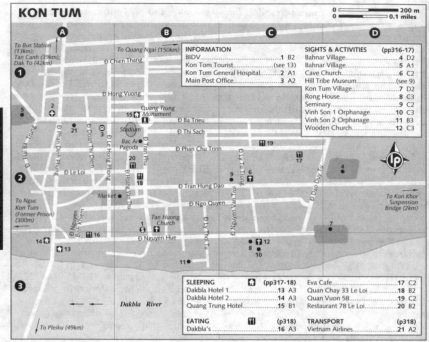

TRAVEL AGENCIES

Kon Tum Tourist (☎ 861 626; www.kontumtourist
.com.vn; 2 Đ Phan Dinh Phung; ☷ 8-11am & 1-4.30pm)
The provincial tourism authority has its main booking
office at the Dakbla Hotel. Staff here can help answer
queries and arrange trekking tours, overnight stays in
villages and boating trips on Yaly Lake and the Dakbla
River. One of their star guides, Mr Huynh, speaks the local
Bahnar language as well as excellent English.

Sights
MONTAGNARD VILLAGES
There are quite a few Montagnard villages
around Kon Tum. In general the local
tribes welcome tourists, but only if you
are not too intrusive with regard to their
lifestyle.

Some of the small villages (or perhaps
we should say 'neighbourhoods') are on the
periphery of Kon Tum and you can even
walk to them from the centre. There are two
Bahnar villages, simply called Lang Bana in
Vietnamese: one is on the east side of town,
the other on the west side.

Also on the east side of Kon Tum is **Kon
Tum village** (Lang Kon Tum). This is, in fact,

the original Kon Tum before it grew up to
become a small Vietnamese city.

If you have time to do a multi-day trek
into the jungle, Kon Tum Tourist (left)
can arrange homestays in outlying villages.
Because the guides here are careful not to
intrude too frequently on any one village,
visitors are always welcomed and traditions
remain intact. Email ahead to schedule a
rare and real look at life in the village.

The Kon Tum police continue to have a
relatively open attitude about tourists visiting local minority villages without permits.
Check in with Kon Tum Tourist for the
latest scoop on the situation.

RONG HOUSE
Kon Tum's **rong house** is the scene of important local events such as meetings, weddings, festivals, prayer sessions and so on.
If you happen to arrive on the day of an
auspicious occasion and stumble upon one
of these activities in progress, it could indeed be interesting.

Rong houses are a type of thatched-roof
community house built on tall stilts. The

original idea of building these on stilts was for protection from elephants, tigers and other overly assertive animals.

There's an attractive old **wooden church** next to the *rong* house.

SEMINARY & HILL-TRIBE MUSEUM

Kon Tum is home to a lovely old Catholic **seminary** that looks as if it was beamed here from a provincial French village. The residents are generally welcoming of visitors, and the **hill-tribe museum** on the 2nd floor is worth stopping to see, if it happens to be open.

Down the road from the seminary gate is a curious little **cave church**.

ORPHANAGES

A short walk from the town centre, these delightful sister orphanages are well worth spending a few hours at. Staff at both the **Vinh Son 1** and **Vinh Son 2** orphanages are welcoming of visitors who come to share some time with the adorable and multi-ethnic resident children.

If you plan to visit, please make a donation to the orphanage; they are very much in need of support. Canned food, clothing or toys for the kids would be appropriate, and monetary contributions are of course appreciated.

Vinh Son 1 is just behind the wooden church on Đ Nguyen Hue. From here you can continue east to visit nearby minority villages. Vinh Son 2, at the southern edge of town and beyond a small Bahnar village, is less visited and more populous (with around 175 children) so is usually in need of more help.

NGUC KON TUM

This **former prison compound** (☺ 7.30-11am & 1-5pm), near the western edge of Kon Tum, is today a quiet park on the banks of the Dakbla River. The prisoners incarcerated here were VC and all were freed in 1975 when the war ended. This was one of the more famous prisons run by the South Vietnamese; VC who survived their internment here were made into heroes after liberation.

There's a small museum at the prison site, but nothing is left of the original buildings. Outside the museum is a memorial statue; inside, you'll find old photos of prisoners and models of the prison cells, but all interpretive signs are in Vietnamese only.

DAK TO & CHARLIE HILL

This obscure **outpost**, 42km north of Kon Tum, was a major battlefield during the American War. In 1972 it was the scene of intense fighting and one of the last big battles before American troops pulled out.

Dak To has become popular with visiting groups of US veterans, but you probably won't find much of interest if you're not a war buff. More intriguingly, those few VC veterans with sufficient free time and money also like to come here to stir their memories.

About 5km south of Dak To is **Charlie Hill**. The hill was a fortified South Vietnamese stronghold before the VC tried to overrun it. The South Vietnamese officer in charge, Colonel Ngoc Minh, decided that he would neither surrender nor retreat and the battle became a fierce fight to the death. Unusually for a guerrilla war, this was a prolonged battle. The VC laid siege to the hill for 1½ months before they managed to kill Colonel Minh and 150 South Vietnamese troops, who had made their last stand here.

Although largely forgotten in the West, the battle is well known, even now, in Vietnam. The reason for this is largely because the fight was commemorated by a popular song, 'Nguoi O Lai Charlie' ('The People Stayed in Charlie').

Not surprisingly, the hill was heavily mined during the war and is still considered unsafe to climb.

There's a **rong house** in Dak To that is worth seeking out.

Sleeping

All three of Kon Tum's hotels are owned and managed by Kon Tum Tourist.

Dakbla Hotel (☎ 863 333; fax 863 336; 2 Đ Phan Dinh Phung; r US$23-30; ⚡) The plushest and priciest of the bunch, Dakbla has a sweet location near the river and is the preferred stop for most travellers. Rates include breakfast, and Kon Tum Tourist is conveniently located adjacent to the lobby.

Dakbla Hotel 2 (☎ 863 335; fax 863 336; 163 Đ Nguyen Hue; r US$6-10; ⚡ P) Across the road from Dakbla, this budget hotel has large but fairly spartan rooms. Rooms starting at US$8 come with air-con, balconies, TV and phone. Though the staff here don't speak much English, they'll bend over backwards to be helpful.

Quang Trung Hotel (☎ 862 249; fax 862 763; 168 Đ Ba Trieu; d 122,000-263,000đ; 🌀) For hardcore backpackers there are a few US$5 fan rooms resembling prison cells. Rooms in the main building are quite a bit more comfortable, with the usual amenities, and include breakfast. The hotel features a sauna, massage and a steam bath. Try booking a room with a view (of the Quang Trung statue) in front.

Eating

Dakbla's (☎ 862 584; 168 Đ Nguyen Hue; mains 30,000đ) With good food and reasonable prices, Dakbla's tends to draw the most travellers. They prepare Vietnamese standards, as well as exotic fare such as wild boar and frog. The owner displays his impressive collection of hill-tribe artefacts on the walls, some of which are for sale.

Quan Vuon 58 (☎ 863 814; 58 Đ Phan Chu Trinh; lau de 50,000đ) This is an indoor-outdoor goat-meat speciality restaurant. Goat *(de)* can be ordered over a dozen ways, such as steamed *(de hap)*, grilled *(de nuong)*, sautéed *(de xao lan)*, curried *(de cari)*, and the ever-popular hotpot *(lau de)*.

Restaurant 78 Le Loi (☎ 864 404; 78 Đ Le Loi; lau 50,000đ) is crowded with locals eating hotpot and drinking beer. Across the road there is good vegetarian food at **Quan Chay 33 Le Loi** (33 Đ Le Loi; mains 15,000đ).

CAFÉS

Eva Café (☎ 862 944; 1 Đ Phan Chu Trinh; coffee 5000đ) A pleasant surprise tucked behind its gate, this unique-looking, three-storey building resembles a local hill-tribe house set in a lovely garden. Vietnamese poetry, sculpture (made by the owner) and stained glass adorn the wooden walls and courtyard. The café seems a little incongruous in simple Kon Tum, but it's a good place for a coffee or cold beer in the evening.

Getting There & Away
AIR
Vietnam Airlines (☎ 862 282; fax 862 455; 129 Đ Ba Trieu; ⏰ 7-11am & 1-5pm Mon-Sat) can handle air-travel bookings; flights from Pleiku go to Danang, HCMC and Hanoi.

BUS
There's a convenient bus service from Kon Tum to HCMC via the scenic Hwy 14 (12 hours). Buses connect Kon Tum to Danang, Pleiku and Buon Ma Thuot. Kon Tum's bus station, however, is inconveniently located about 13km north of the town centre, although many long-distance buses still pass through town, so you can hop off then.

Bus conductors may levy a higher fare for foreigners leaving from Kon Tum; ostensibly, the extra charge is to cover insurance, which is more expensive than for Vietnamese travellers. However, since the price disparity is not clearly quoted anywhere, you'd be wise to bargain a bit.

CAR & MOTORBIKE
The fastest approach to Kon Tum from the coast is on Hwy 19 between Quy Nhon and Pleiku. Hwy 14 between Kon Tum and Buon Ma Thuot is also in good nick. Hwy 24, connecting Quang Ngai with Kon Tum, is particularly scenic and in excellent shape.

Looking at a map, it might seem feasible to drive between Kon Tum and Danang on Hwy 14. Although this is a beautiful drive, unfortunately the road is still in poor condition and only motorbikes and 4WDs can get through. If you've got the right form of transport, this challenging ride on the Ho Chi Minh Trail is surely a great option. It is logical to break the trip, however, in Phuoc Son.

Ho Chi Minh City

319

CONTENTS

At first sight Ho Chi Minh City (HCMC) may seem to be populated with a million bandana-bedecked women bandits on the verge of a giant traffic accident. And in fact, the pattern in the streets reflects a generalised, organised chaos in a city that attracts people from all over the country hoping to better their fortunes. A young office worker manoeuvres her Honda Future through rush-hour traffic, long hair flowing, high heels working the brake pedal. The sweating Chinese businessman chats on his cellular phone, cursing his necktie in the tropical heat. A desperate beggar suddenly grabs your arm, a rude reminder that this is still a developing city, despite the trimmings. It is here that the economic changes sweeping Vietnam – and their negative social implications – are most evident.

Unofficially the city is still called 'Saigon'; officially, 'Saigon' refers only to District 1. Southerners certainly prefer the name Saigon, but if you have to deal with government officials it's best to use HCMC. The city fumes, ferments, bubbles and churns. Yet within this teeming 300-year-old metropolis are timeless traditions and the beauty of an ancient culture. In the pagodas monks pray and incense burns. Artists create masterpieces on canvas or in carved wood. Puppeteers entertain children in the parks while, in the back alleys, acupuncturists treat patients and students learn to play the violin. A seamstress carefully creates an *ao dai*, the graceful Vietnamese costume that might elicit the envy of Parisian fashion designers.

HCMC hums and buzzes with the tenacious will of human beings to survive and improve their lot. Crazy-making and seductive, the city beats with a palpable energy, day and night.

HIGHLIGHTS

- Visit the **War Remnants Museum** (p329) for a view through Vietnamese eyes
- Step off the street and into incense-infused, still air at **Quan Am Pagoda** (p329) and its neighbours in Cholon
- If you can't decide between tapas, tempura or Thai, head to **Đ Dong Du** (p353), close your eyes, point and choose
- Splish-splash a day away at **Dam Sen Water Park** (p346)
- Nurture your Dionysian tendencies in the cool, chic **Q Bar** (p358) or the divier, livelier **Lost in Saigon** (p358).
- Browse **Ben Thanh Market** (p362) for hidden treasure – haute couture or recycled-can helicopters.

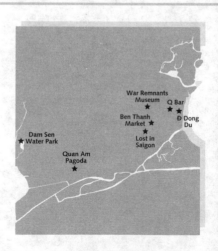

- TELEPHONE CODE: 08
- POPULATION: 6,063,000
- AREA: 2029 SQ KM

HISTORY

The Nguyen dynasty's Saigon was captured by the French in 1859, becoming the capital of the French colony of Cochinchina a few years later. In 1950, the author Norman Lewis described Saigon as follows: 'Its inspiration has been purely commercial and it is therefore without folly, fervour or much ostentation…a pleasant, colourless and characterless French provincial city.' The city served as the capital of the Republic of Vietnam from 1956 until 1975, when it fell to advancing North Vietnamese forces and was renamed Ho Chi Minh City by the Hanoi government.

Nowadays, the official government census counts only those who have official residence permits, and probably a third of the population lives here illegally. Many of these illegal residents actually lived in the city before 1975, but their residence permits were transferred to rural re-education camps after reunification. Not surprisingly, they and their families have simply sneaked back into the city, although without a residence permit they cannot own property or a business.

Explosive growth, part of the effect of *doi moi* (economic reforms) in 1986, is evident in new high-rise buildings, joint-venture hotels

WAR OF THE NAMES

One of the primary battlegrounds for the hearts and minds of the Vietnamese people during the last four decades has been the naming of Vietnam's provinces, districts, cities, towns, streets and institutions. Some places have been known by three or more names since WWII and, in many cases, more than one name is still used.

Urban locations have borne French names (often of the generals, administrators and martyrs who made French colonialism possible); names commemorating the historical figures chosen for veneration by the South Vietnamese government; and the alternative set of heroes selected by the Hanoi government. Buddhist pagodas have formal names as well as one or more popular monikers. In the highlands, both Montagnard and Vietnamese names for mountains, villages and so on are in use. The differences in vocabulary and pronunciation between the north, centre and south sometimes result in the use of different words and spellings (such as 'Pleiku' and 'Playcu').

When French control of Vietnam ended in 1954, almost all French names were replaced in both the North and the South. For example, Rue Catinat in Saigon was renamed Đ Tu Do (Freedom); since reunification it has been known as Đ Dong Khoi (Uprising). In 1956, the names of some provinces and towns in the South were changed as part of an effort to erase from popular memory the Viet Minh's anti-French exploits, which were often known by the places in which they took place. The village-based southern communists, who by this time had gone underground, continued to use the old designations and boundaries in running their regional, district and village organisations. The peasants quickly adapted to this situation, using one set of place names when dealing with the communists and a different set of names when talking to South Vietnamese government representatives.

Later, US soldiers in Vietnam gave nicknames (such as China Beach near Danang) to places whose Vietnamese names they found difficult to remember or pronounce. This helped to make a very foreign land seem a bit more familiar.

After reunification, the first order of Saigon's provisional Municipal Military Management Committee was to change the name of the city to Ho Chi Minh City, a decision confirmed in Hanoi a year later. The new government immediately began changing street names considered inappropriate – an ongoing process – dropping English and French names in favour of Vietnamese ones. The only French names still in use are those of Albert Calmette (1893–1934), developer of a tuberculosis vaccine; Marie Curie (1867–1934), who won the Nobel Prize for her research into radioactivity; Louis Pasteur (1822–95), chemist and bacteriologist; and Alexandre Yersin (1863–1943), discoverer of the plague bacillus.

All this renaming has had mixed results. Streets, districts and provinces are usually known by their new names. As if navigating your way around HCMC wasn't confusing enough, in 2000, when the Municipal People's Committee set out to name 25 new city streets, they also decided to *rename* another 152! Fortunately, most important streets in the city centre have not changed names, and tourist maps of the city are updated annually.

HO CHI MINH CITY

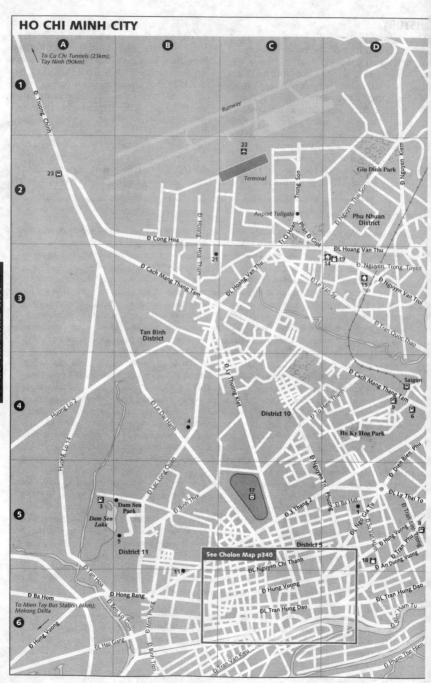

To Cu Chi Tunnels (23km);
Tay Ninh (90km)

Đ Truong Chinh

Runway

23

22

Terminal

Gia Dinh Park

Airport Tollgate

Đ Cong Hoa

Phu Nhuan
District

Đ Hoang Hoa Tham

Đ Cach Mang Thang Tam

21

ĐL Hoang Van Thu

Tr Q Hoan

Phan Đ Giot

Trong Son

Đ Nguyen Thai Son

ĐL Hoang Van Thu

14 19

Đ Nguyen Trong Tuyen

Đ Le Van Sy

15

Đ Nguyen Van Troi

Tan Binh
District

Đ Tran Quoc Thao

Huong Lo 2

Đ Le Dai Hanh

Đ Ly Thuong Kiet

District 10

Đ Cach Mang Thang Tam

Saigon

9

6

4

Đ To Hien Thanh

Ho Ky Hoa Park

Đ Dien Bien Phu

Huong Lo 14

Đ Lac Long Quan

17

Đ Nguyen Tri Phuong

Đ Ba Hat

ĐL Ly Thai To

3

Dam Sen
Park

Đ Binh Thoi

Đ 3 Thang 2

1

Đ Ngo Gia Tu

Đ Su Van Hanh

8

Dam Sen
Lake

5

District 11

11

See Cholon Map p340

Đ Hung Vuong

Đ Tran Phu Trong

Đ Tran Binh Trong

District 5

18

An Duong Vuong

Đ Tran Hoa

ĐL Nguyen Chi Thanh

Đ Hong Bang

Đ Ben Lo Com

Đ Minh Phung

Đ Hung Vuong

ĐL Tran Hung Dao

ĐL Tran Hung Dao

Đ Ba Hom

To Mien Tay Bus Station (4km);
Mekong Delta

Đ Hung Vuong

ĐL Hau Giang

Đ Binh Tien

Đ Tran Van Kieu

Đ Ben Ham Tu

Đ Pham The Hien

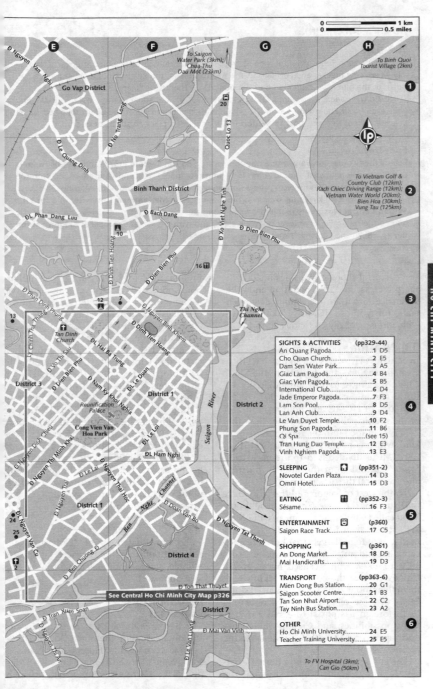

SIGHTS & ACTIVITIES		**(pp329-44)**
An Quang Pagoda	1	D5
Cho Quan Church	2	E5
Dam Sen Water Park	3	A5
Giac Lam Pagoda	4	B4
Giac Vien Pagoda	5	B5
International Club	6	D4
Jade Emperor Pagoda	7	F3
Lam Son Pool	8	D5
Lan Anh Club	9	D4
Le Van Duyet Temple	10	F2
Phung Son Pagoda	11	B6
Qi Spa	(see 15)	
Tran Hung Dao Temple	12	E3
Vinh Nghiem Pagoda	13	E3

SLEEPING	🏠	**(pp351-2)**
Novotel Garden Plaza	14	D3
Omni Hotel	15	D3

EATING	🍽	**(pp352-3)**
Sésame	16	F3

ENTERTAINMENT	🎬	**(p360)**
Saigon Race Track	17	C5

SHOPPING	🛍	**(p361)**
An Dong Market	18	D5
Mai Handicrafts	19	D3

TRANSPORT		**(pp363-6)**
Mien Dong Bus Station	20	G1
Saigon Scooter Centre	21	B3
Tan Son Nhat Airport	22	C2
Tay Ninh Bus Station	23	A2

OTHER		
Ho Chi Minh University	24	E5
Teacher Training University	25	E5

HO CHI MINH CITY IN...

Two Days

Take the Walking Tour (p344) for a good cross-section of HCMC's attractions. Afterwards, take in city views, cool breezes and cocktails at the **rooftop bar** of the Rex Hotel (p351) before heading down to the glut of restaurants on and around Đ Le Thanh Ton (Map p326) for dinner.

Next day, wrangle a *cyclo* into **Cholon** (p339) for a look at some of the ornate pagodas. End your evening in **Pham Ngu Lao** (Map p356), with dinner in one of the alleys followed by an investigation of the bars. **Lost in Saigon** (p358) is a good place to start...or end up.

Four Days

Follow the two-day itinerary with a day trip to the **Cao Dai Temple** (p378) and **Cu Chi Tunnels** (p369). On day four, sniff around some **local markets** (p362) or spend your afternoon (and the contents of your wallet) browsing the sumptuous shops around Dong Khoi (Map pp334-5).

Or spread the walking tour over two days, adding the **Mariamman Hindu Temple** (p3310), **Saigon Central Mosque** (p332) and a walk along the riverfront (Map pp334–5). Rent a bicycle and be the traffic; linger at local sidewalk cafés; end with a decadent cocktail at **Saigon Saigon Bar** (p358), at the Caravelle Hotel.

---

and colourful shops. Downsides include the sharp increase in traffic, pollution and other urban ills, but a more open-minded new generation may infuse HCMC's chaotic growth with a more globally-conscious attitude.

ORIENTATION

In actuality, HCMC is not so much a city as a small province stretching from the South China Sea almost to the Cambodian border. Rural regions make up about 90% of the land area of HCMC and hold around 25% of the municipality's population; the other 75% is crammed into the remaining 10% of land, which constitutes the urban centre.

HCMC is divided into 16 urban districts (*quan*, derived from the French *quartier*) and five rural districts (*huyen*).

To the west of Saigon and the city centre is District 5, the huge Chinese neighbourhood called Cholon, which means 'Big Market'. However, it is decidedly less Chinese than it used to be, largely thanks to the anticapitalist and anti-Chinese campaign from 1978 to 1979, which caused many ethnic Chinese to flee the country – taking with them their money and entrepreneurial skills. Many of these refugees are now returning (with foreign passports) to explore investment possibilities, and Cholon's hotels are once again packed with Chinese-speaking businesspeople.

The city's neoclassical and international-style buildings, and pavement kiosks selling French rolls and croissants, give neighbourhoods such as District 3 an attractive, vaguely French atmosphere. The majority of places and sights described in this chapter are located in District 1.

Making the 7km trip into town from the airport should cost you no more than 60,000d in a metered taxi, or about 30,000d by motorbike taxi (*xe om*). There's also an airport bus (1000d) that drops you right in central HCMC (see p364). From the train station (Ga Sai Gon; Map pp322-3), a *xe om* to Pham Ngu Lao shouldn't cost more than 10,000d. Most *xe om* rides from Saigon's intercity bus stations will run between 10,000d to 20,000d; public buses also pass by the central Ben Thanh Market (3000d), but these usually stop running midafternoon. Open-tour buses will unload you directly into Pham Ngu Lao.

Maps

Good, up-to-date maps of HCMC are available at bookstores in Districts 1 and 3; a reliable, central source is Fahasa Bookshop (see opposite).

INFORMATION
Bookshops

The best area to look for maps, books and stationery is along the north side of ĐL Le Loi, between the Rex Hotel and Đ Nam Ky Khoi Nghia, in the Dong Khoi area (Map pp334-5). There are many small, privately run shops as well as the large government-run ones.

On Đ De Tham, around Pham Ngu Lao (Map p356), there is a handful of shops dealing in used paperbacks and bootleg CDs. Here you can also swap books. Check out the following places.

Fahasa Bookshop Dong Khoi (Map pp334-5; ☎ 822 4670; 185 Đ Dong Khoi); ĐL Nguyen Hue (Map pp334-5; ☎ 822 5446; 40 ĐL Nguyen Hue) One of the best government-run bookshops, with good dictionaries, maps and general books in English and French.
Phuong Nam Bookshop ĐL Le Duan (Map p326; ☎ 822 9650; 2A ĐL Le Duan; ☉ 8am-9.30pm) Carries imported books and magazines in English, French and Chinese, mostly of the instructional variety.
Tiem Sach Bookshop Đ Ho Huan Nghiep (Map pp334-5; 20 Đ Ho Huan Nghiep; ☉ 8.30am-10pm) Not so much a bookshop as a backdrop of used English and French titles for the cosy Bo Gio café.

Cultural Centres
British Council (Map p326; ☎ 823 2862; www.british council.org/vietnam; 25 ĐL Le Duan)
Institute of Cultural Exchange with France (Idecaf; Map pp334-5; ☎ 829 5451; 31 Đ Thai Van Lung)

Emergency
Emergency (☎ 115)
Fire (☎ 114)
Information (☎ 1080)
Police (☎ 113)

Internet Access
Internet access is widely available in HCMC. The largest concentration of Internet cafés is in Pham Ngu Lao (Map p356), with around 30 places along Đ Pham Ngu Lao, Đ De Tham and Đ Bui Vien; just stroll around and take your pick. Most places charge peanuts – just 100d to 200d per minute.

In the downtown area (Map p326), you'll find Internet cafés along Đ Le Thanh Ton and Đ Dong Du.

Media
Hotels, bars and restaurants around HCMC carry the free entertainment magazines the *Guide* and *Time Out*, weekly supplements published by the *Vietnam Economic Times* (*VET*) and the *Vietnam Investment Review* (*VIR*), respectively.

There's also an eclectic selection of slightly stale foreign newspapers and magazines – day-old *Le Monde*, or last week's *Newsweek* –

for sale (be sure to bargain!) by the guys standing on the corner of Đ Dong Khoi and ĐL Le Loi (Map pp334-5), across from the Continental Hotel.

Medical Services
Cho Ray Hospital (Map p340; ☎ 855 4137; fax 855 7267; 201 ĐL Nguyen Chi Thanh, District 5; consultations from US$4; ☉ 24hr) One of the largest medical facilities in Vietnam, with 1000 beds, and a section for foreigners on the 10th floor; about a third of the 200 doctors speak English.
Emergency Centre (Map p326; ☎ 829 2071; 125 ĐL Le Loi; ☉ 24hr) Has doctors that speak English and French.
FV Hospital (Franco-Vietnamese Hospital; Map pp322-3; ☎ 411 3333; www.fvhospital.com; 6 Đ Nguyen Luong Bang, Tan Phu Ward, District 7; ☉ 24hr) French-, Vietnamese- and English-speaking physicians; superb care and equipment.
Grand Dentistry (Map pp334-5; ☎ 821 9446, 24hr emergency ☎ 0903-647 156; Sun Wah Tower, 115 Đ Nguyen Hue) Dental care, emergencies and surgeries.
HCMC Family Medical Practice (Map pp334-5; ☎ 822 7848, 24hr emergency ☎ 0913-234 911; www .doctorkot.com; Diamond Plaza, 34 ĐL Le Duan; consultations from US$50; ☉ 24hr) Run by the well-respected Dr Rafi Kot.
International Medical Centre (Map pp334-5; ☎ 827 2366, 24hr emergency ☎ 865 4025; fac@hcm .vnn.vn; 1 Đ Han Thuyen; consultations US$40-80; ☉ 24hr) A nonprofit organisation billing itself as the least expensive Western health-care centre in the country; has English-speaking French doctors.
International SOS (Map pp334-5; ☎ 829 8424, 24hr emergency ☎ 829 8520; fax 829 8551; 65 Đ Nguyen Du; consultations US$55-65; ☉ 24hr) Has an international team of docs speaking English, French, Japanese and Vietnamese.
Starlight Dental Clinic (Map pp334-5; ☎ 822 2433, 24hr emergency ☎ 0903-834 901; 10C Đ Thai Van Lung)

Money
Just inside the airport terminal, there's an exchange counter run by **Vietindebank-Sasco** (☎ 844 0740), which gives the official exchange rate. Opening hours are irregular, so carry sufficient US$ notes in small denominations to get into the city in case it's closed.

Banks with 24-hour ATMs dispense dong only, to a maximum amount of 2,000,000d per day. Visa or MasterCard cash advances for larger amounts of dong, as well as US dollars, can be handled at bank counters during banking hours. All of these banks also exchange travellers cheques, charging less commission when exchanging for dong. Try the following.

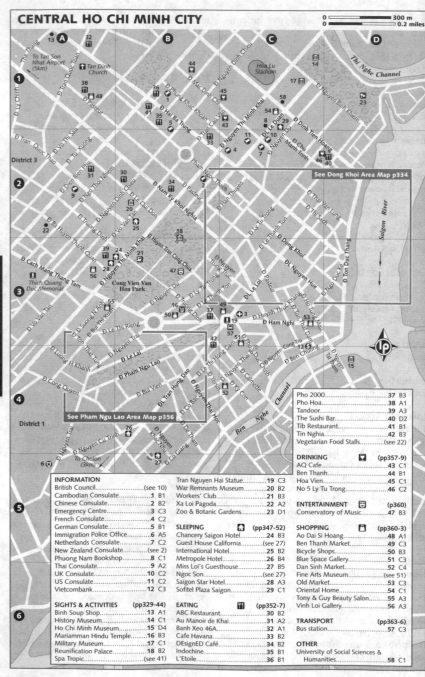

CENTRAL HO CHI MINH CITY

0 — 300 m
0 — 0.2 miles

See Dong Khoi Area Map p334

See Pham Ngu Lao Area Map p356

HO CHÍ MINH CITY

Pho 2000.............................37 B3
Pho Hoa..............................38 A1
Tandoor..............................39 A3
The Sushi Bar.......................40 D2
Tib Restaurant......................41 B1
Tin Nghia............................42 B3
Vegetarian Food Stalls............(see 22)

DRINKING   (pp357-9)
AQ Cafe..............................43 C1
Ben Thanh...........................44 B1
Hoa Vien............................45 C1
No 5 Ly Tu Trong...................46 C2

ENTERTAINMENT   (p360)
Conservatory of Music..............47 B3

SHOPPING   (pp360-3)
Ao Dai Si Hoang....................48 A1
Ben Thanh Market..................49 C3
Bicycle Shops.......................50 B3
Blue Space Gallery..................51 C3
Dan Sinh Market.....................52 C4
Fine Arts Museum.................(see 51)
Old Market..........................53 C1
Oriental Home.......................54 C1
Tony & Guy Beauty Salon..........55 A3
Vinh Loi Gallery.....................56 A3

TRANSPORT   (pp363-6)
Bus station...........................57 C3

OTHER
University of Social Sciences &
    Humanities.......................58 C1

INFORMATION
British Council........................(see 10)
Cambodian Consulate..................1 B1
Chinese Consulate......................2 B2
Emergency Centre......................3 C3
French Consulate.......................4 C2
German Consulate......................5 B1
Immigration Police Office...............6 A5
Netherlands Consulate..................7 C2
New Zealand Consulate.............(see 2)
Phuong Nam Bookshop................8 C1
Thai Consulate..........................9 A2
UK Consulate..........................10 C2
US Consulate..........................11 C2
Vietcombank..........................12 C3

SIGHTS & ACTIVITIES   (pp329-44)
Binh Soup Shop........................13 A1
History Museum.......................14 C1
Ho Chi Minh Museum.................15 D4
Mariamman Hindu Temple............16 B3
Military Museum......................17 C1
Reunification Palace..................18 B2
Spa Tropic...........................(see 41)

Tran Nguyen Hai Statue..............19 C3
War Remnants Museum...............20 B2
Workers' Club........................21 B3
Xa Loi Pagoda........................22 A2
Zoo & Botanic Gardens..............23 D1

SLEEPING   (pp347-52)
Chancery Saigon Hotel...............24 B3
Guest House California............(see 27)
International Hotel....................25 B2
Metropole Hotel......................26 B4
Miss Loi's Guesthouse...............27 B5
Ngoc Son..........................(see 27)
Saigon Star Hotel....................28 A3
Sofitel Plaza Saigon..................29 C1

EATING   (pp352-7)
ABC Restaurant......................30 B2
Au Manoir de Khai...................31 A2
Banh Xeo 46A.......................32 A1
Cafe Havana........................33 B2
DEsignED Café.......................34 B2
Indochine...........................35 B1
L'Etoile.............................36 B1

ANZ Bank (Map pp334-5; ☎ 829 9319; 11 Me Linh Sq) Has a 24-hour ATM.

Fiditourist (Map p356; ☎ 835 3018; 195 Đ Pham Ngu Lao; ☑ 8am-10pm) Keeps late hours in backpackerland, though rates aren't the best.

HSBC (Map pp334-5; ☎ 829 2288; 235 Đ Dong Khoi) With secure 24-hour ATM.

Sacombank (Map p356; ☎ 836 4231; www.sacombank .com; 211 Đ Nguyen Thai Hoc) Conveniently located in the budget-traveller zone, with 24-hour ATM.

Vietcombank (Map p326; ☎ 829 7245; cnr Đ Ben Chuong & Đ Pasteur; ☑ closed Sun & last day of the month) The eastern building is for foreign exchange only, but is also worth a visit just to see the stunningly ornate interior. The bank will accept a wide range of foreign currencies.

Post

HCMC's French-style **main post office** (Map pp334-5; ☎ 829 6555; 2 Cong Xa Paris), with its glass canopy and iron frame, is right next to Notre Dame Cathedral. Built between 1886 and 1891, it is the largest post office in Vietnam and worth visiting just for its architecture.

Customers conduct their post and tele-communications business here under the benevolent gaze of Ho Chi Minh. To your right as you enter the building is the poste restante counter. Pens, envelopes, aero-grams, postcards and stamp collections are sold at the counter to the right of the en-trance, and outside the post office along Đ Nguyen Du.

Countless other post office branches are scattered around town and those in Pham Ngu Lao and Cholon are marked on the relevant maps. Like the main post office, many of these also keep late hours.

The following private carriers operate near the main post office:

DHL (Map pp334-5; ☎ 823 1525; 2 Cong Xa Paris; ☑ 7.30am-4.30pm Mon-Sat)

Federal Express (Map pp334-5; ☎ 829 0995; www .fedex.com; cnr Đ Pasteur & Đ Le Thanh Ton; ☑ 7am-8pm Mon-Fri, 7am-4pm Sat)

Saigon Logistics (Map p356; ☎ 837 3435; 293 Đ Pham Ngu Lao; ☑ 8am-5.30pm Mon-Sat) Deals in freight forwarding, if you've out-shopped yourself.

UPS (Map pp334-5; ☎ 824 3597; www.ups.com; 80 Đ Nguyen Du; ☑ 7.30am-4.30pm Mon-Sat)

Telephone

International and domestic phone calls can be made from post offices and better hotels.

At the post office local calls cost 2000d; hotel prices for local calls vary, so be sure to ask the price beforehand.

International calls can also be made over the Internet at most Internet cafés; rates start around 5000d per minute.

Toilets

In HCMC most places serving travellers have Western-style toilets. However, you may find the occasional squat toilet in local or low-budget restaurants. As in the rest of Vietnam, dispose of toilet paper in the wastebasket provided, as it will choke most plumbing systems.

Tourist Information

Southern Airports Services Company (Sasco; ☎ 848 6711; www.saigonairport.com; ☑ 9am-11pm) Just beyond the baggage carousels, Sasco's Visitors Information & Services counter offers free city maps, tourist literature and an airport timetable, plus transportation, accommodation and tour bookings.

Travel Agencies

HCMC's official government-run travel agency is **Saigon Tourist** (Map pp334-5; ☎ 829 8914; www.saigontourist.net; 49 Đ Le Thanh Ton; ☑ 8-11.30am & 1-5.30pm). The agency owns, or is a joint-venture partner in, more than 70 hotels and numerous restaurants around town, plus a car-rental agency, golf clubs and assorted tourist traps.

There's a plethora of other travel agencies in town, virtually all of them joint ventures between government agencies and private companies. These places can provide cars, book air tickets and extend your visa. Com-petition is keen and you can often undercut Saigon Tourist's tariffs by 50% if you shop around. Many agencies have multilingual guides who speak English, French, Japan-ese etc.

Most tour guides and drivers are paid poorly, so if you're happy with their service, consider tipping them. Many travellers on bus tours to Cu Chi or the Mekong Delta, for example, collect a kitty (say US$1 or US$2 per person) and give it to the guide and driver at the end of the trip.

We recommend visiting several tour oper-ators to see what's being offered to suit your taste and budget. Plenty of cheap tours – of varying quality – are sold around Pham Ngu Lao. One excellent appraisal strategy is to grill other travellers who've just returned from a tour.

Another appealing option is to arrange a customised private tour with your own car, driver and guide. Travelling this way provides maximum flexibility and split between a few people can be surprisingly affordable.

TNK Travel (Map p356; ☎ 837 8276; www.tnktravelvietnam.com; 230 Đ De Tham) has been getting rave reviews from budget travellers lately. It comes recommended for its Mekong Delta tours to Phnom Penh.

For customised tours, **Sinhbalo Adventures** (Map p356; ☎ 837 6766, 836 7682; www.sinhbalo.com; 283/20 Đ Pham Ngu Lao) is one of the best in Vietnam. Sinhbalo specialises in cycling trips, but also arranges innovative special interest journeys to the Mekong Delta, central highlands and further afield. Its programmes range from remote hill-tribe trekking and bird-watching in national parks to motorbiking the Ho Chi Minh Trail. We've been using them for more than 10 years and have yet to hit a snag.

The following agencies can be used as a starting point; see p482 for more options.

BUDGET AGENCIES
Delta Adventure Tours (Map p356; ☎ 836 8542; www.deltaadventuretours.com; 187A Đ Pham Ngu Lao)
Fiditourist (Map p356; ☎ 835 3018; www.fiditour.com; 195 Đ Pham Ngu Lao) A good place to look for domestic and international air tickets.
Kim Travel (Map p356; ☎ 836 9859; www.kimtravel.com; 270 Đ De Tham)
Linh Cafe (Map p356; ☎ 836 0643; linhtravel@hcm.vnn.vn; 291 Đ Pham Ngu Lao)
Mekong Tours (Map p356; ☎ 837 6429; mekongtours@hotmail.com; 272 Đ De Tham)
Sinh Cafe (Map p356; ☎ 836 7338; www.sinhcafé.com; 248 Đ De Tham)
TM Brothers (Map p356; ☎ 836 1791; huuhanhnguyen@yahoo.com; 288 Đ De Tham)

MID-RANGE & TOP-END AGENCIES
Ann Tours (Map p356; ☎ 833 2564; www.anntours.com; 58 Đ Ton That Tung)
Ben Thanh Tourist (Map p356; ☎ 886 0365; fax 836 1953; www.benthanhtour.com; 45 Đ Bui Vien)
Buffalo Tours (Map pp334-5; ☎ 827 9169; www.buffalotours.com; Suite 502, Jardine House, 58 Đ Dong Khoi)
Diethelm Travel (Map pp334-5; ☎ 829 4932; www.diethelm-travel.com; 1A Me Linh Sq)
Saigon Tourist (Map pp334-5; ☎ 829 8914; www.saigontourist.net; 49 Đ Le Thanh Ton)

DANGERS & ANNOYANCES
HCMC is the most theft-ridden city in Vietnam; don't become a statistic. See p457 for advice on how to avoid street crime. Be especially careful in the Dong Khoi area and along the Saigon riverfront, where motorbike 'cowboys' operate.

Scams
We've been receiving more reports lately from travellers getting burned by *cyclo* drivers who demand exorbitant sums at the end of a tour.

Rather than hopping blithely into the *cyclo* when the driver smilingly says, 'Price up to you,' clearly negotiate a fair price up front (consider US$5/10 for a half-day/day tour). If more than one person is travelling make sure you're negotiating the price for both and not a per-passenger fee. It sometimes pays to sketch out numbers and pictures with pen and paper so all parties agree. Unfortunately, 'misunderstandings' do happen; unless the *cyclo* driver has pedalled you to the 21 districts of HCMC, US$25 is not the going rate.

That said, don't just assume the driver is trying to bamboozle you. It's a tough living, especially as the city government tries to phase out the *cyclos* entirely. If you've had a particularly great guide and ride, tip generously.

YOUR FRIENDLY TAXI DRIVER
A minor warning – some airport taxi drivers like to play a little game when it comes to taking you to a hotel. They want the hotel to pay them a commission and they know which hotels pay commissions and which don't. If you want to go to a hotel that does not pay commissions then don't be surprised if the driver claims that place is very dirty, unsafe, expensive or even out of business.

The bottom line is don't *always* believe what your driver tells you. The same thing applies also to drivers of *cyclos*, motorbikes and taxis that are parked at the train station.

SIGHTS

Most of HCMC's major sights are located in District 1. Those with more than a day in the city can take in central HCMC (Map p326) as well as the pagodas in Cholon (Map p340) and other outlying districts.

Central Area

REUNIFICATION PALACE

Striking modern architecture and the eerie feeling you get as you walk through its deserted halls make **Reunification Palace** (Hoi Truong Thong Nhat; Map p326; ☎ 829 4117; 106 Đ Nguyen Du; admission 15,000d; ⏰ 7.30-11am & 1-4pm) one of the most fascinating sights in HCMC. The building, once the symbol of the South Vietnamese government, is preserved almost as it was on that day in April 1975 when the Republic of Vietnam, which hundreds of thousands of Vietnamese and 58,183 Americans had died trying to save, ceased to exist. Some recent additions include a statue of Ho Chi Minh and a viewing room where you can watch a video about Vietnamese history in a variety of languages. The national anthem is played at the end of the tape and you are expected to stand up – it would be rude not to.

It was towards this building – then known as Independence Palace or the Presidential Palace – that the first communist tanks to arrive in Saigon charged on the morning of 30 April 1975. After crashing through the wrought-iron gates – in a dramatic scene recorded by photojournalists and shown around the world – a soldier ran into the building and up the stairs to unfurl a VC flag from the 4th-floor balcony. In an ornate 2nd-floor reception chamber, General Minh, who had become head of state only 43 hours before, waited with his improvised cabinet. 'I have been waiting since early this morning to transfer power to you', Minh said to the VC officer who entered the room. 'There is no question of your transferring power', replied the officer. 'You cannot give up what you do not have.'

In 1868 a residence was built on this site for the French governor-general of Cochinchina and gradually it expanded to become Norodom Palace. When the French departed, the palace became home for South Vietnamese President Ngo Dinh Diem. So hated was Diem that his own air force bombed the palace in 1962 in an unsuccessful attempt to kill him. The president ordered a new residence

to be built on the same site, this time with a sizeable bomb shelter in the basement. Work was completed in 1966, but Diem did not get to see his dream house because he was murdered by his own troops in 1963. The new building was named Independence Palace and was home to South Vietnamese President Nguyen Van Thieu until his hasty departure in 1975.

Norodom Palace, designed by Paris-trained Vietnamese architect Ngo Viet Thu, is an outstanding example of 1960s architecture. It has an airy and open atmosphere and its spacious chambers are tastefully decorated with the finest modern Vietnamese art and crafts. In its grandeur, the building feels worthy of a head of state.

The ground-floor room with the boat-shaped table was often used for conferences. Upstairs in the **Presidential Receiving Room** (Phu Dau Rong, or Dragon's Head Room) – the one with the red chairs in it – the South Vietnamese president received foreign delegations. He sat behind the desk; the chairs with dragons carved into the arms were used by his assistants. The chair facing the desk was reserved for foreign ambassadors. The room with gold-coloured chairs and curtains was used by the vice president. You can sit in the former president's chair and have your photo taken.

In the back of the structure are the president's living quarters. Check out the model boats, horse tails and severed elephants' feet. The 3rd floor has a card-playing room with a bar and a movie-screening chamber. This floor also boasts a terrace with a heliport – there is still a derelict helicopter parked here. The 4th floor has a dance hall and casino.

Perhaps most interesting of all is the basement with its network of tunnels, telecommunications centre and war room (with the best map of Vietnam you'll ever see pasted on the wall).

Reunification Palace is not open to visitors when official receptions or meetings are taking place. English- and French-speaking guides are on duty during opening hours.

WAR REMNANTS MUSEUM

Once known as the Museum of Chinese and American War Crimes, the **War Remnants Museum** (Bao Tang Chung Tich Chien Tranh; Map p326; ☎ 930 5587; 28 Đ Vo Van Tan; admission 10,000d;

7.30-11.45am & 1.30-5.15pm) is now the museum in HCMC most popular with Western tourists. Many of the atrocities documented here were well publicised in the West, but rarely do Westerners have the opportunity to hear the victims of US military action tell their own story.

The museum's name was changed to avoid offending Chinese and American tourists, but the pamphlet *Some Pictures of US Imperialists Aggressive War Crimes in Vietnam*, handed out at reception, pulls no punches.

US armoured vehicles, artillery pieces, bombs and infantry weapons are on display outside. There's also a guillotine used by the French on Viet Minh 'troublemakers'. Many photographs illustrating US atrocities are from US sources, including photos of the infamous My Lai Massacre (see p253). There is a model of the notorious tiger cages used by the South Vietnamese military to house Viet Cong (VC) prisoners on Con Son Island. There are also pictures of deformed babies, their defects attributed to the USA's widespread use of chemical herbicides. An adjacent room has exhibits of 'counter-revolutionary warcrimes' that were committed after 1975 by saboteurs within Vietnam. Counter-revolutionaries are portrayed as being allied with both the US and Chinese imperialists.

Despite the relative one-sidedness of the exhibits, there are few museums in the world that drive home so well the point that war is horribly brutal and that many of its victims are civilians. Even those who supported the war would have a difficult time not being horrified by the photos of children mangled by US bombing and napalming. There are also scenes of torture – it takes a strong stomach to look at these. You'll also have the rare chance to see some of the experimental weapons used in the war, which were at one time military secrets, such as the fléchette (an artillery shell filled with thousands of tiny darts).

The War Remnants Museum is in the former US Information Service building, at the intersection with Đ Le Qui Don. Explanations are in Vietnamese, English and Chinese. Though a bit incongruous with the museum's theme, **water-puppet theatre** is staged in a tent on the museum grounds (see p360).

PEOPLE'S COMMITTEE BUILDING

HCMC's gingerbread **Hôtel de Ville** (Map pp334-5), one of the city's most prominent landmarks, is now somewhat incongruously the home of the Ho Chi Minh City People's Committee. Built between 1901 and 1908, the Hôtel de Ville is situated at the northwestern end of ĐL Nguyen Hue, facing the river. The former hotel is notable for its gardens, ornate facade and elegant interior lit with crystal chandeliers. It's easily the most photographed building in Vietnam. At night, the exterior is usually covered with thousands of geckos feasting on insects.

Unfortunately, you'll have to content yourself with admiring the exterior only. The building is not open to the public and requests by tourists to visit the interior are rudely rebuffed.

MUNICIPAL THEATRE

A grand – and unfortunately, pink – colonial building with a sweeping staircase, the **Municipal Theatre** (Nha Hat Thanh Pho; Map pp334-5; ☎ 829 9976; Lam Son Sq) is hard to miss at the intersection of Đ Dong Khoi and ĐL Le Loi. For information on performances held here, see p360.

HISTORY MUSEUM

The stunning Sino-French–style building that houses the **History Museum** (Bao Tang Lich Su; Map pp322-3; ☎ 829 8146; Đ Nguyen Binh Khiem; admission 10,000d; 8-11am & 1.30-4pm) was built in 1929 by the Société des Études Indochinoises. It's worth a visit just to view the architecture!

The museum has an excellent collection of artefacts illustrating the evolution of the cultures of Vietnam, from the Bronze-Age Dong Son civilisation (13th century BC to 1st century AD) and the Oc-Eo (Funan) civilisation (1st to 6th centuries AD), to the Cham, Khmer and Vietnamese. There are many valuable relics taken from Cambodia's Angkor Wat.

At the back of the building on the 3rd floor is a **research library** (☎ 829 0268; Mon-Sat) with numerous books from the French-colonial period about Indochina.

Across from the entrance to the museum you'll see the elaborate **Temple of King Hung Vuong**. The Hung kings are said to have been the first rulers of the Vietnamese nation, having established their rule in the Red River region before it was invaded by the Chinese.

The museum is just inside the main gate to the city zoo and botanic gardens (p346), where the east end of ĐL Le Duan meets Đ Nguyen Binh Khiem.

Just across Đ Nguyen Binh Khiem is a small **military museum** (Map p326; ☎ 822 9387; 2 ĐL Le Duan) devoted to Ho Chi Minh's campaign to liberate the south. Inside is of minor interest, but some US, Chinese and Soviet war material is on display outdoors, including a Cessna A-37 of the South Vietnamese Air Force and a US-built F-5E Tiger with the 20mm nose gun still loaded. The tank on display is one of the tanks that broke into the grounds of Reunification Palace on 30 April 1975.

FINE ARTS MUSEUM
A classic yellow-and-white building with a modest Chinese influence, the **Fine Arts Museum** (Bao Tang My Thuat; Map p326; ☎ 822 2441; 97A Đ Pho Duc Chinh; admission 10,000d; ☺ 9am-4.30pm Mon-Sat), houses one of the more interesting collections in Vietnam – ranging from lacquer- and enamelware to contemporary oil paintings by Vietnamese and foreign artists. If that doesn't sound enticing, just go to see the huge hall with its Art Nouveau windows and floors. On the 1st floor is a display of officially accepted contemporary art: most of it is just kitsch or desperate attempts to master abstract art, but occasionally something brilliant is displayed here. Most of the recent art is for sale and prices are fair.

The 2nd floor has older politically correct art. Some of it is pretty crude: pictures of heroic figures waving red flags, children with rifles, a wounded soldier joining the Communist Party, innumerable tanks and weaponry, grotesque Americans and God-like reverence for Ho Chi Minh. However, it's worth seeing because Vietnamese artists managed not to be as dull and conformist as their counterparts in Eastern Europe. Once you've passed several paintings and sculptures of Uncle Ho, you will see that those artists who studied before 1975 managed to somehow transfer their own aesthetics onto the world of their prescribed subjects. Most impressive are some drawings of prison riots in 1973 and some remarkable abstract paintings.

The 3rd floor has a good collection of older art, mainly Oc-Eo (Funan) sculptures strongly resembling styles of ancient Greece and Egypt. You will also find here the best Cham pieces outside of Danang. Also interesting are the many pieces of Indian art, such as stone elephant heads. Some pieces clearly originated in Angkor culture.

The garden café in front of the museum is a preferred spot for elderly gentlemen, who like to exchange stamp collections and sip iced tea.

NOTRE DAME CATHEDRAL
Built between 1877 and 1883, **Notre Dame Cathedral** (Map pp334-5; Đ Han Thuyen) is set in the heart of HCMC's government quarter. The cathedral faces Đ Dong Khoi. It is neo-Romanesque with two 40m-high square towers tipped with iron spires, which dominate the city's skyline. In front of the cathedral (in the centre of the square bounded by the main post office) is a statue of the Virgin Mary. If the front gates are locked, try the door on the side of the building that faces Reunification Palace.

Unusually, this cathedral has no stained-glass windows: the glass was a casualty of fighting during WWII. A number of foreign travellers worship here and the priests are allowed to add a short sermon in French or English to their longer presentations in Vietnamese. The 9.30am Sunday mass might be the best one for tourists to attend.

MARIAMMAN HINDU TEMPLE
This is the only **Hindu temple** (Chua Ba Mariamman; Map p326; 45 Đ Truong Dinh) still in use in HCMC and is a little piece of southern India in the centre of town. Though there are only 50 to 60 Hindus in HCMC – all of them Tamils – this temple is also considered sacred by many ethnic Vietnamese and ethnic Chinese. Indeed, it is reputed to have miraculous powers. The temple was built at the end of the 19th century and dedicated to the Hindu goddess Mariamman.

The lion to the left of the entrance used to be carried around the city in a street procession every autumn. In the shrine in the middle of the temple is **Mariamman**, flanked by her guardians Maduraiveeran (to her left) and Pechiamman (to her right). In front of the Mariamman figure are two *linga*. Favourite offerings placed nearby

HO CHI MINH CITY

often include joss sticks, jasmine, lilies and gladioli. The wooden stairs on the left (as you enter the building) lead to the roof, where you'll find two colourful **towers** covered with innumerable figures of lions, goddesses and guardians.

After reunification, the government took over the temple and turned part of it into a factory for joss sticks. Another section was occupied by a company producing seafood for export – the seafood was dried on the roof in the sun. The whole temple is to be returned to the local Hindu community.

Mariamman Temple is only three blocks west of Ben Thanh Market. Take off your shoes before stepping onto the slightly raised platform.

SAIGON CENTRAL MOSQUE

Built by South Indian Muslims in 1935 on the site of an earlier mosque, the **Saigon Central Mosque** (Map pp334-5; 66 Ð Dong Du) is an immaculately clean and well-kept island of calm in the middle of the bustling Dong Khoi area. In front of the sparkling white-and-blue structure, with its four nonfunctional minarets, is a pool for the ritual ablutions required by Islamic law before prayers. Take off your shoes before entering the sanctuary.

The simplicity of the mosque is in marked contrast to the exuberance of Chinese temple decorations, and the rows of figures facing elaborate ritual objects in Buddhist pagodas. Islamic law strictly forbids using human or animal figures for decoration.

Only half a dozen Indian Muslims remain in HCMC; most of the community fled in 1975. As a result, prayers – held five times a day – are sparsely attended, except on Friday, when several dozen worshippers (mainly non-Indian Muslims) are present.

There are 12 other mosques serving the 5000 or so Muslims in HCMC.

XA LOI PAGODA

Famed as the repository of a sacred relic of the Buddha, **Xa Loi Pagoda** (Map p326; 89 Ð Ba Huyen Thanh Quan) was built in 1956. In August 1963 truckloads of armed men under the command of President Ngo Dinh Diem's brother, Ngo Dinh Nhu, attacked Xa Loi Pagoda, which had become a centre of opposition to the Diem government. The pagoda was ransacked and 400 monks and nuns, including the country's 80-year-old Buddhist patriarch, were arrested. This raid and others elsewhere helped solidify opposition among Buddhists to the Diem regime, a crucial factor in the US decision to support the coup against Diem. This pagoda was also the site of several self-immolations by monks protesting against the Diem regime and the American War.

Women enter the main hall of Xa Loi Pagoda by the staircase on the right as you come in the gate; men use the stairs on the left. The walls of the sanctuary are adorned with paintings depicting the Buddha's life.

Xa Loi Pagoda is in District 3 at, near Ð Dien Bien Phu. A monk preaches every Sunday from 8am to 10am. On days of the full moon and new moon, special prayers are held from 7am to 9am and 7pm to 8pm.

AN QUANG PAGODA

This **pagoda** (Map pp322-3; Ð Su Van Hanh) gained some notoriety during the American War as the home of Thich Tri Quang, a powerful monk who led protests against the South Vietnamese government in 1963 and 1966. When the war ended you would have expected the communists to be grateful. Instead, he was placed under house arrest and later thrown into solitary confinement for 16 months. Thich Tri Quang was eventually released and is said to be still living at An Quang Pagoda.

An Quang Pagoda is on Ð Su Van Hanh near the intersection with Ð Ba Hat, in District 10.

MUSEUM OF HO CHI MINH CITY

Housed in a grey, neoclassical structure built in 1886 and once known as Gia Long Palace (later, the Revolutionary Museum), the **Museum of Ho Chi Minh City** (Bao Tang Thanh Pho Ho Chi Minh; Map pp334-5; ☎ 829 9741; 65 Ð Ly Tu Trong; admission US$1; ✆ 8am-4pm) is a singularly beautiful and amazing building.

The museum displays artefacts from the various periods of the communist struggle for power in Vietnam. The photographs of anticolonial activists executed by the French appear out of place in the gilded, 19th century ballrooms, but then again the contrast gives a sense of the immense power and complacency of the colonial French. There are photos of Vietnamese peace demonstrators in Saigon demanding that US roops get out; and a dramatic photo of 'hich Quang Duc, the monk who made eadlines worldwide, when he burned himelf to death in 1963 to protest against the olicies of President Ngo Dinh Diem (see ne 'Thien Mu Pagoda' boxed text, p211).

The information plaques are in Vietnamse only, but some of the exhibits include ocuments in French or English, and many thers are self-explanatory if you know ome basic Vietnamese history (but if you on't, see the History chapter, p24). The xhibitions cover the various periods in the ity's 300-year history.

Among the most interesting artefacts on isplay is a long, narrow rowing boat (ghe) vith a false bottom in which arms were muggled. Nearby is a small diorama of he Cu Chi Tunnels. The adjoining room .as examples of infantry weapons used by he VC and various South Vietnamese and JS medals, hats and plaques. A map shows ommunist advances during the dramatic ollapse of South Vietnam in early 1975. 'here are also photographs of the liberaion of Saigon.

Deep beneath the building is a network ›f reinforced concrete bunkers and fortified orridors. The system, branches of which tretch all the way to Reunification Palace, ncluded living areas, a kitchen and a large neeting hall. In 1963 President Diem and .is brother hid here before fleeing to Cha 'am Church (p341). The network is not urrently open to the public because most ›f the tunnels are flooded, but if you want to ›ring a torch (flashlight), a museum guard night show you around.

In the garden behind the museum is a ioviet tank and a US Huey UH-1 helicopter .nd anti-aircraft gun. In the garden frontng Đ Nam Ky Khoi Nghia is more military ıardware, including the American-built F-ةE jet used by a renegade South Vietnamese ›ilot to bomb the Presidential Palace (now Reunification Palace) on 8 April 1975.

The museum is located a block east of Reunification Palace.

'ON DUC THANG MUSEUM

'his small, seldom-visited **museum** (Bao Tang on Duc Thang; Map pp334-5; ☎ 829 7542; 5 Đ Ton Duc hang; admission US$1; ☒ 7.30-11.30am & 1.30-5pm Tue-ri) is dedicated to Ton Duc Thang, Ho Chi Minh's successor as president of Vietnam,

who was born in Long Xuyen, An Giang province, in 1888. He died in office in 1980. Photos and displays illustrate his role in the Vietnamese Revolution, including a couple of very lifelike exhibits representing the time he spent imprisoned on Con Son Island (p382).

The museum is on the waterfront, half a block north of the Tran Hung Dao statue.

HO CHI MINH MUSEUM

This **museum** (Khu Luu Niem Bac Ho; Map p326; ☎ 840 0647; 1 Đ Nguyen Tat Thanh; admission 5000d; ☒ 7.30-11.30am & 1.30-5pm) is in the old customs house in District 4, just across Ben Nghe Channel from the quayside end of ĐL Ham Nghi. Nicknamed the 'Dragon House' (Nha Rong), it was built in 1863. The tie between Ho Chi Minh and the museum building is tenuous: 21-year-old Ho, having signed on as a stoker and galley boy on a French freighter, left Vietnam from here in 1911 and thus began 30 years of exile in France, the Soviet Union, China and elsewhere.

The museum houses many of Ho's personal effects, including some of his clothing (he was a man of informal dress), sandals, his beloved US-made Zenith radio and other memorabilia. The explanatory signs in the museum are in Vietnamese, but if you know something about Uncle Ho (see p29) you should be able to follow most of the photographs and exhibits.

CONG VIEN VAN HOA PARK

Next to the old Cercle Sportif, which was an elite sporting club during the French-colonial period, the bench-lined walks of **Cong Vien Van Hoa Park** (Map p326) are shaded with avenues of enormous tropical trees.

In the morning, you can often see people here practising the art of thai cuc quyen, or slow-motion shadow boxing. Within the park is also a small-scale model of Nha Trang's most famous Cham towers.

This place still has an active **sports club** that is possible to visit. It has 11 tennis courts, a passable swimming pool and a clubhouse, all of which have a faded colonial feel about them. The tennis courts are available for hire at a reasonable fee and hourly tickets are on sale for use of the pool. The antique dressing rooms are quaint, but there are no lockers.

There are also Roman-style baths and a coffee shop overlooking the colonnaded pool. Other facilities include a gymnasium, table tennis, weights, wrestling mats and ballroom-dancing classes.

Cong Vien Van Hoa Park is adjacent to Reunification Palace. There are entrances across from 115 Đ Nguyen Du and on Đ Nguyen Thi Minh Khai.

Greater HCMC

If you have the time to wander farther afield, the must-sees of Greater HCMC are Binh Soup Shop and a few pagodas. If you're not planning to check out Cholon, investigate the peaceful Giac Lam Pagoda or the Jade Emperor Pagoda for some dazzling architecture and ornamentation.

BINH SOUP SHOP

It might seem strange to introduce a noo-dle-soup restaurant as a sight, but there is more to **Binh Soup Shop** (Map p326; ☎ 848 3775; 7 Đ Ly Chinh Tha Thang, District 3; noodle soup 15,000d) than just the soup. The Binh Soup Shop was the secret headquarters of the VC in Saigon. It

was from here that the VC planned its at tack on the US embassy and other places i Saigon during the Tet Offensive of 1968. On has to wonder how many US soldiers at here, completely unaware that the staff wer all VC infiltrators. By the way, the *pho* isn bad here.

GIAC LAM PAGODA

Believed to be the oldest pagoda in greate HCMC, **Giac Lam Pagoda** (Map pp322-3; 118 Lac Long Quan) dates from 1744. The last re construction here was in 1900, so the ar chitecture, layout and ornamentatio remain almost unaltered by the modernis renovations that have transformed so man of Vietnam's religious structures. Severa monks live at this Vietnamese Buddhis pagoda, which also incorporates aspects o Taoism and Confucianism. It is well wort the trip out here from the city centre.

To the right of the gate to the pagoda com pound are the **tombs** of venerated monk The Bodhi or pipal tree *(bo de)* located in th front garden was the gift of a monk from Sr Lanka. Next to the tree is a gleaming whit

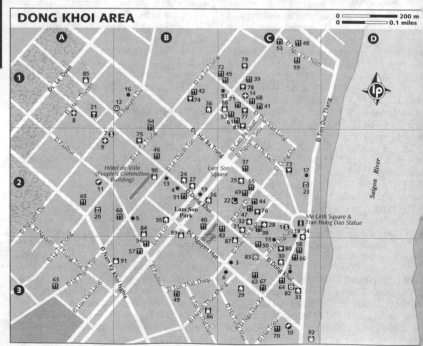

tatue of Quan The Am Bo Tat standing on a lotus blossom – a symbol of purity.

The roof line of the **main building** is decorated both inside and outside with unusual blue-and-white porcelain plates. Through the main entrance is a reception hall lined with funeral tablets and photos of the deceased. Roughly in the centre of the hall, near an old French chandelier, is a figure of the 18-armed Chuan De, another form of the Goddess of Mercy. Note the carved hardwood columns that bear gilded Vietnamese inscriptions written in *nom* characters. The wall to the left is covered with portraits of great monks from previous generations. Their names and other biographical information are recorded on the vertical red tablets in gold *nom* characters. A box for donations sits nearby. Shoes should be removed when passing from the rough red floor tiles to the smaller, white-black-grey tiles.

On the other side of the wall from the monks' funeral tablets is the main **sanctuary**, which is filled with countless gilded figures. On the dais in the centre of the back row sits A Di Da, the Buddha of the Past (Amitabha). Located to his right is Kasyape and to his left Anand; both are disciples of the Thich Ca Buddha (the historical Buddha Sakyamuni, whose real name was Siddhartha Gautama).

Directly in front of A Di Da is a statue of the Thich Ca Buddha, flanked by two guardians. In front is a tiny figure of the Thich Ca Buddha as a child. As always, he is clothed in a yellow robe.

The fat laughing fellow, seated with five children climbing all over him, is Ameda. To his left is Ngoc Hoang, the Taoist Jade Emperor, who presides over a world of innumerable supernatural beings. In the front row is a statue of the Thich Ca Buddha with two Bodhisattvas on each side. On the altars along the side walls of the sanctuary are various Bodhisattvas and the Judges of the 10 Regions of Hell. Each of the judges is holding a scroll resembling the handle of a fork.

HO CHI MINH CITY

The red-and-gold Christmas tree-shaped object is a wooden altar bearing 49 lamps and 49 miniature Bodhisattva statues. People pray for sick relatives or ask for happiness by contributing kerosene for use in the lamps. Petitioners' names and those of ill family members are written on slips of paper, which are attached to the branches of the 'tree'.

The frame of the large bronze bell in the corner looks like a university bulletin board because petitioners have attached to it lists of names: those of people seeking happiness and those of the sick and the dead, placed there by relatives. It is believed that when the bell is rung, the sound will resonate to the heavens above and the underground heavens, carrying with it the attached supplications.

Prayers here consist of chanting to the accompaniment of drums, bells and gongs, and they follow a traditional rite seldom performed these days. Prayers are held daily from 4am to 5am, 11am to noon, 4pm to 5pm and 7pm to 8pm.

Giac Lam Pagoda is about 3km from Cholon in the Tan Binh district. Beware: the numbering of Đ Lac Long Quan is extremely confusing, starting over from '1' several times and at one point jumping to four digits. In many places, odd and even numbers are on the same side of the street.

The best way to get to Giac Lam from Cholon is to take ĐL Nguyen Chi Thanh or ĐL 3 Thang 2 to Đ Le Dai Hanh. Head northwest on Đ Le Dai Hanh and turn right onto Đ Lac Long Quan. Walk 100m and the pagoda gate will be on your left.

GIAC VIEN PAGODA

Architecturally similar to Giac Lam, this **pagoda** (Map pp322-3; Đ Lac Long Quan; ⏰ 7-11.30am & 1.30-7pm) shares with it an atmosphere of scholarly serenity, though Giac Vien, which is right next to Dam Sen Lake in District 11, is in a more rural setting. Giac Vien Pagoda was founded by Hai Tinh Giac Vien about 200 years ago. It is said that Emperor Gia Long, who died in 1819, used to worship at Giac Vien. Today 10 monks live here.

The pagoda is in a relatively poor part of the city. The best way to get here from Cholon is to take ĐL Nguyen Chi Thanh or ĐL 3 Thang 2 to Đ Le Dai Hanh. Turn left (southwest) off Đ Le Dai Hanh onto Đ Binh Thoi and turn right (north) at Đ Lac Long Quan. The gate leading to the pagoda is at 247 Đ Lac Long Quan.

Pass through the gate and go several hundred metres down a potholed dirt road, turning left at the T-junction and right at the fork. You will pass several impressive **tombs** of monks on the right before arriving at the pagoda itself.

The first chamber as you enter the pagoda is lined with funeral tablets. At the back of the second chamber is a statue of Hai Tinh Giac Vien holding a horsetail switch. The nearby portraits are of his disciples and successors as head monk. A donation box sits to the left of the statue. Opposite Hai Tinh Giac Vien is a representation of 18-armed Chuan De, who is flanked by two guardians.

The main **sanctuary** is on the other side of the wall behind the Hai Tinh Giac Vien statue. A Di Da is at the back of the dais. Directly in front of him is the Thich Ca Buddha, flanked by his disciples Anand (on the left) and Kasyape (on the right). To the right of Kasyape is the Ti Lu Buddha; to the left of Anand is the Nhien Dang Buddha. At the foot of the Thich Ca Buddha is a small figure of Thich Ca as a child. Fat, laughing Ameda is seated with children climbing all over him; on either side of him stand guardians. In the front row of the dais is Thich Ca with two Bodhisattvas sitting on each side.

In front of the dais is a fantastic brass incense basin with fierce dragon heads emerging from each side. On the altar to the left of the dais is Dai The Chi Bo Tat; on the altar to the right is Quan The Am Bo Tat. The Guardian of the Pagoda is against the wall opposite the dais. Nearby is a 'Christmas tree' similar to the one in Giac Lam Pagoda (p334). Lining the side walls are the Judges of the 10 Regions of Hell (holding scrolls) and 18 Bodhisattvas.

Giac Vien Pagoda is open during the hours listed, but go before dark as the electricity is often out in the evening. Prayers are held daily from 4am to 5am, 8am to 10am, 2pm to 3pm, 4pm to 5pm and 7pm to 9pm.

JADE EMPEROR PAGODA

Built in 1909 by the Cantonese (Quang Dong) Congregation, the **Jade Emperor Pagoda** (Phuoc Hai Tu or Chua Ngoc Hoang; Map pp322-3; 73 Đ Mai Thi Luu) is truly a gem among Chinese

temples. It is one of the most spectacu-
larly colourful pagodas in HCMC, filled
with statues of phantasmal divinities and
grotesque heroes. The pungent smoke of
burning joss sticks fills the air, obscuring
the exquisite woodcarvings decorated with
gilded Chinese characters. The roof is covered with elaborate tile work. The statues,
which represent characters from both the
Buddhist and Taoist traditions, are made
of reinforced papier-mâché.

As you enter the main doors of the
building, Mon Quan, the God of the Gate,
stands to the right in an elaborately carved
wooden case. Opposite him, in a similar
case, is Tho Than (Tho Dia), the God of
the Land. Straight on is an altar on which
are placed figures of, from left to right: Phat
Mau Chuan De, mother of the five Buddhas
of the cardinal directions; Dia Tang Vuong
Bo Tat (Ksitigartha), the King of Hell; the
Di Lac Buddha (Maitreya), the Buddha of
the Future; Quan The Am Bo Tat; and a
bas-relief portrait of the Thich Ca Buddha. Behind the altar, in a glass case, is the
Duoc Su Buddha, also known as the Nhu
Lai Buddha. The figure is said to be made
of sandalwood.

To either side of the altar, against the
walls, are two especially fierce and menac-
ing figures. On the right (as you face the
altar) is a 4m-high statue of the general who
defeated the Green Dragon. He is stepping
on the vanquished dragon. On the left is
the general who defeated the White Tiger,
which is also being stepped on.

The Taoist Jade Emperor (or King of
Heaven, Ngoc Hoang), draped in luxuri-
ous robes, presides over the **main sanctuary**.
He is flanked by his guardians, the Four Big
Diamonds (Tu Dai Kim Cuong), so named
because they are said to be as hard as dia-
monds. In front of the King of Heaven stand
six figures, three to each side. On the left is
Bac Dau, the Taoist God of the Northern
Polar Star and God of Longevity, flanked by
his two guardians; and on the right is Nam
Tao, the Taoist God of the Southern Polar
Star and God of Happiness, also flanked by
two guardians.

In the case to the right of the Jade Emperor is 18-armed Phat Mau Chuan De.
Two faces, affixed to her head behind each
ear, look to either side. On the wall to her
right, at a height of about 4m, is Dai Minh

Vuong Quang, who was reincarnated as
Sakyamuni, riding on the back of a phoe-
nix. Below are the Tien Nhan (literally the
'God Persons').

In the case to the left of the Jade Emperor
sits Ong Bac De, one of his reincarnations,
holding a sword. One of his feet is resting
on a turtle while the other rests on a snake.
On the wall to the left of Ong Bac De, about
4m off the ground, is Thien Loi, the God
of Lightning, who slays evil people. Below
Thien Loi are the military commanders of
Ong Bac De (on the lower step) and Thien
Loi's guardians (on the upper step). At the
top of the two carved pillars that separate
the three alcoves are the Goddess of the
Moon (on the left) and God of the Sun (on
the right).

Out the door on the left-hand side of the
Jade Emperor's chamber is another room.
The semienclosed area to the right (as you
enter) is presided over by Thanh Hoang,
the Chief of Hell; to the left is his red horse.
Of the six figures lining the walls, the two
closest to Thanh Hoang are Am Quan, the
God of Yin (on the left), and Duong Quan,
the God of Yang (on the right). The other
four figures, the Thuong Thien Phat Ac,
are gods who dispense punishments for evil
acts and rewards for good deeds. Thanh
Hoang faces in the direction of the famous
Hall of the Ten Hells. The carved wooden
panels lining the walls graphically depict
the varied torments awaiting evil people in
each of the Ten Regions of Hell. At the top
of each panel is one of the Judges of the
10 Regions examining a book in which the
deeds of the deceased are inscribed.

On the wall opposite Thanh Hoang is a
bas-relief wood panel depicting Quan Am
Thi Kinh standing on a lotus blossom. On
the panel, Quan Am Thi Kinh is shown
holding her 'son'. To her left is Long Nu,
a very young Buddha who is her protector. To her right is Thien Tai, her guardian
spirit, who knew the real story all along (see
the boxed text 'Quan Am Thi Kinh', p343).
Above her left shoulder is a bird bearing
prayer beads.

To the right of the panel of Quan Am Thi
Kinh is a panel depicting Dia Tang Vuong
Bo Tat, the King of Hell.

On the other side of the wall is a fascinating little room in which the **ceramic
figures** of 12 women, overrun with children

and wearing colourful clothes, sit in two rows of six. Each of the women exemplifies a human characteristic, either good or bad (as in the case of the woman drinking alcohol from a jug). Each figure represents one year in the 12-year Chinese calendar. Presiding over the room is Kim Hoa Thanh Mau, the Chief of All Women.

Off to the right of the main chamber, stairs lead to a 2nd-floor sanctuary and balcony.

The Jade Emperor Pagoda is in a part of the city known as Da Kao (or Da Cao). To get here, go to 20 Đ Dien Bien Phu and walk half a block to the northwest.

LE VAN DUYET TEMPLE

Dedicated to Marshal Le Van Duyet (1763–1831), this **temple** (Map pp322-3) is also the burial place of him and his wife. The marshal was a South Vietnamese general and viceroy who helped put down the Tay Son Rebellion and reunify Vietnam. When the Nguyen dynasty came to power in 1802, he was elevated by Emperor Gia Long to the rank of marshal. Le Van Duyet fell into disfavour with Gia Long's successor, Minh Mang, who tried him posthumously and desecrated his grave. Emperor Thieu Tri, who succeeded Minh Mang, restored the tomb, thus fulfilling a prophesy of its destruction and restoration. Le Van Duyet was considered a national hero in the South before 1975, but is disliked by the communists because of his involvement in the expansion of French influence.

The temple itself was renovated in 1937 and has a distinctly modern feel to it, though since 1975 the government has done little to keep it from becoming dilapidated. Among the items on display are a portrait of Le Van Duyet, some of his personal effects (including European-style crystal goblets) and other antiques. There are two wonderful life-size horse statues on either side of the entrance to the third and last chamber, which is kept locked.

During celebrations of Tet and on the 30th day of the seventh lunar month (the anniversary of Le Van Duyet's death), the tomb is thronged with pilgrims. Vietnamese used to come here to take oaths of good faith if they could not afford the services of a court of justice.

There are tropical fish on sale for visitors. The caged birds that are for sale are bought by pilgrims and freed to earn merit. The birds are often recaptured (and liberated again).

The temple is reached by heading north from the city centre on Đ Dinh Tien Hoang all the way to ĐL Phan Dang Luu; it's easy to spot from the southeast corner.

TRAN HUNG DAO TEMPLE

This small **temple** (Map pp322-3; 36 Đ Vo Thi Sau; 6-11am & 2-6pm Mon-Fri) is dedicated to Tran Hung Dao, a national hero who in 1287 vanquished an invasion force, said to have numbered 300,000 men, that had been dispatched by the Mongol emperor Kubla Khan. The temple is a block northeast of the telecommunication dishes that are between Đ Dien Bien Phu and Đ Vo Thi Sau.

The public park between the dishes and ĐL Hai Ba Trung was built in 1983 on the site of the **Massiges Cemetery**, a burial ground for French soldiers and settlers. The remains of French military personnel were exhumed and repatriated to France. The tomb of the 18th-century French missionary and diplomat Pigneau de Béhaine, Bishop of Adran, which was completely destroyed after reunification, was also here.

VINH NGHIEM PAGODA

Inaugurated in 1971, **Vinh Nghiem Pagoda** (Map pp322-3) is noteworthy for its vast sanctuary and eight-storey tower, each level of which contains a statue of the Buddha. It was built with help from the Japan-Vietnam Friendship Association, which explains the presence of Japanese elements in its architecture. At the base of the tower (open only on holidays) is a shop selling Buddhist ritual objects. Behind the sanctuary is a three-storey tower, which serves as a repository for carefully labelled ceramic urns containing the ashes of people who have been cremated. The pagoda is just off Đ Nguyen Van Troi in District 3.

CHO QUAN CHURCH

Built by the French about 100 years ago, **Cho Quan Church** (Map pp322-3; 133 Đ Tran Binh Trong; 4-7am & 3-6pm Mon-Sat, 4-9am & 1.30-6pm Sun) is one of the largest churches in HCMC. It's the only church we've seen in the city where the figure of Jesus on the altar has a neon halo. The view from the belfry is worth the steep climb. The church is between ĐL

Tran Hung Dao and Đ Nguyen Trai. Sunday masses are held at 5am, 6.30am, 8.30am, 4.30pm and 6pm.

Cholon

A jewel-box of interesting Chinese-style temples awaits in Cholon (District 5) – it's well worth heading over to Chinatown for a half-day or more to explore. Aside from the temples and pagodas, you can sample some excellent Chinese and Vietnamese food – or have a swim at one of the water parks, if you get templed out.

While you're roaming, stroll over to the strip of **traditional herb shops** (Map p340; Đ Hai Thuong Lan Ong) between Đ Luong Nhu Hoc and Đ Trieu Quang Phuc for an olfactory experience you won't soon forget. Here the streets are filled with amazing sights, sounds and, most of all, rich herbal smells.

QUAN AM PAGODA

Founded by the Fujian Congregation, **Quan Am Pagoda** (Map p340; 12 Đ Lao Tu) was built in 1816 and named for Quan The Am Bo Tat, the Goddess of Mercy.

This is the most active pagoda in Cholon and the Chinese influence is obvious. The roof is decorated with fantastic scenes, rendered in ceramic, from traditional Chinese plays and stories. The tableaux include ships, houses, people and several ferocious dragons. The front doors are decorated with gold-and-lacquer panels. On the walls of the porch are murals, in slight relief, of scenes from China around the time of Quan Cong. There are elaborate woodcarvings on roof supports above the porch.

Behind the main altar is A Pho, the Holy Mother Celestial Empress, gilded and in rich raiment. In front of her, in a glass case, are three painted statues of the Thich Ca Buddha, a standing gold Quan The Am Bo Tat, a seated laughing Ameda and, to the far left, a gold figure of Dia Tang Vuong Bo Tat (King of Hell).

In the courtyard behind the main sanctuary, in the pink-tiled altar, is another figure of A Pho. Quan The Am Bo Tat, dressed in white embroidered robes, stands nearby. To the left of the altar is her richly ornamented bed. To the right of the altar is Quan Cong, flanked by his guardians. To the far right, in front of another pink altar, is the black-faced judge Bao Cong.

PHUOC AN HOI QUAN PAGODA

Built in 1902 by the Fujian Congregation, **Phuoc An Hoi Quan Pagoda** (Map p340; 184 Đ Hung Vuong) is one of the most beautifully ornamented pagodas in HCMC. Of special interest are the many small porcelain figures, the elaborate brass ritual objects and the fine woodcarvings on the altars, walls, columns and hanging lanterns. From outside the building you can see the ceramic scenes, each containing innumerable small figurines, which decorate the roof.

To the left of the entrance is a life-size figure of the sacred horse of Quan Cong. Before leaving on a journey, people make offerings to the horse, then stroke its mane and ring the bell around its neck. Behind the main altar, with its stone and brass incense braziers, is Quan Cong, to whom the pagoda is dedicated. Behind the altar to the left is Ong Bon (Guardian Spirit of Happiness and Virtue) and two servants. The altar to the right is occupied by representations of Buddhist (rather than Taoist) personages. In the glass case are a plaster Thich Ca Buddha and two figures of the Goddess of Mercy, one made of porcelain and the other cast in brass.

PHUNG SON PAGODA

This **pagoda** (Map pp322-3; Phung Son Tu & Chua Go; 1408 ĐL 3/2) is extremely rich in statuary made of bronze, wood, ceramic and hammered copper. Some statues are gilded while other beautifully carved ones are painted. This Vietnamese Buddhist pagoda was built between 1802 and 1820 on the site of structures from the Oc-Eo (Funan) period, contemporaneous with early centuries of Christianity. The foundations of Funanese buildings have been discovered here.

Once upon a time, it was decided that Phung Son Pagoda should be moved to a different site. The pagoda's ritual objects – bells, drums, statues – were loaded onto the back of a white elephant, but the elephant slipped because of the great weight and all the precious objects fell into a nearby pond. This event was interpreted as an omen that the pagoda should remain at its original location. All the articles were retrieved except for the bell, which locals say was heard ringing, until about a century ago, whenever there was a full or new moon.

CHOLON

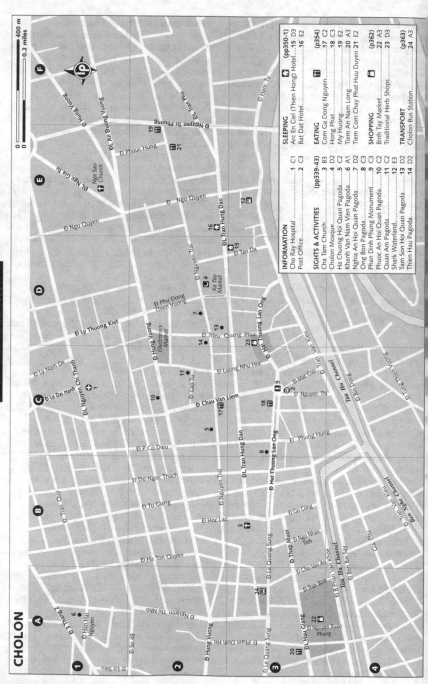

0   400 m
0   0.2 miles

INFORMATION	
Cho Ray Hospital	1 C1
Post Office	2 C3

SIGHTS & ACTIVITIES	(pp339-43)
Cha Tam Church	3 B3
Cholon Mosque	4 D2
Ha Chuong Hoi Quan Pagoda	5 C2
Khanh Van Nam Vien Pagoda	6 A1
Nghia An Hoi Quan Pagoda	7 D2
Ong Bon Pagoda	8 C3
Phan Dinh Phung Monument	9 C3
Phuoc An Hoi Quan Pagoda	10 C2
Quan Am Pagoda	11 C2
Shark Waterland	12 E3
Tam Son Hoi Quan Pagoda	13 D2
Thien Hau Pagoda	14 D2

SLEEPING	(pp350-1)
Arc En Ciel (Thien Hong) Hotel	15 D3
Bat Dat Hotel	16 E2

EATING	(p354)
Com Ga Dong Nguyen	17 C2
Hong Phat	18 C3
My Huong	19 E2
Tiem An Nam Long	20 A3
Tiem Com Chay Phat Huu Duyen	21 E2

SHOPPING	(p362)
Binh Tay Market	22 A3
Traditional Herb Shops	23 D3

TRANSPORT	(p363)
Cholon Bus Station	24 A3

The main dais, with its many levels, is dominated by a gilded A Di Da Buddha seated under a canopy flanked by long mobiles resembling human forms without heads. A Di Da is flanked by Quan The Am Bo Tat (on the left) and Dai The Chi Bo Tat (on the right). To the left of the main dais is an altar with a statue of Bodhidharma, who brought Buddhism from India to China. The statue, which is made of Chinese ceramic, has a face with Indian features.

As you walk from the main sanctuary to the room with the open-air courtyard in the middle, you come to an altar with four statues on it, including a standing bronze Thich Ca Buddha of Thai origin. To the right is an altar with a glass case containing a sandalwood statue claimed to be of Long Vuong (Dragon King), who brings rain. Around the pagoda building are a number of diverse and elaborate monks' tombs.

Phung Son Pagoda is in District 11. Prayers are held three times a day, from 4am to 5am, 4pm to 5pm and 6pm to 7pm. The main entrances are locked most of the time because of problems with theft, but the side entrance (to the left as you approach the building) is open during prayer times.

TAM SON HOI QUAN PAGODA
Built by the Fujian Congregation in the 19th century, **Tam Son Hoi Quan Pagoda** (Map opposite; Chua Ba Chua; 118 Đ Trieu Quang Phuc) retains most of its original rich ornamentation. The pagoda is dedicated to Me Sanh, the Goddess of Fertility. Both men and women – but more of the latter – come here to pray for children.

To the right of the covered courtyard is the deified General Quan Cong with his long black beard; he is flanked by two guardians, the Mandarin General Chau Xuong on the left and the Administrative Mandarin Quan Binh on the right. Next to Chau Xuong is Quan Cong's sacred red horse.

Behind the main altar (directly across the courtyard from the entrance) is Thien Hau. To the right is an ornate case in which Me Sanh, in white, sits surrounded by her daughters. In the case to the left of Thien Hau is Ong Bon. In front of Thien Hau is Quan The Am Bo Tat, enclosed in glass.

Across the courtyard from Quan Cong is a small room containing ossuary jars and memorials in which the dead are repre-

sented by their photographs. Next to this chamber is a small room containing the papier-mâché head of a dragon of the type used by the Fujian Congregation for dragon dancing.

Tam Son Hoi Quan Pagoda is close to 370 ĐL Tran Hung Dao.

CHA TAM CHURCH
President Ngo Dinh Diem and his brother Ngo Dinh Nhu took refuge in **Cha Tam Church** (Map opposite; 25 Đ Hoc Lac) on 2 November 1963, after fleeing the Presidential Palace during a coup attempt. When their efforts to contact loyal military officers (of whom there was almost none) failed, Diem and Nhu agreed to surrender unconditionally and reveal where they were hiding.

The coup leaders sent an M-113 armoured personnel carrier to the church and the two were taken into custody. However, before the vehicle reached central Saigon the soldiers had killed Diem and Nhu by shooting them at point-blank range and then repeatedly stabbing their bodies.

When news of the deaths was broadcast on radio, Saigon exploded with rejoicing. Portraits of the two were torn up and political prisoners, many of whom had been tortured, were set free. The city's nightclubs, which had closed because of the Ngos' conservative Catholic beliefs, were reopened. Three weeks later the US president, John F Kennedy, was assassinated. As his administration had supported the coup against Diem, some conspiracy theorists have speculated that Kennedy was killed by Diem's family in retaliation.

Cha Tam Church, built around the turn of the 19th century, is an attractive white and pastel-yellow structure. The statue in the tower is of François Xavier Tam Assou (1855–1934), a Chinese-born vicar apostolic (delegate of the pope) of Saigon. Today, the church has a very active congregation of 3000 ethnic Vietnamese and 2000 ethnic Chinese.

Masses are held daily. Cha Tam Church is at the western end of ĐL Tran Hung Dao.

THIEN HAU PAGODA
Built by the Cantonese Congregation in the early 19th century, this **pagoda** (Ba Mieu, Pho Mieu or Chua Ba; Map opposite; 710 Đ Nguyen Trai) is dedicated to Thien Hau and is one of the

most active in Cholon. It is said that Thien Hau (also known as Tuc Goi La Ba) can travel over the oceans on a mat and ride the clouds to wherever she pleases. Her mobility allows her to save people in trouble on the high seas.

Thien Hau is very popular in Hong Kong and Taiwan, which might explain why this pagoda is included on so many tour-group agendas.

Though there are guardians to each side of the entrance, it is said that the real protectors of the pagoda are the two land turtles that live here. There are intricate ceramic friezes above the roof line of the interior courtyard. Near the huge braziers are two miniature wooden structures in which a small figure of Thien Hau is paraded around the nearby streets on the 23rd day of the third lunar month.

On the main dais are three figures of Thien Hau, one behind the other, all flanked by two servants or guardians. To the left of the dais is a bed for Thien Hau. To the right is a scale-model boat and on the far right is the Goddess Long Mau, Protector of Mothers and Newborns.

NGHIA AN HOI QUAN PAGODA

Built by the Chaozhou Chinese Congregation, **Nghia An Hoi Quan Pagoda** (Map p340; 678 Đ Nguyen Trai) is noteworthy for its gilded woodwork. There's a carved wooden boat over the entrance, and, inside to the left of the doorway is an enormous representation of Quan Cong's red horse with its groom. To the right of the entrance is an elaborate altar in which a bearded Ong Bon stands holding a stick. Behind the main altar are three glass cases. In the centre is Quan Cong and to either side are his assistants, Chau Xuong (on the left) and Quan Binh (on the right). To the right of Quan Binh is an especially elaborate case holding Thien Hau.

CHOLON MOSQUE

The clean lines and lack of ornamentation of the **Cholon Mosque** (Map p340; 641 Đ Nguyen Trai) contrast starkly with nearby Chinese and Vietnamese Buddhist pagodas. In the courtyard is a pool for ritual ablutions. Note the tiled niche in the wall (mihrab) indicating the direction of prayer, which is towards Mecca. The mosque was built by Tamil Muslims in 1932. Since 1975 it

has served the Malaysian and Indonesian Muslim communities.

ONG BON PAGODA

Built by the Fujian Congregation, **Ong Bon Pagoda** (Chua Ong Bon & Nhi Phu Hoi Quan; Map p340; 264 ĐL Hai Thuong Lan Ong) is dedicated to Ong Bon. The wooden altar is intricately carved and gilded.

As you enter the pagoda, there is a room to the right of the open-air courtyard. In it, behind the table, is a figure of Quan The Am Bo Tat in a glass case. Above the case is the head of a Thich Ca Buddha.

Directly across the courtyard from the pagoda entrance, against the wall, is Ong Bon, to whom people come to pray for general happiness and relief from financial difficulties. He faces a fine carved wooden altar. On the walls of this chamber are rather indistinct murals of five tigers (to the left) and two dragons (to the right).

In the area on the other side of the wall with the mural of the dragons is a furnace for burning paper representations of the wealth that people wish to bestow upon their deceased family members. Diagonally opposite is Quan Cong, flanked by his guardians Chau Xuong and Quan Binh.

HA CHUONG HOI QUAN PAGODA

This typical Fujian **pagoda** (Map p340; 802 Đ Nguyen Trai) is dedicated to Thien Hau, who was born in Fujian. The four carved stone pillars, wrapped in painted dragons, were made in China and brought to Vietnam by boat. There are interesting murals to each side of the main altar. Note the ceramic relief scenes on the roof.

The pagoda becomes extremely active during the Lantern Festival, a Chinese holiday held on the 15th day of the first lunar month (the first full moon of the new lunar year).

KHANH VAN NAM VIEN PAGODA

Built between 1939 and 1942 by the Cantonese Congregation, **Khanh Van Nam Vien Pagoda** (Map p340; 46/5 Đ Lo Sieu) is said to be the only Taoist pagoda in Vietnam. The number of true Taoists in HCMC is estimated at only 4000, though most Chinese practice a mixture of Taoism and Buddhism.

A few metres from the door is a statue of Hoang Linh Quan, chief guardian of the

QUAN AM THI KINH

The legend goes that Quan Am Thi Kinh was a woman unjustly turned out of her home by her husband. She disguised herself as a monk and went to live in a pagoda, where a young woman accused her of fathering her child. She accepted the blame – and the responsibility that went along with it – and again found herself out on the streets, this time with her 'son'. Much later, about to die, she returned to the monastery to confess her secret. When the emperor of China heard of her story, he declared her the Guardian Spirit of Mother and Child.

It is believed that she has the power to bestow male offspring on those who fervently believe in her and as such is extremely popular with childless couples.

pagoda. There is a Yin-and-Yang symbol on the platform on which the incense braziers sit. Behind the main altar are four figures: Quan Cong (on the right) and Lu Tung Pan (on the left) represent Taoism; between them is Van Xuong representing Confucianism; and behind Van Xuong is Quan The Am Bo Tat.

In front of these figures is a glass case containing seven gods and one goddess, all of whom are made of porcelain. In the altars to either side of the four figures are Hoa De (on the left), a famous doctor during the Han dynasty, and Huynh Dai Tien (on the right), a disciple of Laotse (Thai Thuong Lao Quan in Vietnamese).

Upstairs is a 150cm-high statue of Laotse. Behind his head is a halo consisting of a round mirror edged with fluorescent lighting.

Off to the left of Laotse are two stone plaques with instructions for inhalation and exhalation exercises. A schematic drawing represents the human organs as a scene from rural China. The diaphragm, agent of inhalation, is at the bottom; the stomach is represented by a peasant ploughing with a water buffalo. The kidney is marked by four Yin-and-Yang symbols, the liver is shown as a grove of trees and the heart is represented by a circle with a peasant standing in it, above which is a constellation. The tall pagoda represents the throat and the broken rainbow is the mouth. At the top are mountains and a seated figure that represent the brain and imagination, respectively.

The pagoda operates a home for 30 elderly people who have no family. Each of the old folk, most of whom are women, have their own wood stove made of brick and can cook for themselves. Next door, also run by the pagoda, is a free medical clinic, which offers Chinese herbal medicines and acupuncture

treatments to the community. If you would like to support this worthy venture you can leave a donation with the monks.

Prayers are held daily from 8am to 9am. To reach the pagoda, turn off Đ Nguyen Thi Nho, which runs perpendicular to Đ Hung Vuong, between Nos 269B and 271B.

ACTIVITIES
Fitness Clubs & Pools

Even if you don't make it to one of Saigon's water parks (p346) or to Cong Vien Van Hoa Park (p333), there are several fine swimming pools at plush hotels. You needn't stay there to swim, but you'll have to pay an admission fee of US$8 to US$16 per day. Hotels offering access to their pools include the Metropole, Omni, Renaissance Riverside and Rex.

There are a number of less expensive public pools and some of the newer ones are in very good condition. These pools charge by the hour and this works out to be very cheap, if you're staying only a short time.

International Club (Map pp322-3; ☎ 865 7695; 285B Đ Cach Mang Thang Tam, District 10; admission 25,000d; ☯ 9am-midnight) Pool, sauna, steam rooms and gym; 120,000d ticket entitles you to 50-minute rub-down and all-day use of the club's facilities.

Lam Son Pool (Map pp322-3; ☎ 835 8028; 342 Đ Tran Binh Trong, District 5; per hr 5000d, 6000d after 5pm; ☯ 8am-8pm) Has Olympic-sized pool.

Lan Anh Club (Map pp322-3; ☎ 862 7144; 291 Cach Mang Thang Tam, District 10; admission gym/pool 40,000d/25,000d; ☯ pool 6am-9pm) There's a good gym here.

Workers' Club (Map p326; ☎ 930 1819; 55B Đ Nguyen Thi Minh Khai, District 3; admission per hr 10,000d)

If you're interested in martial arts, the best place to see (or try) *thai cuc quyen* is at Cong Vien Van Hoa Park (p333) or in the Cholon district, where there is a large ethnic-Chinese population. Ask the staff at the Arc en Ciel Hotel (p351) to point you in the right direction.

Massage & Spas

Most upmarket hotels offer some kind of massage service…some more legitimate than others. According to local expats, the best massage in town is at the **Duxton Saigon Hotel** (Map pp334–5; ☎ 822 2999; enquiries@saigon.duxton.com.vn; 63 ĐL Nguyen Hue), which charges US$20 for a half-hour massage.

Vietnamese Traditional Massage Institute (Map p356; ☎ 839 6697; 185 Đ Cong Quynh; 35,000-45,000d/hr, sauna 25,000d; ☼ 9am-9pm; ☒) offers one of the best and cheapest rub-downs in town. Here you can enjoy a no-nonsense massage performed by a well-trained blind masseur from the Ho Chi Minh City Association for the Blind. Reservations are not necessary.

Spa Tropic (Map p326; ☎ 822 8895; www.spatropic.com; 187B ĐL Hai Ba Trung, District 3; ☼ 10am-8pm) is a good place to spoil yourself with a top-notch 'proper' massage. This Zen-like beauty spa offers an array of aromatherapy facial treatments (US$28), body treatments (US$20 to US$35) and therapeutic massage (from US$18), from Swedish and deep-tissue to shiatsu. Spa Tropic can be found in the same quiet alley as Tib Restaurant (p352). Call ahead for reservations.

Qi Spa (Map pp322-3; ☼ 10am-11pm) is a brand-new spa offering massage packages (from US$45), including treats such as aromatherapy, Swedish dry sauna and beauty treatments.

Bowling

Diamond Superbowl (Map pp334–5; ☎ 825 7778; Diamond Plaza, 34 ĐL Le Duan; per hr from 120,000d; ☼ 10am-1am) is a state-of-the-art, 32-lane bowling alley smack dab in the centre of town. It's very popular with locals, and is notable for having fluorescent bowling balls and computerised scoring. Attached is a large amusement centre with billiards, a video-game arcade and shops.

Golf

If you're serious about golfing, there are top-notch courses in both Phan Thiet (p282) and Dalat (p297). Visit www.vietnamgolfresorts.com for more information on the courses and reasonably priced golf package tours.

Vietnam Golf and Country Club (Cau Lac Bo Golf Quoc Te Viet Nam; ☎ 733 0124; www.vgccgolf.com; Long Thanh My Village, District 9; driving range/full round US$10/82), about 15km east of central HCMC, was the first in Vietnam to provide night golfing under floodlights. Other facilities include tennis courts and a swimming pool.

Rach Chiec Driving Range (☎ 896 0756; Hwy 1, An Phu Village, District 9; 50 balls 40,000d; ☼ 6am-10pm) is a good place to practise your swing; clubs, shoes and instructors can be hired. It's a 20-minute drive north from central HCMC.

WALKING TOUR

Distance: 5km	
Duration: approximately 7hrs	

HCMC's immense sprawl makes it somewhat impractical to see all of it on foot, though a one-day walking tour around the city centre, District 1 (or 'Saigon'), is certainly possible and highly recommended. For more information on individual sights, refer to the Sights section, earlier.

The **Pham Ngu Lao (1)** backpacker area makes a logical starting point. There are plenty of places around here to fill up on eggs and bacon before the walk, but to soak up a real Vietnamese experience start the walk bright and early with a bowl of *pho* (noodle soup). From Đ Pham Ngu Lao, follow Đ Nguyen Thai Hoc north to the mammoth New World Hotel, turn right and follow Đ Le Lai a few minutes to **Pho 2000 (2**; p357), a good place to sample some noodles – former US President Bill Clinton did, so it can't be that bad!

After your soup, cross the road and enter the vast indoor **Ben Thanh Market (3**; p362), which is at its bustling best in the morning. After exploring the market, cross the large roundabout (carefully!), where you'll see a statue of **Tran Nguyen Hai (4)** on horseback. One short block south, on Đ Pho Duc Chinh, is the praiseworthy **Fine Arts Museum (5**; p331). After touring the exhibits, zigzag east to ĐL Ham Nghi and turn north again on Đ Ton That Dam to stroll through the colourful outdoor **street market (6**; p362). At the northern terminus turn west at the 'T' on Đ Huynh Thuc Khang to Đ Pasteur and out to ĐL Le Loi, the large boulevard leading towards the grand and thoughtfully restored **Municipal Theatre (7**; p320).

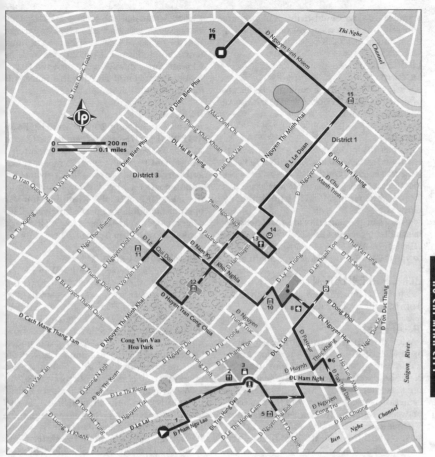

One short block before the theatre, turn left at the **Rex Hotel** (**8**; p351) and head up ĐL Nguyen Hue. Just ahead, at the northern end of the boulevard, is the stately French colonial era **Hôtel de Ville** (**9**; p330). You'll have to admire it from the outside because it's now home to the local People's Committee – requests to visit the interior are usually refused. However, a one-block walk south on Đ Le Thanh Ton will bring you to the **Museum of Ho Chi Minh City** (**10**; p332), where visitors are warmly received.

The popular **War Remnants Museum** (**11**; p329) is just a few blocks away along Đ Nam Ky Khoi Nghia then left on Đ Vo Van Tan. Nearby is **Reunification Palace** (**12**; p329).

Both of these landmarks are must-sees, but keep an eye on your watch because they're both closed around lunchtime.

After lunch, you can stroll north along ĐL Le Duan, stopping to look at **Notre Dame Cathedral** (**13**; p331) and the impressive French-style **post office** (**14**; p327). At the end of the boulevard are the zoo and botanic garden, on the grounds of which is the excellent **History Museum** (**15**; p330).

A few blocks northwest along Đ Nguyen Binh Khiem will bring you to **Jade Emperor Pagoda** (**16**; p336), a colourful way to end your tour. Alternatively, you can head south from here, back toward Dong Khoi.

By this time you will most likely be tired enough to head for your hotel, take a shower, enjoy a cold drink and prepare yourself for a great meal out or for tackling the nightlife of HCMC.

COURSES
Cooking

An array of Vietnamese cooking classes are offered by **Expat Services** (☎ 823 5872; vietnam cookery@hcm.vnn.vn).

Language

The majority of foreign-language students enrol at **Teacher Training University** (Dai Hoc Su Pham; Map pp322-3; ☎ 835 5100; ciecer@hcm.vnn.vn; 280 An Duong Vuong, District 5; private/group class US$4/2.50), a department of Ho Chi Minh City University.

Classes at the **University of Social Sciences & Humanities** (Dai Hoc Khoa Hoc Xa Hoi Va Nhan Van; Map p326; ☎ 822 5009; 12 Dinh Tien Hoang, District 1; group class per hr US$2.80) run on a term schedule.

HCMC FOR CHILDREN

See p359 for information about Binh Quoi Tourist Village, a great place for kids.

Water Parks

A slew of water parks sparkle invitingly around HCMC. Anyone with kids and a half-day to spare will quickly come to appreciate these wet and wonderful playgrounds on a sweltering day. Bring a waterproof camera. The best time to avoid the crowds is between 11am and 2pm on weekdays (most Vietnamese prefer to stay out of the midday sun) – but this is also the best time of day to get sunburnt.

Saigon Water Park (☎ 897 0456; Đ Kha Van Can, Thu Duc district; adult/child 60,000/35,000d, swim-only ticket 35,000d; ☉ 9am-5pm Mon-Fri, 9am-8pm Sat, 8am-8pm Sun & public holidays), a giant oasis in the suburbs, lies on the banks of the Saigon River. It's chock-full of pools and water rides, including loop-the-loop slides, a children's wading pool and even a wave pool. To get here, a meter taxi costs about 50,000d; shuttle buses (every half-hour) from Ben Thanh Market cost 5000d.

Dam Sen Water Park (Map pp322-3; ☎ 858 9991; www.damsenwaterpark.com.vn; 3 Đ Hoa Binh; adult/child 50,000/35,000d; ☉ 9am-6pm Mon-Fri, 8am-7pm Sat, Sun & holidays) is closer to central HCMC than Saigon Water Park. It has water slides, rivers with rapids (or slow currents) and rope swings for flips and fantastic belly flops.

Shark Waterland (Map p340; ☎ 853 7867; 600 Đ Ham Tu, district 5; admission 20,000-45,000d; ☉ 8am-9pm Mon-Fri, 10am-9pm Sat & Sun), despite the ominous name, is a good spot if you happen to be in Cholon. On a smaller scale than the larger water parks around HCMC, this place still has pools and slides.

Ho Ky Hoa Park

Just off ĐL 3 Thang 2 in District 10, **Ho Ky Hoa Park** (Map pp322-3; admission free, boat rental per hr 10,000-15,000d; ☉ 7am-9.30pm; ⛵) is a children's amusement park whose name means 'Lake and Gardens'. There are paddle, rowing and sailing boats for hire. Fishing is allowed in the lakes and a small swimming pool is open to the public for part of the year. The cafés are open year-round. Ho Ky Hoa Park is most crowded on Sunday.

Zoo & Botanic Gardens

One of the first projects undertaken by the French after they established Cochinchina as a colony was to found the **gardens** (Map p326; Thao Cam Vien; ☎ 829 3901; 2 Đ Nguyen Binh Khiem; admission 8000d; ☉ 7am-8pm). Though once one of the finest such gardens in Asia, they're now merely a pleasant place for a stroll under giant tropical trees. The emphasis now is on the fun fair, with kids' rides, a fun house, miniature train, house of mirrors and such.

We strongly recommend against visiting the poorly-kept animals, which live at the usual (ie marginal) Vietnamese standard.

Standing just inside the main zoo gate (Đ Nguyen Binh Khiem on the eastern end of ĐL Le Duan) you'll be flanked by two striking architectural gems, the impressive Temple of King Hung Vuong and the History Museum (p320).

QUIRKY HO CHI MINH CITY

Walls lined with aquariums provide a watery backdrop to the unique **Sango Aquarium Café** (Map pp334-5; ☎ 829 3189; 21 Đ Thai Van Lung; ☉ noon-midnight). Fish-feeding time is frenzied fun; ask the staff if they can give the critters a little snack while you're there. Sango also serves good Asian and Western people food, so you can have a bite while the fish do, too.

TOURS

There are surprisingly few day tours of HCMC itself available, though any local travel agent can come up with something for a fee. Hiring a *cyclo* for a half-day or full day of sightseeing is an interesting option, but be sure to agree on the price before setting out (most drivers charge around US$1 per hour).

There are heaps of organised tours to the outlying areas such as the Cu Chi Tunnels, Tay Ninh and the Mekong Delta. Some tours are day trips and other are overnighters. The cheapest tours by far are available from cafés and agencies in the Pham Ngu Lao area (see p327).

FESTIVALS & EVENTS

Saigon Cyclo Race (mid-March) Professional and nonprofessional *cyclo* drivers find out who's fastest; money raised is donated to local charities.

Festival at Lang Ong (30th day of 7th lunar month) People pray for happiness and the health of the country at the Ong Temple in HCMC's Binh Thanh district; plays and musical performances are staged.

SLEEPING

Each category of traveller has staked out its own turf in this city. Budget travellers tend to congregate around the Pham Ngu Lao area (Map p356) at the western end of District 1; this area has by far the widest range of budget accommodation. Travellers with more cash prefer the upmarket hotels concentrated around Đ Dong Khoi (Map pp334-5), on the eastern side of District 1. French travellers seem to have an affinity for **District 3** (p326), while Cholon (Map p340) attracts plenty of visitors from Hong Kong and Taiwan.

Budget

If you don't really know where you want to stay but are limited by budget, take a taxi into Pham Ngu Lao and proceed on foot. Lugging your bags around makes you a prime target for touts – consider dropping your gear at one of the travellers cafés and walking from there. Most won't mind keeping an eye on it for you and they'll be happy to tell you about their tour programmes. One simple solution is to email or call ahead for reservations; holding a room should not require a deposit, normally. Most hotels will fetch you at the airport for around US$5.

PHAM NGU LAO

Three streets – Đ Pham Ngu Lao, Đ De Tham and Đ Bui Vien – form the heart of the budget-traveller haven. These streets and the adjoining alleys, collectively known as Pham Ngu Lao, contain a treasure-trove of cheap accommodation, restaurants, bars, cafés and travel agents, most catering to the budget end of the market.

At last count there were well over a hundred places to stay in the area, so finding a room is never a problem here. Finding the right one is another story. A few places here have dorms (US$3) and there are countless minihotels (US$6 to US$10) as well as newer, more upmarket ones (US$10 to US$25).

About 100m south of Đ Pham Ngu Lao is Đ Bui Vien, which is rapidly being transformed into a solid string of guesthouses and minihotels. 'Minihotel Alley', flanked by (and addressed as an extension of) Đ Bui Vien and Đ Pham Ngu Lao, has more than a dozen virtually identical places. Most are family-run and range from US$6 to US$20.

Hong Hoa Hotel (Map p356; ☎ 836 1915; www.hong hoavn.com; 185/28 Đ Pham Ngu Lao; r US$12-20; 🔀 🖳) Guests here get two hours free at the Internet café downstairs. Hong Hoa also has a minimarket on Đ De Tham, selling toiletries, alcohol and Western junk food. The staff here are friendly and efficient.

Nga Hoang (Map p356; ☎ 920 3356; 269/19 Đ Pham Ngu Lao; r US$6-20; 🔀) Just off Đ De Tham in a small alley, this very clean, family-run guesthouse is a terrific deal. Breakfast is included, there's satellite TV and the management is very friendly.

Hotel 211 (Map p356; ☎ 836 7353; hotelduy@hotmail .com; 211 Đ Pham Ngu Lao; r US$7-12; 🔀) This large, established budget place has a rooftop terrace. All rooms have private bathroom with hot water and rates include breakfast.

Ha Vy Hotel (Map p356; ☎ 836 9123; havy@saigonnet .vn; 16-18 Đ Do Quang Dau; r US$7-12; 🔀) This family-run minihotel consistently gets good reviews from readers. Rooms here are comfortable and clean, and breakfast is included in the rates.

Chau Long Minihotel (Map p356; ☎ 836 9667; chaulongminihotel@yahoo.com; 185/8 Đ Pham Ngu Lao; r US$6-10; 🔀) A good place in Minihotel Alley, Chau Long offers rooms with hot water at a reasonable price.

Lan Anh Hotel (Map p356; ☎ 836 5197; lan-anh -hotel@hcm.vnn.vn; 252 Đ De Tham; r US$8-15; 🔀) Offering a lift, free breakfast and comfortable rooms, the Lan Anh is a good central choice.

Quyen Thanh Hotel (Map p356; ☎ 836 8570; quyenthanhhotel@hcm.vnn.vn; 212 Đ De Tham; r US$10-14; 🔀) Goofy green granite tubs, a round terrace and plants adorn this older place situated on a noisy corner. There is an excellent souvenir shop on the ground floor, where you'll find locally made lacquerware, snake wine and various other trinkets.

Tan Thanh Thanh Hotel (Map p356; ☎ 837 3595; tanthanhthanh@hcm.fpt.vn; 205 Đ Pham Ngu Lao; dm US$3, r US$5-10; ☒) The first in the neighbourhood to offer dormitory accommodation, this place also offers guests a complimentary breakfast. You can teach language lessons to pay your keep; for more details, ask for Mr Dong.

Other cheap places nearby:

Hotel 265 (Map p356; ☎ 836 7512; hotelduy@hotmail .com; 265 Đ De Tham; dm US$3, r US$7-12; ☒)

Vinh Guesthouse (Map p356; ☎ 836 8585; lelehotel@ hcm.fpt.vn; 269 Đ De Tham; s/d/t US$10/12/15; ☒)

Peace Hotel (Map p356; ☎ 837 2025; hasanvnn@hcm .vnn.vn; 272 Đ De Tham; r US$6-10; ☒)

Giang Son Guesthouse (Map p356; ☎ 837 7547; giangson_guesthouse@hotmail.com; 283/14 Đ Pham Ngu Lao; r US$8-12; ☒) Tucked into an alley off the noisy main street.

Mai Phai Hotel (Map p356; ☎ 836 5868; maiphai hotel@saigonnet.vn; 209 Đ Pham Ngu Lao; r US$10-15) Good reports from travellers; rates include breakfast.

Coco Loco Guesthouse (Map p356; ☎ 837 2647; 373/2 Pham Ngu Lao; r US$10; ☒) An older place down a tiny alley near Thai Binh Market.

CO GIANG AREA

An alternative to Pham Ngu Lao and about 10 minutes' walk south of there, is a string of fine guesthouses in the quiet alley connecting

---

LIFE ON THE STREETS   *Juliet Coombe*

Through the smoke and pollution, groups of battered old men lean against their *cyclos* – three-wheeled rickshaws, operated by pedal-power, with a seat attached to the front.

Before the American War many *cyclo* drivers were doctors, teachers or journalists, but like many of their friends they were punished for siding with the Americans. After the cease-fire, tens of thousands of them were stripped of their citizenship and sent to re-education camps for seven years or more. More than 20 years later, it is still impossible for them to return to the jobs they are qualified to do and, as most do not have an official residence permit (which means they cannot own property or a business), it's technically illegal for them to be in the city. Many of these men have never had families because they could not afford – or were not permitted by the government – a home to live in.

Around the restaurants, hotels, nightclubs and karaoke bars of central HCMC, it's hard to miss them in their worn clothes and sandals tar-stained from years of being caught in the jagged chains of the *cyclos*. The comings and goings at hotels are a constant form of entertainment – and business – for HCMC's *cyclo* drivers. Nothing misses their sharp eyes. Their courteous propositions hide their desire to establish your first name and claim you as 'their property' while you're in town. Once known, cries of your name across crowded streets will hound you as the determined drivers compete for your business.

Cyclo drivers are excellent city guides – they know every corner of the city and can give you a potted history of the key sites. Also, the front seat of a *cyclo* really is one of the best ways to see HCMC – but it does take some getting used to. In heavy traffic it's like riding a roller coaster at a fairground; the traffic races towards you from every direction at startling speeds and, just when you think you are surely going to die, your *cyclo* driver slips into a gap that magically appears in the traffic while you thank the gods that you're still in one piece.

Tourists love to reverse roles and have a go in the saddle, mistakenly thinking that it's easy to spend one's day cycling from place to place, but their opinions quickly change. In most cases they find the *cyclos* too hard to pedal and, if they advance at all, they don't get very far on the uneven, potholed roads.

The drivers' homes are usually a street corner, which are made colourful and interesting by using wooden tables and small, multicoloured, plastic footstools, which support them only inches off the ground. Their floor is broken-up bits of pavement slabs and their 'drinks cabinet' (a street stall or two) nestles just behind them.

After a day's sightseeing, they might invite you to join them for either a whisky in a Coke bottle or the local beer Ba Ba Ba (333) – pronounce it 'baa-baa-baa' slowly because in Vietnamese it can also sound like you are saying 'three old women'! An evening with these guys is always worthwhile.

THE AUTHOR'S CHOICE

Miss Loi's Guesthouse (Map p326; ☎ 837 9589; missloi@hcm.fpt.vn; 178/20 Đ Co Giang; r US$6-20; 🔁) This was the first guesthouse to appear in the neighbourhood and it's probably still the best. Miss Loi and her especially amiable, helpful staff create a warm, low-key familial environment. The free breakfast is served in the pleasant open-air lobby, where fat, happy fish populate the fish pond and a pool table awaits.

Đ Co Giang and Đ Co Bac (Map p326). To reach the guesthouses, walk southwest on Đ Co Bac and turn left after you pass the *nuoc mam* (fish sauce) shops.

Guest House California (Map p326; ☎ 837 8885; guesthousecalifornia-saigon@yahoo.com; 171A Đ Co Bac; r 190,000-250,000d; 🔁) Small and intimate, this homey new guesthouse has a relaxed TV area downstairs and a shared kitchen where you can cook your own meals! It's run by a friendly, relaxed couple who also rent out bikes and motorbikes.

Ngoc Son (Map p326; ☎ 836 4717; ngocsonguest house@yahoo.com; 178/32 Đ Co Giang; r US$6-9; 🔁) A quiet, eight-room guesthouse, Ngoc Son is a family-style place offering rooms with cable TV and fridge. The friendly and helpful family rent motorbikes and will serve you breakfast for US$1 extra.

Mid-Range
PHAM NGU LAO
Canadian Hotel 281 (Map p356; ☎ 837 8666; www .281canadianhotel.com; 281 Đ Pham Ngu Lao; r US$13-28; 🔁 💻) The lobby resembles an airline booking office, with cool, crisp (Canadian?) design. Some rooms have balconies; for US$20 and upwards they have in-room computers with fast ADSL connections. There's a lift and breakfast is included.

Bi/Bee Saigon (Map p356; ☎ 836 0678; www.bi saigon.com; 185/26 & 185/16 Đ Pham Ngu Lao; r US$10-30; 🔁) With two locations in Minihotel Alley, this pair of hotels has comfortable rooms with all the amenities and a good restaurant to boot.

Southern Hotel (Map p356; ☎ 837 0922; www.vn gold.com/hcm/southern; 216 Đ De Tham; r US$12-20; 🔁) At this friendly place the 'special room'

(US$30) has its own private garden terrace; other rooms have nice views of neighbouring rooftops.

Giant Dragon Hotel (Map p356; ☎ 836 1935; gd -hotel@hcm.vnn.vn; 173 Đ Pham Ngu Lao; r/ste US$20/25; 🔁) Fairly fancy, the immaculate rooms at this lift-equipped place have satellite TV, IDD phones, tubs and hair dryers. Super-deluxe rooms have sitting areas and views of town; all room rates include breakfast.

Duna Hotel (Map p356; ☎ 837 3699; dunahotel vn@hcm.vnn.vn; 167 Đ Pham Ngu Lao; r US$13-25; 🔁) Perks at this spotless minihotel include a talking lift, free breakfast and the privilege of paying with a credit card.

Spring House Hotel (Map p356; ☎ 837 8312, 836 8859; hanhhoahotel@hcm.vnn.vn; 221 Đ Pham Ngu Lao; r US$15-20; 🔁) A good-looking place with a lift, the Spring House has pretty bamboo detailing in the lobby. The singles are tiny but cosy.

An An Hotel (Map p356; ☎ 837 8087; www.ananhotel .com; 40 Đ Bui Vien; r US$25-35; 🔁 💻) The usual luxuries such as TV and minibar equip the clean rooms at this slick, newish place. It also offers tours and transportation services.

Le Le Hotel (Map p356; ☎ 836 8686; lelehotel@hcm .fpt.vn; 171 Đ Pham Ngu Lao; r US$12-30) The Le Le boasts a lift and satellite TV; breakfast is included as well. Pricier rooms have unusual sunroom-type sitting areas.

It's worth checking out the trio of superb family-run hotels run by warm-hearted Madam Cuc, a local personality who knows how to make her guests feel safe and at home. All three places feature spotless rooms that are well-appointed and the staff provide a most welcoming reception. There's free tea, coffee and fruit all day; breakfast and a simple dinner are included in the room rates. Virtually identical in size and style, they all share the same email address. They can be found at the following locations:
Hotel 127 (Map p356; ☎ 836 8761; madamcuc@hcm .vnn.vn; 127 Đ Cong Quynh; r US$12-20; 🔁)
Hotel MC 184 (Map p356; ☎ 836 1679; 184 Đ Cong Quynh; 🔁)
Hotel 64 (Map p356; ☎ 836 5073; 64 Đ Bui Vien; 🔁)

More mid-range choices:
Hotel Que Huong (Liberty 3 Hotel; Map p356; ☎ 836 9522; www.quehuonghotel.com; 187 Đ Pham Ngu Lao; r US$25-65; 🔁) Polished wooden furniture, vaguely Art Deco mirrors, and breakfast included; Allez Boo Bar (p358) downstairs.

GAY & LESBIAN HO CHI MINH CITY

Though outright 'out' venues aren't, Saigon's popular bars and clubs are generally gay-friendly and have their own sub-scenes going. Check out **Ben Thanh** (Orient Club; Map p326; 6 Ð Mac Dinh Chi; cover 45,000d) on Monday night if you're into dancing. **Kim Café** (p355) has a queer-friendly vibe.

Saturday and Sunday nights are a great time to check out Ð Dong Khoi on foot or bicycle when all are out and about. Try catching someone's eye and see if you can suss out good hang-outs.

Metropole Hotel (Map p326; ☎ 832 2021; fax 832 2019; 148 ÐL Tran Hung Dao; r US$35-70; ✹ ▣) A fancy Saigon Tourist place with swimming pool.

Hanh Hoa Hotel (Map p356; ☎ 836 0245; hanhhoa hotel@hcm.vnn.vn; 237 Ð Pham Ngu Lao; r US$12-25; ✹) The older sister hotel of the Spring House.

Vien Dong Hotel (Far East Hotel; Map p356; ☎ 836 8941; viendonghotel@hcm.fpt.vn; 275A Ð Pham Ngu Lao; r US$25-60; ✹) A large state-run place with rooftop restaurant and nightclub.

DONG KHOI AREA

If you want to base yourself in the city centre, you'll find a good number of well-appointed hotels along Ð Dong Khoi or near the Saigon River. All of them offer amenities such as air-con and satellite TV.

Spring Hotel (Map pp334-5; ☎ 829 7362; spring hotel@hcm.vnn.vn; 44-46 Ð Le Thanh Ton; d US$32-75; ✹) This tidy place has a subtle Japanese feel to it. Breakfast is complimentary; credit cards are accepted with a 3% fee. All rooms are carpeted and have a small step up from the doorway.

Thang Long Hotel (Map pp334-5; ☎ 822 2595; thanglonghotel@hcm.fpt.vn; 48 Ð Mac Thi Buoi; r US$16-25, ste US$35-40; ✹) A minihotel with a distinctively Chinese look to it, Thang Long abounds with dragons and red décor. Standard rooms are closets, but deluxe ones have good views. Breakfast and mellow atmosphere are included.

Bong Sen Annexe (Map pp334-5; ☎ 823 5818; bongsen2@hcm.vnn.vn; 61-63 ÐL Hai Ba Trung; r & ste US$27-70; ✹) The BS, as it's affectionately known by business travellers, is an attractive choice, with friendly management and staff. All rooms are carpeted and breakfast is included in the rates.

Asian Hotel (Map pp334-5; ☎ 829 6979; asian hotel@hcn.fpt.vn; 150 Ð Dong Khoi; r US$35-55; ✹) Right in the centre of town, this contemporary hotel is notable for its in-house restaurant. Top floor rooms are the best, with big terraces looking northward; all are carpeted.

And a few others in the area:

Huong Sen Hotel (Map pp334-5; ☎ 829 1415; www.vietnamtourism.com/huongsen; 66-70 Ð Dong Khoi; r US$25-95; ✹) Centrally located; call ahead for promotional rates; breakfast included. Doctor on call 24 hours a day.

Kim Long Hotel (Golden Dragon Hotel; Map pp334-5; ☎ 822 8558; annamtour@hcm.fpt.vn; 58 Ð Mac Thi Buoi; s/d US$20/25) The smaller, dumpier, cheerier sister of Thang Long; front rooms have large balconies.

Dong Do Hotel (Map pp334-5; ☎ 827 3637; dongdohotel@hcm.vnn.vn; 35 Ð Mac Thi Buoi; r US$20-40; ✹) Breakfast included, ornate dark décor, smallish rooms, quiet.

Bach Dang Hotel (Map pp334-5; ☎ 825 1501; fax 823 0587; 33 Ð Mac Thi Buoi; r US$39-45) Bright and airy, some rooms with views of Saigon River.

DISTRICT 3

Chancery Saigon Hotel (Map p326; ☎ 930 4088; www .chancerysaigonhotel.com; 196 Ð Nguyen Thi Minh Khai; r US$52-87; ✹ ▣) This modern, luxurious all-suite hotel is brought to you by the US Best Western chain; there's a gym and sauna, as well as a pub and restaurant.

Saigon Star Hotel (Map p326; ☎ 930 6290; saigon starhotel@hcm.vnn.vn; 204 Ð Nguyen Thi Minh Khai; r US$52-98; ✹ ▣) Next door to the Chancery, Saigon Star is also nice and features satellite TV, two restaurants and a coffee shop, a karaoke club and a business centre. Rates include breakfast.

International Hotel (Map p326; ☎ 930 4009; inter national-ht@hcm.vnn.vn; 19 Ð Vo Van Tan; r US$35-58) Maintaining plush standards for the price, the International has rooms fitted with all the usual amenities (satellite TV, minibar, IDD phones and safety-deposit boxes).

CHOLON

Bat Dat Hotel (Map p340; ☎ 855 1662; batdat@hcm .vnn.vn; 238-244 ÐL Tran Hung Dao; r US$35-85; ✹) A good choice in Cholon. Amenities here are of the usual standard, and include 24-hour room service and complimentary breakfast. All rooms have bathtubs.

Arc En Ciel Hotel (Thien Hong Hotel; ☎ 855 2550; thienhong@hcm.vnn.vn; 52-56 Ð Tan Da; r US$25-45; ✹)

The Rainbow is a popular venue for tour groups from Hong Kong and Taiwan, with its Rainbow Disco Karaoke. On the corner of ĐL Tran Hung Dao, it's the sister hotel of Bat Dat. Breakfast is included in the rates, and all rooms are carpeted. The priciest ones come with pretty Chinese carved furniture.

Top End
Nearly all of HCMC's top hotels are concentrated in District 1 and most of them are in the Dong Khoi area. Don't be scared off by the published rates; hefty discounts can often be negotiated. Call or email ahead to ask for the current 'promotional' rates.

Continental Hotel (Map pp334–5; ☎ 829 9252; www.continentalvietnam.com; 132-134 Đ Dong Khoi; r US$60-130; 🌊) One of the city's most historic lodgings, the Continental was the setting for much of the action that occurred in Graham Greene's novel *The Quiet American*. The hotel dates from the turn of the 19th century and received its last renovation in 1989 (unfortunately, at the hands of its aesthetically challenged owner, Saigon Tourist). Panelled wood ceilings with carved detailing accent the carpeted, cavernous rooms.

Rex Hotel (Map pp334–5; ☎ 829 2185; www.rexhotelvietnam.com; 141 ĐL Nguyen Hue; tw & ste US$70-270; 🌊🏊) The giant Rex is another classic central hotel. Its ambience of mellowed kitsch dates from the time it put up US army officers. Amenities include a large gift shop, a tailor, a beauty parlour, massage, acupuncture and a small swimming pool on the 6th floor. There are great views from the rooftop veranda bar, which is decorated with caged birds, plaster elephants and potted animal-shaped topiaries.

Caravelle Hotel (Map pp334–5; ☎ 823 4999; www.caravellehotel.com; 19 Lam Son Sq; r US$219-1127; 🌊🖥🏊) An enormous posh place sitting pretty on the spot once occupied by the Catholic Diocese of Saigon, the centrally located Caravelle is hands-down one of the most luxurious hotels in HCMC. The rooftop Saigon Saigon Bar (p358) is a spectacular place to have a cocktail in the early evening. Phone or fax ahead (don't email) for promotional rates.

Grand Hotel (Map pp334–5; ☎ 823 0163; grand-hotel@fmail.vnn.vn; 8-24 Đ Dong Khoi; r & ste US$85-490;

🌊🖥🏊) Aptly named, the Grand's renovated landmark building is notable for its old-fashioned lift and spacious suites with 4.5m-high ceilings and French windows. Don't bother with modern rooms in the new wing; old-wing rooms are appealing and historic, with parquet wood floors and granite bathrooms. There's also an indoor pool and a gym.

Renaissance Riverside Hotel (Map pp334–5; ☎ 822 0033; rsvn.rrhs@hcm.vnn.vn; 8-15 Đ Ton Duc Thang; r US$104-178d, ste US$334; 🌊🖥🏊) Not to be confused with the Riverside Hotel nearby, this glitzy riverside skyscraper offers a luxurious atmosphere and exceptionally friendly service. Stunning, spectacular, right-there river views are worth the extra cash.

Sofitel Plaza Saigon (Map p326; ☎ 824 1555; www.sofitel.com; 17 ĐL Le Duan; US$150-1500; 🌊🖥🏊) Sleek and sophisticated, the Sofitel is a favourite among business travellers. There are two fine in-house restaurants, and L'Elysée Bar features live jazz and a delightful terrace. Nonguests can use the rooftop swimming pool for US$12.

TAN BINH DISTRICT
This pair of luxury hotels is near the airport and popular with business travellers.

Omni Hotel (Map pp322–3; ☎ 844 9222; www.omnisaigonhotel.com; 253 Đ Nguyen Van Troi; r US$138-575; 🌊🖥🏊) Providing the poshest accommodation in the area, this hotel has everything from a florist and the newly opened Qi Spa (p344), to a gym (available to nonguests for US$15). With lovely accommodation and helpful staff, the Omni also boasts four restaurants serving European and Asian cuisine.

Novotel Garden Plaza (Map pp322-3; ☎ 842 1111; gpnovotel@saigonnet.vn; 309B-311 Đ Nguyen Van Troi; r US$127-288; ⊠ ▯ ☎) Clean design and contemporary Vietnamese art creates a classy atmosphere. Booking 'Orchid Club' rooms garners extra benefits like free airport transfers, breakfast, 24-hour Internet access and entrée to quiet lounge space for working. Traditional music is played in the lobby from 7pm to 9pm nightly.

EATING

Both Vietnamese and Western food are widely available in HCMC and English menus are common. Cholon's speciality is Chinese food. And if you are feeling spring-rolled out, don't fret – there is plenty of superb international food around.

In general, and as a guide to fitting your sightseeing around meals (or vice versa), local restaurants are open from 6am to 9pm; gourmet and international restaurants from 11am to 2pm and 6pm to 11pm; street stalls keep all hours; and markets are open from 6.30am to 5.30pm.

Vietnamese

Quan An Ngon (Map pp334-5; ☎ 829 9449; 138 Đ Nam Ky Khoi Nghia; mains 10,000-60,000d) Two people can sample a feast of traditional, regional Vietnamese food for US$5 to US$6 each. Poke around the outside edge first, where cooks at individual stations make their specialities, and let the lovely fragrances whet your appetite.

Tib Restaurant (Map p326; ☎ 829 7242; 187 ĐL Hai Ba Trung, District 3; mains 45,000-55,000d) Housed in a Sino-French villa down a quiet alleyway, Tib does good Hué-style dishes and a mean jackfruit salad with grilled sesame. It offers a tasty variety of vegetarian specialities as well.

Tan Nam Restaurant (Map pp334-5; ☎ 829 8634; 60-62 Đ Dong Du; mains 30,000d) With appealing traditional décor and fine food, Tan Nam has good atmosphere and service.

Nam Giao (Map pp334-5; ☎ 825 0261; 136/15 Đ Le Thanh Ton; mains 6000-10,000d) Tucked away in an alley of cosmetic shops near Ben Thanh Market, Nam Giao is delicious and always packed

with locals. The food here is Hué-style and superb. There's a simple photo menu.

Bo Tung Xeo (Map pp334-5; ☎ 825 1330; 31 Đ Ly Tu Trong) This popular indoor-outdoor eatery in the city centre serves tasty Vietnamese barbecue. The house speciality is tender marinated beef (30,000d) that you grill over charcoal right at your table. It's served with salad. There are also good seafood dishes on the menu and the cheerful staff speak English.

More good Vietnamese food:

Nam An (Map pp334-5; ☎ 822 0246; 22-36 Đ Nguyen Hue; mains 30,000d) Modelled on a Buddhist temple, with indoor-outdoor seating.

Restaurant 19 (Map pp334-5; ☎ 829 8882; 19 Đ Ngo Duc Ke; mains around 25,000d) Try the very tasty variation on Hanoi's fish cakes (cha ca) and decent Thai dishes.

Restaurant 13 (Map pp334-5; ☎ 823 9314; 13 Đ Ngo Duc Ke) Highly popular with locals and expats alike.

Cool (Map pp334-5; Kinh Bac; ☎ 829 1364; 30 Đ Dong Khoi)

PHAM NGU LAO

Lac Thien (Map p356; ☎ 837 1621; 28/25 Đ Bui Vien; mains 10,000-20,000d) Cloned straight from the trio of travellers restaurants run by deaf people in Hué (p208), Lac Thien serves excellent food. Its Hué-style dishes are recommended.

Pho Bo (Map p356; 96 Đ Bui Vien) A classic hole-in-the-wall that whips up tasty bowls of beef noodle soup (5000d).

Gourmet Vietnamese

Compared to what you would pay for fine Vietnamese food abroad, HCMC's better Vietnamese restaurants are a bargain. It's possible to eat like royalty in a fancy up-market restaurant for around US$10 for lunch – or US$25 for dinner – per person. Aspiring interior designers will enjoy checking out the ethnic décor at many of the better places.

Lemon Grass (Map pp334-5; ☎ 822 0496; 4 Đ Nguyen Thiep) One of the best Vietnamese restaurants in the city centre. You would be hard-pressed to find anything bad on the menu, so if you can't decide what to order just pick something at random. Two women in traditional costume play musical instruments while you eat.

Mandarine (Map pp334-5; ☎ 822 9783; 11A Đ Ngo Van Nam) The fine selection of traditional dishes on offer draws from southern, central and northern cooking styles. The food is superb, and the pleasant décor and traditional music performances make it an all-round good bet. A house speciality worth trying is the Hanoi-style *cha ca*.

Hoi An (Map pp334-5; ☎ 823 7694; hoian@hcm.fpt.vn; 11 Đ Le Thanh Ton) Just down the street from Mandarine – and run by the same people – is this lovely, Chinese-style place decorated in a classical, antique motif. Hoi An specialises in central Vietnamese and imperial Hué-style dishes, and has the heaviest wooden chairs in Vietnam!

Indochine (Map p326; ☎ 823 9256; indochine-sg@hcm.fpt.vn; 32 Đ Pham Ngoc Thach, District 3; set menu US$8-20) Nestled in a French-style villa, with waitstaff dressed in traditional garb, Indochine's atmosphere is serene and elegant. Try the grilled prawn cakes, or the banana-flower salad (*goi bap chuoi*); there's an excellent wine list as well. Traditional music is performed from 7.30pm to 9.30pm Monday, Wednesday and Friday evening.

Other Asian
CENTRAL AREA

Indian and Japanese are the dominant cuisines in the Dong Khoi area.

Chao Thai (Map pp334-5; ☎ 824 1457; 16 Đ Thai Van Lung; set lunch 80,000d) One of Vietnam's best Thai restaurants, Chao Thai offers good-value lunch sets. Recommended dishes include the prawn cakes, Chiang Mai sausages and winged-bean salad.

Sushi Bar (Map pp334-5; ☎ 823 8042; shige@hcm.vnn.vn; 2 Đ Le Thanh Ton; sushi 45,000d) Bristling with life, this sushi bar is full of Japanese people (a good sign) and has a great view of a busy intersection. The restaurant delivers around HCMC until 10pm.

Urvashi (Map pp334-5; ☎ 821 3102; 27 Đ Hai Trieu; set lunch US$3-4) Serving some of the best Indian food in District 1, Urvashi prepares a variety of Indian cooking styles and the *thali* lunch is a guaranteed filler.

Tandoor (Map p326; ☎ 930 4839; 103 Đ Vo Van Tan, District 3; set lunch 52,000d) Tandoor offers excellent North Indian food and also delivers.

For really cheap Indian food, seek out the atmospheric, cult-like **Indian canteen** (Map pp334-5; ☎ 823 2159; 66 Đ Dong Du; dishes 7000d), behind the Saigon Central Mosque. The fish curry (21,000d) is lovely. Meals come with free iced tea and bananas.

Other Dong Khoi area options:
Hakata (Map pp334-5; ☎ 827 5177; 26 Đ Thi Sach; meals 90,000d) Some of the best Japanese fare in town.
Akatonbo (Map pp334-5; ☎ 824 4928; 36-38 ĐL Hai Ba Trung; mains 60,000d) Excellent Japanese food and a picture menu.

Ashoka (Map pp334-5; ☎ 823 1372; 17A/10 Đ Le Thanh Ton; mains 25,000d) Moderately priced Indian place, with a lunch buffet and halal food.

Encore Angkor Plus (☎ 829 8814; 28 Đ Ngo Van Nam; mains 35,000d) Excellent Khmer food makes its encore in a new setting.

CHOLON

District 5 is the place to eat Chinese food.

My Huong (Map p340; ☎ 856 3586; 131 Đ Nguyen Tri Phuong) This is a highly popular indoor-outdoor restaurant serving up all kinds of good food, including superb noodle soup with duck.

Tiem An Nam Long (Map p340; ☎ 969 4659; 47 Đ Pham Dinh Ho; mains US$2) Near the Binh Tay Market, this place is noteworthy for tasty wok-fried dishes and open-air seating. There's an English menu with no prices, but everything is cheap.

Most meals at these restaurants will cost you US$2 or less.

Tiem Com Chay Phat Huu Duyen (Map p340; ☎ 857 7919; 527 Đ Nguyen Trai; mains 18,000d) A tiny but very popular Chinese vegetarian restaurant.

Hong Phat (Map p340; ☎ 856 7172; 206 Đ Hai Thuong Lan Ong) Serves delicious noodle soup with pork.

Com Ga Dong Nguyen (Map p340; ☎ 855 7662; 87-91 Đ Chau Van Liem) Specialises in tasty roast chicken with rice (com ga).

French

HCMC has an astounding selection of great French restaurants, from the casual bistro to the exquisite top-notch restaurant.

Augustin (Map pp334-5; ☎ 829 2941; 10 Đ Nguyen Thiep; mains 50,000d) Many consider Augustin the city's best cheap French restaurant. It serves great bistro-style food.

Bi Bi (Map pp334-5; ☎ 829 5783; 8A/8D2 Đ Thai Van Lung; mains 100,000d) The bright Mediterranean décor at Bi Bi creates a pleasant atmosphere for enjoying casual French bistro fare.

La Fourchette (Map pp334-5; ☎ 829 8143; 9 Đ Ngo Duc Ke; mains US$7) An excellent choice, right in the city centre, La Fourchette serves authentic French food.

Le Jardin (Map pp334-5; ☎ 825 8465; 31 Đ Thai Van Lung; mains 35,000-55,000d) The charming little bistro attached to Idecaf (p325) has a shaded terrace café in the front garden – it's a popular hang-out for local French expats.

L'Etoile (Map p326; ☎ 829 7939; 180 ĐL Hai Ba Trung; set meals 15,000d) L'Etoile serves terrific French food and its all-day 'fast food' menu is good

value. A set meal could be roast chicken with a choice of five sauces, a mini-salad and baguette.

Camargue (Map pp334-5; ☎ 824 3148; 16 Đ Cao Ba Quat; mains US$15) Housed in a beautiful restored villa with an open-air terrace, Camargue is also home to trendy Vasco's bar (p358). The menu includes a variety of gourmet dishes complemented by a well-appointed wine list.

Le Caprice (Map pp334-5; ☎ 822 8337; 5B Đ Ton Duc Thang; set dinner US$40) For those who prefer a fancy French restaurant, this is a high-class place on the top floor of the Landmark building. The river views are stunning.

Au Manoir de Khai (Map p326; ☎ 930 3394; au manoir@hcm.vnn.vn; 251 Đ Dien Bien Phu; set lunch/dinner US$20-50) This five-star Continental restaurant was opened, ironically, by the Vietnamese fashion guru Khai (the brains behind Khai Silk and a string of other superb restaurants and hotels in Vietnam). At least the chef is French. This lavish villa sits in a high-walled enclosure in District 3.

Other European
CENTRAL AREA

Cafe Latin (Map pp334-5; ☎ 822 6363; 19-21 Đ Dong Du; mains 60,000-150,000d) Vietnam's first tapas bar, Cafe Latin carries a superb wine collection and bakes fresh bread daily. On the menu are such offerings as smoked salmon sandwiches on ciabatta, or couscous with roasted vegies and yogurt dressing.

Cafe Havana (Map p326; ☎ 827 9682; www.café havana.biz; 25B Đ Tran Cao Van; mains 30,000d) With three storeys, a wood-fired pizza oven and rooftop terrace, this new café is popular with both locals and expats. Cocktails include Cuban classics like *mojitos*.

Santa Lucia (Map pp334-5; ☎ 822 6562; 14 ĐL Nguyen Hue; mains 60,000d) Santa Lucia dishes up some of the best authentic Italian food in town.

Gartenstadt (Map pp334-5; ☎ 822 3623; 34 Đ Dong Khoi) This cosy little place makes its own bread and German sausages.

Mogambo (Map pp334-5; ☎ 825 1311; 20B Đ Thi Sach; mains 30,000d) Noted for its Polynesian décor and juicy burgers, Mogambo is a restaurant, pub and hotel.

Skewers (Map pp334-5; ☎ 829 2216; 8A/1/D2 Đ Thai Van Lung; mains 35,000d) Skewers specialises in Mediterranean cuisine from Greece to Algeria, notably barbecued skewered meat.

There's a nice atmosphere and an open kitchen so you can watch the cooks at work.

DEsignED Café (Map p326; ☎ 930 2600; 180A Đ Nam Ky Khoi Nghia; mains 45,000-90,000đ) Lunching here on gourmet European and Vietnamese dishes is like dining in a museum café. In fact, upstairs it's an interior design gallery; if you're into Pop Art and sleek Lucite furniture, this is the place for you.

ABC Restaurant (Map p326; ☎ 823 0388; 172H Đ Nguyen Dinh Chieu, District 3; mains 25,000-50,000đ; 🕒 till 3am) A trendy joint for tasty late-night chow, ABC has indoor and outdoor seating and an extensive menu – from noodle soup and fresh seafood to juicy steaks.

Brodard Café (Map pp334-5; ☎ 822 3966; 131 Đ Dong Khoi; mains 25,000-100,000đ) This Parisian-style oldie but goodie is known for good café food at OK prices.

Other central spots:

Annie's Pizza (Map pp334-5; ☎ 823 9044; 45 Đ Mac Thi Buoi; pizzas 40,000-70,000đ) Continuing a yummy pizza tradition, Annie's offers free delivery.

Givral (Map pp334-5; ☎ 824 2750; 169 Đ Dong Khoi) A great, central place to take in views of the Municipal Theatre over pastry (10,000đ) and coffee.

Why Not? (Map pp334-5; ☎ 822 6138; 24 Đ Thai Van Lung; mains around 30,000đ; 🕒 closed Sun) Worth checking out for good European food or a game of darts.

PHAM NGU LAO

Western backpackers tend to easily outnumber the Vietnamese on Đ Pham Ngu Lao and Đ De Tham, which is the axis of HCMC's budget-eatery haven; indeed, the locals have trouble figuring out the menus (banana muesli does not translate well into Vietnamese).

Asian Kitchen (Map p356; ☎ 836 7397; 185/22 Đ Pham Ngu Lao; mains 18,000đ) Tasty budget Indian, Japanese and vegetarian food; eat in the bamboo-walled restaurant or the mosaic patio in front.

Good Morning Vietnam (Map p356; ☎ 837 1894; 197 Đ De Tham; pasta & pizza 30,000-80,000đ) The HCMC branch of this Italian chain serves authentic northern Italian dishes – pasta is served with freshly grated parmesan cheese.

Kim Cafe (☎ 836 8122; cafékim@hcm.vnn.vn; 268 Đ De Tham; mains 20,000đ) A long-running hangout for budget travellers, Kim Cafe is a good place to eat and meet people.

Sinh Cafe (Map p356; ☎ 836 7338; sinhcafévietnam@ hcm.vnn.vn; 246-248 Đ De Tham; mains 20,000đ) Near Kim Cafe, Sinh has a nearly identical setup.

Saigon Cafe (Map p356; 195 Đ Pham Ngu Lao; mains 15,000đ) Saigon Cafe serves cheap breakfasts and has shady tables on the busy corner of Đ De Tham.

Linh Cafe (Map p356; 291 Đ Pham Ngu Lao; mains 20,000đ) Another travellers café run by friendly people. You can also book tours here.

Seafood

Miss Saigon (Map pp334-5; ☎ 823 8174; 86 Đ Le Thanh Ton; mains 35,000-50,000đ) Here you can dine on respectable seafood and Vietnamese dishes in air-con comfort or outside, surrounded by views of past and present – on one side an army tank and on the other a row of tennis courts where HCMC's nouveaux riches swat and sweat.

Vegetarian

The largest concentration of vegetarian restaurants is in and around the Pham Ngu Lao area.

Original Bodhi Tree (Map p356; ☎ 837 1910; bodhitree@hcm.vnn.vn; 175/4 Đ Pham Ngu Lao; mains 12,000đ) In the narrow alley two streets east of Đ De Tham, the vegetarian food at the Original (you'll notice there's a copycat next door) is excellent. It also has rotating art exhibits, sales of which benefit disadvantaged and street children.

Tin Nghia (Map p326; ☎ 821 2538; 9 ĐL Tran Hung Dao; 🕒 7am-8.30pm; mains 8000đ) The owners are strict Buddhists who turn out delicious traditional Vietnamese food, prepared with tofu, mushrooms and other vegetables.

Dinh Y (Map p356; ☎ 836 7715; 171B Đ Cong Quynh; mains 7000đ) Across the road from Thai Binh Market, Dinh Y is run by a friendly Cao Dai family. It serves inexpensive and delicious vegie fare, and has an English menu. The noodle soups are savoury and satisfying.

Zen (Map p356; ☎ 837 3713; 185/30 Đ Pham Ngu Lao; mains 12,000đ) Cheap vegie food in a mellow, family atmosphere in Minihotel Alley.

On the first and 15th days of the lunar month food stalls around the city, especially in the markets, serve vegetarian versions of meaty Vietnamese dishes. While these stalls are quick to serve, they're usually swamped on these special days. Have a little patience; dinner's worth the wait.

Cafés, Coffee Shops & Ice Cream

All of the following establishments are in the Dong Khoi area.

PHAM NGU LAO AREA

HO CHI MINH CITY

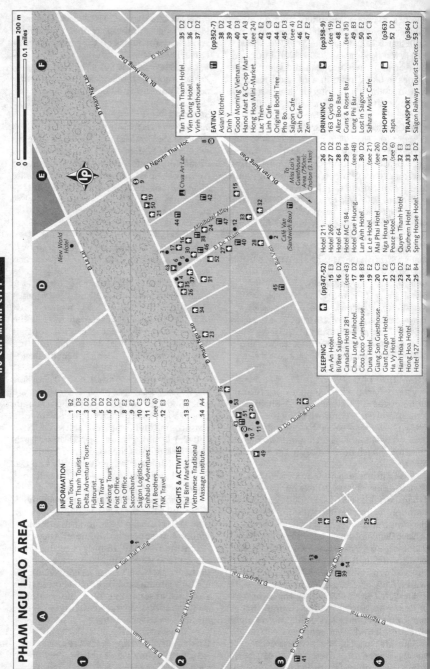

INFORMATION
Ann Tours	1 B2
Ben Thanh Tourist	2 D3
Delta Adventure Tours	3 D2
Fiditourist	4 D2
Kim Travel	5 D2
Mekong Tours	6 D2
Post Office	7 C3
Post Office	8 E2
Sacombank	9 E2
Saigon Logistics	10 C3
Sinhbalo Adventures	11 C3
TM Brothers	(see 6)
TNK Travel	12 E3

SIGHTS & ACTIVITIES
Thai Binh Market	13 B3
Vietnamese Traditional Massage Institute	14 A4

SLEEPING (pp347-52)
An An Hotel	15 E3
Bi/Bee Saigon	16 D2
Canadian Hotel 281	(see 3)
Chau Long Minihotel	17 D2
Coco Loco Guesthouse	18 B3
Duna Hotel	19 E2
Giang Son Guesthouse	20 C3
Giant Dragon Hotel	21 E2
Ha Vy Hotel	22 C3
Hanh Hoa Hotel	23 C3
Hong Hoa Hotel	24 E2
Hotel 127	25 B4
Hotel 211	26 D2
Hotel 265	27 D2
Hotel 64	28 D3
Hotel MC 184	29 B4
Hotel Que Huong	(see 48)
Lan Anh Hotel	30 D2
Le Le Hotel	(see 21)
Mai Phai Hotel	(see 26)
Nga Hoang	31 D2
Peace Hotel	(see 6)
Quyen Thanh Hotel	32 E3
Southern Hotel	33 E3
Spring House Hotel	34 D2
Tan Thanh Thanh Hotel	35 D2
Vien Dong Hotel	36 C2
Vinh Guesthouse	37 D2

EATING (pp352-7)
Asian Kitchen	38 D2
Dinh Y	39 A4
Good Morning Vietnam	40 D3
Hanoi Mart & Co-op Mart	41 A3
Hong Hoa Mini-Market	(see 24)
Lac Thien	42 E2
Linh Cafe	43 C3
Original Bodhi Tree	44 E2
Pho Bo	45 D3
Saigon Cafe	(see 4)
Sinh Cafe	46 D2
Zen	47 E2

DRINKING (pp358-9)
163 Cyclo Bar	(see 19)
Allez Boo Bar	48 D2
Guns & Roses Bar	(see 35)
Long Phi Bar	49 B3
Lost in Saigon	50 E2
Sahara Music Cafe	51 C3

SHOPPING (p363)
Sapa	52 D2

TRANSPORT (p364)
Saigon Railways Tourist Services	53 C3

To Miss Loi's Guesthouse Area (750m); Cholon (3.1km)

Café Van (Sandwich Box)

New World Hotel

Java Coffee Bar (Map pp334-5; ☎ 823 0187; 38-42 Đ Dong Du; ◷ 7.30am-midnight) With espresso bar, excellent café fare and even smoothies (35,000d) made with silken tofu, Java is chic and relaxed – with the comfiest chairs ever.

Fanny (Map pp334-5; ☎ 821 1633; 29-31 Đ Ton That Thiep; ice-cream scoop 6000-15,000d) Established in an attractive French villa, Fanny creates excellent Franco-Vietnamese ice cream of many sublime tropical fruit flavours.

Kem Bach Dang (Map pp334-5; ☎ 829 2707; 26 & 28 Đl Le Loi; ice cream 15,000d) Come here for some of the best ice cream *(kem)* in Vietnam. The twin branches are located across Đ Pasteur from each other and have very reasonable prices. A speciality is ice cream served in a baby coconut with candied fruit on top *(kem trai dua)*.

Chi Lang Cafe (Map pp334-5; cnr Đ Dong Khoi & Đ Le Thanh Ton; coffee 6000d) This long-running coffee shop has a park-like setting and indoor-outdoor seating.

Paris Deli (Map pp334-5; ☎ 829 7533; 31 Đ Dong Khoi) Head here for freshly baked pastries (12,000d) and bread in a charming ambience. There's another **branch** (☎ 821 6127; 65 Đl Le Loi) at the Saigon Centre.

Dong Du Cafe (Map pp334-5; ☎ 823 2414; 31 Đ Dong Du; mains 45,000d) Stick with the desserts and coffee here but consider other restaurants for Italian eats.

Food Stalls

Noodle soup is available all day long at street stalls everywhere. A large bowl of delicious beef-noodle soup usually costs between 7000d and 15,000d. Just look for the signs that say 'pho'.

Pho 2000 (Map p326; ☎ 822 2788; 1-3 Đ Phan Chu Trinh; pho 14,000d; ◷ 6am-2am) Near the Ben Thanh Market, Pho 2000 is a good place to sample your first bowl of *pho* – it was good enough for former US president Bill Clinton to stop in and slurp down a bowl.

Pho Hoa (Map p326; ☎ 829 7943; 260C Đ Pasteur; soup 15,000d) This is another popular place with foreigners in District 3.

Markets always have a side selection of food items, often on the ground floor or in the basement. Clusters of food stalls can be found in Thai Binh, Ben Thanh and An Dong Markets.

Sandwiches with a French look and a very Vietnamese taste are sold by street vendors. Fresh baguettes are stuffed with something resembling pâté (don't ask) and cucumbers seasoned with soy sauce. A sandwich costs between 5000d and 15,000d, depending on what it's filled with. Sandwiches filled with imported French cheese cost a little more. À la carte baguettes usually cost between 500d and 2000d.

Self-Catering

Simple meals can easily be assembled from fruit, vegetables, French bread, croissants, cheese and other delectables sold in the city's markets and at street stalls. But avoid the unrefrigerated chocolate bars – they taste like they were left behind by the Americans in 1975.

If you don't feel like going anywhere, **Chez Guido** (☎ 898 3747, 840 4448; www.chezguido.com; mains 15,000-100,000d; ◷ 9am-11pm) delivers, fast (even wines and desserts)! The menu offers a mind-boggling cornucopia of international cuisine but specialises in Italian food. Download a menu or have one faxed to you.

There are lots of places in the city centre to shop for food and drinks, including supermarkets, shopping malls and small import shops. Two big supermarkets near Pham Ngu Lao are **Hanoi Mart** and **Co-op Mart** (Map opposite; Đ Cong Quynh), just down the street from each other.

Other places to try:

Hong Hoa Mini-Market (Map opposite; Hong Hoa Hotel, 185/28 Đ Pham Ngu Lao) Small but packed with toiletries, alcohol and Western junk food such as chocolate bars.

Veggy's (Map pp334-5; ☎ 823 8526; golden-garden@hcm.vnn.vn; 15 Đ Thai Van Lung) Carries a quality variety of imported foods, wine and sauces, as well as fresh produce and frozen meats.

DRINKING

Wartime Saigon was known for its riotous nightlife. Liberation in 1975 put a real dampener on evening activities, but the pubs and discos have staged a comeback. However, periodic 'crack-down, clean-up' campaigns – allegedly to control drugs, prostitution and excessive noise – continue to keep the city's nightlife on the quiet side.

Pubs & Bars

HCMC's widest and wildest variety of nightlife choices is in the central area, notably around Đ Dong Khoi. In 2001 local authorities, as part of their war against 'social evils,' required all bars and clubs to close by midnight. Enforcement varies from day to day, but you can always depend on the pubs in the Pham Ngu Lao area to stay open till the wee hours.

CENTRAL AREA

Vasco's (Map pp334–5; ☎ 824 3148; 16 Đ Cao Ba Quat; drinks 20,000-70,000d) Much loved by expats, perennially hip Vasco's draws a bigger crowd on weekends when there's live music. There are several nice pool tables indoors and out, and inviting tables in the villa courtyard.

Q Bar (Map pp334–5; ☎ 823 3479; 7 Lam Son Sq; drinks 20,000-70,000d) Attracting a sophisticated clientele for cocktails, Q Bar is where HCMC's fashion-conscious, alternative crowd hangs out. The stylish décor is cool and minimalist, and the music is hip. The bar is on the side of the Municipal Theatre, directly across from the Caravelle Hotel.

Temple Club (Map pp334–5; ☎ 829 9244; 29 Đ Ton That Thiep; drinks 25,000-70,000d) With brick walls and a Chinese atmosphere, this chic spot has a comfy lounge area in the back and a restaurant in the front. Like the décor? You can take some of it home with you – all of the furniture here is for sale!

Hoa Vien (Map p326; ☎ 829 0585; www.hoavener.com; 28 Đ Mac Dinh Chi; half-litre beer 24,000d) Though Hoa Vien is notable for being HCMC's only Czech restaurant, the big drawcard is the draught Czech lager. This is actually a brewery, with shiny copper tanks looming behind the busy bar.

Blue Gecko Bar (Map pp334–5; ☎ 824 3483; 31 Đ Ly Tu Trong) This major Aussie hang-out has the coldest beer in town. The music is good and you can shoot pool or watch sport on the half-dozen or so TVs.

Sheridan's Irish House (Map pp334–5; ☎ 823 0973; 17/13 Đ Le Thanh Ton; ☺ 11am-late) This traditional Irish pub seems beamed straight from the backstreets of Dublin; it has live music nightly and good pub grub.

Saigon Saigon Bar (Map pp334–5; ☎ 823 3479; 10th fl, Caravelle Hotel, 19 Lam Son Sq; drinks 25,000-70,000d; ☺ 11am-late) For the best views in the city centre, stop by Saigon Saigon for a drink around dusk. This fancy bar has live music, cool breezes and a casually upscale feel.

No 5 Ly Tu Trong (Map p326; ☎ 825 6300; 5 Đ Ly Tu Trong; drinks 15,000-70,000d) The décor of this restored French-colonial villa is stylish and

sleek. Good music, tasty food and beer, pool and friendly staff all contribute to the pleasant atmosphere.

Hard Rock Cafe (Map pp334–5; 24 Đ Mac Thi Buoi) This legendary imitation has been around for years. The real Hard Rock had plans to open in town a few years back, but perhaps these guys scared 'em off? You're unlikely to spot any rock stars here, but you can console yourself with a 'Hard Rock Cafe – Saigon' T-shirt.

And if those aren't enough:

Chu (Map pp334–5; ☎ 822 3907; 158 Đ Dong Khoi) Wine, pho and climate-protected Cuban cigars…plus live music on Saturday night.

AQ Cafe (Map p326; ☎ 829 8344; 39 Đ Mac Dinh Chi; beer 15,000d; ☺ 7am-midnight) In a 100-year-old wooden house, this dimly-lit, indoor-outdoor café features a spacious garden and cool jazz music.

Tex-Mex Cantina (Map pp334–5; ☎ 829 5950; 24 Đ Le Thanh Ton; ☺ 11am-midnight) Ceiling sombreros and a pool table liven up this place.

Wild Horse Bar (Map pp334–5; ☎ 825 1901; 8A/D1 Đ Thai Van Lung) Done up in a full-blown cowboy motif.

PHAM NGU LAO

When it comes to nightlife, the Pham Ngu Lao area has several hot spots, in addition to the always jumping travellers-café scene.

Lost in Saigon (Map p356; 169 Đ Pham Ngu Lao; ☺ 8.30am-late) This long-running backpackers' favourite is dark, always packed and serves a mean burger.

Long Phi Bar (Map p356; ☎ 920 3805; 325 Đ Pham Ngu Lao; ☺ 10am-late) Now located at the other end of Pham Ngu Lao, Long Phi has a curvy, hammered-copper bar and retains its relaxed, decadent ambience. Cocktails are good and a limited but satisfying bar menu is also available.

Sahara Music Cafe (Map p356; ☎ 837 8084; 277 Đ Pham Ngu Lao; ☺ 9am-late) More pool-bar than restaurant, Sahara does serve good Western bar food. It's definitely one of the more stylish places in the neighbourhood.

163 Cyclo Bar (Map p356; ☎ 920 1567; 163 Đ Pham Ngu Lao) Bar snacks range from tempura to sandwiches to pho, and live music (every night except for Sunday) covers the gamut from flamenco to pop.

Allez Boo Bar (Map p356; ☎ 837 2505; 187 Đ Pham Ngu Lao; beer from 12,000d) With its prime corner location on Đ De Tham, Allez Boo's open-windowed, bamboo interior is always full.

Guns & Roses Bar (Map p356; 207 Đ Pham Ngu Lao) Pool table, very late hours and a party atmosphere.

ENTERTAINMENT

Pick up the *Guide* or *Time Out* (see p325) to find out what's on during your stay in Saigon. Monthly listings include art shows, live music and theatre performances happening around town. You can also stop by the Municipal Theatre (p360) to see what's brewing there, as it regularly runs worthwhile plays, as well as musical and dance performances.

Binh Quoi Tourist Village (☎ 899 1831, dinner cruise bookings ☎ 829 8914; 1147 Đ Xo Viet Nghe Tinh, Binh Thanh district; boat rides 20,000-840,000đ, dinner adult/child 75,000/45,000đ; ☯ 11am-2pm & 5-8pm Sun & holidays, buffet dinner 5-8pm Sat) This 'village' is essentially a resort run by Saigon Tourist, with boat rides, water-puppet shows, tennis courts and amusements for the kids. The weekend buffet dinner, featuring a dazzling variety of traditional Vietnamese regional specialities, is served along a canal lit with floating lanterns and accompanied by live traditional music. Call for the latest schedule of performances.

The park puts in a plug for Vietnam's ethnic minorities by staging their traditional weddings accompanied by folk music. If you don't mind getting carted around on a tour package, the dinner cruises can be fun and are followed by a traditional music or water puppet performance at the village.

Binh Quoi Tourist Village is 8km north of central HCMC. You can get here by motorbike or taxi (around 60,000đ).

Maxim's Dinner Theatre (Map pp334-5; ☎ 829 6676; 15 Đ Dong Khoi; ☯ 11am-11pm) A Saigon institution next to the Majestic Hotel, this supper club is better recommended for its music performances than for the food. The menu offers Vietnamese, Chinese and Western dishes; though the sea slug may disappoint, the crème caramel definitely won't. The live music goes from Vietnamese folk to show tunes to contemporary pop, and reservations are recommended for dinner.

Cinemas

There are plenty of cinemas *(rap)* in the city centre, but very few films are shown in languages other than Vietnamese.

Foreign-language cinemas:
Diamond Plaza Cinema (Map pp334-5; ☎ 825 7751; Diamond Plaza, 163 Đ Dong Khoi; tickets 30,000-40,000đ) English-language films.
Idecaf (☎ 829 5451; 31 Đ Thai Van Lung) Screens French-language films; videos also available to rent.

Nightclubs

Most of the following dance clubs don't get started until midnight; ask around Pham Ngu Lao bars about the newest hot spots.

Apocalypse Now (Map pp334-5; ☎ 824 1463; 2C Đ Thi Sach) Dance clubs in Vietnam have a tendency to change with the wind, but 'Apo' is one exception to the rule. It's been around forever and gives a good eyeful of the seamier side of international relations. The music is loud, the patrons are from all walks of life and it's apocalyptically rowdy.

Tropical Rainforest Disco (Mua Rung; Map pp334-5; ☎ 825 7783; 5-15 Đ Ho Huan Nghiep; cover US$4) One of the hottest dance spots in the city centre for the younger crowd. The cover charge entitles you to one free drink.

Underground (Map pp334-5; ☎ 829 9079; 69 Đ Dong Khoi; ☯ 10am-midnight) Underground is located in the basement of the Lucky Plaza building and is a popular gathering spot for expats and travellers alike. This spacious London

---

SUNDAY NIGHT LIVE

The Dong Khoi area is the place to be on weekend and holiday nights. The streets are jam-packed with young people cruising *(di troi)* on bicycles and motorbikes. Everyone's dressed to impress. The mass of slow-moving humanity is so thick on Đ Dong Khoi that you may have to wait until dawn to get across the street. It is utter chaos at intersections, where eight, 10 or more lanes of two-wheeled vehicles intersect without the benefit of traffic lights, safety helmets or sanity.

Near the Municipal Theatre, fashionably dressed young people take a break from cruising to watch the endless procession, lining up along the street next to their cycles. The air is electric with the glances of lovers and animated conversations among friends. Everyone is out to see and be seen – it's a sight you shouldn't miss.

tube-theme bar has a good happy hour and great pizza.

Theatre

Municipal Theatre (Nha Hat Thanh Pho; Map pp334-5; ☎ 829 9976; Đ Dong Khoi) Each week the theatre has a different programme, such as Eastern European–style gymnastics, classical music or traditional Vietnamese theatre. Performances typically begin at 8pm; inquire at the theatre or ask at your hotel. And if there's nothing happening when you're in town, you can at least pop into the stylish Q Bar, around the side of the building, for a drink.

Conservatory of Music (Nhac Vien Thanh Pho Ho Chi Minh; Map p326; ☎ 824 3774; 112 Đ Nguyen Du; ⏰ performances 7.30pm Mon-Fri Mar-May & Oct-Dec) Performances of both traditional Vietnamese and Western classical music are held at the conservatory, near Reunification Palace. Students aged seven to 16 attend the conservatory, which performs all the functions of a public school in addition to providing instruction in music. The music teachers here were trained abroad. The school is free, but most of the students come from well-off families who can afford to purchase the prerequisite musical instruments.

Water Puppets

This art really comes from the north, but in recent years has been introduced to the south because it has been such a hit with tourists. There are two venues to see water puppets in HCMC. At the **War Remnants Museum** (☎ 930 5587; 28 Đ Vo Van Tan) and **History Museum** (☎ 829 8146; Đ Nguyen Binh Khiem); schedules vary, but shows tend to start when a group of five or more customers has assembled.

Saigon Race Track

Saigon Race Track (Cau Lac Bo The Thao Phu To; Map pp322-3; ☎ 855 1205; 2 Đ Le Dai Hanh, district 11; admission 1000d; ⏰ 12.30-4.30pm Sat & Sun) When South Vietnam was liberated in 1975, one of the Hanoi government's policies was to ban debauched, capitalistic pastimes such as gambling. Horse-racing tracks – mostly found in the Saigon area – were shut down. However, the government's need for hard cash has caused a rethink. Like the state lottery, the track has proved extremely lucrative.

Dating from around 1900, the track reopened in 1989. But grumbling about just where the money is going has been coupled with widespread allegations about the drugging of horses. The minimum legal age for jockeys is 14 years; most look like they're about 10.

The overwhelming majority of gamblers are Vietnamese though there is no rule prohibiting foreigners from joining in the fun of risking their dong. The minimum legal bet is 2000d and, for the high rollers hoping to become a dong billionaire, the sky's the limit.

Plans to introduce off-track betting have so far not materialised. However, illegal bookmaking (bets can be placed in gold!) does offer one form of competition to the government-owned monopoly.

SHOPPING

The free market in tourist junk has been booming in HCMC – you can pick up a useful item such as a ceramic Buddha that whistles the national anthem. And even if you're not the sort of person who needs a wind-up mechanical monkey that plays the cymbals, there is sure to be something that catches your eye.

In particular, HCMC offers excellent deals on clothing, ceramics, ethnic fabrics and lacquered bamboo. There are also the quirkier gems like the amazing *cyclos* and helicopters made from beer and soda cans – a sure place to find these is at the War Remnants Museum (p329) gift shop.

Central (and thus more expensive) is the Đ Dong Khoi area, which is jam-packed with small boutiques and souvenir shops. Better deals can be found in Pham Ngu Lao, although the selection isn't quite as good. If you're pressed for time, the newly-remodelled **Tax Department Store** (Russian Market; Map pp334-5; cnr Đ Nguyen Hue & Đ Le Loi) is a great place to pick up anything from electronics to clothing to handicrafts.

Arts & Crafts

Đ Dong Khoi is lined with small shops selling all manner of pretty items for adorning the self or the home.

Authentique Interiors (Map pp334-5; ☎ 822 1333; authentique@hcm.vnn.vn; 6 Đ Dong Khoi) Interesting home furnishings, tableware, ceramics, unique embroidery designs on pillowcases, clothing and bags.

Precious Qui (Map pp334-5; quasarkhanh@hcm.vnn
.vn; ☎ 825 6817; 29A Đ Dong Khoi) Ceramics, housewares
and silks in contemporary, minimalist designs.
Oriental Home (Map p326; ☎ 910 0194; www
.madeinvietnamcollection.com; 2A ĐL Le Duan) Furniture,
ceramics, lamps, lanterns and stone carvings, some of
which are antiques; also sells jewellery, clothing and does
custom-made *ao dai*.
Living & Giving (Map pp334-5; ☎ 822 3104;
livinggiving@bdvn.vnd.net; 11 Đ Ngo Duc Ke) Packed with
stylish linens and bedding, furniture and unusual home
décor in iron, wood and ceramic.
Mai Handicrafts (Map pp322-3; ☎ 844 0988;
maivn@hcm.vnn.vn; 298 Đ Nguyen Trong Tuyen, Tan Binh
district) Fair-trade shop dealing in ceramics, ethnic fabrics
and other gift items, in turn supporting disadvantaged
families and street children.

Beauty Salons
Tony & Guy Beauty Salon (Map p326; ☎ 925 0664;
tonyguy68@yahoo.com; 89C Đ Cach Mang Thang Tam) is
run by a friendly Vietnamese-American
stylist, Tony, who trained in Hollywood
and New York before moving back to his
homeland. The salon (not one of the Toni
& Guy group) maintains an international
standard and prices are reasonable: men/
women pay US$7/10 for a wash, head mas-
sage, cut, blow dry and finish. It also offers
beauty treatments.

Carved Seals
No bureaucracy, communist or otherwise,
can exist without the official stamps and
seals that are the *raison d'être* for legions
of clerks. This need is well-catered to by
the numerous shops strung out along the
street just north of the New World Hotel
(opposite side of ĐL Ham Nghi and just
west of Ben Thanh Market). In Cholon you
can find shops making these seals along Đ
Hai Thuong Lan Ong.

Most Vietnamese also own carved seals
bearing their name (an old tradition borrowed from China). You can have one made
too, but ask a local to help translate your
name into Vietnamese. You might want to
get your seal carved in Cholon using Chinese
characters; these are certainly more artistic
(though less practical) than the Romanised
script used by the Vietnamese today.

Clothing
At the budget end of the scale, T-shirts are
available from vendors along ĐL Le Loi in
the city centre, or Đ De Tham in the Pham
Ngu Lao area. Expect to pay about US$2 for
a printed T-shirt and US$3 to US$5 for an
embroidered one.
Ao dai, the silk tunic and trousers (see
the boxed text 'Ca Mau Saves the Ao Dai',
p426), are tailored at shops in and around
Ben Thanh Market and around the Rex and
Continental Hotels. There are also male *ao
dai* available – these are a looser fit and come
with a silk-covered head wrap to match.
Ao Dai Si Hoang (Map p326; ☎ 822 5271; sihoang@
hcm.vnn.vn; 260 Đ Pasteur, District 3) is a good and
reliable place to have *ao dai* made.
The Dong Khoi neighbourhood is awash
with tempting shops selling contemporary
clothing. Some will also custom-tailor clothing and shoes, and turnaround usually takes
a few days. A survey of the neighbourhood
around Đ Pasteur and Đ Le Thanh Ton
yields at least a half-dozen boutiques; Đ
Dong Khoi and Đ Ngo Duc Ke or Đ Dong
Du reveal yet more.
Chi Chi (Map pp334-5; ☎ 824 7812; anhxuanvn@hcm
.fpt.vn; 138 Đ Pasteur) Features well-chosen, lovely fabrics
and fine designs; custom tailoring offered here.
Khai Silk (Map pp334-5; ☎ 829 1146; khaisilksg@hcm
.fpt.vn; 107 Đ Dong Khoi) One branch of this well-established
silk empire; a reliable choice for tailored suits or *ao dai*.

COUTURE SAIGON
Silk shops lace Hanoi's Old Quarter, but the small boutiques scattered around Saigon are arguably
more diverse and untraditional – and usually cheaper. Maybe it's the unruliness of Saigon that
attracts and inspires fashion designers to cut and stitch innovative styles.
Creative contemporary designers from Vietnam and abroad have set up shop around the Dong
Khoi neighbourhood, and their boutiques offer unique, ready-to-wear pieces (most in Westerner
sizes!) at affordable prices. Most designers blend elements from Vietnamese styles with their own
flair and the resulting designs range from elegant to irreverent.
See p361 for a small sampling of boutiques.

HCMC MARKETS

Huynh Thuc Khang Street Market
This **street market** (Map pp334-5; Đ Huynh Thuc Khang & Đ Ton That Dam) in the Dong Khoi area sells everything. The area was known as the 'electronics black market' until early 1989, when it was legalised.

You can still buy electronic goods of all sorts – from mosquito zappers to video cassette recorders – but the market has expanded enormously to include clothing, washing detergent, lacquerware, condoms, pirated cassettes, posters of Ho Chi Minh and Britney Spears, smuggled bottles of Johnny Walker, Chinese-made 'Swiss' army knives and just about everything to satisfy your material needs.

Ben Thanh Market
HCMC has a number of huge indoor markets selling all manner of goods. These are some of the best places to pick up conical hats and ao dai. The most central of these is **Ben Thanh Market** (Cho Ben Thanh; Map p326; cnr ĐL Le Loi, ĐL Ham Nghi, ĐL Tran Hung Dao & Đ Le Lai). The market and surrounding streets make up one of the city's liveliest areas. Everything that's commonly eaten, worn or used by the Saigonese is available here: vegetables, meats, spices, sweets, tobacco, clothing, household items, hardware and so forth. The legendary slogan of US country stores applies equally well here: 'If we don't have it, you don't need it.' There's also a healthy selection of souvenir-worthy items.

Known to the French as Les Halles Centrales, it was built in 1914 from reinforced concrete; the central cupola is 28m in diameter. The main entrance, with its belfry and clock, has become a symbol of HCMC. Opposite the belfry, in the centre of the traffic roundabout, is an equestrian statue of Tran Nguyen Hai, the first person in Vietnam to use carrier pigeons. At the base of it, on a pillar, is a small white bust of Quach Thi Trang, a Buddhist woman killed during antigovernment protests in 1963.

Nearby, food stalls sell inexpensive meals. Ben Thanh Market is 700m southwest of the Rex Hotel.

The Old Market
Despite the name, the **Old Market** (Map p326) is not the place to find antiques. Nor is it the place to look for electronics or machinery (go to Dan Sinh Market for these). Rather, the Old Market is where you can most easily buy imported food, wine, shaving cream, shampoo etc. However, if its Vietnamese name, Cho Cu, is written or pronounced without the correct tones it means 'penis'; your cyclo driver will no doubt be much amused if you say that this is what you're looking for. Perhaps directions would be better – the Old Market is on the north side of ĐL Ham Nghi between Đ Ton That Dam and Đ Ho Tung Mau.

Dan Sinh Market
Also known as the War Surplus Market, this is the place to shop for a chic pair of combat boots or rusty dog tags. It's also the best market for electronics and other types of imported machinery – you could easily renovate a whole villa from the goods on sale.

Dan Sinh Market (Map p326; 104 Đ Yersin) is next to Phung Son Tu Pagoda. The front part is filled with stalls selling automobiles and motorbikes, but directly behind the pagoda building you can find reproductions of what seems to be second-hand military gear.

Stall after stall sells everything from handy gas masks and field stretchers to rain gear and mosquito nets. You can also find canteens, duffel bags, ponchos and boots. Anyone planning on spending time in Rwanda or New York City should consider picking up a second-hand flak jacket (prices are good).

Binh Tay Market
Cholon's main market is **Binh Tay Market** (Map p340; ĐL Hau Giang), a Chinese-style architectural masterpiece with a great clock tower in the centre. Much of the business here is wholesale.

An Dong Market
Cholon's other indoor market, **An Dong** (Map pp322-3), is very close to the intersection of ĐL Tran Phu and ĐL An Duong Vuong. This market is four storeys high and is crammed with shops. The 1st floor carries nothing but clothing, including imported designer jeans from Hong Kong, the latest pumps from Paris and ao dai. The basement is a gourmet's delight of small restaurants – a perfect place to lunch on the cheap.

eda (Map pp334-5; ☎ 827 2695; reda@hcm.vnn.vn; 9 Đ Le Thanh Ton) Notable for its style but also for its adjoining café, for a bite after browsing.

apa (Map p356; vudong@hcm.vnn.vn; ☎ 836 5163; 223 De Tham) Incorporates ethnic fabrics and designs with p style; also sells gifts and jewellery.

ong (Map pp334-5; ☎ 824 6986; www.asiasong esign.com; 76D Đ Le Thanh Ton) A sophisticated, high-nd design house with pieces for both men and women.

ha Ca (Map pp334-5; ☎ 823 4465; 106 Đ Nam Ky Khoi ghia) Wooden sandals, silk cowboy shirts and silver-studded ans are among the funky selections here.

offee

Vietnamese coffee is prime stuff and is amazingly cheap. The best grades are from Buon Ma Thuot and the beans are roasted n butter. Obviously, price varies according o the quality and also with the seasons. You can buy whole beans or have them round for no extra charge.

The city's major markets (opposite) have he best prices and widest selection. We scored some top-grade caffeine in Ben Thanh Market, which is also the best place to find he peculiar coffee-drippers used by the Vietnamese. Get a stainless-steel one because hey are easier to use than the cheaper aluninium ones. Also look in the market for a offee grinder if you're buying whole beans.

Galleries

HCMC is brimming with art galleries. Both **lue Space Gallery** (☎ 821 3695; 1A Đ Le Thi Hong Gam; ⏱ 9am-6pm), inside the Fine Arts Museum p331) and **Vinh Loi Gallery** (Map p326; ☎ 930 006; www.galerievinhloi.com; 41 Đ Ba Huyen Thanh Quan, strict 3; ⏱ 9am-6pm) are top-end galleries.

tamps & Coins

As you enter the **main post office** (Map pp334-5; Cong Xa Paris), immediately to your right is a ounter selling stationery and some decent tamp collections. Also as you face the enrance from the outside, to your right are a ew stalls that have stamp collections and ther goods such as foreign coins and banknotes. You can even find stuff from the ormer South Vietnamese regime. Prices re variable: about 30,000d will get you a espectable set of late-model stamps already nounted in a book, but the older and rarer ollections cost more.

Many bookshops and antique shops long Đ Dong Khoi sell overpriced French Indochinese coins and banknotes as well as packets of Vietnamese stamps.

GETTING THERE & AWAY
Air

Tan Son Nhat Airport was one of the three busiest in the world in the late 1960s. The runways are still lined with lichen-covered, mortar-proof aircraft-retaining walls, hangars and other military structures.

You must reconfirm all reservations for flights out of the country. For more details on international air travel see p468.

Nearly all domestic flights are operated by Vietnam Airlines. Pacific Airlines also flies the HCMC–Hanoi and HCMC–Danang route. See the Transport chapter (p475) for details on routes and schedules.

Boat

Hydrofoils (adult/child US$10/5, 1¼ hours) depart for Vung Tau (p379) almost hourly from the Bach Dang jetty (Map pp334-5) on Đ Ton Duc Thang. For more information contact **Vina Express** (☎ 821 5609) at the jetty.

In Vung Tau you board the hydrofoil at Cau Da pier, opposite the Hai Au Hotel. **Vina Express** (☎ 856 530) has an office in Vung Tau by the pier.

Cargo ferries bound for the Mekong Delta depart from the **dock** (☎ 829 7892) at the river end of ĐL Ham Nghi. There is a daily service to the provinces of An Giang and Vinh Long and to the towns of Ben Tre (8 hours), Ca Mau (30 hours, once every four days), My Tho (six hours, departs 11am) and Phu Chau (Tan Chau). Buy your tickets on the boat. Simple food may be available on board. Be aware that these ancient vessels lack the most elementary safety gear, such as life jackets.

Bus

Intercity buses depart from and arrive at a variety of stations around HCMC. **Cholon bus station** (Map p340; Đ Le Quang Sung) is the most convenient place to get buses to My Tho and other Mekong Delta towns. It's one street north of the sprawling Binh Tay Market.

Less convenient than Cholon, **Mien Tay bus station** (Ben Xe Mien Tay; ☎ 825 5955) nevertheless has even more buses to areas south of HCMC (basically the Mekong Delta). This huge station is about 10km west of HCMC in An Lac, a part of Binh Chanh district (Huyen Binh Chanh). Buses and minibuses from Mien Tay serve most towns in the Mekong Delta.

Buses to points north of HCMC leave from **Mien Dong bus station** (Ben Xe Mien Dong; ☎ 829 4056), in Binh Thanh district about 5km from central HCMC on Hwy 13 (Quoc Lo 13), the continuation of Đ Xo Viet Nghe Tinh. The station is just under 2km north of the intersection of Đ Xo Viet Nghe Tinh and Đ Dien Bien Phu.

There are services from Mien Dong to Buon Ma Thuot (15 hours), Danang (26 hours), Hai Phong (53 hours), Nha Trang (11 hours), Hanoi (49 hours), Hué (29 hours), Pleiku (22 hours), Vinh (42 hours), Quang Ngai (24 hours), Quy Nhon (17 hours), Nam Dinh (47 hours) and Tuy Hoa (12 hours). Most buses leave daily between 5am and 5.30am.

Buses to Tay Ninh, Cu Chi and points northeast of HCMC depart from the **Tay Ninh bus station** (Ben Xe Tay Ninh; Map pp322-3; ☎ 849 5935), in Tan Binh district west of the centre. To get there, head all the way out on Đ Cach Mang Thang Tam. The station is about 1km past where Đ Cach Mang Thang Tam merges with Đ Le Dai Hanh.

Car & Motorbike

Inquire at almost any tourist café, travel agent or your hotel to arrange car rental. The agencies in the Pham Ngu Lao area generally offer the lowest prices.

Train

Trains from **Saigon train station** (Ga Sai Gon; Map pp322-3; ☎ 823 0105; 1 Đ Nguyen Thong, District 3; ticket office ⏲ 7.15-11am & 1-3pm) serve cities along the coast north of HCMC.

Train tickets can be purchased from **Saigon Railways Tourist Services** (Map p356; ☎ 836 7970; fax 836 9031; 275C Đ Pham Ngu Lao; ⏲ 7.30-11.30am & 1-4.30pm) or from most travel agents.

For details on the *Reunification Express* service see p482.

GETTING AROUND
To/From the Airport

Tan Son Nhat Airport is 7km northwest of central HCMC. Metered taxis are your best bet and cost around 60,000d (US$4) between the airport and the city centre. You'll be enthusiastically greeted by a group of taxi drivers after you exit the terminal; mos are OK, but make sure that the driver agree to use the meter and it is switched on *afte* you get in the car. The final fare to centra HCMC shouldn't go much over 60,000d.

Be aware that taxi drivers will probabl recommend a 'good and cheap' hotel, an deliver you to a hotel for a commission; if yo don't know where you're going, this is not bad system per se. Problems may arise, how ever, when you ask a taxi driver to take yo to a place that doesn't pay commission. Th driver may tell you the hotel is closed, burne down, is dirty and dangerous, or anything t steer you somewhere else (see the boxed tex 'Your Friendly Taxi Driver', p328).

If you're travelling solo and withou much baggage, a motorbike taxi is an optio for getting to/from the airport. Drivers han out near the airport car park and typicall ask around US$3 to go to the city centre. I you take a motorbike taxi to Tan Son Nha you may have to walk the short distanc from the airport gate to the terminal. Pri vate cars can bring you into the airport, bu must drop you off at the domestic termina only a minute's walk from the internationa terminal.

To get to the airport you can call a tax (p366). Some cafés in the Pham Ngu La area do runs to the airport – these place even have sign-up sheets where you ca book share-taxis for US$2 per person.

Most economical is the air-conditione airport bus (1000d), No 152, going to an from the airport. Buses leave the airpor approximately every 15 minutes, stop ping briefly at both the international an domestic terminals before heading down town. They then make regular stops along Đ De Tham (Pham Ngu Lao area) and inter national hotels along Đ Dong Khoi, suc as the Caravelle and the Majestic. Buses ar labelled in English, but you might also loo for the words 'Xe Buyt San Bay'.

Bicycle

A bicycle is a great, if slow, way to get aroun the city and see things. Bikes can be rente from a number of places – many hotel cafés and travel agencies can help you.

A good place to buy a decent (ie imported bicycle is at the shops near the New Worl Hotel on Đ Le Thanh Ton, a short walk fron the Pham Ngu Lao area (Map p326).

For on-the-spot bicycle repairs, look for
n upturned army helmet and a hand pump
tting next to the curb.

Bicycle parking lots are usually just
ped-off sections of pavement. For about
000d you can safely leave your bicycle
heft is a big problem). Your bicycle will
ave a number written on the seat in chalk
r stapled to the handlebars and you'll be
ven a reclaim chit – don't lose it! If you
me back and your bicycle is gone, the
arking lot is supposedly required to re-
lace it.

oat

's easy to hire a motorised 5m-long boat
tour the Saigon River. There's always
meone hanging around looking to char-
r a boat. Ask them to bring it to you (they
an easily do this), rather than you going
the boat.

The price should be around US$5 per
our for a small boat or US$10 to US$15
r a larger, faster craft. Interesting destina-
ons for short trips include Cholon (along
en Nghe Channel) and the zoo (along Thi
ghe Channel). Note that both channels
re fascinating, but filthy – raw sewage is
ischarged into the water. Tourists regard
e channels as a major attraction, but the
overnment considers them an eyesore and
as already launched a programme to move
sidents out. The channels will eventually
e filled in and the water diverted into un-
erground sewerage pipes.

For longer trips up the Saigon River, it
worth chartering a fast speedboat from
aigon Tourist. Although these cost US$20
er hour, you'll save money, as a cheap
oat takes at least five times longer for the
ame journey. Splitting the cost between a
mall group of travellers makes sense and
can be more fun boating with others.
lthough cruising the Saigon River can
e interesting, it pales in comparison with
he splendour of the canals in the Mekong
elta.

Since you hire boats by the hour, some
vill go slowly because they know the meter
running. You might want to set a time
imit at the start.

Ferries across the Saigon River leave from
he dock at the foot of ĐL Ham Nghi and
un every half-hour or so between 4.30am
nd 10.30pm.

Bus

Few tourists make use of the city buses; they
are safer than *cyclos*, though less aesthetic.
Now that HCMC's People's Committee has
resolved to phase out *cyclos*, some money
is finally being put into the badly neglected
public-transport system.

At present, there are only a few bus
routes, though more undoubtedly will be
added. No decent bus map is available
and bus stops are mostly unmarked, so it's
worth summarising the main bus lines.

Saigon–Cholon buses depart from Me
Linh Square (by the Saigon River) and
continue along ĐL Tran Hung Dao to
Binh Tay Market in Cholon, then return
along the same route. The buses running
this route have air-con and video movies
and the driver is well dressed! All this for
3000d. Buy your ticket on board from the
attendant.

Mien Dong–Mien Tay buses depart from
Mien Dong bus station (northeast HCMC),
pass through Cholon and terminate at Mien
Tay bus station on the western edge of town.
The fare is 5000d.

Car & Motorbike

Travel agencies, hotels and cafés are all in
the car rental business. Most vehicles are
relatively recent Japanese- or Korean-made
machines – everything from subcompacts
to minibuses. However, it's occasionally
possible to enjoy a ride in a vintage vehicle
from the 1950s or '60s. Not long ago, classic
American cars (complete with tail fins and
impressive chrome fenders) were popular
as 'wedding taxis'. Prestige these days, however, means a white Toyota. Nevertheless,
some of the old vehicles can be hired for
excursions in and around HCMC. You'll
also see the occasional French-built Renault
or Citroën. The former Soviet Union chips
in with Ladas, Moskviches and Volgas.

If you're brave you can rent a motorbike
and really earn your 'I Survived Saigon' T-
shirt. Many say this is the fastest and easiest
way to get around the city – and to the hospital, if you don't know what you're doing.
Even if you're an experienced biker, make
sure you've spent some time observing traffic patterns before putting yourself in it.

Motorbike rentals are ubiquitous in
places where tourists tend to congregate –
the Pham Ngu Lao area is as good as any.

Ask at the cafés. A 100cc motorbike can be rented for US$5 to US$8 per day and your passport may be kept as collateral. Before renting one make sure it's rideable, and if you're wise you'll also rent a helmet (about US$1 per day).

Saigon Scooter Centre (☎ 0903-013 690; www .saigonscootercentre.com; H5A/K300 Đ Cong Hoa, Tan Binh district; ☷ 10am-5pm Mon-Sat) is a reliable source for restored classic Vespa and Lambretta scooters, which are also rented out (as well as a range of other well-maintained bikes). Daily rental rates start from US$10 and discounts are offered for longer rentals. For an extra fee it'll provide a one-way service, with a pick-up of the bikes anywhere in Vietnam.

Cyclo

You can hail a *cyclo* along major thorough-fares almost any time of the day or night. In HCMC, many of the drivers are former South Vietnamese army soldiers and quite a few know at least basic English, while others are quite fluent. Each driver has a story of war, 're-education', persecution and poverty to tell (see the boxed text 'Life on the Streets', p348).

In an effort to control HCMC's rapidly growing traffic problems, there are presently 51 streets on which *cyclos* are prohibited to ride. As a result, your driver must often take a circuitous route to avoid these trouble spots; the police will not hesitate to fine him. For the same reason, the driver may not be able to drop you off at the exact address you want, but will bring you to the nearest side street. Try to have some sympathy since it is not the driver's fault. Perhaps the authorities would have served the city better by allowing the quiet and atmospheric *cyclos* carte blanche and forcing the smoke-spewing cars to take an alternative route.

Short hops around the city centre should cost around 5000d and definitely no more

than 10,000d; District 1 to central Cholo costs about 20,000d. Overcharging touris is the norm, so negotiate a price beforehan and have the exact change ready. You ca rent a *cyclo* for around US$1 per hour, fine idea if you will be doing a lot of tou ing; most *cyclo* drivers around the Pha Ngu Lao area can produce a sample tou programme.

You should enjoy *cyclos* while you can, i the municipal government intends to pha them out.

Taxi

Metered taxis cruise the streets, but it often easier to phone for one. Several con panies in HCMC offer metered taxis an charge almost exactly the same rates. Th flagfall is around 14,000d for the first kilc metre. Most rides in the city centre cost le than 30,000d.

The following contact details are fc HCMC's main taxi companies.
Ben Thanh Taxi (☎ 842 2422)
Mai Linh Taxi (☎ 822 6666)
Red Taxi (☎ 844 6677)
Saigon Taxi (☎ 842 4242)
Vina Taxi (☎ 811 1111)

A quick, if precarious, way around town to ride on the back of a *xe om* (sometime called a *Honda om*). *Xe om* drivers usuall hang out on their parked bikes on stre corners, looking for passengers, and wi usually wave you down first. The accepte rate is comparable to *cyclos*.

Xe Lam

Tiny three-wheeled vehicles, *xe lam* (othe wise known as Lambrettas) connect th various bus stations. There is a useful *x lam* stop on the northwest corner of Pham Ngu Lao and Đ Nguyen Thai Ho (Map p356), where you can catch a ride t the Mien Tay bus station for the Mekon Delta.

Around Ho Chi Minh City

368

Beyond the sprawl of Ho Chi Minh City (HCMC), highways spin away from the metropolitan centre to points less manic. Around the city, there are abundant opportunities for extra-urban exploration. Undoubtedly the most popular excursions cruise a well-travelled road to the Cu Chi Tunnels, where war history is just a trap-door and underground tunnel away. Most of these tours include a visit to the dizzyingly kaleidoscopic colours of the Cao Dai Temple in Tay Ninh, a fascinating place to learn about this singular Vietnamese religion.

Elsewhere in this geographically diverse region, independent travellers can take a break from the coastal tourist trail by escaping to rustic beach villages, where foreigners are almost as rare as wild elephants; or to its national parks, where it's possible to commune with some of Vietnam's non-human inhabitants. Situated off the highway from HCMC to Dalat, Cat Tien National Park makes a superb stop for a few days of hiking and respite from the open-tour circuit. There are also the mangrove marshes of Can Gio and its muddy shore, a good day trip from HCMC for botanists and bivalve (mollusc) diggers.

For travellers with limited time in HCMC and no plans to journey up to coastal resort towns like Nha Trang or Mui Ne, it's easy to hop on a hydrofoil to Vung Tau for a quick-and-dirty beach holiday. Beaches further up the coast from Vung Tau offer lots of coastline and a slow pace but little in the way of resort trimmings. The exception is Binh Chau Hot Springs Resort, worth a stop for mudbaths and hot soaks in mineral water.

Those with deeper pockets and time to spare should consider a helicopter flight to the Con Dao Islands, where clear waters, secluded beaches and remote islands remain – for now – fairly pristine and untainted by mass tourism.

HIGHLIGHTS

- Crawl through the network of narrow tunnels dug by the Viet Cong at **Cu Chi** (p369)

- Observe one of the serene daily worship services against a backdrop of riotous colour at the **Cao Dai Great Temple** (p373) in Tay Ninh

- Detour into the wilds of **Cat Tien National Park** (p388), a bird-watcher's dream

- Journey to the remote **Con Dao Islands** (p382), where prison history meets a natural paradise

- Boil an egg – better yet, soak a travel-weary body – in the mineral hot springs of **Binh Chau** (p387)

- Make a quick getaway to **Vung Tau** (p379) and its long stretch of sandy beach

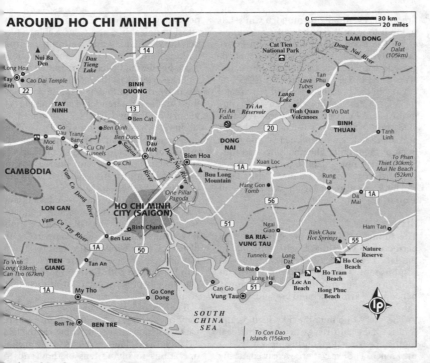

AROUND HO CHI MINH CITY

National Parks

Two notable national parks are found in this southern slice of Vietnam. **Cat Tien National Park** (p388), a few hours from HCMC, makes a lovely detour between HCMC and Dalat for those interested in bird-watching and hiking.

Even more remote is **Con Dao National Park** (p383), located on a string of islands accessible by helicopter (or possibly airplane) from Vung Tau or HCMC. This national park is decidedly off the beaten path, due to cost and time commitments.

Both parks give visitors the opportunity to explore Vietnam's all-too-rare wild side.

CU CHI TUNNELS

The town of Cu Chi is a district of greater HCMC and has a population of about 200,000 (it had about 80,000 residents during the American War). At first glance there is little evidence here to indicate the intense fighting, bombing and destruction that occurred in Cu Chi during the war. To see what went on, you have to dig deeper – underground.

The tunnel network of Cu Chi became legendary during the 1960s for its role in facilitating Viet Cong (VC) control of a large rural area only 30km to 40km from HCMC. At its height the tunnel system stretched from the South Vietnamese capital to the Cambodian border; in the district of Cu Chi alone there were more than 250km of tunnels. The network, parts of which was several storeys deep, included innumerable trap doors, constructed living areas, storage facilities, weapons factories, field hospitals, command centres and kitchens.

The tunnels made possible communication and coordination between the VC-controlled enclaves, isolated from each other by South Vietnamese and American land and air operations. They also allowed the VC to mount surprise attacks wherever the tunnels went – even within the perimeters of the US military base at Dong Du – and to disappear suddenly into hidden trapdoors without a trace. After ground operations against the tunnels claimed large numbers of US casualties and proved ineffective, the Americans resorted to massive firepower, eventually turning Cu Chi's 420 sq km into what the authors of *The Tunnels of Cu Chi* (Tom Mangold and John Penycate) have called 'the most bombed, shelled, gassed, defoliated and generally devastated area in the history of warfare'.

Cu Chi has become a place of pilgrimage for Vietnamese school children and communist-party cadres. Parts of this remarkable tunnel network (which are enlarged and upgraded versions of the real thing) are open to the public. The unadulterated tunnels, though not actually closed to tourists, are hard to get to and are rarely visited.

There are numerous war cemeteries all around Cu Chi.

History

The tunnels of Cu Chi were built over a period of 25 years that began sometime in the late 1940s. They were the improvised response of a poorly equipped peasant army to its enemy's high-tech ordnance, helicopters, artillery, bombers and chemical weapons.

The Viet Minh built the first dugouts and tunnels in the hard, red earth of Cu Chi (ideal for their construction) during the war against the French. The excavations were used mostly for communication between villages and to evade French army sweeps of the area.

When the VC's National Liberation Front (NLF) insurgency began in earnest around 1960, the old Viet Minh tunnels were repaired and new extensions were excavated. Within a few years the tunnel system assumed enormous strategic importance, and most of Cu Chi district and the nearby area came under firm VC control. In addition Cu Chi was used as a base for infiltrating intelligence agents and sabotage teams into Saigon. The stunning attacks in the South Vietnamese capital during the 1968 Tet Offensive were planned and launched from Cu Chi.

In early 1963 the Diem government implemented the botched Strategic Hamlets Program, under which fortified encampments, surrounded by many rows of sharp bamboo spikes, were built to house people who had been 'relocated' from communist-controlled areas. The first strategic hamlet was in Ben Cat district, next to Cu Chi. Not only was the programme carried out with incredible incompetence, alienating the peasantry, but the VC launched a majo effort to defeat it. The VC were able to tun nel into the hamlets and control them from within. By the end of 1963 the first show piece hamlet had been overrun.

The series of setbacks and defeats suf fered by the South Vietnamese forces in the Cu Chi area rendered a complete VC victory by the end of 1965 a distinct pos sibility. In the early months of that year, the guerrillas boldly held a victory parade in the middle of Cu Chi town. VC strength in and around Cu Chi was one of the reasons the Johnson administration decided to involve US troops in the war.

To deal with the threat posed by VC con trol of an area so near the South Vietnam ese capital, one of the USA's first action was to establish a large base camp in Cu Chi district. Unknowingly, they built it right on top of an existing tunnel network. It took months for the 25th Division to figure out why they kept getting shot at in their tent at night.

The US and Australian troops tried a va riety of methods to 'pacify' the area around Cu Chi, which came to be known as the Iron Triangle. They launched large-scale ground operations involving tens of thousands of troops but failed to locate the tunnels. To deny the VC cover and supplies, rice pad dies were defoliated, huge swathes of jungle bulldozed, and villages evacuated and razed The Americans also sprayed chemical defo liants on the area aerially and a few months later ignited the tinder-dry vegetation with gasoline and napalm. But the intense heat interacted with the wet tropical air in such a way as to create cloudbursts that extin guished the fires. The VC remained safe and sound in their tunnels.

Unable to win this battle with chemicals the US army began sending men down into the tunnels. These 'tunnel rats', who were often involved in underground fire fights sustained appallingly high casualty rates.

When the Americans began using Ger man shepherd dogs, trained to use their keen sense of smell to locate trapdoors and guerrillas, the VC began washing with American soap, which gave off a scent the canines identified as friendly. Captured US uniforms were put out to confuse the dogs further. Most importantly, the dogs were not able to spot booby traps. So many dogs were killed or maimed that their horrified handlers then refused to send them into the tunnels.

The USA declared Cu Chi a free-strike zone: little authorisation was needed to shoot at anything in the area, random artillery was fired into the area at night, and pilots were told to drop unused bombs and napalm there before returning to base. But the VC stayed put. Finally, in the late 1960s, American B-52s carpet-bombed the whole area, destroying most of the tunnels along with everything else around. The gesture was militarily useless by then because the USA was already on its way out of the war. The tunnels had served their purpose.

The VC guerrillas serving in the tunnels lived in extremely difficult conditions and suffered horrific casualties. Only about 6000 of the 16,000 cadres who fought in the tunnels survived the war. Thousands of civilians in the area were killed. Their tenacity was extraordinary considering the bombings, the pressures of living underground for weeks or months at a time and the deaths of countless friends and comrades.

The villages of Cu Chi have since been presented with numerous honorific awards, decorations and citations by the government, and many have been declared 'heroic villages'. Since 1975 new hamlets have been established and the population of the area has more than doubled; however, chemical defoliants remain in the soil and water, and crop yields are still poor.

The Tunnels of Cu Chi, by Tom Mangold and John Penycate, is a wonderful work documenting the story of the tunnels and the people involved on both sides.

Sights
THE TUNNELS

Over the years the VC developed simple but effective techniques to make their tunnels difficult to detect or disable. Wooden trapdoors were camouflaged with earth and branches; some were booby-trapped. Hidden underwater entrances from rivers were constructed. To cook they used 'Dien Bien Phu kitchens', which exhausted the smoke through vents many metres away from the cooking site. Trapdoors were installed throughout the network to prevent tear gas, smoke or water from moving from one part of the system to another. Some

sections were even equipped with electric lighting.

Presently two tunnel sites are open to visitors. One is near the village of Ben Dinh and the other is at Ben Duoc.

Ben Dinh

This small, renovated section of the **tunnel system** (admission 65,000d) is near the village of Ben Dinh, 50km from HCMC. In one of the classrooms at the visitors centre, a large map shows the extent of the network; the area shown is in the northwestern corner of greater HCMC. The tunnels are marked in red, VC bases in light grey and the river in light blue (the Saigon River is at the top). Fortified villages held by South Vietnamese and US forces are marked in grey, while blue dots represent the American and South Vietnamese military posts that were supposed to ensure the security of nearby villages. The dark blue area in the centre is the base of the US 25th Infantry Division. Most prearranged tours do not take you to this former base, but it is not off limits and you can arrange a visit if you have your own guide and driver.

To the right of the large map are two cross-section diagrams of the tunnels. The bottom diagram is a reproduction of one used by General William Westmoreland, the commander of US forces in Vietnam (1964–68). For once the Americans seemed to have had their intelligence information right (though the tunnels did not pass under rivers, nor did the guerrillas wear headgear underground).

The section of the tunnel system presently open to visitors is a few hundred metres south of the visitors centre. It snakes up and down through various chambers along its 50m length. The tunnels are about 1.2m high and 80cm across, and are unlit. Some travellers find them too claustrophobic for comfort. A knocked-out M-41 tank and a bomb crater are near the exit, which is in a reforested eucalyptus grove. Be warned that this site tends to get crowded, and it also has the inexplicable added 'attraction' of caged wild animals.

Ben Duoc

These are not the genuine tunnels, but a full **reconstruction** (admission 65,000d) for the benefit of visitors. The emphasis here is more on the fun fair (tourists are given the chance to imagine what it was like to be a guerrilla) and it attracts far more Vietnamese than foreign visitors.

CU CHI WAR HISTORY MUSEUM

The small **Cu Chi War History Museum** (Nha Truyen Thong Huyen Cu Chi; admission US$1) is not actually at the tunnel sites but just off the main highway in the central area of the town of Cu Chi. Almost all of the explanations are in Vietnamese.

There's a collection of some gruesome photos showing civilians who were severely wounded or killed after being attacked by American bombs or burned with napalm. A painting on the wall shows American soldiers armed with rifles being attacked by Vietnamese peasants armed only with sticks.

One wall of the museum contains a long list of names, all VC guerrillas killed in the Cu Chi area. An adjacent room of the museum displays recent photos of prosperous farms and factories, an effort to show the benefits of Vietnam's economic reforms. In the lobby, near the entrance, is a statue of Ho Chi Minh with his right arm raised, waving hello.

This museum is rather disappointing and it gets few visitors. You'll find the War Remnants Museum (p329) in HCMC is much more interesting and informative for foreign visitors.

Tours

An organised tour is the easiest way to visit the Cu Chi tunnels and it's not remotely expensive.

Most of the cafés on Đ Pham Ngu Lao in HCMC run combined full-day tours to the Cu Chi tunnels and Cao Dai Great Temple (p373) for around US$4.

Getting There & Around

Cu Chi district covers a large area, part of which are as close as 30km to central HCMC. The Cu Chi War History Museum is closest to the city, while the Ben Dinh and Ben Duoc tunnels are about 50km and 70km, respectively, from central HCMC by highway. There's a back road that reduces the distance significantly, though it means driving on bumpy dirt roads.

BUS

The buses going to Tay Ninh pass through Cu Chi, but getting from the town of Cu Chi to the tunnels by public transport is impossible – it's 15km, so you'll have to hire a motorbike (see p376).

TAXI

Hiring a taxi in HCMC and driving out to Cu Chi is not all that expensive, especially if the cost is split by several people. The easiest way to do this is to stop by one of the budget travel cafés in Pham Ngu Lao (see p327) and arrange a car, or see if you can flag a taxi in that neighbourhood with a driver who will agree to charge you for driving time only. See p366 for details on local taxi companies.

A visit to the Cu Chi tunnel complex can easily be combined with a stop at the headquarters of the Cao Dai sect in Tay Ninh. A taxi for an all-day excursion to both should cost about US$40.

SHOOT!

Ever wondered what it feels like to fire an AK-47? Well, if you visit the Cu Chi Tunnels, you'll have a chance to find out.

There are target shooting ranges at both the Ben Dinh and Ben Duoc tunnel sites, where tourists line up in droves to handle the military big guns. You can choose from an array of weapons: the M-1, M-3, M-4, M-14, M-16, M-30 and M-60, and the ever-popular Russian AK-47 rifle. If rifles aren't your cup of tea, there are plenty of handguns (including Colt 45s for you Clint Eastwood wannabes), 30-60 machine guns and shotguns to boot.

Hearing protection is mandatory, and the congenial, fatigues-clad firearm staff will provide you with a good pair of DJ-style headphones to wear. Still, if you have a set with you, we recommend you wear a pair of earplugs underneath – these guns are *loud*!

The cost of US$1 per bullet is a relative bargain, considering it's the only opportunity most people will ever get.

AY NINH

☎ 066 / pop 42,000

ay Ninh town, the capital of Tay Ninh
rovince, serves as the headquarters of one
f Vietnam's most interesting indigenous
:ligions, Cao Daism. The Cao Dai Great
emple at the sect's Holy See is one of
ie most striking structures in all of Asia.
uilt between 1933 and 1955, the temple
; a rococo extravaganza combining the
onflicting architectural idiosyncrasies of
French church, a Chinese pagoda, Hong
ong's Tiger Balm Gardens and Madame
ussaud's Wax Museum.

Tay Ninh province, northwest of HCMC,
; bordered by Cambodia on three sides.
he area's dominant geographic feature is
lui Ba Den (Black Lady Mountain), which
owers above the surrounding plains. Tay
linh province's eastern border is formed
y the Saigon River. The Vam Co River
ows from Cambodia through the western
art of the province.

Because of the once-vaunted political
nd military power of the Cao Dai, this
:gion was the scene of prolonged and
eavy fighting during the Franco–Viet
linh War. Tay Ninh province served as a
iajor terminus of the Ho Chi Minh Trail
uring the American War, and in 1969 the
'C captured Tay Ninh town and held it for
:veral days.

During the period of tension between
'ambodia and Vietnam in the late 1970s,
ie Khmer Rouge launched a number of
ross-border raids into Tay Ninh province
nd committed atrocities against civilians.
:everal cemeteries around Tay Ninh are
tark reminders of these events.

nformation

ay Ninh Tourist (☎ 822376; tanitour@hcm.vnn.vn; 210B
30/4) is located in the Hoa Binh Hotel. Tay
linh's **post office** (Đ 30/4) is down the street,
ut it does not offer Internet services.

ights

AO DAI HOLY SEE

he Cao Dai Holy See, founded in 1926,
; 4km east of Tay Ninh, in the village of
.ong Hoa.

The complex houses the **Cao Dai Great Tem-
le** (Thanh That Cao Dai), administrative
ffices, residences for officials and adepts,
nd a hospital of traditional Vietnamese

herbal medicine, to which people from all
over the south travel for treatment. After
reunification the government 'borrowed'
parts of the complex for its own use (and
perhaps to keep an eye on the sect).

Prayers are conducted four times daily in
the Great Temple (suspended during Tet).
It's worth visiting during prayer sessions –
the one at noon is most popular with tour
groups from HCMC - but don't disturb the
worshippers. Only a few hundred priests
participate in weekday prayers, but during
festivals several thousand priests, dressed in
special white garments, may attend.

The Cao Dai clergy has no objection to
your photographing temple objects, but you
cannot photograph people without their
permission, which is seldom granted. However, you can photograph the prayer sessions
from the upstairs balcony, an apparent concession to the troops of tourists who come
here every day.

It's important that guests wear modest
and respectful attire inside the temple; that
means no shorts or sleeveless T-shirts, although sandals are OK since you have to
take them off anyway before you enter.

Set above the front portico of the Great
Temple is the **divine eye**. Americans often
comment that it looks as if it were copied
from the back of a US$1 bill (is this why it's
called 'The Almighty Dollar'?). Lay women
enter the Great Temple through a door at
the base of the tower on the left. Once inside they walk around the outside of the
colonnaded hall in a clockwise direction.
Men enter on the right and walk around
the hall in an anticlockwise direction. Shoes
and hats must be removed upon entering
the building. The area in the centre of the
sanctuary is reserved for Cao Dai priests.

A **mural** in the front entry hall depicts
the three signatories of the 'Third Alliance
Between God and Man': the Chinese states-
man and revolutionary leader Dr Sun Yat-
sen (1866–1925) holds an ink stone; while
the Vietnamese poet Nguyen Binh Khiem
(1492–1587) and French poet and author
Victor Hugo (1802–85) write 'God and Humanity' and 'Love and Justice' in Chinese
and French (Nguyen Binh Khiem writes
with a brush; Victor Hugo uses a quill pen).
Nearby signs in English, French and German each give a slightly different version of
the fundamentals of Cao Daism.

CAO DAISM

Cao Daism (Dai Dao Tam Ky Pho Do) is the outcome of an attempt to create the ideal religion through the fusion of secular and religious philosophies of the East and West. The result is a potpourri that includes aspects of most of the religious philosophies known in Vietnam during the early 20th century: Buddhism, Confucianism, Taoism, native Vietnamese spiritualism, Christianity and Islam. The term Cao Dai (meaning high tower or palace) is a euphemism for God.

History

Cao Daism was founded by the mystic Ngo Minh Chieu (also known as Ngo Van Chieu; born 1878), a civil servant who once served as district chief of Phu Quoc Island. He was widely read in Eastern and Western religious works and became active in séances, at which his presence was said to greatly improve the quality of communication with the spirits. Around 1919 he began to receive a series of revelations from Cao Dai in which the tenets of Cao Dai doctrine were set forth.

Cao Daism was officially founded as a religion in a ceremony held in 1926. Within a year the group had 26,000 followers. By the mid-1950s one in eight Southern Vietnamese was a Cao Dai and the sect was famous worldwide for its imaginative garishness. The Cao Dai had established a virtually independent feudal state in Tay Ninh province and retained enormous influence over its affairs for the next two decades.

The Cao Dai also played a significant political and military role in South Vietnam from 1926 to 1956, when most of the 25,000-strong Cao Dai army, which had been given support by the Japanese and later the French, was incorporated into the South Vietnamese Army.

Having refused to support the VC during the American War – and despite the fact that the Saigon government had barely tolerated them – the Cao Dai feared the worst after Reunification. Indeed, all Cao Dai lands were confiscated by the new communist government and four members of the sect were executed in 1979. However, in 1985 the Holy See and some 400 temples were returned to Cao Dai control.

Cao Daism is strongest in Tay Ninh province and the Mekong Delta, but Cao Dai temples can be found throughout southern and central Vietnam. Today there are an estimated three million followers of Cao Daism.

Philosophy

Much of Cao Dai doctrine is drawn from Mahayana Buddhism, mixed with Taoist and Confucian elements (Vietnam's 'Triple Religion'). Cao Dai ethics are based on the Buddhist ideal of 'the good person' but incorporate traditional Vietnamese taboos and sanctions as well.

The ultimate goal of the Cao Dai disciple is to escape the cycle of reincarnation. This can only be achieved by the performance of certain duties including, first and foremost, the prohibitions against killing, lying, luxurious living, sensuality and stealing.

The main tenets of Cao Daism include believing in one god, the existence of the soul and the use of mediums to communicate with the spiritual world. Some Cao Dai practices include priestly celibacy, vegetarianism, communication with spirits through séances, maintenance of the cult of ancestors, fervent proselytising and sessions of meditative self-cultivation.

Following the Chinese duality of Yin and Yang, there are two principal deities, the female Mother Goddess and the male God (a duality that somewhat complicates the belief in 'one god'). There is a debate among the Cao Dai as to which deity was the primary source of creation.

According to Cao Daism, history is divided into three major periods of divine revelation. During the first period God's truth was revealed to humanity through Laotse (Laozi) and figures associated with Buddhism, Confucianism and Taoism. The human agents of revelation during the second period were Buddha (Sakyamuni), Mohammed, Confucius, Jesus and Moses. The Cao Dai believe that their messages were corrupted because of the human frailty of the messengers and disciples; they also believe that these revelations were limited in scope, intended only to apply to the context in which the messengers lived.

Cao Daism sees itself as the product of the 'Third Alliance Between God and Man', the third and final revelation. Disciples believe that Cao Daism avoids the failures of the first two periods because it is based on divine truth as communicated through the spirits serving as messengers of doctrine. Spirits who have been in touch with the Cao Dai include deceased Cao Dai patriots, warriors, philosophers, poets and political leaders, as well as ordinary people. Among the contacted spirits who lived as Westerners are Joan of Arc, René Descartes, William Shakespeare, Victor Hugo, Louis Pasteur and Vladimir Ilyich Lenin. Because of his frequent appearances to Cao Dai mediums at the Phnom Penh mission, Victor Hugo was posthumously named the chief spirit of foreign missionary works.

Communication with the spirits is done in Vietnamese, Chinese, French and English and the methods of receiving messages from the spirits illustrate the influence of both East Asian and Western spiritualism. Sometimes a medium holds a pen or Chinese calligraphy brush. In the 1920s a wooden staff known as a *corbeille à bec* was used; mediums held one end while a crayon attached to the other wrote out the spirits' messages. The Cao Dai also use what is known as *pneumatographie*, in which a blank slip of paper is sealed in an envelope and hung above the altar; when the envelope is taken down, there is a message on the paper.

Most of Cao Daism's sacred literature consists of messages communicated to its leaders during séances held between 1925 and 1929. From 1927 to 1975 only official séances held at Tay Ninh were considered divinely ordained by the Cao Dai hierarchy, though dissident groups continued to hold séances that produced communications contradicting accepted doctrine.

The clergy is open to both men and women, but women are prevented from reaching the highest levels. When male and female officials of equal rank are serving in the same area, male clergy are in charge. In Cao Dai temples male and female disciples enter on opposite sides; women worship on the left, men on the right.

All Cao Dai temples observe four daily ceremonies, held at 6am, noon, 6pm and midnight. These rituals, during which dignitaries wear ceremonial dress, include offerings of incense, tea, alcohol, fruit and flowers. All Cao Dai altars have the 'divine eye' above them, which became the religion's official symbol after Ngo Minh Chieu saw it in a vision.

The Great Temple is built over nine levels, representing the nine steps to heaven; each level is marked by a pair of columns. At the far end of the sanctuary, eight plaster columns entwined with multicoloured dragons support a dome representing the heavens – as does the rest of the ceiling. Under the dome is a giant star-speckled blue globe with the 'divine eye' on it.

The largest of the seven chairs in front of the globe is reserved for the Cao Dai pope, a position that has remained unfilled since 1933. The next three chairs are for the three men responsible for the religion's law books. The remaining chairs are for the leaders of the three branches of Cao Daism, represented by the colours yellow, blue and red.

On both sides of the area between the columns are two pulpits similar in design to the *minbar* in mosques. During festivals the pulpits are used by officials to address the assembled worshippers. The upstairs balconies are used if the crowd overflows.

Up near the altar are barely discernible portraits of six figures important to Cao Daism: Sakyamuni (Siddhartha Gautama, the founder of Buddhism), Ly Thai Bach (Li Taibai, a fairy from Chinese mythology), Khuong Tu Nha (Jiang Taigong, a Chinese saint), Laozi (the founder of Taoism), Quan Cong (Guangong, Chinese God of War) and Quan Am (Guanyin, the Goddess of Mercy).

LONG HOA MARKET

Several kilometres south of the Cao Dai Holy See complex is **Long Hoa Market** (🕒 5am-6pm). This large market sells meat, food staples, clothing and pretty much everything else you would expect to find in a rural marketplace. Before reunification the Cao Dai sect had the right to collect taxes from the merchants here.

Sleeping & Eating

Hoa Binh Hotel (☎ 821 315; fax 822 345; 210 Đ 30 Thang 4; r 220,000-310,000d; 🗙) This is the main place in town, 5km from the Cao Dai Great Temple, where travellers stay if they do spend the night. It's a classic Russian-style concrete slab; rates include breakfast.

Anh Dao Hotel (☎ 827 306; 146 Đ 30/4; r 170,000-250,000đ) About 500m west of Hoa Binh Hotel, this place is old and rather nondescript, though the rates here also include a decent breakfast.

Both hotels have in-house restaurants, but there's cheaper and better Vietnamese food right next door to the Hoa Binh Hotel at **Thanh Thuy** (☎ 827 606; Đ 30 Thang 40; dishes 25,000-45,000đ). You won't find prices on the menu, but the cost is reasonable and portions are large.

If you're heading to Tay Ninh with your own wheels, one of the better restaurants to look for along Hwy 22 is **Kieu** (☎ 850 357; 9/32 Hwy 22; mains 12,000đ), around 5km from Cao Dai Temple towards HCMC. The food is cheap and good, and the brick kilns out the back are interesting to poke around in after lunch.

Getting There & Away

Tay Ninh is situated on Hwy 22 (Quoc Lo 22), 96km from HCMC. (The road passes through **Trang Bang,** the place where the famous photograph of a severely burnt young girl, screaming and running, was taken by a journalist during a US napalm attack, during the American War.) There are several Cao Dai temples along Hwy 22, including one (which was under construction in 1975) that was heavily damaged by the VC.

BUS

There are buses from HCMC to Tay Ninh that leave from the Tay Ninh bus station (Ben Xe Tay Ninh) in Tan Binh district and Mien Tay bus station in An Lac.

MOTORBIKE

As there's no public transportation to Cu Chi from Tay Ninh, you'll have to hire a motorbike in Tay Ninh. Look for *xe om* drivers in front of the hotels. It will probably cost you around US$5 for a return trip.

TAXI

An easy way to get to Tay Ninh is by chartered taxi, perhaps on a day trip that includes a stop in Cu Chi. An all-day return trip from HCMC to both should cost about US$40.

NUI BA DEN
☎ 066

Fifteen km northeast of Tay Ninh, **Nui Ba De** (Black Lady Mountain; admission adult/child 6000/2000đ) rises 850m above the rice paddies, corr cassava (manioc) and rubber plantations the surrounding countryside. Over the centuries Nui Ba Den has served as a shrine fo various peoples of the area, including th Khmer, Chams, Vietnamese and Chines and there are several interesting **cave temple** on the mountain. The summits of Nui B Den are much cooler than the rest of Ta Ninh province, most of which is only a fe dozen metres above sea level.

Nui Ba Den was used as a staging area b both the Viet Minh and the VC, and was th scene of fierce fighting during the Frenc and American Wars. At one time there wa a US Army firebase and relay station at th summit, which was later, ironically, defol ated and heavily bombed by US aircraft.

The name Black Lady Mountain is de rived from the legend of Huong, a youn woman who married her true love despit the advances of a wealthy Mandarin. Whil her husband was away doing military ser vice, she would visit a magical statue c Buddha at the mountain's summit. On day Huong was attacked by kidnappers bu preferring death to dishonour, she thre herself off a cliff. She then reappeared i the visions of a monk who lived on th mountain, and he told her story.

The hike from the base of the mountai to the main temple complex and back take about 1½ hours. Although steep in parts, it not a difficult walk – plenty of old wome in sandals make the journey to worship a the temple. Around the temple complex few stands sell snacks and drinks.

If you'd like more exercise, a walk to th summit and back takes about six hours. Th fastest, easiest way is via the **chair lift** (one-wa return adult 25,000/45,000đ, child 10,000/20,000đ) tha shuttles the pilgrims up and down the hil

At the base of the mountain there are lake and manicured gardens and, as with man such sacred sites in Asia, a mix of religio and tacky amusement park–style attraction paddle boats for hire; ceramic beaver tras bins; and a choo-choo tram car (ticket 1000đ) to save the weary a bit of walking.

Very few foreign tourists make it to th mountain, but it's a very popular place fo

Vietnamese people. Because of the crowds, visiting on Sunday or during a holiday or festival is a bad idea.

Sleeping & Eating

Nha Nghi Thuy Dong (☎ 624 204; bungalows 120,000d; A-frame platform tents 70,000d) If you get stuck having to overnight at Nui Ba Den, grotty A-frame bungalows and camping options are available here. Bungalows are situated about 500m inside the main entrance gate, on the lakeside. Each bungalow has a basic squat toilet, and showers are outside.

Tent accommodations have shared toilets and cold showers available for 500d; alternatively, you can shower for free at the nearby Trung Pagoda, where the monks will prepare you traditional vegetarian meals with a day's advance notice (the food is free, but a contribution is suggested).

Thuy Dong Restaurant (mains around 15,000d) is attached to the bungalow complex and has nice views of the lake. There are also a few nearby food stalls and kiosks selling cold drinks and souvenirs. Outside the main gate in the parking area, look for the stalls selling locally produced dried fruit and sweets made from coconuts and sugar cane.

Getting There & Away

There is no public transport to Nui Ba Den. If you're not travelling with your own wheels, the easiest way to reach the site is to take a *xe om* from Tay Ninh for around 50,000d.

ONE PILLAR PAGODA
☎ 08

The official name of this interesting pagoda is **Nam Thien Nhat Tru** (Chua Mot Cot Thu Duc; ☎ 896 780; 1/91 Đ Nguyen Du), but everyone calls it the One Pillar Pagoda of Thu Duc.

The One Pillar Pagoda of Thu Duc is modelled after Hanoi's One Pillar Pagoda, though the two structures are not identical. Hanoi's original pagoda was built in the 11th century, destroyed by the French and rebuilt by the Vietnamese in 1954; HCMC's version was constructed in 1958.

When Vietnam was partitioned in 1954, Buddhist monks and Catholic priests wisely fled south to avoid persecution and continued to practise their religion. One monk from Hanoi who travelled south in 1954 was Thich Tri Dung. Just after his arrival in

Saigon, Thich petitioned the South Vietnamese government for permission to construct a replica of Hanoi's famous One Pillar Pagoda. However, President Ngo Dinh Diem was a Catholic with little tolerance for Buddhist clergy and denied permission. Nevertheless, Thich and his supporters raised the funds and built the pagoda in defiance of the president's orders.

At one point the Diem government ordered the monks to tear down the temple, but they refused even though they were threatened with imprisonment for not complying. Faced with significant opposition, the government's dispute with the monks reached a standoff. However, the president's attempts to harass and intimidate the monks in a country that was 90% Buddhist did not go down well and ultimately contributed to Diem's assassination by his own troops in 1963.

During the American War the One Pillar Pagoda of Thu Duc was in possession of an extremely valuable plaque said to weigh 612kg. After liberation the government took it for 'safe-keeping' and brought it to Hanoi. However, none of the monks alive in Hanoi today could say just where it is.

The pagoda is in the Thu Duc district, about 15km northeast of central HCMC. Budget travellers cafés or mid-range travel agencies in HCMC (see p327) should be able to put together a customised tour to the pagoda or to arrange a car and driver for you.

CAN GIO
☎ 08

The only beach within the municipality of HCMC is at Can Gio, a low palm-fringed island, where the Saigon River meets the sea. The island was created by silt washing downstream, so the beach is hard-packed mud rather than the fine white sand sought by sun worshippers. Furthermore, the beach is rather exposed and lashed by strong winds. For these reasons Can Gio gets few visitors and the beach remains entirely undeveloped.

But before you scratch Can Gio off your list of places to visit, it's worth noting that the island does have a wild beauty, plus some good fresh seafood to sample. And, unlike the rest of HCMC, overpopulation is hardly a problem here (chiefly because the island lacks a fresh water supply).

The land here is only about 2m above sea level and the island is basically one big mangrove forest. The salty mud makes most forms of agriculture impossible, but aquaculture is another matter: the most profitable business here is shrimp farming. The hard-packed mud beach also teems with clams and other sea life, which island residents dig up to eat or sell. There is also a small salt industry. Sea water is diverted into shallow ponds and is left to evaporate until a white layer of salt can be harvested. Can Gio has a small port where fishing boats can dock, but the shallow water prevents any large ships from dropping anchor here.

Can Gio is best visited as a day trip, but those wishing to overnight here can arrange to stay at an 'eco-resort' run by **Phu Tho Tourist** (☎ 08-894 008; luhanhphutho@hcm.fpt.vn; 79 Đ Hoa Binh, District 11, HCMC), a nicer alternative to the dumpy accommodation in town.

Sights
CAN GIO MANGROVE PARK
This 70,000-hectare **mangrove forest** (Lam Vien Can Gio; ☎ 874 3069; fax 874 3068; admission 10,000d) was formed by sediment deposits from the Dong Nai and Long Tau Rivers. The **Can Gio Museum**, also in the park, has displays on flora and fauna, as well as exhibits relating to local war history. Near the museum is an area where hundreds of monkeys live. Feeding the monkeys is popular with tourists, but be *very* careful with your belongings: the monkeys here are well practised at swiping bags, pens and sunglasses, and the chances of retrieval are next to none.

CAO DAI TEMPLE
Though much smaller than the Cao Dai Great Temple at Tay Ninh, Can Gio boasts a **Cao Dai temple** of its own. It's near the market and is easy to find.

CAN GIO MARKET
Can Gio has a large **market**, which is made very conspicuous by some rather powerful odours. Seafood and salt are definitely the local specialities. The vegetables, rice and fruit are all imported by boat from HCMC.

WAR MEMORIAL & CEMETERY
Adjacent to the local shrimp hatchery is a large and conspicuous **cemetery and war memorial** (Nghia Trang Liet Si Rung Sac) 2km from Can Gio Market. Like all such sites in Vietnam, the praise for bravery and patriotism goes entirely to the winning side and there is nothing said about the losers. Indeed, all of the former war cemeteries containing remains of South Vietnamese soldiers were bulldozed after liberation – a fact that still causes much bitterness.

CAN GIO BEACH
The southern side of the island faces the sea, creating a beachfront nearly 10km long. Unfortunately a good deal of it is inaccessible because it's been fenced off by shrimp farmers and clam diggers. Nevertheless, there is a point about 4km west of the market where a dirt road leads off the main highway to HCMC, heading towards the beach. The road is easily distinguished by the telephone poles and wires running alongside it. At the beach you'll find a handful of stalls selling food and drinks.

The surface of the beach is as hard as concrete and it is possible to ride a motorbike on it; however, this is not recommended because it damages the local ecology. While the beach may seem dead at first glance it swarms with life just below the surface as the breathing holes in the mud suggest and you can hear the crunch of tiny clam shells as you stroll along. The water here is extremely shallow and you can walk far from shore, but take care – there's a good deal of inhospitable and well-armed sea life in these shallow waters. Stingrays, stonefish and sea urchins are just some of the local residents who can and will retaliate if you step on them.

The hills of the Vung Tau Peninsula are easily visible on a clear day.

Getting There & Away
Can Gio is about 60km southeast of central HCMC, and the fastest way to make the journey is by car or motorbike (about two hours).

There's a ferry crossing (motorbike/car 2000/10,000d) 15km from HCMC at Binh Chanh (Cat Lai), a former US naval base. The road is paved all the way from HCMC to Can Gio. Once you get past the ferry there is very little traffic and both sides of the road are lined with lush mangrove forests.

BUU LONG MOUNTAIN

Since various tourist pamphlets will tell you that **Buu Long Mountain** (admission 5000d) is the 'Halong Bay of the south', you'd be forgiven for thinking that it must be nothing short of stunningly beautiful. In truth Buu Long Mountain is no Halong Bay, but it's a pretty and peaceful place to make a day trip to escape the crowds of HCMC.

The summit is 60m above the car park, and there are several good walking trails. The top of the mountain is marked by a pagoda, from where you can look down and clearly see **Long An** (Dragon Lake). There is some lovely countryside scenery, good bird-watching and sweeping views of the rural farms along the Dong Nai River.

You can buy cold drinks and noodles at a few refreshment shops, but we recommend trying out the food at the small **vegetarian restaurant** (meals around 8000d) at the top of the mountain.

Buu Long Mountain is 32km from central HCMC and is best reached by car or motorbike. It's 2km off the main highway after crossing the bridge that marks the border between HCMC municipality and Dong Nai province.

TRI AN FALLS

An 8m-high and 30m-wide cascade on the Song Be (Be River), the **Tri An Falls** are awesome in the late autumn, when the river's flow is at its greatest. Tri An Falls are in Dong Nai province, 36km from Bien Hoa and 68km northeast of HCMC (via Thu Dau Mot).

Further upstream is **Tri An Reservoir** (Ho Tri An), a large artificial lake fed from the forest highlands around Dalat and created by the Tri An Dam. Completed in the early 1980s with Soviet assistance, the dam and its adjoining hydroelectric station supplies the bulk of HCMC's electric power.

VUNG TAU

☎ 064 / pop 195,400

Vung Tau drones with bass-thumping action on the weekends as visitors from HCMC motor into town; weekdays, however, are blissfully dead. Vung Tau's beaches are easily reached from HCMC, making them a favourite of that city's residents since French colonists first began coming here around 1890.

Known under the French as Cap St Jacques – so-named by Portuguese mariners in honour of their patron saint – Vung Tau is a commercialised beach resort on a peninsula jutting into the South China Sea, about 128km southeast of HCMC (via Bien Hoa). The business of oil-drilling here means the azure horizon is marred by oil tankers, and the population flecked with expats.

The beaches here aren't Vietnam's best, nor is the water pristine due to pollution from oil-drilling, but Vung Tau is an easy, fast beach foray out of HCMC. Beachgoers looking for a tropical-holiday feel might do better making the three-hour trip to beautiful Mui Ne Beach (p283).

Orientation

Vung Tau's peninsula is punctuated by Small Mountain (Nui Nho) to the south and Big Mountain (Nui Lon) in the north. Back Beach (Bai Sau) stretches for kilometres, with a wide, sandy beach and a long strip of guesthouses and hotels. You'll find the downtown action at Front Beach (Bai Truoc), but no beach. If you're looking for a quiet, pebbly beach, head for tranquil Mulberry Beach (Bai Dau).

Information

Ba Ria-Vung Tau Tourist (☎ 856 445; 33-35 Đ Tran Hung Dao). Pick up maps or book tours here. There's also a Vietnam Airlines office next door.
Gossip Internet Café (☎ 818 761; tttt@hcm.vnn .vn; 15A Đ Ly Tu Trong) Fast connections and lots of machines.
International SOS (☎ 858 776; Đ Le Ngoc Han; consultations US$55-65; ☼ 24hr)
Le Loi Hospital (☎ 832 667; 22 Đ Le Loi)
Main post office (8 Đ Hoang Dieu) Located at the ground level of the Petrovietnam Towers building.
Vietcombank (☎ 852 024; 27-29 Đ Tran Hung Dao) Exchanges cash, travellers cheques. Gives credit card advances.

Sights & Activities

Atop **Small Mountain**, a **giant Jesus** (admission free, parking 2000d; ☼ 7.30-11.30am & 1.30-5pm) waits with arms outstretched to embrace the South China Sea – showing off unsightly swallows' nests in His armpits. At His foot is a sad collection of monkeys and snakes in cramped cages.

The nearby 1910 **lighthouse** (admission 2000d; ☼ 7am-5pm) boasts a spectacular 360-degree

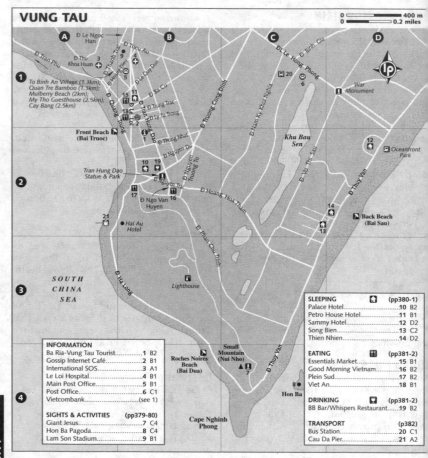

VUNG TAU

```
0                    400 m
0              0.2 miles
```

INFORMATION
Ba Ria-Vung Tau Tourist..............1 B2
Gossip Internet Café....................2 B1
International SOS..........................3 A1
Le Loi Hospital.............................4 B1
Main Post Office...........................5 B1
Post Office....................................6 C1
Vietcombank.........................(see 1)

SIGHTS & ACTIVITIES   (pp379-80)
Giant Jesus....................................7 C4
Hon Ba Pagoda.............................8 C4
Lam Son Stadium..........................9 B1

SLEEPING   (pp380-1)
Palace Hotel.................................10 B2
Petro House Hotel.......................11 B1
Sammy Hotel...............................12 D2
Song Bien.....................................13 C2
Thien Nhien.................................14 D2

EATING   (pp381-2)
Essentials Market........................15 B1
Good Morning Vietnam...............16 B2
Plein Sud......................................17 B2
Viet An...18 B1

DRINKING   (pp381-2)
BB Bar/Whispers Restaurant......19 B2

TRANSPORT   (p382)
Bus Station..................................20 C1
Cau Da Pier.................................21 A2

view sans imprisoned animals. From the
ferry dock on Đ Ha Long, take a sharp right
on the alley north of the Hai Au Hotel, then
roll on up the hill.

Pagodas dot the length of Đ Ha Long,
but prim **Hon Ba pagoda** sits offshore on an
islet – *the* place to be if low tide coincides
with sunrise.

Along Front Beach, heading towards
Mulberry Beach, you'll find café-bars on
the hillside facing the ocean. On weekends
you stand the best chance of hearing local
amateurs belting out the ballads *du jour*,
backed by live bands. It's like karaoke,
only…good.

Oh, one more thing: where else in Vietnam do you think you're gonna see **greyhound**

racing (Lam Son Stadium; ☎ 807 309; www.sesracing.com;
15 Đ Le Loi; admission 20,000d; ☆ 7-10.30pm Sat).

Sleeping

During weekends and holidays, Vung Tau'
hundred or so hotels can get heavily booked
but usually you can find a room.

BACK BEACH

There's a string of older mid-range hotels
on the western side of Small Mountain i
you can't find a room on Back beach. The
following places are across the street from
the sand and South China Sea.

Thien Nhien (☎ 853 481; 145A Đ Thuy Van; d 100,000
200,000d; ☒) This airy, friendly guesthouse is
simple and very clean; some rooms have

Ho Chi Minh statue, Ho Chi Minh City (p319)

JERRY ALEXANDER

Snoozing *cyclo* rider, Ho Chi
Minh City (p319)

CRAIG PERSHOUSE

RICHARD I'ANSON

Sugar-cane vendors in a Ho Chi Minh
City market (p362)

Apocalypse Now (p359), Ho Chi Minh City

GREG ELMS

Cao Dai Great Temple (p373), Tay Ninh

Restaurant kitchen, Ho Chi Minh City (p352)

Cao Dai worshippers, Tay Ninh
(p373)

Dried shrimp, market in Cholon (p362), Ho Chi Minh City

THE AUTHOR'S CHOICE

Binh An Village (☎ 510 016; binhanvillagevt@hcm.vnn.vn; 1 Đ Tran Phu; US$175-290; ✖ ✉) Looking to splurge in Vung Tau? Do it in serious style. There are only five bungalow suites on this serene oceanfront wedge of paradise, each of which is carefully and lavishly decorated with Asian antiques, sliding screens and unique layouts. One has a kitchen, another has an outdoor bathroom and all come with luxuries like airy, sumptuously furnished terraces and DVD players. There are two swimming pools, one ocean-fed and one freshwater, both within spitting distance of the sea.

If these rates break your budget, you could stop by for a meal instead; the cool, open-air **restaurant** (set meals US$15-38) features live jazz on Friday and Saturday nights, and also offers à la carte international and Vietnamese cuisine.

---

lconies, air-con and ocean views, and it's
a side street off the main beach drag.
Song Bien (☎ 523 311; 131A Đ Thuy Van; d 120,000-
0,000d; ✖) Chinese-style décor brightens
is very clean and comfortable place;
oms in front have big ocean views, and
ere's a shared terrace on the top floor.
Sammy Hotel (☎ 854 755; sammyhotel@hcm.vnn
; 157 Đ Thuy Van; r/ste US$60/115; ✖ ▢) Easily
e fanciest place this side of Small Moun-
in, Sammy has an in-house Chinese res-
urant and comfortable rooms with all the
immings. There's a pool at the oceanfront
rk across the street. None of the ocean-
ew rooms have balconies, oddly, though
ountain-view rooms do.

RONT BEACH
tro House Hotel (☎ 852 014; petro.htl@hcm.vnn.vn;
Đ Tran Hung Dao; r/ste US$45/90; ✖ ▢ ✉) De-
ite the unappealing name, Petro House
s an elegant feel to it. Rooms here are
good deal for the price; the hotel has a
isiness centre, a gym and a pool table in
e bar. The in-house French restaurant Ma
aison serves guests 24 hours a day, and
onguests can use the pool for US$5.
Palace Hotel (☎ 856 411; palacevt@hcm.vnn.vn; 1 Đ
uyen Trai; r/ste US$40/95; ✖ ▢ ✉) This cen-
ally located place is well established and
mfortable. Perks include traditional folk
usic performances, tennis courts and well-
pointed rooms. Rates include breakfast.

ULBERRY BEACH
y Tho Guesthouse (☎ 832 035; 47 Đ Tran Phu; s & d
,000-120,000d) The warm couple running this
iesthouse serves delicious, cheap, home-
oked meals on the cosy terrace, and of-
rs free laundry, bicycle hire and friendly
nversation. It has very simple but homey
oms, some of which have squat toilets.

Eating & Drinking
The road along Back Beach, Đ Thuy Van, is crammed with *com* shops and seafood restaurants.

FRONT BEACH
BB Bar/Whispers Restaurant (☎ 856 028; 13-15 Nguyen Trai; ◷ until midnight) Local expats start their evenings at the downtown BB Bar/ Whispers Restaurant with well-prepared Western food and pool tables in a noisy, lively setting.

Plein Sud (☎ 511 570; 152A Đ Ha Long; mains 25,000-150,000d; ▢) Feed your Mediterranean food cravings here. With home-smoked fish and meat, an authentic Italian wood-fired pizza oven and tapas, Plein Sud offers a fixed menu supplemented with rotating specials and freshly baked, home-made French bread. There's a lovely terrace lined with banana trees and even a pool table and a bar.

Viet An (☎ 853 735; 34 Đ Quang Trung; mains 35,000d) On the patio lush with real and fake greenery and a fish pond, this is the place to treat yourself to good halal Indian food.

Good Morning Vietnam (☎ 856 959; 6 Đ Hoang Hoa Tham; mains 40,000d) One more outpost in the coastal chain, this eatery serves up reliably excellent Italian food for lunch and dinner only.

Essentials (☎ 510 099; 6 Đ Le Quy Don; ◷ 7.30am-9pm) Find imported picnic victuals here, from cereals to frozen veal; they also deliver.

MULBERRY BEACH
Mulberry Beach's main road has several good seafood places down on the water.
Cay Bang (☎ 838 522; 69 Đ Tran Phu; mains 40,000d; ◷ 11am-10pm) This local favourite, serving fresh seafood, overlooks the water and is a festive place on weekends.

AROUND HO CHI
MINH CITY

Quan Tre Bamboo (7 Đ Tran Phu; mains 40,000d) Go to this place if you're hankering for lobster or a cocktail with a view of the giant Mary with Baby Jesus statue, best enjoyed from the upstairs terrace.

Getting There & Away

From Mien Dong bus station in HCMC, air-con minibuses (25,000d, two hours, 128km) leave for Vung Tau throughout the day until around 4.30pm. From the **Vung Tau bus station** (192A Đ Nam Ky Khoi Nghia) to Mulberry Beach or Back Beach, a *xe om* should cost around 10,000d.

Should convenience outweigh cost, catch a **Vina Express hydrofoil** (HCMC ☎ 829 7892, Vung Tau ☎ 856 530) to Vung Tau (US$10, 80 minutes) at Bach Dang jetty in HCMC. Boats leave roughly every two hours starting at 6.30am, but check in HCMC for the latest schedule. In Vung Tau the boat leaves from Cau Da pier, opposite the Hai Au Hotel.

Getting Around

Vung Tau is easily traversed on two wheels. Guesthouses can arrange bicycle hire; motorbikes cost US$4 to US$10 per day. Or just make eye contact with that *cyclo* or *xe om* driver on the corner.

CON DAO ISLANDS

☎ 064 / pop 1,650

The Con Dao Archipelago is a remarkable group of 15 islands and islets, 180km (97 nautical miles) south of Vung Tau in the South China Sea.

The largest island in the group, with a total land area of 20 sq km, is the partly forested Con Son Island: ringed with bays, bathing beaches and coral reefs. Con Son Island is also known by its Europeanised Malay name, Iles Poulo Condore (Pulau Kun-dur), which means 'Island of the Squashes'. Local products include teak and pine wood, fruit (grapes, coconuts and mangoes), cashews, pearls, sea turtles, lobster and coral.

For the intrepid traveller, Con Dao offers a rich – if tragic – history (p383), as well as ample pursuits for nature lovers and beach bums. Roughly 80% of the land area in the island chain is part of Con Dao National Park, and there are plenty of great hiking opportunities, as well as deserted beaches.

Con Dao is one of those rare places in Vietnam where there are virtually no struc-

tures over two storeys, and where the traveller's experience is almost hassle-free. There even no need to bargain at the local market Owing to the relatively high cost and th inaccessibility of the islands, mass touris has thankfully been kept to a minimum.

Con Dao is Vietnam's most importa **sea turtle** nesting ground, and since 1995 th World Wide Fund for Nature (WWF) h been working with local park rangers a long-term monitoring programme. Du ing nesting season (March to Septembe the park sets up ranger stations to rescu threatened nests and move them to the sa haven of hatcheries.

Other interesting sea life around Co Dao includes the **dugong**, a rare and seldom seen marine mammal in the same fami as the manatee. Dugongs live as far nor as Japan, and as far south as the subtrop cal coasts of Australia. Their numbers hav been on a steady decline, and increasing efforts are being made to protect the adorable creatures. Major threats includ coastal road development, which caus the destruction of shallow-water beds seagrass, the dugongs' staple diet.

These days most visitors to Con Son a package-tour groups of former VC soldie who were imprisoned on the island. Th Vietnamese government generously subs dises these jaunts as a show of gratitude f their sacrifice. It's safe to say that foreig tourists are few and far between, but as th infrastructure and access improves, this

CON DAO ISLANDS

0 — 6 km
0 — 4 miles

To Vung Tau (177km)

Dong Bac Point

Tre Nho Island
Bai Nho
Tre Lon Island
Con Son National Park
Con Son Island
Ba Island
Bai Dat Doc
Bay Canh Island
Con Son
Ben Dam
Bai Nhat
Cau Island
Ca Map Point
Vung Island
Bai An Hai
Trac Island
Tho Island
SOUTH CHINA SEA

LOVE FOR SALE

The number of Vietnamese women who have, especially in recent years, married foreign men is astounding. Vietnamese women are increasingly being swept off their feet by foreigners and, in many cases, swept away from their homeland to live with their husbands.

Plenty of women have gone to live in Western countries, but Vietnamese brides abound in Asia as well. Perhaps the largest number of Vietnamese wives outside of Vietnam is in Taiwan. In contrast with the thousands who've married Taiwanese men, until recently the number of Vietnamese men married to Taiwanese women could probably have been counted on one hand. But no more, thanks to an entrepreneurial trend in Baria province.

According to local news reports there is a growing number of overweight Taiwanese women, many of whom are considered 'unmarriageable' at home in face-conscious Taiwan, marrying Vietnamese men. So what's the catch? Why would a slender Vietnamese guy want to marry a woman three times his weight, with whom he probably cannot communicate anyhow? The answer: money.

Matchmakers have turned this development into big business, and bridal brokers are making the deals based on the actual size and weight of the prospective brides! Currently, the going rate the Taiwanese bride's family pays to the family of the Vietnamese groom falls between 1.2 to 1.8 million dong per kilo, and the number of such marriages is on the increase. So much for the old adage: this is one case where size *does* matter!

ound to change. Those who make the effort to go now are not likely to regret it.

The best time to visit Con Dao is from November to February. The rainy season lasts from June to September, but there are also northeast and southwest monsoons in autumn that can bring heavy winds. In November 1997 typhoon Linda did a number here: 300 fishing boats were lost, reefs were ripped out and the forests flattened. September and October are the hottest months, though even then the cool island breezes make Con Dao relatively comfortable when compared with HCMC or Vung Tau.

History

occupied at various times by the Khmer, Malays and Vietnamese, Con Son Island also served as an early base for European commercial ventures in the region. The first recorded European arrival was a ship of Portuguese mariners in 1560. The British East India Company maintained a fortified trading post here from 1702 to 1705 – an experiment that ended when the English on the island were massacred in a revolt by the Macassar soldiers they had recruited on the Indonesian island of Sulawesi.

Con Son Island has a strong political and cultural history, and an all-star line-up of Vietnamese revolutionary heroes (many streets are named after them) were incarcerated here. Under the French, Con Son

was used as a major prison for opponents of French colonialism, earning a reputation for the routine mistreatment and torture of prisoners. In 1954 the island was taken over by the South Vietnamese government, which continued to take advantage of its remoteness to hold opponents of the government (including students) in horrifying conditions. During the American War the South Vietnamese were joined here by US forces.

Information

The park **headquarters** (29 Đ Vo Thi Sau) is a good place to get information, although hours tend to be spotty. Since the military controls access to parts of the national park, stop here first to have staff direct you to possible island excursions and hikes. Some hiking trails have interpretive signage in English and Vietnamese. The headquarters also has an exhibition hall with well-presented displays on the diversity of local forest and marine life, threats to the local environment, and local conservation activities.

Sights & Activities
CON DAO NATIONAL PARK

From March to November it's possible to do a beautiful and leisurely two-hour **trek** starting from near the airport runway, but you'll definitely need a local guide to do this (about US$6 for several hours). The walk leads through thick forest and mangroves, and past a hill-top stream to **Bamboo Lagoon** (Dam Tre). This spot is stunning and there's good snorkelling in the bay. You could even consider arranging for a boat to come and pick you up.

CON SON ISLAND

Con Son town is a sleepy seafront spot that would make a perfect location for a period film. All three of the town's hotels are on Đ Ton Duc Thang, along a strip of forlorn single-storey French villas (most are abandoned and in disrepair, but nonetheless photogenic). Nearby is the local **market**, which is busiest between 7am and 8am.

The main sights on Con Son Island are a museum, a prison, prison cages and a cemetery. If you visit the museum first you can buy a ticket for 35,000d that will get you a guided tour of all four – very good value.

The **Revolutionary Museum** (7-11am & 1.30-5pm Mon-Sat) is next to Saigon Con Dao Hotel and has exhibits on Vietnamese resistance to the French, communist opposition to the Republic of Vietnam, and the treatment of political prisoners. There are also some 'nature' displays with some awfully embalmed animals. The most bizarre is a monkey sitting with his legs crossed and smoking a cigarette.

Phu Hai Prison, a short walk from the museum, is the largest of the 11 prisons on the island. Built in 1862, the prison houses several enormous detention buildings, one with about 100 shackled and emaciated mannequins that are all too lifelike. Equally eerie are the empty solitary cells with ankle shackles (the decree on the walls in Vietnamese means 'no killing fleas' – prisoners were not allowed to dirty the walls).

The notorious **Tiger Cages** were built by the French in the 1940s. From 1957 to 1961 nearly 2000 political prisoners were confined in these tiny cells. Here there are 120 chambers with ceiling bars, where guards could watch down on the prisoners like tigers in a zoo, and another 60 solariums with no roof at all.

Over the course of four decades of war, some 20,000 people were killed on Con Son and 1994 of their graves can be seen at **Hang Duong Cemetery**. Sadly, only 700 of these graves bear the name of the victims. Vietnam's most famous heroine, Vo Thi Sau

(1933–1952), was the first woman execut (by a firing squad) on Con Son, on 23 Jan ary 1952. Today's pilgrims come to bu incense at her tomb, and make offerings mirrors and combs (symbolic because s died so young). In the distance behind t cemetery you'll see a huge **monument** sy bolising three giant sticks of incense.

Phu Binh Camp is not part of the ma tour, but is another prison camp that c be visited on Con Son. Built in 1971 by t Americans, this one has 384 chambers a was known as Camp 7 until 1973, when closed following evidence of torture. Aft the Paris Agreements in 1973, the name w changed to Phu Binh Camp.

BEACHES & ISLANDS

On Con Son there are several good beach worth finding. Inquire at the hotels abo snorkelling gear rental for about 50,00(per day.

Bai Dat Doc is one nice beach with beds seagrass and the possibility of sighting du ongs. **Bai Nho** is a quiet and secluded beac but getting there involves trekking over (: around) some large boulders.

Bai Nhat is small and very nice, thoug it's exposed only during low tide. **Bai An H** looks nice, but there are a good numb of fishing boats moored nearby, and a fe too many sandflies. **Bai Loi Voi** is OK as we and shallow, but there can be a fair bit rubbish and lots of sea shells.

The best beaches of all are on the small islands, such as the beautiful white-san beach on **Tre Lon**.

Perhaps the best all-round island to vis is **Bay Canh**, which has lovely beaches, ol growth forest, mangroves, coral reefs (goc snorkelling at low tide) and sea turtles (se sonal). There is a fantastic two-hour walk t a functioning French-built **lighthouse**.

Sleeping

ATC (830 666; atccd@vol.vnn.vn; 16B Đ Ton Duc Thar villa r US$18-20, stilt house r US$25) This family-ru inn is set in a lovely four-room French vil built in 1929. It's decorated with rattan fu niture, and the landscaping features sto walkways through manicured gardens. The are also two attractive stilt houses on sit both relocated here from Hoa Binh in th north. Rates include breakfast. Lunch an dinner fare can also be recommended here

Saigon Con Dao Hotel (☎ 830 366; fax 830 567; 8 Đ Ton Duc Thang; r US$20-30; ❄) Run by Saigon Tourist, this place is just up the street from ATC and is also built around a few old French villas. Inquire at the Saigon Tourist office on Đ Le Thanh Ton in HCMC (p327), which usually offers reasonably priced package tours to the island.

Phi Yen Hotel (☎ 830 168; fax 830 428; r 180,000-22,000d; ❄) This basic mini-hotel has some rooms with partial sea views.

Getting There & Away

With its newly upgraded airport, Con Son Island is now accessible via small plane. At the time of publication, Vasco (Vietnam Air Services Company) had begun offering even weekly flights (one way US$38) between Con Son and HCMC.

You can also still travel to Con Son Island by Russian military helicopter (one way US$75, twice weekly) operated by Vietnam Airlines. However, you must book as far in advance as possible to get a reservation, and even then you may be bumped from your flight if one of the top brass needs your seat.

Getting Around

TO/FROM THE AIRPORT

The tiny Con Son airport is about 15km from the town centre, so it's advisable to book your hotel ahead and arrange to be met at the airport. Otherwise, try a motorbike taxi or a shared taxi.

BICYCLE

Several of the main sites on Con Son, such as the Revolution Museum and Phu Hai Prison, are within walking distance of town, but to get further afield a bicycle is ideal. If you can't bring your own (recommended), all of the hotels rent bikes for about US$2 per day. There are excellent coastal cycling routes such as from town to Bai Nhat and onto Ben Dam), some nice gradual ups and downs and, thankfully, very little motor traffic.

BOAT

If you want to explore the islands by boat, hire one from the national park office. A 2-person boat costs around 1,000,000d per day, which means short of gathering some fellow travellers to share the cost, it's probably not worth the expense. However,

with the advent of fixed-wing flights arriving regularly from HCMC and a bit more tourist traffic, cheaper options may be available when you visit – inquire locally.

LONG HAI
☎ 064

Mass tourism has turned Vung Tau into something of a weekend circus, and many travellers crave a less-commercialised seaside retreat within a couple of hours' drive of HCMC. The fishing village of Long Hai, 30km northeast of Vung Tau, is one such place, but can really only be recommended if you aren't interested in meeting many other Western travellers. Long Hai has little to offer besides its rustic beach and local flavour – which might be all you need. If you require nightlife (or, well, daylife), head to Mui Ne instead (p283).

Backpacker cafés in HCMC can organise trips here, and it's also easy enough to travel to independently.

Sights & Activities

The western end of Long Hai's beach is where fishing boats moor and is therefore none too clean. However, the eastern end is attractive, with a reasonable amount of white sand and palm trees. Some of the nicest municipal beach is in front of Guesthouse 298. You can rent beach chairs here for 10,000d.

After the Tet holiday, Long Hai hosts an annual major **fishermen's pilgrimage festival**, where hundreds of boats come from afar to worship at **Mo Co Temple**.

Apart from the beaches, there are several sites in the area well worth exploring. At Minh Dam, 5km from Long Hai, there are **caves** with historical connections to the Franco–Viet Minh and American Wars. Nearby there is a **mountain-top temple** with great panoramic views of the coastline.

Twenty km away at Dia Dao there are **underground tunnels** (similar, but on a smaller scale, to those at Cu Chi) dating from the American War.

If you are heading to/from Hwy 1, north of Long Hai, a less-travelled route is via the **hot springs** at Binh Chau, just 60km away from Long Hai. There are also plenty of other beaches to seek out as you make your way north or south along the coastal Rte 55.

You could also treat yourself to a day at **Anoasis Beach Resort** (admission weekday/weekend

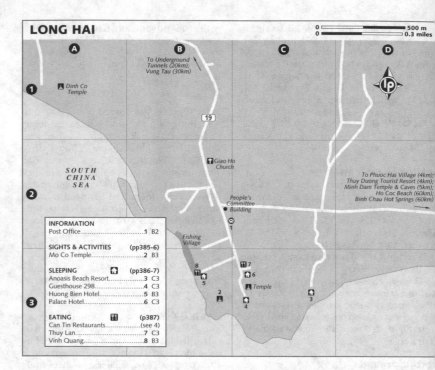

LONG HAI

To Underground
Tunnels (20km);
Vung Tau (30km)

*Dinh Co
Temple*

*Giao Ho
Church*

*SOUTH
CHINA
SEA*

To Phuoc Hai Village (4km);
Thuy Duong Tourist Resort (4km);
Minh Dam Temple & Caves (5km);
Ho Coc Beach (60km);
Binh Chau Hot Springs (60km)

*People's
Committee
Building*

*Fishing
Village*

Temple

INFORMATION	
Post Office	1 B2
SIGHTS & ACTIVITIES	(pp385–6)
Mo Co Temple	2 B3
SLEEPING	(pp386–7)
Anoasis Beach Resort	3 C3
Guesthouse 298	4 C3
Huong Bien Hotel	5 B3
Palace Hotel	6 C3
EATING	(p387)
Can Tin Restaurants	(see 4)
Thuy Lan	7 C3
Vinh Quang	8 B3

US$6/10). The tropically landscaped grounds of this luxury resort were once home to another of Emperor Bao Dai's villas. Day passes entitle nonguests to full use of the recreational facilities, which include a swimming pool, tennis courts, billiards and ping-pong tables and a lovely stretch of private beach.

Sleeping

BUDGET

Palace Hotel (☎ 868 364; d 140,000d) Flanked by frangipani trees, the decaying grandeur of this place, located on the corner of Rte 19 and the road past Thuy Lan (p387), is spookily appealing. Enormous rooms are fan-only and a bit musty but worth a look, with wide windows looking down the palatial terraced stairs.

Huong Bien Hotel (☎ 868 430; Rte 19; bungalows 120,000-180,000d; ✖) Down a signposted dirt driveway off the main drag, Huong Bien has simple concrete bungalows among palms and casuarinas. Most have private bathroom and fan, some have air-con, and all nestle right on the beach.

Guesthouse 298 (☎ 868 316; dead-end of Rte 1 d 100,000-180,000d; ✖) This guesthouse is ru by the navy, which may help explain it prime beach-front location. Rooms here ar clean and comfortable, with hot water; th cheapest rooms are fan-only.

MID-RANGE

Thuy Duong Tourist Resort (☎ 886 215; fax 886 18 bungalows US$20-30, hotel r US$35-60; ✖ 💻) A larg complex in Phuoc Hai village, about 4kr from Long Hai, this vast resort sprawls ou on both sides of the road. Hotel rates in clude breakfast; bungalow rates don't. Tr to avoid the beach bungalows facing th noisy cafés on the beach. Day use of th clean, attractive beach costs 15,000d.

TOP END

Anoasis Beach Resort (☎ 868 227; www.anoasisreso .com.vn; bungalows US$175-250, villas US$340; ✖ 💻) One of Vietnam's loveliest beachsid retreats, this stylish boutique resort is th brainchild of French-Vietnamese helicopte pilot Anoa Dussol-Perran and her husbanc Anoasis offers cosy wooden cottages sprea ut over the landscaped property, and it has beautiful private beach. Recreational opportunities include cycling, fishing, tennis nd, of course, massage.

All rates include a full continental breakfast. Weekend rates are slightly higher than he weekday rates listed above, but discounts re offered for stays of two nights or more.

ating

There's a cluster of good beachside restaurnts called **Can Tin 1**, **2** and **3** (mains around 0,000d) near Guesthouse 298. Opposite the 'alace Hotel, **Thuy Lan** (meals 12,000d) is also ood (and clean), as is the seaside **Vinh Quang** meals 12,000d), near the Huong Bien Hotel.

Getting There & Around

Long Hai is 124km from HCMC and takes bout two hours to reach by car. The 30km oad between Vung Tau and Long Hai is ot served by public transport; a *xe om* ride hould cost around 45,000d.

Motorbike-taxi drivers hang around all he likely tourist spots in the area.

LOC AN BEACH

☎ 064

Heading northeast along the coast from Long Hai to Binh Chau, there's a turn-off onto Rte 328. It's 10km from the turn-off to **Ho Tram Beach**. This beach itself is disappointing, but bout half-way along, there's a right-hand urn. Take this road to a beautiful, seldom-visited beach at **Ben Cat–Loc An**.

Along this road is the tidy **Loc An Resort** (☎ 886 377; locanresort@hcm.vnn.vn; d 190,000-440,000d; 🖧 🖳), a lovely place on a lagoon separating it from the palm-shaded beach. Boats huttle guests to the beach and back for free. The restaurant has a pool table, the place is potless and breakfast is included.

At the fork in the road, there's a sign eading to **Thuy Hoang** (☎ 874 223; bungalows 50,000d; 🖧), which consists of small A-rame beach bungalows. It has an indoor-outdoor restaurant that serves good locally caught seafood and cold beer.

HO COC BEACH

☎ 064

About 45km northeast of Long Hai is the emote and beautiful Ho Coc Beach. It's still very undeveloped area, though the weekends bring crowds of Vietnamese tourists.

The area around the beach is part of an 11,000-hectare rainforest that was designated a nature reserve in 1975. Most of the larger wildlife was exterminated or else relocated for safety reasons (most of the elephants were sent to Thailand), but plenty of birds and monkeys can be spotted in the forest. Guides for the walking trails can be hired for about 50,000d a day. Inquire at Hang Duong Ho Coc (below).

Sleeping & Eating

There are only a few accommodation choices right at the beach, all of which have decent adjoining restaurants serving good seafood.

Saigon-Ho Coc Eco Resort (☎ 791 036; fax 878 175; bungalows 130,000-300,000d) Though it's unclear what's 'eco' about them, these beachfront bamboo bungalows with simple private bathrooms are small and sweet. All rates include a free ticket to Binh Chau Hot Springs, with a 10% discount on mudbaths.

Khu Du Lich Bien Ho Coc (☎ 878 175; fax 871 130; bungalows 120,000d) Each of these five little wooden A-frame bungalows has an attached bathroom with cold water.

Hang Duong Ho Coc (☎ 878 145; fax 873 878; dm 50,000d; d 120,000-160,000d) About 50m south down the beach from Khu Du Lich Bien is this resort with masses of cosy wooden cottages. Rooms have fans and an attached cold-water bathroom.

Getting There & Away

There's no public transport out here, but some of the budget cafés in HCMC offer appealing day and overnight trips to Ho Coc. **Saigon Tourist** (☎ 08-829 8914; www.saigontourist.net; 49 Đ Le Thanh Ton) puts together overnight or multiday trips to Ho Coc that include a visit to Binh Chau Hot Springs Resort (see below). This also makes for a good (but very long) day trip on a motorbike. The 10km unsealed but OK road to Ho Coc takes you through the forest of the local nature reserve.

BINH CHAU HOT SPRINGS

☎ 064

About 150km from HCMC, and 60km northeast of Long Hai, is **Binh Chau Hot Springs** (Suoi Khoang Nong Binh Chau; admission 15,000d). **Binh Chau Hot Springs Resort** (☎ 871 130; www.saigonbinhchauecoresort.com; r US$20-267) offers accommodation and restaurants, as well as massage, mudbaths and soaking facilities.

SPRATLY SPAT

The **Paracel Islands** (Quan Dao Hoang Sa), 300km east of Danang, and the **Spratly Islands** (Quan Dao Truong Sa), 475km southeast of Nha Trang, seem likely to be the source of future conflict between all the nations surrounding the South China Sea.

Several of the Paracel Islands, which historically have been only sporadically occupied, were seized by China in 1951. In the 1960s a few islands were occupied by the South Vietnamese, who were driven out by Chinese forces in 1964, an action protested by both the Saigon and Hanoi governments.

The Spratlys, which consist of hundreds of tiny islets, are closer to Borneo than Vietnam. They have been claimed by virtually every country in the vicinity, including the Philippines, Malaysia, Indonesia, China, Taiwan and Vietnam. In 1988 Vietnam lost two ships and 70 sailors in a clash with China over the Spratlys. In mid-1992 Chinese military patrol boats reportedly opened fire several times on Vietnamese cargo vessels that were leaving Hong Kong, bringing trade between Vietnam and Hong Kong to a near halt. The explanation given was that China was trying to prevent smuggling.

Both archipelagos have little intrinsic value, but the country that has sovereignty over them can claim huge areas of the South China Sea – believed to hold vast oil reserves – as its territorial waters. China pushed tensions to a new high in 1992 by occupying one of the islets claimed by Vietnam, and by signing contracts with a US company (Crestone Corporation) to search for oil in the disputed areas. Vietnam returned the favour in 1996, by signing an oil exploration contract with a competing American company, Conoco. Also in 1996 the Philippine navy destroyed a small Chinese-built radar base on Mischief Reef in the Spratlys.

Some tension was diffused with the 'Declaration on the Conduct of Parties in the South China Sea' signed by Asean nations and China in 2002, but the sovereignty of the islands remains unresolved.

The main drawcard is the outdoor hot-spring baths. All private baths are for rent and each bath is on its own covered wooden platform, complete with a small changing room. The baths range from 37°C to 40°C, and the minerals in the water are said to be beneficial to your bones, muscles and skin, and are also said to improve blood circulation and mental disorders!

The baths come in different sizes/prices. A 3-sq-metre bath for two people costs 60,000d, a 5-sq-metre bath for up to five people costs 100,000d and a 10-sq-metre bath for a party of 10 will set you back 160,000d. A dip in a large, shared swimming pool costs 6000d per person, or 3000d for kids.

Until recently there was wildlife in the area, including tigers and elephants, but it seems humans have nearly won the area over. In 1994 six elephants were captured near the springs, but after a few months of keeping them as pets their captors turned them over to the zoo in HCMC. Nowadays the only wildlife you are likely to spot are ceramic lions, cheetahs and panthers, which decorate the marshes around the springs.

The hottest spring reaches 82°C, which i hot enough to boil an egg in 10 to 15 min utes. Vietnamese visitors like to boil eggs i the bamboo baskets set aside for this pur pose; you'll find a couple of giant chicke statues decorating the springs where you too, can boil up a snack for yourself. Rav eggs are on sale for 2000d each.

Getting There & Away

The resort is in a compound 6km north o the village of Binh Chau. The road connect ing Rte 55 to Binh Chau is a smooth ride thanks to funds donated by the Australia government in the '90s.

Good highway or not, there's no publi transport. You'll need a motorbike or car; i you choose the latter, perhaps you can fin(some travellers to share the expense.

CAT TIEN NATIONAL PARK

☎ 061 / elevation 700m

Straddling the border of three provinces - Lam Dong, Dong Nai and Binh Phuoc - **Cat Tien National Park** (☎ /fax 669 228; admissio 20,000d) is just 150km from HCMC and 40km from Buon Ma Thuot. In the 2nd century

NATIONAL HWY 20: ROADSIDE ATTRACTIONS

Langa Lake
The HCMC–Dalat road (Hwy 20) spans this reservoir, which is crossed by a bridge. Lots of floating houses, where families harvest the fish underneath, can be seen here. It's a very scenic spot for photography, and most tourist vehicles on the HCMC–Dalat road make a short pit-stop here.

Volcanic Craters
Near Dinh Quan on Hwy 20 there are three volcanoes – now extinct, but nonetheless very impressive. The craters date from the late Jurassic period, about 150 million years ago. You'll have to do a little walking to see the crater. One is on the left-hand side of the road, about 2km south of Dinh Quan, and another on the right-hand side about 8km beyond Dinh Quan, towards Dalat.

Underground Lava Tubes
A bit beyond the volcanic craters, towards Dalat, are underground lava tubes. These rare caves were formed as the surface lava cooled and solidified, while the hotter underground lava continued to flow, leaving a hollow space. Lava tubes differ sharply in appearance from limestone caves (the latter are formed by underground springs). While limestone caves have abundant stalactites and stalagmites, the walls of lava caves are smooth.

The easiest way to find the lava tubes is to first find the teak forest on Hwy 20 between the km120 and km124 markers. The children who live around the forest can point you to the entrance of the lava tubes. However, you are strongly advised *not* to go into the tubes by yourself. It's best to have a guide and, furthermore, inform someone responsible where you are going. You definitely need to take a torch (flashlight).

For more information on the waterfalls and other attractions along Hwy 20, see the Central Highlands chapter (p288).

D the Cat Tien area was a religious centre f the Funan empire, and ancient Oc-Eo ultural relics have been discovered in the ark.

Cat Tien was hit hard with defoliants uring the American War, but the large ld-growth trees survived and the smaller lants have recovered. Just as importantly, 1e wildlife has made a comeback and in 002 Unesco added Cat Tien National Park o its list of biosphere reserves.

The 73,878-hectare park is home to 7 types of mammal, 133 freshwater fish pecies, 40 types of reptile, 14 amphibian pecies, plus an incredible array of insects, 1cluding 457 species of butterfly. Many of 1ese creatures are listed as rare and en-angered, but none of them more than the avan rhinoceros. Considered one of the arest mammals in the world, this unusual hino exists only in Cat Tien (there are elieved to be seven or eight living in the ark) and on the island of Java, in Indo-esia. Leopards are also believed to live in 1e park, while another rare creature found ere is a type of wild ox called a gaur.

The jungles of Cat Tien support an astounding variety of bird life (326 species), and avid bird-watchers flock here from around the world. Rare birds in the park include the orange-necked partridge, green peafowl and Siamese fireback. There is also a very healthy population of monkeys. Leeches are another less desirable member of the local fauna so come prepared, especially during the wet season.

Elephants also roam the park, but their presence has caused some controversy. In the early 1990s a herd of 10 hungry elephants fell into a bomb crater, created during the American War, just outside of Cat Tien. Local villagers took pity on the elephants and dug out a ramp to rescue them. Tragically, since then 28 villagers have been killed by rampaging elephants. Theoretically, the problem could have been 'solved' by shooting the elephants, but the Vietnamese government wasn't willing to risk the wrath of international environmental groups. However, none of these organisations has come up with the funds for relocating the elephants, some of which were finally removed to zoos. In the longer term such conflicts are likely to be repeated because of the increasing competition between Vietnam's wildlife and its growing population for the same living space.

Cat Tien also boasts a wide range of evergreen, semideciduous and bamboo forests; some 1800 species of plants thrive in the park.

Cat Tien National Park can be explored on foot, by mountain bike, by 4WD and also by boat along the Dong Nai River. There are several well-established hiking trails in the park. For shorter trips (120,000d) and also to visit **Crocodile Swamp** (Bau Sau, 160,000d), 4WDs can be rented. The latter is a 9km drive from the park headquarters and you have to trek the last 4km to the swamp; the walk takes about three hours round trip. It may be possible for smaller groups (four or less) to spend the night at the ranger's post here. It's a good place to view the wildlife that comes to drink in the swamp.

Hiring a guide in the national park costs 50,000/100,000d per half/full day, or 160,000d to overnight in the jungle.

Sleeping & Eating

There are **bungalows** and **air-con rooms** (☎ /fax 669 228; r/b 150,000/200,000d; 🏠) near the park

headquarters. There's also a small restaurant nearby.

Getting There & Away

The most common approach to the park is from Hwy 20, which connects Dalat with HCMC. To reach the park, follow the narrow 24km road which branches west from Hwy 20 at Talai Junction (Nga Ban Talai, 125km north of HCMC and 175km south of Dalat.

The road to the park is signposted at the junction. With your own wheels getting to the park is easy, but you should call ahead for reservations.

Another approach to Cat Tien National Park is to take a boat across Langa Lake and then go by foot from there. **Dalat Holidays Phat Tire Ventures** (☎ 063-829 422; langbian@hcm .vnn.vn; www.phattireventures.com) is a reputable ecotour operator in Dalat and is a good place to inquire about this and other access options from the central highlands area (including mountain biking to the park from Dalat).

A good place in HCMC to inquire about arranging a customised trip to Cat Tien National Park is **Sinhbalo Adventures** (☎ 08-837 6766, 836 7682; www.sinhbalo.com; 283/20 Đ Pham Ngu Lao).

Mekong Delta

The Mekong Delta vibrates with colour – shimmering fields of bright green rice stalks, fanned-out yellow and electric-pink incense sticks drying along roadsides, and lunchtime traffic jams of white-and-blue-clad schoolkids on bikes. So, too, the rhythm of life along Mekong byways buzzes with slow but constant energy. A trip into the nation's 'rice basket' is a glimpse into the life of Vietnam's agricultural workforce, whose daily toil on this life-sustaining river delta feeds the nation. The Mekong Delta – with the nurturing of its busy inhabitants – produces enough rice to feed the entire country, with a sizable surplus (see the 'Rice Production' boxed text, p395).

The delta was formed by sediment deposited by the Mekong River, a process which continues today; silt deposits extend the delta's shoreline at the mouth of the river by as much as 79m per year. The river itself is so massive that it has two daily tides. Lush with rice paddies and fish farms, this rich delta plain also nourishes the cultivation of sugarcane, fruit, coconut and shrimp. Although the area is primarily rural, it is one of the most densely populated regions and nearly every hectare is intensively farmed.

Travellers to the Mekong can join the languorous clamour by boating into the crush of floating markets or visiting local fruit orchards and fish farms. Those wishing to get away from the hustle and bustle can travel to towns on the eastern edge of the delta, which is notable for having the highest proportion of Khmers in the population despite being the furthest provinces from Cambodia. Tra Vinh and Soc Trang, two such towns, are home to several beautiful Khmer pagodas and are not often visited by foreigners.

For an even more remote experience, head to the western jumping-off point of Rach Gia and catch a boat to peaceful Phu Quoc Island. There is still little commercialisation happening on Phu Quoc, and among the attractions are uncrowded dive sites, deserted beaches and cool freshwater springs.

HIGHLIGHTS

- Cruise the countless canals splintering around **My Tho** (p396) and **Ben Tre** (p400), near the end of the mighty Mekong River
- Explore the delta's bustling floating markets near **Can Tho** (p418)
- Discuss Buddhism with monks at elaborate **Khmer pagodas** (p406)
- Homestay on one of the island fruit orchards around **Vinh Long** (p405)
- Step off the Mekong River boat to check out the **Chau Doc** (p429) area on the way to or from Cambodia
- Relax on the powdery white-sand beaches of remote **Phu Quoc Island** (p445)

Chau Doc ★
Vinh Long ★
★ Phu Quoc Island
Can Tho ★ Tien Giang River (Mekong River)
Khmer Pagodas ★

MEKONG DELTA

History

The Mekong Delta was once part of the Khmer kingdom, and was the last region of modern-day Vietnam to be annexed and settled by the Vietnamese. Cambodians, mindful that they controlled the area until the 18th century, still call the delta 'Lower Cambodia'. The Khmer Rouge tried to follow up on this claim by raiding Vietnamese villages and massacring the inhabitants. This led the Vietnamese army to invade Cambodia in 1979 and oust the Khmer Rouge from power. Most of the current inhabitants of the Mekong Delta are ethnic Vietnamese, but there are also significant populations of ethnic Chinese and Khmer, as well as a few Chams.

When the government introduced collective farming to the delta in 1975, production fell significantly and there were food short-ages in Saigon (although farmers in the delta easily grew enough to feed themselves). People from Saigon would head down to the delta to buy sacks of black-market rice, but to prevent 'profiteering', the police set up checkpoints and confiscated rice from anyone carrying more than 10kg. All this ended in 1986 and farmers in this region have since propelled Vietnam forward to become the world's second-largest rice exporter after Thailand.

Getting There & Around

Most travellers head to the Mekong Delta on an organised tour. With all the cheap and easy-to-book delta tours available now, few people choose to travel independently, particularly those with limited time in Vietnam. The tours can usually save you a good deal of time and money. But those who do

THE RIVER OF NINE DRAGONS

The Mekong River is one of the world's great rivers and its delta is one of the world's largest. The Mekong originates high in the Tibetan plateau, flowing 4500km through China, between Myanmar and Laos, through Laos, along the Laos–Thailand border, and through Cambodia and Vietnam on its way to the South China Sea. At Phnom Penh (Cambodia), the Mekong River splits into two main branches: the Hau Giang (Lower River, also called the Bassac River), which flows via Chau Doc, Long Xuyen and Can Tho to the sea; and the Tien Giang (Upper River), which splits into several branches at Vinh Long and empties into the sea at five points. The numerous branches of the river explain the Vietnamese name for the Mekong: Song Cuu Long (River of Nine Dragons).

The Mekong's flow begins to rise around the end of May and reaches its highest point in September; it ranges from 1900 to 38,000 cubic metres per second depending on the season. A tributary of the river that empties into the Mekong at Phnom Penh drains Cambodia's Tonlé Sap Lake. When the Mekong is at flood stage, this tributary reverses its flow and drains into Tonlé Sap, thereby somewhat reducing the danger of serious flooding in the Mekong Delta. Unfortunately, deforestation in Cambodia is disturbing this delicate balancing act, resulting in more flooding in Vietnam's portion of the Mekong River basin.

In recent years seasonal flooding has claimed the lives of hundreds and forced tens of thousands of the region's residents to evacuate from their homes. In some areas, inhabitants are not able to return to their homes until the waters fully recede several months later. Floods cause hundreds of millions of dollars in damage and have a catastrophic effect on regional rice and coffee crops.

Living on a flood plain presents some technical challenges. Lacking any high ground to escape flooding, many delta residents build their houses on bamboo stilts to avoid the rising waters. Many roads are submerged or turn to muck during floods; all-weather roads have to be built on raised embankments, but this is expensive. The traditional solution has been to build canals and travel by boat. There are thousands of canals in the Mekong Delta – keeping them properly dredged and navigable is a constant but essential chore.

A further challenge is keeping the canals clean. The normal practice of dumping all garbage and sewage directly into the waterways behind the houses that line them is taking its toll. Many of the more populated areas in the Mekong Delta are showing signs of unpleasant waste build-up. One can only hope the government will take stronger measures to curb this pollution.

decide to do it on their own will have more access to areas that are off the beaten track, with many less-visited places to discover.

Travel by express minibuses is cheap, efficient and comfortable (though crowded). The ultimate way to see the delta, however, is by private car, bicycle or rented motorbike. Two-wheeling around the delta is good fun, especially getting lost among the maze of country roads! Real hardcores might investigate hopping a cargo boat from Ho Chi Minh City (HCMC; p363) – a slow but fascinating way to head into the delta.

Since the opening of the river border crossing between Vietnam and Cambodia at Vinh Xuong (near Chau Doc), more and more travellers are choosing this route (see p474) over the land border at Moc Bai. Don't forget, however, that visas for entering Vietnam must be arranged *before* heading to the border.

Wherever you go in the delta (except for My Tho) be prepared for ferry crossings. Fruit, soft drinks and sticky rice-based snacks are sold in the ferry waiting areas.

TOURS

Plenty of inexpensive minibus tours can be booked at travel agents in HCMC (p327). The cheapest ones are sold around the Pham Ngu Lao area. However, before you book, shop around – remember that you usually get what you pay for. This is not to say that

RICE PRODUCTION

The ancient Indian word for rice, *dhanya* ('sustainer of the human race'), is apt when describing the importance of rice to the Vietnamese.

A Vietnamese fable tells of a time when rice did not need to be harvested. Instead, it would be summoned through prayer and arrive in each home from the heavens in the form of a large ball. One day a man ordered his wife to sweep the floor in preparation for the coming of the rice, but she was still sweeping when the huge ball arrived and struck it by accident, causing it to shatter into many pieces. Since then, Vietnamese have had to toil to produce rice by hand.

Rural Vietnam today is in many ways similar to what it would have been centuries ago: women in conical hats *(non bai tho)* irrigating fields by hand, farmers stooping to plant the flooded paddies and water buffalo ploughing seedbeds with harrows.

Despite the labour-intensive production process, rice is the single most important crop in Vietnam and involves 70% of the working population. While always playing an important role in the Vietnamese economy, its production intensified considerably as a result of economic reforms, known as *doi moi*, or 'renovation', in 1986. The reforms shifted agricultural production away from subsistence towards cash cropping, transforming Vietnam from a rice importer to exporter in 1989. In 1997 Vietnam exported over 3.5 million tonnes of rice; for the first time in its history, northern Vietnam had excess rice for export and contributed about 270,000 tonnes. In 1999 rice exports rose to a record 4.5 million tonnes. Since then the yearly average has been hovering around 3.5 million tonnes.

Half of the production and the majority of rice exports from Vietnam come from the Mekong Delta. The Red River Delta is the main rice supplier for the north, although supplies often need to be supplemented by the south. Rice produced in the highlands is an important crop for ethnic minorities, although their output is relatively small compared with the rest of the country. Ironically, it's the powerful rural cartels, which set their own prices for seeds, fertilisers and pesticides, that reap the rewards.

The importance of rice in the diet of the Vietnamese is evident in the many rice dishes available, including rice omelette *(banh xeo)*, rice porridge *(chao)* and extremely potent rice wine *(ruou gao)*, to name a few. Vietnam's ubiquitous *com pho* (rice-noodle soup) restaurants serve white rice *(com)* with a variety of cooked meat and vegetables, as well as rice noodle soup *(pho)*.

In Vietnam the dominant rice-growing system is 'irrigated lowland'. Despite advances in rice production, such as the introduction of new plant varieties and increased use of fertilisers, much of the work involved with growing the plant itself is still carried out without modern machinery. Fields are ploughed and harrowed with the assistance of water buffaloes, seeds are planted by hand, and when the seedlings reach a certain age they have to be individually uprooted and transplanted (again manually) to another field to avoid root rot. This painstaking process is mostly undertaken by women. Irrigation is typically carried out by two workers using woven baskets on rope to transfer water from canals to the fields. When the water level is high enough fish can be raised in the paddies.

Rice plants take three to six months to grow, depending on the type and environment. In Vietnam, the three major cropping seasons are winter-spring, summer-autumn and the wet season. When ready to harvest, the plants are thigh-high and in about 30cm of water. The grains grow in drooping fronds and are cut by hand, then transported by wheelbarrows to thrashing machines that separate the husk from the plant. Other machines are used to 'dehusk' the rice (for brown rice) or 'polish' it (for white rice). A familiar sight at this stage is brown carpets of rice spread along roads to dry before milling. While rice continues to grow in Vietnam, the intensification of production since the start of the 1990s has led to problems such as salinity. In addition there has been a growing infestation of rice-field rats caused by the hunting of snakes (which hunt the rats). Unabated environmental degradation and high population growth are placing further pressure on Vietnam's staple grain supply. This, together with the increasing warnings against high fertilisation, may mean the long-term future of rice production in Vietnam is not guaranteed.

MEKONG DELTA

you need to book a pricey tour, but sometimes 'rock bottom' means all you will get is a brief glance at the delta region. The cost largely depends on how far from HCMC the tour goes. The standard of accommodation, transport, food and the size of the group will be other determining factors.

For private customised tours of the Mekong Delta on two or four wheels, HCMC's **Sinhbalo Adventures** (www.sinhbalo.com) cannot be beaten.

MY THO

☎ 073 / pop 169,300

My Tho, the quiet capital city of Tien Giang province, is the closest city in the Mekong Delta to HCMC, and visitors on whirlwind 10-day Vietnam tours come here for day trips to catch a glimpse of the famous river. In order to visit floating markets, however, you'll need to continue on to Can Tho (p418).

Being located so close to booming HCMC, one would expect My Tho to have profited handsomely from the country's economic reforms. Sadly, this is not the case – My Tho is one of the poorest cities in the Mekong Delta, though it is said to have the richest government and one of the strictest police forces.

My Tho was founded in the 1680s by Chinese refugees fleeing Taiwan for political reasons. The Chinese have virtually all gone now, having been driven out in the late 1970s when their property was seized by the government. The economy – or what's left of it – is based on tourism, fishing and the cultivation of rice, coconuts, bananas, mangoes, longans and citrus fruit.

Orientation

Sprawling along the bank of the northernmost branch of the Mekong River, My Tho is laid out in a fairly regular grid pattern.

The bus station is 3km west of town. Coming from the bus station, you enter My Tho on Đ Ap Bac, which turns into Đ Nguyen Trai (oriented west–east).

Parallel to the Mekong River is Đ 30 Thang 4 (also written as Đ 30/4), named for Saigon Liberation Day.

Information

Tien Giang Tourist (Cong Ty Du Lich Tien Giang; ☎ 873 184; dulichtg@bdvn.vnd.net; 8 Đ 30 Thang 4; ☼ 7am-5pm) is the official tourism authority for Tien

Giang province. There's a **branch office** (☎ 875 189; 25 Đ Nam Ky Khoi Nghia) just up the street.

The post office is located at 59 Đ 30 Thang 4. For medical services, travellers are advised to make the trip back to HCMC.

Sights

MY THO CHURCH & BISHOPRIC

Built about a century ago, **My Tho Church** (32 Đ Hung Vuong; mass 5am & 5pm Mon-Sat, 5am, 7am & 5pm Sun) is a solid pastel-yellow building at the corner of Đ Nguyen Trai. The stone plaques set in the church walls express thanks to various saintly figures.

Today two priests, two nuns and several assistants minister to most of My Tho's 7000 Catholics.

CAO DAI TEMPLE

If you missed the one in Tay Ninh (p373), My Tho has its own smaller **Cao Dai Temple** (Đ Ly Thuong Kiet), which is worth a look. It's west of the town centre between Đ Dong Da and Đ Tran Hung Dao.

MY THO CENTRAL MARKET

This **market** (Đ Trung Trac & Đ Nguyen Hue) is in an area of town that is closed to traffic. The streets are filled with stalls selling everything from fresh food and bulk tobacco to boat propellers. In an attempt to clear these streets, the local government has built a three-storey concrete monstrosity on the riverside, intending to relocate vendors inside. With the high rent and taxes, however, there have been very few takers and the top two floors remain empty.

VINH TRANG PAGODA

The charitable monks at **Vinh Trang Pagoda** (60A Đ Nguyen Trung Truc; admission free; ☼ 9-11.30am & 1.30-5pm), a beautiful and well-maintained sanctuary, provide a home for orphans, disabled and other needy children.

The pagoda is about 1km from the city centre. To get there, take the bridge east across the river on Đ Nguyen Trai and after 400m turn left. The entrance to the sanctuary is about 200m from the turn-off, on the right-hand side of the building as you approach it from the ornate gate.

Tours

Boat trips are the highlight of a visit to My Tho. The small wooden vessels can navigate

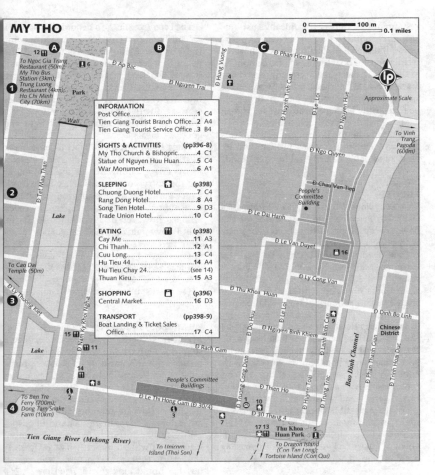

the mighty Mekong (barely), but the target for most trips is cruising past pleasant rural villages through the maze of small canals. Depending on what you book, destinations usually include a coconut-candy workshop, a honey-bee farm (try the banana wine!) and an orchid garden.

The My Tho People's Committee almost has a monopoly on boat travel and its prices are high so you need to be in a large group to make it economical. If you try to rent a boat on your own, you'll pay at least US$25 for a two- to three-hour tour. If you sign up with a tour group in HCMC, it could be as cheap as US$7 per person, including transportation between HCMC and My Tho. When comparing prices, check to see

what you are actually getting – the tours can last anywhere from one to four hours (not including HCMC–My Tho travel time). It would be impossible to do it any cheaper on your own, although many prefer to do it that way.

Tours of the Mekong can be booked at the main riverfront office of Tien Giang Tourist (p396). Several private operators in My Tho defy the authorities by peddling their own trips. They are indeed cheaper than the 'official' rates (per hour around 50,000d), but they are illegal and there's a small chance your boat may be 'pulled over' and you – or more likely your driver – fined by the river cops. The best place to look for these freelancers is near Cuu Long

MEKONG DELTA

restaurant (see right) or, ironically, just outside the doors of the Tien Giang Tourist office. But they'll probably find you first.

Inexpensive boat tours can also be booked at the out-of-the-way but friendly **Viet Phong Travel** (☎ 882 522; vietphongtravel@hcm.vnn.vn; 94 Đ Le Thi Hong Gam; ☺ 8am-5pm); it's best to contact its staff at Trung Luong Restaurant (see right), as its pier office is difficult to find.

See opposite for information about trips to nearby Dragon, Tortoise and Unicorn Islands; and p402 for trips to Phoenix Island.

Sleeping
BUDGET
Rang Dong Hotel (☎ 874 400; 25 Đ 30 Thang 4; s/d $8/12; ☒) Privately run, this is one of the better cheap places in town and is popular with budget travellers.

Song Tien Hotel (☎ 872 009; fax 884 745; 101 Đ Trung Trac; s & d 110,000-250,000d; ☒) The newly refurbished Song Tien has clean, comfortable rooms outfitted with TV, fridge and shared balconies overlooking both the town and channel. There's also a lift here.

Trade Union Hotel (Khach San Cong Doan; ☎ 874 324; congdoantourist@hcm.vnn.vn; 61 Đ 30 Thang 4; s/d 100,000/180,000d; ☒) This ageing but clean government-run hotel is a large place with river views from some of the rooms. Air-con rooms come with a fridge; tour groups book here regularly and the staff is fairly friendly.

Another possible option is to stay overnight in a bungalow on Unicorn Island (Thoi Son; see opposite); inquire at Tien Giang Tourist (p396). There are **homestay** options around Vinh Long (p405).

MID-RANGE
Chuong Duong Hotel (☎ 870 875; fax 874 250; 10 Đ 30 Thang 4; r/ste US$20/30; ☒) My Tho's most luxurious accommodation, this spacious and attractive building boasts a prime riverside location and respectable in-house restaurant. All rooms overlook the Mekong River, making the rates rather reasonable for what you get. Bathrooms in the suites have bathtubs.

Eating
RESTAURANTS
Chi Thanh (☎ 878 428; 19 Đ Ap Bac; mains 15,000-30,000d) A tidy spot for delicious Chinese and Vietnamese fare, Chi Thanh has menus in English.

Cuu Long (☎ 870 779; Đ 30 Thang 4; mains 20,000-30,000d) Though it has the advantage of being right on the Mekong River, the food and decor here leave something to be desired.

Ngoc Gia Trang (☎ 872 742; 196 Đ Ap Bac; set meals US$4-12) A pleasant place on the road into My Tho from HCMC. It's a bit pricey compared with the restaurants in town, but it has a lovely courtyard atmosphere and good set meals.

Trung Luong (☎ 855 441; Hwy 60; mains around 25,000d) Located a few kilometres west of town, Trung Luong is near the gate marking the entry point to My Tho. Here too is a nice garden and the tour groups that stop here appreciate the clean toilets. The caged animals, however, do not add to the charm. Viet Phong Travel (p396) books boat tours from here.

Other good spots with local flavour:
Thuan Kieu (☎ 876 636; 47 Đ Nam Ky Khoi Nghia; mains 10,000-20,000d)
Cay Me (60 Đ Nam Ky Khoi Nghia; mains 10,000-15,000d)

HU TIEU RESTAURANTS
My Tho is known for a special vermicelli soup, *hu tieu my tho*, which is richly garnished with fresh and dried seafood, pork, chicken and fresh herbs. It is served either with broth or dry (with broth on the side) and can also be made vegetarian.

Although *hu tieu* can be found at almost any eatery in town, there's a handful of speciality restaurants (open mornings only). Carnivores will enjoy **Hu Tieu 44** (44 Đ Nam Ky Khoi Nghia; soups 6000d; ☺ 5am-noon), while vegetarians should look for **Hu Tieu Chay 24** (24 Đ Nam Ky Khoi Nghia; soups 3000d; ☺ 6-9am).

Getting There & Around
BICYCLE
You can rent a bicycle from Tien Giang Tourist.

BOAT
The car ferry to Ben Tre province leaves from Ben Pha Rach Mieu station about 1km west of My Tho city centre, near 2/10A Đ Le Thi Hong Gam (the continuation west of Đ 30 Thang 4). The ferry operates between 4am and 10pm and runs at least once an hour (per person/motorbike 2000/4000d). Ten-person trucks shuttle passengers between the ferry terminal and the bus station.

MEKONG DELTA

BUS
My Tho is served by buses leaving HCMC from Mien Tay bus station (p363) and from the bus station in Cholon. Buses from Cholon have the added advantage of dropping passengers right in My Tho, as opposed to the bus station outside of town. The trip takes 1½ hours.

The **My Tho bus station** (Ben Xe Khach Tien Giang; 4am-5pm) is several kilometres west of town. To get there from the city centre, take Ð Ap Bac westward and continue on to Hwy 1 (Quoc Lo 1).

Buses to HCMC (10,000d, two hours) leave when full from the early morning until about 5pm. There are also daily bus services to most points in the Mekong Delta.

CAR & MOTORBIKE
The drive from HCMC to My Tho along Hwy 1, by car or motorbike, takes about two hours.

Road distances from My Tho are 16km to Ben Tre, 104km to Can Tho, 70km to HCMC and 66km to Vinh Long.

AROUND MY THO
Dragon Island
A walk through the well-known **longan orchards** of Dragon Island (Con Tan Long) is pleasant. The lush, palm-fringed shores of the island are lined with wooden fishing boats; some of the residents of the island are shipwrights. There is a small restaurant on the island. Dragon Island is a five-minute boat trip (per person 8000d) from the dock at the southern end of Ð Le Loi.

Other Islands
The other two islands in the vicinity, **Tortoise Island** (Con Qui) and **Unicorn Island** (Thoi Son) are worth a stop to check out the coconut candy and banana wine workshops. For booking a trip to these islands or any of the others, it's cheapest to arrange a day tour from HCMC (p327).

Dong Tam Snake Farm
The **snake farm** (admission 15,000d; 7am-6pm) at Dong Tam, located about 10km from My Tho in the direction of Vinh Long, breeds snakes for eating, for their skins and for producing antivenin. Most of the snakes raised here are pythons and cobras. The king cobras are raised only for exhibit – they are extremely aggressive and are even capable of spitting poison; don't get too close to their cages.

The regular cobras are kept in an open pit and they will generally ignore you if you ignore them, but will strike if they are provoked. On the other hand though, the pythons are docile enough to be taken out of their cages and handled, but be warned that the larger ones are capable of strangling a human.

MONKEY BRIDGES – AN ENDANGERED SPECIES
One of the most endearing sights in the Mekong Delta is a person making their way across one of the fascinating 'monkey bridges' *(cau khi)*. These simple, arch-shaped footbridges are usually built of uneven logs about 30cm to 80cm wide and have only a simple bamboo railing. They are suspended anywhere from 2m to 10m above the canals and connect tiny villages throughout the region to main roads.

At first glance the bridges look more like makeshift scaffolding than a bridge. It's amazing to watch the locals traverse these narrow catwalks with bicycles and heavy loads balanced between their shoulders on bamboo poles. A fall from one of these tightrope bridges could result in serious injury, but the Vietnamese just glide across with ease (and smiles on their faces).

In 1998 the government initiated a programme to begin replacing the region's monkey bridges with safer, 1m-wide wood plank overpasses. In 2000 the plan was amended with a new and improved agenda to do away with *all* of the delta's monkey bridges once and for all, and to replace them with more durable concrete bridges. While the move no doubt is a victory in terms of improvement to the local infrastructure throughout the Mekong Delta, giving local people easier and safer access across the canals, sadly the traditional landscape is suffering an aesthetic loss. The days of seeing these charming bridges everywhere are numbered, but still, with thousands of bridges to dismantle and replace, you can rest assured that there will always be some left to find.

MEKONG DELTA

> **WARNING!**
>
> Besides its snakes, the Dong Tam Snake Farm has wild creatures on display – including monkeys, bears and owls – that are kept in deplorably poor condition.
>
> The farm was formerly run by a retired Viet Cong (VC) colonel named Tu Duoc, who ran the place very efficiently. Unfortunately, after his death in 1990, facilities have gone steadily downhill.
>
> The snake farm is really only to be recommended to those truly charmed by snakes.

Dong Tam also has a collection of mutant turtles and fish on display. The cause of their genetic deformities is almost certainly the spraying of Agent Orange during the American War, which was particularly intensive in the forested parts of the Mekong Delta.

The snake farm is operated by the Vietnamese military for profit and is open to the public. The restaurant here includes cobra on the menu and there's a shop where you can stock up on cobra antivenin.

You'll need your own transport to get to Dong Tam Snake Farm. Coming from HCMC, continue for 3km beyond the turn-off to My Tho and turn left at the Dong Tam Junction (signposted). From the junction, follow the dirt road for 4km, turn right and continue for 1km until you reach the snake farm. To get there from My Tho, follow Đ Le Thi Hong Gam west along the river for around 7km and just beyond the Binh Duc post office turn right and follow the dirt road for 3km to the farm.

BEN TRE
☎ 075 / pop 111,800

The picturesque little province of Ben Tre, just south of My Tho, consists of several large islands in the mouth of the Mekong River. The area gets few visitors because it's off the main highways. The provincial capital is also called Ben Tre and is a friendly sort of place with a few old buildings near the banks of the Mekong.

Ben Tre is a good place for boat trips and, unlike My Tho, Vinh Long and Can Tho, the People's Committee doesn't have a monopoly on the boat tour business so prices have remained low.

Ben Tre is famous for coconut candy (*keo dua*). Many local women work in small factories making coconut sweets, spending their days boiling large cauldrons of sticky mixture, before rolling it out and cutting sections off into squares and wrapping them into paper for sale.

Information

Ben Tre Tourist (☎ 829 618; fax 822 440; 65 Đ Dong Khoi; ⏲ 9am-6pm) also has a branch office adjacent to the Dong Khoi Hotel.

Ben Tre has two **Internet cafés** (per hr 4000d), one on Đ Hung Vuong and the other on Đ Tran Quoc Tuan. There's also Internet access at the **main post office** (☎ 822 161; fax 823 330; 3/1 Đ Dong Khoi; per hr 4000d).

Get cash at **Incombank** (☎ 822 507; 42 Đ Nguyen Dinh Chieu; ⏲ closed weekends).

Sights
VIEN MINH PAGODA

Right in the centre of Ben Tre, this is the head office of the **Buddhist Association of Ben Tre province**. Though the history of the pagoda is vague, the local monks say it is over 100 years old. The original structure was made of wood, but it was torn down to make way for the present building. Reconstruction took place from 1951 to 1958 using bricks and concrete.

An interesting feature of Vien Minh Pagoda is a large white statue of Quan The Am Bo Tat (Goddess of Mercy) set in the front courtyard. The Chinese calligraphy that adorns the pagoda was performed by an old monk. None of the current monks at the pagoda can read Chinese, though some of the local worshippers can.

TRUC GIANG LAKE

Fronting several hotels, Truc Giang Lake is tiny but pleasant and an agreeable place to sit with an iced coffee.

Sleeping
BUDGET

Thao Nhi Guesthouse (☎ 860 009; Hamlet 1, Tan Thach Village; d 150,000d; 🗙) Small and intimate Thao Nhi is 11km north of town in an orchard setting. There's an in-house restaurant, where the excellent elephant-ear fish served with rice paper and fresh greens is recommended. To get here, turn left at the market after disembarking from the My Tho–Ben Tre ferry.

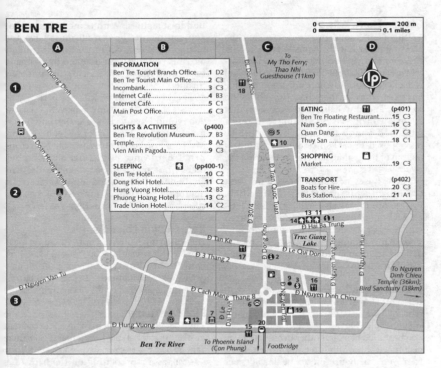

BEN TRE

INFORMATION	
Ben Tre Tourist Branch Office	1 D2
Ben Tre Tourist Main Office	2 C3
Incombank	3 C3
Internet Café	4 B3
Internet Café	5 C1
Main Post Office	6 C3

SIGHTS & ACTIVITIES	(p400)
Ben Tre Revolution Museum	7 B3
Temple	8 A2
Vien Minh Pagoda	9 C3

SLEEPING	(pp400-1)
Ben Tre Hotel	10 C2
Dong Khoi Hotel	11 C2
Hung Vuong Hotel	12 B3
Phuong Hoang Hotel	13 C2
Trade Union Hotel	14 C2

EATING	(p401)
Ben Tre Floating Restaurant	15 C3
Nam Son	16 C3
Quan Dang	17 C3
Thuy San	18 C1

SHOPPING	
Market	19 C3

TRANSPORT	(p402)
Boats for Hire	20 C3
Bus Station	21 A1

A sign will point you the last several hundred metres to the guesthouse gate.

Trade Union Hotel (☎ 825 082; 50 Đ Hai Ba Trung; s & d 130,000-150,000đ; ❄) It's a bit worse for wear, but it's one of the cheapest places in town and centrally located.

Phuong Hoang Hotel (☎ 821 385; 28 Hai Ba Trung; s & d 150,000đ; ❄) This family-run minihotel is a bit dingy, but there's a nice balcony overlooking the lake.

MID-RANGE
Dong Khoi Hotel (☎ 822 501; fax 822 440; 16 Đ Hai Ba Trung; s & d US$10-35; ❄) Popular for wedding parties, this hotel is the best of the three on the lakefront. Clean rooms have big bathrooms with tubs as well as the usual amenities. On Saturday night a band entertains the guests at the restaurant here, the most upmarket eatery in town.

Hung Vuong Hotel (☎ 822 408; 166 Đ Hung Vuong; old-/new-wing r US$10-37; ❄) One of Ben Tre's nicest places to stay and the only one on the riverfront. Rooms in the new wing have hot water, bathtubs and TVs. It also has a big restaurant.

Ben Tre Hotel (☎ 825 332; 8/2 Đ Tran Quoc Tuan; s & d US$13-23; ❄) All the bright, spacious rooms here have hot water and clean bathrooms. There's an Internet café nearby.

Eating
Nam Son (☎ 822 873; 40 42 Đ Phan Ngoc Tong; mains 15,000-30,000đ) Popular for its Vietnamese fare, Nam Son is usually packed with locals feasting on roast chicken and drinking draught beer.

Ben Tre Floating Restaurant (mains around 35,000đ) Ben Tre is anchored on the south side of town near the market. The food and décor here is unremarkable, but you can't beat the location.

For fresh river fish, seafood and Vietnamese fare:
Quan Dang (☎ 829 889; 1 Đ Tan Ke; mains 15,000đ)
Thuy San (☎ 825 548; 210B ĐL Dong Khoi; mains 15,000đ)

If you're travelling on the cheap, just head over to the market, which has plenty of **food stalls** (rice plates around 7000đ) where you can fill up for peanuts.

Getting There & Away

As this is an island province, crossing the Mekong River is a prerequisite for reaching Ben Tre. The My Tho–Ben Tre ferry (motorbike/person 5000/600d, 25 minutes one way) is the fastest option. There are other possible ferry crossings further south but these are so slow and unreliable that you shouldn't count on them. Ferry crossings are much quicker if you're travelling by motorbike (as opposed to car) since there are numerous small boats that can take you across the river.

Public buses stop at the bus station west of the town centre on Đ Doan Hoang Minh. Private minibuses also make the Ben Tre–HCMC run daily. They operate on no fixed schedule, so you'll need to inquire locally. Try asking around the market, or by the petrol station on Đ Dong Khoi (where some vans leave from).

Getting Around

Ben Tre Tourist has a high-speed boat for rent for US$35 per hour. It can hold about eight people. Slower and larger boats can also be rented here, but other bargains can be negotiated at the public pier near the market. Here you can figure on about 25,000d per hour, with a minimum of two hours cruising the local canals. Check with the boat drivers who hang around near the end of the footbridge.

AROUND BEN TRE
Phoenix Island

Until his imprisonment by the communists for his antigovernment activities and the consequent dispersion of his flock, the Coconut Monk (Ong Dao Dua; see 'The Coconut Monk' boxed text, opposite) led a small community on Phoenix Island (Con Phung), a few kilometres from My Tho. In its heyday, the island was dominated by a fantastic open-air **sanctuary** (admission 10,000d; 8-11.30am & 1.30-6pm) that looked a bit like a cross between a cheaply built copy of Disneyland and the Tiger Balm Gardens of Singapore. The dragon-enwrapped columns and the multiplatformed tower, with its huge metal globe, must have once been brightly painted, but these days the whole place is faded, rickety and silent. Nevertheless, it's good kitsch – there's even a model of the Apollo rocket set among the

Buddhist statues! With some imagination, you can picture how it all must have appeared as the Coconut Monk presided over his congregation, flanked by elephant tusks and seated on a richly ornamented throne.

The My Tho police will not permit you to visit this island using a private boat, so you would have to hire a government one for at least US$25 in order to get here from My Tho. You could hire a private boat from Ben Tre province just across the river, but there's not much to see to make the trip worthwhile. Instead, you might keep an eye out for the Coconut Monk's complex as you chug by on the My Tho–Ben Tre ferry.

Nguyen Dinh Chieu Temple

Dedicated to Nguyen Dinh Chieu, a local scholar, this **temple** (7.30-11.30am & 1.30-6.30pm) is in Ba Tri district, which is a 30-minute drive (36km) from Ben Tre. It's a very charming temple, excellent for photography.

Bird Sanctuary

The locals make much of the storks that nest at the local bird sanctuary, **San Chim Vam Ho** (☎ 858 669; admission 10,000d; 7-11am & 1-7pm), as a stork sitting on the back of a water buffalo is a quintessential image of the Mekong waterways. The sanctuary is 38km east of Ben Tre town. Ben Tre Tourist has speedboats that can make the round trip in about two hours, or slow boats that take about five hours. You can check the going rates at Ben Tre Tourist and compare them with what the freelance boat operators are charging.

To get there overland, follow Đ Nguyen Dinh Chieu east out of town for 20km to Giong Tram. Turn left onto the windy, rural dirt road leading to Trai Tu K-20 (Prison K-20); you'll reach the prison after travelling 11km (you may see hundreds of prisoners out tilling the fields) – turn right and drive the final 7km to Vam Ho.

VINH LONG
☎ 070 / pop 124,600

A medium-sized town along the banks of the Mekong River, Vinh Long is the capital of Vinh Long province and about midway between My Tho and Can Tho. Trips to the river islands are the big attraction for visitors to Vinh Long.

Information
Cuu Long Tourist (☎ 823 616; cuulongtourist1@hcm
.vnn.vn; 1 Đ 1 Thang 5) is one of the more capable
state-run tour outfits located in the Mekong Delta region and can arrange homestays at an orchard (see the boxed text 'A
Home Away from Home', p405). It also
has a small booking office near the Phuong
Thuy restaurant (p406), which can rent out
bicycles (per day US$2) and motorbikes
(US$8).

Internet access can be found at **@lpha**
(☎ 829 905; 78 Đ Trung Nu Vuong; per min 100d).

Vietincombank (☎ 823 109; 143 Đ Le Thai To) has
two branches in town and can exchange
cash and travellers cheques.

Sights
MEKONG RIVER ISLANDS
What makes a trip to Vinh Long worthwhile is not the town itself but the beautiful
small islands in the river. The islands are totally given over to agriculture, especially the
growing of tropical fruit, which are shipped
to markets in HCMC.

To visit the islands you have to charter a
boat through Cuu Long Tourist (see above).
Small boats cost around US$10 per person
for a three-hour journey (four people). The
tours include an English- or French-speaking
Vietnamese guide.

One way to bypass the government monopoly is to take the public ferry (3000d) to
one of the islands and then walk around
on your own; however, this is not nearly as
interesting as a boat tour, since you will not
cruise the narrow canals.

Some of the more popular islands to visit
include **Binh Hoa Phuoc** and **An Binh Island**, but
there are many others. This low-lying region is as much water as land and houses
are generally built on stilts. Bring plenty of
film because there are photo opportunities
in every direction.

CAI BE FLOATING MARKET
This bustling **river market** (5am-5pm) is
worth including on a boat tour from Vinh
Long. It is best to go early in the morning.
Wholesalers on big boats moor here, each
specialising in one or a few types of fruit or
vegetable. Customers cruise the market in
smaller boats and can easily find what they're
looking for, as the larger boats hang samples
of their goods from tall wooden poles.

One interesting thing you won't see at
other floating markets is the huge Catholic
cathedral on the riverside – a popular and
fantastic backdrop for photographs.

It takes about an hour to reach the market from Vinh Long, but most people make
detours on the way there or back to see the
canals or visit orchards.

MILITARY MUSEUM
It might not be up to the standard of the
military museums in HCMC and Hanoi, but
there is a **military museum** (Bao Tang Quan Su; Đ Phan
Boi Chau; 8-10am & 7-9pm Sat & Sun) close to the
Cuu Long Hotel. It was being overhauled at
the time we visited, but there shouldn't be
any surprises in the way of subject matter –
expect the usual lionisation of Ho Chi Minh
and the Vietnamese military.

THE COCONUT MONK
The Coconut Monk was so named because he once ate only coconuts for three years; others
claim he only drank coconut juice and ate fresh young corn. Whatever the story, he was born
Nguyen Thanh Nam in 1909, in what is now Ben Tre province. He studied chemistry and phys-
ics in France at Lyon, Caen and Rouen from 1928 until 1935, when he returned to Vietnam, got
married and had a daughter.

In 1945 the Coconut Monk left his family in order to pursue a monastic life. For three years
he sat on a stone slab under a flagpole and meditated day and night. He was repeatedly imprisoned by successive South Vietnamese governments, which were infuriated by his philosophy of
achieving reunification through peaceful means. He died in 1990.

Plaques on the 3.5m-high porcelain jar (created in 1972) on Con Phung tell all about the
Coconut Monk. He founded a religion, Tinh Do Cu Si, which was a mixture of Buddhism and
Christianity. Representations of Jesus and the Buddha appeared together, as did the Virgin Mary
and eminent Buddhist women, and the cross and Buddhist symbols. Today, only the symbols
remain, as the Tinh Do Cu Si community has dissolved from the island.

VAN THANH MIEU TEMPLE

A big surprise in Vinh Long is the large and beautiful **Van Thanh Mieu Temple** (Phan Thanh Gian Temple; Đ Tran Phu) by the river. It's unusual as far as Vietnamese temples go. To begin with, it's a Confucian temple, which is very rare in southern Vietnam. Another oddity is that while the rear hall is dedicated to Confucius, the front hall was built in honour of the local hero Phan Thanh Gian. A plaque outside the temple entrance briefly tells his story – Phan Thanh Gian led an uprising in 1930 against the French colonists. When it became obvious that his revolt was doomed, Phan killed himself rather than be captured by the colonial army. No-one is quite certain exactly when the hall honour-

ing Phan was built, but it seems as if it must have been some time after 1975.

The rear hall, built in 1866, has a portrait of Confucius above the altar. The building was designed in the Confucian style and looks like it was lifted straight out of China.

Van Thanh Mieu Temple is 3km southeast of town. Don't confuse it with the much smaller Quoc Cong Pagoda on Đ Tran Phu, which you will pass along the way.

Tours

Cuu Long Tourist (p403) offers a variety of boat tours ranging from three to five hours in length, as well as overnight excursions. Tour destinations include small canals, fruit orchards, brick kilns, a conical

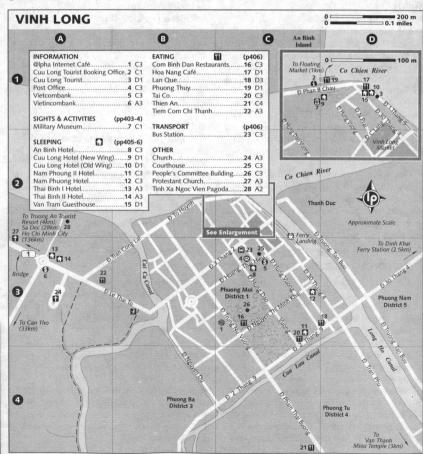

VINH LONG

0 _____ 200 m
0 _____ 0.1 miles

INFORMATION	
@lpha Internet Café	1 C3
Cuu Long Tourist Booking Office	2 C1
Cuu Long Tourist	3 D1
Post Office	4 C3
Vietcombank	5 C3
Vietincombank	6 A3

SIGHTS & ACTIVITIES	(pp403-4)
Military Museum	7 C1

SLEEPING	(pp405-6)
An Binh Hotel	8 C3
Cuu Long Hotel (New Wing)	9 D1
Cuu Long Hotel (Old Wing)	10 D1
Nam Phuong II Hotel	11 C3
Nam Phuong Hotel	12 C3
Thai Binh I Hotel	13 A3
Thai Binh II Hotel	14 A3
Van Tram Guesthouse	15 D1

EATING	(p406)
Com Binh Dan Restaurants	16 C3
Hoa Nang Café	17 D1
Lan Que	18 D3
Phuong Thuy	19 D1
Tai Co	20 C3
Thien An	21 C4
Tiem Com Chi Thanh	22 A3

TRANSPORT	(p406)
Bus Station	23 C3

OTHER	
Church	24 A3
Courthouse	25 C3
People's Committee Building	26 C3
Protestant Church	27 A3
Tinh Xa Ngoc Vien Pagoda	28 A2

An Binh Island

To Floating Market (1km)

Co Chien River

Đ Phan B Chau

Đ Hung Phu Vuong

Đ Hung Dao Vuong

Đ Hung Vuong

Đ Phan C Lang

Đ 30 Thang 5

Vinh Long Market

Co Chien River

Thanh Duc

Approximate Scale

To Truong An Tourist Resort (4km);
Sa Dec (28km);
Ho Chi Minh City (136km)

Đ To Huynh

Đ Truong An

See Enlargement

Ferry Landing

Đ Truong Tan Buu

To Dinh Khai Ferry Station (2.5km)

Đ Tran Cong Lai

Đ 3 Thang 2

Bridge

Đ Cai Ca Canal

Đ Le Thai To

Đ Hoang Thai Hieu

Đ Hung Vuong

Đ 30 Thang 4

Đ 30 Thang 4

Phuong Nam District 5

To Can Tho (33km)

Phuong Moi District 1

Đ Nguyen Thi Minh Khai

Đ 1 Thang 9

Đ Tran Phu

Đ Long Ho Canal

Đ Nguyen Du

Đ Tung Nu Vuong

Cau Lau Canal

Đ 2 Thang 9

Phuong Ba District 3

Đ Pham Thai Buong

Phuong Tu District 4

To Van Thanh Mieu Temple (3km)

A HOME AWAY FROM HOME

A homestay among the people of the Mekong Delta is an unforgettable experience and can give you a unique insight into the day-to-day lives of the local people. The bulk of the local people here make their living from growing fruit or cultivating rice.

Many of the homes that are open to Western visitors are on the banks of the Mekong River. When you reach the home of your host family, you should remove your shoes. Most families also prefer women to be well covered up.

In traditional houses, the sleeping area is open plan and has hammocks and wooden beds with mosquito nets hanging overhead (before the last rays of the sun disappear slap on plenty of repellent, as mosquitoes are rampant throughout the area).

A typical supper is the local favourite, elephant-ear fish, served bolt upright on a bed of greens with flourishes of carrots shaped as water flowers. The flesh of the fish is pulled off in chunks with chopsticks and wrapped into a rice-paper pancake and dipped into sauce. This is accompanied by crispy spring rolls, followed by soup and rice (Mekong rice is considered the most flavoursome).

After dinner some families exchange stories and songs over bottles of rice wine long into the night, while others cluster around the TV.

The morning starts as the first lights flicker across the water. Before breakfast, everyone takes a bath with the family. Splashing around in the muddy Mekong, fully dressed, can leave you feeling dirtier than when you started! After a hearty breakfast you say your goodbyes and head back to Vinh Long via the floating market.

The easiest way to arrange such a visit is through a travel agent in HCMC or through **Cuu Long Tourist** (☎ 823 616; cuulongtourist1@hcm.vnn.vn; Đ 1 Thang 5) in Vinh Long. However, independent travellers can usually make arrangements with freelance agents at the An Binh boat station on arrival in Vinh Long. Rates are typically US$7 to US$10 per night.

palm hat workshop and the Cai Be Floating Market (p403).

As is the case in most of the Mekong Delta, if you're travelling independently you will need to organise at least a few people to go with you in order to make the prices of these tours reasonable.

Sleeping

Van Tram Guesthouse (☎ 823 820; 4 Đ 1 Thang 5; s/d 150,000-200,000đ; 🛏) The five rooms at this very clean and comfortable family-run place are spacious, with hot water, TV and balconies.

Nam Phuong II Hotel (Đ 2 Thang 9; r 100,000-150,000đ; 🛏) Small and safe, this friendly family-run hotel has hot water and rooms with TV. A more upmarket branch on Đ 30 Thang 4 was being remodelled when we visited and is well situated near the river and market.

Cuu Long Hotel (☎ 823 656; cuulonghotelvl@hcm .vnn.vn; 1 Đ 1 Thang 5; r old wing US$10-25, new wing US$25-40; 🛏) This hotel has two branches right on the riverfront; the new wing address is given here (note that you can book old-wing rooms at the new wing). The cav-

ernous old wing has spacious, vaguely dingy rooms with balconies; river-view rooms top out at US$25. New-wing rooms are slightly more modern but have less character. All rooms have satellite TV and rates include breakfast.

An Binh Hotel (☎ 823 190; fax 822 231; 3 Đ Hoang Thai Hieu; r US$12-14; 🛏) Facilities here include a decent restaurant, tennis courts and a massage service, but the place isn't favoured by travellers because it's away from the scenic riverfront.

Thai Binh I Hotel (☎ 827 161; fax 822 213; 190-202 Đ Le Thai To; r US$7-10; 🛏) On the outskirts of town, the Thai Binh is a simple, cheap option. Fan rooms have cold water only. There's a cheaper, grubbier branch down the street if you're short of cash.

Truong An Tourist Resort (☎ 823 161; r US$25) Midway on the 8km stretch of road between Vinh Long and the My Thuan bridge, this is a quiet place to stay if you don't mind being away from town. There are cottages here, but not much to do except sit by the river and enjoy the park-like surroundings.

Cuu Long Tourist can arrange for you to spend the night at one of four island farmhouses (see the boxed text 'A Home Away from Home', p405). Options include staying in a colonial-style house or brick house, or a cottage in a large bonsai garden. Perhaps the most interesting choice is the house built on stilts above the river in traditional Mekong Delta style. All of these places are peaceful, but they are isolated – commuting to town involves a boat trip. The overnight cost is about US$35 per person, including the boat trip, guide, meals and a stop at the Cai Be floating market.

Eating

Thien Tan (☎ 824 001; 56/1 Đ Pham Thai Buong; mains 40,000-50,000d) Specialising in barbecued dishes, this is considered the best eatery in town. Recommended is the fish cooked in bamboo *(ca loc nuong tre)* and chicken cooked in clay *(ga nuong dat set)*. If you're feeling brave, consider the roasted rice-field rat *(chout quay)*.

Tiem Com Chi Thanh (☎ 823 457; 64 Đ Le Thai To; mains 10,000d) Rice steamed in tiny clay bowls is served with excellent Chinese dishes ranging from tofu and shiitakes to frog to pork intestine.

Lan Que (☎ 823 262; Đ 2 Thang 9; mains around 15,000d) This popular local joint serves up genuine Vietnamese food, including good turtle and frog dishes.

Tai Co (☎ 824 845; 40A Đ 2 Thang 9; hotpot 30,000d) *Lau* (hotpot) is the speciality here, but it also serves good Chinese fare.

There are a string of local point-and-eat *com binh dan* **restaurants** (rice plates 7000d) along Đ Nguyen Thi Minh Khai that are worth checking out.

Hoa Nang Café Enjoy an iced coffee on the riverfront.

Phuong Thuy Another establishment with OK food and fine river views.

Vinh Long Market Sample some delicious local fruit and take in the scenery.

Getting There & Away
BOAT
It may be possible to travel by cargo boat from Vinh Long all the way to Chau Doc (near the Cambodian border), but you'll probably need a Vietnamese person to help you decide if you want to attempt this.

BUS
There are buses between Vinh Long and HCMC (three hours), which leave HCMC

from Cholon bus station (p363) in District 5, and from Mien Tay bus station (p363). You can also get to Vinh Long by bus from My Tho, Tra Vinh, Can Tho, Chau Doc and other points on the Mekong Delta. Vinh Long's bus station is conveniently located smack in the middle of town.

CAR & MOTORBIKE
Vinh Long is just off Hwy 1, 66km from My Tho, 33km from Can Tho and 136km from HCMC.

TRA VINH
☎ 074 / pop 70,000
Bordered by the Tien and Hau branches of the Mekong, Tra Vinh's location on a peninsula makes it somewhat isolated. Getting there is a straight up and back trip, because no car ferries cross the rivers here (motorbikes can be ferried by small boats). Western tourists are few, though there are several very worthwhile things to see here.

About 300,000 ethnic Khmer live in Tra Vinh province. At first glance, they might seem to be an invisible minority since they all speak fluent Vietnamese and there's nothing outwardly distinguishing about their clothing or lifestyle. However, digging a little deeper quickly reveals that Khmer culture is alive and well in this part of Vietnam. There are over 140 Khmer pagodas in Tra Vinh province, compared with 50 Vietnamese and five Chinese pagodas. The pagodas have schools to teach the Khmer language – most of the locals in Tra Vinh can read and write Khmer at least as well as Vietnamese.

Vietnam's Khmer minority are almost all followers of Theravada Buddhism. If you've visited monasteries in Cambodia, you may have observed that Khmer monks are not involved in growing food and rely on donations from the strictly religious locals. Here in Tra Vinh, Vietnamese guides will proudly point out the monks' rice harvest as one of the accomplishments of liberation. To the Vietnamese government, nonworking monks were parasites. The Khmers don't necessarily see it the same way and continue to donate funds to the monasteries surreptitiously.

Between the ages of 15 and 20, most boys set aside a few months or years to

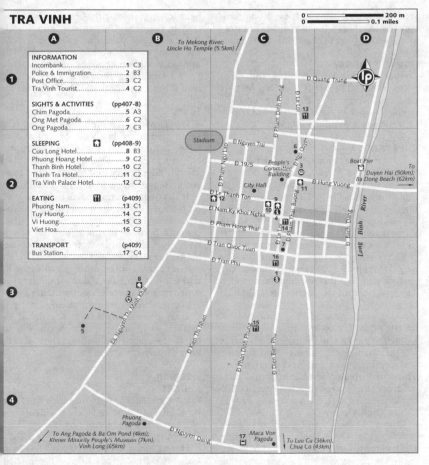

TRA VINH

0 _____ 200 m
0 _____ 0.1 miles

INFORMATION
Incombank..............................1 C3
Police & Immigration.............2 B3
Post Office.............................3 C2
Tra Vinh Tourist.....................4 C2

SIGHTS & ACTIVITIES (pp407-8)
Chim Pagoda.........................5 A3
Ong Met Pagoda....................6 C2
Ong Pagoda..........................7 C3

SLEEPING (pp408-9)
Cuu Long Hotel......................8 B3
Phuong Hoang Hotel..............9 C2
Thanh Binh Hotel.................10 C2
Thanh Tra Hotel...................11 C2
Tra Vinh Palace Hotel...........12 C2

EATING (p409)
Phuong Nam.........................13 C1
Tuy Huong...........................14 C2
Vi Huong.............................15 C3
Viet Hoa..............................16 C3

TRANSPORT (p409)
Bus Station..........................17 C4

live as monks (they decide themselves on the length of service). Khmer monks are allowed to eat meat, although they cannot kill animals.

There is also a small but active Chinese community in Tra Vinh, one of the few remaining in the Mekong Delta region.

Information

Tra Vinh Tourist (☎ 862 559; fax 866 768; 64-6 Đ Le Loi; ☼ 8am-6pm) has a monopoly here. The staff can book various trips to sites around the province, though the boat trips prove to be the most interesting.

Incombank (☎ 863 827; fax 863 886; 15A Đ Dien Bien Phu) can exchange foreign currencies and handles Visa cash advances.

Sights
ONG PAGODA

The very ornate, brightly painted **Ong Pagoda** (Chua Ong & Chua Tau; cnr Đ Pham Thai Buong & Đ Tran Quoc Tuan) is – rarely for the Mekong Delta region – a 100% Chinese pagoda and still a very active place of worship. The red-faced god on the altar is deified general Quan Cong (in Chinese, Guangong, Guandi or Guanyu). Quan Cong is believed to offer protection against war and is based on an historical figure, a soldier of the 3rd century. You can read more about him in the Chinese classic *The Romance of the Three Kingdoms*.

The Ong Pagoda was founded in 1556 by the Fujian Chinese Congregation, but has been rebuilt a number of times. Recent

MEKONG DELTA

visitors from Taiwan and Hong Kong have contributed money for the pagoda's restoration, which is why it is in such fine shape.

ONG MET PAGODA
The chief reason for visiting the large Khmer **Ong Met Pagoda** (Chua Ong Met) is its accessibility – it's right in the centre of town. The monks at are friendly and happy to show you around the interior.

CHIM PAGODA
An interesting monastery, **Chim Pagoda** (Chua Chim) sees few visitors because you have to wind your way along dirt roads to find it. It's actually just 1km off the main highway to Vinh Long in the southwest part of town. Probably the best way to get there, if you don't have your own wheels, is to get a local to take you on a motorbike.

The friendly monks here claim that the pagoda was built 500 years ago, though the present structure is obviously much newer. There are about 20 monks in residence here.

BA OM POND & ANG PAGODA
Known as Ao Ba Om (Square Lake), this is a spiritual site for the Khmers and a picnic and drinking spot for local Vietnamese. The square-shaped pond is surrounded by tall trees and is pleasant if not spectacular.

More interesting is the nearby Ang Pagoda (Chua An in Vietnamese; Angkor Rek Borei in Khmer), a beautiful and venerable Khmer-style pagoda. There is also an interesting **Khmer Minority People's Museum** (Bao Tang Van Hoa Dan Tac; admission free; 7.30-11am & 1.30-4.30pm Mon-Fri) of Khmer culture on the far side of the lake, though little is labelled in English.

Ba Om Pond is 7km southwest from Tra Vinh along the highway towards Vinh Long.

UNCLE HO TEMPLE
Sometimes Vietnam throws something totally unexpected at you. Tra Vinh chips in with the **Uncle Ho Temple** (Den Tho Bac), dedicated, of course, to the late president Ho Chi Minh. Perhaps Tra Vinh's enterprising People's Committee was looking for a way to distinguish its fine town and put it on the tourist circuit. If so, it may have succeeded – although no monks have taken up residence, 'worshippers' continue to flock

here (Communist Party brass arrive regularly in their chauffeur-driven limousines). A local tourist pamphlet calls the temple the 'pride of Tra Vinh's inhabitants'. Ho himself would no doubt be horrified.

The Uncle Ho Temple is at Long Duc commune, 5km north of Tra Vinh town.

Tours
The narrow Long Binh River meanders southward from Tra Vinh town for over 10km before reaching a **spillway**. This was built to prevent sea water from intruding at high tide; otherwise the salt would contaminate the river and kill the crops.

It is possible to hire boats from the pier on the east side of town to take you downstream to the spillway. Tra Vinh Tourist can also book you onto these trips, which typically take about 1½ hours by speedboat, longer for a slower boat.

Tours can also be arranged to **Oyster Island** (Con Ngao), an offshore mud flat that supports a small contingent of oyster farmers (of limited interest for most). Tra Vinh Tourist offers trips for US$100 per boat regardless of group size, though you should be able to negotiate something cheaper with boat drivers at the pier.

Sleeping
BUDGET
Thanh Binh Hotel (858 120; fax 858 906; 1 Đ Le Thanh Ton; r 60,000-130,000đ;) It's definitely old, but fairly clean and tidy. Small, blue-tiled rooms come with hot water and TV.

Phuong Hoang Hotel (858 270; 1 Đ Le Thanh Ton; r 50,000-176,000đ;) Rooms behind the thin bamboo doors are a bit dingy but OK. There's no hot water at this hotel.

MID-RANGE
Tra Vinh Palace Hotel (864 999; fax 863 005; 3 Đ Le Thanh Ton; r US$17-26;) A big dose of the colour pink, lots of plants in the courtyard, and spotless rooms with heavy carved furniture and bathtubs make this the most pleasant place to stay in Tra Vinh.

Cuu Long Hotel (862 615; cuulonghoteltravinh@hcm.vnn.vn; 999 Đ Nguyen Thi Minh Khai; r/ste US$20/35;) The Cuu Long offers the usual mid-range amenities. In addition to balconies, fridges and TVs, rooms are decorated with pretty wood furniture and bamboo details. Suites are huge, with tubs in the bathrooms.

Thanh Tra Hotel (☎ 853 621; fax 853 769; 1 Đ Pham Thai Buong; r US$13-27; 🔀) Most tour groups are put up here for the night, as it's big and central. Comfortable and clean rooms are large, and there are pool tables on the 2nd floor.

Eating
Phuong Nam (☎ 853 511; Đ Chau Van Tiep; mains 12,000đ) The spot for excellent barbecued and clay-pot dishes.

Viet Hoa (☎ 863 046; 80 Đ Tran Phu; mains 10,000đ) Run by a friendly Chinese family, this is one of the best places to eat in town.

Vi Huong (Đ Phan Dinh Phung; mains 10,000đ) A very cheap place doing simple rice dishes.

Tuy Huong (☎ 858 312; Đ Pham Thai Buong; mains 9000đ) Another good place to sample local Vietnamese fare.

Getting There & Away
Tra Vinh is 65km from Vinh Long and 205km from HCMC. Either Vinh Long or Can Tho would be logical places to catch buses to Tra Vinh. Tra Vinh's intercity bus station is on Đ Nguyen Dang, on the south side of town.

AROUND TRA VINH
Chua Co
A Khmer monastery, Chua Co is particularly interesting because the grounds form a bird sanctuary. Several types of stork and ibis arrive here in large numbers just before sunset to spend the night here. Of course, there are many nests here and you must take care not to disturb them.

Chua Co is 43km from Tra Vinh. Travel 36km to Tra Cu then follow the sandy road for 7km to the monastery.

Luu Cu
Some **ancient ruins** are to be found at Luu Cu, south of Tra Vinh near the shores of the Hau Giang River. The ruins include brick foundations similar to those found at Cham temples. There have been a series of archaeological digs here and the site is now protected. The site is 10km from the town of Tra Cu (36km from Tra Vinh).

Ba Dong Beach
This yellow-sand beach is not bad compared with other 'beaches' in the Mekong Delta, but the main attraction at Ba Dong

Beach is the peace and quiet – it sees very few visitors. **Tra Vinh Tourist** (☎ 862 559) runs a restaurant and some simple bungalows by the beach – it is possible to stay overnight for around US$5.

To get to Ba Dong Beach from Tra Vinh, head 50km along the paved road to Duyen Hai and follow the bumpy dirt road for 12km until you reach the beach.

SA DEC
☎ 067 / pop 101,800
The former capital of Dong Thap province, Sa Dec gained as some small fame as the setting for *The Lover*, a film based on the novel by Marguerite Duras. Two of the classic French villas used in the film can be seen across the river from the outdoor market area.

Sa Dec is famous for its many nurseries that cultivate flowers and bonsai trees. The flowers are picked almost daily and transported fresh to shops in HCMC. These nurseries are a major sightseeing attraction for domestic tourists, especially around the Tet festival holiday.

Groups doing a whirlwind tour of the Mekong Delta often make a lunch stop here and drop in on the nurseries.

Information
There's an **Internet service** (☎ 862 010; Đ Hung Vuong) next door to the **post office** (cnr Đ Hung Vuong & Quoc Lo 80). Hwy 80 is also known as Đ Nguyen Sinh Sac as it passes through town.

Sights
HUONG TU PAGODA
Of classic Chinese design is the **Huong Tu Pagoda** (Chua Co Huong Tu), where a bright white statue of Quan The Am Bo Tat standing on a pedestal adorns the grounds. Don't confuse this place with the adjacent Buu Quang Pagoda, which is somewhat less glamorous.

NURSERIES
The **nurseries** (vuon hoa; 🕑 8-11am & 1-5pm) operate year-round, though they are practically stripped bare of their flowers just before Tet. You're welcome to have a look around, but don't pick any flowers unless you plan on buying them. Photography is permitted – indeed, the flower farmers are used to it.

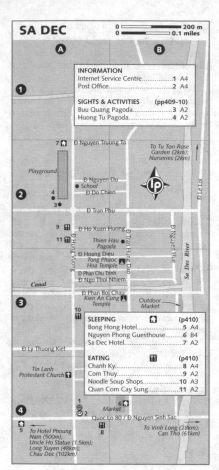

The nurseries don't belong to one person. There are many small operators here, each with a different speciality. The most famous garden is called the **Tu Ton Rose Garden** (Vuon Hong Tu Ton; ☺ 8-11am & 1-5pm), which has over 500 different kinds of rose in 50 different shades and colours.

UNCLE HO STATUE
We're not being facetious – they really do call it 'Uncle Ho Statue' (Tuong Bac Ho) in Vietnamese. Ho Chi Minh didn't live in Sa Dec, but his father did. To commemorate this bit of historical consequence, a large statue of Ho Chi Minh (but not his father!) has been erected about 1.5km west of town. You'll need a motorbike to get out there, as

it's probably too far for a *cyclo* unless you have a lot of time and patience.

Sleeping
Not many foreigners overnight in Sa Dec because nearby Cao Lanh, Long Xuyen and Vinh Long all tend to siphon off the tourists. Still, Sa Dec is a pleasant, if not very exciting, place to spend an evening.

Sa Dec Hotel (☎ 861 430; fax 862 828; 108/5A Đ Hung Vuong; r US$8-18; 🛇) The main tourist accommodation in town, this hotel has comfortable rooms with balconies, and bathtubs with hot water to go in them.

Hotel Phuong Nam (☎ 867 867; phuongnam384@ yahoo.com; 384A Đ Nguyen Sinh Sac; s/d 100,000/150,000d; 🛇) Wood floors and a quiet atmosphere set this place apart. Bathrooms can be slightly musty, but the place is otherwise very clean.

Bong Hong Hotel (☎ 868 288; fax 868 289; 251A Đ Nguyen Sinh Sac; r & ste US$6-16; 🛇) A newish hotel with less personality than the Sa Dec, its rooms have amenities like fridge, bathtub, phone and TV.

Nguyen Phong Guesthouse (☎ 866 515; 1/A2 Đ Tran Hung Dao; s & d 120,000d; 🛇) Very clean and fairly basic, the Nguyen Phong is Sa Dec's cheapest option. Rooms have hot water and TV.

Eating
Chanh Ky (☎ 864 065; 192 Đ Nguyen Sinh Sac; mains 15,000d) Rice dishes, *chao* and tasty noodle soups like *mi quang* are served here.

Com Thuy (☎ 861 644; 439 Đ Hung Vuong; mains 15,000d) This is a local eatery worth trying. The food is good, but the bizarre facial expressions on the fish in the big tank are even better!

Quan Com Cay Sung (☎ 861 749; 437 Đ Hung Vuong; mains 15,000d) is next door to Thuy and also serves respectable Vietnamese fare.

A bit further south on Đ Hung Vuong are a few good **noodle soup shops** (soups around 5000d).

Getting There & Away
Sa Dec is midway between Vinh Long and Long Xuyen and accessible by bus, minibus and car.

CAO LANH
☎ 067 / pop 139,100
A new town carved from the jungles and swamps of the Mekong Delta region, Cao Lanh's up-and-coming status has much

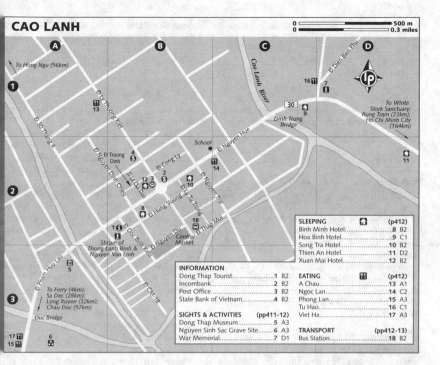

CAO LANH

0 _____ 500 m
0 _____ 0.3 miles

To Hong Ngu (56km)

Cao Lanh River

To White
Stork Sanctuary;
Rung Tram (23km);
Ho Chi Minh City
(164km)

Dinh Trung
Bridge

School

Đ Nguyen Hue

Statue of
Thong Lanh Binh &
Nguyen Van Linh

Central
Market

To Ferry (4km);
Sa Dec (28km);
Long Xuyen (32km);
Chau Doc (57km)

Duc Bridge

INFORMATION	
Dong Thap Tourist	1 B2
Incombank	2 B2
Post Office	3 B2
State Bank of Vietnam	4 B2

SIGHTS & ACTIVITIES	(pp411-12)
Dong Thap Museum	5 A3
Nguyen Sinh Sac Grave Site	6 A3
War Memorial	7 D1

SLEEPING		(p412)
Binh Minh Hotel	8	B2
Hoa Binh Hotel	9	C1
Song Tra Hotel	10	B2
Thien An Hotel	11	D2
Xuan Mai Hotel	12	B2

EATING		(p412)
A Chau	13	A1
Ngoc Lan	14	C2
Phong Lan	15	A3
Tu Hao	16	C1
Viet Ha	17	A3

TRANSPORT	(pp412-13)
Bus Station	18 B2

to do with its designation as the provincial capital of Dong Thap province. Boat tours of bird sanctuaries and Rung Tram (Tram Forest) are major attractions in this region.

Information

Dong Thap Tourist (☎ /fax 855 637; dothatour@hcm .vnn.vn; 2 Đ Doc Binh Kieu) deserves kudos for being so helpful. This is the best place to inquire about boat tours of the surrounding area. A boat-station **branch office** (☎ 821054) handles boat tours from a landing in My Hiep village.

Public **Internet access** (per hr 15,000d) is available at the Xuan Mai Hotel (p412). The post office is at 85 Đ Nguyen Hue. Exchange cash at the **Incombank** (☎ 822 030; Đ Nguyen Hue) or the **State Bank of Vietnam** (☎ 852 198; 50 Đ Ly Thuong Kiet).

Sights

DONG THAP MUSEUM

The well-designed **Dong Thap Museum** (admission free; ☼ 7-11am & 1-4pm) is the best museum in the Mekong Delta. The 1st floor displays

an anthropological history of Dong Thap province, with exhibits of tools, sculpture, models of traditional houses and a few stuffed animals. The 2nd floor is devoted to war history and, of course, to Ho Chi Minh. All interpretive signs are in Vietnamese.

WAR MEMORIAL

On the eastern edge of town off Hwy 30, the **War Memorial** (Dai Liet Si) is Cao Lanh's most prominent landmark. This masterpiece of socialist-style sculpture boasts a clamshell-shaped building displaying a large Vietnamese star alongside a hammer and sickle. In front of this are several concrete statues of victorious peasants and soldiers with upraised fists and brandishing weapons. The surrounding grounds are decked out with the graves of over 3000 VC who died while fighting in the American War.

Construction of the War Memorial began in 1977 and finished in 1984.

NGUYEN SINH SAC GRAVE SITE

Another significant **tomb** here is that of Nguyen Sinh Sac (1862-1929). Nguyen's main contribution to Vietnamese history was being Ho Chi Minh's father. His tomb (Lang Cu Nguyen Sinh Sac) occupies one hectare about 1km southwest of Cao Lanh.

Although there are various plaques (in Vietnamese) and tourist pamphlets extolling Nguyen Sinh Sac as a great revolutionary, there is little evidence to suggest that he was involved in the anticolonial struggle against the French.

Sleeping
BUDGET

Binh Minh Hotel (☎ 853 423; 157 Đ Hung Vuong; r US$3-8; 🔀) Owned by a friendly local school teacher, this is one of the cheapest places in town and is recommended. A few new rooms were under construction when we visited; current bathrooms have squat toilets only.

Thien An Hotel (☎ 853 041; 177 Quoc Lo 30; r US$10; 🔀) A couple of the rooms here have river views and all have hot water, making this a decent value. It's about 500m from the War Memorial.

MID-RANGE

Hoa Binh Hotel (☎ 851 469; fax 851 218; Quoc Lo 30; r/ste US$15/20; 🔀) Opposite the War Memorial, this is the city's most upmarket hotel. Rooms have satellite TV and heavy hardwood furniture. Try to book a room in the pleasant villa at the rear – it's conveniently located near the in-house beer garden!

Xuan Mai Hotel (☎ 852 852; fax 856 776; 33 Đ Le Qui Don; d US$16-20; 🔀 🖳) Behind the post office, the Xuan Mai has a restaurant, and all rooms have hot water and bathtubs.

Song Tra Hotel (☎ 852 624; fax 852 623; 178 Đ Nguyen Hue; r & ste US$14-20; 🔀) Staff at this government-run hotel are friendly, and the place is equipped with lift and satellite TV.

Eating

Cao Lanh is famous for rice-field rats (chuot dong) and it's as good a place as any to sample the local delicacy!

A Chau (☎ 852 202; 105B Đ Ly Thuong Kiet; mains 15,000-40,000d) This place specialises in fried pancakes (banh xeo) that you roll up and dip in fish sauce. The goat hotpot (lau de) is also yummy.

Tu Hao (☎ 852 589; Đ Dien Bien Phu; mains 25,000-45,000d) One of the best eateries in town, Tu Hao serves all kinds of barbecued food, including rice-field rats and the snakes who like to eat them! The house special are the fresh spring rolls (cuon banh trang).

Ngoc Lan (☎ 851 498; 208 Đ Nguyen Hue; mains 15,000d) If you're after something local, dine at Ngoc Lan. You might try the shredded frog, or better yet, the 'raw dish bowel'.

Viet Ha (☎ 851 639; 206 Đ Pham Huu Lau; mains 20,000d) Serving good Vietnamese food, Viet Ha is on the road to the ferry, just south of the Duc Bridge.

Phong Lan (Orchid Garden; ☎ 851 294; mains 30,000d) Near Viet Ha, Phong Lan is a tastier but slightly more expensive option.

In a pinch there are decent restaurants in both the Song Tra and Hoa Binh Hotels (see above and left, respectively).

Getting There & Around

The road between Cao Lanh and Long Xuyen is beautiful but has few buses. You'll

---

ONE IN EVERY COUNTRY

One of the world's commonalities, something shared by urbanites of all nationalities in their own language, is a somewhat derogatory term for rural folk. English speakers call them country bumpkins, rednecks or hicks, while the Japanese, for example, say inaka mon.

In Vietnam, however, the word for countryside is nha que and this is the term they use in the north. But in the 'rice basket' of the Mekong Delta, the regional articulation of choice is hai lua. Literally 'second rice', hai lua refers to when the customarily not-so-clever second son of a rice farming family (the guy with no street savvy) visits the big city. Remember Crocodile Dundee?

Hai lua, pronounced high loo-ah, can be a handy phrase to learn before heading into the Mekong Delta. Now, we're not suggesting here that you attempt to go around insulting the locals. Rather, using this expression in a self-deprecating way, or perhaps aiming the slur at your travel companion, will surely get a rise out of the locals. It would be like saying, 'Please forgive the stupidity of my feeble-witted friend.' Just remember not to use it towards people you don't know!

JOHN ELK III

Rural houses, Chau Doc (p429), Mekong Delta

Rice paddy, Mekong Delta
(p391)

RICHARD I'ANSON

MASON FLORENCE

Khmer school children, Tra Vinh (p406),
Mekong Delta

ANDERS BLOMQVIST

View of Chau Doc from Sam Mountain (p434),
Mekong Delta

Bassac River, Mekong Delta (p391)

Floating market along the Mekong Delta (p391)

JOHN ELK III

Tay An Pagoda (p434), Sam Mountain, Mekong Delta

JOHN BANAGAN

NICK WELLMAN

Local, Ha Tien (p440)

obably need to hire your own vehicle to
ke that route, but try your luck at the bus
ation next to the market.

The sights around Cao Lanh are best
sited by river. Although you could pos-
bly arrange something privately with boat
wners, you'll probably find it easier to deal
ith Dong Thap Tourist (p411).

There are too many different combin-
ions of boat sizes and possible destinations
list them all, but a group of 15 people
ould be charged about US$2 per person
r a half-day tour, including all transport.
group of five might pay US$5 each for the
me thing. You may not be travelling with
companions, but you can try rounding
other travellers at the hotels in town.

ROUND CAO LANH
hite Stork Sanctuary

o the northeast of Cao Lanh is a bird
nctuary (Vuon Co Thap Muoi) for white
orks. A white stork standing on the back of
water buffalo is the symbol of the Mekong
elta and you probably have more chance
f seeing a stork here than anywhere else.
he sanctuary only covers two hectares,
t the birds seem mostly undisturbed by
e nearby farmers (who have been sternly
arned not to hunt them).

The storks are accustomed to people and
re fairly easy to spot, as they feed in the
angrove and bamboo forests. They live in
airs and don't migrate with the seasons, so
ou can see them at any time of year. The
irds live on freshwater crabs and other tit-
its that they catch in the canals.

There are no roads as such to the bird
nctuary, so getting there requires a trip by
oat. Dong Thap Tourist (p411) can arrange
is, though you may be able to arrange it
sewhere. A speedboat costs US$25 per hour
nd the ride takes 50 minutes. A slow boat
osts US$4 per person (with 20 people) and
kes three hours to make the return journey.
the dry season, you have to plan your boat
ip according to the two daily tides – at low
de the canals can become impassable.

Many travellers include a trip to White
tork Sanctuary with a visit to Rung Tram
Tram Forest; see below).

ung Tram

outheast of Cao Lanh and accessible by
oat tour is the 46-hectare Rung Tram near
My Long village. The area is one vast swamp
with a beautiful thick canopy of tall trees
and vines. It's one of the last natural forests left in the Mekong Delta and by now
probably would have been turned into a
rice paddy were it not for its historical significance. During the American War, the
VC had a base here called Xeo Quit, where
top-brass VC lived in underground bunkers.
But don't mistake this for another Cu Chi
Tunnels – it's very different.

Only about 10 VC were here at any given
time. They were all generals who directed
the war from here, just 2km from a US
military base. The Americans never realised
that the VC generals were living right under
their noses. Of course, they were suspicious
about that patch of forest and periodically
dropped some bombs in it just to reassure
themselves, but the VC remained safe in
their underground bunkers.

Access to the area is most popular by boat
and many visitors combine a visit with a trip
to White Stork Sanctuary. A speedboat from
Cao Lanh to Rung Tram takes only a few
minutes, but a slow boat takes around 30
minutes (depending on the tides). It is also
possible now to reach the forest by road if
you are travelling by car or motorbike.

Beware of the exceedingly mean red ants
here: they are huge, fast and aggressive.

Tram Chim Nature Reserve

Due north of Cao Lanh in Tam Nong
(Dong Thap province) is Tram Chim National Wetland Reserve (Tram Chim Tam
Nong), which is notable for its **eastern sarus
cranes** (Grus antigone sharpii). Over 220
species of bird have been identified within
the reserve, but ornithologists will be most
interested in the rare red-headed cranes,
which grow to over 1.5m high.

The birds nest here from about December to June; from July to November they
migrate to Cambodia, so schedule your visit
to coordinate with the birds' travel itinerary if you want to see them. Also, the birds
are early risers – early morning is the best
time to see them, though you might get
a glimpse when they return home in the
evening. During the day, the birds are engaged in the important business of eating.

Seeing these birds requires a considerable
commitment (time, effort and money), so
it's really a special-interest tour. Because

you'll need to be up at the crack of dawn, staying in Cao Lanh doesn't work out too well – you would have to head out at 4.30am and travel in the dark over an unlit dirt road. This is not advisable, so you really need to stay at the government guesthouse in Tam Nong, which is much closer to where the birds are.

Tam Nong is a sleepy town 45km from Cao Lanh. The one-way drive takes about 1½ hours by car; it's also possible to get there by boat. A speedboat takes only one hour, but costs US$25 per hour to rent. A slow boat (per person US$4) can be arranged from Dong Thap Tourist (p411), but the one-way journey takes four hours and requires 20 people to make it economically viable. From the guesthouse in Tam Nong it takes another hour by small boat (per hour US$15) to reach the area where the cranes live and another hour to return. Add to this whatever time you spend (perhaps an hour) staring at your feathered friends through binoculars (bring your own), and then the requisite one to four hours to return to Cao Lanh, depending on your mode of transport.

The state-run **guesthouse** (r with fan US$10) in Tam Nong is just before the bridge, heading into town. We found the guesthouse deplorable; not only were the rooms filthy, the place was overrun with thousands of bugs and the staff had no insecticide. If you're going to stay here, you may want to stock up on toxic chemicals in Cao Lanh, or try to score a can of bug killer in town.

Tam Nong shuts down early – if you want to eat dinner here, make arrangements before 5pm and remember to bring insect repellent.

Phuong Chi (☎ 827 230; 537 Thi Tran Tram Chim) is a good restaurant close to the market in the town centre. Meals can be served later if you book in advance, but you will have to pay extra.

CAN THO

☎ 071 / pop 330,100

Can Tho, the (relatively) cosmopolitan capital of Can Tho province, is the political, economic, cultural and transportation centre of the Mekong Delta, as well as the largest city in the region. Rice-husking mills provide a major local industry.

This friendly, bustling city is connected to most other population centres in the Mekong Delta by a system of rivers and canals. These waterways and the colourful floating markets around the city are the major tourist drawcard in Can Tho – travellers come here to do economical boat trips.

Information

EMERGENCY
Hospital (Khoa Khan Benh; ☎ 820 071; 4 Đ Chau V Liem)

INTERNET ACCESS
Nu Hoang Internet Service (☎ 821 531; 9 Đ Chau Van Liem; ☾ 7.30am-11.30pm)

MONEY
Indovina Bank (☎ 827 368; fax 827 361; 59A Đ Phan Dinh Phung) Foreign-currency exchange.
Sacombank (☎ 810 519; fax 810 523; 13A Đ Phan Din Phung) Credit card advances can be done here.
Vietcombank (Ngan Hang Ngoai Thuong Viet Nam; ☎ 820 445; fax 820 694; 7 ĐL Hoa Binh) Has foreign-currency exchange and 24hr ATM.

POST
Post office (2 ĐL Hoa Binh)

TOURIST INFORMATION
Can Tho Tourist (☎ 821 852; fax 822 719; 20 Đ Hai Ba Trung; ☾ 7am-5pm & 6-8pm) Staff at this provincial tourism authority are pleasant and well equipped to serve tourists; they can also speak English, French and Japanese.
Vietnam Airlines (☎ 824 088) Has booking desk at the Can Tho Tourist office.

Sights

MUNIRANGSYARAM PAGODA
The ornamentation of **Munirangsyaram Pagoda** (36 ĐL Hoa Binh) is typical of Khmer Hinayana Buddhist pagodas: it doesn't have any of the multiple Bodhisattvas and Taoist spirits common in Vietnamese Mahayana pagodas. In the upstairs sanctuary, a 1.5m high representation of Siddhartha Gautama, the historical Buddha, sits serenely under a Bodhi Tree.

Built in 1946, the Munirangsyaram Pagoda serves the Khmer community of Can Tho, which numbers about 2000. Khmer monks hold daily prayers here.

CANTONESE CONGREGATION PAGODA
This small **Chinese pagoda** (Quan Cong Hoi Quan; Đ H Ba Trung) was built by the Cantonese Congregation. The original one was constructed on

CAN THO

0 _____ 200 m
0 _____ 0.1 miles

A **B** **C** **D**

Khai Luong Canal

Xang Canal

To Vinh Long (34km);
My Tho (96km);
Ho Chi Minh City (165km)

Hau River

Stadium

To Binh Thuy Temple
(5km); Vuon Co Stork
Garden (47km);
Long Xuyen (62km)

Đ Tran Phu

Cai Khe
Market

Đ Nguyen Trai

39
1

Đ Hung Vuong

To Short-Distance
Bus Depot (750m);
Phong Dien Floating
Market (20.5km);
Soc Trang (62.5km)

Cai Rang
Floating
Market
(5.5km)

Cai Khe Canal

INFORMATION
Cai Khe Post Office......................1 A2
Can Tho Tourist..........................2 C5
Hospital.....................................3 A6
Indovina Bank............................4 C6
Main Post Office.........................5 C4
Nu Hoang Internet Service...........6 C6
Sacombank................................7 C5
Vietcombank..............................8 B5

SIGHTS & ACTIVITIES   (pp414-16)
Can Tho Museum........................9 C5
Can Tho Water Park...................10 D2
Cantonese Congregation
  Pagoda..................................11 C5
Central Market..........................12 C5
Church....................................13 C4
Ho Chi Minh Museum.................14 B5
Ho Chi Minh Statue...................15 C5
Munirangsyaram Pagoda............16 B5
Provincial People's Committee
  Building.................................17 C4

SLEEPING   🛏 (pp416-17)
Asia Hotel................................18 B6
Can Tho Hotel...........................19 C6
Doan 30 Can Tho Hotel..............20 B3
Golf Hotel Can Tho....................21 C4
Hau Giang A Hotel.....................22 B5
Hien Guesthouse.......................23 C6
Hoa Binh Hotel.........................24 B5
Hotel-Restaurant 31...................25 C6
Huy Hoang Hotel.......................26 C6
Ngan Ha Hotel..........................27 C5
Ninh Kieu Hotel........................28 D4
Phong Nha Hotel.......................29 B6
Quoc Te Hotel..........................30 C5
Saigon-Can Tho Hotel................31 C5
Tay Do Hotel............................32 B6
Victoria Can Tho Hotel...............33 D4

EATING   🍴 (pp417-18)
Local Cafés..............................34 D2
Mekong...................................35 C5
Nam Bo...................................36 C5
Phuong Nam...........................(see 35)
Restaurant Alley........................37 C6
Thien Hoa................................38 C5

TRANSPORT   (p418)
Can Tho Bus Station...................39 A2
Vietnam Airlines.......................(see 2)

Approximate Scale

Shuttle Boat
Route

Hydrofoil Boat
Landing

Đ Nguyen Trai

20

13

Đ Xo Viet Nghe Tinh

Đ Vo Thi Sau

Fountain

17

5

Đ Ngo Quyen

14
9

Vietnamese
Pagoda

16

24

Đ Hoa Binh

8

Đ Ngo Quyen

Đ Ngo Van So

Đ Nguyen Thai Hoc

Đ Vo Van Tan

Đ Phan Dinh Phung

Đ Le Thanh Ton

27

7

22

31

12

Đ Ly Thuong Kiet

30
2
38
35
36

15

Local
Boat
Pier

Local
People's
Committee
Building

33

28

21

Lưu Hữu
Phuoc Park

Đ Phan Van Tri

3

Đ 30 Thang 4

Đ Nam Ky Khoi Nghia

Đ Nguyen An Ninh

Đ Chau Van Liem

Đ Dien Bien Phu

37

4

Đ Hai Ba Trung

Can Tho River

18 29   32 19

23

Đ Ngo Duc Ke

6

Đ Hai Thuong
Lan Ong

26 25

To Thanh
Thuy (3km)

To Phung Hiep
Floating Market (35.5km)

MEKONG DELTA

different site about 70 years ago. The current pagoda was built with funds donated by overseas Chinese more recently. Can Tho used to have a large ethnic-Chinese population, but most of them fled after the anti-Chinese persecutions (1978–79).

The pagoda occupies a splendid location facing the Can Tho River.

CENTRAL MARKET

Many local farmers and wholesalers arrive at this **market** (Đ Hai Ba Trung) by boat to buy and sell. The fruit section, near the intersection of Đ Hai Ba Trung and Đ Ngo Quyen, is particularly colourful and stays open until late evening.

HO CHI MINH MUSEUM

This is the only **museum** (☎ 823 591; fax 822 581; 6 ĐL Hoa Binh; admission free; ✆ 8-11am & 2-4.30pm Tue-Sat) in the Mekong Delta devoted to Ho Chi Minh and it's a bit of a mystery as to why it was built here, because Ho Chi Minh never lived in Can Tho. When we visited it had been closed 'temporarily' for a year already, but if you'd like to have a look, it's inside a gated courtyard near the main post office.

CAN THO MUSEUM

The enormous **Can Tho Museum** (☎ 813 890; 1 ĐL Hoa Binh; ✆ 8-11am & 2-5pm Tue, Wed & Thu; 8-11am & 6.30-9pm Sat, Sun & holidays) has locally-focused exhibits of historical and social interest.

Can Tho for Children
CAN THO WATER PARK

Let the kids – or your inner child – run amok in glorious chlorinated water at **Can Tho Water Park** (☎ 763 373; fax 761 730; Cai Khe Ward; adult/child 40,000/25,000đ; ✆ 9am-6pm Mon-Fri, 8am-7pm Sat & Sun). Among the fun attractions are water slides and a wave pool. Children under 80cm tall are admitted free.

Tours

The most interesting thing to do in Can Tho is take a boat ride through the canals and visit a floating market. The cost is around US$3 per hour for a small boat, which can carry two or three passengers. You won't have to look hard for boats – they will be looking for you. Just wander by the riverside near the market and you'll have plenty of offers. You can also book through Can

Tho Tourist, but this leaves little room fo negotiation. Most of the boats are operate by women.

Bring your camera, but keep it in a plas tic bag when it's not in use because it's eas to get splashed by the wake of motorise boats. The paddle boats only go on th smaller canals (which are actually more in teresting), where the current is weaker.

Larger motorboats can go further afiel and it's worth hiring one to make a tour c the Mekong River itself. Check the goin rates at Can Tho Tourist then see what's o offer at the pier by the Ninh Kieu Hotel (se opposite). For a three-hour tour of the ca nals and Cai Rang floating market expect t pay around 120,000đ for a small boat (on to four people), or 150,000đ for a larger on (five to 12 people). The cost of a five-hou boat trip to the Phong Dien floating marke (one to 10 people) is around 200,000đ. Th name of the game is negotiate.

For more on the area's floating markets see p418.

Sleeping

Can Tho boasts the best range of accom modation in the Mekong Delta.

BUDGET

Hien Guesthouse (☎ 812 718; hien_gh@yahoo.com 118/10 Đ Phan Dinh Phung; r US$4-10; ✖) Thi friendly, family-run guesthouse is tucke down a narrow (and quiet) alley a few min utes' walk from the city centre. Small, clear rooms come with floor-level mattresses i the older half of the building; proper bed are installed in the new rooms. Dependabl motorbikes can be rented here for aroun US$5 a day.

Huy Hoang Hotel (☎ 825 833; 35 Đ Ngo Duc Ke r 80,000-150,000đ; ✖) Another popular spot fo the backpacker crowd, the Huy Hoang i centrally located and has nice views from the common balcony.

Hotel-Restaurant 31 (☎ 825 287; 31 Đ Ngo Duc Ke r 70,000-150,000đ; ✖) This very clean hotel i next door to Huy Hoang and the restauran is recommended for good meals.

Phong Nha Hotel (☎ 821 615; 75 Đ Chau Van Liem r 60,000-150,000đ; ✖) It's cheap and sort o cosy here, with slatted wood doors and a low-key, family atmosphere. But the toilets are not the cleanest and it's on a noisy stree with many motorbikes.

Ngan Ha Hotel (☎ 821 024; fax 813 396; 39-41 Đ Ngo Quyen; r 70,000-200,000d; ✷) In a convenient but noisy location, this private hotel gets decent sun. All rooms have hot water and rates include breakfast.

MID-RANGE
Ninh Kieu Hotel (☎ 821 171; fax 821 104; 2 Đ Hai Ba Trung; r & ste US$25-35; ✷) This hotel belongs to the army and occupies a terrific location on the riverfront. Rooms with balconies and carpet have breakfast included in the rates. Expect higher rates in the new building, which was under construction when we visited.

Hoa Binh Hotel (☎ 810 218; hoabinhct@hcm.vnn.vn; 5 ĐL Hoa Binh; r US$18-31, ste US$52; ✷ ▭) Rooms have carpeting, IDD phones and satellite TV. With its elegant wood furniture, it's one of the better deals for this price range. Breakfast is included.

Saigon-Can Tho Hotel (☎ 825 831; www.saigon-cantho.com; 55 Đ Phan Dinh Phung; r US$38-50; ✷ ▭) All rooms are carpeted at this three-star place, which also has a restaurant, massage service, sauna and karaoke. Rates include breakfast.

Tay Do Hotel (☎ 827 009; taydoct@hcm.vnn.vn; 61 Đ Chau Van Liem; r US$27-35; ✷) The lobby may blind you with its shiny surfaces, but perhaps that can be fixed with a massage or soak in the sauna. Rooms come with amenities like satellite TV; the ones at the back are quieter and cheaper.

Doan 30 Can Tho Hotel (☎ 823 623; fax 811 140; 80A Đ Nguyen Trai; r & ste US$10-30; ✷) At the northern end of town, this army-owned place has an outdoor café on the riverside. Some rooms have balconies and river views, as well as huge bathrooms. Rates include a simple breakfast.

Quoc Te Hotel (International Hotel; ☎ 822 080; ksquocte-ct@hcm.vnn.vn; 12 Đ Hai Ba Trung; r & ste US$17-71; ✷) The expensive suites at the ageing Quoc Te have an excellent view of the river, but the budget rooms are a bad deal. Breakfast is included in the room rates. All rooms are carpeted.

Other mid-range possibilities:
Asia Hotel (Khach San A Chau; ☎ 812 800; asiahotel@hcm.vnn.vn; 91 Đ Chau Van Liem; r US$20-28; ✷) A nice place with large balconies; rates include breakfast.
Can Tho Hotel (☎ 811 770; fax 820 356; 41 Đ Chau Van Liem; r US$16-25; ✷) All the mid-range amenities, but slightly dingier than the above.

Hau Giang A Hotel (☎ 821 851; fax 821 139; 34-36 Đ Nam Ky Khoi Nghia; ✷) Attached restaurant, lift and the usual amenities; comfortable and clean.

TOP END
Victoria Can Tho Hotel (☎ 810 111; Cai Khe Ward; www.victoriahotels-asia.com; r US$135-250; ✷ ▭ ▣) This lovely place is Can Tho's *crème de la crème* and is right on the riverfront. There are rooms with garden or river views and eight spacious suites. Rates are exclusive of breakfast, tax and service. Facilities include two fine restaurants, an open-air bar, tennis courts and a swimming pool; even if you're not staying at the resort, it's worth coughing up US$5 for day use of the pool. The shuttle boat across the river is free. The hotel offers **boat trips** (2½ hr; per person US$25), which link the Victoria Can Tho and Chau Doc resorts; stopovers can be arranged en route.

Golf Hotel Can Tho (☎ 812 210; golfcanthohtl@hcm.vnn.vn; 2 Đ Hai Ba Trung; r US$50-149, ste US$185-200; ✷ ▭ ▣) The enormous and glitzy riverside Golf Hotel is near the Ninh Kieu pier. Tastefully decorated rooms are furnished to a 'T' and there are incredible views from the upper-floor balconies. Hotel facilities include a health club and a beauty salon; room rates include tax, service and breakfast.

Eating
Along the Can Tho River waterfront there are several café-restaurants, most serving Mekong specialities such as fish, frog and turtle, as well as standard backpacker fare.

Nam Bo (☎ 823 908; nambo@hcm.vnn.vn; 50 Đ Hai Ba Trung; mains 25,000-50,000d) Housed in a thoughtfully restored, classic French villa, Nam Bo offers excellent European and Vietnamese cuisine in a delightful atmosphere. The view of the local fruit market from the 2nd-storey terrace can't be beat. If you can't decide what to order, the pizzas are recommended.

Mekong (☎ 821 646; 38 Đ Hai Ba Trung; mains 15,000-25,000d) Mekong is always packed, for good reason: good Vietnamese food at reasonable prices.

Phuong Nam (☎ 812 077; 48 Đ Hai Ba Trung; mains 25,000d) As with Mekong, Phuong Nam is a delicious deal.

Other popular eateries line the riverfront strip, across from the huge Uncle Ho statue (which bears a curious resemblance to the Tin Man in *The Wizard of Oz*).

Thien Hoa (☎ 821 942; 26 Đ Hai Ba Trung; mains 15,000-25,000đ) The speciality of the house are delicious Hué-style spring rolls (dac biet cha gio re).

Thanh Thuy (☎ 840 207; 149 Đ 30 Thang 4; mains 20,000-40,000đ) This goat-meat speciality restaurant is run by a Frenchman, formerly a chef in Toulouse. Try the curried goat, or if you're feeling adventurous, the goat-scrotum hotpot. It also does good standard Vietnamese fare. The restaurant is a few kilometres out of town, just beyond the local university. Look for the sign on your left, just beyond the junction with Đ Tran Hoang Na.

Restaurant Alley (Đ Nam Ky Khoi Nghia; mains around 15,000đ) This is a good spot to escape the tourist scene on the riverfront. Situated in an alley between Đ Dien Bien Phu and Đ Phan Dinh Phung, there are about a dozen local restaurants scattered on both sides of the street.

Getting There & Away
BUS
There are buses leaving HCMC from Mien Tay bus station (p363; about 30,000đ, five hours). Express minibuses make the same trip in about the same time.

The main bus station in Can Tho is about a kilometre north of town at the intersection of Đ Nguyen Trai and Đ Tran Phu. There is another short-haul bus depot about 300m south of the intersection of Đ 30 Thang 4 and Đ Mau Than, which is good for getting to Soc Trang and the Phung Hiep floating market.

CAR & MOTORBIKE
Whether you travel by car or motorbike, the ride from HCMC to Can Tho along Hwy 1 takes about four hours. There is one ferry crossing at Binh Minh (in Can Tho). The Can Tho ferry runs from 4am to 2am.

To get from ĐL Hoa Binh in Can Tho to the ferry crossing, go along Đ Nguyen Trai to the main bus station and turn right onto Đ Tran Phu.

Getting Around
XE LOI
Unique to the Mekong Delta, these makeshift vehicles are the main form of transport around Can Tho. A xe loi is essentially a two-wheeled wagon attached to the rear of a motorbike, creating what resembles a

motorised cyclo, but with four wheels touching the ground rather than two. Fares around town should be about 3000đ per person (they can carry two, or sometimes more), a bit higher for trips to outlying areas.

AROUND CAN THO
Perhaps the biggest drawcard of the delta is its colourful **floating markets**. Unlike the floating markets you may have seen in Thailand, where small wooden boats thread narrow canals, most floating markets here are on the banks of wide stretches of river. Most begin early to avoid the daytime heat, so try to visit between 6am and 8am. The tides, however, are also a factor as bigger boats must often wait until the water is high enough for them to navigate.

Some of the smaller, rural floating markets are disappearing, largely because of improved roads and access to private and public transport. Many of the larger markets near urban areas, however, are still going strong.

Rural areas of Can Tho province, renowned for their durian, mangosteen and orange orchards, can easily be reached from Can Tho by boat or bicycle.

Cai Rang Floating Market
Just 6km from Can Tho in the direction of Soc Trang is Cai Rang, the biggest floating market in the Mekong Delta. There is a bridge here that serves as a great vantage point for photography. The market is best before 9am and, although some vendors hang out until noon, it's less lively by then.

Cai Rang can be seen from the road, but getting there is far more interesting by boat. From the market area in Can Tho it takes about an hour by river, or you can drive to the Cau Dau Sau boat landing (by the Dau Sau Bridge), from where it takes only about 10 minutes to reach the market.

Phong Dien Floating Market
Perhaps the best floating market in the Mekong Delta, Phong Dien has fewer motorised craft and more stand-up rowing boats. It's less crowded than Cai Rang and there are far fewer tourists. The market is at its bustling best between 6am and 8am. It is 20km southwest of Can Tho and most get there by road.

It is theoretically possible to do a whirlwind boat trip here, visiting the small canals on the way and finishing back at the Cai Rang floating market. This journey should take approximately five hours return from Can Tho.

Phung Hiep Floating Market

Until recently, the small town of Phung Hiep was notable for its eerie snake market. In 1998, however, a new national law banned the capture and sale of snakes in an effort to control the rapidly multiplying rat population (due to a relative absence of snakes) which had been devastating rice crops. Snake sellers throughout the country are now forced to operate underground.

These days the cages that used to swell with cobras and pythons are empty, and Phung Hiep is back to being a regular (yet interesting) market. There is a small-scale floating market under the bridge and boats can be hired here for a tour along the river.

Phung Hiep is right on Hwy 1, 35km from Can Tho in the direction of Soc Trang.

Stork Garden

On the road between Can Tho and Long Xuyen, **Vuon Co** (admission 2000d; ⏰ 5am-6pm) is a 1.3-hectare stork sanctuary. It is a popular stop for group tours who come to view the thousands of storks that reside here. There is a tall wooden viewing platform and the best times of day to see the birds are from 5am to 6am, and again between 4pm and 6pm.

Vuon Co is in the Thot Not district, about 15km southeast of Long Xuyen. Look for a sign in the hamlet of Thoi An: 'Ap Von Hoa'; coming from Can Tho the sign is on the west side of the road, immediately after a small bridge. It is a few kilometres off the main highway. Walk to it in about 30 minutes, or hire a motorbike taxi for about 5000d.

SOC TRANG

☎ 079 / pop 110,800

Soc Trang is the capital of Soc Trang province. Khmer people make up about 28% of the population. The town itself isn't much, but the Khmers have built some very impressive temples in the area. Furthermore, there is a very colourful annual festival (usually in December) and, if you're in the vicinity at the right time, it's very much worth your while to catch it.

Soc Trang Tourist (☎ 821 498; soctrangtourism. com; 131 Đ Nguyen Chi Thanh; ⏰ 8-11am & 1.30-5pm)

is adjacent to the Phong Lan 2 Hotel. The staff are friendly enough, but speak little English and are not all that accustomed to walk-in tourists.

The **post office** (☎ 820 051) is at 1 ĐL Tran Hung Dao.

Sights
KH'LEANG PAGODA

Except for the bright orange paint job, this **pagoda** (Chua Kh'leang) looks like it's been transported straight from Cambodia. Originally built from bamboo in 1533, it had a complete rebuild in 1905 (this time using concrete). There are seven religious festivals held here every year that are worth seeing – people come from outlying areas of the province for these events. Even outside of festival times, Khmer people drop in regularly to bring donations and pray.

Several monks reside in the pagoda, which also serves as a base for over 150 student monks who come from around the Mekong Delta to study at Soc Trang's College of Buddhist Education across the street. The monks are friendly and happy to show you around the pagoda and discuss Buddhism.

KHMER MUSEUM

This **museum** (Bao Tang Tinh Soc Trang; ☎ 822 983; 23 Đ Nguyen Chi Thanh; admission free; ⏰ 7-11am & 1-5pm Mon-Fri) is dedicated to the history and culture of Vietnam's Khmer minority. Indeed, it serves as a sort of cultural centre, and traditional dance and music shows are periodically staged here. There's no regular schedule of performances; however, something could be arranged for a group provided a little advance notice is given.

The Khmer Museum is opposite Kh'leang Pagoda and often appears closed; you may have to roust someone to let you in.

CLAY PAGODA

Buu Son Tu (Precious Mountain Temple) was founded over 200 years ago by a Chinese family named Ngo. Today the temple is better known as **Chua Dat Set** (Đ Mau Than 68), or Clay Pagoda.

Unassuming from the outside, this pagoda is highly unusual in that nearly everything inside is made entirely of clay. These objects were hand-sculpted by the monk Ngo Kim Tong. From age 20 until his death at 62, Tong, a genius artisan, dedicated his

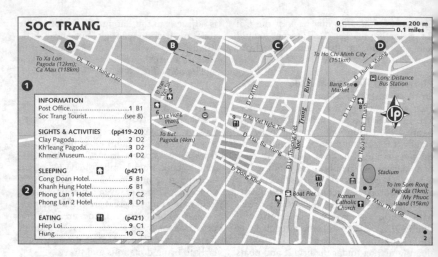

SOC TRANG

0 ————— 200 m
0 ————— 0.1 miles

INFORMATION
Post Office.................................1 B1
Soc Trang Tourist...................(see 8)

SIGHTS & ACTIVITIES (pp419-20)
Clay Pagoda.............................2 D2
Kh'leang Pagoda.......................3 D2
Khmer Museum.........................4 D2

SLEEPING (p421)
Cong Doan Hotel.......................5 B1
Khanh Hung Hotel.....................6 B1
Phong Lan 1 Hotel.....................7 C2
Phong Lan 2 Hotel.....................8 D1

EATING (p421)
Hiep Loi....................................9 C1
Hung.......................................10 C2

life to decorating the pagoda. He made the hundreds of statues and sculptures that adorn the interior today.

Entering the pagoda, visitors are greeted by one of Ngo's greatest creations – a six-tusked clay elephant (which is said to have appeared in a dream of Buddha's mother). Behind this is the centre altar, which alone was built from over five tonnes of clay. In the altar are a thousand Buddhas seated on lotus petals. Other highlights include a 13-storey Chinese-style tower over 4m tall. The tower features 208 cubby-holes, each with a mini-Buddha figure inside, and is decorated with 156 dragons.

Two giant candles have been burning here unceasingly since the clay artist died in 1970. To get an idea of how big these were to begin with (200kg and 260cm tall), there is another pair waiting to be lit when the current ones (expected to burn until 2005) are spent.

Though some of the stuff here is bordering on kitsch – our favourites are the lions with red light bulbs for eyeballs – the pagoda is an active place of worship, and totally different from the Khmer and Vietnamese Buddhist pagodas found elsewhere in Soc Trang. The resident monk, Ngo Kim Giang, is the younger brother of the artist and a delightful old man to chat with about the pagoda. He speaks excellent French although very little English.

The Clay Pagoda is within walking distance of the town centre. Needless to say, the clay objects in the pagoda are fragile – do not touch.

IM SOM RONG PAGODA

This large, beautiful **Khmer pagoda** was built in 1961 and is notable for its well-kept gardens. A plaque on the grounds honours the man who donated the funds to build the pagoda. There are many monks in residence here, most of whom are very friendly and happy to chat.

Im Som Rong Pagoda is over 1km east of Soc Trang on the road to My Phuoc Island. When you reach the main gate it's a 300m walk along a dirt track to the pagoda itself.

Festivals & Events
OC BOM BOC FESTIVAL

Once a year, the Khmer community turns out for the **Oc Bom Boc Festival**, with longboat races on the Soc Trang River. This event attracts visitors from all over Vietnam and even Cambodia. First prize is over US$1000, so it's not difficult to see why competition is so fierce.

The races are held according to the lunar calendar on the 15th day of the 10th moon, which roughly means December. The races start at noon, but things get jumping in Soc Trang the evening before. Not surprisingly, hotel space is at a premium during the festival and travellers without a prepaid hotel reservation will probably have to sleep in a car or minibus.

Sleeping

Phong Lan 2 Hotel (☎ 821 757; phonglan2@soctrang
tourism.com; 133 Đ Nguyen Chi Thanh; r US$8-17; ❄)
Though a bit run-down, this is still an OK
place to stay, with very friendly staff. Rates
include breakfast, and the place is notable
for its massage and sauna service.

Khanh Hung Hotel (☎ 821 027; ksankhanhhung@
hcm.vnn.vn; 15 ĐL Tran Hung Dao; r US$8-30; ❄) The
Khanh Hung boasts a large indoor-outdoor
café. There is satellite TV, but it only shows
Indian soap operas and movies; all rooms
have balconies.

Phong Lan 1 Hotel (☎ 821 619; phonglan1@soc
trangtourism.com; 124 Đ Dong Khoi; r US$16-21; ❄)
This riverside hotel is a bit pricey by local
standards, though rates include breakfast. If
you're with a group it can arrange a traditional Khmer music and dance show.

Cong Doan Hotel (☎ 825 614; fax 829 008; 4 Đ Tran
Van Sac; r 60,000-120,000d; ❄) Despite being on
the new side, this is a rather dingy state-
run hotel.

Eating

Most restaurants in Soc Trang do not have
English menus, nor are meal prices written
anywhere, so you will have to work it out in
this town like the Vietnamese do.

Hung (☎ 822 268; 74-76 Đ Mau Than 68; mains
20,000d) One of the best places in town, Hung
is open from breakfast until late into the
evening and always seems to be busy.

Hiep Loi (☎ 821 301; 11 Đ CMT8; mains 15,000d)
This spot is another popular local eatery
worth trying for Vietnamese food.

Getting There & Away

Long-distance buses stop at the station
on Đ Nguyen Chi Thanh, just down the
street from Soc Trang Tourist. Buses run
between Soc Trang and most Mekong cities,
including Can Tho and Ca Mau.

AROUND SOC TRANG
Bat Pagoda

This is one of the Mekong Delta's most
unusual sights and has become a favourite stopoff for both foreign and domestic
tourists. The Bat Pagoda (Chua Doi) is a
large monastery compound. Upon entering
through an archway, you'll almost immediately hear the eerie screeching of the large
colony of fruit bats residing here. There are
thousands of these creatures hanging from

the fruit trees. The largest bats weigh about
1kg and have a wingspan of about 1.5m.

Fruit bats make plenty of noise – in the
morning the din is incredible (likewise the
smell). The bats are not toilet trained, so
watch out when standing under a tree or
bring an umbrella. In the evening, the bats
spread their wings and fly out to invade
orchards all over the Mekong Delta, much
to the consternation of farmers, who are
known to trap the bats and eat them. Inside
the monastery the creatures are protected
and the bats seem to know this – no doubt
this is why they stay.

Locals tend to show excessive zeal
in shaking the trees to make the bats fly
around so that tourists can take photos,
but it's better to leave the poor things in
peace. You can easily get a photo of the
bats hanging off a branch if you have a good
telephoto lens. The best times for visiting
are early morning and at least an hour before sunset, when the bats are most active.
Around dusk, hundreds of bats swoop out
of the trees to go foraging.

The monks are very friendly and don't
ask for money, though it doesn't hurt to
leave a donation. The pagoda is decorated
with gilt Buddhas and murals paid for by
overseas-Vietnamese contributors. In one
room there's a life-size statue of the monk
who was the former head of the complex.
There's also a beautifully painted Khmer
longboat here of the type used at the Oc
Bom Boc Festival.

Behind the pagoda is an odd tomb
painted with the image of a pig. It was
erected in memory of a pig with five toenails (usually pigs have only four toenails).
It died in 1996, but two other rare pigs with
five toenails have survived and are being
raised by the monks. These pigs are not for
eating – they are pets.

Little kids hang around the front gate and
beg from the tourists, but they aren't allowed
inside the monastery grounds. We didn't give
money but handed over a packet of biscuits –
the kids devoured them as if they hadn't
eaten in over a week. Perhaps they hadn't.

There's a small restaurant just opposite
the Bat Pagoda.

The Bat Pagoda is about 4km west of Soc
Trang. You can catch a motorbike taxi or
easily walk there in under an hour. About
3km out of town towards the pagoda the

road splits into two – take the right fork and continue for 1km.

Xa Lon (Sa Lon) Pagoda

This magnificent, classic **Khmer pagoda** is 12km from Soc Trang, towards Ca Mau, on Hwy 1. The original structure was built over 200 years ago from wooden materials. In 1923 it was completely rebuilt, but proved to be too small. From 1969 to 1985, the present-day large pagoda was slowly built as funds trickled in from donations. The ceramic tiles on the exterior of the pagoda are particularly stunning.

As at other pagodas, the monks lead an austere life. They eat breakfast at 6am and beg for contributions until 11am, when they hold a one-hour worship. They eat again at noon and study in the afternoon – they do not eat dinner.

At present, around 25 monks reside here. The pagoda also operates a school for the study of Buddhism and Sanskrit. The reason for studying Sanskrit, as the monks explained, is that all original books about Buddhism were written in this ancient language.

My Phuoc Island

A 15km journey east of Soc Trang brings you to the Hau Giang River. From there it's a short boat ride to My Phuoc Island. It's an isolated spot very suitable for growing fruit. The local government tourist agency likes to bring foreigners here for tours of the orchards. You can do it yourself, though this is a little complicated since you'll need a motorbike to get to the river.

BAC LIEU

☎ 0781 / pop 129,300

The capital of southern Bac Lieu province, Bac Lieu is 280km from HCMC. Of the 800,000 people living in the province, about 8% are of Chinese or Cambodian origin.

The town has a few elegant but forlorn French colonial buildings, like the impressive **Fop House** (now used as a community sports centre), but not much else.

Farming is a difficult occupation here because of saltwater intrusion, which means that the town has remained fairly poor. The province is, however, known for its healthy longan orchards. In addition to this, the enterprising locals eke out a living from fishing, oyster collection and shrimp farm-

ing, as well as salt production (obtained from evaporating saltwater ponds that form immense salt flats).

For the Vietnamese people, Bac Lieu's main claim to fame is the grave site of Cao Van Lau (1892–1976), famed composer of 'Dai Coa Hoai Long' ('Night Song of the Missing Husband').

Most foreigners give the tomb a miss and instead use Bac Lieu as a springboard to reach the outstanding bird sanctuary out of town. If you're keen on seeing it, head out on Đ Cao Van Lau towards the bird sanctuary for about 1km, turn right and follow the dirt road for 150m to the grave.

Information

The sleepy **Bac Lieu tourist office** (☎ 824 272; fax 824 273; 2 Đ Hoang Van Thu; ﹀ 7-11am & 1-5pm) is next to the Bac Lieu Hotel; though little English is spoken here, all staff are as helpful as can be.

The **post office** (☎ 824 242; 20 Đ Tran Phu) is off the main roundabout downtown; up the same street is **Sacombank** (☎ 932 200; fax 932 201; B2 Đ Tran Phu), which can exchange currency.

Sleeping & Eating

Most hotels in town are near the roundabout where the roads fork off to Soc Trang and Ca Mau.

Bac Lieu Guest House (☎ 823 815; 8 Đ Ly Tu Trong; d US$6-8; 🍴) A real budget special – cheap rooms have fan and shared bath, while pricier ones come with air-con and private bath. There's a pleasant tiled sitting area on the 2nd storey.

Bac Lieu Hotel (☎ 822 437; fax 823 655; 4-6 Đ Hoang Van Thu; r US$16-25; 🍴) Rooms at this fancier place have TV, fridge and air-con; more expensive ones have balconies and tubs.

Hoang Cung Hotel (☎ 823 362; 1B/5 Đ Tran Phu; r 80,000-250,000d; 🍴) About 1km from the roundabout in the direction of Soc Trang (across from the Khmer pagoda gate), this hotel offers clean and comfortable rooms.

There is an OK **restaurant** (mains 30,000d) in the Bac Lieu Hotel, but you're better off looking outside for local **seafood restaurants** (mains around 10,000d).

AROUND BAC LIEU
Bac Lieu Bird Sanctuary

Five kilometres south of town, **Bac Lieu Bird Sanctuary** (Vuon Chim Bac Lieu; ☎ 835 991; admission

10,000d; ⏰ 7.30am-dusk) is most notable for its 50-odd species of bird, including a large population of graceful white herons. This is one of the most interesting sights in the Mekong Delta and is surprisingly popular with Vietnamese tourists. Foreign visitors are rare, probably because Bac Lieu is in such an out-of-the-way place.

Whether or not you see any birds depends on what time of year you visit. Bird populations are at their peak in the rainy season – approximately May to October. The birds hang around to nest until about January, then fly off in search of greener pastures. There are basically no birds here from February until the rainy season begins again.

Because of flooding, most travellers try to avoid the Mekong Delta during the rainy season, so it's better to aim for a December visit.

Although the drive is only 5km, the road is in bad shape. The rest of the trek is through dense jungle. Bring plenty of repellent as there are lots of mosquitoes. There is also some mud to slog through so don't wear your expensive Italian shoes. You should also bring bottled drinking water, binoculars, film and a camera (with a powerful telephoto lens if you have one).

Pay the admission fee when you reach the entrance of the bird sanctuary. You can (and should) hire a guide here – you'll probably get lost without one. The guides aren't supposed to take any money, so give them a tip (US$2 is enough) discreetly; most guides do not speak English. Transport and guides can also be arranged at the Bac Lieu tourist office (see opposite), but hiring a guide there will cost you around US$8.

Bac Lieu Beach

The same road leading to the Bac Lieu Bird Sanctuary eventually terminates 10km from Bac Lieu at this beach (Bai Bien Bac Lieu). Don't expect white sand – it's all hard-packed Mekong Delta mud. Quite a few shellfish and other slimy things crawl around where the muck meets the sea. Tide pool enthusiasts might be impressed. Locals may be willing to take you for a walk on the tidal flats where they harvest oysters.

Moi Hoa Binh Pagoda

This **Khmer pagoda** (Chua Moi Hoa Binh or Se Rey Vongsa) is 13km south of Bac Lieu along Hwy 1 (look to your left while driving to Ca Mau).

The pagoda is uniquely designed and chances are good that the monastery's enormous tower will catch your eye even if you're not looking for it. As pagodas in Vietnam go, it's relatively new, having first been built in 1952. The tower was added in 1990 and is used to store the bones of the deceased. There is a large and impressive meeting hall in front of the tower.

Most Khmer people in the area head for monastery schools in Soc Trang in order to receive a Khmer education. Apart from the small contingent of student monks, very few students study at the Moi Hoa Binh Pagoda.

CA MAU

☎ 0780 / pop 173,300

Built on the swampy shores of the Ganh Hao River, Ca Mau is the capital and largest city in Ca Mau province, which has a total population of 1.7 million. It occupies the southern tip of the Mekong Delta – a wasteland for centuries, the area was first cultivated in the late 17th century. The population of Ca Mau includes many ethnic Khmers.

Owing to the boggy terrain, this area has the lowest population density in southern Vietnam. Ca Mau lies in the middle of Vietnam's largest swamp. The area is known for mosquitoes the size of hummingbirds – during the rainy season you might need a shotgun to keep them at bay. The mosquitoes come out in force just after dark.

Ca Mau has developed rapidly in recent years, but the town itself is rather dull. The main attractions here are the nearby swamps and forests, which can be explored by boat. Bird-watchers and aspiring botanists are reportedly enthralled with the area for its stork-sighting opportunities and swamp ecology. We recommend consulting the folks at Ca Mau Tourist before undertaking trips to these outlying attractions to get the latest information on visiting.

Unfortunately, high hotel prices, the long distance from HCMC and the vampire mosquitoes all conspire to keep the number of foreigners to a minimum. Still, the local tourist literature tries hard: 'Ca Mau – people and nature still remain innocent, generous and of specialty fit stature.'

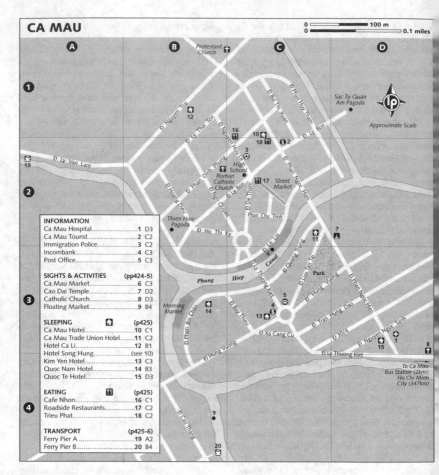

CA MAU

INFORMATION
Ca Mau Hospital.........................**1**	D3
Ca Mau Tourist..........................**2**	C2
Immigration Police....................**3**	C2
Incombank................................**4**	C3
Post Office................................**5**	C3

SIGHTS & ACTIVITIES (pp424-5)
Ca Mau Market..........................**6**	C3
Cao Dai Temple.........................**7**	D2
Catholic Church.........................**8**	D3
Floating Market.........................**9**	B4

SLEEPING (p425)
Ca Mau Hotel...........................**10**	C1
Ca Mau Trade Union Hotel.......**11**	C2
Hotel Ca Li...............................**12**	B1
Hotel Song Hung.................(see 10)	
Kim Yen Hotel..........................**13**	C3
Quoc Nam Hotel......................**14**	B3
Quoc Te Hotel..........................**15**	D3

EATING (p425)
Cafe Nhon...............................**16**	C1
Roadside Restaurants..............**17**	C2
Trieu Phat...............................**18**	C2

TRANSPORT (p425-6)
Ferry Pier A **19**	A2
Ferry Pier B.............................**20**	B4

Information

Interesting boat trips – two days and two nights to Nam Can, Dat Mui (Cape Ca Mau), the Da Bac Islands and the U-Minh Forest – can be organised at **Ca Mau Tourist** (Cong Ty Du Lich Minh Hai; ☎ 831 238; 3-5 Đ Ly Bon; ⏰ 8-11am & 1-5pm). Other services available here include foreign-currency exchange, car and boat rentals and visa extensions.

Near the post office, **Incombank** (☎ 838 677; icbcamau@hcm.vnn.vn; 94 Đ Ly Thuong Kiet), offers foreign-currency exchange and cash advances for Visa and MasterCard, as well as cashing travellers cheques.

In an emergency, seek medical help at **Ca Mau Hospital** (Benh Vien Ca Mau; ☎ 831 015; Đ Ly Thuong Kiet).

Sights
CA MAU MARKET

This is a wholesale **market** (⏰ 6am-6pm) and not really a place for people to shop. The animal life on display – such as fish and turtles – is cleaned, packed into crates, frozen and sent to HCMC by truck. It's an interesting place to wander around – it certainly bears little resemblance to the supermarkets at home. However, proponents of animal rights will not be pleased.

There's also a **floating market** (⏰ 6am–mid-afternoon) here.

CAO DAI TEMPLE
Though not as large as the one in Tay Ninh (p373), the **Cao Dai Temple** (Đ Phan Ngoc Hien) is

still an impressive place and it's staffed by friendly monks. The temple was built in 1966 and seems to be fairly active.

Sleeping

By the standards of most other Mekong Delta cities, Ca Mau's hotels tend to be a bit pricey for what you get.

BUDGET

Kim Yen Hotel (☎ 827 308; fax 831 249; 20A Đ Hung Vuong; r 70,000-250,000d; 🔁) Near the post office, you'll find comfortable rooms in this very clean minihotel. There's also a lift here.

Ca Mau Hotel (☎ 831 165; fax 835 075; 20 Đ Phan Ngoc Hien; r 120,000-220,000d; 🔁) Spacious, well-outfitted rooms here have bathrooms with tubs. Rates include breakfast.

Ca Mau Trade Union Hotel (☎ 833 245; fax 830 873; 9 Đ Luu Tan Tai; r 100,000-200,000d; 🔁) Almost opposite the Cao Dai Temple, this hotel has rooms on the small side, but they're clean and cosy. Fan rooms have balconies, mosquito nets and cold water.

MID-RANGE

Quoc Te Hotel (International Hotel; ☎ 826 745; ksquocte@hcm.vnn.vn; 179 Đ Phan Ngoc Hien; r 100,000-350,000d; 🔁) Boasting a lift, a restaurant and massage service, the Quoc Te is a solid mid-range choice. The priciest rooms have big views of the city; breakfast is included in most room rates.

Quoc Nam Hotel (☎ 827 281; 23 Đ Phan Boi Chau; r 150,000-250,000d; 🔁) Another good private hotel with a similar standard to the Quoc Te, this one has the added bonus of a pleasant café on the top floor with great views of the market and canal.

Hotel Ca Li (☎ 829 405; calihotel82@hotmail.com; 121A Đ Nguyen Trai; r 180,000-250,000d; 🔁) Conveniently near the minibus station, this is a very comfortable minihotel run by a friendly family. Some rooms have balconies.

Hotel Song Hung (☎ 822 822; fax 831 790; 28 Đ Phan Ngoc Hien; r 140,000-220,000d; 🔁) The family-run Song Hung offers smallish but clean rooms decorated with heavily varnished inlay furniture and pink tile, as well as the usual TV, fridge and phone.

Eating

Ca Mau's speciality is shrimp, which are raised in ponds and mangrove forests.

Trieu Phat (☎ 832 766; 26 Đ Phan Ngoc Hien; mains 25,000d) This is a decent spot for local seafood, next to the Ca Mau Hotel.

Cafe Nhon (☎ 830 737; cafénhon@yahoo.com; 443/2A Đ Nguyen Huu Le; coffee 5000d) The garden setting makes this a nice place for sipping coffee and watching street life.

There is a cluster of small roadside restaurants on Đ Ly Bon, at the entrance to the street market. They are very cheap and the food is OK. The friendly outdoor restaurant in the Ca Mau Trade Union Hotel is not bad and certainly more aesthetically pleasing than eating in the market.

Getting There & Away

BOAT

Approximately once every four days, cargo boats run between Ca Mau and HCMC. The trip takes 30 hours and is certainly not comfortable. You'll find that the cost is totally negotiable; paying about 30,000d is not unreasonable, and you must bring your own food and water.

Of more interest is the boat from Ca Mau north to Rach Gia (the boat docks in Rach Soi, about 10km from Rach Gia). This departs from Ferry Pier B daily around 5.15am (20,000d, 10 hours) Bicycles/motorbikes can be taken on board for 10,000/15,000d. Hammocks can be rented for 5000d. Ferry Pier B is also the spot where you can catch the speedboats heading south to Ngoc Hien.

Also popular are the boats to U-Minh Forest (p426). These depart from Ferry Pier A. You'll have to do some negotiating to arrange a tour here. It's also worth asking staff at the hotels as they may be able to arrange a whole group.

BUS

The buses from HCMC to Ca Mau leave from Mien Tay bus station (p363). The trip takes 11 hours by regular bus and eight hours by express bus (around 65,000d). There are several daily express buses to HCMC leaving between 5am and 10.30am.

The Ca Mau bus station is 2.5km from the centre of town, along Hwy 1 towards HCMC.

CAR & MOTORBIKE

Ca Mau is the end of the line for Hwy 1; it's the southernmost point in Vietnam that's accessible by car and bus. Drivers who

CA MAU SAVES THE *AO DAI*

The graceful national dress of Vietnamese women is known as the *ao dai* (pronounced ow-zai in the north and ow-yai in the south). An *ao dai* consists of a close-fitting tunic with long panels at the front and back, which is worn over loose trousers. The outfit was designed for the Vietnamese hot weather and for that reason is much more common in the south, especially in HCMC and the Mekong Delta. Although *ao dai* are impractical for women working in the rice paddies, they're considered appropriate for office workers and students.

In years past, men also wore *ao dai*, but these days you are likely to see this only in traditional operas or wedding ceremonies. The male *ao dai* is shorter and looser than the female version. Before the end of dynastic rule, the colours of the brocade and embroidery indicated the rank of the wearer; gold brocade with embroidered dragons was reserved for the emperor. High-ranking mandarins wore purple, while lower-ranking mandarins had to settle for blue.

Ao dai are versatile and are even considered appropriate for funerals. Mourners usually wear either white or black *ao dai* (white is the traditional colour of mourning in Vietnam). *Ao dai* can also be worn more happily to weddings (bright colours with embroidery on the shirt is appropriate).

The famous 'black pyjamas' of the Viet Cong (VC), immortalised in numerous Hollywood movies, were not *ao dai* but actually a common form of rural dress. You will see plenty of people in the countryside wearing these, though they are not always black.

From 1975 to 1985, *ao dai* were no longer considered politically correct. Chic baggy military uniforms were all the rage and the *ao dai* disappeared everywhere in Vietnam.

Beauty contests – a symbol of bourgeois capitalism – were banned by the communists but were finally permitted again in HCMC in 1989. Swimsuit competitions were not permitted, but many of the contestants did wear their best designer jeans. However, the Ca Mau team stole the show – they wore *ao dai*. Suddenly, there was a nationwide boom in *ao dai* production.

boldly attempt to drive on the 'highway' south of Ca Mau will soon find their vehicles sinking into a quagmire of mud and mangroves.

Ca Mau is 178km from Can Tho (three hours) and 347km from HCMC (eight hours).

Getting Around

There are plenty of water taxis along the canal at the back of Ca Mau Market. For longer trips upriver, larger longboats collect at the cluster of jetties just outside the market area. You can either join the throngs of passengers going downriver or hire the whole boat for about 50,000d an hour.

AROUND CA MAU
U-Minh Forest

The town of Ca Mau borders the U-Minh Forest, a huge mangrove forest covering 1000 sq km of Ca Mau and Kien Giang provinces. Local people use certain species of mangrove as a source of timber, charcoal, thatch and tannin. When the mangroves flower, bees feed on the blossoms, provid-

ing both honey and wax. The area is an important habitat for waterfowl.

The U-Minh Forest, which is the largest mangrove forest in the world outside of the Amazon basin, was a favourite hideout for the VC during the American War. US patrol boats were frequently ambushed here and the VC regularly planted mines in the canals. The Americans responded with chemical defoliation, which made their enemy more visible at the same time as doing enormous damage to the forests. Replanting efforts at first failed because the soil was so toxic, but gradually the heavy rainfall has washed the dioxin out to sea and the forest is returning. Many eucalyptus trees have also been planted here because they have proved to be relatively resistant to dioxin.

Unfortunately the mangrove forests are being further damaged by clearing for shrimp-farming ponds, charcoal production and woodchipping. The government has tried to limit these activities, but the conflict between nature and humans continues. The conflict will probably get worse before it gets better, because Vietnam's population is still growing rapidly.

The area is known for its birdlife, but these creatures have also taken a beating. Nevertheless, ornithologists will derive much joy from taking boat trips around Ca Mau – though the swarms of birds aren't nearly as ubiquitous as the swarms of mosquitoes.

Ca Mau Tourist (p424) offers all-day tours of the forest by boat. It costs US$135 per boat (maximum 10 people), though bargaining is possible. You can also talk to the locals down at Ferry Pier A to see if you can find a better deal.

Bird Sanctuary

The **Bird Sanctuary** (Vuon Chim; admission 10,000d; ◯ dawn-dusk) is about 45km southeast of Ca Mau. Storks are the largest and most easily spotted birds here, making their nests in the tall trees. Remember, however, that birds will be birds – they don't like humans to get too close and they leave their nests early in the morning in search of food.

Ca Mau Tourist offers a full-day tour by boat to the sanctuary for US$120 (one to 10 people).

NAM CAN

☎ 0780

Except for a minuscule fishing hamlet (Tran De) and an offshore island (Hon Khoai), Nam Can stakes its claim as the southernmost town in Vietnam. Few tourists come to this isolated community, which survives mainly from the shrimp industry.

At the southern tip of the delta is the **Ca Mau Nature Reserve**, sometimes referred to as Ngoc Hien Bird Sanctuary. It's one of the least developed and most protected parts of the Mekong Delta region. Shrimp farming is prohibited here. Access is by boat.

At the southern end of the reserve is the tiny fishing village of Tran De. A public ferry connects Tran De to Nam Can. If you are obsessed with reaching Vietnam's southern tip, you'll have to take a boat from Tran De to Hon Khoai Island.

If you're looking to visit another remote spot, you can hire a boat to take you to Dat Mui (Cape Ca Mau), the southwestern tip of Vietnam. However, few people find this worthwhile.

Sleeping

Nam Can Hotel (☎ 877 039; r US$16; ✷) This is the only decent accommodation option in

Nam Can, so you'll have little choice unless you plan on camping.

Getting There & Away

A road connecting Ca Mau to Nam Can is shown on most maps of Vietnam, but it's little more than wishful thinking. Basically, it's a muddy track that's under water most of the time, though some have attempted it by motorbike.

The trip to Nam Can from Ca Mau is best done by speedboat (around 30,000d, four hours). These boats are readily available in Ca Mau.

From Nam Can south to Tran De takes another four hours.

LONG XUYEN

☎ 076 / pop 238,100

The capital of An Giang province, Long Xuyen was once a stronghold of the Hoa Hao sect. Founded in 1939, the sect emphasises simplicity in worship and does not believe in temples or intermediaries between humans and the Supreme Being. Until 1956 the Hoa Hao had an army and constituted a major military force in this region.

The town's big claim to fame is being the birthplace of Vietnam's second president, Ton Duc Thang. There is a museum in town dedicated to Bac Ton (Uncle Ton) as well as a large statue bearing his likeness.

Long Xuyen is a moderately prosperous town, and the surrounding area does a good trade in agriculture, fish processing and cashew nuts. There are a few sights to see around town, but for travellers its value is mainly as a transit point with good accommodation and a foreign-exchange bank (change travellers cheques here if you're heading to Chau Doc; there is no place in Chau Doc to do so). The market along the riverside is colourful and lively, and boats can be hired here for about 50,000d per hour.

Information

An Giang Tourist (☎ 841 036; angiangtour@hcm .vnn.vn; 17 Ð Nguyen Van Cung; ◯ 7-11am & 1-5pm) is beside the Long Xuyen Hotel. The staff can speak some English and are courteous enough, but beyond selling tours they are of little use to visitors.

Vietcombank (☎ 841 075; 1 Ð Hung Vuong; ◯ closed weekends) gives cash advances on credit cards and also exchanges travellers cheques. There's also an **Incombank** (☎ 841 704; 20-22 Ngo Gia Tu) near the post office.

Sights

LONG XUYEN CATHOLIC CHURCH
One of the largest churches in the Mekong Delta region, **Long Xuyen Catholic Church** (☯ 7.30am-5.30pm) is an impressive modern structure that boasts a 50m-high bell tower. It was constructed between 1966 and 1973, and can seat 1000 worshippers. Mass is held daily.

AN GIANG MUSEUM
This sleepy little **museum** (Bao Tang An Giang; ☎ 841 251; 77 Đ Thoai Ngoc Hau; admission free; ☯ 7.30-10.30am Tue, Thu, Sat & Sun, 2-4.30pm Sat & Sun) is a proud highlight of An Giang province and features photographs and personal effects of the former president, Ton Duc Thang. There are also some artefacts from the Oc-Eo site near Rach Gia (see p439) and displays that detail the history of this region from the 1930s to the present day.

LONG XUYEN PROTESTANT CHURCH
This **Protestant church** (4 Đ Hung Vuong; prayers 10am-noon Sun) is a small, modern structure.

CHO MOI DISTRICT
Across the river from Long Xuyen, **Cho Moi district** is known for its rich groves of fruit such as bananas, durians, guava, jackfruit, longans, mangoes, mangosteens and plums.

The women here are said to be the most beautiful in the Mekong Delta.

Cho Moi district can be reached by boat from the ferry terminal at the foot of Đ Nguyen Hue.

Sleeping
Thai Binh Hotel II (☎ 847 078; fax 846 451; 4-8 Đ Nguyen Hue A; r 70,000-220,000d; ❄) Musty fan rooms are OK at this older, privately-run place, and the air-con quarters are spacious and quite comfortable. Friendly staff are a bonus.

Long Xuyen Hotel (☎ 841 927; longxuyenhotel@hcm. vnn.vn; 19 Đ Nguyen Van Cung; r US$9-16; ❄) Rooms come with shared balconies and baths with hot water; breakfast is included. Optional life insurance is sold at reception for US11¢

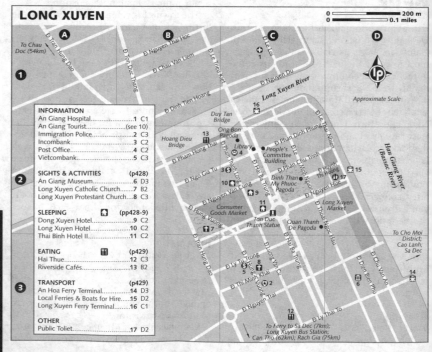

LONG XUYEN

0 — 200 m
0 — 0.1 miles

Approximate Scale

INFORMATION	
An Giang Hospital	1 C1
An Giang Tourist	(see 10)
Immigration Police	2 C3
Incombank	3 C2
Post Office	4 C2
Vietcombank	5 C3

SIGHTS & ACTIVITIES	(p428)
An Giang Museum	6 D3
Long Xuyen Catholic Church	7 B2
Long Xuyen Protestant Church	8 C3

SLEEPING	(pp428-9)
Dong Xuyen Hotel	9 C2
Long Xuyen Hotel	10 C2
Thai Binh Hotel II	11 C2

EATING	(p429)
Hai Thue	12 C3
Riverside Cafés	13 B2

TRANSPORT	(p429)
An Hoa Ferry Terminal	14 D3
Local Ferries & Boats for Hire	15 D2
Long Xuyen Ferry Terminal	16 C1

OTHER	
Public Toilet	17 D2

To Chau Doc (54km)

Long Xuyen River

Hau Giang River (Bassac River)

Duy Tan Bridge

Ong Bon Pagoda

Hoang Dieu Bridge

Library

People's Committee Building

Dinh Than My Phuoc Pagoda

Long Xuyen Market

Consumer Goods Market

Ton Duc Thanh Statue

Quan Thanh De Pagoda

To Cho Moi District; Cao Lanh; Sa Dec

To Ferry to Sa Dec (7km); Long Xuyen Bus Station; Can Tho (62km); Rach Gia (75km)

MEKONG DELTA

per day! Staff may be too busy chatting on mobile phones to book you into a room.

Dong Xuyen Hotel (☎ 942 260; dongxuyenhotel@ hcm.vnn.vn; Đ 9A Luong Van Cu; d 300,000-450,000d, ste 600,000d; ❄) Long Xuyen's fanciest digs are located right in the centre of town. Well-appointed rooms (satellite TV, minibar etc) are matched by facilities and services like massage and steam bath. Even the staff sparkle with friendliness and good English skills.

Eating
Besides the hotel restaurants, it's slim pickings for decent places to eat in Long Xuyen.

Hai Thue (☎ 845 573; 245/3 Đ Luong Van Cu; mains 10,000d) Serves up excellent and cheap Vietnamese food.

There's good coffee and a happening scene at the **riverside cafés** (coffee 4000d) on Đ Pham Hong Thai.

Getting There & Away
BOAT
To get to the Long Xuyen ferry dock from Đ Pham Hong Thai, cross Duy Tan Bridge and turn right. Passenger ferries leave from here to Cho Vam, Dong Tien, Hong Ngu, Kien Luong, Lai Vung, Rach Gia, Sa Dec and Phu Chau (Tan Chau). Boats to Rach Gia (15,000d, nine hours) leave at 6.30am and/ or 8am. You can also catch boats from here to Sa Dec (10,000d, four hours) at noon.

From the An Hoa ferry terminal you can also catch boats to Cao Lanh and Sa Dec.

BUS
The buses heading from HCMC to Long Xuyen leave from the Mien Tay bus station (p363; around 35,000d).

Long Xuyen bus station (Ben Xe Long Xuyen; ☎ 852 125; opposite 96/3B Đ Tran Hung Dao) is at the southern end of town. Buses from Long Xuyen to Ca Mau, Can Tho, Chau Doc, Ha Tien, HCMC and Rach Gia leave from here.

CAR & MOTORBIKE
Long Xuyen is 62km from Can Tho, 126km from My Tho and 189km from HCMC.

Getting Around
The best way to get around Long Xuyen is to take a *cyclo*, *xe dap loi* (a two-wheeled wagon pulled by a bicycle) or a *xe loi*.

Car ferries from Long Xuyen to Cho Moi district (across the river) leave from the ferry terminal near the market every half-hour between 4am and 6.30pm.

CHAU DOC
☎ 076 / pop 100,000
Perched on the banks of the Bassac River, Chau Doc is a pleasant little town near the Cambodian border. Chau Doc has quite sizable Chinese, Cham and Khmer communities, each of which has built distinctive temples that are worth a visit. The city was once known for its dugout-canoe races.

Since the opening of the nearby Vinh Xuong and Tinh Bien borders (see p471 for information on border crossings) between Vietnam and Cambodia, more and more travellers are finding their way to Chau Doc. Both border crossings can issue Cambodian visas on arrival (US$25). Those who are not rushing in one direction or another will discover it's a nice place to chill out for a few days. There are a good many places to explore, especially in the outlying areas of town (see p433).

Be aware that there is no place to change travellers cheques or get cash advances in Chau Doc; you should take care of exchanging money before you arrive. Nearby Long Xuyen (p427) is a popular place to do this.

Information
There's an **Internet service** (per hr 4000d; ☺ 7am-9pm) in the courtyard of Chau Doc's main **post office** (☎ 869 200; 2 Đ Le Loi). Foreign currency – but not travellers cheques – can be exchanged at **Incombank** (☎ 866 497; 68-70 Đ Nguyen Huu Canh).

Though not officially a tourist office, there's a travel information desk at **Vinh Phuoc Hotel** (p431) where objective, pressure-free travel advice is dispensed. Tours and onward travel arrangements are sold at reasonable prices. Check here first for up-to-date reports on hydrofoils to Phu Quoc Island, border crossing information, slow cargo boats and bus schedules.

Sights
CHAU PHU TEMPLE
In 1926 the **Chau Phu Temple** (Dinh Than Chau Phu; cnr Đ Nguyen Van Thoai & Đ Gia Long) was built to worship the Nguyen dynasty official Thoai Ngoc Hau, who is buried at Sam Mountain (p434). The

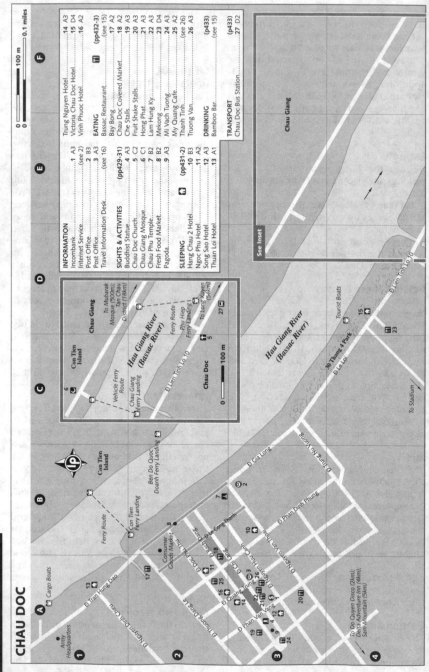

CHAU DOC

MEKONG DELTA

0   100 m
0   0.1 miles

Chau Giang

See Inset

Con Tien Island

Chau Giang

To Mubarak
Mosque (500m);
Tan Chau
District (18km)

Hau Giang River
(Bassac River)

Ferry Route
Vehicle Ferry
Route

Phu Hiep
Ferry Landing

To Long Xuyen
(54km)

Chau Giang
Ferry Landing

D Lien Tinh Lo 10

Chau Doc

0   100 m

Con Tien Island

Ferry Route

Ben Do Quoc
Doanh Ferry Landing

Con Tien
Ferry Landing

Cargo Boats

Army
Headquarters

D Nguyen Dinh Chieu

D Tran Hung Dao

D Truong Dinh

Consumer
Goods Market

Fresh Food Market

D Thu Khoa Nghia

D Phan Van Vang

D Quang Trung

D Nguyen Van Thoai

D Phan Dinh Phung

D Gia Long

D Phan Van Vang

D Chi Lang

D Nguyen Huu Canh

D Doc Phu Thu

D Le Loi

Hau Giang River
(Bassac River)

30 Thang 4 Park

Tourist Boats

D Truong Nu Vuong

D Le Loi

D Lien Tinh Lo 10

To Stadium

To Do Quyen Disco (2km);
Delta Adventure Inn (4km);
Sam Mountain (5km)

FISH FARMING

Fish farming constitutes some 15% of Vietnam's total seafood output and is widely practised in An Giang province, in the region near the Cambodian border. The highest concentration of 'floating houses' with fish cages can be observed on the banks of the Bassac River in Chau Doc, near its confluence with the mighty Mekong.

The primary fish farmed here are two members of the Asian catfish family, *Pangasius bocourti* and *P hypophthalmus*. It is interesting to note that even with two tides a day here, there is no salt water in the river. Around 15,000 tonnes of fish are exported annually, primarily to European and American markets (about 5% makes it to Australia and Japan), in the form of frozen white fish fillets.

The two-step production cycle starts with capturing fish eggs from the wild, followed by raising the fish to a marketable size – usually about 1kg. Fish are fed on a kind of dough made by the farmers from cereal, vegetables and fish scraps. The largest cage measures 2000 cubic metres and can produce up to 400 tonnes of raw fish in each 10-month production cycle.

Since 1994 the French Institute for International Agronomic Research and Development (Cirad) has been carrying out a project to develop an artificial reproduction method for the two species. The first successful attempt was in 1995 and by 2000 production was up to 700 million larvae for each species. Further research is being conducted in Chau Doc on the nutrition and reproduction of the fish.

structure is decorated with both Vietnamese and Chinese motifs. Inside are funeral tablets bearing the names of the deceased and some biographical information about them.

CHAU DOC CHURCH
This small **Catholic church** (opposite 459 Đ Lien Tinh Lo 10; ☺ mass 5pm) was constructed in 1920 and is not far from Phu Hiep ferry landing.

MOSQUES
Domed and arched **Chau Giang Mosque**, in the hamlet of Chau Giang, serves the local Cham Muslims. To get there, take the car ferry from Chau Giang ferry landing in Chau Doc across the Hau Giang River. From the ferry landing, walk away from the river for 30m, turn left and walk 50m.

The **Mubarak Mosque** (Thanh Duong Hoi Giao), where children study the Koran in Arabic script, is also on the river bank opposite Chau Doc. Visitors are permitted, but you should avoid entering during the calls to prayer (five times daily) unless you are a Muslim.

There are other small mosques in the Chau Doc area. They are accessible by boat, but you'll need a local guide to find them all.

FLOATING HOUSES
These houses, whose floats consist of empty metal drums, are both a place to live and a livelihood for their residents. Under each house, fish are raised in suspended metal nets: the fish flourish in their natural river habitat; the family can feed them whatever scraps are handy; and catching the fish requires less exertion than fishing. You can find these houses floating around Chau Doc and get a close-up by hiring a boat (please be respectful of their privacy though). To learn more about the workings of these fish cages, see the boxed text above.

Sleeping
BUDGET
Vinh Phuoc Hotel (☎ 866 242, 562 265; 12-14 Đ Quang Trung; r US$4; ☒) A great budget deal, this place is run by an amiable Brit who is an excellent source of local travel information. The in-house restaurant serves good Vietnamese and Western food at backpacker prices (mains around 25,000d).

Thuan Loi Hotel (☎ 866 134; hotelthuanloi@hcm .vnn.vn; 18 Đ Tran Hung Dao; d US$6-10; ☒) Commanding a great location on the riverside, this pleasant place has friendly staff and a relaxed atmosphere. The 3rd-floor terrace is a great place to watch life on the river go by. Fan rooms have flimsier plastic accessories (like the bathroom doors).

Ngoc Phu Hotel (☎ 866 484; 17 Đ Doc Phu Thu; r 90,000-150,000d; ☒) Even the fan rooms at this large, liveable place have hot water, TV and fridge. The staff here are particularly cheery and helpful.

PASSPORT WARNING

Other towns might be more lax about passports, but the Chau Doc police require hotels to show them the passports of foreign guests. If you don't feel comfortable leaving yours at your hotel, a good photocopy that includes your Vietnam visa is usually acceptable.

Delta Adventure Inn (Nha Khach Long Chau; Map p434; ☎ 861 249; deltaadventureinn@hotmail.com; r US$7-10; ⚡) This cosy terra cotta-tiled compound sits amid the beautiful rice paddies about 4km from Chau Doc. The views of Sam Mountain are lovely from the island café-restaurant in the centre of the property.

MID-RANGE

Trung Nguyen Hotel (☎ 866 158; trunghotel@yahoo. com; 86 Đ Bach Dang; r US$10-18; ⚡) An excellent deal, this shiny minihotel is run by friendly, helpful management. Smallish but very comfortable rooms have hot water, TV and minibar, and the hotel is right near the market.

Song Sao Hotel (☎ 561 777; songsaohotel@yahoo. com; 12-13 Đ Nguyen Huu Canh; r US$12-16; ⚡) All rooms are well-outfitted with the usual amenities, with lovely wooden furnishings. Some rooms have balconies; all are very clean. Continental breakfast is US$2 extra.

Hang Chau 2 Hotel (☎ 868891; hangchau2agg@hcm. vnn.vn; 10 Đ Nguyen Van Thoai; r 120,000-200,000đ; ⚡) Spacious, well-appointed rooms also boast carved wooden furniture and wood fixtures in bathrooms; the 'special' room even has wood floors and a balcony.

TOP END

Victoria Chau Doc Hotel (☎ 865 010; www.victoria hotels-asia.com; 32 Đ Le Loi; r US$115-196; Internet rates US$92-144; ⚡ ▯ ⚡) Set right on the riverside, the Victoria is by far the swishest place in town. All rooms have wood floors, bathtubs and gorgeous decor. The hotel's Bassac Restaurant (p432) is superb and the top-floor massage salon offers the best river views around.

Nonguests can indulge themselves with day use of the swimming pool and fitness centre for US$5, or have a sauna and massage for US$8. The hotel offers boat trips linking the Victoria Can Tho and Chau Doc

resorts (US$25/person; 2½ hours); stopovers can be arranged en route. Victoria boats also cruise between Chau Doc and Phnom Penh (see opposite).

Eating
RESTAURANTS
Chau Doc has some truly excellent restaurants on offer.

Bay Bong (☎ 867 271; 22 Đ Thuong Dang Le; mains 35,000đ) Among the town's excellent restaurants, Bay Bong specialises in hotpots and soups, as well as fresh fish dishes. Try the stewed fish in a clay pot *(ca kho to)* or sweet-and-sour soup *(canh chua)*.

Mekong (☎ 867 381; 41 Đ Le Loi; mains 35,000đ) Just across the road from the Victoria Chau Doc Hotel, Mekong is worthy of a plug. Set outdoors in front of a classic old French villa, it's a lovely place for lunch or dinner.

Bassac Restaurant (☎ 865 010; 32 Đ Le Loi; mains US$7-12; ⏱ 6-11am & 6-11pm) Sophisticated dining is paired with a relaxed colonial ambience at Le Bassac. It also has good snack food such as burgers, sandwiches, spicy chicken wings and pizza at the hotel's poolside Bamboo Bar.

Lam Hung Ky (☎ 866 745; 71 Đ Chi Lang; mains 40,000đ) This joint serves up good Chinese and Vietnamese food, with misleadingly unappetizing menu items like 'instant boiled assorted meats'.

Hong Phat (☎ 866 950; 79 Đ Chi Lang; mains 40,000đ) Similar in standard and fare to Lam Hung Ky.

Other options nearby:

Mi Vach Tuong (Đ Thu Khoa Nghia; noodles 7000đ) Literally meaning 'noodles along the wall', this is a great breakfast noodle joint beside the local basketball court.

My Quang Cafe (☎ 560 398; 25 Đ Doc Phu Thu; mains 12,000đ) Another popular eatery well known for its friendly service.

Thanh Tinh (☎ 865 064; 13 Đ Quang Trung; mains 15,000đ) Great vegetarian food at the place whose name means 'to calm the body down'.

Truong Van (☎ 866 567; 15 Đ Quang Trung; mains 15,000đ) Good Vietnamese food at decent prices.

QUICK EATS
If you'd like to sample the best fruit shakes *(sinh to)* in town, look out for the stalls on the corner of Đ Phan Van Vang and Đ Nguyen Van Thoai.

At night, you can also try a variety of cool dessert soups *(che)* at stalls on Đ Bach Dang, next to the pagoda.

The **Chau Doc Covered Market** (Đ Bach Dang) has excellent Vietnamese food.

Sampling these street treats will cost you a cool 3000d to 10,000d.

Drinking & Entertainment

Chau Doc is a fairly sleepy town and tends to shut down early.

Do Quyen (☎ 865 565; 7 Đ Truong Dua; admission free; 8-11pm most nights) This is a fun little local disco about 2km from Chau Doc on the way to Sam Mountain.

There's another dance hall nearby that's popular with the locals, called **An Tuong 2** (admission 20,000d; 8-11pm, closed Mon & Wed). The entry fee includes one drink.

The Lobby Bar in the Victoria Chau Doc Hotel is a nice, 'civilised' place for a drink or a game of pool.

Getting There & Away
BOAT

Daily boat services (via the Mekong River) run between Chau Doc and Phnom Penh (Cambodia) – a fascinating way to enter or exit this part of Vietnam. Departures in either direction are at around 8am and the trip takes the better part of a day. Most local guesthouses and hotels can organise tickets (US$10 to US$15 one way). Be aware that you must arrange your Vietnamese visa beforehand – Vietnamese visas cannot be issued at the border but can easily be arranged, usually within a few days, in Phnom Penh or HCMC. The Victoria Hotel also runs a fancier boat (per person US$35, 3½ hours) between Chau Doc and Phnom Penh, Cambodia.

No-frills cargo boats run daily between Chau Doc and Ha Tien via the Vinh Te Canal (US$5, 13 hours); it's an interesting 95km trip. The canal, which straddles the Cambodian border, is named after Vinh Te, the wife of Thoai Ngoc Hau, who built it. Departures are at 4am.

Cargo boats also travel to/from Vinh Long.

BUS

The buses from HCMC to Chau Doc leave from the Mien Tay bus station (p363); the express bus can make the run in six hours and costs around 50,000d.

The Chau Doc bus station (Ben Xe Chau Doc) is east of town towards Long Xuyen.

Buses from Chau Doc leave here for Ca Mau, Can Tho, Ha Tien, Long Xuyen, My Tho, HCMC, Soc Trang and Tra Vinh.

CAR & MOTORBIKE

By road, Chau Doc is approximately 117km from Can Tho, 181km from My Tho and 245km from HCMC.

The Chau Doc–Ha Tien road is 100km in length and is now in decent shape. As you approach Ha Tien, the land turns into a mangrove forest that is infertile and almost uninhabited.

This area is considered reasonably safe during the day, but it's not advisable to be out here after dark due to the risk of robbery in this remote, unlit area.

The drive takes about three hours, and it's possible to visit Ba Chuc and Tup Duc en route. If you don't plan to drive yourself, *xe om* drivers typically charge about US$12.

Getting Around

Xe loi can be hired around town for a few thousand dong.

Boats to Chau Giang district (across the Hau Giang River) leave from two docks: vehicle ferries depart from Chau Giang ferry landing (Ben Pha Chau Giang), opposite 419 Đ Le Loi; smaller, more frequent boats leave from Phu Hiep ferry landing (Ben Pha FB Phu Hiep), a little further south.

Vehicle ferries to Con Tien Island depart from the Con Tien ferry landing (Ben Pha Con Tien) at the river end of Đ Thuong Dang Le; you can catch boats to Chau Giang and Phu Chau (Tan Chau) from the Ben Do Quoc Doanh ferry landing on Đ Gia Long, opposite the post office.

Private boats (per hour 10,000d), which are rowed standing up, can be hired from either of these spots, and are highly recommended for seeing the floating houses and visiting nearby Cham minority villages and mosques.

Prices for all of the public ferries (per person 500d, motorbike or bicycle 1000d) are doubled at night; bicycles or motorbikes require their own ticket.

AROUND CHAU DOC
Phu Chau (Tan Chau) District

Traditional silk making has made Phu Chau (Tan Chau) district famous all over southern Vietnam. The **market** in Phu Chau has a selection of competitively priced Thai and Cambodian goods.

To get to Phu Chau district from Chau Doc, take a boat across the Hau Giang River from the Phu Hiep ferry landing, then catch a ride on the back of a *xe om* (about 10,000d) for the 18km trip to Phu Chau district.

Sam Mountain

There are dozens of pagodas and temples, many of them set in caves, around Sam Mountain (Nui Sam), which is about 6km southwest of Chau Doc out on Đ Bao Ho Thoai. The Chinese influence is obvious and Sam Mountain is a favourite spot for ethnic Chinese (both pilgrims from Vietnam and abroad).

Climbing the peak is, of course, the highlight of a visit to Sam Mountain. The views from the top are spectacular (weather permitting) and you can easily look out over Cambodia. There's a military outpost on the summit, a legacy of the days when the Khmer Rouge made cross-border raids and massacred Vietnamese civilians. The outpost is still functional and the soldiers are quite used to tourists taking photos now; however, you should ask permission and perhaps ply the soldiers with cigarettes before taking photos of them or anything that could be considered militarily sensitive.

Walking down is easier than walking up, so if you want to cheat, have a motorbike take you to the summit. The road to the top is on the east side of the mountain. You can walk down along a peaceful, traffic-free trail on the north side which will bring you to the main temple area. The summit road has been decorated with amusement-park ceramic dinosaurs and the like. But there are also some small shrines and pavilions, which add a bit of charm and also remind you that this is indeed Vietnam and not Disneyland.

TAY AN PAGODA

This pagoda (Chua Tay An) is renowned for the fine carving of its hundreds of religious figures, most of which are made of wood. Aspects of the building's architecture reflect Hindu and Islamic influences. The first chief monk of Tay An Pagoda (founded in 1847) came from Giac Lam Pagoda in Saigon. Tay An was last rebuilt in 1958.

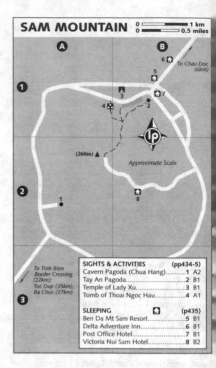

SAM MOUNTAIN

SIGHTS & ACTIVITIES	(pp434-5)
Cavern Pagoda (Chua Hang)	1 A2
Tay An Pagoda	2 B1
Temple of Lady Xu	3 B1
Tomb of Thoai Ngoc Hau	4 A1

SLEEPING	(p435)
Ben Da Mt Sam Resort	5 B1
Delta Adventure Inn	6 B1
Post Office Hotel	7 B1
Victoria Nui Sam Hotel	8 B2

The main gate is of traditional Vietnamese design. Above the bi-level roof are figures of lions and two dragons fighting for possession of pearls, chrysanthemums, apricot trees and lotus blossoms. Nearby is a statue of Quan Am Thi Kinh, the Guardian Spirit of Mother and Child (see the boxed text 'Quan Am Thi Kinh', p343).

In front of the pagoda are statues of a black elephant with two tusks and a white elephant with six tusks. Around the pagoda are monks' tombs. Inside are Buddha statues adorned with psychedelic disco lights.

TEMPLE OF LADY XU

Founded in the 1820s, the Temple of Lady Xu (Mieu Ba Chua Xu) stands facing Sam Mountain, not far from Tay An Pagoda. The first building here was made of bamboo and leaves; the last reconstruction took place in 1972.

According to legend, the statue of Lady Xu used to stand at the summit of Sam Mountain. In the early 19th century, Siamese troops invaded the area and, impressed with the statue, decided to take it back to Thailand. But as they carried the statue down the hill, it became heavier and heavier, and they were forced to abandon it by the side of the path.

One day some villagers who were cutting wood came upon the statue and decided to bring it back to their village in order to build a temple for it; but it weighed too much for them to budge. Suddenly, there appeared a girl who, possessed by a spirit, declared herself to be Lady Xu. She announced to them that 40 virgins were to be brought and that they would be able to transport the statue down the mountainside. The 40 virgins were then summoned and carried the statue down the slope, but when they reached the plain, it became too heavy and they had to set it down. The people concluded that the site where the virgins halted had been selected by Lady Xu for the temple construction and it's here that the Temple of Lady Xu stands to this day.

Another story claims that the wife of Thoai Ngoc Hau, builder of the Vinh Te Canal, swore to erect a temple when the canal, whose construction had claimed many lives, was completed. She died before being able to carry out her oath, but Thoai Ngoc Hau implemented her plans by building the Temple of Lady Xu.

Offerings of roast whole pigs are frequently made here, providing an interesting photo opportunity. The temple's most important festival is held from the 23rd to the 26th day of the fourth lunar month. During this time, pilgrims flock here, sleeping on mats in the large rooms of the two-storey resthouse next to the temple.

TOMB OF THOAI NGOC HAU
A high-ranking official, Thoai Ngoc Hau (1761–1829) served the Nguyen Lords and, later, the Nguyen dynasty. In early 1829, Thoai Ngoc Hau ordered that a tomb be constructed for himself at the foot of Sam Mountain. The site he chose is not far from Tay An Pagoda.

The steps are made of red 'beehive' stone (da ong) brought from the southeastern part of Vietnam. In the middle of the platform is the tomb of Thoai Ngoc Hau and those of his wives, Chau Thi Te and Truong Thi Miet. Nearby are several dozen other tombs where officials who served under Thoai Ngoc Hau are buried.

CAVERN PAGODA
The Cavern Pagoda (Chua Hang, also known as Phuoc Dien Tu) is about halfway up the western side of Sam Mountain. The lower part of the pagoda includes monks' quarters and two hexagonal tombs in which the founder of the pagoda, a female tailor named Le Thi Tho, and a former head monk, Thich Hue Thien, are buried.

The upper section has two parts: the main sanctuary, in which there are statues of A Di Da (the Buddha of the Past) and Thich Ca Buddha (Sakyamuni, the Historical Buddha); and the cavern. At the back of the cave behind the sanctuary building is a shrine dedicated to Quan The Am Bo Tat.

According to legend, Le Thi Tho came from Tay An Pagoda to this site half a century ago to lead a quiet, meditative life. When she arrived, she found two enormous snakes, one white and the other dark green. Le Thi Tho soon converted the snakes, who thereafter led pious lives. Upon her death, the snakes disappeared.

Sleeping & Eating
For details on the Delta Adventure Inn between Chau Doc and Sam Mountain, see p432.

Ben Da Mt Sam Resort (☎ 076-861 745; bendanuisam@hcm.vnn.vn; Quoc Lo 91; r 250,000d;) Though a bit lacking in charisma, this clean hotel offers the standard amenities, plus steam bath, massage and sauna. Breakfast is included and there's an outdoor restaurant here.

Post Office Hotel (Khach San Buu Dien; ☎ 076-861 999; ksnhnsag@hcm.vnn.vn; Quoc Lo 91; d/q US$20/25;) Across the road from Tay An Pagoda, this popular hotel shares the building with the local post office, so you can take care of any philatelic needs in the lobby. Rooms are clean and rates include breakfast.

BA CHUC
Close to the Cambodian border, just inside Vietnam, is Ba Chuc, otherwise known as the Bone Pagoda. The pagoda stands as a grisly reminder of the horrors perpetrated by the Khmer Rouge. Between 1975 and 1978 Khmer Rouge guerrillas regularly crossed the border into Vietnam and slaughtered civilians. And this is to say nothing of the million or so Cambodians who were also killed.

Between 12 April and 30 April 1978, the Khmer Rouge killed 3157 people at Ba Chuc. Only two people are known to have survived. Many of the victims were tortured to death. The Vietnamese government might have had other motives for invading Cambodia at the end of 1978, but certainly outrage at the Ba Chuc massacre was a major reason.

Two other notable pagodas at Ba Chuc are Chua Tam Buu and Chua Phi Lai. The 'bone' pagoda has a common tomb housing the skulls and bones of over 1100 victims. This resembles Cambodia's Choeung Ek killing fields, where thousands of skulls of Khmer Rouge victims are on display. Near the skull collection is a temple that displays gruesome photos taken shortly after the massacre. The display is both fascinating and horrifying – you'll need a strong stomach to visit.

To reach Ba Chuc follow the road that runs along the canal from Chau Doc to Ha Tien. Turn off this main road onto Hwy 3T and follow it for 4km.

TUC DUP HILL
elevation 216m
Because of its network of connecting caves, Tuc Dup Hill served as a strategic base of operations during the American War. *Tuc dup* is Khmer for 'water runs at night' and it is also known locally as 'Two Million Dollar Hill', in reference to the amount of money the Americans sank into securing it. Tuc Dup is 35km from Chau Doc and 64km from Long Xuyen.

This is a place of historical interest but there isn't much to see. It's worth a trip if you're visiting Ba Chuc.

RACH GIA
☎ 077 / pop 172,400
The capital of Kien Giang province, Rach Gia is a booming port city on the Gulf of Thailand. The population includes significant numbers of both ethnic Chinese and ethnic Khmers.

Fishing and agriculture have made the town reasonably prosperous. Easy access to the sea and the proximity of Cambodia and Thailand have also made smuggling a profitable business. The Rach Gia area was once famous for the large feathers used to make ceremonial fans for the Imperial Court.

Visitors' main interest in Rach Gia is to catch the ferry to Phu Quoc Island (p445).

Information
The provincial tourism authority is **Kien Giang Tourist** (Cong Ty Du Lich Kien Giang; ☎ 862 081, fax 862 111; 12 Đ Ly Tu Trong).

Rach Gia is the last place to exchange money before Ha Tien or Phu Quoc Island **Vietcombank** (☎ 863 178; fax 866 243; 2 Đ Mac Cuu) has a 24-hour ATM.

On the road towards Long Xuyen, **Rach Gia Internet Café** (130 Đ Nguyen Trung Truc) has a pretty fast connection. The **post office** (☎ 873008; 2 Đ Mau Than) is centrally located near the river.

Sights
RACH GIA MUSEUM
The **Rach Gia Museum** (☎ 863 727; 21 Đ Nguyen Van Troi; admission free; ✆ 7-11am Mon-Fri, or by appointment) was recently restored and is worth a visit to see the Oc-Eo artefacts and pottery.

NGUYEN TRUNG TRUC TEMPLE
This **temple** (18 Đ Nguyen Cong Tru) is dedicated to Nguyen Trung Truc, a leader of the resistance campaign of the 1860s against the newly arrived French. Among other exploits, he led the raid that resulted in the burning of the French warship *Espérance*. Despite repeated attempts to capture him, Nguyen Trung Truc continued to fight until 1868, when the French took his mother and a number of civilians hostage and threatened to kill them if he did not surrender. Nguyen Trung Truc turned himself in and was executed by the French in the marketplace of Rach Gia on 27 October 1868.

The first temple structure was a simple building with a thatched roof; over the years it has been enlarged and rebuilt several times. The last reconstruction took place between 1964 and 1970. In the centre of the main hall is a portrait of Nguyen Trung Truc on an altar.

PHAT LON PAGODA
This large **Cambodian Hinayana Buddhist pagoda**, whose name means Big Buddha, was founded about two centuries ago. Though all of the three dozen monks who live here are ethnic Khmers, ethnic Vietnamese also frequent the pagoda.

Inside the sanctuary (*vihara*), figures of the Thich Ca Buddha wear Cambodian- and

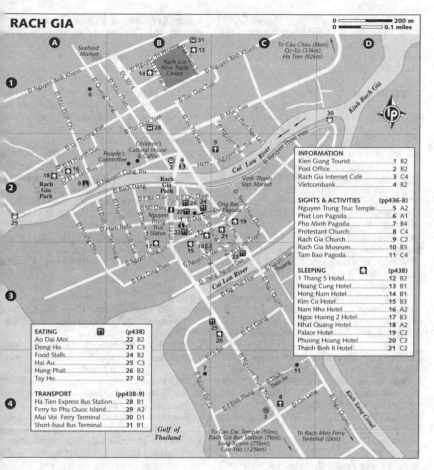

RACH GIA

Thai-style pointed hats. Around the exterior of the main hall are eight small altars.

The two towers near the main entrance are used to cremate the bodies of deceased monks. Near the pagoda are the tombs of about two dozen monks.

Prayers are held here daily from 4am to 5am and 5pm to 7pm. The pagoda, off Đ Quang Trung, is officially open during the seventh, eighth and ninth lunar months (summer season), but guests are welcome all year round.

PHO MINH PAGODA

Only a handful of Buddhist nuns live at Pho Minh Pagoda (cnr Đ Co Bac & Đ Nguyen Van Cu; prayers 3.30-4.30am & 6.30-7.30pm). This small

pagoda was built in 1967 and contains a large Thai-style Thich Ca Buddha that was donated by a Buddhist organisation based in Thailand. Near the Thai-style Buddha there is a Vietnamese-style Thich Ca Buddha. The nuns living here reside in a building located behind the main hall. The pagoda is open to visitors and prayers are held daily.

TAM BAO PAGODA

This **pagoda** (prayers 4.30-5.30am & 5.30-6.30pm), which dates from the early 19th century, is near the corner of Đ Thich Thien An and Đ Ngo Quyen; it was last rebuilt in 1913. The garden contains numerous trees sculpted as dragons, deer and other animals.

MEKONG DELTA

CAO DAI TEMPLE
This small **Cao Dai Temple** (189 Đ Nguyen Trung Truc) was constructed in 1969 and is worth a peek if you missed the Great Temple in Tay Ninh.

CHURCHES
Rach Gia Church (Nha Tho Chanh Toa Rach Gia), a red-brick structure built in 1918, is in Vinh Thanh Van subdistrict, across the channel from Vinh Thanh Van Market. Mass is held daily.

Services are held every Sunday from 10am to noon at the **Protestant Church** (133 Đ Nguyen Trung Truc), built in 1972.

Sleeping
BUDGET
Nhat Quang Hotel (☎ 863 433, 879 687; 16 Đ Tu Do; r 60,000-150,000đ; 🌀) Although the walls are thin and the rooms smallish, this is a very friendly place on a pleasant street near the river mouth.

Thanh Binh II Hotel (☎ 861 921; 37 Đ Hung Vuong; r 50,000-120,000đ; 🌀) The Thanh Binh is nothing to write home about, except for a postscript about the presence of urinals rather than toilets (there's a shared regular toilet). Each room has a cold bath and shower, and some of the tiny rooms have balconies.

Ngoc Huong 2 Hotel (☎ 863 499; 150 Đ Nguyen Hung Son; r 60,000-150,000đ; 🌀) Another OK budget option, this place could be a little cleaner. Not much English is spoken here, but the rates are low.

MID-RANGE
Phuong Hoang Hotel (☎ /fax 866 525, 866 078; 6 Đ Nguyen Trung Truc; s & tw 200,000-250,000đ; 🌀) One of a handful of private minihotels in town, the Phuong Hoang has smallish but very comfortable rooms equipped with amenities like hot water, TV and fridge. There are tubs in the bathrooms and everything is spotless.

Kim Co Hotel (☎ 879 610; fax 879 611; 141 Đ Nguyen Hung Son; s/tw 160,000/200,000đ; 🌀) With a cheery, colourful interior, this hotel offers the usual conveniences. Try to get a room with a view of the street or the small courtyard.

Palace Hotel (☎ 863 049, 867 423; 243 Đ Tran Phu; r US$12-23; 🌀) Surprisingly, the cheapest rooms on the top floor are the ones with balconies; however, all rooms are of the same class. This place is majestically clean.

Hong Nam Hotel (☎ 873 090; Đ Ly Thai To; r 150,000-250,000đ; 🌀) This minihotel offers sparkly spacious rooms decked out with all the modern comforts. It's near the Rach Gia Trade Centre.

Hoang Cung Hotel (☎ 872 655; 26-27 Đ Le Thanh Ton; r 150,000-250,000đ) Similar in standard and near the Hong Nam, the pricier rooms at this place have bathtubs and funky bas-reliefs gracing the bedroom walls.

Nam Nho Hotel (☎ 866 644, 879 879; 21 Đ Tran Phu; r 160,000-180,000đ; 🌀) This small, simple guesthouse is clean and comfortable, with 'careful, whole-hearted and polite service'. Some rooms have balconies.

1 Thang 5 Hotel (☎ 862 103; fax 866 917; 137 Đ Nguyen Hung Son; d/tr 150,000/190,000đ; 🌀) Named after the date of International Workers' Day, the hotel has declined – much like the festival's importance. The place is tidy, but some rooms smell faintly musty. It does have a lift.

Eating
Rach Gia is known for its seafood, dried cuttlefish, dried fish slices (ca thieu), fish sauce and black pepper.

Hung Phat (☎ 867 599; 7 Đ Nguyen Du; meals 25,000đ) Come here for excellent sweet-and-sour soups and a good vegetarian fried rice.

Tay Ho (☎ 863 031; 6 Đ Nguyen Du; meals 25,000đ) Serves good Chinese and Vietnamese food for about the same prices as Hung Phat.

Dong Ho (124 Đ Tran Phu; mains 18,000đ) Run by the same family as Tay Ho, this place serves Chinese, Vietnamese and Western dishes.

Ao Dai Moi (☎ 866 295; 26 Đ Ly Tu Trong; soups 8,000đ) The name means 'new ao dai' and Ao Dai Moi is run by a local tailor. It does very good pho and won ton soup in the morning.

Hai Au (☎ 863 740; fax 876 4192 Đ Nguyen Trung Truc; mains 45,000đ) For standard Vietnamese dishes; it's by the Cai Lon River.

Cheap, tasty Vietnamese food is sold from food stalls along Đ Hung Vuong between Đ Bach Dang and Đ Le Hong Phong.

Vinh Thanh Van Market, Rach Gia's main market area, stretches east of Đ Tran Phu along Đ Nguyen Thoai Hau, Đ Trinh Hoai Duc and Đ Thu Khoa Nghia.

Getting There & Away
AIR
Vietnam Airlines flies between HCMC and Rach Gia twice weekly; see p475 for more

details. The same flight carries on to Phu Quoc Island (p450).

BOAT

At the western end of Đ Nguyen Cong Tru is Rach Gia Park, where you catch the ferries across to Phu Quoc Island (p445).

Mui Voi ferry terminal (*mui* means nose and *voi* means elephant – so named because of the shape of the island) is at the northeastern end of Đ Nguyen Thoai Hau. Cargo boats (15,000d, 9 hours) running from here make daily trips to Long Xuyen (p427) at 8am.

Boats for Ca Mau leave at 5am from the **Rach Meo ferry terminal** (☎ 811 306; 747 Đ Ngo Quyen), about 2km south of town.

BUS

Buses from HCMC to Rach Gia leave from the Mien Tay bus station (p363); the express bus takes six to seven hours (around 90,000d). Night buses leave Rach Gia for HCMC between 7pm and 11pm.

The main **Rach Gia bus station** (Ben Xe Rach Soi; 78 Đ Nguyen Trung Truc) is 7km south of the city (towards Long Xuyen and Can Tho). Buses link Rach Gia with Can Tho, Dong Thap, Ha Tien, Long Xuyen and HCMC.

The **Ha Tien Express Bus Station** (Ben Xe Ha Tien; Tran Quoc Toan) is closer to town and offers daily express services to Long Xuyen, Sa Dec and HCMC.

The short-haul bus terminal, next to Rach Gia New Trade Centre, is where you can catch buses to Hon Chong and Ha Tien.

CAR & MOTORBIKE

Rach Gia is 92km from Ha Tien, 125km from Can Tho and 248km from HCMC.

AROUND RACH GIA
Ancient City of Oc-Eo

During the 1st to 6th centuries AD, when southern Vietnam, much of southern Cambodia and the Malay peninsula were ruled by Funan, the Indian-influenced empire, Oc-Eo was a major trading city. Much of what is known about the Funan empire, which reached its height during the 5th century AD, comes from contemporary Chinese sources and the excavations at Oc-Eo. The excavations have uncovered evidence of contact between Oc-Eo and what is now Thailand, Malaysia and Indonesia, as well as Persia and the Roman Empire.

An elaborate system of canals around Oc-Eo was once used for both irrigation and transportation, prompting Chinese travellers of the time to write about 'sailing across Funan' on their way to the Malay peninsula. Most of the buildings of Oc-Eo were built on piles and pieces of these structures indicate the high degree of refinement achieved by Funanese civilisation. Artefacts found at Oc-Eo are on display in HCMC at the History Museum (p330) and Fine Arts Museum (p331), in Hanoi at the History Museum (p90) and in Long Xuyen at the An Giang Museum (p428).

Though there is in fact very little to see here, the remains of Oc-Eo are not far from

---

IT COULD BE YOU

Asians love to gamble and the Vietnamese are no exception. Lottery madness has swept Vietnam, with tickets being issued in some 40 different provincial areas. While Vietnam's lottery is a legitimate, government-sanctioned cash cow, frequently reported ticket forgeries, as well as occasional printing mistakes, add a whole other element to the game.

Tickets come in three basic varieties, each costing 2000d. The most popular style is roughly fashioned on paper currency and features chic 1970s motifs like cherry-red sports cars, flowers or voluptuous Vietnamese supermodels. Less popular are instant tickets, sealed in a perforated paper packet and checked on the spot with the vendors who hold the day's winning numbers. Finally there are instant win scratch cards, which are most popular in the central provinces and typically decorated with exotic African wildlife.

Tickets are primarily peddled on the street by young children and the elderly, who clear a 10% commission on each ticket sold (less than US1¢). Daily winning numbers, announced each afternoon, can be checked with the vendors (earning you the unspoken obligation to buy another one) or in local newspapers the following day. Cash prizes, determined by winning numbers sequentially matching the six-digit number on your ticket, max out at 50 million dong, about US$350. Winners have one month to make claims.

Rach Gia. The nearest site is Cau Chau, a hill 11km inland that is littered with potsherds and shells. It's near the village of Vong The, which can be reached by 4WD, bicycle or motorbike from Hue Duc village (about 8km away). Head 3km towards Ha Tien, cross on the local ferry and continue for 5km more.

Oc-Eo is most accessible during the dry season. Special permission may be required to visit; for more information, contact Kien Giang Tourist (p436). You might also inquire at the Hong Nam Hotel (p438); ask for Mr Duong Quang, a local English teacher who may be able to guide you to Oc-Eo.

HA TIEN

☎ 077 / pop 90,100

Just 8km from the Cambodian border, Ha Tien is on the Gulf of Thailand in an area known for the production of seafood, black pepper and items made from the shells of sea turtles. All around the area are lovely, towering limestone formations that give this place a very different appearance from the rest of the Mekong Delta. The rock formations support a network of caves, many of which have been turned into temples. Plantations of pepper trees cling to the hillsides. On a clear day, Phu Quoc Island (p445) is easily visible to the west.

Ha Tien was a province of Cambodia until 1708. However, in the face of attacks by the Thais, the Khmer-appointed governor, a Chinese immigrant named Mac Cuu, turned to the Vietnamese for protection and assistance. Mac Cuu thereafter governed this area as a fiefdom under the protection of the Nguyen Lords. He was succeeded as ruler by his son, Mac Thien Tu. During the 18th century the area was invaded and pillaged several times by the Thais. Rach Gia and the southern tip of the Mekong Delta came under direct Nguyen rule in 1798.

During the Khmer Rouge regime, their forces repeatedly attacked the Vietnamese territory and massacred thousands of civilians here. The entire populations of Ha Tien and nearby villages (in fact, tens of thousands of people) fled their homes. Also during this period, areas north of Ha Tien (along the Cambodian border) were sown with mines and booby traps, which have yet to be cleared.

Though the government has designated Ha Tien a 'frontier economic zone', the border crossing here is not yet open to tourists. Rumours are circulating, however, that it is just a matter of time. Check with travel agencies and the local English-language magazines.

Information

The **post office** (☎ 852 190; 3 Đ To Chau; ⏲ 6.30am–9pm) also has Internet access for 4000d per hour.

There's an **Agricultural Bank** (Ngan Hang Nong Nhiep; ☎ 852 055; fax 851 888; 37 Đ Lam Son) near the market area.

Sights

MAC CUU FAMILY TOMBS

On a low ridge not far from town are the **Mac Cuu Family Tombs** (Lang Mac Cuu). They are known locally as Nui Lang, the Hill of the Tombs. Several dozen relatives of Mac Cuu are buried here in traditional Chinese tombs decorated with figures of dragons, phoenixes, lions and guardians.

The largest tomb is that of Mac Cuu himself; it was constructed in 1809 on the orders of Emperor Gia Long and is decorated with finely carved figures of Thanh Long (Green Dragon) and Bach Ho (White Tiger). The tomb of Mac Cuu's first wife is flanked by dragons and phoenixes. At the bottom of the ridge is a shrine dedicated to the Mac family.

TAM BAO PAGODA

Founded by Mac Cuu in 1730 is the **Tam Bao Pagoda** (Sac Tu Tam Bao Tu; 328 Đ Phuong Thanh; ⏲ prayers 8-9am & 2-3pm). It is now home to several Buddhist nuns. In front of the pagoda is a statue of Quan The Am Bo Tat standing on a lotus blossom in the middle of a pond. Inside the sanctuary, the largest statue on the dais is of A Di Da, the Buddha of the Past. It is made of bronze, but has been painted. Outside the building are the tombs of 16 monks.

Near Tam Bao Pagoda is a section of the city wall dating from the early 18th century.

PHU DUNG PAGODA

This **pagoda** (Phu Cu Am Tu; ⏲ prayers 4-5am & 7-8pm) was founded in the mid-18th century by Mac Thien Tich's wife, Nguyen Thi Xuan. It is now home to one monk.

In the middle of the main hall is a statue of nine dragons embracing a newly born Thich Ca Buddha. The most interesting statue on the main dais is a bronze Thich Ca Buddha from China. On the hillside behind the main hall are the tombs of Nguyen Thi Xuan and one of her female servants; nearby are four monks' tombs.

Behind the main hall is a small temple, Dien Ngoc Hoang, dedicated to the Taoist Jade Emperor. The figures inside are of Ngoc Hoang flanked by Nam Tao, the Taoist God of the Southern Polar Star and the God of Happiness (on the right); and Bac Dao, the Taoist God of the Northern Polar Star and the God of Longevity (on the

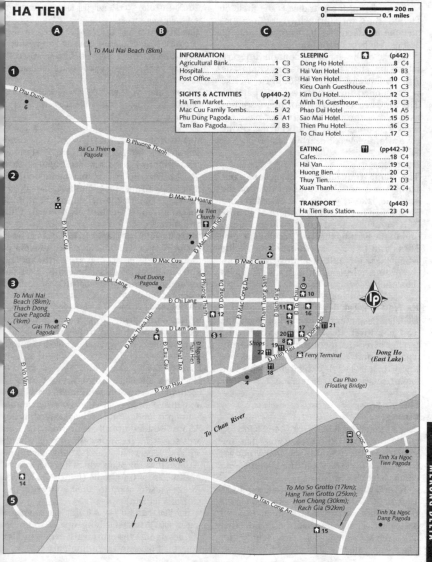

HA TIEN

0		200 m
0		0.1 miles

INFORMATION
Agricultural Bank	1 C3
Hospital	2 C3
Post Office	3 C3

SIGHTS & ACTIVITIES (pp440-2)
Ha Tien Market	4 C4
Mac Cuu Family Tombs	5 A2
Phu Dung Pagoda	6 A1
Tam Bao Pagoda	7 B3

SLEEPING (p442)
Dong Ho Hotel	8 C4
Hai Van Hotel	9 B3
Hai Yen Hotel	10 C3
Kieu Oanh Guesthouse	11 C3
Kim Du Hotel	12 C3
Minh Tri Guesthouse	13 C3
Phao Dai Hotel	14 A5
Sao Mai Hotel	15 D5
Thien Phu Hotel	16 C3
To Chau Hotel	17 C3

EATING (pp442-3)
Cafes	18 C4
Hai Van	19 C4
Huong Bien	20 C3
Thuy Tien	21 D3
Xuan Thanh	22 C4

TRANSPORT (p443)
Ha Tien Bus Station	23 D4

MEKONG DELTA

left). The statues are made of papier-mâché moulded over bamboo frames.

To get to Phu Dung Pagoda, turn off Đ Phuong Thanh at No 374.

THACH DONG CAVE PAGODA

Also known as Chua Thanh Van, this is a subterranean **Buddhist temple** 4km from town.

To the left of the entrance is the Stele of Hatred (Bia Cam Thu), which commemorates the massacre by the Khmer Rouge of 130 people here on 14 March 1978.

Several of the chambers contain funerary tablets and altars to Ngoc Hoang, Quan The Am Bo Tat and the two Buddhist monks who founded the temples of this pagoda. The wind here creates extraordinary sounds as it blows through the grotto's passageways. Openings in several branches of the cave afford views of nearby Cambodia.

Dong Ho

The name translates as East Lake, but Dong Ho is not a lake but an inlet of the sea. The 'lake' is just east of Ha Tien, and is bounded to the east by a chain of granite hills known as the Ngu Ho (Five Tigers) and to the west by the To Chan hills. Dong Ho is said to be most beautiful on nights when there is a full or almost-full moon. According to legend, on such nights fairies dance here.

Ha Tien Market

Ha Tien has an excellent market along the To Chau River. It's well worth your while to stop here – many of the goods are from Thailand and Cambodia, and prices are lower than in HCMC. Cigarette smuggling is particularly big business.

Sleeping

BUDGET

Dong Ho Hotel (☎ 851 031; fax 852 141; 2 Đ Tran Hau; r 50,000-160,000đ; ✷) This breezy hotel near the river offers little charms like slatted windows, friendly staff and well-outfitted rooms. Fan rooms have shared bath.

Thien Phu Hotel (☎ 851 144; 3 Đ Chi Lang; r 80,000-180,000đ; ✷) Fairly simple, the singles at this friendly spot are particularly small but cool and quiet. There is a three-bed room that can sleep six people. It's a cosy, family-run place with pale blue and green tiles.

Phao Dai Hotel (☎ 851 849; r 80,000-140,000đ; ✷) On a hill in the far southwest of town, the Phao Dai is a relatively quiet place. Aircon rooms have ocean views filled with lots of colourful boats; large common terraces have views. Facilities include massage, a karaoke bar and a restaurant.

Other budget choices:

Kieu Oanh Guesthouse (☎ 852 748; 14-20 Đ To Chau; r 80,000-120,000đ; ✷) Measures up to a similar standard as Minh Tri, with extra smiles.

Minh Tri Guesthouse (☎ 852 724; 22 Đ To Chau; r 100,000-120,000đ; ✷) Simple, family-run accommodation.

Sao Mai Hotel (☎ 852 740; Đ Tran Cong An; r 80,000-150,000đ; ✷) A nice friendly place south of the floating bridge.

To Chau Hotel (☎ 852 277; Đ To Chau; r 100,000-150,000đ; ✷) A decent state-owned hotel; staff aren't overly helpful.

MID-RANGE

Hai Van Hotel (☎ 852 001; fax 851 685; 55 Đ Lam Son; r old wing 70,000-150,000đ, new wing 250,000-400,000đ; ✷ ▭) The super-nice management here, coupled with pleasant, comfortable rooms make the Hai Van Hotel an excellent deal. Spacious rooms in the new wing include breakfast.

Kim Du Hotel (☎ 851 929; fax 852 119; 14 Đ Phuong Thanh; r US$14-23; ✷) This is a pleasant place, though third-class rooms are a little musty. Rates include breakfast and the in-house restaurant is good. It has a lift.

Hai Yen Hotel (☎ 851 580; 15 Đ To Chau; r 200,000-250,000đ; ✷) Hai Yen is another private hotel worth considering. All rooms have hot water, TV, phone and fridge; the more expensive ones are bigger and have balconies.

Eating

Ha Tien's speciality is an unusual variety of coconut that can only be found in Cambodia and this part of Vietnam. These coconuts contain no milk, but the delicate flesh is delicious. Restaurants all around the Ha Tien area serve the coconut flesh in a glass with ice and sugar. The Cambodians have long claimed that any place which has these coconuts is part of Cambodia (hence the Khmer Rouge's justification for their attacks on this part of Vietnam).

Hai Van (☎ 850 344; 4 Đ Tran Hau; soups/lunch specials 7000/10,000đ) Dishing up Vietnamese, Chinese and Western meals; Hai Van also does birthdays and wedding parties.

Xuan Thanh (☎ 852 197; 20 Đ Tran Hau; mains 5,000d) This friendly place serves some of the best grub in Ha Tien. Opposite the market, it has tasty food and the most salubrious surroundings in town.

Huong Bien (☎ 852 072; 974 Đ To Chau; mains 0,000d) Another excellent place to eat.

Thuy Tien (☎ 851 828; Đ Dong Ho; coffee 3000d) For a cuppa accompanied by a scenic lakeside location, stop by this low-key café.

For a more lively backdrop try the cafés along the waterfront.

Getting There & Away

BOAT
Passenger ferries dock at the ferry terminal, which is not far from the To Chau Hotel near the floating bridge. Daily ferries depart for Chau Doc (three hours) at 6am. You can travel by boat all the way from HCMC to Ha Tien with a change of boats in Chau Doc, but it's a very long journey and the boats are anything but luxurious.

BUS
Buses from HCMC to Ha Tien leave from the Mien Tay bus station (p363); the trip around 90,000d) takes nine to 10 hours.

Ha Tien bus station (Ben Xe Ha Tien) is on the other side of the floating toll bridge from the centre of town. Buses leave from here to An Giang province, Can Tho 5.50am and 9.10am), Vinh Long province, HCMC (68,000d, eight hours, 7am and 9am) and Rach Gia (five hours, five daily departures).

Buses also run to Rach Gia (20,000d, 1½ hours, 5am and 5pm).

CAR & MOTORBIKE
Ha Tien is 92km from Rach Gia, 95km from Chau Doc, 206km from Can Tho and 338km from HCMC.

AROUND HA TIEN
There are many other islands off the coast between Rach Gia and the Cambodian border. Some locals make a living gathering swiftlet nests (the most important ingredient of that famous Chinese delicacy, bird's-nest soup), on the islands' rocky cliffs.

Beaches
The beaches in this part of Vietnam face the Gulf of Thailand. The water is incredibly warm and calm here, like a placid lake. The beaches are OK for bathing and diving but hopeless for surfing.

Mui Nai (Stag's Head Peninsula) is 8km west of Ha Tien; it supposedly resembles the head of a stag with its mouth pointing upward. On top is a lighthouse and there are sand beaches on both sides of the peninsula. Mui Nai is accessible by road from both Ha Tien and from Thach Dong Cave Pagoda.

No Beach (Bai No), lined with coconut palms, and shady **Bang Beach** (Bai Bang), are several kilometres west of Ha Tien and can be reached from the road to Mui Nai Beach.

Mo So Grotto
About 17km towards Rach Gia from Ha Tien, and 3km from the road, Mo So Grotto consists of three large rooms and a labyrinth of tunnels. Sadly, the local Morning Star cement factory has carted away a substantial amount of limestone and managed to cause irreparable damage to the grotto. The cave is accessible on foot during the dry season and by small boat during the wet season. Visitors should take torches (flashlights) and a local guide.

Hang Tien Grotto
About 25km towards Rach Gia from Ha Tien, Hang Tien Grotto served as a hideout for Nguyen Anh (later Emperor Gia Long) in 1784, when he was being pursued by the Tay Son Rebels. His fighters found zinc coins buried here, a discovery that gave the cave its name, Coin Grotto. Hang Tien Grotto is accessible by boat (15,000d) from the ferry terminal in Ha Tien. The trip takes about an hour.

Hon Giang Island
About 15km from Ha Tien and accessible by small boat, Hon Giang Island has a lovely, secluded beach.

HON CHONG
☎ 077
This small and secluded village beach resort has the most scenic stretch of coastline on the Mekong Delta mainland. It is a peaceful place most of the year and worth chilling out in for a few days. Hon Chong (also called Binh An) is seldom visited by foreign travellers.

The big attractions here are Chua Hang Grotto, Duong Beach and Nghe Island. Though they are a far cry from the stunning 3000-plus islands and grottoes of Halong Bay (p127), the stone formations here are indeed photogenic. Aside from the three gargantuan cement factories that spew out smoke along the road from Ha Tien, the coastal drive there boasts some beautiful landscape.

Hon Chong lies along both sides of the road from Ba Hon, curving along the coast. Hotels and resorts dot the road, which terminates at Chua Hang Grotto and the temple there.

Chua Hang Grotto

Chua Hang Grotto is entered through a Buddhist temple set against the base of a hill. The temple is called **Hai Son Tu** (Sea Mountain Temple). Visitors light incense and offer prayers here before entering the grotto itself, whose entrance is located behind the altar. Inside is a statue of Quan The Am Bo Tat. The thick stalactites are hollow and resonate like bells when tapped.

Duong Beach

Running north from Chua Hang Grotto, this beach (Bai Duong) is named for its long-needled pine trees *(duong)*. The southern area can get busy with Vietnamese tourists – and their beloved karaoke – but otherwise the 3km stretch of coast is quite tranquil.

Although this is easily the prettiest beach in the Mekong Delta, don't expect any white sand. The waters around the delta contain heavy concentrations of silt (and now cement dust), so the beach sand tends to be hard while in the water it's muddy. Still, the water is reasonably clear here and this is the only beach south of HCMC (excluding those on Phu Quoc Island) that looks appealing to swimmers. The beach is known for its spectacular sunsets.

From the busy southern end of the beach (near Chua Hang Grotto), you can see **Father and Son Isle** (Hon Phu Tu) several hundred metres offshore; it is said to be shaped like a father embracing his son. The island, a column of stone, is perched on a 'foot' worn away by the pounding of the waves; the foot is almost fully exposed at low tide. Boats can be hired at the shore to row out for a closer look.

Nghe Island

This is the most beautiful island in the area and is a favourite pilgrimage spot for Buddhists. The island contains a **cave temple** (Chua Hang) next to a large statue of Quan The Am Bo Tat, which faces the sea. The area where you'll find the cave temple and statue is called Doc Lau Chuong.

Finding a boat to the island is not too difficult, though it is much cheaper if you round up a group. Inquire at the Hon Trem Guesthouse (see below); a full-day, three island boat trip costs around US$60 and the boat can hold 15 people. The boat ride to the island usually takes about one to two hours. There is also a speedboat (half-/full-day US$50/100) for hire at the waterside Doi Xanh restaurant, 4.5km from the Chua Hang Grotto back towards Ha Tien. The boat can carry around 20 people for island hopping.

At the time of writing, tourists were not permitted to stay on the island.

Sleeping

A word of warning: the hotels are completely packed out when Buddhists arrive to worship 15 days before and one month after Tet. Another worship deluge occurs in March and April.

BUDGET

Binh An Hotel (☎ 854 332; fax 854 533; 1030 Hamlet 3; r 80,000-160,000d; ✷) On the same road as the Green Hill Guesthouse (see opposite), 1km towards Chua Hang Grotto, this fine place is in a large quiet compound surrounded by a wall with gardens. All rooms have a private bath. The old-wing fan rooms are grotty but cheap, while rooms in the new wing feature air-con and are much nicer.

Huong Bien Guesthouse (☎ 854 537; Hamlet 3, tv 70,000-150,000d; ✷) Huong Bien has moved further down the road from the noisy entrance gate to the Chua Hang Grotto. It's now conveniently sited across the street from the little restaurant row.

Hon Trem Guesthouse (☎ /fax 854 331; r from 130,000d; ✷) This is a state-owned place near the bend in the road, about 1km before the beach gate. It features rooms in a large cottage or in the main building. The hotel can prepare meals on request.

Phuong Thao Guesthouse (☎ 854 357; r 80,000-120,000d; ✷) Two hundred metres beyond

...e Green Hill is this simple guesthouse
...ith thin-walled, bungalow-style rooms.
...'s mildly grubby but friendly, with chick-
...ns and turkeys roaming the yard.

MID-RANGE

...reen Hill Guesthouse (☎ 854 369; 905 Hon Chong;
US$13-20; ❄) This lovely villa on the hill
... the first place you'll see upon arriving
... Hon Chong. Perched on a knoll over-
...oking Duong Beach, this friendly, family-
...n guesthouse has comfortable, spacious
...ooms. The 2nd-storey balcony, festooned
...ith orchids and bougainvillea, has terrific
...ews of Hon Phu Tu. Try booking the
...Hollywood Room' on the top floor, with
...s neat conical ceiling and private terrace.

An Hai Son Resort (☎ 759 226; anhaison@hcm
...nn.vn; Bai Gieng Hamlet; r 200,000-250,000d; ❄ 🖥)
...uite a deal, the bungalows and villa rooms
... this landscaped resort are equipped with
...ll the amenities. Villa rooms are smaller,
...heaper and nicer, with stylish furniture.
...ooms on the 2nd storey have sea views.

My Lan Hotel (☎ 759 044; fax 759 040; r 150,000-
...0,000d; ❄) The My Lan is a recommend-
...ble hotel that was invested in by overseas
...ietnamese from Milan, Italy (hence the
...ame). Rooms are nondescript but immac-
...late; showers even have shower curtains!

...ating

...side from special orders prepared at your
...otel, there are **food stalls** (mains around 8000d)
...ust near the entrance of Chua Hang Grotto.
...or only a few dollars, you can point to one
...f the live chickens, which will be summar-
...y executed and barbecued for you.

Hong Ngoc (coconuts around 3000d), just near the
...ntrance gate to the Chua Hang Grotto, is
... good place to sample delicious Ha Tien
...oconuts.

...etting There & Away

...Chua Hang Grotto and Duong Beach are
...2km from Ha Tien towards Rach Gia. The
...ccess road branches off the Rach Gia–Ha
...ien highway at the small town of Ba Hon,
...hich is just west of the cement factory at
...ien Luong. Buses can drop you off at Ba
...Hon, from where you can hire a motorbike
... get around.

There's also a direct bus service from
...ach Gia to Hon Chong (15,000d, four
...ours). It departs from the **Ben Xe Ha Tien**
bus station (Đ 30 Thang 4) in Rach Gia at 10am
and leaves again from Hon Chong (outside
the Huong Bien Guesthouse) to Rach Gia
at 4am.

PHU QUOC ISLAND
☎ 077 / pop 52,700

Mountainous and forested Phu Quoc Island is in the Gulf of Thailand, 45km west
of Ha Tien and 15km south of the coast of
Cambodia. This tear-shaped island, which
is 48km long and has an area of 1320 sq
km, is ringed with some of the most beautiful beaches in Vietnam. There are fantastic
views of marine life through transparent
blue-green waters.

Phu Quoc is claimed by Cambodia; its
Khmer name is Ko Tral. Needless to say,
the Vietnamese view it very differently and
have built a substantial military base covering much of the northern end of the island.
Phu Quoc is governed as a district of Kien
Giang province.

Phu Quoc Island served as a base for the
French missionary Pigneau de Behaine during the 1760s and 1780s. Prince Nguyen
Anh, who later became Emperor Gia Long,
was sheltered here by Behaine when he was
being hunted by the Tay Son Rebels.

Phu Quoc is not really part of the Mekong Delta and doesn't share the delta's
extraordinary ability to produce rice. The
most valuable crop is black pepper, but the
islanders here have traditionally earned
their living from the sea. Phu Quoc is also
famous in Vietnam for its production of
high-quality fish sauce (nuoc mam).

The island is also known for Phu Quoc
hunting dogs. The dogs have been a great
success – with their help, the islanders have
decimated most of the island's wildlife.
These dogs are said to be able to pick up
the scent of their master from over 1km
away. The classic Phu Quoc pooch has a
ridgeback, curly tail and blue tongue.

Phu Quoc has tremendous tourism potential, but although it is beginning to ramp
up it is mostly unrealised. Transport difficulties, not to mention some of the best
beaches being occupied by military bases,
have contributed to keeping the visitors
away. But since it became a national park in
2001, the island is gaining more attention.
Phu Quoc National Park covers close to 70% of
the island, an area of 31,422 hectares.

PHU QUOC ISLAND

0	10 km
0	6 miles

Hon Ban

CAMBODIA

(319m)

Bai Thom

(365m)

(683m)

Hon Doi Moi (Turtle Island)

Bai Dai

Phu Quoc National Park

Cua Can River

(539m)

Bai Bung

(333m)

Bai Cua Can

Ong Lang Beach

Khu Tuong

Ong Thay

Duong Dong River

Phu Quoc Airport

Van Nguyen Hotel

Suoi Da Ban

(365m)

Duong Dong

(410m)

Suoi Tranh

Cai Lap River

Ham Ninh

Long Beach

(242m)

Old Military Base

SIGHTS & ACTIVITIES (pp447-9)
Coconut Prison.........................1 C5
Rainbow Divers......................(see 5)

SLEEPING (pp449-50)
Bo Resort................................(see 4)
Kim Hoa Resort........................2 C3
Kim Linh Hotel.........................3 C3
Nam Phuong Guesthouse.........(see 2)
Nhat Lan.................................(see 6)
Phu Quoc Resort Thang Loi......4 B3
Saigon-Phu Quoc Resort..........5 C3
Thanh Hai...............................6 C3
Thousand Stars Resort.............7 C4
Tropicana Resort......................8 C3

DRINKING (p450)
Rainbow Bar............................9 C3

Gulf of Thailand

Bai Dam

Cau Sau Hamlet

Bai Sao

Bai Khem

An Thoi

To Rach Gia (138km)

Hon Dam Trong

Hon Dua

Hon Dam Ngoai

Hon Roi

Hon Thom

An Thoi Islands

Hon Vong

Hon Vang

Chan Qui

Hon Xuong

Hon May Rut

Hon Mong Tay

MEKONG DELTA

Phu Quoc's rainy season is from July to November. The peak season for tourism is mid-winter, when the sky is blue and the sea is calm; however, when it's not raining it's stinking hot. Bring sunglasses and plenty of sunblock. Don't set out to explore the island unless you've got at least two litres of water in your day-pack or you'll dehydrate.

Orientation

The main shipping port is **An Thoi** at the southern tip of Phu Quoc Island. This town is not blessed with scenic sights, though the market here is definitely worth a peek. This is the embarkation point for Rach Gia (p436), or for day trips to the An Thoi Islands (p448).

The island's chief fishing port is Duong Dong, on the central west coast. The airport and most of the hotels are here.

The town is not that exciting, though the markets are mildly interesting. The bridge nearby is a good vantage point to photograph the island's fishing fleet – you'll notice that this tiny harbour is anything but clean.

Information

The post office and **Agricultural Bank** (closed weekends) are in downtown Duong Dong. The bank can change dollars but not much else; the safer route is to exchange money in Rach Gia before coming to Phu Quoc.

Internet access is rare; you might try seeking access at the Tropicana Resort.

Sights & Activities

BEACHES

Bai Dai & Bai Thom (Map p446)

These are both remote beaches: **Bai Dai** is in the far northwest and **Bai Thom** is on the northeastern coast. A new road to Bai Dai cuts down on motorbike time and red dust in your face. You can rest assured that neither beach is crowded.

Both are in military areas, but Bai Dai is open to the public and has a couple of restaurants. The military usually opens Bai Thom to civilians on Sunday but you must leave your passport with the military receptionist while you're on the base. In any event, do not try to sneak onto the beaches: make local inquiries and obey the rules.

Bai Cua Can & Long Beach (Map p446)

The most accessible beach, **Bai Cua Can** is in the northwest. It's 11km from Duong Dong.

Long Beach (Bai Truong) is one, well, *long* spectacular stretch of sand from Duong Dong southward along the west coast, almost to An Thoi port (20km). The southern end of the beach is known as Tau Ru Bay (Khoe Tau Ru). The water is crystal clear and the beach is lined with coconut palms.

Long Beach is easily accessible on foot (just walk south from Duong Dong's Cau Castle), but you will need a motorbike or bicycle to reach some of the remote stretches towards the southern end of the island. The beach around the family-run guesthouse area is a particularly popular spot. There are a few bamboo huts where you can buy drinks, but bring water if you're planning a long hike along this beach.

Bai Sao & Bai Dam (Map p446)

Two beautiful white-sand beaches along the southeastern part of the island are **Bai Sao** and **Bai Dam**, just a few kilometres from An Thoi. There are a couple of beachfront restaurants at Bai Sao.

Just south of these beaches is undeveloped Bai Khem, one of the most beautiful beaches on the island and also, sadly, a military area that was closed to the public at the time of writing.

SUOI DA BAN (MAP P446)

Compared with the waterlogged Mekong Delta, Phu Quoc has very little surface moisture; however, several springs originate in the hills. The most accessible of these is **Suoi Da Ban** (Stony Surface Spring). Basically, it's a white-water creek tumbling across some attractive large granite boulders. There are deep pools and it's pleasant enough for a swim. Bring plenty of mosquito repellent.

The stream is in the south-central part of the island. There is no admission charge, though there is a 4000d fee for parking a motorbike.

FOREST RESERVE

Phu Quoc's poor soil and lack of surface water have disappointed farmers for generations, although their grief has been the island's environmental salvation. About 90% of the island is forested and the trees now enjoy official protection. Indeed, this is the last large stand of forest in the south.

The **forest** is most dense in the northern half of the island. The area is a forest

DUONG DONG

INFORMATION
Agricultural Bank	1 B4
Post Office	2 B4

SIGHTS & ACTIVITIES (pp447-9)
Cau Castle	3 A3
Dry Goods Market	4 B2
Fish Sauce Factory	5 B2

SLEEPING (pp449-50)
Duong Dong Hotel	6 C2
Nha Tro Quoc Tuan	7 C2

EATING (p450)
Food Stalls	8 B2
Gop Gio	9 B2
Le Giang	10 C4
Tuoi Tham	11 C4

TRANSPORT (pp450-1)
Ferry Landing (Steel Ships)	12 B3
Ferry Landing (Wooden Boats)	13 B2

reserve (Khu Rung Nguyen Sinh). You'll need a motorbike or mountain bike to get into the reserve. There are a few primitive dirt roads, but no real hiking trails.

AN THOI ISLANDS

Off the southern tip of Phu Quoc are the tiny **An Thoi Islands** (Quan Dao An Thoi; Map p446). These 15 islands and islets can be visited by chartered boat, and it's a fine area for sightseeing, fishing, swimming and snorkelling. Hon Thom (Pineapple Island) is about 3km in length and is the largest island in the group. Other islands here include Hon Dua (Coconut Island), Hon Roi (Lamp Island), Hon Vang (Echo Island), Hon May Rut (Cold Cloud Island), Hon Dam (Shadow

Island), Chan Qui (Yellow Tortoise) and Hon Mong Tay (Short Gun Island).

Most boats depart from An Thoi on Phu Quoc, but you can make arrangements through hotels in Duong Dong. The Tropicana Resort has a large boat for charter that can make the trip directly from Long Beach. The Kim Linh also has two boats for day hire, one that can carry eight to 10 passengers (US$35) and a larger one that can carry 15 to 20 people (US$65). Boat charters are seasonal and generally do not run during the rainy season.

DIVING

Though Nha Trang (p261) gets the heaviest billing as Vietnam's best dive destination

living opportunities also abound around
Phu Quoc. The reputable **Rainbow Divers** (Map
p446; ☎ 0913-400 964; www.divevietnam.com; ⏰ 7am-
10pm) has a dive centre on the island. Find it
at Saigon-Phu Quoc Resort (see below).

COCONUT TREE PRISON

Being an island and an economically marginal area of Vietnam, Phu Quoc was useful
to the French colonial administration –
chiefly as a prison. The Americans took
over where the French left off and as a
consequence Phu Quoc was used to house
about 40,000 VC prisoners.

The island's main penal colony was known
as the **Coconut Tree Prison** (Nha Lao Cay Dua; Map p446)
and is near An Thoi town. Though it's considered an historic site, plans to open a museum here have been stalled. It's still used as a
prison, so not surprisingly, few visitors come
to check it out.

CAU CASTLE (DINH CAU)

According to tourist brochures, Duong
Dong's main attraction is **Cau Castle** (Dinh
Cau; Map p448; admission free). In fact, it's not so
much a castle as a combination temple and
lighthouse. It was built in 1937 to honour
Thien Hau (Goddess of the Sea), who protects sailors and fishermen. The castle is
worth a quick look and gives you a good
view of the harbour entrance.

FISH SAUCE FACTORY

OK, so it's not your average sightseeing
attraction, but more than a few have en-
joyed a visit to the **distillery** (Map p448; admission
free; ⏰ 8-11am & 1-5pm) of Nuoc Mam Hung
Thanh, the largest of Phu Quoc's fish-sauce
makers. At first glance, the giant wooden
vats may make you think you've arrived for
a wine tasting, but one sniff of the festering
nuoc mam essence brings you right back to
reality (it's actually not so bad after a few
minutes).

Most of the sauce produced is exported
to the mainland for domestic consumption, though a surprising amount finds its
way abroad to kitchens in Japan, the USA,
Canada and France.

The factory is a short walk from the **markets** in Duong Dong. There is no admission charge to visit, though you'd be best
off taking a guide along unless you speak
Vietnamese.

Tours

Your best bet for booking tours is through
your hotel, as there's no local tourism authority in Duong Dong. Most travellers
get around the island by hired motorbike.
There are a handful of English-speaking
motorbike guides on the island, the most
notorious of whom is **Tony** (☎ 846 144).
Raised by a US military family, Tony speaks
a distinctive breed of Al Pacino English that
could easily land him a role in the next
sequel to *The Godfather*. He's easy to find
(more likely he'll find you) or you can call
him if you want to book ahead.

Sleeping

Depending on the tourist load, prices for
Phu Quoc's hotels and resorts are very
much negotiable. Between late December
and early January, accommodation fills up
fast, so it's highly advisable to book well
in advance.

LONG BEACH

Tropicana Resort (Map p446; ☎ 847 127; www.vngold
.com/pq/tropicana; km2; d US$15, bungalows US$35-70;
❌ 🖳) The unassumingly pretty Tropicana
is the kind of oasis you might need after
a rough ferry ride. Friendly English- and
French-speaking staff hire out sailboards,
kayaks and motorbikes, but you might prefer to simply sit on the terrace and soak
up the view. Rates include breakfast and
airport pick-up.

Saigon-Phu Quoc Resort (Map p446; ☎ 846 510;
www.sgphuquocresort.com.vn; r US$56-161, family house
US$507; ❌ 🖳) Attractive rooms here are in
villa-type houses, with names like Tarzan
Villa, and have good views overlooking
the beautiful beach. Rooms come complete with IDD phones, satellite TV and
minibars. Rates include free airport trans-
fers and buffet breakfast; book through the
website for significant deals.

Thousand Stars Resort (Khu Du Lich Ngan Sao; Map
p446; ☎ 848 203; hungthanhphuquoc@hcm.vnn.vn; km3;
d 220,000d, bungalows 300,000-600,000d; ❌) There's
a beautiful beach here, with delightful plaster animals (not live ones, for a change)
welcoming guests along the entry path. The
beachfront restaurant is a superb place for
drinks or a seafood dinner at sunset.

Kim Hoa Resort (Map p446; ☎ 847 039; km1.5;
d 225,000-270,000d, bungalows 180,000d; ❌) This
popular guesthouse has lots of bungalows

and a busy restaurant above the beach; it seems to be the preferred venue for local wedding parties (all-day affairs). While the accommodation is comfortable enough, staff are inattentive and unfriendly.

Several family-run guesthouses line Long Beach:

Beach Club (☎ 980 998; r US$8-15) A new French-run place, offering yoga, movie nights and DJ nights.

Nam Phuong Guesthouse (Map p446; ☎ 846 319; km1.5; d 105,000-120,000d, bungalows 225,000d) With bungalows near the beach and a breezy café.

Nhat Lan (Map p446; ☎ 847 663; km1.7; d 120,000-180,000d) Kind family, comfortable concrete bungalows and excellent hammocks.

Thanh Hai (Map p446; ☎ 847 482; km1.7; d 120,000d) A very peaceful, family-run spot in the woods; only six rooms available.

ONG LANG BEACH
Although it is rockier and less beautiful than Long Beach, Ong Lang Beach, 7km north of Duong Dong near the hamlet of Ong Lang, is unquestionably less crowded and quieter.

Phu Quoc Resort Thang Loi (Map p446; ☎ 0918-073 494, 0908-297 413; www.phu-quoc.de; bungalows US$11-17) A lovely resort, the Thang Loi has 12 wooden bungalows in a vast open garden setting, under the shade of cashew nut, palm and mango trees. The staff are friendly and the restaurant is cosy. Room rates vary depending on the size. Email ahead for reservations.

Bo Resort (Map p446; ☎ 0913-640 520; boresort@yahoo.com; bungalows US$15-20) Recommended by travellers, this resort with a good restaurant is run by a French-Vietnamese couple.

DUONG DONG
Most travellers prefer to put up at the beach, though there are a few cheapie options in Duong Dong town.

Duong Dong Hotel (Map p448; ☎ 846 106; r with/without bath 50,000/35,000d) This hotel near Duong Dong Market has rooms that are dark boxes, but the management is friendly.

Nha Tro Quoc Tuan (Map p448; ☎ 847 552; r 50,000d) With eight rooms, this place is slightly better than the Duong Dong Hotel.

AN THOI
Although few travellers care to stay in the township of An Thoi (Map p446), it's worth considering if you arrive late on the ferry

or will be taking the ferry early the next morning.

Duy Khoa (☎ 844 832; www.vngold.com/pc/duykhoa; r 70,000-150,000d; 🗙) The most appealing minihotel in An Thoi, rooms here are small but tidy. It's a short walk from the ferry pier.

Eating
Gop Gio (Map p448; ☎ 847 057; 145 Đ Bach Dang; mains 15,000d) Near the ferry landing in Duong Dong, this casual eatery wins hands down for the freshest (and cheapest) seafood in town.

Tuoi Tham (Map p448; ☎ 846 368; Đ Tran Hung Dao) and **Le Giang** (Map p448; ☎ 846 444; 289 Đ Tran Hung Dao) are two more local places with good food (mains around 10,000d) on the way from Duong Dong to Long Beach.

For atmosphere and fine food, check out the seafront terrace restaurants at the **Tropicana Resort** (Map p446) and the **Kim Hoa Resort** (Map p446).

For something a bit more local (and loud), try the outdoor beachside restaurants near the small guesthouses on Long Beach (Map p446).

There are heaps of cheap food stalls (Map p448) all around the market area in Duong Dong.

Drinking
Run by the same great crew who made this erstwhile Nha Trang institution a legendary good time, the friendly **Rainbow Bar** (Map p446) is located between the Saigon-Phu Quoc and Kim Hoa resorts.

Getting There & Away
AIR
Vietnam Airlines has four flights weekly between HCMC and Duong Dong, Phu Quoc's main town; see p475 for more details. Some flights make a stop en route at Rach Gia, on the mainland.

A popular round trip between HCMC and Phu Quoc is to travel overland through the Mekong Delta, taking a ferry to the island (or a flight for US$32) from Rach Gia and, when you're finally tanned and rested, taking the short one-hour flight (US$46) back to HCMC.

BOAT
The fastest boats to Phu Quoc Island are hydrofoils (adult/child 130,000/70,000d

2½ hours, 8.30am/1.30pm from Rach Gia/
An Thoi), travelling daily between Rach Gia
and Phu Quoc. Tickets must be purchased
in advance. Fast boats between Ba Hon and
Phu Quoc were being phased out at the
time of research.

All passenger ferries departing and arriving at Phu Quoc use the port of An Thoi on
the southern tip of the island.

There are **ferries** (☎ 863 242) to An Thoi
(66,000d, eight hours, 9am). Departure time
may vary depending on the tides and passenger load. In any case, it's best to be there
early, not only to be assured passage, but
also to stake out a good spot to sit or lie
down on. On the smaller ferry boats, avoid
the cosy-looking platform over the engine
unless you fancy being slow-roasted during
the trip! Be sure to stock up on snacks and
water in town or at the docks.

None of the boats in the fleet – vintage steel
vessels and wooden fishing boats – are very
comfortable. They are usually packed with
too many passengers (who string hammocks
across every possible nook and cranny) and
cargo (including noisy fighting cocks and
other exotic animals). Although we haven't
heard of any mishaps, it can be a rough ride
and concerned parties might consider flying.
Boats cannot dock at Rach Gia when the tide
is low – passengers and cargo have to be ferried offshore in a small shuttle boat.

The ride to An Thoi takes about eight
hours and most travellers jump off here to
catch a motorbike to Duong Dong. However, if you're not in a rush to reach your
hotel by sundown, it's possible to pay an
extra 15,000d when you buy your ticket and
stay on board right up to Duong Dong. This
extra leg adds another 2½ hours to your
trip, what with the stop in An Thoi and the
(ideally, moonlit) cruise up the coast.

There are on-again, off-again rickety
boats between Ham Tinh – on the east
coast of Phu Quoc – and Ha Tien on the
mainland, but these are considered to be
dangerous and not worth the risk.

Getting Around
TO/FROM THE AIRPORT
Phu Quoc's airport is almost in central
Duong Dong. Unless your luggage is really
heavy, you can easily walk the few hundred
metres to the centre of town. If you're heading for one of the hotels on Long Beach,
just walk down the beach from the Huong
Bien Hotel.

The motorbike drivers at the airport will
charge you about US$1 to most hotels, but
are notorious for trying to cart people off
to where they can collect a commission. If
you know where you want to go, tell them
you've already got a reservation.

BICYCLE
If you can ride a bicycle in the tropical heat
over these dusty, bumpy roads, more power
to you. Bicycle rentals are available through
most hotels for about US$1 per day.

BUS
There is a skeletal bus service between An
Thoi and Duong Dong. Buses run perhaps
once every hour or two. A bus (tickets
10,000d) waits for the ferry at An Thoi to
take passengers to Duong Dong.

MOTORBIKE
You'll hardly have to look for the motorbike
taxis – they'll be looking for you. Some polite bargaining may be necessary. For most
short runs within the town itself, 5000d
should be sufficient. Otherwise, figure
on around 10,000d for about 5km. From
Duong Dong to An Thoi should cost you
about 30,000d.

Motorbikes can be hired for US$7 per
day. Add another US$5 if you want a driver
as well. This should be sufficient to get you
anywhere on the island. If interested, ask
at your hotel.

There are few paved roads on the island
and after a day of motorbike riding you
can expect to be covered from head to toe
with red dust.

Directory

CONTENTS

ACCOMMODATION

Vietnam has something for everyone – from the fleapit to the five star – and we cover them all! Most hotels in Vietnam quote prices in a mix of Vietnamese dong and US dollars. In the provinces the lower dong price is usually reserved for locals, while foreigners pay the higher dollar price. Prices are quoted in dong or dollars throughout this book based on the preferred currency.

Talking about budget, we mean guesthouses or hotels where the majority of rooms cost less than US$15. These are usually family-run guesthouses, mini-hotels or, traditionally the least-appealing choice, government-run guesthouses that time forgot. Budget rooms generally come well equipped for the money, so don't be surprised to find air-con, hot water and a TV for less than 10 bucks.

Moving on to mid-range, you're looking at the US$15 to US$50 range, which buys some pretty tasty extras in Vietnam. At the lower end of this bracket, many of the hotels are similar to budget hotels but with bigger rooms or balconies. Flash a bit more cash and three-star touches are available, like access to a swimming pool and a hairdryer hidden away somewhere.

At the top end are a host of international-standard hotels and resorts that charge from US$50 a room to US$500 a suite. Some of these are fairly faceless business hotels, while others ooze opulence or resonate with history. There are some real bargains when compared with the Hong Kongs and Singapores of this world, so if you fancy indulging yourself, Vietnam is a good place to do it. Most hotels at the top end levy a tax of 10% and a service charge of 5%, displayed as ++ ('plus plus') on the bill.

Peak tourist demand for hotel rooms comes at Christmas and New Year, when prices may rise by as much as 25%. There is also a surge in many cities during Tet, when half of Vietnam is on the move. Try and make a reservation at these times so as not to get caught out. During quiet periods it is often possible to negotiate a discount, whether by email in advance or over the counter on arrival, as there is now a surplus of hotel beds in many destinations.

Passports are almost always requested on arrival at a hotel. It is not absolutely essential to hand over your actual passport, but at the very least you need to hand over a photocopy of the passport details, visa and departure card. Most people end up handing over their passports, but make sure it comes back with the yellow departure card.

Accommodation prices listed are high-season prices for rooms with attached bathroom, unless stated otherwise. An icon is included if air-con is available; otherwise, assume that a fan will be provided.

PRACTICALITIES

- **Electricity** The usual voltage is 220V, 50 cycles, but sometimes you encounter 110V, also at 50 cycles, just to confuse things. Electrical sockets are usually two-prong.

- **Laundry** Most guesthouses and hotels have cheap laundry services, but check they have a dryer if the weather is bad. There are dry-cleaning outlets in every town.

- **Newspapers & Magazines** *Vietnam News* and the *Saigon Times* are popular English-language dailies. Good magazines include the *Vietnam Economic Times,* plus its listings mag, the *Guide,* and the *Vietnam Investment Review.*

- **Radio & TV** *Voice of Vietnam* hogs the airwaves all day and is pumped through loudspeakers in many smaller towns. There are seven TV channels and a steady diet of satellite stuff.

- **Weights & Measures** The Vietnamese use the metric system for everything except precious metals and gems, where they use the Chinese system.

Camping

Perhaps because so many Vietnamese spent much of the war years living in tents, as either soldiers or refugees, camping is not the popular pastime it is in the West.

Some innovative private travel agencies in Ho Chi Minh City (HCMC) and Hanoi offer organised camping trips to national parks, plus camping out in beauty spots like Halong Bay (p127). See under Travel Agencies in Hanoi (p79) and HCMC (p327).

Guesthouses & Hotels

Many of the large hotels (*khach san*) and guesthouses (*nha khach* or *nha nghi*) are government-owned or joint ventures. There has also been a mushrooming of mini-hotels – small, smart private hotels that represent good value for money. The international hotel chains are now well represented in Hanoi and HCMC.

There is considerable confusion over the terms 'singles', 'doubles', 'double occupancy' and 'twins', so let's set the record straight here. A single contains one bed, even if two people sleep in it. If there are two beds in the room, that is a twin, even if only one person occupies it. If two people stay in the same room, that is double occupancy. In some hotels 'doubles' means twin beds, while in others it means double occupancy.

While many of the newer hotels have lifts, older hotels often don't and the cheapest rooms are at the end of several flights of stairs. It's a win-win situation: cheaper rooms, a bit of exercise and better views!

Many hotels post a small sign warning guests not to leave cameras, passports and other valuables in the room. Most places have a safety deposit system of some kind, but if leaving cash (not recommended) or travellers cheques, be sure to seal the loot in an envelope and have it counter-signed by staff.

ACTIVITIES

If you are looking for action, Vietnam can increasingly deliver. Biking and hiking are taking off up and down the country, while offshore there is kayaking and surfing above the water and diving and snorkelling beneath. If it all sounds like too much hard work, rent a motorbike and let the engine take the strain.

Cycling

For distances near and far, cycling is an excellent way to experience Vietnam. A bicycle can be rented in most tourist centres for around US$1 a day.

The flatlands of the Mekong Delta region are an ideal place for a long-distance ride through the back roads. The entire coastal route along Hwy 1 is an alluring achievement, but the insane traffic makes it tough going and dangerous. Better is the new inland trunk road Hwy 14, also known as the Ho Chi Minh Rd, which offers stunning scenery and little traffic.

North of the old Demilitarised Zone (DMZ), cycling is a bad idea in the winter months, particularly if heading from south to north, thanks to the massive monsoon winds, which blow from the north.

For some laughs, as well as the lowdown on cycling in Vietnam, visit the website www.mrpumpy.net.

Diving & Snorkelling
The most popular scuba-diving area in Vietnam is around Nha Trang (p270). There are several reputable dive operators here, whose equipment and training is up to international standards. It is also possible to hire snorkelling gear and scuba equipment at several beach resorts along the coast, including Ca Na (p281) and China Beach (p226). Phu Quoc Island (p445) has the potential to be the next big thing in underwater exploration, but there are no dive operators on the island just yet.

Golf
Mark Twain once said that playing golf was 'a waste of a good walk' and apparently Ho Chi Minh agreed with him. Times have changed and government officials can often be seen fraternising on the fairways.

All over East Asia playing golf wins considerable points in the 'face game', even if you never hit a ball. For maximum snob value you need to join a country club, and in Vietnam memberships start at around US$20,000. Most golf clubs will allow you to simply pay a guest fee.

The best golf courses in Vietnam are located in Dalat (p297) and Phan Thiet (p282), but there are also courses in and around Hanoi and HCMC.

For information about golf package deals visit www.vietnamgolfresorts.com.

Kayaking
Kayaking has taken off around Halong Bay in the past few years, following in the footsteps of Krabi in Thailand. Several companies offer kayaking itineraries around the majestic limestone pinnacles, including overnights on islands in the bay.

Motorbiking
Motorbiking Vietnam's 'deep north' is unforgettable. For those seeking true adventure there is no better way to go. If you are not confident riding a motorbike, it's comparatively cheap to hire someone to drive it for you. Four-wheel-drive trips in the north are also highly recommended, though the mobility of two wheels is unrivalled.

Rock Climbing
Well, it's still early days, but with the sheer range of limestone karsts found up and down the country, it is only a matter of time before the word gets out. For now, it is likely to be Halong Bay (p127) that emerges as the premier spot, but in time Ninh Binh (p174) and Phong Nha (p185) could offer some competition.

Surfing & Windsurfing
Surfing and windsurfing have only recently arrived on the scene, but they are quickly catching on. The best place to practice these pursuits is at Mui Ne Beach (p283), but experienced surfers head for China Beach in Danang (p226).

Trekking
Vietnam offers some excellent trekking opportunities, notably in its growing array of national parks and nature reserves. There are ample opportunities to hike to minority villages in the northwest, northeast and central highlands regions. Anything is possible, from half-day hikes to a six-day ascent of Fansipan, Vietnam's highest mountain. The best bases from which to arrange treks are Sapa (p163), Bac Ha (p169) and Cat Ba (p131), all in northern Vietnam; Bach Ma National Park (p216) in central Vietnam; and Cat Tien (p388) and Yok Don (p311) National Parks in the south. Tour operators in Hanoi and HCMC offer a variety of programmes that feature hiking and trekking.

Bear in mind that you may need to arrange special permits, especially if you want to spend the night in remote mountain villages where there are no hotels.

BUSINESS HOURS
Vietnamese people rise early and consider sleeping in to be a sure indication of illness. Offices, museums and many shops open between 7am and 8am and close between 4pm and 5pm. Post offices keep longer hours and are generally open from 6.30am to 9pm. Banks are generally open from 8am to 11.30am and 1pm to 4pm during the week and 8am to 11.30am on Saturday.

Most government offices are open on Saturday until noon but are closed on Sunday. Most museums are closed on Monday while temples and pagodas are usually open every day from around 5am to 9pm.

Many of the small privately owned shops, restaurants and street stalls stay open seven days a week, often until late at night.

Lunch is taken very seriously and virtually everything shuts down between noon and 1.30pm. Government workers tend to take longer breaks, so figure on getting nothing done between 11.30am and 2pm.

CHILDREN

Children get to have a good time in Vietnam, mainly because of the overwhelming amount of attention they attract and the fact that almost everybody wants to play with them! For the full picture on surviving and thriving on the road, check out Lonely Planet's *Travel with Children* by Cathy Lanigan, with a rundown on health precautions for kids and advice on travel during pregnancy.

Practicalities

When it comes to feeding and caring for babies, almost anything and everything is available in the major cities of Vietnam, but supplies dry up quickly in the countryside. Cot beds are available in international-standard mid-range and top-end hotels, but not elsewhere. There are no safety seats in rented cars or taxis, but some Western restaurants can usually find a highchair when it comes to eating.

Breastfeeding in public is very common in Vietnam, so there is no need to worry about crossing a cultural boundary. But there are few facilities for changing babies other than the usual bathrooms, so pack a baby bag everywhere you go. For kiddies who are too young to handle chopsticks, most restaurants also have knives and forks.

Sights & Activities

There is plenty to do in big cities to keep kids interested, though in most smaller towns and rural areas you will probably encounter the boredom factor. The zoos, parks and some of the best ice-cream shops in the region are usually winners. Children visiting the south should not miss HCMC's water parks (p346), while Hanoi's two *musts* are the circus (p106) and a water-puppet performance (p107).

Nature lovers with children can hike in one of Vietnam's expansive national parks or nature reserves. Cuc Phuong National Park (p177) is home to the excellent Endangered Primate Rescue Centre, where endangered species of monkeys are protected and bred. This is a great place to see gibbons gallivanting about their safe houses and to learn about the plight of our furry friends.

With such a long coast, there are some great beaches for young children to enjoy, but pay close attention to any playtime in the sea, as there are some big riptides at many of the most popular beaches.

CLIMATE CHARTS

The climate of Vietnam varies considerably from region to region. Although the entire country lies in the tropics and subtropics, local conditions vary from frosty winters in the far northern hills to year-round, subequatorial warmth in the Mekong Delta.

For more climatic kudos, take a look at the When to Go information (p13).

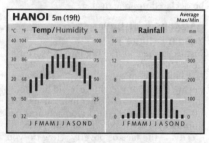

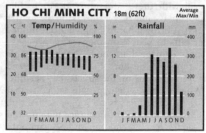

COURSES
Cooking

For the full story on cooking courses, check out the Food & Drink chapter (p69).

Language

If you want to brush up on your Vietnamese, there are courses offered in HCMC, Hanoi and elsewhere. To qualify for student-visa status you need to enrol at a bona fide university, as opposed to a private language centre or with a tutor. Lessons usually last for two hours per day, and cost from US$3 to US$7 per hour.

It is important to decide on whether to study Vietnamese in Hanoi or HCMC, as the northern and southern dialects are quite different. Many have been dismayed to discover that if they studied in one city they could not communicate in the other. For more details, see under Language Courses in Hanoi (p94) and Ho Chi Minh City (p346).

CUSTOMS

Enter Vietnam by air and the whole procedure only takes a few minutes. If you enter overland expect a bit more attention.

Duty free allowances are the standard 200 cigarettes and a bottle of booze variety. Visitors can bring unlimited foreign currency into Vietnam, but large sums must be declared upon arrival.

DANGERS & ANNOYANCES
Beggar Fatigue

Just as you're about to dig into the scrumptious Vietnamese meal you've ordered, you feel a tug on your shirt sleeve. This latest 'annoyance' is a bony, eight-year-old boy holding his three-year-old sister in his arms. The little girl has a distended stomach and her hungry eyes are fixed on your full plate.

This is the face of poverty. How do you deal with these situations? If you're like most of us, not very well. Taking the matter into your own hands by giving out money or gifts to people on the streets can cause more damage than good. The more people are given hand-outs, the more reliant and attracted to life on the streets they become. When money is tight, people recognise that life on the streets is no longer so fruitful. This will hopefully discourage parents and 'leaders' forcing children and beggars onto the streets.

One way to contribute and help improve the situation is to invest just a few hours to find out about local organisations that work with disadvantaged people; these groups are far more likely to make sure contributions are used in the most effective way possible to help those who need it.

However, if you want to do something on the spot, at least avoid giving money or anything that can be sold. The elderly and the young are easily controlled and are ideal begging tools.

So if you are going to give something directly to a beggar, it's better to give food than money; take them to a market or stall and buy them a nutritious meal or some fruit to be sure they are the only beneficiaries.

Noise

Not just any noise, but a whole lot of noises that just never seem to stop. At night there is most often a competing cacophony from motorbikes, discos, cafés, video arcades, karaoke lounges and restaurants; if your hotel is near any or all of these, it may be difficult to sleep.

Fortunately most noise subsides around 10pm or 11pm, as few places stay open much later than that. Unfortunately, however, Vietnamese are up and about from around 5am onwards. This not only means that traffic noise starts early, but you may be woken up by the crackle of loud speakers as the Voice of Vietnam cranks into life at 5am in small towns. It's worth trying to get a room at the back of a hotel.

One last thing…don't forget the earplugs!

Prostitution

Karaoke and massage signs are ubiquitous throughout Vietnam. Sometimes this may mean an orchestra without instruments, or a healthy massage to ease a stiff body. However, more often than not, both of these terms are euphemisms for some sort of prostitution. There may be some singing or a bit of shoulder tweaking going on, but ultimately it is just a polite introduction to something naughtier. Legitimate karaoke and legitimate massage do exist in the bigger cities, but as a general rule of thumb, if the place looks small and sleazy, it most probably is.

Scams

Con artists and thieves are always seeking new tricks to separate naive tourists from their money and are becoming more savvy in their ways. We can't warn you about every trick you might encounter, so maintain a healthy scepticism and be prepared to argue when unnecessary demands are made for your money.

Beware of a motorbike-rental scam that some travellers have encountered in HCMC. Rent a motorbike and the owner supplies an excellent lock, insisting you use it. What he doesn't tell you is that he has another key and that somebody will follow you and 'steal' the bike at the first opportunity. You then have to pay for a new bike.

More common is when your motorbike won't start after you parked it in a 'safe' area with a guard. But yes, the guard knows somebody who can repair your bike. The mechanic shows up and quickly reinstalls the parts they removed earlier and the bike works again. That will be US$10, please.

Beware of massage boys who, after a price has been agreed upon, try to extort money from you afterwards by threatening to set the police on you (these threats are generally empty ones).

Despite an array of scams, however, it is important to keep in mind the Vietnamese are not always out to get you. One concerning trend we're noticing in Vietnam, relative to neighbouring countries such as Cambodia and Laos, is a general lack of trust in the locals on the part of foreigners. Try to differentiate between who is good and bad and not close yourself off to every person you encounter.

This is not always an easy thing to do. Even one of the original authors of this book, a veteran travel writer and Vietnam hand, was duped by a long-time Vietnamese friend who, unbeknown to him, had tried to collect fees from hotels and restaurants that wished to be included in this guide!

One final word of advice: we're seeing an awful lot of travellers in Vietnam with their noses dug too deep inside guidebooks. The paranoia people develop from being hassled so much seems to result in many refusing to believe anyone if it's 'not in the book'. For better or worse, often it's not. Try to keep an open mind, be aware of what can happen and what things 'should' cost, and then use this information in conjunction with your own better judgment.

Sea Creatures

If you plan to spend your time swimming, snorkelling and scuba diving, familiarise yourself with the various hazards. The list of dangerous creatures that are found in seas off Vietnam is extensive and includes sharks, jellyfish, stonefish, scorpion fish, sea snakes and stingrays. However, there is little cause for alarm as most of these

creatures avoid humans, or humans avoid them, so the number of people injured or killed is fairly small.

Jellyfish tend to travel in groups, so as long as you look before you leap into the sea, avoiding them should not be too hard. Stonefish, scorpion fish and stingrays tend to hang out in shallow water along the ocean floor and can be very difficult to see. One way to protect against these nasties is to wear shoes in the sea.

Theft

The Vietnamese are convinced that their cities are full of criminals. Street crime is commonplace in HCMC and Nha Trang, but it doesn't hurt to keep the antennae up wherever you are.

HCMC is the place to really keep your wits about you. Don't have anything dangling from your body that you are not ready to part with, including bags and jewellery, which might tempt a robber. Keep an eye out for drive-by thieves on motorbikes – they specialise in snatching handbags and cameras from tourists on foot and riding *cyclos* in the city.

Pickpocketing, which often involves kids, women with babies and newspaper vendors, is also a serious problem, especially in the tourist areas of HCMC. Many of the street kids, adorable as they may be, are very skilled at liberating people from their wallets.

Avoid putting things down while you're eating, or at least take the precaution of fastening these items to your seat with a strap or chain. Remember, any luggage that you leave unattended for even a moment may grow legs and vanish.

There are also 'taxi girls' (sometimes transvestites) who approach Western men, give them a big hug, sometimes more, and ask if they'd like 'a good time'. Then they suddenly change their mind and depart, along with a wristwatch and wallet.

We have also had reports of people being drugged and robbed on long-distance buses. It usually starts with a friendly passenger offering a free Coke, which turns out to be a chloral-hydrate cocktail. You wake up hours later to find your valuables and new-found 'friend' gone.

Despite all this, don't be overly paranoid. Although crime certainly exists and you need to be aware of it, theft in Vietnam does not seem to be any worse than what you'd expect anywhere else. Don't assume that everyone's a thief – most Vietnamese are poor, but honest.

Undetonated Explosives
Four armies expended untold energy and resources for more than three decades mining, booby-trapping, rocketing, strafing, mortaring and bombarding wide areas of Vietnam. When the fighting stopped most of this ordnance remained exactly where it had landed or been laid; American estimates at the end of the war placed the quantity of unexploded ordnance at 150,000 tonnes.

Since 1975 about 40,000 Vietnamese have been maimed or killed by this leftover ordnance. While cities, cultivated areas and well-travelled rural roads and paths are safe for travel, straying from these areas could land you in the middle of a minefield that is completely unmarked.

Never touch any rockets, artillery shells, mortars, mines or other relics of war you may come across. Such objects can remain lethal for decades. And don't climb inside bomb craters – you never know what undetonated explosive device is at the bottom.

You can learn more about the issue of landmines from the Nobel Peace Prize–winning **International Campaign to Ban Landmines** (ICBL; www.icbl.org).

DISABLED TRAVELLERS
Vietnam is not the easiest of places for disabled travellers, despite the fact that many Vietnamese are disabled as a result of war injuries. Tactical problems include the crazy traffic, a lack of pedestrian footpaths, a lack of lifts in smaller hotels and the ubiquitous squat toilets.

That said, with some careful planning it is possible to have a relatively stress-free trip to Vietnam. Find a reliable company to make the travel arrangements and don't be afraid to double-check things with hotels and restaurants yourself. In the major cities many hotels have lifts and disabled access is improving. Bus and train travel is not really geared up for disabled travellers, but rent a private vehicle with a driver and almost anywhere becomes instantly accessible. As long as you are not too proud about how you get in and out of a boat or up some stairs,

anything is possible, as the Vietnamese are always willing to help.

You might try contacting the following organisations:
Mobility International USA (☎ 54-1343 1284; www.miusa.org)
Royal Association for Disability and Rehabilitation (Radar; ☎ 020-7250 3222; www.radar.org.uk)
Society for Accessible Travel & Hospitality (SATH; ☎ 212-447 7284; www.sath.org)

Lonely Planet's **Thorn Tree** (www.lonelyplanet.com) is a good place to seek the advice of other travellers.

DISCOUNT CARDS
Senior Cards
There are no 'senior citizen' discounts for pensioners, as all foreigners who can afford to fly to Vietnam are considered rich enough to pay the full whack.

Student & Youth Cards
Ditto for student cards. Carry one if you are travelling through the region, but it will gather dust in your wallet while you are visiting Vietnam.

EMBASSIES & CONSULATES
Vietnamese Embassies & Consulates
The following are Vietnamese diplomatic representations abroad:
Australia Canberra (☎ 02-6286 6059; embassy@webone.com.au; 6 Timbarra Crescent, O'Malley, ACT 2606); Sydney (☎ 02-9327 2539; tlssyd@auco.net.au; 489 New South Head Rd, Double Bay, NSW 2028)
Cambodia Phnom Penh (☎ 023-362531; 436 Monivong Blvd)
Canada Ottawa (☎ 613-236 0772; www.vietnamembassy-canada.ca; 470 Wilbrod St, ON K1N 6M8)
China Beijing (☎ 010-6532 1125; vnaemba@mailhost.cinet.co.cn; 32 Guanghua Lu, 100600); Guangzhou (☎ 020-8652 7908; Jin Yanf Hotel, 92 Huanshi Western Rd)
France Paris (☎ 01 44 14 6400; 62-66 Rue Boileau, 75016)
Germany Bonn 2 (☎ 228-357 021; Konstantinstrasse 37, 5300)
Hong Kong Wan Chai (☎ 22-591 4510; 15th fl, Great Smart Tower, 230 Wan Chai Rd)
Italy Rome (☎ 06-854 3223; 34 Via Clituno, 00198)
Japan Tokyo (☎ 03-3466 3311; 50-11 Moto Yoyogi-Cho, Shibuya-ku, 151); Osaka (☎ 06-263 1600; 10th fl, Estate Bakurocho Bldg, 1-4-10 Bakurocho, Chuo-ku)
Laos Vientiane (☎ 214-13409; dsqvn@laotel.net; Thap Luang Rd); Savannakhet (☎ 412-12239; 418 Sisavang Vong)

Philippines Metro Manila (☎ 2-500 364; 54 Victor Cruz, Malate)

Thailand Bangkok (☎ 2-251 7202; 83/1 Wireless Rd 10500)

UK London (☎ 020-7937 1912; www.vietnamembassy .org.uk; 12-14 Victoria Rd, W8 5RD)

USA Washington (☎ 202-861 0737; www.vietnamem bassy-usa.org; 1233 20th St NW, Ste 400, DC 20036); San Francisco (☎ 415-922 1707; www.vietnamconsulate -sf.org; 1700 California St, Ste 430, CA 94109)

Embassies & Consulates in Vietnam

With the exception of those for Cambodia, China and Laos, Hanoi's embassies and HCMC's consulates do very little visa business for non-Vietnamese.

It's important to realise what your country's embassy can and can't do to help if you get into trouble. Generally speaking, it won't be much help if the trouble you're in is remotely your own fault. Remember that you are bound by the laws of the country you are in. Your embassy won't be sympathetic if you end up in jail after committing a crime, even if such actions are legal in your own country.

In genuine emergencies you might get some assistance, but only if other channels have been exhausted. If you have all your money and documents stolen, it might assist with getting a new passport, but a loan for onward travel is out of the question.

The following are some of the embassies and consulates found in Vietnam.

Australia (www.ausinvn.com) Hanoi (Map p77; ☎ 831 7755; 8 Duong Dao Tan, Ba Dinh District); HCMC (Map p334; ☎ 829 6035; 5th fl, 5B Đ Ton Duc Thang)

Cambodia Hanoi (Map pp80-1; ☎ 825 3788; 71A Pho Tran Hung Dao); HCMC (Map p326; ☎ 829 2751; cambocg@hcm.vnn.vn; 41 Đ Phung Khac Khoan)

Canada (www.dfait-maeci.gc.ca/vietnam) Hanoi (Map pp80-1; ☎ 823 5500; 31 Pho Hung Vuong); HCMC (Map p334; ☎ 824 5025; 10th fl, 235 Đ Dong Khoi)

China Hanoi (Map pp80-1; ☎ 845 3736; Pho Hoang Dieu); HCMC (Map p326; ☎ 829 2457; chinaconsul_hcm _vn@mfa.gov.cn; 39 Đ Nguyen Thi Minh Khai)

France Hanoi (Map pp80-1; ☎ 943 7719; Pho Tran Hung Dao); HCMC (Map p326; ☎ 829 7231; 27 Đ Nguyen Thi Minh Khai)

Germany Hanoi (Map pp80-1; ☎ 845 3836; 29 Đ Tran Phu); HCMC (Map p326; ☎ 829 1967; 126 Đ Nguyen Dinh Chieu)

Japan Hanoi (Map p77; ☎ 846 3000; 27 Pho Lieu Giai, Ba Dinh District); HCMC (Map p334; ☎ 822 5314; 13-17 ĐL Nguyen Hue)

Laos Hanoi (Map pp80-1; ☎ 825 4576; 22 Pho Tran Dinh Trong); HCMC (Map p334; ☎ 829 9272; 93 Đ Pasteur); Danang (Map p222; 16 Đ Tran Qui Cap)

Netherlands HCMC (Map pp80-1; ☎ 823 5932; hcm-ca@minbuza.nl; 29 ĐL Le Duan)

New Zealand Hanoi (Map p84; ☎ 824 1481; nzembhan@fpt.vn; Level 5, 63 Pho Ly Thai To); HCMC (Map p326; ☎ 822 6907; 5th fl, 41 Đ Nguyen Thi Minh Khai)

Philippines Hanoi (Map pp80-1; ☎ 825 7948; 27B Pho Tran Hung Dao)

Singapore Hanoi (Map pp80-1; ☎ 823 3965; 41-43 Đ Tran Phu)

Sweden Hanoi (Map p77; ☎ 726 0400; 2 Đ Nui Truc)

Thailand Hanoi (Map pp80-1; ☎ 823 5092; 63-65 Pho Hoang Dieu); HCMC (Map p326; ☎ 822 2637; 77 Đ Tran Quoc Thao)

UK (www.uk-vietnam.org) Hanoi (Map p84; ☎ 936 0500; Central Bldg, 31 Pho Hai Ba Trung); HCMC (Map p326; ☎ 823 2862; 25 ĐL Le Duan)

US (http://usembassy.state.gov/vietnam) Hanoi (Map p77; ☎ 772 1500; 7 Pho Lang Ha, Ba Dinh District); HCMC (Map p326; ☎ 822 9433; 4 ĐL Le Duan)

FESTIVALS & EVENTS

Major religious festivals in Vietnam have lunar dates; check against any Vietnamese calendar for the Gregorian dates. If you know when Tet kicks off, simply count from there.

Special prayers are held at Vietnamese and Chinese pagodas when the moon is full or just the thinnest sliver. Many Buddhists eat only vegetarian food on these days, which, according to the Chinese lunar calendar, fall on the 14th and 15th days of the month and from the last day of the month to the first day of the next month.

Tet (Tet Nguyen Dan) The Big One! The Vietnamese Lunar New Year is Christmas, New Year and birthdays all rolled into one. Lasting from the first to seventh days of the first moon, the Tet Festival falls in late January or early February.

Holiday of the Dead (Thanh Minh) It's time to honour the ancestors with a visit to graves of deceased relatives. Fifth day of the third moon.

Buddha's Birth, Enlightenment and Death A big celebration at Buddhist temples and pagodas with lively processions. Eighth day of the fourth moon.

Summer Solstice Day (Tiet Doan Ngo) Keep the epidemics at bay with offerings to the spirits, ghosts and the God of Death. Fifth day of the fifth moon.

Wandering Souls Day (Trung Nguyen) Second in the pecking order to Tet, offerings are made for the wandering souls of the forgotten dead. Fifteenth day of the seventh moon.

Mid-Autumn Festival (Trung Thu) A fine time for foodies with moon cakes of sticky rice filled with lotus seeds, watermelon seeds, peanuts, the yolks of duck eggs, raisins and other treats. Fifteenth day of the eighth moon.
Confucius' Birthday Happy birthday to China's leading philosophical export. Twenty-eighth day of the ninth moon.

FOOD
Vietnamese cuisine has become a favourite throughout the Western world and a journey through Vietnam is a gastronomic treat. For the full story on Vietnamese cuisine, see the Food & Drink chapter (p62).

GAY & LESBIAN TRAVELLERS
Vietnam is a relatively hassle-free place for homosexuals. There are no official laws on same-sex relationships in Vietnam, nor much in the way of individual harassment.

That said, the government is notorious for clamping down on gay venues, and places that are covered in the mass media are 'coincidentally' closed down days later. Most gay venues keep a fairly low profile. There is, however, a healthy gay scene in Hanoi and HCMC, evidenced by unabashed cruising around certain lakes in Hanoi (p95) and the thriving café scene in HCMC (p350).

Homosexuality is still far from accepted in the wider community, though the lack of any laws keeps things fairly safe. Major headlines were made in 1997 with Vietnam's first gay marriage, and again in 1998 at the country's first lesbian wedding, in the Mekong Delta. However, displaying peculiar double standards, two weeks later government officials broke up the marriage of the women and the couple signed an agreement promising not to live together again.

With the vast number of same-sex travel partners – gay or otherwise – checking into hotels throughout Vietnam, there is little scrutiny over how travelling foreigners are related. However, it would be prudent not to flaunt your sexuality. As with heterosexual couples, passionate public displays of affection are considered a basic no-no.

Utopia (www.utopia-asia.com) features gay travel information and contacts, including detailed sections on the legality of homosexuality in Vietnam and some local gay terminology.

HOLIDAYS
Politics affects everything, including public holidays. After a 15-year lapse, religious holidays were re-established in 1990. The following are public holidays in Vietnam:
New Year's Day (Tet Duong Lich) 1 January
Anniversary of the Founding of the Vietnamese Communist Party (Thanh Lap Dang CSVN) 3 February – the date the party was founded in 1930.
Liberation Day (Saigon Giai Phong) 30 April – the date on which Saigon surrendered is commemorated nationwide as Liberation Day.
International Workers' Day (Quoc Te Lao Dong) 1 May
Ho Chi Minh's Birthday (Sinh Nhat Bac Ho) 19 May
Buddha's Birthday (Phat Dan) Eighth day of the fourth moon (usually June).
National Day (Quoc Khanh) 2 September – commemorates the Declaration of Independence by Ho Chi Minh in 1945.
Christmas Day (Giang Sinh) 25 December

INSURANCE
Insurance is a *must* for Vietnam, as the cost of major medical treatment is prohibitive. Although you may have medical insurance in your own country, it is probably not valid while you are in Vietnam. A travel insurance policy to cover theft, loss and medical problems is the best bet.

There is a wide variety of policies available, so check the small print. Some insurance policies specifically exclude such 'dangerous activities' as riding motorbikes, diving and even trekking. Check that the policy covers an emergency evacuation in the event of serious injury.

INTERNET ACCESS
Today the Internet is widely available throughout towns and cities in Vietnam. There is everything from trendy cybercafés to computer terminals in the lobbies of hotels and guesthouses, plus public Internet access in many Vietnamese post offices.

The cost of Internet access generally ranges from 50d to 500d per minute, depending on where you are and what the competition is like. Printing usually costs around 1000d per page and scanning about 2000d a page.

If you're travelling with a notebook or hand-held computer, be aware that your modem may not work once you leave your home country. The safest option is to buy a reputable 'global' modem before you leave home, or buy a local PC-card modem if you're spending an extended time in Vietnam. For more information on travelling with a portable computer, see www.teleadapt.com.

Remember that the power supply voltage will vary from that at home, risking damage to your equipment. The best investment is a universal AC adapter, which will enable you to plug it in anywhere without frying the innards.

A major boon for laptop travellers is the recent debut of prepaid Internet-access cards that can provide you with nationwide dial up to the Net. **FPT** (☎ 08-821 4160; www.fpt .com.vn) is one of Vietnam's largest ISPs, and its Internet card is sold in most cities.

LAUNDRY

It is easy to get your laundry done at guesthouses and cheaper hotels for just a few US dollars. There have, however, been a number of reports of gross overcharging at certain hotels, so make sure you ask the price beforehand.

Budget hotels do not have clothes dryers as they rely on the sunshine – so allow at least a day and a half for washing and drying, especially during the wet season.

LEGAL MATTERS
Civil Law

On paper it looks good, but in practice the rule of law in Vietnam is a fickle beast. Local officials interpret the law any way it suits them, often against the wishes of Hanoi. There is no independent judiciary. Not surprisingly, most legal disputes are settled out of court. In general, you can accomplish more with a carton of cigarettes and a bottle of good cognac than you can with a lawyer.

Drugs

The drug trade has made a comeback in Vietnam. The country has a very serious problem with heroin these days and the authorities are clamping down hard: in 2001 alone, the government executed 55 people for drug offences.

Marijuana and, in the northwest, opium are readily available, but giving in to this temptation is a risk. There are many plainclothes police in Vietnam and, if arrested, the result might be a long prison term and/ or a large fine.

Police

Vietnamese police are the best that money can buy. Police corruption is an everyday reality and has been acknowledged in official newspapers. If something does go wrong, or if something is stolen, the police can't do much more than prepare an insurance report for a fee.

Hanoi has warned all provincial governments that any police caught shaking down foreign tourists will be fired and arrested. The crackdown has dented the enthusiasm of the police to confront foreigners directly with demands for bribes, but it still happens in more out-of-the-way places.

MAPS

Most bookshops in Vietnam stock a good range of maps. A *must* for its detailed road maps of every province is the *Viet Nam Administrative Atlas,* published by Ban Do. It is perfect for cyclists or motorbikers looking for roads less travelled and costs 68,000d.

Ban Do also publishes reasonable tourist maps of HCMC, Hanoi, Danang, Hué and a few other cities. Unfortunately, maps of smaller towns are practically nonexistent. Most of the listings mags produced in Vietnam have good city maps of Hanoi and HCMC, and there are a couple of good hand-drawn 3D maps of Hué and Sapa available from Covit, a local publisher.

Vietnamese street names are preceded with the words Pho, Duong and Dai Lo – on the maps in this book, they appear respectively as P, Đ and ĐL.

MONEY

The first currency of Vietnam is the dong, which is abbreviated to 'd'. Banknotes come in denominations of 200d, 500d, 1000d, 2000d, 5000d, 10,000d, 20,000d, 50,000d and 100,000d. Now that Ho Chi Minh has been canonised (against his wishes), his picture is on *every* banknote. Coins have recently come into circulation, including 500d, 1000d and 5000d. The second currency is the US dollar and that needs no introduction.

The dong has experienced its ups and downs. The late 1990s Asian economic crisis, which wreaked severe havoc on the regional currencies, caused the dong to lose about 15% of its US-dollar value. Since then the dong has slowly weakened, but is pretty stable at around 16,000d to the US dollar.

Where prices are quoted in dong, we quote them in this book in dong. Likewise, when prices are quoted in dollars, we follow suit. While this may seem inconsistent, this is the way it's done in Vietnam and the sooner you get used to thinking comparatively in dong and dollars, the easier your travels will be.

For a smattering of exchange rates at the time of going to print, see the Quick Reference section on the inside front cover of this book.

ATMs
It used to be just a couple of foreign banks in Hanoi and HCMC that offered ATMs, but Vietnamese banks have now got into this game in a big way. Vietcombank has the best network in the country, including most of the major tourist destinations and all the big cities. Every branch stocks a useful leaflet with a list of their nationwide ATMs. Withdrawals are issued in dong, and there is a daily limit of 2,000,000d (about US$125). Cash advances for larger amounts of dong, as well as US dollars, can be arranged over the counter during office hours.

Black Market
The black market is Vietnam's unofficial banking system that is almost everywhere and operates quite openly. Private individuals and some shops and restaurants will exchange US dollars for dong and vice versa. While the practice is technically illegal, law enforcement is virtually nonexistent. Ironically, black market exchange rates are usually *worse* than the official exchange rates, so the only advantage is the convenience of changing money when and where you like.

If people approach you on the street with offers to change money at rates better than the official one, you can rest assured that you are being set up for a rip-off. Don't even think about trying it! Remember, if an offer seems too good to be true, that's because it probably is.

Cash
Most major currencies can be exchanged at leading banks in Vietnam, but away from the tourist centres the US dollar remains king. Vietcombank is the most organised of the local banks for changing cash and can

deal with euros, pounds and pretty much anything else you are packing. The US dollar exchange rate worsens the further you get from the tourist trail, so stock up on dong if you are heading into remote areas.

The relatively low value of Vietnamese banknotes means that almost any currency exchange will leave you with piles of banknotes to count; changing US$100 will make you an instant millionaire! In small towns it can be difficult to get change for the larger notes, so keep a stack of smaller bills handy.

It's a good idea to check that any big dollar bills you take do not have any small tears or look too tatty, as no-one will want to touch them in Vietnam.

You cannot legally take the dong out of Vietnam but you can reconvert reasonable amounts of it into dollars on departure.

Credit Cards
Visa, MasterCard and JCB cards are now widely acceptable in all major cities and many tourist centres. However, a 3% commission charge on every transaction is pretty common; check first, as some charge higher commissions than others. Some merchants also accept Amex, but the surcharge is typically 4%. Better hotels and restaurants do not usually slap on an additional charge.

Getting a cash advance from Visa, Master Card and JCB is possible at Vietcombank in most cities, as well as at some foreign banks in HCMC and Hanoi. Banks generally charge a 3% commission for this service. This is handy if you want to get out large sums, as the ATMs have low daily limits.

Tipping
Tipping is not expected in Vietnam, but it is enormously appreciated. For a person who earns US$50 per month, a US$1 tip is about half a day's wages. Upmarket hotels and some restaurants may levy a 5% service charge, but this may not make it to the staff. If you stay a couple of days in the same hotel, try and remember to tip the staff who clean your room.

You should also consider tipping drivers and guides – after all, the time they spend on the road with you means time away from home and family. Typically, travellers on minibus tours will pool together to collect a communal tip to be split between the guide and driver. About US$1 per day (per tourist) is standard.

It is considered proper to make a small donation at the end of a visit to a pagoda, especially if a monk has shown you around; most pagodas have contribution boxes for this purpose.

Travellers Cheques

It is wise not to rely entirely on travellers cheques by keeping a reasonable stash of US dollars on hand. Travellers cheques can only be exchanged at authorised foreign-exchange banks, but these aren't found throughout Vietnam. Strangely, there are no banks at most of the land border crossings. The only way to change money at these places is on the black market.

If you only have travellers cheques, stock up on US dollars at a bank, which will usually charge anywhere from 1.25% to 3% commission to change them into cash. Vietcombank charges no commission for exchanging travellers cheques for dong.

If your travellers cheques are in currencies other than US dollars, they may be useless beyond the major cities. Hefty commissions are the norm if they can be exchanged at all.

PHOTOGRAPHY & VIDEO

Colour print film is widely available and prices are pretty reasonable at about US$2.50 for a roll of 36 print film. Slide film can be bought in Hanoi and HCMC, but don't count on it elsewhere. Supplies of black-and-white film are rapidly disappearing, so bring your own.

Photo-processing shops are located all over Vietnam and developing costs are about US$5 per roll depending on the print size selected. The quality is generally very good. Processing slide film is best saved for somewhere else.

Cameras are fairly expensive in Vietnam and the selection is limited. Happily, batteries and digital-camera memory cards are readily available in large cities.

The Vietnamese police usually don't care what you photograph, but on occasion they get pernickety. Obviously, don't photograph sensitive sites such as airports and border checkpoints. Don't even think of trying to get a snapshot of Ho Chi Minh in his glass sarcophagus!

Photographing anyone, particularly hill-tribe people, demands patience and the utmost respect for local customs. Photograph with discretion and manners. It's always polite to ask first and if the person says no, don't take the photo. For endless tips on better travel photography, pick up a copy of Lonely Planet's *Travel Photography*.

POST

Every city, town, village and rural subdistrict in Vietnam has some sort of post office *(buu dien)*. Post offices all over the country keep long hours, from about 6.30am to 9pm including weekends and public holidays (even Tet).

Vietnam has a pretty reliable post service these days. International postal rates are similar to those in European countries. Postcards cost from 7000d to 9000d depending on the destination.

Items mailed from anywhere other than large towns and cities might take a month to arrive at their international destination. Airmail service from HCMC and Hanoi takes approximately five to 10 days to get to most Western countries. Express-mail service (EMS), available in the larger cities, is twice as fast as regular airmail and everything is registered.

Private couriers such as FedEx, DHL and UPS are reliable for small parcels or documents. See under Post in Hanoi (p78) and HCMC (p327) for listings.

Poste restante works well in post offices in Hanoi and HCMC. Foreigners must pay a 500d service charge for each letter received through the poste restante.

Receiving even a small package from abroad can cause a headache and large ones will produce a migraine. If the parcel contains books, documents, video tapes, computer disks or dangerous goods it's possible that a lengthy inspection will be required, which could take anywhere from a few days to a few weeks.

SHOPPING

Vietnam has some fantastic shopping opportunities so it is well worth setting aside half a day or so to properly peruse. Hotspots include Hanoi, Hoi An and HCMC, each of which has a tempting selection of everything from avant-garde art to sumptuous silk suits. Some of the best buys on the block include gorgeous glazed pottery, classic lanterns, 'almost' antiques, embroidered tablecloths, fine furnishings, and lavish silk and linen creations in designer boutiques.

Art & Antiques
There are several good shops to hunt for art and antiques, but Vietnam has strict regulations on the export of real antiques, so be sure the items are allowed out of the country. Most reputable shops can provide the necessary paperwork.

Both traditional and modern paintings are a popular item. Cheaper mass-produced stuff is touted in souvenir shops and by street vendors. More sophisticated works are displayed in art galleries, with paintings from US$50 to US$500, but some of the hottest Vietnamese artists now fetch up to 10 times that. It's important to know that there are forgeries around – just because you spot a painting by a 'famous Vietnamese artist' does not mean that it's an original.

A Vietnamese speciality is the 'instant antique', such as a teapot or ceramic dinner plate, with a price tag of around US$2. Of course, it's OK to buy fake antiques as long as you aren't paying genuine-antique prices.

Clothing
Forget the rubber sandals and pith helmets, Vietnam is emerging as a regional design centre and there are some extravagant creations in the boutiques of Hanoi and HCMC. Beautiful silk dresses cost a fraction of what they would at home, and men can get in on the action with some flamboyant shirts or sharp suits.

Ao dai (ow-zai in the north, ow-yai in the south) is the national dress for Vietnamese women and is a popular item to take home. Ready-made ao dai cost from US$10 to US$20, but custom numbers can cost a lot more. There are ao dai tailors nationwide, but those in the tourist centres are more familiar with foreigners.

These days more and more hill-tribe gear is winding its way to shops in Hanoi and HCMC. It is brightly patterned stuff, but you may need to set the dyes yourself so those colours don't bleed all over the rest of your clothes.

Women all over the country wear conical hats to keep the sun off their faces, though

they also function as umbrellas in the rain. The best-quality conical hats are produced in the Hué area.

T-shirts are ever popular items with travellers. A printed shirt costs around 20,000d while an embroidered design will cost about 50,000d.

Handicrafts
Hot items on the tourist market include lacquerware, boxes and wooden screens with mother-of-pearl inlay, ceramics (check out the elephants), colourful embroidery, silk greeting cards, wood-block prints, oil paintings, watercolours, blinds made of hanging bamboo beads, reed mats, carpets, jewellery and leatherwork.

War Souvenirs
In places frequented by tourists, it's easy to buy what looks like equipment left over from the American War. However, almost all of these items are reproductions and your chances of finding anything original are slim.

The fake Zippo lighters engraved with platoon philosophy are still one of the hottest-selling items. You can pay extra to get one that's been beat up to look like a war relic, or just buy a brand-new shiny one for less.

Bargaining
Some bargaining is essential in most tourist transactions. Remember that in Asia 'saving face' is important, so bargaining should be good-natured. Smile and don't get angry or argue. In some cases you will be able to get a 50% discount or more, at other times this may only be 10%. And once the money is accepted, the deal is done – if you harbour hard feelings because you later find out that someone else got it cheaper, the only one you are hurting is yourself.

TELEPHONE & FAX
For the all-important numbers like emergency services and the international access code, check out the Quick Reference section on the inside cover of this book.

Every city has a **general information service** (☎ 1080) that provides everything from phone numbers and train and air timetables to exchange rates and the latest football scores. It even provides marriage counselling or bedtime lullabies for your child – no kidding! You can usually be connected to an operator who speaks English or French.

Domestic Calls

Phone numbers in Hanoi and HCMC have seven digits. Elsewhere around the country phone numbers have six digits. Telephone area codes are assigned according to the province.

Local calls can usually be made from any hotel or restaurant phone and are often free. Confirm this with the hotel so you don't receive any unpleasant surprises when you check out. Domestic long-distance calls are reasonably priced and cheaper if you dial direct. Save up to 20% by calling between 10pm and 5am.

International Calls

Charges for international calls from Vietnam have dropped significantly in the past few years. With the introduction of Voice Over Internet Protocol, international phone calls to most countries cost a flat rate of just US$1.30 per minute, less than half of the previous cheapest rate. The service is easy to use from any phone in the country; just dial ☎ 17100, the country code and the number.

International and domestic long-distance calls can be made at hotels, but it's expensive. A cheaper alternative is to make these calls from the post office, which have handy displays telling you the cost of the call.

Reverse charges or collect calls are possible to most, but not all, Western countries including Australia, Canada, France, Japan, New Zealand, the UK and the USA.

Mobile (Cellular) Phones

Vietnam is putting a lot of money into its cellular network. Vietnam uses GSM 900/1800, which is compatible with most of Asia, Europe and Australia but not with North America.

If your phone has roaming, it is easy enough, if expensive, to make calls in Vietnam. Another option is to buy a SIM card with a local number to use in Vietnam.

Rival companies Vina Phone and Mobi Phone battle it out in the mobile-phone market with gimmicks galore to attract new customers. Both of these companies have offices and branches nationwide.

Be aware that mobile-phone numbers in Vietnam start with the prefixes ☎ 0903 or

☎ 0913, and cost more to call than a local number.

Fax

Most post offices and hotels offer fax services. Hotels charge considerably more than the post office.

TIME

Vietnam is seven hours ahead of Greenwich Mean Time/Universal Time Coordinated (GMT/UTC). Because of its proximity to the equator, Vietnam does not have daylight-saving or summer time. When it's noon in Vietnam it is 9pm the previous day in Vancouver, midnight in New York, 5am in London, 1pm in Perth and 3pm in Sydney.

TOILETS

The issue of toilets and what to do with used toilet paper causes some concern. In general, if there's a wastepaper basket next to the toilet, that is where the toilet paper goes, as many sewage systems cannot handle toilet paper.

Toilet paper is seldom provided in the toilets at bus and train stations or in other public buildings. You'd be wise to keep a stash of your own with you at all times while on the move.

Another thing to be mentally prepared for is squat toilets. For the uninitiated, a squat toilet has no seat for you to sit on while reading this guidebook; it's a hole in the floor. The only way to flush it is to fill the conveniently placed bucket with water and pour it into the hole. Most hotels will have Western-style loos, but squats are the norm in older hotels and public places.

The scarcity of public toilets is more of a problem for women than for men. Vietnamese men often urinate in public. Women might find road-side toilet stops easier if wearing a sarong.

TOURIST INFORMATION

Tourist offices in Vietnam have a different philosophy from the majority of tourist offices worldwide. These government-owned enterprises are really travel agencies whose primary interests are booking tours and turning a profit. Don't come here hoping for freebies.

Vietnam Tourism and Saigon Tourist are old examples of this genre, but nowadays every province has at least one such organisation. Travel cafés, budget agencies and your fellow travellers are a much better source of information than any of the so-called 'tourist offices'.

VISAS

Tourist visas allow visitors to enter and exit Vietnam at Hanoi, HCMC and Danang airports or at any of its nine land borders, three each with Cambodia, China and Laos.

Tourist visas are valid for a single 30-day stay. The government periodically talks about issuing visas on arrival to certain favoured nationalities, but as yet this sensible scheme has failed to materialise. Arranging the necessary paperwork for a Vietnamese visa has become fairly straightforward, but it remains quite expensive and unnecessarily time-consuming. Processing a tourist-visa application typically takes four or five working days in countries in the West.

In Asia the best place to pick up a Vietnamese visa is Cambodia, where it costs just US$30 and takes as little as 15 minutes. Bangkok is also a popular place as many agents offer cheap packages with an air ticket and visa thrown in.

If you plan to spend more than a month in Vietnam, or if you plan to exit Vietnam and enter again from Cambodia or Laos, arrange a three-month multiple-entry visa. These cost around US$70 in Cambodia, but are not available from all Vietnamese embassies.

In our experience personal appearance influences the reception you receive from airport immigration – if you wear shorts or scruffy clothing, look dirty or unshaven, you can expect problems. Try your best to look 'respectable'.

Business Visas

Business visas are usually valid for three or six months, allow multiple entries and the right to work. Getting a business visa has now become fairly easy. The main drawback is the cost – a business visa is about four times the cost of a tourist visa. It is generally much easier to apply for a business visa once in Vietnam.

Student Visas

A student visa is usually arranged after your arrival. It's acceptable to enter Vietnam on a tourist visa, enrol in a Vietnamese language course and then apply at the immigration police for a change in status.

Visa Extensions

If you've got the dollars, they've got the rubber stamp. Tourist-visa extensions cost around US$20, but it is easier to pay more and sort this out through a travel agency. The procedure takes two or three days and you can only extend one time for 30 days.

In theory you should be able to extend your visa in any provincial capital. In practice it goes smoothest in major cities, such as HCMC, Hanoi, Danang and Hué, which cater to mass tourism. In Hué the place to arrange a visa extension is at the **immigration police** (Map pp200-1; Đ Hung Vuong).

Re-Entry Visas

It's possible to enter Cambodia, Laos or any other country from Vietnam and then re-enter without having to apply for another visa. However, you must apply for a re-entry visa *before* you leave Vietnam. If you do not have a re-entry visa, you will have to go through the whole Vietnamese visa nonsense again.

Re-entry visas are easiest to arrange in Hanoi or HCMC, but you will almost certainly have to ask a travel agent to do the paperwork for you. Travel agents charge about US$25 for this service and can complete the procedure in a day or two.

VOLUNTEERING

For information on volunteer work opportunities, chase up the full list of non-government organisations (NGOs) at the **NGO Resource Centre** (☎ 04-832 8570; ngocentr@netnam.org.vn; Hotel La Thanh, 218 Pho Doi Can, Hanoi), which keeps a database of all of the NGOs assisting Vietnam.

Try contacting the following organisations if you want to help in some way:

15 May School (www.15mayschool.org) A school in HCMC for disadvantaged children, which provides free education and vocational training.

Idealist.org (www.idealist.org) Look up volunteer opportunities with nonprofit organisations worldwide.

Street Voices (www.streetvoices.com.au) Donate your skills, time or money to help give street children career opportunities. Street Voices' primary project is KOTO Restaurant (p99); check their website to see what you can do to help in Vietnam or Australia.

WOMEN TRAVELLERS

Like Thailand and other predominantly Buddhist countries, Vietnam is relatively free of serious hassles for Western women. But it is a different story for some Asian women, particularly those who are young. It's not uncommon for an Asian woman accompanied by a Western male to be stereotyped as a Vietnamese prostitute. The fact that the couple could be married, or friends, doesn't seem to occur to everyone, or that the woman may not be Vietnamese at all. Asian women travelling in Vietnam with a Western male companion have occasionally reported verbal abuse.

However, there's no need to be overly paranoid, as locals are becoming more accustomed to seeing Asian women. Things have improved as more Vietnamese people are exposed to foreign visitors.

Sanitary napkins are widely available in larger cities, though tampons are harder to find.

WORK

Vietnam's opening up to capitalist countries has suddenly created all sorts of work opportunities for Westerners. The best-paid Westerners living in Vietnam are those working for international organisations or foreign companies, but most of these jobs are secured before arrival in the country.

Foreigners who look like Rambo have occasionally been approached by Vietnamese talent scouts wanting to recruit them to work as extras in war movies, but for most travellers the main work opportunities are teaching a foreign language.

English is by far the most popular foreign language with Vietnamese students, but some students also want to learn French. There is also a limited demand for teachers of Japanese, German, Spanish and Korean.

Government-run universities in Vietnam hire some foreign teachers. Pay is generally around US$5 per hour, but benefits such as free housing and unlimited visa renewals are usually thrown in.

There is also a budding free market in private language centres and home tutoring; this is where most newly arrived foreigners seek work. Pay in the private sector is slightly better, at about US$6 to US$10 per hour, but these private schools won't offer the same extras as a government-run school. Private tutoring usually pays even better, at around US$10 to US$15 per hour.

Finding teaching jobs is quite easy in places such as HCMC and Hanoi, and is sometimes possible in towns that have universities. Pay in the smaller towns tends to be lower and work opportunities fewer.

Looking for employment is a matter of asking around – jobs are rarely advertised. The longer you stay, the easier it is to find work – travellers hoping to land a quick job and depart two months later will be disappointed.

Transport

CONTENTS

GETTING THERE & AWAY

ENTERING VIETNAM

Entering Vietnam used to be something of a bureaucratic nightmare, but has become much more straightforward in recent years.

Formalities at Vietnam's international airports are generally smoother than at land borders, as the volume of traffic is greater. That said, crossing overland from Cambodia, China or Laos, is now relatively stress-free.

It's possible to enter Vietnam by train, plane, automobile and other forms of transport. Air is popular for those holidaying in Vietnam, while bus is the most common route for those travelling extensively in the region. Anyone planning on arriving from China should seriously consider the spectacular train ride from Kunming to Hanoi.

When entering Vietnam you will be issued with a yellow slip of paper, which doubles up as a departure card for the country. If you lose this you will likely be 'fined' US$20 or so by obliging immigration officials.

THINGS CHANGE...

The information in this chapter is particularly vulnerable to change. Check directly with the airline or a travel agent to make sure you understand how a fare (and ticket you may buy) works and be aware of the security requirements for international travel. Shop carefully. The details given in this chapter should be regarded as pointers and are not a substitute for your own careful, up-to-date research.

Passport

There are no 'suspect' stamps that will prevent foreigners from visiting Vietnam, but some overseas Vietnamese may be given a harder time by immigration and customs than non-Vietnamese visitors. Arranging a visa remains essential before arrival in Vietnam, but these are easy to obtain from embassies at home or in the region (see p466).

AIR

Airports & Airlines

There are three international airports in Vietnam. **Tan Son Nhat airport** (SGN; ☎ 08-848 5383) serves Ho Chi Minh City (HCMC) and is Vietnam's busiest international air hub. Hanoi's **Noi Bai airport** (HAN; ☎ 04-886 6527) is the destination of choice for those concentrating on north Vietnam, while a handful of international flights also serve **Danang airport** (DAD; ☎ 0511-830 339), a useful gateway to the charms of central Vietnam.

Vietnam Airlines (☎ 04-943 9660 in Hanoi, ☎ 08-829 2118 in HCMC; www.vietnamair.com.vn) is the state-owned flag carrier, and the majority of flights into and out of Vietnam are joint operations between Vietnam Airlines and foreign airlines.

Vietnam Airlines has a modern fleet of Airbuses and Boeings and the level of service on its international flights is starting to catch up with its bigger rivals. However, on the domestic front, cancellations and late flights are common.

Many international flights leaving Hanoi connect through HCMC, but it's a pain. Passengers have to pay a domestic departure

ax, fly to HCMC, claim their bags, check
n again, and pay an international departure tax before boarding the international
light. Ugh!

AIRLINES FLYING TO & FROM VIETNAM

All phone numbers are in Hanoi (area code
04) unless otherwise stated.

Aeroflot (airline code SU; ☎ 825 6742; www.aeroflot
.com; hub Moscow)

Air France (airline code AF; ☎ 825 6742; www
.airfrance.fr; hub Paris)

All Nippon Airways (airline code NH; ☎ 934 7237;
www.ana.co.jp; hub Tokyo)

Asiana Airlines (airline code OZ; ☎ 822 2671; www
.us.flyasiana.com; hub Seoul)

Cathay Pacific (airline code CX; ☎ 826 7298; www
.cathaypacific.com; hub Hong Kong)

China Airlines (airline code CI; ☎ 824 2688; www
.china-airlines.com; hub Taipei)

China Southern Airlines (airline code CZ; ☎ 771 6611;
www.cs-air.com; hub Guangzhou)

Japan Airlines (airline code JL; ☎ 826 6693; www.jal
.co.jp; hub Tokyo)

Korean Air (airline code KE; ☎ 934 7236; www.korean
air.com; hub Seoul)

Lao Airlines (airline code QV; ☎ 846 4873; www
.laoairlines.com; hub Vientiane)

Lion Air (airline code JT; www.lionair.co.id; hub Jakarta)

Lufthansa (airline code LH; in HCMC ☎ 08-829 8529;
www.lufthansa.com; hub Frankfurt)

Malaysia Airlines (airline code MY; ☎ 826 8820; www
.malaysiaairlines.com; hub Kuala Lumpur)

Philippine Airlines (airline code PR; in HCMC
☎ 08-822 2241; www.philippineair.com; hub Manila)

Qantas (airline code QF; ☎ 934 7238; www.qantas.com
.au; hubs Sydney & Melbourne)

Siem Reap Airways (airline code FT; in HCMC
☎ 08-914 0296; www.siemreapair.com; hub Phnom Penh)

Singapore Airlines (airline code SQ; ☎ 826 8888;
www.singaporeair.com; hub Singapore)

Thai Airways (airline code TG; ☎ 826 6893; www
.thaiair.com; hub Bangkok)

Tickets

Shop around and it is possible to find some
good deals to Vietnam. If there are no obvious bargains to Hanoi or HCMC, then consider buying a discounted ticket to Bangkok
or Hong Kong and picking up a flight on to
Vietnam from there.

There are some good offers to Vietnam,
but they are often through smaller, specialised agencies which concentrate on Southeast
Asia.

> **DEPARTURE TAX**
>
> There is an international departure tax of
> US$14 from Hanoi, US$12 from HCMC and
> US$8 from Danang.

Discounted flights are available into Vietnam, but Vietnam Airlines will not allow
foreign carriers to sell cheap outbound
tickets from Vietnam. For example, a ticket
from Bangkok to Hanoi or HCMC costs
almost half the price of a Vietnam Airlines'
flight, if it's purchased in Bangkok. This
also means that for anyone planning to purchase a long-haul flight in the region, Vietnam is not the place to do it with Bangkok
just a short hop away.

It's hard to get reservations for flights to/
from Vietnam during holidays, especially
the Tet Festival, which falls between late
January and mid-February. If you will be
in Vietnam during Tet, make reservations
in advance or you may find yourself ma-
rooned in a regional airport along the way.
The chaos begins a week before Tet and can
last for about two weeks after it.

Be aware that Vietnam is not the only
country to celebrate the Lunar New Year,
as it falls at the same time as Chinese New
Year. Many people hit the road at this time,
resulting in overbooked airlines, trains and
hotels all over Asia.

REGIONAL TICKETS

An interesting new development for those
planning extensive air travel around the
region is the Asean Hip Hop Pass. This
allows for three international flights within
the Asean region for just US$399, plus three
optional sectors at US$150 each. It doesn't
work well if you are touring Indochina
where the regional flights are quite cheap,
but if you are travelling right across the region it can make for significant savings.

Asia

Although many Asian countries now offer
competitive deals, Bangkok, Singapore and
Hong Kong are still the best places to shop
around for discount tickets.

CAMBODIA

Vietnam Airlines as well as Siem Reap
Airways serve the Phnom Penh to HCMC

route several times a day. Vietnam Airlines also offers numerous services daily between Siem Reap and HCMC and one expensive flight a day direct to Hanoi.

There are direct flights from Danang to Siem Reap several times a week with Siem Reap Airways, but *not* from Siem Reap to Danang.

One of the most reliable travel agencies in Cambodia is **Hanuman Tourism** (www.hanu mantourism.com; ☎ 023-218 356), based in Phnom Penh.

CHINA
Vietnam Airlines now offers links from Hanoi to several major cities in China, including Beijing, Guangzhou and Kunming. These routes are shared with Air China, China Southern Airlines and China Yunnan Airlines, respectively. The only direct flight between HCMC and mainland China is through Guangzhou.

HONG KONG
Vietnam Airlines and Cathay Pacific jointly operate daily services between Hong Kong and both Hanoi and HCMC. The open-jaw option is a popular deal, allowing you to fly into one and out of the other.

Reliable travel agents in Hong Kong:
Four Seas Tours (☎ 2200 7760; www.fourseastravel .com)
Phoenix Services (☎ 2722 7378)
STA (☎ 2736 1618; www.statravel.com.hk)

JAPAN
ANA, Japan Airlines and Vietnam Airlines connect Hanoi and HCMC with Osaka and Tokyo. Cheaper indirect flights are available via other Asian capitals.

Recommended travel agents in Japan:
No 1 Travel (☎ 03-3205 6073; www.no1-travel.com)
STA (☎ 03-5391 2922; www.statravel.co.jp)

LAOS
Both Lao Airlines and Vietnam Airlines operate daily flights between Vientiane and Hanoi or HCMC.

SINGAPORE
Singapore Airlines and Vietnam Airlines have daily flights from Singapore to both Hanoi and HCMC. For reliable fares from Singapore to Vietnam, contact **STA Travel** (☎ 6737 7188; www.statravel.com.sg).

SOUTH KOREA
Asiana Airlines, Korean Air and Vietnam Airlines all fly the Seoul–HCMC route, so there's at least one flight offered per day. There are also several direct Seoul–Hanoi flights per week.

A good agent for ticketing in Seoul is **Joy Travel Service** (☎ 02-776 9871).

TAIWAN
Airlines flying from Taipei include China Airlines, Eva Air and Vietnam Airlines.

A long-running discount travel agent with a good reputation is **Jenny Su Travel** (☎ 02-2594 7733; jennysu@tpe.atti.net.tw).

THAILAND
Bangkok is still the most popular gateway to Vietnam. Air France, Thai Airways and Vietnam Airlines offer daily connections from Bangkok to Hanoi and HCMC.

One popular option is an open-jaw ticket that involves a flight to either HCMC or Hanoi, an overland journey to the other city and a flight back to Bangkok.

Khao San Rd in Bangkok is the budget-travellers headquarters. If some of the agents there look too fly-by-night, try **STA Travel** (☎ 0 2236 0262; www.statravel.co.th).

Australia
Fares between Australia and Asia are relatively expensive considering the distances involved. Most cheaper flights between Australia and Vietnam involve stopovers at Kuala Lumpur, Bangkok or Singapore, but Qantas and Vietnam Airlines have services linking Brisbane, Melbourne, Perth and Sydney with either Hanoi or HCMC.

The following are good places to pick up tickets in Australia:
STA Travel (☎ 1300 733 035; www.statravel.com.au)
Flight Centre (☎ 133 133; www.flightcentre.com.au)

Canada
Discount tickets from Canada tend to cost about 10% more than those sold in the USA. For the lowdown on cheap fares, contact **Travel Cuts** (☎ 800-667 2887; www.travelcuts.com), with offices across the country.

Continental Europe
Although London is the discount-travel capital of Europe, major airlines and big

travel agents usually have offers from all the major cities on the continent.

Recommended agents with branches across France:

Nouvelles Frontières (☎ 08 25 00 07 47; www .nouvelles-frontieres.fr)

OTU Voyages (www.otu.fr) This agency specialises in student and youth travel.

Voyageurs du Monde (☎ 01 40 15 11 15; www.vdm .com)

Reliable agencies flying out of Germany:

Just Travel (☎ 089-747 33 30; www.justtravel.de)

STA Travel (☎ 0180-545 64 22; www.statravel.de)

From other countries in Europe, try the following agencies in Italy, Netherlands and Spain.

Airfair (☎ 0206-20 51 21; www.airfair.nl; Netherlands)

Barcelo Viajes (☎ 902 11 62 26; www.barceloviajes .com; Spain)

CTS Viaggi (☎ 064 62 04 31; www.cts.it; Italy)

NBBS Reizen (☎ 0206-20 50 71; www.nbbs.nl; Netherlands)

Nouvelles Frontières (☎ 902 17 09 79; www.nouvelles-frontieres.es; Spain)

New Zealand

The best way to get from New Zealand to Vietnam is to use one of the leading Asian carriers like Malaysian, Singapore or Thai. Good agencies to start shopping around for tickets:

Flight Centre (☎ 0800 243 544; www.flightcentre .co.nz)

STA Travel (☎ 0508 782 872; www.statravel.co.nz)

UK & Ireland

From London there are some great fares to Asia, although prices to Vietnam are nowhere near as cheap as to Bangkok or Hong Kong. There are no direct flights from the UK to Vietnam, although expansionist Vietnam Airlines will more than likely start a service during the lifetime of this book.

There are oodles of agencies in the UK. Some of the best bets:

Flightbookers (☎ 087-0010 7000; www.ebookers.com)

North-South Travel (☎ 01245-608291; www.northsouthtravel.co.uk) North-South Travel donates part of its profit to projects in the developing world.

STA Travel (☎ 087-0160 0599; www.statravel.co.uk)

Trailfinders (☎ 084-5050 5891; www.trailfinders.co.uk)

Travel Bag (☎ 087-0890 1456; www.travelbag.co.uk)

USA

Discount travel agents in the USA are known as consolidators, although you won't see a sign on the door saying 'Consolidator'. San Francisco is the ticket-consolidator capital of America, although some good deals can be found in Los Angeles, New York and other big cities.

Useful online options in the USA:

- www.cheaptickets.com
- www.itn.net
- www.lowestfare.com
- www.sta.com
- www.travelocity.com

LAND

Vietnam shares land borders with Cambodia, China and Laos and there are three border crossings open to foreigners with each neighbour, a big improvement on a few years ago.

Border Crossings

It is essential to have a Vietnam visa before rocking up to the border, as they are not issued at land crossings. There are currently nine international land borders: three each with Cambodia, China and Laos.

There are few legal money-changing facilities on the Vietnamese side of these crossings, so be sure to have some small denomination US dollars handy. The black market is also an option for local currencies – Vietnamese dong, Chinese renminbi, Lao kip and Cambodian riel. Remember that black marketeers have a well-deserved reputation for short-changing and outright theft.

Vietnamese police at the land-border crossings, especially the Lao borders, have a bad reputation for petty extortion. Most travellers find that it's much easier to exit Vietnam overland than it is to enter. Travellers at the border crossings are occasionally asked for an 'immigration fee' of some kind.

CAMBODIA

The Moc Bai–Bavet border is the traditional favourite for a cheap and quick way between HCMC and Phnom Penh. For those willing to take their time, it is much nicer to meander through the Mekong Delta and travel by river between Chau Doc and Phnom Penh. One-month Cambodian visas are issued on arrival at Bavet and Kaam Samnor for US$20, but they are not yet available at Phnom Den.

TRANSPORT

TRANSPORT

BORDER CROSSINGS

Country	Border Crossing	Nearest Towns
Cambodia	Bavet/Moc Bai	Svay Rieng/Tay Ninh
	Kaam Samnor/Vinh Xuong	Neak Luong/Chau Doc
	Phnom Den/Tinh Bien	Takeo/Chau Doc
China	Youyi Guan/Huu Nghi Quan (Friendship Pass)	Pingxiang/Lang Son
	Hekou/Lao Cai	Hekou/Lao Cai
	Dongxing/Mong Cai	Dongxing/Mong Cai
Laos	Donsavanh/Lao Bao	Sepon/Dong Ha
	Nam Phao/Cau Treo	Tha Kaek/Vinh
	Na Meo/Nam Can	Phonsavan/Vinh

Moc Bai–Bavet

The most popular border crossing between Cambodia and Vietnam is Moc Bai, which connects Vietnam's Tay Ninh province with Cambodia's Svay Rieng province. There are several buses daily between Phnom Penh and HCMC (via Moc Bai), usually departing around 8am, taking about seven hours and costing a paltry US$6. The cheapest tickets are sold at the travellers cafés in HCMC's Pham Ngu Lao area (see p327), or try **Capitol Guesthouse** (☎ 023-364104) or **Narin Guesthouse** (☎ 023-982554) in Phnom Penh.

Vinh Xuong–Kaam Samnor

A more pleasurable alternative to the Moc Bai crossing is the Vinh Xuong border near Chau Doc. This offers the advantage of a leisurely look at the Mekong delta without the boredom of backtracking to HCMC. There are several companies offering daily boats between Chau Doc and Phnom Penh, departing around 9am and costing about US$8. It takes about six hours including a slow border check.

For something faster, consider the **Victoria Hotels express boats** (www.victoriahotels-asia.com), which run from the Victoria Chau Doc Hotel to Phnom Penh several times a week. It is pretty pricey at about US$65 per person, but very comfortable.

Finally there are two companies that offer luxury boat cruises between HCMC and Siem Reap via this border: the international player **Pandaw Cruises** (www.pandaw.com) and Cambodian company **Toum Teav Cruises**

(cfm@online.com.kh). Pandaw is an expensive option favoured by high-end tour companies, while Tum Teav is smaller and is well regarded for the personal service and excellent food.

Tinh Bien–Phnom Den

This border crossing point sees little traffic, as anyone in Chau Doc tends to use the river crossing direct to Phnom Penh. It's pretty remote and the roads are in bad shape so give it a miss for now.

CHINA

There are currently three border check points where foreigners are permitted to cross between Vietnam and China: the Friendship Pass, Lao Cai and Mong Cai. It is necessary to arrange a Chinese visa in advance (US$35 for one month) through the embassy in Hanoi (p459; ☒ 8.30-11.30am for visas).

The Vietnam–China border-crossing hours are 7am to 4pm (Vietnam time). Set your watch when you cross the border as the time in China is one hour behind.

Friendship Pass

The busiest border crossing is located at the Vietnamese town of Dong Dang, 164km northeast of Hanoi. There is a 600m walk between the Vietnamese and Chinese border posts.

Dong Dang is an obscure town, about 18km north of Lang Son (p139). Buses between Hanoi and Lang Son are frequent. The fastest way to cover the 18km between

Dong Dang and Lang Son is to hire a motorbike (30,000d). There are also mini-buses cruising the streets looking for passengers. Just make sure they take you to Huu Nghi Quan, as there are other checkpoints for locals only.

On the Chinese side, it's a 20-minute drive from the border to Pingxiang by bus or a shared taxi. Pingxiang is connected by train and bus to Nanning, the capital of China's Guangxi province.

There is a twice-weekly international train between Beijing and Hanoi that stops at Friendship Pass. You can board or get off at numerous stations in China. The entire Hanoi–Beijing run is about 2951km and takes approximately 48 hours, including a three-hour delay (if you are lucky) at the border checkpoint.

Train tickets to China are more expensive in Hanoi, so some travellers prefer to buy a ticket to Dong Dang, cross the border and then buy another ticket on the Chinese side. While this plan involves a motorbike to the border and a bus or taxi on to Pingxiang, it is a good way to go as it avoids the three-hour delay while the international train is given the once over.

Lao Cai–Hekou

There's a 762km railway linking Hanoi with Kunming in China's Yunnan province. The border town on the Vietnamese side is Lao Cai (p167), 294km from Hanoi. On the Chinese side, the border town is Hekou, 468km south of Kunming.

There are currently no direct train services between Hanoi and Kunming. There are three trains a day from Hanoi to Lao Cai, so it is easy to combine a stop at Sapa (p160) when crossing this way. On the Chinese side, the Hekou–Kunming trip takes approximately 17 hours.

From the border crossing to Lao Cai train station is about 3km, so it's best to take a motorbike (10,000d).

Mong Cai–Dongxing

Vietnam's third (but seldom-used) border crossing to China can be found at Mong Cai (p137) in the northeast of the country, opposite the Chinese city of Dongxing. It might be useful for anyone planning to travel between Halong Bay and Hainan Island, but otherwise is out of the way.

LAOS

There are three overland crossings between Laos and Vietnam – Lao Bao, Cau Treo and the latest, but not greatest, option of Na Meo. At all three border crossings, 15-day Lao visas are now available. We have received scores of letters complaining about immigration and local-transport hassles on the Vietnamese side of these borders, but the situation is slowly improving.

Keep your ears open for news on the Tay Trang border near Dien Bien Phu (northwestern Vietnam) opening up to foreigners.

Lao Bao–Donsavanh

The border town of Lao Bao is on Hwy 9, 80km west of Dong Ha. Just across the border is the southern Lao province of Savannakhet, but there is no town on that side of the border. An international bus runs between Danang (Vietnam) and the city of Savannakhet daily, but at US$25 for foreigners, it is a poor deal. Better is the service from Hué to Savannakhet (US$15, 13 hours, departing at 6am and 6pm daily). Coming in the other direction, there is a daily 10pm bus from Savannakhet that is much cheaper, serving Dong Ha (US$7, 329km), Hué (US$9, 409km) or Danang (US$11, 508km).

For details on the ins and outs of local transport for this border, see the boxed text on p198.

Cau Treo–Nam Phao

Vietnam's Hwy 8 hits Laos at Keo Nua Pass (734m), known as Cau Treo in Vietnamese, Kaew Neua in Lao.

The nearest Vietnamese city of any importance is Vinh, 96km east of the border. On the Lao side it's about 200km from the border to Tha Khaek. Most people use this border when travelling on the direct buses between Hanoi and Vientiane, but this is no picnic. In fact it's a set menu from hell. The journey takes about 24 hours and the buses get progressively more dangerous and overcrowded. The bus hardly stops for bathrooms or meals, but stops randomly when the driver fancies a sleep. Invariably the bus arrives at the border at an ungodly hour. Almost everyone ends up wishing they had flown! If you are a sucker for punishment, travel agents and guesthouses in Hanoi and Vientiane can help set you up, literally, for somewhere in the region of US$12 to US$25.

For the lowdown on the local transport linking Laos and Vietnam in this neck of the woods, see the boxed text p183.

Nam Can–Na Meo

This is only for hardcore border aficionados. The border crossing is more than 200km northwest of Vinh and drops you in the middle of nowhere in Laos. The nearest town on the Lao side is Phonsavan, about 80km west of here. The roads are quite good, but public transport is infrequent.

For the full story on crossing this most remote of borders, see the boxed text p180.

Bus

It is possible to cross into Vietnam by bus from Cambodia or Laos. The most popular way from Cambodia is a cheap tourist shuttle via the Bavet–Moc Bai border crossing (see p471). From Laos, most travellers take the nightmare bus from Vientiane to Hanoi via the Cau Treo crossing or the easier route from Savannakhet in southern Laos to Hué in central Vietnam via the Lao Bao border crossing.

Car & Motorbike

It is possible to travel in and out of Vietnam by car or motorbike, but only through borders shared with Cambodia and Laos. It is currently not possible to take any sort of vehicle into China from Vietnam.

Drivers of cars and riders of motorbikes will need the vehicle's registration papers, liability insurance and an International Driving Permit, in addition to a domestic licence. Most important is a *carnet de passage en douane*, which is effectively a passport for the vehicle and acts as a temporary waiver of import duty.

Train

Several international trains link China and Vietnam. The most scenic stretch of railway is between Hanoi and Kunming via Lao Cai, but the mammoth journey from Hanoi to Beijing via Lang Son is also a possibility. There are no railway lines linking Vietnam to Cambodia or Laos.

RIVER

There is a river border crossing between Cambodia and Vietnam on the banks of the Mekong. Regular passenger boats ply the route between Phnom Penh in Cambodia and Chau Doc in Vietnam, with a change at the Vinh Xuong–Kaam Samnor border (see p471). There is also a luxury fast boat service and two river boats running all the way to the temples of Angkor at Siem Reap in Cambodia (see p471).

TOURS

Package tours to Vietnam are offered by travel agencies worldwide. Nearly all these tours follow one of a dozen or so set itineraries. Tours come in every shape and size, from budget trips to ultimate indulgences. Tours booked outside Vietnam are not bad value when you tally everything up (flights, hotels, transport), but then again it's a cheap country in which to travel.

It's easy enough to fly into Vietnam and make the travel arrangements after arrival (see p481). The main saving through booking before arrival is time, and if time is more precious than money, a pre-booked package tour is probably right for you.

Almost any reputable travel agency can book you on a standard mad-dash minibus tour around Vietnam. More noteworthy are the adventure tours arranged for people with a particular passion. These include speciality tours for cyclists, trekkers, bird watchers, war veterans, culture vultures and gourmet travellers.

For a rewarding trip to Vietnam, consider contacting the following speciality travel outfits:

Australia

Adventure World (☎ 02-8913 0755; www.adventure world.com.au)
Griswalds Vietnamese Vacations (☎ 02-9564 5040; www.vietnamvacations.com.au)
Intrepid Travel (☎ 1300 360 667; www.intrepidtravel .com.au)
Peregrine (☎ 02-9290 2770, www.peregrine.net.au)

France

Compagnie des Indes & Orients (☎ 01 53 63 33 40; www.compagniesdumonde.com)
Intermedes (☎ 01 45 61 90 90; www.intermedes.com)
La Route des Indes (☎ 01 42 60 60 90; www.laroutedesindes.com)

New Zealand

Adventure World (☎ 09-524 5118; www.adventure world.co.nz)

UK
Audley Travel (☎ 01604-234855; www.audleytravel
.com)
Tales Worldwide (☎ 087-0241 3208; www
.talesworldwide.com)
Exodus (☎ 020-8675 5550; www.exodus.co.uk)
Mekong Travel (☎ 01494-674456; www.mekong
travel.com)
Regent Holidays (☎ 01179-211711; www.regent
holidays.com)
Symbiosis (☎ 020-7924 5906; www.symbiosis-travel
.com)

USA
Asia Transpacific Journeys (☎ 800-642 2742, www
.asiatranspacific.com)
Asian Pacific Adventures (☎ 800-825 1680)
Geographic Expeditions (☎ 800-777 8183; www
.geoex.com)
Global Spectrum (☎ 800-419 4446; www.asian
passages.com)

John Gray's Sea Canoe (www.seacanoe.com)
Wild Card Adventures (☎ 800-590 3776; www
.awildcard.com)

GETTING AROUND

AIR
Airlines in Vietnam
Vietnam Airlines (www.vietnamairlines.com.vn) has a monopoly on domestic flights, as it owns the only rival, **Pacific Airlines** (www.pacificairlines
.com.vn), which flies the Hanoi–HCMC route and the HCMC–Danang route.

Most travel agents do not charge any more than when you book directly with the airline. A passport is required to make a booking on all domestic flights.

Vietnam Airlines has come a long way and many (but not all) branch offices accept credit cards for ticket purchases. The airline

TRANSPORT

DOMESTIC AIRLINE SCHEDULES
VIETNAM AIRLINES

From	To	Frequency	Economy
Danang	Buon Ma Thuot	3 weekly	500,000d
	Hai Phong	3 weekly	800,000d
	Nha Trang	3 weekly	550,000d
	Pleiku	1 daily	400,000d
	Vinh	3 weekly	500,000d
Hanoi	Danang	3 daily	800,000d
	Dien Bien Phu	1 daily	465,000d
	HCMC	7 daily	1,500,000d
	Hué	1 daily	800,000d
	Son La	2 weekly	390,000d
Ho Chi Minh City	Buon Ma Thuot	3 daily	400,000d
	Dalat	6 weekly	400,000d
	Danang	3 daily	800,000d
	Hai Phong	2 daily	1,500,000d
	Hanoi	7 daily	1,500,000d
	Hué	1 daily	800,000d
	Nha Trang	2 daily	550,000d
	Phu Quoc	3 weekly	500,000d
	Pleiku	3 daily	550,000d
	Quy Nhon	6 weekly	550,000d
	Rach Gia	5 weekly	570,000d

PACIFIC AIRLINES

From	To	Frequency	Economy
Ho Chi Minh City	Danang	1 daily	800,000d
Ho Chi Minh City	Hanoi	3 daily	1,500,000d

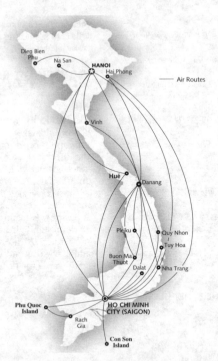

Air Routes

has retired its ancient Soviet-built fleet (thank heavens!) and purchased new Western-made aircraft.

See the Air Routes map above, and Domestic Airline Schedules (p475), for routes available within Vietnam.

There's a helicopter charter service from Hanoi to Halong Bay (see p129).

BICYCLE

A great way to get around Vietnam's towns and cities is to do as the locals do and ride a bicycle. During rush hours, urban thoroughfares approach gridlock, as rushing streams of cyclists force their way through intersections without the benefit of traffic lights. In the countryside, Westerners on bicycles are often greeted enthusiastically by locals who don't see many foreigners pedalling around.

DEPARTURE TAX

Domestic departure tax is 25,000d, but is included when you buy the ticket.

Long-distance cycling is popular in Vietnam. Much of the country is flat or only moderately hilly, and the major roads are in good shape. Safety, however, is a considerable concern. Bicycles can be transported around the country on the top of buses or in train baggage compartments. Lonely Planet's *Cycling Vietnam, Laos & Cambodia* gives the lowdown on cycling through Vietnam.

Decent bikes can be bought at a few speciality shops in Hanoi and HCMC, but it's better to bring your own if you plan on cycling over long distances. Mountain bikes are preferable, as large potholes or unsealed roads are rough on the rims. Basic cycling safety equipment and authentic spare parts are also in short supply, so bring all this from home. A bell is mandatory – the louder the better.

Hotels and some travel agencies rent bicycles from 10,000d to US$1 per day and is a great way to explore some of the smaller cities like Hué or Nha Trang. There are innumerable bicycle-repair stands along the side of the roads in every city and town in Vietnam.

Groups of foreign cyclists touring Vietnam ... e a common sight these days, and there are ... veral tour companies that specialise in bi- ... ... cling trips. See p474 and p481 for details.

OAT

... ietnam has an enormous number of rivers ... at are at least partly navigable, but the ... ... ost important by far is the Mekong River ... ... d its tributaries. Scenic day trips by boat ... e possible on rivers in Hoi An, Danang, ... ué, Tam Coc and even HCMC, but only ... the Mekong Delta are boats used as a ... actical means of transport.

Boat trips are also possible on the sea – a ... uise to the islands off the coast of Nha ... rang is a particularly popular trip. If you ... sit Halong Bay, a cruise to the islands in ... at region is a must.

In some parts of Vietnam, particularly ... e Mekong Delta, there are frequent ferry ... rossings. Don't stand between parked ... ehicles on the ferry as they can roll and ... ou could wind up as the meat in the ... ndwich.

US

... ietnam has an extensive network of dirt- ... heap buses that reach the far-flung corners ... f the country. Traditionally, few foreign ... avellers have used them because of safety ... oncerns and overcharging, but the situation ... improving with modern buses and fixed- ... rice ticket offices at most bus stations.

Bus fleets are being upgraded as fast as ... e roads, so the old French, American and ... ussian buses from the '50s, '60s and '70s ... re becoming increasingly rare. On most ... opular routes, modern Korean buses are ... e flavour of the day. Most of these offer ... ir-con and comfortable seats, but on the ... ipside most of them are equipped with ... Vs and dreaded karaoke machines. You ... an ignore the crazy kung fu videos by ... losing your eyes (or wearing a blindfold), ... ut you'd need to be deaf to sleep through ... e karaoke sessions – ear plugs are recom- ... ended!

Figuring out the bus system is not easy. ... any cities have several bus stations, and ... esponsibilities are divided according to ... e location of the destination (whether it ... s north or south of the city) and the type ... f service being offered (local or long dis- ... nce, express or nonexpress).

Short-distance buses, mostly minibuses, depart when full (ie jam-packed with people and luggage). They often operate throughout the day, but don't count on many leaving after about 4pm.

Nonexpress buses and minibuses drop off and pick up as many passengers as possible along the route, so try to avoid these. The frequent stops to pick up and drop off (and arrange luggage and chickens) can make for a slow journey.

Express buses make a beeline from place to place. This is the deluxe class and you can usually be certain of there being enough space to sit comfortably. Such luxury comes at a price, but it's very cheap by anyone's standards.

It is also perfectly feasible (and highly recommended) to kick in with some fellow travellers and charter your own minibus. See p478 for details.

If possible, try to travel during daylight hours only. Many drivers refuse to drive after dark because the unlit highways tend to have gaping potholes and lots of bicycles and pedestrians who seem oblivious to the traffic. However, if you like living dangerously, there are some overnight buses.

Be aware that luggage is easily pilfered at toilet stops unless someone is looking after it. Bound to the rooftop, it should be safe from swift hands, but try keeping the bags in sight. A distinct disadvantage of having your gear on top is that it will be exposed to constant dust and sometimes heavy rain.

No matter how honest your fellow passengers might seem, *never* accept drinks from them, as there is a chance you may be drugged and robbed.

Reservations & Costs

Reservations aren't required for most of the frequent, popular services between towns and cities, but it doesn't hurt to purchase the ticket the day before if you're set on a departure time. Most major bus stations now have ticket offices with official prices clearly displayed. Always buy a ticket from the office, as bus drivers are notorious overchargers.

Costs are negligible, though on rural runs foreigners are typically charged anywhere from twice to 10 times the going rate. If you have to battle it out with the bus driver, it is helpful to determine the cost of the ticket for locals before starting negotiations.

Open Tours
In backpacker haunts throughout Vietnam, you'll see lots of signs advertising 'Open Tour', 'Open Date Ticket' or 'Open Ticket'. This is a bus service catering mostly to foreign budget travellers, not to Vietnamese. These air-con buses run between HCMC and Hanoi and people can hop on and hop off the bus at any major city along the route.

Competition has driven the price of these tours so low that it would practically only be cheaper if you walked. Sample prices from HCMC are as follows:

Route	Price
Ho Chi Minh City–Dalat	US$5
Ho Chi Minh City–Mui Ne	US$6
Ho Chi Minh City–Nha Trang	US$7
Ho Chi Minh City–Hoi An	US$13
Ho Chi Minh City–Hué	US$14
Ho Chi Minh City–Hanoi	US$21

Some would argue they should *raise* the cost of the tickets and, by actually making money on the bus fare, allow passengers some freedom of choice on arrival at a destination. Unfortunately, they depend on kickbacks from a very elaborate and well-established network of sister hotels and restaurants along the way, making the whole experience feel like you are part of a herd.

However, bear in mind that if they weren't collecting commissions by delivering travellers to selected hotels or restaurants, the ticket would never be so cheap. Trying to avoid the commission circus will not only waste time that you've gained by using these relatively speedy buses, but it can make your hair turn grey (or fall out!).

As cheap and popular as it is, the open-tour deal is not the ideal way to experience Vietnam. Once you've bought the ticket, you're stuck with it. It really isolates you from Vietnam – you should try to have at least some contact with the locals. Buying shorter point-to-point tickets on the open-tour buses costs a bit more but you achieve more flexibility, including the chance to take a train, rent a motorbike or simply change plans.

Nevertheless, cheap open-tour tickets are a temptation and many people go for them. A couple of shorter routes to try are HCMC–Dalat and HCMC–Mui Ne Beach, two places that are not serviced by train.

If you are set on open-tour tickets, look for them at budget cafés in HCMC and Hanoi. From the original Sinh Café concept a decade ago, there are now lots of companies in on this game. Buses vary in size and standard, so a good rule of thumb is to turn up and check out the bus before committing to a company.

CAR & MOTORBIKE
The discomfort and unreliability of Vietnam's public transport combined with the relative affordability of vehicle hire make the latter a popular option. Having your own set of wheels gives you maximum flexibility to visit remote regions and stop where and where you please.

Driving Licence
In order to drive a car in Vietnam, you need a domestic licence and an International Driving Permit, usually issued by your automobile association back home. When it comes to renting motorbikes, it's a case of no licence required.

Fuel & Spare Parts
Fuel is pretty cheap in Vietnam, at around 6000d a litre. Fuel is readily available throughout the country, but prices rise in rural areas. Even the most isolated communities usually have someone selling petrol out of Fanta or Johnnie Walker bottles. Some sellers mix the fuel with kerosene to make a quick profit; use it sparingly, in emergencies only.

When it comes to spare parts, Vietnam is awash with Japanese motorbikes, so it is easy to get parts for Hondas, Yamahas or Suzukis, but finding a part for a Harley or Ducati is another matter. Likewise for cars; spares for Japanese cars are easy to come by, as are spares for international brands manufactured in Vietnam like Ford and Mercedes. But if you are driving something obscure, whether with two wheels or four, bring substantial spares.

Hire
The major considerations are safety, the mechanical condition of the vehicle, reliability of the rental agency and your budget. Don't think about driving a car yourself in Vietnam; a motorbike is challenging enough, and moreover, hire charges include a driver.

ROAD DISTANCES (KM)

	Can Tho	Chau Doc	Dalat	Danang	Dong Ha	Dien Bien Phu	Hai Phong	Halong City	Hanoi	Ho Chi Minh City	Hoi An	Hue	Lang Son	Kon Tum	Mui Ne	Nha Trang	Qui Nhon	Sapa
Can Tho	---																	
Chau Doc	116	---																
Dalat	477	593	---															
Danang	1141	1257	746	---														
Dong Ha	1331	1447	936	190	---													
Dien Bien Phu	2418	2534	1979	1233	1043	---												
Hai Phong	1971	2087	1532	826	636	573	---											
Halong City	2026	2142	1587	881	691	635	55	---										
Hanoi	1948	2064	1509	763	617	470	103	165	---									
Ho Chi Minh City	169	285	308	972	1169	2180	1733	1788	1710	---								
Hoi An	1111	1227	716	30	220	1263	856	911	793	942	---							
Hué	1229	1445	854	108	72	1128	718	773	658	1097	138	---						
Lang Son	2094	2210	1655	909	763	616	249	311	146	1856	939	804	---					
Kon Tum	1053	1169	641	274	464	1507	1100	1155	1037	896	258	380	1183	---				
Mui Ne	379	495	257	762	952	1995	1548	1603	1525	210	732	870	1671	646	---			
Nha Trang	617	733	205	541	731	1774	1327	1383	1304	448	511	649	1450	436	238	---		
Qui Nhon	855	971	453	303	493	1536	1089	1144	1066	686	273	411	1212	198	979	470	---	
Sapa	2271	2388	1833	1087	897	253	427	489	324	2034	1117	979	470	1361	1849	1628	1390	---
Vinh	1629	1745	1190	484	294	789	342	397	319	1391	514	376	465	758	1206	985	747	643

TRANSPORT

AR & MINIBUS

elf-drive rental cars have yet to make their
ebut in Vietnam, which is a blessing in dis-
uise given traffic conditions, but cars with
rivers are popular and plentiful. Renting a
ehicle with a driver and guide is a realistic
ption even for budget travellers, providing
ou have friends to share the cost.

Hanoi and HCMC have an especially
vide selection of travel agencies that rent
ehicles. For sightseeing trips around
ICMC or Hanoi, a car with driver can also
e rented by the day. It costs about US$20
› US$30 per day, depending on the car.

Renting a minibus (van) is good value for
arger groups, as they hold between eight
nd 15 passengers. They are also a smart

option for groups of three or four set on
travelling long distances at night, as everyone can stretch out.

For the really bad roads of northwestern
Vietnam, the only reasonably safe vehicle is
a 4WD. Without one, the muddy mountain
roads can be deadly. In Vietnam, 4WDs
come in different flavours – the cheapest
(and least comfortable) are Russian made,
while more cushy Korean and Japanese
vehicles with air-con are about twice the
price.

MOTORBIKE

Motorbikes can be rented from cafés, hotels, motorbike shops and travel agencies. If
you don't fancy self-drive, there are plenty

of local drivers willing to act as a chauffeur and guide for around US$6 to US$10 per day.

Renting a 100cc moped is cheap at around US$6 per day, usually with unlimited mileage. For more on renting a mighty Minsk to take on the mountains of the far northwest, see p110.

Most places will ask to keep your passport until you return the bike. Try and sign some sort of agreement – preferably in a language you understand – clearly stating what you are renting, how much it costs, the extent of compensation and so on.

Insurance

If you are travelling in a tourist vehicle with a driver, then it is almost guaranteed to be insured. When it comes to motorbikes, many rental bikes are not insured and you will have to sign a contract agreeing to a valuation for the bike if it is stolen. Make sure you have a strong lock and always leave it in guarded parking where available.

Do not even consider renting a motorbike if you are daft enough to be travelling in Vietnam without insurance. The cost of treating serious injuries is bankrupting for budget travellers.

Road Conditions & Hazards

Road safety is definitely not one of Vietnam's strong points. The intercity road network of two-lane highways is becoming more and more dangerous. High-speed, head-on collisions between buses, trucks and other smaller vehicles (such as motorbikes and bicycles) have become a sickeningly familiar sight on the major highways. Vietnam does not have an efficient emergency-rescue system, so if something happens on the road, it could be hours until even rudimentary medical treatment.

In general, the major highways are hard surfaced and reasonably well maintained, but seasonal flooding can be a problem. A big typhoon can create potholes the size of bomb craters. In remote areas roads are not surfaced and will become a sea of mud if the weather turns bad – such roads are best tackled with a 4WD vehicle or motorbike. Mountain roads are particularly dangerous: those landslides, falling rocks and runaway vehicles can add an unwelcome edge to your journey. The occasional roadside cemetery

often indicates where a bus has plunged over the edge.

For motorbikers, serious sunburn is major risk and well worth preventing. The cooling breeze prevents you from realising how badly you are burning until it's too late. Cover up exposed skin or wear sun screen. Bikers also must consider the opposite problem – occasional heavy rain. A rainsuit or poncho is essential, especially during the monsoon season.

Road Rules

Basically, there aren't any. Size matters and the biggest vehicle wins by default. Be particularly careful about children on the road; you'll find kids playing hopscotch in the middle of a major highway. Livestock on the road is also a menace; hit a cow on motorbike and you'll both be hamburger.

Although the police frequently stop drivers and fine them for all sorts of real and imagined offences, nobody gets stopped for speeding. Rally driving is the norm and everyone seems to be in the race. In cities there is a rule that you cannot turn right on a red light. It's easy to run afoul of this law in Vietnam and the police will fine you for this offence.

Honking at all pedestrians and bicycles (to warn them of your approach) is considered a basic element of safe driving; larger trucks and buses might as well have dynamo-driven horn.

There is no national seat-belt law and the locals often laugh at foreigners who insist on using seat belts. Helmets are now required for motorbike riders on national highways and, although this is not always enforced, it's wise to make it a personal rule. Decent helmets are available in HCMC and Hanoi for around US$20.

Legally a motorbike can carry only two people, but we've seen up to seven on one vehicle…plus luggage! This law is enforced in major cities, but ignored in rural areas.

HITCHING

Hitching is never entirely safe in any country in the world, and we don't recommend it. Travellers who decide to hitch should understand that they are taking a potentially serious risk. People who do choose to hitch will be safer if they travel in pairs and let someone know where they are planning to go.

In Vietnam, locals do flag down private and public vehicles for a lift, but a small fee is usually expected. Foreigners are expected to pay more.

LOCAL TRANSPORT

Bus
The bus systems in Hanoi and HCMC have improved in the past few years but are light years behind Hong Kong and Bangkok and, in general, buses are not a practical way to get around town. Fortunately there are many other fast and economical options, such as meter taxis, *cyclos* and motorbike taxis.

Cyclo
The *cyclo* (*xich lo*), from the French *cyclo-pousse*, is the best invention since sliced bread. *Cyclos* offer cheap and environmentally friendly transportation around Vietnam's sprawling cities.

Groups of *cyclo* drivers always hang out near major hotels and markets, and many speak at least broken English. To make sure the driver understands where you want to go, it's useful to bring a city map. Bargaining is imperative. Settle on a fare *before* going anywhere or you're likely to get stiffed.

As a basic rule, short rides around town should cost about 5000d. For a longer ride or a night ride, expect to pay double that or more. It pays to have the exact change when taking a *cyclo*, as drivers may claim they don't have change. *Cyclos* are cheaper by time rather than distance. A typical price is US$1 per hour.

There have been many stories of travellers being mugged by their *cyclo* drivers in HCMC so, as a general rule of thumb, hire *cyclos* only during the day. When leaving a bar late at night, take a meter taxi.

Taxi
Western-style taxis with meters, found in most major cities, are very, very cheap by international standards and a safe way to travel around at night. Average tariffs are about 10,000d per kilometre.

Xe Dap Loi & Xe Loi
The two forms of transport used mostly in the Mekong Delta are the *xe dap loi*, which is a wagon pulled by a bicycle, and the *xe loi*, a wagon pulled by a motorbike.

Xe Lam
Xe lam are tiny, three-wheeled trucks used for short-haul passenger and freight transport (similar to the Indonesian *bajaj*). They tend to have whining two-stroke 'lawn-mower' engines with no mufflers and emit copious quantities of blue exhaust smoke.

Xe Om
The *xe om* (zay-ohm) is a motorbike that carries one passenger, like a two-wheeled taxi. *Xe* means motorbike, and *om* means hug (or hold), so you probably get the picture. Getting around by *xe om* is easy, as long as you don't have a lot of luggage.

Fares are comparable with those for a *cyclo*, but negotiate the price beforehand. There are plenty of *xe om* drivers hanging around street corners, markets, hotels and bus stations. They will find you before you find them!

TOURS
We get loads of letters complaining about the quality of bottom-end budget tours being peddled in HCMC and Hanoi. Some are better than others, but remember the old adage that 'you get what you pay for'. Tour-operator gimmicks like 'one free beer' or 'ten minutes of Internet' are not a good sign.

Renting a car with a driver and guide gives you the chance to design a tailor-made itinerary for you and your companions. Seeing the country this way is almost like independent travel, except that it's more comfortable, less time-consuming and allows for stops anywhere, or everywhere, along the way.

The cost varies considerably. At the high end are tours booked through government travel agencies like Saigon Tourist and upmarket tour companies, while budget and mid-range companies can usually arrange something just as enjoyable at a cheaper price.

The price typically includes accommodation, a guide, a driver and a car. The cost of the car depends largely on the type of vehicle you choose.

Once you've settled on an itinerary, get a copy from the travel agency. If you find that your guide is making it up as they go along, ignoring the agreed itinerary, that piece of paper is your most effective leverage.

A good guide can be your translator and travelling companion, and can usually save you as much money along the way as they

TRANSPORT

cost you. A bad guide can ruin your trip. If possible, you should meet your guide before starting out – make sure that this is someone you can travel with.

Travelling with a freelance guide, you are usually responsible for their travel expenses, but if you pay for a package through a company, any expenses for the guide and driver should be included.

For trips in and around big cities like HCMC and Hanoi, you'll often find women working as guides. However, it seems relatively few women are employed as guides on long-distance trips.

The following are Vietnam-based travel agencies who offer premium tours throughout Vietnam and Indochina:

Buffalo Tours (☎ 04-828 0702; www.buffalotours.com; 11 Pho Hang Muoi, Hanoi)

Destination Asia (☎ 08-844 8071; www.destination -asia.com; 143 Đ Nguyen Van Troi, Phu Nhuan district, HCMC)

Exotissimo (☎ 04-828 2150; www.exotissimo.com; 26 Tran Nhat Duat, Hanoi)

Phoenix Voyages (☎ 04-716 1956; www.phoenix vietnam.com; 52 Pho Nguyen Khac Hieu, Hanoi)

Sinhbalo Adventures (☎ 08-837 6766; www .sinhbalo.com; 283/20 Đ Pham Ngu Lao, District 1, HCMC)

Sisters Tours (☎ 04-562 2733; www.sisterstours vietnam.com; 37 Đ Thai Thinh, Hanoi)

Vidotour (☎ 08-933 0457; www.vidotour.com; 145 Đ Nam Ky Khoi Nghia, HCMC)

TRAIN

The 2600km Vietnamese railway system operated by **Vietnam Railways** (Duong Sat Vie Nam; ☎ 04-747 0308; www.vr.com.vn), runs along the coast between HCMC and Hanoi, and links the capital with Hai Phong and northern towns. While sometimes even slower than buses, trains offer a more relaxing way to get around and more leg and body room than the jam-packed buses. The trains are also much safer than the country's kamikaze bus fleet.

Vietnam's railway authority has been rapidly upgrading trains and facilities – with air-con sleeping berths and dining cars available now on express trains – and lowering the price for foreigners. Foreigners and Vietnamese are now charged the same price, a big change from a few years ago when foreigners were charged 400% more!

The quickest train journey between Hanoi and HCMC takes 30 hours. The slowest express train on this route takes 41 hours. There are also local trains that only cover short routes, but these can crawl along at 15km/h, as there is only one track

THE REUNIFICATION EXPRESS

Construction of the 1726km-long Hanoi–Saigon railway, the Transindochinois, began in 1899 and was completed in 1936. In the late 1930s, the trip from Hanoi to Saigon took 40 hours and 20 minutes at an average speed of 43km/h. During WWII the Japanese made extensive use of the rail system, resulting in Viet Minh sabotage on the ground and US bombing from the air. After WWII efforts were made to repair the Transindochinois, major parts of which were either damaged or had become overgrown.

During the Franco–Viet Minh War, the Viet Minh engaged in sabotage against the rail system. At night the Viet Minh made off with rails to create a 300km network of tracks (between Ninh Hoa and Danang) in an area wholly under their control – the French quickly responded with their own sabotage.

In the late 1950s, the South, with US funding, reconstructed the track between Saigon and Hué, a distance of 1041km. But between 1961 and 1964 alone, 795 Viet Cong attacks were launched on the rail system, forcing the abandonment of large sections of track (including the Dalat spur).

By 1960 the North had repaired 1000km of track, mostly between Hanoi and China. During the US air war against the North, the northern rail network was repeatedly bombed. Even now clusters of bomb craters can be seen around virtually every rail bridge and train station in the north.

After reunification, the government immediately set about re-establishing the Hanoi–Ho Chi Minh City (HCMC) rail link as a symbol of Vietnamese unity. By the time the *Reunification Express* trains were inaugurated on 31 December 1976, 1334 bridges, 27 tunnels, 158 stations and 1370 shunts (switches) had been repaired.

Today the *Reunification Express* chugs along slightly faster than the trains did in the 1930s, at an average of 48km/h.

REUNIFICATION EXPRESS FARES FROM HANOI

Hanoi–HCMC (S1 Express Train); 33 hours

station	hard seat	soft seat a/c	bottom hard a/c (6 berth)	bottom soft a/c (4 berth)
Vinh	85,000d	103,000d	152,000d	171,000d
Dong Hoi	148,000d	179,000d	264,000d	296,000d
Hué	195,000d	235,000d	348,000d	390,000d
Danang	224,000d	271,000d	400,000d	448,000d
Nha Trang	386,000d	466,000d	689,000d	773,000d
HCMC	460,000d	556,000d	822,000d	922,000d

with many passing points and local trains have the lowest priority.

Petty crime is a problem on Vietnamese trains. While there doesn't seem to be organised pack-nipping gangs, such as those in India, thieves have become proficient at grabbing packs through the windows as trains pull out of stations. Always keep your bag nearby and lock or tie it to something, especially at night.

Another hazard is children throwing rocks at the train. Passengers have been severely injured this way and many conductors insist that you keep down the metal window shield. Unfortunately, however, these shields also obstruct the view.

Bicycles and motorbikes must travel in the freight car. Just make sure that the train you are on has a freight car (most have) or your bike will arrive later than you do.

Eating is easy, as there are vendors at every station who board the train and practically stuff food, drinks and cigarettes into your pockets. However, the food supplied by the railway company, included in the ticket price on some long journeys, isn't Michelin rated. It's a good idea to stock up on your favourite munchies before taking a long trip.

Odd-numbered trains travel south and even-numbered ones travel north. The fastest train service is provided by the *Reunification Express*, which runs between HCMC and Hanoi, making only a few short stops en route. If you want to stop at some obscure point between the major towns, use one of the slower local trains.

Aside from the main HCMC–Hanoi run, three rail-spur lines link Hanoi with the other parts of northern Vietnam. One runs east to the port city of Hai Phong. A second

heads northeast to Lang Son, crosses the border and continues to Nanning, China. A third goes northwest to Lao Cai and on to Kunming, China.

Four *Reunification Express* trains depart from HCMC's Saigon station between 9am and 10.30pm every day. The same number of trains depart from Hanoi between 5am and 6.40pm daily.

The train schedules change frequently. The timetables for all trains are posted on the Vietnam Railway website and at major stations. Most travel agents and some hotels keep a copy of the latest schedule on hand. In HCMC call or visit the **Saigon Railways Tourist Service** (☎ 08-836 7640; 275C Đ Pham Ngu Lao, District 1) in the Pham Ngu Lao area.

It's important to realise that the train schedule is 'bare-bones' during the Tet festival. The *Reunification Express* is suspended for nine days, beginning four days before Tet and continuing for four days afterwards.

Classes

There are four main classes of train travel in Vietnam: hard seat, soft seat, hard sleeper and soft sleeper. The latter three are also split into air-con and nonair-con options; presently, air-con is only available on the fastest express trains. Since it's all that many Vietnamese can afford, hard-seat class is usually packed. Hard seat is tolerable for day travel, but overnight it is worse than the bus. Soft-seat carriages have vinyl-covered seats rather than the uncomfortable hard benches.

A hard sleeper has three tiers of beds (six beds per compartment). Because the Vietnamese don't seem to like climbing up, the upper berth is cheapest, followed by the

TRANSPORT

middle berth and finally the lower berth. There is no door to separate the compartment from the corridor. Soft sleeper has two tiers (four beds per compartment) and all bunks are priced the same. These compartments have a door.

Costs

Ticket prices vary depending on the train, and the fastest trains are naturally the most expensive. See the following table for some sample fares from Hanoi to stations south. For all the details on trains from Hanoi to Hai Phong (p124), Lao Cai (p168) and Lang Son (p141), see the relevant sections.

Reservations

The supply of train seats is often insufficient to meet demand. Reservations for all trips should be made at least one day in advance. For sleeping berths, it is wise to book several days before the date of departure. Bring your passport when buying train tickets.

Many travel agencies, hotels and café sell train tickets for a small commission and this can save considerable time and trouble. It's a good idea to make reservations for onward travel as soon as you arrive in a city.

WALKING

If you don't want to wind up like a bug on a windshield, pay close attention to a few pedestrian survival rules, especially on the streets of motorbike-crazed HCMC and Hanoi. Foreigners frequently make the mistake of thinking that the best way to cross a busy street in Vietnam is to run quickly across it. This does not always work, and could get you creamed. Most Vietnamese cross the street slowly – very slowly – giving the motorbike drivers sufficient time to judge their position so they can pass on either side. They won't stop or even slow down, but they will try to avoid hitting you. Just don't make any sudden moves. Good luck!

Health Dr Trish Batchelor

CONTENTS

Health issues and the quality of medical facilities vary enormously depending on where and how you travel in Vietnam. Many of the major cities are now very well developed, although travel to rural areas can expose you to a variety of health risks and inadequate medical care.

Travellers tend to worry about contracting infectious diseases when in the tropics, but infections are a rare cause of serious illness or death in travellers. Pre-existing medical conditions such as heart disease, and accidental injury (especially traffic accidents), account for most life-threatening problems.

Becoming ill in some way, however, is a relatively common thing. Fortunately most common illnesses can either be prevented with some common-sense behaviour or be treated easily with a well-stocked traveller's medical kit.

The following advice is a general guide only and does not replace the advice of a doctor trained in travel medicine.

BEFORE YOU GO

Pack medications in their original, clearly labelled, containers. A signed and dated letter from your physician describing your

---

HEALTH ADVISORIES

It's usually a good idea to consult your government's travel-health website before departure, if one is available:
Australia (www.dfat.gov.au/travel/)
Canada (www.travelhealth.gc.ca)
New Zealand (www.mfat.govt.nz/travel)
UK (www.doh.gov.uk/traveladvice/)
US (www.cdc.gov/travel/)

---

medical conditions and medications, including generic names, is also a good idea. If carrying syringes or needles, be sure to have a physician's letter documenting their medical necessity. If you have a heart condition bring a copy of your ECG taken just prior to travelling.

If you happen to take any regular medication bring double your needs in case of loss or theft. In most Southeast Asian countries you can buy many medications over the counter without a doctor's prescription, but it can be difficult to find some of the newer drugs, particularly the latest antidepressant drugs, blood pressure medications and contraceptive pills.

INSURANCE

Even if you are fit and healthy, don't travel without health insurance – accidents do happen. Declare any existing medical conditions you have – the insurance company *will* check if your problem is pre-existing and will not cover you if it is undeclared. You may require extra cover for adventure activities such as rock climbing. If your health insurance doesn't cover you for medical expenses abroad, consider getting extra insurance – check **LonelyPlanet.com** (www.lonelyplanet.com) for more information. If you're uninsured, emergency evacuation is expensive; bills of over US$100,000 are not uncommon.

You should find out in advance if your insurance plan will make payments directly to providers or if they reimburse you later for overseas health expenditures. (Note that in many countries doctors expect payment in cash.) Some policies offer lower and higher medical-expense options; the higher ones are chiefly for countries that have extremely high medical costs, such as the USA.

You may prefer a policy that pays doctors or hospitals directly rather than you having to pay on the spot and claim later. If you have to claim later, make sure you keep all documentation. Some policies ask you to call back (reverse charges) to a centre in your home country where an immediate assessment of your problem is made.

VACCINATIONS

The only vaccine required by international regulations is yellow fever. Proof of vaccination will only be required if you have visited a country in the yellow-fever zone within the six days prior to entering Vietnam. If you are travelling to Vietnam from Africa or South America you should check to see if you require proof of vaccination.

Specialised travel-medicine clinics are your best source of information; they stock

RECOMMENDED VACCINATIONS

The World Health Organization (WHO) recommends the following vaccinations for travellers to Southeast Asia:

- Adult diphtheria and tetanus – single booster recommended if you've had none in the previous 10 years. Side effects include a sore arm and fever.
- Hepatitis A – provides almost 100% protection for up to a year; a booster after 12 months provides at least another 20 years' protection. Mild side effects such as headache and a sore arm occur for between 5% and 10% of people.
- Hepatitis B – now considered routine for most travellers. Given as three shots over six months. A rapid schedule is also available, as is a combined vaccination with Hepatitis A. Side effects are mild and uncommon, usually a headache and sore arm. Lifetime protection occurs in 95% of people.
- Measles, mumps and rubella – two doses of MMR required unless you have had the diseases. Occasionally a rash and flulike illness can develop a week after receiving the vaccine. Many young adults require a booster.
- Polio – in 2002, no countries in Southeast Asia reported cases of polio. Only one booster is required as an adult for lifetime protection. Inactivated polio vaccine is safe during pregnancy.
- Typhoid – recommended unless your trip is less than a week and only to developed cities. The vaccine offers around 70% protection, lasts for two or three years and comes as a single shot. Tablets are also available; however, the injection is usually recommended as it has fewer side effects. Sore arm and fever may occur.
- Varicella – if you haven't had chickenpox, discuss this vaccination with your doctor.

Long-term travellers

These vaccinations are recommended for people travelling more than one month, or those at special risk:

- Japanese B Encephalitis – three injections in all. Booster recommended after two years. A sore arm and headache are the most common side effects. Rarely, an allergic reaction comprising hives and swelling can occur up to 10 days after any of the three doses.
- Meningitis – single injection. There are two types of vaccination: the quadrivalent vaccine gives two to three years protection; meningitis group C vaccine gives around 10 years protection. Recommended for long-term travellers aged under 25.
- Rabies – three injections in all. A booster after one year will provide 10 years of protection. Side effects are rare – occasionally a headache and sore arm.
- Tuberculosis – adult long-term travellers are usually recommended to have a TB skin test before and after travel, rather than vaccination. Only one vaccine is given in a lifetime.

ll available vaccines and will be able to give specific recommendations for you and your trip. The doctors will take into account factors such as past vaccination history, the length of your trip, activities you may be undertaking, and underlying medical conditions, such as pregnancy.

Most vaccines don't produce immunity until at least two weeks after they're given, so visit a doctor four to eight weeks before departure. Ask your doctor for an International Certificate of Vaccination (otherwise known as the yellow booklet), which will list all the vaccinations you've received. In the US, the yellow booklet is no longer issued, but it is highly unlikely the Vietnam authorities will ask for proof of vaccinations (unless you have recently been in a yellow-fever affected country).

For info on current immunisation recommendations for Vietnam, contact the international team of doctors at the **Family Medical Practice** (www.doctorkot.com) in Hanoi (p78) and HCMC (p325). They can provide the latest information on vaccinations, malaria and dengue-fever status, and offer general medical advice regarding Vietnam. See the boxed text opposite for possible vaccinations.

MEDICAL CHECKLIST

Recommended items for a personal medical kit:

- antifungal cream, eg Clotrimazole
- antibacterial cream, eg Muciprocin
- antibiotics for skin infections, eg Amoxicillin/Clavulanate or Cephalexin
- antibiotics for diarrhoea, eg Norfloxacin or Ciprofloxacin; Azithromycin for bacterial diarrhoea; and Tinidazole for giardiasis or amoebic dysentery
- antihistamines for allergies, eg Cetrizine for daytime and Promethazine for night
- anti-inflammatories, eg Ibuprofen
- antinausea medication, eg Prochlorperazine
- antiseptic for cuts and scrapes, eg Betadine
- antispasmodic for stomach cramps, eg Buscopa
- contraceptives
- decongestant for colds and flus, eg Pseudoephedrine
- DEET-based insect repellent
- diarrhoea 'stopper', eg Loperamide

- first-aid items such as scissors, plasters (Band Aids), bandages, gauze, thermometer (electronic, not mercury), sterile needles and syringes, safety pins and tweezers
- indigestion medication, eg Quick Eze or Mylanta
- iodine tablets (unless you are pregnant or have a thyroid problem) to purify water
- laxative, eg Coloxyl
- migraine medication (your personal brand), if a migraine sufferer
- oral-rehydration solution for diarrhoea, eg Gastrolyte
- paracetamol for pain
- permethrin (to impregnate clothing and mosquito nets) for repelling insects
- steroid cream for allergic/itchy rashes, eg 1% to 2% hydrocortisone
- sunscreen and hat
- throat lozenges
- thrush (vaginal yeast infection) treatment, eg Clotrimazole pessaries or Diflucan tablet
- urine alkalisation agent, eg Ural, if you're prone to urinary tract infections.

INTERNET RESOURCES

There is a wealth of travel health advice on the Internet. For further information, **LonelyPlanet.com** (www.lonelyplanet.com) is a good place to start. The **World Health Organization** (WHO; www.who.int/ith/) publishes a superb book called *International Travel & Health*, which is revised annually and is available free on line. Another website of general interest is **MD Travel Health** (www.mdtravelhealth .com), which provides complete travel health recommendations for every country and is updated daily. The **Centers for Disease Control and Prevention** (CDC; www.cdc.gov) website also has good general information.

FURTHER READING

Lonely Planet's *Healthy Travel – Asia & India* is a handy pocket-size book that is packed with useful information including pretrip planning, emergency first aid, immunisation and disease information and what to do if you get sick on the road.

Other good recommended references include *Traveller's Health* by Dr Richard Dawood as well as *Travelling Well* by Dr Deborah Mills – check out the website (www.travellingwell.com.au).

HEALTH

IN TRANSIT

DEEP VEIN THROMBOSIS (DVT)

Deep vein thrombosis (DVT) occurs when blood clots form in the legs during plane flights, chiefly because of prolonged immobility. The longer the flight, the greater the risk. Though most blood clots are reabsorbed uneventfully, some may break off and travel through the blood vessels to the lungs, where they may cause life-threatening complications.

The chief symptom of DVT is swelling or pain of the foot, ankle, or calf, usually on just one side. When a blood clot travels to the lungs, it may cause chest pain and difficulty in breathing. Travellers with any of these symptoms should immediately seek medical attention.

To prevent the development of DVT on long flights you should walk about the cabin, perform isometric compressions of the leg muscles (ie contract the leg muscles while sitting), drink plenty of fluids, and avoid alcohol and tobacco.

JET LAG & MOTION SICKNESS

Jet lag is common when crossing more than five time zones; it results in insomnia, fatigue, malaise or nausea. To avoid jet lag try drinking plenty of fluids (nonalcoholic) and eating light meals. Upon arrival, seek exposure to natural sunlight and readjust your schedule (for meals, sleep etc) as soon as possible.

Antihistamines such as dimenhydrinate (Dramamine) and meclizine (Antivert, Bonine) are usually the first choice for treating motion sickness. Their main side effect is drowsiness. A herbal alternative is ginger, which works like a charm for some people.

IN VIETNAM

AVAILABILITY OF HEALTH CARE

The significant improvement in Vietnam's economy has brought with it some major advances in public health. Rural areas can still pose a problem when it comes to finding good health care, however; although foreigners with hard cash will receive the best treatment available, even bars of gold cannot buy blood tests or X-rays when the local clinic doesn't even have a thermom-

eter or any aspirin. If you become seriously ill in rural Vietnam, get to Ho Chi Minh City (HCMC) or Hanoi as quickly as you can. If you need any type of surgery or other extensive treatment, don't hesitate to fly to Bangkok, Hong Kong or another renowned medical centre as soon as possible.

Government hospitals in Vietnam are overcrowded and basic. In order to treat foreigners, a facility needs to obtain a special license and so far only a few have been provided. The private clinics in Hanoi and HCMC should be your first port of call. They are familiar with the local resources and can organise evacuations if necessary. The contact details of the best medical facilities in Vietnam are listed in the HCMC (p78) and Hanoi (p325) chapters. These are the only cities where you are likely to find health facilities that come close to meeting the standard of developed countries.

Self-treatment may be appropriate if your problem is minor (eg traveller's diarrhoea), you are carrying the appropriate medication and you cannot attend a recommended clinic. If you think you may have a serious disease, especially malaria, do not waste time – travel to the nearest quality facility to receive attention. It is always better to be assessed by a doctor than to rely on self-treatment.

Buying medication over the counter is not recommended, as fake medication and poorly stored or out-of-date drugs are common. Check the expiry dates on any medicines you buy. If you need special medication then take it with you.

INFECTIOUS DISEASES
Dengue

This mosquito-borne disease is becoming increasingly problematic throughout Southeast Asia, especially in the cities. As there is no vaccine available it can only be prevented by avoiding mosquito bites. The mosquito that carries dengue bites day and night, so use insect avoidance measures at all times. Symptoms include high fever, severe headache and body ache (dengue was previously known as 'breakbone fever'). Some people develop a rash and experience diarrhoea. There is no specific treatment, just rest and paracetamol – do not take aspirin as it increases the likelihood of haemorrhaging. See a doctor to be diagnosed and monitored.

Filariasis

This is a mosquito-borne disease that is very common in the local population, yet very rare in travellers. Mosquito-avoidance measures are the best way to prevent this disease.

Hepatitis A

A problem throughout the region, this food- and water-borne virus infects the liver, causing jaundice (yellow skin and eyes), nausea and lethargy. There is no specific treatment for hepatitis A, you just need to allow time for the liver to heal. All travellers to Southeast Asia should be vaccinated against hepatitis A.

Hepatitis B

The only sexually transmitted disease that can be prevented by vaccination, hepatitis B is spread by body fluids, including sexual contact. In some parts of Southeast Asia up to 20% of the population are carriers of hepatitis B, and usually are unaware of this. The long-term consequences can include liver cancer and cirrhosis.

Hepatitis E

Hepatitis E is transmitted through contaminated food and water and has similar symptoms to hepatitis A, but is far less common. It is a severe problem in pregnant women and can result in the death of both mother and baby. There is currently no vaccine, and prevention is by following safe eating and drinking guidelines.

HIV

The official figures on the number of people with HIV/AIDS in Vietnam are vague, but they are on the rise. Health-education messages relating to HIV/AIDS can be seen all over the countryside, however the official line is that infection is largely limited to sex workers and drug users. Condoms are widely available throughout Vietnam.

Influenza

Present year-round in the tropics, influenza (flu) symptoms include high fever, muscle aches, runny nose, cough and sore throat. It can be very severe in people over the age of 65 or in those with underlying medical conditions such as heart disease or diabetes; vaccination is recommended for these indi-viduals. There is no specific treatment, just rest and paracetamol.

Japanese B Encephalitis

While a rare disease in travellers, at least 50,000 locals are infected with Japanese B Encephalitis each year in Southeast Asia. This viral disease is transmitted by mosquitoes. Most cases occur in rural areas and vaccination is recommended for travellers spending more than one month outside of cities. There is no treatment, and a third of infected people will die while another third will suffer permanent brain damage.

Malaria

For such a serious and potentially deadly disease, there is an enormous amount of misinformation concerning malaria. You must get expert advice as to whether your trip actually puts you at risk. Many parts of Vietnam, particularly city and resort areas, have minimal to no risk of malaria, and the risk of side effects from the tablets may outweigh the risk of getting the disease. For most rural areas, however, the risk of contracting the disease far outweighs the risk of any tablet side effects. Travellers to isolated areas in high-risk regions such as Ca Mau (p423) and Bac Lieu (p422) provinces, and the rural south, may like to carry a treatment dose of medication for use if symptoms occur. Remember that malaria can be fatal. Before you travel, seek medical advice on the right medication and dosage for you.

Malaria is caused by a parasite transmitted by the bite of an infected mosquito. The most important symptom of malaria is fever, but general symptoms such as headache, diarrhoea, cough, or chills may also occur. Diagnosis can only be made by taking a blood sample.

Two strategies should be combined to prevent malaria – mosquito avoidance, and antimalarial medications. Most people who catch malaria are taking inadequate or no antimalarial medication.

Travellers are advised to prevent mosquito bites by taking these steps:

- Choose accommodation with screens and fans (if not air-conditioned).
- Impregnate clothing with Permethrin in high-risk areas.
- Sleep under a mosquito net impregnated with Permethrin.

HEALTH

- Spray your room with insect repellent before going out for your evening meal.
- Use a DEET-containing insect repellent on exposed skin. Wash this off at night, as long as you are sleeping under a mosquito net. Natural repellents such as Citronella can be effective, but must be applied more frequently than products containing DEET.
- Use mosquito coils.
- Wear long sleeves and trousers in light colours.

MALARIA MEDICATION
There are a variety of medications available. The effectiveness of the Chloroquine and Paludrine combination is now limited in most of Southeast Asia. Common side effects include nausea (40% of people) and mouth ulcers. It is generally not recommended.

Lariam (Mefloquine) has received much bad press, some of it justified, some not. This weekly tablet suits many people. Serious side effects are rare but include depression, anxiety, psychosis and seizures. Anyone with a history of depression, anxiety, other psychological disorder, or epilepsy should not take Lariam. It is considered safe in the second and third trimesters of pregnancy. It is around 90% effective in most parts of Southeast Asia, but there is significant resistance in parts of northern Thailand, Laos and Cambodia. Tablets must be taken for four weeks after leaving the risk area.

Doxycycline, taken as a daily tablet, is a broad-spectrum antibiotic that has the added benefit of helping to prevent a variety of tropical diseases, including leptospirosis, tick-borne disease, typhus and melioidosis. The potential side effects include photosensitivity (a tendency to sunburn), thrush in women, indigestion, heartburn, nausea and interference with the contraceptive pill. More serious side effects include ulceration of the oesophagus – you can help prevent this by taking your tablet with a meal and a large glass of water, and never lying down within half an hour of taking it. It must be taken for four weeks after leaving the risk area.

Malarone is a new drug combining Atovaquone and Proguanil. Side effects are uncommon and mild, most commonly nausea and headaches. It is the best tablet for scuba divers and for those on short trips to high-risk areas. It must be taken for one week after leaving the risk area.

Derivatives of Artesunate are not suitable as a preventive medication. They are useful treatments under medical supervision.

A final option is to take no preventive medication but to have a supply of emergency medication should you develop the symptoms of malaria. This is less than ideal and you'll need to get to a good medical facility within 24 hours of developing a fever. If you choose this option the most effective and safest treatment is Malarone (four tablets once daily for three days). Other options include Mefloquine and Quinine but the side effects of these drugs at treatment doses make them less desirable. Fansidar is no longer recommended.

Measles
Measles remains a problem in some parts of Vietnam. This highly contagious bacterial infection is spread via coughing and sneezing. Many people born before 1966 are immune as they had the disease in childhood. Measles starts with a high fever and rash and can be complicated by pneumonia and brain disease. There is no specific treatment.

Rabies
This uniformly fatal disease is spread by the bite or lick of an infected animal – most commonly a dog or monkey. You should seek medical advice immediately after any animal bite and commence post-exposure treatment. Having a pretravel vaccination means the postbite treatment is greatly simplified. If an animal bites you, gently wash the wound with soap and water, and apply iodine based antiseptic. If you are not vaccinated you will need to receive rabies immunoglobulin as soon as possible.

Schistosomiasis
Schistosomiasis (also called bilharzia) is a tiny parasite that enters your skin after you've been swimming in contaminated water – travellers usually only get a light infection and hence have no symptoms. If you are concerned, you can be tested three months after exposure. On rare occasions travellers may develop 'Katayama fever' – this occurs some weeks after exposure, as the parasite passes through the lungs and causes an allergic reaction – symptoms are

SARS

In March 2003 the world's attention was drawn to the outbreak of an apparently new and serious respiratory illness that became known as SARS (Severe Acute Respiratory Syndrome). At the time of writing SARS appears to have been brought under control. Since the outbreak commenced, 8500 cases were confirmed, resulting in 800 deaths. The peak of disease activity was in early May 2003, when over 200 new cases were being reported daily. The outbreak started in the Chinese province of Guangdong in November 2002. By mid-March numerous cases of an unusually virulent respiratory virus were being reported in Hong Kong, Vietnam, Singapore and Canada. The World Health Organization (WHO) soon issued a global alert to health authorities and the public. Although this helped to bring the disease under control, it also resulted in widespread panic, and the cost of SARS to countries in the Far East as a result of lost tourism and trade was estimated as at least US$30 billion.

The cause of SARS was identified in April 2003 – a new virus unlike any other previously known in humans or animals. The symptoms of SARS are identical to many other respiratory infections, namely high fever and cough. The case definition of SARS is a person with fever and cough who has travelled to an infected area or had close contact with an infected individual within the previous 10 days. There is no specific quick test for SARS but certain blood test and chest X-ray results offer support for the diagnosis. There is no specific treatment available and death from respiratory failure occurs in around 10% of patients. Fortunately it appears it is not as easy to catch SARS as was initially thought. Wearing masks has limited effectiveness and is not generally recommended.

The risk of contracting SARS is extremely low. However, there are still fundamental questions to be answered about SARS – where did it come from, will it come back and can we develop a rapid test or treatment for it? At least another year will be needed to see whether SARS has become established in our ecosystem.

oughing and fever. Schistosomiasis is easy treated with medications.

TDs

exually transmitted diseases include erpes, warts, syphilis, gonorrhoea and hlamydia. People carrying these diseases ften have no signs of infection. Condoms ill prevent gonorrhoea and chlamydia but ot warts or herpes. If after a sexual encounter you develop any rash, lumps, discharge r pain when passing urine seek immediate nedical attention. If you have been sexully active during your travels have an STD heck on your return home.

While abstinence from sexual contact is ne only 100% effective prevention, using ondoms is also effective. Condoms are idely available throughout Vietnam; when urchasing, ensure the package hasn't been :ored in the sun as the rubber could have eteriorated.

uberculosis

uberculosis (TB) is rare in short-term -avellers. Medical and aid workers, and ong-term travellers who have significant

contact with the local population should take precautions, however. Vaccination is usually only given to children under the age of five, but adults at risk are recommended pre- and post-travel TB testing. The main symptoms are fever, cough, weight loss, night sweats and tiredness.

Typhoid

This serious bacterial infection is spread via food and water. It gives a high, slowly progressive fever and headache, and may be accompanied by a dry cough and stomach pain. It is diagnosed by blood tests and treated with antibiotics. Vaccination is recommended for all travellers spending more than a week in Southeast Asia, or travelling outside of the major cities. Be aware that vaccination is not 100% effective so you must still be careful with what you eat and drink.

Typhus

Murine typhus is spread by the bite of a flea whereas scrub typhus is spread via a mite. These diseases are rare in travellers. Symptoms include fever, muscle pains and

---

DRINKING WATER

The number one rule is *be careful of the water*. Ice can be particularly risky; if you don't know for certain that the water is safe, assume the worst. However, a lot of the ice in Vietnam comes from factories introduced by the French, so it is as safe as the bottled water. Following these rules will help you avoid water-borne diseases.

■ Never drink tap water.

■ Bottled water is generally safe – check the seal is intact at purchase.

■ Avoid fresh juices – they may have been watered down.

■ Boiling water is the most efficient method of purifying it.

■ The best chemical purifier is iodine. It should not be used by pregnant women or those people who suffer with thyroid problems.

■ Water filters should filter out viruses. Ensure your filter has a chemical barrier such as iodine and a small pore size, ie less than four microns.

---

a rash. You can avoid these diseases by following general insect-avoidance measures. Doxycycline will also prevent them.

TRAVELLER'S DIARRHOEA

Traveller's diarrhoea is by far the most common problem affecting travellers – between 30% and 50% of people will suffer from it within two weeks of starting their trip. In over 80% of cases, traveller's diarrhoea is caused by a bacteria (there are numerous potential culprits), and therefore responds promptly to treatment with antibiotics. Treatment with antibiotics will depend on your situation – how sick you are, how quickly you need to get better, where you are etc.

Traveller's diarrhoea is defined as the passage of more than three watery bowel-actions within 24 hours, plus at least one other symptom such as fever, cramps, nausea, vomiting or feeling generally unwell.

Treatment consists of staying well-hydrated. Rehydration solutions like Gastrolyte are the best for this. Antibiotics such as Norfloxacin, Ciprofloxacin or Azithromycin will kill the bacteria quickly.

Loperamide is just a 'stopper' and doesn't get to the cause of the problem. It can be helpful, for example if you have to go on a long bus ride. Don't take Loperamide if you have a fever, or blood in your stools. Seek medical attention quickly if you do not respond to an appropriate antibiotic.

Amoebic Dysentery

Amoebic dysentery is very rare in travellers but is often misdiagnosed by poor-quality

labs in Southeast Asia. Symptoms are similar to bacterial diarrhoea, ie fever, blood diarrhoea and generally feeling unwell. You should always seek reliable medical care if you have blood in your diarrhoea. Treatment involves two drugs: Tinidazole or Metroniadzole to kill the parasite in your gut and then a second drug to kill the cysts. If left untreated complications such as liver or gut abscesses can occur.

Giardiasis

Giardia lamblia is a parasite that is relatively common in travellers. Symptoms include nausea, bloating, excess gas, fatigue and intermittent diarrhoea. 'Eggy' burps are often attributed solely to giardiasis, but work in Nepal has shown that they are not specific to this infection. The parasite will eventually go away if left untreated but this can take months. The treatment of choice is Tinidazole, with Metronidazole being a second line option.

ENVIRONMENTAL HAZARDS
Air Pollution

Air pollution, particularly vehicle pollution, is an increasing problem in most of Southeast Asia's major cities. If you have severe respiratory problems speak with your doctor before travelling to any heavily polluted urban centres.

This pollution also causes minor respiratory problems such as sinusitis, dry throat and irritated eyes. If troubled by the pollution leave the city for a few days and get some fresh air.

ood

ating in restaurants is the biggest risk
ctor for contracting traveller's diar-
loea. Ways to avoid it include eating only
eshly cooked food, and avoiding shellfish
nd food that has been sitting around in
uffets. Peel all fruit, cook vegetables, and
oak salads in iodine water for at least 20
inutes. Eat in busy restaurants with a high
rnover of customers.

eat

 any parts of Southeast Asia are hot and
umid throughout the year. For most people
takes at least two weeks to adapt to the
ot climate. Swelling of the feet and ankles
common, as are muscle cramps caused by
xcessive sweating. Prevent these by avoid-
g dehydration and excessive activity in
e heat. Take it easy when you first arrive.
on't eat salt tablets (they aggravate the
ut) but do drink rehydration solution and
at salty food. Treat cramps by stopping
ctivity, resting, rehydrating with double-
rength rehydration solution and gently
retching.

Dehydration is the main contributor to
eat exhaustion. Symptoms include feel-
g weak, headache, irritability, nausea or
omiting, sweaty skin, a fast, weak pulse
nd a normal or slightly elevated body tem-
erature. Treatment involves getting out of
e heat and/or sun, fanning the victim and
pplying cool wet cloths to the skin, laying
e victim flat with their legs raised and
hydrating with water containing a quarter
f a teaspoon of salt per litre. Recovery is
sually rapid, though it is common to feel
eak for some days afterwards.

Heatstroke is a serious medical emer-
ency. Symptoms come on suddenly and
clude weakness, nausea, a hot dry body
ith a body temperature of over 41°C,
izziness, confusion, loss of coordination,
eizures and eventually collapse and loss
f consciousness. Seek medical help and
ommence cooling by getting the person
ut of the heat, removing their clothes, fan-
ing them and applying cool wet cloths or
e to their body, especially to the groin
nd armpits.

Prickly heat is a common skin rash in
e tropics, caused by sweat being trapped
nder the skin. The result is an itchy rash
f tiny lumps. Treat by moving out of the

heat and into an air-conditioned area for
a few hours and by having cool showers.
Creams and ointments clog the skin so they
should be avoided. Locally bought prickly
heat powder can be helpful.

Tropical fatigue is common in long-term
expats based in the tropics. It's rarely due
to disease and is caused by the climate,
inadequate mental rest, excessive alcohol
intake and the demands of daily work in a
different culture.

Insect Bites & Stings

Bedbugs don't carry disease but their bites
are very itchy. They live in the cracks of
furniture and walls and then migrate to the
bed at night to feed on you. You can treat
the itch with an antihistamine. Lice inhabit
various parts of your body but most commonly your head and pubic area. Transmis-
sion is via close contact with an infected
person, although body lice can come from
contaminated bedclothes. They can be difficult to treat and you may need numerous
applications of an antilice shampoo such as
Permethrin, or in the case of body lice, with
medicated creams or ointments. Pubic lice
are usually contracted from sexual contact.

Ticks are contracted during walks in
rural areas. They are commonly found behind the ears, on the belly and in armpits.
If you have had a tick bite and experience
symptoms such as a rash (at the site of the
bite or elsewhere), fever or muscle aches
you should see a doctor. Doxycycline prevents tick-borne diseases.

Leeches are found in humid forest areas.
They do not transmit any disease but their
bites are often intensely itchy for weeks
afterwards and can easily become infected.
Apply an iodine-based antiseptic to any
leech bite to help prevent infection.

Bee and wasp stings mainly cause problems for people who are allergic to them.
Anyone with a serious bee or wasp allergy
should carry an injection of adrenaline (eg
an Epipen) for emergency treatment. For
others pain is the main problem – apply ice
to the sting and take painkillers.

Most jellyfish in Southeast Asian waters
are not dangerous, just irritating. First aid
for jellyfish stings involves pouring vinegar
onto the affected area to neutralise the poison. Do not rub sand or water onto the
stings. Take painkillers, and anyone who

feels ill in any way after being stung should seek medical advice. Take local advice if there are dangerous jellyfish around and keep out of the water.

Parasites

Numerous parasites are common in local populations in Southeast Asia; however, most of these are rare in travellers. The two rules to follow if you wish to avoid parasitic infections are to wear shoes and to avoid eating raw food, especially fish, pork and vegetables. A number of parasites are transmitted via the skin by walking barefoot including strongyloides, hookworm and cutaneous larva migrans.

Skin Problems

Fungal rashes are common in humid climates. There are two common fungal rashes that affect travellers. The first occurs in moist areas that get less air such as the groin, armpits and between the toes. It starts as a red patch that slowly spreads and is usually itchy. Treatment involves keeping the skin dry, avoiding chafing and using an antifungal cream such as Clotrimazole or Lamisil. *Tinea versicolor* is also common – this fungus causes small, light-coloured patches, most commonly on the back, chest and shoulders. Consult a doctor.

Cuts and scratches become easily infected in humid climates. Take meticulous care of any cuts and scratches to prevent complications such as abscesses. Immediately wash all wounds in clean water and apply antiseptic. If you develop signs of infection (increasing pain and redness) see a doctor. Divers and surfers should be particularly careful with coral cuts as they become easily infected.

Snakes

Southeast Asia is home to many species of both poisonous and harmless snakes. Assume all snakes are poisonous and never try to catch one. Always wear boots and long pants if walking in an area that may have snakes. First-aid in the event of a snakebite involves pressure immobilisation via an elastic bandage firmly wrapped around the affected limb, starting at the bite site and working up towards the chest. The bandage should not be so tight that the circulation is cut off, and the fingers or toes should be kept free so the circulation can be checke Immobilise the limb with a splint and carr the victim to medical attention. Do not us tourniquets or try to suck the venom ou Antivenom is available for most species.

Sunburn

Even on a cloudy day sunburn can occu rapidly. Always use a strong sunscreen (a least factor 30), making sure to reapply afte a swim, and always wear a wide-brimme hat and sunglasses outdoors. Avoid lying i the sun during the hottest part of the da (from 10am to 2pm). If you become sun burnt stay out of the sun until you hav recovered, apply cool compresses and tak painkillers for the discomfort. One percen hydrocortisone cream applied twice daily also helpful.

WOMEN'S HEALTH

Pregnant women should receive specialise advice before travelling. The ideal time t travel is in the second trimester (betwee 16 and 28 weeks), during which the risk o pregnancy-related problems is at its lowe and pregnant women generally feel at thei best. During the first trimester there is risk of miscarriage and in the third trimes ter complications such as premature labou and high blood pressure are possible. It wise to travel with a companion.

Always carry a list of quality medic facilities available at your destination an ensure you continue your standard ante natal care at these facilities. Avoid rur travel in areas with poor transportation an medical facilities. Most of all, ensure trav insurance covers all pregnancy-related pos sibilities, including premature labour.

Malaria is a high-risk disease in preg nancy. WHO recommends that pregnar women do *not* travel to areas that hav Chloroquine-resistant malaria. None the more effective antimalarial drugs ar completely safe in pregnancy.

Traveller's diarrhoea can quickly lead t dehydration and result in inadequate bloo flow to the placenta. Many of the drug used to treat various diarrhoea bugs are n recommended in pregnancy. Azithromyci is considered safe.

In the urban areas of Southeast Asi supplies of sanitary products are readil available. Birth control options may b

mited so bring adequate supplies of con-
traception. Heat, humidity and antibiotics
can all contribute to thrush. Treatment is
with antifungal creams and pessaries such
as Clotrimazole. A practical alternative is a
single tablet of Fluconazole (Diflucan). Urin-
ry tract infections can be precipitated by
dehydration or long bus journeys without
toilet stops; bring suitable antibiotics.

TRADITIONAL MEDICINE

A number of traditional medical treatments
are practised in Vietnam. Herbal medicine,
much of it imported from China, is widely
available and sometimes very effective. As
with Western medicine, self-diagnosis is
not advisable – see a doctor. Traditional
Chinese doctors are found wherever a
large Chinese community exists, including
HCMC, Hanoi and Hoi An.

If you visit traditional Chinese doctors,
you might be surprised by what they discover about your body. For example, the
doctor will almost certainly take your
pulse and then may perhaps tell you that
you have a 'slippery' or 'thready' pulse.
They have identified more than 30 different kinds of pulse. A pulse could be empty,
prison, leisurely, bowstring, irregular or
even regularly irregular. The doctor may
then examine your tongue to see if it is slippery, dry, pale, greasy, has a thick coating
or possibly no coating at all. The doctor,
having discovered your ailment, such as wet
heat, as evidenced by a slippery pulse and a
red greasy tongue, will prescribe the proper
herbs for your condition.

Once you have a diagnosis you may be
treated by moxibustion, a traditional treatment whereby various types of herbs, rolled
into what looks like a ball of fluffy cotton,
are held near the skin and ignited. A slight
variation of this method is to place the herb
on a slice of ginger and then ignite it. The
idea is to apply the maximum amount of
heat possible without burning the patient.
This heat treatment is supposed to be very
good for diseases such as arthritis.

It is common to see Vietnamese people
with long bands of red welts on their necks,
foreheads and backs. Don't worry, this is
not some kind of hideous skin disease, but
rather a treatment known as cao gio, literally 'scrape wind'. In traditional Vietnamese
folk medicine, many illnesses are attributed
to 'poisonous wind', which can be released
by applying eucalyptus oil or tiger balm
and scraping the skin with a spoon or coin,
thus raising the welts. The results aren't
pretty, but the locals say this treatment is
good for the common cold, fatigue, headaches and other ailments. Whether the cure
hurts less than the disease is something one
can only judge from experience.

Another technique to battle bad breezes
is called giac hoi. This one employs suction
cups, typically made of bamboo or glass,
which are placed on the patient's skin. A
burning piece of alcohol-soaked cotton is
briefly put inside the cup to drive out the
air before it is applied. As the cup cools,
a partial vacuum is produced, leaving a
nasty-looking but harmless red circular
mark on the skin, which goes away in a
few days. Looks pretty weird on the forehead though!

There is some solid evidence attesting to
the efficacy of acupuncture. Some major
surgical operations have been performed
using acupuncture as the only anaesthetic
(this works best on the head). In this case,
a small electric current (from batteries) is
passed through the needles.

If done properly the practice doesn't
hurt. Knowing where to insert the needle
is crucial. Acupuncturists have identified
more than 2000 insertion points, but only
about 150 are commonly used. The exact
mechanism by which it works is not fully
understood. Practitioners talk of energy
channels or meridians that connect the needle insertion point to the particular organ,
gland or joint being treated. The acupuncture point is sometimes quite far from the
area of the body being treated.

Nonsterile acupuncture needles pose a
genuine health risk in this era of AIDS. You
would be wise to purchase your own acupuncture needles if you plan on having this
treatment in Vietnam.

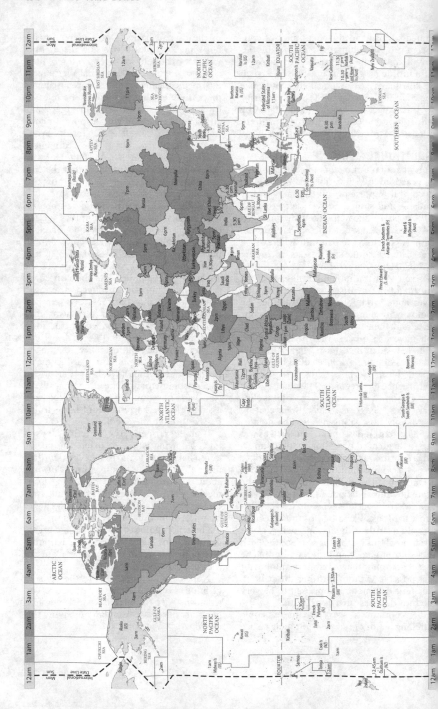

Language

CONTENTS

LANGUAGES IN VIETNAM

Vietnamese is the official language of Vietnam, and it is spoken throughout the country. There are dialectical differences between the north, central and southern regions. There are also dozens of different languages spoken by the various ethnic minorities, particularly in the Central Highlands and in the far north of the country. Khmer, the Cambodian language, is spoken in parts of the Mekong Delta, and Lao and various Chinese dialects are evident in areas bordering Laos and China.

The Vietnamese people's knowledge of foreign languages reflects their country's relationship with foreign powers – cordial or otherwise – in recent history.

Much of Vietnam's elder generation still speak French, while many middle-aged Vietnamese speak Russian and other Eastern

European languages – many of these people spent time in countries like Russia, Bulgaria and the former East Germany during the Cold War (at least until it thawed in the late 1980s). Today, however, Vietnam's youth has fully embraced the English language. A fair number of young people also study Japanese, French and other Western European languages.

The most widely spoken foreign languages in Vietnam are Chinese (Cantonese and Mandarin), English and French, more or less in that order. People in their 50s and older (who grew up during the colonial period) are much more likely to understand some French than southerners of the successive generation, for whom English was indispensable for professional and commercial contacts with the Americans. Some southern Vietnamese men – former combat interpreters – speak a quaint form of English peppered with all sorts of charming southern-American expressions such as 'y'all come back' and 'it ain't worth didley squat', pronounced with a perceptible drawl. Apparently, they worked with Americans from the deep south, carefully studied their pronunciation and diligently learned every nuance.

Many of the Vietnamese who can speak English – especially former South Vietnamese soldiers and officials – learned it while working with the Americans during the war. After reunification, almost all of them spent periods of time ranging from a few months to 15 years in 're-education camps'. Many of these former South Vietnamese soldiers and officials will be delighted to renew contact with Americans, with whose compatriots they spent so much time, often in very difficult circumstances, more than half a lifetime ago.

These days, almost everyone has a desire to learn English. If you're looking to make contacts with English students, the best place is at the basic food stalls in university areas.

Spoken Chinese (both Cantonese and Mandarin) is making a definite comeback after years of being supressed. The large number of free-spending tourists and investors from Taiwan and Hong Kong provide the chief motivation for studying Chinese. In addition, cross-border trade with mainland China has been increasing rapidly and those who are able to speak Chinese are well positioned to profit from it.

After reunification, the teaching of Russian was stressed all over the country. With the collapse of the USSR in 1991, all interest in studying Russian ground to a screeching halt. Most Vietnamese who bothered to learn the language have either forgotten it or are in the process of forgetting it.

VIETNAMESE

The Vietnamese language *(Kinh)* is a fusion of Mon-Khmer, Tai and Chinese elements. Vietnamese derived a significant percentage of its basic words from the non-tonal Mon-Khmer languages. From the Tai languages, came certain grammatical elements and tonality. Chinese gave Vietnamese most of its literary, technical and governmental vocabulary, as well as its traditional writing system.

The following list of words and phrases will help get you started. If you'd like a more comprehensive guide to the language, pick up a copy of Lonely Planet's pocket-sized *Vietnamese Phrasebook*.

The variations in vocabulary between the Vietnamese of the north and that of the south is indicated in this chapter by (N) and (S) respectively.

WRITTEN VIETNAMESE

For centuries, the Vietnamese language was written in standard Chinese characters *(chữ nho)*. Around the 13th century, the Vietnamese devised their own writing system called *chữ nôm* (or just *nôm*), which was created by combining two Chinese words or by using single Chinese characters for their phonetic value. Both writing systems were in use until the 20th century – official business and scholarship was conducted in *chữ nho*, while *chữ nôm* was used for popular literature. The Latin-based *quốc ngữ* script, widely used since WWI, was developed in the 17th century by Alexandre de Rhodes (see the box on this page). *Quốc ngữ* served to undermine the position of

ALEXANDRE DE RHODES

One of the most illustrious of the early missionaries was the brilliant French Jesuit scholar Alexandre de Rhodes (1591–1660). De Rhodes first preached in Vietnamese only six months after arriving in the country in 1627, and he is most recognised for his work in devising *quốc ngữ*, the Latin-based phonetic alphabet in which Vietnamese is written to this day. By replacing Chinese characters with *quốc ngữ*, de Rhodes facilitated the propagation of the gospel to a wide audience.

Over the course of his long career, de Rhodes travelled back and forth between Hanoi, Macau, Rome and Paris, seeking support and funding for his missionary activities and battling both Portuguese colonial opposition and the intractable Vatican bureaucracy. In 1645, he was sentenced to death for illegally entering Vietnam to proselytise, but was expelled instead; two of the priests with him were beheaded.

For his contributions, de Rhodes gained the highest respect from the Vietnamese (in the south, anyway), who called him *cha caả* (father). A memorial statue of de Rhodes stands in central Saigon.

Mandarin officials, whose power was based on traditional scholarship in *chữ nho* and *chữ nôm*, scripts that were largely inaccessible to the masses.

The Vietnamese treat every syllable as an independent word, so 'Saigon' is spelt 'Sai Gon' and 'Vietnam' is written as 'Viet Nam'. Foreigners aren't too comfortable with this system – we prefer to read 'London' rather than 'Lon Don'. This leads to the notion that Vietnamese is a 'monosyllabic language', where every syllable represents an independent word. This idea appears to hark back to the Chinese writing system, where every syllable is represented by an independent character and each character is treated as a meaningful word in its own right. In reality, Vietnamese appears to be polysyllabic, like English. However, writing systems do influence people's perceptions of their own language, so the Vietnamese themselves will insist that their language is monosyllabic – it's a debate probably not worth pursuing.

PRONUNCIATION

Most of the names of the letters of the *quốc ngữ* alphabet are pronounced like the letters of the French alphabet. Dictionaries are alphabetised as in English except that each vowel/tone combination is treated as a different letter.

Most of the consonants of the Romanised Vietnamese alphabet are pronounced more or less as they are in English with a few exceptions, and Vietnamese makes no use of the English letters 'f', 'j', 'w' and 'z'.

To help you make sense of what is (for non-Vietnamese) a very tricky writing system, the words and phrases in this language guide include pronunciations that use a written form more familiar to English speakers. For example, Vietnamese **d** and **gi-** are represented with 'z', **đ** with 'd', **ph-** with 'f', **x** with 's', **-ng** with 'm', **-nh** with 'ny' etc.

The same symbols as *quốc ngữ* are used for marking the tones.

c	as an unaspirated 'k'
đ	(with crossbar) a hard 'd' as in 'do'
d	(without crossbar) as the 'z' in 'zoo' (north); as the 'y' in 'yes' (south)
gi-	as a 'z' (north); as 'y' (south)
kh-	as the 'ch' in German *buch*
ng-	as the '-nga-' sound in 'long ago'
nh-	as the 'ni' in 'onion'
ph-	as in 'pharmacy'
r	as 'z' (north); as 'r' (south)
s	as 's' (north); as 'sh' (south)
tr-	as 'ch' (north); as 'tr' (south)
th-	a strongly aspirated 't'
x	like an 's'
-ch	like a 'k'
-ng	as the 'ng' in 'long' but with the lips closed; sounds like English 'm'
-nh	as the 'ng' in 'sing'

TONES

The hardest part of studying Vietnamese for westerners is learning to differentiate between the tones. There are six tones in spoken Vietnamese. Thus, every syllable in Vietnamese can be pronounced six different ways. For example, depending on the tones, the word *ma* can be read to mean 'phantom', 'but', 'mother', 'rice seedling', 'tomb' or 'horse'.

The six tones of spoken Vietnamese are represented by five diacritical marks in the written language (the first tone is left unmarked). These should not be confused with the four other diacritical marks that are used to indicate special consonants and vowels.

The following examples show the six different tone representations:

TONE NAME		EXAMPLE	
dấu ngang	*ma*		'ghost'
dấu sắc	*má*		'mother'
dấu huyền	*mà*		'which'
dấu nặng	*mạ*		'rice seedling'
dấu hỏi	*mả*		'tomb'
dấu ngã	*mã*		'horse'

A visual representation looks something like this:

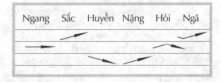

GRAMMAR

Vietnamese grammar is fairly straightforward, with a wide variety of possible sentence structures. Nouns have no masculine, feminine or plural forms and verbs have only one form regardless of gender, person or tense. Instead, tool words and classifiers are used to show a word's relationship to its neighbours. For example, in the expression *con mèo (của) tôi* (my cat), *con* is the classifier, *mèo* is the noun, *của* means 'of/belong to' (and can be omitted), and *tôi* is the personal pronoun 'I'.

PROPER NAMES

Most Vietnamese names consist of a family name, a middle name and a given name, in that order. Thus, if Henry David Thoreau had been Vietnamese, he would have been named Thoreau David Henry and would have been addressed as Mr Henry – people are called by their given name, but to do this without using the title Mr, Mrs or Miss is considered as expressing either great intimacy or arrogance of the sort a superior would use with his or her inferior.

In Vietnamese, Mr is *Ông* if the man is of your grandparents' generation, *Bác* if he is of your parents' age, *Chú* if he is younger than your parents and *Anh* if he is in his teens or early 20s. Mrs is *Bà* if the woman is of your grandparents' age and *Bác* if she is of your parents' generation or younger. Miss is *Chị* or *Em* unless the woman is very young, in which case *Cô* might be more appropriate. Other titles of respect are *Thầy* (Buddhist monk or male teacher), *Bà* (Buddhist nun), *Cha* (Catholic priest) and *Cô* (Catholic nun).

There are 300 or so family names in use in Vietnam, the most common of which is Nguyen (which is pronounced something like 'nwee-en'). About half of all Vietnamese have the surname Nguyen! When women marry, they usually (but not always) take their husband's family name. The middle name may be purely ornamental, may indicate the sex of its bearer or may be used by all the male members of a given family. A person's given name is carefully chosen to form a harmonious and meaningful ensemble with their family and middle names and with the names of other family members.

PRONOUNS
I
| *tôi* | doy |

you
ông (to an older man)	om
bà (to an older woman)	bà
anh (to a man your own age)	ang
chị (to a woman your own age)	chẹe

he
| *anh ấy* | ang áy |

she
| *chị ấy/cô ấy* | chẹe áy/ko áy |

we
| *chúng tôi* | chóom doy |

they
| *họ* | hạw |

ACCOMMODATION
Where is there a (cheap) ...?
đâu có ... (rẻ tiền)?
dow káw ... (rải dee-èn)?

camping ground
| *đất trại* | dút trại |

hotel
| *khách sạn* | kát sạn |

guesthouse
| *nhà khách* | nyà kát |

What is the address?
Địa chỉ là gì?
dee-ạ chée là zèe?

Could you write the address down, please?
Bạn có thể viết giùm địa chỉ được không?
bạn káw tảy vee-ét zòom dee-ạ chée dur-ẹrk kom?

I need to leave at ... o'clock (tomorrow morning).
Tôi phải đi lúc ... giờ (sáng mai).
doy fải dee lóop ... zèr (sáng mai)

How much does a room cost?
Giá một phòng là bao nhiêu?
zá mọt fòm là bow nyoo?

I'd like (a) ...
Tôi muốn ...
doy moón ...

bed
| *cái giường* | gái zur-èrng |

single room
| *phòng đơn* | fòm dern |

double-bed
| *giường đôi* | zur-èrng do-ee |

room
| *phòng* | fòm |

room with two beds
| *phòng gồm hai giường ngủ* | fòm gòm hai zur-èrng ngòo |

room with a bathroom
| *phòng có phòng tắm* | fòm kó fòm túm |

to share a dorm
| *ở chung phòng nội trú* | ẻr choom fòm nọ-ee tróo |

air-conditioning
| *máy lạnh* | máy lạng |

bathroom
| *phòng tắm* | fòm dúm |

blanket
| *mền* | mèn |

fan
| *quạt máy* | gwạt máy |

hot water
| *nước nóng* | nur-érk nóm |

laundry
| *giặt ủi* | zạt óo-ee |

mosquito net
| *màng* | màng |

reception
| *tiếp tân* | dee-ép tun |

MAKING A RESERVATION
(for written and phone inquiries)

To ...
| *Đến ...* | dén ... |

From ...
| *Từ ...* | tùr ... |

Date
| *ngày tháng* | ngày táng |

I'd like to book ...
| *Làm ơn cho tôi* | làm ern jaw doy |
| *đặt trước một ...* | dụt trur-érk mọt ... |

in the name of ...
| *tên là ...* | den là ... |

from ...
| *Từ ...* | tùr ... |

to ...
| *Đến ...* | dén ... |

credit card
| *thẻ tín dụng* | táir dín zọom |

number
| *số* | só |

expiry date
| *hết hàng* | hét hàng |

---

room
| *phòng* | fòm |

room key
| *chìa khóa phòng* | chèe-a kwá fòm |

1st class room
| *phòng loại 1* | fòm lwại mọt |

2nd class room
| *phòng loại 2* | fòm lwại hai |

sheet
| *ra trải giường* | ra trãi zur-èrng |

toilet
| *nhà vệ sinh* | nyà vạy sing |

toilet paper
| *giấy vệ sinh* | záy vạy sing |

towel
| *khăn tắm* | kún dúm |

How much is it ...?
| *Giá bao nhiêu ...?* | zá bow nyoo ...? |

per night
| *mọt đêm* | một dem |

per person
| *mọt người* | một ngùr-ee |

May I see it?
Tôi có thể xem phòng được không?
doy kó tảy sem fòm dur-ẹrk kom?

Where is the bathroom?
Phòng tắm ở đâu?
fòm dúm ẻr dow?

Where is the toilet?
Nhà vệ sinh ở đâu?
nyà vạy sing ẻr dow?

I'm leaving today.
Hôm nay tôi rời đay.
hom nay doy rèr-ee day

We're leaving tomorrow.
Ngày mai chúng tôi rời đay.
ngày mai chóom doy rèr-ee day

CONVERSATION & ESSENTIALS

Hello.
| *Xin chào.* | sin jòw |

Goodbye.
| *Tạm biệt.* | dụm bee-ẹt |

Yes.
| *Vâng.* (N)/*Dạ.* (S) | vang/yạ |

No.
| *Không.* | kom |

Please.
| *Làm ơn.* | làm ern |

Thank you.
| *Cảm ơn.* | kảm ern |

You're welcome.
| *Không có chi.* | kom kó chee |

Excuse me. (often used before questions)
| *Xin lỗi.* | sin lõ-ee |

Sorry.
| *Xin lỗi.* | sin lõ-ee |

How are you?
| *Có khỏe không?* | káw kwảỉr kom? |

Fine, thank you.
| *Khỏe, cảm ơn.* | kwảỉr kảm ern |

Good night.
| *Chúc ngủ ngon.* | chóop ngỏo ngon |

What's your name?
| *Tên là gì?* | den là zèe? |

My name is ...
| *Tên tôi là ...* | den doy là ... |

Where are you from?
| *Bạn từ đâu đến?* | bạn tùr dow dén? |

I'm from ...
| *Tôi đến từ ...* | doy dén tùr ... |

I like ...
| *Tôi thích ...* | doy tít |

I don't like ...
| *Tôi không thích ...* | doy kom tít |

I want ...
| *Tôi muốn ...* | doy móon ... |

I don't want ...
| *Tôi không muốn ...* | doy kom móon ... |

DIRECTIONS

Where is ...?
| *ở đâu ...?* | ẻr dow ...? |

EMERGENCIES

Help!
Cứu tôi! cứr-oo doy!
There's been an accident!
Có tai nạn! káw tai nạn!
I'm lost.
Tôi bị lạc đường. doi bẹc lạk dur-èrng
Leave me alone!
Thôi! toy!
Thief!
Ăn cắp! un gúp!
Pickpocket!
Móc túi! móp tóo-ee

Please call ...
Làm ơn gọi ... làm ern gọi ...
  an ambulance
  xe cứu thương sair cứr-oo tur-erng
  a doctor
  bác sĩ bák sẽe
  the police
  công an gom an

Go straight ahead.
Thẳng tới trước. tủng dér-ee trur-érk
Turn left.
Sang trái. sang trái
Turn right.
Sang phải. sang fải
at the corner
ở góc đường ẻr góp dur-èrng
at the traffic lights
tại đèn giao thông tại dèn zow tom
behind
đằng sau dùng sow
in front of
đằng trước dùng trur-érk
far
xa sa
near (to)
gần gùn
opposite
đối diện dó-ee zee-ẹn

beach
bãi biển bãi bee-én
bridge
cầu ków
island
đảo dỏw
main square
quảng trường gwảng trur-èrng
  chính jíng

market
chợ trường jẹr trur-èrng
mountain
núi nóo-ee
quay
bến tàu bén dòw
river
sông som
sea
biển bee-én
square (in a city)
công viên gom vee-en
temple
chùa chòo-a
boulevard
đại lộ dại lọ
street
phố/đường (N/S) fó/dur-èrng
north
bắc búk
south
nam nam
east
đông dom
west
tây day

SIGNS

Lối Vào	Entrance
Lối Ra	Exit
Hướng Dẫn	Information
Mở	Open
Đóng	Closed
Cấm	Prohibited
Cảnh Sát/Công An	Police
Nhà Vệ Sinh	Toilets/WC
Đàn Ông	Men
Phụ Nữ	Women

HEALTH

I'm sick.
Tôi bị đau.
doy bẹc dow
It hurts here.
Chỗ bị đau ở đây.
jõ bẹc dow ẻr day
Please take me to the hospital.
Làm ơn đưa tôi bệnh viện.
làm ern dur-a doy bẹn vee-ẹn

dentist
nha sĩ nya sẽe

doctor
bác sĩ — bák sẽe
pharmacy
nhà thuốc tây — nyà tóok day

I'm ...
Tôi bị ... — doy bẹe ...
  asthmatic
  suyễn — swee-ẽn
  diabetic
  bệnh đái đường — bẹn dái dur-èrng
  epileptic
  động kinh — dọm king

I'm allergic to ...
Tôi bị dị ứng với ... — doy bẹe zẹe úrng vér-ee ...
  antibiotics
  thuốc kháng sinh — tóok káng sing
  aspirin
  thuốc cảm/át pi rin — tóok kảm/át pi rin
  penicillin
  trụ sinh — trọo sing
  bees
  ong — om
  peanuts
  đậu phộng — dọw fọm

backache
đau lưng — dow lưrng
diarrhoea
tiêu chảy — dee-oo chảy
dizziness
chóng mặt — chóm mụt
fever
bệnh sốt — bẹn sót
headache
nhức đầu — nyúrk dow
malaria
sốt rét — sót rét
nausea
buồn nôn — bòon non
stomachache
đau bụng — dow bọom
toothache
nhức răng — nyúrk rung
vomiting
ói — óy
antiseptic
thuốc khử trùng — tóok kùr tròong
condoms
bao dương vật — bao zur-erng vạt
contraceptive
cách ngừa thai — kák ngùr-a tai
insect repellent
thuốc chống muỗi — tóok chóm mõo-ee

medicine
y thuốc — ee tóok
mosquito coils
hương đốt chống muỗi (N) — hur-erng dért chóm mõo-ee
nhang chống muỗi (S) — nyang chóm mõo-ee
sanitary pads
băng vệ sinh — bung vệ sinh
sunblock cream
kem chống nắng — kem chóm núng
tampons
ống băng vệ sinh — óm bung vệ sinh

LANGUAGE DIFFICULTIES
Do you speak English?
Bạn có nói được tiếng Anh không?
Bạn káw nóy dur-ẹrk tíng ang kom?
Does anyone here speak English?
Có ai biết nói tiếng Anh không?
káw ai bee-ét nóy tíng ang kom?
What does that mean?
Nghĩa là gì?
ngẽe-a là zèe?
I (don't) understand.
Tôi (không) hiểu.
doy (kom) hée-oo
Could you write it down, please?
Xin viết ra giùm tôi.
sin vee-ét ra zòom doy
Can you show me (on the map)?
Xin chỉ giùm (trên bản đồ này).
sin chée zòom (tren bản dò này)

NUMBERS
1	*một*	mọt
2	*hai*	hai
3	*ba*	ba
4	*bốn*	bón
5	*năm*	num
6	*sáu*	sów
7	*bảy*	bảy
8	*tám*	dúm
9	*chín*	jín
10	*mười*	mùr-ee
11	*mười một*	mùr-ee mọt
19	*mười chín*	mùr-ee
20	*hai mươi*	hai mur-ee
21	*hai mươi mốt*	hai mur-ee mót
22	*hai mươi hai*	hai mur-ee hai
30	*ba mươi*	ba mur-ee
90	*chín mươi*	jín mur-ee
100	*một trăm*	mọt chum
200	*hai trăm*	hai chum
900	*chín trăm*	jín chum

1000	*một nghìn* (N)	mọt ngìn
	một ngàn (S)	mọt ngàn
10,000	*mười nghìn* (N)	mùr-ee ngìn
	mười ngàn (S)	mùr-ee ngàn
one million	*một triệu*	mọt chee-ọo
two million	*hai triệu*	hai chee-ọo
first	*thứ nhất*	túr nyút
second	*thứ hai*	túr hai

PAPERWORK

name
  tên   den
nationality
  quốc gia   gwók za
address
  địa chỉ   dẹe-a chée
date/place of birth
  ngày/nơi sinh   ngày/ner-ee sing
sex/gender
  giới tính   zér-ee tíng
passport (number)
  (số) hộ chiếu   (só) họ chee-óo
visa
  thị thực   tẹe tựrk

QUESTION WORDS

Who?
  Ái?   ái?
What?
  Cái gì?   kái zèe?
What is it?
  Cái này là cái gì?   kái này là kái zèe?
When?
  Khi nào?   kee nòw?
Where?
  Ở đâu?   ér dow?
Which?
  Cái nào?   kái nòw?
Why?
  Tại sao?   tại sow?
How?
  Làm sao?   làm sow?

SHOPPING & SERVICES

I'd like to buy ...
  Tôi muốn mua ...
  dọy móon moo-a ...
How much is this?
  Cái này giá bao nhiêu?
  kái này zá bow nyoo?
I want to pay in dong.
  Tôi muốn trả bằng tiền Việt Nam.
  dọy móon trả bùng dee-èn vyẹt nam

I don't like it.
  Tôi không thích nó.
  dọy kom tít náw
May I look at it?
  Tôi có thể xem được không?
  dọy káw tảy sem dur-ẹrk kom?
I'm just looking.
  Tôi chỉ ngắm xem.
  dọy chée ngúm sem
It's cheap.
  Cái này rẻ.
  kái này rẻir
It's too expensive.
  Cái này quá mắc.
  kái này gwá múk
I'll take it.
  Tôi lấy cái này.
  dọy láy kái này

Do you accept ...?
  Bạn có nhận ... không?
  bạn káw nyụn ... kom?
  credit cards
    thẻ tín dụng   tảir dín zọom
  travellers cheques
    xét du lịch   sét zoo lịt

more	*nhiều hơn*	nyòo hern
less	*ít hơn*	ít hern
smaller	*nhỏ hơn*	nyỏ hern
bigger	*lớn hơn*	lérn hern

I'm looking for ...
  Tôi tìm ...
  dọy dìm ...
  a bank
    ngân hàng   ngun hàng
  the church
    nhà thờ   nyà tèr
  the city centre
    trung tâm thành phố   troom dum tàng fó
  the ... embassy
    sự quan ...   sự gwan ...
  the hospital
    nhà thương   nyà tur-erng
  my hotel
    khách sạn của tôi   kát sạn kỏo-a dọy
  the market
    chợ   jẹr
  the museum
    viện bảo tàng   vee-ẹn bỏw tàng
  the police
    cảnh sát   kảng sát
  the post office
    bưu điện   bur-oo dee-ẹn

a public phone
phòng điện thoại   fòm dee-ẹn twại
a restaurant
nhà hàng   nyà hàng
a public toilet
phòng vệ sinh   fòm vạy sing
tourist office
văn phòng hướng   vun fòm hur-érng
  dẫn du lịch   zũn zoo lịt

TIME & DATES
What time is it?
Mấy giờ rồi?   máy zèr ròy?
It's (8) o'clock.
Bây giờ là (mười)   bay zèr là (mùr-ee)
  giờ.   zèr
When?
Khi nào?   kee nòw?
now
bây giờ   bay zèr
in the morning
sáng   sáng
in the afternoon
chiều   chee-òo
in the evening
tối   dóy
today
hôm nay   hom nay
tomorrow
ngày mai   ngày mai

Monday	*thứ hai*	túr hai
Tuesday	*thứ ba*	túr ba
Wednesday	*thứ tư*	túr dur
Thursday	*thứ năm*	túr num
Friday	*thứ sáu*	túr sów
Saturday	*thứ bảy*	túr bảy
Sunday	*chủ nhật*	chỏo nhụt

January	*tháng giêng*	táng zee-eng
February	*tháng hai*	táng hai
March	*tháng ba*	táng ba
April	*tháng tư*	táng tur
May	*tháng năm*	táng num
June	*tháng sáu*	táng sów
July	*tháng bảy*	táng bảy
August	*tháng tám*	táng dúm
September	*tháng chín*	táng jín
October	*tháng mười*	táng mùr-ee
November	*tháng mười*	táng mùr-ee
	một	mọt
December	*tháng mười*	táng mùr-ee
	hai	hai

TRANSPORT
Public Transport
What time does the (first)... leave/arrive?
Chuyến ... (sớm nhất) chạy lúc mấy giờ?
chwee-én ... (sérm nhút) chạy lóop máy zèr?
boat
tàu/thuyền   tòw/twee-èn
bus
xe buýt   sair béet
plane
máy bay   máy bay
train
xe lửa   sair lủr-a

I'd like a ... ticket.
Tôi muốn vé ...
doy móon váir ...
one·way
đi một chiều   dee mọt chee-òo
return
khứ hồi   kúr hò-ee
1st class
hạng nhất   hạng nyút
2nd class
hạng nhì   hạng nyèe

I want to go to ...
Tôi muốn đi ...
doy móon dee ...
How long does the trip take?
Chuyến đi sẽ mất bao lâu?
chwee-én dee sãir mút bow low?
What time does it arrive?
Mấy giờ đến?
máy zèr dén?
The train has been cancelled.
Chuyến xe lửa bị hủy bỏ.
chwee-én sair lủr-a bẹ hwée bảw

the first
đầu tiên   dòw dee-en
the last
cuối cùng   kóo-ee kòom
bus station
bến xe   bén sair
ticket office
phòng bán vé   fòm bán váir
timetable
thời biểu   tèr-ee bee-ỏo
sleeping berth
giường ngủ   zùrng ngỏo
railway station
ga xe lửa   ga sair lủr-a

Private Transport

I'd like to hire a ...
Tôi muốn thuê ...(N) doy móon tway ...
Tôi muốn mướn ...(S) doy móon mứrn ...

car
xe hơi sair her-ee
motorbike
xe moto sair mo-to
bicycle
xe đạp sair dạp
cyclo (pedicab)
xe xích lô sair sík lo

ROAD SIGNS

Nguy Hiểm	Danger
Cấm Đậu Xe	No Parking
Quành Lại	Detour
Lối Vào	Entry
Cấm Vượt Qua	No Overtaking
Chạy Chậm Lại	Slow Down
Cấm Vào	No Entry
Đường Một Chiều	One Way
Lối Ra	Exit

Is this the road to ...?
Con đường nầy có dẫn đến ...?
kon dur-èrng này káw zũn dén ...?
How many kilometres to ...?
... cách đây bao nhiêu ki-lô-mét?
... kák sa bow nyoo kee-lo-mét?
Where's a service station?
Trạm xăng ở đâu?
trạm sung ẻr dow?
Please fill it up.
Làm ơn đổ đầy bình.
làm ern dỏ dày bìng
I'd like ... litres.
Tôi muốn ... lít.
doy móon ... léet

diesel
dầu diesel zòw dee-sel
leaded petrol
dầu xăng có chì zòw sung káw chèe
unleaded petrol
dầu xăng zòw sung
highway
xa lộ sa lọ
National Highway 1
Quốc Lộ 1 gwók lọ mọt
map
bản đồ bản dò

(How long) Can I park here?
Chúng tôi có thể đậu được (bao lâu)?
chóom doy káw tảy dọw dur-ẹrk (bow low)?
Where do I pay?
Trả tiền ở đâu?
trả dee-èn ẻr dow?
I need a mechanic.
Chúng tôi cần thợ sửa xe.
chóom doy gùn tẹr súr-a sair
The car/motorbike has broken down (at ...)
Xe bị hư (tại ...).
sair bẹe hur (tại ...)
The car/motorbike won't start.
(Xe hơi/Xe moto) không để được.
(sair her-ee/sair mo-to) kom dày dur-ẹrk
I have a flat tyre.
Bánh xe tôi bị xì.
báng sair doy bẹe sèe
I've run out of petrol.
Tôi bị hết dầu/xăng.
doy bẹe hét zòw/sung

TRAVEL WITH CHILDREN

Is there a/an ...?
Ở đây có ...? ẻr day káw ...?
I need a/an ...
Tôi cần ... doy kùn ...

baby change room
phòng thay quần áo fòm tay gwùn ów
cho em bé jaw em báir
car baby seat
ghế ngồi trong xe gáy ngò-ee trom sair
cho em bé jaw em báir
child-minding service
dịch vụ giữ trẻ em zịt vọo zũr tráir em
children's menu
thực đơn cho trẻ em tựrk dern jaw tráir em
disposable nappies/diapers
tã lót tã lót
(English-speaking) babysitter
người giữ trẻ em ngừr-ee zũr tráir em
nói tiếng Anh nóy tíng ang
highchair
ghế cao cho em bé gáy kow jaw em báir
potty
bô cho trẻ em bo jaw tráir em
stroller
xe đẩy cho em bé sair day jaw em báir

Do you mind if I breastfeed here?
Xin lỗi tôi có thể cho con tôi bú ở đây không?
sin lõy doy káw tảy jaw kon doy bóo ẻr day kom?
Are children allowed?
Trẻ em có được phép không?
tráir em káw dur-ẹk fép kom?

HILL TRIBE LANGUAGES

The task of neatly classifying the different hill tribe groups of Vietnam is not an easy one. Ethnologists typically classify the Montagnards by linguistic distinction and commonly refer to three main groups (which further splinter into vast and quite complex sub-groupings). The Austro-Asian family includes the Viet-Muong, Mon-Khmer, Tay-Tai and Meo-Dzao language groups; the Austronesian family includes Malayo-Polynesian languages; and the Sino-Tibetan family encompasses the Chinese and Tibeto-Burmese language groups. In addition, within a single spoken language, there are often myriad dialectical variations.

The following words and phrases should prove useful when visiting members of the larger Vietnamese hill tribes. If you're planning on spending a lot of time within hill tribe areas, consider taking Lonely Planet's *Hill Tribes Phrasebook* with you. For more information on hill tribes and the areas they inhabit see pp42–5.

TAY

Also known as the Ngan, Pa Di, Phen, Thu Lao and Tho, the Tay belong to the Tay-Thai language group.

Hello.	*Pá prama.*
Goodbye.	*Pá paynó.*
Yes.	*Mi.*
No.	*Boomi.*
Thank you.	*Ðay fon.*
What's your name?	*Ten múng le xăng ma?*

Where are you from?	*Mu'ng du' te là ma?*
How much does this cost?	*Ău ni ki lai tiên?*

H'MONG

The H'mong are also known as Meo, Mieu, Mong Do (White H'mong), Mong Du (Black H'mong), Mong Lenh (Flower H'mong), Mong Si (Red H'mong). They belong to the H'mong-Dzao language group, but their spoken language resembles Mandarin Chinese.

Hello.	*Ti nấu/Caó cu.*
Goodbye.	*Caó mun'g chè.*
Yes.	*Có mua.*
No.	*Chúi muá.*
Thank you.	*Ô chờ.*
What's your name?	*Caó be hua chan'g?*
Where are you from?	*Caó nhao từ tuá?*
How much does this cost?	*Pổ chố chá?*

DZAO

Also known as Coc Mun, Coc Ngang, Dai Ban, Diu Mien, Dong, Kim Mien, lan Ten, Lu Gang, Tieu Ban, Trai and Xa, this tribe belongs to the Mong Dzao language group.

Hello.	*Puang tọi.*
Goodbye.	*Puang tọi.*
Yes.	*Mái.*
No.	*Mái mái.*
Thank you.	*Tờ dun.*
What's your name?	*Mang nhi búa chiên nay?*
Where are you from?	*May hải đo?*
How much does this cost?	*Pchiá nhăng?*

LANGUAGE

Glossary

For food and drink terms, see Eat Your Words on p70. For information on the Vietnamese language, and pronunciation, see the Language chapter (p497).

A Di Da – Buddha of the Past
agent orange – toxic, carcinogenic chemical herbicide used extensively during the *American War*
am duong – Vietnamese equivalent of Yin and Yang
Amerasians – children borne of unions between Asian women and US servicemen during the *American War*
American War – Vietnamese name for what is also known as the 'Vietnam War'
Annam – old Chinese name for Vietnam, meaning 'Pacified South'
Annamites – term used by the French to describe the Vietnamese
ao dai – Vietnamese national dress
apsaras – heavenly maidens
arhat – anyone who has attained nirvana
ARVN – Army of the Republic of Vietnam (former South Vietnamese army)

ba mu – 12 'midwives', each of whom teaches newborns a different skill necessary for the first year of life: smiling, sucking, lying on their stomachs and so forth
Ba Tay – a term used to refer to Western women, meaning 'Mrs Westerner'
ban – village
bang – congregation (in the Chinese community)
bar om – literally 'holding' bars associated with the sex industry; also known as 'karaoke om'
bat trang – tiles
binh dinh vo – traditional martial art performed with a bamboo stick
Black Flags – a semi-autonomous army of Chinese, Vietnamese and hill-tribe troops
bo de – Bodhi tree, or pipal tree
bonze – Vietnamese Buddhist monk
buu dien – post office

cai luong – modern theatre
can – 10-year cycle
Cao Daism – indigenous Vietnamese religion
cay son – tree from whose resin lacquer is made
Cham – ethnic minority descended from the people of *Champa*
cham chu – acupuncture
Champa – Hindu kingdom dating from the late 2nd century AD
Charlie – nickname for the *VC*, used by US soldiers

choi ga – cock fighting
chu nho – standard Chinese characters (script)
chu nom – Vietnamese script; also called *nom*
Cochinchina – the southern part of Vietnam during the French-colonial era
com pho – rice-noodle soup; common sign on restaurants
cong – gong
corbeille à bec – wooden staff with a crayon attached for writing messages from spirits
cowboys – motorbike-riding thieves
crachin – fine drizzle
crémaillère – cog railway
cu ly – fern stems used to stop bleeding; also known as *kim mao cau tich*
cyclo – pedicab or bicycle rickshaw

Dai The Chi Bo Tat – an assistant of *A Di Da*
dan bau – single-stringed lute that generates an astounding magnitude of tones
dan tranh – 16-stringed zither
danh de – illegal numbers game
dau – oil
Di Lac Buddha – Buddha of the Future
dikpalaka – gods of the directions of the compass
dinh – communal meeting hall
DMZ – the misnamed Demilitarised Zone, a strip of land that once separated North and South Vietnam
doi moi – economic restructuring or reform
dong – natural caves
dong chi – comrade
DRV – Democratic Republic of Vietnam (the old North Vietnam)

ecocide – term used to describe the devastating effects of the herbicides sprayed over Vietnam during the *American War*

feng shui – see *phong thuy*
flechette – experimental US weapon; an artillery shell containing thousands of darts
fu – talisman
Funan – see *Oc-Eo*

garuda – Sanskrit term for griffin-like sky beings who feed on *naga*
ghe – long, narrow rowboat
giay phep di lai – internal travel permit
gom – ceramics

hai dang – lighthouse

hai lua – literally 'second rice,' but a derogatory way in the Mekong Delta region to call someone a country bumpkin. Also see *nha que*.
han viet – Sino-Vietnamese literature
hat boi – classical theatre in the south
hat cheo – popular theatre
hat tuong – classical theatre in the north
hieu – filial piety
ho ca – aquarium
Ho Chi Minh Trail – route used by the *NVA* and *VC* to move supplies to guerrillas in the South
ho khau – residence permit needed for everything (eg school, employment, land ownership, vehicle registration, home and business ownership)
Hoa – ethnic-Chinese, the largest single minority group in Vietnam
hoi – 60-year period (used in calendars)
hoi quan – Chinese congregational assembly halls
Honda Dream – most popular model of Honda motor-scooter sold in Vietnam
Honda om – motorbike taxi, also called *xe om*
huong – perfume
huyen – rural district

Indochina – Vietnam, Cambodia and Laos. The name derives from Indian and Chinese influences.

kala-makara – sea-monster god
kalan – a religious sanctuary
ken doi – musical instrument made from two seven-holed bamboo flutes
khach san – hotel
Khmer – ethnic-Cambodians
Khong Tu – Confucius
kich noi – spoken drama
kim mao cau tich – fern used to stop bleeding in traditional Chinese medicine; also known as *cu ly*
Kinh – Vietnamese language
Kuomintang – Nationalist Party, also known as KMT. The KMT controlled China between 1925 and 1949 until defeated by the communists.
ky – 12-year cycle (used in calendars)

lang – hereditary noble family who rules the communal land and collects the benefits of labour and tax through its use by locals
lang tam – tombs
li xi – lucky money
liberation – 1975 takeover of the South by the North; what most foreigners call 'reunification'
Lien Xo – literally, Soviet Union; used to call attention to a foreigner
linga – stylised phallus which represents the Hindu god Shiva

MAAG – Military Assistance Advisory Group, set up to instruct troops receiving US weapons on how to use them
mandapa – meditation hall
mang dang – bamboo-shoot soup
manushi-buddha – Buddha who appeared in human form
mat cua – 'watchful eyes', supposed to protect the residents of a house from harm
MIA – missing in action
mihrab – niche in a mosque wall indicating the direction of Mecca
minbar – feature of mosques
moi – derogatory word meaning 'savages', mostly used by ethnic-Vietnamese to describe hill-tribe people
Montagnards – term meaning highlanders or mountain people, used to refer to the ethnic minorities who inhabit remote areas of Vietnam
muong – large village unit made up of *quel*

naga – Sanskrit term for a mythical serpent being with divine powers; often depicted forming a kind of shelter over the Buddha
nam phai – for men
napalm – jellied petrol (gasoline) dropped and lit from aircraft; used by US forces with devastating effect during the *American War*
NGO – nongovernment organisation
nha hang – restaurant
nha khach – hotel; guesthouse
nha nghi – guesthouse
nha que – literally 'countryside,' but used in a derogatory way (mainly in the north) to refer to someone as a country bumpkin. See also *hai lua*.
nha-rong – large stilt house, used by hill tribes as a kind of community centre
nha tro – dormitory
NLF – National Liberation Front; official name for the *VC*
nom – Vietnamese script
nu phai – for women
nui – mountain
nuoc mam – fish sauce, added to almost every dish in Vietnam
NVA – North Vietnamese Army

Oc-Eo – Indianised kingdom (also called Funan) in southern Vietnam between the 1st and 6th centuries
Ong Bon – Guardian Spirit of Happiness and Virtue
Ong Tay – a term used to refer to Western men, meaning 'Mr Westerner'
Orderly Departure Program (ODP) – carried out under the auspices of the *UNHCR*, designed to allow orderly resettlement of Vietnamese political refugees
OSS – US Office of Strategic Services; the predecessor of the CIA

pagoda – traditionally an eight-sided Buddhist tower, but in Vietnam the word is commonly used to denote a temple
Phoenix Program – also known as Operation Phoenix; a controversial program run by the CIA, aimed at eliminating VC cadres by assassination, capture or defection
phong thuy – literally, 'wind water'; used to describe geomancy. Also known by its Chinese name, feng shui.
piastre – the local currency in the days of French Indochina
pneumatographie – Cao Dai ritual in which a blank slip of paper is sealed in an envelope and hung above an altar. When it is taken down, there is a message on the paper.
Politburo – Political Bureau; about a dozen members overseeing the Party's day-to-day functioning with the power to issue directives to the government
POW – prisoner of war
PRG – Provisional Revolutionary Government, the temporary Communist government set up by the VC in the South. It existed from 1969 to 1976.

quan – urban district
Quan Cong – Chinese God of War
quan lai – mandarins
Quan The Am Bo Tat – Goddess of Mercy
quel – small stilt-house hamlets
quoc am – modern Vietnamese literature
quoc ngu – Latin-based phonetic alphabet in which Vietnamese is written

rap – cinema
Revolutionary Youth League – first Marxist group in Vietnam and predecessor of the Communist Party
roi can – conventional puppetry
roi nuoc – water puppetry
rong – communal houses
RVN – Republic of Vietnam (the old South Vietnam)

salangane – swiftlet
sao – wooden flute
sao la – antelope-like creature
shakti – feminine manifestation of Shiva
social evils – campaign to prevent evil ideas from the West 'polluting' Vietnamese society
song – river
SRV – Socialist Republic of Vietnam (Vietnam's official name)
Strategic Hamlets Program – programme (by South Vietnam and the USA) of forcibly moving peasants into fortified villages to deny the VC bases of support

sung – fig-tree timber

Tam Giao – literally, 'triple religion'; Confucianism, Taoism and Buddhism fused over time with popular Chinese beliefs and ancient Vietnamese animism
Tao – the Way; the essence of which all things are made
Tet – Vietnamese Lunar New Year
thai cuc quyen – Vietnamese for t'ai chi
Thich Ca Buddha – the historical Buddha Sakyamuni, whose real name was Siddhartha Gautama
Thien Hau Thanh Mau – Goddess of the Sea and Protector of Fishermen and Sailors
thong nhat – express train
thung chai – gigantic round wicket baskets sealed with pitch; used as rowboats
thuoc bac – Chinese medicine
to rung – large bamboo xylophone
toc hanh – express bus
Tonkin – the northern part of Vietnam during the French-colonial era; also the name of a body of water in the north (Tonkin Gulf)
trong com – cylindrical drums
truyen khau – traditional oral literature
tu sat – dominoes

UNHCR – United Nations High Commission for Refugees

VC – Viet Cong or Vietnamese Communists
Viet Kieu – overseas Vietnamese
Viet Minh – League for the Independence of Vietnam, a nationalistic movement that fought the Japanese and French but later became Communist-dominated
VNQDD – Viet Nam Quoc Dan Dang; largely middle-class nationalist party

xang – petrol
xe dap loi – wagon pulled by a bicycle
xe Honda loi – wagon pulled by a motorbike
xe lam – tiny three-wheeled trucks used for short-haul passenger and freight transport
xe loi – wagon pulled by a motorbike in the Mekong Delta region
xe om – motorbike taxi, also called *Honda om*
xich lo – *cyclo*, from the French *cyclo-pousse*
xo so – state lottery

yang – genie

Behind the Scenes

THIS BOOK

This is the 8th edition of *Vietnam*. Nick Ray was the coordinating author and was ably assisted by Wendy Yanagihara. Nick and Wendy worked with text researched by Mason Florence and Virginia Jealous for *Vietnam 7*. The 6th edition of the book was written by Mason Florence. The Food & Drink chapter was written by Nick, with text from *World Food Vietnam* by Richard Sterling. Dr Trish Batchelor provided text for the Health chapter in this edition of *Vietnam*.

THANKS from the Authors

Nick Ray As always, so many people have been instrumental in helping to put this book together. First thanks to my wonderful wife Kulikar Sotho who has joined me on many a trip to Vietnam, and to our young son Julian who timed his arrival to perfection, earlier than expected but he gave me time to get there, just! Thanks to Mum and Dad for the support and encouragement that carried me to faraway lands from a young age.

In Vietnam, thanks to fellow Cambodia resident John McGeoghan and fellow author Neal Bedford for joining me in the mountains of the northwest. Vinh, Linh and Thanh at Handspan were good company on the Hanoi nightshift, as were Dida, Tim, Digby, Dan, Maeve and Marcus. Thanks also to Digby for those superb roads that only a Minsk could make it through in the northwest. Thanks to Minh Ly for helping with logistics in remote places and thanks to Hoang and Thanh for last-minute extras.

A big thanks also to Le Van Sinh for all the effort he put into early editions of this book and a major

thanks to Mason Florence for all his good work on the last three incarnations of this book.

Wendy Yanagihara I am forever indebted to Diem & Adrien; my Vietnamese family Me, Bo, Quynh & Quan; Chau and her wonderful family; new-mama Quyen; and pool-playing Son, for their friendship and so very much more.

A truckload of thanks to the fabulous Sinh, who kept police off my trail and my notes abundant. Many thanks also go out to Dung in HCMC, Xuan in Dalat, Barbara in Quy Nhon, Thanh for safely motoring us down all those dusty Mekong trails, and Tam for getting me through the central highlands in record time.

Gracias, otra vez, to Paul Wellman for shooting the author photo. And to my family, thank you for your continued love and support.

CREDITS

Vietnam 8 was commissioned and developed in Lonely Planet's Melbourne office by Mary Neighbour and Kalya Ryan. Emma Koch assisted in assessing the manuscript. Cartography for this guide was developed by Anthony Phelan. Editing was coordinated by Carolyn Boicos, and Jacqueline Nguyen coordinated the mapping. Michael Ruff laid the book out and put together the colour wraps.

Assisting editors and proofers included David Andrew, Yvonne Byron, Andrea Dobbin, Bruce Evans, Diana Saad, Suzannah Shwer and Jane Thompson. Assisting Carolyn with editorial layout checks were Louise McGregor, Kate McLeod

THE LONELY PLANET STORY

The story begins with a classic travel adventure: Tony and Maureen Wheeler's 1972 journey across Europe and Asia to Australia. There was no useful information about the overland trail then, so Tony and Maureen published the first Lonely Planet guidebook to meet a growing need.

From a kitchen table, Lonely Planet has grown to become the largest independent travel publisher in the world, with offices in Melbourne (Australia), Oakland (USA) and London (UK). Today Lonely Planet guidebooks cover the globe. There is an ever-growing list of books and information in a variety of media. Some things haven't changed. The main aim is still to make it possible for adventurous travellers to get out there – to explore and better understand the world.

At Lonely Planet we believe travellers can make a positive contribution to the countries they visit – if they respect their host communities and spend their money wisely. Every year 5% of company profit is donated to charities around the world.

BEHIND THE SCENES

and Meg Worby. Quentin Frayne compiled the Language chapter and Ben Handicott took care of fonts and translations for the Food & Drink chapter. Bonnie Wintle assisted with cartography. Index tagging and cross-referencing was done by Jacqui Saunders and Michael Ruff, with assistance from Jim Hsu, Adam Bextream and Wibowo Rusli.

Chris Love managed the project, with assistance from Andrew Weatherill, and overseeing production were Darren O'Connell and Louise McGregor (managing editors) and Corie Waddell (managing cartographer). Cover design was by James Hardy, and Wendy Wright did the cover art and series design. Thanks to Gerard Walker, Claire Gibson and Glenn Beanland in LPI; Kate McDonald, Adriana Mammarella, Sally Darmody and Jacqui Saunders for layout checks and Jennifer Mundy-Nordin for the readers thanks list.

THANKS from Lonely Planet

Many thanks to the following travellers who used the last edition and wrote to us with helpful hints, useful advice and interesting anecdotes.

A Gep Aadriaanse, Marianne Abadie, Kyoko Abe, Andray Abrahamian, Garry Adams, Philip Adey, Adria Aguado, Brett Alexander, Miguel Almirall, Ingrid Alten, Bruce Anderson, Claire Anderson, Craig T Anderson, Simon Anderson, Corinne Angehrn, Martin Angiset, Kirsty Archer, Matthew Archer, Dr Andreas Arkades, Chris Arthur, Warren Askew, Karen Aslett, James Aurelius, Nicky Avery, Scott Avery **B** Nicole Baccini, Stefan Backlund, Julie Baker, Chas Barter, Kelly Batstone, Brad Baurain, Steve Beatson, Geoff Beattie, Sarah Beck, Stefan & Tanya Becker, Charles Bendon, Nicola Bennett, Richard Bennett, Sonya Bennett, Jessica Bent, Julien Benta, Klaus Bettenhausen, Nicholas Bias, Elise Bigelow, Amanda Bird, Dennis Bird, Daniel Bishop, John Bishop, Georgia & Charlie Blake, Pippa & Bill Blakemore, Alfred Blok, Andreas Blom, Stephen Blow, Randi Blutstein, Alex Bodmann, Traci R Bogan, Stephane Bone, Tony & Veronica Boniface, Ian Booth, Jo Anne Border, Michele Boscia, Allan Bowman, Inga Brabrand, Kate Bradbury, Audrey & Roy Bradford, Jonathan Bradley, William J Bradshaw, Josh Brann, Bart Braun, Adam Bray, John Brehney, Iris Breutz, Simon Briggs, Erwin Broschinski, Alden Brown, Frank Brown, Joshua Samuel Brown, Nancy Brown, Thomas Brown, Kevin Brubaker, Mary Bryant, Nicola Bryne, Daniel Buckler, Mark Burns, Wolfgang Burr, Roger Burrows, Georgine Burton, Cynthia Butler, Jo Butler, Magnus Byrod **C** Silvio Caligaris, Kirsty Cambridge, Martin Caminada, Geoff Campbell, Jon Canada, Nigel Canavan, Steve Capelin, Susie Carr, Heino Caspelherr, Claudio Cavallari, Ursula Ceresa, Raegan Cerisano, Wilmar Ceton, Matt Chalmers, Brook Chambers, Candy Chan, Esther Chasse, Lucy Chesser, Nikos Chimonides, Loretta Chou, Anthony Chrisite, Henrik Christensen, Anthony Christie, Mindy Christie, Meredith Christie-Ling, Barbara Clifford, Johan & Clara Collier, Georgia Collins, Judy Collins, Lorna Connelly, Joshua Conway, Kathryn Cook, Trevor Cook, JA Coombs, Roy Cooper, Sharon Chen Cooper, Helena Cooper Thomas, Marie Eve Cote, David Cotterill, Lisa Coulton, David Court,

Graeme Cowans, Oliver Craig, Mark Crawford, Susan Crawford, Laura Creasey, Catherine Cregan, Peter A Cromie, Philip Crosby, Cheri Cross, Gabor Csonka, Emma Curson **D** Jason Dance, Howard A Daniel III, Laura D'Antonio, Jessica Davey, Amanda Davies, Caroline Davies, Barry Davis, Julie & Brad Davis, Amber Dawson, Sanne de Graaf, Sharon de Groot, Barry de Vent, Suzanne de Visser, Colin Dealney, Peter Dekkers, Jonathan Del Mar, John Derraugh, Padraigin Ni Dhonghaile, Ben Di Maggio, Doron Dinstein, Fredrik Divall, Chris Doherty, Audra Dore, Julia Dorn, Jenny Drezin, Blandine du Pradel, Sophie Dubillot, Aoife Duggan, Andrew Duke, Ray Dunn, Tu Duong, Dan Dutfield, Peter Dwyer, Trish Dwyer **E** Gary Edgar, Camilla Edlund, Rotem Einav, Magnus Ekstrom, Pascal Endstra, David Engstrom, Johanna Eriksson, Petra Essenfelder, Allun Evans, Tim Evans **F** Guido Faes, Bear Falugo, Erin Farnbach, Gabrielle Farran, Heather Fedchuk, Karen Ferguson, Yoni Fernhout, Martin Fitzpatrick, Blythe Fitzwiliam, Desirée Fleer, Jody Foege, Jenny Forbes, Peter Forbes, Iris Fox, Shaun Fox, Victor Fraile, Dutty Francis, Eric Frantz, Graeme Fraser, Maureen Fraser, Walt Fraser, Graziano Freschi, Rachel Friedlander, Grace Frith, Jo-Anne Fryer, Marianne & Fabio Fukushima **G** Rebecca Gardner, Heather Garry, Thomas Gay, Lia Genovese, Nguyen Thu Giang, Emma Giesen, Linda Gillespie, George Girling, Stian Giskeodegard, Sandra Gisler, Amanda Glasson, Marco Glueck, Tobias Gnamm, Jonathan Godfray, Lori Gold, Ted Golden, Johneen Goltermann, Lily Goncalves, Kady Gotlieb, Elise, Jacob & Martin Gottliebsen, Frances Gow, Martha J Graham, Sarah Grams, Michael Grant, Emma Gray, Fiona & Bard Green, Bob Greer, Macgregor Greer, Beat Gregoric, Michael Griffin, Ed Griffith, Martin Griffith, Eelko-Jan Groenevelt, David Gualtieri **H** Klaus Haertel, Nathalie Hagestein, Andrew Hale, Allan Hall, Nina Hall, Keith Hanson, Hennie Harink, Amy Harris, Graham Harris, Paul Harris, Bruce Hart, Klaus Hartel, Frida Harvig, Wendlandt Hasselle, Una Hassett, Lucy Hayes, Alberta Heagney, Lynne Healey, Marie-Claude Hebert, N Henley, Brenda Henry, Mick Henrys, Adria Hertzmark, Jonathan Hess, Mark Hewitt, Denise Hilhorst, Peter Hill, Kathrina Hiller, Claire Hindson, Bonnie Hittmann, Thao Ho, Julia Hodgkinson, Kerstin Hoff, Michael Hohn, Rolien Hollaar, BJ Hoogland, Corne de Hoon, David Hope, David Hopkinson, Elizabeth Horn, Stephen Horn, Jill Ho-You, Isabelle Huchett, Thomas Hudson, Doris Hug, Karen & Brian Humes, Alicia Hunt, Chris Hunt, Laura Huntley, Carolyn & Jarrod Hunt-Wackett, Moz Hussain, Stephen Hussey, Annette Hutton, Huynh Huu Hoi, Oliver Hynek **I** Blanche Iberg, Margaret Ingram **J** Con Jackson, Suzanne Jacobs, Mark Jaffray, Cameron James, F James, Bruce Jefferies, Michael Jennings, Ricardo Jobin, Fiona Johnston, Tony Johnston, Tania Johnstone, Andrew Jones, James W Jones, Jason Jones, Norma Jones, Richard F Jones, Stephen Jones, Victoria Jones, Wally Jones, Karolien Joossens, Anne Judson, Linda Juris **K** Patricia Kaaij, Anna Kaipainen, Richie Kalwarczyk, Marc & Margareth Kampinga, Sonja Kappler, Judith Karena, Pius Karena, Alexandra Karl, Simon Karsties, Samira Katib, Jason Keen, Liz Keen, Melanie Kelleher, Chris Kelly, Bas Kempen, Barbara Kenny, Michael Kent, Miriam Kersten, Jason Khoo, Markus Kiesling, Collette Kilty, James & Kasia Kilvington, Hatty Kingsley-Miller, Charles Kivette, Willem Klaassen, Fran Knowles, Justus Koek, Yeong Haur Kok, Pazu Kong, Maaike Koops, Erik Koornneef, H F Kop, Karl Kreiner, Marieke Krijnen, Nick

Kromer, Stefan & Charlotte Kunz **L** Robert Laffaire, Noel Lahart, Thien-Kieu Lam, John Lancaster, Darryl Lang, Dita Langenberg, Zoe Langridge, Frida Lauri, Jennifer Laws, Chinh Le, Chinh & Jeri Le, Sebastian Le, Nguyen Le Bac, Alan & Gill Le Serve, Dat Le Tan, John Lee, Theresa Lee, Francois Legendre, Diane Leighton, Jean Lennane, Isaac Lennox, Mary Lermitte, Robyn Les, Julie Leung, Omer & Dafna Levin, Elton Levingston, Gillian Levitan, Rasmus Levy, Robert Lewis, Timothy Lillfommen, Bas Linders, Selena Liss, Daphne Liu, Erika & Brad Lloyd, Nguyen Tran Dinh Loc, Neil & Kim Locker, Edward Long, Mike Longley, Steve Lopes, Sonia Lopez, Kim Lord, Nathan Lorentz, Maria Lorenzo, Andrew Love, Richard Love, Gary Lowe, Ron & Elaine Lowe, Kim Luckie, Carsten Ludvigsen, Clive Lundquist, Maria Luptakova, Jerry Lvinson **M** Baerbel Maessen, Ruth Maguire, Josefin Mandorsson, Maree Marmion, Lucy Marshall, Stéphane Martel, Jeff Martin, Nanne Martinus, Nikola Lee Matcham, Helen Mather, Schmid Mathias, Lindy & Stan Matthews, Silvia Maurer, Peter Maxey, John McDermott, Laura McEndoo, John McEwan, Ralph McLean, John McLennan, David McManamon, Gary McWilliam, Kevin Meadowcroft, Helen Meadows, Maya Mehta, Christine Meier, Denise Meier, Kim Meijer, Stefan Meivers, Phil Mellifont, Jefri Metheany, Nicolai Meyendorff, Mary Meyer, Eithne Ni Mhorain, Henry Milczuk, Anna Miles, Tim Miller, Stephan Miond, Milorad Misina, Robert mmarvin, Mia Moawad, Justin Mogg, Paul Moir, Marie-Loe Molenaar, Hans Mommer, Egbert Mone, Kimberley Amber Monsma, Kevin Montague, Rainer Moor, Vivien Moore, Sean Morgan, Lee Morley, Nick Morley, Julie Morrice, Jason Morris, Gaye Morrison, Terence Moylan, Peter Mueller, Lynn Muench, Hilda Mulcahy, Sebastian Mulder, Kara Louise Munn, Jude & Joe Murless, Clodagh Murphy, Patrick Murphy, Jan Murray, Phil & Rhonda Murray, Anton Myhra **N** Gordana Najdanovic, Katy Napier Ford, Deborah Nash, Jose Antonio Navarro, Elena, Eloy & Alberto Navarro, Carol & Peter Nelson, Lindsay Nelson, Chris & Cathy Newby, Minh Nguyen, T Nguyen, Trung Dung Nguyen, Helena Nicklasson, Brad Nieder, Bernt Nielsen, Phil Nizette, Yvonne Nolan, Jolein Noppen, Kim Nottle, Al Nuttall **O** Aisling O Connell, Paul O Sullivan, Ingrid Ochodek, Matthew O'Connor, Dieter Oelschlaeger, Sebastian Oergel, Asger Olesen, Deborah Olie, David Oppenheim, Derek O'Reilly, Ian O'Reilly, Noey O'Rielly, Ros Osborne, Karina Osgood, Mr D Owen **P** Aldo Paeffgen, Ralph Palim, Chris & Damaris Palmer, Nick Park, Lesley & Ron Parker, Joanna Parkes, Pedro Pastrano, Kong Pazu, Anders Persson, Lana Peth, Walter Pfeiffer, Tony O Pham, Marilyn Phillips, Madeleine Pidgeon, Maureen Pierre, Joachim Pietsch, Clare Pilkington, Michael Poesen, Anne Pomery, Doreen Pon, Jane Power, Robert Poyntz, Jessie Price, Mark Princi, Michael Puls, Catherine Purvis **R** Dierk Rade, Rowan Rafferty, Art & Connie Ramsay, Steve Rayson, Sally Reader, Paul Reardon, Emma Redshaw, Bob Richards, Jeff Richardson, Matthew Ridd, Alison Rigby, Peter & Yumiko Riley, Chris Ripke, Danielle Ripley, Craig Ritchie, Christian Ritz, Meryl Roberts, Claire Robinson, Scott Robinson, Greg Rocke, Aldo Rodenhaeuser, Peter Rodgers, Julie Rogers, Tanya Rogers, Esther Roling, Jerry Rolls, Alexander Rose, Jessica Rosenberg, Lee Roskin, Anne Rote, Belinda Roy, Maggie Roy, Jochen Rundholz, Patricia Anne Russell, Olive Ryan, Nurit Sadan, Peter Salenbauch, Bruno Salvaudon, Peter Sand, Monica Santiago, Glen Sauer, Linda Sawyer, Andre Schaarschmidt, Jeroen Schilt, Manuela Schmed, Tom Schneider, Jeannette Schoenau, Falk Schoenlebe, Jane Schou-Clarke, Dan Schulstad, Jaap Schuurman, Raymond Schweichert, Ralph Schwer, Nicola Schwytz, Jerry Sciarine, Karen & Martin Scott, Tom Sebald, Blandine Sebileau, William Seccombe, Stephanie Seding, Beate Selbig, Jon Senior, Heidi Sequenz, Lasse Settem, Vicky Seville, Gavin Sexton, Andrew Sharp, Wendy Sharples, Meredith Shore, Pierre Simard, David Sindall, Al Slagle, Alexander Slingeland, Dan Slyper, Max & Val Smerdon, Gerben Smit, Alex Smith, Brendan Smith, Carrie Smith, Daniel I Smith, Derek Smith, Jason Smith, Nick Smith, Sean Smith, EA Snook, Aity Soekidjo, Emma Soichet, Per Sonnvik, Laura & Brian Sorensen, Bronwyn Spiteri, Gary & Brunni Spohr, Fabian Stadler, Katja Sterger, Samantha Stess, Simon Stockdale, Eduard Stomp, Philip Storer, Rosie Stowell, Edwina Strachen, Jennie Strickland, Chris Stump, Jean Sturge, Belinda Suendermann, Aity Sukidjo, Sally Supplee, John & Blanca Swanson, Rob & Jane Swell **T** Neil Ta, Wendy Tabor, Hiroya Takano, Julie Talbot, Brett Tandy, Tilo Tappesser, Emanuela Tasinato, JR Tattis, Jeanette A Taudin Chabot, Rene Tayeb, Genevieve Tearle, Liz Teuma, Thai Thanh, Nguyen Thi Viet, Burghard Thiele, Gared Thomas, Jodie Thomas, Paul Thomas, Stephen Thomas, Kate Thompson, Nanna Thomsen, Regis Titeca, Daniel Tompsett, Dan Ton, Sarah Toomey, Jan Trabandt, Han Tran, Hue Tran, Matt Tranter, Vangelio Trova, Kevin Troy, Jon Tuck **U** Roland Ullram, Elle

SEND US YOUR FEEDBACK

We love to hear from travellers – your comments keep us on our toes and help make our books better. Our well-travelled team reads every word on what you loved or loathed about this book. Although we cannot reply individually to postal submissions, we always guarantee that your feedback goes straight to the appropriate authors, in time for the next edition. Each person who sends us information is thanked in the next edition – and the most useful submissions are rewarded with a free book.

To send us your updates – and find out about Lonely Planet events, newsletters and travel news – visit our award-winning website: **www.lonelyplanet.com/feedback**.

Note: We may edit, reproduce and incorporate your comments in Lonely Planet products such as guidebooks, websites and digital products, so let us know if you don't want your comments reproduced or your name acknowledged. For a copy of our privacy policy visit www.lonelyplanet.com/privacy.

BEHIND THE SCENES

Umbers, Susan Ussher **V** Henk van Bourgonje, Reinout van den Bergh, Hedwig van den Heuvel, Karlijn van der Hoeven, Huub van der Linden, Jaap van der Marel, Jeroen Kroon van Diest, Suzan van Echtelt, Eva van Ingen, Karina van Leeuwen, Teun van Metelen, Sef van Nieuwenborg, Colleen Van Onselen, Richard van Schip, Ineke Van Severen, Gerco van Vulpen, Lodewijk van Wersch, Paul Vasquez, Ben Verhoef, Clem Vetters, Sebastian Vieregg, Laura Villemoes, Don Vinh, Chris Virtue, Marinus Vlugter, Tobias von Platen **W** Kevin Wafer, Kieran Wales, Eilidh Walker, Smurf Walker, Mari Walters, Ross E Walton, Clare Ward-Smith, Domenic Wasescha, Roman & Colleen Washyn, Ben Watkins, John Webb, Xuess Wee, Jerray Wei, John Welch, John & Annie Welch, Mike Welch, Pauline Wennett, Ernst Weyhe, Maxine Wheller, Simon White, Lynda Whittle, Sid James Whitworth, Augustinus Wibowo, Dan Wigmore, Nina Wiio, Briant William, Todd Williams, Miles Willis, Karen Wilson, Lisa Wilson, Mira Wilson, Howard Wolff, Jane Wood, Dennis Wu **Y** Kent Yeoman, Cecilia Yong, John Young, Misima Yukio **Z** Gabriella Zipper, Todd Zwillich

ACKNOWLEDGMENTS

Many thanks to the following for the use of their content:
Globe on back cover © Mountain High Maps 1993 Digital Wisdom, Inc.

Index

INDEX

000 Map pages
000 Location of colour photographs

524

MAP LEGEND

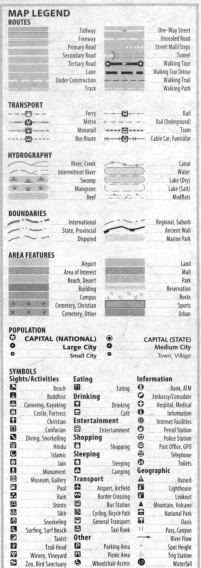

LONELY PLANET OFFICES

Australia
Head Office
Locked Bag 1, Footscray, Victoria 3011
☎ 03 8379 8000, fax 03 8379 8111
talk2us@lonelyplanet.com.au

USA
150 Linden St, Oakland, CA 94607
☎ 510 893 8555, toll free 800 275 8555
fax 510 893 8572, info@lonelyplanet.com

UK
72–82 Rosebery Ave,
Clerkenwell, London EC1R 4RW
☎ 020 7841 9000, fax 020 7841 9001
go@lonelyplanet.co.uk

Published by Lonely Planet Publications Pty Ltd
ABN 36 005 607 983

© Lonely Planet 2005

© photographers as indicated 2005

Cover photographs by Lonely Planet Images: drying candy products in Ho Chi Minh City, Keren Su (front); bike riders sheltering from a downpour on the road to Quang Ngai, Greg Elms (back). Many of the images in this guide are available for licensing from Lonely Planet Images: www.lonelyplanetimages.com